Math 050

Muskegon Community College

Alan S. Tussy

CENGAGE
Learning·

Australia • Brazil • Japan • Korea • Mexico • Singapore • Spain • United Kingdom • United States

Math 050: Muskegon Community College

Source:

Elementary and Intermediate Algebra, 5th Edition
Alan S. Tussy - Citrus College
R. David Gustafson - Rock Valley College (Emeritus)
© 2013 Cengage Learning. All rights reserved.

Executive Editors:
 Maureen Staudt
 Michael Stranz

Senior Project Development Manager:
 Linda deStefano

Marketing Specialist:
 Courtney Sheldon

Senior Production/Manufacturing Manager:
 Donna M. Brown

Production Editorial Manager:
 Kim Fry

Sr. Rights Acquisition Account Manager:
 Todd Osborne

For product information and technology assistance, contact us at
Cengage Learning Customer & Sales Support, 1-800-354-9706
For permission to use material from this text or product, submit all requests online at **cengage.com/permissions**
Further permissions questions can be emailed to
permissionrequest@cengage.com

This book contains select works from existing Cengage Learning resources and was produced by Cengage Learning Custom Solutions for collegiate use. As such, those adopting and/or contributing to this work are responsible for editorial content accuracy, continuity and completeness.

Compilation © 2012 Cengage Learning
ISBN-13: 978-1-285-12446-9

ISBN-10: 1-285-12446-4

Cengage Learning
5191 Natorp Boulevard
Mason, Ohio 45040
USA
Cengage Learning is a leading provider of customized learning solutions with office locations around the globe, including Singapore, the United Kingdom, Australia, Mexico, Brazil, and Japan. Locate your local office at:
international.cengage.com/region.

Cengage Learning products are represented in Canada by Nelson Education, Ltd.
For your lifelong learning solutions, visit **www.cengage.com/custom.**
Visit our corporate website at **www.cengage.com.**

Printed in the United States of America

Brief Contents

Transition to Intermediate Algebra

8

©Ronen/Shutterstock.com

from Campus to Careers

Webmaster

If you use the Internet, then you have seen firsthand what webmasters do. They design and maintain websites for individuals and companies on the World Wide Web. The job of webmaster requires excellent computer and technical skills. A background in business, art, and design is also helpful. Since webmasters are often called on to be troubleshooters when technical difficulties arise, those considering entering the field are encouraged to study mathematics to strengthen their problem-solving abilities.

Problem 113 in Study Set 8.1, **problem 107** in Study Set 8.2, and **problem 33** in Study Set 8.9 involve situations that a webmaster might encounter on the job. The mathematical concepts discussed in this chapter can be used to solve those problems.

JOB TITLE:
Webmaster

EDUCATION:
Many webmasters have college degrees. However, some have only a year or two of college training.

JOB OUTLOOK:
Excellent—job opportunities are expected to increase between 18% and 26% through the year 2014.

ANNUAL EARNINGS:
Average salary $73,830

FOR MORE INFORMATION:
http://www.bls.gov/k12/computers05.htm

Since a student's level of effort is significantly influenced by his or her attitude, you should strive to maintain a positive mental outlook for the entire term. Here are three suggestions to help you do that:

PERSONAL REMINDERS: From time to time, remind yourself of the ways in which you will benefit by passing the course.

DON'T DWELL ON THE NEGATIVE: Counterproductive feelings of stress and math anxiety often can be overcome with extra preparation, support services, and even relaxation techniques.

ACCOMPLISH GOALS AND EARN REWARDS: Reward yourself after studying, learning a difficult concept, or completing a homework assignment. The reward can be small, like listening to music, reading a novel, playing a sport, or spending some time with friends.

Now Try This ▶

1. List six ways in which you will benefit by passing this course. For example, it will get you one step closer to a college degree or it will improve your problem-solving abilities.

2. List three ways in which you can to respond to feelings of stress or math anxiety, should they arise during the term.

3. List some simple ways that you can reward yourself when you complete one of the class goals that you set for yourself.

SECTION 8.1

Review of Solving Linear Equations, Formulas, and Linear Inequalities; Applications

OBJECTIVES

1. Use properties of equality to solve linear equations.
2. Identify identities and contradictions.
3. Solve formulas for a specified variable.
4. Solve linear inequalities.
5. Use equations and inequalities to solve application problems.

ARE YOU READY?

The following problems review some basic skills that are needed when solving equations and inequalities.

1. Simplify: $5m - 2(8m - 4)$

2. Multiply: $21\left(\dfrac{6}{7}n\right)$

3. Multiply: $100 \cdot 0.27$

4. True or false: $-15 \leq -15$

5. Graph the set of real numbers greater than or equal to -2 on a number line.

6. Express the fact that $6 > x$ using an $<$ symbol.

One of the most useful concepts in algebra is the equation. Writing and then solving an equation is a powerful problem-solving strategy.

The Language of Algebra

It is important to know the difference between an **equation** and an **expression**. An equation contains an = symbol; an expression does not.

1 Use Properties of Equality to Solve Linear Equations.

Recall that an **equation** is a statement indicating that two expressions are equal. A number that makes an equation true when substituted for the variable is called a **solution,** and it is said to *satisfy* the equation. The **solution set** of an equation is the set of all numbers that make the equation true.

In this section, we will solve *linear equations in one variable.*

Linear Equations in One Variable

A linear equation in one variable can be written in the form $ax + b = c$, where a, b, and c are real numbers, and $a \neq 0$.

Some examples of linear equations in one variable are

$$5a + 2 = 8, \qquad \frac{7}{3}y = -28, \qquad \text{and} \qquad 3(2x - 1) = 8x + 9 - 6x$$

We can solve a linear equation in one variable by using the following **properties of equality** to replace it with simpler **equivalent equations** that have the same solution set. We continue this process until the variable is isolated on one side of the $=$ symbol.

Success Tip

You may want to review the more detailed explanations of the properties of equality on pages 103, 105, 106, and 108.

Properties of Equality

1. Adding the same number to, or subtracting the same number from, both sides of an equation does not change its solution.

2. Multiplying or dividing both sides of an equation by the same nonzero number does not change its solution.

When solving equations, we should simplify the expressions that make up the left and right sides before applying any properties of equality. Often that involves using the **distributive property** to remove parentheses and/or **combining like terms.**

EXAMPLE 1

Solve: $3(2x - 1) = 8x + 9 - 6x$

Strategy We will use the distributive property on the left side of the equation and combine like terms on the right side.

Why It's best to simplify each side of an equation before using a property of equality. This makes it easier to determine the steps needed to get all the terms containing x on the same side of the equation.

Solution

Success Tip

Since division by 4 is the same as multiplication by $\frac{1}{4}$, we can solve $4x = 12$ using the multiplication property of equality by multiplying both sides by the *multiplicative inverse* of 4, which is $\frac{1}{4}$.

$$\frac{1}{4} \cdot 4x = \frac{1}{4} \cdot 12$$

$$x = 3$$

$3(2x - 1) = 8x + 9 - 6x$	This is the equation to solve.
$6x - 3 = 2x + 9$	On the left side, distribute the multiplication by 3. On the right side, combine like terms: $8x - 6x = 2x$.
$6x - 3 - 2x = 2x + 9 - 2x$	To eliminate $2x$ from the right side, subtract $2x$ from both sides.
$4x - 3 = 9$	Combine like terms: $6x - 2x = 4x$ and $2x - 2x = 0$.
$4x - 3 + 3 = 9 + 3$	To isolate the variable term $4x$, undo the subtraction of 3 on the left side by adding 3 to both sides.
$4x = 12$	Combine like terms: $-3 + 3 = 0$.
$x = 3$	To isolate the variable x, undo the multiplication by 4 by dividing both sides by 4.

Check: We substitute 3 for x in the original equation to see whether it satisfies the equation.

The Language of Algebra

Read $\stackrel{?}{=}$ as "is possibly equal to."

Evaluate the expression on the left side.

Evaluate the expression on the right side.

$$3(2x - 1) = 8x + 9 - 6x$$
$$3(2 \cdot 3 - 1) \stackrel{?}{=} 8 \cdot 3 + 9 - 6 \cdot 3$$
$$3(5) \stackrel{?}{=} 24 + 9 - 18$$
$$15 = 15 \quad \text{True}$$

Since the resulting statement $15 = 15$ is true, 3 satisfies the equation, and we say that 3 is a solution of $3(2x - 1) = 8x + 9 - 6x$. The solution set is $\{3\}$.

Self Check 1 Solve: $2(3x - 2) = 10x - 13 - 7x$

Now Try ▶ Problem 21

In general, we will follow these steps to solve linear equations in one variable. Not every step is needed to solve every equation.

Strategy for Solving Linear Equations in One Variable

1. **Clear the equation of fractions or decimals:** Multiply both sides by the LCD to clear fractions or multiply both sides by a power of 10 to clear decimals.

2. **Simplify each side of the equation:** Use the distributive property to remove parentheses and combine like terms on each side.

3. **Isolate the variable term on one side:** Add (or subtract) to get the variable term on one side of the equation and a number on the other using the addition (or subtraction) property of equality.

4. **Isolate the variable:** Multiply (or divide) to isolate the variable using the multiplication (or division) property of equality.

5. **Check the result:** Substitute the possible solution for the variable in the *original* equation to see if a true statement results.

EXAMPLE 2   Solve: $\dfrac{1}{3}(6x + 17) = \dfrac{3}{2}(x + 2) - 2$

Strategy   We will follow the strategy for solving equations.

Why   This is the most efficient way to solve a linear equation in one variable.

Solution   **Step 1:** We can clear the equation of fractions by multiplying both sides by the least common denominator (LCD) of $\frac{1}{3}$ and $\frac{3}{2}$. The LCD of these fractions is the smallest number that can be divided by both 2 and 3 exactly. That number is 6.

$$\frac{1}{3}(6x + 17) = \frac{3}{2}(x + 2) - 2$$ This is the equation to solve.

Success Tip

Before multiplying both sides of an equation by the LCD, frame the left side and frame the right side with parentheses or brackets.

$$6\left[\frac{1}{3}(6x + 17)\right] = 6\left[\frac{3}{2}(x + 2) - 2\right]$$ To eliminate the fractions, multiply both sides by the LCD, 6.

$$2(6x + 17) = 6 \cdot \frac{3}{2}(x + 2) - 6 \cdot 2$$ On the left side, perform the multiplication: $6 \cdot \frac{1}{3} = 2$. On the right side, distribute the multiplication by 6.

$$2(6x + 17) = 9(x + 2) - 12$$ Multiply on the right side: $6 \cdot \frac{3}{2} = 9$ and $6 \cdot 2 = 12$. Don't forget the parentheses shown in blue.

Step 2: Simplify the expressions on each side of the equation.

$$12x + 34 = 9x + 18 - 12$$ Distribute the multiplication by 2 and the multiplication by 9.

$$12x + 34 = 9x + 6$$ Combine like terms: $18 - 12 = 6$.

Step 3: To get the variable term on the left side of the equation and the constant on the right side, subtract $9x$ and 34 from both sides.

$$12x + 34 - 9x - 34 = 9x + 6 - 9x - 34$$

$$3x = -28$$ On each side, combine like terms.

Step 4: To isolate x, we undo the multiplication by 3 by dividing both sides by 3.

$$\frac{3x}{3} = \frac{-28}{3}$$

$$x = -\frac{28}{3}$$

Step 5: Verify that $-\frac{28}{3}$ is the solution by substituting it into the original equation and evaluating each side.

> **Self Check 2**   Solve: $\frac{1}{3}(2x - 5) = \frac{3}{4}(5x + 1) + 2$
>
> **Now Try** ▶ Problem 29

2 | Identify Identities and Contradictions.

The equations discussed so far are called **conditional equations.** For these equations, some real numbers satisfy the equation and others do not. Other equations are made true by *any* permissible replacement value for the variable. Such an equation is called an **identity.** Still other equations are false for *all* replacement values for the variable. We call such an equation a **contradiction.**

EXAMPLE 3   Solve: **a.** $-2(x - 1) - 4 = -4(1 + x) + 2x + 2$
b. $-6.2(-x - 1) - 4 = 4.2x - (-2x)$

Strategy   In each case, we will follow the strategy for solving equations.

Why   This is the most efficient way to solve a linear equation in one variable.

Solution   **a.** Since there are no fractions to clear, we will begin by using the distributive property to remove the parentheses on the left and right sides of the equation.

Success Tip

We know the given equation is an identity because we see in Step 3 that it is equivalent to the equation $-2x - 2 = -2x - 2$, which is true for all values of x.

$$-2(x - 1) - 4 = -4(1 + x) + 2x + 2 \qquad \text{This is the equation to solve.}$$
$$-2x + 2 - 4 = -4 - 4x + 2x + 2 \qquad \text{On each side, use the distributive property.}$$
$$-2x - 2 = -2x - 2 \qquad \text{On each side, combine like terms.}$$
$$-2x - 2 + 2x = -2x - 2 + 2x \qquad \text{To attempt to isolate the variable on one side of the equation, add } 2x \text{ to both sides.}$$
$$-2 = -2 \qquad \text{True}$$

In the solution process, the terms involving x drop out. The resulting true statement indicates that the original equation is true for every permissible value of x. Therefore, *all real numbers* are solutions and this equation is an identity. Its solution set is written as {all real numbers} or using the symbol $\mathbb{R}$.

b.

The Language of Algebra

Contradiction is a form of the word *contradict,* meaning conflicting ideas. During a trial, evidence might be introduced that contradicts the testimony of a witness.

$$-6.2(-x - 1) - 4 = 4.2x - (-2x) \qquad \text{This is the equation to solve.}$$
$$-6.2(-x - 1) - 4 = 4.2x + 2x \qquad \text{Simplify: } -(-2x) = 2x.$$
$$10[-6.2(-x - 1) - 4] = 10(4.2x + 2x) \qquad \text{To clear the decimals, multiply both sides by 10.}$$
$$10(-6.2)(-x - 1) - 10 \cdot 4 = 10 \cdot 4.2x + 10 \cdot 2x \qquad \text{On each side, distribute the multiplication by 10.}$$
$$-62(-x - 1) - 40 = 42x + 20x \qquad \text{Perform each multiplication by 10.}$$
$$62x + 62 - 40 = 42x + 20x \qquad \text{On the left side, distribute } -62.$$
$$62x + 22 = 62x \qquad \text{On each side, combine like terms.}$$
$$62x + 22 - 62x = 62x - 62x \qquad \text{To attempt to isolate the variable on one side of the equation, subtract } 62x \text{ from both sides.}$$
$$22 = 0 \qquad \text{False}$$

In the solution process, the terms involving x drop out. The resulting false statement indicates that no value for x makes the original equation true. Therefore, this equation has *no solution* and it is a contradiction. Its solution set is the empty set, which is written as { } or using the symbol $\varnothing$.

Self Check 3   Solve: **a.** $3(a + 1) - (20 + a) = 5(a - 1) - 3(a + 4)$

b. $0.3(a + 4) + 0.2 = 0.2(a - 1) + 0.1a + 1.9$

Now Try ▶ Problems 31 and 35

3 Solve Formulas for a Specified Variable.

Real-world applications sometimes call for a formula solved for one variable to be solved for a different variable. **To solve a formula for a specified variable** means to isolate that variable on one side of the equal symbol, with all other variables and constants on the other side.

EXAMPLE 4

Banking.   The formula $A = P + Prt$ gives the amount of money in an account at the end of a specific time t. A represents the amount, P the principal, and r the simple rate of interest. Solve the formula for t.

Strategy   To solve for t, we treat it as if it were the only variable in the equation. To isolate t, we will use the same strategy that we used to solve linear equations in one variable.

Why   We can solve this formula as if it were an equation in one variable because all the other variables, A, P, and r, are treated as if they were numbers (constants).

Solution

┌─ To solve for t, we will isolate it on this side of the equation.

$A = P + Prt$

The Language of Algebra

We say the formula is **solved for** t because t is alone on one side of the equation and the other side does not contain t.

$A - P = Prt$ To isolate the term involving t, subtract P from both sides. This step is done mentally.

$\dfrac{A - P}{Pr} = \dfrac{Prt}{Pr}$ To isolate t, divide both sides by Pr (or multiply both sides by $\frac{1}{Pr}$).

$\dfrac{A - P}{Pr} = t$ On the right side, remove the common factors: $\dfrac{\overset{1}{\cancel{Pr}}t}{\underset{1}{\cancel{Pr}}}$.

$t = \dfrac{A - P}{Pr}$ It is common practice to write the equation so that the specified variable, in this case t, is on the left side.

Self Check 4   Solve $A = P + Prt$ for r.

Now Try ▶ Problem 39

EXAMPLE 5

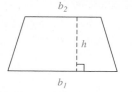

b_2

h

b_1

Trapezoid

Geometry.   The formula for the area of a trapezoid is $A = \frac{1}{2}h(b_1 + b_2)$. Solve the formula for b_1.

Strategy   To solve for b_1, we will treat it as if it were the only variable in the equation. To isolate b_1, we will use the same strategy that we used to solve linear equations in one variable.

Why   We can solve the formula as if it were an equation in one variable because all the other variables, A, h, and b_2, are treated as if they were numbers (constants).

Solution

To solve for b_1, we will isolate b_1 on this side of the equation.

$$A = \frac{1}{2}h(b_1 + b_2)$$ Read b_1 as "b-sub-one" and b_2 as "b-sub-two."

$$2 \cdot A = 2 \cdot \frac{1}{2}h(b_1 + b_2)$$ Multiply both sides by 2 to clear the equation of the fraction.

$$2A = h(b_1 + b_2)$$ Simplify each side of the equation.

$$2A = hb_1 + hb_2$$ Distribute the multiplication by h.

$$2A - hb_2 = hb_1$$ Subtract hb_2 from both sides to isolate the variable term hb_1 on the right side. This step is done mentally.

$$\frac{2A - hb_2}{h} = \frac{hb_1}{h}$$ To isolate b_1, undo the multiplication by h by dividing both sides by h.

$$\frac{2A - b_2h}{h} = b_1$$ On the right side, remove the common factor of h: $\frac{\overset{1}{\cancel{h}}b_1}{\underset{1}{\cancel{h}}}$.

$$b_1 = \frac{2A - hb_2}{h}$$ Reverse the sides of the equation so that b_1 is on the left.

When solving formulas for a specified variable, there is often more than one way to express the result. In this case, we could perform the division by h on the right side term-by-term: $b_1 = \frac{2A}{h} - \frac{hb_2}{h}$. After removing the common factor of h in the numerator and denominator of the second fraction, we obtain the following equivalent form of the result: $b_1 = \frac{2A}{h} - b_2$.

Caution

Do not try to simplify the result in the following way. It is incorrect because h is not a factor of the entire numerator.

$$b_1 = \frac{\cancel{2A - hb_2}}{\underset{1}{\cancel{h}}}$$

Self Check 5 Solve $S = \frac{180(t - 2)}{7}$ for t.

Now Try ▶ Problem 47

4 Solve Linear Inequalities.

Inequalities are statements indicating that two quantities are unequal and they contain one or more of the following symbols.

Inequality Symbols

$<$ is less than $>$ is greater than $\neq$ is not equal to
$\leq$ is less than or equal to $\geq$ is greater than or equal to

In this section, we will solve *linear inequalities in one variable*. A linear *inequality* in one variable is similar to a linear *equation* in one variable except that the equal symbol is replaced with an inequality symbol.

Linear Inequalities

A linear inequality in one variable (say, x) is any inequality that can be expressed in one of the following forms, where a, b, and c represent real numbers and $a \neq 0$.

$$ax + b < c \qquad ax + b \leq c \qquad ax + b > c \qquad ax + b \geq c$$

Some examples of linear inequalities are

$$3(2x - 9) < 9, \qquad -11x - 8.2 \leq x + 32.2, \qquad \text{and} \qquad 3x > 0$$

Success Tip

You may want to review the more detailed explanations of properties of inequality on pages 165 and 166.

To **solve a linear inequality** means to find all values that, when substituted for the variable, make the inequality true. The set of all solutions of an inequality is called its **solution set.** Most inequalities that we will solve have infinitely many solutions. To represent such solutions, we can use the graph of an **interval** on the number line and two special types of notation: **interval notation** and **set-builder notation.**

We use the following properties to solve inequalities.

Properties of Inequality

1. Adding the same number to, or subtracting the same number from, both sides of an inequality does not change the solutions.

2. Multiplying or dividing both sides of an inequality by the same positive number does not change the solutions.

3. If we multiply or divide both sides of an inequality by a negative number, the direction of the inequality symbol must be *reversed* for the inequalities to have the same solutions.

After applying one of these properties, the resulting inequality is equivalent to the original one. Like equivalent equations, **equivalent inequalities** have the same solution set.

EXAMPLE 6 Solve $3(2x - 9) < 9$. Graph the solution set and write it using interval notation.

Strategy We will use the properties of inequality and the same strategy for solving equations to isolate x on one side of the inequality.

Why Once we have obtained an equivalent inequality, with the variable isolated on one side, the solution set will be obvious.

Solution

$3(2x - 9) < 9$	This is the inequality to solve.
$6x - 27 < 9$	Distribute the multiplication by 3.
$6x < 36$	To isolate the variable term 6x, undo the subtraction of 27 by adding 27 to both sides: 9 + 27 = 36.
$x < 6$	To isolate x, undo the multiplication by 6 by dividing both sides by 6.

The solution set is the interval $(-\infty, 6)$, whose graph is shown. We also can write the solution set using set-builder notation: $\{x \mid x < 6\}$. We read this notation as "the set of all real numbers x such that x is less than 6."

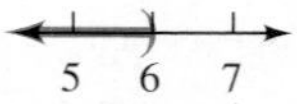

Notation

When graphing solution sets on a number line, parentheses are used to exclude endpoints and brackets are used to include endpoints.

Since the solution set contains infinitely many real numbers, we cannot check all of them to see whether they satisfy the original inequality. However, as an informal check, we can pick one number in the graph, near the endpoint, such as 5, and see whether it satisfies the inequality. We also can pick one number not in the graph, but near the endpoint, such as 7, and see whether it fails to satisfy the inequality.

Check a value in the graph: $x = 5$	*Check a value not in the graph: $x = 7$*
$3(2x - 9) < 9$	$3(2x - 9) < 9$
$3[2(5) - 9] \overset{?}{<} 9$	$3[2(7) - 9] \overset{?}{<} 9$
$3(10 - 9) \overset{?}{<} 9$	$3(14 - 9) \overset{?}{<} 9$
$3(1) \overset{?}{<} 9$	$3(5) \overset{?}{<} 9$
$3 < 9$ True	$15 < 9$ False

Since 5 satisfies $3(2x - 9) < 9$ and 7 does not, the solution set appears to be correct.

Self Check 6 Solve $2(3x + 2) > -44$. Graph the solution set and write it using interval notation.

Now Try ▶ Problem 53

EXAMPLE 7   Solve $-11x + 8.2 \leq x + 32.2$. Graph the solution set and write it using interval notation.

Strategy   We will use the properties of inequality and the same strategy for solving equations to isolate x on one side of the inequality.

Why   Once we have obtained an equivalent inequality, with the variable isolated on one side, the solution set will be obvious.

Solution

$-11x + 8.2 \leq x + 32.2$	This is the inequality to solve.
$-12x + 8.2 \leq 32.2$	To eliminate x from the right side, subtract x from both sides.
$-12x \leq 24$	To isolate the variable term $-12x$, undo the addition of 8.2 by subtracting 8.2 from both sides: $32.2 - 8.2 = 24$.
$\dfrac{-12x}{-12} \geq \dfrac{24}{-12}$	To isolate the x, undo the multiplication by -12 by dividing both sides by -12. Because we are dividing by a negative number, reverse the $\leq$ symbol.
$x \geq -2$	Do the division.

Success Tip

We must remember to reverse the inequality symbol every time we multiply or divide both sides by a negative number.

The solution set is $\{x \mid x \geq -2\}$ or the interval $[-2, \infty)$, whose graph is shown.

$$\xrightarrow{\hspace{0.5cm}\underset{-3}{\mid}\hspace{0.5cm}\underset{-2}{[}\hspace{0.5cm}\underset{-1}{\mid}\hspace{0.5cm}}$$

Self Check 7   Solve: $-5x + 6 \leq x$. Graph the solution set and write it using interval notation.

Now Try ▶ Problem 59

EXAMPLE 8   Solve $3a - 4 < 3(a + 5)$. Graph the solution set and write it using interval notation.

Strategy   We will use the properties of inequality and the same strategy for solving equations to isolate a on one side of the inequality.

Why   Once we have obtained an equivalent inequality, with the variable isolated on one side, the solution set is obvious.

Solution

$3a - 4 < 3(a + 5)$	This is the inequality to solve.
$3a - 4 < 3a + 15$	Distribute the multiplication by 3.
$3a - 4 - 3a < 3a + 15 - 3a$	To eliminate $3a$ on the right side, subtract $3a$ from both sides.
$-4 < 15$	True

Success Tip

If the terms involving the variable drop out when solving an inequality and the result is false, the solution set contains no elements and is denoted by $\emptyset$.

In the solution process, the terms involving a drop out. The resulting true statement indicates that the original inequality is true for every permissible value of a. Therefore, *all real numbers* are solutions and this inequality is an identity. Its solution set is the set of real numbers, written as $(-\infty, \infty)$ or $\mathbb{R}$, and its graph is as shown.

Self Check 8   Solve $-8n + 10 \geq 1 - 2(4n - 2)$. Graph the solution set and write it using interval notation.

Now Try ▶ Problem 67

---

5 Use Equations and Inequalities to Solve Application Problems.

To become a good problem solver, you need a plan to follow such as the following six-step problem-solving strategy: **Analyze** the problem, **Assign** a variable, **Form** an equation (or inequality), **Solve** the equation (or inequality), **State** the conclusion, **Check** the result.

EXAMPLE 9

Travel Promotions.   The price of a 7-day Alaskan cruise, normally $2,752 per person, is reduced by $1.75 per person for large groups traveling together. How large a group is needed for the price to be $2,500 per person?

Analyze   It is often helpful to consider some specific situations before attempting to form an equation. For a group of, say, 20 people, the price of the cruise would be reduced by 20($1.75), and each person would pay $2,752 − 20($1.75). For a group of 30 people, the price of the cruise would be reduced by 30($1.75), and each person would pay $2,752 − 30($1.75).

Assign   We let x = the group size necessary for the price of the cruise to be $2,500 per person.

Form   We can form the following equation:

The price of the cruise	is	$2,752	minus	the number of people in the group	times	$1.75.
2,500	=	2,752	−	x	·	1.75

Solve

$$2,500 = 2,752 - 1.75x$$

$$2,500 - \mathbf{2{,}752} = 2,752 - 1.75x - \mathbf{2{,}752}$$ To isolate the variable term −1.75x, subtract 2,752 from both sides.

$$-252 = -1.75x$$ Do the subtraction.

$$\frac{-252}{-1.75} = \frac{-1.75x}{-1.75}$$ To isolate x, divide both sides by −1.75.

$$144 = x$$ Use a calculator to do the division. This is the required size of the group.

State   If 144 people travel together, the price will be $2,500 per person.

Check   For 144 people, the cruise cost of $2,752 will be reduced by 144($1.75) = $252. If we subtract, $2,752 − $252 = $2,500. The result checks.

Self Check 9   **Broadway Shows.**   Tickets to a Broadway show normally sell for $90 per person. This price is reduced by $0.50 per person for large groups. How large a group is needed for the price to be $75 per person?

Now Try ▶ Problem 107

To determine whether to use an equation or an inequality to solve a problem, look for key words and phrases. For example, phrases like *does not exceed, is no more than,* and *is at least* translate into inequalities.

EXAMPLE 10

Communication.   A satellite phone is a mobile phone that sends and receives calls using satellites instead of cellular broadcasting towers. Satellite phone calls can be made from anywhere, such as the Sahara desert or the top of Mount Everest. If a satellite telephone company charges callers $5.50 for the first three minutes and 88¢ for each additional minute, for how many minutes can a call last if the cost is not to exceed $20?

Analyze   We are given the rate at which a call is billed. Since the cost of a call is not to exceed $20, the cost must be *less than or equal to* $20. This phrase indicates that we should write an inequality to find how long a call can last.

Assign   We will let x = the total number of minutes that a call can last.

Form If the call lasts x minutes, then the cost of a call will be $5.50 for the first three minutes plus 88¢ times the number of additional minutes, where the number of *additional* minutes is $x - 3$ (the total number of minutes minus the first 3 minutes). With this information, we can form an inequality.

The cost of the first three minutes	plus	the cost of the additional minutes	is not to exceed	$20.
5.50	+	$0.88(x - 3)$	$\leq$	20

Solve First, we clear the inequality of decimals.

$$5.50 + 0.88(x - 3) \leq 20 \qquad \textit{Write 88¢ as \$0.88.}$$
$$550 + 88(x - 3) \leq 2{,}000 \qquad \textit{To eliminate the decimals, multiply both sides by 100.}$$
$$550 + 88x - 264 \leq 2{,}000 \qquad \textit{Distribute the multiplication by 88.}$$
$$88x + 286 \leq 2{,}000 \qquad \textit{Combine like terms: } 550 - 264 = 286.$$
$$88x \leq 1{,}714 \qquad \textit{To isolate 88x, subtract 286 from both sides.}$$
$$x \leq 19.4772727\ldots \qquad \textit{To isolate x, divide both sides by 88.}$$
$$\textit{Use a calculator.}$$

State Since the phone company doesn't bill for part of a minute, the longest time a call can last is 19 minutes. If a call lasts for $x = 19.4772727\ldots$ minutes, it will be charged as a 20-minute call, and the cost will be $5.50 + \$0.88(17) = \$20.46$.

Check If the call lasts 19 minutes, the cost will be $5.50 + \$0.88(16) = \$19.58$. This is less than $20. The result checks.

Self Check 10 **Renting Cars.** Great Value Car Rental charges $12 a day and $0.15 per mile to rent a Ford Fusion. Be Thrifty Car Rental's daily charge for the same car is $15 and $0.12 per mile. If a businessman wants to rent the car for one day, for what range of miles driven is the Be Thrifty rental plan better?

Now Try ▶ Problem 115

SECTION 8.1 ▶ STUDY SET

VOCABULARY

Fill in the blanks.

1. An _____ is a statement indicating that two expressions are equal.
2. $2x + 1 = 4$ is an example of a _____ equation in one variable.
3. A number that makes an equation true when substituted for the variable is called a _____.
4. If two equations have the same solution set, they are called _____ equations.
5. An equation that is made true by any permissible replacement value for the variable is called an _____.
6. An equation that is false for all replacement values for the variable is called a _____.
7. $<$, $>$, $\leq$, and $\geq$ are _____ symbols.
8. To _____ an inequality means to find all values of the variable that make the inequality true.

CONCEPTS

Fill in the blanks.

9. **a.** Adding the _____ number to, or subtracting the same number from, both sides of an equation does not change its solution.

   b. Multiplying or dividing both sides of an equation by the _____ nonzero number does not change its solution.

10. If we multiply both sides of an inequality by a negative number, the direction of the inequality must be _____ for the inequalities to have the same solutions.

11. Use a check to determine whether -5 is a solution of the following equation and inequality.
    a. $5(2x + 7) = 2x - 4$ \qquad **b.** $3x + 6 \leq -9$

12. The solution set of a linear inequality in x is graphed on the right. Determine whether a true or false statement results when

 a. -4 is substituted for x.

 b. -3 is substituted for x.

 c. 0 is substituted for x.

NOTATION

13. Match each interval with its graph.

 a. $(-\infty, -1]$ b. $(-\infty, 1)$ c. $[-1, \infty)$

 i.   ii.   iii.

14. a. Suppose that when solving a linear equation, the variable drops out, and the result is $7 = -1$. What is the solution set?

 b. Suppose that when solving a linear inequality, the variable drops out, and the result is $6 \leq 10$. Write the solution set in interval notation and graph it.

GUIDED PRACTICE

Solve each equation. Check the result. See Example 1.

15. $4x + 1 = 13$
16. $4x - 8 = 16$
17. $3(x + 1) = 15$
18. $-2(x + 5) = 30$
19. $2x + 6(2x + 3) = -10$
20. $3(2y - 4) - 6 = 3y$
21. $7(a + 2) = 11a + 17 - 7a$
22. $5(5 - a) = 4a + 37 - 6a$

Solve each equation. Check the result. See Example 2.

23. $\frac{1}{2}x - 4 = -1 + 2x$
24. $2x + 3 = \frac{2}{3}x - 1$
25. $\frac{x}{2} - \frac{x}{3} = 4$
26. $\frac{x}{2} + \frac{x}{3} = 10$
27. $\frac{1}{6}(x + 12) + 1 = \frac{x}{3}$
28. $\frac{3}{2}(y + 4) = \frac{20 - y}{2}$
29. $\frac{1}{5}(x + 6) = \frac{5}{8}(2x - 1) + 2$
30. $\frac{2}{3}(x - 3) = \frac{1}{6}(7x + 29) + 3$

Solve each equation. If an equation is an identity or a contradiction, so indicate. See Example 3.

31. $2x - 6 = -2x + 4(x - 2)$
32. $-3x = -2x + 1 - (5 + x)$
33. $2y + 1 = 5(0.2y + 1) - (4 - y)$
34. $4(2 - 3t) + 6t = -6t + 8$
35. $\frac{7}{2}(y - 1) + \frac{1}{2} = \frac{1}{2}(7y - 6)$
36. $2(x - 3) = \frac{3}{2}(x - 4) + \frac{x}{2}$
37. $0.3(x - 4) + 0.6 = -0.2(x + 4) + 0.5x$
38. $0.5(y + 2) + 0.7 - 0.3y = 0.2(y + 9)$

Solve each formula for the specified variable. See Examples 4 and 5.

39. $P = 2l + 2w$ for w
40. $P = 2l + 2w$ for l
41. $V = \frac{1}{3}Bh$ for B
42. $A = \frac{1}{2}bh$ for b
43. $T - W = ma$ for W
44. $G = U - TS + PV$ for S
45. $z = \frac{x - \mu}{\sigma}$ for x
46. $P = L + \frac{s}{f}i$ for s
47. $S = \frac{n(a + l)}{2}$ for l
48. $h = 48t + \frac{1}{2}at^2$ for a
49. $l = a + (n - 1)d$ for d
50. $P = 2(w + h + l)$ for h

Solve each inequality. Graph the solution set and write it in interval notation. See Example 6.

51. $5x - 3 > 7$
52. $7x - 9 < 5$
53. $9a + 11 \leq 29$
54. $3b - 26 \geq 4$
55. $3(z - 2) \leq 2(z + 7)$
56. $5(3 + z) > -3(z + 3)$
57. $2x + 4 + 6x > 2 - 3x + 2$
58. $5x + 6 + 2x \geq 2 - x + 4$

Solve each inequality. Write the solution set in interval notation and then graph it. See Example 7.

59. $-3x - 1 \leq 5$
60. $-2x + 6 \geq 16$
61. $-5t + 3 \leq 5$
62. $-9t + 6 \geq 16$
63. $-7y + 5 > -5y - 1$
64. $8 - 9y \geq -y$
65. $t + 1 - 3t \geq t - 20$
66. $a + 4 - 10a > a - 16$

Solve each inequality. Graph the solution set and write it in interval notation. See Example 8 and the Success Tip in the margin.

67. $2(5x - 6) > 4x - 15 + 6x$
68. $3(4x - 2) > 14x - 7 - 2x$
69. $\frac{3b + 7}{3} \leq \frac{2b - 9}{2}$
70. $-\frac{5x}{4} > \frac{3 - 5x}{4}$

TRY IT YOURSELF

Solve each equation. If an equation is an identity or a contradiction, so indicate.

71. $2r - 5 = 1 - r$
72. $5s - 13 = s - 1$
73. $0.2(a - 5) - 0.1(3a + 1) = 0$
74. $0.8(3a - 5) - 0.4(2a + 3) = 1.2$

75. $-\dfrac{4}{5}s = 2$

76. $-\dfrac{9}{8}s = 3$

77. $\dfrac{1}{2}(3y + 2) - \dfrac{5}{8} = \dfrac{3}{4}y$

78. $-\dfrac{3}{4}(4c - 3) + \dfrac{7}{8}c = \dfrac{19}{16}$

79. $8x + 3(2 - x) = 5x + 6$

80. $2(2a + 1) - 1 = 4a + 1$

81. $12 + 3(x - 4) - 21 = 5[5 - 4(4 - x)]$

82. $1 + 3[-2 + 6(4 - 2x)] = -(x + 3)$

83. $\dfrac{3 + p}{3} - 4p = 1 - \dfrac{p + 7}{2}$

84. $\dfrac{4 - t}{2} - \dfrac{3t}{5} = 2 + \dfrac{t + 1}{3}$

85. $5x + 10 = 5x$

86. $4(t - 2) - t = -(9 - 3t)$

87. $0.06(a + 200) + 0.1a = 172$

88. $0.03x + 0.05(6,000 - x) = 280$

89. $-4[p - (3 - p)] = 3(6p - 2)$

90. $2[5(4 - a) + 2(a - 1)] = 3 - a$

Solve each inequality. Graph the solution set and write it in interval notation.

91. $-3(a + 2) > 2(a + 1)$

92. $-4(y - 1) < y + 8$

93. $\dfrac{x - 7}{2} - \dfrac{x - 1}{5} \le -\dfrac{x}{4}$

94. $\dfrac{3a + 1}{3} - \dfrac{4 - 3a}{5} \le -\dfrac{1}{15}$

95. $5(2n + 2) - n > 3n - 3(1 - 2n)$

96. $-1 + 4(y - 1) + 2y \le \dfrac{1}{2}(12y - 30) + 15$

97. $0.4x + 0.4 \le 0.1x + 0.85$

98. $0.05 + 0.8x \le 0.5x - 0.7$

99. $\dfrac{1}{2}y + 2 \ge \dfrac{1}{3}y - 4$

100. $\dfrac{1}{4}x - \dfrac{1}{3} \le x + 2$

101. $7 < \dfrac{5}{3}a - 3$

102. $5 > \dfrac{7}{2}a - 9$

Look Alikes . . .

Simplify each expression and solve each equation.

103. a. $\dfrac{1}{2}(6x + 8) - 10 - \dfrac{2}{3}(6x - 9)$

b. $\dfrac{1}{2}(6x + 8) - 10 = -\dfrac{2}{3}(6x - 9)$

104. a. $6.31w + 9.22 + 5(7.21w - 1.13)$

b. $6.31w + 9.22 = 5(7.21w - 1.13)$

Solve the inequality in part a. Graph the solution set and write it in interval notation. Then use your answer to part a to determine the solution set for the inequality in part b. (No new work is necessary!) Graph the solution set and write it in interval notation.

105. a. $12x - 33.16 \le 5.84$

b. $12x - 33.16 > 5.84$

106. a. $-\dfrac{3}{4}x > -\dfrac{21}{32}$

b. $-\dfrac{3}{4}x \le -\dfrac{21}{32}$

APPLICATIONS

107. Spring Tours. A group of junior high students will be touring Washington, D.C. Their chaperons will have the $1,810 cost of the tour reduced by $15.50 for each student they supervise. How many students will a chaperon have to supervise so that his or her cost to take the tour will be $1,500?

108. Machining. Each pass through a lumber plane shaves off 0.015 inch of thickness from a board. How many times must a board, originally 0.875 inch thick, be run through the planer if a board of thickness 0.74 inch is desired?

109. Moving Expenses. To help move his furniture, a man rents a truck for $41.50 per day plus 35¢ per mile. If he has budgeted $150 for transportation expenses, how many miles will he be able to drive the truck if the move takes 1 day?

110. Computing Salaries. A student working for a delivery company earns $57.50 per day plus $4.75 for each package she delivers. How many deliveries must she make each day to earn $200 a day?

111. Fencing Pens. A man has 150 feet of fencing to build the two-part pen shown in the illustration. If one end is a square and the other a rectangle, find the outside dimensions of the pen.

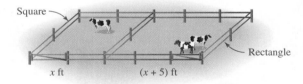

Square

Rectangle

x ft $(x + 5)$ ft

112. Fencing Pastures. A farmer has 624 feet of fencing to enclose a pasture. Because a river runs along one side, fencing will be needed on only three sides. Find the dimensions of the pasture if its length is double its width.

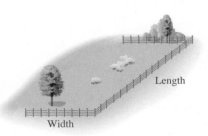

Length

Width

©Ronen/Shutterstock.com

from Campus to Careers

113. ▶ Webmaster

One of the most important duties that a webmaster has is to monitor the web traffic of the site that he or she oversees. Suppose a counter for a news organization website has recorded 650,568,999 *views* for April 1 through April 29. How many views does the site need on the last day of the month (April 30) to average 22,000,000 daily visitors?

114. Averaging Grades.   A student has scores of 70, 77, and 85 on three government exams. What score does she need on a fourth exam to give her an average of 80 or better?

115. Fundraising.   A school PTA wants to rent a dunking tank for its annual school fundraising carnival. The cost is $85.00 for the first 3 hours and then $19.50 for each additional hour or part thereof. How long can the tank be rented if up to $185 is budgeted for this expense?

116. Work Schedules.   A student works two part-time jobs. He earns $8 an hour for working at the college library and $15 an hour for construction work. To save time for study, he limits his work to 25 hours a week. If he enjoys the work at the library more, how many hours can he work at the library and still earn at least $300 a week?

117. Scheduling Equipment.   An excavating company charges $300 an hour for the use of a backhoe and $500 an hour for the use of a bulldozer. (Part of an hour counts as a full hour.) The company employs one operator for 40 hours per week to operate the machinery. If the company wants to bring in at least $18,500 each week from equipment rental, how many hours per week can it schedule the operator to use a backhoe?

118. Video Game Systems.   A student who can afford to spend up to $1,000 sees the ad shown in the illustration. If she decides to buy the video game system, find the greatest number of video games that she also can purchase. (Disregard sales tax.)

VIDEO GAME SYSTEM
only $449^{99}

YOUR FAVORITE GAMES
only $45^{99} each

WRITING

119. Explain why the equation $x = x + 1$ doesn't have a real-number solution.

120. Explain what is wrong with the following statement:

When solving inequalities involving negative numbers, the direction of the inequality symbol must be reversed.

REVIEW

Simplify each expression. Write answers using only positive exponents.

121. $\left(\dfrac{t^3t^5t^{-6}}{t^2t^{-4}}\right)^{-3}$

122. $\left(\dfrac{a^{-2}b^3a^5b^{-2}}{a^6b^{-5}}\right)^{-4}$

CHALLENGE PROBLEMS

123. Find the value of k that makes 4 a solution of the following linear equation in x.

$$k + 3x - 6 = 3kx - k + 16$$

124. Solve: $0.75(x - 5) - \dfrac{4}{5} = \dfrac{1}{6}(3x + 1) + 3.2$

125. Consider the following "solution" of the inequality $\frac{1}{3} > \frac{1}{x}$ where it appears that the solution set is the interval $(3, \infty)$.

$$\frac{1}{3} > \frac{1}{x}$$

$$3x\left(\frac{1}{3}\right) > 3x\left(\frac{1}{x}\right)$$

$$x > 3$$

a. Show that $x = -1$ makes the original inequality true.

b. If $x = -1$ makes the original inequality true, there must be an error in the "solution." Where is it?

126. Medical Plans.   A college provides its employees with a choice of the two medical plans shown in the following table. For what size hospital bills is Plan 2 better for the employee than Plan 1? (*Hint:* The cost to the employee includes both the deductible payment and the employee's coinsurance payment.)

Plan 1	Plan 2
Employee pays $100	Employee pays $200
Plan pays 70% of the rest	Plan pays 80% of the rest

©Chris Howey/Shutterstock.com

SECTION 8.2

OBJECTIVES

1 Define relation, domain, and range.

2 Identify functions.

3 Use function notation.

4 Find the domain of a function.

5 Graph linear functions.

6 Write equations of linear functions.

7 Evaluate polynomial functions.

Functions

ARE YOU READY?

The following problems review some basic skills that are needed when working with functions.

1. Which of the ordered pairs in the following set have the same x-coordinate: $\{(3, 5), (2, 9), (6, -7), (-1, 5), (3, 0), (1, 9)\}$?

2. Substitute 8 for x in $y = \dfrac{1}{2}x + 3$ and find y.

3. What are the slope and the y-intercept of the line described by the equation $y = 3x - 8$?

4. What is the slope of a line perpendicular to the graph of the line that is described by the equation $y = \dfrac{2}{3}x + 1$?

The concept of a *function* is one of the most important ideas in all of mathematics. To introduce this topic, we will begin with a table that might be seen on television or printed in a newspaper.

1 Define Relation, Domain, and Range.

The following table shows the number of women serving in the U.S. House of Representatives for several recent sessions of Congress.

Women in the U.S. House of Representatives							
Session of Congress	105th	106th	107th	108th	109th	110th	111th
Number of Women Representatives	54	56	59	59	68	71	78

Source: womenincongress.house.gov

We can display the data in the table as a set of ordered pairs, where the **first component** represents the session of Congress and the **second component** represents the number of women representatives serving during that session:

$$\{(105, 54), \quad (106, 56), \quad (107, 59), \quad (108, 59), \quad (109, 68), \quad (110, 71), \quad (111, 78)\}$$

Sets of ordered pairs like this are called **relations.** The set of all first components is called the **domain of the relation,** and the set of all second components is called the **range of the relation.** A relation may consist of a finite (countable) number of ordered pairs or an infinite (unlimited) number of ordered pairs.

EXAMPLE 1   Find the domain and range of the relation: $\{(3, 2), (5, -7), (-8, 2), (9, 0)\}$

Strategy   We will identify the first components and the second components of the ordered pairs.

Why   The set of all first components is the domain of the relation, and the set of all second components is the range.

Solution   The first components of the ordered pairs are highlighted in red, and the second components are highlighted in blue: $\{(\mathbf{3}, 2), (\mathbf{5}, -7), (-\mathbf{8}, 2), (\mathbf{9}, 0)\}$. When listing the elements of the domain and range, they are usually written in increasing order, and if a value is repeated, it is listed only once.

The domain of the relation is $\{-8, 3, 5, 9\}$ and the range of the relation is $\{-7, 0, 2\}$.

Self Check 1   Find the domain and range of the relation:
$$\{(5, 6), (-12, 4), (8, 6), (-6, -6), (5, 4)\}$$

Now Try ▶ Problem 19

2 Identify Functions.

The relation in Example 1 was defined by a set of ordered pairs. Relations also can be defined using an **arrow** or **mapping diagram**. The data from the U.S. House of Representatives example is presented on the right in that form. Relations are also often defined using **two-column tables.**

Notice that to each session of Congress, there corresponds exactly one number of women representatives. That is, to each member of the domain, there corresponds exactly one member of the range. Relations that have this characteristic are called *functions.*

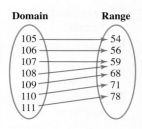

Function, Domain, Range	▼	A **function** is a set of ordered pairs (a relation) in which to each first component there corresponds exactly one second component. The set of first components is called the **domain of the function**, and the set of second components is called the **range of the function.**

Since we often will work with sets of ordered pairs of the form (x, y), it is helpful to define a function using the variables x and y.

y Is a Function of x	▼	Given a relation in x and y, if to each value of x in the domain there corresponds exactly one value of y in the range, then y is said to be a function of x.

In the previous definition, since y depends on x, we call x the **independent variable** and y the **dependent variable.** The set of all possible values that can be used for the independent variable is the **domain** of the function, and the set of all values of the dependent variable is the **range** of the function.

EXAMPLE 2   Determine whether the relation defines y to be a function of x.

a.

x	y
5	4
7	6
11	10

b.

x	y
8	2
1	4
8	3
9	9

c. $\{(-2, 3), (-1, 3), (0, 3), (1, 3)\}$

Strategy   We will determine whether there is more than one value of y that corresponds to a single value of x.

Why   If to any x-value there corresponds more than one y-value, then y is not a function of x.

Solution   **a.** The arrow diagram defines a function because to each value of x there corresponds exactly one value of y.

- 5→4   To the x-value 5, there corresponds exactly one y-value, 4.
- 7→6   To the x-value 7, there corresponds exactly one y-value, 6.
- 11→10   To the x-value 11, there corresponds exactly one y-value, 10.

b. The table does not define a function, because to the x-value 8 there corresponds more than one y-value.

- In the first row, to the x-value 8, there corresponds the y-value 2.
- In the third row, to the same x-value 8, there corresponds a different y-value, 3.

When the correspondence in the table is written as a set of ordered pairs, it is apparent that the relation does not define a function:

The same x-value

$\{(\mathbf{8}, 2), (1, 4), (\mathbf{8}, 3), (9, 9)\}$ This is not a function.

Different y-values

c. Since to each value of x, there corresponds exactly one value of y, the set of ordered pairs defines y to be a function of x.

- $(-2, 3)$ To the x-value -2, there corresponds exactly one y-value, 3.
- $(-1, 3)$ To the x-value -1, there corresponds exactly one y-value, 3.
- $(0, 3)$ To the x-value 0, there corresponds exactly one y-value, 3.
- $(1, 3)$ To the x-value 1, there corresponds exactly one y-value, 3.

In this case, the same y-value, 3, corresponds to each x-value.

The results from parts (b) and (c) illustrate an important fact: *Two different ordered pairs of a function can have the same y-value, but they cannot have the same x-value.*

Self Check 2   Determine whether the relation defines y to be a function of x.

a.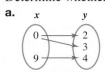

b.

x	y
-1	-60
0	55
3	0

c. $\{(4, -1), (9, 2), (16, 15), (4, 4)\}$
d. $\{(9,5), (10,5), (11,5), (12,5)\}$

Now Try ▶ Problems 23, 27, and 31

A function also can be defined by an equation. For example, $y = \frac{1}{2}x + 3$ sets up a rule in which to each value of x there corresponds exactly one value of y. To find the y-value (called an **output**) that corresponds to the x-value 4 (called an **input**), we substitute 4 for x and evaluate the right side of the equation.

$$y = \frac{1}{2}x + 3$$

$y = \frac{1}{2}(4) + 3$ Substitute 4 for x. The input is 4.

$y = 2 + 3$ Do the multiplication: $\frac{1}{2}(4) = 2$.

$y = 5$ Do the addition. This is the output.

For the function defined by $y = \frac{1}{2}x + 3$, a y-value of 5 corresponds to an x-value of 4.

Not all equations define functions, as we will see in the next example.

EXAMPLE 3   Determine whether each equation defines y to be a function of x.
a. $y = 2x - 5$ **b.** $y^2 = x$

Strategy   In each case, we will determine whether there is more than one value of y that corresponds to a single value of x.

Why   If to any x-value there corresponds more than one y-value, then y is not a function of x.

Solution   **a.** To find the output value y that corresponds to an input value x, we multiply x by 2 and subtract 5. Since this arithmetic gives one result, to each value of x there corresponds exactly one value of y. Thus, $y = 2x - 5$ defines y to be a function of x.

b. The equation $y^2 = x$ does not define y to be a function of x, because more than one value of y corresponds to a single value of x. For example, if x is 16, then the equation becomes $y^2 = 16$ and y can be either 4 or -4. This is because $4^2 = 16$ and $(-4)^2 = 16$.

x	y
16	4
16	-4

Self Check 3   Determine whether each equation defines y to be a function of x.

a. $y = -x + 1$ **b.** $\left| \dfrac{1}{2}y \right| = x$

Now Try ▶ Problems 35 and 39

---

3 Use Function Notation.

A special notation is used to name functions that are defined by equations.

Function Notation	The notation $y = f(x)$ indicates that y is a function of x.

If y is a function of x, the symbols y and $f(x)$ are interchangeable. In Example 3a, we saw that $y = 2x - 5$ defines y to be a function of x. To write this equation using function notation, we replace y with $f(x)$ to get $f(x) = 2x - 5$. This is read as "f of x is equal to $2x$ minus 5." In this notation, the parentheses do not indicate multiplication.

Caution

The symbol $f(x)$ denotes a function. It does not mean f times x.

This variable represents the input.
↓
$$f(x) = \underline{2x - 5}$$
This is the name of the function. ⎬ This expression shows how to obtain an output from a given input.

Function notation provides a compact way of representing the output value that corresponds to some input value. For example, if $f(x) = 2x - 5$, the value that corresponds to $x = 6$ is represented by $f(6)$.

$f(x) = 2x - 5$
$f(6) = 2(6) - 5$ Substitute 6 for each x. (The input is 6.)
$\quad\ \ = 12 - 5$ Do the multiplication.
$\quad\ \ = 7$ Do the subtraction. This is the output.

The Language of Algebra

Another way to read $f(6) = 7$ is to say "the value of f at 6 is 7."

Thus, $f(6) = 7$.

We read this result as "f of 6 equals 7." It means that when $x = 6$, $f(x)$ or y is 7. The output 7 is called a **function value**. The input, 6, and output, 7, also can be written as an ordered pair of the form $(6, 7)$.

To see why function notation is useful, we consider two sentences that ask you to do the same thing:

1. If $y = 2x - 5$, find the value of y when x is 6.
2. If $f(x) = 2x - 5$, find $f(6)$.

Statement 2, which uses $f(x)$ notation, is more compact.

The letter f used in the notation $f(x)$ represents the word *function*. However, other letters are often used to name functions. For example, in $g(x) = -5x + 15$, the name of the function is g and in $h(x) = x^3 - 7x + 9$, the name of the function is h.

Letters other than x can be used to represent the input of a function. Examples are $f(a) = 4a$, $g(t) = t^2 - 2t$, and $h(n) = -\dfrac{n^2 + 2}{2}$.

EXAMPLE 4   Let $f(x) = 4x + 3$ and $g(t) = t^2 - 2t$. Find: **a.** $f(3)$ **b.** $f(-1)$ **c.** $f(r + 1)$ **d.** $g(-2.4)$

Strategy   We will substitute 3, -1, and $r + 1$ for each x in $f(x) = 4x + 3$ and evaluate the right side. We will substitute -2.4 for each t in $g(t) = t^2 - 2t$ and evaluate the right side.

Why   Whatever appears within the parentheses in $f(\ )$ is to be substituted for each x in $f(x) = 4x + 3$. Whatever appears within the parentheses in $g(\ )$ is to be substituted for each t in $g(t) = t^2 - 2t$.

Solution   **a.** To find $f(3)$, we replace each x with 3.   **b.** To find $f(-1)$, we replace each x with -1:

$f(x) = 4x + 3$	$f(x) = 4x + 3$
$f(3) = 4(3) + 3$	$f(-1) = 4(-1) + 3$
$\quad = 12 + 3$	$\quad = -4 + 3$
$\quad = 15$	$\quad = -1$

Thus, $f(3) = 15$ and the corresponding ordered pair is $(3, 15)$.

Thus, $f(-1) = -1$ and the corresponding ordered pair is $(-1, -1)$.

> **Notation**
>
> Note how function notation and ordered pair notation are related:
> $$f(3) = 15$$
> $$\uparrow \qquad \uparrow$$
> $$x \qquad y$$
> $$\downarrow \qquad \downarrow$$
> $$(3, \quad 15)$$

c. To find $f(r + 1)$, we replace each x with $r + 1$:

$$f(x) = 4x + 3$$
$$f(r + 1) = 4(r + 1) + 3$$
$$= 4r + 4 + 3$$
$$= 4r + 7$$

d. To find $g(-2.4)$, we replace each t with -2.4:

$$g(t) = t^2 - 2t \qquad \text{Read as "g of t."}$$
$$g(-2.4) = (-2.4)^2 - 2(-2.4)$$
$$= 5.76 + 4.8$$
$$= 10.56$$

> **The Language of Algebra**
>
> In part (d), if we use $g(t) = t^2 - 2t$ or $g(x) = x^2 - 2x$ or $g(a) = a^2 - 2a$, the results are the same: $g(-2.4) = 10.56$. The independent variable is really just a place holder, and for this reason, the letter that is used is often referred to as a **dummy variable**.

Self Check 4   If $f(x) = -2x - 1$ and $h(n) = -\dfrac{n^2 + 2n}{2}$, find: **a.** $f(2)$ **b.** $f(-3)$ **c.** $f(-t)$ **d.** $h(-0.6)$

Now Try ▶   Problems 47, 67, and 71

In the next example, we are asked to find the input of a function when we are given the corresponding output.

EXAMPLE 5   Let $f(x) = 5x + 4$. For what value of x is $f(x) = -26$?

Strategy   We will substitute -26 for $f(x)$ and solve for x.

Why   In the equation, there are two unknowns, x and $f(x)$. If we replace $f(x)$ with -26, we can use our equation-solving skills to find x.

Solution

$$f(x) = 5x + 4 \qquad \text{This is the given function.}$$
$$-26 = 5x + 4 \qquad \text{Substitute } -26 \text{ for } f(x).$$
$$-30 = 5x \qquad \text{To isolate the variable term 5x, subtract 4 from both sides.}$$
$$-6 = x \qquad \text{To isolate x, divide both sides by 5.}$$

We have found that $f(x) = -26$ when $x = -6$. To check this result, we can substitute -6 for x and verify that $f(-6) = -26$.

$$f(x) = 5x + 4 \qquad \text{This is the given function.}$$
$$f(-6) = 5(-6) + 4 \qquad \text{Substitute } -6 \text{ for x.}$$
$$= -30 + 4 \qquad \text{Do the multiplication.}$$
$$= -26 \qquad \text{This is the desired output.}$$

Self Check 5   Let $f(x) = 7x + 200$. For what value of x is $f(x) = 11$?

Now Try ▶ Problem 75

4 Find the Domain of a Function.

We can think of a function as a machine that takes some input x and turns it into some output $f(x)$, as shown in figure (a). The machine shown in figure (b) turns the input -6 into the output -11. The set of numbers that we put into the machine is the domain of the function, and the set of numbers that comes out is the range.

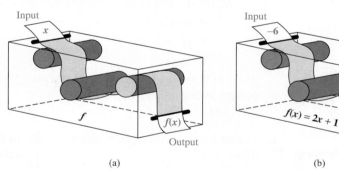

(a)   (b)

Success Tip

To find the domain of a function defined by an equation, we must identify all the values of the input variable that produce a real-number output.

EXAMPLE 6   Find the domain of each function: **a.** $f(x) = 3x + 1$ **b.** $f(x) = \dfrac{x}{3x - 6}$

Strategy   We will ask, "What values of x are permissible replacements for x in $3x + 1$ and $\dfrac{x}{3x - 6}$?"

Why   These values of x form the domain of the function.

Solution   **a.** We will be able to evaluate $3x + 1$ for any value of x that is a real number. Thus, the domain of the function is *the set of real numbers,* which can be represented by the symbol $\mathbb{R}$.

The Language of Algebra

The last two letters in the word *domain* help us remember that it is the set of all *inputs* of a function.

b. Since division by 0 is undefined, we will not be able to evaluate $\dfrac{x}{3x - 6}$ for any number x that makes the denominator equal to 0. To find such x-values, we set the denominator equal to 0 and solve for x.

$$3x - 6 = 0$$
$$3x = 6 \qquad \text{To isolate the variable term 3x, add 6 to both sides.}$$
$$x = 2 \qquad \text{To isolate the variable, divide both sides by 3.}$$

Success Tip

Notice that to determine the domain of $f(x) = \dfrac{x}{3x - 6}$, we don't have to examine the numerator. It can be any value, including 0.

We have found that 2 must be excluded from the domain of the function because it makes the denominator 0. However, all other real numbers are permissible replacements for x. Thus, the domain of the function *is the set of all real numbers except* 2.

> **Self Check 6** Find the domain of each function: **a.** $f(x) = 2x - 6$
>
> **b.** $f(x) = \dfrac{2}{-4x - 12}$
>
> **Now Try ▶** Problem 79

5 Graph Linear Functions.

In this course, we will study several important "families" of functions. We will begin here with the most basic family, *linear functions*.

Linear Functions	A **linear function** is a function that can be defined by an equation of the form $f(x) = mx + b$, where m and b are real numbers. The graph of a linear function is a straight line with slope m and y-intercept $(0, b)$.

Some examples of linear functions are:

$$f(x) = \frac{1}{2}x + 3, \qquad f(x) = -6x - 10, \qquad \text{and} \qquad f(x) = x$$

The input-output pairs that a linear function such as $f(x) = \frac{1}{2}x + 3$ generates can be plotted on a rectangular coordinate system to get the **graph of the function.** Since the symbols y and $f(x)$ are interchangeable, we can graph $f(x) = \frac{1}{2}x + 3$ as we would $y = \frac{1}{2}x + 3$, using the methods of Sections 3.2, 3.3, and 3.5.

To use the **point-plotting method** to graph $f(x) = \frac{1}{2}x + 3$, we begin by constructing a table of function values. To make the table, we select several values for x, and find the corresponding values of $f(x)$. Then we plot the ordered pairs and draw a straight line through the points to get the graph of the function, as shown on the next page.

To use the **slope–intercept method** to graph $f(x) = \frac{1}{2}x + 3$, we begin by identifying m and b in the equation. Then we plot the y-intercept and use the slope to determine a second point on the line. Finally, we draw a line through the points to obtain a graph like that shown on the next page.

$$f(x) = \frac{1}{2}x + 3$$

Slope ⎯⏐   ⎿⎯ y-intercept: (0, 3)

To use the **intercept method** to graph $f(x) = \frac{1}{2}x + 3$, we begin by identifying b in the equation to determine the y-intercept. Then we let y, which in this case is $f(x)$, equal 0 and solve for x to find the x-intercept.

Find the y-intercept: Identify b	*Find the x-intercept: Let $f(x) = 0$*
$f(x) = \dfrac{1}{2}x + 3$ ↑ The y-intercept is (0, 3).	$f(x) = \dfrac{1}{2}x + 3$ $0 = \dfrac{1}{2}x + 3$ $-3 = \dfrac{1}{2}x$ $-6 = x$ The x-intercept is $(-6, 0)$.

When we plot the intercepts $(0, 3)$ and $(-6, 0)$ and draw a straight line through them, we obtain a graph like that on the next page.

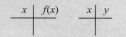
$f(x) = \frac{1}{2}x + 3$

x	$f(x)$
-2	2	$\longrightarrow$ $(-2, 2)$
0	3	$\longrightarrow$ $(0, 3)$
2	4	$\longrightarrow$ $(2, 4)$

$\uparrow$ $\uparrow$ $\uparrow$
Select x.   Find f(x).   Plot.

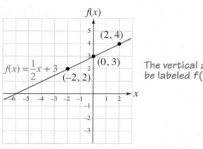

The vertical axis can be labeled f(x) or y.

The most basic linear function is $f(x) = x$. It is called the **identity function** because it assigns each real number to itself. The graph of the identity function is a line with slope 1 and y-intercept $(0, 0)$, as shown below in figure (a).

A linear function defined by $f(x) = b$ is called a **constant function,** because for any input x, the output is the constant b. The graph of a constant function is a horizontal line. The graph of $f(x) = 2$ is shown below in figure (b).

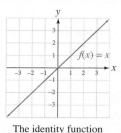

The identity function

(a)

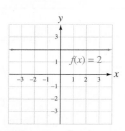

A constant function

(b)

6 Write Equations of Linear Functions.

The slope–intercept and point–slope forms for the equation of a line that we studied in Sections 3.5 and 3.6 can be adapted to write equations of linear functions.

EXAMPLE 7

a. Write an equation for the linear function whose graph has slope $-\dfrac{3}{4}$ and y-intercept $(0, 2)$.

b. Write an equation for the linear function whose graph passes through $(6, 4)$ with slope 5.

c. Write an equation for the linear function whose graph passes through $(-16, -12)$ and is perpendicular to the graph of $g(x) = -8x - 1$.

Strategy We will use either the slope–intercept or point–slope form to write each equation.

Why Writing equations of linear functions is similar to writing equations of linear equations in two variables, except that we replace y with $f(x)$.

Solution

a. If the slope is $-\frac{3}{4}$ and the y-intercept is $(0, 2)$, then $m = -\frac{3}{4}$ and $b = 2$.

$$f(x) = mx + b \qquad \text{This is the slope–intercept form in which y is replaced with f(x).}$$

$$f(x) = -\frac{3}{4}x + 2 \qquad \text{Substitute } -\tfrac{3}{4} \text{ for m and 2 for b.}$$

b. If the slope is 5 and the graph passes through $(6, 4)$, then $m = 5$ and $(x_1, y_1) = (6, 4)$.

$$f(x) - y_1 = m(x - x_1) \qquad \text{This is the point–slope form in which y is replaced with f(x).}$$
$$f(x) - 4 = 5(x - 6) \qquad \text{Substitute 4 for } y_1, \text{ 5 for m, and 6 for } x_1.$$
$$f(x) - 4 = 5x - 30 \qquad \text{Distribute the multiplication by 5.}$$
$$f(x) = 5x - 26 \qquad \text{To isolate f(x), add 4 to both sides.}$$

c. The slope of the line represented by $g(x) = -8x - 1$ is the coefficient of x: -8. Since the desired function is to have a graph that is perpendicular to the graph of $g(x) = -8x - 1$, its slope must be the negative reciprocal of -8, which is $\frac{1}{8}$.

$$f(x) - y_1 = m(x - x_1)$$ This is the point-slope form in which y is replaced with f(x).

$$f(x) - (-12) = \frac{1}{8}[x - (-16)]$$ Substitute −12 for y_1, $\frac{1}{8}$ for m, and −16 for x_1.

$$f(x) + 12 = \frac{1}{8}(x + 16)$$ Simplify each side.

$$f(x) + 12 = \frac{1}{8}x + 2$$ Distribute the multiplication by $\frac{1}{8}$: $\frac{1}{8} \cdot 16 = 2$.

$$f(x) = \frac{1}{8}x - 10$$ To isolate f(x), subtract 12 from both sides.

Self Check 7   **a.** Write an equation for the linear function whose graph has slope $-\frac{1}{5}$ and y-intercept $(0, 9)$.   **b.** Write an equation for the linear function whose graph passes through $(7, 1)$ with slope 2.   **c.** Write an equation for the linear function whose graph passes through $(-20, -4)$ and is perpendicular to the graph of $g(x) = -10x$.

Now Try ▶ Problems 95, 97, and 103

EXAMPLE 8

The Language of Algebra

The phrase **constant rate** indicates that a linear function should be used to model the situation.

Alzheimer's Disease. The graph on the right is from a recent Alzheimer's Association report. It shows how the number of people in the United States with Alzheimer's disease is expected to increase steadily at a constant rate. The report estimated there were 4,800,000 people with Alzheimer's in 2005 and 5,100,000 with the disease in 2010. (Source: Medill Reports)

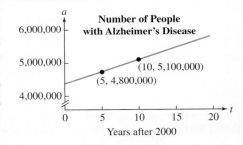

a. Write the linear function that models this situation. **b.** Use the function to estimate the number of people who will have Alzheimer's disease in 2025, assuming the trend continues.

Strategy We will use the point–slope form to write a linear function.

Why We are given two points that lie on the graph of the function.

Solution Let a represent the approximate number of people in the U.S. with Alzheimer's disease and t represent the number of years after 2000. Two ordered pairs of the form (t, a) that lie on the graph of the function are:

- $(5, 4,800,000)$ Since the year 2005 is 5 years after 2000, t = 5.
- $(10, 5,100,00)$ Since the year 2010 is 10 years after 2000, t = 10.

Since we know two points that lie on the graph, we can write its equation. First, we find the slope of the line. If we write the slope formula using the variables t and a, and let $(t_1, a_1) = (5, 4,800,000)$ and $(t_2, a_2) = (10, 5,100,000)$, we have:

$$m = \frac{a_2 - a_1}{t_2 - t_1} = \frac{5,100,000 - 4,800,000}{10 - 5} = \frac{300,000}{5} = 60,000$$

The result indicates the number of people with Alzheimer's disease will increase at a rate of 60,000 per year.

a. To find the linear function, we substitute 60,000 for m, 5 for t_1, and 4,800,000 for a_1 in the point–slope form and simplify.

$$a(t) - a_1 = m(t - t_1)$$ This is the point–slope form using the variable t and replacing a with $a(t)$.

$$a(t) - 4{,}800{,}000 = 60{,}000(t - 5)$$ Substitute for m, t_1, and a_1.

$$a(t) - 4{,}800{,}000 = 60{,}000t - 300{,}000$$ Distribute the multiplication by 60,000.

$$a(t) = 60{,}000t + 4{,}500{,}000$$ To isolate $a(t)$, add 4,800,000 to both sides.

The approximate number of people with Alzheimer's disease t years after 2000 is given by $a(t) = 60{,}000t + 4{,}500{,}000$.

b. To estimate the number of people who will have Alzheimer's disease in 2025, which is 25 years after 2000, we find $a(25)$.

$$a(t) = 60{,}000t + 4{,}500{,}000$$ This is the linear function model.

$$a(25) = 60{,}000(25) + 4{,}500{,}000$$ Substitute 25 for t.

$$= 1{,}500{,}000 + 4{,}500{,}000$$ Do the multiplication.

$$= 6{,}000{,}000$$ Do the addition.

In 2025, there will be approximately 6,000,000 people in the U.S. with Alzheimer's disease.

Self Check 8   **Energy.** The world's annual energy consumption can be modeled by a linear function. In 2004, the world consumed about 430 quadrillion Btu. By the year 2006, that number had increased to about 446 quadrillion Btu. (Source: Energy Information Administration)
a. Let t be the number of years after 2000 and E be the amount of energy (in quadrillion Btu). Write a linear function $E(t)$ to model the situation.   **b.** Predict the world's energy consumption in 2030, if the trend continues.

Now Try ▶ Problem 111

Using Your Calculator ▶ Evaluating Functions

We can use a graphing calculator to find function values. For example, suppose the linear function $f(c) = 12c - 18$ gives the daily income earned by a cosmetologist from serving c customers.

To find the income she earns for different numbers of customers, we first graph the income function $f(c) = 12c - 18$ as $y = 12x - 18$, using window settings of $[0, 10]$ for x and $[0, 100]$ for y to obtain figure (a). To find her income when she serves seven customers, we trace and move the cursor until the x-coordinate on the screen is nearly 7, as in figure (b). From the screen, we see that her income is about $66.26.

To find her income when she serves nine customers, we trace and move the cursor until the x-coordinate is nearly 9, as in figure (c). From the screen, we see that her income is about $90.51.

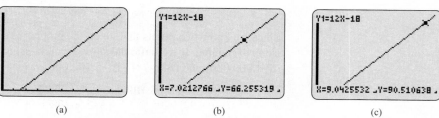

(a)   (b)   (c)

With some graphing calculator models, we can evaluate a function by entering function notation. To find $f(15)$, the income earned by the cosmetologist if she serves 15 customers, we use the following steps on a TI-84 Plus calculator.

With $f(c) = 12c - 18$ entered as $Y_1 = 12x - 18$, we call up the home screen by pressing 2nd QUIT . Then we enter VARS ▶ 1 ENTER . The symbolism Y_1 will be displayed. See figure (a). Next, we enter the input value 15 within parentheses, as shown in figure (b), and press ENTER . In figure (c) we see that $Y_1(15) = 162$. That is, $f(15) = 162$. The cosmetologist will earn \$162 if she serves 15 customers in one day.

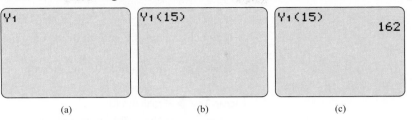

(a)	(b)	(c)

7 Evaluate Polynomial Functions.

We have seen that linear functions are defined by equations of the form $f(x) = mx + b$. Some examples of linear functions are

$$f(x) = 8x - 10, \qquad g(x) = -\frac{1}{2}x + 1, \qquad \text{and} \qquad h(x) = 5x$$

In each case, the right side of the equation is a polynomial. For this reason, linear functions are members of a larger class of functions known as *polynomial functions*.

Polynomial Functions	▼ A **polynomial function** is a function whose equation is defined by a polynomial in one variable.

Another example of a polynomial function is $f(x) = x^2 + 6x - 8$. This is a second-degree polynomial function, called a **quadratic function.** Quadratic functions are of the form $f(x) = ax^2 + bx + c$, where $a \neq 0$.

An example of a third-degree polynomial function is $f(x) = x^3 - 3x^2 - 9x + 2$. Third-degree polynomial functions, also called **cubic functions,** are of the form $f(x) = ax^3 + bx^2 + cx + d$, where $a \neq 0$.

Success Tip

Recall that a polynomial is a single term or the sum of terms in which all variables have whole-number exponents. No variable appears in the denominator.

Polynomial functions can be used to model many real-life situations. If we are given a polynomial function model, we can learn more about the situation by evaluating the function at specific values. To **evaluate a polynomial function** at a specific value, we replace the variable in the defining equation with that value, called the *input*. Then we simplify the resulting expression to find the *output*.

EXAMPLE 9

Packaging.   To make boxes, a manufacturer cuts equal-sized squares from each corner of 10 in. × 12 in. pieces of cardboard and then folds up the sides. The polynomial function $f(x) = 4x^3 - 44x^2 + 120x$ gives the volume (in cubic inches) of the resulting box when a square with sides x inches long is cut from each corner. Find the volume of a box if 3-inch squares are cut out.

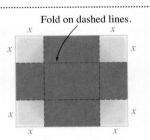

Fold on dashed lines.

Strategy   We will find $f(3)$.

Why   The notation $f(3)$ represents the volume of the box when 3-inch squares are cut out of the corners of the piece of cardboard.

Solution

$$f(x) = 4x^3 - 44x^2 + 120x \qquad \text{This is the given function.}$$

$$f(3) = 4(3)^3 - 44(3)^2 + 120(3) \qquad \text{Substitute 3 for each } x. \text{ (The input is 3.)}$$

$$= 4(27) - 44(9) + 120(3) \qquad \text{Evaluate the exponential expressions.}$$

$$= 108 - 396 + 360 \qquad \text{Do the multiplication.}$$

$$= 72 \qquad \text{The output is 72.}$$

If 3-inch squares are cut out of the corners, the resulting box has a volume of 72 in.³.

Self Check 9 In Example 9, find the volume of a box if 2-inch squares are cut out.

Now Try ▶ **Problem 119**

SECTION 8.2 ▶ STUDY SET

VOCABULARY

Fill in the blanks.

1. A set of ordered pairs is called a _____. The set of all first components of the ordered pairs is called the _____ and the set of all second components is called the _____.

2. A _____ is a set of ordered pairs (a relation) in which to each first component there corresponds exactly one second component.

3. Given a relation in x and y, if to each value of x in the domain there corresponds exactly one value of y in the range, y is said to be a _____ of x. We call x the independent _____ and y the _____ variable.

4. For a function, the set of all possible values that can be used for the independent variable is called the _____. The set of all values of the dependent variable is called the _____.

5. A _____ function is a function that can be defined by an equation of the form $f(x) = mx + b$. A polynomial function is a function whose equation is defined by a polynomial in _____ variable.

6. We call $f(x) = x$ the _____ function because it assigns each real number to itself. We call $f(x) = 2$ a _____ function, because for any input x, the output is always 2.

CONCEPTS

7. **U.S. Recycling.** The following table gives the approximate number of aluminum cans (in billions) collected each year for the years 2000–2006.

   a. Display the data in the table as a relation, that is, as a set of ordered pairs.

   b. Find the domain and range of the relation.

   c. Use an arrow diagram to show how members of the range correspond to members of the domain.

Year	2000	2001	2002	2003	2004	2005	2006
Billions of aluminum cans	63	56	54	50	52	51	51

Source: Aluminum Association of America, U.S. Dept. of Commerce

8. For the given input, what value will the function machine output?

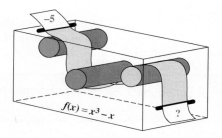

9. Explain why -4 is not in the domain of $f(x) = \dfrac{1}{x + 4}$.

10. Consider the linear function $y = -\dfrac{4}{5}x + 3$.
    a. What is the slope of its graph?
    b. What is the y-intercept of its graph?

11. Consider the linear function $f(x) = -6x - 4$.
    a. What is the y-intercept of its graph?
    b. What is the x-intercept of its graph?

12. The graphing calculator display shows a table of values for a function f. Fill in the blanks:

    $$f(-1) = \boxed{} \qquad f(3) = \boxed{}$$

X	Y₁
-2	10
-1	1
0	-4
1	-5
2	-2
3	5
4	16
X=-2	

NOTATION

Fill in the blanks.

13. a. We read $f(x) = 5x - 6$ as "f __ x is equal to $5x$ minus 6."
    b. We read $g(t) = t + 9$ as "g __ t is equal to t plus 9."

14. This variable represents the ____.

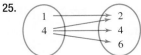

$$f(x) = 2x - 5$$

This is the ____ of the function. Use this expression to find the ____.

15. Fill in the blank so that the following statements are equivalent:
- If $y = 5x + 1$, find the value of y when $x = 8$.
- If $f(x) = 5x + 1$, find ____.

16. If $f(2) = 7$, the input 2 and the output 7 can be written as the ordered pair (,).

17. When graphing $f(x) = -x + 5$, the vertical axis of the rectangular coordinate system can be labeled ____ or ____.

18. To write the slope–intercept form $y = mx + b$ and the point–slope form $y - y_1 = m(x - x_1)$ using function notation, we simply replace y with ____.

GUIDED PRACTICE

Find the domain and range of each relation. See Example 1.

19. $\{(7, -1), (-1, -11), (-5, 3), (8, -6)\}$

20. $\{(15, -3), (0, 0), (4, 6), (-3, -8)\}$

21. $\{(0, 1), (-23, 35), (7, 1)\}$

22. $\{(1, -12), (-6, 8), (5, 8), (0, 0), (1, 4)\}$

Determine whether the relation defines y to be a function of x. If it does not, find two ordered pairs where more than one value of y corresponds to a single value of x. See Example 2.

23.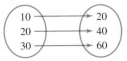

24.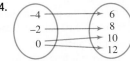

25.

26.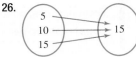

27. $\{(3, 4), (3, -4), (4, 3), (4, -3)\}$

28. $\{(-1, 1), (-3, 1), (-5, 1), (-7, 1), (-9, 1)\}$

29. $\{(-2, 7), (-1, 10), (0, 13), (1, 16)\}$

30. $\{(-2, 4), (-3, 8), (-3, 12), (-4, 16)\}$

31.

x	y
1	7
2	15
3	23
4	16
5	8

32.

x	y
30	2
30	4
30	6
30	8
30	10

33.

x	y
-4	6
-1	0
0	-3
2	4
-1	2

34.

x	y
1	1
2	1
3	1
4	1

Determine whether each equation defines y to be a function of x. If it does not, find two ordered pairs where more than one value of y corresponds to a single value of x. See Example 3.

35. $y = 2x + 3$

36. $y = 4x - 1$

37. $y = 4x^2$

38. $y^2 = x$

39. $y^4 = x$

40. $y = \dfrac{1}{x}$

41. $xy = 9$

42. $y = |x|$

43. $y = \dfrac{1}{x^2}$

44. $x + 1 = |y|$

45. $x = |y|$

46. $xy = -4$

Find f(3) and f(-1). See Example 4.

47. $f(x) = 3x$

48. $f(x) = -4x$

49. $f(x) = 2x - 3$

50. $f(x) = 3x - 5$

Find g(2) and g(3). See Example 4.

51. $g(x) = x^2 - 10$

52. $g(x) = x^2 - 2$

53. $g(x) = -x^3 + x$

54. $g(x) = x^3 - x$

55. $g(x) = (x + 1)^2$

56. $g(x) = (x - 3)^2$

57. $g(x) = 2x^2 - x + 1$

58. $g(x) = 5x^2 + 2x + 2$

Find h(5) and h(-2). See Example 4.

59. $h(x) = |x| + 2$

60. $h(x) = |x| - 5$

61. $h(x) = \dfrac{1}{x + 3}$

62. $h(x) = \dfrac{3}{x - 4}$

63. $h(x) = \dfrac{x}{x - 3}$

64. $h(x) = \dfrac{x}{x^2 + 2}$

65. $h(x) = \dfrac{x^2 + 2x - 35}{x^2 + 5x + 6}$

66. $h(x) = \dfrac{x^2 + x - 2}{x^2 - 5x}$

Complete each table. See Example 4.

67. $f(t) = |t - 2|$

t	f(t)
-1.7	
0.9	
5.4	

68. $f(r) = -2r^2 + 1$

Input	Output
-1.7	
0.9	
5.4	

69. $g(a) = a^3$

Input	Output
$-\frac{3}{4}$	
$\frac{1}{6}$	
$\frac{5}{2}$	

70. $g(b) = 2\left(-b - \frac{1}{4}\right)$

b	g(b)
$-\frac{3}{4}$	
$\frac{1}{6}$	
$\frac{5}{2}$	

Find g(w) and g(w + 1). **See Example 4.**

71. $g(x) = 2x$

72. $g(x) = -3x$

73. $g(x) = 3x - 5$

74. $g(x) = 2x - 7$

Let f(x) = −2x + 5. For what value of x does function f have the given value? **See Example 5.**

75. $f(x) = 5$

76. $f(x) = -7$

Let f(x) = $\frac{3}{2}$x − 2. For what value of x does function f have the given value? **See Example 5.**

77. $f(x) = -\frac{1}{2}$

78. $f(x) = \frac{2}{3}$

Find the domain of each function. **See Example 6.**

79. **a.** $h(x) = 3x + 6$

 b. $f(x) = \frac{1}{x - 4}$

80. **a.** $g(x) = |x - 7|$

 b. $f(x) = \frac{5}{x + 1}$

81. **a.** $f(x) = x^2$

 b. $s(x) = \frac{9}{2x + 1}$

82. **a.** $h(x) = x^3$

 b. $t(x) = \frac{15}{1 - 3x}$

Graph each function. **See Objective 5.**

83. $f(x) = 2x - 1$

84. $f(x) = -x + 2$

85. $f(x) = -\frac{3}{2}x - 3$

86. $f(x) = \frac{2}{3}x - 2$

87. $f(x) = x$

88. $f(x) = -x$

89. $f(x) = -4$

90. $f(x) = 2$

91. $g(x) = 0.75x$

92. $g(x) = -0.25x$

93. $s(x) = \frac{7}{8}x + 2$

94. $s(x) = -\frac{4}{5}x + 3$

Write an equation for a linear function whose graph has the given characteristics. **See Example 7.**

95. Slope 5, *y*-intercept $(0, -3)$

96. Slope 2, *y*-intercept $(0, 11)$

97. Slope $\frac{1}{5}$, passes through $(10, 1)$

98. Slope $\frac{1}{4}$, passes through $(8, 1)$

99. Passes through $(1, 7)$ and $(-2, 1)$

100. Passes through $(-2, 2)$ and $(2, -8)$

101. Passes through $(3, 0)$, parallel to the graph of $g(x) = -\frac{2}{3}x - 4$

102. Passes through $(2, 20)$, parallel to the graph of $g(x) = 8x + 1$

103. Passes through $(1, 2)$, perpendicular to the graph of $g(x) = -\frac{x}{6} + 1$

104. Passes through $(54, 0)$, perpendicular to the graph of $g(x) = 9x + 5$

105. Horizontal, passes through $(-8, 12)$

106. Horizontal, passes through $(9, -32)$

APPLICATIONS

107. from **Campus to Careers**

Webmaster

According to data from *Netcraft Web Server Survey,* the total number of active websites available over the Internet (in millions) is approximated by the function $w(t) = 12.67t + 29.15$, where *t* is the number of years after 2005. Approximately how many active websites were there in 2011?

108. Decongestants. The temperature in degrees Celsius that is equivalent to a temperature in degrees Fahrenheit is given by the linear function $C(F) = \frac{5}{9}(F - 32)$. Refer to the label from a bottle of decongestant shown below. Use this function to find the low and high temperature extremes, in degrees Celsius, in which the bottle should be stored.

DIRECTIONS: Adults and children 12 years of age and over: Two teaspoons every 4 hours. DO NOT EXCEED 6 DOSES IN A 24-HOUR PERIOD. Store at a controlled room temperature between 68°F and 77°F.

109. Concessionaires. A baseball club pays a vendor $125 per game for selling bags of peanuts for $4.75 each.

 a. Write a linear function that describes the profit the vendor makes for the baseball club during a game if she sells *b* bags of peanuts.

 b. Find the profit the baseball club will make if the vendor sells 110 bags of peanuts during a game.

110. Home Construction. In a proposal to some clients, a housing contractor listed the following costs:

Fees, permits, miscellaneous	$12,000
Construction, per square foot	$95

 a. Write a linear function that the clients could use to determine the cost of building a home having *f* square feet.

 b. Find the cost to build a home having 1,950 square feet.

111. Nurses. The demand for full-time registered nurses in the United States can be modeled by a linear function. In 2005, approximately 2,175,500 nurses were needed. By the year 2015, that number is expected to increase to about 2,586,500. (Source: National Center for Health Workforce Analysis)

 a. Let *t* be the number of years after 2000 and *N* be the number of full-time registered nurses needed in the U.S. Write a linear function $N(t)$ to model the demand for nurses.

 b. Use your answer to part a to predict the number of full-time registered nurses that will be needed in 2025, if the trend continues.

112. Wood Production. The total world wood production can be modeled by a linear function. In 1960, approximately 2,400 million cubic feet of wood were produced. Since then, the amount of increase has been approximately 25.5 million cubic feet per year. (Source: Earth Policy Institute)

a. Let t be the number of years after 1960 and W be the number of million cubic feet of wood produced. Write a linear function $W(t)$ to model the production of wood.

b. Use your answer to part a to estimate how many million cubic feet of wood the world produced in 2010.

113. Breathing Capacity. When fitness instructors prescribe exercise workouts for elderly patients, they must take into account age-related loss of lung function. Studies show that the percent of remaining breathing capacity for someone over 30 years old can be modeled by a linear function. (Source: alsearsmd.com)

a. At 35 years of age, approximately 90% of maximal breathing capacity remains and at 55 years of age, approximately 66% of maximal breathing capacity remains. Let a be the age of a patient and L be the percent of her maximal breathing capacity that remains. Write a linear function $L(a)$ to model this situation.

b. Use your answer to part a to estimate the percent of maximal breathing capacity that remains in an 80-year-old.

114. Chemical Reactions. When students mixed solutions of acetone and chloroform, they found that heat was generated. However, as time passed, the mixture cooled down. The graph shows data points of the form (time, temperature) taken by the students.

a. The linear function $T(t) = -\frac{t}{240} + 30$ models the relationship between the elapsed time t since the solutions were combined and the temperature $T(t)$ of the mixture. Graph the function.

b. Predict the temperature of the mixture immediately after the two solutions are combined.

c. Is $T(180)$ more or less than the temperature recorded by the students for $t = 300$?

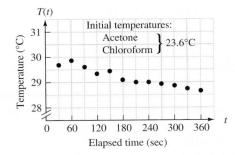

115. Taxes. The function

$$T(a) = 837.50 + 0.15(a - 8,375)$$

(where a is adjusted gross income) is a model of the instructions given on the first line of the following tax rate Schedule X.

a. Find $T(25,000)$ and interpret the result.

b. Write a function that models the second line on Schedule X.

Schedule X–Use if your filing status is **Single**	2010		
If your adjusted gross income is: *Over —*	*But not over —*	Your tax is	of the amount over —
$ 8,375	$34,000	$ 837.50 + 15%	$ 8,375
$34,000	$82,400	$4,681.25 + 25%	$34,000

116. Storage Tanks. The volume $V(r)$ of the gasoline storage tank, in cubic feet, is given by the polynomial function $V(r) = 4.2r^3 + 37.7r^2$, where r is the radius in

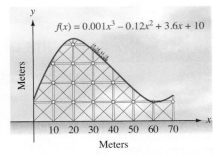

feet of the cylindrical part of the tank. What is the capacity of the tank if its radius is 4 feet?

117. Roller Coasters. The polynomial function $f(x) = 0.001x^3 - 0.12x^2 + 3.6x + 10$ models the path of a portion of the track of a roller coaster. Use the function equation to find the height of the track for $x = 0, 20, 40,$ and 60.

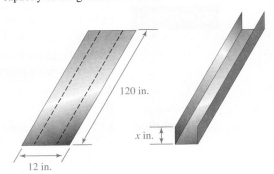

118. Customer Service. A software service hotline has found that on Mondays, the polynomial function $C(t) = -0.0625t^4 + t^3 - 6t^2 + 16t$ approximates the number of callers to the hotline at any one time. Here, t represents the time, in hours, since the hotline opened at 8:00 A.M. How many service technicians should be on duty on Mondays at noon if the company doesn't want any callers to the hotline waiting to be helped by a technician?

119. Rain Gutters. A rectangular sheet of metal will be used to make a rain gutter by bending up its sides, as shown. If the ends are covered, the capacity $f(x)$ of the gutter is a polynomial function of x: $f(x) = -240x^2 + 1,440x$. Find the capacity of the gutter if x is 3 inches.

120. Stopping Distances. The number of feet that a car travels before stopping depends on the driver's reaction time and the braking distance. For one driver, the stopping distance $d(v)$, in feet, is given by the polynomial function $d(v) = 0.04v^2 + 0.9v$, where v is the velocity of the car in mph. Find the stopping distance at 60 mph.

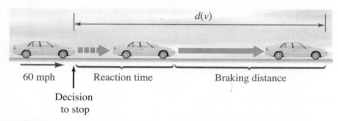

60 mph | Reaction time | Braking distance
Decision to stop

WRITING

121. Explain why 8 is not in the domain of the function $f(x) = \dfrac{5x - 7}{x - 8}$.

122. Explain why we can think of a function as a machine.

123. Consider the function defined by $y = 6x + 4$. Why do you think x is called the *independent* variable and y the *dependent* variable?

124. A website selling nutritional supplements contains the following sentence: "Health is a *function* of proper nutrition." Explain what this statement means.

REVIEW

Solve each equation. If the equation is an identity or a contradiction, so indicate.

125. $-2(t + 4) + 5t + 1 = 3(t - 4) + 7$

126. $\dfrac{3}{2}(a - 4) = 2(a - 3) - \dfrac{a}{2}$

CHALLENGE PROBLEMS

127. Let $f(x) = 4x + 6$, function g be defined by $\{(4, 6), (6, 8), (8, 4)\}$, and function h be defined by the arrow diagram below. Find $\dfrac{f(8) + g(8)}{h(8)}$.

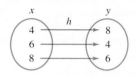

128. Find the domain of $f(x) = \dfrac{1}{5[9(x - 2) - 6(x - 3) + 3]}$.

SECTION 8.3

Graphs of Functions

OBJECTIVES

1. Find function values graphically.

2. Find the domain and range of a function graphically.

3. Graph nonlinear functions.

4. Translate graphs of functions.

5. Reflect graphs of functions.

6. Find function values and the domain and range of polynomial functions graphically.

7. Use the vertical line test.

ARE YOU READY?

The following problems review some basic skills that are needed when graphing functions.

1. Fill in the blanks: $f(3) = 9$ corresponds to the ordered pair (⬚ , ⬚).
2. If $f(x) = x^2$, find $f(-1)$ and $f(1)$.
3. If $f(x) = x^3$, find $f(-2)$ and $f(2)$.
4. If $f(x) = |x|$, find $f(-4)$ and $f(4)$.

Since a graph is often the best way to describe a function, we need to know how to construct and interpret their graphs.

1 Find Function Values Graphically.

From the graph of a function, we can determine function values. In general, the value of $f(a)$ is given by the y-coordinate of a point on the graph of function f with x-coordinate a.

EXAMPLE 1 Refer to the graph of function f in figure (a) on the next page.
a. Find $f(-3)$ **b.** Find the value of x for which $f(x) = -2$.

Strategy In each case, we will use the information provided by the function notation to locate a specific point on the graph and determine its x- and y-coordinates.

Why Once we locate the specific point, one of its coordinates will equal the value that we are asked to find.

Solution **a.** To find $f(-3)$, we need to find the y-coordinate of the point on the graph of f whose x-coordinate is -3. If we draw a vertical line through -3 on the x-axis, as shown in figure (b), the line intersects the graph of f at $(-3, 5)$. Therefore, 5 corresponds to -3, and it follows that $f(-3) = 5$.

b. To find the input value x that has an output value $f(x) = -2$, we draw a horizontal line through -2 on the y-axis, as shown in figure (c) and note that it intersects the graph of f at $(4, -2)$. Since -2 corresponds to 4, it follows that $f(x) = -2$ if $x = 4$.

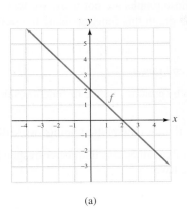

(a)

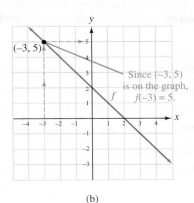

(b)

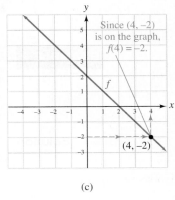

(c)

Self Check 1   Refer to the graph of function g on the right.
a. Find $g(-3)$.   **b.** Find the x-value for which $g(x) = 2$.

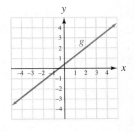

Now Try ▶ Problem 17

---

2 Find the Domain and Range of a Function Graphically.

We can find the domain and range of a function from its graph. For example, to find the domain of the linear function graphed in figure (a), we *project* the graph onto the x-axis. Because the graph of the function extends indefinitely to the left and to the right, the projection includes all the real numbers. Therefore, the domain of the function is the set of real numbers.

   To find the range of the same linear function, we project the graph onto the y-axis, as shown in figure (b). Because the graph of the function extends indefinitely upward and downward, the projection includes all the real numbers. Therefore, the range of the function is the set of real numbers.

The Language of Algebra

Think of the **projection** of a graph on an axis as the "shadow" that the graph makes on the axis.

Project the graph onto the x-axis.

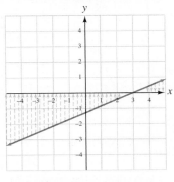

Domain: all real numbers

(a)

Project the graph onto the y-axis.

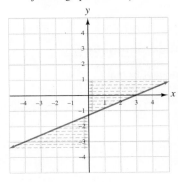

Range: all real numbers

(b)

3 Graph Nonlinear Functions.

We have seen that the graph of a linear function is a line. We will now consider several examples of **nonlinear functions** whose graphs are not lines. We will begin with $f(x) = x^2$, called the **squaring function.** We can graph this function using the **point-plotting method.**

EXAMPLE 2   Graph $f(x) = x^2$ and find its domain and range.

Strategy   We will graph the function by creating a table of function values and plotting the corresponding ordered pairs.

Why   After drawing a smooth curve through the plotted points, we will have the graph.

Solution   To graph the function, we select several x-values and find the corresponding values of $f(x)$. For example, if we select -3 for x, we have

$$f(x) = x^2 \qquad \text{This is the function to graph.}$$
$$f(-3) = (-3)^2 \qquad \text{Substitute } -3 \text{ for each } x.$$
$$= 9$$

Since $f(-3) = 9$, the ordered pair $(-3, 9)$ lies on the graph of f. In a similar manner, we find the corresponding values of $f(x)$ for six other x-values and list the ordered pairs in the table of values. Then we plot the points and draw a smooth curve through them to get the graph, called a **parabola.**

The Language of Algebra

The cuplike shape of a **parabola** has many real-life applications. For example, a satellite TV dish is called a **parabolic** dish.

$$f(x) = x^2$$

x	$f(x)$	
-3	9	$\longrightarrow (-3, 9)$
-2	4	$\longrightarrow (-2, 4)$
-1	1	$\longrightarrow (-1, 1)$
0	0	$\longrightarrow (0, 0)$
1	1	$\longrightarrow (1, 1)$
2	4	$\longrightarrow (2, 4)$
3	9	$\longrightarrow (3, 9)$

↑ Select x.   ↑ Find f(x).   ↑ Plot the point.

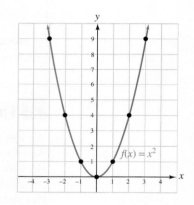

Because the graph extends indefinitely to the left and to the right, the projection of the graph onto the x-axis includes all the real numbers. See figure (a). This means that the domain of the squaring function is the set of real numbers.

The Language of Algebra

The set of **nonnegative real numbers** is the set of real numbers greater than or equal to 0.

Project the graph onto the x-axis.

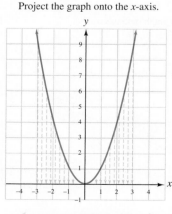

Domain: all real numbers

(a)

Project the graph onto the y-axis.

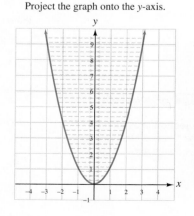

Range: nonnegative real numbers

(b)

Because the graph extends upward indefinitely from the point (0, 0), the projection of the graph on the y-axis includes only positive real numbers and 0. See figure (b) on the previous page. This means that the range of the squaring function is the set of nonnegative real numbers.

Self Check 2 Graph $g(x) = x^2 - 2$ by plotting points. Then find its domain and range. Compare the graph to the graph of $f(x) = x^2$.

Now Try ▶ Problem 29

Another important nonlinear function is $f(x) = x^3$, called the **cubing function.**

EXAMPLE 3   Graph $f(x) = x^3$ and find its domain and range.

Strategy   We will graph the function by creating a table of function values and plotting the corresponding ordered pairs.

Why   After drawing a smooth curve through the plotted points, we will have the graph.

Solution   To graph the function, we select several values for x and find the corresponding values of $f(x)$. For example, if we select -2 for x, we have

$$f(x) = x^3 \qquad \text{This is the function to graph.}$$
$$f(-2) = (-2)^3 \qquad \text{Substitute } -2 \text{ for each } x.$$
$$= -8$$

Since $f(-2) = -8$, the ordered pair $(-2, -8)$ lies on the graph of f. In a similar manner, we find the corresponding values of $f(x)$ for four other x-values and list the ordered pairs in the table. Then we plot the points and draw a smooth curve through them to get the graph.

Success Tip

To graph a linear function, it is recommended that you find three points on the line to draw its graph. Because the graphs of nonlinear functions are more complicated, more work is required. You need to find a sufficient number of points on the graph so that its entire shape is revealed. At least five well-chosen input values are recommended.

$$f(x) = x^3$$

x	$f(x)$	
-2	-8	→ $(-2, -8)$
-1	-1	→ $(-1, -1)$
0	0	→ $(0, 0)$
1	1	→ $(1, 1)$
2	8	→ $(2, 8)$

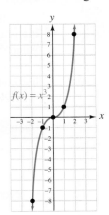

Because the graph of the function extends indefinitely to the left and to the right, the projection includes all the real numbers. Therefore, the domain of the cubing function is the set of real numbers.

Because the graph of the function extends indefinitely upward and downward, the projection includes all the real numbers. Therefore, the range of the cubing function is the set of real numbers.

Self Check 3 Graph $g(x) = x^3 + 1$ by plotting points. Then find its domain and range. Compare the graph to the graph of $f(x) = x^3$.

Now Try ▶ Problem 31

A third nonlinear function is $f(x) = |x|$, called the **absolute value function.**

EXAMPLE 4 Graph $f(x) = |x|$ and find its domain and range.

Strategy We will graph the function by creating a table of function values and plotting the corresponding ordered pairs.

Why After drawing straight lines through the plotted points, we will have the graph.

Solution To graph the function, we select several x-values and find the corresponding values for $f(x)$. For example, if we choose -3 for x, we have

$$f(x) = |x| \qquad \text{This is the function to graph.}$$
$$f(-3) = |-3| \qquad \text{Substitute } -3 \text{ for each } x.$$
$$= 3$$

Since $f(-3) = 3$, the ordered pair $(-3, 3)$ lies on the graph of f. In a similar manner, we find the corresponding values of $f(x)$ for six other x-values and list the ordered pairs in the table. Then we plot the points and connect them to get the following V-shaped graph.

Success Tip

To determine the entire shape of the graph, several positive and negative values, along with 0, were selected as x-values when constructing the table of values.

$$f(x) = |x|$$

x	$f(x)$	
-3	3	$\longrightarrow$ $(-3, 3)$
-2	2	$\longrightarrow$ $(-2, 2)$
-1	1	$\longrightarrow$ $(-1, 1)$
0	0	$\longrightarrow$ $(0, 0)$
1	1	$\longrightarrow$ $(1, 1)$
2	2	$\longrightarrow$ $(2, 2)$
3	3	$\longrightarrow$ $(3, 3)$

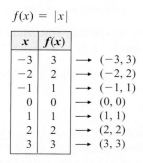
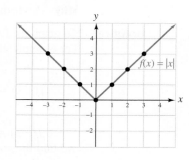

Because the graph extends indefinitely to the left and to the right, the projection of the graph onto the x-axis includes all the real numbers. Thus, the domain of the absolute value function is the set of real numbers.

Because the graph extends upward indefinitely from the point $(0, 0)$, the projection of the graph on the y-axis includes only positive real numbers and 0. Thus, the range of the absolute value function is the set of nonnegative real numbers.

Self Check 4 Graph $g(x) = |x - 2|$ by plotting points. Then find its domain and range. Compare the graph to the graph of $f(x) = |x|$.

Now Try ▶ Problem 33

Using Your Calculator ▶ **Graphing Functions**

We can graph nonlinear functions with a graphing calculator. For example, to graph $f(x) = x^2$ in a standard window of $[-10, 10]$ for x and $[-10, 10]$ for y, we first press $\boxed{Y =}$. Then we enter the function by typing $x \,^\wedge\, 2$ (or x followed by $\boxed{x^2}$), and press the $\boxed{\text{GRAPH}}$ key. We will obtain the graph shown in figure (a).

To graph $f(x) = x^3$, we enter the function by typing $x \,^\wedge\, 3$ and then press the $\boxed{\text{GRAPH}}$ key to obtain the graph in figure (b). To graph $f(x) = |x|$, we enter the function by selecting abs(from the NUM option within the MATH menu, typing x, and pressing the $\boxed{\text{GRAPH}}$ key to obtain the graph in figure (c).

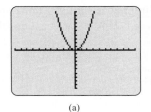
(a)

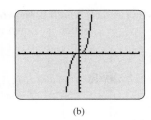
(b)

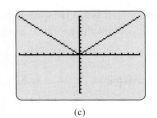
(c)

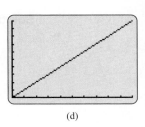
(d)

When using a graphing calculator, we must be sure that the viewing window does not show a misleading graph. For example, if we graph $f(x) = |x|$ in the window $[0, 10]$ for x and $[0, 10]$ for y, we will obtain a misleading graph that looks like a line. See figure (d). This is not correct. The proper graph is the V-shaped graph shown in figure (c). One of the challenges of using graphing calculators is finding an appropriate viewing window.

4 Translate Graphs of Functions.

Examples 2, 3, and 4 and their Self Checks suggest that the graphs of different functions may be identical except for their positions in the coordinate plane. For example, the figure on the right shows the graph of $f(x) = x^2 + k$ for three different values of k. If $k = 0$, we get the graph of $f(x) = x^2$, shown in red. If $k = 3$, we get the graph of $f(x) = x^2 + 3$, shown in blue. Note that it is identical to the graph of $f(x) = x^2$ except that it is shifted 3 units upward. If $k = -4$, we get the graph of $f(x) = x^2 - 4$, shown in green. It is identical to the graph of $f(x) = x^2$ except that it is shifted 4 units downward. These shifts are called **vertical translations.**

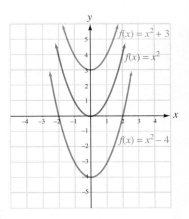

In general, we can make these observations.

| **Vertical Translations** | If f is a function and k represents a positive number, then

 ■ The graph of $y = f(x) + k$ is identical to the graph of $y = f(x)$ except that it is translated k units upward.

 ■ The graph of $y = f(x) - k$ is identical to the graph of $y = f(x)$ except that it is translated k units downward. | 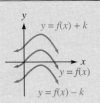 |

EXAMPLE 5   Graph: $g(x) = |x| + 2$

Strategy   We will graph $g(x) = |x| + 2$ by translating (shifting) the graph of $f(x) = |x|$ upward 2 units.

Why   The addition of 2 in $g(x) = |x| + 2$ causes a vertical shift of the graph of the absolute value function 2 units upward.

Solution   Each point used to graph $f(x) = |x|$, which is shown in gray, is shifted 2 units upward to obtain the graph of $g(x) = |x| + 2$, which is shown in red. This is a vertical translation.

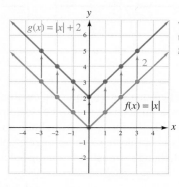

To graph $g(x) = |x| + 2$, translate each point on the graph of $f(x) = |x|$ up 2 units.

Self Check 5   Graph: $g(x) = |x| - 3$

Now Try ▶ Problem 37

The figure on the right shows the graph of $f(x) = (x + h)^2$ for three different values of h. If $h = 0$, we get the graph of $f(x) = x^2$, shown in red. The graph of $f(x) = (x - 3)^2$ shown in green is identical to the graph of $f(x) = x^2$ except that it is shifted 3 units to the right. The graph of $f(x) = (x + 2)^2$ shown in blue is identical to the graph of $f(x) = x^2$ except that it is shifted 2 units to the left. These shifts are called **horizontal translations.**

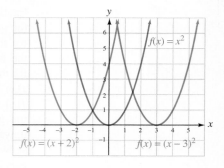

In general, we can make these observations.

Horizontal Translations

If f is a function and h is a positive number, then

- The graph of $y = f(x - h)$ is identical to the graph of $y = f(x)$ except that it is translated h units to the right.

- The graph of $y = f(x + h)$ is identical to the graph of $y = f(x)$ except that it is translated h units to the left.

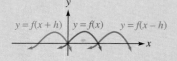

EXAMPLE 6   Graph: $g(x) = (x + 3)^3$

Success Tip

To determine the direction of the horizontal translation, find the value of x that makes the expression within the parentheses, in this case, $x + 3$, equal to 0. Since -3 makes $x + 3 = 0$, the translation is 3 units to the left.

Strategy   We will graph $g(x) = (x + 3)^3$ by translating (shifting) the graph of $f(x) = x^3$ to the left 3 units.

Why   The addition of 3 to x in $g(x) = (x + 3)^3$ causes a horizontal shift of the graph of the cubing function 3 units to the left.

To graph $g(x) = (x + 3)^3$, translate each point on the graph of $f(x) = x^3$ to the left 3 units.

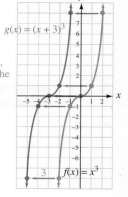

Solution   Each point used to graph $f(x) = x^3$, which is shown in gray, is shifted 3 units to the left to obtain the graph of $g(x) = (x + 3)^3$, which is shown in red. This is a horizontal translation.

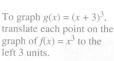

Self Check 6   Graph: $g(x) = (x - 2)^2$

Now Try ▶ Problem 47

The graphs of some functions involve horizontal and vertical translations.

EXAMPLE 7   Graph: $g(x) = (x - 5)^2 - 2$

Strategy   To graph $g(x) = (x - 5)^2 - 2$, we will perform two translations by shifting the graph of $f(x) = x^2$ to the right 5 units and then 2 units downward.

Why   The subtraction of 5 from x in $g(x) = (x - 5)^2 - 2$ causes a horizontal shift of the graph of the squaring function 5 units to the right. The subtraction of 2 causes a vertical shift of the graph 2 units downward.

Solution   Each point used to graph $f(x) = x^2$, which is shown in gray, is shifted 5 units to the right and 2 units downward to obtain the graph of $g(x) = (x - 5)^2 - 2$, which is shown in red. This is a horizontal and vertical translation.

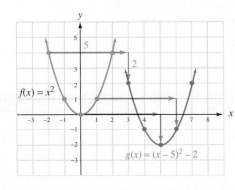

To graph $g(x) = (x - 5)^2 - 2$, translate each point on the graph of $f(x) = x^2$ to the right 5 units and then 2 units downward.

Self Check 7   Graph: $g(x) = |x + 2| - 3$

Now Try ▶ Problem 53

5 Reflect Graphs of Functions.

The following figure shows a table of values for $f(x) = x^2$ and for $g(x) = -x^2$. We note that for a given value of x, the corresponding y-value in the tables are opposites. When graphed, we see that the $-$ sign in $g(x) = -x^2$ has the effect of flipping the graph of $f(x) = x^2$ over the x-axis so that the parabola opens downward. We say that the graph of $g(x) = -x^2$ is a **reflection** of the graph of $f(x) = x^2$ about the x-axis.

$f(x) = x^2$

x	$f(x)$
-2	4
-1	1
0	0
1	1
2	4

→ $(-2, 4)$
→ $(-1, 1)$
→ $(0, 0)$
→ $(1, 1)$
→ $(2, 4)$

$g(x) = -x^2$

x	$g(x)$
-2	-4
-1	-1
0	0
1	-1
2	-4

→ $(-2, -4)$
→ $(-1, -1)$
→ $(0, 0)$
→ $(1, -1)$
→ $(2, -4)$

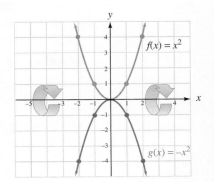

Reflection of a Graph	▼	The graph of $y = -f(x)$ is the graph of $y = f(x)$ reflected about the x-axis.

EXAMPLE 8   Graph: $g(x) = -x^3$

Strategy   We will graph $g(x) = -x^3$ by reflecting the graph of $f(x) = x^3$ about the x-axis.

Why   Because of the $-$ sign in $g(x) = -x^3$, the y-coordinate of each point on the graph of function g is the opposite of the y-coordinate of the corresponding point on the graph $f(x) = x^3$.

Solution   To graph $g(x) = -x^3$, we use the graph of $f(x) = x^3$ from Example 3. First, we reflect the portion of the graph of $f(x) = x^3$ in quadrant I to quadrant IV, as shown. Then we reflect the portion of the graph of $f(x) = x^3$ in quadrant III to quadrant II.

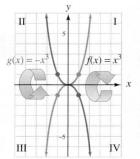

Self Check 8   Graph: $g(x) = -|x|$

Now Try   Problem 63

6   Find Function Values and the Domain and Range of Polynomial Functions Graphically.

We have seen that the graphs of polynomial functions of degree 1, such as $f(x) = 4x - 1$ or $f(x) = \frac{1}{2}x + 3$, are straight lines and the graphs of polynomial functions of degree 2, such as $f(x) = x^2$ or $f(x) = x^2 - 2$, are parabolas. The graphs of polynomial functions of degree 3 or higher are often more complicated. Such graphs are always *smooth* and *continuous*. That is, they consist of only rounded curves with no sharp corners, and there are no breaks.

We can obtain important information about a polynomial function from its graph.

EXAMPLE 9   Refer to the graph of polynomial function $f(x) = x^3 - 3x^2 - 9x + 2$ in figure (a) on the next page.   **a.** Find $f(2)$.   **b.** Find any values of x for which $f(x) = -25$.   **c.** Find the domain and range of f.

Strategy   For parts a and b, we will use the information provided by the function notation to locate a specific point on the graph and determine its x- and y-coordinates. For part c, we will project the graph onto each axis.

Why   Once we locate the specific point, one of its coordinates will equal the value that we are asked to find. Projecting the graph onto the x-axis gives the domain and projecting it onto the y-axis gives the range.

Solution   **a.** To find $f(2)$, we need to find the y-coordinate of the point on the graph of f whose x-coordinate is 2. If we draw a vertical line downward, from 2 on the x-axis, as shown in figure (b) on the next page, the line intersects the graph of f at $(2, -20)$. Therefore, -20 corresponds to 2, and it follows that $f(2) = -20$.

   b. To find any input value x that has an output value $f(x) = -25$, we draw a horizontal line through -25 on the y-axis, as shown in figure (c) on the next page, and note that it intersects the graph of f at $(-3, -25)$ and $(3, -25)$. Therefore, $f(-3) = -25$ and $f(3) = -25$. It follows that the values of x for which $f(x) = -25$ are -3 and 3.

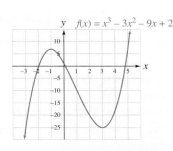

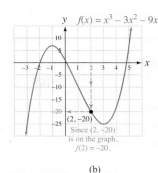

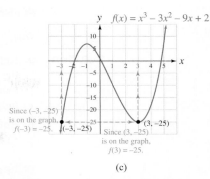

(a)   (b)   (c)

c. To find the domain of $f(x) = x^3 - 3x^2 - 9x + 2$, we project its graph onto the x-axis as shown in figure (d) below. Because the graph extends indefinitely to the left and right, the projection includes all real numbers. Therefore, the domain of the function is the set of real numbers, which can be written in interval notation as $(-\infty, \infty)$.

To determine the range of the same polynomial function, we project the graph onto the y-axis, as shown in figure (e) below. Because the graph of the function extends indefinitely upward and downward, the projection includes all real numbers. Therefore the range of the function is the set of real numbers, written $(-\infty, \infty)$.

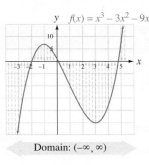

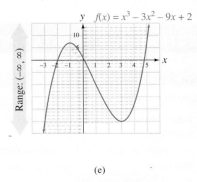

(d)   (e)

Self Check 9 Refer to the graph of function f in Example 9. Estimate each of the following: **a.** $f(1)$ **b.** Any x-values for which $f(x) = 0$

Now Try ▶ Problem 65

7 Use the Vertical Line Test.

Some graphs define functions and some do not. If a vertical line intersects a graph more than once, the graph does not represent a function, because to one value of x there would correspond more than one value of y.

The Vertical Line Test   If a vertical line intersects a graph in more than one point, the graph is not the graph of a function.

EXAMPLE 10   Determine whether the graph in figure (a) and figure (c) is the graph of a function.

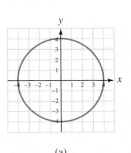

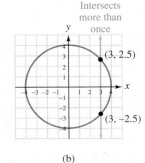

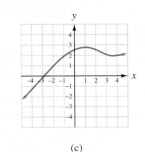

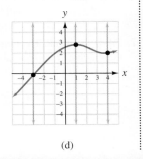

(a)   (b)   (c)   (d)

Strategy   We will check to see whether any vertical lines intersect the graph more than once.

Why   If any vertical line intersects the graph more than once, it is not the graph of a function.

Solution   **a.** Refer to figure (b) on the previous page. The graph shown in red is not the graph of a function because a vertical line intersects the graph more than once. The points of intersection of the graph and the vertical line indicate that two values of y (2.5 and -2.5) correspond to the x-value 3.

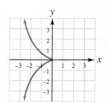

x	y
3	2.5
3	-2.5

b. Refer to figure (d) on the previous page. The graph shown in red is the graph of a function, because no vertical line intersects the graph more than once.

Self Check 10   Determine whether the following graph is the graph of a function.

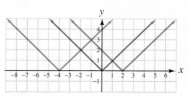

Now Try ▶ Problems 69 and 71

SECTION **8.3** ▶ STUDY SET

VOCABULARY

Fill in the blanks.

1. Functions whose graphs are not lines are called _____ functions.
2. The graph of $f(x) = x^2$ is a cuplike shape called a _____.
3. The set of _____ real numbers is the set of real numbers greater than or equal to 0.
4. A shift of the graph of a function upward or downward is called a vertical _____.

CONCEPTS

5. Graph each basic function by plotting points and give its name.

   a. $f(x) = x^2$
   b. $f(x) = x^3$
   c. $f(x) = |x|$

6. Complete each sentence about finding function values graphically.

   a. To find $f(-3)$, we find the y-coordinate of the point on the graph whose x-coordinate is ____.
   b. To find the value of x for which $f(x) = -2$, we find the x-coordinate of the point(s) on the graph whose y-coordinate is
       ____.
   c. Suppose for a function f that $f(5) = 9$. The corresponding ordered pair that will be on the graph of the function is (__ , __).

7. Fill in the blank. The graph of $g(x) = -x^2$ is the _____ of the graph of $f(x) = x^2$ about the x-axis.

8. Fill in the blanks. The illustration shows the projection of the graph of function f on the _____. We see that the _____ of f is the set of real numbers less than or equal to 0.

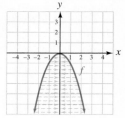

9. Consider the graph of the function f.
   a. Label each arrow in the illustration with the appropriate term: *domain* or *range*.
   b. Give the domain and range of f.

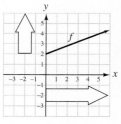

10. The graph of $f(x) = x^2 + k$ for three values of k is shown on the right. Find the value of k for
    a. the blue graph
    b. the red graph
    c. the green graph

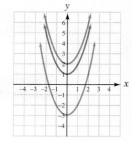

11. The graph of $f(x) = |x + h|$ for three values of h is shown. Find the value of h for
    a. the blue graph
    b. the red graph
    c. the green graph

12. a. Translate each point plotted on the graph below to the left 5 units and then up 1 unit. **b.** Translate each point plotted on the graph below to the right 4 units and then down 3 units.

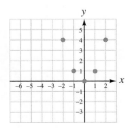

13. a. Give the coordinates of the points where the given vertical line intersects the graph in red.

b. Is this the graph of a function? Explain.

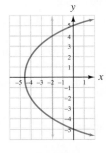

NOTATION

Fill in the blanks.

14. Fill in the blanks. The _____ line test: If a vertical line intersects a graph in more than one point, the graph is not the graph of a _____.

15. a. The graph of $f(x) = (x + 4)^3$ is the same as the graph of $f(x) = x^3$ except that it is shifted ___ units to the ____.
   b. The graph of $f(x) = x^3 + 4$ is the same as the graph of $f(x) = x^3$ except that it is shifted ___ units ____.

16. a. The graph of $f(x) = |x| - 5$ is the same as the graph of $f(x) = |x|$ except that it is shifted ___ units _____.
   b. The graph of $f(x) = |x - 5|$ is the same as the graph of $f(x) = |x|$ except that it is shifted ___ units to the ____.

GUIDED PRACTICE

Refer to the given graph to find each value. See Example 1.

17. a. $f(-2)$
   b. $f(0)$
   c. The value of x for which $f(x) = 4$
   d. The value of x for which $f(x) = -2$

18. a. $s(-3)$
   b. $s(3)$
   c. The values of x for which $s(x) = 0$
   d. The values of x for which $s(x) = 3$

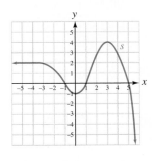

19. a. $g(-2)$
   b. $g(0)$
   c. The value of x for which $g(x) = 3$
   d. The values of x for which $g(x) = -1$

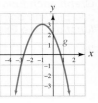

20. a. $h(-3)$
   b. $h(4)$
   c. The values of x for which $h(x) = 1$
   d. The value of x for which $h(x) = 0$

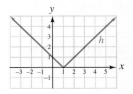

Find the domain and range of each function. See Objective 2 and Example 2.

21.

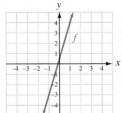

22.

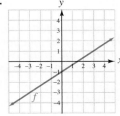

23.

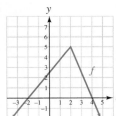

24.

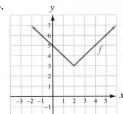

25.

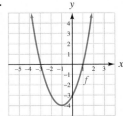

26.

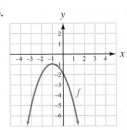

27.

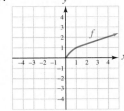

28.

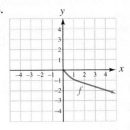

Graph each function by creating a table of function values and plotting points. Give the domain and range of the function. See Examples 2, 3, and 4.

29. $f(x) = x^2 + 2$

30. $f(x) = x^2 - 4$

31. $f(x) = x^3 - 3$

32. $f(x) = x^3 + 2$

33. $f(x) = |x - 1|$

34. $f(x) = |x + 4|$

35. $f(x) = (x + 4)^2$

36. $f(x) = (x - 1)^3$

For each of the following functions, first sketch the graph of its associated function, $f(x) = x^2$, $f(x) = x^3$, or $f(x) = |x|$. Then draw the graph of function g using a translation and give its domain and range. See Examples 5 and 6.

37. $g(x) = |x| - 2$

38. $g(x) = |x + 2|$

39. $g(x) = (x + 1)^3$

40. $g(x) = x^3 + 5$

41. $g(x) = x^2 - 3$

42. $g(x) = (x - 6)^2$

43. $g(x) = (x - 4)^3$

44. $g(x) = |x| + 1$

45. $g(x) = x^3 + 4$

46. $g(x) = x^2 - 5$

47. $g(x) = (x + 4)^2$

48. $g(x) = (x - 1)^3$

For each of the following functions, first sketch the graph of its associated function, $f(x) = x^2$, $f(x) = x^3$, or $f(x) = |x|$. Then draw the graph of function g using translations and/or a reflection. See Examples 7 and 8.

49. $g(x) = |x - 2| - 1$

50. $g(x) = (x + 2)^2 - 1$

51. $g(x) = (x + 1)^3 - 2$

52. $g(x) = |x + 4| + 3$

53. $g(x) = (x - 2)^2 + 4$

54. $g(x) = (x - 4)^2 + 3$

55. $g(x) = |x + 3| + 5$

56. $g(x) = (x - 3)^2 - 2$

57. $g(x) = -x^3$

58. $g(x) = -|x|$

59. $g(x) = -x^2$

60. $g(x) = -(x + 1)^2$

61. $g(x) = -|x + 5|$

62. $g(x) = -(x + 4)^3$

63. $g(x) = -x^2 + 3$

64. $g(x) = -|x| - 4$

Use the graph of the function to find each of the following. See Example 9.

65. Find:
a. $f(1)$
b. $f(-3)$
c. The values of x for which $f(x) = 0$
d. The domain and range of f

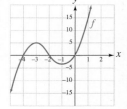

66. Find:
a. $f(-1)$
b. $f(0)$
c. The values of x for which $f(x) = 3$
d. The domain and range of f

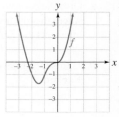

67. Find:
a. $g(1)$
b. $g(-4)$
c. The values of x for which $g(x) = 4$
d. The domain and range of g

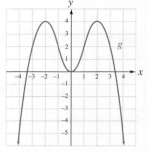

68. Find:
a. $h(0.5)$
b. $h(-0.5)$
c. The values of x for which $h(x) = -1.5$
d. The domain and range of h

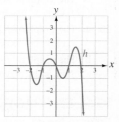

Determine whether each graph is the graph of a function. If it is not, find two ordered pairs where more than one value of y corresponds to a single value of x. See Example 10.

69.

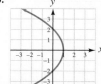

70.

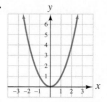

71.

72.

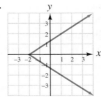

73.

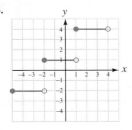

74.

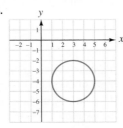

75.

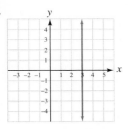

76.

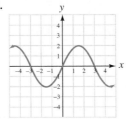

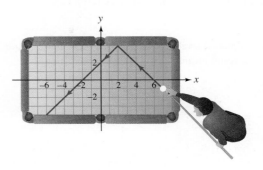

Graph each function using window settings of [−4, 4] for x and [−4, 4] for y. The graph is not what it appears to be. Pick a better viewing window and find a better representation of the true graph. **See Using Your Calculator: Graphing Functions.**

77. $f(x) = x^2 + 8$ **78.** $f(x) = x^3 - 8$

79. $f(x) = |x + 5|$ **80.** $f(x) = |x - 5|$

81. $f(x) = (x - 6)^2$ **82.** $f(x) = (x + 9)^2$

83. $f(x) = x^3 + 8$ **84.** $f(x) = x^3 - 12$

APPLICATIONS

85. Optics. See the illustration. The **law of reflection** states that the angle of reflection is equal to the angle of incidence. What function studied in this section models the path of the reflected light beam with an angle of incidence measuring 45°?

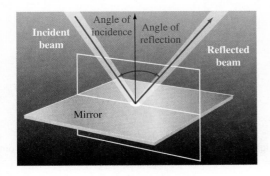

86. Billiards. In the illustration, a rectangular coordinate system has been superimposed over a billiard table. Write a function that models the path of the ball that is shown banking off of the cushion.

87. Center of Gravity. See the illustration. As a diver performs a $1\frac{1}{2}$-somersault in the tuck position, her center of gravity follows a path that can be described by a graph shape studied in this section. What graph shape is that?

88 Earth's Atmosphere. The illustration below shows a graph of the temperatures of the atmosphere at various altitudes above Earth's surface. The temperature is expressed in degrees Kelvin, a scale widely used in scientific work.

a. Estimate the coordinates of three points on the graph that have an x-coordinate of 200.

b. Explain why this is not the graph of a function.

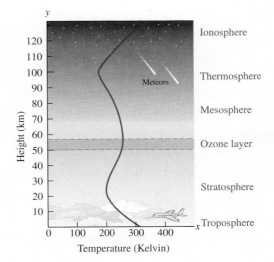

89. Labor Statistics. The polynomial function that is graphed below approximates the number of manufacturing jobs (in millions) in the United States, where x is the number of years after 2000. Use the graph to answer the following questions.

a. Estimate $J(9)$. Explain what the result means.

b. Estimate the value of x for which $J(x) = 14.5$. Explain what the result means.

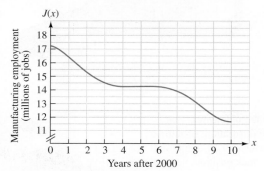

(Source: Bureau of Labor Statistics)

90. Transportation Engineering. The polynomial function A that is graphed below approximates the number of accidents per mile in one year on a 4-lane interstate, where x is the average daily traffic in number of vehicles. Use the graph to answer the following questions.

a. Estimate $A(20,000)$. Explain what the result means.

b. Estimate the value of x for which $A(x) = 2$. Explain what the result means.

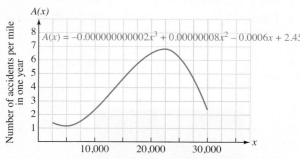

Source: Highway Safety Manual, Colorado Department of Transportation

WRITING

91. Explain how to graph a function by plotting points.

92. Explain how to *project* the graph of a function onto the x-axis. Give an example.

93. a. What does it mean to translate a graph vertically?

b. What does it mean to horizontally translate a graph?

c. What does it mean to reflect the graph of a function about the x-axis?

94. A student was asked to determine whether the graph shown below is the graph of a function. What is wrong with the following reasoning?

When I draw a vertical line through the graph, it intersects the graph only once. By the vertical line test, this is the graph of a function.

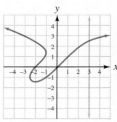

95. Explain why the graph of $g(x) = (x - 2)^2$ is two units to the right of the graph of $f(x) = x^2$.

96. Explain why the range of the polynomial function graphed below is not $(-\infty, \infty)$.

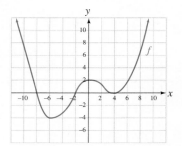

REVIEW

Solve each formula for the indicated variable.

97. $T - W = ma$ for W

98. $a + (n - 1)d = l$ for n

99. $s = \dfrac{1}{2}gt^2 + vt$ for g

100. $e = mc^2$ for m

CHALLENGE PROBLEMS

Graph each function.

101. $f(x) = \begin{cases} |x| & \text{for } x \geq 0 \\ x^3 & \text{for } x < 0 \end{cases}$

102. $f(x) = \begin{cases} x^2 & \text{for } x \geq 0 \\ |x| & \text{for } x < 0 \end{cases}$

Find the domain and range of each function.

103. a.

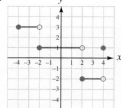

b.

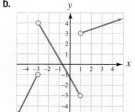

104. Light. Light beams coming from a bulb are reflected outward by a parabolic mirror as parallel rays.

a. The cross-section of a parabolic mirror is given by the function $f(x) = x^2$ for the following values of x: -0.7, -0.6, -0.5, -0.4, -0.3, -0.2, -0.1, 0, 0.1, 0.2, 0.3, 0.4, 0.5, 0.6, 0.7. Sketch the parabolic mirror using the following grid.

b. From the lightbulb filament at $(0, 0.25)$, draw a line segment representing a beam of light that strikes the mirror at $(-0.4, 0.16)$ and then reflects outward, parallel to the y-axis.

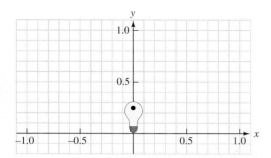

Complete the table and then graph the polynomial function.

105.

$f(x) = 2x^3 - 3x^2 - 11x + 6$

x	$f(x)$
-3	
-2	
-1	
0	
1	
2	
3	
4	

106.

$f(x) = -x^3 - x^2 + 6x$

x	$f(x)$
-4	
-3	
-2	
-1	
0	
1	
2	
3	

SECTION 8.4

Solving Compound Inequalities

OBJECTIVES

1 Find the intersection and the union of two sets.

2 Solve compound inequalities containing the word *and*.

3 Solve double linear inequalities.

4 Solve compound inequalities containing the word *or*.

ARE YOU READY?

The following problems review some basic skills that are needed to solve inequalities.

1. Let $A = \{-6, 1, 2, 3, 4\}$ and $B = \{0, 3, 4, 5, 6\}$. What numbers do sets A and B have in common?

2. Solve $6x + 8 + x \geq 5(x - 3) + 9$. Graph the solution set and write it in interval notation.

3. Consider the statements $x > 4$ and $x < 8$. Does the number 7 make both inequalities true?

4. Graph the solution set for $x > 2$ and the solution set for $x \leq -1$ on the same number line.

A label on a first-aid cream warns the user about the temperature at which the medication should be stored. A careful reading reveals that the storage instructions consist of two parts:

The storage temperature should be at least 59°F

and

the storage temperature should be at most 77°F

First Aid Cream

Store at 59° to 77° F

When the word *and* or the word *or* is used to connect pairs of inequalities, we call the statement a **compound inequality**. To solve compound inequalities, we need to know how to find the *intersection* and *union* of two sets.

1 Find the Intersection and the Union of Two Sets.

Just as operations such as addition and multiplication are performed on real numbers, operations also can be performed on sets. The operation of intersection of two sets produces a new third set that consists of all of the elements that the two given sets have in common.

The Intersection of Two Sets ▼	The **intersection of set A and set B,** written $A \cap B$, is the set of all elements that are common to set A and set B.

The operation of union of two sets produces a third set that is a combination of all of the elements of the two given sets.

The Union of Two Sets ▼	The **union of set A and set B,** written $A \cup B$, is the set of elements that belong to set A or set B or both.

Venn diagrams can be used to illustrate the intersection and union of sets. The area shown in purple in figure (a) represents $A \cap B$ and the area shown in both shades of red in figure (b) represents $A \cup B$.

The Language of Algebra

The **union** of two sets is the collection of elements that belong to either set. The concept is similar to that of a family *reunion,* which brings together the members of several families.

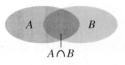

$A \cap B$

Read as "A intersect B."

(a)

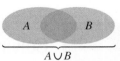

$A \cup B$

Read as "A union B."

(b)

EXAMPLE 1 Let $A = \{0, 1, 2, 3, 4, 5, 6\}$ and $B = \{-4, -2, 0, 2, 4\}$.
a. Find $A \cap B$. **b.** Find $A \cup B$.

Strategy In part (a), we will find the elements that sets A and B have in common, and in part (b), we will find the elements that are in one set, or the other set, or both.

Why The symbol $\cap$ means intersection, and the symbol $\cup$ means union.

Solution **a.** Since the numbers 0, 2, and 4 are common to both sets A and B, we have

The Language of Algebra

The **intersection** of two sets is the collection of elements that they have in common. When two streets cross, we call the area of pavement that they have in common an *intersection.*

$A \cap B = \{0, 2, 4\}$ Since the intersection is, itself, a set, braces are used.

b. Since the numbers in either or both sets are $-4, -2, 0, 1, 2, 3, 4, 5,$ and 6, we have

$A \cup B = \{-4, -2, 0, 1, 2, 3, 4, 5, 6\}$ 0, 2, and 4 are not listed twice.

Self Check 1 Let $C = \{8, 9, 10, 11\}$ and $D = \{3, 6, 9, 12, 15\}$.
a. Find $C \cap D$. **b.** Find $C \cup D$.

Now Try ▶ Problems 17 and 21

---

2 Solve Compound Inequalities Containing the Word *And.*

When two inequalities are joined with the word *and,* we call the statement a **compound inequality.** Some examples are

The Language of Algebra

Compound means composed of two or more parts, as in *compound* inequalities, chemical *compounds,* and *compound* sentences.

$$x \geq -3 \qquad \text{and} \qquad x \leq 6$$

$$\frac{x}{2} + 1 > 0 \qquad \text{and} \qquad 2x - 3 < 5$$

$$x + 3 \leq 2x - 1 \qquad \text{and} \qquad 3x - 2 < 5x - 4$$

The **solution set of a compound inequality containing the word *and*** includes all numbers that make both of the inequalities true. That is, it is the intersection of their solution sets. We can find the solution set of the compound inequality $x \geq -3$ and $x \leq 6$, for example, by graphing the solution sets of each inequality on the same number line and looking for the numbers common to both graphs.

In the following figure, the graph of the solution set of $x \geq -3$ is shown in red, and the graph of the solution set of $x \leq 6$ is shown in blue.

Preliminary work to determine the graph of the solution set

The figure below shows the graph of the solution of the compound inequality $x \geq -3$ and $x \leq 6$. The purple shaded interval, where the red and blue graphs intersect (or overlap), represents the real numbers that are common to the graphs of $x \geq -3$ and $x \leq 6$.

The graph of the solution set

The solution set of $x \geq -3$ and $x \leq 6$ is the **bounded interval** $[-3, 6]$, where the brackets indicate that the endpoints, -3 and 6, are included. It represents all real numbers between -3 and 6, including -3 and 6. Intervals such as this, which contain both endpoints, are called **closed intervals.**

Since the solution set of $x \geq -3$ and $x \leq 6$ is the intersection of the solution sets of the two inequalities, we can write

$$[-3, \infty) \cap (-\infty, 6] = [-3, 6]$$

The solution set of the compound inequality $x \geq -3$ and $x \leq 6$ can be expressed in several ways:

1. As a graph:
2. In words: all real numbers from -3 to 6
3. In interval notation: $[-3, 6]$
4. Using set-builder notation: $\{x \mid x \geq -3 \text{ and } x \leq 6\}$

EXAMPLE 2

Solve $\dfrac{x}{2} + 1 > 0$ and $2x - 3 < 5$. Graph the solution set and write it using interval notation and set-builder notation.

Strategy We will solve each inequality separately. Then we will graph the two solution sets on the same number line and determine their intersection.

Why The solution set of a compound inequality containing the word *and* is the intersection of the solution sets of the two inequalities.

Solution In each case, we can use properties of inequality to isolate the variable on one side of the inequality.

$$\dfrac{x}{2} + 1 > 0 \qquad \text{and} \qquad 2x - 3 < 5 \qquad \text{This is the compound inequality to solve.}$$

$$\dfrac{x}{2} > -1 \qquad\qquad\qquad 2x < 8$$

$$x > -2 \qquad\qquad\qquad x < 4$$

Notation

When graphing on a number line, $(-2, 4)$ represents an *interval*. When graphing on a rectangular coordinate system, $(-2, 4)$ is an *ordered pair* that gives the coordinates of a point.

Next, we graph the solutions of each inequality on the same number line and determine their intersection.

Preliminary work to determine the graph of the solution set

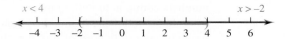

We see that the intersection of the graphs is the set of all real numbers between -2 and 4. The solution set of the compound inequality is the interval $(-2, 4)$, whose graph is shown below. This bounded interval, which does not include either endpoint, is called an **open interval.** Written using set-builder notation, the solution set is $\{x \mid x > -2 \text{ and } x < 4\}$.

The graph of the solution set

Self Check 2 Solve $3x > -18$ and $\frac{x}{5} - 1 \le 1$. Graph the solution set and write it using interval notation.

Now Try ▶ Problem 27

The solution of the compound inequality in the Self Check of Example 2 is the interval $(-6, 10]$. A bounded interval such as this, which includes only one endpoint, is called a **half-open interval.** The following chart shows the various types of bounded intervals, along with the inequalities and interval notation that describe them.

Intervals		
Open intervals	The interval (a, b) includes all real numbers x such that $a < x < b$.	
Half-open intervals	The interval $[a, b)$ includes all real numbers x such that $a \le x < b$.	
	The interval $(a, b]$ includes all real numbers x such that $a < x \le b$.	
Closed intervals	The interval $[a, b]$ includes all real numbers x such that $a \le x \le b$.	

EXAMPLE 3 Solve $x + 3 \le 2x - 1$ and $3x - 2 < 5x - 4$. Graph the solution set and write it using interval notation and set-builder notation.

Strategy We will solve each inequality separately. Then we will graph the two solution sets on the same number line and determine their intersection.

Why The solution set of a compound inequality containing the word *and* is the intersection of the solution sets of the two inequalities.

Solution In each case, we can use properties of inequality to isolate the variable on one side.

$$
\begin{array}{lll}
x + 3 \le 2x - 1 & \text{and} & 3x - 2 < 5x - 4 \qquad \text{This is the compound inequality to solve.} \\
\quad\quad 4 \le x & & \quad\quad 2 < 2x \\
\quad\quad x \ge 4 & & \quad\quad 1 < x \\
& & \quad\quad x > 1
\end{array}
$$

The graph of $x \geq 4$ is shown below in red and the graph of $x > 1$ is shown below in blue.

Preliminary work to determine the graph of the solution set

Only those values of x where $x \geq 4$ and $x > 1$ are in the solution set of the compound inequality. Since all numbers greater than or equal to 4 are also greater than 1, the solutions are the numbers x where $x \geq 4$. The solution set is the interval $[4, \infty)$, whose graph is shown below. Written using set-builder notation, the solution set is $\{x \mid x \geq 4\}$.

The graph of the solution set

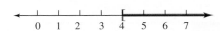

Self Check 3	Solve $2x + 3 < 4x + 2$ and $3x + 1 < 5x + 3$. Graph the solution set and write it using interval notation.
Now Try ▶	**Problem 29**

EXAMPLE 4   Solve $x - 1 > -3$ and $2x < -8$, if possible.

Strategy   We will solve each inequality separately. Then we will graph the two solution sets on the same number line and determine their intersection, if any.

Why   The solution set of a compound inequality containing the word *and* is the intersection of the solution sets of the two inequalities.

Solution   In each case, we can use properties of inequality to isolate the variable on one side.

$$x - 1 > -3 \quad \text{and} \quad 2x < -8 \quad \text{This is the compound inequality to solve.}$$
$$x > -2 \qquad\qquad\qquad x < -4$$

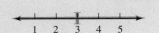

The graphs of the solution sets shown below do not intersect. Since there are no numbers that make both parts of the original compound inequality true, $x - 1 > -3$ and $2x < -8$ has no solution.

Preliminary work to determine the graph of the solution set

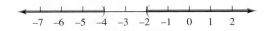

The solution set of the compound inequality is the empty set, which can be written as $\varnothing$. Since there is no solution, a graph is not needed.

Self Check 4	Solve $2x - 3 < x - 2$ and $0 < x - 3.5$, if possible.
Now Try ▶	**Problem 31**

---

3 Solve Double Linear Inequalities.

Inequalities that contain exactly two inequality symbols are called **double inequalities.** An example is

$$-3 \leq 2x + 5 < 7 \quad \text{Read as "-3 is less than or equal to $2x + 5$ and $2x + 5$ is less than 7."}$$

Any double linear inequality can be written as a compound inequality containing the word *and.* In general, the following is true.

| **Double Linear Inequalities** ▼ | The compound inequality $c < x < d$ is equivalent to $c < x$ and $x < d$. |

Thus, the double inequality $-3 \le 2x + 5 < 7$ is a shorter form for the compound inequality

$$-3 \le 2x + 5 \quad \text{and} \quad 2x + 5 < 7$$

As you will see in Example 5, it is easier to solve the double inequality because it enables us to solve both inequalities at once.

EXAMPLE 5   Solve $-3 \le 2x + 5 < 7$. Graph the solution set and write it using interval notation and set-builder notation.

Strategy   We will solve the double inequality by applying properties of inequality to *all three of its parts* to isolate x in the middle.

Why   This double inequality $-3 \le 2x + 5 < 7$ means that $-3 \le 2x + 5$ and $2x + 5 < 7$. We can solve it more easily by leaving it in its original form.

Solution   The objective is to isolate x in the middle of the double inequality.

Notation

Note that the two inequality symbols in $-3 \le 2x + 5 < 7$ point in the same direction and point to the smaller number. And in $-4 \le x < 1$, the numbers -4 and 1 appear in the same order as they do on a number line.

$$-3 \le 2x + 5 < 7 \qquad \text{This is the double inequality to solve.}$$

$$-3 - 5 \le 2x + 5 - 5 < 7 - 5 \qquad \text{To undo the addition of 5, subtract} \\ \text{5 from all three parts.}$$

$$-8 \le 2x < 2 \qquad \text{Perform the subtractions.}$$

$$\frac{-8}{2} \le \frac{2x}{2} < \frac{2}{2} \qquad \text{To isolate } x, \text{ undo the multiplication by 2} \\ \text{by dividing all three parts by 2.}$$

$$-4 \le x < 1 \qquad \text{Perform the divisions.}$$

The solution set of the double linear inequality is the half-open interval $[-4, 1)$, whose graph is shown below. Written using set-builder notation, the solution set is $\{x \,|\, -4 \le x < 1\}$.

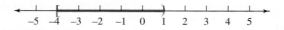

Self Check 5   Solve $-5 \le 3x - 8 \le 7$. Graph the solution set and write it using interval notation.

Now Try ▶ **Problem 35**

CAUTION   When multiplying or dividing all three parts of a double inequality by a negative number, don't forget to reverse the direction of both inequalities. As an example, we solve $-15 < -5x \le 25$.

$$-15 < -5x \le 25$$

$$\frac{-15}{-5} > \frac{-5x}{-5} \ge \frac{25}{-5} \qquad \text{Divide all three parts by } -5 \text{ to isolate } x \text{ in} \\ \text{the middle. Reverse both inequality signs.}$$

$$3 > x \ge -5 \qquad \text{Perform the divisions.}$$

$$-5 \le x < 3 \qquad \text{Write an equivalent double inequality with} \\ \text{the smaller number, } -5, \text{ on the left.}$$

4 Solve Compound Inequalities Containing the Word *Or.*

A warning on the water temperature gauge of a commercial dishwasher cautions the operator to shut down the unit if

> The water temperature goes below 140°
>
> or
>
> The water temperature goes above 160°

When two inequalities are joined with the word *or,* we also call the statement a compound inequality. Some examples are

$$x < 140 \quad \text{or} \quad x > 160$$
$$x \le -3 \quad \text{or} \quad x \ge 2$$
$$\frac{x}{3} > \frac{2}{3} \quad \text{or} \quad -(x - 2) > 3$$

The **solution set of a compound inequality containing the word** *or* includes all numbers that make one or the other or both inequalities true. That is, it is the union of their solution sets. We can find the solution set of $x \le -3$ or $x \ge 2$, for example, by drawing the graphs of each inequality on the same number line.

In the following figure, the graph of the solution set of $x \le -3$ is shown in red, and the graph of the solution set of $x \ge 2$ is shown in blue.

Preliminary work to determine the graph of the solution set

$x \le -3$ $x \ge 2$

```
←——●———+———+———+———+———+———●———+———+———+——→
   -6  -5  -4  -3  -2  -1   0   1   2   3   4   5
```

The figure below shows the graph of the solution set of $x \le -3$ or $x \ge 2$. This graph is a union of the graph of $x \le -3$ with the graph of $x \ge 2$.

The graph of the solution set

```
←——+———+———●———+———+———+———[———+———+———+——→
   -6  -5  -4  -3  -2  -1   0   1   2   3   4   5
```

For the compound inequality $x \le -3$ or $x \ge 2$, we can write the solution set as the union of two intervals:

$$(-\infty, -3] \cup [2, \infty)$$

We can express the solution set of the compound inequality $x \le -3$ or $x \ge 2$ in several ways:

1. As a graph: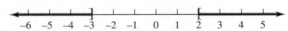

2. In words: all real numbers less than or equal to -3 *or* greater than or equal to 2

3. As the union of two intervals: $(-\infty, -3] \cup [2, \infty)$

4. Using set-builder notation: $\{x \mid x \le -3 \text{ or } x \ge 2\}$

EXAMPLE 6

Solve $\dfrac{x}{3} > \dfrac{2}{3}$ or $-(x - 2) > 3$. Graph the solution set and write it using interval notation and set-builder notation.

Strategy We will solve each inequality separately. Then we will graph the two solution sets on the same number line to show their union.

Why The solution set of a compound inequality containing the word *or* is the union of the solution sets of the two inequalities.

Solution To solve each inequality, we proceed as follows:

$$\frac{x}{3} > \frac{2}{3} \quad \text{or} \quad -(x - 2) > 3 \quad \textsf{This is the compound inequality to solve.}$$

$$x > 2 \quad \Big| \quad -x + 2 > 3$$
$$-x > 1$$
$$x < -1$$

The Language of Algebra

The meaning of the word **or** in a compound inequality differs from our everyday use of the word. For example, when we say, "I will go shopping today *or* tomorrow," we mean that we will go one day or the other, but *not* both. With compound inequalities, *or* includes one possibility, or the other, or both.

Next, we graph the solutions of each inequality on the same number line and determine their union.

Preliminary work to determine the graph of the solution set

The union of the two solution sets consists of all real numbers less than -1 or greater than 2. The solution set of the compound inequality is the union of two intervals: $(-\infty, -1) \cup (2, \infty)$. Its graph appears below. Written using set-builder notation, the solution set is $\{x \mid x > 2 \text{ or } x < -1\}$.

The graph of the solution set

Self Check 6 Solve $\frac{x}{2} > 2$ or $-3(x - 2) > 0$. Graph the solution set and write it using interval notation.

Now Try ▶ Problem 41

EXAMPLE 7 Solve $x + 3 \geq -3$ or $-x > 0$. Graph the solution set and write it using interval notation and set-builder notation.

Strategy We will solve each inequality separately. Then we will graph the two solution sets on the same number line to show their union.

Why The solution set of a compound inequality containing the word *or* is the union of the solution sets of the two inequalities.

Solution To solve each inequality, we proceed as follows:

$$x + 3 \geq -3 \quad \text{or} \quad -x > 0 \quad \textsf{This is the compound inequality to solve.}$$
$$x \geq -6 \quad \Big| \quad x < 0$$

We graph the solution set of each inequality on the same number line and determine their union.

Preliminary work to determine the graph of the solution set

Since the entire number line is shaded, all real numbers satisfy the original compound inequality and the solution set is denoted as $(-\infty, \infty)$ or $\mathbb{R}$. Its graph is shown below. Written using set-builder notation, the solution set is $\{x \mid x \text{ is a real number}\}$.

The graph of the solution set

Self Check 7 Solve $x - 1 < 5$ or $-2x \leq 10$. Graph the solution set and write it using interval notation.

Now Try ▶ Problem 43

Solving Compound Inequalities

1. Solve each inequality separately and graph their solution sets in different colors on the same number line.

2. If the inequalities are connected with the word *and*, find the intersection of the two solution sets. If the inequalities are connected with the word *or*, find the union of the two solution sets.

3. Write the solution set of the compound inequality using interval notation or set-builder notation, and graph it on a new number line.

SECTION 8.4 ▶ STUDY SET

VOCABULARY

Fill in the blanks.

1. The _____ of two sets is the set of elements that are common to both sets and the _____ of two sets is the set of elements that are in one set, or the other, or both.

2. $x \geq 3$ and $x < 4$ is a _____ inequality.

3. $-6 < x + 1 \leq 1$ is a _____ linear inequality.

4. $(2, 8)$ is an example of an open _____, $[-4, 0]$ is an example of a _____ interval, and $(0, 9]$ is an example of a half-_____ interval.

CONCEPTS

Fill in the blanks.

5. **a.** The solution set of a compound inequality containing the word *and* includes all numbers that make _____ inequalities true.

   b. The solution set of a compound inequality containing the word *or* includes all numbers that make _____, or the other, or _____ inequalities true.

6. The double inequality $4 < 3x + 5 \leq 15$ is equivalent to $4 < 3x + 5$ _____ $3x + 5 \leq 15$.

7. **a.** When solving a compound inequality containing the word *and*, the solution set is the _____ of the solution sets of the inequalities.

   b. When solving a compound inequality containing the word *or*, the solution set is the _____ of the solution sets of the inequalities.

8. When multiplying or dividing all three parts of a double inequality by a negative number, the direction of both inequality symbols must be _____.

9. Use a check to determine whether -3 is a solution of the compound inequality.

   a. $\dfrac{x}{3} + 1 \geq 0$ and $2x - 3 < -10$

   b. $2x \leq 0$ or $-3x < -5$

10. Use a check to determine whether -3 is a solution of the double linear inequality.

    a. $-1 < -3x + 4 < 12$

    b. $-1 < -3x + 4 < 14$

11. Use interval notation, if possible, to describe the intersection of each pair of graphs.

    a.
    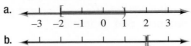

    b.

    c.

12. Use interval notation to describe the union of each pair of graphs.

    a.
    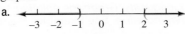

    b.

    c.

NOTATION

13. Fill in the blanks: We read $\cup$ as _____ and $\cap$ as _____.

14. Match each interval with its corresponding graph.

    a. $[2, 3)$ **i.**
    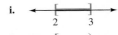

    b. $(2, 3)$ **ii.**

    c. $[2, 3]$ **iii.**
    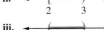

15. What set is represented by the interval notation $(-\infty, \infty)$? Graph it.

16. **a.** Graph: $(-\infty, 2) \cup [3, \infty)$

    b. Graph: $(-\infty, 3) \cap [-2, \infty)$

GUIDED PRACTICE

Let $A = \{0, 1, 2, 3, 4, 5, 6\}$, $B = \{4, 6, 8, 10\}$,
$C = \{-3, -1, 0, 1, 2\}$, and $D = \{-3, 1, 2, 5, 8\}$.
Find each set. See Example 1.

17. $A \cap B$ **18.** $A \cap D$

19. $C \cap D$ **20.** $B \cap C$

21. $B \cup C$ **22.** $A \cup C$

23. $A \cup D$ **24.** $C \cup D$

Solve each compound inequality, if possible. Graph the
solution set (if one exists) and write it using interval
notation. See Examples 2–4.

25. $x > -2$ and $x \le 5$
26. $x \le -4$ and $x \ge -7$
27. $2x - 1 > 3$ and $x + 8 \le 11$
28. $5x - 3 \ge 2$ and $6 \ge 4x - 3$
29. $6x + 1 < 5x - 3$ and $\dfrac{x}{2} + 9 \le 6$
30. $\dfrac{2}{3}x + 1 > -9$ and $\dfrac{3}{4}x - 1 > -10$
31. $x + 2 < -\dfrac{1}{3}x$ and $-6x < 9x$
32. $\dfrac{3}{2}x + \dfrac{1}{5} < 5$ and $2x + 1 > 9$

Solve each double inequality. Graph the solution set and
write it using interval notation. See Example 5.

33. $4 \le x + 3 \le 7$ **34.** $-5.3 \le x - 2.3 \le -1.3$

35. $0.9 < 2x - 0.7 < 1.5$ **36.** $7 < 3x - 2 < 25$

Solve each compound inequality. Graph the solution set
and write it using interval notation. See Examples 6 and 7.

37. $x \le -2$ or $x > 6$
38. $x \ge -1$ or $x \le -3$
39. $x - 3 < -4$ or $-x + 2 < 0$
40. $4x < -12$ or $\dfrac{x}{2} > 4$
41. $3x + 2 < 8$ or $2x - 3 > 11$
42. $3x + 4 < -2$ or $3x + 4 > 10$
43. $2x > x + 3$ or $\dfrac{x}{8} + 1 < \dfrac{13}{8}$
44. $2(x + 2) < x - 11$ or $-\dfrac{x}{5} < 20$

TRY IT YOURSELF

Solve each compound inequality, if possible. Graph the
solution set (if one exists) and write it using interval
notation.

45. $-4(x + 2) \ge 12$ or $3x + 8 < 11$
46. $4.5x - 1 < -10$ or $6 - 2x \ge 12$

47. $2.2x < -19.8$ and $-4x < 40$
48. $\dfrac{1}{2}x \le 2$ and $0.75x \ge -6$
49. $-2 < -b + 3 < 5$
50. $2 < -t - 2 < 9$
51. $4.5x - 2 > 2.5$ or $\dfrac{1}{2}x \le 1$
52. $0 < x$ or $3x - 5 > 4x - 7$
53. $5(x - 2) \ge 0$ and $-3x < 9$
54. $x - 1 \le 2(x + 2)$ and $x \le 2x - 5$
55. $-x < -2x$ and $3x > 2x$
56. $-\dfrac{x}{4} > -2.5$ and $9x > 2(4x + 5)$
57. $-6 < -3(x - 4) \le 24$
58. $-4 \le -2(x + 8) < 8$
59. $2x + 1 \ge 5$ and $-3(x + 1) \ge -9$
60. $2(-2) \le 3x - 1$ and $3x - 1 \le -1 - 3$
61. $\dfrac{4.5x - 12}{2} < x$ or $-15.3 > -3(x - 1.4)$
62. $y + 0.52 < 1.05y$ or $9.8 - 15y > -15.7$
63. $\dfrac{x}{0.7} + 5 > 4$ and $-4.8 \le \dfrac{3x}{-0.125}$
64. $5(x + 1) \le 4(x + 3)$ and $x + 12 < -3$
65. $-24 < \dfrac{3}{2}x - 6 \le -15$
66. $-4 > \dfrac{2}{3}x - 2 > -6$
67. $\dfrac{x}{3} - \dfrac{x}{4} > \dfrac{1}{6}$ or $\dfrac{x}{2} + \dfrac{2}{3} \le \dfrac{3}{4}$
68. $\dfrac{a}{2} + \dfrac{7}{4} > 5$ or $\dfrac{3}{8} + \dfrac{a}{3} \le \dfrac{5}{12}$
69. $0 \le \dfrac{4 - x}{3} \le 2$
70. $-2 \le \dfrac{5 - 3x}{2} \le 2$
71. $x \le 6 - \dfrac{1}{2}x$ and $\dfrac{1}{2}x + 1 \ge 3$
72. $3\left(x + \dfrac{2}{3}\right) \le -7$ and $2(x + 2) \ge -2$
73. $-6 < f(x) \le 0$ where $f(x) = 3x - 9$
74. $-3 < f(x) < 7$ where $f(x) = \dfrac{2}{3}x - \dfrac{1}{3}$
75. Let $f(x) = 5x + 14$ and $g(x) = 2x + 8$. Find all values of x for which $f(x) > 29$ and $g(x) < 20$.
76. Let $f(x) = x - 2$. Find all values of x for which $f(x) > 5$ or $f(x) < -1$.

Look Alikes . . .

Solve the inequality in part a. Graph the solution set and
write it in interval notation. Then use your work from part a
to determine the solution set for the compound inequality
in part b. (No new work is necessary!) Graph the solution
set and write it in interval notation.

77. **a.** $3x - 2 \ge 4$ and $x + 6 \ge 12$
      b. $3x - 2 \ge 4$ or $x + 6 \ge 12$

78. a. $x + 2 \leq 10$ or $x - 3 \geq 2$
   b. $x + 2 \leq 10$ and $x - 3 \geq 2$
79. a. $2x + 1 \leq 7$ and $3x + 5 \geq 23$
   b. $2x + 1 \leq 7$ or $3x + 5 \geq 23$
80. a. $7 \leq 4x + 1 < 23$

   b. $7 < 4x + 1 \leq 23$

APPLICATIONS

81. Baby Furniture. Refer to the illustration. A company manufactures various sizes of play yard cribs having perimeters between 128 and 192 inches, inclusive.

a. Complete the double inequality that describes the range of the perimeters of the play yard shown.

$$\boxed{} \leq 4s \leq \boxed{}$$

b. Solve the double inequality to find the range of the side lengths of the play yard.

82. Trucking. The distance that a truck can travel in 8 hours, at a constant rate of r mph, is given by $8r$. A trucker wants to travel at least 350 miles, and company regulations don't allow him to exceed 450 miles in one 8-hour shift.

a. Complete the double inequality that describes the mileage range of the truck.

$$\boxed{} \leq 8r \leq \boxed{}$$

b. Solve the double inequality to find the range of the average rate (speed) of the truck for the 8-hour trip.

83. Thermostats. During business hours, as shown in figure (a), the *Temp range* control in an office is set at 5. This means that the heater comes on when the room temperature gets 5 degrees below the *Temp setting* and the air conditioner comes on when the room temperature gets 5 degrees above the *Temp setting*.

a. Use interval notation to describe the temperature range when neither the heater nor the air conditioner will come on during business hours.

b. After business hours, the *Temp range* setting is changed to save energy. See figure (b). Use interval notation to describe the after-business-hours temperature range when neither the heater nor the air conditioner will come on.

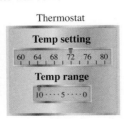

Thermostat	Thermostat
During business hours (a)	After business hours (b)

84. Treating Fevers. Use the flow chart to determine what action should be taken for a 13-month-old child who has had a 99.8° temperature for 3 days and is not suffering any other symptoms. T represents the child's temperature, A the child's age in months, and S the number of hours the child has experienced the symptoms.

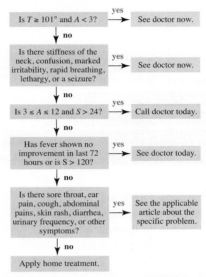

Based on information from *Take Care of Yourself* (Addison-Wesley, 1993)

85. U.S. Health Care. Refer to the following graph. Let P represent the percent of children covered by private insurance, M the percent covered by Medicaid, and N the percent not covered. For what years are the following true?

a. $P \geq 63$ and $M \geq 26$
b. $P > 60$ or $M \geq 29$
c. $M \geq 29$ and $N \leq 10$
d. $M \geq 30$ or $N < 9.2$

U.S. Health Care Coverage for People Under 18 Years of Age (in percent)

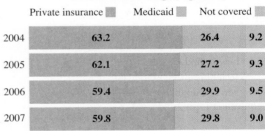

	Private insurance	Medicaid	Not covered
2004	63.2	26.4	9.2
2005	62.1	27.2	9.3
2006	59.4	29.9	9.5
2007	59.8	29.8	9.0

Source: U.S. Department of Health and Human Services

(The small percent of people covered each year by some nonstandard program is not shown.)

86. Polls. For each response to the poll question shown below, the *margin of error* is $+/-$ (read as "plus or minus") 2.8%. This means that for the statistical methods used to do the polling, the actual response could be as much as 2.8 points more or 2.8 points less than shown. Use interval notation to describe the possible interval (in percent) for each response.

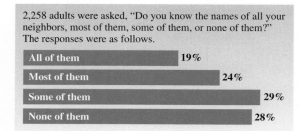

2,258 adults were asked, "Do you know the names of all your neighbors, most of them, some of them, or none of them?" The responses were as follows.

All of them	19%
Most of them	24%
Some of them	29%
None of them	28%

87. Street Intersections. Refer to figure (a) below.

   a. Shade the area that represents the intersection of the two streets shown in the illustration.

   b. Shade the area that represents the union of the two streets.

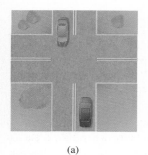

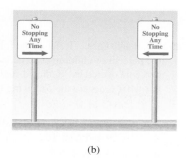

(a)   (b)

88. Traffic Signs. The pair of signs shown in figure (b) above are a real-life example of which concept discussed in this section?

WRITING

89. Explain how to find the union and how to find the intersection of $(-\infty, 5)$ and $(-2, \infty)$ graphically.

90. Explain why the double inequality $2 < x < 8$ can be written in the equivalent form $2 < x$ and $x < 8$.

91. Explain the meaning of the notation $(-1, 2)$ for each type of graph.

   a.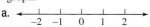

   b.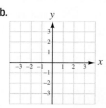

92. The meaning of the word *or* in a compound inequality differs from our everyday use of the word. Explain the difference.

93. Describe each set in words.

   a. $(-3, 3)$ **b.** $[7, 12]$

   c. $(-\infty, 5] \cup (6, \infty)$

94. What is incorrect about the double inequality $3 < -3x + 4 < -3$?

REVIEW

95. Airplanes. Together, a Delta B747 and a Delta B777 seat 681 passengers. If the B777 seats 125 less people than the B747, how many passengers does each seat? (Source: deltaskymag.com)

96. Denzel. As of October 2010, Denzel Washington's three top domestic grossing films, *American Gangster, Remember the Titans,* and *The Pelican Brief,* had earned a total of $346.7 million. If *American Gangster* earned $14.5 million more than *Remember the Titans,* and if *Remember the Titans* earned $14.9 million more than *The Pelican Brief,* how much did each film earn as of that date? (Source: boxofficemojo.com)

CHALLENGE PROBLEMS

Solve each compound inequality. Graph the solution set and write it in interval notation.

97. $-5 < \dfrac{x + 2}{-2} < 0$ or $2x + 10 \geq 30$

98. $-2 \leq \dfrac{x - 4}{3} \leq 0$ and $\dfrac{x - 5}{2} \geq -3$

99. $x - 12 < 4x < 2x + 16$

100. $6(x - 3) \leq 3(3x + 2) \leq 4(2x + 3)$

SECTION **8.5**

Solving Absolute Value Equations and Inequalities

OBJECTIVES

1 Solve equations of the form $|X| = k$.

2 Solve equations with two absolute values.

3 Solve inequalities of the form $|X| < k$.

4 Solve inequalities of the form $|X| > k$.

ARE YOU READY?

The following problems review some basic skills that are needed to solve absolute value equations and inequalities.

1. Find each absolute value.

    a. $|12|$ **b.** $|-7.5|$

2. Tell whether each statement is true or false.

    a. $|-3| \geq 2$ **b.** $|-26| < -27$

3. Solve $3x + 6 \leq -3$ or $3x + 6 \geq 9$. Graph the solution set and write it using interval notation.

4. Solve $-8 < 2x + 8 < 16$. Graph the solution set and write it using interval notation.

Many quantities studied in mathematics, science, and engineering are expressed as positive numbers. To guarantee that a quantity is positive, we often use absolute value. In this section, we will consider equations and inequalities involving the absolute value of an algebraic expression. Some examples are

$$|3x - 2| = 5, \qquad |2x - 3| < 9, \qquad \text{and} \qquad \left| \frac{3 - x}{5} \right| \geq 6$$

To solve these *absolute value equations* and *inequalities,* we write and then solve equivalent compound equations and inequalities.

1 Solve Equations of the Form $|X| = k$.

Recall that the absolute value of a real number is its distance from 0 on a number line. To solve the **absolute value equation** $|x| = 5$, we must find all real numbers x whose distance from 0 on the number line is 5. There are two such numbers: 5 and -5. It follows that the solutions of $|x| = 5$ are 5 and -5 and the solution set is $\{5, -5\}$.

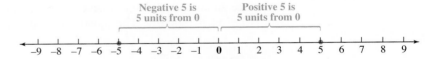

The results from this example suggest the following approach for solving absolute value equations.

Solving Absolute Value Equations	For any positive number k and any algebraic expression X: To solve $|X| = k$, solve the equivalent compound equation $X = k$ or $X = -k$

The statement $X = k$ or $X = -k$ is called a **compound equation** because it consists of two equations joined with the word *or.*

EXAMPLE 1   Solve: **a.** $|s| = 0.003$ **b.** $|3x - 2| = 5$ **c.** $|10 - x| = -40$

Strategy   To solve the first two equations, we will write and then solve an equivalent compound equation. We will solve the third equation by inspection.

Why All three of the equations are of the form $|X| = k$. However, the standard method for solving absolute value equations cannot be applied to $|10 - x| = -40$ because k is negative.

Solution

a. The absolute value equation $|s| = 0.003$ is equivalent to the compound equation

$$s = 0.003 \qquad \text{or} \qquad s = -0.003$$

> **The Language of Algebra**
>
> When we say that the absolute value equation and a compound equation are **equivalent,** we mean that they have the same solution(s).

Therefore, the solutions of $|s| = 0.003$ are 0.003 and -0.003, and the solution set is $\{0.003, -0.003\}$.

b. The equation-solving method used in part a can be extended to equations where the expression within absolute value bars is more complicated than a single variable. The absolute value equation $|3x - 2| = 5$ is equivalent to the compound equation

$$3x - 2 = 5 \qquad \text{or} \qquad 3x - 2 = -5$$

Now we solve each equation for x:

$$
\begin{array}{ccc}
3x - 2 = 5 & \text{or} & 3x - 2 = -5 \\
3x = 7 & & 3x = -3 \\
x = \dfrac{7}{3} & & x = -1
\end{array}
$$

> **Caution**
>
> When you see the word *solve,* you probably think of steps such as combining like terms, distributing, or doing something to both sides. However, to solve absolute value equations of the form $|X| = k$, those familiar steps are not used until an equivalent compound equation is written.

The results must be checked separately to see whether each of them produces a true statement. We substitute $\frac{7}{3}$ for x and then -1 for x in the original equation.

Check:

For $x = \dfrac{7}{3}$

$$|3x - 2| = 5$$
$$\left|3\left(\frac{7}{3}\right) - 2\right| \stackrel{?}{=} 5$$
$$|7 - 2| \stackrel{?}{=} 5$$
$$|5| \stackrel{?}{=} 5$$
$$5 = 5 \quad \text{True}$$

For $x = -1$

$$|3x - 2| = 5$$
$$|3(-1) - 2| \stackrel{?}{=} 5$$
$$|-3 - 2| \stackrel{?}{=} 5$$
$$|-5| \stackrel{?}{=} 5$$
$$5 = 5 \quad \text{True}$$

The resulting true statements indicate that the equation has two solutions: $\frac{7}{3}$ and -1. The solution set is $\left\{\frac{7}{3}, -1\right\}$.

c. Since an absolute value can never be negative, there are no real numbers x that make $|10 - x| = -40$ true. The equation has no solution and the solution set is $\varnothing$.

Self Check 1 Solve: **a.** $|x| = \frac{1}{2}$ **b.** $|2x - 3| = 7$

c. $\left|\frac{x}{4} - 1\right| = -3$

Now Try Problems 19, 23, and 29

When solving absolute value equations (or inequalities), we must **isolate the absolute value expression on one side** before writing the equivalent compound statement.

EXAMPLE 2 Solve: $\left|\dfrac{2}{3}x + 3\right| + 4 = 10$

Strategy We will first isolate $\left|\frac{2}{3}x + 3\right|$ on the left side of the equation and then write and solve an equivalent compound equation.

Why After isolating the absolute value expression on the left, the resulting equation will have the desired form $|X| = k$.

Solution

$$\left|\frac{2}{3}x + 3\right| + 4 = 10 \qquad \text{This is the equation to solve.}$$

$$\left|\frac{2}{3}x + 3\right| = 6 \qquad \begin{array}{l}\text{To isolate the absolute value expression, subtract 4 from both} \\ \text{sides. The resulting equation is in the form } |X| = k.\end{array}$$

Caution

A common error when solving absolute value equations is to forget to isolate the absolute value expression first. Note:

$$\left|\frac{2}{3}x + 3\right| + 4 = 10$$

does not mean

$$\frac{2}{3}x + 3 + 4 = 10$$

or

$$\frac{2}{3}x + 3 + 4 = -10$$

With the absolute value now isolated, we can solve $\left|\frac{2}{3}x + 3\right| = 6$ by writing and solving an equivalent compound equation:

$$\frac{2}{3}x + 3 = 6 \qquad \text{or} \qquad \frac{2}{3}x + 3 = -6$$

Now we solve each equation for x:

$$
\begin{array}{ccc}
\dfrac{2}{3}x + 3 = 6 & \text{or} & \dfrac{2}{3}x + 3 = -6 \\[2mm]
\dfrac{2}{3}x = 3 & & \dfrac{2}{3}x = -9 \\[2mm]
2x = 9 & & 2x = -27 \\[2mm]
x = \dfrac{9}{2} & & x = -\dfrac{27}{2}
\end{array}
$$

Verify that both $\frac{9}{2}$ and $-\frac{27}{2}$ are solutions by substituting them into the original equation.

Self Check 2 Solve: $|0.4x - 2| - 0.6 = 0.4$

Now Try ▶ Problem 33

EXAMPLE 3 Solve: $3\left|\frac{1}{2}x - 5\right| - 4 = -4$

Strategy We will first isolate $\left|\frac{1}{2}x - 5\right|$ on the left side of the equation and then write and solve an equivalent compound equation.

Why After isolating the absolute value expression, the resulting equation will have the desired form $|X| = k$.

Solution

Success Tip

To solve most absolute value equations, we must consider two cases. However, if an absolute value is equal to 0, we need only consider one: the case when the expression within the absolute value bars is equal to 0.

$$3\left|\frac{1}{2}x - 5\right| - 4 = -4 \qquad \text{This is the equation to solve.}$$

$$3\left|\frac{1}{2}x - 5\right| = 0 \qquad \begin{array}{l}\text{To isolate the absolute value expression } \left|\frac{1}{2}x - 5\right|, \\ \text{we first add 4 to both sides.}\end{array}$$

$$\left|\frac{1}{2}x - 5\right| = 0 \qquad \begin{array}{l}\text{To complete the process to isolate the absolute value expression,} \\ \text{divide both sides by 3. The resulting equation is in the form } |X| = k.\end{array}$$

Since 0 is the only number whose absolute value is 0, the expression $\frac{1}{2}x - 5$ must be 0.

$$\frac{1}{2}x - 5 = 0 \qquad \begin{array}{l}\text{Set the expression within the absolute value bars equal to 0 and solve for x.}\end{array}$$

$$\frac{1}{2}x = 5 \qquad \text{To isolate the variable term } \tfrac{1}{2}x, \text{ add 5 to both sides.}$$

$$x = 10 \qquad \text{To isolate x, multiply both sides by 2.}$$

The solution is 10 and the solution set is $\{10\}$. Verify that it satisfies the original equation.

Self Check 3 Solve: $-5\left|\frac{2}{3}x + 4\right| + 1 = 1$

Now Try ▶ Problem 39

In Section 8.3 we discussed absolute value functions and their graphs. If we are given an output of an absolute value function, we can work in reverse to find the corresponding input(s).

EXAMPLE 4 Let $f(x) = |x + 4|$. For what value(s) of x is $f(x) = 20$?

Strategy We will substitute 20 for $f(x)$ and solve for x.

Why In the equation, there are two unknowns, x and $f(x)$. If we replace $f(x)$ with 20, we can solve the resulting absolute value equation for x.

Solution

$$f(x) = |x + 4| \qquad \text{This is the given function.}$$

$$20 = |x + 4| \qquad \text{Substitute 20 for } f(x).$$

$$|x + 4| = 20 \qquad \text{Rewrite the equation so that the absolute value expression is on the left side.}$$

To solve $|x + 4| = 20$, we write and then solve an equivalent compound equation:

$$x + 4 = 20 \qquad \text{or} \qquad x + 4 = -20$$

Now we solve each equation for x:

$$x + 4 = 20 \qquad \text{or} \qquad x + 4 = -20$$
$$x = 16 \qquad | \qquad \qquad x = -24$$

The values of x for which $f(x) = 20$ are 16 and -24. To check, find $f(16)$ and $f(-24)$, and verify that the result is 20 in each case.

Self Check 4 Let $f(x) = |x + 4|$. For what value(s) of x is $f(x) = 11$?

Now Try ▶ Problem 71

2 Solve Equations with Two Absolute Values.

Equations can contain two absolute value expressions. To develop a strategy to solve them, consider the following four true statements.

$$|3| = |3| \qquad \text{or} \qquad |-3| = |-3| \qquad \text{or} \qquad |3| = |-3| \qquad \text{or} \qquad |-3| = |3|$$

The numbers are the same.   The numbers are the same.   The numbers are opposites.   The numbers are opposites.

These four possible cases are really just two cases: *Two absolute value expressions are equal when the expressions within the absolute value bars are equal to or opposites of each other.* This observation suggests the following approach for solving equations having two absolute value expressions.

Solving Equations with Two Absolute Values

For any algebraic expressions X and Y:

To solve $|X| = |Y|$, solve the compound equation $X = Y$ or $X = -Y$.

EXAMPLE 5   Solve: $|5x + 3| = |3x + 25|$

Strategy   To solve this equation, we will write and then solve an equivalent compound equation.

Why   We can use this approach because the equation is of the form $|X| = |Y|$.

Solution   The equation $|5x + 3| = |3x + 25|$, with the two absolute value expressions, is equivalent to the following compound equation:

The expressions within the absolute value symbols are equal

$$5x + 3 = 3x + 25$$
$$2x = 22$$
$$x = 11$$

or

The expressions within the absolute value symbols are opposites

$$5x + 3 = -(3x + 25)$$
$$5x + 3 = -3x - 25 \quad \text{Solve each equation.}$$
$$8x = -28$$
$$x = -\frac{28}{8}$$
$$x = -\frac{7}{2} \quad \text{Simplify the fraction.}$$

> **Caution**
>
> Don't forget to use parentheses to write the opposite of expressions that have more than one term.
>
> | Expression | Opposite |
> |---|---|
> | $3x + 25$ | $-(3x + 25)$ |

Verify that both solutions, 11 and $-\frac{7}{2}$, check by substituting them into the original equation. The solution set is $\left\{11, -\frac{7}{2}\right\}$.

Self Check 5   Solve: $|2x - 3| = |4x + 9|$

Now Try ▶ Problem 47

---

3 Solve Inequalities of the Form $|X| < k$.

To solve the **absolute value inequality** $|x| < 5$, we must find all real numbers x whose distance from 0 on the number line is less than 5. From the graph, we see that there are many such numbers. For example, -4.999, -3, -2.4, $-1\frac{7}{8}$, $-\frac{3}{4}$, 0, 1, 2.8, 3.001, and 4.999 all meet this requirement. We conclude that the solution set is all numbers between -5 and 5, which can be written in interval notation as $(-5, 5)$.

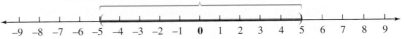

The real numbers in this interval are less than 5 units from 0

Since x is between -5 and 5, it follows that $|x| < 5$ is equivalent to $-5 < x < 5$. This observation suggests the following approach for solving absolute value inequalities of the form $|X| < k$ and $|X| \le k$.

Solving $|X| < k$ and $|X| \le k$

For any positive number k and any algebraic expression X:

To solve $|X| < k$, solve the equivalent double inequality $-k < X < k$.

To solve $|X| \le k$, solve the equivalent double inequality $-k \le X \le k$.

EXAMPLE 6   Solve $|2x - 3| < 9$ and graph the solution set.

Strategy   To solve this absolute value inequality, we will write and solve an equivalent double inequality.

Why   We can use this approach because the inequality is of the form $|X| < k$, and k is positive.

Solution   The absolute value inequality $|2x - 3| < 9$ is equivalent to the double inequality

$$-9 < 2x - 3 < 9$$

which we can solve for x:

$$-9 < 2x - 3 < 9$$
$$-6 < 2x < 12 \qquad \text{To isolate the variable term 2x, add 3 to all three parts.}$$
$$-3 < x < 6 \qquad \text{To isolate x, divide all parts by 2.}$$

Any number between -3 and 6 is in the solution set, which can be written as $\{x \mid -3 < x < 6\}$. This is the interval $(-3, 6)$; its graph is shown on the right.

Self Check 6   Solve $|3x + 2| < 4$ and graph the solution set.

Now Try   Problems 55 and 59

Because it is related to distance, absolute value can be used to describe the amount of error involved when measurements are taken.

EXAMPLE 7   **Tolerances.**   When manufactured parts are inspected by a quality control engineer, they are classified as acceptable if each dimension falls within a given **tolerance range** of the dimensions listed on the blueprint. For the bracket shown in the margin, the distance between the two drilled holes is given as 2.900 inches. Because the tolerance is ± 0.015 inch, this distance can be as much as 0.015 inch longer or 0.015 inch shorter, and the part will be considered acceptable. The acceptable distance d between holes can be represented by the absolute value inequality $|d - 2.900| \leq 0.015$. Solve the inequality and explain the result.

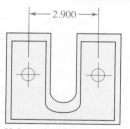

Unless otherwise specified, dimensions are in inches.
Tolerances ±0.015

Strategy   To solve $|d - 2.900| \leq 0.015$, we will write and solve an equivalent double inequality.

Why   We can use this approach because the inequality is of the form $|X| \leq k$, and k is positive.

Solution   The absolute value inequality $|d - 2.900| \leq 0.015$ is equivalent to the double inequality

$$-0.015 \leq d - 2.900 \leq 0.015$$

which we can solve for d:

$$-0.015 \leq d - 2.900 \leq 0.015$$
$$2.885 \leq d \leq 2.915 \qquad \text{To isolate d, add 2.900 to all three parts.}$$

The solution set is the interval $[2.885, 2.915]$. This means that the distance between the two holes should be between 2.885 and 2.915 inches, inclusive. If the distance is less than 2.885 inches or more than 2.915 inches, the part should be rejected.

Self Check 7   **Tolerances.**   Refer to Example 7. Find the tolerance range if the tolerance is ±0.0015.

Now Try   Problem 105

EXAMPLE 8   Solve: $|4x - 5| < -2$

Strategy   We will solve this inequality by inspection.

Why   The inequality $|4x - 5| < -2$ is of the form $|X| < k$. However, the standard method for solving such inequalities cannot be used because k (in this case, -2) is not positive.

Solution   Since $|4x - 5|$ is always greater than or equal to 0 for any real number x, this absolute value inequality has no solution. The solution set is $\varnothing$.

> **Self Check 8**   Solve: $|6x + 24| < -51$
>
> **Now Try** ▶ Problem 61

4 Solve Inequalities of the Form $|X| > k$.

To solve the absolute value inequality $|x| > 5$, we must find all real numbers x whose distance from 0 on the number line is greater than 5. From the following graph, we see that there are many such numbers. For example, -5.001, -6, -7.5, and $-8\frac{3}{8}$, as well as 5.001, 6.2, 7, 8, and $9\frac{1}{2}$ all meet this requirement. We conclude that the solution set is all numbers less than -5 or greater than 5, which can be written as the union of two intervals: $(-\infty, -5) \cup (5, \infty)$.

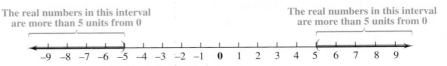

Since x is less than -5 or greater than 5, it follows that $|x| > 5$ is equivalent to $x < -5$ or $x > 5$. This observation suggests the following approach for solving absolute value inequalities of the form $|X| > k$ and $|X| \geq k$.

Solving $\|X\| > k$ and $\|X\| \geq k$	For any positive number k and any algebraic expression X:
	To solve $|X| > k$, solve the equivalent compound inequality $X < -k$ or $X > k$.
	To solve $|X| \geq k$, solve the equivalent compound inequality $X \leq -k$ or $X \geq k$.

EXAMPLE 9   Solve $\left| \dfrac{3 - x}{5} \right| \geq 6$ and graph the solution set.

Strategy   To solve this absolute value inequality, we will write and solve an equivalent compound inequality.

Why   We can use this approach because the inequality is of the form $|X| \geq k$, and k is positive.

Solution   The absolute value inequality $\left| \dfrac{3 - x}{5} \right| \geq 6$ is equivalent to the compound inequality

$$\frac{3 - x}{5} \leq -6 \qquad \text{or} \qquad \frac{3 - x}{5} \geq 6$$

Now we solve each inequality for x:

$$\frac{3-x}{5} \le -6 \quad \text{or} \quad \frac{3-x}{5} \ge 6$$

$3 - x \le -30$	$3 - x \ge 30$
$-x \le -33$	$-x \ge 27$
$x \ge 33$	$x \le -27$

To clear the fraction, multiply both sides by 5.

To isolate the variable term $-x$, subtract 3 from both sides.

To isolate x, divide both sides by -1 and reverse the direction of the inequality symbol.

The solution set is the union of two intervals: $(-\infty, -27] \cup [33, \infty)$. Using set-builder notation, the solution set is written as $\{x \mid x \le -27 \text{ or } x \ge 33\}$. Its graph appears on the right.

Self Check 9 Solve $\left|\frac{2-x}{4}\right| \ge 1$ and graph the solution set.

Now Try ▶ Problems 63 and 65

EXAMPLE 10 Solve $6 < \left|\frac{2}{3}x - 2\right| - 3$ and graph the solution set.

Strategy We will first write the inequality in an equivalent form with the absolute value on the left side.

Why It's usually easier to solve an absolute value inequality if the absolute value appears on the left side of the inequality.

Solution

$$6 < \left|\frac{2}{3}x - 2\right| - 3 \quad \text{This is the inequality to solve.}$$

$$\left|\frac{2}{3}x - 2\right| - 3 > 6 \quad \text{Write the inequality with the absolute value on the left side.}$$

$$\left|\frac{2}{3}x - 2\right| > 9 \quad \text{Add 3 to both sides to isolate the absolute value expression.}$$

After isolating the absolute value expression on the left side, the resulting inequality has the form $|X| > k$. To solve this absolute value inequality, we write and solve an equivalent compound inequality:

$$\frac{2}{3}x - 2 < -9 \quad \text{or} \quad \frac{2}{3}x - 2 > 9$$

$\frac{2}{3}x < -7$	$\frac{2}{3}x > 11$
$2x < -21$	$2x > 33$
$x < -\frac{21}{2}$	$x > \frac{33}{2}$

Add 2 to both sides.

Multiply both sides by 3.

To isolate x, divide both sides by 2.

The solution set is the union of two intervals: $\left(-\infty, -\frac{21}{2}\right) \cup \left(\frac{33}{2}, \infty\right)$. Its graph appears on the right. Using set-builder notation, the solution set can be written as $\left\{x \mid x < -\frac{21}{2} \text{ or } x > \frac{33}{2}\right\}$.

Self Check 10   Solve $3 < \left|\frac{3}{4}x + 2\right| - 1$ and graph the solution set.

Now Try ▶ Problem 67

EXAMPLE 11   Solve $\left|\frac{x}{8} - 1\right| \ge -4$ and graph the solution set.

Strategy   We will solve this inequality by inspection.

Why   The inequality $\left|\frac{x}{8} - 1\right| \ge -4$ is of the form $|x| \ge k$. However, the standard method for solving such inequalities cannot be used because k is not positive.

Solution   Since $\left|\frac{x}{8} - 1\right|$ is always greater than or equal to 0 for any real number x it will also be greater than or equal to -4 for any real number x. Therefore, this absolute value inequality is true for all real numbers. The solution set is the interval $(-\infty, \infty)$ or $\mathbb{R}$. Its graph appears on the right.

Self Check 11   Solve $|-x - 9| > -0.5$ and graph the solution set.

Now Try ▶ Problem 69

The following summary shows how we can interpret absolute value in three ways. Assume $k > 0$.

Geometric description	*Graphic description*	*Algebraic description*
1. $|x| = k$ means that x is k units from 0 on the number line.	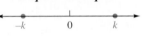	$|x| = k$ is equivalent to $x = k$ or $x = -k$.
2. $|x| < k$ means that x is less than k units from 0 on the number line.	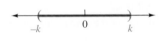	$|x| < k$ is equivalent to $-k < x < k$.
3. $|x| > k$ means that x is more than k units from 0 on the number line.		$|x| > k$ is equivalent to $x > k$ or $x < -k$.

Using Your Calculator ▶ Solving Absolute Value Equations and Inequalities

We can solve absolute value equations and inequalities with a graphing calculator. For example, to solve $|2x - 3| = 9$, we graph the equations $y = |2x - 3|$ and $y = 9$ on the same coordinate system, as shown in the figure. The equation $|2x - 3| = 9$ will be true for all x-coordinates of points that lie on *both* graphs. Using the TRACE or the INTERSECT feature, we can see that the graphs intersect at the points $(-3, 9)$ and $(6, 9)$. Thus, the solutions of the absolute value equation are -3 and 6.

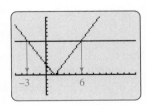

The inequality $|2x - 3| < 9$ will be true for all x-coordinates of points that lie on the graph of $y = |2x - 3|$ and *below* the graph of $y = 9$. We see that these values of x are between -3 and 6. Thus, the solution set is the interval $(-3, 6)$.

The inequality $|2x - 3| > 9$ will be true for all x-coordinates of points that lie on the graph of $y = |2x - 3|$ and *above* the graph of $y = 9$. We see that these values of x are less than -3 or greater than 6. Thus, the solution set is the union of two intervals: $(-\infty, -3) \cup (6, \infty)$.

SECTION 8.5 **STUDY SET**

VOCABULARY

Fill in the blanks.

1. The _____ _____ of a number is its distance from 0 on a number line.

2. $|2x - 1| = 10$ is an absolute value _____ and $|2x - 1| > 10$ is an absolute value _____.

3. To _____ the absolute value in $|3 - x| - 4 = 5$, we add 4 to both sides.

4. When we say that the absolute value equation and a compound equation are equivalent, we mean that they have the same _____.

5. When two equations are joined by the word *or*, such as $x + 1 = 5$ or $x + 1 = -5$, we call the statement a _____ equation.

6. $f(x) = |6x - 2|$ is called an absolute value _____.

CONCEPTS

Fill in the blanks.

7. To solve absolute value equations and inequalities, we write and solve equivalent _____ equations and inequalities.

8. Two absolute value expressions are equal when the expressions within the absolute value bars are equal to or _____ of each other.

9. Consider the following real numbers:
   $-3, -2.01, -2, -1.99, -1, 0, 1, 1.99, 2, 2.01, 3$
   a. Which of them make $|x| = 2$ true?
   b. Which of them make $|x| < 2$ true?
   c. Which of them make $|x| > 2$ true?

10. Determine whether -3 is a solution of the given equation or inequality.
    a. $|x - 1| = 4$ b. $|x - 1| > 4$
    c. $|x - 1| \leq 4$ d. $|5 - x| = |x + 12|$

11. For each absolute value equation, write an equivalent compound equation.
    a. $|x - 7| = 8$ is equivalent to
       $$x - 7 = \boxed{} \quad \text{or} \quad x - 7 = \boxed{}$$
    b. $|x + 10| = |x - 3|$ is equivalent to
       $$x + 10 = \boxed{} \quad \text{or} \quad x + 10 = \boxed{}$$

12. For each absolute value inequality, write an equivalent compound inequality.
    a. $|x + 5| < 1$ is equivalent to
       $$\boxed{} < x + 5 < \boxed{}$$
    b. $|x - 6| \geq 3$ is equivalent to
       $$x - 6 \leq \boxed{} \quad \text{or} \quad x - 6 \geq \boxed{}$$

13. For each absolute value equation or inequality, write an equivalent compound equation or inequality.
    a. $|x| = 8$ b. $|x| \geq 8$
    c. $|x| \leq 8$ d. $|5x - 1| = |x + 3|$

14. Perform the necessary steps to isolate the absolute value expression on one side of the equation. *Do not solve.*
    a. $|3x + 2| - 7 = -5$
    b. $6 + 2|5x - 19| \leq 40$

15. Determine the solution set of each absolute value equation or inequality by inspection. (No work is necessary.) Your answer should be either *all real numbers* or *no solution*.
    a. $|7x + 6| = -8$ b. $|7x + 6| \leq -8$

    c. $|7x + 6| \geq -8$

16. Write the inequality $10 > |16x - 3|$ in an equivalent form with the absolute value expression on the left side.

NOTATION

17. Match each equation or inequality with its graph.
    a. $|x| = 1$ i.
    b. $|x| > 1$ ii.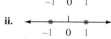
    c. $|x| < 1$ iii.

18. Describe the set graphed below using interval notation.

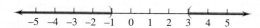

GUIDED PRACTICE

Solve each equation. See Example 1.

19. $|x| = 23$ 20. $|x| = 90$

21. $|x - 5| = 8$ 22. $|x - 7| = 4$

23. $|3x + 2| = 16$ 24. $|5x - 3| = 22$

25. $\left|\dfrac{x}{5}\right| = 10$ 26. $\left|\dfrac{x}{7}\right| = 2$

27. $|2x + 3.6| = 9.8$ 28. $|4x - 24.8| = 32.4$

29. $\left|\dfrac{7}{2}x + 3\right| = -5$ 30. $|x - 2.1| = -16.3$

Solve each equation. **See Example 2.**

31. $|x - 3| - 19 = 3$

32. $|x - 10| + 30 = 50$

33. $|3x - 7| + 8 = 22$

34. $|6x - 3| + 7 = 28$

35. $|3 - 4x| + 1 = 6$

36. $|8 - 5x| - 8 = 10$

37. $\left|\frac{7}{8}x + 5\right| - 2 = 7$

38. $\left|\frac{3}{4}x + 4\right| - 5 = 11$

Solve each equation. **See Example 3.**

39. $\left|\frac{1}{5}x + 2\right| - 8 = -8$

40. $\left|\frac{1}{9}x + 4\right| + 25 = 25$

41. $2|3x + 24| = 0$

42. $8\left|\frac{2x}{3} + 10\right| = 0$

43. $-5|2x - 9| + 14 = 14$

44. $-10|16x + 4| - 3 = -3$

45. $6 - 3|10x + 5| = 6$

46. $15 - |12x + 12| = 15$

Solve each equation. **See Example 5.**

47. $|5x - 12| = |4x - 16|$

48. $|4x - 7| = |3x - 21|$

49. $|10x| = |x - 18|$

50. $|6x| = |x + 45|$

51. $|2 - x| = |3x + 2|$

52. $|4x + 3| = |9 - 2x|$

53. $|5x - 7| = |4(x + 1)|$

54. $|2x + 1| = |3(x + 1)|$

Solve each inequality. Graph the solution set and write it using interval notation. **See Examples 6 and 8.**

55. $|x| < 4$

56. $|x| < 9$

57. $|x + 9| \le 12$

58. $|x - 8| \le 12$

59. $|3x - 2| < 10$

60. $|4 - 3x| \le 13$

61. $|5x - 12| < -5$

62. $|3x + 2| \le -3$

Solve each inequality. Graph the solution set and write it using interval notation. **See Examples 9–11.**

63. $|x| > 3$

64. $|x| > 7$

65. $|x - 12| > 24$

66. $|x + 5| \ge 7$

67. $0 \le |5x - 1| - 2$

68. $0 \le |6x - 3| - 5$

69. $|4x + 3| \ge -5$

70. $|7x + 2| \ge -8$

See Examples 4, 6, and 9.

71. Let $f(x) = |x + 3|$. For what value(s) of x is $f(x) = 3$?

72. Let $g(x) = |2 - x|$. For what value(s) of x is $g(x) = 2$?

73. Let $f(x) = |2(x - 1) + 4|$. For what value(s) of x is $f(x) < 4$?

74. Let $h(x) = \left|\frac{x}{5} - \frac{1}{2}\right|$. For what value(s) of x is $h(x) > \frac{9}{10}$?

TRY IT YOURSELF

Solve each equation and inequality. For the inequalities, graph the solution set and write it using interval notation.

75. $|3x + 2| + 1 > 15$

76. $|2x - 5| - 5 > 20$

77. $6\left|\frac{x - 2}{3}\right| \le 24$

78. $8\left|\frac{x - 2}{3}\right| > 32$

79. $-7 = 2 - |0.3x - 3|$

80. $-1 = 1 - |0.1x + 8|$

81. $|2 - 3x| \ge -8$

82. $|-1 - 2x| > 5$

83. $|7x + 12| = |x - 6|$

84. $|8 - x| = |x + 2|$

85. $2 \ge 3|2 - 3x| + 2$

86. $7 \ge |15x - 45| + 7$

87. $-14 = |x - 3|$

88. $-75 = |x + 4|$

89. $\frac{6}{5} = \left|\frac{3x}{5} + \frac{x}{2}\right|$

90. $\frac{11}{12} = \left|\frac{x}{3} - \frac{3x}{4}\right|$

91. $-|2x - 3| < -7$

92. $-|3x + 1| < -8$

93. $|0.5x + 1| < -23$

94. $15 \ge 7 - |1.4x + 9|$

Look Alikes . . .

95. a. $\frac{x}{10} - 1 = 1$ **b.** $\left|\frac{x}{10} - 1\right| = 1$

    c. $\frac{x}{10} - 1 > 1$ **d.** $\left|\frac{x}{10} - 1\right| > 1$

96. a. $4x - 5 = 15$ **b.** $|4x - 5| = 15$

    c. $4x - 5 \le 15$ **d.** $|4x - 5| \le 15$

97. a. $0.9 - 0.3x = 8.4$ **b.** $|0.9 - 0.3x| = 8.4$

    c. $0.9 - 0.3x > 8.4$ **d.** $|0.9 - 0.3x| > 8.4$

98. a. $8(x - 4) = 6x - 44$

    b. $|8(x - 4)| = |6x - 44|$

Solve the absolute value inequality in part a. Graph the solution set and write it in interval notation. Then use your work from part a to determine the solution set for the absolute value inequality in part b. (No new work is necessary!) Graph the solution set and write it in interval notation.

99. a. $|8x - 40| \le 16$ **b.** $|8x - 40| \ge 16$

100. a. $0 \le |14 - 27x|$ **b.** $0 > |14 - 27x|$

101. a. $\left|\dfrac{4x - 4}{3}\right| - 1 > 11$

b. $\left|\dfrac{4x - 4}{3}\right| - 1 \le 11$

102. a. $\left|-\dfrac{1}{2}x - 3\right| + 2 > 7$

b. $\left|-\dfrac{1}{2}x - 3\right| + 2 < 7$

APPLICATIONS

103. Temperature Ranges.   The temperatures on a sunny summer day satisfied the inequality $|t - 78°| \le 8°$, where t is a temperature in degrees Fahrenheit. Solve this inequality and express the range of temperatures as a double inequality.

104. Operating Temperatures.   A car CD player has an operating temperature of $|t - 40°| < 80°$, where t is a temperature in degrees Fahrenheit. Solve the inequality and express this range of temperatures as an interval.

105. Auto Mechanics.   On most cars, the bottoms of the front wheels are closer together than the tops, creating a *camber angle*. This lessens road shock to the steering system. (See the illustration.) The specifications for a certain car state that the camber angle c of its wheels should be $0.6° \pm 0.5°$.

a. Express the range with an inequality containing absolute value symbols.

b. Solve the inequality and express this range of camber angles as an interval.

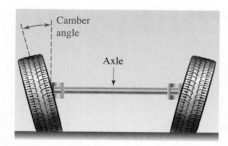

106. Steel Production.   A sheet of steel is to be 0.250 inch thick with a tolerance of 0.025 inch.

a. Express this specification with an inequality containing absolute value symbols, using x to represent the thickness of a sheet of steel.

b. Solve the inequality and express the range of thickness as an interval.

107. Error Analysis.   In a lab, students measured the percent of copper p in a sample of copper sulfate. The students know that copper sulfate is actually 25.46% copper by mass. They are to compare their results to the actual value and find the amount of *experimental error*. Which measurements shown in the illustration satisfy the absolute value inequality $|p - 25.46| \le 1.00$?

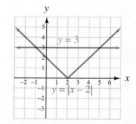

Lab 4	Section A
Title:	
"Percent copper (Cu) in	
copper sulfate (CuSO$_4$·5H$_2$O)"	

Results

	% Copper
Trial #1:	22.91%
Trial #2:	26.45%
Trial #3:	26.49%
Trial #4:	24.76%

108. Error Analysis.   See Exercise 107. Which measurements satisfy the absolute value inequality $|p - 25.46| > 1.00$?

WRITING

109. Explain the error.

Solve: $|x| + 2 = 6$

~~$x + 2 = 6$~~   or   ~~$x + 2 = -6$~~

~~$x = 4$~~ | ~~$x = -8$~~

110. Explain why the equation $|x - 4| = -5$ has no solution.

111. Explain the differences between the solution sets of $|x| = 8$, $|x| < 8$, and $|x| > 8$.

112. Explain how to use the graph in the illustration to solve the following.

a. $|x - 2| = 3$

b. $|x - 2| \le 3$

c. $|x - 2| \ge 3$

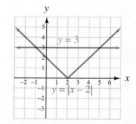

REVIEW

113. Flutes.   When it is assembled, a flute is 29 inches long. The middle piece is 4 inches less than twice as long as the first piece. The last piece is two-thirds as long as the first piece. Find the length of each piece of the flute.

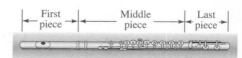

114. Commercials.   For the typical "one-hour" prime-time television slot, the number of minutes of commercials is $\frac{3}{7}$ of the number of minutes of the actual program. Determine how many minutes of the program are shown in that one hour.

CHALLENGE PROBLEMS

115. a. For what values of k does $|x| + k = 0$ have exactly two solutions?

b. For what values of k does $|x| + k = 0$ have exactly one solution?

116. Solve: $2^{|2x-3|} = 64$

Solution set for: $x + 6 < 8$

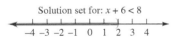

Solution set for: $5x + 3 \geq 4x$

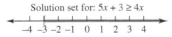

Graphing Linear Inequalities

ARE YOU READY?

The following problems review some basic skills that are needed when graphing linear inequalities.

1. True or false: $2(-3) + 1 > -4$

2. True or false: $8 \leq 8$

3. Graph: $2x - 3y = 6$

4. Determine whether each of the following points lies *above, below,* or *on* the line graphed in problem 3.

    a. $(2, -4)$ **b.** $(-3, -4)$ **c.** $(0, 0)$

Recall that an **inequality** is a statement that contains one of the symbols $<$, $\leq$, $>$, or $\geq$. Inequalities in one variable, such as $x + 6 < 8$ and $5x + 3 \geq 4x$, were solved in Section 2.7. Because they have an infinite number of solutions, we represented their solution sets graphically, by shading intervals on a number line. Two examples of this type of shading are shown in the left margin.

We now extend that concept to linear inequalities *in two variables,* as we introduce a procedure that is used to graph their solution sets.

1 Determine Whether an Ordered Pair Is a Solution of an Inequality.

If the $=$ symbol in a linear equation in two variables is replaced with an inequality symbol, we have a **linear inequality in two variables.**

Linear Inequalities ▼	A **linear inequality in two variables** is an inequality that can be written in one of the forms
	$$Ax + By > C, \qquad Ax + By < C, \qquad Ax + By \geq C, \qquad \text{or} \qquad Ax + By \leq C$$
	where A, B, and C are real numbers and A and B are not both 0.

Some examples of linear inequalities in two variables are

$$x - y \leq 5, \qquad 4x + 3y < -6, \qquad y > 2x \qquad \text{and} \qquad x < -3$$

As with linear equations, an ordered pair (x, y) is a **solution of an inequality** in x and y if a true statement results when the values of the variables are substituted into the inequality.

EXAMPLE 1 Determine whether each ordered pair is a solution of $x - y \leq 5$. Then graph each solution:
a. $(4, 2)$ **b.** $(0, -6)$ **c.** $(1, -4)$

Strategy We will substitute each ordered pair of coordinates into the inequality.

Why If the resulting statement is true, the ordered pair is a solution.

Solution

a. For $(4, 2)$:

$$x - y \leq 5 \qquad \text{This is the given inequality.}$$
$$4 - 2 \overset{?}{\leq} 5 \qquad \text{Substitute 4 for x and 2 for y.}$$
$$2 \leq 5 \qquad \text{True}$$

Because $2 \leq 5$ is true, $(4, 2)$ is a solution of $x - y \leq 5$. We say that $(4, 2)$ *satisfies* the inequality. This solution is graphed as shown on the right.

> **Notation**
>
> The symbol $\overset{?}{\leq}$ is read as "is possibly less than or equal to."

Two solutions of $x - y \leq 5$.

b. For $(0, -6)$:

$$x - y \leq 5 \qquad \text{This is the given inequality.}$$
$$0 - (-6) \overset{?}{\leq} 5 \qquad \text{Substitute 0 for x and } -6 \text{ for y.}$$
$$6 \leq 5 \qquad \text{False}$$

Because $6 \leq 5$ is false, $(0, -6)$ is not a solution.

c. For $(1, -4)$:

$$x - y \leq 5 \qquad \text{This is the given inequality.}$$
$$1 - (-4) \overset{?}{\leq} 5 \qquad \text{Substitute 1 for x and } -4 \text{ for y.}$$
$$5 \leq 5 \qquad \text{True}$$

Because $5 \leq 5$ is true, $(1, -4)$ is a solution, and we graph it as shown.

Self Check 1 Using the inequality in Example 1, determine whether each ordered pair is a solution: **a.** $(8, 2)$ **b.** $(4, -1)$ **c.** $(-2, 4)$ **d.** $(-3, -5)$

Now Try ▶ Problem 19

In Example 1, we graphed two of the solutions of $x - y \leq 5$. Since there are infinitely more ordered pairs (x, y) that make the inequality true, it would not be reasonable to plot all of them. Fortunately, there is an easier way to show all of the solutions.

2 Graph a Linear Inequality in Two Variables.

The graph of a linear inequality is a picture that represents the set of all points whose coordinates satisfy the inequality. In general, such graphs are regions bounded by a line. We call those regions **half-planes,** and we use a two-step procedure to find them.

EXAMPLE 2   Graph: $x - y \leq 5$

Strategy   We will graph the **related equation** $x - y = 5$ to establish a boundary line between two regions of the coordinate plane. Then we will determine which region contains points whose coordinates satisfy the given inequality.

Why   The graph of a linear inequality in two variables is a region of the coordinate plane on one side of a boundary line.

Solution   Since the inequality symbol $\leq$ includes an equal symbol, the graph of $x - y \leq 5$ includes the graph of $x - y = 5$.

Step 1:   To graph $x - y = 5$, we use the intercept method, as shown in part (a) of the illustration below. The resulting line, called a **boundary line,** divides the coordinate plane into two half-planes. To show that the points on the boundary line are solutions of $x - y \leq 5$, we draw it as a solid line.

The inequality $x - y \leq 5$ means

$$x - y = 5 \quad \text{or} \quad x - y < 5$$

A table of solutions to graph the boundary

$$x - y = 5$$

x	y	(x, y)
0	−5	(0, −5)
5	0	(5, 0)
6	1	(6, 1)

Let $x = 0$ and find y.
Let $y = 0$ and find x.
As a check, let $x = 6$ and find y.

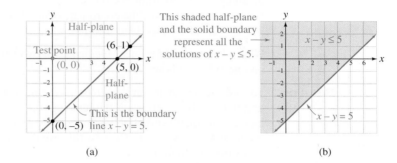

(a)   (b)

Step 2:   Since the inequality $x - y \leq 5$ also allows $x - y$ to be less than 5, other ordered pairs, besides those on the boundary, satisfy the inequality. For example, consider the origin, with coordinates (0, 0). If we substitute 0 for x and 0 for y in the given inequality, we have

$$x - y \leq 5 \quad \text{This is the given inequality.}$$
$$0 - 0 \stackrel{?}{\leq} 5 \quad \text{Substitute.}$$
$$0 \leq 5 \quad \text{True}$$

Because $0 \leq 5$, the coordinates of the origin satisfy $x - y \leq 5$. In fact, the coordinates of every point on the same side of the boundary as the origin satisfy the inequality. To indicate this, we shade in red the half-plane that contains the test point (0, 0), as shown in part (b). Every point in the shaded half-plane and every point on the boundary line satisfies $x - y \leq 5$. On the other hand, the points in the unshaded half-plane *do not* satisfy $x - y \leq 5$.

As an informal check, we can pick an ordered pair that lies in the shaded region and one that does not lie in the shaded region. When we substitute their coordinates into the inequality, we should obtain a true statement and then a false statement.

Success Tip

All the points in the unshaded region below the boundary line have coordinates that satisfy $x - y > 5$.

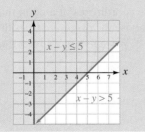

For (3, 1), in the shaded region:

$$x - y \leq 5$$
$$3 - 1 \stackrel{?}{\leq} 5 \quad \text{Substitute.}$$
$$2 \leq 5 \quad \text{True}$$

For (5, −4), not in the shaded region:

$$x - y \leq 5$$
$$5 - (-4) \stackrel{?}{\leq} 5 \quad \text{Substitute.}$$
$$9 \leq 5 \quad \text{False}$$

Self Check 2   Graph: $x - y \leq 2$

Now Try ▶ Problem 35

The previous example suggests the following **test-point method** to graph linear inequalities in two variables.

Graphing Linear Inequalities in Two Variables

1. Replace the inequality symbol with an equal symbol $=$ and graph the boundary line of the region. If the original inequality allows the possibility of equality (the symbol is either $\le$ or $\ge$), draw the boundary line as a solid line. If equality is not allowed ($<$ or $>$), draw the boundary line as a dashed line.

2. Pick a test point that is on one side of the boundary line. (Use the origin if possible.) Replace x and y in the inequality with the coordinates of that point. If a true statement results, shade the side that contains that point. If a false statement results, shade the other side of the boundary.

EXAMPLE 3   Graph: $4x + 3y < -6$

Strategy   We will graph the related equation $4x + 3y = -6$ to establish the boundary line between two regions of the coordinate plane. Then we will determine which region contains points that satisfy the given inequality.

Why   The graph of a linear inequality in two variables is a region of the coordinate plane on one side of a boundary line.

Solution   To find the boundary line, we replace the inequality symbol with an equal symbol $=$ and graph $4x + 3y = -6$ using the intercept method. Since the inequality symbol $<$ does not include an equal symbol, the points on the graph of $4x + 3y = -6$ will not be part of the graph of $4x + 3y < -6$. To show this, we draw the boundary line as a dashed line. See part (a) of the illustration below.

A table of solutions to graph the boundary

$$4x + 3y = -6$$

x	y	(x, y)
0	-2	$(0, -2)$
$-\frac{3}{2}$	0	$\left(-\frac{3}{2}, 0\right)$
-3	2	$(-3, 2)$

Let $x = 0$ and find y.
Let $y = 0$ and find x.
As a check, let $x = -3$ and find y.

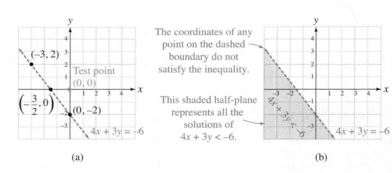

(a)   The coordinates of any point on the dashed boundary do not satisfy the inequality. This shaded half-plane represents all the solutions of $4x + 3y < -6$.   (b)

To determine which half-plane to shade, we substitute the coordinates of a point that lies on one side of the boundary line into $4x + 3y < -6$. We choose the origin $(0, 0)$ as the test point because the calculations are easy when they involve 0. We substitute 0 for x and 0 for y in the inequality.

Caution

When using a test point to determine which half-plane to shade, remember to substitute the coordinates into the given inequality, not the equation for the boundary.

$$4(0) + 3(0) = -6$$

$$4x + 3y < -6 \qquad \text{This is the given inequality.}$$
$$4(0) + 3(0) \stackrel{?}{<} -6 \qquad \text{The symbol } \stackrel{?}{<} \text{ is read as "is possibly less than."}$$
$$0 + 0 \stackrel{?}{<} -6$$
$$0 < -6 \qquad \text{False}$$

Since $0 < -6$ is a false statement, the point $(0, 0)$ does not satisfy the inequality. In fact, no point in the half-plane containing $(0, 0)$ is a solution. Therefore, we shade the other side of the boundary line—the half-plane that does not contain $(0, 0)$. The graph of the solution set of $4x + 3y < -6$ is the half-plane below the dashed line, as shown in part (b).

Self Check 3   Graph: $5x + 6y < -15$

Now Try ▶   Problem 37

3 Graph Inequalities with a Boundary through the Origin.

In the next example, the boundary line passes through the origin. In such cases, the ordered pair $(0, 0)$ should not be used as a test point to determine which half-plane to shade.

EXAMPLE 4 Graph: $y > 2x$

Strategy We will graph the related equation $y = 2x$ to establish the boundary line between two regions of the coordinate plane. Then we will determine which region contains points that satisfy the given inequality.

Why The graph of a linear inequality in two variables is a region of the coordinate plane on one side of a boundary line.

Solution To find the boundary line, we graph $y = 2x$. Since the symbol $>$ does *not* include an equal symbol, the points on the graph of $y = 2x$ are not part of the graph of $y > 2x$. Therefore, the boundary line should be dashed, as shown in part (a) of the illustration below.

Success Tip

Draw a solid boundary line if the inequality has $\leq$ or $\geq$. Draw a dashed line if the inequality has $<$ or $>$.

A table of solutions to graph the boundary

$y = 2x$

x	y	(x, y)
0	0	$(0, 0)$
-1	-2	$(-1, -2)$
1	2	$(1, 2)$

Select three values for x and find the corresponding values of y.

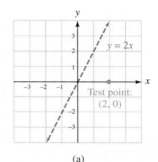

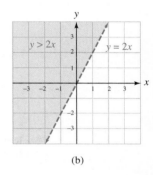

(a)   (b)

Success Tip

The origin $(0, 0)$ is a smart choice for a test point because calculations involving 0 are usually easy. If the origin is on the boundary, choose a test point not on the boundary that has one coordinate that is 0, such as $(0, 1)$ or $(2, 0)$.

To determine which half-plane to shade, we substitute the coordinates of a point that lies on one side of the boundary line into $y > 2x$. Since the origin is on the boundary, it cannot serve as a test point. One of the many possible choices for a test point is $(2, 0)$, because it does not lie on the boundary line. To see whether it satisfies $y > 2x$, we substitute 2 for x and 0 for y in the inequality.

$y > 2x$ This is the given inequality.

$0 \overset{?}{>} 2(2)$ The symbol $\overset{?}{>}$ is read as "is possibly greater than."

$0 > 4$ False

Since $0 > 4$ is a false statement, the point $(2, 0)$ does not satisfy the inequality. We shade the half-plane that does not contain $(2, 0)$, as shown in part (b).

Self Check 4 Graph: $y < 3x$

Now Try Problem 55

The graphs of some linear inequalities in two variables have boundary lines that are horizontal or vertical.

EXAMPLE 5 Graph each linear inequality: **a.** $x < -3$ **b.** $y \geq 0$

Strategy We will use the procedure for graphing linear inequalities in two variables.

Why Since the inequalities can be written as $x + 0y < -3$ and $0x + y \geq 0$, they are linear inequalities in two variables.

Solution **a.** Because $x < -3$ contains an $<$ symbol, we draw the boundary, $x = -3$, as a dashed vertical line. See figure (a) below. We can use $(0, 0)$ as the test point.

$x < -3$ This is the given inequality.

$0 < -3$ Substitute 0 for x. The y-coordinate of the test point (0, 0) is not used.

Since the result is false, we shade the half-plane that does not contain $(0, 0)$, as shown in figure (b) below. Note that the solution consists of all points that have an x-coordinate that is less than -3.

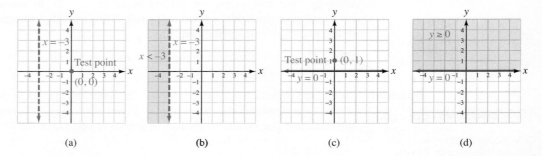

(a)   (b)   (c)   (d)

b. Because $y \geq 0$ contains an $\geq$ symbol, we draw the boundary, $y = 0$, as a solid horizontal line. (Recall that the graph of $y = 0$ is the x-axis. See figure (c) above.) Next, we choose a test point not on the boundary. The point $(0, 1)$ is a convenient choice. See figure (c) above.

$y \geq 0$ This is the given inequality.

$1 \geq 0$ Substitute 1 for y. The x-coordinate of the test point (0, 1) is not used.

Since the result is true, we shade the half-plane that contains $(0, 1)$, as shown in part (d) above. Note that the solution consists of all points that have a y-coordinate that is greater than or equal to 0.

Self Check 5   Graph each linear inequality: **a.** $x \geq 2$ **b.** $y < 4$

Now Try ▶   Problems 63 and 65

4 Solve Applied Problems Involving Linear Inequalities in Two Variables.

When solving applied problems, phrases such as *at least*, *at most*, and *should not exceed* indicate that an inequality should be used.

EXAMPLE 6   **Working Two Jobs.**   Carlos has two part-time jobs, one paying $10 per hour and another paying $12 per hour. If x represents the number of hours he works on the first job, and y represents the number of hours he works on the second, the graph of $10x + 12y \geq 240$ shows the possible ways he can schedule his time to earn at least $240 per week to pay his college expenses. Find four possible combinations of hours he can work to achieve his financial goal.

Strategy   We will graph the inequality and find four points whose coordinates satisfy the inequality.

Why   The coordinates of these points will give four possible combinations.

Solution The graph of the inequality is shown below in part (a) of the illustration. Any point in the shaded region represents a possible way Carlos can schedule his time and earn $240 or more per week. If each shift is a whole number of hours long, the red highlighted points in part (b) represent four of the many acceptable combinations.

(6, 24):	6 hours on the first job, 24 hours on the second job
(12, 12):	12 hours on the first job, 12 hours on the second job
(22, 4):	22 hours on the first job, 4 hours on the second job
(26, 20):	26 hours on the first job, 20 hours on the second job

To verify one combination, suppose Carlos works 22 hours on the first job and 4 hours on the second job. He will earn

$$\$10(22) + \$12(4) = \$220 + \$48$$
$$= \$268 \qquad \text{This is at least \$240 per week.}$$

A table of solutions to graph the boundary

$$10x + 12y = 240$$

x	y	(x, y)
0	20	(0, 20)
24	0	(24, 0)

Let $x = 0$ and find y.
Let $y = 0$ and find x.

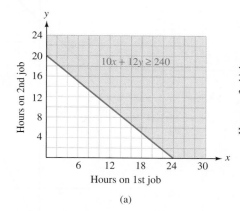

(a)

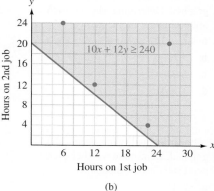

(b)

Self Check 6 **iTunes.** Brianna and Ashley pool their money to purchase some songs and movies on iTunes. If songs cost $1 and movies cost $15, write an inequality to represent the number of songs and movies they can buy if they want to spend $150 or less.

Now Try Problem 79

SECTION 3.7 **STUDY SET**

VOCABULARY

Fill in the blanks.

1. $2x - y \le 4$ is a linear _____ in two variables.

2. An ordered pair (x, y) is a _____ of a linear inequality in two variables if a true statement results when the values of the variables are substituted into the inequality.

3. (7, 2) is a solution of $x - y > 1$. We say that (7, 2) _____ the inequality.

4. In the graph, the line $2x - y = 4$ is the _____ line.

5. In the graph, the line $2x - y = 4$ divides the coordinate plane into two _____.

6. When graphing a linear inequality, we determine which half-plane to shade by substituting the coordinates of a test _____ into the inequality.

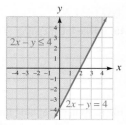

CONCEPTS

7. Determine whether $(-3, -5)$ is a solution of $5x - 3y \ge 0$.

8. Determine whether $(3, -1)$ is a solution of $x + 4y < -1$.

9. Fill in the blanks: A _____ line indicates that points on the boundary are not solutions and a _____ line indicates that points on the boundary are solutions.

10. The boundary for the graph of a linear inequality is shown. Why can't the origin be used as a test point to decide which side to shade?

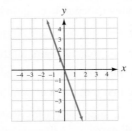

11. If a false statement results when the coordinates of a test point are substituted into a linear inequality, which half-plane should be shaded to represent the solution of the inequality?

12. A linear inequality has been graphed. Determine whether each point satisfies the inequality.
    a. $(1, -3)$
    b. $(-2, -1)$
    c. $(2, 3)$
    d. $(3, -4)$

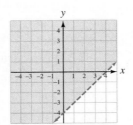

13. A linear inequality has been graphed. Determine whether each point satisfies the inequality.
    a. $(2, 1)$
    b. $(-2, -4)$
    c. $(4, -2)$
    d. $(-3, 4)$

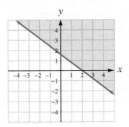

14. To graph linear inequalities, we must be able to graph boundary lines. Complete the table of solutions for each given boundary line.

    a. $5x - 3y = 15$

x	y	(x, y)
0		
	0	
1		

    b. $y = 3x - 2$

x	y	(x, y)
-1		
0		
2		

NOTATION

15. Write the meaning of each symbol in words.
    a. $<$
    b. $\geq$
    c. $\leq$
    d. $\overset{?}{>}$

16. a. When graphing linear inequalities, which inequality symbols are associated with a dashed boundary line?
    b. When graphing linear inequalities, which inequality symbols are associated with a solid boundary line?

17. Fill in the blanks: The inequality $4x + 2y \leq 9$ means $4x + 2y$ ▢ 9 or $4x + 2y$ ▢ 9.

18. Fill in the blanks: The inequality $-x + 8y \geq 1$ means $-x + 8y$ ▢ 1 or $-x + 8y$ ▢ 1.

Determine whether each ordered pair is a solution of the given inequality. See Example 1.

19. $2x + y > 6; (3, 2)$
20. $4x - 2y \geq -6; (-2, 1)$
21. $-5x - 8y < 8; (-8, 4)$
22. $x + 3y > 14; (-3, 8)$
23. $4x - y \leq 0; \left(\frac{1}{2}, 1\right)$
24. $9x - y \leq 2; \left(\frac{1}{3}, 1\right)$
25. $-5x + 2y > -4; (0.8, 0.6)$
26. $6x - 2y < -7; (-0.2, 1.5)$

Complete the graph by shading the correct side of the boundary. See Example 2.

27. $x - y \geq -2$

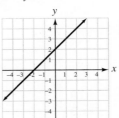

28. $x - y < 3$

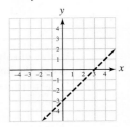

29. $y > 2x - 4$

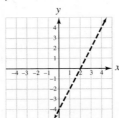

30. $y \leq -x + 1$

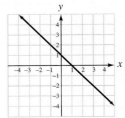

31. $x - 2y \geq 4$

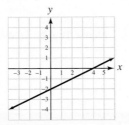

32. $3x + 2y > 12$

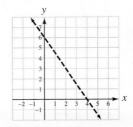

33. $y \leq 4x$

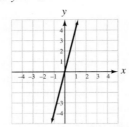

34. $y + 2x < 0$

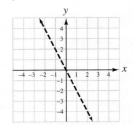

Graph each inequality. See Examples 2 and 3.

35. $x + y \geq 3$
36. $x + y < 2$
37. $3x - 4y > 12$
38. $5x + 4y \geq 20$
39. $2x + 3y \leq -12$
40. $3x - 2y > 6$
41. $y < 2x - 1$
42. $y > x + 1$
43. $y < -3x + 2$
44. $y \geq -2x + 5$

45. $y \geq -\dfrac{3}{2}x + 1$ 46. $y < \dfrac{x}{3} - 1$

47. $x - 2y \geq 4$ 48. $4x + y \geq -4$

49. $2y - x < 8$ 50. $y + 9x \geq 3$

51. $7x - 2y < 21$ 52. $3x - 3y \geq -10$

53. $2x - 3y \geq 4$ 54. $4x + 3y < 6$

Graph each inequality. See Example 4.

55. $y \geq 2x$ 56. $y < 3x$

57. $y < -\dfrac{x}{2}$ 58. $y \geq x$

59. $y + x < 0$ 60. $y - x < 0$

61. $5x + 3y < 0$ 62. $2x + 5y > 0$

Graph each inequality. See Example 5.

63. $x < 2$ 64. $y > -3$

65. $y \leq 1$ 66. $x \geq -4$

67. $y + 2.5 > 0$ 68. $x - 1.5 \leq 0$

69. $x \leq 0$ 70. $y < 0$

TRY IT YOURSELF

Look Alikes . . .

Graph the given inequality in part a. Then use your answer to part a to help you quickly graph the associated inequality in part b. (Hint: If you spot the relationship between the inequalities, the graph in part b can be completed without having to use the test-point method.)

71. **a.** $5x - 3y \geq -15$ **b.** $5x - 3y < -15$

72. **a.** $y > -\dfrac{2}{3}x + 2$ **b.** $y \leq -\dfrac{2}{3}x + 2$

73. **a.** $y + 2x < 0$ **b.** $y + 2x \geq 0$

74. **a.** $y \leq \dfrac{1}{4}x$ **b.** $y > \dfrac{1}{4}x$

APPLICATIONS

75. **Deliveries.** To decide the number x of pallets and the number y of barrels that a truck can hold, a driver refers to the graph below. Can a truck make a delivery of 4 pallets and 10 barrels in one trip?

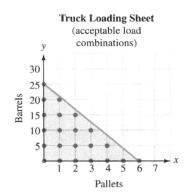

Truck Loading Sheet
(acceptable load combinations)

76. **Zoos.** To determine the allowable number of juvenile chimpanzees x and adult chimpanzees y that can live in an

enclosure, a zookeeper refers to the graph. Can 6 juvenile and 4 adult chimps be kept in the enclosure?

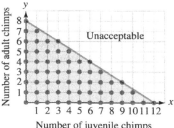

Number of adult chimps

Unacceptable

Number of juvenile chimps

77. ▶ **from Campus to Careers**

Dental Assistant

A dentist's office schedules 1-hour long appointments for adults and $\frac{3}{4}$-hour long appointments for children. The appointment times do not overlap. Let c represent the number of appointments scheduled for children and a represent the number of appointments scheduled for adults. The graph of $\frac{3}{4}c + a \leq 9$ shows the possible ways the time for seeing patients can be scheduled so that it does not exceed 9 hours per day. Graph the inequality. Label the horizontal axis c and the vertical axis a. Then find three possible combinations of children/adult appointments.

78. **Rolling Dice.** The points on the graph represent all of the possible outcomes when two fair dice are rolled a single time. For example, (5, 2), shown in red, represents a 5 on the first die and a 2 on the second. Which of the following sentences best describes the outcomes that lie in the shaded area?

   (i) Their sum is at most 6.   **(ii)** Their sum exceeds 6.

   (iii) Their sum does not exceed 6.   **(iv)** Their sum is at least 6.

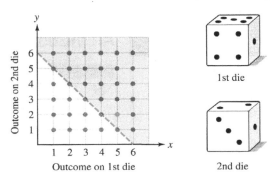

Outcome on 2nd die

Outcome on 1st die

1st die

2nd die

79. **Production Planning.** It costs a bakery $3 to make a cake and $4 to make a pie. If x represents the number of cakes made, and y represents the number of pies made, the graph of $3x + 4y \leq 120$ shows the possible combinations of cakes and pies that can be produced so that costs do not exceed $120 per day. Graph the inequality. Then find three possible combinations of cakes and pies that can be made so that the daily costs are not exceeded.

80. **Hiring Babysitters.**   Mrs. Cansino has a choice of two babysitters. Sitter 1 charges $6 per hour, and Sitter 2 charges $7 per hour. If x represents the number of hours she uses Sitter 1 and y represents the number of hours she uses Sitter 2, the graph of $6x + 7y \leq 42$ shows the possible ways she can hire the sitters and not spend more than $42 per week. Graph the inequality. Then find three possible ways she can hire the babysitters so that her weekly budget for babysitting is not exceeded.

81. **Inventories.**   A clothing store advertises that it maintains an inventory of at least $4,400 worth of men's jackets at all times. At the store, leather jackets cost $100 and nylon jackets cost $88. If x represents the number of leather jackets in stock and y represents the number of nylon jackets in stock, the graph of $100x + 88y \geq 4,400$ shows the possible ways the jackets can be stocked. Graph the inequality. Then find three possible combinations of leather and nylon jackets so that the store lives up to its advertising claim.

82. **Making Sporting Goods.**   A sporting goods manufacturer allocates at least 2,400 units of production time per day to make baseballs and footballs. It takes 20 units of time to make a baseball and 30 units of time to make a football. If x represents the number of baseballs made and y represents the number of footballs made, the graph of $20x + 30y \geq 2,400$ shows the possible ways to schedule the production time. Graph the inequality. Then find three possible combinations of production time for the company to make baseballs and footballs.

WRITING

83. Explain how to decide which side of the boundary line to shade when graphing a linear inequality in two variables.

84. Why is the origin usually a good test point to choose when graphing a linear inequality?

85. Why is the $(0, 0)$ not an acceptable choice for a test point when graphing a linear inequality whose boundary passes through the origin?

86. Explain the difference between the graph of the solution set of $x + 1 > 8$, an inequality in one variable, and the graph of $x + y > 8$, an inequality in two variables.

REVIEW

87. Solve $A = P + Prt$ for t.

88. What is the sum of the measures of the three angles of any triangle?

89. Simplify: $40\left(\dfrac{3}{8}x - \dfrac{1}{4}\right) + 40\left(\dfrac{4}{5}\right)$

90. Evaluate: $-4 + 5 - (-3) - 13$

CHALLENGE PROBLEMS

91. Find a linear inequality that has the graph shown.

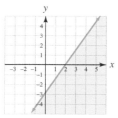

92. Graph the inequality: $4x - 3(x + 2y - 1) \geq -6\left(y - \dfrac{1}{2}\right)$

OBJECTIVES

1 Factor out the greatest common factor.

2 Factor by grouping.

3 Use factoring to solve formulas for a specified variable.

4 Factor trinomials.

5 Use substitution to factor trinomials.

6 Use the grouping method to factor trinomials.

Review of Factoring Methods: GCF, Grouping, Trinomials

ARE YOU READY?

The following problems review some basic skills that are needed when factoring expressions.

1. Find the prime factorization of 108.

2. Multiply: $6b(b^3 + 2b + 4)$

3. Multiply: $(x + 8)(x - 6)$

4. Multiply and simplify:
$m(m + 2) - 5(m + 2)$

5. Find two integers whose product is 10 and whose sum is 7.

6. Find two integers whose product is -18 and whose sum is 3.

In Chapter 6, we discussed how to factor polynomials. In this section, we will review that material.

1 Factor Out the Greatest Common Factor.

Recall that *when we factor a polynomial, we write a sum of terms as a product of factors.* To perform the most basic type of factoring, we determine whether the terms of the given polynomial have any common factors. This process, called **factoring out the greatest common factor,** is based on the distributive property.

EXAMPLE 1

Factor: $3xy^2z^3 + 6xz^2 - 9xyz^4$

Strategy We will determine the GCF of the terms of the polynomial. Then we will write each term of the polynomial as the product of the GCF and one other factor.

Why We can then use the distributive property to factor out the GCF.

Solution We begin by factoring each term:

$$\left. \begin{array}{l} 3xy^2z^3 = 3 \cdot x \cdot y \cdot y \cdot z \cdot z \cdot z \\ 6xz^2 = 2 \cdot 3 \cdot x \cdot z \cdot z \\ 9xyz^4 = 3 \cdot 3 \cdot x \cdot y \cdot z \cdot z \cdot z \cdot z \end{array} \right\} \text{GCF} = 3 \cdot x \cdot z \cdot z = 3xz^2$$

Since each term has one factor of 3, one factor of x, and two factors of z, and there are no other common factors, $3xz^2$ is the greatest common factor of the three terms. We write each term as the product of the GCF, $3xz^2$, and one other factor and proceed as follows:

$$3xy^2z^3 + 6xz^2 - 9xyz^4 = 3xz^2 \cdot y^2z + 3xz^2 \cdot 2 - 3xz^2 \cdot 3yz^2 \qquad \text{This can be done mentally.}$$
$$= 3xz^2(y^2z + 2 - 3yz^2) \qquad \text{Factor out the GCF, } 3xz^2.$$

We can check the factorization using multiplication.

$$3xz^2(y^2z + 2 - 3yz^2) = 3xy^2z^3 + 6xz^2 - 9xyz^4 \qquad \text{This is the original polynomial.}$$

Self Check 1 Factor: $6a^2b^2 - 4ab^3 + 2ab^2$

Now Try Problem 25

Success Tip

Always verify a factorization by performing the indicated multiplication. The result should be the original polynomial.

When asked to factor a polynomial whose leading coefficient is negative, we factor out the *opposite of the GCF.*

EXAMPLE 2   Factor out the opposite of the GCF from $-6u^2v^3 + 8u^3v^2$.

Strategy   We will determine the GCF of the terms of the polynomial. Then we will write each term as the product of the opposite of the GCF and one other factor.

Why   We can then use the distributive property to factor out the opposite of the GCF.

Solution   Because the greatest common factor of the two terms is $2u^2v^2$, the opposite of the greatest common factor is $-2u^2v^2$. To factor out $-2u^2v^2$, we proceed as follows:

$$-6u^2v^3 + 8u^3v^2 = -2u^2v^2 \cdot 3v - (-2u^2v^2)4u \quad \text{This can be done mentally.}$$
$$= -2u^2v^2(3v - 4u)$$

The leading coefficient of the polynomial within the parentheses is positive.

> **Success Tip**
>
> It is standard practice to factor in such a way that the leading coefficient of the polynomial within the parentheses is positive.

Self Check 2   Factor out the opposite of the GCF: $-3p^3q + 6p^2q^2$

Now Try ▶ Problem 35

A polynomial that cannot be factored is called a **prime polynomial** or an **irreducible polynomial**. For example, $9x + 16$ is a prime polynomial because its two terms, $9x$ and 16, have no common factors other than 1.

In the next example, we see that a common factor can have more than one term.

EXAMPLE 3   Factor: $a(x - y + z) - b(x - y + z) + 3(x - y + z)$

Strategy   We will factor out the trinomial $x - y + z$ from each term.

Why $x - y + z$ is the GCF of each term of the given expression.

Solution $a(x - y + z) - b(x - y + z) + 3(x - y + z) = (x - y + z)(a - b + 3)$

Self Check 3   Factor: $c^2(y^2 + 1) + d^2(y^2 + 1)$

Now Try ▶ Problem 41

2 Factor by Grouping.

Although the terms of many polynomials don't have a common factor, other than 1, it is possible to factor some of them by arranging their terms in convenient groups. This method is called **factoring by grouping.**

EXAMPLE 4   Factor: $2c - 2d + cd - d^2$

Strategy   Since the four terms of the polynomial do not have a common factor (other than 1), we will attempt to factor the polynomial by grouping. We will factor out a common factor from the first two terms and from the last two terms.

Why   This will produce a common binomial factor that can be factored out.

Solution

Success Tip

You may want to review the steps in the process of factoring by grouping on page 438.

If we group the terms as highlighted in blue, the first two terms have a common factor, 2, and the last two terms have a common factor, d. When we factor out the common factor from each group, a common binomial factor $c - d$ appears.

$$2c - 2d \;+\; cd - d^2 = 2(c - d) + d(c - d) \qquad \text{Factor out 2 from } 2c - 2d \text{ and } d \text{ from } cd - d^2. \text{ Don't forget the } + \text{ sign.}$$

$$= (c - d)(2 + d) \qquad \text{Factor out the common binomial factor, } c - d.$$

We can check by multiplying:

$$(c - d)(2 + d) = 2c + cd - 2d - d^2$$
$$= 2c - 2d + cd - d^2 \qquad \text{Rearrange the terms to get the original polynomial.}$$

Self Check 4 Factor: $7m - 7n + mn - n^2$

Now Try ▶ Problems 43 and 47

The instruction "Factor" means to factor the given expression completely. Each factor of a completely factored expression will be prime.

To factor a polynomial, it is often necessary to factor more than once. When factoring a polynomial, *always look for a common factor first*.

EXAMPLE 5 Factor: $3x^3y - 4x^2y^2 - 6x^2y + 8xy^2$

Strategy Since all four terms have a common factor of xy, we factor it out first. Then we will attempt to factor the resulting polynomial by grouping.

Why Factoring out the GCF first makes factoring by any method easier.

Solution We begin by factoring out the common factor xy.

$$3x^3y - 4x^2y^2 - 6x^2y + 8xy^2 = xy(3x^2 - 4xy - 6x + 8y)$$

We can now factor the resulting four-term polynomial $3x^2 - 4xy - 6x + 8y$ by grouping:

$$3x^3y - 4x^2y^2 - 6x^2y + 8xy^2$$
$$= xy(3x^2 - 4xy - 6x + 8y)$$
$$= xy[x(3x - 4y) - 2(3x - 4y)] \qquad \text{Brackets are needed to enclose the factoring by grouping steps. Factor } x \text{ from } 3x^2 - 4xy \text{ and } -2 \text{ from } -6x + 8y.$$

$$= xy(3x - 4y)(x - 2) \qquad \text{Factor out } 3x - 4y. \text{ The brackets are no longer needed.}$$

Because xy, $3x - 4y$, and $x - 2$ are prime, no further factoring can be done; the factorization is complete.

Self Check 5 Factor: $3a^3b + 3a^2b - 2a^2b^2 - 2ab^2$

Now Try ▶ Problem 51

3 Use Factoring to Solve Formulas for a Specified Variable.

Factoring is often required to solve a formula for one of its variables.

EXAMPLE 6

Electronics. The formula $r_1r_2 = rr_2 + rr_1$ is used in electronics to relate the combined resistance, r, of two resistors wired in parallel. The variable r_1 represents the resistance of the first resistor, and the variable r_2 represents the resistance of the second. Solve for r_2.

Strategy To isolate r_2 on one side of the equation, we will get all the terms involving r_2 on the left side and all the terms not involving r_2 on the right side.

Why To *solve a formula for a specified variable* means to isolate that variable on one side of the equation, with all other variables and constants on the opposite side.

Solution

We want to isolate this variable on one side of the equation.

$$r_1r_2 = rr_2 + rr_1$$

$$r_1r_2 - rr_2 = rr_1 \qquad \text{To eliminate } rr_2 \text{ on the right side, subtract } rr_2 \text{ from both sides.}$$

$$r_2(r_1 - r) = rr_1 \qquad \text{On the left side, factor out the GCF } r_2 \text{ from } r_1r_2 - rr_2.$$

$$\frac{r_2(\overset{1}{\cancel{r_1 - r}})}{\underset{1}{\cancel{r_1 - r}}} = \frac{rr_1}{r_1 - r} \qquad \text{To isolate } r_2 \text{ on the left side, divide both sides by } r_1 - r.$$

$$r_2 = \frac{rr_1}{r_1 - r} \qquad \text{Simplify the left side by removing the common factor } r_1 - r \text{ from the numerator and denominator.}$$

Self Check 6 Solve $f_1f_2 = ff_1 + ff_2$ for f_1.

Now Try ▶ Problem 57

4 Factor Trinomials.

Recall that many trinomials factor as the product of two binomials.

EXAMPLE 7

Factor: $x^2 - 6x + 8$

Strategy We will assume that this trinomial is the product of two binomials. We must find the terms of the binomials.

Why Since the terms of $x^2 - 6x + 8$ do not have a common factor (other than 1), the only option is to try to factor it as the product of two binomials.

Solution We represent the binomials using two sets of parentheses. Since the first term of the trinomial is x^2, we enter x and x as the first terms of the binomial factors.

$$x^2 - 6x + 8 = \left(x \,\boxed{}\right)\left(x \,\boxed{}\right) \qquad \text{Because } x \cdot x \text{ will give } x^2.$$

The second terms of the binomials must be two integers whose product is 8 and whose sum is -6. We list all possible integer-pair factors of 8 in the table.

Factors of 8	Sum of the factors of 8
$1(8) = 8$	$1 + 8 = 9$
$2(4) = 8$	$2 + 4 = 6$
$-1(-8) = 8$	$-1 + (-8) = -9$
$-2(-4) = 8$	$-2 + (-4) = -6$ ← This is the pair to choose.

The fourth row of the table contains the correct pair of integers -2 and -4, whose product is 8 and whose sum is -6. To complete the factorization, we enter -2 and -4 as the second terms of the binomial factors.

$$x^2 - 6x + 8 = (x - 2)(x - 4)$$

Success Tip

You may want to review the procedure for factoring trinomials whose leading coefficient is 1 on page 447.

The Language of Algebra

Make sure you understand the following vocabulary: *Many trinomials factor as the product of two binomials.*

Trinomial $\quad$ Product of two binomials

$$\overbrace{x^2 - 6x + 8}^{\text{Trinomial}} = \overbrace{(x - 2)(x - 4)}^{\text{Product of two binomials}}$$

Check: We can verify the factorization by multiplication:

$$(x - 2)(x - 4) = x^2 - 4x - 2x + 8 \quad \text{Use the FOIL method.}$$
$$= x^2 - 6x + 8 \quad \text{This is the original trinomial.}$$

Self Check 7   Factor: $a^2 - 7a + 12$

Now Try ▶ Problem 63

EXAMPLE 8   Factor: $2a^2 + 4ab - 30b^2$

Strategy   We will factor out the GCF, 2, first. Then we will factor the resulting trinomial.

Why   The first step in factoring any polynomial is to factor out the GCF. Factoring out the GCF first makes factoring by any method easier.

Solution   Each term in this trinomial has a common factor of 2, which can be factored out.

$$2a^2 + 4ab - 30b^2 = 2(a^2 + 2ab - 15b^2)$$

Next, we factor $a^2 + 2ab - 15b^2$. Since the first term of the trinomial is a^2, the first term of each binomial factor must be a. Since the third term contains b^2, the last term of each binomial factor must contain b. To complete the factorization, we need to determine the coefficient of each b-term.

$$a^2 + 2ab - 15b^2 = \left(a \boxed{} b\right)\left(a \boxed{} b\right) \quad \begin{array}{l} \text{Because } a \cdot a \text{ will give } a^2 \\ \text{and } b \cdot b \text{ will give } b^2. \end{array}$$

The coefficients of b must be two integers whose product is -15 and whose sum is 2. We list the factors of -15 and find the pair whose sum is 2.

This is the pair to choose.
↓

$$1(-15) \qquad 3(-5) \qquad 5(-3) \qquad 15(-1)$$

Caution

Be sure to include all factors in the final answer. Here, a common error is to forget to write the GCF, which is 2.

The only factorization where the sum of the factors is 2 (which is the coefficient of the middle term of $a^2 + 2ab - 15b^2$) is $5(-3)$. Thus,

$$2a^2 + 4ab - 30b^2 = 2(a^2 + 2ab - 15b^2)$$
$$= 2(a + 5b)(a - 3b)$$

Verify this result by multiplication.

Self Check 8   Factor: $3p^2 + 6pq - 24q^2$

Now Try ▶ Problem 67

There are more combinations of coefficients to consider when factoring trinomials with leading coefficients other than 1. Because it is not easy to give specific rules for factoring such trinomials, we will use a method called the **trial-and-check method.**

EXAMPLE 9   Factor: $3p^2 - 4p - 4$

Strategy   We will assume that this trinomial is the product of two binomials. To find their terms, we will make educated guesses and then check them using multiplication.

Why   Since the terms of the trinomial do not have a common factor (other than 1), the only option is to try to factor it as the product of two binomials.

Solution   To factor the trinomial, we note that the first terms of the binomial factors must be $3p$ and p to give the first term of $3p^2$.

$$3p^2 - 4p - 4 = \left(3p\boxed{}\right)\left(p\boxed{}\right)$$ Because $3p \cdot p$ will give $3p^2$.

The second terms of the binomials must be two integers whose product is -4. There are three such pairs: $1(-4)$, $-1(4)$, and $-2(2)$. When these pairs are entered, and then reversed, as second terms of the binomials, there are six possibilities to consider.

Success Tip

You may want to review the procedure for factoring trinomials using the trial-and-check method on page 458.

For 1 and −4: $(3p + 1)(p - 4)$ or $(3p - 4)(p + 1)$

$-12p + p = -11p$ $3p + (-4p) = -p$

For −1 and 4: $(3p - 1)(p + 4)$ or $(3p + 4)(p - 1)$

$12p + (-p) = 11p$ $-3p + 4p = p$

Notation

By the commutative property of multiplication, the factors of a trinomial can be written in either order. Thus, we also could write:

$3p^2 - 4p - 4 = (p - 2)(3p + 2)$

For −2 and 2: $(3p - 2)(p + 2)$ or $(3p + 2)(p - 2)$

$6p + (-2p) = 4p$ $-6p + 2p = -4p$

Of these possibilities, only the one in blue gives the required middle term of $-4p$. Thus,

$$3p^2 - 4p - 4 = (3p + 2)(p - 2)$$

Self Check 9   Factor: $4q^2 - 9q - 9$

Now Try ▶ Problem 75

EXAMPLE 10   Factor: $6y^3 + 13x^2y^3 + 6x^4y^3$

Strategy   We write the expression in descending powers of x.

Why   It is easier to factor a trinomial if its terms are written in descending powers of one variable.

Solution   We write the expression in descending powers of x and factor out the greatest common factor, y^3.

$$6y^3 + 13x^2y^3 + 6x^4y^3 = 6x^4y^3 + 13x^2y^3 + 6y^3$$
$$= y^3(6x^4 + 13x^2 + 6)$$

Success Tip

Always write the terms of a trinomial in descending powers of one variable before attempting to factor it.

To factor $6x^4 + 13x^2 + 6$, we examine its terms.

■ Since the first term is $6x^4$, the first terms of the binomial factors must be either $2x^2$ and $3x^2$ or x^2 and $6x^2$.

$$6x^4 + 13x^2 + 6 = \left(2x^2\boxed{}\right)\left(3x^2\boxed{}\right) \text{ or } \left(x^2\boxed{}\right)\left(6x^2\boxed{}\right)$$

- Since the signs of the middle term and the last term of the trinomial are positive, the signs within each binomial factor will be positive.
- Since the product of the last terms of the binomial factors must be 6, we must find two numbers whose product is 6 that will lead to a middle term of $13x^2$.

After trying some combinations, we find the one that works.

$$6x^4y^3 + 13x^2y^3 + 6y^3 = y^3(6x^4 + 13x^2 + 6)$$
$$= y^3(2x^2 + 3)(3x^2 + 2)$$

Self Check 10   Factor: $4b + 11a^2b + 6a^4b$

Now Try ▶ Problem 87

---

5 Use Substitution to Factor Trinomials.

For more complicated expressions, especially those involving a quantity within parentheses, a substitution sometimes helps to simplify the factoring process.

EXAMPLE 11   Factor: $(x + y)^2 + 7(x + y) + 12$

Strategy   We will use a substitution where we will replace each expression $x + y$ with the variable z and factor the resulting trinomial.

Why   The resulting trinomial will be easier to factor because it will be in only one variable, z.

Solution   If we use the substitution $z = x + y$, we obtain

$$(x + y)^2 + 7(x + y) + 12 = z^2 + 7z + 12 \qquad \text{Replace } x + y \text{ with } z.$$
$$= (z + 4)(z + 3) \qquad \text{Factor the trinomial.}$$

To find the factorization of $(x + y)^2 + 7(x + y) + 12$, we substitute $x + y$ for each z in the expression $(z + 4)(z + 3)$.

$$(z + 4)(z + 3) = (x + y + 4)(x + y + 3)$$

Thus, $(x + y)^2 + 7(x + y) + 12 = (x + y + 4)(x + y + 3)$.

Self Check 11   Factor: $(a + b)^2 - 3(a + b) - 10$

Now Try ▶ Problem 95

---

6 Use the Grouping Method to Factor Trinomials.

Another way to factor trinomials is to write them as equivalent four-termed polynomials and factor by grouping.

EXAMPLE 12   Factor by grouping: **a.** $x^2 + 8x + 15$ **b.** $10x^2 + 13xy - 3y^2$

Strategy   In each case, we will express the middle term of the trinomial as the sum of two terms.

Why   We want to produce an equivalent four-termed polynomial that can be factored by grouping.

Solution

a. Since $x^2 + 8x + 15 = 1x^2 + 8x + 15$, we identify a as 1, b as 8, and c as 15. The **key number** is $ac = 1(15) = 15$. We must find two integers whose product is the key number 15 and whose sum is $b = 8$. Since the integers must have a positive product and a positive sum, we consider only positive factors of 15.

Key number = 15	$b = 8$
Positive factors of 15	**Sum of the factors of 15**
$1 \cdot 15 = 15$	$1 + 15 = 16$
$3 \cdot 5 = 15$	$3 + 5 = 8$

The second row of the table contains the correct pair of integers 3 and 5, whose product is 15 and whose sum is 8.

We can express the middle term, $8x$, of the trinomial as the *sum of two terms,* using the integers 3 and 5 as coefficients of the two terms and factor the equivalent four-termed polynomial by grouping:

$$x^2 + 8x + 15 = x^2 + 3x + 5x + 15 \qquad \text{Express 8x as 3x + 5x.}$$
$$x^2 + 3x + 5x + 15 = x(x + 3) + 5(x + 3) \qquad \begin{array}{l}\text{Factor x out of } x^2 + 3x \\ \text{and 5 out of 5x + 15.}\end{array}$$
$$= (x + 3)(x + 5) \qquad \text{Factor out the GCF, x + 3.}$$

Check the factorization by multiplying.

b. In $10x^2 + 13xy - 3y^2$, we have $a = 10$, $b = 13$, and $c = -3$. The key number is $ac = 10(-3) = -30$. We must find a factorization of -30 such that the sum of the factors is $b = 13$. Since the factors must have a negative product, their signs must be different. The possible factor pairs are listed in the table.

Key number = −30	$b = 13$
Factors of −30	**Sum of the factors of −30**
$1(-30) = -30$	$1 + (-30) = -29$
$2(-15) = -30$	$2 + (-15) = -13$
$3(-10) = -30$	$3 + (-10) = -7$
$5(-6) = -30$	$5 + (-6) = -1$
$6(-5) = -30$	$6 + (-5) = 1$
$10(-3) = -30$	$10 + (-3) = 7$
15(−2) = −30	**15 + (−2) = 13**
$30(-1) = -30$	$30 + (-1) = 29$

The seventh row contains the correct pair of numbers 15 and -2, whose product is -30 and whose sum is 13. They serve as the coefficients of two terms, $15xy$ and $-2xy$, that we place between $10x^2$ and $-3y^2$.

$$10x^2 + 13xy - 3y^2 = 10x^2 + 15xy - 2xy - 3y^2 \qquad \text{Express 13xy as 15xy − 2xy.}$$

We factor the resulting four-term polynomial by grouping.

$$10x^2 + 15xy - 2xy - 3y^2 = 5x(2x + 3y) - y(2x + 3y) \qquad \begin{array}{l}\text{Factor out 5x from} \\ 10x^2 + 15xy. \text{ Factor out} \\ -y \text{ from } -2xy - 3y^2.\end{array}$$
$$= (2x + 3y)(5x - y) \qquad \begin{array}{l}\text{Factor out the} \\ \text{GCF, 2x + 3y.}\end{array}$$

Thus, $10x^2 + 13xy - 3y^2 = (2x + 3y)(5x - y)$. Check by multiplying.

Self Check 12 Factor by grouping: **a.** $m^2 + 13m + 42$
b. $15a^2 + 17ab - 4b^2$

Now Try ▶ Problems 63 and 75

SECTION 8.6 ▶ STUDY SET

VOCABULARY

Fill in the blanks.

1. When we write $2x + 4$ as $2(x + 2)$, we say that we have _____ $2x + 4$.

2. When we factor a polynomial, we write a sum of terms as a _____ of factors.

3. The abbreviation GCF stands for _____ _____ _____.

4. If a polynomial cannot be factored, it is called a _____ polynomial or an irreducible polynomial.

5. To factor $ab + 6a + 2b + 12$ by _____, we begin by factoring out a from the first two terms and 2 from the last two terms.

6. The trinomial $4a^2 - 5a - 6$ is written in _____ powers of a.

7. The _____ coefficient of $x^2 - 3x + 2$ is 1, the _____ of the middle term is -3, and the last term is ___.

8. The statement $x^2 - x - 12 = (x - 4)(x + 3)$ shows that $x^2 - x - 12$ factors into the _____ of two binomials.

CONCEPTS

9. The prime factorizations of three terms are shown here. Find their GCF.

$$2 \cdot 2 \cdot 3 \cdot x \cdot x \cdot y \cdot y \cdot y$$
$$2 \cdot 3 \cdot 3 \cdot x \cdot y \cdot y \cdot y \cdot y$$
$$2 \cdot 3 \cdot 3 \cdot 7 \cdot x \cdot x \cdot x \cdot y \cdot y$$

10. Use multiplication to determine whether $(3t - 1)(5t - 6)$ is the correct factorization of $15t^2 - 19t + 6$.

11. Complete the table.

Factors of 8	Sum of the factors of 8
$1(8) = 8$	
$2(4) = 8$	
$-1(-8) = 8$	
$-2(-4) = 8$	

12. Find two integers whose
    a. product is 10 and whose sum is 7.
    b. product is 8 and whose sum is -6.
    c. product is -6 and whose sum is 1.
    d. product is -9 and whose sum is -8.

13. Complete the key number table.

   Key number $= 12$ $b = -7$

Negative factors of 12	Sum of the factors of 12
$-1(-12) = 12$	
$-3(-4) = 12$	

14. Use the substitution $x = a + b$ to rewrite the trinomial $6(a + b)^2 - 17(a + b) - 3$.

NOTATION

Complete each factorization.

15. $15c^3d^4 - 25c^2d^4 + 5c^3d^6 = $ _____ $(3c - 5 + cd^2)$

16. $x^3 - x^2 + 2x - 2 = $ ___ $(x - 1) + $ ___ $(x - 1)$
    $= ($ ___ $)(x^2 + 2)$

17. $6m^2 + 7m - 3 = ($ ___ $- 1)(2m + $ ___ $)$

18. $2y^2 + 10y + 12 = $ ___ $(y^2 + 5y + 6)$
    $= 2(y + $ ___ $)($ ___ $+ 2)$

GUIDED PRACTICE

Factor each polynomial. **See Example 1.**

19. $2x^2 - 6x$

20. $3y^3 + 3y^2$

21. $15x^2y - 10x^2y^2$

22. $63x^3y^2 + 81x^2y^4$

23. $27z^3 + 12z^2 + 3z$

24. $25t^6 - 10t^3 + 5t^2$

25. $24s^3 - 12s^2t + 6st^2$

26. $18y^2z^2 + 12y^2z^3 - 24y^4z^3$

27. $11x^3 - 12y$

28. $14s^3 + 15t^6$

29. $23a^2b^3 + 4x^3y^2$

30. $18p^3q^2 - 5t^5$

Factor each polynomial by factoring out the opposite of the GCF. **See Example 2.**

31. $-8a - 16$

32. $-6b - 30$

33. $-6x^2 - 3xy$

34. $-15y^3 - 25y^2$

35. $-18a^2b + 12ab^2$

36. $-21t^5 + 28t^3$

37. $-8a^4c^8 + 28a^3c^8 - 20a^2c^9$

38. $-30x^{10}y + 24x^9y^2 - 60x^8y^2$

Factor. **See Example 3.**

39. $(x + y)u + (x + y)v$

40. $4(x + y) + t(x + y)$

41. $5(a - b + c) - t(a - b + c)$

42. $(a - b - c)r - (a - b - c)s$

Factor by grouping. **See Example 4.**

43. $ax + bx + ay + by$

44. $ar - br + as - bs$

45. $x^2 + yx - x - y$

46. $d^2 + cd + c + d$

47. $t^3 - 3t^2 - 7t + 21$

48. $b^3 - 4b^2 - 3b + 12$

49. $a^2 - 4b + ab - 4a$

50. $3c - cd + 3d - c^2$

Factor. **See Example 5.**

51. $6x^3 - 6x^2 + 12x - 12$

52. $3x^3 - 6x^2 + 15x - 30$

53. $28a^3b^3c + 14a^3c - 4b^3c - 2c$

54. $12x^3z + 12xy^2z - 8x^2yz - 8y^3z$

Solve for the specified variable or expression. **See Example 6.**

55. $2g = ch + dh$ for h

56. $d_1d_2 = fd_2 + fd_1$ for f

57. $r_1r_2 = rr_2 + rr_1$ for r_1

58. $rx - ty = by$ for y

59. $b^2x^2 + a^2y^2 = a^2b^2$ for a^2

60. $b^2x^2 + a^2y^2 = a^2b^2$ for b^2

61. $Sn = (n - 2)180$ for n

62. $S(1 - r) = a - lr$ for r

Factor. See Example 7 or 12.

63. $x^2 - 5x + 6$

64. $y^2 + 7y + 6$

65. $x^2 + x - 30$

66. $c^2 + 3c - 28$

Factor. See Example 8.

67. $3x^2 + 12xy - 63y^2$

68. $2y^2 + 4yz - 48z^2$

69. $6a^2 - 30ab + 24b^2$

70. $4b^2 + 12bc - 16c^2$

71. $n^4 - 28n^3t - 60n^2t^2$

72. $c^4 - 16c^3d - 80c^2d^2$

73. $-3x^2 + 15xy - 18y^2$

74. $-2y^2 - 16yt + 40t^2$

Factor. See Example 9 or 12.

75. $5x^2 + 13x + 6$

76. $5x^2 + 18x + 9$

77. $7a^2 + 12a + 5$

78. $7a^2 + 36a + 5$

79. $11y^2 + 32y - 3$

80. $2y^2 - 9y - 18$

81. $8x^2 - 22x + 5$

82. $4z^2 - 13z + 3$

83. $6y^2 - 13y + 6$

84. $6x^2 - 11x + 3$

85. $15b^2 + 4b - 4$

86. $8a^2 + 6a - 9$

Factor each expression. See Example 10.

87. $30x^4 - 25x^2 - 20$

88. $14x^4 + 77x^2 + 84$

89. $32x^4 - 96x^2 + 72$

90. $20a^4 + 60a^2 + 45$

91. $64h^5 - 4h + 24h^3$

92. $9x^5 - 24x + 30x^3$

93. $-3a^4 - 5a^2b^2 - 2b^4$

94. $-2x^4 + 3x^2y^2 + 5y^4$

Factor by using a substitution. See Example 11.

95. $(a + b)^2 - 2(a + b) - 24$

96. $(x - y)^2 + 3(x - y) - 10$

97. $(x + a)^2 + 2(x + a) + 1$

98. $(a + b)^2 - 2(a + b) + 1$

TRY IT YOURSELF

Factor completely. Factor out all common factors first including −1 *if the first term is negative. If an expression is prime, so indicate.*

99. $3(m + n + p) + x(m + n + p)$

100. $x(x - y - z) + y(x - y - z)$

101. $-63u^3v^6 + 28u^2v^7 - 21u^3v^3$

102. $-56x^4y^3 - 72x^3y^4 + 80xy^2$

103. $b^4x^2 - 12b^2x^2 + 35x^2$

104. $c^3x^4 + 11c^3x^2 - 42c^3$

105. $1 - n - m + mn$

106. $a^2x^2 - 10 - 2x^2 + 5a^2$

107. $-x^2 + 4xy + 21y^2$

108. $-a^2 - 4ab + 5b^2$

109. $a^2x + bx - a^2 - b$

110. $x^2y - ax - xy + a$

111. $4y^2 + 4y + 1$

112. $9x^2 + 6x + 1$

113. $b^2 + 8b + 18$

114. $x^2 + 4x - 28$

115. $13r + 3r^2 - 10$

116. $-r + 3r^2 - 10$

117. $y^3 - 12 + 3y - 4y^2$

118. $h^3 - 8 + h - 8h^2$

119. $2y^5 - 26y^3 + 60y$

120. $2y^5 - 26y^3 + 84y$

121. $14(q - r)^2 - 17(q - r) - 6$

122. $8(h + s)^2 + 34(h + s) + 35$

APPLICATIONS

123. Crayons.   The amount of colored wax used to make the crayon shown in the illustration can be found by computing its volume using the formula

$$V = \pi r^2 h_1 + \frac{1}{3}\pi r^2 h_2$$

Factor the expression on the right side of this equation.

124. Packaging.   The amount of cardboard needed to make the following cereal box can be found by finding the area A, which is given by the formula

$$A = 2wh + 4wl + 2lh$$

where w is the width, h the height, and l the length. Solve the equation for the width.

125. Ice.   The surface area of the ice cube is represented by the expression $6x^2 + 36x + 54$. Use factoring to find the length of an edge of the cube.

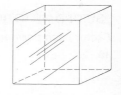

126. Checkers. The area of the checkerboard is represented by the expression $25x^2 - 40x + 16$. Use factoring to find the length of each side.

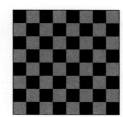

130. Determine whether each equation defines y to be a function of x. If it does not, find two ordered pairs where more than one value of y corresponds to a single value of x.
  a. $x = |y|$
  b. $y = x^2$
  c. $y^2 = x$

CHALLENGE PROBLEMS

Factor out the specified factor.

131. t^{-3} from $t^5 + 4t^{-6}$

132. $7x^{-3n}$ from $21x^{6n} + 7x^{3n} + 14$

Factor. Assume that n is a natural number.

133. $x^{2n} + 2x^n + 1$ **134.** $2a^{6n} - 3a^{3n} - 2$

135. $x^{4n} + 2x^{2n}y^{2n} + y^{4n}$ **136.** $6x^{2n} + 7x^n - 3$

WRITING

127. Explain the error in the following solution.

  Solve for r_1: $r_1 r_2 = rr_2 + rr_1$

$$\frac{r_1 r_2}{r_2} = \frac{rr_2 + rr_1}{r_2}$$

$$\cancel{r_1 = \frac{rr_2 + rr_1}{r_2}}$$

128. Explain the error.

  Factor: $\cancel{2x^2 - 4x - 6 = (2x + 2)(x - 3)}$

REVIEW

129. Use the graph to find:
  a. $s(-5)$
  b. $s(4)$
  c. The values of x for which $s(x) = 0$
  d. The value of x for which $s(x) = 4$

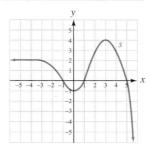

OBJECTIVES

1 Factor the difference of two squares.

2 Factor the sum and difference of two cubes.

Review of Factoring Methods: The Difference of Two Squares; the Sum and Difference of Two Cubes

ARE YOU READY?

The following problems review some basic skills that are needed when factoring certain types of binomials.

1. Multiply: $(n + 9)(n - 9)$ **2.** Simplify: $(8d)^2$

3. Evaluate: **a.** 3^3 **b.** 6^3 **4.** Simplify: $(4a)^3$

5. Multiply: $(b + 4)(b^2 - 4b + 16)$ **6.** Multiply: $(2a - 1)(4a^2 + 2a + 1)$

We will now review how to factor the difference of two squares and the sum and difference of two cubes.

1 **Factor the Difference of Two Squares.**

Recall the special-product rule for multiplying the sum and difference of the same two terms:

$$(A + B)(A - B) = A^2 - B^2$$

The binomial $A^2 - B^2$ is called a **difference of two squares,** because A^2 is the square of A and B^2 is the square of B. If we reverse this rule, we obtain a method for factoring a difference of two squares.

The Language of Algebra

The expression $A^2 - B^2$ is a **difference of two squares,** whereas $(A - B)^2$ is the **square of a difference.** They are not equivalent because $(A - B)^2 \neq A^2 - B^2$.

Factoring a Difference of Two Squares	To factor the square of a First quantity minus the square of a Last quantity, multiply the First plus the Last by the First minus the Last. $$F^2 - L^2 = (F + L)(F - L)$$

To factor the difference of two squares, it is helpful to know the first twenty **perfect-square integers.** The number 400, for example, is a perfect square, because $400 = 20^2$.

$1 = 1^2$	$25 = 5^2$	$81 = 9^2$	$169 = 13^2$	$289 = 17^2$
$4 = 2^2$	$36 = 6^2$	$100 = 10^2$	$196 = 14^2$	$324 = 18^2$
$9 = 3^2$	$49 = 7^2$	$121 = 11^2$	$225 = 15^2$	$361 = 19^2$
$16 = 4^2$	$64 = 8^2$	$144 = 12^2$	$256 = 16^2$	$400 = 20^2$

EXAMPLE 1 Factor: $49x^2 - 16$

Strategy The terms of this binomial do not have a common factor (other than 1). The only option is to attempt to factor it as a difference of two squares.

Why If a binomial is a difference of two squares, we can factor it using a special product.

Solution $49x^2 - 16$ is the difference of two squares because it can be written as $(7x)^2 - (4)^2$. We can match it to the rule for factoring a difference of two squares to find the factorization.

$$\begin{array}{cccccc} F^2 & - & L^2 & = (F & + & L)(F & - & L) \\ \downarrow & & \downarrow & \downarrow & & \downarrow & \downarrow & \downarrow \\ (7x)^2 & - & (4)^2 & = (7x & + & 4)(7x & - & 4) \end{array}$$

Therefore, $49x^2 - 16 = (7x + 4)(7x - 4)$. We can verify this result using multiplication.

$$(7x + 4)(7x - 4) = 49x^2 - 28x + 28x - 16$$
$$= 49x^2 - 16 \quad \text{This is the original binomial.}$$

Success Tip

Always verify a factorization by doing the indicated multiplication. The result should be the original polynomial.

Self Check 1 Factor: $81p^2 - 25$

Now Try ▶ Problems 11 and 17

Expressions such as a^4 and x^6y^8 are also perfect squares, because they can be written as the square of another quantity:

$$a^4 = (a^2)^2, \qquad 81b^4 = (9b^2)^2, \qquad \text{and} \qquad x^6y^8 = (x^3y^4)^2$$

EXAMPLE 2 Factor: $64a^4 - 25b^2$

Strategy The terms of this binomial do not have a common factor (other than 1). The only option is to attempt to factor it as a difference of two squares.

Why If a binomial is a difference of two squares, we can factor it using a special-product rule.

Solution We can write $64a^4 - 25b^2$ in the form $(8a^2)^2 - (5b)^2$ and use the rule for factoring the difference of two squares.

Notation

By the commutative property of multiplication, this factorization could be written

$$(8a^2 - 5b)(8a^2 + 5b)$$

$$\begin{array}{cccccc} F^2 & - & L^2 & = (F & + & L)(F & - & L) \\ \downarrow & & \downarrow & \downarrow & & \downarrow & \downarrow & \downarrow \\ (8a^2)^2 & - & (5b)^2 & = (8a^2 & + & 5b)(8a^2 & - & 5b) \end{array}$$

Therefore, $64a^4 - 25b^2 = (8a^2 + 5b)(8a^2 - 5b)$.

Self Check 2   Factor: $36r^4 - s^2$

Now Try ▶ Problems 21 and 25

EXAMPLE 3   Factor: $x^4 - 1$

Strategy   The terms of $x^4 - 1$ do not have a common factor (other than 1). To factor this binomial, we will write it in a form that shows it is a difference of two squares.

Why   We can then use a special-product rule to factor it.

Solution   Because the binomial is the difference of the squares of x^2 and 1, it factors into the sum of x^2 and 1 and the difference of x^2 and 1.

$$x^4 - 1 = (x^2)^2 - (1)^2$$
$$= (x^2 + 1)(x^2 - 1)$$
$$\text{A prime polynomial}$$

> **Caution**
>
> The binomial $x^2 + 1$ is the **sum of two squares.** In general, after removing any common factor, a sum of two squares cannot be factored using real numbers.

The factor $x^2 + 1$ is the sum of two quantities and is prime. However, the factor $x^2 - 1$ is the difference of two squares and can be factored as $(x + 1)(x - 1)$. Thus,

$$x^4 - 1 = (x^2 + 1)(x^2 - 1)$$
$$= (x^2 + 1)(x + 1)(x - 1)   \quad \text{Don't forget to write } (x^2 + 1).$$

Self Check 3   Factor: $a^4 - 81$

Now Try ▶ Problem 29

At times, a **substitution** can be helpful in simplifying the factorization process.

EXAMPLE 4   Factor: $(x + y)^4 - z^4$

Strategy   We will use a substitution to factor this difference of two squares.

Why   For more complicated expressions, especially those involving a quantity within parentheses, a substitution often helps simplify the factoring process.

Solution   If we use the substitution $a = x + y$, we obtain

$$(x + y)^4 - z^4 = a^4 - z^4   \qquad \text{Replace } x + y \text{ with } a.$$
$$= (a^2 + z^2)(a^2 - z^2)   \qquad \text{Factor the difference of two squares.}$$
$$= (a^2 + z^2)(a + z)(a - z)   \quad \text{Factor } a^2 - z^2.\ a^2 + z^2 \text{ is prime.}$$

> **Caution**
>
> A common error after making a substitution is to forget to "undo" or "reverse" it. In this example, if you are to factor an expression in x, y, and z, your answer must involve only x, y, and z. It should not contain the variable a.

To find the factorization of $(x + y)^4 - z^4$, we "reverse" substitute $x + y$ for each a in the expression $(a^2 + z^2)(a + z)(a - z)$.

$$(a^2 + z^2)(a + z)(a - z) = [(x + y)^2 + z^2](x + y + z)(x + y - z)$$

Thus, $(x + y)^4 - z^4 = [(x + y)^2 + z^2](x + y + z)(x + y - z)$.

> **Caution**
>
> When factoring a polynomial, be sure to factor it completely. Always check to see whether any of the factors of your result can be factored further.

If we square the binomial within the brackets, we have

$$(x + y)^4 - z^4 = [x^2 + 2xy + y^2 + z^2](x + y + z)(x + y - z)$$

Self Check 4   Factor: $(a - b)^4 - c^4$

Now Try ▶ Problem 35

When possible, we always factor out a common factor before factoring the difference of two squares. The factoring process is easier when all common factors are factored out first.

EXAMPLE 5   Factor: $2x^4y - 32y$

Strategy   We will factor out the GCF of $2y$ and factor the resulting difference of two squares.

Why   The first step in factoring any polynomial is to factor out the GCF.

Solution

$$
\begin{aligned}
2x^4y - 32y &= 2y(x^4 - 16) &&\text{Factor out the GCF, which is } 2y.\\
&= 2y(x^2 + 4)(x^2 - 4) &&\text{Factor } x^4 - 16.\\
&= 2y(x^2 + 4)(x + 2)(x - 2) &&\text{Factor } x^2 - 4.\ x^2 + 4 \text{ is prime.}
\end{aligned}
$$

Success Tip

Remember that a **difference of two squares** is a binomial. Each term is a square and the terms have different signs. The powers of the variables in the terms must be even.

Self Check 5   Factor: $3a^4 - 3$

Now Try ▶ Problems 37 and 43

To factor some expressions, we need to use some creative grouping to begin the process.

EXAMPLE 6   Factor: **a.** $x^2 - y^2 + x - y$ **b.** $x^2 + 6x + 9 - z^2$

Strategy   The terms of each expression do not have a common factor (other than 1) and traditional factoring by grouping will not work. Instead, in part a, we will group only the first two terms of the polynomial and in part b we will group the first three terms.

Why   Hopefully, those steps will produce equivalent expressions that can be factored.

Solution   We group the first two terms, factor them as a difference of two squares, and look for a common factor.

a. $\boxed{x^2 - y^2} + x - y = \boxed{(x + y)(x - y)} + (x - y)$ Factor $x^2 - y^2$. The terms of the resulting expression have a common binomial factor, $x - y$, that can be factored out later.

$$= (x + y)(x - y) + 1(x - y) \qquad \text{Factor out 1 from } x - y.$$

$$= (x - y)(x + y + 1) \qquad \text{Factor out the GCF, } x - y.\ \text{Don't forget the 1.}$$

b. We group the first three terms and factor that trinomial to get:

$$\boxed{x^2 + 6x + 9} - z^2 = \boxed{(x + 3)(x + 3)} - z^2 \qquad x^2 + 6x + 9 \text{ is a perfect-square trinomial.}$$

Success Tip

We could use a substitution to factor $(x + 3)^2 - z^2$.

$$= (x + 3)^2 - z^2 \qquad \text{Write } (x + 3)(x + 3) \text{ as } (x + 3)^2.\ \text{The expression that results is a difference of two squares.}$$

$$= (x + 3 + z)(x + 3 - z) \qquad \text{Factor the difference of two squares.}$$

Self Check 6   Factor: **a.** $a^2 - b^2 + a + b$
                                  b. $a^2 + 4a + 4 - b^2$

Now Try ▶ Problems 45 and 49

2 Factor the Sum and Difference of Two Cubes.

The number 64 is called a perfect cube, because $4^3 = 64$. To factor the sum or difference of two cubes, it is helpful to know the first ten **perfect-cube integers:**

$1 = 1^3$	$27 = 3^3$	$125 = 5^3$	$343 = 7^3$	$729 = 9^3$
$8 = 2^3$	$64 = 4^3$	$216 = 6^3$	$512 = 8^3$	$1,000 = 10^3$

Expressions such as b^6 and $64x^9y^{12}$ are also perfect cubes, because they can be written as the cube of another quantity:

$$b^6 = (b^2)^3 \quad \text{and} \quad 64x^9y^{12} = (4x^3y^4)^3$$

To find rules for factoring the sum of two cubes and the difference of two cubes, we need to find the products shown below. Note that each term of the trinomial is multiplied by each term of the binomial.

$$(x + y)(x^2 - xy + y^2) = x^3 - x^2y + xy^2 + x^2y - xy^2 + y^3$$
$$= x^3 + y^3 \qquad \text{Combine like terms.}$$

$$(x - y)(x^2 + xy + y^2) = x^3 + x^2y + xy^2 - x^2y - xy^2 - y^3$$
$$= x^3 - y^3 \qquad \text{Combine like terms.}$$

We have found that

$$x^3 + y^3 = (x + y)(x^2 - xy + y^2) \quad \text{and} \quad x^3 - y^3 = (x - y)(x^2 + xy + y^2)$$

The Language of Algebra

The expression $x^3 + y^3$ is a **sum of two cubes,** whereas $(x + y)^3$ is the **cube of a sum.** If you expand $(x + y)^3$, you will see that they are not equivalent.

The binomial $x^3 + y^3$ is called the **sum of two cubes,** because x^3 represents the cube of x, y^3 represents the cube of y, and $x^3 + y^3$ represents the sum of these cubes. Similarly, $x^3 - y^3$ is called the **difference of two cubes.**

These results justify the rules for factoring the **sum and difference of two cubes.** They are easier to remember if we think of a sum (or a difference) of two cubes as the cube of a First quantity plus (or minus) the cube of the Last quantity.

Factoring the Sum and Difference of Two Cubes

To factor the cube of a First quantity plus the cube of a Last quantity, multiply the First plus the Last by the First squared, minus the First times the Last, plus the Last squared.

$$F^3 + L^3 = (F + L)(F^2 - FL + L^2)$$

To factor the cube of a First quantity minus the cube of a Last quantity, multiply the First minus the Last by the First squared, plus the First times the Last, plus the Last squared.

$$F^3 - L^3 = (F - L)(F^2 + FL + L^2)$$

EXAMPLE 7   Factor: $a^3 + 8$

Strategy   We will write the binomial in a form that shows it is the sum of two cubes.

Why   We can then use the rule for factoring the sum of two cubes.

Solution Since $a^3 + 8$ can be written as $a^3 + 2^3$, it is a sum of two cubes, which factors as follows:

$$\mathbf{F}^3 + \mathbf{L}^3 = (\mathbf{F} + \mathbf{L})(\mathbf{F}^2 - \mathbf{FL} + \mathbf{L}^2)$$
$$a^3 + 2^3 = (a + 2)(a^2 - a\,2 + 2^2)$$
$$= (a + 2)(a^2 - 2a + 4) \qquad a^2 - 2a + 4 \text{ does not factor, it is prime.}$$

Therefore, $a^3 + 8 = (a + 2)(a^2 - 2a + 4)$.

We can check by multiplying.

$$(a + 2)(a^2 - 2a + 4) = a^3 - 2a^2 + 4a + 2a^2 - 4a + 8$$
$$= a^3 + 8 \qquad \text{This is the original binomial.}$$

Self Check 7 Factor: $p^3 + 27$

Now Try ▶ Problem 53

You should memorize the rules for factoring the sum and the difference of two cubes. Note that each has the form

(a binomial)(a trinomial)

and that there is a relationship between the signs that appear in these forms.

The Sum of Cubes

The same sign

$$\mathbf{F}^3 + \mathbf{L}^3 = (\mathbf{F} + \mathbf{L})(\mathbf{F}^2 - \mathbf{FL} + \mathbf{L}^2)$$

Opposite   Always plus
signs

The Difference of Cubes

The same sign

$$\mathbf{F}^3 - \mathbf{L}^3 = (\mathbf{F} - \mathbf{L})(\mathbf{F}^2 + \mathbf{FL} + \mathbf{L}^2)$$

Opposite   Always plus
signs

EXAMPLE 8 Factor: $27a^3 - 64b^6$

Strategy We will write the binomial in a form that shows it is the difference of two cubes.

Why We can then use the rule for factoring the difference of two cubes.

Solution Since $27a^3 - 64b^6$ can be written as $(3a)^3 - (4b^2)^3$, it is a difference of two cubes, which factors as follows:

$$\mathbf{F}^3 - \mathbf{L}^3 = (\mathbf{F} - \mathbf{L})(\mathbf{F}^2 + \mathbf{F}\,\mathbf{L} + \mathbf{L}^2)$$
$$(3a)^3 - (4b^2)^3 = (3a - 4b^2)[(3a)^2 + (3a)(4b^2) + (4b^2)^2]$$
$$= (3a - 4b^2)(9a^2 + 12ab^2 + 16b^4)$$

Thus, $27a^3 - 64b^6 = (3a - 4b^2)(9a^2 + 12ab^2 + 16b^4)$. Multiply to check.

Self Check 8 Factor: $8c^6 - 125d^3$

Now Try ▶ Problem 57

EXAMPLE 9 Factor: $a^3 - (c + d)^3$

Strategy To factor this expression, we will use the rule for factoring the difference of two cubes.

Why The terms a^3 and $(c + d)^3$ are perfect cubes.

Solution

$$F^3 \;-\; L^3 \;=\; (F \;-\; L\;)(F^2 \;+\; F\;L \;+\; L^2\;)$$
$$\downarrow \qquad \downarrow \qquad \downarrow \qquad \downarrow \qquad \downarrow \quad \downarrow \qquad \downarrow$$
$$a^3 \;-\; (c + d)^3 \;=\; [a \;-\; (c + d)][a^2 \;+\; a(c + d) \;+\; (c + d)^2]$$

Success Tip

We could also use the substitution $x = c + d$, factor $a^3 - x^3$ as $(a - x)(a^2 + ax + x^2)$, and then replace each x with $c + d$.

Now we simplify the expressions within both sets of brackets. Thus,

$$a^3 \;-\; (c + d)^3 \;=\; (a - c - d)(a^2 + ac + ad + c^2 + 2cd + d^2)$$

Self Check 9 Factor: $(p + q)^3 - r^3$

Now Try ▶ Problem 61

EXAMPLE 10 Factor: $x^6 - 64$

Strategy This binomial is both the difference of two squares and the difference of two cubes. We will write it in a form that shows it is a difference of two squares to begin the factoring process.

Why It is easier to factor it as the difference of two squares first.

Solution
$$x^6 - 64 = (x^3)^2 - 8^2$$
$$= (x^3 + 8)(x^3 - 8)$$

Each of these binomial factors can be factored further. The first is the sum of two cubes and the second is the difference of two cubes. Thus,

$$x^6 - 64 = (x + 2)(x^2 - 2x + 4)(x - 2)(x^2 + 2x + 4)$$

Self Check 10 Factor: $1 - x^6$

Now Try ▶ Problem 65

EXAMPLE 11 Factor: $2a^5 + 250a^2$

Strategy We will factor out the GCF $2a^2$ and then factor the resulting sum of two cubes.

Why The first step in factoring any polynomial is to factor out the GCF.

Solution We first factor out the common factor $2a^2$ to obtain

$$2a^5 + 250a^2 = 2a^2(a^3 + 125)$$

Then we factor $a^3 + 125$ as the sum of two cubes to obtain

$$2a^5 + 250a^2 = 2a^2(a + 5)(a^2 - 5a + 25) \qquad a^2 - 5a + 25 \text{ is prime.}$$

Self Check 11 Factor: $3x^5 + 24x^2$

Now Try ▶ Problem 69

SECTION 8.7 ▶ **STUDY SET**

VOCABULARY

Fill in the blanks.

1. When the polynomial $4x^2 - 25$ is written as $(2x)^2 - (5)^2$, we see that it is the difference of two _____.

2. When the polynomial $8x^3 + 125$ is written as $(2x)^3 + (5)^3$, we see that it is the sum of two _____.

CONCEPTS

3. **a.** Write the first ten perfect-square integers.

   b. Write the first ten perfect-cube integers.

4. **a.** Use multiplication to verify that the sum of two squares $x^2 + 25$ does not factor as $(x + 5)(x + 5)$.

   b. Use multiplication to verify that the difference of two squares $x^2 - 25$ factors as $(x + 5)(x - 5)$.

5. Complete each factorization.
   a. $F^2 - L^2 = (F + L)()$
   b. $F^3 + L^3 = (F + L)()$
   c. $F^3 - L^3 = (F - L)()$

6. Factor each binomial.
   a. $5p^2 + 20$
   b. $5p^2 - 20$
   c. $5p^3 + 20$
   d. $5p^3 + 40$

NOTATION

7. Give an example of each.
   a. a difference of two squares
   b. a square of a difference
   c. a sum of two squares
   d. a sum of two cubes
   e. a cube of a sum

8. Fill in the blanks.
   a. $36y^2 - 49m^4 = ()^2 - ()^2$

   b. $125h^3 - 27k^6 = ()^3 - ()^3$

GUIDED PRACTICE

Factor. See Example 1.

9. $x^2 - 16$

10. $y^2 - 49$

11. $9y^2 - 64$

12. $16x^2 - 81$

13. $144 - c^2$

14. $25 - t^2$

15. $100m^2 - 1$

16. $144x^2 - 1$

17. $81a^2 - 49b^2$

18. $64r^2 - 121s^2$

19. $x^2 + 25$

20. $a^2 + 36$

Factor each difference of two squares. See Example 2.

21. $9r^4 - 121s^2$

22. $81a^4 - 16b^2$

23. $16t^2 - 25w^4$

24. $9r^2 - 25s^4$

25. $100r^2s^4 - t^4$

26. $400x^2z^4 - a^4$

27. $36x^4y^2 - 49z^6$

28. $4a^2b^4 - 9d^6$

Factor completely. See Example 3.

29. $x^4 - y^4$

30. $16n^4 - 1$

31. $16a^4 - 81b^4$

32. $81m^4 - 256n^4$

Factor. See Example 4.

33. $(x + y)^2 - z^2$

34. $a^2 - (b - c)^2$

35. $(r - s)^2 - t^4$

36. $(m + n)^2 - p^4$

Factor each expression. Factor out any GCF first. See Example 5.

37. $2x^2 - 288$

38. $8x^2 - 72$

39. $3x^3 - 243x$

40. $2x^3 - 32x$

41. $5ab^4 - 5a$

42. $3ac^4 - 243a$

43. $64b - 4b^5$

44. $1{,}250n - 2n^5$

Factor by first grouping the appropriate terms. See Example 6.

45. $c^2 - d^2 + c + d$

46. $s^2 - t^2 + s - t$

47. $a^2 - b^2 + 2a - 2b$

48. $m^2 - n^2 + 3m + 3n$

49. $x^2 + 12x + 36 - y^2$

50. $x^2 - 6x + 9 - 4y^2$

51. $x^2 - 2x + 1 - 9z^2$

52. $x^2 + 10x + 25 - 16z^2$

Factor each sum of cubes. See Example 7.

53. $a^3 + 125$

54. $b^3 + 64$

55. $8r^3 + s^3$

56. $27t^3 + u^3$

Factor each difference of cubes. See Example 8.

57. $64t^6 - 27v^3$

58. $125m^3 - x^6$

59. $x^3 - 216y^6$

60. $8c^6 - 343w^3$

Factor. See Example 9.

61. $(a - b)^3 + 27$

62. $(b - c)^3 - 1{,}000$

63. $64 - (a + b)^3$

64. $1 - (x + y)^3$

Factor each expression completely. Factor a difference of two squares first. See Example 10.

65. $x^6 - 1$

66. $x^6 - y^6$

67. $x^{12} - y^6$

68. $a^{12} - 64$

Factor each sum or difference of cubes. Factor out the GCF first. See Example 11.

69. $5x^3 + 625$

70. $2x^3 - 128$

71. $4x^5 - 256x^2$

72. $2x^6 + 54x^3$

TRY IT YOURSELF

Factor each expression.

73. $64a^3 - 125b^6$

74. $8x^6 - 27y^3$

75. $288b^2 - 2b^6$

76. $98x - 2x^5$

77. $x^2 - y^2 + 8x + 8y$

78. $5m - 5n + m^2 - n^2$

79. $x^9 + y^9$

80. $x^6 + y^6$

81. $144a^2t^2 - 169b^6$

82. $25x^6 - 81y^2z^2$

83. $100a^2 + 9b^2$

84. $25s^4 + 16t^2$

85. $81c^4d^4 - 16t^4$

86. $256x^4 - 81y^4$

87. $128u^2v^3 - 2t^3u^2$

88. $56rs^2t^3 + 7rs^2v^6$

89. $y^2 - (2x - t)^2$

90. $(15 - r)^2 - s^2$

91. $x^2 + 20x + 100 - 9z^2$

92. $49a^2 - b^2 - 14b - 49$

93. $(c - d)^3 + 216$

94. $1 - (x + y)^3$

95. $\dfrac{1}{36} - y^4$

96. $\dfrac{4}{81} - m^4$

97. $m^6 - 64$

98. $1 - y^6$

99. $(a + b)x^3 + 27(a + b)$

100. $(c - d)r^3 - (c - d)s^3$

101. $x^9 - y^{12}z^{15}$

102. $r^{12} + s^{18}t^{24}$

Look Alikes . . .

103. a. $q^2 - 64$ **b.** $q^3 - 64$

104. a. $a^2 - b^2$ **b.** $a^3 - b^3$

105. a. $d^2 - 25$ **b.** $d^3 - 125$

106. a. $m^2 + 27$ **b.** $m^3 + 27$

Factor the expression in part a. Then use your answer from part a to give the factorization of the expression in part b. (No new work is necessary!)

107. a. $a^6 - b^3$ **b.** $a^6 + b^3$

108. a. $c^3 - \dfrac{1}{8}$ **b.** $c^3 + \dfrac{1}{8}$

109. a. $125m^3 + 8n^3$ **b.** $125m^3 - 8n^3$

110. a. $w^3 + 0.001$ **b.** $w^3 - 0.001$

APPLICATIONS

111. Candy.   To find the amount of chocolate used in the outer coating of the malted-milk ball shown, we can find the volume V of the chocolate shell using the formula

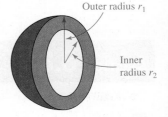
Outer radius r_1
Inner radius r_2

$$V = \frac{4}{3}\pi r_1^3 - \frac{4}{3}\pi r_2^3$$

Factor the expression on the right side of the formula.

112. Movie Stunts.   The function that gives the distance a stuntwoman is above the ground t seconds after she falls over the side of a 144-foot tall building is $h(t) = 144 - 16t^2$. Factor the right side.

WRITING

113. Explain how the patterns used to factor the sum and difference of two cubes are similar and how they differ.

114. Explain why the factorization is not complete.

Factor: $1 - t^8 = (1 + t^4)(1 - t^4)$

115. Explain the error.

Factor: $4g^2 - 16 = \cancel{(2g + 4)(2g - 4)}$

116. When asked to factor $81t^2 - 16$, one student answered $(9t - 4)(9t + 4)$, and another answered $(9t + 4)(9t - 4)$. Explain why both students are correct.

REVIEW

For each of the following purchases, determine the better buy.

117. Flute lessons: 45 minutes for $25 or 1 hour for $35.

118. Tissue paper: 15 sheets for $1.39 or a dozen sheets for $1.10.

CHALLENGE PROBLEMS

Factor. Assume all variables represent natural numbers.

119. $4x^{2n} - 9y^{2n}$

120. $25 - x^{6n}$

121. $a^{3b} - c^{3b}$

122. $27x^{3n} + y^{3n}$

123. Factor: $x^{32} - y^{32}$

124. Find the error in this proof that $2 = 1$.

$$x = y$$
$$x^2 = xy$$
$$x^2 - y^2 = xy - y^2$$
$$(x + y)(x - y) = y(x - y)$$
$$\frac{(x + y)(x - y)}{(x - y)} = \frac{y(x - y)}{(x - y)}$$
$$x + y = y$$
$$y + y = y$$
$$2y = y$$
$$\frac{2y}{y} = \frac{y}{y}$$
$$2 = 1$$

SECTION 8.8

OBJECTIVES

1. Evaluate rational functions.
2. Find the domain of a rational function.
3. Recognize the graphs of rational functions.
4. Simplify rational expressions.
5. Multiply and divide rational expressions.
6. Add and subtract rational expressions.
7. Solve rational equations.

Review of Rational Expressions and Rational Equations; Rational Functions

ARE YOU READY?

The following problems review some basic skills that are needed when working with rational expressions.

1. Evaluate: **a.** $\dfrac{0}{10}$ **b.** $\dfrac{10}{0}$

2. Simplify: $\dfrac{36}{28}$

3. Simplify: $\dfrac{x(x + 5)(x - 7)}{4x(x - 5)(x - 7)}$

4. What is the reciprocal of $\dfrac{2}{3x}$?

5. a. Multiply: $\dfrac{3}{8} \cdot \dfrac{1}{7}$

    b. Divide: $\dfrac{21}{25} \div \dfrac{7}{15}$

6. a. Add: $\dfrac{5}{11} + \dfrac{3}{11}$

    b. Subtract: $\dfrac{2}{3} - \dfrac{1}{5}$

Recall that rational expressions are algebraic fractions with polynomial numerators and denominators.

Rational Expressions ▼

A **rational expression** is an expression of the form $\dfrac{A}{B}$, where A and B are polynomials and B does not equal 0.

Caution

Since division by 0 is undefined, the value of a polynomial in the denominator of a rational expression cannot be 0. For example, x cannot be 7 in the rational expression $\frac{3x}{x-7}$, because the value of the denominator would be 0.

Some examples of rational expressions are

$$\frac{3x}{x - 7}, \qquad \frac{8yz^4}{6y^2z^2}, \qquad \frac{5m + n}{m^2 + 4mn + 4n^2}, \qquad \text{and} \qquad \frac{6a^2 - 13a + 6}{a^3 + 3a^2 + a - 2}$$

The rational expression $\dfrac{3x}{x - 7}$ is the quotient of the monomial $3x$ and the binomial $x - 7$. It is in one variable, x. The rational expression $\dfrac{5m + n}{m^2 + 4mn + 4n^2}$ is the quotient of the binomial $5m + n$ and the trinomial $m^2 + 4mn + 4n^2$. It is in two variables, m and n.

Rational expressions in one variable are used to define *rational functions*.

1 Evaluate Rational Functions.

We have previously studied linear and polynomial functions. In this section, we introduce another family of functions known as *rational functions*.

Rational Functions	▼ A **rational function** is a function whose equation is defined by a rational expression in one variable, where the value of the polynomial in the denominator is never zero.

The Language of Algebra

Rational functions get their name from the fact that their defining equation contains a *ratio* (fraction) of two polynomials.

Two examples of rational functions are

$$f(x) = \frac{1}{x + 8}$$ The rational expression $\frac{1}{x+8}$ that defines function f is in one variable, x.

$$s(t) = \frac{5t^2 + t}{t^2 + 6t - 1}$$ The rational expression $\frac{5t^2 + t}{t^2 + 6t - 1}$ that defines function s is in one variable, t.

Rational functions can be used to model many types of real-world situations.

EXAMPLE 1

Internet Research. The cost of subscribing to an online research network is $6 a month plus $1.50 per hour of access time. The rational function $c(n) = \frac{1.50n + 6}{n}$ gives the average hourly cost $c(n)$ of using the network for n hours a month. Find the average hourly cost for

a. a student who used the network for 2 hours in a month.

b. an instructor who used the network for 18 hours in a month.

Strategy We will find $c(2)$ and $c(18)$.

Why The notation $c(2)$ represents the average hourly cost for using the network for 2 hours in a month and $c(18)$ represents the average hourly cost for using the network for 18 hours in a month.

Solution **a.** To find the average hourly cost the student paid for 2 hours of access time in a month, we find $c(2)$.

$$c(2) = \frac{1.50(2) + 6}{2} = 4.5$$ Substitute 2 for n and evaluate the right side.

The student paid $4.50 per hour to use the online research network for 2 hours.

b. To find the average hourly cost for 18 hours of access time in a month, we find $c(18)$.

$$c(18) = \frac{1.50(18) + 6}{18} = 1.833333333$$ Substitute 18 for n and evaluate the right side.

The instructor paid approximately $1.83 per hour to use the online research network for 18 hours.

Self Check 1 **Internet Research.** Find the average hourly cost when the online research network in Example 1 is used for 100 hours in a month.

Now Try ▶ Problem 127

2 Find the Domain of a Rational Function.

Recall that the **domain** of a function is the set of all permissible input values for the variable. Since division by 0 is undefined, any input values that make the denominator 0 in a rational function must be excluded from the domain of the function.

EXAMPLE 2 Find the domain of the function: $f(x) = \dfrac{3x + 2}{x^2 + x - 6}$

Strategy We will set $x^2 + x - 6$ equal to 0 and solve for x.

Why We don't need to examine the numerator of the rational expression; it can be any value, including 0. The domain of the function includes all real numbers, except those that make the *denominator equal to* 0.

Solution

$$x^2 + x - 6 = 0 \qquad \text{Set the denominator equal to 0.}$$
$$(x + 3)(x - 2) = 0 \qquad \text{Factor the trinomial.}$$
$$x + 3 = 0 \quad \text{or} \quad x - 2 = 0 \qquad \text{Set each factor equal to 0.}$$
$$x = -3 \quad | \quad x = 2 \qquad \text{Solve each linear equation.}$$

> **The Language of Algebra**
>
> Two other ways that Example 2 could be phrased are:
> - **State the restrictions** on the variable.
> - Find the values of x for which the function is **undefined**.

Thus, the domain of the function is the set of all real numbers except -3 and 2. Using set-builder notation we can describe the domain as $\{x \mid x$ is a real number and $x \neq -3, x \neq 2\}$. In interval notation, the domain is $(-\infty, -3) \cup (-3, 2) \cup (2, \infty)$.

To check the answers, substitute -3 and 2 for x in $x^2 + x - 6$ and verify that the result is 0 for each.

Self Check 2 Find the domain of the function: $f(x) = \dfrac{x^2 + 1}{x^2 - 49}$

Now Try ▶ Problem 31

3 Recognize the Graphs of Rational Functions.

The simplest of all rational functions, $f(x) = \dfrac{1}{x}$, is called the **reciprocal function.** We can use the point-plotting method to graph it. Because of the complex shape of the graph, we must select a large number of x-values, including positive and negative fractions, to determine how it looks. After plotting all of the ordered pairs, we draw a smooth curve through the points that form a "branch" on the left and a smooth curve through the points that form a "branch" on the right. Since 0 is not in the domain of the function, there is no point on the graph for $x = 0$.

$f(x) = \dfrac{1}{x}$

x	$f(x)$	
-4	$-\dfrac{1}{4}$	$\rightarrow \left(-4, -\dfrac{1}{4}\right)$
-3	$-\dfrac{1}{3}$	$\rightarrow \left(-3, -\dfrac{1}{3}\right)$
-2	$-\dfrac{1}{2}$	$\rightarrow \left(-2, -\dfrac{1}{2}\right)$
-1	-1	$\rightarrow (-1, -1)$
$-\dfrac{1}{2}$	-2	$\rightarrow \left(-\dfrac{1}{2}, -2\right)$
$-\dfrac{1}{3}$	-3	$\rightarrow \left(-\dfrac{1}{3}, -3\right)$
$-\dfrac{1}{4}$	-4	$\rightarrow \left(-\dfrac{1}{4}, -4\right)$

↑ Select x. ↑ Find the reciprocal. ↑ Plot the point.

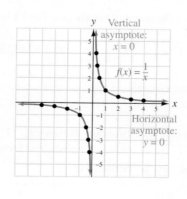

$f(x) = \dfrac{1}{x}$

x	$f(x)$	
4	$\dfrac{1}{4}$	$\rightarrow \left(4, \dfrac{1}{4}\right)$
3	$\dfrac{1}{3}$	$\rightarrow \left(3, \dfrac{1}{3}\right)$
2	$\dfrac{1}{2}$	$\rightarrow \left(2, \dfrac{1}{2}\right)$
1	1	$\rightarrow (1, 1)$
$\dfrac{1}{2}$	2	$\rightarrow \left(\dfrac{1}{2}, 2\right)$
$\dfrac{1}{3}$	3	$\rightarrow \left(\dfrac{1}{3}, 3\right)$
$\dfrac{1}{4}$	4	$\rightarrow \left(\dfrac{1}{4}, 4\right)$

↑ Select x. ↑ Find the reciprocal. ↑ Plot the point.

When a graph approaches a line, we call the line an **asymptote.** In this case, as x gets smaller and approaches 0, the graph of $f(x) = \frac{1}{x}$ approaches the y-axis. We say that the y-axis is a **vertical asymptote** of the graph.

On the far left and far right, the graph gets steadily closer to the x-axis. We say that the x-axis is a **horizontal asymptote** of the graph.

4   Simplify Rational Expressions.

To **simplify a rational expression** means to write it so that the numerator and denominator have no common factors other than 1.

Simplifying Rational Expressions	1. Factor the numerator and denominator completely to determine their common factors.
	2. Remove factors equal to 1 by replacing each pair of factors common to the numerator and denominator with the equivalent fraction $\frac{1}{1}$.
	3. Multiply the remaining factors in the numerator and in the denominator.

EXAMPLE 3   Simplify: $\dfrac{8yz^4}{6y^2z^2}$

Strategy   We will begin by writing the numerator and denominator in factored form. Then we will remove any factors common to the numerator and denominator.

Why   The rational expression is simplified when the numerator and denominator have no common factors other than 1.

Solution

The Language of Algebra

When a rational expression is simplified, the result is an **equivalent expression.**

$$\frac{8yz^4}{6y^2z^2} = \frac{2 \cdot 2 \cdot 2 \cdot y \cdot z \cdot z \cdot z \cdot z}{2 \cdot 3 \cdot y \cdot y \cdot z \cdot z}$$

To prepare to simplify the rational expression, factor $8yz^4$ and $6y^2z^2$ completely.

$$= \frac{\overset{1}{2} \cdot 2 \cdot 2 \cdot \overset{1}{\cancel{y}} \cdot \overset{1}{\cancel{z}} \cdot \overset{1}{\cancel{z}} \cdot z \cdot z}{\underset{1}{2} \cdot 3 \cdot \underset{1}{\cancel{y}} \cdot y \cdot \underset{1}{\cancel{z}} \cdot \underset{1}{\cancel{z}}}$$

Replace $\frac{2}{2}, \frac{y}{y},$ and $\frac{z}{z}$ with $\frac{1}{1}$. This removes the factor $\frac{2 \cdot y \cdot z \cdot z}{2 \cdot y \cdot z \cdot z} = 1$.

$$= \frac{4z^2}{3y}$$

Multiply the remaining factors in the numerator.
Multiply the remaining factors in the denominator.

Caution

Unless otherwise stated, we will now assume that the variables in rational expressions represent real numbers for which the denominator is not zero. Therefore, as we simplify rational expressions, warnings like the "provided $y \ne 0$ and $z \ne 0$" statement in this example are not necessary.

Since $\frac{8yz^4}{6y^2z^2}$ is undefined for $y = 0$ and $z = 0$, the expressions $\frac{8yz^4}{6y^2z^2}$ and $\frac{4z^2}{3y}$ are equal only if $y \ne 0$ and $z \ne 0$. That is,

$$\frac{8yz^4}{6y^2z^2} = \frac{4z^2}{3y} \qquad \text{provided } y \ne 0 \text{ and } z \ne 0.$$

An alternate approach is to use the rules for exponents to simplify the rational expressions that are the quotient of two monomials.

$$\frac{8yz^4}{6y^2z^2} = \frac{\overset{1}{\cancel{2}} \cdot 2 \cdot 2 \cdot y^{1-2}z^{4-2}}{\underset{1}{\cancel{2}} \cdot 3} = \frac{4y^{-1}z^2}{3} = \frac{4z^2}{3y}$$

To divide exponential expressions with the same base, keep the base and subtract the exponents.

Self Check 3   Simplify: $\dfrac{12a^4b^2}{20ab^4}$

Now Try   Problems 33 and 35

To simplify rational expressions, we often make use of the factoring methods discussed in Sections 8.6 and 8.7. We also often use the following property about polynomials and their opposites.

The Quotient of Opposites ▼ The quotient of any nonzero polynomials and its opposite is -1.

EXAMPLE 4   Simplify: **a.** $\dfrac{2x^2 + 11x + 12}{3x^2 + 11x - 4}$ **b.** $\dfrac{3x^2 - 10xy - 8y^2}{4y^2 - xy}$

Strategy   We will begin by factoring the numerator and denominator completely. Then we will remove any factors common to the numerator and denominator.

Why   We need to make sure that the numerator and denominator have no common factors other than 1. If that is the case, then the rational expression is simplified.

Solution   **a.** $\dfrac{2x^2 + 11x + 12}{3x^2 + 11x - 4} = \dfrac{(2x + 3)\overset{1}{\cancel{(x + 4)}}}{(3x - 1)\underset{1}{\cancel{(x + 4)}}}$ *Factor the numerator and denominator.*

                                            Remove a factor equal to 1: $\frac{x + 4}{x + 4} = 1$.

                    $= \dfrac{2x + 3}{3x - 1}$ *This expression does not simplify further.*

b. $\dfrac{3x^2 - 10xy - 8y^2}{4y^2 - xy} = \dfrac{(3x + 2y)\overset{-1}{\cancel{(x - 4y)}}}{y\underset{1}{\cancel{(4y - x)}}}$ *Factor the numerator and denominator.*

                                     Since $x - 4y$ and $4y - x$ are opposites,
                                     simplify by replacing $\frac{x - 4y}{4y - x}$ with the
                                     equivalent fraction $\frac{-1}{1} = -1$.

                    $= \dfrac{-(3x + 2y)}{y}$

This result can also be written as $-\dfrac{3x + 2y}{y}$ or $\dfrac{-3x - 2y}{y}$.

Self Check 4   Simplify: **a.** $\frac{2x^2 + 5x + 2}{3x^2 + 5x - 2}$
                           b. $\frac{2a^2 - 3ab - 9b^2}{3b^2 - ab}$

Now Try ▶ Problems 39 and 43

> **Caution**
>
> In Example 4, do not remove the x's in the result $\frac{2x + 3}{3x - 1}$. The x in the numerator is not a factor of the entire numerator. Likewise, the x in the denominator is not a factor of the entire denominator.
>
> $\dfrac{\overset{1}{\cancel{2}x} + 3}{\underset{1}{\cancel{3}x} - 1} = \dfrac{2 + 3}{3 - 1} = \dfrac{5}{2}$

> **Caution**
>
> A $-$ symbol in front of a fraction may be placed in the numerator or the denominator, but not in both. For example,
>
> $-\dfrac{3x + 2y}{y} \neq \dfrac{-3x - 2y}{-y}$

---

5   **Multiply and Divide Rational Expressions.**

Recall that to multiply two fractions, we multiply the numerators and multiply the denominators. We use the same strategy to multiply rational expressions.

Multiplying Rational Expressions ▼ To multiply rational expressions, multiply their numerators and their denominators. Then, if possible, factor and simplify.

For any two rational expressions, $\frac{A}{B}$ and $\frac{C}{D}$,

$$\frac{A}{B} \cdot \frac{C}{D} = \frac{AC}{BD}$$

EXAMPLE 5   Multiply: **a.** $\dfrac{x^2 - 6x + 9}{20x} \cdot \dfrac{5x^2}{x^2 - 9}$ **b.** $(2x - x^2) \cdot \dfrac{x}{x^2 - xb - 2x + 2b}$

Strategy   To find the product, we will use the rule for multiplying rational expressions. In the process, we must be prepared to factor the numerators and denominators so that any common factors can be removed.

Why   We want to give the result in simplified form.

Solution   **a.** $\dfrac{x^2 - 6x + 9}{20x} \cdot \dfrac{5x^2}{x^2 - 9} = \dfrac{(x^2 - 6x + 9)5x^2}{20x(x^2 - 9)}$

Multiply the numerators.
Multiply the denominators.

$= \dfrac{(x - 3)(x - 3)5 \cdot x \cdot x}{4 \cdot 5 \cdot x(x + 3)(x - 3)}$

To prepare to simplify, factor the numerator and factor the denominator.

> **Caution**
>
> When multiplying rational expressions, always write the result in simplest form by removing any factors common to the numerator and denominator.

$= \dfrac{\overset{1}{\cancel{(x - 3)}}(x - 3)\overset{1}{\cancel{5}} \cdot \overset{1}{\cancel{x}} \cdot x}{4 \cdot \underset{1}{\cancel{5}} \cdot \underset{1}{\cancel{x}}(x + 3)\underset{1}{\cancel{(x - 3)}}}$

Simplify by removing common factors of the numerator and denominator.

$= \dfrac{x(x - 3)}{4(x + 3)}$

We could distribute in the numerator and/or denominator and write the result as $\dfrac{x^2 - 3x}{4(x + 3)}$ or $\dfrac{x^2 - 3x}{4x + 12}$. Check with your instructor to see which form of the result he or she prefers.

b.   Writing $2x - x^2$ as $\dfrac{2x - x^2}{1}$ is helpful during the multiplication process when we multiply numerators and multiply denominators.

$(2x - x^2) \cdot \dfrac{x}{x^2 - xb - 2x + 2b}$

$= \dfrac{2x - x^2}{1} \cdot \dfrac{x}{x^2 - xb - 2x + 2b}$

Write $2x - x^2$ as $\dfrac{2x - x^2}{1}$.

$= \dfrac{(2x - x^2)x}{1(x^2 - xb - 2x + 2b)}$

Multiply the numerators.
Multiply the denominators.

> **Success Tip**
>
> We would obtain the same answer if we had factored the numerators and denominators first and simplified before we multiplied.

$= \dfrac{x(2 - x)x}{1[x(x - b) - 2(x - b)]}$

To prepare to simplify, factor out x in the numerator. In the denominator, begin factoring by grouping.

$= \dfrac{x(2 - x)x}{1(x - b)(x - 2)}$

In the denominator, complete the factoring by grouping. The brackets [ ] are no longer needed.

$= \dfrac{x\overset{-1}{\cancel{(2 - x)}}x}{1(x - b)\underset{1}{\cancel{(x - 2)}}}$

Simplify: The quotient of any nonzero quantity and its opposite is -1: $\dfrac{2 - x}{x - 2} = -1$.

$= -\dfrac{x^2}{x - b}$

Self Check 5   Multiply: **a.** $\dfrac{a^2 + 6a + 9}{18a} \cdot \dfrac{3a^3}{a + 3}$

b. $\dfrac{x^2 + 5x + 6}{4x + 8 - x^2 - 2x}(x^2 - 4x)$

Now Try ▶ Problems 51 and 53

Recall that to divide fractions, we multiply the first fraction by the reciprocal of the second fraction. We use the same strategy to divide rational expressions.

Dividing Rational Expressions	To divide two rational expressions, multiply the first by the reciprocal of the second. Then, if possible, factor and simplify.

For any two rational expressions, $\frac{A}{B}$ and $\frac{C}{D}$, where $\frac{C}{D} \neq 0$,

$$\frac{A}{B} \div \frac{C}{D} = \frac{A}{B} \cdot \frac{D}{C} = \frac{AD}{BC}$$

EXAMPLE 6   Divide: $\dfrac{x^3 + 8}{4x + 4} \div \dfrac{x^2 - 2x + 4}{2x^2 - 2}$

Strategy   To find the quotient, we will use the rule for dividing rational expressions. After multiplying by the reciprocal, we will factor each polynomial that is not prime and remove any common factors of the numerator and denominator.

Why   We want to give the result in simplified form.

Solution

$$\frac{x^3 + 8}{4x + 4} \div \frac{x^2 - 2x + 4}{2x^2 - 2}$$

$$= \frac{x^3 + 8}{4x + 4} \cdot \frac{2x^2 - 2}{x^2 - 2x + 4}$$

Multiply the first rational expression by the reciprocal of the second.

$$= \frac{(x^3 + 8)(2x^2 - 2)}{(4x + 4)(x^2 - 2x + 4)}$$

Multiply the numerators.
Multiply the denominators.

$$= \frac{(x + 2)(\overset{1}{\cancel{x^2 - 2x + 4}})2(\overset{1}{\cancel{x + 1}})(x - 1)}{2 \cdot 2(\underset{1}{\cancel{x + 1}})(\underset{1}{\cancel{x^2 - 2x + 4}})}$$

To prepare to simplify, factor completely. Note that $x^2 - 2x + 4$ is prime. Then simplify.

$$= \frac{(x + 2)(x - 1)}{2}$$

Multiply the remaining monomial factors in the numerator: $1 \cdot 1 \cdot 1 = 1$. Multiply the remaining factors in the denominator: $2 \cdot 1 \cdot 1 \cdot 1 = 2$.

Caution

When dividing rational expressions, always write the result in simplest form by removing any factors common to the numerator and denominator.

Self Check 6   Divide: $\dfrac{x^3 - 8}{9x - 9} \div \dfrac{x^2 + 2x + 4}{3x^2 - 3x}$

Now Try ▶ **Problem 61**

6   Add and Subtract Rational Expressions.

To add (or subtract) fractions with like denominators, we add (or subtract) the numerators and keep the same denominator. We use the same strategy to add (or subtract) rational expressions with like denominators.

Adding and Subtracting Rational Expressions That Have the Same Denominator	To add (or subtract) rational expressions that have same denominator, add (or subtract) their numerators and write the sum (or difference) over the common denominator. Then, if possible, factor and simplify.

If $\frac{A}{D}$ and $\frac{B}{D}$ are rational expressions,

$$\frac{A}{D} + \frac{B}{D} = \frac{A + B}{D} \qquad \text{and} \qquad \frac{A}{D} - \frac{B}{D} = \frac{A - B}{D}$$

EXAMPLE 7 Add $\dfrac{a^2}{a^2 - 36} + \dfrac{6a}{a^2 - 36}$ and simplify the result.

Strategy We will add the numerators and write the sum over the common denominator.

Why This is the rule for adding rational expressions that have the *same* denominator.

Solution

$\dfrac{a^2}{a^2 - 36} + \dfrac{6a}{a^2 - 36} = \dfrac{a^2 + 6a}{a^2 - 36}$ Add the numerators. Write the sum over the common denominator, $a^2 - 36$.

$= \dfrac{a(a + 6)}{(a + 6)(a - 6)}$ To prepare to simplify, factor the numerator and denominator.

$= \dfrac{\overset{1}{a\cancel{(a + 6)}}}{\underset{1}{\cancel{(a + 6)}(a - 6)}}$ Simplify by removing the common factor of $a + 6$.

$= \dfrac{a}{a - 6}$

Caution

When adding or subtracting rational expressions, always write the result in simplest form by removing any factors common to the numerator and denominator.

Self Check 7 Add: $\dfrac{2b}{b^2 - 4} + \dfrac{b^2}{b^2 - 4}$

Now Try ▶ Problem 65

To add or subtract rational expressions with unlike denominators, we build them to rational expressions with the same denominator.

Building Rational Expressions

To build a rational expression, multiply it by 1 in the form of $\dfrac{c}{c}$, where c is any nonzero number or expression.

When adding (or subtracting) rational expressions with unlike denominators, we will write the rational expressions with the smallest common denominator possible, called the **least** (or lowest) **common denominator (LCD).** To find the least common denominator of several rational expressions, we follow these steps.

Finding the LCD

1. Factor each denominator completely.
2. The LCD is a product that uses each different factor obtained in step 1 the greatest number of times it appears in any one factorization.

EXAMPLE 8 Add: $\dfrac{5a}{24b} + \dfrac{11a}{18b^2}$

Strategy We will find the LCD of these rational expressions. Then we will build the rational expressions so each one has the LCD as its denominator.

Why Since the denominators are different, we cannot add these rational expressions in their present form.

Solution To find the LCD, we write each denominator as the product of prime numbers and variables.

$24b = 2 \cdot 2 \cdot 2 \cdot 3 \cdot b = 2^3 \cdot 3 \cdot b$

$18b^2 = 2 \cdot 3 \cdot 3 \cdot b \cdot b = 2 \cdot 3^2 \cdot b^2$

Then we form a product using each of these factors the greatest number of times it appears in any one factorization.

Success Tip

Note that the highest power of each factor is used to form the LCD:

$$24b = 2^{\textcircled{3}} \cdot 3 \cdot b$$
$$18b^2 = 2 \cdot 3^{\textcircled{2}} \cdot b^{\textcircled{2}}$$
$$LCD = 2^3 \cdot 3^2 \cdot b^2 = 72b^2$$

The greatest number of times the factor 2 appears is three times.
The greatest number of times the factor 3 appears is twice.
The greatest number of times the factor b appears is twice.

$$LCD = 2 \cdot 2 \cdot 2 \cdot 3 \cdot 3 \cdot b \cdot b$$
$$= 72b^2$$

We now multiply the numerator and denominator of each rational expression by whatever it takes to build their denominators to $72b^2$.

Success Tip

You may want to review the procedure for adding and subtracting rational expressions that have unlike denominators on page 541.

$$\frac{5a}{24b} + \frac{11a}{18b^2} = \frac{5a}{24b} \cdot \frac{3b}{3b} + \frac{11a}{18b^2} \cdot \frac{4}{4}$$

Build each rational expression by multiplying it by a form of 1.

$$= \frac{15ab}{72b^2} + \frac{44a}{72b^2}$$

Multiply the numerators. Multiply the denominators. Note that the expressions now have like denominators.

$$= \frac{15ab + 44a}{72b^2}$$

Add the numerators. Write the sum over the common denominator. The result does not simplify.

Self Check 8 Add: $\frac{3}{28z^3} + \frac{5x}{21z}$

Now Try ▶ Problem 73

EXAMPLE 9 Subtract: $\dfrac{x+1}{x^2 - 2x + 1} - \dfrac{x-4}{x^2 - 1}$

Strategy We will factor each denominator, find the LCD, and build the rational expressions so each one has the LCD as its denominator.

Why Since the denominators are different, we cannot subtract these rational expressions in their present form.

Solution We factor each denominator to find the LCD:

$$x^2 - 2x + 1 = (x-1)(x-1) = (x-1)^2$$
$$x^2 - 1 = (x+1)(x-1)$$

The greatest number of times $x - 1$ appears is twice.
The greatest number of times $x + 1$ appears is once.

The LCD is $(x-1)^2(x+1)$ or $(x-1)(x-1)(x+1)$.

We now write each rational expression with its denominator in factored form. Then we multiply each numerator and denominator by the missing factor, so that each rational expression has a denominator of $(x-1)(x-1)(x+1)$.

$$\frac{x+1}{x^2 - 2x + 1} - \frac{x-4}{x^2 - 1}$$

$$= \frac{x+1}{(x-1)(x-1)} - \frac{x-4}{(x+1)(x-1)}$$

Write each denominator in factored form.

$$= \frac{x+1}{(x-1)(x-1)} \cdot \frac{x+1}{x+1} - \frac{x-4}{(x+1)(x-1)} \cdot \frac{x-1}{x-1}$$

Build each rational expression.

Multiply the numerators using the FOIL method to prepare to combine like terms.

$$= \frac{x^2 + 2x + 1}{(x-1)(x-1)(x+1)} - \frac{x^2 - 5x + 4}{(x-1)(x-1)(x+1)}$$

Multiply the numerators. The denominators are now the same.

Don't multiply the denominators. Leave them in factored form to possibly simplify the result later.

$$= \frac{x^2 + 2x + 1 - (x^2 - 5x + 4)}{(x - 1)(x - 1)(x + 1)}$$

Subtract the numerators. Write the difference over the common denominator. Don't forget the parentheses shown in blue.

$$= \frac{x^2 + 2x + 1 - x^2 + 5x - 4}{(x - 1)(x - 1)(x + 1)}$$

To subtract in the numerator, change the signs of x^2, $-5x$, and 4, and drop the parentheses.

$$= \frac{7x - 3}{(x - 1)(x - 1)(x + 1)}$$

Combine like terms in the numerator. The result does not simplify.

Self Check 9   Subtract: $\dfrac{a + 2}{a^2 - 4a + 4} - \dfrac{a - 3}{a^2 - 4}$

Now Try ▶ Problem 81

7   Solve Rational Equations.

If an equation contains one or more rational expressions, it is called a **rational equation.** Recall that we use a fraction-clearing strategy to solve rational equations. All possible solutions of a rational equation must be checked. Multiplying both sides of an equation by an expression that contains a variable can lead to **extraneous solutions,** which must be discarded.

EXAMPLE 10   Solve: $1 + \dfrac{8a}{a^2 + 3a} = \dfrac{3}{a}$

Strategy   We will find the LCD of the rational expressions in the equation and multiply both sides by the LCD.

Why   This will clear the equation of fractions.

Solution   Since the binomial $a^2 + 3a$ factors as $a(a + 3)$, we can write the given equation as:

Success Tip

You may want to review the procedure for solving rational equations on page 558.

$$1 + \frac{8a}{a(a + 3)} = \frac{3}{a}   \quad \text{Factor } a^2 + 3a.$$

We see that 0 and -3 cannot be solutions of the equation, because they make rational expressions in the equation undefined.

We can clear the equation of fractions by multiplying both sides by $a(a + 3)$, which is the LCD of the two rational expressions $\dfrac{8a}{a^2 + 3a}$ and $\dfrac{3}{a}$.

Caution

After multiplying both sides by the LCD and simplifying, the equation should not contain any fractions. If it does, check for an algebraic error, or perhaps your LCD is incorrect.

$$a(a + 3)\left[1 + \frac{8a}{a(a + 3)} \right] = a(a + 3)\left(\frac{3}{a} \right)$$

Multiply both sides by the LCD.

$$a(a + 3)1 + a(a + 3)\frac{8a}{a(a + 3)} = a(a + 3)\left(\frac{3}{a} \right)$$

On the left side, distribute the multiplication by $a(a + 3)$.

$$a(a + 3)1 + \overset{1}{\cancel{a}}\overset{1}{(\cancel{a + 3})}\frac{8a}{\underset{1}{\cancel{a}}\underset{1}{(\cancel{a + 3})}} = \overset{1}{\cancel{a}}(a + 3)\left(\frac{3}{\underset{1}{\cancel{a}}} \right)$$

Remove common factors of the numerator and denominator.

$$a^2 + 3a + 8a = 3a + 9$$

Simplify each side. The resulting quadratic equation does not contain any fractions.

$$a^2 + 8a - 9 = 0$$

To get 0 on the right side, subtract $3a$ and 9 from both sides.

$$(a + 9)(a - 1) = 0$$

Factor the left side.

$$a + 9 = 0 \quad \text{or} \quad a - 1 = 0$$

Set each factor equal to 0.

$$a = -9 \quad | \quad a = 1$$

Solve each equation.

The solutions are -9 and 1. Verify that both satisfy the original equation.

Self Check 10 Solve: $1 + \dfrac{2}{2b + 1} = \dfrac{5}{2b^2 + b}$

Now Try ▶ Problem 95

SECTION 8.8 STUDY SET

VOCABULARY

Fill in the blanks.

1. A quotient of two polynomials, such as $\dfrac{x^2 + x}{x^2 - 3x}$, is called a _____ expression.

2. A _____ function, such as $f(x) = \dfrac{x - 7}{x^2 - x - 6}$, is a function whose equation is defined by a rational expression in one variable.

3. The _____ of a function is the set of all permissible input values for the variable.

4. The rational function $f(x) = \dfrac{9x}{x - 10}$ is _____ for $x = 10$. In other words, there is a _____ on the domain of the function: $x \neq 10$.

5. To _____ a rational expression, we remove factors common to the numerator and denominator.

6. The quotient of _____ is -1. For example, $\dfrac{x - 8}{8 - x} = -1$.

7. In the rational expression $\dfrac{(x + 2)(3x - 1)}{(x + 2)(4x + 2)}$, the binomial $x + 2$ is a common _____ of the numerator and the denominator.

8. The least _____ _____ of $\dfrac{x - 8}{x + 6}$ and $\dfrac{6 - 5x}{x}$ is $x(x + 6)$.

9. To _____ a rational expression, we multiply it by a form of 1. For example, $\dfrac{2}{n^2} \cdot \dfrac{8}{8} = \dfrac{16}{8n^2}$.

10. Equations that contain one or more rational expressions, such as $\dfrac{x}{x + 2} = 4 + \dfrac{10}{x + 1}$, are called _____ equations.

CONCEPTS

11. Let $f(x) = \dfrac{2x + 1}{x^2 + 3x - 4}$. Find

   a. $f(0)$ **b.** $f(2)$ **c.** $f(1)$

12. For what value(s) of x is each function undefined?

   a. $f(x) = \dfrac{x - 7}{x}$ **b.** $f(x) = \dfrac{x + 1}{x - 3}$

   c. $f(x) = \dfrac{x^2 - 2}{x(x + 8)}$ **d.** $f(x) = \dfrac{8x}{(x - 1)(x + 1)}$

13. The graph of rational function f is shown. Find each of the following.

   a. $f(1)$
   b. $f(4)$
   c. The value of x for which $f(x) = -2$
   d. The value of x for which $f(x) = 1$

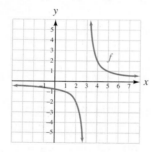

14. Match each function with the correct graph shown below.

   a. $f(x) = 2$ **b.** $f(x) = x$ **c.** $f(x) = x^2$

   d. $f(x) = x^3$ **e.** $f(x) = |x|$ **f.** $f(x) = \dfrac{1}{x}$

i.   ii.   iii.

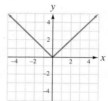
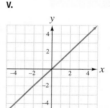
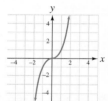

iv.   v.   vi.

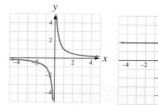

Fill in the blanks.

15. To multiply rational expressions, multiply their _____ and multiply their _____. To divide two rational expressions, multiply the first by the _____ of the second.

16. To add or subtract rational expressions that have the same denominator, add or subtract the _____ and write the sum or difference over the common _____.

17. To find the least common denominator of several rational expressions, _____ each denominator completely. The LCD is a product that uses each different factor the _____ number of times it appears in any one factorization.

18. The expression $4 - y$ must be multiplied by [ ] to obtain $y - 4$.

19. Consider the following factorizations.

$$18x - 36 = 2 \cdot 3 \cdot 3 \cdot (x - 2)$$
$$3x^2 - 3x - 6 = 3(x - 2)(x + 1)$$

   a. What is the greatest number of times the factor 3 appears in any one factorization?

   b. What is the greatest number of times the factor $x - 2$ appears in any one factorization?

20. The LCD for $\frac{2x+1}{x^2+5x+6}$ and $\frac{3x}{x^2-4}$ is

$$\text{LCD} = (x+2)(x+3)(x-2)$$

If we want to subtract these rational expressions, what form of 1 should be used

a. to build $\frac{2x+1}{x^2+5x+6}$?

b. to build $\frac{3x}{x^2-4}$?

21. To clear the following equations of fractions, by what should both sides be multiplied?

a. $\frac{1}{a} = \frac{1}{3} - \frac{2}{3a}$

b. $\frac{2}{x-2} + \frac{10}{x+5} = \frac{2x}{x^2+3x-10}$

22. Perform each multiplication.

a. $4x\left(\frac{3}{4x}\right)$

b. $(x+6)(x-2)\left(\frac{3}{x-2}\right)$

c. $8(x+4)\left[\frac{7x}{2(x+4)}\right]$

d. $6(m-5)\left(\frac{7}{5-m}\right)$

NOTATION

23. a. Write $5x^2 + 35x$ as a fraction.

b. What is the reciprocal of $5x^2 + 35x$?

24. What numbers are not included in each set of real numbers represented using interval notation?

a. $(-\infty, 4) \cup (4, \infty)$

b. $(-\infty, -8) \cup (-8, 0) \cup (0, \infty)$

GUIDED PRACTICE

Find the domain of each rational function. Express your answer in words and using interval notation. See Example 2.

25. $f(x) = \dfrac{2}{x}$

26. $f(x) = \dfrac{8}{x-1}$

27. $f(x) = \dfrac{2x}{x+2}$

28. $f(x) = \dfrac{2x+1}{x^2-2x}$

29. $f(x) = \dfrac{3x-1}{x-x^2}$

30. $f(x) = \dfrac{x^2+36}{x^2-36}$

31. $f(x) = \dfrac{x^2+3x+2}{x^2-x-56}$

32. $f(x) = \dfrac{2x^2-3x-2}{x^2+2x-24}$

Simplify each rational expression. See Example 3.

33. $\dfrac{15a^2}{25a^8}$

34. $\dfrac{12x}{16x^7}$

35. $\dfrac{24x^3y^4}{54x^4y^3}$

36. $\dfrac{15a^5b^4}{21a^2b^5}$

Simplify each rational expression. See Example 4.

37. $\dfrac{5x^2-10x}{x^2-4x+4}$

38. $\dfrac{x^2+6x+9}{2x^2+6x}$

39. $\dfrac{6x^2-7x-5}{2x^2+5x+2}$

40. $\dfrac{6x^2+x-2}{8x^2+2x-3}$

41. $\dfrac{4-x^2}{x^2-x-2}$

42. $\dfrac{x^2-2x-15}{25-x^2}$

43. $\dfrac{p^3+p^2q-2pq^2}{pq^2+p^2q-2p^3}$

44. $\dfrac{m^3-mn^2}{mn^2+m^2n-2m^3}$

Perform the operations and simplify, if possible. See Example 5.

45. $\dfrac{10a^2}{3b^4} \cdot \dfrac{12b^3}{5a^2}$

46. $\dfrac{16c^3}{5d^2} \cdot \dfrac{25d}{12c}$

47. $\dfrac{3p^2}{6p+24} \cdot \dfrac{p^2-16}{6p}$

48. $\dfrac{y^2+6y+9}{15y} \cdot \dfrac{3y^2}{2y+6}$

49. $\dfrac{x^2+2x+1}{9x} \cdot \dfrac{2x^2-2x}{2x^2-2}$

50. $\dfrac{a+6}{a^2-16} \cdot \dfrac{3a-12}{3a+18}$

51. $\dfrac{2x^2-x-3}{x^2-1} \cdot \dfrac{x^2+x-2}{2x^2+x-6}$

52. $\dfrac{2p^2-5p-3}{p^2-9} \cdot \dfrac{2p^2+5p-3}{2p^2+5p+2}$

53. $(6a-a^2) \cdot \dfrac{a^3}{a^3-6a^2+3a-18}$

54. $(10n-n^2) \cdot \dfrac{n^6}{n^3-10n^2-2n+20}$

55. $(x^2+x-2cx-2c) \cdot \dfrac{x^2+3x+2}{4c^2-x^2}$

56. $(2ax-10x-a+5) \cdot \dfrac{x}{x-2x^2}$

Perform the operations and simplify, if possible. See Example 6.

57. $\dfrac{m^2n}{4} \div \dfrac{mn^3}{6}$

58. $\dfrac{a^4b}{14} \div \dfrac{a^3b^2}{21}$

59. $\dfrac{x^2-16}{x^2-25} \div \dfrac{x+4}{x-5}$

60. $\dfrac{a^2-9}{a^2-49} \div \dfrac{a+3}{a+7}$

61. $\dfrac{5c+1}{6} \div \dfrac{125c^3+1}{6c+6}$

62. $\dfrac{6m-8}{9m^3} \div \dfrac{27m^3-64}{9m+9}$

63. $\dfrac{3n^2+5n-2}{12n^2-13n+3} \div \dfrac{n^2+3n+2}{4n^2+5n-6}$

64. $\dfrac{8y^2 - 14y - 15}{6y^2 - 11y - 10} \div \dfrac{4y^2 - 9y - 9}{3y^2 - 7y - 6}$

Perform the operations and simplify, if possible. See Example 7.

65. $\dfrac{3x}{x^2 - 9} - \dfrac{9}{x^2 - 9}$

66. $\dfrac{9x}{x^2 - 1} - \dfrac{9}{x^2 - 1}$

67. $\dfrac{3y - 2}{2y + 6} - \dfrac{2y - 5}{2y + 6}$

68. $\dfrac{5x + 8}{3x + 15} - \dfrac{3x - 2}{3x + 15}$

Perform the operations and simplify, if possible. See Example 8.

69. $\dfrac{3}{4x} + \dfrac{2}{3x}$

70. $\dfrac{2}{5a} + \dfrac{3}{2a}$

71. $\dfrac{8}{9y^2} + \dfrac{1}{6y^4}$

72. $\dfrac{5}{6a^3} + \dfrac{7}{8a^2}$

73. $\dfrac{3}{4ab^2} - \dfrac{5}{2a^2b}$

74. $\dfrac{1}{5xy^3} - \dfrac{2}{15x^2y}$

75. $\dfrac{y - 7}{y^2} - \dfrac{y + 7}{2y}$

76. $\dfrac{x + 5}{xy} - \dfrac{x - 1}{x^2y}$

Perform the operations and simplify, if possible. See Example 9.

77. $\dfrac{3}{x + 2} + \dfrac{5}{x - 4}$

78. $\dfrac{2}{a + 4} - \dfrac{6}{a + 3}$

79. $\dfrac{x + 2}{x + 5} - \dfrac{x - 3}{x + 7}$

80. $\dfrac{7}{x + 3} + \dfrac{4x}{x + 6}$

81. $\dfrac{x}{x^2 + 5x + 6} + \dfrac{x}{x^2 - 4}$

82. $\dfrac{x}{x^2 + 2x + 1} + \dfrac{x}{x^2 - 1}$

83. $\dfrac{4}{x^2 - 2x - 3} - \dfrac{x}{3x^2 - 7x - 6}$

84. $\dfrac{5}{x^2 + 5x - 6} - \dfrac{x}{2x^2 + 7x - 30}$

85. $\dfrac{6}{5d^2 - 5d} - \dfrac{3}{5d - 5}$

86. $\dfrac{9}{2r^2 - 2r} - \dfrac{5}{2r - 2}$

87. $\dfrac{m}{m^2 + 9m + 20} - \dfrac{4}{m^2 + 7m + 12}$

88. $\dfrac{x + 3}{2x^2 - 5x + 2} - \dfrac{3x - 1}{x^2 - x - 2}$

Solve each equation. See Example 10.

89. $\dfrac{3}{y} + \dfrac{7}{2y} = 13$

90. $\dfrac{2}{x} + \dfrac{1}{2} = \dfrac{7}{2x}$

91. $\dfrac{2}{x} + \dfrac{1}{2} = \dfrac{9}{4x} - \dfrac{1}{2x}$

92. $\dfrac{7}{5x} - \dfrac{1}{2} = \dfrac{5}{6x} + \dfrac{1}{3}$

93. $\dfrac{a}{2} = \dfrac{a - 6}{3a - 9} - \dfrac{1}{3}$

94. $\dfrac{b}{5} = \dfrac{b - 14}{2b - 16} - \dfrac{1}{2}$

95. $\dfrac{2}{5x - 5} + \dfrac{x - 2}{15} = \dfrac{4}{5x - 5}$

96. $\dfrac{3}{2x + 4} = \dfrac{x - 2}{2} + \dfrac{x - 5}{2x + 4}$

Simplify each function. List any restrictions on the domain.

97. $f(x) = \dfrac{x^2 + 6x - 16}{x^2 - 4}$

98. $f(x) = \dfrac{5x^2 + 50x}{x^5 + 10x^4}$

99. $g(x) = \dfrac{x^3 + 64}{x^3 + 4x^2 + 3x + 12}$

100. $h(t) = \dfrac{t^3 - 5t^2 - 5t + 25}{t^3 - 125}$

In the following problems, simplify each expression by performing the indicated operations and solve each equation.

101. $\dfrac{p^3 - q^3}{q^2 - p^2} \cdot \dfrac{q^2 + pq}{p^3 + p^2q + pq^2}$

102. $\dfrac{x^3 + y^3}{x^3 - y^3} \div \dfrac{x^2 - xy + y^2}{x^2 + xy + y^2}$

103. $\dfrac{t}{t^2 + 5t + 6} - \dfrac{2}{t^2 + 3t + 2}$

104. $\dfrac{2a}{a^2 - 2a - 8} + \dfrac{3}{a^2 - 5a + 4}$

105. $\dfrac{4}{m^2 - 9} + \dfrac{5}{m^2 - m - 12} = \dfrac{7}{m^2 - 7m + 12}$

106. $\dfrac{34}{x^2} + \dfrac{13}{20x} = \dfrac{3}{2x}$

107. $\dfrac{2}{x - 1} - \dfrac{2x}{x^2 - 1} - \dfrac{x}{x^2 + 2x + 1}$

108. $\dfrac{x - 2}{x^2 - 3x} + \dfrac{2x - 1}{x^2 + 3x} - \dfrac{2}{x^2 - 9}$

109. $(2x^2 - 15x + 25) \div \dfrac{2x^2 - 3x - 5}{x + 1}$

110. $(x^2 - 6x + 9) \div \dfrac{x^2 - 9}{x + 3}$

111. $\dfrac{y^3 - x^3}{2x^2 + 2xy + x + y} \cdot \dfrac{2x^2 - 5x - 3}{yx - 3y - x^2 + 3x}$

112. $\dfrac{ax + ay + bx + by}{x^3 - 27} \cdot \dfrac{x^2 + 3x + 9}{xc + xd + yc + yd}$

113. $\dfrac{24n^4}{16n^4 + 24n^3}$

114. $\dfrac{18m^4}{36m^4 - 9m^3}$

115. $1 + x - \dfrac{x}{x - 5}$

116. $2 - x + \dfrac{3}{x - 9}$

117. $\dfrac{ax + by + ay + bx}{a^2 - b^2}$

118. $\dfrac{3x^2 - 3y^2}{x^2 + 2y + 2x + yx}$

119. $\dfrac{3}{s - 2} + \dfrac{s - 14}{2s^2 - 3s - 2} - \dfrac{4}{2s + 1} = 0$

120. $\dfrac{1}{y^2 - 2y - 3} + \dfrac{1}{y^2 - 4y + 3} - \dfrac{1}{y^2 - 1} = 0$

121. $\dfrac{5}{x + 4} + \dfrac{1}{x + 4} = x - 1$

122. $\dfrac{5}{3x + 12} - \dfrac{1}{9} = \dfrac{x - 1}{3x}$

123. $\dfrac{5x}{x-3} + \dfrac{4x}{3-x}$

124. $\dfrac{8x}{x-4} - \dfrac{10x}{4-x}$

APPLICATIONS

125. Environmental Cleanup. Suppose the cost (in dollars) of removing $p\%$ of the pollution in a river is given by the rational function

$$f(p) = \frac{50,000p}{100-p} \quad \text{where } 0 \le p < 100$$

Find the cost of removing each percent of pollution.

a. 50%   **b.** 80%

126. Directory Costs. The average (mean) cost for a service club to publish a directory of its members is given by the rational function

$$f(x) = \frac{1.25x + 700}{x}$$

where x is the number of directories printed. Find the average cost per directory if

a. 500 directories are printed.

b. 2,000 directories are printed.

127. Utility Costs. An electric company charges $7.50 per month plus 9¢ for each kilowatt hour (kwh) of electricity used.

a. Find a linear function that gives the total cost of n kwh of electricity. (*Hint:* See Example 1.)

b. Find a rational function that gives the average cost per kwh when using n kwh.

c. Find the average cost per kwh when 775 kwh are used.

128. Drafting. Among the tools used in drafting are $45° - 45° - 90°$ and $30° - 60° - 90°$ triangles. Find the perimeter of each triangle and express each result as a rational expression.

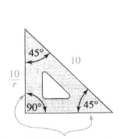

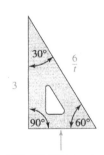

For a 45°–45°–90° triangle, these two sides are the same length.   For a 30°–60°–90° triangle, this side is half as long as the hypotenuse.

WRITING

129. A student compared his answer, $\dfrac{a-3b}{2b-a}$, with the answer, $\dfrac{3b-a}{a-2b}$, in the back of the text. Is the student's work correct? Explain.

130. Explain the error that is made in the following work:

$$\frac{3x^2 + 1}{3y} = \frac{\cancel{3}x^2 + 1}{\cancel{3}y} = \frac{x^2 + 1}{y}$$

131. Write some comments to the student who wrote the following solution, explaining his misunderstanding.

$$\text{Multiply:} \quad \frac{1}{x} \cdot \frac{3}{2} = \frac{1}{x} \cdot \frac{2}{2} \cdot \frac{3}{2} \cdot \frac{x}{x}$$

$$= \frac{2}{2x} \cdot \frac{3x}{2x}$$

$$= \frac{6x}{4x^2}$$

132. Would you use the same approach to answer the following problems? Explain why or why not.

$$\text{Simplify:} \quad \frac{x^2 - 10}{x^2 - 1} - \frac{3x}{x - 1} - \frac{2x}{x + 1}$$

$$\text{Solve:} \quad \frac{x^2 - 10}{x^2 - 1} - \frac{3x}{x - 1} = -\frac{2x}{x + 1}$$

REVIEW

Solve each equation.

133. $-10|16h + 4| - 3 = -3$

134. $-5|2a - 9| + 14 = 14$

CHALLENGE PROBLEMS

135. Simplify: $\dfrac{a^6 - 64}{(a^2 + 2a + 4)(a^2 - 2a + 4)}$

136. Add: $x^{-1} + x^{-2} + x^{-3} + x^{-4} + x^{-5}$

137. Simplify: $[(x^{-1} + 1)^{-1} + 1]^{-1}$

138. Find two rational expressions, each with denominator $x^2 + 5x + 6$, such that their sum is $\dfrac{1}{x + 2}$.

Graph each rational function. Show the vertical asymptote as a dashed line and label it.

139. $f(x) = \dfrac{1}{x - 1}$ **140.** $f(x) = \dfrac{1}{x + 4}$

Perform the operations and simplify.

141. $\dfrac{6a^2 - 7a - 3}{2a^2 - 2} \div \dfrac{4a^2 - 12a + 9}{a^2 - 1} \cdot \dfrac{2a^2 - a - 3}{3a^2 - 2a - 1}$

142. $\dfrac{2x^2 - 2x - 4}{x^2 + 2x - 8} \cdot \dfrac{3x^2 + 15x}{x + 1} \div \dfrac{100 - 4x^2}{x^2 - x - 20}$

143. $\dfrac{\dfrac{h}{h^2 + 3h + 2}}{\dfrac{4}{h + 2} - \dfrac{4}{h + 1}}$

144. $\dfrac{\dfrac{2}{y - 1} - \dfrac{2}{y}}{\dfrac{3}{y - 1} - \dfrac{1}{1 - y}}$

8 ▶ Summary & Review

SECTION 8.1 ▶ Review of Solving Linear Equations, Formulas, and Linear Inequalities; Applications

DEFINITIONS AND CONCEPTS	EXAMPLES
Strategy for Solving Linear Equations in One Variable 1. Clear the equation of fractions or decimals. 2. Simplify each side of the equation by removing all sets of parentheses and combining like terms. 3. Isolate the variable term on one side of the equation. 4. Isolate the variable. 5. Check the result in the original equation.	Solve: $\dfrac{x-1}{6} + x = \dfrac{2}{3} - \dfrac{x+2}{6}$

$$6\left(\frac{x-1}{6} + x\right) = 6\left(\frac{2}{3} - \frac{x+2}{6}\right) \qquad \text{Multiply both sides by 6 to clear the fractions.}$$

$$6 \cdot \frac{x-1}{6} + 6 \cdot x = 6 \cdot \frac{2}{3} - 6 \cdot \frac{x+2}{6} \qquad \text{Distribute 6 on both sides.}$$

$$x - 1 + 6x = 4 - (x + 2) \qquad \text{Simplify. Don't forget the parentheses.}$$

$$x - 1 + 6x = 4 - x - 2 \qquad \text{Remove parentheses.}$$

$$7x - 1 = 2 - x \qquad \text{Combine like terms on each side.}$$

$$7x - 1 + x = 2 - x + x \qquad \text{To eliminate } -x \text{ on the right side, add } x \text{ to both sides.}$$

$$8x - 1 = 2 \qquad \text{Combine like terms on each side.}$$

$$8x - 1 + 1 = 2 + 1 \qquad \text{To isolate the variable term } 8x, \text{ add 1 to both sides.}$$

$$8x = 3 \qquad \text{Simplify each side.}$$

$$\frac{8x}{8} = \frac{3}{8} \qquad \text{Isolate the variable } x \text{ by dividing both sides by 8.}$$

$$x = \frac{3}{8}$$

The solution is $\frac{3}{8}$ and the solution set is $\left\{\frac{3}{8}\right\}$. Check this result to verify that it satisfies the *original* equation.

An equation that is satisfied by every number for which both sides are defined is called an **identity**.

A **contradiction** is an equation that is never true.

When we solve $x + 5 + x = 2x + 5$, the variables drop out and we obtain a true statement $5 = 5$. All real numbers are solutions. The solution set is the set of real numbers written as $\mathbb{R}$.

When we solve $y + 2 = y$, the variables drop out and we obtain a false statement $2 = 0$. The equation has no solutions. The solution set contains no elements and can be written as the **empty set** $\{\ \ \}$ or the **null set** $\varnothing$.

To **solve a formula for a specified variable** means to isolate that variable on one side of the equation, with all other variables and constants on the opposite side.

Solve $\quad F = \dfrac{mMg}{r^2}$ for M.

$$Fr^2 = mMg \qquad \text{To clear the fraction, multiply both sides by } r^2.$$

$$\frac{Fr^2}{mg} = M \qquad \text{To isolate M, divide both sides by mg.}$$

$$M = \frac{Fr^2}{mg} \qquad \text{Write M on the left side.}$$

To **solve a linear inequality** in one variable, we use **properties of inequality** to find the values of its variable that make the inequality true.

If we multiply or divide both sides of an inequality by a negative number, the direction of the **inequality symbol must be reversed** for the inequalities to have the same solutions.

The set of all solutions of an inequality is called its **solution set**.

Solve: $\quad -5x + 7 > 22$

$$-5x + 7 - 7 > 22 - 7 \qquad \text{Subtract 7 from both sides.}$$

$$-5x > 15$$

$$\frac{-5x}{-5} < \frac{15}{-5} \qquad \text{Divide both sides by } -5 \text{ and reverse the direction of the inequality symbol.}$$

$$x < -3$$

The solution set is:

Graph	Interval notation	Set-builder notation
	$(-\infty, -3)$	$\{x \mid x < -3\}$

-4 -3 -2

REVIEW EXERCISES

Solve each equation. If an equation is an identity or a contradiction, so indicate.

1. $5x + 12 = 0$

2. $-3x - 7 + x = 6x + 20 - 5x$

3. $4(y - 1) = 28$ 　　　**4.** $2 - 13(x - 1) = 4 - 6x$

5. $\dfrac{8}{3}(x - 5) = \dfrac{2}{5}(x - 4)$ 　　**6.** $\dfrac{3y}{4} - 14 = -\dfrac{y}{3} - 1$

7. $2x + 4 = 2(x + 3) - 2$ 　　**8.** $3x - 2 - x = 2(x - 4)$

9. $-\dfrac{5}{4}p = 10$ 　　　**10.** $\dfrac{4t + 1}{3} - \dfrac{t + 5}{6} = \dfrac{t - 3}{6}$

Solve each formula for the indicated variable.

11. $V = \pi r^2 h$ for h

12. $v = \dfrac{1}{6}ab(x + y)$ for x

Solve each inequality. Give each solution set in interval notation and graph it.

13. $0.3x - 0.4 \geq 1.2 - 0.1x$

14. $\dfrac{7}{4}(x + 3) < \dfrac{3}{8}(x - 3)$

15. $-16 < -\dfrac{4}{5}x$

16. $5(2n + 2) - n > 3n - 3(1 - 2n)$

Use the six-step problem-solving strategy for each of the following application problems.

17. Carpentry. A carpenter wants to cut a 20-foot rafter so that one piece is 3 times as long as the other. Where should he cut the board?

18. Geometry. A rectangle is 4 meters longer than it is wide. If the perimeter of the rectangle is 28 meters, find its length and width.

SECTION 8.2 ▶ Functions

DEFINITIONS AND CONCEPTS	EXAMPLES
A **relation** is a set of ordered pairs. The set of first components is called the **domain** of the relation and the set of second components is called the **range.**	The relation $\{(2, 5), (7, -3), (4, 6)\}$ has domain $\{2, 4, 7\}$ and range $\{-3, 5, 6\}$.
A **function** is a set of ordered pairs (a relation) in which to each first component there corresponds exactly one second component. Since we often work with sets of ordered pairs of the form (x, y), it is helpful to define a function using the variables x and y: **y is a function of x**: Given a relation in x and y, if to each value of x in the domain there corresponds exactly one value of y in the range, then y is said to be a function of x. Since y depends on x, we call x the **independent variable** and y the **dependent variable.**	The relation $\{(2, 5), (7, -3), (4, 6)\}$ defines a function because to each first component there corresponds exactly one second component. The relation $\{(-9, 1), (3, 8), (0, 0), (3, 24)\}$ *does not* define a function because to the first component 3 there corresponds two second components, 8 and 24. The arrow diagram *does not* define y as a function of x because to the x-value 4 there corresponds more than one y-value: 2 and 6. The table defines a function and illustrates an important point: *Two different ordered pairs of a function can have the same y-value.* x $\quad\quad$ y 4 → 2 0 → 6 $\begin{array}{c\|c} x & y \\ \hline 1 & 9 \\ 2 & 9 \\ 3 & 9 \end{array}$
A function can be defined by an equation, however not all equations in two variables define functions.	The equation $y = 2x - 7$ defines y as a function of x because to each value of x there corresponds exactly one value of y. The equation $x = \|y\|$ does not define y as a function of x because more than one value of y corresponds to a single value of x. If x is 2, for example, the equation becomes $2 = \|y\|$ and y can be either 2 or -2.
The **function notation** $y = f(x)$ indicates that the variable y is a function of x. It is read as "f of x." Think of a function as a machine that takes some **input** x and turns it into some **output** $f(x)$, called a **function value.**	If $f(x) = 2x + 1$, find $f(-2)$ and $f(n + 1)$. $\begin{aligned} f(x) &= 2x + 1 \\ f(-2) &= 2(-2) + 1 \\ &= -4 + 1 \\ &= -3 \end{aligned}$ $\quad\quad$ $\begin{aligned} f(x) &= 2x + 1 \\ f(n + 1) &= 2(n + 1) + 1 \\ &= 2n + 2 + 1 \\ &= 2n + 3 \end{aligned}$ Thus, $f(-2) = -3$. $\quad\quad$ Thus, $f(n + 1) = 2n + 3$.
The input-output pairs that a function generates can be written as ordered pairs and plotted on a rectangular coordinate system to give the **graph of the function.** A **linear function** is a function that can be defined by an equation of the form $f(x) = mx + b$. The graph of a linear function is a straight line. Linear functions can be graphed using the **point-plotting method,** the **intercept method,** or the **slope–intercept method.**	To graph the linear function $f(x) = -4x - 2$, we make a table of values, plot the points, and draw the graph. 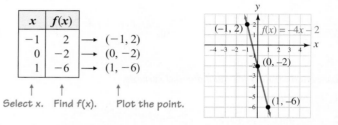 $\begin{array}{c\|c} x & f(x) \\ \hline -1 & 2 \\ 0 & -2 \\ 1 & -6 \end{array}$ → $(-1, 2)$ → $(0, -2)$ → $(1, -6)$ ↑ Select x. $\quad$ ↑ Find $f(x)$. $\quad$ ↑ Plot the point.
The **domain** of a function is the set of input values. The **range** is the set of output values. To find the domain of a function defined by an equation, we must identify all the values of the input variable that produce a real-number output.	Find the domain of $f(x) = \dfrac{10}{x + 3}$. The number -3 cannot be substituted for x, because that would make the denominator equal to 0. Since any real number except -3 can be substituted for x, the domain is *the set of all real numbers except* -3.

To write equations of linear functions, we can use:	Write an equation for the linear function whose graph has slope -4 and passes through $(1, 8)$.
slope–intercept form: $f(x) = mx + b$ **point–slope form:** $f(x) - y_1 = m(x - x_1)$	$\begin{aligned} f(x) - y_1 &= m(x - x_1) &\text{This is point–slope form.}\\ f(x) - 8 &= -4(x - 1) &\text{Substitute for } m, y_1, \text{ and } x_1.\\ f(x) - 8 &= -4x + 4 &\text{Distribute.}\\ f(x) &= -4x + 12 &\text{Solve for } f(x). \end{aligned}$
A **polynomial function** is a function whose equation is defined by a polynomial in one variable. To **evaluate a polynomial function,** we replace the variable in the defining equation with its value, called the **input.** Then we simplify to find the **output.**	Let $f(x) = x^3 - 3x^2 - 9x + 2$. Find $f(2)$. $\begin{aligned} f(x) &= x^3 - 3x^2 - 9x + 2\\ f(2) &= (2)^3 - 3(2)^2 - 9(2) + 2 &\text{Substitute 2 for } x.\\ &= 8 - 3(4) - 18 + 2\\ &= -20 &\text{The output is } -20. \end{aligned}$

REVIEW EXERCISES

19. Find the domain and the range of the relation:
   $\{(-4, 0), (5, 16), (2, -2), (-1, -2)\}$

20. Fill in the blanks.
   a. A _____ is a set of ordered pairs (a relation) in which to each first component there corresponds exactly one second component.
   b. Given a relation in x and y, if to each value of x in the domain there corresponds exactly one value of y in the range, y is said to be a _____ of x. We call x the independent _____ and y the _____ variable.

Determine whether the relation defines y as a function of x. If it does not, find two ordered pairs where more than one value of y corresponds to a single value of x.

21. a.

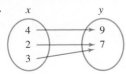

b.

x	y
-1	8
0	5
4	1
-1	9

   c. $\{(14, 6), (-1, 14), (6, 0), (-3, 8)\}$

22. For the given input, what value will the function machine output?

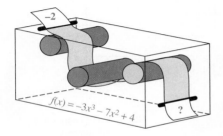

Determine whether each equation defines y as a function of x. If it does not, find two ordered pairs where more than one value of y corresponds to a single value of x.

23. $y = 6x - 4$

24. $y = 4 - x^2$

25. $y^2 = x$

26. $|y| = x + 1$

Let $f(x) = 3x + 2$ and $g(a) = \dfrac{a^2 - 4a + 4}{2}$. Find each function value.

27. $f(-3)$

28. $g(8)$

29. $g(-2)$

30. $f(t + 2)$

31. Let $f(x) = -5x + 7$. For what value of x is $f(x) = -8$?

32. Let $g(t) = \frac{3}{4}t - 1$. For what value of t is $g(t) = 0$?

Find the domain of each function.

33. $f(x) = 4x - 1$

34. $s(t) = t^2 + 1$

35. $h(x) = \dfrac{4}{2 - x}$

36. $g(b) = \dfrac{12}{5b + 25}$

37. What are the slope and the y-intercept of the graph of $g(x) = -2x - 16$?

38. Graph: $f(x) = \frac{2}{3}x - 2$

Write an equation for a linear function whose graph has the given characteristics.

39. Slope: $\dfrac{9}{10}$, y-intercept: $\left(0, \dfrac{7}{8}\right)$

40. Slope: $\dfrac{1}{5}$, passes through $(10, 1)$

41. Horizontal, passes through $(-8, 12)$

42. Passes through $(2, 5)$, parallel to the graph of $g(x) = 4x - 7$

43. Passes through $(-6, 3)$, perpendicular to the graph of $g(x) = -3x - 12$

44. Electricity. The relationship between the electrical resistance R of a coil of wire and its temperature t can be modeled with a linear function.

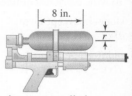

a. Use the following data in the table to write a function that describes this relationship.

b. Use the answer to part (a) to predict the resistance if the temperature of the coil of wire is 100° Celsius.

t (in degrees Celsius)	10	30
R (in milliohms)	5.25	5.65

45. Squirt Guns. The volume of the reservoir on top of the squirt gun is given by the polynomial function $V(r) = 4.19r^3 + 25.13r^2$, where r is the radius in inches. Find $V(2)$ to the nearest cubic inch.

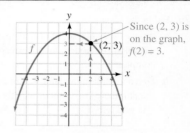

46. Calculus. In the advanced mathematics course called Calculus, an important polynomial function is:

$$f(x) = 1 + x + \frac{x^2}{2} + \frac{x^3}{6} + \frac{x^4}{24}$$

Find $f(1)$.

SECTION 8.3 ▶ Graphs of Functions

DEFINITIONS AND CONCEPTS	EXAMPLES
From the graph of a function, we can determine function values. For the example, the value of $f(2)$ is given by the y-coordinate of a point on the graph of f with x-coordinate 2.	To find $f(2)$ from the graph, draw a vertical line through 2 on the x-axis. It intersects the graph at $(2, 3)$. Therefore, 3 corresponds to 2 and it follows that $f(2) = 3$. 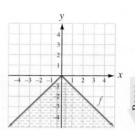 Since $(2, 3)$ is on the graph, $f(2) = 3$.
These three basic functions are used so often in algebra that you should memorize their names and their graphs. They are called **nonlinear functions** because their graphs are not lines.	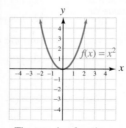 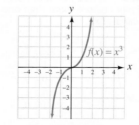 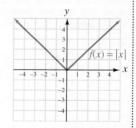 The squaring function The cubing function The absolute value function
We can find the domain and range of a function from its graph. The **domain of a function** is the projection of its graph onto the x-axis. **The range of a function** is the projection of its graph onto the y-axis.	Find the domain and range of function f. 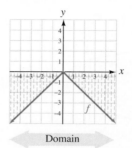 ◀ Domain ▶ R: The set of nonpositive real numbers D: The set of real numbers

A **vertical translation** shifts a graph upward or downward. A **horizontal translation** shifts a graph left or right. A **reflection** "flips" a graph about the x-axis.	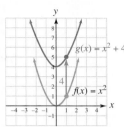 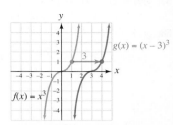
	To graph $g(x) = x^2 + 4$, translate each point on the graph of $f(x) = x^2$ up 4 units. To graph $g(x) = (x - 3)^3$, translate each point on the graph of $f(x) = x^3$ to the right 3 units.
The **vertical line test:** If a vertical line intersects a graph in more than one point, the graph is not the graph of a function.	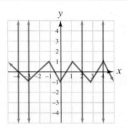 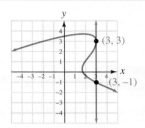
	The graph of a function Not the graph of a function

REVIEW EXERCISES

47. Use the graph to find each value.
  a. $f(-2)$
  b. $f(3)$
  c. The value of x for which $f(x) = 0$.

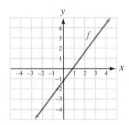

48. Use the graph to find each value.
  a. $g(0)$
  b. $g(-3)$
  c. The value(s) of x for which $g(x) = -4$.

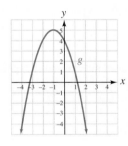

49. Use the graph of function f to find each of the following.
  a. $f(0)$
  b. The values of x for which $f(x) = 0$
  c. Write the domain and range of f in interval notation.

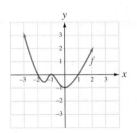

50. What are the nonnegative real numbers?

Give the domain and range of each function graphed below.

51.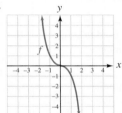

52.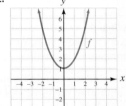

53. Graph $f(x) = |x + 2|$ by creating a table of function values and plotting points. Give the domain and range of the function.

54. Fill in the blanks.
  a. The graph of $f(x) = x^2 + 6$ is the same as the graph of $f(x) = x^2$ except that it is shifted ___ units ___.
  b. The graph of $f(x) = (x + 6)^2$ is the same as the graph of $f(x) = x^2$ except that it is shifted ___ units to the ____.

For each of the following functions, first sketch the graph of its associated function, $f(x) = x^2$, $f(x) = x^3$, or $f(x) = |x|$. Then draw the graph of function g using a translation and/or a reflection and give its domain and range.

55. $g(x) = x^2 - 3$

56. $g(x) = |x - 4|$

57. $g(x) = (x - 2)^3 + 1$

58. $g(x) = -x^3$

Determine whether each graph is the graph of a function. If it is not, find two ordered pairs where more than one value of y corresponds to a single value of x.

59.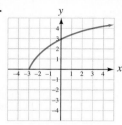

60.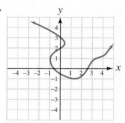

SECTION 8.4   ▶ **Solving Compound Inequalities**

DEFINITIONS AND CONCEPTS	EXAMPLES
The **intersection** of two sets A and B, written $A \cap B$, is the set of all elements that are common to set A and set B. The **union** of two sets A and B, written $A \cup B$, is the set of all elements that are in set A, set B, or both.	Let $A = \{-2, 0, 3, 5\}$ and $B = \{-3, 0, 5, 7\}$. $A \cap B = \{0, 5\}$ The intersection contains the elements that the sets have in common. $A \cup B = \{-3, -2, 0, 3, 5, 7\}$ The union contains the elements that are in one or the other set, or both.
When the word *and* or the word *or* is used to connect pairs of inequalities, we call the statement a **compound inequality.** The solution set of a **compound inequality containing the word *and*** includes all numbers that make both of the inequalities true. That is, it is the intersection of their solution sets.	Solve: $2x - 1 \leq 5$ and $5x + 1 > 4$ We solve each inequality separately. Then we graph the two solution sets (one in red, the other in blue) on the same number line and determine their intersection. $2x - 1 \leq 5$ and $5x + 1 > 4$ ***Preliminary Work:*** $\quad\quad 2x \leq 6 \quad\quad\quad\quad 5x > 3$ $\quad\quad\quad x \leq 3 \quad\quad\quad\quad x > \dfrac{3}{5}$ 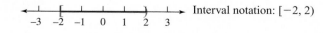 The purple-shaded interval shown below is where the red and blue graphs overlap. Thus, the solution set is: Interval notation: $\left(\dfrac{3}{5}, 3\right]$
Inequalities that contain exactly two inequality symbols are called **double inequalities.** Any double linear inequality can be written as a compound inequality containing the word *and*. For example: $c < x < d$ is equivalent to $c < x$ and $x < d$	Solve: $-7 \leq 3x - 1 < 5$ We apply properties of inequality to *all three of its parts* to isolate x in the middle. $-7 \leq 3x - 1 < 5$ $-7 + 1 \leq 3x - 1 + 1 < 5 + 1$ Add 1 to all three parts. $-6 \leq 3x < 6$ $\dfrac{-6}{3} \leq \dfrac{3x}{3} < \dfrac{6}{3}$ Divide each part by 3. $-2 \leq x < 2$ The solution set is: Interval notation: $[-2, 2)$

The solution set of a **compound inequality containing the word** *or* includes all numbers that make one or the other, or both, inequalities true. That is, it is the union of their solution sets.

Solve: $2x - 1 > 5$ or $-(5x - 7) \geq 2$

We solve each inequality separately. Then we graph the two solution sets on the same number line to show their union.

$$
\begin{array}{c|c}
2x - 1 > 5 \quad \text{or} & -(5x - 7) \geq 2 \\
2x > 6 & -5x + 7 \geq 2 \\
x > 3 & -5x \geq -5 \\
& x \leq 1
\end{array}
$$

The solution set is:

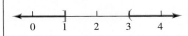

Interval notation: $(-\infty, 1] \cup (3, \infty)$
This is the union of two intervals.

REVIEW EXERCISES

Let $A = \{-6, -3, 0, 3, 6\}$ and $B = \{-5, -3, 3, 8\}$.

61. Find $A \cap B$.

62. Find $A \cup B$.

Check to determine whether −4 is a solution of the compound inequality.

63. $x < 0$ and $x > -5$

64. $x + 3 < -3x - 1$ and $4x - 3 > 3x$

Graph each set.

65. $(-3, 3) \cup [1, 6]$

66. $(-\infty, 2] \cap [1, 4)$

Solve each compound inequality. Graph the solution set and write it using interval notation.

67. $-2x > 8$ and $x + 4 \geq -6$

68. $5(x + 2) \leq 4(x + 1)$ and $11 + x < 0$

69. $\dfrac{2}{5}x - 2 < -\dfrac{4}{5}$ and $-\dfrac{x}{3} < -1$

70. $4\left(x - \dfrac{1}{4}\right) \leq 3x - 1$ and $x \geq 0$

Solve each double inequality. Graph the solution set and write it using interval notation.

71. $3 < 3x + 4 < 10$

72. $-2 \leq \dfrac{5 - x}{2} \leq 2$

Check to determine whether −4 is a solution of the compound inequality.

73. $x < 1.6$ or $x > -3.9$

74. $x + 1 < 2x - 1$ or $4x - 3 > 3x$

Solve each compound inequality. Graph the solution set and write it using interval notation.

75. $x + 1 < -4$ or $x - 4 > 0$

76. $\dfrac{x}{2} + 3 > -2$ or $4 - x > 4$

77. Rugs.   A manufacturer makes a line of decorator rugs that are 4 feet wide and of varying lengths x (in feet). The floor area covered by the rugs ranges from 17 ft^2 to 25 ft^2. Write and then solve a double linear inequality to find the range of the lengths of the rugs.

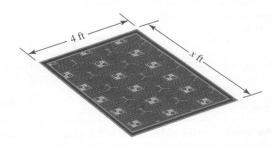

78. Match each word in Column I with *two* associated items in Column II.

Column I	Column II
a. or	**i.** $\cap$
	ii. $\cup$
b. and	**iii.** intersection
	iv. union

79. Let $f(x) = \dfrac{5}{4}x - 140$. Find all values of x for which $f(x) < -48$ or $f(x) \geq 32$.

80. Let $f(x) = 3x - 5$. Find all values of x for which $-4 \geq f(x) > -12$.

SECTION 8.5 ▶ Solving Absolute Value Equations and Inequalities

DEFINITIONS AND CONCEPTS	EXAMPLES
To **solve absolute value equations** of the form $\lvert X \rvert = k$, where $k > 0$, solve the equivalent **compound equation** $X = k$ or $X = -k$ If k is negative, then $\lvert X \rvert = k$ has no solution. Recall that **equivalent equations** have the same solutions.	Solve: $\lvert 2x + 1 \rvert = 7$ This absolute value equation is equivalent to the following compound equation: $\quad 2x + 1 = 7$ or $2x + 1 = -7$ $\qquad 2x = 6 \qquad\qquad 2x = -8$ $\qquad\ x = 3 \qquad\qquad\ x = -4$ This equation has two solutions: 3 and -4. The solution set is $\{-4, 3\}$.
Since absolute value expresses distance, the absolute value of a number is always positive or zero, but never negative.	Solve: $\lvert 4x - 5 \rvert = -3$ Since an absolute value can never be negative, there are no real numbers x that make $\lvert 4x - 5 \rvert = -3$ true. The equation has no solution and the solution set is $\varnothing$.
To **solve absolute value equations** of the form $\lvert X \rvert = \lvert Y \rvert$, solve the compound equation $\quad X = Y$ or $X = -Y$ The expressions within the absolute value symbols are equal, or they are opposites.	Solve: $\lvert 3x - 2 \rvert = \lvert 2x + 4 \rvert$ This equation is equivalent to the following compound equation: $\quad 3x - 2 = 2x + 4$ or $3x - 2 = -(2x + 4)$ $\qquad\ x - 2 = 4 \qquad\qquad 3x - 2 = -2x - 4$ $\qquad\quad\ x = 6 \qquad\qquad\ 5x - 2 = -4$ $\qquad\qquad\qquad\qquad\qquad\quad 5x = -2$ $\qquad\qquad\qquad\qquad\qquad\quad\ x = -\dfrac{2}{5}$ This equation has two solutions: 6 and $-\frac{2}{5}$. The solution set is $\left\{ -\frac{2}{5}, 6 \right\}$.
To **solve absolute value inequalities** of the form $\lvert X \rvert < k$, where $k > 0$, solve the equivalent double inequality $-k < X < k$. Use a similar approach to solve $\lvert X \rvert \le k$. When solving absolute value equations or inequalities, **isolate the absolute value expression** on one side **before** writing the equivalent compound statement.	Solve: $\lvert 4x - 3 \rvert - 2 < 7$ $\qquad\ \lvert 4x - 3 \rvert - 2 + 2 < 7 + 2$ To isolate the absolute value, $\qquad\qquad\qquad\qquad\qquad\qquad\qquad$ add 2 to both sides. $\qquad\qquad\quad \lvert 4x - 3 \rvert < 9$ The resulting inequality is equivalent to the following double inequality: $\quad -9 < 4x - 3 < 9$ $\quad -6 < 4x < 12 \qquad$ Add 3 to all three parts. $\quad -\dfrac{3}{2} < x < 3 \qquad$ Divide each part by 4 and simplify. The solution set is: Interval notation: $\left(-\frac{3}{2}, 3 \right)$ Set builder: $\left\{ x \mid -\frac{3}{2} < x < 3 \right\}$

To **solve absolute value inequalities** of the form $|X| \geq k$, where $k > 0$, solve the equivalent compound inequality $X \leq -k$ or $X \geq k$.

Use a similar approach to solve $|X| > k$.

Solve: $\quad |3x + 1| \geq 7$

This inequality is equivalent to the following compound inequality:

$$3x + 1 \leq -7 \quad \text{or} \quad 3x + 1 \geq 7$$
$$3x \leq -8 \qquad\qquad 3x \geq 6$$
$$x \leq -\frac{8}{3} \qquad\qquad x \geq 2$$

Interval notation: $\left(-\infty, -\frac{8}{3}\right] \cup [2, \infty)$

This is the union of two intervals.

Set builder: $\left\{ x \mid x \leq -\frac{8}{3} \text{ or } x > 2 \right\}$

REVIEW EXERCISES

Solve each absolute value equation.

81. $|4x| = 8$

82. $2|3x + 1| - 1 = 19$

83. $\left|\dfrac{3}{2}x - 4\right| - 10 = -1$

84. $\left|\dfrac{2 - x}{3}\right| = -4$

85. $|-4(2x - 6)| = 0$

86. $\left|\dfrac{3}{8} + \dfrac{x}{3}\right| = \dfrac{5}{12}$

87. $|3x + 2| = |2x - 3|$

88. $\left|\dfrac{2(1 - x) + 1}{2}\right| = \left|\dfrac{3x - 2}{3}\right|$

Solve each absolute value inequality. Graph the solution set and write it using interval notation.

89. $|x| \leq 3$

90. $|2x + 7| < 3$

91. $2|5 - 3x| \leq 28$

92. $\left|\dfrac{2}{3}x + 14\right| + 6 < 6$

93. $|x| > 1$

94. $\left|\dfrac{1 - 5x}{3}\right| \geq 7$

95. $|3x - 8| - 4 > 0$

96. $\left|\dfrac{3}{2}x - 14\right| \geq 0$

97. Produce. Before packing, freshly picked tomatoes are weighed on the scale shown. Tomatoes having a weight w (in ounces) that falls within the highlighted range are sold to grocery stores.

a. Complete the following absolute value inequality that expresses the acceptable weight range:

$|w - | \leq $

b. Solve the inequality from part (a) and express the acceptable weight range using interval notation.

98. Let $f(x) = \frac{1}{3}|6x| - 1$. For what value(s) of x is $f(x) = 5$?

99. Let $f(x) = 2|3(x + 4)| + 1.5$. Find all values of x for which $f(x) = 25.5$.

100. Let $f(x) = |7 - x|$. Find all values of x for which $f(x) < 5$.

101. Explain why $|0.04x - 8.8| < -2$ has no solution.

102. Explain why the solution set of $\left|\dfrac{3x}{50} + \dfrac{1}{45}\right| \geq -\dfrac{4}{5}$ is the set of all real numbers.

SECTION 8.6 ▶ Review of Factoring Methods: GCF, Grouping, Trinomials

DEFINITIONS AND CONCEPTS	EXAMPLES
The first step of factoring a polynomial is to see whether the terms of the polynomial have a common factor. If they do, **factor out the GCF.**	Factor: $\quad 14a^4 + 35a^3 - 56a^2 = 7a^2(2a^2 + 5a - 8) \quad$ *Factor out the GCF, $7a^2$.* Use multiplication to check the factorization: $\quad 7a^2(2a^2 + 5a - 8) = 14a^4 + 35a^3 - 56a^2 \quad$ *This is the original polynomial.*

If an expression has four or more terms, try to factor the expression by **grouping.**	Factor: $ax - 2x + 3a - 6$ $ax - 2x + 3a - 6 =$ $ax - 2x$ $+$ $3a - 6$ Group the terms. $= x(a - 2) + 3(a - 2)$ Factor x from ax − 2x. Factor 3 from 3a − 6. $= (a - 2)(x + 3)$ Factor out the GCF, a − 2.
Many trinomials factor as the product of two binomials. To **factor a trinomial** of the form $x^2 + bx + c$, whose **leading coefficient is 1,** find two integers whose product is c and whose sum is b.	Factor: $p^2 + 14p + 45$ We must find two integers whose product is 45 and whose sum is 14. Since $5 \cdot 9 = 45$ and $5 + 9 = 14$, two such numbers are **5** and **9**, and we have $p^2 + 14p + 45 = (p + 5)(p + 9)$ ***Check:*** $(p + 5)(p + 9) = p^2 + 9p + 5p + 45 = p^2 + 14p + 45$
We can use the **trial-and-check method** to factor trinomials with **leading coefficients other than 1.** Write the trinomial as the product of two binomials and determine four integers.	Factor: $2x^2 - 5x - 12$ Since the first term is $2x^2$, the first terms of the binomial factors must be $2x$ and x. $(2x\ \boxed{\ \ }\ )(x\ \boxed{\ \ }\ )$ Because 2x · x will give 2x² The second terms of the binomials must be two integers whose product is -12. There are six such pairs: $1(-12),\ \ 2(-6),\ \ \mathbf{3(-4)},\ \ 4(-3),\ \ 6(-2),\ \ \text{and}\ \ 12(-1)$ The pair in blue gives the correct middle term, $-5x$, when placed in the binomial factors shown above. We use the FOIL method to check: Outer: −8x $(2x + 3)(x - 4)$ Combine like terms: −8x + 3x = −5x. Inner: 3x Thus, $2x^2 - 5x - 12 = (2x + 3)(x - 4)$.
To factor $ax^2 + bx + c$ by **grouping,** write it as an equivalent four-term polynomial: $ax^2 + \boxed{\ \ }\,x + \boxed{\ \ }\,x + c$ The product of these numbers must be ac, and their sum must be b. Then factor the four-term polynomial by grouping. Use the FOIL method to check.	Factor by grouping: $2x^2 - 5x - 12$ We must find two integers whose product is $ac = 2(-12) = -24$ and whose sum is $b = -5$. Two such numbers are -8 and 3. They serve as the coefficients of $-8x$ and $3x$, the two terms that we use to represent the middle term, $-5x$, of the trinomial. $2x^2 - 5x - 12 = 2x^2 - 8x + 3x - 12$ Express −5x as −8x + 3x. $= 2x(x - 4) + 3(x - 4)$ $= (x - 4)(2x + 3)$ Factor out the GCF, (x − 4).

REVIEW EXERCISES

Factor, if possible.

103. $z^2 - 11z + 30$ **104.** $x^4 + 4x^2 + x^2y + 4y$

105. $4a^2 - 5a + 1$

106. $27x^3y^3z^3 + 81x^4y^5z^2 - 90x^2y^3z^7$

107. $15b^2 + 4b - 4$ **108.** $-x^2 - 3x + 28$

109. $15x^2 - 57xy - 12y^2$ **110.** $w^8 - w^4 - 90$

111. $r^2y - ar - ry + a + r - 1$ **112.** $49a^6 + 84a^3b^2 + 36b^4$

113. $3b^2 + 2b + 1$ **114.** $2a^4 + 4a^3 - 6a^2$

115. Use a substitution to factor: $(s + t)^2 - 2(s + t) + 1$

116. Solve $m_1m_2 = mm_2 + mm_1$ for m_1.

▶ Review of Factoring Methods: The Difference of Two Squares;
the Sum and Difference of Two Cubes

DEFINITIONS AND CONCEPTS	EXAMPLES
The **difference of two squares:** To factor the square of a First quantity minus the square of a Last quantity, multiply the First plus the Last by the First minus the Last. $F^2 - L^2 = (F + L)(F - L)$	Factor: $x^2y^2 - 100$ $x^2y^2 - 100 = (xy)^2 - 10^2$ *This is a difference of two squares.* $= (xy + 10)(xy - 10)$
In general, the **sum of two squares** (with no common factor other than 1) cannot be factored using real numbers.	$x^2 + 100$ and $36y^2 + 49z^4$ are prime polynomials.
The **sum of two cubes:** To factor the cube of a First quantity plus the cube of a Last quantity, multiply the First plus the Last by the First squared, minus the First times the Last, plus the Last squared. $F^3 + L^3 = (F + L)(F^2 - FL + L^2)$	Factor: $y^3 + 27z^6$ $y^3 + 27z^6 = y^3 + (3z^2)^3$ *This is a sum of two cubes.* $= (y + 3z^2)[y^2 - y \cdot 3z^2 + (3z^2)^2]$ $= (y + 3z^2)(y^2 - 3yz^2 + 9z^4)$
The **difference of two cubes:** To factor the cube of a First quantity minus the cube of a Last quantity, multiply the First minus the Last by the First squared, plus the First times the Last, plus the Last squared. $F^3 - L^3 = (F - L)(F^2 + FL + L^2)$	Factor: $125s^3 - 64$ $125s^3 - 64 = (5s)^3 - 4^3$ *This is a difference of two cubes.* $= (5s - 4)[(5s)^2 + 5s \cdot 4 + 4^2]$ $= (5s - 4)(25s^2 + 20s + 16)$

REVIEW EXERCISES

Factor, if possible.

117. $z^2 - 16$

118. $x^2y^4 - 64z^6$

119. $a^2b^2 + c^2$

120. $c^2 - (a + b)^2$

121. $32a^4c - 162b^4c$

122. $k^2 + 2k + 1 - 9m^2$

123. $m^2 - n^2 - m - n$

124. $t^3 + 64$

125. $8a^3 - 125b^9$

126. Spanish Roof Tile.   The amount of clay used to make a roof tile is given by

$$V = \frac{\pi}{2}r_1^2h - \frac{\pi}{2}r_2^2h$$

Factor the right side of the formula completely.

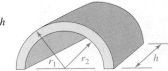

▶ Review of Rational Expressions and Rational Equations; Rational Functions

DEFINITIONS AND CONCEPTS	EXAMPLES
A **rational expression** is an expression of the form $\frac{A}{B}$, where A and B are polynomials and B does not equal 0.	Rational expressions: $\dfrac{3x^2}{xy}$, $\dfrac{5b - 15}{b^2 - 25}$, and $\dfrac{a + 2}{a^2 - 3a - 4}$
A **rational function** is a function whose equation is defined by a rational expression in one variable.	Rational functions: $f(x) = \dfrac{6x}{x - 2}$ and $f(n) = \dfrac{n + 3}{n^3 + 2n - 9}$

Since division by 0 is undefined, any values that make the denominator 0 in a rational function must be excluded from the **domain** of the function.

When finding the domain of a rational function, we *don't need to examine the numerator* of the expression; it can be any value, including 0.

Find the domain of the rational function: $f(x) = \dfrac{x + 3}{x^2 - 4}$

$x^2 - 4 = 0$ Set the denominator equal to 0.

$(x + 2)(x - 2) = 0$ Factor the difference of two squares.

$x + 2 = 0$ or $x - 2 = 0$ Set each factor equal to 0.

$x = -2$ | $x = 2$ Solve each equation.

The domain of the function is the set of all real numbers except -2 and 2. In interval notation, the domain is $(-\infty, -2) \cup (-2, 2) \cup (2, \infty)$.

To simplify a rational expression:

1. Factor the numerator and denominator completely.

2. Remove factors equal to 1 by replacing each pair of factors common to the numerator and denominator with the equivalent fraction $\frac{1}{1}$.

3. Multiply the remaining factors in the numerator and in the denominator.

Simplify: $\dfrac{x^2 - 4}{2x + 4} = \dfrac{\overset{1}{\cancel{(x + 2)}}(x - 2)}{2\underset{1}{\cancel{(x + 2)}}} = \dfrac{x - 2}{2}$

Simplify: $\dfrac{2a^3 - 5a^2 - 12a}{2a^3 - 11a^2 + 12a} = \dfrac{\overset{1}{\cancel{a}}(2a + 3)\overset{1}{\cancel{(a - 4)}}}{\underset{1}{\cancel{a}}(2a - 3)\underset{1}{\cancel{(a - 4)}}} = \dfrac{2a + 3}{2a - 3}$

To **multiply rational expressions,** multiply the numerators and multiply the denominators.

$$\dfrac{A}{B} \cdot \dfrac{C}{D} = \dfrac{AC}{BD}$$

Then simplify, if possible.

Multiply, and then simplify, if possible.

$\dfrac{x^2 - 4}{x + 3} \cdot \dfrac{3x + 9}{x + 2} = \dfrac{(x^2 - 4)(3x + 9)}{(x + 3)(x + 2)}$ Multiply the numerators. Multiply the denominators.

$= \dfrac{\overset{1}{\cancel{(x + 2)}}(x - 2) \cdot 3 \cdot \overset{1}{\cancel{(x + 3)}}}{\underset{1}{\cancel{(x + 3)}}\underset{1}{\cancel{(x + 2)}}}$ Factor completely and then simplify.

$= 3(x - 2)$

To **divide rational expressions,** multiply the first by the reciprocal of the second.

$$\dfrac{A}{B} \div \dfrac{C}{D} = \dfrac{A}{B} \cdot \dfrac{D}{C} = \dfrac{AD}{BC}$$

Then simplify, if possible.

Divide, and then simplify, if possible.

$\dfrac{x^2 + 4x + 3}{x^2 + 3x} \div \dfrac{3}{x} = \dfrac{x^2 + 4x + 3}{x^2 + 3x} \cdot \dfrac{x}{3}$ Multiply the first rational expression by the reciprocal of the second.

$= \dfrac{(x^2 + 4x + 3) \cdot x}{(x^2 + 3x) \cdot 3}$ Multiply the numerators. Multiply the denominators.

$= \dfrac{(x + 1)\overset{1}{\cancel{(x + 3)}} \cdot \overset{1}{\cancel{x}}}{\underset{1}{\cancel{x}}\underset{1}{\cancel{(x + 3)}} \cdot 3}$ Factor completely and then simplify.

$= \dfrac{x + 1}{3}$ Multiply the remaining factors in the numerator. Multiply the remaining factors in the denominator.

To **add (or subtract) two rational expressions with like denominators,** add (or subtract) the numerators and keep the common denominator. Then, if possibe, factor and simplify.

Add:

$\dfrac{x^2 - 26}{x - 5} + \dfrac{1}{x - 5} = \dfrac{x^2 - 26 + 1}{x - 5}$ Add the numerators. Write the sum over the common denominator, $x - 5$.

$= \dfrac{x^2 - 25}{x - 5}$ Combine like terms.

$= \dfrac{(x + 5)\overset{1}{\cancel{(x - 5)}}}{\underset{1}{\cancel{x - 5}}}$ To simplify the result, factor the numerator and remove the factor common to the numerator and denominator.

$= x + 5$

To **add or subtract rational expressions with unlike denominators,** find the LCD and express each rational expression with a denominator that is the LCD. Add (or subtract) the resulting fractions and simplify the result, if possible.

To **build a rational expression,** multiply it by 1 in the form of $\dfrac{c}{c}$, where c is any nonzero number or expression.

Subtract:

$$\frac{2x}{x+5} - \frac{1}{x} = \frac{2x}{x+5} \cdot \frac{x}{x} - \frac{1}{x} \cdot \frac{x+5}{x+5}$$

Build each rational expression to have the LCD of $x(x+5)$.

$$= \frac{2x^2}{x(x+5)} - \frac{x+5}{x(x+5)}$$

Multiply the numerators.
Multiply the denominators.

$$= \frac{2x^2 - (x+5)}{x(x+5)}$$

Subtract the numerators.
Write the difference over the common denominator.

$$= \frac{2x^2 - x - 5}{x(x+5)}$$

The result does not simplify.

To **solve a rational equation:**

1. Factor all denominators.

2. Determine which numbers cannot be solutions of the equation.

3. Multiply both sides of the equation by the LCD of all rational expressions in the equation.

4. Use the distributive property to remove parentheses, remove any factors equal to 1, and write the result in simplified form.

5. Solve the resulting equation.

6. Check all possible solutions in the original equation.

All possible solutions of a rational equation must be checked. Multiplying both sides of an equation by an expression that contains a variable can lead to **extraneous solutions,** which must be discarded.

Solve: $\dfrac{3}{2} + \dfrac{1}{a-4} = \dfrac{5}{2a-8}$

If we factor the last denominator, the equation can be written as:

$$\frac{3}{2} + \frac{1}{a-4} = \frac{5}{2(a-4)}$$

We see that 4 cannot be a solution of the equation, because it makes at least one of the rational expressions in the equation undefined.

We can clear the equation of fractions by multiplying both sides by $2(a-4)$, which is the LCD of the three rational expressions.

$$2(a-4)\left(\frac{3}{2} + \frac{1}{a-4}\right) = 2(a-4)\left[\frac{5}{2(a-4)}\right]$$

Multiply both sides by the LCD.

$$2(a-4)\left(\frac{3}{2}\right) + 2(a-4)\left(\frac{1}{a-4}\right) = 2(a-4)\left[\frac{5}{2(a-4)}\right]$$

Distribute.

$$\overset{1}{2}(a-4)\left(\frac{3}{\underset{1}{2}}\right) + \overset{1}{2}(a-\overset{1}{4})\left(\frac{1}{a-4}\right) = \overset{1}{2}(a-\overset{1}{4})\left[\frac{5}{2(a-4)}\right]$$

Remove common factors.

$$(a-4)3 + 2 = 5 \qquad \text{Simplify.}$$
$$3a - 12 + 2 = 5 \qquad \text{Distribute.}$$
$$3a - 10 = 5 \qquad \text{Combine like terms.}$$
$$3a = 15$$
$$a = 5$$

The solution is 5. Verify that it satisfies the original equation.

REVIEW EXERCISES

127. Use the graph of function f to find each of the following:

   a. $f(2)$

   b. $f(-1)$

   c. The value of x for which $f(x) = -1$

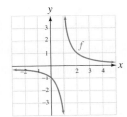

128. Find the domain of the rational function $f(x) = \dfrac{2x^2 + 8x}{x^2 + 2x - 24}$. Express your answer in words and using interval notation.

129. **Injections.** A hospital patient was given an injection for pain. The rational function

$$n(t) = \frac{28t}{t^2 + 1}$$

gives the number of milligrams n of pain medication per liter in the patient's bloodstream, where t is the number of hours since the injection. Find $n(3)$ and explain its meaning.

130. Let $f(x) = \dfrac{4x^2 - 6x + 7}{3x^2 - 27}$. Find $f(3)$.

Simplify each rational expression.

131. $\dfrac{62x^2y}{144xy^2}$

132. $\dfrac{2m - 2n}{n - m}$

Perform the operations and simplify, if possible.

133. $\dfrac{3x^3y^4}{c^2d} \cdot \dfrac{c^3d^2}{21x^5y^4}$

134. $\dfrac{2a^2 - 5a - 3}{a^2 - 9} \div \dfrac{2a^2 + 5a + 2}{2a^2 + 5a - 3}$

135. $\dfrac{m^2 + 3m + 9}{m^2 + mp + mr + pr} \div \dfrac{m^3 - 27}{am + ar + bm + br}$

136. $\dfrac{x^3 + 3x^2 + 2x}{2x^2 - 2x - 12} \cdot \dfrac{3x^2 - 3x}{x^3 - 3x^2 - 4x} \div \dfrac{x^2 + 3x + 2}{2x^2 - 4x - 16}$

137. $\dfrac{d^2}{c^3 - d^3} + \dfrac{c^2 + cd}{c^3 - d^3}$

138. $\dfrac{4}{t - 3} + \dfrac{6}{3 - t}$

139. $\dfrac{5x}{14z^2} + \dfrac{y^2}{16z}$

140. $\dfrac{4}{3xy - 6y} - \dfrac{4}{10 - 5x}$

141. $\dfrac{y + 7}{y + 3} - \dfrac{y - 3}{y + 7}$

142. $\dfrac{2x}{x + 1} + \dfrac{3x}{x + 2} + \dfrac{4x}{x^2 + 3x + 2}$

Solve each equation. If a solution is extraneous, so indicate.

143. $\dfrac{4}{x} - \dfrac{1}{10} = \dfrac{7}{2x}$

144. $\dfrac{3}{y} - \dfrac{2}{y + 1} = \dfrac{1}{2}$

145. $\dfrac{2}{3x + 15} - \dfrac{1}{18} = \dfrac{1}{3x + 12}$

146. $\dfrac{3}{x + 2} = \dfrac{1}{2 - x} + \dfrac{2}{x^2 - 4}$

147. $\dfrac{x + 3}{x - 5} + \dfrac{2x^2 + 6}{x^2 - 7x + 10} = \dfrac{3x}{x - 2}$

148. $\dfrac{5a}{a - 3} - 7 = \dfrac{15}{a - 3}$

SECTION 8.9 ▶ Variation

DEFINITIONS AND CONCEPTS	EXAMPLES
The words **y varies directly as x** or **y is directly proportional to x** mean that $y = kx$ for some nonzero constant k, called the **constant of variation**. The words **y varies inversely as x** or **y is inversely proportional to x** mean that $y = \dfrac{k}{x}$ for some nonzero constant k.	The distance d that a spring stretches **varies directly** as the force f attached to the spring: $d = kf$. If the voltage in an electric circuit is kept constant, the current I **varies inversely** as the resistance R: $$I = \dfrac{k}{R}$$
Strategy for solving variation problems 1. Translate the verbal model into an equation. 2. Substitute the first set of values into the equation from step 1 to determine the value of k. 3. Substitute the value of k into the equation from step 1. 4. Substitute the remaining set of values into the equation from step 3 and solve for the unknown.	Suppose d varies inversely as h. If $d = 5$ when $h = 4$, find d when $h = 10$. 1. The words d *varies inversely as* h translate to $d = \dfrac{k}{h}$. 2. If we substitute 5 for d and 4 for h, we have $$5 = \dfrac{k}{4}$$ $$20 = k \quad \text{To find } k, \text{ multiply both sides by 4.}$$ This is the constant of variation. 3. Since $k = 20$, the inverse variation equation is $d = \dfrac{20}{h}$. 4. To answer the final question, we substitute 10 for h in the inverse variation model: $$d = \dfrac{20}{10} = 2$$
Joint variation: One variable varies as the product of several variables. For example, $y = kxz$ (k is a constant).	The number of gallons g of oil that can be stored in a cylindrical tank **varies jointly** as the height h of the tank and the square of the radius r of its base: $g = khr^2$.

Combined variation: A combination of direct and inverse variation. For example,

$$y = \frac{kx}{z} \quad (k \text{ is a constant})$$

The gravitational force F between two objects with masses m_1 and m_2 *varies directly* as the product of their masses and *inversely* as the square of the distance d between them:

$$F = \frac{km_1m_2}{d^2}$$

REVIEW EXERCISES

149. **Property Tax.** The property tax in a certain county varies directly as assessed valuation. If a tax of $1,575 is charged on a single-family home assessed at $90,000, determine the property tax on an apartment complex assessed at $312,000.

150. **Electricity.** For a fixed voltage, the current in an electrical circuit varies inversely as the resistance in the circuit. If a certain circuit has a current of $2\frac{1}{2}$ amps when the resistance is 150 ohms, find the current in the circuit when the resistance is doubled.

151. Assume that y varies jointly with x and z. Find the constant of variation if $x = 24$ when $y = 3$ and $z = 4$.

152. **Hurricane Winds.** The wind force on a vertical surface varies jointly as the area of the surface and the square of the wind's velocity. If a 10-mph wind exerts a force of 1.98 pounds on the sign shown in the next column, find the force on the sign when the wind is blowing at 80 mph.

153. Does the graph on the right show direct or inverse variation?

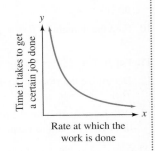

154. Assume that x_1 varies directly with the third power of t and inversely with x_2. Find the constant of variation if $x_1 = 1.6$ when $t = 8$ and $x_2 = 64$.

---

8 ▶ Chapter Test

1. Fill in the blanks.

   a. To _____ an equation means to find all of the values of the variable that make the equation true.

   b. $<$, $>$, $\leq$, and $\geq$ are _____ symbols.

   c. The statement $x^2 - x - 12 = (x - 4)(x + 3)$ shows that the trinomial $x^2 - x - 12$ _____ as the product of two binomials.

   d. The _____ of $\frac{x+1}{x-7}$ is $\frac{x-7}{x+1}$.

   e. Given a relation in x and y, if to each value of x in the domain there corresponds exactly one value of y in the range, y is said to be a _____ of x.

   f. For a function, the set of all possible values that can be used for the independent variable is called the _____. The set of all values of the dependent variable is called the _____.

2. Use a check to determine whether 6.7 is a solution of $1.6y + (-3) = y + 1.02$.

Solve each equation.

3. $t + 18 = 5t - 3 + t$

4. $\frac{2}{3}(2s + 2) = \frac{1}{6}(5s + 29) - 4$

5. $6 - (x - 3) - 5x = 3[1 - 2(x + 2)]$

6. Solve $y - y_1 = m(x - x_1)$ for x_1.

7. **Hand Tools.** With each pass that a craftsman makes with a sander over a piece of fiberglass, he removes 0.03125 inch of thickness. If the fiberglass was originally 0.9375 inch thick, how many passes are needed to obtain the desired thickness of 0.6875 inch?

8. Averaging Grades. Use the information from the gradebook to determine what score Karen Nelson-Sims needs on the fifth exam so that her exam average exceeds 80.

Sociology 101 8:00-10:00 pm MW	Exam 1	Exam 2	Exam 3	Exam 4	Exam 5
Nelson-Sims, Karen	70	79	85	88	

9. Determine whether the relation defines y to be a function of x. If it does not, explain why.

a.

b.

x	y
-3	4
4	-3
1	5
5	1

c. $\left\{\left(0, \frac{1}{2}\right), \left(-10, \frac{1}{2}\right), \left(-20, \frac{1}{2}\right), \left(-30, \frac{1}{2}\right)\right\}$

d. $|y| = x$

10. Find the domain of $f(x) = \dfrac{15}{12 - 2x}$.

11. Let $f(x) = -\frac{4}{5}x - 12$. For what value of x is $f(x) = 4$?

12. Determine the slope and y-intercept of the graph of $f(x) = 8x - 9$.

13. Write an equation for the linear function whose graph passes through $(2, 0)$ and is perpendicular to the graph of $g(x) = \frac{4}{5}x + \frac{1}{9}$.

14. Vehicle Performance. The average fleet-wide performance of light-duty trucks has made constant improvement since 1980. For example, the time for the average 1980 model light-duty truck to accelerate from 0 to 60 mph was about 14.5 seconds. For 2005 models, that time was only 10.5 seconds. (Source: United States EPA)

a. Let m be the model year of a light-duty truck and T be the time in seconds for it to accelerate from 0 to 60 mph. Write a linear function $T(m)$ to model the situation.

b. Use your answer to part a to predict the time it will take the average light-duty truck to accelerate from 0 to 60 mph in 2015, if the trend continues.

Let $f(x) = 3x + 1$ and $g(t) = t^2 - 2t + 1$. Find each value.

15. $f(3)$

16. $g(-6)$

17. $g\left(\dfrac{1}{4}\right)$

18. $f(r + 8)$

19. Boating. The height (in feet) of a warning flare from the surface of the ocean t seconds after being shot into the air is approximated by the polynomial function $h(t) = -16t^2 + 80t + 10$. What is the height of the flare 2.5 seconds after being fired?

20. Use the graph of function f to find each of the following.

a. $f(4)$

b. The values of x for which $f(x) = 2$.

c. The domain and range of f.

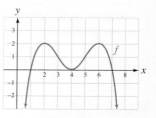

Determine whether each graph is the graph of a function. If it is not, explain why.

21.

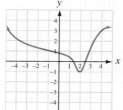

22.

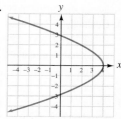

23. Graph $f(x) = |x| + 3$ by creating a table of function values and plotting points. Give the domain and range of the function.

24. Draw the graph of $g(x) = (x - 4)^3 + 1$ using a translation by first sketching the graph of its associated function. Then give the domain and range of function g.

Solve each inequality. Write the solution set in interval notation and graph it.

25. $-2(2x + 3) \geq 14$

26. $-2 < \dfrac{x - 4}{3} < 4$

27. $3x \geq -2x + 5$ and $7 \geq 4x - 2$

28. $3x < -9$ or $-\dfrac{x}{4} < -2$

29. $|2x - 4| > 22$

30. $2|3(x - 2)| \leq 4$

Solve each equation.

31. $|2x + 3| - 19 = 0$

32. $|3x + 4| = |x + 12|$

Factor.

33. $12a^3b^2c - 3a^2b^2c^2 + 6abc^3$

34. $4y^4 - 64$

35. $b^3 + 125$

36. $6u^2 + 9u - 6$

37. $ax - xy + ay - y^2$

38. $25m^8 - 60m^4n + 36n^2$

39. $144b^2 + 25$

40. $x^2 + 6x + 9 - y^2$

41. $64a^3 - 125b^6$

42. $(x - y)^2 + 3(x - y) - 10$

43. Refer to the graph of function f on the right. Find

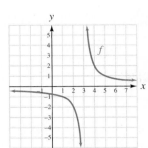

    a. $f(5)$

    b. $f(-1)$

    c. $f(1)$

    d. The value of x for which $f(x) = -2$

44. Wildlife. The number of prairie dogs p living in a given area of land is approximated by the rational function

$$p(t) = \frac{200t}{t + 1}$$

where t is the time, in months, since the first of the year. Find the number of prairie dogs in that area by the end of July.

45. Are the expressions $\dfrac{x - 4}{x^2 + x - 18}$ and $-\dfrac{x + 4}{x^2 + x - 18}$ equivalent?

46. Find the domain of the rational function $f(x) = \frac{x^2 + 6x + 5}{x - x^2}$. Express it using words and interval notation.

Simplify each rational expression.

47. $\dfrac{3y - 6z}{2z - y}$

48. $\dfrac{2x^2 + 7xy + 3y^2}{4xy + 12y^2}$

Perform the operations and simplify, if possible.

49. $\dfrac{x^3 + y^3}{4} \div \dfrac{x^2 - xy + y^2}{2x + 2y}$

50. $\dfrac{xu + 2u + 3x + 6}{u^2 - 9} \cdot \dfrac{13u - 39}{x^2 + 3x + 2}$

51. $\dfrac{-3t + 4}{t^2 + t - 20} + \dfrac{5t + 6}{t^2 + t - 20}$

52. $\dfrac{a + 3}{a^2 - a - 2} - \dfrac{a - 4}{a^2 - 2a - 3}$

Solve each equation.

53. $\dfrac{34}{a^2} = \dfrac{3}{2a} - \dfrac{13}{20a}$

54. $\dfrac{u - 2}{u - 3} + 3 = u + \dfrac{u - 4}{3 - u}$

55. $\dfrac{3}{x - 2} = \dfrac{x + 3}{2x}$

56. $\dfrac{4}{x^2 - 9} = \dfrac{7}{x^2 - 7x + 12} - \dfrac{5}{x^2 - x - 12}$

57. Assume that y varies directly with x. If $x = 30$ when $y = 4$, find y when $x = 9$.

58. Sound. Sound intensity (loudness) varies inversely as the square of the distance from the source. If a rock band has a sound intensity of 100 decibels 30 feet away from the amplifier, find the sound intensity 60 feet away from the amplifier.

Group Project

VENN DIAGRAMS

Overview: In this activity, we will discuss several of the fundamental concepts of what is known as *set theory.*

Instructions: *Venn diagrams* are a convenient way to visualize relationships between sets and operations on sets. They were invented by the English mathematician John Venn (1834–1923). To draw a Venn diagram, we begin with a large rectangle, called the *universal set*. Ovals or circles are then drawn in the interior of the rectangle to represent subsets of the universal set.

Form groups of 2 or 3 students. Study the following figures, which illustrate three set operations: union, intersection, and complement.

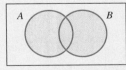

$A \cup B$
The shaded region is the *union* of set A and set B.

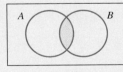

$A \cap B$
The shaded region is the *intersection* of set A and set B.

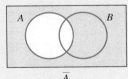

$\overline{A}$
The shaded region is the complement of set A.

For each of the following exercises, sketch the following blank Venn diagram and then shade the indicated region.

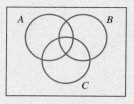

1. $A \cup B$

2. $A \cap B$

3. $A \cap C$

4. $A \cup C$

5. $A \cup B \cup C$

6. $A \cap B \cap C$

7. $(B \cup C) \cap A$

8. $C \cup (A \cap B)$

9. $\overline{A}$

10. $\overline{B} \cup \overline{C}$

11. $\overline{B} \cap \overline{C}$

12. $\overline{A \cup B}$

Radical Expressions and Equations

9

©Goodluz/Shutterstock.com

from Campus to Careers

General Contractor

The growing popularity of remodeling has created a boom for general contractors. If it's an additional bedroom you need or a makeover of a dated kitchen or bathroom, they can provide design and construction expertise, as well as knowledge of local building code requirements. From the planning stages of a project through its completion, general contractors use mathematics every step of the way.

Problem 141 in **Study Set 9.2**, **problem 113** in **Study Set 9.3**, and **problem 109** in **Study Set 9.5** involve situations that a general contractor encounters on the job. The mathematical concepts in this chapter can be used to solve those problems.

JOB TITLE:
General Contractor

EDUCATION:
Courses in mathematics, science, drafting, business math, and English are important. Certificate programs are also available.

JOB OUTLOOK:
In general, employment is expected to increase by about 19% through the year 2018.

ANNUAL EARNINGS:
Mean annual salary $86,850

FOR MORE INFORMATION:
http://www.careers.stateuniversity.com

Many Students attempt to learn algebra by rote memorization. Unfortunately, as the term progresses, they find that does not work. When they encounter problem types slightly different from those that they have memorized, they experience great difficulty. Remember, memorization only provides a superficial grasp of the concepts. When learning a new algebraic procedure, it is most important that you:

UNDERSTAND "WHY":   Be able to exaplin the purpose for each stp in the procedure and why they are applied in that order.

UNDERSTAND "WHEN":   Be able to explain what types of problems are solved using the procedure and what types are not.

Now Try This ▶

1. Choose five problems in the Guided Practice section of a Study Set to solve. Write a *Strategy* and *Why* statement for each solution in your own words.
2. Select a procedure that is introduced in this chapter and explain when it should be used. Write a *Caution* statement that warns of a possible pitfall when using it. Give an example of an application problem that can be solved using the procedure.

SECTION 9.1

Radical Expressions and Radical Functions

OBJECTIVES

1 Find square roots.
2 Find square roots of expressions containing variables.
3 Graph the square root function.
4 Evaluate radical functions.
5 Find cube roots.
6 Graph the cube root function.
7 Find nth roots.

ARE YOU READY?

The following problems review some basic skills that are needed when working with radical expressions and radical functions.

1. Evaluate: **a.** 15^2 **b.** 4^3

2. Evaluate: **a.** $\left(\dfrac{7}{5}\right)^2$ **b.** $(0.2)^2$

3. Evaluate: **a.** $(-6)^3$ **b.** 3^4

4. Simplify: **a.** $a^4 \cdot a^4$ **b.** $x^3 \cdot x^3 \cdot x^3$

5. Multiply: $(x + 8)(x + 8)$

6. Let $f(x) = |2x - 3|$. Find $f(4)$.

In this section, we will reverse the squaring process and learn how to find *square roots* of numbers. Then we will generalize the concept of root and consider cube roots, fourth roots, and so on. We will also discuss a new family of functions, called *radical functions*.

1   Find Square Roots.

When we raise a number to the second power, we are squaring it, or finding its **square.**

- The square of 5 is 25 because $5^2 = 25$.
- The square of -5 is 25, because $(-5)^2 = 25$.

We can reverse the squaring process to find **square roots** of numbers. For example, to find the square roots of 25, we ask ourselves "What number, when squared, is equal to 25?" There are two possible answers.

- 5 is a square root of 25, because $5^2 = 25$.
- -5 is also a square root of 25, because $(-5)^2 = 25$.

In general, we have the following definition.

Square Root of a

The number b is a **square root** of the number a if $b^2 = a$.

Every positive number has two square roots, one positive and one negative. For example, the two square roots of 9 are 3 and −3, and the two square roots of 144 are 12 and −12. The number 0 is the only real number with exactly one square root. In fact, it is its own square root, because $0^2 = 0$.

A **radical symbol** $\sqrt{}$ represents the **positive** or **principal square root** of a number. Since 3 is the positive square root of 9, we can write

$$\sqrt{9} = 3 \quad \text{Read as "the square root of 9."}$$

The symbol $-\sqrt{}$ represents the **negative square root** of a number. It is the opposite of the principal square root. Since −12 is the negative square root of 144, we can write

$$-\sqrt{144} = -12 \quad \text{Read as "the negative square root of 144 is −12" or} $$
"the opposite of the square root of 144 is −12."

Square Root Notation

If a is a positive real number,

1. $\sqrt{a}$ represents the **positive** or **principal square root** of a. It is the positive number we square to get a.

2. $-\sqrt{a}$ represents the **negative square root** of a. It is the opposite of the principal square root of a: $-\sqrt{a} = -1 \cdot \sqrt{a}$.

3. The principal square root of 0 is 0: $\sqrt{0} = 0$.

The number or variable expression under a radical symbol is called the **radicand.** Together, the radical symbol and radicand are called a **radical.** An algebraic expression containing a radical is called a **radical expression.**

Radical symbol

$\sqrt{81} \leftarrow$ Radicand

Radical

Read $\sqrt{81}$ as "the square root of 81" or as "radical 81."

Some more examples of radical expressions are:

$$\sqrt{100}, \quad \sqrt{2} + 3, \quad \sqrt{x^2}, \quad \text{and} \quad \sqrt{\dfrac{a-1}{49b^2}}$$

To evaluate (find the value of) square root radical expressions, you need to quickly recognize each of the natural-number **perfect squares** shown below in red.

$1 = 1^2$	$25 = 5^2$	$81 = 9^2$	$169 = 13^2$	$289 = 17^2$
$4 = 2^2$	$36 = 6^2$	$100 = 10^2$	$196 = 14^2$	$324 = 18^2$
$9 = 3^2$	$49 = 7^2$	$121 = 11^2$	$225 = 15^2$	$361 = 19^2$
$16 = 4^2$	$64 = 8^2$	$144 = 12^2$	$256 = 16^2$	$400 = 20^2$

EXAMPLE 1 Evaluate: **a.** $\sqrt{81}$ **b.** $-\sqrt{225}$ **c.** $\sqrt{\dfrac{49}{4}}$ **d.** $\sqrt{0.36}$

Strategy In each case, we will determine what positive number, when squared, produces the radicand.

Why The symbol $\sqrt{}$ indicates that the positive square root of the number written under it should be found.

Solution **a.** $\sqrt{81} = 9$ Because $9^2 = 81$ **b.** $-\sqrt{225} = -15$ Because $-\sqrt{225} = -1 \cdot \sqrt{225}$

c. $\sqrt{\dfrac{49}{4}} = \dfrac{7}{2}$ *Because* $\left(\dfrac{7}{2}\right)^2 = \dfrac{49}{4}$ **d.** $\sqrt{0.36} = 0.6$ *Because* $(0.6)^2 = 0.36$

Self Check 1   Evaluate: **a.** $\sqrt{64}$ **b.** $-\sqrt{1}$ **c.** $\sqrt{\dfrac{1}{16}}$

d. $\sqrt{0.09}$

Now Try ▶   Problems 23, 27, and 29

A number, such as 81, 225, $\dfrac{49}{4}$, and 0.36, that is the square of some rational number, is called a **perfect square.** In Example 1, we saw that the square root of a perfect square is a rational number.

If a positive number is not a perfect square, its square root is irrational. For example, $\sqrt{83}$ is an irrational number because 83 is not a perfect square. Since $\sqrt{83}$ is irrational, its decimal representation is nonterminating and nonrepeating. We can find a rational-number approximation of $\sqrt{83}$ using the square root key $\boxed{\sqrt{}}$ on a calculator or from the table of square roots found in Appendix I at the back of the book.

$$\sqrt{83} \approx 9.110433579 \quad \text{or} \quad \sqrt{83} \approx 9.11 \quad \text{\textit{Round to the nearest hundredth.}}$$

CAUTION   Square roots of negative numbers are not real numbers. For example, $\sqrt{-9}$ is not a real number, because no real number squared equals -9. Square roots of negative numbers come from a set called the **imaginary numbers,** which we will discuss later in this chapter. If we attempt to evaluate $\sqrt{-9}$ using a calculator, we will get an error message.

Scientific calculator   Graphing calculator

We summarize three important facts about square roots as follows.

Square Roots

1. If a is a perfect square, then $\sqrt{a}$ is rational.

2. If a is a positive number that is not a perfect square, then $\sqrt{a}$ is irrational.

3. If a is a negative number, then $\sqrt{a}$ is not a real number.

---

2 Find Square Roots of Expressions Containing Variables.

If $x \neq 0$, the positive number x^2 has x and $-x$ for its two square roots. To denote the positive square root of $\sqrt{x^2}$, we must know whether x is positive or negative.

If x is positive, we can write

$$\sqrt{x^2} = x \qquad \sqrt{x^2} \text{ represents the positive square root of } x^2, \text{ which is } x.$$

If x is negative, then $-x$ is positive and we can write

$$\sqrt{x^2} = -x \qquad \sqrt{x^2} \text{ represents the positive square root of } x^2, \text{ which is } -x.$$

If we don't know whether x is positive or negative, we can use absolute value symbols to ensure that $\sqrt{x^2}$ is not negative.

Simplifying $\sqrt{x^2}$

For any real number x,

$$\sqrt{x^2} = |x|$$ The principal square root of x squared is equal to the absolute value of x.

We use this definition to *simplify* square root radical expressions.

EXAMPLE 2

Simplify. Assume all variables are unrestricted. **a.** $\sqrt{16x^2}$ **b.** $\sqrt{t^2 + 2t + 1}$ **c.** $\sqrt{m^6}$ **d.** $\sqrt{49r^8}$

Strategy In each case, we will determine what positive expression, when squared, produces the radicand.

Why The symbol $\sqrt{}$ indicates that the positive square root of the expression written under it should be found.

Solution If x, t, m, and r can be any real number, we have

The Language of Algebra

The phrase **"assume all variables are unrestricted"** in the instructions for Example 2 reminds us that negative numbers are permissible replacement values for the variables. Therefore, absolute value symbols may be necessary to ensure the answer is not negative.

a. $\sqrt{16x^2} = |4x|$ Because $(4x)^2 = 16x^2$. Since 4x could be negative (for example, when x = −5, the expression 4x is −20), absolute value symbols are needed to ensure that the result is not negative.

$\phantom{\sqrt{16x^2}} = 4|x|$ Since 4 is a positive constant in the product 4x, we can write it outside the absolute value symbols.

b. $\sqrt{t^2 + 2t + 1} = \sqrt{(t + 1)^2}$ Factor the radicand: $t^2 + 2t + 1 = (t + 1)^2$.

$\phantom{\sqrt{t^2 + 2t + 1}} = |t + 1|$ Since t + 1 can be negative (for example, when t = −5, the expression t + 1 is −4), absolute value symbols are needed to ensure that the result is not negative.

c. $\sqrt{m^6} = |m^3|$ Because $(m^3)^2 = m^6$. Since m^3 can be negative (for example, when m = −3, the expression m^3 is −27), absolute value symbols are needed to ensure that the result is not negative.

d. $\sqrt{49r^8} = 7r^4$ Because $(7r^4)^2 = 49r^8$. Since r^4 is never negative for any value of r, no absolute value symbols are needed.

Self Check 2 Simplify. Assume all variables are unrestricted. **a.** $\sqrt{25a^2}$ **b.** $\sqrt{b^{14}}$ **c.** $\sqrt{x^2 - 18x + 81}$ **d.** $\sqrt{100n^8}$

Now Try Problems 39, 41, 45, and 47

If we know that x, t, and m are positive in Example 2, we don't need to use absolute value symbols in the answers. For example,

$\sqrt{16x^2} = 4x$ If x is positive, 4x is positive.

$\sqrt{m^6} = m^3$ If m is positive, m^3 is positive.

$\sqrt{t^2 + 2t + 1} = t + 1$ If t is positive, t + 1 is positive.

The Language of Algebra

If we are told **"All variables represent positive real numbers,"** then absolute value symbols are not needed when simplifying square root radical expressions.

3 Graph the Square Root Function.

Since there is one principal square root for every nonnegative real number x, the equation $f(x) = \sqrt{x}$ determines a function, called a **square root function**. Square root functions belong to a larger family of functions known as **radical functions**.

EXAMPLE 3 Graph $f(x) = \sqrt{x}$ and find the domain and range of the function.

Strategy We will graph the function by creating a table of function values and plotting the corresponding ordered pairs.

Why After drawing a smooth curve through the plotted points, we will have the graph.

Solution To graph the function, we select several values for x that are perfect squares, such as 0, 1, 4, and 9, and find the corresponding values of $f(x)$. We begin with $x = 0$, since 0 is the smallest input for which $\sqrt{x}$ is defined.

$f(x) = \sqrt{x}$	$f(x) = \sqrt{x}$	$f(x) = \sqrt{x}$	$f(x) = \sqrt{x}$
$f(0) = \sqrt{0}$	$f(1) = \sqrt{1}$	$f(4) = \sqrt{4}$	$f(9) = \sqrt{9}$
$= 0$	$= 1$	$= 2$	$= 3$

We also can select values of x that are not perfect squares when creating a table of function values. For example, if $x = 6$, then $f(6) = \sqrt{6}$, and it follows that the point $\left(2, \sqrt{6}\right)$ is on the graph. To help locate this point on the coordinate system, it is helpful to approximate: $\sqrt{6} \approx 2.45$.

We enter each value of x and its corresponding value of $f(x)$ in the table below. After plotting the ordered pairs, we draw a smooth curve through the points to get the graph shown in figure (a). Since the equation defines a function, its graph passes the vertical line test.

To find the domain of the function graphically, we project the graph onto the x-axis, as shown in figure (b). Because the graph begins at $(0, 0)$ and extends indefinitely to the right, the projection includes 0 and all positive real numbers. Thus, the domain of $f(x) = \sqrt{x}$ is the set of nonnegative real numbers, which can be written in interval notation as $[0, \infty)$.

To find the range of the function graphically, we project the graph onto the y-axis, as shown in figure (b). Because the graph of the function begins at $(0, 0)$ and extends indefinitely upward, the projection includes all nonnegative real numbers. Therefore, the range of the function is $[0, \infty)$.

The Language of Algebra

Together, 0 and the positive real numbers are called the **nonnegative real numbers.**

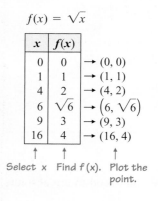

$f(x) = \sqrt{x}$

x	$f(x)$	
0	0	→ (0, 0)
1	1	→ (1, 1)
4	2	→ (4, 2)
6	$\sqrt{6}$	→ $\left(6, \sqrt{6}\right)$
9	3	→ (9, 3)
16	4	→ (16, 4)

↑   ↑   ↑
Select x Find $f(x)$.   Plot the point.

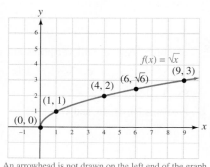

An arrowhead is not drawn on the left end of the graph because it does not extend indefinitely in that direction.

(a)

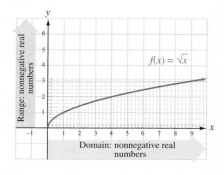

(b)

Self Check 3 Graph: $g(x) = \sqrt{x} + 2$. Then give its domain and range and compare it with the graph of $f(x) = \sqrt{x}$.

Now Try ▶ Problem 51

EXAMPLE 4 Let $g(x) = \sqrt{x + 3}$. **a.** Find its domain algebraically. **b.** Graph the function.
c. Find its range.

Strategy We will determine the domain algebraically by finding all the values of x for which $x + 3 \geq 0$.

Why Since the expression $\sqrt{x + 3}$ is not a real number when $x + 3$ is negative, we must require that $x + 3 \geq 0$.

Solution **a.** To determine the domain of the function, we solve the following inequality:

$$x + 3 \geq 0 \qquad \text{Because we cannot find the square root of a negative number}$$

$$x \geq -3 \qquad \text{To solve for x, subtract 3 from both sides.}$$

The x-inputs must be real numbers greater than or equal to -3. Thus, the domain of $g(x) = \sqrt{x + 3}$ is the interval $[-3, \infty)$.

b. To graph the function, we construct a table of function values. We begin by selecting $x = -3$, since -3 is the smallest input for which $\sqrt{x + 3}$ is defined. Then we let $x = -2, 1,$ and 6 and list each corresponding function value $g(x)$ in the table.

$$g(x) = \sqrt{x + 3} \qquad g(x) = \sqrt{x + 3} \qquad g(x) = \sqrt{x + 3} \qquad g(x) = \sqrt{x + 3}$$

$$g(-3) = \sqrt{-3 + 3} \qquad g(-2) = \sqrt{-2 + 3} \qquad g(1) = \sqrt{1 + 3} \qquad g(6) = \sqrt{6 + 3}$$

$$= \sqrt{0} \qquad\qquad = \sqrt{1} \qquad\qquad = \sqrt{4} \qquad\qquad = \sqrt{9}$$

$$= 0 \qquad\qquad = 1 \qquad\qquad = 2 \qquad\qquad = 3$$

After plotting the ordered pairs, we draw a smooth curve through the points to get the graph shown in figure (a). In figure (b), we see that the graph of $g(x) = \sqrt{x + 3}$ is the graph of $f(x) = \sqrt{x}$, translated 3 units to the left.

$g(x) = \sqrt{x + 3}$

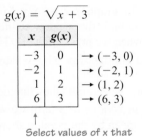

x	$g(x)$	
-3	0	$\rightarrow (-3, 0)$
-2	1	$\rightarrow (-2, 1)$
1	2	$\rightarrow (1, 2)$
6	3	$\rightarrow (6, 3)$

↑
Select values of x that
make x + 3 a perfect square.

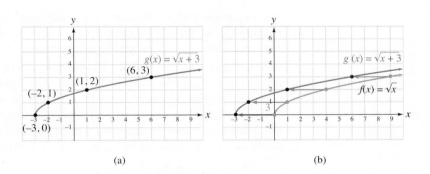

(a)   (b)

c. From the graph in figure (a), we see that the range of $g(x) = \sqrt{x + 3}$ is $[0, \infty)$.

Self Check 4 Let $h(x) = \sqrt{x - 2}$. **a.** Find its domain algebraically.
b. Graph the function. **c.** Find its range.

Now Try ▶ Problems 53 and 55

4 Evaluate Radical Functions.

Radical functions can be used to model certain real-life situations that exhibit growth that eventually levels off. A calculator is often helpful when evaluating a radical function for a given value of the input variable.

EXAMPLE 5 **Pendulums.** The **period of a pendulum** is the time required for the pendulum to swing back and forth to complete one cycle. The period (in seconds) is a function of the pendulum's length L (in feet) and is given by $f(L) = 2\pi\sqrt{\dfrac{L}{32}}$. Find the period of the 5-foot-long pendulum of a clock. Round the result to the nearest tenth.

Strategy To find the period of the pendulum we will find $f(5)$.

Why The notation $f(5)$ represents the period (in seconds) of a pendulum whose length L is 5 feet.

Solution

$$f(L) = 2\pi\sqrt{\dfrac{L}{32}}$$

$$f(5) = 2\pi\sqrt{\dfrac{5}{32}} \qquad \text{Substitute 5 for } L.$$

$$\approx 2.483647066 \qquad \text{Evaluate the radical expression. Use a calculator to find an approximation. } 2\pi\sqrt{\tfrac{5}{32}} \text{ means } 2 \cdot \pi \cdot \sqrt{\tfrac{5}{32}}.$$

The period is approximately 2.5 seconds.

Self Check 5 **Pendulums.** Find the period of a pendulum that is 3 feet long. Round the result to the nearest hundredth.

Now Try ▶ Problem 123

Using Your Calculator ▶ **Graphing and Evaluating a Square Root Function**

We can graph radical functions on a graphing calculator. To graph $f(x) = \sqrt{x}$ from Example 3, we press Y = and enter the right side of the equation. If the window settings for x and y are $[-1, 9]$, we get the graph shown in figure (a) when we press GRAPH. The function $g(x) = \sqrt{x + 3}$ from Example 4 is graphed in a similar way with window settings of $[-4, 10]$ for x and $[-1, 9]$ for y. See figure (b).

To answer Example 5 with a graphing calculator, we graph the function $f(x) = 2\pi\sqrt{\dfrac{x}{32}}$. We then trace and move the cursor toward an x-value of 5 until we see the coordinates shown in figure (c). The pendulum's period is given by the y-value shown on the screen. By zooming in, we can get better results.

After entering $Y_1 = 2\pi\sqrt{\dfrac{x}{32}}$, we can also use the TABLE mode to find $f(5)$. See figure (d).

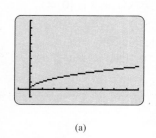

(a)

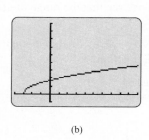

(b)

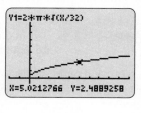

(c)

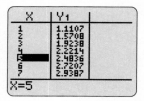

(d)

---

5 Find Cube Roots.

When we raise a number to the third power, we are cubing it, or finding its **cube.** We can reverse the cubing process to find **cube roots** of numbers. To find the cube root of 8, we ask "What number, when cubed, is equal to 8?" It follows that 2 is a cube root of 8, because $2^3 = 8$.

In general, we have this definition.

Cube Root of a   The number b is a **cube root** of the real number a if $b^3 = a$.

All real numbers have one real cube root. A positive number has a positive cube root, a negative number has a negative cube root, and the cube root of 0 is 0.

Cube Root Notation   The **cube root of a** is written as $\sqrt[3]{a}$. By definition,

$$\sqrt[3]{a} = b \qquad \text{if} \qquad b^3 = a$$

Earlier, we determined that the cube root of 8 is 2. In symbols, we can write: $\sqrt[3]{8} = 2$. The number 3 is called the **index,** 8 is called the **radicand,** and the entire expression is called a **radical.**

Index
$\downarrow$
$\sqrt[3]{8} \leftarrow$ Radicand   Read as "the cube root of 8."
Radical

A number, such as 125, $\frac{1}{64}$, -27, and -8, that is the cube of some rational number is called a **perfect cube.**

To simplify cube root radical expressions, you need to quickly recognize each of the following natural-number perfect cubes shown in blue.

$1 = 1^3$	$27 = 3^3$	$125 = 5^3$	$343 = 7^3$	$729 = 9^3$
$8 = 2^3$	$64 = 4^3$	$216 = 6^3$	$512 = 8^3$	$1{,}000 = 10^3$

The following property is also used to simplify cube root radical expressions.

Simplifying $\sqrt[3]{x^3}$ For any real number x,

$$\sqrt[3]{x^3} = x$$

EXAMPLE 6   Simplify: **a.** $\sqrt[3]{125}$ **b.** $\sqrt[3]{-\dfrac{1}{64}}$ **c.** $\sqrt[3]{27x^3}$ **d.** $\sqrt[3]{-8a^9b^6}$

Strategy   In each case, we will determine what number or expression, when cubed, produces the radicand.

Why   The symbol $\sqrt[3]{}$ indicates that the cube root of the number written under it should be found.

Solution   **a.** $\sqrt[3]{125} = 5$ Because $5^3 = 5 \cdot 5 \cdot 5 = 125$

b. $\sqrt[3]{-\dfrac{1}{64}} = -\dfrac{1}{4}$ Because $\left(-\frac{1}{4}\right)^3 = \left(-\frac{1}{4}\right)\left(-\frac{1}{4}\right)\left(-\frac{1}{4}\right) = -\frac{1}{64}$

c. $\sqrt[3]{27x^3} = 3x$ Because $(3x)^3 = (3x)(3x)(3x) = 27x^3$. No absolute value symbols are needed.

d. $\sqrt[3]{-8a^9b^6} = -2a^3b^2$ Because $(-2a^3b^2)^3 = (-2a^3b^2)(-2a^3b^2)(-2a^3b^2) = -8a^9b^6$.

6 Graph the Cube Root Function.

Since there is one cube root for every real number x, the equation $f(x) = \sqrt[3]{x}$ defines a function, called the **cube root function.** Like square root functions, cube root functions belong to the family of radical functions.

EXAMPLE 7   Consider $f(x) = \sqrt[3]{x}$.   **a.** Graph the function.   **b.** Find its domain and range.
c. Graph: $g(x) = \sqrt[3]{x} - 2$

Strategy   We will graph the function by creating a table of function values and plotting the corresponding ordered pairs.

Why   After drawing a smooth curve through the plotted points, we will have the graph. The answers to parts (b) and (c) can then be determined from the graph.

Solution   **a.** To graph the function, we select several values for x, that are perfect cubes, such as $-8, -1, 0, 1,$ and 8, and find the corresponding values of $f(x)$. The results are entered in the table below.

$$
\begin{array}{c|c|c|c|c}
\begin{array}{l} f(x) = \sqrt[3]{x} \\ f(-8) = \sqrt[3]{-8} \\ = -2 \end{array} &
\begin{array}{l} f(x) = \sqrt[3]{x} \\ f(-1) = \sqrt[3]{-1} \\ = -1 \end{array} &
\begin{array}{l} f(x) = \sqrt[3]{x} \\ f(0) = \sqrt[3]{0} \\ = 0 \end{array} &
\begin{array}{l} f(x) = \sqrt[3]{x} \\ f(1) = \sqrt[3]{1} \\ = 1 \end{array} &
\begin{array}{l} f(x) = \sqrt[3]{x} \\ f(8) = \sqrt[3]{8} \\ = 2 \end{array}
\end{array}
$$

After plotting the ordered pairs, we draw a smooth curve through the points to get the graph shown in figure (a).

$f(x) = \sqrt[3]{x}$

x	$f(x)$	
-8	-2	→ $(-8, -2)$
-1	-1	→ $(-1, -1)$
0	0	→ $(0, 0)$
1	1	→ $(1, 1)$
8	2	→ $(8, 2)$

↑
Select values of x that
are perfect cubes.

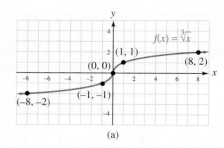

(a)

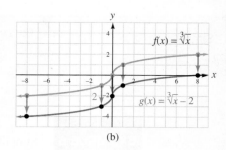

(b)

b. If we project the graph in figure (a) onto the x- and y-axes, we see that the domain and the range of the function are the set of real numbers. Thus, the domain is $(-\infty, \infty)$ and the range is $(-\infty, \infty)$.

c. Refer to figure (b). The graph of $g(x) = \sqrt[3]{x} - 2$ is the graph of $f(x) = \sqrt[3]{x}$, translated 2 units downward.

7 Find *n*th Roots.

Just as there are square roots and cube roots, there are fourth roots, fifth roots, sixth roots, and so on. In general, we have the following definition.

---

nth Roots of *a*

The **nth root of *a*** is written as $\sqrt[n]{a}$, and

$$\sqrt[n]{a} = b \quad \text{if} \quad b^n = a$$

The number n is called the **index** (or **order**) of the radical. If n is an even natural number, a must be positive or zero, and b must be positive.

When n is an odd natural number, the expression $\sqrt[n]{x}$, where $n > 1$, represents an **odd root**. Since every real number has just one real nth root when n is odd, we don't need absolute value symbols when finding odd roots. For example,

$$\sqrt[5]{243} = 3 \qquad \text{Because } 3^5 = 243$$

$$\sqrt[5]{-32x^5} = -2x \qquad \text{Because } (-2x)^5 = -32x^5$$

When n is an even natural number, the expression $\sqrt[n]{x}$, where $x > 0$, represents an **even root**. In this case, there will be one positive and one negative real nth root. For example, the real sixth roots of 729 are 3 and -3, because $3^6 = 729$ and $(-3)^6 = 729$. When finding even roots, we can use absolute value symbols to guarantee that the nth root is positive.

$$\sqrt[4]{(-3)^4} = |-3| = 3 \qquad \text{We also could simplify this as follows: } \sqrt[4]{(-3)^4} = \sqrt[4]{81} = 3.$$

$$\sqrt[6]{729x^6} = |3x| = 3|x| \qquad \text{Because } (3x)^6 = 729x^6. \text{ The absolute value symbols ensure that the result is positive.}$$

In general, we have the following rules.

Simplifying $\sqrt[n]{x^n}$

If x is a real number and $n > 1$, then

If n is an odd natural number, $\sqrt[n]{x^n} = x$.

If n is an even natural number, $\sqrt[n]{x^n} = |x|$.

EXAMPLE 8 Evaluate: **a.** $\sqrt[4]{625}$ **b.** $\sqrt[4]{-1}$ **c.** $\sqrt[5]{-32}$ **d.** $\sqrt[6]{\dfrac{1}{64}}$

Strategy In each case, we will determine what number, when raised to the fourth, fifth, or sixth power, produces the radicand.

Why The symbols $\sqrt[4]{}$, $\sqrt[5]{}$, and $\sqrt[6]{}$ indicate that the fourth, fifth, or sixth root of the number written under it should be found.

Solution

a. $\sqrt[4]{625} = 5$, because $5^4 = 625$.   Read $\sqrt[4]{625}$ as "the fourth root of 625."

b. $\sqrt[4]{-1}$ is not a real number.   An even root of a negative number is not a real number.

c. $\sqrt[5]{-32} = -2$, because $(-2)^5 = -32$.   Read $\sqrt[5]{-32}$ as "the fifth root of -32."

d. $\sqrt[6]{\dfrac{1}{64}} = \dfrac{1}{2}$, because $\left(\dfrac{1}{2}\right)^6 = \dfrac{1}{64}$.   Read $\sqrt[6]{\dfrac{1}{64}}$ as "the sixth root of $\dfrac{1}{64}$."

Self Check 8   Evaluate: **a.** $\sqrt[4]{\dfrac{1}{81}}$ **b.** $\sqrt[5]{10^5}$ **c.** $\sqrt[6]{-64}$

Now Try ▶ Problems 87, 91, and 93

Using Your **Calculator** ▶ Finding Roots

The square root key $\boxed{\sqrt{}}$ on a reverse entry scientific calculator can be used to evaluate square roots. To evaluate roots with an index greater than 2, we can use the root key $\boxed{\sqrt[x]{y}}$. For example, the function $r(V) = \sqrt[3]{\dfrac{3V}{4\pi}}$ gives the radius of a sphere with volume V. To find the radius of the spherical propane tank shown on the left, we substitute 113 for V to get:

$$r(113) = \sqrt[3]{\dfrac{3(113)}{4\pi}}$$

To evaluate a root, we enter the radicand and press the root key $\boxed{\sqrt[x]{y}}$ followed by the index of the radical, which in this case is 3.

$\boxed{3}\ \boxed{\times}\ \boxed{113}\ \boxed{\div}\ \boxed{(}\ \boxed{4}\ \boxed{\times}\ \boxed{\pi}\ \boxed{)}\ \boxed{=}\ \boxed{2\text{nd}}\ \boxed{\sqrt[x]{y}}\ \boxed{3}\ \boxed{=}$ 2.999139118

To evaluate the cube root of $\dfrac{3(113)}{4\pi}$ using a direct entry calculator, we enter:

$\boxed{3}\ \boxed{2\text{nd}}\ \boxed{\sqrt[x]{y}}\ \boxed{(}\ \boxed{3}\ \boxed{\times}\ \boxed{113}\ \boxed{\div}\ \boxed{(}\ \boxed{4}\ \boxed{\times}\ \boxed{\pi}\ \boxed{)}\ \boxed{)}\ \boxed{\text{ENTER}}$

To evaluate the cube root of $\dfrac{3(113)}{4\pi}$ with a graphing calculator, we enter:

$\boxed{\text{MATH}}\ \boxed{4}\ \boxed{(}\ \boxed{3}\ \boxed{\times}\ \boxed{113}\ \boxed{)}\ \boxed{\div}\ \boxed{(}\ \boxed{4}\ \boxed{\times}\ \boxed{2\text{nd}}\ \boxed{\pi}\ \boxed{)}\ \boxed{)}\ \boxed{\text{ENTER}}$

```
³√((3*113)/(4*π)
)
        2.999139118
```

If we round the result to the nearest foot, we see that the radius of the propane tank is about 3 feet.

EXAMPLE 9   Simplify each radical expression. Assume that x can be any real number.
  a. $\sqrt[5]{x^5}$ **b.** $\sqrt[4]{16x^4}$ **c.** $\sqrt[6]{(x+4)^6}$ **d.** $\sqrt[4]{81x^8}$

Strategy   When the index n is odd, we will determine what expression, when raised to the nth power, produces the radicand. When the index n is even, we will determine what positive expression, when raised to the nth power, produces the radicand.

Why   This is the definition of nth root.

Solution   **a.** $\sqrt[5]{x^5} = x$ Since n is odd, absolute value symbols aren't needed.

The Language of Algebra

Another way to say that x can be any real number is to say that **the variable is unrestricted.**

b. $\sqrt[4]{16x^4} = |2x| = 2|x|$ Since n is even and x can be negative, absolute value symbols are needed to ensure that the result is positive.

c. $\sqrt[6]{(x+4)^6} = |x+4|$ Absolute value symbols are needed to ensure that the result is positive.

d. $\sqrt[4]{81x^8} = 3x^2$ Because $(3x^2)^4 = 81x^8$. Since $3x^2 \geq 0$ for any value of x, no absolute value symbols are needed.

Self Check 9   Simplify. Assume all variables are unrestricted.
  a. $\sqrt[6]{x^6}$ **b.** $\sqrt[5]{(a+5)^5}$ **c.** $\sqrt[4]{16a^8}$

Now Try ▶ Problems 95, 97, 99, and 101

If we know that x is positive in parts (b) and (c) of Example 9, we don't need to use absolute value symbols. For example, if $x > 0$, then

$$\sqrt[4]{16x^4} = 2x \qquad \text{If x is positive, 2x is positive.}$$

$$\sqrt[6]{(x + 4)^6} = x + 4 \qquad \text{If x is positive, x + 4 is positive.}$$

We now summarize the definitions concerning nth roots.

Summary of the Definitions of $\sqrt[n]{x}$	If n is a natural number greater than 1 and x is a real number,
	If $x > 0$, then $\sqrt[n]{x}$ is the positive number such that $\left(\sqrt[n]{x}\right)^n = x$.
	If $x = 0$, then $\sqrt[n]{x} = 0$.
	If $x < 0$ $\begin{cases} \text{and } n \text{ is odd, then } \sqrt[n]{x} \text{ is the negative number such that } \left(\sqrt[n]{x}\right)^n = x. \\ \text{and } n \text{ is even, then } \sqrt[n]{x} \text{ is not a real number.} \end{cases}$

SECTION 9.1 ▶ STUDY SET

VOCABULARY

Fill in the blanks.

1. $5x^2$ is the _____ root of $25x^4$ because $(5x^2)^2 = 25x^4$. The _____ root of 216 is 6 because $6^3 = 216$.

2. The symbol $\sqrt{}$ is called a _____ symbol or a _____ root symbol.

3. A radical symbol $\sqrt{}$ represents the _____ or principal square root of a number.

4. The number 4 has two square roots, -2 and 2. When we speak of *the* square root of 4, we mean only the _____ square root of 4, which is 2.

5. The number 100 has two square roots. The positive or _____ square root of 100 is 10.

6. In the expression $\sqrt[3]{27x^6}$, the _____ is 3 and $27x^6$ is the _____.

7. When we write $\sqrt{b^4} = b^2$, we say that we have _____ the radical expression.

8. When n is an odd number, $\sqrt[n]{x}$ represents an _____ root. When n is an _____ number, $\sqrt[n]{x}$ represents an even root.

9. $f(x) = \sqrt{x}$ and $g(x) = \sqrt[3]{x}$ are _____ functions.

10. Together, 0 and the positive real numbers are called the _____ real numbers.

CONCEPTS

Fill in the blanks.

11. b is a square root of a if $b^2 =$ ▢.

12. $\sqrt{0} =$ ▢ and $\sqrt[3]{0} =$ ▢.

13. $\sqrt{-4}$ is not a real number, because no real number _____ equals -4.

14. $\sqrt[3]{x} = y$ if $y^3 =$ ▢.

15. $\sqrt{x^2} =$ ▢ and $\sqrt[3]{x^3} =$ ▢

16. **a.** The graph of $g(x) = \sqrt{x} + 3$ is the graph of $f(x) = \sqrt{x}$ translated ▢ units ____.

   b. The graph of $g(x) = \sqrt{x + 5}$ is the graph of $f(x) = \sqrt{x}$ translated ▢ units to the ____.

17. The graph of a square root function f is shown below. Find each of the following, if possible.

   a. $f(11)$ **b.** $f(2)$

   c. $f(-1)$

   d. The value of x for which $f(x) = 2$

   e. The value of x for which $f(x) = -1$

   f. The domain and range of f (Use interval notation.)

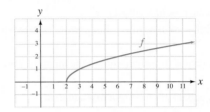

18. Refer to the graph in problem 17. Estimate each of the following function values.

   a. $f(4)$ **b.** $f(10)$

19. The graph of a cube root function f is shown below. Find each of the following.

a. $f(-8)$　　　　　　　　**b.** $f(0)$

c. The value of x for which $f(x) = -2$

d. The domain and range of f
(Use interval notation.)

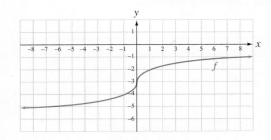

20. Match each function with the correct graph shown below.

a. $f(x) = x - 1$　　　　　**b.** $f(x) = \sqrt{x} - 1$

c. $f(x) = x^2 - 1$　　　　　**d.** $f(x) = \sqrt[3]{x} - 1$

e. $f(x) = |x| - 1$　　　　　**f.** $f(x) = \dfrac{1}{x - 1}$

i. 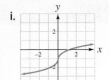　　**ii.** 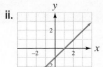　　**iii.**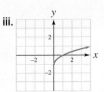

iv. 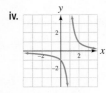　　**v.** 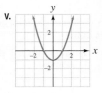　　**vi.**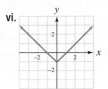

NOTATION

Translate each sentence into mathematical symbols.

21. a. The square root of x squared is the absolute value of x.

b. The cube root of x cubed is x.

c. The fifth root of negative thirty-two is negative two.

22. a. f of x equals the square root of the quantity x minus five.

b. g of x equals the cube root of x squared.

GUIDED PRACTICE

Evaluate each square root without using a calculator. See Objective 1 and Example 1.

23. $\sqrt{100}$　　**24.** $\sqrt{49}$　　**25.** $-\sqrt{64}$　　**26.** $-\sqrt{1}$

27. $\sqrt{\dfrac{1}{9}}$　　**28.** $\sqrt{\dfrac{4}{25}}$　　**29.** $\sqrt{0.25}$　　**30.** $\sqrt{0.16}$

31. $\sqrt{-81}$　　**32.** $-\sqrt{-49}$　　**33.** $\sqrt{121}$　　**34.** $\sqrt{144}$

Use a calculator to find each square root. Give each answer to four decimal places. See Objective 1.

35. $\sqrt{12}$　　　　　　　**36.** $\sqrt{340}$

37. $\sqrt{679.25}$　　　　　**38.** $\sqrt{0.0063}$

Simplify each expression. Assume that all variables are unrestricted and use absolute value symbols when necessary. See Example 2.

39. $\sqrt{4x^2}$　　　　　　　**40.** $\sqrt{64t^2}$

41. $\sqrt{81h^4}$　　　　　　**42.** $\sqrt{36y^4}$

43. $\sqrt{36s^6}$　　　　　　**44.** $\sqrt{9y^6}$

45. $\sqrt{144m^8}$　　　　　**46.** $\sqrt{4n^8}$

47. $\sqrt{y^2 - 2y + 1}$　　　**48.** $\sqrt{b^2 - 14b + 49}$

49. $\sqrt{a^4 + 6a^2 + 9}$　　**50.** $\sqrt{x^4 + 10x^2 + 25}$

Complete each table and then graph the function. Give the domain and range. See Examples 3 and 4.

51. $f(x) = -\sqrt{x}$

x	y
0	
1	
4	
9	
16	

52. $f(x) = \sqrt{x} + 2$

x	y
0	
1	
4	
9	
16	

Graph each function. Give the domain and range. See Examples 3 and 4.

53. $f(x) = \sqrt{x + 4}$　　　**54.** $f(x) = \sqrt{x} - 1$

Find the domain of each function. See Example 4.

55. $f(x) = \sqrt{x + 6}$　　　**56.** $g(x) = \sqrt{x + 12}$

57. $g(x) = \sqrt{8 - 2x}$　　**58.** $h(x) = \sqrt{35 - 5x}$

59. $s(t) = \sqrt{9t - 4}$　　　**60.** $T(a) = \sqrt{3a + 17}$

61. $c(x) = \sqrt{0.5x - 20}$　　**62.** $H(b) = \sqrt{0.4b - 36}$

Find each function value, if possible. Do not use a calculator. See Example 5.

63. $f(x) = \sqrt{3x + 1}$
　　a. $f(8)$　　　　　　**b.** $f(-2)$

64. $h(t) = \sqrt{t^2 + t - 3}$
　　a. $h(-4)$　　　　　**b.** $h(-1)$

65. $g(x) = \sqrt[3]{x - 4}$
　　a. $g(12)$　　　　　**b.** $g(-23)$

66. $s(a) = -\sqrt[3]{32s}$
　　a. $s(-2)$　　　　　**b.** $s(2)$

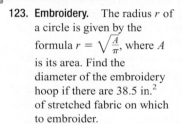

Use a calculator to find each function value. Round to the nearest ten-thousandth. See Example 5 and Using Your Calculator.

67. $f(x) = \sqrt{x^2 + 1}$

    a. $f(4)$ **b.** $f(2.35)$

68. $g(x) = \sqrt{7 - 4x}$

    a. $g(-\pi)$ **b.** $g(0.5)$

69. $g(x) = \sqrt[3]{x^2 + 1}$

    a. $g(6)$ **b.** $g(21.57)$

70. $h(t) = \sqrt[3]{2.1t + 11}$

    a. $h(-0.4)$ **b.** $h(15)$

Simplify each cube root. See Example 6.

71. $\sqrt[3]{1}$ **72.** $\sqrt[3]{8}$

73. $\sqrt[3]{-125}$ **74.** $\sqrt[3]{-27}$

75. $\sqrt[3]{\dfrac{8}{27}}$ **76.** $\sqrt[3]{\dfrac{125}{64}}$

77. $\sqrt[3]{64}$ **78.** $\sqrt[3]{1,000}$

79. $\sqrt[3]{-216a^3}$ **80.** $\sqrt[3]{-512x^3}$

81. $\sqrt[3]{-1,000p^6q^3}$ **82.** $\sqrt[3]{-343a^6b^3}$

Complete each table and then graph the function. Give the domain and range. See Example 7.

83. $f(x) = \sqrt[3]{x} - 3$

x	y
-8	
-1	
0	
1	
8	

84. $f(x) = -\sqrt[3]{x}$

x	y
-8	
-1	
0	
1	
8	

Graph each function. Give the domain and range. See Example 7.

85. $f(x) = \sqrt[3]{x} - 3$ **86.** $f(x) = \sqrt[3]{x} + 3$

Evaluate each radical expression, if possible, without using a calculator. See Example 8.

87. $\sqrt[4]{81}$ **88.** $\sqrt[6]{64}$

89. $-\sqrt[5]{243}$ **90.** $-\sqrt[4]{625}$

91. $\sqrt[6]{-256}$ **92.** $\sqrt[6]{-729}$

93. $\sqrt[5]{-\dfrac{1}{32}}$ **94.** $\sqrt[5]{-\dfrac{243}{32}}$

Simplify each radical expression. Assume all variables are unrestricted. See Example 9.

95. $\sqrt[5]{32a^5}$ **96.** $\sqrt[5]{-32x^5}$

97. $\sqrt[4]{81a^4}$ **98.** $\sqrt[8]{t^8}$

99. $\sqrt[6]{k^{12}}$ **100.** $\sqrt[6]{64b^6}$

101. $\sqrt[4]{(m + 4)^8}$ **102.** $\sqrt[4]{(x - 7)^8}$

TRY IT YOURSELF

Simplify each radical expression, if possible. Assume all variables are unrestricted.

103. $\sqrt[3]{64s^9t^6}$ **104.** $\sqrt[3]{1,000a^6b^6}$

105. $-\sqrt{49b^8}$ **106.** $-\sqrt{144t^4}$

107. $-\sqrt[5]{\dfrac{1}{32}}$ **108.** $-\sqrt[5]{-243}$

109. $\sqrt[3]{-125m^6}$ **110.** $\sqrt[3]{-216z^9}$

111. $\sqrt{400m^{16}n^2}$ **112.** $\sqrt{169p^4q^2}$

113. $\sqrt[6]{64a^6b^6}$ **114** $\sqrt[6]{(x + 4)^6}$

115. $\sqrt[4]{-81}$ **116.** $\sqrt[6]{-1}$

117. $\sqrt{n^2 + 12n + 36}$ **118.** $\sqrt{s^2 - 20s + 100}$

Look Alikes . . .

119. a. $\sqrt{64}$ **b.** $\sqrt[3]{64}$ **120. a.** $\sqrt{-64}$ **b.** $\sqrt[3]{-64}$

121. a. $\sqrt{81}$ **b.** $\sqrt[4]{81}$ **122. a.** $\sqrt{16}$ **b.** $\sqrt[4]{16}$

APPLICATIONS

Use a calculator to solve each problem. Round answers to the nearest tenth.

123. Embroidery. The radius r of a circle is given by the formula $r = \sqrt{\dfrac{A}{\pi}}$, where A is its area. Find the diameter of the embroidery hoop if there are 38.5 in.^{2} of stretched fabric on which to embroider.

124. Pendulums. Find the period of a pendulum with length 1 foot. *See Example 5.*

125. Shoelaces. The formula

$$S = 2\left[H + L + (p - 1)\sqrt{H^2 + V^2}\right]$$ can be used to

calculate the correct shoelace length for the criss-cross lacing pattern shown in the illustration, where p represents the number of *pairs* of eyelets. Find the correct shoelace length if H(horizontal distance) = 50 mm, L (length of end) = 250 mm, and V(vertical distance) = 20 mm. Round to the nearest tenth. (*Source:* Ian's Shoelace Site at www.fieggen.com)

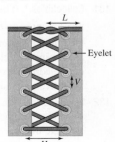

126. Baseball. The length of a diagonal of a square is given by the function $d(s) = \sqrt{2s^2}$, where s is the length of a side of the square. Find the distance from home plate to second base on a softball diamond and on a baseball diamond. Round to the nearest tenth. The illustration gives the dimensions of each type of infield.

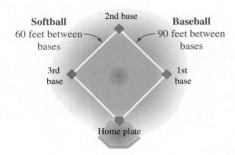

127. Pulse Rates. The approximate pulse rate (in beats per minute) of an adult who is t inches tall is given by the function $p(t) = \frac{590}{\sqrt{t}}$. The *Guinness Book of World Records 2008* lists Leonid Stadnyk of Ukraine as the tallest living man, at 8 feet, 5.5 inches. Find his approximate pulse rate as predicted by the function.

128. The Grand Canyon. The time t (in seconds) that it takes for an object to fall a distance of s feet is given by the formula $t = \frac{\sqrt{s}}{4}$. In some places, the Grand Canyon is one mile (5,280 feet) deep. How long would it take a stone dropped over the edge of the canyon to hit bottom?

129. Biology. Scientists will place five rats inside a clear plastic hemisphere and control the environment to study the rats' behavior. The function $d(V) = \sqrt[3]{12\left(\frac{V}{\pi}\right)}$ gives the diameter of a hemisphere with volume V. Use the function to determine the diameter of the base of the hemisphere, if each rat requires 125 cubic feet of living space.

130. Aquariums. The function $s(g) = \sqrt[3]{\frac{g}{7.5}}$ determines how long (in feet) an edge of a cube-shaped tank must be if it is to hold g gallons of water. What dimensions should a cube-shaped aquarium have if it is to hold 1,250 gallons of water?

131. Collectibles. The *effective rate of interest* r earned by an investment is given by the formula $r = \sqrt[n]{\frac{A}{P}} - 1$, where P is the initial investment that grows to value A after n years. Determine the effective rate of interest earned by a collector on a Lladró porcelain figurine purchased for $800 and sold for $950 five years later.

132. Law Enforcement. The graphs of the two radical functions shown in the illustration in the next column can be used to estimate the speed (in mph) of a car involved in an accident. Suppose a police accident report listed skid marks to be 220 feet long but failed to give the road conditions. Estimate the possible speeds the car was traveling prior to the brakes being applied.

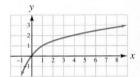

WRITING

133. If x is any real number, that is, if x is unrestricted, then $\sqrt{x^2} = x$ is not correct. Explain why.

134. Explain why $\sqrt{36}$ is just 6, and not also -6.

135. Explain what is wrong with the graph in the illustration if it is supposed to be the graph of $f(x) = \sqrt{x}$.

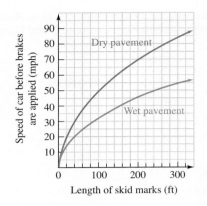

136. Explain how to estimate the domain and range of the radical function whose graph is shown here.

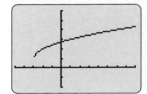

REVIEW

Perform the operations and simplify when possible.

137. $\dfrac{x^2 - 3xy - 4y^2}{x^2 + cx - 2yx - 2cy} \div \dfrac{x^2 - 2xy - 3y^2}{x^2 + cx - 4yx - 4cy}$

138. $\dfrac{2x + 3}{3x - 1} - \dfrac{x - 4}{2x + 1}$

CHALLENGE PROBLEMS

139. Graph $f(x) = -\sqrt{x - 2} + 3$ and find the domain and range.

140. Simplify $\sqrt{9a^{16} + 12a^8b^{25} + 4b^{50}}$ and assume that $a > 0$ and $b > 0$.

SECTION 9.2

Rational Exponents

OBJECTIVES

1 Simplify expressions of the form $a^{1/n}$.

2 Simplify expressions of the form $a^{m/n}$.

3 Convert between radicals and rational exponents.

4 Simplify expressions with negative rational exponents.

5 Use rules for exponents to simplify expressions.

6 Simplify radical expressions.

ARE YOU READY?

▼ *The following problems review some basic skills that are needed when working with rational exponents.*

1. Evaluate: **a.** $\sqrt{64}$ **b.** $\sqrt[3]{-64}$ **2.** Evaluate: **a.** $\sqrt[4]{81}$ **b.** $\sqrt[5]{\dfrac{1}{32}}$

3. Simplify: **a.** $\sqrt{(x+5)^2}$ **4.** Evaluate: $\left(\sqrt{36}\right)^3$
b. $\sqrt[3]{27a^6}$

5. Simplify: 7^{-2} **6.** Simplify: $\dfrac{x^5 x^7}{x^3}$

In this section, we will extend the definition of exponent to include rational (fractional) exponents. We will see how expressions such as $9^{1/2}$, $\left(\frac{1}{16}\right)^{3/4}$, and $(-32x^5)^{-2/5}$ can be simplified by writing them in an equivalent radical form using two new rules for exponents.

1 Simplify Expressions of the Form $a^{1/n}$.

The Language of Algebra

Rational exponents are also called **fractional exponents.**

It is possible to raise numbers to fractional powers. To give meaning to rational exponents, we first consider $\sqrt{7}$. Because $\sqrt{7}$ is the positive number whose square is 7, we have

$$\left(\sqrt{7}\right)^2 = 7$$

We now consider the notation $7^{1/2}$, which is read as "7 to the one-half power." If rational exponents are to follow the same rules as integer exponents, the square of $7^{1/2}$ must be 7, because

$$(7^{1/2})^2 = 7^{1/2 \cdot 2} \quad \text{Keep the base and multiply the exponents.}$$
$$= 7^1 \quad \text{Do the multiplication: } \tfrac{1}{2} \cdot 2 = 1.$$
$$= 7$$

Since the square of $7^{1/2}$ and the square of $\sqrt{7}$ are both equal to 7, we define $7^{1/2}$ to be $\sqrt{7}$. Similarly,

$$7^{1/3} = \sqrt[3]{7}, \qquad 7^{1/4} = \sqrt[4]{7}, \qquad \text{and} \qquad 7^{1/5} = \sqrt[5]{7}$$

In general, we have the following definition.

The Definition of $x^{1/n}$

A rational exponent of $\dfrac{1}{n}$ indicates the *n*th root of its base.
If *n* represents a positive integer greater than 1 and $\sqrt[n]{x}$ represents a real number,

$$x^{1/n} = \sqrt[n]{x} \quad \text{Read as "x to the } \tfrac{1}{n} \text{ power equals the nth root of x."}$$

We can use this definition to simplify exponential expressions that have rational exponents with a numerator of 1. For example, to simplify $8^{1/3}$, we write it as an equivalent expression in radical form and proceed as follows:

Index

$$8^{1/3} = \sqrt[3]{8} = 2 \quad \text{The base of the exponential expression, 8, is the radicand of the radical expression. The denominator of the fractional exponent, 3, is the index of the radical.}$$

Radicand

Thus, $8^{1/3} = 2$.

EXAMPLE 1 Evaluate: **a.** $9^{1/2}$ **b.** $(-64)^{1/3}$ **c.** $16^{1/4}$ **d.** $-\left(\dfrac{1}{32}\right)^{1/5}$

Strategy First, we will identify the base and the exponent of the exponential expression. Then we will write the expression in an equivalent radical form using the rule for rational exponents $x^{1/n} = \sqrt[n]{x}$.

Why We can then use the methods from Section 7.1 to evaluate the resulting square root, cube root, fourth root, and fifth root.

Solution
a. $9^{1/2} = \sqrt{9} = 3$ *The base is 9 and the exponent is $\frac{1}{2}$.*
Because the denominator of the exponent $\frac{1}{2}$ is 2, find the square root of the base, 9.

Success Tip

One key to successfully simplifying the exponential expressions in this section is this: When you see an exponent, always ask yourself, "What is the base?"

b. $(-64)^{1/3} = \sqrt[3]{-64} = -4$ *Read as " −64 to the one-third power." Because the denominator of the exponent $\frac{1}{3}$ is 3, find the cube root of the base, −64.*

c. $16^{1/4} = \sqrt[4]{16} = 2$ *Because the denominator of the exponent $\frac{1}{4}$ is 4, find the fourth root of the base, 16.*

d. $-\left(\dfrac{1}{32}\right)^{1/5} = -\sqrt[5]{\dfrac{1}{32}} = -\dfrac{1}{2}$ *Read as "the opposite of the one-fifth power of $\frac{1}{32}$." Because the denominator of the exponent $\frac{1}{5}$ is 5, find the fifth root of the base, $\frac{1}{32}$.*

Self Check 1 Evaluate: **a.** $16^{1/2}$ **b.** $\left(-\dfrac{27}{8}\right)^{1/3}$ **c.** $-(81)^{1/4}$ **d.** $1^{1/5}$

Now Try ▶ Problems 19, 23, 25, and 27

As with radicals, when n is an *odd natural number* in the expression $x^{1/n}$, where $n > 1$, there is exactly one real nth root, and we don't need to use absolute value symbols.

When n is an *even natural number,* there are two nth roots. Since we want the expression $x^{1/n}$ to represent the positive nth root, we often must use absolute value symbols to ensure that the simplified result is positive. Thus, if n is even,

$$(x^n)^{1/n} = |x|$$

When n is even and x is negative, the expression $x^{1/n}$ is not a real number.

EXAMPLE 2 Simplify. Assume that the variables are unrestricted. **a.** $(-27x^3)^{1/3}$ **b.** $(256a^8)^{1/8}$
c. $[(y + 4)^2]^{1/2}$ **d.** $(25b^4)^{1/2}$ **e.** $(-256)^{1/4}$

Strategy We will write each exponential expression in an equivalent radical form using the rule for rational exponents $x^{1/n} = \sqrt[n]{x}$.

Why We can then use the methods of Section 7.1 to simplify the resulting radical expression.

Solution
a. $(-27x^3)^{1/3} = \sqrt[3]{-27x^3} = -3x$ *Read as "the quantity $-27x^3$ raised to the one-third power." Because $(-3x)^3 = -27x^3$. Since n is odd, no absolute value symbols are needed.*

The Language of Algebra

The phrase **"assume that the variables are unrestricted"** in the instructions for Example 2 reminds us that negative numbers are permissible replacement values for the variables. Therefore, absolute value symbols may be necessary to ensure the answer is not negative.

b. $(256a^8)^{1/8} = \sqrt[8]{256a^8} = 2|a|$ *Because $(2a)^8 = 256a^8$. Since n is even and a can be any real number, $2a$ can be negative. Thus, absolute value symbols are needed.*

c. $\left[(y + 4)^2\right]^{1/2} = \sqrt{(y + 4)^2} = |y + 4|$ *Because $|y + 4|^2 = (y + 4)^2$. Since n is even and y can be any real number, $y + 4$ can be negative. Thus, absolute value symbols are needed.*

d. $(25b^4)^{1/2} = \sqrt{25b^4} = 5b^2$ Because $(5b^2)^2 = 25b^4$. Since $b^2 \geq 0$, no absolute value symbols are needed.

e. $(-256)^{1/4} = \sqrt[4]{-256}$, which is not a real number.   Because no real number raised to the 4th power is -256.

> **Self Check 2** Simplify. Assume that the variables are unrestricted.
> **a.** $(-8n^3)^{1/3}$ **b.** $(625a^4)^{1/4}$ **c.** $(b^4)^{1/2}$ **d.** $(-64)^{1/6}$
>
> **Now Try ▶** Problems 29, 35, 37, and 39

If we were told that the variables represent positive real numbers in parts (b) and (c) of Example 2, the absolute value symbols in the answers would not be needed.

$(256a^8)^{1/8} = 2a$ If a represents a positive real number, then $2a$ is positive.

$[(y + 4)^2]^{1/2} = y + 4$ If y represents a positive real number, then $y + 4$ is positive.

We summarize the cases as follows.

Summary of the Definitions of $x^{1/n}$

If n is a natural number greater than 1 and x is a real number,

If $x > 0$, then $x^{1/n}$ is the real number such that $(x^{1/n})^n = x$.

If $x = 0$, then $x^{1/n} = 0$.

If $x < 0$ $\begin{cases} \text{and } n \text{ is odd, then } x^{1/n} \text{ is the negative number such that } (x^{1/n})^n = x. \\ \text{and } n \text{ is even, then } x^{1/n} \text{ is not a real number.} \end{cases}$

2   Simplify Expressions of the Form $a^{m/n}$.

We can extend the definition of $x^{1/n}$ to include fractional exponents with numerators other than 1. For example, since $8^{2/3}$ can be written as $(8^{1/3})^2$, we have

$8^{2/3} = (8^{1/3})^2$ Read $8^{2/3}$ as "8 to the two-thirds power."

$\quad\ = (\sqrt[3]{8})^2$ Write $8^{1/3}$ in radical form.

$\quad\ = 2^2$ Find the cube root first: $\sqrt[3]{8} = 2$.

$\quad\ = 4$ Then find the power.

Thus, we can simplify $8^{2/3}$ by finding the second power of the cube root of 8.

The numerator of the rational exponent is the power.

$$8^{2/3} = (\sqrt[3]{8})^2$$ The base of the exponential expression is the radicand.

The denominator of the rational exponent is the index of the radical.

We also can simplify $8^{2/3}$ by taking the cube root of 8 squared.

$8^{2/3} = (8^2)^{1/3}$

$\quad\ = 64^{1/3}$ Find the power first: $8^2 = 64$.

$\quad\ = \sqrt[3]{64}$ Write $64^{1/3}$ in radical form.

$\quad\ = 4$ Now find the cube root.

In general, we have the following definition.

The Definition of $x^{m/n}$

If m and n represent positive integers ($n \neq 1$) and $\sqrt[n]{x}$ represents a real number,

$$x^{m/n} = \left(\sqrt[n]{x}\right)^m \qquad \text{and} \qquad x^{m/n} = \sqrt[n]{x^m}$$

We read the first definition given above as "x to the m divided by n power equals the nth root of x, raised to the mth power."

Because of the previous definition, we can interpret $x^{m/n}$ in two ways:

1. $x^{m/n}$ means the nth root of the mth power of x.
2. $x^{m/n}$ means the mth power of the nth root of x.

We can use this definition to evaluate exponential expressions that have rational exponents with a numerator that is not 1. To avoid large numbers, we usually find the root of the base first and then calculate the power using the rule $x^{m/n} = \left(\sqrt[n]{x}\right)^m$.

EXAMPLE 3 Evaluate: **a.** $32^{2/5}$ **b.** $81^{3/4}$ **c.** $(-64)^{2/3}$ **d.** $-\left(\dfrac{1}{25}\right)^{3/2}$

Strategy First, we will identify the base and the exponent of the exponential expression. Then we will write the expression in an equivalent radical form using the rule for rational exponents $x^{m/n} = \left(\sqrt[n]{x}\right)^m$.

Why We know how to evaluate square roots, cube roots, fourth roots, and fifth roots.

Solution **a.** To evaluate $32^{2/5}$, we write it in an equivalent radical form. The denominator of the rational exponent is the same as the index of the corresponding radical. The numerator of the rational exponent indicates the power to which the radical base is raised.

$$32^{2/5} = \left(\sqrt[5]{32}\right)^2 = (2)^2 = 4$$

Power / Root

Read as "32 to the two-fifths power." Because the exponent is 2/5, find the fifth root of the base, 32, to get 2. Then find the second power of 2.

b. $81^{3/4} = \left(\sqrt[4]{81}\right)^3 = (3)^3 = 27$

Power / Root

Read as "81 to the three-fourths power." Because the exponent is 3/4, find the fourth root of the base, 81, to get 3. Then find the third power of 3.

c. For $(-64)^{2/3}$, the base is -64.

$$(-64)^{2/3} = \left(\sqrt[3]{-64}\right)^2 = (-4)^2 = 16$$

Power / Root

Read as "-64 to the two-thirds power." Because the exponent is 2/3, find the cube root of the base, -64, to get -4. Then find the second power of -4.

d. For $-\left(\dfrac{1}{25}\right)^{3/2}$, the base is $\dfrac{1}{25}$, not $-\dfrac{1}{25}$.

$$-\left(\dfrac{1}{25}\right)^{3/2} = -\left(\sqrt[2]{\dfrac{1}{25}}\right)^3 = -\left(\dfrac{1}{5}\right)^3 = -\dfrac{1}{125}$$

Power / Root

Read as "the opposite of the three-halves power of $\dfrac{1}{25}$." Because the exponent is 3/2, find the square root of the base, $\dfrac{1}{25}$, to get $\dfrac{1}{5}$. Then find the third power of $\dfrac{1}{5}$.

Caution

We also can evaluate $x^{m/n}$ using $\sqrt[n]{x^m}$. However, the resulting radicand is often extremely large. For example,

$$81^{3/4} = \sqrt[4]{81^3}$$
$$= \sqrt[4]{531,441}$$
$$= 27$$

Self Check 3 Evaluate: **a.** $16^{3/2}$ **b.** $125^{4/3}$ **c.** $(-216)^{2/3}$ **d.** $-\left(\dfrac{1}{32}\right)^{4/5}$

Now Try ▶ Problems 41, 45, and 47

EXAMPLE 4 Simplify. All variables represent positive real numbers. **a.** $(36m^4)^{3/2}$ **b.** $(-8x^3)^{4/3}$ **c.** $-(x^5y^5)^{2/5}$

Strategy We will write each exponential expression in an equivalent radical form using the rule for rational exponents $x^{m/n} = \left(\sqrt[n]{x}\right)^m$.

Why We can then use the methods of Section 9.1 to simplify the resulting radical expression.

Power
Root

Solution **a.** $(36m^4)^{3/2} = \left(\sqrt[2]{36m^4}\right)^3 = (6m^2)^3 = 216m^6$

Read as "the quantity of $36m^4$ raised to the three-halves power." Because the exponent is 3/2, find the square root of the base, $36m^4$, to get $6m^2$. Then find the third power of $6m^2$.

Power
Root

b. $(-8x^3)^{4/3} = \left(\sqrt[3]{-8x^3}\right)^4 = (-2x)^4 = 16x^4$

Read as "the quantity of $-8x^3$ raised to the four-thirds power." Because the exponent is 4/3, find the cube root of the base, $-8x^3$, to get $-2x$. Then find the fourth power of $-2x$.

Power
Root

c. $-(x^5y^5)^{2/5} = -\left(\sqrt[5]{x^5y^5}\right)^2 = -(xy)^2 = -x^2y^2$

Read as "the opposite of the two-fifths power of the quantity x^5y^5." Because the exponent is 2/5, find the fifth root of the base, x^5y^5, to get xy. Then find the second power of xy.

Self Check 4 Simplify. All variables represent positive real numbers. **a.** $(4c^4)^{3/2}$ **b.** $(-27m^3n^3)^{2/3}$ **c.** $-(32a^{10})^{3/5}$

Now Try ▶ Problems 49 and 51

Using Your Calculator ▶ **Rational Exponents**

We can evaluate expressions containing rational exponents using the exponential key $\boxed{y^x}$ or $\boxed{x^y}$ on a scientific calculator. For example, to evaluate $10^{2/3}$, we enter

10 $\boxed{y^x}$ $\boxed{(}$ 2 $\boxed{\div}$ 3 $\boxed{)}$ $\boxed{=}$ $\boxed{4.641588834}$

Note that parentheses were used when entering the power. Without them, the calculator would interpret the entry as $10^2 \div 3$.

To evaluate the exponential expression using a direct entry or graphing calculator, we use the $\boxed{\wedge}$ key, which raises a base to a power. Again, we use parentheses when entering the power.

10 $\boxed{\wedge}$ $\boxed{(}$ 2 $\boxed{\div}$ 3 $\boxed{)}$ $\boxed{\text{ENTER}}$

```
10^(2/3)
        4.641588834
```

To the nearest hundredth, $10^{2/3} \approx 4.64$.

3 Convert Between Radicals and Rational Exponents.

We can use the rules for rational exponents to convert expressions from radical form to exponential form, and vice versa.

EXAMPLE 5 Write $\sqrt{5xyz}$ as an exponential expression with a rational exponent.

Strategy We will use the first rule for rational exponents in reverse: $\sqrt[n]{x} = x^{1/n}$.

Why We are given a radical expression and we want to write an equivalent exponential expression.

Solution The radicand is $5xyz$, so the base of the exponential expression is $5xyz$. The index of the radical is an understood 2, so the denominator of the fractional exponent is 2.

$$\sqrt{5xyz} = (5xyz)^{1/2} \quad \text{Recall: } \sqrt[2]{5xyz} = \sqrt{5xyz}.$$

Self Check 5 Write $\sqrt[6]{7ab}$ as an exponential expression with a rational exponent.

Now Try Problem 57

Rational exponents appear in formulas used in many disciplines, such as science and engineering.

EXAMPLE 6 **Satellites.** The formula $r = \left(\frac{GMP^2}{4\pi^2}\right)^{1/3}$ gives the orbital radius (in meters) of a satellite circling Earth, where G and M are constants and P is the time in seconds for the satellite to make one complete revolution. Write the formula using a radical.

Strategy We will use the first rule for rational exponents: $x^{1/n} = \sqrt[n]{x}$.

Why We are given an exponential expression involving a rational exponent with a numerator of 1 and we want to write an equivalent radical expression.

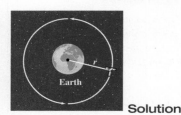

Earth

Solution The fractional exponent $\frac{1}{3}$, with a numerator of 1 and a denominator of 3, indicates that we are to find the cube root of the base of the exponential expression. So we have

$$r = \sqrt[3]{\frac{GMP^2}{4\pi^2}}$$

Self Check 6 **Statistics.** The formula $\sigma = \left(\frac{\Sigma(x - \mu)^2}{N}\right)^{1/2}$ gives the population standard deviation. Write the formula using a radical.

Now Try Problem 61

4 Simplify Expressions with Negative Rational Exponents.

To be consistent with the definition of negative integer exponents, we define $x^{-m/n}$ as follows.

Definition of $x^{-m/n}$ If m and n are positive integers, $\frac{m}{n}$ is in simplified form, and $x^{1/n}$ is a real number, then

$$x^{-m/n} = \frac{1}{x^{m/n}} \quad \text{and} \quad \frac{1}{x^{-m/n}} = x^{m/n} \quad (x \neq 0)$$

From the definition, we see that another way to write $x^{-m/n}$ is to write its reciprocal and change the sign of the exponent.

EXAMPLE 7 Simplify. Assume that x can represent any nonzero real number.

a. $64^{-1/2}$ **b.** $(-16)^{-5/4}$ **c.** $-625^{-3/4}$ **d.** $(-32x^5)^{-2/5}$ **e.** $\dfrac{1}{25^{-3/2}}$

Strategy We will use one of the rules $x^{-m/n} = \dfrac{1}{x^{m/n}}$ or $\dfrac{1}{x^{-m/n}} = x^{m/n}$ to write the reciprocal of each exponential expression and change the exponent's sign to positive.

Why If we can produce an equivalent expression having a positive rational exponent, we can use the methods of this section to simplify it.

Solution **a.**
$$64^{-1/2} = \frac{1}{64^{1/2}} = \frac{1}{\sqrt{64}} = \frac{1}{8}$$

Reciprocal / Change sign

Read as "64 to the negative one-half power." Because the exponent is negative, write the reciprocal of $64^{-1/2}$, and change the sign of the exponent.

Caution

A negative exponent does not, itself, indicate a negative number. For example,

$$64^{-1/2} = \frac{1}{8}$$

b. $(-16)^{-5/4}$ is read as "-16 to the negative five-fourths power." It is not a real number because $(-16)^{1/4}$ is not a real number.

c. In $-625^{-3/4}$, the base is 625.

$$-625^{-3/4} = -\frac{1}{625^{3/4}} = -\frac{1}{\left(\sqrt[4]{625}\right)^3} = -\frac{1}{(5)^3} = -\frac{1}{125}$$

d. This is read as "the quantity of $-32x^5$, raised to the negative two-fifths power."

$$(-32x^5)^{-2/5} = \frac{1}{(-32x^5)^{2/5}} = \frac{1}{\left(\sqrt[5]{-32x^5}\right)^2} = \frac{1}{(-2x)^2} = \frac{1}{4x^2}$$

Caution

A base of 0 raised to a negative power is undefined. For example, $0^{-2} = \frac{1}{0^2}$ is undefined because we cannot divide by 0.

e. This is read as "1 over 25 to the negative three-halves power."

$$\frac{1}{25^{-3/2}} = 25^{3/2} = \left(\sqrt{25}\right)^3 = (5)^3 = 125$$

Because the exponent is negative, write the reciprocal of $\frac{1}{25^{-3/2}}$, and change the sign of the exponent.

Self Check 7 Simplify. Assume that a can represent any nonzero real number.
a. $9^{-1/2}$ **b.** $(36)^{-3/2}$ **c.** $(-27a^3)^{-2/3}$ **d.** $-\dfrac{1}{81^{-3/4}}$

Now Try ▶ Problems 65, 69, and 75

5 Use Rules for Exponents to Simplify Expressions.

We can use the rules for exponents to simplify many expressions with fractional exponents. If all variables represent positive real numbers, absolute value symbols are not needed.

EXAMPLE 8 Simplify. All variables represent positive real numbers. Write all answers using positive exponents only. **a.** $5^{2/7} \cdot 5^{3/7}$ **b.** $(11^{2/7})^3$ **c.** $(a^{2/3}b^{1/2})^6$ **d.** $\dfrac{a^{8/3}a^{1/3}}{a^2}$

Strategy We will use the product, power, and quotient rules for exponents to simplify each expression.

Why The familiar rules for exponents discussed in Chapter 5 are valid for rational exponents.

Solution

a. $5^{2/7} \cdot 5^{3/7} = 5^{2/7+3/7}$ Use the rule $x^m x^n = x^{m+n}$. Do not multiply the bases.

$= 5^{5/7}$ Add the exponents: $\frac{2}{7} + \frac{3}{7} = \frac{5}{7}$.

b. $(11^{2/7})^3 = 11^{(2/7)(3)}$ Use the rule $(x^m)^n = x^{mn}$.

$= 11^{6/7}$ Multiply the exponents: $\frac{2}{7}(3) = \frac{6}{7}$.

c. $(a^{2/3}b^{1/2})^6 = (a^{2/3})^6(b^{1/2})^6$ Use the rule $(xy)^n = x^n y^n$.

$= a^{12/3}b^{6/2}$ Use the rule $(x^m)^n = x^{mn}$ twice. Multiply the exponents.

$= a^4 b^3$ Simplify the exponents.

d. $\dfrac{a^{8/3}a^{1/3}}{a^2} = a^{8/3+1/3-2}$ Use the rules $x^m x^n = x^{m+n}$ and $\frac{x^m}{x^n} = x^{m-n}$.

$= a^{8/3+1/3-6/3}$ To establish an LCD, write -2 as $-\frac{6}{3}$.

$= a^{3/3}$ Simplify: $\frac{8}{3} + \frac{1}{3} - \frac{6}{3} = \frac{3}{3}$.

$= a$ Simplify: $\frac{3}{3} = 1$.

Self Check 8   Simplify. All variables represent positive real numbers.

a. $2^{1/5} \cdot 2^{2/5}$ **b.** $(12^{1/3})^4$ **c.** $(x^{1/3}y^{3/2})^6$ **d.** $\dfrac{x^{5/3}x^{2/3}}{x^{1/3}}$

Now Try ▶ Problems 77, 81, and 85

EXAMPLE 9   Perform each multiplication and simplify when possible. Assume all variables represent positive real numbers. Write all answers using positive exponents only.

a. $a^{4/5}(a^{1/5} + a^{3/5})$ **b.** $x^{1/2}(x^{-1/2} - x^{1/2})$

Strategy   We will use the distributive property and multiply each term within the parentheses by the term outside the parentheses.

Why   The first expression has the form $a(b + c)$ and the second has the form $a(b - c)$.

Solution

a. $a^{4/5}(a^{1/5} + a^{3/5}) = a^{4/5}a^{1/5} + a^{4/5}a^{3/5}$ Use the distributive property.

$= a^{4/5+1/5} + a^{4/5+3/5}$ Use the rule $x^m x^n = x^{m+n}$.

$= a^{5/5} + a^{7/5}$ Add the exponents.

$= a + a^{7/5}$ We cannot add these terms because they are not like terms.

b. $x^{1/2}(x^{-1/2} - x^{1/2}) = x^{1/2}x^{-1/2} - x^{1/2}x^{1/2}$ Use the distributive property.

$= x^{1/2+(-1/2)} - x^{1/2+1/2}$ Use the rule $x^m x^n = x^{m+n}$.

$= x^0 - x^1$ Add the exponents.

$= 1 - x$ Simplify: $x^0 = 1$.

Self Check 9   Simplify: $t^{5/8}(t^{3/8} - t^{-5/8})$. Assume t represents a positive real number.

Now Try ▶ Problem 91

6 Simplify Radical Expressions.

We can simplify many radical expressions by using the following steps.

Using Rational Exponents to Simplify Radicals	1. Change the radical expression into an exponential expression.
	2. Simplify the rational exponents.
	3. Change the exponential expression back into a radical.

EXAMPLE 10   Simplify: **a.** $\sqrt[4]{3^2}$ **b.** $\sqrt[8]{x^6}$ **c.** $\sqrt[9]{27x^6y^3}$ **d.** $\sqrt[5]{\sqrt[3]{t}}$

Strategy   We will write each radical expression as an equivalent exponential expression and use rules for exponents to simplify it. Then we will change that result back into a radical.

Why   When the given expression is written in an equivalent exponential form, we can use rules for exponents and our arithmetic skills with fractions to simplify the exponents.

Solution   **a.** $\sqrt[4]{3^2} = 3^{2/4}$ Use the rule $\sqrt[n]{x^m} = x^{m/n}$.

$= 3^{1/2}$ Simplify the fractional exponent: $\frac{2}{4} = \frac{1}{2}$.

$= \sqrt{3}$ Change back to radical form.

b. $\sqrt[8]{x^6} = x^{6/8}$ Use the rule $\sqrt[n]{x^m} = x^{m/n}$.

$= x^{3/4}$ Simplify the fractional exponent: $\frac{6}{8} = \frac{3}{4}$.

$= (x^3)^{1/4}$ Write $\frac{3}{4}$ as $3\left(\frac{1}{4}\right)$.

$= \sqrt[4]{x^3}$ Change back to radical form.

c. $\sqrt[9]{27x^6y^3} = (3^3x^6y^3)^{1/9}$ Write 27 as 3^3 and change the radical to an exponential expression.

$= 3^{3/9}x^{6/9}y^{3/9}$ Raise each factor to the $\frac{1}{9}$ power by multiplying the fractional exponents.

$= 3^{1/3}x^{2/3}y^{1/3}$ Simplify each fractional exponent.

$= (3x^2y)^{1/3}$ Use the rule $(xy)^n = x^ny^n$.

$= \sqrt[3]{3x^2y}$ Change back to radical form.

d. $\sqrt[5]{\sqrt[3]{t}} = \sqrt[5]{t^{1/3}}$ Change the radical $\sqrt[3]{t}$ to exponential notation.

$= (t^{1/3})^{1/5}$ Change the radical $\sqrt[5]{t^{1/3}}$ to exponential notation.

$= t^{1/15}$ Use the rule $(x^m)^n = x^{mn}$. Multiply: $\frac{1}{3} \cdot \frac{1}{5} = \frac{1}{15}$.

$= \sqrt[15]{t}$ Change back to radical form.

Self Check 10   Simplify: **a.** $\sqrt[6]{3^3}$ **b.** $\sqrt[4]{49x^2y^2}$ **c.** $\sqrt[3]{\sqrt[4]{m}}$

Now Try ▶   Problems 93, 99, and 101

SECTION **9.2**   STUDY SET

VOCABULARY

Fill in the blanks.

1. The expressions $4^{1/2}$ and $(-8)^{-2/3}$ have _____ exponents.

2. We read $16^{3/2}$ as "16 to the three-_____ power."

3. We read $27^{-1/3}$ as "27 to the _____ one-third power."

4. We read $(-64a^5)^{4/5}$ as "the quantity of $-64a^5$, _____ to the four-fifths power."

5. In the radical expression $\sqrt[4]{16x^8}$, 4 is the _____, and $16x^8$ is the _____.

6. $32^{4/5}$ means the fourth _____ of the fifth _____ of 32.

CONCEPTS

7. Complete the table by writing the given expression in the alternate form. Also give the base and exponent for the exponential form.

Radical form	Exponential form	Base	Exponent
$\sqrt[5]{25}$			
	$(-27)^{2/3}$		
$\left(\sqrt[4]{16}\right)^{-3}$			
	$81^{3/2}$		
$-\sqrt{\frac{9}{64}}$			

8. In your own words, explain the three rules for rational exponents illustrated in the diagrams below.

a. $(-32)^{1/5} = \sqrt[5]{-32}$

b. $125^{4/3} = (\sqrt[3]{125})^4$

c. $8^{-1/3} = \dfrac{1}{8^{1/3}}$

9. Graph the following real numbers on a number line.

$$\left\{ 8^{2/3}, \quad (-125)^{1/3}, \quad -16^{-1/4}, \quad 4^{3/2}, \quad -\left(\frac{9}{100}\right)^{-1/2} \right\}$$

10. a. Evaluate $25^{3/2}$ by writing it in the form $(25^{1/2})^3$.
    b. Evaluate $25^{3/2}$ by writing it in the form $(25^3)^{1/2}$.
    c. Which way was easier?

Complete each rule for exponents.

11. $x^{1/n} = \boxed{}$

12. $x^{m/n} = \boxed{} = \sqrt[n]{x^m}$

13. $x^{-m/n} = \boxed{}$

14. $\dfrac{1}{x^{-m/n}} = \boxed{}$

NOTATION

Complete each solution.

15. Simplify:
$$(100a^4)^{3/2} = \left(\sqrt{\boxed{}}\right)^3$$
$$= \left(\boxed{}\right)^3$$
$$= 1{,}000a^6$$

16. Simplify:
$$(m^{1/3}n^{1/2})^6 = \left(\boxed{}\right)^6 (n^{1/2})^6$$
$$= m^{\boxed{}} n^{6/2}$$
$$= m^2 n^3$$

GUIDED PRACTICE

Evaluate each expression. See Example 1.

17. $125^{1/3}$
18. $8^{1/3}$
19. $81^{1/4}$
20. $625^{1/4}$
21. $32^{1/5}$
22. $0^{1/5}$
23. $(-216)^{1/3}$
24. $(-1{,}000)^{1/3}$
25. $-16^{1/4}$
26. $-125^{1/3}$
27. $\left(\dfrac{1}{4}\right)^{1/2}$
28. $\left(\dfrac{1}{16}\right)^{1/2}$

Simplify each expression. Assume that the variables can be any real number, and use absolute value symbols when necessary. See Example 2.

29. $(4x^4)^{1/2}$
30. $(25a^8)^{1/2}$
31. $(x^2)^{1/2}$
32. $(x^3)^{1/3}$
33. $(-64p^8)^{1/2}$
34. $(-16q^4)^{1/2}$
35. $(-27n^9)^{1/3}$
36. $(-64t^9)^{1/3}$
37. $(-64x^8)^{1/8}$
38. $(243x^{10})^{1/5}$
39. $[(x+1)^6]^{1/6}$
40. $[(x+5)^8]^{1/8}$

Evaluate each expression. See Example 3.

41. $36^{3/2}$
42. $27^{2/3}$
43. $16^{3/4}$
44. $-100^{3/2}$
45. $\left(-\dfrac{1}{216}\right)^{2/3}$
46. $\left(\dfrac{4}{9}\right)^{3/2}$

47. $-4^{5/2}$
48. $(-125)^{4/3}$

Simplify each expression. All variables represent positive real numbers. See Example 4.

49. $(25x^4)^{3/2}$
50. $(27a^3b^3)^{2/3}$
51. $(-8x^6y^3)^{2/3}$
52. $(-32x^{10}y^5)^{4/5}$
53. $(81x^4y^8)^{3/4}$
54. $\left(\dfrac{1}{16}x^8y^4\right)^{3/4}$
55. $-\left(\dfrac{x^5}{32}\right)^{4/5}$
56. $-\left(\dfrac{27}{64y^6}\right)^{2/3}$

Change each radical to an exponential expression. See Example 5.

57. $\sqrt[5]{8abc}$
58. $\sqrt{7p^2q}$
59. $\sqrt[3]{a^2 - b^2}$
60. $\sqrt{x^2 + y^2}$

Change each exponential expression to a radical. See Example 6.

61. $(6x^3y)^{1/4}$
62. $(7a^2b^2)^{1/5}$
63. $(2s^2 - t^2)^{1/2}$
64. $(x^3 + y^3)^{1/3}$

Simplify each expression. All variables represent positive real numbers. See Example 7.

65. $4^{-1/2}$
66. $49^{-1/2}$
67. $125^{-1/3}$
68. $8^{-1/3}$
69. $-(1{,}000y^3)^{-2/3}$
70. $-(81c^4)^{-3/2}$
71. $\left(-\dfrac{27}{8}\right)^{-4/3}$
72. $\left(\dfrac{25}{49}\right)^{-3/2}$
73. $\left(\dfrac{16}{81y^4}\right)^{-3/4}$
74. $\left(-\dfrac{8x^3}{27}\right)^{-1/3}$
75. $\dfrac{1}{9^{-5/2}}$
76. $\dfrac{1}{16^{-5/2}}$

Simplify each expression. Write the answers without negative exponents. All variables represent positive real numbers. See Example 8.

77. $9^{3/7} \cdot 9^{2/7}$
78. $4^{2/5} \cdot 4^{2/5}$
79. $6^{-2/3}6^{-4/3}$
80. $5^{1/3}5^{-5/3}$
81. $(m^{2/3}m^{1/3})^6$
82. $(b^{3/5}b^{2/5})^8$
83. $(a^{1/2}b^{1/3})^{3/2}$
84. $(mn^{-2/3})^{-3/5}$
85. $\dfrac{3^{4/3}3^{1/3}}{3^{2/3}}$
86. $\dfrac{2^{5/6}2^{1/3}}{2^{1/2}}$
87. $\dfrac{a^{3/4}a^{3/4}}{a^{1/2}}$
88. $\dfrac{b^{4/5}b^{4/5}}{b^{3/5}}$

Perform the multiplications. All variables represent positive real numbers. See Example 9.

89. $y^{1/3}(y^{2/3} + y^{5/3})$
90. $y^{2/5}(y^{-2/5} + y^{3/5})$
91. $x^{3/5}(x^{7/5} - x^{-3/5} + 1)$
92. $x^{4/3}(x^{2/3} + 3x^{5/3} - 4)$

Use rational exponents to simplify each radical. All variables represent positive real numbers. See Example 10.

93. $\sqrt[4]{5^2}$
94. $\sqrt[6]{7^3}$
95. $\sqrt[9]{11^3}$
96. $\sqrt[12]{13^4}$
97. $\sqrt[6]{p^3}$
98. $\sqrt[8]{q^2}$

99. $\sqrt[10]{x^2y^2}$

100. $\sqrt[6]{x^2y^2}$

101. $\sqrt[9]{\sqrt{c}}$

102. $\sqrt[4]{\sqrt{x}}$

103. $\sqrt[5]{\sqrt[3]{7m}}$

104. $\sqrt[3]{\sqrt[4]{21x}}$

 Use a calculator to evaluate each expression. Round to the nearest hundredth. See **Using Your Calculator: Rational Exponents.**

105. $15^{1/3}$

106. $(50.5)^{1/4}$

107. $(1.045)^{2/5}$

108. $(-1,000)^{3/5}$

TRY IT YOURSELF

Simplify each expression. All variables represent positive real numbers.

109. $(25y^2)^{1/2}$

110. $(-27x^3)^{1/3}$

111. $-\left(\dfrac{a^4}{81}\right)^{3/4}$

112. $-\left(\dfrac{b^8}{625}\right)^{3/4}$

113. $16^{-3/2}$

114. $(16)^{-5/4}$

115. $\dfrac{p^{8/5}p^{7/5}}{p^2}$

116. $\dfrac{c^{2/3}c^{2/3}}{c^{1/3}}$

117. $(-27x^6)^{-1/3}$

118. $(16a^4)^{-1/2}$

119. $\dfrac{1}{32^{-1/5}}$

120. $\dfrac{1}{64^{-1/6}}$

121. $n^{1/5}(n^{2/5} - n^{-1/5})$

122. $t^{4/3}(t^{5/3} + t^{-4/3})$

123. $\dfrac{1}{4^{-5/2}}$

124. $\dfrac{1}{100^{-5/2}}$

125. $(m^4)^{1/2}$

126. $(a^4)^{1/4}$

127. $\sqrt[4]{25b^2}$

128. $\sqrt[9]{8x^6}$

129. $(16x^4)^{1/4}$

130. $(-x^4)^{1/4}$

131. $-(8a^3b^6)^{-2/3}$

132. $-(25s^4t^6)^{-3/2}$

Look Alikes . . .

133. a. $-125^{2/3}$

   b. $(-125)^{2/3}$

   c. $-125^{-2/3}$

   d. $\dfrac{1}{(-125)^{-2/3}}$

134. a. $81^{1/4}$

   b. $81^{-1/4}$

   c. $-81^{1/4}$

   d. $\dfrac{1}{81^{-1/4}}$

135. a. $(64a^4)^{1/2}$

   b. $(64a^4)^{-1/2}$

   c. $-(64a^4)^{1/2}$

   d. $\dfrac{1}{(64a^4)^{1/2}}$

136. a. $r^{1/3} \cdot r^{1/5}$

   b. $(r^{1/3})^{1/5}$

   c. $r^{1/3} \cdot r^{-1/5}$

   d. $(r^{-1/3})^{-1/5}$

APPLICATIONS

137. **Ballistic Pendulums.** The formula $v = \dfrac{m + M}{m}(2gh)^{1/2}$ gives the velocity (in ft/sec) of a bullet with weight m fired into a block with weight M, that raises the height of the block h feet after the collision. See the illustration in the next column. The letter g represents a constant, 32. Find the velocity of the bullet to the nearest ft/sec.

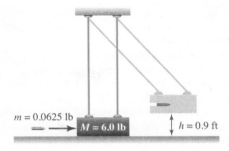

$m = 0.0625\ \text{lb}$ $M = 6.0\ \text{lb}$ $h = 0.9\ \text{ft}$

138. **Geography.** The formula $A = [s(s - a)(s - b)(s - c)]^{1/2}$ gives the area of a triangle with sides of length a, b, and c, where s is one-half of the perimeter. Estimate the area of Virginia (to the nearest square mile) using the data given in the illustration.

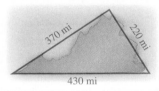

370 mi   220 mi   430 mi

139. **Relativity.** One concept of relativity theory is that an object moving past an observer at a speed near the speed of light appears to have a larger mass because of its motion. If the mass of the object is m_0 when the object is at rest relative to the observer, its mass m will be given by the formula $m = m_0\left(1 - \dfrac{v^2}{c^2}\right)^{-1/2}$ when it is moving with speed v (in miles per second) past the observer. The variable c is the speed of light, 186,000 mi/sec. If a proton with a rest mass of 1 unit is accelerated by a nuclear accelerator to a speed of 160,000 mi/sec, what mass will the technicians observe it to have? Round to the nearest hundredth.

140. **Logging.** The width w and height h of the strongest rectangular beam that can be cut from a cylindrical log of radius a are given by $w = \dfrac{2a}{3}\left(3^{1/2}\right)$ and $h = a\left(\dfrac{8}{3}\right)^{1/2}$. Find the width, height, and cross-sectional area of the strongest beam that can be cut from a log with *diameter* 4 feet. Round to the nearest hundredth.

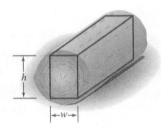

141. ▶ from **Campus to Careers**

General Contractor

The length L of the longest board that can be carried horizontally around the right-angle corner of two intersecting hallways is given by the formula $L = (a^{2/3} + b^{2/3})^{3/2}$, where a and b represent the widths of the hallways. Find the longest shelf that a carpenter can carry around the corner if $a = 40$ in. and $b = 64$ in. Give your result in inches and in feet. In each case, round to the nearest tenth.

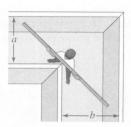

142. Cubicles. The area of the base of a cube is given by the function $A(V) = V^{2/3}$, where V is the volume of the cube. In a preschool room, 18 children's cubicles like the one shown are placed on the floor around the room. Estimate how much floor space is lost to the cubicles. Give your answer in square inches and in square feet.

Mary S.

Storage capacity 4,096 in.³

WRITING

143. What is a rational exponent? Give some examples.

144. Explain how the root key $\boxed{\sqrt[x]{y}}$ on a scientific calculator can be used in combination with other keys to evaluate the expression $16^{3/4}$.

REVIEW

145. Commuting Time. The time it takes a car to travel a certain distance varies inversely with its rate of speed. If a certain trip takes 3 hours at 50 miles per hour, how long will the trip take at 60 miles per hour?

146. Bankruptcy. After filing for bankruptcy, a company was able to pay its creditors only 15 cents on the dollar. If the company owed a lumberyard \$9,712, how much could the lumberyard expect to be paid?

CHALLENGE PROBLEMS

147. The fraction $\frac{2}{4}$ is equal to $\frac{1}{2}$. Is $16^{2/4}$ equal to $16^{1/2}$? Explain.

148. Explain how would you evaluate an expression with a mixed-number exponent. For example, what is $8^{1\frac{1}{3}}$? What is $25^{2\frac{1}{2}}$?

SECTION 9.3

Simplifying and Combining Radical Expressions

OBJECTIVES

1 Use the product rule to simplify radical expressions.

2 Use prime factorization to simplify radical expressions.

3 Use the quotient rule to simplify radical expressions.

4 Add and subtract radical expressions.

ARE YOU READY?

▼ *The following problems review some basic skills that are needed when adding and subtracting radical expressions.*

1. Complete each factorization:
   a. $28 = \boxed{} \cdot 7$ **b.** $54 = \boxed{} \cdot 2$

2. Simplify:
   a. $\sqrt[3]{-8}$ **b.** $\sqrt[4]{16}$

3. Multiply: $3 \cdot 3 \cdot 3 \cdot a^4 \cdot b^8$

4. Which of the following are like terms?

   $7x$ $3x^2$ $9x$ $2x^3$

5. Combine like terms:
   $15m^2 + 5m - m^2 - 6m$

6. Simplify: $\dfrac{\sqrt{25}}{\sqrt{36}}$

In algebra, it is often helpful to replace an expression with a simpler equivalent expression. This is certainly true when working with radicals. In most cases, radical expressions should be written in simplified form. We use two rules for radicals to do this.

1 Use the Product Rule to Simplify Radical Expressions.

To introduce the product rule for radicals, we will find $\sqrt{4 \cdot 25}$ and $\sqrt{4}\sqrt{25}$, and compare the results.

Square root of a product	*Product of square roots*
$\sqrt{4 \cdot 25} = \sqrt{100}$	$\sqrt{4}\sqrt{25} = 2 \cdot 5$
$= 10$	$= 10$

In each case, the answer is 10. Thus, $\sqrt{4 \cdot 25} = \sqrt{4}\sqrt{25}$.

Similarly, we will find $\sqrt[3]{8 \cdot 27}$ and $\sqrt[3]{8}\sqrt[3]{27}$ and compare the results.

Cube root of a product	*Product of cube roots*
$\sqrt[3]{8 \cdot 27} = \sqrt[3]{216}$	$\sqrt[3]{8}\sqrt[3]{27} = 2 \cdot 3$
$= 6$	$= 6$

In each case, the answer is 6. Thus, $\sqrt[3]{8 \cdot 27} = \sqrt[3]{8}\sqrt[3]{27}$. These results illustrate the *product rule for radicals*.

Notation

The products $\sqrt{4}\sqrt{25}$ and $\sqrt[3]{8}\sqrt[3]{27}$ also can be written using a raised dot:

$$\sqrt{4} \cdot \sqrt{25} \qquad \sqrt[3]{8} \cdot \sqrt[3]{27}$$

The Product Rule for Radicals	The *n*th root of the product of two numbers is equal to the product of their *n*th roots. If $\sqrt[n]{a}$ and $\sqrt[n]{b}$ are real numbers, $$\sqrt[n]{ab} = \sqrt[n]{a}\sqrt[n]{b}$$ Read as "the *n*th root of a times b equals the *n*th root of a times the *n*th root of b."

CAUTION   The product rule for radicals applies to the *n*th root of a product. There is no such property for sums or differences. For example,

$\sqrt{9 + 4} \neq \sqrt{9} + \sqrt{4}$	$\sqrt{9 - 4} \neq \sqrt{9} - \sqrt{4}$
$\sqrt{13} \neq 3 + 2$	$\sqrt{5} \neq 3 - 2$
$\sqrt{13} \neq 5$	$\sqrt{5} \neq 1$

Thus, $\sqrt{a + b} \neq \sqrt{a} + \sqrt{b}$ and $\sqrt{a - b} \neq \sqrt{a} - \sqrt{b}$.

The product rule for radicals can be used to simplify radical expressions. When a radical expression is written in **simplified form,** each of the following is true.

Simplified Form of a Radical Expression	1. Each factor in the radicand is to a power that is less than the index of the radical.
	2. The radicand contains no fractions or negative numbers.
	3. No radicals appear in the denominator of a fraction.

To simplify radical expressions, we must often factor the radicand using two natural-number factors. Since one factor should be a perfect square, perfect cube, perfect-fourth power, and so/on, it is helpful to memorize the following lists.

Perfect squares: **1, 4, 9, 16, 25, 36, 49, 64, 81, 100, 121, 144, 169, 196, 225,** . . .

Perfect cubes: **1, 8, 27, 64, 125, 216, 343, 512, 729, 1,000,** . . .

Perfect-fourth powers: **1, 16, 81, 256, 625,** . . .

Perfect-fifth powers: **1, 32, 243, 1,024,** . . .

EXAMPLE 1 Simplify: **a.** $\sqrt{12}$ **b.** $\sqrt{98}$ **c.** $5\sqrt[3]{54}$ **d.** $-\sqrt[4]{48}$

Strategy We will factor each radicand into two factors, one of which is a perfect square, perfect cube, or perfect-fourth power, depending on the index of the radical. Then we can use the product rule for radicals to simplify the expression.

Why Factoring the radicand in this way leads to a square root, cube root, or fourth root of a perfect square, perfect cube, or perfect-fourth power that we can easily simplify.

Solution

a. To simplify $\sqrt{12}$, we first factor 12 so that one factor is the largest perfect square that divides 12. Since 4 is the largest perfect-square factor of 12, we write 12 as $4 \cdot 3$, use the product rule for radicals, and simplify.

$$\sqrt{12} = \sqrt{4 \cdot 3} \quad \text{Write 12 as } 12 = 4 \cdot 3.$$
$$\qquad\qquad \text{Write the perfect-square factor first.}$$
$$= \sqrt{4}\sqrt{3} \quad \text{The square root of a product is equal to the product of the square roots.}$$
$$= 2\sqrt{3} \quad \text{Evaluate } \sqrt{4}. \text{ Read as "2 times the square root of 3" or as "2 radical 3."}$$

We say that $2\sqrt{3}$ is the simplified form of $\sqrt{12}$. Note that $\sqrt{12}$ and $2\sqrt{3}$ are just different representations of the same number. When we compare calculator approximations of each, that fact seems reasonable.

$$\sqrt{12} \approx 3.464101615 \qquad 2\sqrt{3} \approx 3.464101615$$

b. The largest perfect-square factor of 98 is 49. Thus,

$$\sqrt{98} = \sqrt{49 \cdot 2} \quad \text{Write 98 in factored form: } 98 = 49 \cdot 2.$$
$$= \sqrt{49}\sqrt{2} \quad \text{The square root of a product is equal to the product of the square roots: } \sqrt{49 \cdot 2} = \sqrt{49}\sqrt{2}.$$
$$= 7\sqrt{2} \quad \text{Evaluate } \sqrt{49}.$$

c. Since the largest perfect-cube factor of 54 is 27, we have

$$5\sqrt[3]{54} = 5\sqrt[3]{27 \cdot 2} \quad \text{Write 54 as } 27 \cdot 2.$$
$$= 5\sqrt[3]{27}\sqrt[3]{2} \quad \text{The cube root of a product is equal to the product of the cube roots: } \sqrt[3]{27 \cdot 2} = \sqrt[3]{27}\sqrt[3]{2}.$$
$$= 5 \cdot 3\sqrt[3]{2} \quad \text{Evaluate } \sqrt[3]{27}.$$
$$= 15\sqrt[3]{2} \quad \text{Multiply: } 5 \cdot 3 = 15.$$

d. The largest perfect-fourth power factor of 48 is 16. Thus,

$$-\sqrt[4]{48} = -\sqrt[4]{16 \cdot 3} \quad \text{Write 48 as } 16 \cdot 3.$$
$$= -\sqrt[4]{16}\sqrt[4]{3} \quad \text{The fourth root of a product is equal to the product of the fourth roots: } \sqrt[4]{16 \cdot 3} = \sqrt[4]{16} \cdot \sqrt[4]{3}.$$
$$= -2\sqrt[4]{3} \quad \text{Evaluate } \sqrt[4]{16}.$$

Self Check 1 Simplify: **a.** $\sqrt{18}$ **b.** $7\sqrt[3]{24}$ **c.** $\sqrt[4]{32}$ **d.** $\sqrt[5]{128}$

Now Try ▶ Problems 13, 17, and 19

The Language of Algebra

The instructions **simplify** and **approximate** do not mean the same thing.

Simplify: $\sqrt{12} = 2\sqrt{3}$ (exact)

Approximate:

$$\sqrt{12} \approx 3.464 \text{ (not exact)}$$

When referring to a square root, the instruction *simplify* means to remove any perfect-square factors from the radicand.

The Language of Algebra

In Example 1, a radical of a product is written as a product of radicals:

$$\sqrt[n]{ab} = \sqrt[n]{a}\sqrt[n]{b}$$

Variable expressions also can be perfect squares, perfect cubes, perfect-fourth powers, and so on. For example,

Perfect squares: $x^2, x^4, x^6, x^8, x^{10}, \ldots$
Perfect cubes: $x^3, x^6, x^9, x^{12}, x^{15}, \ldots$
Perfect-fourth powers: $x^4, x^8, x^{12}, x^{16}, x^{20}, \ldots$
Perfect-fifth powers: $x^5, x^{10}, x^{15}, x^{20}, x^{25}, \ldots$

EXAMPLE 2   Simplify. All variables represent positive real numbers.

    a. $\sqrt{m^9}$ **b.** $10\sqrt{128a^5}$ **c.** $\sqrt[3]{-24x^5}$ **d.** $\sqrt[5]{a^9b^5}$

Strategy   We will factor each radicand into two factors, one of which is a perfect nth power.

Why   We can then apply the rule *the nth root of a product is the product of the nth roots* to simplify the radical expression.

Solution   **a.** The largest perfect-square factor of m^9 is m^8.

$$\sqrt{m^9} = \sqrt{m^8 \cdot m} \qquad \text{Write } m^9 \text{ in factored form as } m^8 \cdot m.$$
$$= \sqrt{m^8}\sqrt{m} \qquad \text{Use the product rule for radicals.}$$
$$= m^4\sqrt{m} \qquad \text{Simplify } \sqrt{m^8}.$$

b. Since the largest perfect-square factor of 128 is 64 and the largest perfect-square factor of a^5 is a^4, the largest perfect-square factor of $128a^5$ is $64a^4$. We write $128a^5$ as $64a^4 \cdot 2a$ and proceed as follows:

$$10\sqrt{128a^5} = 10\sqrt{64a^4 \cdot 2a} \qquad \text{Write } 128a^5 \text{ in factored form as } 64a^4 \cdot 2a.$$
$$= 10\sqrt{64a^4}\sqrt{2a} \qquad \text{Use the product rule for radicals.}$$
$$= 10 \cdot 8a^2\sqrt{2a} \qquad \text{Simplify } \sqrt{64a^4}.$$
$$= 80a^2\sqrt{2a} \qquad \text{Multiply: } 10 \cdot 8 = 80.$$

c. We write $-24x^5$ as $-8x^3 \cdot 3x^2$ and proceed as follows:

$$\sqrt[3]{-24x^5} = \sqrt[3]{-8x^3 \cdot 3x^2} \qquad 8x^3 \text{ is the largest perfect-cube factor of } 24x^5. \text{ Since}$$
$$\text{the radicand is negative, we factor it using } -8x^3.$$
$$= \sqrt[3]{-8x^3}\sqrt[3]{3x^2} \qquad \text{Use the product rule for radicals.}$$
$$= -2x\sqrt[3]{3x^2} \qquad \text{Simplify } \sqrt[3]{-8x^3}.$$

d. The largest perfect-fifth power factor of a^9 is a^5, and b^5 is a perfect-fifth power.

$$\sqrt[5]{a^9b^5} = \sqrt[5]{a^5b^5 \cdot a^4} \qquad a^5b^5 \text{ is the largest perfect-fifth power factor of } a^9b^5.$$
$$= \sqrt[5]{a^5b^5}\sqrt[5]{a^4} \qquad \text{Use the product rule for radicals.}$$
$$= ab\sqrt[5]{a^4} \qquad \text{Simplify } \sqrt[5]{a^5b^5}.$$

Caution

$\sqrt{m^9} \neq m^3$ because $(m^3)^2 \neq m^9$. By the power rule for exponents, $(m^3)^2 = m^6$. Similarly, $\sqrt{y^{25}} \neq y^5$ because $(y^5)^2 \neq y^{25}$.

Caution

$\sqrt[3]{-24x^5} = -2x\sqrt[3]{3x^2}$

$\uparrow$

In simplified form, the radicand should not have any perfect-cube factors.

Self Check 2   Simplify. All variables represent positive real numbers.

    a. $6\sqrt{98b^3}$ **b.** $\sqrt[3]{-54y^5}$ **c.** $\sqrt[4]{t^8u^{15}}$

Now Try ▶ Problems 21, 25, and 27

---

2 Use Prime Factorization to Simplify Radical Expressions.

When simplifying radical expressions, prime factorization can be helpful in determining how to factor the radicand.

EXAMPLE 3   Simplify. All variables represent positive real numbers.

    a. $\sqrt{150}$ **b.** $\sqrt[3]{297b^4}$ **c.** $\sqrt[4]{224s^8t^7}$

Strategy   In each case, the way to factor the radicand is not obvious. Another approach is to prime-factor the coefficient of the radicand and look for groups of like factors.

Why   Identifying groups of like factors of the radicand leads to a factorization of the radicand that can be easily simplified.

Solution

a. $\sqrt{150} = \sqrt{2 \cdot 3 \cdot 5 \cdot 5}$ Write 150 in prime-factored form.

$= \sqrt{2 \cdot 3}\sqrt{5 \cdot 5}$ Group the pair of like factors together and use the product rule for radicals.

$= \sqrt{2 \cdot 3}\sqrt{5^2}$ Write $5 \cdot 5$ as 5^2.

$= \sqrt{6} \cdot 5$ Evaluate $\sqrt{5^2}$.

$= 5\sqrt{6}$ Write the factor 5 first.

$$\begin{array}{r|l} 2 & 150 \\ \hline 3 & 75 \\ \hline 5 & 25 \\ \hline & 5 \end{array}$$

> ### Caution
>
> To simplify $\sqrt{150}$, we could have factored 150 as $10 \cdot 15$. However, neither of the resulting radical expressions is the square root of a perfect square.
>
> $\sqrt{150} = \sqrt{10}\sqrt{15}$

b. $\sqrt[3]{297b^4} = \sqrt[3]{3 \cdot 3 \cdot 3 \cdot 11 \cdot b^3 \cdot b}$ Write 297 in prime-factored form. The largest perfect-cube factor of b^4 is b^3.

$= \sqrt[3]{3 \cdot 3 \cdot 3 \cdot b^3}\sqrt[3]{11b}$ Group the three like factors of 3 together and use the product rule for radicals.

$= \sqrt[3]{3^3 b^3}\sqrt[3]{11b}$ Write $3 \cdot 3 \cdot 3$ as 3^3.

$= 3b\sqrt[3]{11b}$ Simplify $\sqrt[3]{3^3 b^3}$.

$$\begin{array}{r|l} 3 & 297 \\ \hline 3 & 99 \\ \hline 3 & 33 \\ \hline & 11 \end{array}$$

c. $\sqrt[4]{224s^8t^7} = \sqrt[4]{2 \cdot 2 \cdot 2 \cdot 2 \cdot 2 \cdot 7 \cdot s^8 \cdot t^4 \cdot t^3}$ Write 224 in prime-factored form. The largest perfect-fourth power factor of t^7 is t^4.

$= \sqrt[4]{2 \cdot 2 \cdot 2 \cdot 2 \cdot s^8 \cdot t^4}\sqrt[4]{2 \cdot 7 \cdot t^3}$ Group the four like factors of 2 together and use the product rule for radicals.

$= \sqrt[4]{2^4 s^8 t^4}\sqrt[4]{2 \cdot 7 \cdot t^3}$ Write $2 \cdot 2 \cdot 2 \cdot 2$ as 2^4.

$= 2s^2t\sqrt[4]{14t^3}$ Simplify $\sqrt[4]{2^4 s^8 t^4}$.

$$\begin{array}{r|l} 2 & 224 \\ \hline 2 & 112 \\ \hline 2 & 56 \\ \hline 2 & 28 \\ \hline 2 & 14 \\ \hline & 7 \end{array}$$

> **Self Check 3**   Simplify. All variables represent positive real numbers.
>
> **a.** $\sqrt{275}$ **b.** $\sqrt[3]{189c^4d^3}$ **c.** $\sqrt[4]{1,250x^8y^6}$
>
> **Now Try** ▶ Problems 29 and 35

3   Use the Quotient Rule to Simplify Radical Expressions.

To introduce the quotient rule for radicals, we will find $\sqrt{\dfrac{100}{4}}$ and $\dfrac{\sqrt{100}}{\sqrt{4}}$ and compare the results.

Square root of a quotient	***Quotient of square roots***
$\sqrt{\dfrac{100}{4}} = \sqrt{25}$	$\dfrac{\sqrt{100}}{\sqrt{4}} = \dfrac{10}{2}$
$= 5$	$= 5$

Since the answer is 5 in each case, $\sqrt{\dfrac{100}{4}} = \dfrac{\sqrt{100}}{\sqrt{4}}$.

Similarly, we will find $\sqrt[3]{\dfrac{64}{8}}$ and $\dfrac{\sqrt[3]{64}}{\sqrt[3]{8}}$, and compare the results.

Cube root of a quotient	***Quotient of cube roots***
$\sqrt[3]{\dfrac{64}{8}} = \sqrt[3]{8}$	$\dfrac{\sqrt[3]{64}}{\sqrt[3]{8}} = \dfrac{4}{2}$
$= 2$	$= 2$

Since the answer is 2 in each case, $\sqrt[3]{\dfrac{64}{8}} = \dfrac{\sqrt[3]{64}}{\sqrt[3]{8}}$. These results illustrate the *quotient rule for radicals.*

The Quotient Rule for Radicals	The nth root of the quotient of two numbers is equal to the quotient of their nth roots. If $\sqrt[n]{a}$ and $\sqrt[n]{b}$ are real numbers, then

$$\sqrt[n]{\frac{a}{b}} = \frac{\sqrt[n]{a}}{\sqrt[n]{b}} \qquad (b \neq 0) \qquad$$ Read as "the nth root of a divided by b equals the nth root of a divided by the nth root of b."

In the following examples, variables appear in the denominators of radical expressions. To avoid undefined situations, we will assume *all variables represent positive real numbers.*

EXAMPLE 4 Simplify each expression: **a.** $\sqrt{\dfrac{7}{64}}$ **b.** $\sqrt{\dfrac{15}{49x^2}}$ **c.** $\sqrt[3]{\dfrac{10x^2}{27y^6}}$

Strategy In each case, the radical is not in simplified form because the radicand contains a fraction. To write each of these expressions in simplified form, we will use the quotient rule for radicals.

Why Writing these expressions in $\dfrac{\sqrt[n]{a}}{\sqrt[n]{b}}$ form leads to square roots of perfect squares and cube roots of perfect cubes that we can easily simplify.

Solution **a.** We can use the quotient rule for radicals to simplify each expression.

The Language of Algebra

In Example 4, a **radical of a quotient** is written as a **quotient of radicals**:

$$\sqrt[n]{\frac{a}{b}} = \frac{\sqrt[n]{a}}{\sqrt[n]{b}}$$

$$\sqrt{\frac{7}{64}} = \frac{\sqrt{7}}{\sqrt{64}} \qquad$$ The square root of a quotient is equal to the quotient of the square roots.

$$= \frac{\sqrt{7}}{8} \qquad$$ Evaluate $\sqrt{64}$.

b. $\sqrt{\dfrac{15}{49x^2}} = \dfrac{\sqrt{15}}{\sqrt{49x^2}} \qquad$ The square root of a quotient is equal to the quotient of the square roots.

$$= \frac{\sqrt{15}}{7x} \qquad$$ Simplify the denominator: $\sqrt{49x^2} = 7x$.

c. $\sqrt[3]{\dfrac{10x^2}{27y^6}} = \dfrac{\sqrt[3]{10x^2}}{\sqrt[3]{27y^6}} \qquad$ The cube root of a quotient is equal to the quotient of the cube roots.

$$= \frac{\sqrt[3]{10x^2}}{3y^2} \qquad$$ Simplify the denominator.

Self Check 4 Simplify: **a.** $\sqrt[3]{\dfrac{25}{27}}$ **b.** $\sqrt{\dfrac{11}{36a^2}}$ **c.** $\sqrt[4]{\dfrac{a^3}{625y^{12}}}$

Now Try ▶ Problems 37, 39, and 43

EXAMPLE 5 Simplify: **a.** $\dfrac{\sqrt{45xy^2}}{\sqrt{5x}}$ **b.** $\dfrac{\sqrt[3]{-432x^5}}{\sqrt[3]{8x}}$

Strategy We will use the quotient rule for radicals in reverse: $\dfrac{\sqrt[n]{a}}{\sqrt[n]{b}} = \sqrt[n]{\dfrac{a}{b}}$

Why When the radicands are written under a single radical symbol, the result is a rational expression. Our hope is that the rational expression can be simplified.

Solution

a. We can write the quotient of the square roots as the square root of a quotient.

$$\frac{\sqrt{45xy^2}}{\sqrt{5x}} = \sqrt{\frac{45xy^2}{5x}} \qquad \text{Use the quotient rule for radicals. Note that the resulting radicand is a rational expression.}$$

$$= \sqrt{9y^2} \qquad \text{Simplify the radicand: } \frac{45xy^2}{5x} = \frac{\overset{1}{\cancel{5}} \cdot 9 \cdot \overset{1}{\cancel{x}} \cdot y^2}{\underset{1}{\cancel{5}} \cdot \underset{1}{\cancel{x}}} = 9y^2.$$

$$= 3y \qquad \text{Simplify the radical.}$$

b. We can write the quotient of the cube roots as the cube root of a quotient.

$$\frac{\sqrt[3]{-432x^5}}{\sqrt[3]{8x}} = \sqrt[3]{-\frac{432x^5}{8x}} \qquad \text{Use the quotient rule for radicals. Note that the resulting radicand is a rational expression.}$$

$$= \sqrt[3]{-54x^4} \qquad \text{Simplify the radicand: } -\frac{432x^5}{8x} = -54x^4.$$

$$= \sqrt[3]{-27x^3 \cdot 2x} \qquad 27x^3 \text{ is the largest perfect cube that divides } 54x^4.$$

$$= \sqrt[3]{-27x^3}\sqrt[3]{2x} \qquad \text{Use the product rule for radicals.}$$

$$= -3x\sqrt[3]{2x} \qquad \text{Simplify: } \sqrt[3]{-27x^3} = -3x.$$

Self Check 5 Simplify: **a.** $\dfrac{\sqrt{50ab^2}}{\sqrt{2a}}$ **b.** $\dfrac{\sqrt[3]{-2{,}000x^5v^3}}{\sqrt[3]{2x}}$

Now Try ▶ Problems 47 and 51

4 Add and Subtract Radical Expressions.

Radical expressions with the same index and the same radicand are called **like** or **similar radicals**. For example, $3\sqrt{2}$ and $2\sqrt{2}$ are like radicals. However,

- $3\sqrt{5}$ and $4\sqrt{2}$ are not like radicals, because the radicands are different.
- $3\sqrt[4]{5}$ and $2\sqrt[3]{5}$ are not like radicals, because the indices are different.

For an expression with two or more radical terms, we should attempt to combine like radicals, if possible. For example, to simplify the expression $3\sqrt{2} + 2\sqrt{2}$, we use the distributive property to factor out $\sqrt{2}$ and simplify.

$$3\sqrt{2} + 2\sqrt{2} = (3 + 2)\sqrt{2} \qquad \text{Factor out } \sqrt{2}.$$

$$= 5\sqrt{2} \qquad \text{Do the addition.}$$

Radicals with the same index but different radicands often can be written as like radicals. For example, to simplify the expression $\sqrt{75} - \sqrt{27}$, we simplify both radicals first and then combine the like radicals.

$$\sqrt{75} - \sqrt{27} = \sqrt{25 \cdot 3} - \sqrt{9 \cdot 3} \qquad \text{Write 75 and 27 in factored form.}$$

$$= \sqrt{25}\sqrt{3} - \sqrt{9}\sqrt{3} \qquad \text{Use the product rule for radicals.}$$

$$= 5\sqrt{3} - 3\sqrt{3} \qquad \text{Evaluate } \sqrt{25} \text{ and } \sqrt{9}.$$

$$= (5 - 3)\sqrt{3} \qquad \text{Factor out } \sqrt{3}.$$

$$= 2\sqrt{3} \qquad \text{Do the subtraction.}$$

As the previous examples suggest, we can add or subtract radicals as follows.

Adding and Subtracting Radicals   ▼   To add or subtract radicals, simplify each radical, if possible, and combine like radicals.

EXAMPLE 6   Simplify: **a.** $18 + 2\sqrt{12} - 3\sqrt{48} + 9$ **b.** $\sqrt[3]{16} + \sqrt[3]{54} - \sqrt[3]{24}$

Strategy   Since the radicals in each part are unlike radicals, we cannot add or subtract them in their current form. However, we will simplify the radicals and hope that like radicals result.

Why   Like radicals can be combined.

Solution   **a.** We begin by simplifying each radical expression:

$$18 + 2\sqrt{12} - 3\sqrt{48} + 9 = 18 + 2\sqrt{4 \cdot 3} - 3\sqrt{16 \cdot 3} + 9 \quad \text{Factor the radicands, 12 and 48.}$$
$$= 18 + 2\sqrt{4}\sqrt{3} - 3\sqrt{16}\sqrt{3} + 9 \quad \text{Use the product rule for radicals.}$$
$$= 18 + 2(2)\sqrt{3} - 3(4)\sqrt{3} + 9 \quad \text{Evaluate } \sqrt{4} \text{ and } \sqrt{16}.$$
$$= 18 + 4\sqrt{3} - 12\sqrt{3} + 9 \quad \text{Both radicals now have the same index, 2, and radicand, 3.}$$
$$= (4 - 12)\sqrt{3} + 27 \quad \text{Add the constants: } 18 + 9 = 27. \text{ Combine like radicals.}$$
$$= -8\sqrt{3} + 27 \quad \text{Do the subtraction.}$$

b. We begin by simplifying each radical expression:

$$\sqrt[3]{16} + \sqrt[3]{54} - \sqrt[3]{24} = \sqrt[3]{8 \cdot 2} + \sqrt[3]{27 \cdot 2} - \sqrt[3]{8 \cdot 3} \quad \text{Factor the radicands.}$$
$$= \sqrt[3]{8}\sqrt[3]{2} + \sqrt[3]{27}\sqrt[3]{2} - \sqrt[3]{8}\sqrt[3]{3} \quad \text{Use the product rule.}$$
$$= 2\sqrt[3]{2} + 3\sqrt[3]{2} - 2\sqrt[3]{3} \quad \text{Evaluate } \sqrt[3]{8} \text{ and } \sqrt[3]{27}.$$
$$= (2 + 3)\sqrt[3]{2} - 2\sqrt[3]{3} \quad \text{Combine the first two radical expressions because they have the same index and radicand.}$$
$$= 5\sqrt[3]{2} - 2\sqrt[3]{3} \quad \text{Do the addition.}$$

CAUTION   Even though the expressions $5\sqrt[3]{2}$ and $2\sqrt[3]{3}$ have the same index, we cannot combine them, because their radicands are different. Neither can we combine radical expressions having the same radicand but a different index. For example, the expression $\sqrt[3]{2} + \sqrt[4]{2}$ cannot be simplified.

Self Check 6   Simplify: **a.** $14 + 3\sqrt{75} - 2\sqrt{12} + 2\sqrt{48} - 8$
                              b. $\sqrt[3]{24} - \sqrt[3]{16} + \sqrt[3]{54}$

Now Try ▶ Problems 57 and 63

EXAMPLE 7   Simplify: $\sqrt[3]{16x^4} + 4\sqrt[3]{54x^4} - x\sqrt[3]{-128x}$

Strategy   Since the radicals are unlike radicals, we cannot add or subtract them in their current form. However, we will simplify the radicals and hope that like radicals result.

Why   Like radicals can be combined.

Solution   We begin by simplifying each radical expression.

$$\sqrt[3]{16x^4} + 4\sqrt[3]{54x^4} - x\sqrt[3]{-128x}$$
$$= \sqrt[3]{8x^3 \cdot 2x} + 4\sqrt[3]{27x^3 \cdot 2x} - x\sqrt[3]{-64 \cdot 2x}$$
$$= \sqrt[3]{8x^3}\sqrt[3]{2x} + 4\sqrt[3]{27x^3}\sqrt[3]{2x} - x\sqrt[3]{-64}\sqrt[3]{2x}$$
$$= 2x\sqrt[3]{2x} + 4 \cdot 3x\sqrt[3]{2x} + x \cdot 4\sqrt[3]{2x} \quad \text{All three radicals have the same index and radicand.}$$
$$= 2x\sqrt[3]{2x} + 12x\sqrt[3]{2x} + 4x\sqrt[3]{2x} \quad \text{Combine like radicals.}$$
$$= (2x + 12x + 4x)\sqrt[3]{2x} \quad \text{Multiply: } 4 \cdot 3x = 12x \text{ and } x \cdot 4 = 4x.$$
$$= 18x\sqrt[3]{2x} \quad \text{Within the parentheses, combine like terms: } 2x + 12x + 4x = 18x.$$

Self Check 7 Simplify: $\sqrt{32x^3} + 4\sqrt{50x^3} - x\sqrt{18x}$

Now Try Problems 67 and 69

SECTION 9.3 STUDY SET

VOCABULARY

Fill in the blanks.

1. Radical expressions such as $\sqrt[3]{4}$ and $6\sqrt[3]{4}$ with the same index and the same radicand are called _____ radicals.
2. Numbers such as 1, 4, 9, 16, 25, and 36 are called perfect _____. Numbers such as 1, 8, 27, 64, and 125 are called perfect _____. Numbers such as 1, 16, 81, 256, and 625 are called perfect-fourth _____.
3. The largest perfect-square _____ of 27 is 9. The largest _____-cube factor of 16 is 8.
4. To _____ $\sqrt{24}$ means to write it as $2\sqrt{6}$.

CONCEPTS

Fill in the blanks.

5. The product rule for radicals: $\sqrt[n]{ab} = $ _____. In words, the nth root of the _____ of two numbers is equal to the product of their nth _____.
6. The quotient rule for radicals: $\sqrt[n]{\dfrac{a}{b}} = $ _____. In words, the nth root of the _____ of two numbers is equal to the quotient of their nth _____.
7. Consider the expressions $\sqrt{4\cdot 5}$ and $\sqrt{4}\sqrt{5}$. Which expression is
   a. the square root of a product?
   b. the product of square roots?
   c. How are these two expressions related?
8. Consider $\dfrac{\sqrt[3]{a}}{\sqrt[3]{x^2}}$ and $\sqrt[3]{\dfrac{a}{x^2}}$. Which expression is
   a. the cube root of a quotient?
   b. the quotient of cube roots?
   c. How are these two expressions related?
9. a. Write two radical expressions that have the same radicand but a different index. Can the expressions be added?
   b. Write two radical expressions that have the same index but a different radicand. Can the expressions be added?
10. Fill in the blanks.
   a. $5\sqrt{6} + 3\sqrt{6} = \left(\;\;+\;\;\right)\sqrt{6} = \;\;\sqrt{6}$
   b. $9\sqrt[3]{n} - 2\sqrt[3]{n} = \left(\;\;-\;\;\right)\sqrt[3]{n} = 7$

NOTATION

Complete each solution.

11. Simplify:
$$\sqrt[3]{32k^4} = \sqrt[3]{\quad}\cdot 4k$$
$$= \sqrt[3]{\quad}\,\sqrt[3]{4k}$$
$$= \quad\sqrt[3]{4k}$$

12. Simplify:
$$\frac{\sqrt{80s^2t^4}}{\sqrt{5s^2}} = \sqrt{\frac{80s^2t^4}{\quad}}$$
$$= \sqrt{\quad}$$
$$= \quad$$

GUIDED PRACTICE

Simplify each expression. See Example 1.

13. $\sqrt{50}$
14. $\sqrt{28}$
15. $8\sqrt{45}$
16. $9\sqrt{54}$
17. $\sqrt[3]{32}$
18. $\sqrt[3]{40}$
19. $\sqrt[4]{48}$
20. $\sqrt[4]{32}$

Simplify each radical expression. All variables represent positive real numbers. See Example 2.

21. $\sqrt{75a^2}$
22. $\sqrt{50x^2}$
23. $\sqrt{128a^3b^5}$
24. $\sqrt{75b^8c}$
25. $2\sqrt[3]{-54x^6}$
26. $4\sqrt[3]{-81a^3}$
27. $\sqrt[4]{32x^{12}y^4}$
28. $\sqrt[5]{64x^{10}y^5}$

Simplify each radical expression. All variables represent positive real numbers. See Example 3.

29. $\sqrt{242}$
30. $\sqrt{363}$
31. $\sqrt{112a^3}$
32. $\sqrt{147a^5}$
33. $-\sqrt[5]{96a^4}$
34. $-\sqrt{256t^6}$
35. $\sqrt[3]{405x^{12}y^4}$
36. $\sqrt[3]{280a^5b^6}$

Simplify each radical expression. All variables represent positive real numbers. See Example 4.

37. $\sqrt{\dfrac{11}{9}}$
38. $\sqrt{\dfrac{3}{4}}$
39. $\sqrt[4]{\dfrac{3}{625}}$
40. $\sqrt[5]{\dfrac{2}{243}}$
41. $\sqrt[5]{\dfrac{3x^{10}}{32}}$
42. $\sqrt[6]{\dfrac{5y^{12}}{64}}$
43. $\sqrt{\dfrac{z^2}{16x^2}}$
44. $\sqrt{\dfrac{b^4}{64a^8}}$

Simplify each expression. All variables represent positive real numbers. **See Example 5.**

45. $\dfrac{\sqrt{500}}{\sqrt{5}}$

46. $\dfrac{\sqrt{128}}{\sqrt{2}}$

47. $\dfrac{\sqrt{98x^3}}{\sqrt{2x}}$

48. $\dfrac{\sqrt{75y^5}}{\sqrt{3y}}$

49. $\dfrac{\sqrt[3]{48x^7}}{\sqrt[3]{6x}}$

50. $\dfrac{\sqrt[3]{64y^8}}{\sqrt[3]{8y^2}}$

51. $\dfrac{\sqrt[3]{189a^5}}{\sqrt[3]{7a}}$

52. $\dfrac{\sqrt[3]{243x^8}}{\sqrt[3]{9x}}$

Simplify by combining like radicals. **See Objective 4 and Example 6.**

53. $5\sqrt{7} + 3\sqrt{7}$

54. $11\sqrt{3} + 2\sqrt{3}$

55. $20\sqrt[3]{4} - 15\sqrt[3]{4}$

56. $30\sqrt[3]{6} - 10\sqrt[3]{6}$

57. $4 + \sqrt{8} + \sqrt{2} + 8$

58. $9 + \sqrt{45} + \sqrt{20} + 16$

59. $\sqrt{98} - \sqrt{50} - \sqrt{72}$

60. $\sqrt{20} + \sqrt{125} - \sqrt{80}$

61. $8 + \sqrt[3]{32} - \sqrt[3]{108} - 7$

62. $12 + \sqrt[3]{80} - \sqrt[3]{10,000} + 4$

63. $14\sqrt[4]{32} - 15\sqrt[4]{2}$

64. $23\sqrt[4]{3} + \sqrt[4]{48}$

Simplify by combining like radicals. All variables represent positive real numbers. **See Example 7.**

65. $4\sqrt{2x} + 6\sqrt{2x}$

66. $6\sqrt[3]{5y} + 3\sqrt[3]{5y}$

67. $\sqrt{18t} + \sqrt{300t} - \sqrt{243t}$

68. $\sqrt{80m} - \sqrt{128m} + \sqrt{288m}$

69. $2\sqrt[3]{16} - \sqrt[3]{54} - 3\sqrt[3]{128}$

70. $\sqrt[3]{250} - 4\sqrt[3]{5} + \sqrt[3]{16}$

71. $\sqrt[4]{32} + 5\sqrt[4]{2} - \sqrt[4]{162}$

72. $\sqrt[4]{48} - \sqrt[4]{243} - \sqrt[4]{768}$

TRY IT YOURSELF

Simplify each expression, if possible. All variables represent positive real numbers.

73. $\sqrt[6]{m^{11}}$

74. $\sqrt[6]{n^{13}}$

75. $2\sqrt[3]{64a} + 2\sqrt[3]{8a}$

76. $3\sqrt[4]{x^4y} - 2\sqrt[4]{x^4y}$

77. $\sqrt{8y^7} + \sqrt{32y^7} - \sqrt{2y^7}$

78. $\sqrt{y^5} - \sqrt{9y^5} - \sqrt{25y^5}$

79. $\sqrt{32b}$

80. $\sqrt{80c}$

81. $\sqrt{\dfrac{125n^5}{64n}}$

82. $\sqrt{\dfrac{72q^7}{25q^3}}$

83. $2\sqrt[3]{125} - 5\sqrt[3]{64}$

84. $3\sqrt[3]{27} + 12\sqrt[3]{216}$

85. $\sqrt{300xy}$

86. $\sqrt{200x^2y}$

87. $\sqrt[4]{\dfrac{5x}{16z^4}}$

88. $\sqrt[3]{\dfrac{11a^2}{125b^6}}$

89. $8\sqrt[5]{7a^2} - 7\sqrt[5]{7a^2}$

90. $10\sqrt[6]{12xy} - \sqrt[6]{12xy}$

91. $\sqrt[5]{x^6y^2} + \sqrt[5]{32x^6y^2} + \sqrt[5]{x^6y^2}$

92. $\sqrt[3]{xy^4} + \sqrt[3]{8xy^4} - \sqrt[3]{27xy^4}$

93. $\sqrt[4]{208m^4n}$

94. $\sqrt[4]{128p^8q^3}$

95. $\sqrt[3]{\dfrac{a^7}{64a}}$

96. $\sqrt[3]{\dfrac{b^3c^8}{125c^5}}$

97. $\sqrt[3]{\dfrac{7}{64}}$

98. $\sqrt[3]{\dfrac{4}{125}}$

99. $\sqrt{80} + \sqrt{45} - \sqrt{27}$

100. $\sqrt{63} + \sqrt{72} - \sqrt{28}$

101. $\sqrt[5]{64t^{11}}$

102. $\sqrt[5]{243r^{22}}$

103. $\sqrt[3]{24x} + \sqrt[3]{3x}$

104. $\sqrt[3]{16y} + \sqrt[3]{128y}$

Look Alikes . . .

105. a. $\sqrt{20} + \sqrt{20}$ **b.** $\sqrt{21} + \sqrt{21}$

106. a. $\sqrt{2} + \sqrt{18}$ **b.** $\sqrt{2} + \sqrt{19}$

107. a. $\sqrt{9x^2} - \sqrt{25x^2} + \sqrt{16x^2}$
b. $\sqrt{9x^3} - \sqrt{25x^3} + \sqrt{16x^3}$

108. a. $2\sqrt{5} - \sqrt[3]{5} + 4\sqrt{5} - 6\sqrt[3]{5}$
b. $2\sqrt[3]{5} - \sqrt[3]{5} + 4\sqrt[3]{5} - 6\sqrt[3]{5}$

109. a. $3\sqrt{16} + \sqrt{54}$ **b.** $3\sqrt[3]{16} + \sqrt[3]{54}$

110. a. $\sqrt[3]{27} - 5\sqrt[3]{8}$ **b.** $\sqrt{27} - 5\sqrt{8}$

111. a. $24\sqrt[5]{6x} + 16\sqrt[5]{6x}$ **b.** $24\sqrt[4]{6x} + 16\sqrt[4]{6x}$

112. a. $x\sqrt[3]{64x^6} - x\sqrt[3]{x^6}$ **b.** $x\sqrt{64x^6} - x\sqrt{x^6}$

APPLICATIONS

First give the exact answer, expressed as a simplified radical expression. Then give an approximation, rounded to the nearest tenth.

113.

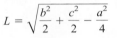

from **Campus to Careers**

General Contractor

Structural engineers have determined that two additional supports (shown in red) need to be added to strengthen the truss shown below. Find the length L of a support using the formula

$$L = \sqrt{\dfrac{b^2}{2} + \dfrac{c^2}{2} - \dfrac{a^2}{4}}$$

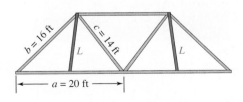

$b = 16$ ft $c = 14$ ft L L

$a = 20$ ft

114. Unbrellas. The surface area of a cone is given by the formula $S = \pi r \sqrt{r^2 + h^2}$, where r is the radius of the base and h is its height. Use this formula to find the number of square feet of waterproof cloth used to make the umbrella shown.

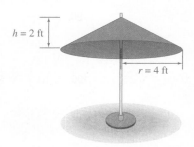

$h = 2$ ft

$r = 4$ ft

115. Blow Dryers. The current I (in amps), the power P (in watts), and the resistance R (in ohms) are related by the formula $I = \sqrt{\frac{P}{R}}$. What current is needed for a 1,200-watt hair dryer if the resistance is 16 ohms?

116. Communications Satellites. Engineers have determined that a spherical communications satellite needs to have a capacity of 565.2 cubic feet to house all of its operating systems. The volume V of a sphere is related to its radius r by the formula $r = \sqrt[3]{\frac{3V}{4\pi}}$. What radius must the satellite have to meet the engineer's specification? Use 3.14 as an approximation of π.

117. Ductwork. The following pattern is laid out on a sheet of galvanized tin. Then it is cut out and bent on the dashed lines to make an air conditioning duct connection. Find the total length of the cut that must be made. (All measurements are in inches.)

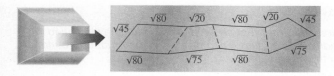

118. Outdoor Cooking. The diameter of a circle is given by the function $d(A) = 2\sqrt{\frac{A}{\pi}}$, where A is the area of the circle. Find the difference between the diameters of the barbecue grills.

Cooking area 147π in.^{3}

Cooking area 48π in.^{3}

119. Explain why each expression is not in simplified form.

    a. $\sqrt[3]{9x^4}$ **b.** $\sqrt{\dfrac{24m}{25}}$ **c.** $\dfrac{\sqrt[4]{c^3}}{\sqrt[4]{16}}$

120. How are the procedures used to simplify $3x + 4x$ and $3\sqrt{x} + 4\sqrt{x}$ similar?

121. Explain the mistake in the student's solution shown below. Simplify: $\sqrt[3]{54}$

$$\sqrt[3]{54} = \sqrt[3]{27 + 27}$$
$$= \sqrt[3]{27} + \sqrt[3]{27}$$
$$= 3 + 3$$
$$= 6$$

122. Explain how the graphs of $Y_1 = 3\sqrt{24x} + \sqrt{54x}$ (on the left) and $Y_1 = 9\sqrt{6x}$ (on the right) can be used to verify the simplification $3\sqrt{24x} + \sqrt{54x} = 9\sqrt{6x}$. In each graph, settings of $[-5, 20]$ for x and $[-5, 100]$ for y were used.

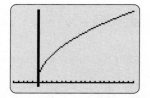 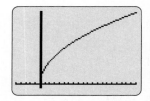

Perform each operation.

123. $3x^2y^3(-5x^3y^{-4})$

124. $(2x^2 - 9x - 5) \cdot \dfrac{x}{2x^2 + x}$

125. $2p - 5\overline{)6p^2 - 7p - 25}$

126. $\dfrac{xy}{\dfrac{1}{x} - \dfrac{1}{y}}$

Simplify each expression. All variables represent positive real numbers.

127. $\dfrac{\sqrt{24}}{3} + \dfrac{\sqrt{6}}{5}$

128. $\sqrt{3} + \sqrt{3^2} + \sqrt{3^3} + \sqrt{3^4} + \sqrt{3^5}$

129. $\sqrt[3]{\dfrac{3b}{8}} - 9\sqrt[3]{3b}$

130. $\dfrac{\sqrt[4]{32}}{3y} - \dfrac{3\sqrt[4]{2}}{7y}$

131. $\sqrt{25x + 25} - \sqrt{x + 1}$

132. $\sqrt[3]{216m^4} + \sqrt[3]{125m}$

SECTION 9.4

Multiplying and Dividing Radical Expressions

OBJECTIVES

1 Multiply radical expressions.

2 Find powers of radical expressions.

3 Rationalize denominators.

4 Rationalize denominators that have two terms.

5 Rationalize numerators.

ARE YOU READY?

▼ *The following problems review some basic skills that are needed when multiplying and dividing radical expressions.*

Perform the indicated operations and simplify, if possible.

1. $(5a^6)^2$

2. $9t^3(6t^3 + 2t^2)$

3. $(2x + 3)(x - 1)$

4. $7 - 3\sqrt{14} + \sqrt{14} - 6$

5. $(x + 10)(x - 10)$

6. Build an equivalent fraction for $\dfrac{2}{3a}$ with a denominator of $27a$.

In this section, we will discuss the methods we can use to multiply and divide radical expressions.

1 Multiply Radical Expressions.

We have used the *product rule for radicals* to write radical expressions in simplified form. We also can use this rule to multiply radical expressions that have the same index.

The Product Rule for Radicals	The product of the nth roots of two nonnegative numbers is equal to the nth root of the product of those numbers.
	If $\sqrt[n]{a}$ and $\sqrt[n]{b}$ are real numbers,
	$$\sqrt[n]{a} \cdot \sqrt[n]{b} = \sqrt[n]{a \cdot b}$$

EXAMPLE 1 Multiply and then simplify: **a.** $\sqrt{5}\sqrt{10}$ **b.** $3\sqrt{6}(2\sqrt{3})$ **c.** $-2\sqrt[3]{7x} \cdot 6\sqrt[3]{49x^2}$

Strategy In each expression, we will use the product rule for radicals to multiply factors of the form $\sqrt[n]{a}$ and $\sqrt[n]{b}$.

Why The product rule for radicals is used to multiply radicals that have the same index.

Solution

a. $\sqrt{5}\sqrt{10} = \sqrt{5 \cdot 10}$ Use the product rule for radicals.

$= \sqrt{50}$ Multiply under the radical. Note that $\sqrt{50}$ can be simplified.

$= \sqrt{25 \cdot 2}$ Prepare to simplify: factor 50.

$= 5\sqrt{2}$ Simplify: $\sqrt{25 \cdot 2} = \sqrt{25}\sqrt{2} = 5\sqrt{2}$.

Success Tip

Here we use the product rule for radicals in two ways: to *multiply* and to *simplify* the result.

b. We use the commutative and associative properties of multiplication to multiply the integer factors and the radicals separately. Then we simplify any radicals in the product, if possible.

$3\sqrt{6}(2\sqrt{3}) = 3(2)\sqrt{6}\sqrt{3}$ Multiply the integer factors, 3 and 2, and multiply the radicals.

$= 6\sqrt{18}$ Use the product rule for radicals.

$= 6\sqrt{9}\sqrt{2}$ Simplify: $\sqrt{18} = \sqrt{9 \cdot 2} = \sqrt{9}\sqrt{2}$.

$= 6(3)\sqrt{2}$ Evaluate: $\sqrt{9} = 3$.

$= 18\sqrt{2}$ Multiply 6 and 3 to get 18.

Notation

Multiplication of radicals can be shown in several ways:

$\sqrt{5} \cdot \sqrt{10} = \sqrt{5}(\sqrt{10}) = \sqrt{5}\sqrt{10}$

c. $-2\sqrt[3]{7x} \cdot 6\sqrt[3]{49x^2} = -2(6)\sqrt[3]{7x}\sqrt[3]{49x^2}$ Write the integer factors together and the radicals together.

$$= -12\sqrt[3]{7x \cdot 49x^2}$$ Multiply the integer factors, -2 and 6, and multiply the radicals.

$$= -12\sqrt[3]{7x \cdot 7^2 x^2}$$ Write 49 as 7^2.

$$= -12\sqrt[3]{7^3 x^3}$$ Prepare to simplify: write $7x \cdot 7^2 x^2$ as $7^3 x^3$.

$$= -12(7x)$$ Simplify: $\sqrt[3]{7^3 x^3} = 7x$.

$$= -84x$$ Multiply.

Caution

Note that to multiply radical expressions, they must have the same index.

$$\sqrt[n]{a} \cdot \sqrt[n]{b} = \sqrt[n]{a \cdot b}$$

Self Check 1   Multiply and then simplify: **a.** $\sqrt{7}\sqrt{14}$
b. $-2\sqrt[3]{2}\left(5\sqrt[3]{12}\right)$ **c.** $\sqrt[4]{4x^3} \cdot 9\sqrt[4]{8x^2}$

Now Try   Problems 15, 23, and 25

Recall that to multiply a polynomial by a monomial, we use the distributive property. We use the same technique to multiply a radical expression that has two or more terms by a radical expression that has only one term.

EXAMPLE 2   Multiply and then simplify: $3\sqrt{3}\left(4\sqrt{8} - 5\sqrt{10}\right)$

Strategy   We will use the distributive property and multiply each term within the parentheses by the term outside the parentheses.

Why   The given expression has the form $a(b - c)$.

Solution

$$3\sqrt{3}\left(4\sqrt{8} - 5\sqrt{10}\right)$$

$$= 3\sqrt{3} \cdot 4\sqrt{8} - 3\sqrt{3} \cdot 5\sqrt{10}$$ Distribute the multiplication by $3\sqrt{3}$.

$$= 12\sqrt{24} - 15\sqrt{30}$$ Multiply the integer factors and use the product rule to multiply the radicals.

$$= 12\sqrt{4}\sqrt{6} - 15\sqrt{30}$$ Simplify: $\sqrt{24} = \sqrt{4 \cdot 6} = \sqrt{4}\sqrt{6}$.

$$= 12(2)\sqrt{6} - 15\sqrt{30}$$ Evaluate: $\sqrt{4} = 2$.

$$= 24\sqrt{6} - 15\sqrt{30}$$ Multiply 12 and 2 to get 24.

Self Check 2   Multiply and then simplify: $4\sqrt{2}\left(3\sqrt{5} - 2\sqrt{8}\right)$

Now Try   Problems 31 and 33

Recall that to multiply two binomials, we multiply each term of one binomial by each term of the other binomial and simplify. We multiply two radical expressions, each having two terms, in the same way.

EXAMPLE 3   Multiply and then simplify: **a.** $\left(\sqrt{7} + \sqrt{2}\right)\left(\sqrt{7} - 9\sqrt{2}\right)$
b. $\left(\sqrt[3]{x^2} - 4\sqrt[3]{5}\right)\left(\sqrt[3]{x} + \sqrt[3]{2}\right)$

Strategy   As with binomials, we will multiply each term within the first set of parentheses by each term within the second set of parentheses.

Why   This is an application of the FOIL method for multiplying binomials.

Solution   **a.** $\left(\sqrt{7} + \sqrt{2}\right)\left(\sqrt{7} - 9\sqrt{2}\right)$

$$\begin{array}{cccc} F & O & I & L \end{array}$$
$$= \sqrt{7}\sqrt{7} - 9\sqrt{7}\sqrt{2} + \sqrt{2}\sqrt{7} - 9\sqrt{2}\sqrt{2} \quad \text{Use the FOIL method.}$$
$$= 7 - 9\sqrt{14} + \sqrt{14} - 9(2) \quad \text{Perform each multiplication.}$$
$$= 7 - 8\sqrt{14} - 18 \quad \text{Combine like radicals: } -9\sqrt{14} + \sqrt{14} = -8\sqrt{14}.$$
$$= -11 - 8\sqrt{14} \quad \text{Combine like terms: } 7 - 18 = -11.$$

> **Caution**
>
> A common error is to "simplify" incorrectly by subtracting:
> $$-11 - 8\sqrt{14} \neq -19\sqrt{14}$$

b. $\left(\sqrt[3]{x^2} - 4\sqrt[3]{5}\right)\left(\sqrt[3]{x} + \sqrt[3]{2}\right)$

$$= \sqrt[3]{x^2}\sqrt[3]{x} + \sqrt[3]{x^2}\sqrt[3]{2} - 4\sqrt[3]{5}\sqrt[3]{x} - 4\sqrt[3]{5}\sqrt[3]{2} \quad \text{Use the FOIL method.}$$
$$= \sqrt[3]{x^3} + \sqrt[3]{2x^2} - 4\sqrt[3]{5x} - 4\sqrt[3]{10} \quad \text{Perform each multiplication.}$$
$$= x + \sqrt[3]{2x^2} - 4\sqrt[3]{5x} - 4\sqrt[3]{10} \quad \begin{array}{l}\text{Simplify the first term. There are no like} \\ \text{radicals or terms to combine.}\end{array}$$

> **Self Check 3**   Multiply and then simplify:
> **a.** $\left(\sqrt{5} + 2\sqrt{3}\right)\left(\sqrt{5} - \sqrt{3}\right)$
> **b.** $\left(\sqrt[3]{a} + 9\sqrt[3]{2}\right)\left(\sqrt[3]{a^2} - \sqrt[3]{3}\right)$
>
> **Now Try**   Problems 37 and 41

2 Find Powers of Radical Expressions.

To find the power of a radical expression, such as $\left(\sqrt{5}\right)^2$ or $\left(\sqrt[3]{2}\right)^3$, we can use the definition of exponent and the product rule for radicals.

$$\begin{aligned} \left(\sqrt{5}\right)^2 &= \sqrt{5}\sqrt{5} \\ &= \sqrt{25} \\ &= 5 \end{aligned} \qquad\qquad \begin{aligned} \left(\sqrt[3]{2}\right)^3 &= \sqrt[3]{2} \cdot \sqrt[3]{2} \cdot \sqrt[3]{2} \\ &= \sqrt[3]{8} \\ &= 2 \end{aligned}$$

These results illustrate the following property of radicals.

The nth Power of the nth Root	If $\sqrt[n]{a}$ is a real number, $$\left(\sqrt[n]{a}\right)^n = a$$

EXAMPLE 4   Find: **a.** $\left(\sqrt{5}\right)^2$ **b.** $\left(2\sqrt[3]{7x^2}\right)^3$ **c.** $\left(8 - \sqrt{3}\right)^2$ **d.** $\left(\sqrt{m+1} + 2\right)^2$

Strategy   In part (a), we will use the definition of square root. In part (b), we will use a power rule for exponents. In parts (c) and (d), we will use the FOIL method.

Why   Part (a) is the square of a square root, part (b) has the form $(xy)^n$, and part (c) has the form $(x + y)^2$.

Solution   **a.** $\left(\sqrt{5}\right)^2 = 5$ Because the square of the square root of 5 is 5

b. We can use the power of a product rule for exponents to find $\left(2\sqrt[3]{7x^2}\right)^3$.

$$\left(2\sqrt[3]{7x^2}\right)^3 = 2^3\left(\sqrt[3]{7x^2}\right)^3 \quad \text{Raise each factor of } 2\sqrt[3]{7x^2} \text{ to the 3rd power.}$$
$$= 8(7x^2) \quad \text{Evaluate: } 2^3 = 8. \text{ Use } \left(\sqrt[n]{a}\right)^n = a.$$
$$= 56x^2 \quad \text{Multiply: } 8 \cdot 7 = 56.$$

Success Tip

Since $\left(8 - \sqrt{3}\right)^2$ has the form $(x - y)^2$, we could also use a special-product rule to find this square of a difference quickly.

c. $\left(8 - \sqrt{3}\right)^2 = \left(8 - \sqrt{3}\right)\left(8 - \sqrt{3}\right)$ *Write the base $8 - \sqrt{3}$ as a factor twice.*

$= 64 - 8\sqrt{3} - 8\sqrt{3} + \sqrt{3}\sqrt{3}$ *Use the FOIL method.*

$= 64 - 16\sqrt{3} + 3$ *Combine like radicals: $-8\sqrt{3} - 8\sqrt{3} = -16\sqrt{3}$.*

$= 67 - 16\sqrt{3}$ *Combine like terms: $64 + 3 = 67$.*

Caution

A common error when squaring a two-term expression is to simply square the first term and square the last term, and forget the middle term of the product.

$\left(\sqrt{m + 1} + 2\right)^2 = \left(\sqrt{m + 1}\right)^2 + 2^2$
$= m + 1 + 4$

d. We can use the FOIL method to find the product.

$\left(\sqrt{m + 1} + 2\right)^2 = \left(\sqrt{m + 1} + 2\right)\left(\sqrt{m + 1} + 2\right)$

$= \left(\sqrt{m + 1}\right)^2 + 2\sqrt{m + 1} + 2\sqrt{m + 1} + 2 \cdot 2$

$= m + 1 + 2\sqrt{m + 1} + 2\sqrt{m + 1} + 4$ *Use $\left(\sqrt[n]{a}\right)^n = a$.*

$= m + 4\sqrt{m + 1} + 5$ *Combine like terms.*

Self Check 4   Find: **a.** $\left(\sqrt{11}\right)^2$ **b.** $\left(3\sqrt[3]{4y}\right)^3$ **c.** $\left(\sqrt{3} + 4\right)^2$

         d. $\left(\sqrt{x - 8} - 5\right)^2$

Now Try ▶ Problems 43, 49, and 53

3   Rationalize Denominators.

We have seen that when a radical expression is written in simplified form, each of the following statements is true.

Simplified Form of a Radical Expression	1. Each factor in the radicand is to a power that is less than the index of the radical.
	2. The radicand contains no fractions or negative numbers.
	3. No radicals appear in the denominator of a fraction.

The Language of Algebra

Since $\sqrt{3}$ is an irrational number, $\dfrac{\sqrt{5}}{\sqrt{3}}$ has an **irrational denominator**. Since 3 is a rational number, $\dfrac{\sqrt{15}}{3}$ has a **rational denominator**.

We now consider radical expressions that do not satisfy requirements 2 or 3. We will introduce an algebraic technique, called **rationalizing the denominator,** that is used to write such expressions in an equivalent simplified form. In this process, we multiply the expression by a form of 1 and use the fact that $\sqrt[n]{a^n} = a$.

As an example, let's consider the following expression:

$\dfrac{\sqrt{5}}{\sqrt{3}}$ *This radical expression is not in simplified form, because a radical appears in the denominator. It doesn't satisfy requirement 3 listed above.*

We want to find a fraction equivalent to $\dfrac{\sqrt{5}}{\sqrt{3}}$ that does not have a radical in its denominator. If we multiply $\dfrac{\sqrt{5}}{\sqrt{3}}$ by $\dfrac{\sqrt{3}}{\sqrt{3}}$, the denominator becomes $\sqrt{3} \cdot \sqrt{3} = 3$, a rational number.

Success Tip

As an informal check, we can use a calculator to approximate the value of each expression.

$\dfrac{\sqrt{5}}{\sqrt{3}} \approx 1.290994449$

$\dfrac{\sqrt{15}}{3} \approx 1.290994449$

$\dfrac{\sqrt{5}}{\sqrt{3}} = \dfrac{\sqrt{5}}{\sqrt{3}} \cdot \dfrac{\sqrt{3}}{\sqrt{3}}$ *To build an equivalent fraction, multiply by a form of 1: $\dfrac{\sqrt{3}}{\sqrt{3}} = 1$.*

$= \dfrac{\sqrt{15}}{3}$ *Multiply the numerators: $\sqrt{5} \cdot \sqrt{3} = \sqrt{15}$. Multiply the denominators: $\sqrt{3} \cdot \sqrt{3} = \left(\sqrt{3}\right)^2 = 3$. The denominator is now a rational number, 3.*

Thus, $\dfrac{\sqrt{5}}{\sqrt{3}} = \dfrac{\sqrt{15}}{3}$. These equivalent fractions represent the same number, but have different forms. Since there is no radical in the denominator, and $\sqrt{15}$ is in simplest form, the expression $\dfrac{\sqrt{15}}{3}$ is in simplified form. We say that we have *rationalized the denominator* of $\dfrac{\sqrt{5}}{\sqrt{3}}$.

EXAMPLE 5   Rationalize the denominator: **a.** $\sqrt{\dfrac{20}{7}}$ **b.** $\dfrac{4}{\sqrt[3]{2}}$

Strategy   We look at each denominator and ask, "By what must we multiply it to obtain a rational number?" Then we will multiply each expression by a carefully chosen form of 1.

Why   We want to produce an equivalent expression that does not have a radical in its denominator.

Solution   **a.** This radical expression is not in simplified form, because the radicand contains a fraction. (It doesn't satisfy requirement 2.) We begin by writing the square root of the quotient as the quotient of two square roots:

$$\sqrt{\dfrac{20}{7}} = \dfrac{\sqrt{20}}{\sqrt{7}} \qquad \text{Use the division property of radicals: } \sqrt[n]{\dfrac{a}{b}} = \dfrac{\sqrt[n]{a}}{\sqrt[n]{b}}.$$

To rationalize the denominator, we proceed as follows:

$$\dfrac{\sqrt{20}}{\sqrt{7}} = \dfrac{\sqrt{20}}{\sqrt{7}} \cdot \boxed{\dfrac{\sqrt{7}}{\sqrt{7}}} \qquad \text{To build an equivalent fraction, multiply by } \dfrac{\sqrt{7}}{\sqrt{7}} = 1.$$

$$= \dfrac{\sqrt{140}}{7} \qquad \text{Multiply the numerators. Multiply the denominators: } \sqrt{7} \cdot \sqrt{7} = \left(\sqrt{7}\right)^2 = 7. \text{ The denominator is now a rational number, 7.}$$

$$= \dfrac{2\sqrt{35}}{7} \qquad \text{Simplify: } \sqrt{140} = \sqrt{4 \cdot 35} = \sqrt{4}\sqrt{35} = 2\sqrt{35}.$$

> **Caution**
>
> Do not attempt to remove a common factor of 7 from the numerator and denominator of $\dfrac{2\sqrt{35}}{7}$. The numerator, $2\sqrt{35}$, does not have a factor of 7.
>
> $$\dfrac{2\sqrt{35}}{7} = \dfrac{2 \cdot \sqrt{5 \cdot 7}}{7}$$

b. This expression is not in simplified form because a radical appears in the denominator of a fraction. (It doesn't satisfy requirement 3.) Here, we must rationalize a denominator that is a cube root. We multiply the numerator and the denominator by a number that will give a perfect cube under the radical. Since $2 \cdot 4 = 8$ is a perfect cube, $\sqrt[3]{4}$ is such a number.

$$\dfrac{4}{\sqrt[3]{2}} = \dfrac{4}{\sqrt[3]{2}} \cdot \boxed{\dfrac{\sqrt[3]{4}}{\sqrt[3]{4}}} \qquad \text{To build an equivalent fraction, multiply by } \dfrac{\sqrt[3]{4}}{\sqrt[3]{4}} = 1.$$

$$= \dfrac{4\sqrt[3]{4}}{\sqrt[3]{8}} \qquad \text{Multiply the numerators. Multiply the denominators. This radicand is now a perfect cube.}$$

$$= \dfrac{4\sqrt[3]{4}}{2} \qquad \text{Evaluate the denominator: } \sqrt[3]{8} = 2. \text{ The denominator is now a rational number, 2.}$$

$$= 2\sqrt[3]{4} \qquad \text{Simplify the fraction: } \dfrac{4\sqrt[3]{4}}{2} = \dfrac{\overset{1}{\cancel{2}} \cdot 2\sqrt[3]{4}}{\underset{1}{\cancel{2}}} = 2\sqrt[3]{4}.$$

> **Caution**
>
> Multiplying $\dfrac{4}{\sqrt[3]{2}}$ by $\dfrac{\sqrt[3]{2}}{\sqrt[3]{2}}$ does not rationalize the denominator.
>
> $$\dfrac{4}{\sqrt[3]{2}} \cdot \dfrac{\sqrt[3]{2}}{\sqrt[3]{2}} = \dfrac{4\sqrt[3]{2}}{\underset{\uparrow}{\sqrt[3]{4}}}$$
>
> Since 4 is not a perfect cube, this radical does not simplify.

An alternate way to rationalize the denominator is to use the equivalent form $\dfrac{\sqrt[3]{2^2}}{\sqrt[3]{2^2}}$ instead of $\dfrac{\sqrt[3]{4}}{\sqrt[3]{4}}$ to build an equivalent fraction:

$$\dfrac{4}{\sqrt[3]{2}} \cdot \dfrac{\sqrt[3]{2^2}}{\sqrt[3]{2^2}} = \dfrac{4\sqrt[3]{2^2}}{\sqrt[3]{2^3}} \qquad \text{Multiply the numerators. Multiply the denominators. In the denominator, the radicand is now a perfect cube because } 2 \cdot 2^2 = 2^3.$$

$$= \dfrac{4\sqrt[3]{4}}{2} \qquad \text{In the numerator, } 2^2 = 4. \text{ Simplify in the denominator, } \sqrt[3]{2^3} = 2.$$

$$= 2\sqrt[3]{4} \qquad \text{Simplify the fraction: } \dfrac{4\sqrt[3]{4}}{2} = \dfrac{\overset{1}{\cancel{2}} \cdot 2\sqrt[3]{4}}{\underset{1}{\cancel{2}}} = 2\sqrt[3]{4}.$$

Self Check 5 Rationalize the denominator: **a.** $\sqrt{\dfrac{8}{5}}$ **b.** $\dfrac{5}{\sqrt[3]{9}}$

Now Try ▶ Problems 57, 59, and 63

EXAMPLE 6 Rationalize the denominator: $\dfrac{\sqrt{5xy^2}}{\sqrt{xy^3}}$

Strategy We will begin by using the quotient rule for radicals in reverse: $\dfrac{\sqrt[n]{a}}{\sqrt[n]{b}} = \sqrt[n]{\dfrac{a}{b}}$

Why When the radicands are written under a single radical symbol, the result is a rational expression. Our hope is that the rational expression can be simplified, which could possibly make rationalizing the denominator easier.

Solution There are two methods we can use to rationalize the denominator. In each method, we simplify the rational expression $\dfrac{5xy^2}{xy^3}$ that appears in the radicand first.

> **Caution**
>
> We will assume that all of the variables appearing in the following examples represent positive numbers.

Method 1

$$\dfrac{\sqrt{5xy^2}}{\sqrt{xy^3}} = \sqrt{\dfrac{5xy^2}{xy^3}}$$

$$= \sqrt{\dfrac{5}{y}} \qquad \text{Simplify the radicand.}$$

$$= \dfrac{\sqrt{5}}{\sqrt{y}} \qquad \text{Use the quotient rule.}$$

$$= \dfrac{\sqrt{5}}{\sqrt{y}} \cdot \dfrac{\sqrt{y}}{\sqrt{y}} \qquad \text{Multiply outside the radical.}$$

$$= \dfrac{\sqrt{5y}}{y} \qquad \text{Multiply the numerators and the denominators.}$$

Method 2

$$\dfrac{\sqrt{5xy^2}}{\sqrt{xy^3}} = \sqrt{\dfrac{5xy^2}{xy^3}}$$

$$= \sqrt{\dfrac{5}{y}} \qquad \text{Simplify the radicand.}$$

$$= \sqrt{\dfrac{5}{y} \cdot \dfrac{y}{y}} \qquad \text{Multiply within the radical.}$$

$$= \dfrac{\sqrt{5y}}{\sqrt{y^2}} \qquad \text{Use the quotient rule.}$$

$$= \dfrac{\sqrt{5y}}{y} \qquad \text{Simplify the denominator.}$$

Self Check 6 Rationalize the denominator: $\dfrac{\sqrt{4ab^3}}{\sqrt{2a^2b^2}}$

Now Try ▶ Problems 67 and 73

EXAMPLE 7 Rationalize the denominator: $\dfrac{11}{\sqrt{20q^5}}$

Strategy We will simplify the radical expression in the denominator before rationalizing the denominator.

Why We could begin by multiplying $\dfrac{11}{\sqrt{20q^5}}$ by $\dfrac{\sqrt{20q^5}}{\sqrt{20q^5}}$. However, to work with smaller numbers and simpler radical expressions, it is easier if we simplify $\sqrt{20q^5}$ first, and then rationalize the denominator.

Solution

$$\dfrac{11}{\sqrt{20q^5}} = \dfrac{11}{\sqrt{4q^4 \cdot 5q}} \qquad \text{To prepare to simplify } \sqrt{20q^5}, \text{ factor } 20q^5 \text{ as } 4q^4 \cdot 5q.$$

$$= \dfrac{11}{2q^2\sqrt{5q}} \qquad \text{Simplify: } \sqrt{4q^4 \cdot 5q} = \sqrt{4q^4}\sqrt{5q} = 2q^2\sqrt{5q}.$$

Success Tip

We usually simplify a radical expression before rationalizing the denominator.

$$= \frac{11}{2q^2\sqrt{5q}} \cdot \frac{\sqrt{5q}}{\sqrt{5q}} \qquad \text{To rationalize the denominator, multiply by } \frac{\sqrt{5q}}{\sqrt{5q}} = 1.$$

$$= \frac{11\sqrt{5q}}{2q^2(5q)} \qquad \begin{array}{l}\text{Multiply the numerators.} \\ \text{Multiply the denominators: } \sqrt{5q} \cdot \sqrt{5q} = \left(\sqrt{5q}\right)^2 = 5q.\end{array}$$

$$= \frac{11\sqrt{5q}}{10q^3} \qquad \text{Multiply in the denominator: } 2 \cdot 5 = 10 \text{ and } q^2 \cdot q = q^3.$$

Self Check 7   Rationalize the denominator: $\dfrac{7}{\sqrt{18c^3}}$

Now Try ▶   Problems 75 and 81

EXAMPLE 8   Rationalize each denominator: **a.** $\dfrac{5}{\sqrt[3]{6n^2}}$ **b.** $\dfrac{\sqrt[4]{2}}{\sqrt[4]{3a}}$

Strategy   In part (a), we will examine the radicand in the denominator and ask, "By what must we multiply it to obtain a perfect cube?" In part (b), we will examine the radicand in the denominator and ask, "By what must we multiply it to obtain a perfect-fourth power?"

Why   The answers to those questions will determine what form of 1 we use to rationalize each denominator.

Solution   **a.** To rationalize the denominator $\sqrt[3]{6n^2}$, we need the radicand to be a perfect cube. Since $6n^2 = 6 \cdot n \cdot n$, the radicand needs two more factors of 6 and one more factor of n.
It follows that we should multiply the given expression by $\dfrac{\sqrt[3]{6^2 n}}{\sqrt[3]{6^2 n}}$.

Success Tip

An alternate form of 1 that can be used to rationalize the denominator is $\dfrac{\sqrt[3]{36n}}{\sqrt[3]{36n}}$.

$$\frac{5}{\sqrt[3]{6n^2}} = \frac{5}{\sqrt[3]{6n^2}} \cdot \frac{\sqrt[3]{6^2 n}}{\sqrt[3]{6^2 n}} \qquad \text{Multiply by a form of 1 to rationalize the denominator.}$$

$$= \frac{5\sqrt[3]{36n}}{\sqrt[3]{6^3 n^3}} \qquad \begin{array}{l}\text{Multiply the numerators. Multiply the denominators.} \\ \leftarrow \text{This radicand is now a perfect cube.}\end{array}$$

$$= \frac{5\sqrt[3]{36n}}{6n} \qquad \text{Simplify the denominator: } \sqrt[3]{6^3 n^3} = 6n.$$

b. To rationalize the denominator $\sqrt[4]{3a}$, we need the radicand to be a perfect-fourth power. Since $3a = 3 \cdot a$, the radicand needs three more factors of 3 and three more factors of a. It follows that we should multiply the given expression by $\dfrac{\sqrt[4]{3^3 a^3}}{\sqrt[4]{3^3 a^3}}$.

Success Tip

An alternate form of 1 that can be used to rationalize the denominator is $\dfrac{\sqrt[4]{27a^3}}{\sqrt[4]{27a^3}}$.

$$\frac{\sqrt[4]{2}}{\sqrt[4]{3a}} = \frac{\sqrt[4]{2}}{\sqrt[4]{3a}} \cdot \frac{\sqrt[4]{3^3 a^3}}{\sqrt[4]{3^3 a^3}} \qquad \text{Multiply by a form of 1 to rationalize the denominator.}$$

$$= \frac{\sqrt[4]{54a^3}}{\sqrt[4]{3^4 a^4}} \qquad \begin{array}{l}\text{Multiply the numerators: } 2 \cdot 27 = 54. \text{ Multiply the} \\ \leftarrow \text{denominators. This radicand is now a perfect-fourth power.}\end{array}$$

$$= \frac{\sqrt[4]{54a^3}}{3a} \qquad \text{Simplify the denominator: } \sqrt[4]{3^4 a^4} = 3a.$$

Self Check 8   Rationalize each denominator: **a.** $\dfrac{27}{\sqrt[3]{100a}}$

b. $\dfrac{\sqrt[4]{3}}{\sqrt[4]{4y^2}}$

Now Try ▶   Problems 83 and 87

4 Rationalize Denominators That Have Two Terms.

So far, we have rationalized denominators that have only one term. We will now discuss a method to rationalize denominators that have two terms.

One-termed denominators

$$\dfrac{\sqrt{5}}{\sqrt{3}} \qquad \dfrac{11}{\sqrt{20q^5}} \qquad \dfrac{4}{\sqrt[3]{2}}$$

Two-termed denominators

$$\dfrac{1}{\sqrt{2}+1} \qquad \dfrac{\sqrt{x}+\sqrt{2}}{\sqrt{x}-\sqrt{2}}$$

To rationalize the denominator of $\dfrac{1}{\sqrt{2}+1}$, for example, we multiply the numerator and denominator by $\sqrt{2}-1$, because the product $\left(\sqrt{2}+1\right)\left(\sqrt{2}-1\right)$ contains no radicals.

$$\left(\sqrt{2}+1\right)\left(\sqrt{2}-1\right) = \left(\sqrt{2}\right)^2 - (1)^2 \quad \text{\small Use a special-product rule.}$$
$$= 2 - 1$$
$$= 1$$

Radical expressions that involve the sum and difference of the same two terms, such as $\sqrt{2}+1$ and $\sqrt{2}-1$, are called **conjugates.**

EXAMPLE 9   Rationalize the denominator: **a.** $\dfrac{1}{\sqrt{2}+1}$ **b.** $\dfrac{\sqrt{x}+\sqrt{2}}{\sqrt{x}-\sqrt{2}}$

Strategy   In each part, we will rationalize the denominator by multiplying the numerator and the denominator by the conjugate of the denominator.

Why   Multiplying each denominator by its conjugate will produce a new denominator that does not contain radicals.

Solution   **a.** To find a fraction equivalent to $\dfrac{1}{\sqrt{2}+1}$ that does not have a radical in its denominator, we multiply $\dfrac{1}{\sqrt{2}+1}$ by a form of 1 that uses the conjugate of $\sqrt{2}+1$.

$$\dfrac{1}{\sqrt{2}+1} = \dfrac{1}{\sqrt{2}+1} \cdot \dfrac{\sqrt{2}-1}{\sqrt{2}-1}$$

$$= \dfrac{\sqrt{2}-1}{\left(\sqrt{2}\right)^2 - (1)^2} \qquad \text{\small Multiply the numerators. Multiply the denominators using a special-product rule.}$$

$$= \dfrac{\sqrt{2}-1}{2-1} \qquad \text{\small In the denominator, } \left(\sqrt{2}\right)^2 = 2.$$

$$= \dfrac{\sqrt{2}-1}{1}$$

$$= \sqrt{2}-1$$

> **Success Tip**
>
> In the denominator, we can use the special-product rule $(A+B)(A-B) = A^2 - B^2$ to multiply $\sqrt{2}+1$ and $\sqrt{2}-1$ quickly.

b. We multiply the numerator and denominator by $\sqrt{x}+\sqrt{2}$, which is the conjugate of $\sqrt{x}-\sqrt{2}$, and simplify.

$$\dfrac{\sqrt{x}+\sqrt{2}}{\sqrt{x}-\sqrt{2}} = \dfrac{\sqrt{x}+\sqrt{2}}{\sqrt{x}-\sqrt{2}} \cdot \dfrac{\sqrt{x}+\sqrt{2}}{\sqrt{x}+\sqrt{2}}$$

$$= \dfrac{x + \sqrt{2x} + \sqrt{2x} + 2}{\left(\sqrt{x}\right)^2 - \left(\sqrt{2}\right)^2} \qquad \text{\small Multiply the numerators. Multiply the denominators using a special-product formula.}$$

$$= \dfrac{x + \sqrt{2x} + \sqrt{2x} + 2}{x - 2} \qquad \text{\small In the denominator, } \left(\sqrt{x}\right)^2 = x \text{ and } \left(\sqrt{2}\right)^2 = 2.$$

$$= \dfrac{x + 2\sqrt{2x} + 2}{x - 2} \qquad \text{\small In the numerator, combine like radicals: } \sqrt{2x} + \sqrt{2x} = 2\sqrt{2x}.$$

Self Check 9 Rationalize the denominator: $\dfrac{\sqrt{x} - \sqrt{2}}{\sqrt{x} + \sqrt{2}}$

Now Try ▶ Problems 91 and 97

5 Rationalize Numerators.

In some advanced mathematics courses, like calculus, we sometimes have to rationalize a numerator by multiplying the numerator and denominator of the fraction by the conjugate of the numerator.

EXAMPLE 10 Rationalize the numerator: $\dfrac{\sqrt{x} - 3}{\sqrt{x}}$

Strategy To rationalize the numerator, we will multiply the numerator and the denominator by the conjugate of the numerator.

Why After rationalizing the numerator, we can simplify the expression. Although the result will not be in simplified form, this nonsimplified form is often desirable in calculus.

Solution We multiply the numerator and denominator by $\sqrt{x} + 3$, which is the conjugate of the numerator.

$$\frac{\sqrt{x} - 3}{\sqrt{x}} = \frac{\sqrt{x} - 3}{\sqrt{x}} \cdot \frac{\sqrt{x} + 3}{\sqrt{x} + 3} \qquad \text{Multiply by a form of 1 to rationalize the numerator.}$$

$$= \frac{\left(\sqrt{x}\right)^2 - 3^2}{x + 3\sqrt{x}} \qquad \text{Multiply the numerators using a special-product rule.} \\ \text{Multiply the denominators using the distributive property.}$$

$$= \frac{x - 9}{x + 3\sqrt{x}} \qquad \text{In the numerator, } \left(\sqrt{x}\right)^2 = x \text{ and } 3^2 = 9.$$

Self Check 10 Rationalize the numerator: $\dfrac{\sqrt{x} + 3}{\sqrt{x}}$

Now Try ▶ Problem 101

SECTION 9.4 ▶ STUDY SET

VOCABULARY

Fill in the blanks.

1. In this section, we used the _____ rule for radicals in reverse: $\sqrt[n]{a} \cdot \sqrt[n]{b} = \sqrt[n]{ab}$.

2. To multiply $2\sqrt{5}\left(3\sqrt{8} + \sqrt{3}\right)$, use the _____ property.

3. To _____ the denominator of $\dfrac{4}{\sqrt{5}}$, we multiply the fraction by $\dfrac{\sqrt{5}}{\sqrt{5}}$.

4. The denominator of the fraction $\dfrac{4}{\sqrt{5}}$ is an _____ number.

5. To obtain a _____-cube radicand in the denominator of $\dfrac{\sqrt[3]{7}}{\sqrt[3]{5n}}$, we multiply the fraction by $\dfrac{\sqrt[3]{25n^2}}{\sqrt[3]{25n^2}}$.

6. The _____ of $\sqrt{x} + 1$ is $\sqrt{x} - 1$.

CONCEPTS

7. Tell why each of the following expressions is not in simplified radical form. Then simplify it. Finally, use a calculator to approximate its value.

	Why isn't it in simplified form?	Simplified form	Approximation
$\dfrac{3}{\sqrt{2}}$			
$\dfrac{\sqrt{18}}{2}$			
$\sqrt{\dfrac{9}{2}}$			

8. Fill in the blank: To rationalize the denominator of $\dfrac{3}{\sqrt{2}}$, we multiply it by $\dfrac{\sqrt{2}}{\sqrt{2}}$, which is a form of $\boxed{}$.

9. Fill in the blanks to complete this special product:

$$\left(5 - \sqrt{x}\right)^2 = \left(\boxed{}\right)^2 - \boxed{}(5)\left(\sqrt{x}\right) + \left(\boxed{}\right)^2$$

$$= \boxed{} - 10\sqrt{x} + \boxed{}$$

10. Fill in the blanks to complete this special product:

$$\left(\sqrt{7} + 2\right)\left(\sqrt{7} - 2\right) = \left(\sqrt{7}\right)^{\boxed{}} - (2)^{\boxed{}}$$

$$= \boxed{} - 4$$

$$= \boxed{}$$

11. Perform each operation, if possible.

a. $4\sqrt{6} + 2\sqrt{6}$ b. $4\sqrt{6}\left(2\sqrt{6}\right)$

c. $3\sqrt{2} - 2\sqrt{3}$ d. $3\sqrt{2}\left(-2\sqrt{3}\right)$

12. Perform each operation, if possible.

a. $5 + 6\sqrt[3]{6}$ b. $5\left(6\sqrt[3]{6}\right)$

c. $\dfrac{30\sqrt[3]{15}}{5}$ d. $\dfrac{\sqrt[3]{15}}{5}$

NOTATION

Fill in the blanks.

13. Multiply:

$$5\sqrt{8} \cdot 7\sqrt{6} = 5(7)\sqrt{8\,\boxed{}}$$

$$= 35\sqrt{\boxed{}}$$

$$= 35\sqrt{\boxed{} \cdot 3}$$

$$= 35\left(\boxed{}\right)\sqrt{3}$$

$$= 140\sqrt{3}$$

14. Rationalize the denominator:

$$\frac{9}{\sqrt[3]{4a^2}} = \frac{9}{\sqrt[3]{4a^2}} \cdot \frac{\sqrt[3]{2a}}{\boxed{}}$$

$$= \frac{9\sqrt[3]{2a}}{\sqrt[3]{\boxed{}}}$$

$$= \frac{9\sqrt[3]{2a}}{\boxed{}}$$

GUIDED PRACTICE

Multiply and simplify. All variables represent positive real numbers. See Example 1.

15. $\sqrt{3}\sqrt{15}$ **16.** $\sqrt{5}\sqrt{15}$

17. $2\sqrt{3}\sqrt{6}$ **18.** $-3\sqrt{11}\sqrt{33}$

19. $\left(3\sqrt[3]{9}\right)\left(2\sqrt[3]{3}\right)$ **20.** $\left(2\sqrt[3]{16}\right)\left(-\sqrt[3]{4}\right)$

21. $\sqrt[3]{2} \cdot \sqrt[3]{12}$ **22.** $\sqrt[3]{3} \cdot \sqrt[3]{18}$

23. $6\sqrt{ab^3}\left(8\sqrt{ab}\right)$ **24.** $3\sqrt{8x}\left(2\sqrt{2x^3y}\right)$

25. $\sqrt[4]{5a^3}\sqrt[4]{125a^2}$ **26.** $\sqrt[4]{2r^3}\sqrt[4]{8r^2}$

Multiply and simplify. All variables represent positive real numbers. See Example 2.

27. $3\sqrt{5}\left(4 - \sqrt{5}\right)$ **28.** $2\sqrt{7}\left(3 - \sqrt{7}\right)$

29. $\sqrt{2}\left(4\sqrt{6} + 2\sqrt{7}\right)$ **30.** $-\sqrt{3}\left(\sqrt{7} - \sqrt{15}\right)$

31. $-2\sqrt{5x}\left(4\sqrt{2x} - 3\sqrt{3}\right)$ **32.** $3\sqrt{7t}\left(2\sqrt{7t} + 3\sqrt{3t^2}\right)$

33. $\sqrt[3]{2}\left(4\sqrt[3]{4} + \sqrt[3]{12}\right)$ **34.** $\sqrt[3]{3}\left(2\sqrt[3]{9} + \sqrt[3]{18}\right)$

Multiply and simplify. All variables represent positive real numbers. See Example 3.

35. $\left(\sqrt{2} + 1\right)\left(\sqrt{2} - 3\right)$
36. $\left(2\sqrt{3} + 1\right)\left(\sqrt{3} - 1\right)$
37. $\left(\sqrt{3x} - \sqrt{2y}\right)\left(\sqrt{3x} + \sqrt{2y}\right)$
38. $\left(\sqrt{3m} + \sqrt{2n}\right)\left(\sqrt{3m} - \sqrt{2n}\right)$
39. $\left(2\sqrt[3]{4} - 3\sqrt[3]{2}\right)\left(3\sqrt[3]{4} + 2\sqrt[3]{10}\right)$

40. $\left(4\sqrt[3]{9} - 3\sqrt[3]{3}\right)\left(4\sqrt[3]{3} + 2\sqrt[3]{6}\right)$
41. $\left(\sqrt[3]{5z} + \sqrt[3]{3}\right)\left(\sqrt[3]{5z} + 2\sqrt[3]{3}\right)$
42. $\left(\sqrt[3]{3p} - 2\sqrt[3]{2}\right)\left(\sqrt[3]{3p} + \sqrt[3]{2}\right)$

Square or cube each quantity and simplify the result. See Example 4.

43. $\left(\sqrt{7}\right)^2$ **44.** $\left(\sqrt{11}\right)^2$
45. $\left(\sqrt[3]{12}\right)^3$ **46.** $\left(\sqrt[3]{9}\right)^3$
47. $\left(3\sqrt{2}\right)^2$ **48.** $\left(2\sqrt{5}\right)^2$

49. $\left(-2\sqrt[3]{2x^2}\right)^3$

50. $\left(-3\sqrt[3]{10y^3}\right)^3$

51. $\left(6 - \sqrt{3}\right)^2$

52. $\left(9 - \sqrt{11}\right)^2$

53. $\left(\sqrt{3x} + \sqrt{3}\right)^2$

54. $\left(\sqrt{5x} - \sqrt{3}\right)^2$

Rationalize each denominator. See Example 5.

55. $\sqrt{\dfrac{2}{7}}$

56. $\sqrt{\dfrac{5}{3}}$

57. $\sqrt{\dfrac{8}{3}}$

58. $\sqrt{\dfrac{8}{7}}$

59. $\dfrac{4}{\sqrt{6}}$

60. $\dfrac{8}{\sqrt{10}}$

61. $\dfrac{1}{\sqrt[3]{2}}$

62. $\dfrac{2}{\sqrt[3]{6}}$

63. $\dfrac{3}{\sqrt[3]{9}}$

64. $\dfrac{2}{\sqrt[3]{a}}$

65. $\dfrac{1}{\sqrt[4]{8}}$

66. $\dfrac{1}{\sqrt[5]{2}}$

Rationalize each denominator. All variables represent positive real numbers. See Example 6.

67. $\dfrac{\sqrt{10y^2}}{\sqrt{2y^3}}$

68. $\dfrac{\sqrt{15b^2}}{\sqrt{5b^3}}$

69. $\dfrac{\sqrt{48x^2}}{\sqrt{8x^2y}}$

70. $\dfrac{\sqrt{9xy}}{\sqrt{3x^2y}}$

71. $\dfrac{\sqrt[3]{12t^3}}{\sqrt[3]{54t^2}}$

72. $\dfrac{\sqrt[3]{15m^4}}{\sqrt[3]{12m^3}}$

73. $\dfrac{\sqrt[3]{4a^6}}{\sqrt[3]{2a^5b}}$

74. $\dfrac{\sqrt[3]{9x^5y^4}}{\sqrt[3]{3x^5y^5}}$

Rationalize each denominator. All variables represent positive real numbers. See Example 7.

75. $\dfrac{23}{\sqrt{50p^5}}$

76. $\dfrac{11}{\sqrt{75s^5}}$

77. $\dfrac{7}{\sqrt{24b^3}}$

78. $\dfrac{13}{\sqrt{32n^3}}$

Rationalize each denominator. All variables represent positive real numbers. See Example 8.

79. $\sqrt[3]{\dfrac{5}{16}}$

80. $\sqrt[3]{\dfrac{2}{81}}$

81. $\sqrt[3]{\dfrac{4}{81}}$

82. $\sqrt[3]{\dfrac{7}{16}}$

83. $\dfrac{19}{\sqrt[3]{5c^2}}$

84. $\dfrac{1}{\sqrt[3]{4m^2}}$

85. $\dfrac{\sqrt[3]{3}}{\sqrt[3]{2r}}$

86. $\dfrac{\sqrt[3]{7}}{\sqrt[3]{100s}}$

87. $\dfrac{\sqrt[4]{2}}{\sqrt[4]{3t^2}}$

88. $\dfrac{\sqrt[4]{3}}{\sqrt[4]{5b^3}}$

89. $\dfrac{25}{\sqrt[4]{8a}}$

90. $\dfrac{4}{\sqrt[4]{9t}}$

Rationalize each denominator. All variables represent positive real numbers. See Example 9.

91. $\dfrac{\sqrt{2}}{\sqrt{5} + 3}$

92. $\dfrac{\sqrt{3}}{\sqrt{3} - 2}$

93. $\dfrac{2}{\sqrt{x} + 1}$

94. $\dfrac{3}{\sqrt{x} - 2}$

95. $\dfrac{\sqrt{7} - \sqrt{2}}{\sqrt{2} + \sqrt{7}}$

96. $\dfrac{\sqrt{3} + \sqrt{2}}{\sqrt{3} - \sqrt{2}}$

97. $\dfrac{\sqrt{x} - \sqrt{y}}{\sqrt{x} + \sqrt{y}}$

98. $\dfrac{\sqrt{x} + \sqrt{y}}{\sqrt{x} - \sqrt{y}}$

Rationalize each numerator. All variables represent positive real numbers. See Example 10.

99. $\dfrac{\sqrt{x} + 3}{x}$

100. $\dfrac{2 + \sqrt{x}}{5x}$

101. $\dfrac{\sqrt{x} + \sqrt{y}}{\sqrt{x}}$

102. $\dfrac{\sqrt{x} - \sqrt{y}}{\sqrt{x} + \sqrt{y}}$

TRY IT YOURSELF

The following problems involve addition, subtraction, and multiplication of radical expressions, as well as rationalizing the denominator. Perform the operations and simplify, if possible. All variables represent positive real numbers.

103. $\sqrt{x}\left(\sqrt{14x} + \sqrt{2}\right)$

104. $2\sqrt[3]{16} - 3\sqrt[3]{128} - \sqrt[3]{54}$

105. $\dfrac{3\sqrt{2} - 5\sqrt{3}}{2\sqrt{3} - 3\sqrt{2}}$

106. $\dfrac{3\sqrt{6} + 5\sqrt{5}}{2\sqrt{5} - 3\sqrt{6}}$

107. $\left(10\sqrt[3]{2x}\right)^3$

108. $\dfrac{\sqrt{3}}{\sqrt{98x^2}}$

109. $-4\sqrt[3]{5r^2s}\left(5\sqrt[3]{2r}\right)$

110. $-\sqrt[3]{3xy^2}\left(-\sqrt[3]{9x^3}\right)$

111. $\left(3p + \sqrt{5}\right)^2$

112. $\sqrt{288t} + \sqrt{80t} - \sqrt{128t}$

113. $\sqrt{\dfrac{72m^8}{25m^3}}$

114. $\left(\sqrt{14x} + \sqrt{3}\right)\left(\sqrt{14x} - \sqrt{3}\right)$

115. $\sqrt[4]{3n^2}\,\sqrt[4]{27n^3}$

116. $\dfrac{\sqrt{y} - 2}{\sqrt{y} + 3}$

117. $\dfrac{\sqrt[3]{x}}{\sqrt[3]{9}}$

118. $\sqrt[5]{\dfrac{2}{243}}$

119. $\left(3\sqrt{2r} - 2\right)^2$

120. $\left(2\sqrt{3t} + 5\right)^2$

121. $\sqrt{x(x+3)}\sqrt{x^3(x+3)}$

122. $\sqrt{y^2(x+y)}\sqrt{(x+y)^3}$

123. $\dfrac{2z-1}{\sqrt{2z-1}}$

(*Hint:* Do not perform the multiplication of the numerators.)

124. $\dfrac{3t-1}{\sqrt{3t+1}}$

(*Hint:* Do not perform the multiplication of the numerators.)

Look Alikes . . .

125. a. $\left(3\sqrt{a}\right)^2$ **b.** $\left(3 + \sqrt{a}\right)^2$

126. a. $\left(9\sqrt{x-5}\right)^2$ **b.** $\left(9 + \sqrt{x-5}\right)^2$

127. a. $\left(\sqrt{m-6}\right)^2$ **b.** $\left(\sqrt{m} - 6\right)^2$

128. a. $\dfrac{1}{\sqrt{xy}}$ **b.** $\dfrac{1}{\sqrt{x}+\sqrt{y}}$

APPLICATIONS

129. Statistics. An example of a normal distribution curve, or *bell-shaped* curve, is shown. A fraction that is part of the equation that models this curve

is $\dfrac{1}{\sigma\sqrt{2\pi}}$, where σ is a letter from the Greek alphabet. Rationalize the denominator of the fraction.

130. Analytical Geometry. The length of the perpendicular segment drawn from $(-2, 2)$ to the line with equation $2x - 4y = 4$ is given by

$$L = \frac{|2(-2) + (-4)(2) + (-4)|}{\sqrt{(2)^2 + (-4)^2}}$$

Find L. Express the result in simplified radical form. Then give an approximation to the nearest tenth.

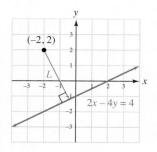

131. Trigonometry. In trigonometry, we often must find the ratio of the lengths of two sides of right triangles. Use the information in the illustration to find the ratio

$$\frac{\text{length of side } AC}{\text{length of side } AB}$$

Write the result in simplified radical form.

132. Engineering. Refer to the illustration below that shows a block connected to two walls by springs. A measure of how fast the block will oscillate when the spring system is set in motion is given by the formula $\omega = \sqrt{\dfrac{k_1 + k_2}{m}}$ where k_1 and k_2 indicate the stiffness of the springs and m is the mass of the block. Rationalize the right side and restate the formula.

WRITING

133. Consider $\dfrac{\sqrt{3}}{\sqrt{7}} = \dfrac{\sqrt{3}}{\sqrt{7}} \cdot \dfrac{\sqrt{7}}{\sqrt{7}}$. Explain why the expressions on the left side and the right side of the equation are equal.

134. To rationalize the denominator of $\dfrac{\sqrt[4]{12}}{\sqrt[4]{3}}$, why wouldn't we multiply the numerator and denominator by $\dfrac{\sqrt[4]{3}}{\sqrt[4]{3}}$?

135. Explain why $\dfrac{\sqrt[3]{12}}{\sqrt[3]{5}}$ is not in simplified form.

136. Explain why $\sqrt{\dfrac{3a}{11k}}$ is not in simplified form.

137. Explain why $\sqrt{m} \cdot \sqrt{m} = m$ but $\sqrt[3]{m} \cdot \sqrt[3]{m} \neq m$. Assume that m represents a positive number.

138. Explain why the product of $\sqrt{m} + 3$ and $\sqrt{m} - 3$ does not contain a radical.

REVIEW

Solve each equation.

139. $\dfrac{8}{b-2} + \dfrac{3}{2-b} = -\dfrac{1}{b}$

140. $\dfrac{2}{x-2} + \dfrac{1}{x+1} = \dfrac{1}{(x+1)(x-2)}$

CHALLENGE PROBLEMS

141. Multiply: $\sqrt{2} \cdot \sqrt[3]{2}$. (*Hint:* Keep in mind two things. The indices (plural for *index*) must be the same to use the product rule for radicals, and radical expressions can be written using rational exponents.)

142. Show that $\dfrac{\sqrt[3]{a^2} + \sqrt[3]{a}\sqrt[3]{b} + \sqrt[3]{b^2}}{\sqrt[3]{a^2} + \sqrt[3]{a}\sqrt[3]{b} + \sqrt[3]{b^2}}$ can be used to rationalize the denominator of $\dfrac{1}{\sqrt[3]{a} - \sqrt[3]{b}}$.

SECTION 9.5

OBJECTIVES

1 Solve equations containing one radical.

2 Solve equations containing two radicals.

3 Solve formulas containing radicals.

Solving Radical Equations

ARE YOU READY?

The following problems review some basic skills that are needed when solving radical equations.

1. Simplify: **a.** $\left(\sqrt{x-1}\right)^2$
   b. $\left(\sqrt[3]{x^3+7}\right)^3$

2. Simplify: $\left(3\sqrt{2x+5}\right)^2$

3. Expand: $(x-4)^2$

4. Solve: $x^2 - 6x - 27 = 0$

5. Expand: $(x+2)^3$

6. Multiply: $\left(2-\sqrt{x}\right)^2$

When we solve equations containing fractions, we clear them of the fractions by multiplying both sides by the LCD. To solve equations containing radical expressions, we take a similar approach. The first step is to clear them of the radicals by raising both sides to a power.

1 Solve Equations Containing One Radical.

Radical equations contain at least one radical expression with a variable in the radicand. Some examples are

$$\sqrt{x+3} = 4 \qquad \sqrt[3]{x^3+7} = x+1 \qquad \sqrt{x} + \sqrt{x+2} = 2$$

To **solve a radical equation,** we find all the values of the variable that make the equation true. The goal when solving a radical equation is to use the following **power rule** to find an equivalent equation that we already know how to solve, such as a linear equation in one variable or a quadratic equation.

The Power Rule for Solving Radical Equations

If we raise two equal quantities to the same power, the results are equal quantities.
If x, y, and n are real numbers and $x = y$, then

$$x^n = y^n \quad \text{for any exponent } n.$$

If both sides of an equation are raised to the same power, all solutions of the original equation are also solutions of the new equation. However, the resulting equation might not be equivalent to the original equation. For example, if we square both sides of the equation $x = 3$ with a solution set of $\{3\}$, we obtain the equation $x^2 = 9$ with a solution set of $\{3, -3\}$.

The equations $x = 3$ and $x^2 = 9$ are not equivalent, because they have different solution sets. The solution -3 of $x^2 = 9$ does not satisfy the equation $x = 3$. Since raising both sides of an equation to the same power can produce an equation with proposed solutions that don't satisfy the original equation, **we must always check each proposed solution in the original equation** and discard any **extraneous solutions.**

When we use the power rule to solve square root radical equations, it produces expressions of the form $\left(\sqrt{a}\right)^2$. We have seen that when this expression is simplified, the radical symbol is removed.

Caution

A similar warning about checking proposed solutions was given in Chapter 7 when we solved rational equations, such as:

$$\frac{11x}{x-5} = 6 + \frac{55}{x-5}$$

The Square of a Square Root

For any nonnegative real number a, $\left(\sqrt{a}\right)^2 = a$.

Here are some examples of the square of a square root. Notice how squaring such an expression *removes the square root symbol.*

$$\left(\sqrt{4n}\right)^2 = 4n, \qquad \left(\sqrt{x-3}\right)^2 = x-3, \qquad \text{and} \qquad \left(\sqrt{5a+8}\right)^2 = 5a+8$$

EXAMPLE 1   Solve: $\sqrt{x+3} = 4$

Strategy   We will use the power rule and square both sides of the equation.

Why   Squaring both sides will produce, on the left side, the expression $\left(\sqrt{x+3}\right)^2$ that simplifies to $x+3$. This step clears the equation of the radical.

Solution

$\sqrt{x+3} = 4$	This is the equation to solve.
$\left(\sqrt{x+3}\right)^2 = (4)^2$	To clear the equation of the square root, square both sides.
$x + 3 = 16$	Perform the operations on each side.
$x = 13$	Solve the resulting linear equation by subtracting 3 from both sides.

The Language of Algebra

When we square both sides of an equation, we are **raising both sides to the second power.**

We must check the proposed solution 13 to see whether it satisfies the original equation.

The Language of Algebra

Proposed solutions are also called **potential** or **possible** solutions.

Evaluate the left side. Do not square both sides when checking!

Check:

$\sqrt{x+3} = 4$	This is the original equation.
$\sqrt{13+3} \overset{?}{=} 4$	Substitute 13 for x.
$\sqrt{16} \overset{?}{=} 4$	
$4 = 4$	True

Since 13 satisfies the original equation, it is the solution. The solution set is {13}.

Self Check 1   Solve: $\sqrt{a-2} = 3$

Now Try ▶ Problems 15 and 19

The method used in Example 1 to solve a radical equation containing a square root can be generalized, as follows.

Solving an Equation Containing Radicals

1. Isolate a radical term on one side of the equation.
2. Raise both sides of the equation to the power that is the same as the index of the radical.
3. If it still contains a radical, go back to step 1. If it does not contain a radical, solve the resulting equation.
4. Check the proposed solutions in the original equation.

EXAMPLE 2   **Free Fall.**   The distance d in feet that an object will fall in t seconds is given by the formula $t = \sqrt{\frac{d}{16}}$. If the designers of the amusement park attraction want the riders to experience 3 seconds of vertical free fall, what length of vertical drop is needed?

Strategy   We will begin by substituting 3 for the time t in the formula.

Why   We can then solve the resulting radical equation in one variable to find the unknown distance d.

Solution

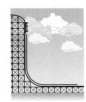

$$t = \sqrt{\dfrac{d}{16}}$$ This is the given formula.

$$3 = \sqrt{\dfrac{d}{16}}$$ Substitute 3 for t. Here the radical is isolated on the right side.

$$(3)^2 = \left(\sqrt{\dfrac{d}{16}}\right)^2$$ To clear the equation of the square root, square both sides.

$$9 = \dfrac{d}{16}$$ Perform the operations on each side.

$$144 = d$$ Solve the resulting equation by multiplying both sides by 16.

The amount of vertical drop needs to be 144 feet.

Caution

When using the power rule, don't forget to raise both sides to the same power. For this example, a common error would be to write

$$3 = \left(\sqrt{\dfrac{d}{16}}\right)^2$$

Self Check 2   **Free Fall.**   How long a vertical drop is needed if the riders are to free fall for 3.5 seconds?

Now Try ▶ Problem 105

When solving radical equations, always isolate a radical term before using the power rule.

EXAMPLE 3   Solve: $\sqrt{3x + 1} + 1 = x$

Strategy   Since 1 is outside the square root symbol, there are two terms on the left side of the equation. To isolate the radical term, we will subtract 1 from both sides.

Why   This will put the equation in a form in which we can square both sides to clear the radical.

Solution

$$\sqrt{3x + 1} + 1 = x$$ This is the equation to solve.

$$\sqrt{3x + 1} = x - 1$$ To isolate the radical on the left side, subtract 1 from both sides.

$$\left(\sqrt{3x + 1}\right)^2 = (x - 1)^2$$ Square both sides to eliminate the square root. Don't forget the parentheses.

$$3x + 1 = x^2 - 2x + 1$$ On the right side, use a special-product formula to square the binomial: $(x - 1)^2 = x^2 - 2x + 1$. The resulting equation is quadratic.

$$0 = x^2 - 5x$$ To get 0 on the left side, subtract 3x and 1 from both sides.

$$0 = x(x - 5)$$ Factor out the GCF, x.

$$x = 0 \quad \text{or} \quad x - 5 = 0$$ Set each factor equal to 0.

$$x = 0 \quad | \quad \quad x = 5$$

Caution

If both sides of the equation in Example 3 are squared, as is, the radical is not cleared. In fact, the equation becomes more complicated.

$$\left(\sqrt{3x + 1} + 1\right)^2 = (x)^2$$
$$3x + 1 + 2\sqrt{3x + 1} + 1 = x^2$$

We must check each proposed solution to see whether it satisfies the original equation.

Success Tip

Even if you are certain that no algebraic mistakes were made when solving a radical equation, you must still check your solutions. Raising both sides to an even power can introduce extraneous solutions that must be discarded.

This is the check for **0**:

$$\sqrt{3x + 1} + 1 = x$$
$$\sqrt{3(0) + 1} + 1 \overset{?}{=} 0$$
$$\sqrt{1} + 1 \overset{?}{=} 0$$
$$2 = 0 \quad \text{False}$$

This is the check for **5**:

$$\sqrt{3x + 1} + 1 = x$$ This is the original equation.
$$\sqrt{3(5) + 1} + 1 \overset{?}{=} 5$$
$$\sqrt{16} + 1 \overset{?}{=} 5$$
$$5 = 5 \quad \text{True}$$

The proposed solution 0 does not check; it must be discarded. Since the only solution is 5, the solution set is $\{5\}$.

Self Check 3   Solve: $\sqrt{4x + 1} + 1 = x$

Now Try ▶ Problems 23 and 27

Using Your Calculator ▶ Solving Radical Equations

To find solutions for $\sqrt{3x + 1} + 1 = x$ with a graphing calculator, we graph the functions $f(x) = \sqrt{3x + 1} + 1$ and $g(x) = x$, as in figure (a). We then trace to find the approximate x-coordinate of their intersection point, as in figure (b). After repeated zooms, we will see that $x = 5$.

We also can use the INTERSECT feature to approximate the point of intersection of the graphs. See figure (c). The intersection point of (**5**, 5), with x-coordinate **5**, implies that 5 is a solution of the radical equation.

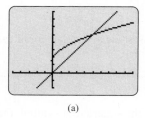
(a)

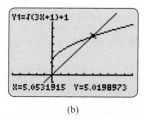
(b)

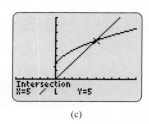
(c)

EXAMPLE 4   Solve: $\sqrt{3x} + 8 = 2$

Strategy   Since 8 is outside the square root symbol, there are two terms on the left side of the equation. To isolate the radical, we will subtract 8 from both sides.

Why   This will put the equation in a form in which we can square both sides to clear the radical.

Solution

$$\sqrt{3x} + 8 = 2 \qquad \text{This is the equation to solve.}$$
$$\sqrt{3x} = -6 \qquad \text{To isolate the radical on the left side, subtract 8 from both sides.}$$
$$\left(\sqrt{3x}\right)^2 = (-6)^2 \qquad \text{Square both sides to eliminate the square root.}$$
$$3x = 36 \qquad \text{Perform the operations on each side.}$$
$$x = 12 \qquad \text{To solve the resulting linear equation, divide both sides by 3.}$$

Success Tip

After isolating the radical, we obtained the equation $\sqrt{3x} = -6$. Since the principal square root of a number cannot be negative, we immediately know that $\sqrt{3x} + 8 = 2$ has no solution.

We check the proposed solution 12 in the original equation.

$$\sqrt{3x} + 8 = 2$$
$$\sqrt{3(12)} + 8 \overset{?}{=} 2 \qquad \text{Substitute 12 for } x.$$
$$\sqrt{36} + 8 \overset{?}{=} 2$$
$$6 + 8 \overset{?}{=} 2$$
$$14 = 2 \quad \text{False}$$

Since 12 does not satisfy the original equation, it is extraneous. The equation $\sqrt{3x} + 8 = 2$ has no solution. The solution set is $\varnothing$.

Self Check 4   Solve: $\sqrt{a - 9} + 3 = 0$

Now Try ▶ Problem 31

Recall the following property of radicals from Section 9.4.

The *n*th Power of the *n*th Root	If $\sqrt[n]{a}$ is a real number, $$\left(\sqrt[n]{a}\right)^n = a$$

Here are some examples of the cube of a cube root, and the fourth power of a fourth root. Notice how raising each expression to the appropriate power *removes the radical symbol.*

$$\left(\sqrt[3]{5x}\right)^3 = 5x \qquad \left(\sqrt[3]{2a-11}\right)^3 = 2a - 11 \qquad \left(\sqrt[4]{6-y}\right)^4 = 6 - y$$

The power rule and the *n*th power of the *n*th root property can be used in combination to solve radical equations that involve cube roots, fourth roots, fifth roots, and so on.

EXAMPLE 5 Solve: $(x^3 + 7)^{1/3} = x + 1$

Strategy We will use the definition of a fractional exponent with numerator 1 to rewrite the given equation as an equivalent radical equation.

Why Then we can use the equation-solving strategy of this section to find the solution(s).

Solution Recall from Section 9.2 that $x^{1/n} = \sqrt[n]{x}$. Thus, we can replace $(x^3 + 7)^{1/3}$ on the left side of the given equation with $\sqrt[3]{x^3 + 7}$.

Success Tip

Be careful cubing the binomial $x + 1$.
$$(x+1)^3 \neq x^3 + 1^3$$

$(x^3 + 7)^{1/3} = x + 1$	This is the equation to solve.
$\sqrt[3]{x^3 + 7} = x + 1$	Write $(x^3 + 7)^{1/3}$ using radical notation.
$\left(\sqrt[3]{x^3 + 7}\right)^3 = (x + 1)^3$	Cube both sides to eliminate the cube root. Don't forget the parentheses.
$x^3 + 7 = x^3 + 3x^2 + 3x + 1$	Perform the operations on each side. On the right: $(x + 1)^3 = (x + 1)(x + 1)^2$.
$0 = 3x^2 + 3x - 6$	To get 0 on the left side, subtract x^3 and 7 from both sides. This is a quadratic equation.
$0 = x^2 + x - 2$	Divide both sides by 3.
$0 = (x + 2)(x - 1)$	Factor the trinomial.
$x + 2 = 0 \quad$ or $\quad x - 1 = 0$	Set each factor equal to 0.
$x = -2 \qquad\qquad x = 1$	Solve each linear equation.

Success Tip

Raising both sides of an equation to an even power may not produce an equivalent equation. Raising both sides to an odd power does produce an equivalent equation and, in such cases, there will be no extraneous solutions. However, it is still recommended that all proposed solutions be checked regardless of the type of root involved.

We check each proposed solution, -2 and 1, to see whether they satisfy the original equation.

Check:

$$(x^3 + 7)^{1/3} = x + 1 \qquad\qquad (x^3 + 7)^{1/3} = x + 1$$
$$\sqrt[3]{x^3 + 7} = x + 1 \qquad\qquad \sqrt[3]{x^3 + 7} = x + 1$$
$$\sqrt[3]{(-2)^3 + 7} \overset{?}{=} -2 + 1 \qquad\qquad \sqrt[3]{1^3 + 7} \overset{?}{=} 1 + 1$$
$$\sqrt[3]{-8 + 7} \overset{?}{=} -1 \qquad\qquad \sqrt[3]{1 + 7} \overset{?}{=} 2$$
$$\sqrt[3]{-1} \overset{?}{=} -1 \qquad\qquad \sqrt[3]{8} \overset{?}{=} 2$$
$$-1 = -1 \quad \text{True} \qquad\qquad 2 = 2 \quad \text{True}$$

Both -2 and 1 satisfy the original equation. Thus, the solution set is $\{-2, 1\}$.

Self Check 5 Solve: $(x^3 + 8)^{1/3} = x + 2$

Now Try ▶ Problems 35 and 39

EXAMPLE 6 Let $f(x) = \sqrt[4]{2x + 1}$. For what value(s) of x is $f(x) = 5$?

Strategy We will substitute 5 for $f(x)$ and solve the equation $5 = \sqrt[4]{2x + 1}$. To do so, we will raise both sides of the equation to the fourth power.

Why Raising both sides to the fourth power will produce, on the right side, the expression $\left(\sqrt[4]{2x + 1}\right)^4$ that simplifies to $2x + 1$. This step clears the equation of the radical.

Solution To find the value(s) for which $f(x) = 5$, we substitute 5 for $f(x)$ and solve for x.

$$f(x) = \sqrt[4]{2x + 1}$$

$$5 = \sqrt[4]{2x + 1} \qquad \text{This is the equation to solve.}$$

Since the equation contains a fourth root, we raise both sides to the fourth power to solve for x.

$$(5)^4 = \left(\sqrt[4]{2x + 1}\right)^4 \qquad \text{Use the power rule to clear the radical.}$$

$$625 = 2x + 1 \qquad \text{Perform the operations on each side.}$$

$$624 = 2x \qquad \text{To solve the resulting equation, subtract 1 from both sides.}$$

$$312 = x \qquad \text{Divide both sides by 2.}$$

If $x = 312$, then $f(x) = 5$. Verify this by evaluating $f(312)$ using a calculator, if necessary.

Self Check 6 Let $g(x) = \sqrt[5]{10x + 1}$. For what value(s) of x is $g(x) = 1$?

Now Try ▶ Problem 43

2 Solve Equations Containing Two Radicals.

To solve an equation containing two radicals, we want to have one radical on the left side and one radical on the right side.

EXAMPLE 7 Solve: $\sqrt{5x + 9} = 2\sqrt{3x + 4}$

Strategy We will square both sides to clear the equation of both radicals.

Why We can square both sides immediately since each radical is isolated on one side of the equation.

Solution

$$\sqrt{5x + 9} = 2\sqrt{3x + 4} \qquad \text{This is the equation to solve.}$$

$$\left(\sqrt{5x + 9}\right)^2 = \left(2\sqrt{3x + 4}\right)^2 \qquad \text{Square both sides to eliminate the radicals.}$$

$$5x + 9 = 2^2\left(\sqrt{3x + 4}\right)^2 \qquad \text{Simplify on the left. On the right, raise each factor of the product } 2\sqrt{3x + 4} \text{ to the second power.}$$

$$5x + 9 = 4(3x + 4) \qquad \text{Perform the operations on the right.}$$

$$5x + 9 = 12x + 16 \qquad \text{To solve the resulting linear equation, distribute the multiplication by 4.}$$

$$-7 = 7x \qquad \text{Subtract 5x and 16 from both sides.}$$

$$-1 = x \qquad \text{Divide both sides by 7.}$$

Caution

When finding $\left(2\sqrt{3x + 4}\right)^2$, remember to square both of the factors, 2 and $\sqrt{3x + 4}$, to get:

$$2^2\left(\sqrt{3x + 4}\right)^2$$

This is an application of the power of a product rule for exponents:

$$(xy)^n = x^n y^n$$

We check the solution by substituting -1 for x in the original equation.

$$\sqrt{5x + 9} = 2\sqrt{3x + 4}$$

$$\sqrt{5(-1) + 9} \stackrel{?}{=} 2\sqrt{3(-1) + 4} \qquad \text{Substitute } -1 \text{ for } x.$$

$$\sqrt{4} \stackrel{?}{=} 2\sqrt{1}$$

$$2 = 2 \qquad \text{True}$$

The solution is -1 and the solution set is $\{-1\}$.

Self Check 7   Solve: $\sqrt{x-4} = 2\sqrt{x-16}$

Now Try ▶ Problem 49

When more than one radical appears in an equation, we often must use the power rule more than once.

EXAMPLE 8   Solve: $\sqrt{x} + \sqrt{x+2} = 2$

Strategy   We will isolate $\sqrt{x+2}$ on the left side of the equation and square both sides to eliminate it. After simplifying the resulting equation, we will isolate the remaining radical term and square both sides a second time to eliminate it.

Why   Each time that we square both sides, we are able to clear the equation of one radical.

Solution

$$\sqrt{x} + \sqrt{x+2} = 2 \qquad \text{This is the equation to solve.}$$

$$\sqrt{x+2} = 2 - \sqrt{x} \qquad \text{To isolate } \sqrt{x+2}, \text{ subtract } \sqrt{x} \text{ from both sides.}$$

$$\left(\sqrt{x+2}\right)^2 = \left(2 - \sqrt{x}\right)^2 \qquad \text{Square both sides to eliminate the square root on the left side.}$$

$$x + 2 = \left(2 - \sqrt{x}\right)^2 \qquad \text{Perform the operation on the left side.}$$

Success Tip

Note in this example that we isolate the more complicated radical term, $\sqrt{x+2}$. As a result, we work with the less complicated radical term $\sqrt{x}$ when applying the special-product rule.

Caution

When finding $\left(2 - \sqrt{x}\right)^2$, it is like squaring a binomial. Remember to use a special-product rule (or FOIL). **Do not just square the first term and the last term.**

$$\left(2 - \sqrt{x}\right)^2 \neq 4 + x$$

To square the expression $2 - \sqrt{x}$ on the right side, we can use a special-product rule:

$$x + 2 = \underbrace{2^2}_{\substack{\text{Square} \\ \text{the first} \\ \text{term, 2.}}} - \underbrace{2(2)\left(\sqrt{x}\right)}_{\substack{\text{Twice the} \\ \text{product of} \\ \text{both terms.}}} + \underbrace{\left(\sqrt{x}\right)^2}_{\substack{\text{Square the} \\ \text{last term,} \\ \sqrt{x}.}}$$

$$x + 2 = 4 - 4\sqrt{x} + x$$

Since the equation still contains a radical, we need to square both sides again. Before doing that, we must isolate the radical on one side.

$$2 = 4 - 4\sqrt{x} \qquad \text{Subtract } x \text{ from both sides.}$$

$$-2 = -4\sqrt{x} \qquad \text{To isolate the radical term } -4\sqrt{x}, \text{ subtract 4 from both sides.}$$

$$\frac{1}{2} = \sqrt{x} \qquad \text{To isolate the radical, divide both sides by } -4.$$

$$\left(\frac{1}{2}\right)^2 = \left(\sqrt{x}\right)^2 \qquad \text{To eliminate the radical, square both sides again.}$$

$$\frac{1}{4} = x \qquad \text{Perform the operations on each side.}$$

Check:
$$\sqrt{x} + \sqrt{x+2} = 2 \qquad \text{This is the original equation.}$$

$$\sqrt{\frac{1}{4}} + \sqrt{\frac{1}{4} + 2} \stackrel{?}{=} 2 \qquad \text{Substitute } \tfrac{1}{4} \text{ for } x.$$

$$\frac{1}{2} + \sqrt{\frac{9}{4}} \stackrel{?}{=} 2 \qquad \text{Think of 2 as } \tfrac{8}{4} \text{ and add: } \tfrac{1}{4} + \tfrac{8}{4} = \tfrac{9}{4}.$$

$$\frac{1}{2} + \frac{3}{2} \stackrel{?}{=} 2 \qquad \text{Evaluate } \sqrt{\tfrac{9}{4}}.$$

$$2 = 2 \qquad \text{True}$$

The result $\frac{1}{4}$ checks. The solution set is $\left\{\frac{1}{4}\right\}$.

Self Check 8 Solve: $\sqrt{a} + \sqrt{a + 3} = 3$

Now Try ▶ Problems 55 and 59

Using Your Calculator ▶ **Solving Radical Equations**

To find solutions for $\sqrt{x} + \sqrt{x + 2} = 4$ (an equation similar to Example 8) with a graphing calculator, we graph the functions $f(x) = \sqrt{x} + \sqrt{x + 2}$ and $g(x) = 4$. We then trace to find an approximation of the x-coordinate of their intersection point, as in figure (a). From the figure, we can see that $x \approx 2.98$. We can zoom to get better results.

Figure (b) shows that the INTERSECT feature gives the approximate coordinates of the point of intersection of the two graphs as (3.06, 4). Therefore, an approximate solution of the radical equation is 3.06. Check its reasonableness.

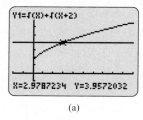
(a)

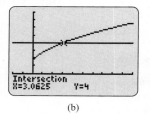
(b)

---

3 Solve Formulas Containing Radicals.

To *solve a formula for a variable* means to isolate that variable on one side of the equation, with all other quantities on the other side.

EXAMPLE 9 **Depreciation Rates.** Some office equipment that is now worth V dollars originally cost C dollars 3 years ago. The rate r at which it has depreciated is given by $r = 1 - \sqrt[3]{\dfrac{V}{C}}$. Solve the formula for C.

Strategy To isolate the radical, we will subtract 1 from both sides. We can then eliminate the radical by cubing both sides.

Why Cubing both sides will produce, on the right, the expression $\left(\sqrt[3]{\dfrac{V}{C}}\right)^3$ that simplifies to $\dfrac{V}{C}$. This step clears the equation of the radical.

Solution We begin by isolating the cube root on the right side of the equation.

$$r = 1 - \sqrt[3]{\frac{V}{C}} \qquad \text{This is the depreciation model.}$$

$$r - 1 = -\sqrt[3]{\frac{V}{C}} \qquad \text{Subtract 1 from both sides to isolate the radical.}$$

$$(r - 1)^3 = \left(-\sqrt[3]{\frac{V}{C}}\right)^3 \qquad \text{To eliminate the radical, cube both sides.}$$

$$(r - 1)^3 = -\frac{V}{C} \qquad \text{Simplify the right side.}$$

$$C(r - 1)^3 = -V \qquad \text{To clear the equation of the fraction, multiply both sides by } C.$$

$$C = -\frac{V}{(r - 1)^3} \qquad \text{To isolate } C, \text{ divide both sides by } (r - 1)^3.$$

Self Check 9 **Statistics.** A formula used in statistics to determine the size of a sample to obtain a desired degree of accuracy is $E = z_0 \sqrt{\frac{pq}{n}}$. Solve the formula for n.

Now Try ▶ Problem 67

SECTION 9.5 **STUDY SET**

VOCABULARY

Fill in the blanks.

1. Equations such as $\sqrt{x + 4} - 4 = 5$ and $\sqrt[3]{x + 1} = 12$ are called _____ equations.
2. To solve a radical equation, we find all the values of the variable that make the equation _____
3. When we square both sides of a radical equation, we say we are _____ both sides to the second power.
4. When solving equations containing radicals, first we _____ one radical expression on one side of the equation.
5. Proposed solutions of a radical equation that don't satisfy it are called _____ solutions.
6. To _____ a proposed solution means to substitute it into the original equation and see whether a true statement results.

CONCEPTS

7. Fill in the blanks.
   a. The power rule for solving radical equations states that if x, y, and n are real numbers and $x = y$, then
      $$x^{\square} = y^{\square}$$
   b. If $\sqrt[n]{a}$ is a real number, then $\left(\sqrt[n]{a}\right)^n = \square$.
8. Determine whether 6 is a solution of each radical equation.
   a. $\sqrt{x + 3} = x - 3$ b. $\sqrt[3]{5x - 3} + 9 = x$
9. What is the first step in solving each equation?
   a. $\sqrt{x + 11} = 5$
   b. $\sqrt[3]{5x + 4} + 3 = 30$
   c. $\sqrt{x + 8} - \sqrt{2x} = 1$
10. Simplify each expression.
   a. $\left(\sqrt{x}\right)^2$ b. $\left(\sqrt{x - 5}\right)^2$
   c. $\left(\sqrt[3]{4x - 8}\right)^3$ d. $\left(\sqrt[4]{8x}\right)^4$
   e. $\left(4\sqrt{2x}\right)^2$ f. $\left(3\sqrt[3]{x + 1}\right)^3$
11. Find: $\left(\sqrt{x} - 3\right)^2$
12. Find: $\left(\sqrt{5x + 2} - 4\right)^2$

NOTATION

Complete each solution.

13. Solve: $\sqrt{3x + 3} - 1 = 5$
   $$\sqrt{3x + 3} = \square$$
   $$\left(\sqrt{3x + 3}\right)^{\square} = (6)^{\square}$$
   $$\square = 36$$
   $$3x = \square$$
   $$x = \square$$

   Does the proposed solution check?

14. Fill in the blanks. Write each radical equation using a rational exponent.
   a. $\sqrt{x + 10} + 5 = 15$ can be written $(x + 10)^{\square} + 5 = 15$
   b. $\sqrt[3]{2t + 4} = t - 1$ can be written $(2t + 4)^{\square} = t - 1$

GUIDED PRACTICE

Solve each equation. See Example 1.

15. $\sqrt{a - 3} = 1$ 16. $\sqrt{x - 10} = 1$
17. $\sqrt{4x + 5} = 5$ 18. $\sqrt{5x - 6} = 2$
19. $\sqrt{6x + 13} = 7$ 20. $\sqrt{6x + 1} = 5$
21. $\sqrt{\frac{1}{3}x - 2} = 8$ 22. $\sqrt{\frac{1}{2}x + 3} = 6$

Solve each equation. Write all proposed solutions. Cross out those that are extraneous. See Example 3.

23. $\sqrt{2x + 11} + 2 = x$ 24. $\sqrt{2a - 3} + 3 = a$
25. $\sqrt{2r - 3} + 9 = r$ 26. $\sqrt{-x + 2} + 2 = x$
27. $\sqrt{3t + 7} - t = 1$ 28. $\sqrt{t + 3} - t = 1$
29. $\sqrt{9 - a} - a = 3$ 30. $\sqrt{4 - a} - a = 2$

Solve each equation. Write all proposed solutions. Cross out those that are extraneous. See Example 4.

31. $\sqrt{5x + 10} = 8$ 32. $\sqrt{3x + 5} = 2$

33. $\sqrt{5 - x} + 10 = 9$ 34. $1 = 2 + \sqrt{4x + 75}$

Solve each equation. See Example 5.

35. $\sqrt[3]{7n - 1} = 3$ 36. $\sqrt[3]{12m + 4} = 4$

37. $\sqrt[3]{x^3 - 7} = x - 1$ 38. $\sqrt[3]{b^3 - 63} = b - 3$

39. $(m^3 + 26)^{1/3} = m + 2$ **40.** $(x^3 + 56)^{1/3} = x + 2$

41. $(5r + 14)^{1/3} = 4$ **42.** $(2b + 29)^{1/3} = 3$

See Example 6.

43. Let $f(x) = \sqrt[4]{3x + 1}$. For what value(s) of x is $f(x) = 4$?

44. Let $f(x) = \sqrt{2x^2 - 7x}$. For what value(s) of x is $f(x) = 2$?

45. Let $f(x) = \sqrt[3]{3x - 6}$. For what value(s) of x is $f(x) = -3$?

46. Let $f(x) = \sqrt[5]{4x - 4}$. For what value(s) of x is $f(x) = -2$?

Solve each equation. See Example 7.

47. $\sqrt{3x + 12} = \sqrt{5x - 12}$ **48.** $\sqrt{m + 4} = \sqrt{2m - 5}$

49. $2\sqrt{4x + 1} = \sqrt{x + 4}$ **50.** $\sqrt{6 - 2x} = 4\sqrt{x - 3}$

51. $\sqrt{6t + 9} = 3\sqrt{t}$ **52.** $\sqrt{12x + 24} = 6\sqrt{x}$

53. $(34x + 26)^{1/3} = 4(x - 1)^{1/3}$ **54.** $(a^2 + 2a)^{1/3} = 2(a - 1)^{1/3}$

Solve each equation. Write all proposed solutions. Cross out those that are extraneous. See Example 8.

55. $\sqrt{x - 5} + \sqrt{x} = 5$ **56.** $\sqrt{x - 7} + \sqrt{x} = 7$

57. $\sqrt{z + 3} - \sqrt{z} = 1$ **58.** $\sqrt{x + 12} + \sqrt{x} = 6$

59. $3 = \sqrt{y + 4} - \sqrt{y + 7}$ **60.** $3 = \sqrt{u - 3} - \sqrt{u}$

61. $2 = \sqrt{2u + 7} - \sqrt{u}$ **62.** $1 = \sqrt{4s + 5} - \sqrt{2s + 2}$

Solve each equation for the specified variable or expression. See Example 9.

63. $v = \sqrt{2gh}$ for h **64.** $d = 1.4\sqrt{h}$ for h

65. $T = 2\pi\sqrt{\dfrac{l}{32}}$ for l **66.** $d = \sqrt[3]{\dfrac{12V}{\pi}}$ for V

67. $r = \sqrt[3]{\dfrac{A}{P}} - 1$ for A **68.** $r = \sqrt[3]{\dfrac{A}{P}} - 1$ for P

69. $L_A = L_B\sqrt{1 - \dfrac{v^2}{c^2}}$ for v^2 **70.** $R_1 = \sqrt{\dfrac{A}{\pi} - R_2{}^2}$ for A

TRY IT YOURSELF

Solve each equation. Write all proposed solutions. Cross out those that are extraneous.

71. $2\sqrt{x} = \sqrt{5x - 16}$ **72.** $3\sqrt{x} = \sqrt{3x + 54}$

73. $\sqrt{x + 5} + \sqrt{x - 3} = 4$ **74.** $\sqrt{b + 7} - \sqrt{b - 5} = 2$

75. $n = (n^3 + n^2 - 1)^{1/3}$ **76.** $(m^4 + m^2 - 25)^{1/4} = m$

77. $\sqrt{y + 2} + y = 4$ **78.** $\sqrt{22y + 86} - y = 9$

79. $\sqrt[3]{x + 8} = -2$ **80.** $\sqrt[3]{x + 4} = -1$

81. $2 = \sqrt{x + 5} - \sqrt{x} + 1$ **82.** $4 = \sqrt{x + 8} - \sqrt{x} + 2$

83. $x = \dfrac{\sqrt{12x - 5}}{2}$ **84.** $x = \dfrac{\sqrt{16x - 12}}{2}$

85. $(n^2 + 6n + 3)^{1/2} = (n^2 - 6n - 3)^{1/2}$

86. $(m^2 - 12m - 3)^{1/2} = (m^2 + 12m + 3)^{1/2}$

87. $\sqrt{x - 5} - \sqrt{x + 3} = 4$ **88.** $\sqrt{x + 8} - \sqrt{x - 4} = -2$

89. $\sqrt[4]{10y + 6} = 2\sqrt[4]{y}$ **90.** $\sqrt[4]{21a + 39} = 3\sqrt[4]{a - 1}$

91. $\sqrt{-5x + 24} = 6 - x$ **92.** $-s - 3 = 2\sqrt{5 - s}$

93. $\sqrt{2x + 5} = 1$ **94.** $\sqrt{3x + 10} = 1$

95. $\sqrt{6x + 2} - \sqrt{5x + 3} = 0$ **96.** $\sqrt{5x + 2} - \sqrt{x + 10} = 0$

97. Let $f(x) = \sqrt{x + 16}$ and $g(x) = 7 - \sqrt{x + 9}$. Find all values of x for which $f(x) = g(x)$.

98. Let $s(t) = \sqrt{t + 8}$ and $h(t) = 6 - \sqrt{t - 4}$. Find all values of t for which $s(t) = h(t)$.

99. Let $f(x) = \sqrt[4]{x + 8} - \sqrt[4]{2x}$. Find all values of x for which $f(x) = 0$.

100. Let $h(a) = \sqrt[4]{a + 11} - \sqrt[4]{2a + 6}$. Find all values of a for which $h(a) = 0$.

Look Alikes . . .

101. a. $3\sqrt{5n - 9} = \sqrt{5n}$ **b.** $3 + \sqrt{5n - 9} = \sqrt{5n}$

102. a. $\sqrt{8 + a} = 2\sqrt{a}$ **b.** $\sqrt{8 + a} = 2 + \sqrt{a}$

103. a. $\sqrt{2x} - 10 = 0$ **b.** $\sqrt{2x} + 10 = 0$

104. a. $x^{1/2} + 6 = 8$ **b.** $x^{1/4} + 6 = 8$

APPLICATIONS

105. Highway Design. A curved road will accommodate traffic traveling s mph if the radius of the curve is r feet, according to the formula $s = 3\sqrt{r}$. If engineers expect 40-mph traffic, what radius should they specify? Give the result to the nearest foot.

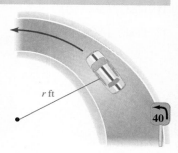

106. Forestry. The taller a lookout tower, the farther an observer can see. That distance d (called the *horizon distance,* measured in miles) is related to the height h of the observer (measured in feet) by the formula $d = 1.22\sqrt{h}$. How tall must a lookout tower be to see the edge of the forest, 25 miles away? (Round to the nearest foot.)

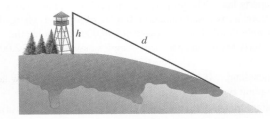

107. Wind Power. The power generated by a windmill is related to the velocity of the wind by the formula $v = \sqrt[3]{\dfrac{P}{0.02}}$ where P is the power (in watts) and v is the velocity of the wind (in mph). Find how much power the windmill is generating when the wind is 29 mph.

108. Diamonds. The *effective rate of interest* r earned by an investment is given by the formula $r = \sqrt[n]{\dfrac{A}{P}} - 1$ where P is the initial investment that grows to value A after n years. If a diamond buyer got \$4,000 for a 1.73-carat diamond that he had purchased 4 years earlier, and earned an annual rate of return of 6.5% on the investment, what did he originally pay for the diamond?

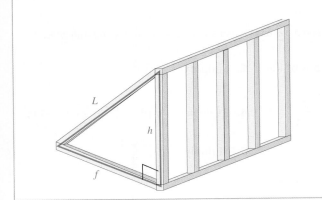

109.

from **Campus to Careers**

General Contractor

During construction, carpenters often brace walls as shown in the illustration, where the length L of the brace is given by the formula $L = \sqrt{f^2 + h^2}$. If a carpenter nails a 10-ft brace to the wall 6 feet above the floor, how far from the base of the wall should he nail the brace to the floor?

110. Theater Productions. The ropes, pulleys, and sandbags shown in the illustration are part of a mechanical system used to raise and lower scenery for a stage play. For the scenery to be in the proper position, the following formula must apply: $w_2 = \sqrt{w_1^2 + w_3^2}$. If $w_2 = 12.5$ lb and $w_3 = 7.5$ lb, find w_1.

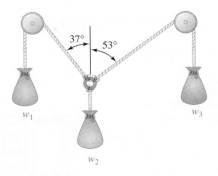

111. Supply and Demand. The number of wrenches that will be produced at a given price can be predicted by the formula $s = \sqrt{5x}$, where s is the supply (in thousands) and x is the price (in dollars). The demand d for wrenches can be predicted by the formula $d = \sqrt{100 - 3x^2}$. Find the equilibrium price—that is, find the price at which supply will equal demand.

112. Supply and Demand. The number of mirrors that will be produced at a given price can be predicted by the formula $s = \sqrt{23x}$, where s is the supply (in thousands) and x is the price (in dollars). The demand d for mirrors can be predicted by the formula $d = \sqrt{312 - 2x^2}$. Find the equilibrium price—that is, find the price at which supply will equal demand.

WRITING

113. What is wrong with the work shown below?

$$\text{Solve:} \quad \sqrt[3]{x+1} - 3 = 8$$
$$\sqrt[3]{x+1} = 11$$
$$\left(\sqrt[3]{x+1}\right)^3 = 11$$
$$x + 1 = 11$$
$$x = 10$$

114. The first step of a student's solution is shown below. What is a better way to begin the solution?

$$\text{Solve:} \quad \sqrt{x} + \sqrt{x+22} = 12$$
$$\left(\sqrt{x} + \sqrt{x+22}\right)^2 = 12^2$$

115. Explain the error in the following work.

$$\text{Solve:} \quad \sqrt{2y+1} = \sqrt{y+7} + 3$$
$$\left(\sqrt{2y+1}\right)^2 = \left(\sqrt{y+7} + 3\right)^2$$
$$2y + 1 = y + 7 + 9$$

116. Explain why it is immediately apparent that $\sqrt{8x - 7} = -2$ has no solution.

117. To solve the equation $\sqrt{2x + 7} = \sqrt{x}$ we need only square both sides once. To solve the equation $\sqrt{2x + 7} = \sqrt{x} + 2$ we have to square both sides twice. Why does the second equation require more work?

118. Explain how to solve $\sqrt{x-2} + 2 = 4$ using the graphs below.

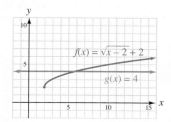

119. Explain how the table can be used to solve
$\sqrt{4x-3} - 2 = \sqrt{2x-5}$ if
$Y_1 = \sqrt{4x-3} - 2$ and
$Y_2 = \sqrt{2x-5}$.

X	Y1	Y2
2	.23607	ERROR
3	1	1
4	1.6056	1.7321
5	2.1231	2.2361
6	2.5826	2.6458
7	3	3
8	3.3852	3.3166

X=2

120. Explain how to use the graph of $f(x) = \sqrt[3]{x - 0.5} - 1$, shown in the illustration, to approximate the solution of
$\sqrt[3]{x - 0.5} = 1$.

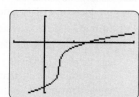

REVIEW

121. Lighting. The intensity of light from a lightbulb varies inversely as the square of the distance from the bulb. If you are 5 feet away from a bulb and the intensity is 40 foot-candles, what will the intensity be if you move 20 feet away from the bulb?

122. Property Tax. The property tax in a certain county varies directly as assessed valuation. If a tax of $1,575 is charged on a single-family home assessed at $90,000, determine the property tax on an apartment complex assessed at $312,000.

123. Typesetting. If 12-point type is 0.166044 inch tall, how tall is 30-point type?

124. Guitar Strings. The frequency of vibration of a string varies directly as the square root of the tension and inversely as the length of the string. Suppose a string 2.5 feet long, under a tension of 16 pounds, vibrates 25 times per second. Find k, the constant of proportionality.

CHALLENGE PROBLEMS

Solve each equation. Write all proposed solutions. Cross out those that are extraneous.

125. $\sqrt[4]{x} = \sqrt{\dfrac{x}{4}}$

126. $\sqrt[3]{2x} = \sqrt{x}$

127. $\sqrt{x+2} + \sqrt{2x} = \sqrt{18-x}$

128. $\sqrt{8-x} - \sqrt{3x-8} = \sqrt{x-4}$

129. $\sqrt{2\sqrt{x+1}} = \sqrt{16-4x}$

130. $(2x-1)^{2/3} = x^{1/3}$

SECTION 9.6

Geometric Applications of Radicals

OBJECTIVES

1 Use the Pythagorean theorem to solve problems.

2 Solve problems involving 45°–45°–90° triangles.

3 Solve problems involving 30°–60°–90° triangles.

4 Use the distance formula to solve problems.

5 Find the midpoint of a line segment.

ARE YOU READY?

The following problems review some basic skills that are needed when working with special triangles.

1. What is the sum of the measures of the angles of any triangle?

2. Simplify: $\sqrt{3a^2}$

3. Rationalize the denominator: $\dfrac{25}{\sqrt{3}}$

4. Evaluate: $\sqrt{(9-4)^2 + (-1-11)^2}$

5. Approximate to the nearest hundredth: $2\sqrt{3}$

6. Multiply: $2 \cdot \dfrac{7\sqrt{3}}{3}$

We will now consider applications of square roots in geometry. Then we will find the distance between two points on a rectangular coordinate system, using a formula that contains a square root. We begin by considering an important theorem about right triangles.

1 Use the Pythagorean Theorem to Solve Problems.

If we know the lengths of two legs of a right triangle, we can find the length of the **hypotenuse** (the side opposite the 90° angle) by using the **Pythagorean theorem.**

The Pythagorean Theorem

If a and b are the lengths of two legs of a right triangle and c is the length of the hypotenuse,

$$a^2 + b^2 = c^2$$

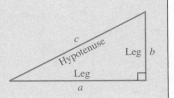

In words, the Pythagorean theorem is expressed as follows:

In a right triangle, the sum of the squares of the lengths of two legs is equal to the square of the length of the hypotenuse.

Suppose the right triangle shown in the margin has legs of length 3 and 4 units. To find the length of the hypotenuse, we use the **Pythagorean equation.**

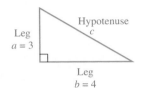

$$a^2 + b^2 = c^2$$
$$3^2 + 4^2 = c^2 \quad \text{Substitute 3 for } a \text{ and 4 for } b.$$
$$9 + 16 = c^2$$
$$25 = c^2$$

To find c, we ask "What number, when squared, is equal to 25?" There are two such numbers: the positive square root of 25 and the negative square root of 25. Since c represents the length of the hypotenuse, and it cannot be negative, it follows that c is the positive square root of 25.

$$\sqrt{25} = c \quad \text{Recall that a radical symbol } \sqrt{} \text{ is used to represent}$$
$$\text{the positive, or principal, square root of a number.}$$
$$5 = c$$

The length of the hypotenuse is 5 units.

The Language of Algebra

A **theorem** is a mathematical statement that can be proved. The Pythagorean theorem is named after Pythagoras, a Greek mathematician who lived about 2,500 years ago. He is thought to have been the first to prove the theorem.

EXAMPLE 1

Firefighting. To fight a fire, the forestry department plans to clear a rectangular firebreak around the fire, as shown in the illustration on the left. Crews are equipped with mobile communications that have a 3,000-yard range. Can crews at points A and B remain in radio contact?

Strategy We will use the Pythagorean theorem to find the distance between points A and B.

Why If this distance is less than 3,000 yards, they can communicate. If it is greater than 3,000 yards, they cannot communicate.

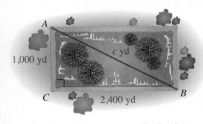

Solution The line segments connecting points A, B, and C form a right triangle. To find the distance c from point A to point B, we can use the Pythagorean theorem, substituting 2,400 for a and 1,000 for b and solving for c.

$$a^2 + b^2 = c^2 \quad \text{This is the Pythagorean equation.}$$
$$2,400^2 + 1,000^2 = c^2 \quad \text{Substitute for } a \text{ and } b.$$
$$5,760,000 + 1,000,000 = c^2 \quad \text{Evaluate each exponential expression.}$$
$$6,760,000 = c^2 \quad \text{Do the addition.}$$
$$\sqrt{6,760,000} = c \quad \text{If } c^2 = 6,760,000, \text{ then } c \text{ must be a square root of}$$
$$\text{6,760,000. Because } c \text{ represents a length, it must}$$
$$\text{be the positive square root of 6,760,000.}$$
$$2,600 = c \quad \text{Use a calculator to find the square root.}$$

Caution

When using the Pythagorean equation $a^2 + b^2 = c^2$, we can let a represent the length of either leg of the right triangle. We then let b represent the length of the other leg. The variable c must always represent the length of the hypotenuse.

The two crews are 2,600 yards apart. Because this distance is less than the 3,000-yard range of the radios, they can communicate by radio.

Self Check 1 **Firefighting.** In Example 1, can the crews communicate if $b = 1,500$ yards?

Now Try ▶ Problems 15 and 55

2 Solve Problems Involving 45°–45°–90° Triangles.

An **isosceles right triangle** is a right triangle with two legs of equal length. Isosceles right triangles have angle measures of 45°, 45°, and 90°. If we know the length of one leg of an isosceles right triangle, we can use the Pythagorean theorem to find the length of the hypotenuse. Since the triangle shown in the margin is a right triangle, we have

$$c^2 = a^2 + b^2 \qquad \text{This is the Pythagorean equation.}$$

$$c^2 = a^2 + a^2 \qquad \text{Both legs are } a \text{ units long, so replace } b \text{ with } a.$$

$$c^2 = 2a^2 \qquad \text{Combine like terms.}$$

$$c = \sqrt{2a^2} \qquad \text{If } c^2 = 2a^2, \text{ then } c \text{ must be a square root of } 2a^2. \text{ Because } c \text{ represents a length, it must be the positive square root of } 2a^2.$$

$$c = a\sqrt{2} \qquad \text{Simplify the radical: } \sqrt{2a^2} = \sqrt{2}\sqrt{a^2} = \sqrt{2}a = a\sqrt{2}.$$

Thus, **in an isosceles right triangle, the length of the hypotenuse is $\sqrt{2}$ times the length of one leg.**

EXAMPLE 2 If one leg of an isosceles right triangle is 10 feet long, find the exact length of the hypotenuse. Then approximate the length to two decimal places.

Strategy We will multiply the length of the known leg by $\sqrt{2}$.

Why The length of the hypotenuse of an isosceles right triangle is $\sqrt{2}$ times the length of one leg.

Solution Since the length of the hypotenuse is the length of a leg times $\sqrt{2}$, we have

$$c = 10\sqrt{2}$$

The exact length of the hypotenuse is $10\sqrt{2}$ feet. If we approximate to two decimal places, the length is 14.14 feet.

Self Check 2 Find the exact length of the hypotenuse of an isosceles right triangle if one leg is 12 meters long. Then approximate the length to two decimal places.

Now Try ▶ Problem 23

EXAMPLE 3 Find the exact length of each leg of the isosceles right triangle shown in the margin. Then approximate the lengths to two decimal places.

Strategy We will find the length of each leg of the triangle by substituting 25 for c in the formula $c = a\sqrt{2}$ and solving for a.

Why The variable a represents the unknown length of each leg of the triangle.

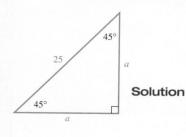

Solution

$$c = a\sqrt{2} \qquad \text{This is the formula for the length of the hypotenuse of an isosceles right triangle.}$$

$$25 = a\sqrt{2} \qquad \text{Substitute 25 for } c, \text{ the length of the hypotenuse.}$$

$$\frac{25}{\sqrt{2}} = \frac{a\sqrt{2}}{\sqrt{2}} \qquad \text{To isolate } a, \text{ undo the multiplication by } \sqrt{2} \text{ by dividing both sides by } \sqrt{2}.$$

$$\frac{25}{\sqrt{2}} = a \qquad \text{Simplify the right side.}$$

$$a = \frac{25}{\sqrt{2}} \qquad \text{Reverse the sides of the equation so that } a \text{ is on the left.}$$

$$a = \frac{25}{\sqrt{2}} \cdot \frac{\sqrt{2}}{\sqrt{2}} \qquad \text{Rationalize the denominator.}$$

$$a = \frac{25\sqrt{2}}{2} \qquad \text{Simplify the denominator: } \sqrt{2} \cdot \sqrt{2} = 2.$$

The exact length of each leg is $\frac{25\sqrt{2}}{2}$ units. If we approximate to two decimal places, the length is 17.68 units.

> **Self Check 3** Find the exact length of each leg of an isosceles right triangle if the length of the hypotenuse is 9 inches. Then approximate the lengths to two decimal places.
>
> **Now Try** ▶ Problem 27

3 Solve Problems Involving 30°–60°–90° Triangles.

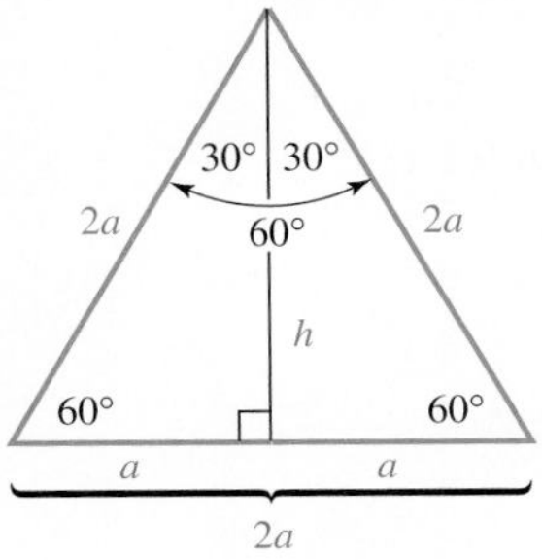

From geometry, we know that an **equilateral triangle** is a triangle with three sides of equal length and three 60° angles. Each side of the equilateral triangle shown in the margin is $2a$ units long. If an **altitude** (height) is drawn to its base, the altitude divides the base into two segments of equal length and divides the equilateral triangle into two 30°–60°–90° triangles. From the figure, we can see that the shorter leg of each 30°–60°–90° triangle (the side *opposite* the 30° angle) is a units long. Thus,

> **The length of the hypotenuse of a 30°–60°–90° triangle is twice as long as the shorter leg.**

We can discover another relationship between the legs of a 30°–60°–90° triangle if we find the length of the altitude h in the figure. We begin by applying the Pythagorean theorem to one of the 30°–60°–90° triangles.

$$a^2 + b^2 = c^2 \qquad \text{This is the Pythagorean equation.}$$

$$a^2 + h^2 = (2a)^2 \qquad \begin{array}{l} \text{The altitude is } h \text{ units long, so replace } b \text{ with } h. \\ \text{The hypotenuse is } 2a \text{ units long, so replace } c \text{ with } 2a. \end{array}$$

$$a^2 + h^2 = 4a^2 \qquad (2a)^2 = (2a)(2a) = 4a^2.$$

$$h^2 = 3a^2 \qquad \text{Subtract } a^2 \text{ from both sides.}$$

$$h = \sqrt{3a^2} \qquad \text{If } h^2 = 3a^2, \text{ then } h \text{ must be the positive square root of } 3a^2.$$

$$h = a\sqrt{3} \qquad \text{Simplify the radical: } \sqrt{3a^2} = \sqrt{3}\sqrt{a^2} = a\sqrt{3}.$$

We see that the altitude—the longer leg of the 30°–60°–90° triangle—is $\sqrt{3}$ times as long as the shorter leg. Thus,

> **The length of the longer leg of a 30°–60°–90° triangle is $\sqrt{3}$ times the length of the shorter leg.**

EXAMPLE 4 Find the length of the hypotenuse and the length of the longer leg of the 30°–60°–90° triangle shown in the margin.

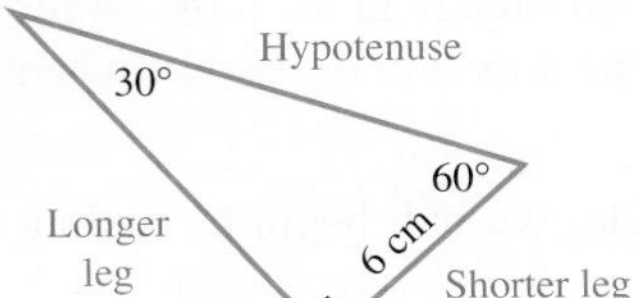

Strategy To find the length of the hypotenuse, we will multiply the length of the shorter leg by 2. To find the length of the longer leg, we will multiply the length of the shorter leg by $\sqrt{3}$.

Why These side-length relationships are true for any 30°–60°–90° triangle.

Solution Since the length of the hypotenuse of a 30°–60°–90° triangle is twice as long as the shorter leg, and the length of the shorter leg is 6 cm, the hypotenuse is $2 \cdot 6 = 12$ cm.

Since the length of the longer leg is $\sqrt{3}$ times the length of the shorter leg, and the length of the shorter leg is 6 cm, the longer leg is $6\sqrt{3}$ cm (about 10.39 cm).

Self Check 4 Find the length of the hypotenuse and the longer leg of a 30°–60°–90° triangle if the shorter leg is 8 centimeters long.

Now Try ▶ Problem 31

EXAMPLE 5 Find the length of the hypotenuse and the length of the shorter leg of the 30°–60°–90° triangle shown in the margin. Then approximate the lengths to two decimal places.

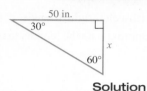

Strategy We will find the length of the shorter leg first.

Why Once we know the length of the shorter leg, we can multiply it by 2 to find the length of the hypotenuse.

Solution If we let $x =$ the length in inches of the shorter leg of the triangle, we can form an equation by translating the following statement:

The length of the longer leg of a 30°–60°–90° triangle	is	$\sqrt{3}$	times	the length of the shorter leg.
50	=	$\sqrt{3}$	$\cdot$	x

To find the length of the shorter leg, we solve the equation for x.

$$50 = \sqrt{3}x$$

$$\frac{50}{\sqrt{3}} = \frac{\sqrt{3}x}{\sqrt{3}} \quad \text{To isolate } x, \text{ divide both sides by } \sqrt{3}.$$

$$\frac{50}{\sqrt{3}} = x$$

The length of the shorter leg is exactly $\dfrac{50}{\sqrt{3}}$ inches. To write this number in simplified radical form, we rationalize the denominator.

$$\frac{50}{\sqrt{3}} \cdot \frac{\sqrt{3}}{\sqrt{3}} = \frac{50\sqrt{3}}{3}$$

Thus, the length of the shorter leg is exactly $\dfrac{50\sqrt{3}}{3}$ inches (about 28.87 inches).

Since the length of the hypotenuse of a 30°–60°–90° triangle is twice as long as the shorter leg, the hypotenuse is $2 \cdot \dfrac{50\sqrt{3}}{3} = \dfrac{100\sqrt{3}}{3}$ inches (about 57.74 inches).

Self Check 5 Find the length of the hypotenuse and the shorter leg of a 30°–60°–90° triangle if the longer leg is 15 feet long. Then approximate the lengths to two decimal places.

Now Try ▶ Problem 35

> **Success Tip**
>
> In a 30°–60°–90° triangle, the side opposite the 30° angle is the shorter leg, the side opposite the 60° angle is the longer leg, and the hypotenuse is opposite the 90° angle.

EXAMPLE 6 **Stretching Exercises.** A doctor prescribed the exercise shown in figure (a) on the next page. The patient was instructed to raise his leg to an angle of 60° and hold the position for 10 seconds. If the patient's leg is 36 inches long, how high off the floor will his foot be when his leg is held at the proper angle?

Strategy This situation is modeled by a 30°–60°–90° triangle. We will begin by finding the length of the shorter leg.

Why Once we know the length of the shorter leg, we can easily find the length of the longer leg, which represents the distance the patient's foot is off the ground.

Solution In figure (b), we see right triangle ABC, which models the situation. Since the length of the hypotenuse is twice as long as the side opposite the 30° angle, side AC is half as long as the hypotenuse. Since the hypotenuse is given to be 36 inches long, side AC must be 18 inches long.

Since the length of the longer leg (the leg opposite the 60° angle) is $\sqrt{3}$ times the length of the shorter leg (side AC), side BC is $18\sqrt{3}$, or about 31 inches long. So the patient's foot will be about 31 inches from the floor when his leg is in the proper position.

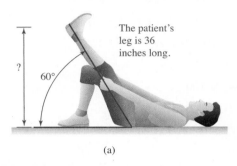

The patient's leg is 36 inches long.

(a)

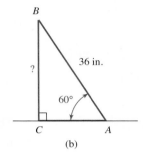

(b)

Self Check 6 **Stretching Exercises.** Refer to Example 6. The doctor prescribed the same exercise for a patient whose leg is 29 inches long. Find how high off the floor this patient's foot is when her leg is held at the proper angle.

Now Try ▶ Problems 39 and 61

4 Use the Distance Formula to Solve Problems.

With the **distance formula,** we can find the distance between any two points graphed on a rectangular coordinate system. To find the distance d between points $P(x_1, y_1)$ and $Q(x_2, y_2)$ shown in the figure on the right, we construct the right triangle PRQ. The distance between P and R is $|x_2 - x_1|$, and the distance between R and Q is $|y_2 - y_1|$. We apply the Pythagorean theorem to the right triangle PRQ to get

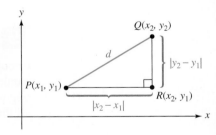

$$d^2 = |x_2 - x_1|^2 + |y_2 - y_1|^2$$
$$= (x_2 - x_1)^2 + (y_2 - y_1)^2 \qquad \text{Because } |x_2 - x_1|^2 = (x_2 - x_1)^2 \text{ and } |y_2 - y_1|^2 = (y_2 - y_1)^2$$

Because d represents the distance between two points, it must be equal to the positive square root of $(x_2 - x_1)^2 + (y_2 - y_1)^2$.

$$d = \sqrt{(x_2 - x_1)^2 + (y_2 - y_1)^2}$$

We call this result the *distance formula.*

Distance Formula ▼ The distance d between two points with coordinates (x_1, y_1) and (x_2, y_2) is given by
$$d = \sqrt{(x_2 - x_1)^2 + (y_2 - y_1)^2}$$

EXAMPLE 7   Find the distance between the points: **a.** $(-2, 3)$ and $(4, -5)$ **b.** $(27, 46)$ and $(33, 50)$

Strategy   We will use the distance formula.

Why   We know the x- and y-coordinates of both points.

Solution   **a.** To find the distance, we can use the distance formula by substituting 4 for x_2, -2 for x_1, -5 for y_2, and 3 for y_1.

$$d = \sqrt{(x_2 - x_1)^2 + (y_2 - y_1)^2}$$ This is the distance formula.

$$= \sqrt{[4 - (-2)]^2 + (-5 - 3)^2}$$ Substitute for x_1, x_2, y_1, and y_2.

$$= \sqrt{(4 + 2)^2 + (-5 - 3)^2}$$ Simplify within the parentheses.

$$= \sqrt{6^2 + (-8)^2}$$ Do the addition and subtraction.

$$= \sqrt{36 + 64}$$ Evaluate each exponential expression.

$$= \sqrt{100}$$ Do the addition.

$$= 10$$ Evaluate the square root.

The distance between the points is 10 units.

b. $$d = \sqrt{(x_2 - x_1)^2 + (y_2 - y_1)^2}$$ This is the distance formula.

$$d = \sqrt{(33 - 27)^2 + (50 - 46)^2}$$ Substitute 33 for x_2, 27 for x_1, 50 for y_2, and 46 for y_1.

$$= \sqrt{6^2 + 4^2}$$ Do the subtraction.

$$= \sqrt{52}$$ Evaluate: $6^2 + 4^2 = 36 + 16 = 52$.

$$= 2\sqrt{13}$$ Simplify: $\sqrt{52} = \sqrt{4 \cdot 13} = 2\sqrt{13}$.

The distance between the points is exactly $2\sqrt{13}$ units, which is about 7.21 units.

Self Check 7   Find the distance between the points: **a.** $(-2, -2)$ and $(3, 10)$
b. $(55, 29)$ and $(61, 32)$

Now Try ▶   Problems 47 and 49

5   Find the Midpoint of a Line Segment.

If point M in the figure on the right lies midway between point P and point Q, it is called the **midpoint** of line segment PQ. We call the points P and Q, the **endpoints** of the segment.

To distinguish between the coordinates of the endpoints of a line segment, we can use *subscript notation*. In the figure, the point P with coordinates (x_1, y_1) is read as "point P with coordinates x sub 1 and y sub 1," and the point Q with coordinates (x_2, y_2) is read as "point Q with coordinates x sub 2 and y sub 2."

To find the coordinates of point M, we find the average of the x-coordinates and the average of the y-coordinates of points P and Q. Using subscript notation, we can write the midpoint formula in the following way.

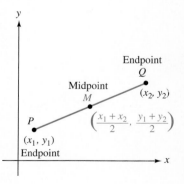

The Midpoint Formula   ▼   The **midpoint** of a line segment with endpoints (x_1, y_1) and (x_2, y_2) is the point with coordinates

$$\left(\frac{x_1 + x_2}{2}, \frac{y_1 + y_2}{2} \right)$$

EXAMPLE 8   Find the midpoint of the line segment with endpoints $(-2, 5)$ and $(4, -2)$.

Strategy   To find the coordinates of the midpoint, we find the average of the x-coordinates and the average of the y-coordinates of the endpoints.

Why   This is what is called for by the expressions $\frac{x_1 + x_2}{2}$ and $\frac{y_1 + y_2}{2}$ of the midpoint formula.

Solution   We can let $(x_1, y_1) = (-2, 5)$ and $(x_2, y_2) = (4, -2)$. After substituting these values into the expressions for the x- and y-coordinates in the midpoint formula, we evaluate each expression to find the coordinates of the midpoint.

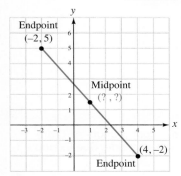

Find the x-coordinate of the midpoint:

$$\frac{x_1 + x_2}{2} = \frac{-2 + 4}{2}$$
$$= \frac{2}{2}$$
$$= 1$$

Find the y-coordinate of the midpoint:

$$\frac{y_1 + y_2}{2} = \frac{5 + (-2)}{2}$$
$$= \frac{3}{2}$$

Thus, the midpoint is $\left(1, \frac{3}{2}\right)$.

Self Check 8   Find the midpoint of the line segment with endpoints $(-1, 8)$ and $(5, 2)$.

Now Try ▶ Problem 57

EXAMPLE 9   The midpoint of the line segment joining $(-5, -3)$ and a point Q is the point $(-1, 2)$. Find the coordinates of point Q.

Strategy   As in Example 8, we will use the midpoint formula to find the unknown coordinates. However, this time, we need to find x_2 and y_2.

Why   We want to find the coordinates of one of the endpoints.

Solution   We can let $(x_1, y_1) = (-5, -3)$ and $(x_M, y_M) = (-1, 2)$, where x_M represents the x-coordinate and y_M represents the y-coordinate of the midpoint. To find the coordinates of point Q, we substitute for x_1, x_M, y_1, and y_M in the expressions for the coordinates in the midpoint formula and solve the resulting equations for x_2 and y_2.

$$x_M = \frac{x_1 + x_2}{2}$$

$$-1 = \frac{-5 + x_2}{2} \quad \text{Substitute.}$$

$$-2 = -5 + x_2 \quad \text{Multiply both sides by 2.}$$

$$3 = x_2 \quad \text{Add 5 to both sides.}$$

$$y_M = \frac{y_1 + y_2}{2} \quad \text{Read } x_M \text{ as "x sub M" and } y_M \text{ as "y sub M."}$$

$$2 = \frac{-3 + y_2}{2} \quad \text{Substitute.}$$

$$4 = -3 + y_2 \quad \text{Multiply both sides by 2.}$$

$$7 = y_2 \quad \text{Add 3 to both sides.}$$

Since $x_2 = 3$ and $y_2 = 7$, the coordinates of point Q are $(3, 7)$.

Self Check 9   The midpoint of the line segment joining $(-5, -3)$ and a point P is the point $(-2, 5)$. Find the coordinates of point P.

Now Try ▶ Problem 63

SECTION 9.6 **STUDY SET**

VOCABULARY

Fill in the blanks.

1. In a right triangle, the side opposite the 90° angle is called the

   _____ .

2. An _____ right triangle is a right triangle with two legs of equal length.

3. The _____ theorem states that in a right triangle, the sum of the squares of the lengths of the two legs is equal to the square of the hypotenuse.

4. An _____ triangle has three sides of equal length and three 60° angles.

CONCEPTS

Fill in the blanks.

5. If a and b are the lengths of the legs of a right triangle and c is the length of the hypotenuse, then ☐ + ☐ = ☐. This is called the Pythagorean _____ .

6. In any right triangle, the square of the hypotenuse is equal to the _____ of the squares of the two _____ .

7. In an isosceles right triangle, the length of the hypotenuse is ☐ times the length of one leg.

8. The shorter leg of a 30°–60°–90° triangle is _____ as long as the hypotenuse.

9. The length of the longer leg of a 30°–60°–90° triangle is ☐ times the length of the shorter leg.

10. In a 30°–60°–90° triangle, the shorter leg is opposite the ☐ angle, and the longer leg is opposite the ☐ angle.

11. The formula to find the distance between points (x_1, y_1) and (x_2, y_2) is $d = \sqrt{\boxed{} + \boxed{}}$.

12. Solve for c, where c represents the length of the hypotenuse of a right triangle. Simplify the result, if possible.

    a. $c^2 = 64$

    b. $c^2 = 15$

    c. $c^2 = 24$

NOTATION

Complete each solution.

13. Evaluate. Approximate to two decimal places.

$$\sqrt{(-1 - 3)^2 + [2 - (-4)]^2} = \sqrt{(-4)^2 + [\ \ ]^2}$$
$$= \sqrt{\boxed{}}$$
$$= \sqrt{\boxed{} \cdot 13}$$
$$= \boxed{}\sqrt{13}$$
$$\approx \boxed{}$$

14. Solve $8^2 + 4^2 = c^2$ and assume $c > 0$. Approximate to two decimal places.

$$\boxed{} + 16 = c^2$$
$$\boxed{} = c^2$$
$$\sqrt{\boxed{}} = \boxed{}$$
$$\sqrt{\boxed{} \cdot 5} = c$$
$$\boxed{}\sqrt{5} = c$$
$$c \ \boxed{} \ 8.94$$

GUIDED PRACTICE

The lengths of two sides of the right triangle ABC are given. Find the length of the missing side. See Example 1.

15. $a = 6$ ft and $b = 8$ ft

16. $a = 5$ in. and $b = 12$ in.

17. $a = 8$ ft and $b = 15$ ft

18. $a = 24$ yd and $b = 7$ yd

19. $b = 9$ ft and $c = 41$ ft

20. $b = 18$ m and $c = 82$ m

21. $a = 10$ cm and $c = 26$ cm

22. $a = 14$ in. and $c = 50$ in.

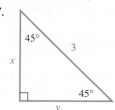

Find the missing side lengths in each triangle. Give the exact answer and then an approximation to two decimal places when appropriate. See Example 2.

23.

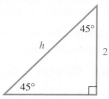

24.

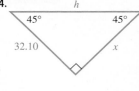

25. One leg of an isosceles right triangle is 3.2 feet long. Find the length of its hypotenuse. Give the exact answer and then an approximation to two decimal places.

26. One side of a square is $5\frac{1}{2}$ in. long. Find the length of its diagonal. Give the exact answer and then an approximation to two decimal places.

Find the missing side lengths in each triangle. Give the exact answer and then an approximation to two decimal places. See Example 3.

27.

28.

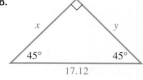

29. Photographs. The diagonal of a square photograph measures 10 inches. Find the length of one of its sides. Give the exact answer and then an approximation to two decimal places.

30. Parking Lots. The diagonal of a square parking lot is approximately 1,414 feet long.

    a. Find the length of one side of the parking lot. Round to the nearest foot.

    b. Find the approximate area of the parking lot.

Find the missing side lengths in each triangle. Give the exact answer and then an approximation to two decimal places, when appropriate. **See Example 4.**

31.

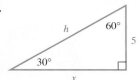

32.

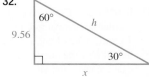

33. In a 30°–60°–90° triangle, the length of the leg opposite the 30° angle is 75 cm. Find the length of the leg opposite the 60° angle and the length of the hypotenuse. Give the exact answer and then an approximation to two decimal places, when appropriate.

34. In a 30°–60°–90° triangle, the length of the shorter leg is $5\sqrt{2}$ inches. Find the length of the hypotenuse and the length of the longer leg. Give the exact answer and then an approximation to two decimal places.

Find the missing lengths in each triangle. Give the exact answer and then an approximation to two decimal places. **See Example 5.**

35.

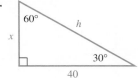

36.

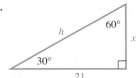

37. In a 30°–60°–90° right triangle, the length of the leg opposite the 60° angle is 55 millimeters. Find the length of the leg opposite the 30° angle and the length of the hypotenuse. Give the exact answer and then an approximation to two decimal places.

38. In a 30°–60°–90° right triangle, the length of the longer leg is 24 yards. Find the length of the hypotenuse and the length of the shorter leg. Give the exact answer and then an approximation to two decimal places.

Find the missing lengths in each triangle. Give the exact answer and then an approximation to two decimal places, when appropriate. **See Example 6.**

39.

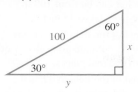

40.

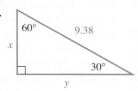

41. In a 30°–60°–90° right triangle, the length of the hypotenuse is 1.5 feet. To the nearest hundredth, find the length of the shorter leg and the length of the longer leg. Give the exact answer and then an approximation to two decimal places, when appropriate.

42. In a 30°–60°–90° right triangle, the length of the hypotenuse is $12\sqrt{3}$ inches. Find the length of the leg opposite the 30° angle and the length of the leg opposite the 60° angle. Give the exact answer and then an approximation to two decimal places, when appropriate.

Find the exact distance between each pair of points. **See Example 7.**

43. $(0, 0), (3, -4)$ **44.** $(0, 0), (-12, 16)$

45. $(-2, -8), (3, 4)$ **46.** $(-5, -2), (7, 3)$

47. $(6, 8), (12, 16)$ **48.** $(10, 4), (2, -2)$

49. $(-2, 1), (3, 4)$ **50.** $(2, -3), (4, -8)$

51. $(-1, -6), (3, -4)$ **52.** $(-3, 5), (-5, -5)$

53. $(-2, -1), (-5, 8)$ **54.** $(4, 7), (-4, -5)$

Find the midpoint of the line segment with the given endpoints. **See Example 8.**

55. $(0, 0), (6, 8)$ **56.** $(10, 12), (0, 0)$

57. $(6, 8), (12, 16)$ **58.** $(10, 4), (2, -2)$

59. $(-2, -8), (3, -8)$ **60.** $(-5, -2), (7, 3)$

61. $(7, 1), (-10, 4)$ **62.** $(-4, -3), (4, -8)$

Solve each problem. **See Example 9.**

63. If $(-2, 3)$ is the midpoint of segment PQ and the coordinates of P are $(-8, 5)$, find the coordinates of Q.

64. If $(6, -5)$ is the midpoint of segment PQ and the coordinates of Q are $(-5, -8)$, find the coordinates of P.

65. If $(-7, -3)$ is the midpoint of segment QP and the coordinates of Q are $(6, -3)$, find the coordinates of P.

66. If $\left(\frac{1}{2}, -2\right)$ is the midpoint of segment QP and the coordinates of P are $\left(-\frac{5}{2}, 5\right)$, find the coordinates of Q.

APPLICATIONS

67. Soccer. The allowable length of a rectangular soccer field used for international adult matches can be from 100 to 110 meters and the width can be from 64 to 75 meters.

  a. Find the length of the diagonal of the field that has the minimum allowable length and minimum allowable width. Give an approximation to two decimal places.

  b. Find the length of the diagonal of the field that has the maximum allowable length and maximum allowable width. Give the exact answer and an approximation to two decimal places.

68. Cubes. Find the exact length of the diagonal (in blue) of one of the *faces* of the cube shown here.

69. Cubes. Find the exact length of the diagonal (in green) of the cube shown here.

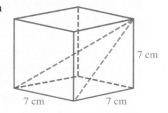

7 cm

7 cm   7 cm

70. Geometry. Use the distance formula to show that a triangle with vertices $(-2, 4)$, $(2, 8)$, and $(6, 4)$ is isosceles.

71. Washington, D.C. The square in the map shows the 100-square-mile site selected by George Washington in 1790 to serve as a permanent capital for the United States. In 1847, the part of the district lying on the west bank of the Potomac was returned to Virginia. Find the exact coordinates of each corner of the original square that outlined the District of Columbia and approximations to two decimal places.

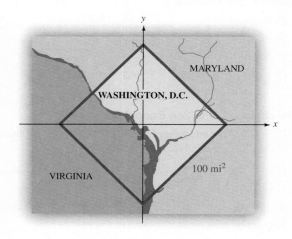

72. Paper Airplanes. The illustration gives the directions for making a paper airplane from a square piece of paper with sides 8 inches long. Find the length l of the plane when it is completed. Give the exact answer and an approximation to two decimal places.

Step 1:
Fold up.

Step 2:
Fold to make wing.

Step 3:
Fold up tip of wing.

l

73. Hardware. The sides of a regular hexagonal nut are 10 millimeters long. Find the height h of the nut. Give the exact answer and an approximation to two decimal places.

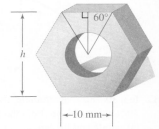

60°

h

←10 mm→

74. Ironing Boards. Find the height h of the ironing board shown in the illustration. Give the exact answer and an approximation to two decimal places.

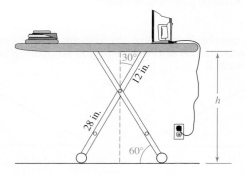

30°

12 in.

28 in.

60°

h

75. Baseball. A baseball diamond is a square, 90 feet on a side. If the third baseman fields a ground ball 10 feet directly behind third base, how far must he throw the ball to throw a runner out at first base? Give the exact answer and an approximation to two decimal places.

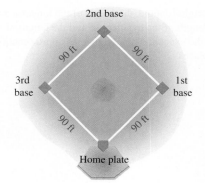

2nd base

90 ft   90 ft

3rd base   1st base

90 ft   90 ft

Home plate

76. Baseball. A shortstop fields a grounder at a point one-third of the way from second base to third base. How far will he have to throw the ball to make an out at first base? Give the exact answer and an approximation to two decimal places.

77. Clotheslines. A pair of damp jeans are hung on a clothesline to dry. They pull the center down 1 foot. By how much is the line stretched? Give an approximation to two decimal places.

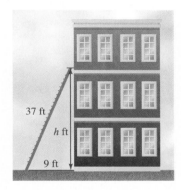

78. Firefighting. The base of the 37-foot ladder is 9 feet from the wall. Will the top reach a window ledge that is 35 feet above the ground? Verify your result.

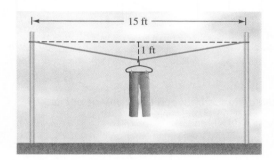

79. Art History. A figure displaying some of the characteristics of Egyptian art is shown in the illustration. Use the distance formula to find the following dimensions of the drawing. Round your answers to two decimal places.

  a. From the foot to the eye
  b. From the belt to the hand holding the staff
  c. From the shoulder to the symbol held in the hand

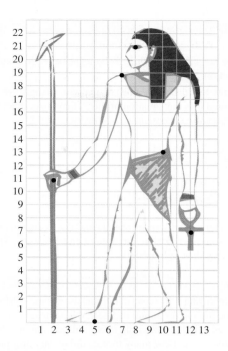

80. Packaging. The diagonal d of a rectangular box with dimensions $a \times b \times c$ is given by $d = \sqrt{a^2 + b^2 + c^2}$. Will the umbrella fit in the shipping carton in the illustration? Verify your result.

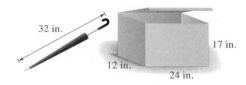

81. Packaging. An archaeologist wants to ship a 34-inch femur bone. Will it fit in a 4-inch-tall box that has a square base with sides 24 inches long? (See Exercise 68.) Verify your result.

82. Telephone. The telephone cable in the illustration runs from A to B to C to D. How much cable is required to run from A to D directly?

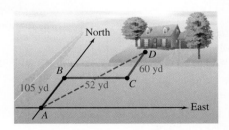

WRITING

83. State the Pythagorean theorem in words.

84. List the facts that you learned about special right triangles in this section.

85. When the lengths of the sides of a certain triangle are substituted into the equation of the Pythagorean theorem, the result is a false statement. Explain why.

$$a^2 + b^2 = c^2$$
$$2^2 + 4^2 = 5^2$$
$$4 + 16 = 25$$
$$20 = 25 \quad \text{False}$$

86. Explain how the distance formula and the Pythagorean theorem can be used to show that a triangle with vertices $(2, 3)$, $(-3, 4)$, and $(1, -2)$ is a right triangle.

REVIEW

87. Discount Buying. A repairman purchased some washing-machine motors for a total of $224. When the unit cost decreased by $4, he was able to buy one extra motor for the same total price. How many motors did he buy originally?

88. Aviation. An airplane can fly 650 miles with the wind in the same amount of time as it can fly 475 miles against the wind. If the wind speed is 40 mph, find the speed of the plane in still air.

CHALLENGE PROBLEMS

89. Find the length of the diagonal of the cube shown in figure (a) below.

90. Show that the length of the diagonal of the rectangular solid shown in figure (b) below is $\sqrt{a^2 + b^2 + c^2}$ cm.

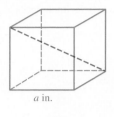
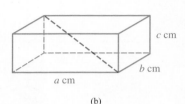

(a)   (b)

Find the distance between each pair of points.

91. $\left(\sqrt{48}, \sqrt{150}\right)$ and $\left(\sqrt{12}, \sqrt{24}\right)$

92. $\left(\sqrt{8}, -\sqrt{20}\right)$ and $\left(\sqrt{50}, -\sqrt{45}\right)$

SECTION 9.7

Complex Numbers

OBJECTIVES

1 Express square roots of negative numbers in terms of *i*.

2 Write complex numbers in the form *a + bi*.

3 Add and subtract complex numbers.

4 Multiply complex numbers.

5 Divide complex numbers.

6 Perform operations involving powers of *i*.

ARE YOU READY?

The following problems review some basic skills that are needed when working with complex numbers.

1. Explain why $\sqrt{-16}$ is not a real number.

2. Simplify: $(x^2 + 8x) + (5x^2 - 10x)$

3. Multiply: $(2n + 3)(7n - 1)$

4. Simplify: $\sqrt{63}$

5. Rationalize the denominator:

$$\frac{7}{\sqrt{x} + 4}$$

6. Divide and give the remainder: $4\overline{)87}$

Recall that the square root of a negative number is not a real number. However, an expanded number system, called the *complex number system,* gives meaning to square roots of negative numbers, such as $\sqrt{-9}$ and $\sqrt{-25}$. To define complex numbers, we use a number that is denoted by the letter *i*.

1 Express Square Roots of Negative Numbers in Terms of *i*.

Some equations do not have real-number solutions. For example, $x^2 = -1$ has no real-number solutions because the square of a real number is never negative. To provide a solution to this equation, mathematicians have defined the number i so that $i^2 = -1$.

The Number *i* ▼

The **imaginary number *i*** is defined as

$$i = \sqrt{-1}$$

From the definition, it follows that $i^2 = -1$.

This definition enables us to write the square root of any negative number in terms of i. We can use extensions of the product and quotient rules for radicals to write the square root of a negative number as the product of a real number and i.

EXAMPLE 1   Write each expression in terms of i: **a.** $\sqrt{-9}$ **b.** $\sqrt{-7}$ **c.** $-\sqrt{-18}$
d. $\sqrt{-\dfrac{24}{49}}$

Strategy   We will write each radicand as the product of -1 and a positive number. Then we will apply the appropriate rules for radicals.

Why   We want our work to produce a factor of $\sqrt{-1}$ so that we can replace it with i.

Solution   After factoring the radicand, we use an extension of the product rule for radicals.

a. $\sqrt{-9} = \sqrt{-1 \cdot 9} = \sqrt{-1}\sqrt{9} = i \cdot 3 = 3i$ Replace $\sqrt{-1}$ with i.

b. $\sqrt{-7} = \sqrt{-1 \cdot 7} = \sqrt{-1}\sqrt{7} = i\sqrt{7}$ or $\sqrt{7}i$ Replace $\sqrt{-1}$ with i.

c. $-\sqrt{-18} = -\sqrt{-1 \cdot 9 \cdot 2} = -\sqrt{-1}\sqrt{9}\sqrt{2} = -i \cdot 3 \cdot \sqrt{2} = -3i\sqrt{2}$ or $-3\sqrt{2}i$

d. After factoring the radicand, use an extension of the product and quotient rules for radicals.

$$\sqrt{-\frac{24}{49}} = \sqrt{-1 \cdot \frac{24}{49}} = \frac{\sqrt{-1 \cdot 24}}{\sqrt{49}} = \frac{\sqrt{-1}\sqrt{4}\sqrt{6}}{\sqrt{49}} = \frac{2i\sqrt{6}}{7} \text{ or } \frac{2\sqrt{6}}{7}i$$

Notation

Since it is easy to confuse $\sqrt{b}i$ with $\sqrt{bi}$, we usually write i first so that it is clear that the i is not under the radical symbol. However, both $i\sqrt{b}$ and $\sqrt{b}i$ are correct. For example: $i\sqrt{7} = \sqrt{7}i$.

Self Check 1   Write each expression in terms of i: **a.** $\sqrt{-25}$
b. $-\sqrt{-19}$ **c.** $\sqrt{-45}$ **d.** $\sqrt{-\dfrac{50}{81}}$

Now Try ▶   Problems 19, 21, and 27

The results from Example 1 illustrate a rule for simplifying square roots of negative numbers.

Square Root of a Negative Number ▼

For any positive real number b,

$$\sqrt{-b} = i\sqrt{b}$$

To justify this rule, we use the fact that $\sqrt{-1} = i$.

$$\sqrt{-b} = \sqrt{-1 \cdot b}$$
$$= \sqrt{-1}\sqrt{b}$$
$$= i\sqrt{b}$$

2 Write Complex Numbers in the Form $a + bi$.

The imaginary number i is used to define *complex numbers*.

Complex Numbers

A **complex number** is any number that can be written in the form $a + bi$, where a and b are real numbers and $i = \sqrt{-1}$.

Complex numbers of the form $a + bi$, where $b \neq 0$, are also called **imaginary numbers.***

*Some textbooks define imaginary numbers as complex numbers with $a = 0$ and $b \neq 0$.

Notation

It is acceptable to use $a - bi$ as a substitute for the form $a + bi$. For example:

$$6 - 9i = 6 + (-9)i$$

For a complex number written in the **standard form** $a + bi$, we call a the **real part** and b the **imaginary part.** Some examples of complex numbers written in standard form are

$2 + 11i$	$6 - 9i$	$-\dfrac{1}{2} + 0i$	$0 + i\sqrt{3}$
$a = 2, b = 11$	$a = 6, b = -9$	$a = -\frac{1}{2}, b = 0$	$a = 0, b = \sqrt{3}$

Two complex numbers $a + bi$ and $c + di$ are equal if and only if $a = c$ and $b = d$. Thus, $0.5 + 0.9i = \frac{1}{2} + \frac{9}{10}i$ because $0.5 = \frac{1}{2}$ and $0.9 = \frac{9}{10}$.

EXAMPLE 2   Write each number in the form $a + bi$:   **a.** 6   **b.** $\sqrt{-64}$ **c.** $-2 + \sqrt{-63}$

Strategy   We will determine a, the real part, and we will simplify the radical (if necessary) to determine the bi part.

Why   We can put the two parts together to produce the desired $a + bi$ form.

Solution

a. $6 = 6 + 0i$ The real part a is 6. The imaginary part b is 0.

Caution

Use i only when working with the *square root* of a negative number. It does not apply to cube roots.

$$\sqrt{-64} = 8i \quad \text{and} \quad \sqrt[3]{-64} = -4$$

b. $\sqrt{-64} = 0 + 8i$ The real part a is 0. Simplify: $\sqrt{-64} = \sqrt{-1}\sqrt{64} = 8i$. Thus, b is 8.

c. $-2 + \sqrt{-63} = -2 + 3i\sqrt{7}$ The real part a is -2.
Simplify: $\sqrt{-63} = \sqrt{-1}\sqrt{63} = \sqrt{-1}\sqrt{9}\sqrt{7} = 3i\sqrt{7}$.
Thus, $b = 3\sqrt{7}$.

Self Check 2   Write each number in the form $a + bi$:   **a.** -18
b. $\sqrt{-36}$ **c.** $1 + \sqrt{-24}$

Now Try ▶   Problems 29 and 33

The following illustration shows the relationship between the real numbers, the imaginary numbers, and the complex numbers.

The complex numbers: $a + bi$

The real numbers: $a + bi$ where $b = 0$				The imaginary numbers: $a + bi$ where $b \neq 0$		
-6	$\dfrac{5}{16}$	-1.75	π	$9 + 7i$	$-2i$	$\dfrac{1}{4} - \dfrac{3}{4}i$
$48 + 0i$	0	$-\sqrt{10}$	$-\dfrac{7}{2}$	$0.56i$	$\sqrt{-10}$	$6 + i\sqrt{3}$
$\sqrt[3]{-10}$	$4 + \pi$	$15\dfrac{5}{8}$	$\sqrt[4]{99}$	$25i\sqrt{5}$	$\dfrac{7}{8}i$	$\sqrt{3} + 3i\sqrt{2}$

Success Tip

Just as real numbers are either rational or irrational, but not both, complex numbers are either real or imaginary, but not both.

3 Add and Subtract Complex Numbers.

Adding and subtracting complex numbers is similar to adding and subtracting polynomials.

Addition and Subtraction of Complex Numbers	1. To add complex numbers, add their real parts and add their imaginary parts. 2. To subtract complex numbers, add the opposite of the complex number being subtracted.

EXAMPLE 3

Perform each operation. Write the answers in the form $a + bi$. **a.** $(8 + 4i) + (12 + 8i)$
b. $(-6 + 4i) - (3 + 2i)$ **c.** $\left(7 - \sqrt{-16}\right) + \left(9 + \sqrt{-4}\right)$

Strategy   To add the complex numbers, we will add their real parts and add their imaginary parts. To subtract the complex numbers, we will add the opposite of the complex number to be subtracted.

Why   We perform the indicated operations as if the complex numbers were polynomials with i as a variable.

Solution

a. $(8 + 4i) + (12 + 8i) = (8 + 12) + (4 + 8)i$

↑ The sum of the imaginary parts
The sum of the real parts

$$= 20 + 12i$$

b. $(-6 + 4i) - (3 + 2i) = (-6 + 4i) + (-3 - 2i)$ To find the opposite, change the sign of each term of $3 + 2i$.

the opposite

$$= [-6 + (-3)] + [4 + (-2)]i$$ Add the real parts. Add the imaginary parts.

$$= -9 + 2i$$

c. $\left(7 - \sqrt{-16}\right) + \left(9 + \sqrt{-4}\right)$

$$= (7 - 4i) + (9 + 2i)$$ Write $\sqrt{-16}$ and $\sqrt{-4}$ in terms of i.

$$= (7 + 9) + (-4 + 2)i$$ Add the real parts. Add the imaginary parts.

$$= 16 - 2i$$ Write $16 + (-2i)$ in the form $16 - 2i$.

Self Check 3   Perform the operations. Write the answers in the form $a + bi$.
a. $(3 - 5i) + (-2 + 7i)$
b. $\left(3 - \sqrt{-25}\right) - \left(-2 + \sqrt{-49}\right)$

Now Try ▶   Problems 37 and 43

The Language of Algebra

For years, mathematicians thought numbers like $\sqrt{-4}$ and $\sqrt{-16}$ were useless. In the 17th century, French mathematician René Descartes (1596–1650) called them **imaginary numbers.** Today they have important uses such as describing alternating electric current.

Success Tip

Always express square roots of negative numbers in terms of i before performing any operations.

4 Multiply Complex Numbers.

Since imaginary numbers are not real numbers, some properties of real numbers do not apply to imaginary numbers. For example, we cannot use the product rule for radicals to multiply two imaginary numbers.

CAUTION   If a and b are both negative, then $\sqrt{a}\sqrt{b} \neq \sqrt{ab}$. For example, if $a = -4$ and $b = -9$,

$$\sqrt{-4} \cdot \sqrt{-9} = \sqrt{-4(-9)} = \sqrt{36} = 6 \qquad \sqrt{-4}\sqrt{-9} = 2i(3i) = 6i^2 = 6(-1) = -6$$

EXAMPLE 4   Multiply: $\sqrt{-2} \cdot \sqrt{-20}$

Strategy   To multiply the imaginary numbers, first we will write $\sqrt{-2}$ and $\sqrt{-20}$ in $i\sqrt{b}$ form. Then we will use the product rule for radicals.

Why   We cannot use the product rule for radicals immediately because it does not apply when both radicands are negative.

Solution

$$\sqrt{-2} \cdot \sqrt{-20} = \left(i\sqrt{2}\right)\left(2i\sqrt{5}\right) \quad \text{Simplify: } \sqrt{-20} = i\sqrt{20} = 2i\sqrt{5}.$$
$$= 2i^2\sqrt{2 \cdot 5} \qquad \text{Multiply: } i \cdot 2i = 2i^2. \text{ Use the product rule for radicals.}$$
$$= 2i^2\sqrt{10}$$
$$= 2(-1)\sqrt{10} \qquad \text{Replace } i^2 \text{ with } -1.$$
$$= -2\sqrt{10} \qquad \text{Multiply.}$$

Success Tip

The algebraic methods we have used with polynomials and rational expressions (such as combining like terms, distributive property, FOIL, and building fractions) are also used with complex numbers. However, when you encounter i^2 in your work, remember to replace it with -1.

Self Check 4   Multiply: $\sqrt{-3} \cdot \sqrt{-32}$

Now Try ▶ Problem 47

Multiplying complex numbers is similar to multiplying polynomials.

EXAMPLE 5   Multiply. Write the answers in the form $a + bi$.   **a.** $6(2 + 9i)$ **b.** $-5i(4 - 8i)$

Strategy   We will use the distributive property to find the products.

Why   We perform the indicated operations as if the complex numbers were polynomials with i as a variable.

Solution   **a.** $6(2 + 9i) = 6(2) + 6(9i)$ Use the distributive property.
$$= 12 + 54i \qquad \text{Perform each multiplication.}$$

Caution

A common mistake is to replace i with -1. Remember, $i \neq -1$. By definition, $i = \sqrt{-1}$ and $i^2 = -1$.

b. $-5i(4 - 8i) = -5i(4) - (-5i)8i$ Use the distributive property.
$$= -20i + 40i^2 \qquad \text{Perform each multiplication.}$$
$$= -20i + 40(-1) \qquad \text{Replace } i^2 \text{ with } -1.$$
$$= -20i - 40 \qquad \text{Multiply.}$$
$$= -40 - 20i \qquad \text{Write the real part, } -40, \text{ as the first term.}$$

Self Check 5   Multiply. Write the answers in the form $a + bi$.
   a. $-2(-9 - i)$ **b.** $10i(7 + 4i)$

Now Try ▶ Problems 49 and 55

EXAMPLE 6   Multiply. Write the answers in the form $a + bi$.   **a.** $(2 + 3i)(3 - 2i)$
b. $(-4 + 2i)(2 + i)$

Strategy   We will use the FOIL method to multiply the two complex numbers.

Why   We perform the indicated operations as if the complex numbers were binomials with i as a variable.

F   O   I   L

Solution   **a.** $(2 + 3i)(3 - 2i) = 6 - 4i + 9i - 6i^2$ Use the FOIL method.

$= 6 + 5i - 6(-1)$ Combine the imaginary terms: $-4i + 9i = 5i$. Replace i^2 with -1.

$= 6 + 5i + 6$ Simplify the last term.

$= 12 + 5i$ Combine like terms.

b. $(-4 + 2i)(2 + i) = -8 - 4i + 4i + 2i^2$ Use the FOIL method.

$= -8 + 0i + 2(-1)$ Combine like terms: $-4i + 4i = 0i$. Replace i^2 with -1.

$= -8 + 0i - 2$ Multiply.

$= -10 + 0i$ Combine like terms.

> **Self Check 6**   Multiply. Write the answers in the form $a + bi$. $(-2 + 3i)(3 - 2i)$
>
> **Now Try** ▶ Problem 59

5 Divide Complex Numbers.

Before we can discuss division of complex numbers, we must introduce an important fact about *complex conjugates*.

▼

Complex Conjugates   The complex numbers $a + bi$ and $a - bi$ are called **complex conjugates**.

For example,

- $7 + 4i$ and $7 - 4i$ are complex conjugates.
- $5 - i$ and $5 + i$ are complex conjugates.
- $-6i$ and $6i$ are complex conjugates, because $-6i = 0 - 6i$ and $6i = 0 + 6i$.

In general, the product of the complex number $a + bi$ and its complex conjugate $a - bi$ is the real number $a^2 + b^2$, as the following work shows:

$(a + bi)(a - bi) = a^2 - abi + abi - b^2i^2$ Use the FOIL method.

$= a^2 - b^2(-1)$ $-abi + abi = 0$. Replace i^2 with -1.

$= a^2 + b^2$

EXAMPLE 7   Find the product of $3 + 5i$ and its complex conjugate.

Strategy   The complex conjugate of $3 + 5i$ is $3 - 5i$. We will find their product by using the FOIL method.

Why   We perform the indicated operations as if the complex numbers were binomials with i as a variable.

Solution We can find the product as follows:

$$(3 + 5i)(3 - 5i) = 9 - 15i + 15i - 25i^2 \quad \text{Use the FOIL method.}$$

$$= 9 - 25i^2 \quad \text{Combine like terms: } -15i + 15i = 0.$$

$$= 9 - 25(-1) \quad \text{Replace } i^2 \text{ with } -1.$$

$$= 9 + 25$$

$$= 34$$

The product of $3 + 5i$ and its complex conjugate $3 - 5i$ is the real number 34.

> **Self Check 7** Multiply: $(2 + 3i)(2 - 3i)$
>
> **Now Try** ▶ Problem 65

Recall that to divide *radical expressions,* we rationalized the denominator. We will use a similar approach to divide complex numbers. To divide two complex numbers when the divisor has two terms, we use the following strategy.

Division of Complex Numbers	▼ To divide complex numbers, multiply the numerator and denominator by the complex conjugate of the denominator.

EXAMPLE 8 Divide. Write the answers in the form $a + bi$. **a.** $\dfrac{3}{6 + i}$ **b.** $\dfrac{1 + 2i}{3 - 4i}$

Strategy We will build each fraction by multiplying it by a form of 1 that uses the conjugate of the denominator.

Why This step produces a *real number* in the denominator so that the result then can be written in the form $a + bi$.

Solution **a.** We want to build a fraction equivalent to $\dfrac{3}{6 + i}$ that does not have i in the denominator. To make the denominator, $6 + i$, a real number, we need to multiply it by its complex conjugate, $6 - i$. It follows that $\dfrac{6 - i}{6 - i}$ should be the form of 1 that is used to build $\dfrac{3}{6 + i}$.

$$\frac{3}{6 + i} = \frac{3}{6 + i} \cdot \frac{6 - i}{6 - i} \qquad \text{To build an equivalent fraction, multiply by } \tfrac{6 - i}{6 - i} = 1.$$

$$= \frac{18 - 3i}{36 - 6i + 6i - i^2} \qquad \text{To multiply the numerators, distribute the multiplication by 3. Use the FOIL method to multiply the denominators.}$$

$$= \frac{18 - 3i}{36 - (-1)} \qquad \text{Combine like terms: } -6i + 6i = 0. \text{ Replace } i^2 \text{ with } -1. \\ \text{Note that the denominator no longer contains } i.$$

$$= \frac{18 - 3i}{37} \qquad \text{Simplify the denominator. This notation represents the difference of two fractions that have the common denominator 37: } \tfrac{18}{37} \text{ and } \tfrac{3i}{37}.$$

$$= \frac{18}{37} - \frac{3}{37}i \qquad \text{Write the complex number in the form } a + bi.$$

Success Tip

When multiplying the denominator and its complex conjugate, we can use the special-product rule for the sum and difference of the same two terms to simplify the calculations:

$$(3-4i)(3+4i) = 3^2 - (4i)^2$$
$$= 9 - 16i^2$$

b. We can make the denominator of $\frac{1+2i}{3-4i}$ a real number by multiplying it by the complex conjugate of $3-4i$, which is $3+4i$. It follows that $\frac{3+4i}{3+4i}$ should be the form of 1 that is used to build $\frac{1+2i}{3-4i}$.

$$\frac{1+2i}{3-4i} = \frac{1+2i}{3-4i} \cdot \frac{3+4i}{3+4i} \qquad \text{To build an equivalent fraction, multiply by } \frac{3+4i}{3+4i} = 1.$$

$$= \frac{3+4i+6i+8i^2}{9+12i-12i-16i^2} \qquad \text{Use the FOIL method to multiply the numerators and the denominators.}$$

$$= \frac{3+10i+8(-1)}{9-16(-1)} \qquad \text{Combine like terms in the numerator and denominator. Replace } i^2 \text{ with } -1. \text{ The denominator is now a real number.}$$

$$= \frac{3+10i-8}{9+16} \qquad \text{Simplify the numerator and denominator.}$$

$$= \frac{-5+10i}{25} \qquad \text{Combine like terms in the numerator and denominator.}$$

$$= \frac{\overset{1}{\cancel{5}}(-1+2i)}{\underset{1}{\cancel{5} \cdot 5}} \qquad \text{Factor out 5 in the numerator and remove the common factor of 5.}$$

$$= \frac{-1+2i}{5} \qquad \text{Simplify. This notation represents the sum of two fractions that have the common denominator 5.}$$

$$= -\frac{1}{5} + \frac{2}{5}i \qquad \text{Write the complex number in the form } a+bi.$$

Caution

Remember, we can remove only factors common to the entire numerator and denominator. Don't make the mistake of removing a common term, as shown below:

$$\frac{\cancel{-5} + 10i}{\underset{5}{\cancel{25}}}$$

Self Check 8 Divide. Write the answers in the form $a+bi$. **a.** $\frac{6}{5+2i}$

b. $\frac{2-4i}{5-3i}$

Now Try ▶ Problems 71 and 77

EXAMPLE 9 Divide and write the answer in the form $a+bi$: $\dfrac{4+\sqrt{-16}}{2+\sqrt{-4}}$

Strategy We will begin by writing $\sqrt{-16}$ and $\sqrt{-4}$ in $i\sqrt{b}$ form.

Why To perform any operations, the numerator and denominator should be written in the form $a+bi$.

Solution
$$\frac{4+\sqrt{-16}}{2+\sqrt{-4}} = \frac{4+4i}{2+2i} \qquad \text{Simplify: } \sqrt{-16} = \sqrt{-1}\sqrt{16} = 4i \text{ and } \sqrt{-4} = \sqrt{-1}\sqrt{4} = 2i.$$

$$= \frac{\overset{1}{2(\cancel{2+2i})}}{\underset{1}{\cancel{2+2i}}} \qquad \text{Factor out 2 in the numerator and remove the common factor of } 2+2i.$$

$$= 2$$

$$= 2 + 0i \qquad \text{Write 2 in the form } a+bi.$$

Self Check 9 Divide and write the answer in the form $a+bi$: $\dfrac{21-\sqrt{-49}}{3-\sqrt{-1}}$

Now Try ▶ Problem 81

EXAMPLE 10 Divide and write the result in the form $a + bi$: $\dfrac{7}{2i}$

Strategy We will use $\dfrac{-2i}{-2i}$ as the form of 1 to build $\dfrac{7}{2i}$.

Why Since the denominator $2i$ can be expressed as $0 + 2i$, its complex conjugate is $0 - 2i$. However, instead of building with $\dfrac{0 - 2i}{0 - 2i}$, we will drop the zeros and just use $\dfrac{-2i}{-2i}$.

Solution

$$\frac{7}{2i} = \frac{7}{2i} \cdot \frac{-2i}{-2i} \qquad \text{To build an equivalent fraction, multiply by } \tfrac{-2i}{-2i} = 1.$$

$$= \frac{-14i}{-4i^2} \qquad \text{Multiply the numerators and multiply the denominators.}$$

$$= \frac{-14i}{-4(-1)} \qquad \text{Replace } i^2 \text{ with } -1. \text{ The denominator is now a real number.}$$

$$= \frac{-14i}{4} \qquad \text{Simplify the denominator.}$$

$$= -\frac{7i}{2} \qquad \text{Simplify the fraction: } -\dfrac{\overset{1}{\cancel{2}} \cdot 7i}{\underset{1}{\cancel{2}} \cdot 2}.$$

$$= 0 - \frac{7}{2}i \qquad \text{Write in the form } a + bi.$$

> **Success Tip**
>
> In this example, the denominator of $\dfrac{7}{2i}$ is of the form bi. In such cases, we can eliminate i in the denominator by simply multiplying by $\dfrac{i}{i}$.
>
> $$\frac{7}{2i} = \frac{7}{2i} \cdot \frac{i}{i} = \frac{7i}{2i^2} = -\frac{7}{2}i$$

Self Check 10 Divide and write the result in the form $a + bi$: $\dfrac{3}{4i}$

Now Try Problem 85

6 Perform Operations Involving Powers of i.

The powers of i produce an interesting pattern:

$$i = \sqrt{-1} = i \qquad\qquad i^5 = i^4 i = 1i = i$$
$$i^2 = \left(\sqrt{-1}\right)^2 = -1 \qquad i^6 = i^4 i^2 = 1(-1) = -1$$
$$i^3 = i^2 i = -1i = -i \qquad i^7 = i^4 i^3 = 1(-i) = -i$$
$$i^4 = i^2 i^2 = (-1)(-1) = 1 \qquad i^8 = i^4 i^4 = (1)(1) = 1$$

The pattern continues: $i, -1, -i, 1, \ldots$.

> **Success Tip**
>
> Note that the powers of i cycle through four possible outcomes:
>
>

Larger powers of i can be simplified by using the fact that $i^4 = 1$. For example, to simplify i^{29}, we note that 29 divided by 4 gives a quotient of 7 and a remainder of 1. Thus, $29 = 4 \cdot 7 + 1$ and

$$i^{29} = i^{4 \cdot 7 + 1} \qquad 4 \cdot 7 = 28.$$

$$= \left(i^4\right)^7 \cdot i^1 \qquad \text{Use the rules for exponents } x^{m \cdot n} = (x^m)^n \text{ and } x^{m+n} = x^m \cdot x^n.$$

$$= 1^7 \cdot i \qquad \text{Simplify: } i^4 = 1.$$

$$= i \qquad \text{Simplify: } 1 \cdot i = i.$$

The result of this example illustrates the following fact.

Powers of i ▼ If n is a natural number that has a remainder of R when divided by 4, then

$$i^n = i^R$$

EXAMPLE 11 Simplify: **a.** i^{55} **b.** i^{98}

Strategy We will examine the remainder when we divide the exponents 55 and 98 by 4.

Why The remainder determines the power to which i is raised in the simplified form.

Solution

a. We divide 55 by 4 and get a remainder of 3. Therefore,

$$i^{55} = i^3 = -i$$

$$\begin{array}{r} 13\ R\ 3 \\ 4\overline{)55} \\ \underline{-4} \\ 15 \\ \underline{-12} \\ 3 \end{array}$$

b. We divide 98 by 4 and get a remainder of 2. Therefore,

$$i^{98} = i^2 = -1$$

$$\begin{array}{r} 24\ R\ 2 \\ 4\overline{)98} \\ \underline{-8} \\ 18 \\ \underline{-16} \\ 2 \end{array}$$

Success Tip

If we divide the natural number exponent n of a power of i by 4, the remainder indicates the simplified form of i^n:

R = 1: i
R = 2: -1
R = 3: $-i$
R = 0: 1

Self Check 11 Simplify: **a.** i^{62} **b.** i^{105}

Now Try ▶ Problem 91

SECTION **9.7** ▶ STUDY SET

VOCABULARY

Fill in the blanks.

1. The _____ number i is defined as $i = \sqrt{-1}$. We call i^{25} a _____ of i.

2. A _____ number is any number that can be written in the form $a + bi$, where a and b are real numbers and $i = \sqrt{-1}$.

3. For the complex number $2 + 5i$, we call 2 the _____ part and 5 the _____ part.

4. $6 + 3i$ and $6 - 3i$ are called complex _____.

CONCEPTS

Fill in the blanks.

5. **a.** $i =$ ▢ **b.** $i^2 =$ ▢

   c. $i^3 =$ ▢ **d.** $i^4 =$ ▢

   e. In general, the powers of i cycle through _____ possible outcomes.

6. Simplify:

   $$\sqrt{-36} = \sqrt{ \cdot 36} = \sqrt{}\sqrt{36} = 6$$

7. **a.** To add (or subtract) complex numbers, add (or subtract) their _____ parts and add (or subtract) their _____ parts.

   b. To multiply two complex numbers, such as $(2 + 3i)(3 + 5i)$, we can use the _____ method.

8. To divide $6 + 7i$ by $1 - 8i$, we multiply $\frac{6 + 7i}{1 - 8i}$ by 1 in the form of $\frac{}{}$.

9. Give the complex conjugate of each number.
   a. $2 - 3i$ **b.** 2 **c.** $-3i$

10. Factor each numerator. Then remove the factor common to the numerator and denominator. Write the result in the form $a + bi$.

    a. $\dfrac{3 + 6i}{3}$ **b.** $\dfrac{15 + 25i}{10}$

11. Complete the illustration. Label the *real numbers,* the *imaginary numbers,* the *complex numbers,* the *rational numbers,* and the *irrational numbers.*

    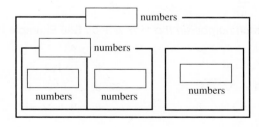

12. Determine whether each statement is true or false.

    a. Every complex number is a real number.

    b. Every real number is a complex number.

    c. i is a real number.

    d. The square root of a negative number is an imaginary number.

    e. The product of a complex number and its complex conjugate is always a real number.

NOTATION

Complete each solution.

13. $(3 + 2i)(3 - i) = \boxed{} - 3i + \boxed{} - 2i^2$

$\qquad = 9 + 3i + \boxed{}$

$\qquad = \boxed{} + 3i$

14. $\dfrac{3}{2 - i} = \dfrac{3}{2 - i} \cdot \dfrac{\boxed{}}{\boxed{}}$

$\qquad = \dfrac{6 + \boxed{}}{4 - \boxed{}}$

$\qquad = \dfrac{6 + 3i}{\boxed{}}$

$\qquad = \dfrac{\boxed{}}{\boxed{}} + \dfrac{3}{5}i$

15. Determine whether each statement is true or false.

   a. $\sqrt{6}i = i\sqrt{6}$ **b.** $\sqrt{8}i = \sqrt{8i}$

   c. $\sqrt{-25} = -\sqrt{25}$ **d.** $-i = i$

16. Write each number in the form $a + bi$.

   a. $\dfrac{9 + 11i}{4}$ **b.** $\dfrac{1 - i}{18}$

GUIDED PRACTICE

Express each number in terms of i. See Example 1.

17. $\sqrt{-9}$ **18.** $\sqrt{-4}$

19. $\sqrt{-7}$ **20.** $\sqrt{-11}$

21. $\sqrt{-24}$ **22.** $\sqrt{-28}$

23. $-\sqrt{-72}$ **24.** $-\sqrt{-24}$

25. $5\sqrt{-81}$ **26.** $6\sqrt{-49}$

27. $\sqrt{-\dfrac{25}{9}}$ **28.** $-\sqrt{-\dfrac{121}{144}}$

Write each number in the form $a + bi$. See Example 2.

29. a. 5 **30. a.** -43

    b. $\sqrt{-49}$ **b.** $\sqrt{-169}$

31. a. $1 + \sqrt{-25}$ **32. a.** $21 + \sqrt{-16}$

    b. $-3 + \sqrt{-8}$ **b.** $-9 + \sqrt{-12}$

33. a. $76 - \sqrt{-54}$ **34. a.** $88 - \sqrt{-98}$

    b. $-7 + \sqrt{-19}$ **b.** $-2 + \sqrt{-35}$

35. a. $-6 - \sqrt{-9}$ **36. a.** $-45 - \sqrt{-81}$

    b. $3 + \sqrt{-6}$ **b.** $8 + \sqrt{-7}$

Perform the operations. Write all answers in the form $a + bi$. See Example 3.

37. $(3 + 4i) + (5 - 6i)$ **38.** $(8 + 3i) + (-7 - 2i)$

39. $(6 - i) + (9 + 3i)$ **40.** $(5 + 3i) - (6 - 9i)$

41. $(7 - 3i) - (4 + 2i)$ **42.** $(5 - 4i) - (3 + 2i)$

43. $\left(8 + \sqrt{-25}\right) - \left(7 + \sqrt{-4}\right)$

44. $\left(-7 + \sqrt{-81}\right) - \left(-2 - \sqrt{-64}\right)$

Multiply. See Example 4.

45. $\sqrt{-1} \cdot \sqrt{-36}$ **46.** $\sqrt{-9} \cdot \sqrt{-100}$

47. $\sqrt{-2}\sqrt{-12}$ **48.** $\sqrt{-3}\sqrt{-45}$

Multiply. Write all answers in the form $a + bi$. See Example 5.

49. $3(2 - 9i)$ **50.** $-4(3 + 4i)$

51. $7(5 - 4i)$ **52.** $-5(3 + 2i)$

53. $2i(7 - 3i)$ **54.** $i(8 + 2i)$

55. $-5i(5 - 5i)$ **56.** $2i(7 + 2i)$

Multiply. Write all answers in the form $a + bi$. See Example 6.

57. $(2 + i)(3 - i)$ **58.** $(4 - i)(2 + i)$

59. $(3 - 2i)(2 + 3i)$ **60.** $(3 - i)(2 + 3i)$

61. $\left(4 + \sqrt{-1}\right)\left(3 - \sqrt{-1}\right)$ **62.** $\left(1 - \sqrt{-25}\right)\left(1 - \sqrt{-16}\right)$

63. $(2 + i)^2$ **64.** $(3 - 2i)^2$

Find the product of the given complex number and its conjugate. See Example 7.

65. $2 + 6i$ **66.** $5 + 2i$

67. $-4 - 7i$ **68.** $-10 - 9i$

Divide. Write all answers in the form $a + bi$. See Example 8.

69. $\dfrac{9}{5 + i}$ **70.** $\dfrac{4}{2 - i}$

71. $\dfrac{11i}{4 - 7i}$ **72.** $\dfrac{2i}{3 + 8i}$

73. $\dfrac{3 - 2i}{4 - i}$ **74.** $\dfrac{6 - i}{2 + i}$

75. $\dfrac{7 + 4i}{2 - 5i}$ **76.** $\dfrac{2 + 3i}{2 - 3i}$

77. $\dfrac{7 + 3i}{4 - 2i}$ **78.** $\dfrac{5 - 3i}{4 + 2i}$

79. $\dfrac{1 - 3i}{3 + i}$ **80.** $\dfrac{3 + 5i}{1 - i}$

Divide. Write all answers in the form $a + bi$. See Example 9. (Hint: Factor the numerator.)

81. $\dfrac{8 + \sqrt{-144}}{2 + \sqrt{-9}}$ **82.** $\dfrac{3 + \sqrt{-36}}{1 + \sqrt{-4}}$

83. $\dfrac{-4 - \sqrt{-4}}{2 + \sqrt{-1}}$ **84.** $\dfrac{-5 - \sqrt{-25}}{1 + \sqrt{-1}}$

Divide. Write all answers in the form $a + bi$. See Example 10.

85. $\dfrac{5}{3i}$ **86.** $\dfrac{3}{8i}$

87. $-\dfrac{2}{7i}$ **88.** $-\dfrac{8}{5i}$

Simplify each expression. See Example 11.

89. i^{21} **90.** i^{19} **91.** i^{27} **92.** i^{22}

93. i^{100} **94.** i^{97} **95.** i^{42} **96.** i^{200}

TRY IT YOURSELF

Perform the operations. Write all answers in the form a + bi.

97. $(3 - i) - (-1 + 10i)$ **98.** $(14 + 4i) - (-9 - i)$

99. $\left(2 - \sqrt{-16}\right)\left(3 + \sqrt{-4}\right)$ **100.** $\left(3 - \sqrt{-4}\right)\left(4 - \sqrt{-9}\right)$

101. $(-6 - 9i) + (4 + 3i)$ **102.** $(-3 + 11i) + (-1 - 6i)$

103. $\dfrac{-2i}{3 + 2i}$ **104.** $\dfrac{-4i}{2 - 6i}$

105. $6i(2 - 3i)$ **106.** $-9i(4 - 6i)$

107. $\dfrac{4}{5i^{35}}$ **108.** $\dfrac{3}{2i^{17}}$

109. $\left(2 + i\sqrt{2}\right)\left(3 - i\sqrt{2}\right)$ **110.** $\left(5 + i\sqrt{3}\right)\left(2 - i\sqrt{3}\right)$

111. $\dfrac{5 + 9i}{1 - i}$ **112.** $\dfrac{5 - i}{3 + 2i}$

113. $(4 - 8i)^2$ **114.** $(7 - 3i)^2$

115. $\dfrac{\sqrt{5} - i\sqrt{3}}{\sqrt{5} + i\sqrt{3}}$ **116.** $\dfrac{\sqrt{3} + i\sqrt{2}}{\sqrt{3} - i\sqrt{2}}$

Look Alikes . . .

117. a. $\sqrt{-8}$ **b.** $\sqrt[3]{-8}$

118. a. $(3 + i) + (2 + 4i)$ **b.** $(3 + i)(2 + 4i)$

119. a. $(2i)^2$ **b.** $(2 + i)^2$

120. a. $\sqrt{-9}\sqrt{-16}$ **b.** $\sqrt{9}\sqrt{16}$

APPLICATIONS

121. Fractals. Complex numbers are fundamental in the creation of the intricate geometric shape shown below, called a *fractal*. The process of creating this image is based on the following sequence of steps, which begins by picking any complex number, which we will call z.

  1. Square z, and then add that result to z.

  2. Square the result from step 1, and then add it to z.

  3. Square the result from step 2, and then add it to z.

If we begin with the complex number i, what is the result after performing steps 1, 2, and 3?

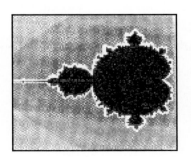

122. Electronics. The impedance Z in an AC (alternating current) circuit is a measure of how much the circuit impedes (hinders) the flow of current through it. The impedance is related to the voltage V and the current I by the formula $V = IZ$. If a circuit has a current of $(0.5 + 2.0i)$ amps and an impedance of $(0.4 - 3.0i)$ ohms, find the voltage.

WRITING

123. What is an imaginary number? What is a complex number?

124. The method used to divide complex numbers is similar to the method used to divide radical expressions. Explain why. Give an example.

125. Explain the error. Then find the correct result.

  a. Add: $\cancel{\sqrt{-16} + \sqrt{-9} = \sqrt{-25}}$

  b. Multiply: $\cancel{\sqrt{-2}\sqrt{-3} = \sqrt{-2(-3)} = \sqrt{6}}$

126. Determine whether the pair of complex numbers are equal. Explain your reasoning.

  a. $4 - \dfrac{2}{5}i,\ \dfrac{8}{2} - 0.4i$ **b.** $0.25 + 0.7i,\ \dfrac{1}{4} + \dfrac{7}{10}i$

REVIEW

127. Wind Speeds. A plane that can fly 200 mph in still air makes a 330-mile flight with a tail wind and returns, flying into the same wind. Find the speed of the wind if the total flying time is $3\frac{1}{3}$ hours.

128. Finding Rates. A student drove a distance of 135 miles at an average speed of 50 mph. How much faster would she have to drive on the return trip to save 30 minutes of driving time?

CHALLENGE PROBLEMS

129. Simplify: $\left(i^{349}\right)^{-i^{456}}$

130. Simplify $(2 + 3i)^{-2}$ and write the result in the form $a + bi$.

9 ▶ Summary & Review

SECTION 9.1 ▶ Radical Expressions and Radical Functions

DEFINITIONS AND CONCEPTS	EXAMPLES
The number b is a **square root of a** if $b^2 = a$. Every positive real number has two square roots.	7 is a square root of 49 because $7^2 = 49$. -7 is also a square root of 49 because $(-7)^2 = 49$.
A **radical symbol** $\sqrt{}$ represents the **positive** or **principal square root** of a number. For any real number x, $\sqrt{x^2} = \lvert x \rvert$ The symbol $-\sqrt{}$ represents the **negative square root** of a number. Review the list of perfect squares on page 729.	$\sqrt{25} = 5$ because $5^2 = 25$. $\sqrt{36x^2} = \lvert 6x \rvert = 6\lvert x \rvert$ because $(6x)^2 = 36x^2$. *Since x could be negative, absolute value symbols ensure that the result is not negative.* $\sqrt{\dfrac{r^8}{100}} = \dfrac{r^4}{10}$ because $\left(\dfrac{r^4}{10}\right)^2 = \dfrac{r^8}{100}$. *Since $\frac{r^4}{10}$ cannot be negative, no absolute value symbols are needed.* $-\sqrt{81} = -9$ and $\sqrt{-81}$ is not a real number.
A function of the form $f(x) = \sqrt{x}$ is called a **square root function.** Review its graph on page 732.	Let $f(x) = \sqrt{x - 2}$. Find $f(38)$. $f(38) = \sqrt{38 - 2} = \sqrt{36} = 6$
The **domain of a square root function** is the set of all real numbers for which the radicand is nonnegative. To find the domain, set the radicand greater than or equal to 0 and solve for the variable.	Find the domain of $g(x) = \sqrt{2x - 4}$. Since $\sqrt{2x - 4}$ is not a real number when $2x - 4$ is negative, we must require that $2x - 4 \geq 0$ *Because we cannot find the square root of a negative number* $2x \geq 4$ *Solve for x.* $x \geq 2$ The domain of g is $[2, \infty)$.
The **cube root** of x is denoted as $\sqrt[3]{x}$ and is defined as $\sqrt[3]{x} = y$ if $y^3 = x$ Review the list of perfect cubes on page 735.	$\sqrt[3]{8} = 2$ because $2^3 = 8$. $\sqrt[3]{-64} = -4$ because $(-4)^3 = -64$. $\sqrt[3]{-27a^6} = -3a^2$ because $(-3a^2)^3 = -27a^6$.
A function of the form $f(x) = \sqrt[3]{x}$ is called a **cube root function.** Review its graph on page 736.	Let $f(x) = \sqrt[3]{x + 4}$. Find $f(23)$. $f(23) = \sqrt[3]{23 + 4} = \sqrt[3]{27} = 3$
The ***n*th root of x** is denoted as $\sqrt[n]{x}$. Index $\searrow$ $\sqrt[4]{16a^8}$ ← Radicand If x is a real number and $n > 1$, then: $\begin{cases} \text{If } n \text{ is an odd natural number, } \sqrt[n]{x^n} = x. \\ \text{If } n \text{ is an even natural number, } \sqrt[n]{x^n} = \lvert x \rvert. \end{cases}$	$\sqrt[4]{81x^4} = \lvert 3x \rvert = 3\lvert x \rvert$ because $(3x)^4 = 81x^4$. $\sqrt[4]{-16}$ *Not a real number* $\sqrt[5]{32a^{10}} = 2a^2$ because $(2a^2)^5 = 32a^{10}$. *No absolute value symbols are needed.* $\sqrt[6]{(m - 4)^6} = \lvert m - 4 \rvert$ because $(m - 4)^6 = (m - 4)^6$.

REVIEW EXERCISES

1. The graph of a square root function f is shown here. Find each of the following:

   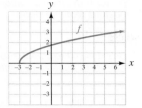

   a. $f(1)$
   b. $f(-3)$
   c. The value of x for which $f(x) = 3$
   d. The domain and range of f

2. a. Simplify $\sqrt{100a^2}$. Assume that the variable a is unrestricted.

   b. Simplify $\sqrt{100a^2}$. Assume that the variable a is a positive real number.

Simplify each expression. Assume that all variables are unrestricted and use absolute value symbols when necessary.

3. $\sqrt{49}$

4. $-\sqrt{121}$

5. $\sqrt{\dfrac{225}{49}}$

6. $\sqrt{-4}$

7. $\sqrt{100a^{12}}$

8. $\sqrt{25x^2}$

9. $\sqrt{x^8}$

10. $\sqrt{x^2 + 4x + 4}$

11. $\sqrt[3]{-27}$

12. $-\sqrt[3]{216}$

13. $\sqrt[3]{64x^6 y^3}$

14. $\sqrt[3]{\dfrac{x^9}{125}}$

15. $\sqrt[6]{64}$

16. $\sqrt[5]{-32}$

17. $\sqrt[4]{256x^8 y^4}$

18. $\sqrt[5]{(x+1)^5}$

19. $-\sqrt[4]{\dfrac{1}{16}}$

20. $\sqrt[4]{-81}$

21. $\sqrt[6]{-1}$

22. $\sqrt[3]{0}$

23. Find the domain of $f(x) = \sqrt{3x + 15}$.

24. **Geometry.**   The side of a square with area A square feet is given by the function $s(A) = \sqrt{A}$. Find the length of one side of a square that has an area of 169 ft^2.

25. **Cubes.**   The total surface area of a cube is related to its volume V by the function $A(V) = 6\sqrt[3]{V^2}$. Find the surface area of a cube with a volume of 8 cm^3.

26. Let $g(x) = \sqrt[3]{x^2} + 9$. Use a calculator fo find $g(-1.9)$ to four decimal places.

Graph each function. Find the domain and range.

27. $f(x) = \sqrt{x}$

28. $f(x) = \sqrt[3]{x}$

29. $f(x) = \sqrt{x + 2}$

30. $f(x) = -\sqrt[3]{x} + 3$

SECTION 9.2 ▶ Rational Exponents

DEFINITIONS AND CONCEPTS	EXAMPLES
To simplify exponential expressions involving **rational (fractional) exponents,** use the following rules to write the expressions in an equivalent radical form. $$x^{1/n} = \sqrt[n]{x} \qquad x^{m/n} = \left(\sqrt[n]{x}\right)^m = \sqrt[n]{x^m}$$	Simplify. All variables represent positive real numbers. $$25^{1/2} = \sqrt{25} = 5 \qquad \left(\dfrac{256}{d^4}\right)^{1/4} = \sqrt[4]{\dfrac{256}{d^4}} = \dfrac{4}{d}$$ $$8^{2/3} = \left(\sqrt[3]{8}\right)^2 = (2)^2 = 4 \qquad \left(t^{10}\right)^{6/5} = \left(\sqrt[5]{t^{10}}\right)^6 = \left(t^2\right)^6 = t^{12}$$
To be consistent with the definition of negative integer exponents, we define $x^{-m/n}$ as follows. $$x^{-m/n} = \dfrac{1}{x^{m/n}}$$ $$\dfrac{1}{x^{-m/n}} = x^{m/n}$$	Simplify. All variables represent positive real numbers. $$(125)^{-2/3} = \dfrac{1}{(125)^{2/3}} = \dfrac{1}{\left(\sqrt[3]{125}\right)^2} = \dfrac{1}{25}$$ $$\dfrac{1}{(-32x^5)^{-3/5}} = (-32x^5)^{3/5} = \left(\sqrt[5]{-32x^5}\right)^3 = -8x^3$$
The **rules for exponents** can be used to simplify expressions with rational (fractional) exponents.	Simplify: $$\dfrac{p^{5/3} p^{8/3}}{p^4} = p^{5/3 + 8/3 - 4} = p^{5/3 + 8/3 - 12/3} = p^{1/3}$$
We can write certain radical expressions as an equivalent exponential expression and use rules for exponents to simplify it. Then we can change that result back into a radical.	Simplify: $$\sqrt[4]{9} = \sqrt[4]{3^2} = 3^{2/4} = 3^{1/2} = \sqrt{3}$$

REVIEW EXERCISES

Write each expression in radical form.

31. $t^{1/2}$

32. $(5xy^3)^{1/4}$

Simplify each expression, if possible. Assume that all variables represent positive real numbers.

33. $25^{1/2}$

34. $-36^{1/2}$

35. $(-36)^{1/2}$

36. $1^{1/5}$

37. $\left(\dfrac{9}{x^2}\right)^{1/2}$

38. $(-8)^{1/3}$

39. $625^{1/4}$

40. $(81c^4d^4)^{1/4}$

41. $9^{3/2}$

42. $8^{-2/3}$

43. $-49^{5/2}$

44. $\dfrac{1}{100^{-1/2}}$

45. $\left(\dfrac{4}{9}\right)^{-3/2}$

46. $\dfrac{1}{25^{5/2}}$

47. $(25x^2y^4)^{3/2}$

48. $(8u^6v^3)^{-2/3}$

Perform the operations. Write answers without negative exponents. Assume that all variables represent positive real numbers.

49. $5^{1/4} \cdot 5^{1/2}$

50. $a^{3/7}a^{-2/7}$

51. $(k^{4/5})^{10}$

52. $\dfrac{3^{5/6}3^{1/3}}{3^{1/2}}$

Perform the multiplications. Assume all variables represent positive real numbers.

53. $u^{1/2}(u^{1/2} - u^{-1/2})$

54. $v^{2/3}(v^{1/3} + v^{4/3})$

Use rational exponents to simplify each radical. All variables represent positive real numbers.

55. $\sqrt[4]{a^2}$

56. $\sqrt[3]{\sqrt{c}}$

57. Visibility. The distance d in miles a person in an airplane can see to the horizon on a clear day is given by the formula $d = 1.22a^{1/2}$, where a is the altitude of the plane in feet. Find d.

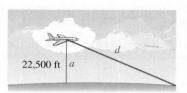

22,500 ft | a | d

58. Substitute the x- and y-coordinates of each point labeled in the graph into the equation

$$x^{2/3} + y^{2/3} = 32$$

Show that each one satisfies the equation.

$(-64, 64)$ $(64, 64)$

DEFINITIONS AND CONCEPTS	EXAMPLES
Product rule for radicals: $$\sqrt[n]{ab} = \sqrt[n]{a}\,\sqrt[n]{b}$$ The product rule for radicals can be used to simplify radical expressions. **Simplified form** of a radical: 1. Except for 1, the radicand has no perfect-square factors. 2. No fraction appears in the radicand. 3. No radical appears in the denominator. Review the lists of perfect squares, cubes, fourth powers, and fifth powers on pages 755 and 756.	Simplify: $\sqrt{98} = \sqrt{49 \cdot 2}$ Write 98 as the product of its greatest perfect-square factor and one other factor. $\quad = \sqrt{49}\sqrt{2}$ The square root of a product is equal to the product of the square roots. $\quad = 7\sqrt{2}$ Evaluate $\sqrt{49}$. Simplify: $\sqrt[3]{16x^4} = \sqrt[3]{8x^3 \cdot 2x}$ Write $16x^4$ as the product of its greatest perfect-cube factor and one other factor. $\quad = \sqrt[3]{8x^3}\sqrt[3]{2x}$ The cube root of a product is equal to the product of the cube roots. $\quad = 2x\sqrt[3]{2x}$ Simplify $\sqrt[3]{8x^3}$.

Quotient rule for radicals: $$\sqrt[n]{\dfrac{a}{b}} = \dfrac{\sqrt[n]{a}}{\sqrt[n]{b}}$$	Simplify: $$\sqrt{\dfrac{10}{25x^4}} = \dfrac{\sqrt{10}}{\sqrt{25x^4}} = \dfrac{\sqrt{10}}{5x^2}$$ Simplify: $$\sqrt[3]{\dfrac{16y^3}{125a^3}} = \dfrac{\sqrt[3]{16y^3}}{\sqrt[3]{125a^3}} = \dfrac{\sqrt[3]{8y^3}\sqrt[3]{2}}{5a} = \dfrac{2y\sqrt[3]{2}}{5a}$$
Radical expressions with the same index and radicand are called **like radicals.** Like radicals can be combined by addition and subtraction. To **combine like radicals,** we use the distributive property in reverse.	Add: $3\sqrt{6} + 5\sqrt{6} = (3 + 5)\sqrt{6} = 8\sqrt{6}$ Subtract: $8\sqrt[4]{2y} - 9\sqrt[4]{2y} = (8 - 9)\sqrt[4]{2y} = -\sqrt[4]{2y}$
If a sum or difference involves unlike radicals, make sure that each one is written in simplified form. After doing so, like radicals may result that can be combined.	Simplify: $$\begin{aligned}\sqrt[3]{54a^4} - \sqrt[3]{16a^4} &= \sqrt[3]{27a^3 \cdot 2a} - \sqrt[3]{8a^3 \cdot 2a}\\ &= \sqrt[3]{27a^3}\sqrt[3]{2a} - \sqrt[3]{8a^3}\sqrt[3]{2a}\\ &= 3a\sqrt[3]{2a} - 2a\sqrt[3]{2a}\\ &= (3a - 2a)\sqrt[3]{2a}\\ &= a\sqrt[3]{2a}\end{aligned}$$

REVIEW EXERCISES

Simplify each expression. All variables represent positive real numbers.

59. $\sqrt{80}$

60. $\sqrt[3]{54}$

61. $\sqrt[4]{160}$

62. $\sqrt[5]{-96}$

63. $\sqrt{8x^5}$

64. $\sqrt[4]{r^{17}}$

65. $\sqrt[3]{-27j^7k}$

66. $\sqrt[3]{-16x^5y^4}$

67. $\sqrt{\dfrac{m}{144n^{12}}}$

68. $\sqrt{\dfrac{17xy}{64a^4}}$

69. $\dfrac{\sqrt[5]{64x^8}}{\sqrt[5]{2x^3}}$

70. $\dfrac{\sqrt[5]{243x^{16}}}{\sqrt[5]{x}}$

Simplify and combine like radicals. All variables represent positive real numbers.

71. $\sqrt{2} + 2\sqrt{2}$

72. $6\sqrt{20} - \sqrt{5}$

73. $2\sqrt[3]{3} - \sqrt[3]{24}$

74. $-\sqrt[4]{32a^5} - 2\sqrt[4]{162a^5}$

75. $2x\sqrt{8} + 2\sqrt{200x^2} + \sqrt{50x^2}$

76. $\sqrt[3]{54x^3} - 3\sqrt[3]{16x^3} + 4\sqrt[3]{128x^3}$

77. $2\sqrt[4]{32t^3} - 8\sqrt[4]{6t^3} + 5\sqrt[4]{2t^3}$

78. $10\sqrt[4]{16x^9} - 8x^2\sqrt[4]{x} + 5\sqrt[4]{x^5}$

79. Explain the error in each simplification.

a. $2\sqrt{5x} + 3\sqrt{5x} = 5\sqrt{10x}$ ✗

b. $30 + 30\sqrt[4]{2} = 60\sqrt[4]{2}$ ✗

c. $7\sqrt[3]{y^2} - 5\sqrt[3]{y^2} = 2$ ✗

d. $6\sqrt{11ab} - 3\sqrt{5ab} = 3\sqrt{6ab}$ ✗

80. Sewing. A corner of fabric is folded over to form a collar and stitched down as shown. From the dimensions given in the figure, determine the exact number of inches of stitching that must be made. Then give an approximation to one decimal place. (All measurements are in inches.)

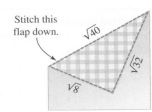

Stitch this flap down. $\sqrt{40}$ $\sqrt{32}$ $\sqrt{8}$

SECTION 9.4 ▶ Multiplying and Dividing Radical Expressions

DEFINITIONS AND CONCEPTS	EXAMPLES
We can use the product rule for radicals to **multiply radical expressions** that have the same index: $$\sqrt[n]{a}\,\sqrt[n]{b} = \sqrt[n]{ab}$$ provided $\sqrt[n]{a}$ and $\sqrt[n]{b}$ are real numbers.	Multiply and then simplify, if possible: $$\sqrt{6}\sqrt{8} = \sqrt{6\cdot 8} = \sqrt{48} = \sqrt{16\cdot 3} = \sqrt{16}\sqrt{3} = 4\sqrt{3}$$ $$\sqrt[3]{9x^4}\,\sqrt[3]{3x^2} = \sqrt[3]{9x^4\cdot 3x^2} = \sqrt[3]{27x^6} = 3x^2$$
We can use the **distributive property** to multiply a radical expression with two or more terms by a radical expression with one term.	Multiply and then simplify, if possible: $$2\sqrt{3}\left(4\sqrt{5} - 5\sqrt{2}\right) = 2\sqrt{3}\cdot 4\sqrt{5} - 2\sqrt{3}\cdot 5\sqrt{2}$$ $$= 2\cdot 4\sqrt{3\cdot 5} - 2\cdot 5\sqrt{3\cdot 2}$$ $$= 8\sqrt{15} - 10\sqrt{6}$$
We can use the **FOIL method** to multiply a radical expression with two terms by another radical expression with two terms.	Multiply and then simplify, if possible: $$\left(\sqrt[3]{x} - \sqrt[3]{3}\right)\left(\sqrt[3]{x} + \sqrt[3]{9}\right) = \overset{F}{\sqrt[3]{x}\sqrt[3]{x}} + \overset{O}{\sqrt[3]{x}\sqrt[3]{9}} - \overset{I}{\sqrt[3]{3}\sqrt[3]{x}} - \overset{L}{\sqrt[3]{3}\sqrt[3]{9}}$$ $$= \sqrt[3]{x^2} + \sqrt[3]{9x} - \sqrt[3]{3x} - \sqrt[3]{27}$$ $$= \sqrt[3]{x^2} + \sqrt[3]{9x} - \sqrt[3]{3x} - 3$$
If a radical appears in a denominator of a fraction, or if a radicand contains a fraction, we can write the radical in simplest form by **rationalizing the denominator.** To rationalize a denominator, we multiply the given expression by a carefully chosen form of 1.	Rationalize the denominator: $$\sqrt{\dfrac{10}{3}} = \dfrac{\sqrt{10}}{\sqrt{3}}\cdot\dfrac{\sqrt{3}}{\sqrt{3}} \qquad \sqrt[3]{\dfrac{5}{2p^2}} = \dfrac{\sqrt[3]{5}}{\sqrt[3]{2p^2}}\cdot\dfrac{\sqrt[3]{4p}}{\sqrt[3]{4p}}$$ $$= \dfrac{\sqrt{30}}{3} \qquad\qquad\qquad = \dfrac{\sqrt[3]{20p}}{\sqrt[3]{8p^3}}$$ $$\qquad\qquad\qquad\qquad\qquad = \dfrac{\sqrt[3]{20p}}{2p}$$
Radical expressions that involve the sum and difference of the same two terms are called **conjugates.**	Conjugates: $\sqrt{2x} + 3$ and $\sqrt{2x} - 3$
To **rationalize a two-termed denominator** of a fraction, multiply the numerator and the denominator by the **conjugate** of the denominator.	Rationalize the denominator: $$\dfrac{\sqrt{x} - 2}{\sqrt{x} + 2} = \dfrac{\sqrt{x} - 2}{\sqrt{x} + 2}\cdot\dfrac{\sqrt{x} - 2}{\sqrt{x} - 2}$$ $$= \dfrac{\sqrt{x}\sqrt{x} - 2\sqrt{x} - 2\sqrt{x} + 4}{\sqrt{x}\sqrt{x} - 2\sqrt{x} + 2\sqrt{x} - 4}$$ $$= \dfrac{x - 4\sqrt{x} + 4}{x - 4}$$

REVIEW EXERCISES

Simplify each expression. All variables represent positive real numbers.

81. $\sqrt{7}\sqrt{7}$

82. $(2\sqrt{5})(3\sqrt{2})$

83. $(-2\sqrt{8})^2$

84. $2\sqrt{6}\sqrt{15}$

85. $\sqrt{9x}\sqrt{x}$

86. $(\sqrt[3]{x+1})^3$

87. $-\sqrt[3]{2x^2}\sqrt[3]{4x^8}$

88. $\sqrt[5]{9}\cdot\sqrt[5]{27}$

89. $3\sqrt{7t}(2\sqrt{7t}+3\sqrt{3t^2})$

90. $-\sqrt[4]{4x^5y^{11}}\sqrt[4]{8x^9y^3}$

91. $(\sqrt{3b}+\sqrt{3})^2$

92. $(\sqrt[3]{3p}-2\sqrt[3]{2})(\sqrt[3]{3p}+\sqrt[3]{2})$

Rationalize each denominator. All variables represent positive real numbers.

93. $\dfrac{10}{\sqrt{3}}$

94. $\sqrt{\dfrac{3}{5xy}}$

95. $\dfrac{\sqrt[3]{6u}}{\sqrt[3]{u^5}}$

96. $\dfrac{\sqrt[4]{a}}{\sqrt[4]{3b^2}}$

97. $\dfrac{2}{\sqrt{2}-1}$

98. $\dfrac{4\sqrt{x}-2\sqrt{z}}{\sqrt{z}+4\sqrt{x}}$

99. Rationalize the numerator: $\dfrac{\sqrt{a}-\sqrt{b}}{\sqrt{a}}$

100. Volume. The formula relating the radius r of a sphere and its volume V is $r=\sqrt[3]{\dfrac{3V}{4\pi}}$. Write the radical in simplest form.

SECTION 9.5 ▶ Solving Radical Equations

DEFINITIONS AND CONCEPTS	EXAMPLES
We can use the **power rule** to solve radical equations. If $x=y$, then $x^n=y^n$. **To solve equations containing radicals:** 1. Isolate one radical expression on one side of the equation. 2. Raise both sides of the equation to the power that is the same as the index. 3. If it still contains a radical, go back to step 1. If it does not contain a radical, solve the resulting equation. 4. Check the proposed solutions in the original equation to eliminate **extraneous** solutions.	Solve each equation. $\sqrt{2x-2}+1=x$ $\sqrt{2x-2}=x-1$ $(\sqrt{2x-2})^2=(x-1)^2$ $2x-2=x^2-2x+1$ $0=x^2-4x+3$ $0=(x-3)(x-1)$ $x-3=0$ or $x-1=0$ $x=3$ | $x=1$ The solutions are 3 and 1. Verify that each satisfies the original equation. $\sqrt[3]{x+2}=3$ $(\sqrt[3]{x+2})^3=3^3$ $x+2=27$ $x=25$ The solution is 25. Verify that it satisfies the original equation.
When **more than one radical** appears in an equation, we often must use the power rule more than once to solve the equation. The **special-product rules** are often helpful when squaring expressions containing two terms, such as $(5-\sqrt{x})^2$. Warning: The result is not $25+x$.	Solve: $\sqrt{x}+\sqrt{x+5}=5$ $\sqrt{x+5}=5-\sqrt{x}$ To isolate one radical, subtract $\sqrt{x}$ from both sides. $(\sqrt{x+5})^2=(5-\sqrt{x})^2$ To eliminate one radical, square both sides. $x+5=25-10\sqrt{x}+x$ Perform the operations on each side. $-20=-10\sqrt{x}$ To isolate the radical term, subtract 25 and x from both sides. $2=\sqrt{x}$ To isolate the radical, divide both sides by -10. $(2)^2=(\sqrt{x})^2$ To eliminate the radical, square both sides again. $4=x$ The solution is 4. Verify that it satisfies the original equation.

REVIEW EXERCISES

Solve each equation. Write all proposed solutions. Cross out those that are extraneous.

101. $\sqrt{7x - 10} - 1 = 11$

102. $u = \sqrt{25u - 144}$

103. $2\sqrt{y - 3} = \sqrt{2y + 1}$

104. $\sqrt{z + 1} + \sqrt{z} = 2$

105. $\sqrt[3]{x^3 + 56} - 2 = x$

106. $a = \sqrt{a^2 + 5a - 35}$

107. $(x + 2)^{1/2} - (4 - x)^{1/2} = 0$ **108.** $\sqrt{b^2 + b} = \sqrt{3 - b^2}$

109. $\sqrt[4]{8x - 8} + 2 = 0$

110. $\sqrt{2m + 4} - \sqrt{m + 3} = 1$

111. Let $f(x) = \sqrt{5x + 1}$ and $g(x) = x + 1$. For what values of x is $f(x) = g(x)$?

112. Let $f(x) = \sqrt{2x^2 - 7x}$. For what value(s) of x is $f(x) = 2$?

Solve each equation for the specified variable.

113. $r = \sqrt{\dfrac{A}{P} - 1}$ for P

114. $h = \sqrt[3]{\dfrac{12I}{b}}$ for I

SECTION 9.6 ▶ Geometric Applications of Radicals

DEFINITIONS AND CONCEPTS	EXAMPLES

The Pythagorean theorem:
 	
If a and b are the lengths of the **legs** of a right triangle and c is the length of the **hypotenuse,** then $a^2 + b^2 = c^2$.
 	
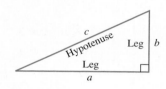
	Find the length of the third side of the right triangle.
	
	$a^2 + b^2 = c^2$ This is the Pythagorean equation.
	$6^2 + b^2 = 10^2$ Substitute 6 for a and 10 for c.
	$36 + b^2 = 100$
	    $b^2 = 64$ To isolate b^2, subtract 36 from both sides.
	    $b = \sqrt{64}$ Since b must be positive, find the positive square root of 64.
	    $b = 8$
	
	The length of the third side of the triangle is 8 ft.

In an **isosceles right triangle,** the length of the hypotenuse is $\sqrt{2}$ times the length of one leg.	If the length of one leg of an isosceles right triangle is 7 feet, the length of the hypotenuse is $7\sqrt{2}$ feet. 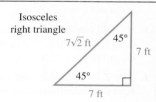
The hypotenuse of a **30°–60°–90° triangle** is twice as long as the shorter leg (the leg opposite the 30° angle.) The length of the longer leg (the leg opposite the 60° angle) is $\sqrt{3}$ times the length of the shorter leg.	If the shorter leg of a 30°–60°–90° triangle is 9 inches long: 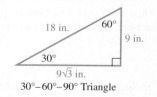 ■ The length of the hypotenuse is $2 \cdot 9 = 18$ inches. ■ The length of the longer leg is $\sqrt{3} \cdot 9 = 9\sqrt{3}$ inches.
The distance d between two points with coordinates (x_1, y_1) and (x_2, y_2) is given by **the distance formula:** $$d = \sqrt{(x_2 - x_1)^2 + (y_2 - y_1)^2}$$	The distance between points $(-2, 3)$ and $(1, 7)$ is: $\begin{aligned} d &= \sqrt{(x_2 - x_1)^2 + (y_2 - y_1)^2} \\ &= \sqrt{[1 - (-2)]^2 + (7 - 3)^2} \\ &= \sqrt{3^2 + 4^2} \\ &= \sqrt{9 + 16} \\ &= \sqrt{25} \\ &= 5 \end{aligned}$

The **midpoint** of a line segment with endpoints (x_1, y_1) and (x_2, y_2) is the point with coordinates $$\left(\frac{x_1 + x_2}{2}, \frac{y_1 + y_2}{2}\right)$$	Find the midpoint of the segment joining $(-3, 7)$ and $(5, -8)$. We let $(x_1, y_1) = (-3, 7)$ and $(x_2, y_2) = (5, -8)$ and substitute the coordinates into the midpoint formula. $$\left(\frac{x_1 + x_2}{2}, \frac{y_1 + y_2}{2}\right) = \left(\frac{-3 + 5}{2}, \frac{7 + (-8)}{2}\right)$$ $$= \left(1, -\frac{1}{2}\right) \qquad \text{This is the midpoint.}$$

REVIEW EXERCISES

115. Carpentry. The gable end of the roof shown below is divided in half by a vertical brace, 8 feet in height. Find the length of the roof line.

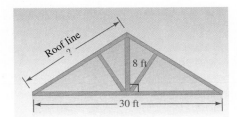

116. Sailing. A technique called *tacking* allows a sailboat to make progress into the wind. A sailboat follows the course shown below. Find d, the distance the boat advances into the wind after tacking.

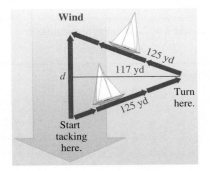

For problems 117–122, give the exact answer and then an approximation to two decimal places, when appropriate.

117. Find the length of the hypotenuse of an isosceles right triangle if the length of one leg is 7 meters.

118. The length of the hypotenuse of an isosceles right triangle is 15 yards. Find the length of one leg of the triangle.

119. The length of the hypotenuse of a 30°–60°–90° triangle is 12 centimeters. Find the length of each leg.

120. In a 30°–60°–90° triangle, the length of the longer leg is 60 feet. Find the length of the hypotenuse and the length of the shorter leg.

121. Find x and y.

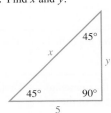

122. Find x and y.

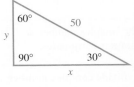

Find the distance between the points.

123. $(1, 3)$ and $(6, -9)$

124. $(-4, 6)$ and $(-2, 8)$

125. Find the midpoint of the segment joining $(8, -2)$ and $(6, -4)$.

126. If $(6, 1)$ is the midpoint of segment PQ and the coordinates of P are $(10, 4)$, find the coordinates of Q.

SECTION 9.7 ▶ **Complex Numbers**

DEFINITIONS AND CONCEPTS	EXAMPLES
The **imaginary number** i is defined as $$i = \sqrt{-1}$$ From the definition, it follows that $i^2 = -1$.	Write each expression in terms of i: $$\sqrt{-81} = \sqrt{-1 \cdot 81} \qquad \sqrt{-24} = \sqrt{-1 \cdot 24}$$ $$= \sqrt{-1}\sqrt{81} \qquad\qquad = \sqrt{-1}\sqrt{24}$$ $$= i \cdot 9 \qquad\qquad\qquad = i\sqrt{4}\sqrt{6}$$ $$= 9i \qquad\qquad\qquad = 2i\sqrt{6} \quad \text{or} \quad 2\sqrt{6}i$$

A **complex number** is any number that can be written in the form $a + bi$, where a and b are real numbers and $i = \sqrt{-1}$. We call a the **real part** and b the **imaginary part.**	Complex numbers: $5 + 3i$ 5 is the real part a and 3 is the imaginary part b. $16 = 16 + 0i$ 16 is the real part a and 0 is the imaginary part b. $9i = 0 + 9i$ 0 is the real part a and 9 is the imaginary part b.
Adding and subtracting complex numbers is similar to adding and subtracting polynomials. To **add two complex numbers,** add their real parts and add their imaginary parts. To **subtract two complex numbers,** add the opposite of the complex number being subtracted.	Add. Write the answer in the form $a + bi$. $\begin{aligned}(7 - 5i) + (3 + 9i) &= (7 + 3) + (-5 + 9)i \\ &= 10 + 4i\end{aligned}$ Add the real parts. Add the imaginary parts. Subtract. Write the answer in the form $a + bi$. $(8 - i) - (-1 + 6i) = (8 - i) + (1 - 6i)$ Add the opposite of $-1 + 6i$. $\qquad\qquad\qquad = (8 + 1) + [-1 + (-6)]i$ Add the real parts. Add the imaginary parts. $\qquad\qquad\qquad = 9 - 7i$
Multiplying complex numbers is similar to multiplying polynomials.	Multiply. Write the answers in the form $a + bi$. $\begin{aligned}3i(6 - 4i) &= 18i - 12i^2 \\ &= 18i - 12(-1) \\ &= 18i + 12 \\ &= 12 + 18i\end{aligned}$ $\begin{aligned}(4 + 7i)(2 - i) &= 8 - 4i + 14i - 7i^2 \\ &= 8 + 10i - 7(-1) \\ &= 8 + 10i + 7 \\ &= 15 + 10i\end{aligned}$
The complex numbers $a + bi$ and $a - bi$ are called **complex conjugates.**	The complex numbers $7 - 2i$ and $7 + 2i$ are complex conjugates.
To **divide complex numbers,** multiply the numerator and denominator by the complex conjugate of the denominator. The process is similar to rationalizing denominators.	Divide. Write the answers in the form $a + bi$. $\begin{aligned}\frac{3}{1 + i} \cdot \frac{1 - i}{1 - i} &= \frac{3(1 - i)}{1 - i + i - i^2} \\ &= \frac{3(1 - i)}{1 - (-1)} \\ &= \frac{3 - 3i}{2} \\ &= \frac{3}{2} - \frac{3}{2}i\end{aligned}$ $\begin{aligned}\frac{6 + i}{2 - i} \cdot \frac{2 + i}{2 + i} &= \frac{12 + 6i + 2i + i^2}{4 + 2i - 2i - i^2} \\ &= \frac{12 + 8i + (-1)}{4 - (-1)} \\ &= \frac{11 + 8i}{5} \\ &= \frac{11}{5} + \frac{8}{5}i\end{aligned}$
The **powers of i** cycle through four possible outcomes: i, -1, $-i$, and 1. $i^1 = \boxed{i} = i^5 = i^9 = \ldots$ $R = 1$ $i^2 = \boxed{-1} = i^6 = i^{10} = \ldots$ $R = 2$ $i^3 = \boxed{-i} = i^7 = i^{11} = \ldots$ $R = 3$ $i^4 = \boxed{1} = i^8 = i^{12} = \ldots$ $R = 0$	Simplify: i^{66} We divide 66 by 4 to get a remainder of 2. The remainder determines the power to which i is raised in the simplified form. Thus, $i^{66} = i^2 = -1$. $\begin{array}{r} 16\ \text{R}2 \\ 4\overline{)66} \\ \underline{-4} \\ 26 \\ \underline{-24} \\ 2 \end{array}$

REVIEW EXERCISES

Write each expression in terms of i.

127. $\sqrt{-25}$ **128.** $\sqrt{-18}$

129. $-\sqrt{-6}$ **130.** $\sqrt{-\dfrac{9}{64}}$

131. Complete the diagram.

Complex numbers

_____ numbers	_____ numbers

132. Determine whether each statement is true or false.

   a. Every real number is a complex number.

   b. $3 - 4i$ is a complex number.

   c. $\sqrt{-4}$ is a real number.

   d. i is a real number.

Give the complex conjugate of each number.

133. a. $3 + 6i$ **134. a.** $-1 - 7i$

     b. $19i$ **b.** $-i$

Perform the operations. Write all answers in the form a + bi.

135. $(3 + 4i) + (5 - 6i)$ **136.** $\left(7 - \sqrt{-9}\right) - \left(4 + \sqrt{-4}\right)$

137. $3i(2 - i)$ **138.** $(2 - 7i)(-3 + 4i)$

139. $\sqrt{-3} \cdot \sqrt{-9}$ **140.** $(9i)^2$

141. $\dfrac{5 + 14i}{2 + 3i}$ **142.** $\dfrac{3}{11i}$

Simplify each expression.

143. i^{42} **144.** i^{97}

---

9 ▶ Chapter Test

1. Fill in the blanks.

   a. The symbol $\sqrt{}$ is called a _____ symbol.

   b. The _____ number i is defined as $i = \sqrt{-1}$.

   c. Squaring both sides of an equation can introduce _____ solutions.

   d. An _____ right triangle is a right triangle with two legs of equal length.

   e. To _____ the denominator of $\dfrac{4}{\sqrt{5}}$, we multiply the fraction by $\dfrac{\sqrt{5}}{\sqrt{5}}$.

   f. A _____ number is any number that can be written in the form $a + bi$, where a and b are real numbers and $i = \sqrt{-1}$.

2. a. State the product rule for radicals.

   b. State the quotient rule for radicals.

   c. Explain why $\sqrt[4]{-16}$ is not a real number.

3. Graph $f(x) = \sqrt{x - 1}$. Find the domain and range of the function.

4. Diving. Refer to the illustration in the next column. The velocity v of an object in feet per second after it has fallen a distance of d feet is approximated by the function $v(d) = \sqrt{64.4d}$. Olympic diving platforms are 10 meters tall (approximately 32.8 feet). Estimate the velocity at which a diver hits the water from this height. Round to the nearest foot per second.

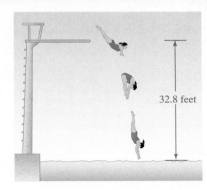

32.8 feet

5. Use the graph of function f below to find each of the following.

   a. $f(-1)$ **b.** $f(8)$

   c. The value of x for which $f(x) = 1$

   d. The domain and range of f

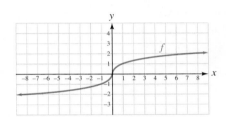

6. Find the domain of $f(x) = \sqrt{10x + 50}$.

Simplify each expression. All variables represent positive real numbers. Write answers without using negative exponents.

7. $(49x^4)^{1/2}$

8. $-27^{2/3}$

9. $36^{-3/2}$

10. $\left(-\dfrac{8}{125n^6}\right)^{-2/3}$

11. $\dfrac{2^{5/3}2^{1/6}}{2^{1/2}}$

12. $(a^{2/3})^{1/6}$

Simplify each expression. The variables are unrestricted.

13. $\sqrt{x^2}$

14. $\sqrt{y^2 - 10y + 25}$

Simplify each expression. All variables represent positive real numbers.

15. $\sqrt[3]{-64x^3y^6}$

16. $\sqrt{\dfrac{4a^2}{9}}$

17. $\sqrt[5]{(t + 8)^5}$

18. $\sqrt{540x^3y^5}$

19. $\dfrac{\sqrt[3]{24x^{15}y^4}}{\sqrt[3]{y}}$

20. $\sqrt[4]{32}$

Perform the operations and simplify. All variables represent positive real numbers.

21. $2\sqrt{48y^5} - 3y\sqrt{12y^3}$

22. $2\sqrt[3]{40} - \sqrt[3]{5,000} + 4\sqrt[3]{625}$

23. $\sqrt[4]{243z^{13}} + z\sqrt[4]{48z^9}$

24. $-2\sqrt{xy}\left(3\sqrt{x} + \sqrt{xy^3}\right)$

25. $\left(3\sqrt{2} + \sqrt{3}\right)\left(2\sqrt{2} - 3\sqrt{3}\right)$

26. $\left(\sqrt[3]{2a} + 9\right)^2$

27. $\dfrac{8}{\sqrt{10}}$

28. $\dfrac{\sqrt{x} + \sqrt{y}}{\sqrt{x} - \sqrt{y}}$

29. $\sqrt[3]{\dfrac{9}{4a}}$

30. Rationalize the numerator: $\dfrac{\sqrt{5} + 3}{-4\sqrt{2}}$

Solve each equation. Write all proposed solutions. Cross out those that are extraneous.

31. $4\sqrt{x} = \sqrt{x + 1}$

32. $\sqrt[3]{6n + 4} - 4 = 0$

33. $1 = \sqrt{u - 3} + \sqrt{u}$

34. $(2m^2 - 9)^{1/2} = m$

35. $\sqrt{t - 2} - t + 2 = 0$

36. $\sqrt{x - 8} + 10 = 0$

37. Let $f(x) = \sqrt[4]{15 - x}$ and $g(x) = \sqrt[4]{13 - 2x}$. Find all values of x for which $f(x) = g(x)$.

38. Solve $r = \sqrt[3]{\dfrac{GMt^2}{4\pi^2}}$ for G.

Find the missing side lengths in each triangle. Give the exact answer and then an approximation to two decimal places, when appropriate.

39.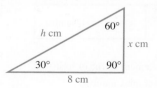

40.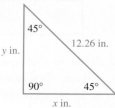

41. Find the distance between $(-2, 5)$ and $(22, 12)$.

42. Find the coordinates of the midpoint of the line segment joining $(-2, -5)$ and $(7, -11)$.

43. If $(3, 0)$ is the midpoint of segment PQ and the coordinates of P are $(-1, -3)$, find the coordinates of Q.

44. **Shipping Crates.** The diagonal brace on the shipping crate in the illustration is 53 inches. Find the height h of the crate.

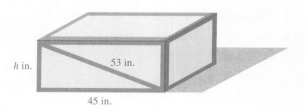

45. Express $\sqrt{-45}$ in terms of i.

46. Simplify: i^{106}

Perform the operations. Write all answers in the form $a + bi$.

47. $(9 + 4i) + (-13 + 7i)$

48. $\left(3 - \sqrt{-9}\right) - \left(-1 + \sqrt{-16}\right)$

49. $15i(3 - 5i)$

50. $(8 + 10i)(-7 - i)$

51. $\dfrac{1}{i\sqrt{2}}$

52. $\dfrac{2 + i}{3 - i}$

Group Project

A Spiral of Roots

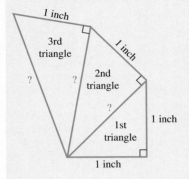

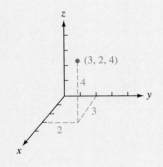

Overview: In this activity, you will create a visual representation of a collection of square roots.

Instructions: Form groups of 2 or 3 students. You will need a piece of unlined paper, a protractor, a ruler, and a pencil. Begin by drawing an isosceles right triangle with legs of length 1 inch in the middle of the paper. (See the illustration.) Use the Pythagorean theorem to determine the length of the hypotenuse. Draw a second right triangle using the hypotenuse of the first right triangle as one leg. Draw its second leg with length 1 inch. Find the length of the hypotenuse of the second triangle.

Continue creating right triangles, using the previous hypotenuse as one leg and drawing a new second leg of length 1 inch each time. Calculate the length of each resulting hypotenuse. When the figure begins to spiral onto itself, you may stop the process. Make a list of the lengths of each hypotenuse. What pattern do you see?

Graphing in Three Dimensions

Overview: In this activity, you will find the distance between two points that lie in three-dimensional space.

Instructions: Form groups of 2 or 3 students. In a three-dimensional Cartesian coordinate system, the positive x-axis is horizontal and pointing toward the viewer (out of the page), the positive y-axis is also horizontal and pointing to the right, and the positive z-axis is vertical, pointing up. A point is located by plotting an ordered triple of numbers (x, y, z). In the illustration, the point $(3, 2, 4)$ is plotted.

In three dimensions, the distance formula is

$$d = \sqrt{(x_2 - x_1)^2 + (y_2 - y_1)^2 + (z_2 - z_1)^2}$$

1. Copy the illustration shown. Then plot the point $(1, 4, 3)$. Use the distance formula to find the distance between these two points.
2. Draw another three-dimensional coordinate system and plot the points $(-3, 3, -4)$ and $(2, -3, 2)$. Use the distance formula to find the distance between these two points.

Quadratic Equations, Functions, and Inequalities

© Robert E Daemmrich/Getty Images

from Campus to Careers

Police Patrol Officer

The responsibilities of a police patrol officer are extremely broad. Quite often, he or she must make a split-second decision while under enormous pressure. One internet vocational website cautions anyone considering such a career to "pay attention in your mathematics and science classes. Those classes help sharpen your ability to think things through and solve problems—an important part of police work."

Problem 93 in **Study Set 10.2**, **problem 87** in **Study Set 10.3**, and **problem 89** in **Study Set 10.4** involve situations that a police patrol officer encounters on the job. The mathematical concepts discussed in this chapter can be used to solve those problems.

JOB TITLE:
Police Patrol Officer

EDUCATION:
A basic high school education is required, however, an associate's or bachelor's degree is recommended.

JOB OUTLOOK:
In general, employment is expected to increase approximately 10% through the year 2018.

ANNUAL EARNINGS:
Mean annual base salary $55,180 with an opportunity for overtime pay

FOR MORE INFORMATION:
www.bls.gov/oco/ocos160.htm

If you're like most students, your algebra notebook could probably use some attention at this stage of the course. You will definitely appreciate a well-organized notebook when it comes time to study for the final exam. Here are some suggestions to put it in tip-top shape.

ORGANIZE YOUR NOTEBOOK INTO SECTIONS: Create a separate section in the notebook for each chapter (or unit of study) that your class has covered this term.

ORGANIZE THE PAPERS WITHIN EACH SECTION: One recommended order is to begin each section with your class notes, followed by your completed homework assignments, then any study sheets or handouts, and, finally, all graded quizzes and tests.

Now Try This ▶

1. Organize your algebra notebook using the guidelines given above.
2. Write a Table of Contents to place at the beginning of your notebook. List each chapter (or unit of study) and include the dates over which the material was covered.
3. Compare your completed notebook with those of other students in your class. Have you overlooked any important items that would be useful when studying for the final exam?

SECTION 10.1

The Square Root Property and Completing the Square

OBJECTIVES

1 Use the square root property to solve quadratic equations.

2 Solve quadratic equations by completing the square.

ARE YOU READY?

The following problems review some basic skills that are needed when using the square root property and completing the square.

1. Simplify: **a.** $\sqrt{28}$
                b. $\sqrt{-36}$

2. Rationalize: $\sqrt{\dfrac{5}{6}}$

3. What is one-half of 9?

4. Find the square of $\dfrac{7}{2}$.

5. Fill in the blank: $1 + \dfrac{25}{144} = \dfrac{}{144}$

6. Factor: $x^2 - 8x + 16$

Recall that a *quadratic equation* is an equation of the form $ax^2 + bx + c = 0$, where a, b, and c are real numbers and $a \ne 0$. We have solved quadratic equations, such as $6x^2 - 7x - 3 = 0$, using factoring and the zero-factor property as shown below.

$$6x^2 - 7x - 3 = 0$$
$$(2x - 3)(3x + 1) = 0 \qquad \text{Factor the trinomial.}$$
$$2x - 3 = 0 \quad \text{or} \quad 3x + 1 = 0 \qquad \text{Set each factor equal to 0.}$$
$$x = \frac{3}{2} \qquad\qquad x = -\frac{1}{3} \qquad \text{Solve each linear equation.}$$

The solutions are $-\frac{1}{3}$ and $\frac{3}{2}$.

Many expressions do not factor as easily as $6x^2 - 7x - 3$. For example, it would be difficult to solve $2x^2 + 4x + 1 = 0$ by factoring, because $2x^2 + 4x + 1$ cannot be factored by using only integers. In this section and the next, we will develop more general methods that enable us to solve any quadratic equation. Those methods are based on the *square root property*.

1 Use the Square Root Property to Solve Quadratic Equations.

To develop general methods for solving quadratic equations, we first consider the equation $x^2 = c$. If $c \geq 0$, we can find the real solutions of $x^2 = c$ as follows:

$$x^2 = c$$

$$x^2 - c = 0 \qquad \text{Subtract } c \text{ from both sides.}$$

$$x^2 - \left(\sqrt{c}\right)^2 = 0 \qquad \text{Replace } c \text{ with } \left(\sqrt{c}\right)^2, \text{ since } c = \left(\sqrt{c}\right)^2.$$

$$\left(x + \sqrt{c}\right)\left(x - \sqrt{c}\right) = 0 \qquad \text{Factor the difference of two squares.}$$

$$x + \sqrt{c} = 0 \qquad \text{or} \qquad x - \sqrt{c} = 0 \qquad \text{Set each factor equal to 0.}$$

$$x = -\sqrt{c} \qquad \Big| \qquad x = \sqrt{c} \qquad \text{Solve each linear equation.}$$

The solutions of $x^2 = c$ are $\sqrt{c}$ and $-\sqrt{c}$.

The Square Root Property	For any nonnegative real number c, if $x^2 = c$, then $$x = \sqrt{c} \qquad \text{or} \qquad x = -\sqrt{c}$$

The Language of Algebra

The ± symbol is often seen in political polls. A candidate with 48% (± 4%) support could be between 48 + 4 = 52% and 48 − 4 = 44%

We can write the conclusion of the square root property in a more compact form, called **double-sign notation.**

$$x = \pm\sqrt{c} \qquad \text{This is formally read as "x equals the positive or negative square root of } c\text{."}$$
$$\text{However, it is often read more informally as "x equals plus or minus the square root of } c\text{."}$$

EXAMPLE 1 Solve: $x^2 - 12 = 0$

Strategy Since $x^2 - 12$ does not factor as a difference of two integer squares, we must take an alternate approach. We will add 12 to both sides of the equation and use the square root property to solve for x.

Why After adding 12 to both sides, the resulting equivalent equation will have the desired form $x^2 = c$.

Solution

$$x^2 - 12 = 0 \qquad \text{This is the equation to solve. It is a quadratic equation that is missing an x-term.}$$

$$x^2 = 12 \qquad \text{To isolate } x^2 \text{ on the left side, add 12 to both sides.}$$

$$x = \sqrt{12} \quad \text{or} \quad x = -\sqrt{12} \qquad \text{Use the square root property.}$$

$$x = 2\sqrt{3} \quad \Big| \quad x = -2\sqrt{3} \qquad \text{Simplify: } \sqrt{12} = \sqrt{4}\sqrt{3} = 2\sqrt{3}.$$

Check:

$$x^2 - 12 = 0 \qquad\qquad x^2 - 12 = 0$$

$$\left(2\sqrt{3}\right)^2 - 12 \stackrel{?}{=} 0 \qquad\qquad \left(-2\sqrt{3}\right)^2 - 12 \stackrel{?}{=} 0$$

$$12 - 12 \stackrel{?}{=} 0 \qquad\qquad 12 - 12 \stackrel{?}{=} 0$$

$$0 = 0 \quad \text{True} \qquad\qquad 0 = 0 \quad \text{True}$$

The exact solutions are $2\sqrt{3}$ and $-2\sqrt{3}$, which can be written using double-sign notation as $\pm 2\sqrt{3}$. The solution set is $\left\{-2\sqrt{3}, 2\sqrt{3}\right\}$. We can use a calculator to approximate the solutions. To the nearest hundredth, they are ± 3.46.

Self Check 1   Solve: $x^2 - 18 = 0$

Now Try ▶ Problems 15 and 19

EXAMPLE 2   **Phonograph Records.**   Before compact discs, music was recorded on thin vinyl discs. The discs used for long-playing records had a surface area of about 111 square inches per side. Find the radius of a long-playing record to the nearest tenth of an inch.

CD ◀—r—▶

Strategy   The area A of a circle with radius r is given by the formula $A = \pi r^2$. We will find the radius of a record by substituting 111 for A and dividing both sides by π. Then we will use the square root property to solve for r.

Why   After substituting 111 for A and dividing both sides by π, the resulting equivalent equation will have the desired form $r^2 = c$.

Solution

$$A = \pi r^2 \qquad \text{This is the formula for the area of a circle.}$$

$$111 = \pi r^2 \qquad \text{Substitute 111 for A.}$$

$$\frac{111}{\pi} = r^2 \qquad \text{To undo the multiplication by } \pi, \text{ divide both sides by } \pi.$$

$$r = \sqrt{\frac{111}{\pi}} \quad \text{or} \quad r = -\sqrt{\frac{111}{\pi}} \qquad \begin{array}{l}\text{Use the square root property. Since the radius of the} \\ \text{record cannot be negative, discard the second solution.}\end{array}$$

The radius of a long-playing record is $\sqrt{\frac{111}{\pi}}$ inches—to the nearest tenth, 5.9 inches.

Self Check 2   **Restaurant Seating.**   A restaurant requires 14 square feet of floor area for one of their round tables. Find the radius of a table. Round to the nearest hundredth.

Now Try ▶ Problems 35 and 103

Some quadratic equations have solutions that are not real numbers.

EXAMPLE 3   Solve: $4x^2 + 25 = 0$

Strategy   We will subtract 25 from both sides of the equation and divide both sides by 4. Then we will use the square root property to solve for x.

Why   After subtracting 25 from both sides and dividing both sides by 4, the resulting equivalent equation will have the desired form $x^2 = $ a constant.

Solution

$$4x^2 + 25 = 0 \qquad \text{This is the equation to solve.}$$

$$x^2 = -\frac{25}{4} \qquad \text{To isolate } x^2, \text{ subtract 25 from both sides and divide both sides by 4.}$$

$$x = \pm\sqrt{-\frac{25}{4}} \qquad \begin{array}{l}\text{Use the square root property and write the result using double-} \\ \text{sign notation.}\end{array}$$

$$x = \pm\frac{5}{2}i \qquad \text{Simplify the radical: } \sqrt{-\frac{25}{4}} = \sqrt{-1 \cdot \frac{25}{4}} = \sqrt{-1}\frac{\sqrt{25}}{\sqrt{4}} = \frac{5}{2}i$$

Since the solutions are $\frac{5}{2}i$ and $-\frac{5}{2}i$, the solution set is $\left\{\frac{5}{2}i, -\frac{5}{2}i\right\}$.

Check:

$$4x^2 + 25 = 0 \qquad\qquad 4x^2 + 25 = 0$$

$$4\left(\frac{5}{2}i\right)^2 + 25 \overset{?}{=} 0 \qquad\qquad 4\left(-\frac{5}{2}i\right)^2 + 25 \overset{?}{=} 0$$

$$4\left(\frac{25}{4}\right)i^2 + 25 \overset{?}{=} 0 \qquad\qquad 4\left(\frac{25}{4}\right)i^2 + 25 \overset{?}{=} 0$$

$$25(-1) + 25 \overset{?}{=} 0 \qquad\qquad 25(-1) + 25 \overset{?}{=} 0$$

$$0 = 0 \quad \text{True} \qquad\qquad 0 = 0 \quad \text{True}$$

> **Self Check 3** Solve: $16x^2 + 49 = 0$
>
> **Now Try** ▶ Problem 27

We can extend the square root property to solve equations that involve the square of a binomial and a constant.

EXAMPLE 4 Use the square root property to solve $(x - 1)^2 = 16$.

Strategy Instead of a variable squared on the left side, we have a quantity squared. We still use the square root property to solve the equation.

Why We want to eliminate the square on the binomial, so that we can eventually isolate the variable on one side of the equation.

Solution

$$(x - 1)^2 = 16 \qquad \text{This is the equation to solve.}$$

$$x - 1 = \pm\sqrt{16} \qquad \text{Use the square root property and write the result using double-sign notation.}$$

$$x - 1 = \pm 4 \qquad \text{Simplify: } \sqrt{16} = 4.$$

$$x = 1 \pm 4 \qquad \text{To isolate } x, \text{ add 1 to both sides. It is standard practice to write the addition of the 1 in front of the } \pm \text{ symbol. Read as "one plus or minus four."}$$

$$x = 1 + 4 \quad \text{or} \quad x = 1 - 4 \qquad \text{To find one solution, use +. To find the other, use −.}$$

$$x = 5 \qquad\qquad x = -3 \qquad \text{Add (subtract).}$$

Verify that 5 and −3 satisfy the original equation.

> **Caution**
>
> It might be tempting to square the binomial on the left side of $(x - 1)^2 = 16$. However, that causes unnecessary, additional steps to solve the equation another way.
>
> $$(x - 1)^2 = 16$$
>
> $$x^2 - 2x + 1 = 16$$

> **Self Check 4** Use the square root property to solve $(x + 2)^2 = 9$.
>
> **Now Try** ▶ Problems 31 and 33

EXAMPLE 5 Let $f(x) = (3x + 8)^2$. For what value(s) of x is $f(x) = 6$?

Strategy We will substitute 6 for $f(x)$ and solve for x.

Why In the equation, there are two unknowns, x and $f(x)$. If we replace $f(x)$ with 6, we can use equation-solving techniques to find x.

Solution

$$f(x) = (3x + 8)^2 \qquad \text{This is the given function.}$$

$$6 = (3x + 8)^2 \qquad \text{Substitute 6 for } f(x).$$

$$\pm \sqrt{6} = 3x + 8 \qquad \begin{array}{l}\text{Use the square root property and write}\\\text{the result using double-sign notation.}\end{array}$$

$$-8 \pm \sqrt{6} = 3x \qquad \begin{array}{l}\text{To isolate the variable term } 3x, \text{ subtract 8 from both sides. It is}\\\text{standard practice to write the subtraction of } -8 \text{ in front of the } \pm.\end{array}$$

$$\frac{-8 \pm \sqrt{6}}{3} = x \qquad \text{To isolate } x, \text{ undo the multiplication by 3 by dividing both sides by 3.}$$

We have found that $f(x) = 6$ when $x = \dfrac{-8 - \sqrt{6}}{3}$ or $x = \dfrac{-8 + \sqrt{6}}{3}$. To check, verify that $f\left(\dfrac{-8 - \sqrt{6}}{3}\right) = 6$ and $f\left(\dfrac{-8 + \sqrt{6}}{3}\right) = 6$.

> **Self Check 5**   Let $f(x) = (4x + 11)^2$. For what values of x is $f(x) = 3$?
>
> **Now Try** ▶ Problem 35

2   Solve Quadratic Equations by Completing the Square.

When the polynomial in a quadratic equation doesn't factor easily, we can solve the equation by **completing the square.** This method is based on the following perfect-square trinomials (with leading coefficients of 1) and their factored forms:

$$x^2 + 2bx + b^2 = (x + b)^2 \qquad \text{and} \qquad x^2 - 2bx + b^2 = (x - b)^2$$

The Language of Algebra

Recall that trinomials that are the square of a binomial are called **perfect-square trinomials**.

In each of these perfect-square trinomials, the third term is the square of one-half of the coefficient of x.

- In $x^2 + 2bx + b^2$, the coefficient of x is $2b$. If we find $\frac{1}{2} \cdot 2b$, which is b, and square it, we get the third term, b^2.

- In $x^2 - 2bx + b^2$, the coefficient of x is $-2b$. If we find $\frac{1}{2}(-2b)$, which is $-b$, and square it, we get the third term: $(-b)^2 = b^2$.

We can use these observations to change certain binomials into perfect-square trinomials using a 3-step process. For example, to change $x^2 + 12x$ into a perfect-square trinomial, we find one-half of the coefficient of x, square the result, and add the square to $x^2 + 12x$.

$$x^2 + 12x + \boxed{}$$

Step 1: Find one-half of the coefficient of x.   Step 3: Add the square to the binomial.

$$\frac{1}{2} \cdot 12 = 6 \qquad 6^2 = 36$$

Step 2: Square the result.

We obtain the perfect-square trinomial $x^2 + 12x + 36$, which factors as $(x + 6)^2$. By adding 36 to $x^2 + 12x$, we say that we have *completed the square on* $x^2 + 12x$.

Completing the Square

To complete the square on $x^2 + bx$, add the square of one-half of the coefficient of x:

$$x^2 + bx + \left(\frac{1}{2}b\right)^2$$

EXAMPLE 6   Complete the square and factor the resulting perfect-square trinomial: **a.** $x^2 + 10x$

b. $x^2 - 11x$ **c.** $x^2 + \dfrac{7}{3}x$

Strategy   We will add the square of one-half of the coefficient of x to the given binomial.

Why   Adding such a term will change the binomial into a perfect-square trinomial that will factor.

Solution   **a.** To make $x^2 + 10x$ a perfect-square trinomial, we find one-half of 10, square it, and add the result to $x^2 + 10x$.

$$x^2 + 10x + 25 \quad \text{\small $\frac{1}{2} \cdot 10 = 5$ and $5^2 = 25$. Add 25 to the given binomial.}$$

This trinomial factors as $(x + 5)^2$. To check, we square $x + 5$ and verify that the result is $x^2 + 10x + 25$.

b. To make $x^2 - 11x$ a perfect-square trinomial, we find one-half of -11, square it, and add the result to $x^2 - 11x$.

$$x^2 - 11x + \frac{121}{4} \quad \text{\small $\frac{1}{2}(-11) = -\frac{11}{2}$ and $\left(-\frac{11}{2}\right)^2 = \frac{121}{4}$. Add $\frac{121}{4}$ to the given binomial.}$$

This trinomial factors as $\left(x - \dfrac{11}{2}\right)^2$. Check using multiplication or using a special-product rule.

c. To make $x^2 + \dfrac{7}{3}x$ a perfect-square trinomial, we find one-half of $\dfrac{7}{3}$, square it, and add the result to $x^2 + \dfrac{7}{3}x$.

$$x^2 + \frac{7}{3}x + \frac{49}{36} \quad \text{\small To complete the square: $\frac{1}{2}\left(\frac{7}{3}\right) = \frac{7}{6}$ and $\left(\frac{7}{6}\right)^2 = \frac{49}{36}$.}$$
$$\text{\small Add $\frac{49}{36}$ to the given binomial.}$$

The trinomial factors as $\left(x + \dfrac{7}{6}\right)^2$.

Caution

Realize that when we complete the square on a binomial, we are not writing an equivalent trinomial expression. Since the result is a completely different polynomial, it would be incorrect to use an $=$ symbol between the two.

$$x^2 + 10x = x^2 + 10x + 25$$

The Language of Algebra

When we add $\frac{121}{4}$ to $x^2 - 11x$, we say we have **completed the square** on $x^2 - 11x$. For that reason, binomials such as $x^2 - 11x$ are often called **incomplete squares**.

Self Check 6   Complete the square on $a^2 - 5a$ and factor the resulting trinomial.

Now Try ▶ Problems 39 and 41

To solve an equation of the form $ax^2 + bx + c = 0$ by completing the square, we use the following steps.

Completing the Square to Solve a Quadratic Equation in x

1. If the coefficient of x^2 is 1, go to step 2. If it is not, make it 1 by dividing both sides of the equation by the coefficient of x^2.

2. Get all variable terms on one side of the equation and constants on the other side.

3. Complete the square by finding one-half of the coefficient of x, squaring the result, and adding the square to both sides of the equation.

4. Factor the perfect-square trinomial as the square of a binomial.

5. Solve the resulting equation using the square root property.

6. Check your answers in the original equation.

EXAMPLE 7 Solve by completing the square: $x^2 - 8x - 5 = 0$. Approximate the solutions to the nearest hundredth.

Strategy We will use the addition property of equality and add 5 to both sides. Then we will complete the square to solve for x.

Why To prepare to complete the square, we need to isolate the variable terms, x^2 and $-8x$, on the left side of the equation and the constant term on the right side.

Solution

$$x^2 - 8x - 5 = 0 \quad \text{This is the equation to solve.}$$
$$x^2 - 8x \quad\ \ = 5 \quad \text{Add 5 to both sides so that the constant term is on the right side.}$$

The Language of Algebra

For $x^2 - 8x - 5$, we call x^2 the **leading term,** the **first term,** or the **quadratic term.** We call $-8x$ the **second term** or the **linear term.** Together, x^2 and $-8x$ are called **variable terms.** We call -5 the **constant term** or the **third term.**

In $x^2 - 8x$, the coefficient of x is -8. One-half of -8 is -4, and $(-4)^2 = 16$. If we add 16 to $x^2 - 8x$, it becomes a perfect-square trinomial.

$$x^2 - 8x + \mathbf{16} = 5 + \mathbf{16} \qquad \begin{array}{l}\text{To complete the square on the}\\ \text{left side, add 16 to both sides.}\end{array}$$

$$(x - 4)^2 = 21 \qquad \text{Factor the perfect-square trinomial. Add on the right side.}$$

$$x - 4 = \pm\sqrt{21} \qquad \begin{array}{l}\text{By the square root property, } x - 4 = \sqrt{21} \text{ or}\\ x - 4 = -\sqrt{21}. \text{ Use double-sign notation to show this.}\end{array}$$

$$x = 4 \pm \sqrt{21} \qquad \begin{array}{l}\text{To isolate } x, \text{ add 4 to both sides. It is common practice to}\\ \text{write the 4 in front of the } \pm \text{ symbol.}\end{array}$$

The exact solutions of $x^2 - 8x - 5 = 0$ are two irrational numbers, $4 + \sqrt{21}$ and $4 - \sqrt{21}$.

We also can approximate each solution by using the decimal approximation of $\sqrt{21}$, which is 4.582575695:

$$4 + \sqrt{21} \approx 4 + 4.582575695 \qquad\qquad 4 - \sqrt{21} \approx 4 - 4.582575695$$
$$\approx 8.58 \qquad\qquad\qquad\qquad\qquad\qquad \approx -0.58$$

To the nearest hundredth, the solutions are 8.58 and -0.58. These approximations can be used to check the exact solutions informally by substituting each of them into the original equation.

Self Check 7 Solve by completing the square: $x^2 - 10x - 4 = 0$. Approximate the solutions to the nearest hundredth.

Now Try ▶ Problem 47

If the coefficient of the squared variable (called the **leading coefficient**) of a quadratic equation is not 1, we must make it 1 before we can complete the square.

EXAMPLE 8 Solve $6x^2 + 5x - 6 = 0$ by completing the square.

Strategy We will begin by dividing both sides of the equation by 6.

Why This will create a leading coefficient that is 1 so that we can proceed to complete the square to solve the equation.

Solution **Step 1:** To make the coefficient of x^2 equal to 1, we divide both sides of the equation by 6.

$$6x^2 + 5x - 6 = 0 \qquad \text{This is the equation to solve.}$$

$$\frac{6x^2}{6} + \frac{5x}{6} - \frac{6}{6} = \frac{0}{6} \qquad \text{Divide both sides by 6, term-by-term.}$$

$$x^2 + \frac{5}{6}x - 1 = 0 \qquad \text{Simplify. The coefficient of } x^2 \text{ is now 1.}$$

Step 2: To have the constant term on one side of the equation and the variable terms on the other, add 1 to both sides.

$$x^2 + \frac{5}{6}x \qquad = 1$$ *Some students find it helpful to leave additional space here to prepare for completing the square.*

Step 3: The coefficient of x is $\frac{5}{6}$, one-half of $\frac{5}{6}$ is $\frac{5}{12}$, and $\left(\frac{5}{12}\right)^2 = \frac{25}{144}$. To complete the square, we add $\frac{25}{144}$ to both sides.

$$x^2 + \frac{5}{6}x + \frac{25}{144} = 1 + \frac{25}{144}$$

$$x^2 + \frac{5}{6}x + \frac{25}{144} = \frac{169}{144}$$ *On the right side, add: $1 + \frac{25}{144} = \frac{144}{144} + \frac{25}{144} = \frac{169}{144}$.*

Step 4: Factor the left side of the equation.

$$\left(x + \frac{5}{12}\right)^2 = \frac{169}{144}$$ *$x^2 + \frac{5}{6}x + \frac{25}{144}$ is a perfect-square trinomial.*

Step 5: We can solve the resulting equation by using the square root property.

$$x + \frac{5}{12} = \pm\sqrt{\frac{169}{144}}$$ *Don't forget to write the $\pm$ symbol.*

$$x + \frac{5}{12} = \pm\frac{13}{12}$$ *Simplify: $\pm\sqrt{\frac{169}{144}} = \pm\frac{13}{12}$.*

$$x = -\frac{5}{12} \pm \frac{13}{12}$$ *To isolate x, subtract $\frac{5}{12}$ from both sides. These are like terms that can be added and subtracted.*

To find the first solution, we evaluate the expression using the $+$ symbol. To find the second solution, we evaluate the expression using the $-$ symbol.

$$x = -\frac{5}{12} + \frac{13}{12} \quad \text{or} \quad x = -\frac{5}{12} - \frac{13}{12}$$

$$x = \frac{8}{12} \qquad\qquad x = -\frac{18}{12}$$ *Add (subtract) the fractions.*

$$x = \frac{2}{3} \qquad\qquad x = -\frac{3}{2}$$ *Simplify each fraction. The solutions are two rational numbers.*

Step 6: Check each solution, $\frac{2}{3}$ and $-\frac{3}{2}$, in the original equation.

Self Check 8   Solve by completing the square: $3x^2 + 2x - 8 = 0$

Now Try ▶ Problem 55

EXAMPLE 9   Solve: $2x^2 + 4x + 1 = 0$. Approximate the solutions to the nearest hundredth.

Strategy   We will follow the steps for solving a quadratic equation by completing the square.

Why   Since the trinomial $2x^2 + 4x + 1$ cannot be factored using only integers, solving the equation by completing the square is our only option at this time.

Solution

$$2x^2 + 4x + 1 = 0$$ This is the equation to solve.

$$x^2 + 2x + \frac{1}{2} = 0$$ Divide both sides by 2 to make the coefficient of x^2 equal to 1.

$$x^2 + 2x \qquad = -\frac{1}{2}$$ Subtract $\frac{1}{2}$ from both sides so that the constant term is on the right side.

$$x^2 + 2x + 1 = -\frac{1}{2} + 1$$ To complete the square, square one-half of the coefficient of x and add it to both sides.

$$(x + 1)^2 = \frac{1}{2}$$ Factor on the left side and do the addition on the right side.

$$x + 1 = \pm\sqrt{\frac{1}{2}}$$ Use the square root property. Don't forget the $\pm$ symbol.

$$x = -1 \pm \sqrt{\frac{1}{2}}$$ To isolate x, subtract 1 from both sides.

To write $\sqrt{\frac{1}{2}}$ in simplified radical form, we use the quotient rule for radicals and then rationalize the denominator.

$$x = -1 + \frac{\sqrt{2}}{2} \quad \text{or} \quad x = -1 - \frac{\sqrt{2}}{2}$$ Rationalize: $\sqrt{\frac{1}{2}} = \frac{\sqrt{1}}{\sqrt{2}} = \frac{1 \cdot \sqrt{2}}{\sqrt{2}\sqrt{2}} = \frac{\sqrt{2}}{2}$.

We can express each solution in an alternate form if we write -1 as a fraction with a denominator of 2.

$$x = -\frac{2}{2} + \frac{\sqrt{2}}{2} \quad \text{or} \quad x = -\frac{2}{2} - \frac{\sqrt{2}}{2}$$ Write -1 as $-\frac{2}{2}$.

$$x = \frac{-2 + \sqrt{2}}{2} \quad \bigg| \quad x = \frac{-2 - \sqrt{2}}{2}$$ Add (subtract) the numerators and keep the common denominator 2.

The exact solutions are $\frac{-2 + \sqrt{2}}{2}$ and $\frac{-2 - \sqrt{2}}{2}$, or simply, $\frac{-2 \pm \sqrt{2}}{2}$. We can use a calculator to approximate them. To the nearest hundredth, they are -0.29 and -1.71.

Self Check 9   Solve: $3x^2 + 6x + 1 = 0$. Approximate the solutions to the nearest hundredth.

Now Try ▶ Problem 59

Using Your Calculator ▶ **Checking Solutions of Quadratic Equations**

We can use a graphing calculator to check the solutions of the quadratic equation $2x^2 + 4x + 1 = 0$ found in Example 9. After entering $Y_1 = 2x^2 + 4x + 1$, we call up the home screen by pressing 2nd QUIT. Then we press VARS, arrow to Y-VARS, press ENTER, and enter 1 to get the display shown in figure (a). We evaluate $2x^2 + 4x + 1$ for $x = \frac{-2 + \sqrt{2}}{2}$ by entering the solution using function notation, as shown in figure (b). When ENTER is pressed, the result of 0 is confirmation that $x = \frac{-2 + \sqrt{2}}{2}$ is a solution of the equation.

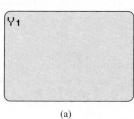

(a)

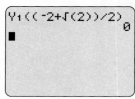

(b)

The solutions of some quadratic equations are complex numbers that contain i.

EXAMPLE 10   Solve: **a.** $x^2 - 4x + 16 = 0$ **b.** $x^2 + \dfrac{2}{3}x + 6 = 0$

Strategy   We will follow the steps for solving a quadratic equation by completing the square.

Why   Since the trinomials $x^2 - 4x + 16$ and $x^2 + \dfrac{2}{3}x + 6 = 0$ cannot be factored using only integers, solving the equation by completing the square is our only option.

Solution   **a.**

$x^2 - 4x + 16 = 0$	This is the equation to solve.
$x^2 - 4x = -16$	Subtract 16 from both sides so that the constant term is on the right side.
$x^2 - 4x + 4 = -16 + 4$	Complete the square: $\frac{1}{2}(-4) = -2$ and $(-2)^2 = 4$. Add 4 to both sides.
$(x - 2)^2 = -12$	Factor the left side. On the right side, add.
$x - 2 = \pm\sqrt{-12}$	Use the square root property. Don't forget the $\pm$ symbol.
$x = 2 \pm \sqrt{-12}$	To isolate x, add 2 to both sides.
$x = 2 \pm 2i\sqrt{3}$	Simplify the radical: $\sqrt{-12} = \sqrt{-1 \cdot 4 \cdot 3} = \sqrt{-1}\sqrt{4}\sqrt{3} = 2i\sqrt{3}$.

Success Tip

Example 8 can be solved by factoring. However, Examples 7, 9, and 10 cannot. This illustrates an important fact: completing the square can be used to solve any quadratic equation.

There are two complex number solutions involving i: $2 + 2i\sqrt{3}$ and $2 - 2i\sqrt{3}$. Verify this by checking them in the original equation.

b.

$x^2 + \dfrac{2}{3}x + 6 = 0$	This is the equation to solve.
$x^2 + \dfrac{2}{3}x \phantom{+ \frac{1}{9}} = -6$	Subtract 6 from both sides so that the constant term is on the right side.
$x^2 + \dfrac{2}{3}x + \dfrac{1}{9} = \dfrac{1}{9} - 6$	Complete the square: $\frac{1}{2} \cdot \frac{2}{3} = \frac{1}{3}$ and $\left(\frac{1}{3}\right)^2 = \frac{1}{9}$. Add $\frac{1}{9}$ to both sides.
$\left(x + \dfrac{1}{3}\right)^2 = \dfrac{1}{9} - \dfrac{6}{1} \cdot \dfrac{9}{9}$	Factor the left side. On the right side, prepare to subtract. Write 6 as $\frac{6}{1}$ and multiply by $\frac{9}{9}$ to build an equivalent fraction with denominator 9.
$\left(x + \dfrac{1}{3}\right)^2 = \dfrac{1}{9} - \dfrac{54}{9}$	On the right side, multiply the numerators. Multiply the denominators.
$\left(x + \dfrac{1}{3}\right)^2 = -\dfrac{53}{9}$	On the right side, subtract the fractions.
$x + \dfrac{1}{3} = \pm\sqrt{-\dfrac{53}{9}}$	Use the square root property. Don't forget the $\pm$ symbol.
$x = -\dfrac{1}{3} \pm \sqrt{-\dfrac{53}{9}}$	To isolate x, subtract $\frac{1}{3}$ from both sides.
$x = -\dfrac{1}{3} \pm \dfrac{\sqrt{53}}{3}i$	Simplify the radical: $\sqrt{-\frac{53}{9}} = \sqrt{-1}\dfrac{\sqrt{53}}{\sqrt{9}} = \dfrac{\sqrt{53}}{3}i$.

Success Tip

Notice how we multiply $\frac{6}{1}$ by a form of 1 to build an equivalent fraction with a denominator 9:

$$\dfrac{6}{1} \cdot \dfrac{9}{9}$$

Notation

The solutions are written in complex number form $a + bi$. They also could be written as

$$\dfrac{-1 \pm i\sqrt{53}}{3}$$

The solutions are $-\dfrac{1}{3} + \dfrac{\sqrt{53}}{3}i$ and $-\dfrac{1}{3} - \dfrac{\sqrt{53}}{3}i$.

Self Check 10   Solve: **a.** $x^2 - 6x + 27 = 0$ **b.** $x^2 + \dfrac{2}{5}x + 3 = 0$

Now Try ▶   Problems 63 and 67

SECTION 10.1 ▶ STUDY SET

VOCABULARY

Fill in the blanks.

1. An equation of the form $ax^2 + bx + c = 0$, where $a \neq 0$, is called a _____ equation.
2. $x^2 + 6x + 9$ is called a _____-square trinomial because it factors as $(x + 3)^2$.
3. When we add 16 to $x^2 + 8x$, we say that we have completed the _____ on $x^2 + 8x$.
4. The _____ coefficient of $5x^2 - 2x + 7$ is 5 and the _____ term is 7.

CONCEPTS

Fill in the blanks.

5. For any nonnegative number c, if $x^2 = c$, then $x =$ [ ] or $x =$ [ ].
6. To complete the square on $x^2 + 10x$, add the square of _____ of the coefficient of x.
7. Find one-half of the given number and square the result.
   a. 12   b. -5
8. Fill in the blanks to factor the perfect-square trinomial.
   a. $x^2 + 8x + 16 = (x + \ )^2$
   b. $x^2 - 9x + \dfrac{81}{4} = \left(x - \ \right)^2$
9. What is the first step to solve each equation by completing the square? **Do not solve.**
   a. $x^2 + 9x + 7 = 0$
   b. $4x^2 + 5x - 16 = 0$
10. Divide both sides of the equation by the proper number to make the coefficient of x^2 equal to 1. **Do not solve.**
    a. $2x^2 - 3x + 6 = 0$
    b. $3x^2 + 6x - 4 = 0$
11. Use a check to determine whether $-2 + \sqrt{2}$ is a solution of $x^2 + 4x + 2 = 0$.
12. Determine whether each statement is true or false.
    a. Any quadratic equation can be solved by the factoring method.
    b. Any quadratic equation can be solved by completing the square.

NOTATION

13. We read $8 \pm \sqrt{3}$ as "eight _____ ___ _____ the square root of 3."
14. When solving a quadratic equation, a student obtains $x = \dfrac{-5 \pm \sqrt{7}}{3}$.
    a. How many solutions are represented by this notation? List them.
    b. Approximate the solutions to the nearest hundredth.

GUIDED PRACTICE

Use the square root property to solve each equation. See Example 1.

15. $t^2 - 11 = 0$ 16. $w^2 - 47 = 0$
17. $x^2 - 35 = 0$ 18. $x^2 - 101 = 0$
19. $z^2 - 50 = 0$ 20. $u^2 - 24 = 0$
21. $3x^2 - 16 = 0$ 22. $5x^2 - 49 = 0$

Use the square root property to solve each equation. See Example 3.

23. $p^2 = -16$ 24. $q^2 = -25$
25. $a^2 + 8 = 0$ 26. $m^2 + 18 = 0$
27. $4m^2 + 81 = 0$ 28. $9n^2 + 121 = 0$
29. $6b^2 + 144 = 0$ 30. $9n^2 + 288 = 0$

Use the square root property to solve each equation. See Example 4.

31. $(x + 5)^2 = 9$ 32. $(x - 1)^2 = 4$
33. $(t + 4)^2 = 16$ 34. $(s - 7)^2 = 9$

See Example 5.

35. Let $f(x) = (x + 5)^2$. For what value(s) of x is $f(x) = 3$?

36. Let $f(x) = (x + 3)^2$. For what value(s) of x is $f(x) = 7$?

37. Let $g(a) = (7a - 2)^2$. For what value(s) of a is $g(a) = 8$?

38. Let $h(c) = (11c - 2)^2$. For what value(s) of c is $h(c) = 12$?

Complete the square and factor the resulting perfect-square trinomial. See Example 6.

39. $x^2 + 24x$
40. $y^2 - 18y$
41. $a^2 - 7a$
42. $b^2 + 11b$
43. $x^2 + \dfrac{2}{3}x$ 44. $x^2 + \dfrac{2}{5}x$
45. $m^2 - \dfrac{5}{6}m$ 46. $n^2 - \dfrac{5}{3}n$

Use completing the square to solve each equation. Approximate each solution to the nearest hundredth. See Example 7.

47. $x^2 - 4x - 2 = 0$ 48. $x^2 - 6x - 4 = 0$
49. $x^2 - 12x + 1 = 0$ 50. $x^2 - 18x + 2 = 0$
51. $t^2 + 20t + 25 = 0$ 52. $t^2 + 22t + 93 = 0$

53. $t^2 + 16t - 16 = 0$ **54.** $t^2 + 14t - 7 = 0$

Use completing the square to solve each equation. See Example 8.

55. $2x^2 - x - 1 = 0$ **56.** $2x^2 - 5x + 2 = 0$

57. $12t^2 - 5t - 3 = 0$ **58.** $5m^2 + 13m - 6 = 0$

Use completing the square to solve each equation. Approximate each solution to the nearest hundredth. See Example 9.

59. $3x^2 - 12x + 1 = 0$ **60.** $6x^2 - 12x + 1 = 0$

61. $2x^2 + 5x - 2 = 0$ **62.** $2x^2 - 8x + 5 = 0$

Use completing the square to solve each equation. See Example 10.

63. $p^2 + 2p + 2 = 0$ **64.** $x^2 - 6x + 10 = 0$

65. $y^2 + 8y + 18 = 0$ **66.** $n^2 + 10n + 28 = 0$

67. $x^2 + \dfrac{2}{3}x + 7 = 0$ **68.** $x^2 + \dfrac{2}{5}x + 6 = 0$

69. $a^2 - \dfrac{1}{2}a + 1 = 0$ **70.** $b^2 - \dfrac{1}{4}b + 1 = 0$

TRY IT YOURSELF

Solve each equation. Approximate the solutions to the nearest hundredth when appropriate.

71. $(3x - 1)^2 = 25$ **72.** $(5x - 2)^2 = 64$

73. $3x^2 - 6x = 1$ **74.** $2x^2 - 6x = -3$

75. $x^2 + 8x + 6 = 0$ **76.** $x^2 + 6x + 4 = 0$

77. $6x^2 + 72 = 0$ **78.** $5x^2 + 40 = 0$

79. $x^2 - 2x = 17$ **80.** $x^2 + 10x = 7$

81. $m^2 - 7m + 3 = 0$ **82.** $m^2 - 5m + 3 = 0$

83. $7h^2 = 35$ **84.** $9n^2 = 99$

85. $\dfrac{7x + 1}{5} = -x^2$ **86.** $\dfrac{3}{8}x^2 = \dfrac{1}{8} - x$

87. $t^2 + t + 3 = 0$ **88.** $b^2 - b + 5 = 0$

89. $(8x + 5)^2 = 24$ **90.** $(3y - 2)^2 = 18$

91. $r^2 - 6r - 27 = 0$ **92.** $s^2 - 6s - 40 = 0$

93. $4p^2 + 2p + 3 = 0$ **94.** $3m^2 - 2m + 3 = 0$

Look Alikes . . .

95. a. $x^2 - 24 = 0$ **b.** $x^2 + 24 = 0$

96. a. $x^2 + 7x - 8 = 0$ **b.** $x^2 + 7x - 9 = 0$

97. a. $2m^2 - 8m = 0$ **b.** $2m^2 - 8m = 1$

98. a. $a^2 + a - 7 = 0$ **b.** $a^2 - a - 7 = 0$

99. a. $x^2 - 4x + 20 = 0$ **b.** $x^2 - 4x - 20 = 0$

100. a. $a^2 = 6a - 3$ **b.** $n^2 = 6n + 3$

101. a. $2r^2 - 4r + 3 = 0$ **b.** $2r^2 - 4r - 3 = 0$

102. a. $5y^2 + 15y + 12 = 0$ **b.** $5y^2 + 15y - 12 = 0$

APPLICATIONS

103. Movie Stunts.   According to the *Guinness Book of World Records,* stuntman Dan Koko fell a distance of 312 feet into an airbag after jumping from the Vegas World Hotel and Casino. The distance d in feet traveled by a free-falling object in t seconds is given by the formula $d = 16t^2$. To the nearest tenth of a second, how long did the fall last?

104. Geography.   The surface area S of a sphere is given by the formula $S = 4\pi r^2$, where r is the radius of the sphere. An almanac lists the surface area of the Earth as 196,938,800 square miles. Assuming the Earth to be spherical, what is its radius to the nearest mile?

105. Accidents.   The height h (in feet) of an object that is dropped from a height of s feet is given by the formula $h = s - 16t^2$, where t is the time the object has been falling. A 5-foot-tall woman on a sidewalk looks directly overhead and sees a window washer drop a bottle from four stories up. How long does she have to get out of the way? Round to the nearest tenth. (A story is 12 feet.)

106. Flags.   In 1912, an order by President Taft fixed the width and length of the U.S. flag in the ratio 1 to 1.9. If 100 square feet of cloth are to be used to make a U.S. flag, estimate its dimensions to the nearest $\frac{1}{4}$ foot.

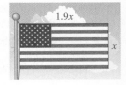

107. Automobile Engines. As the piston shown moves upward, it pushes a cylinder of a gasoline/air mixture that is ignited by the spark plug. The formula that gives the volume of a cylinder is $V = \pi r^2 h$, where r is the radius and h the height. Find the radius of the piston (to the nearest hundredth of an inch) if it displaces 47.75 cubic inches of gasoline/air mixture as it moves from its lowest to its highest point.

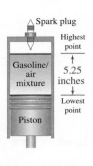

Spark plug

Highest point

Gasoline/ air mixture

5.25 inches

Lowest point

Piston

108. Investments. If P dollars are deposited in an account that pays an annual rate of interest r, then in n years, the amount of money A in the account is given by the formula $A = P(1 + r)^n$. A savings account was opened on January 3, 2006, with a deposit of \$10,000 and closed on January 2, 2008, with an ending balance of \$11,772.25. Find the rate of interest.

109. Physics. Albert Einstein discovered a connection between energy and mass. This relationship (*energy equals mass times the velocity of light squared*) is expressed in the equation $E = mc^2$. Solve for c.

110. Right Triangles. The Pythagorean theorem relates the lengths of the sides in a right triangle: $a^2 + b^2 = c^2$, where a and b represent the lengths of the legs and c represents the length of the hypotenuse. Solve for b.

WRITING

111. Give an example of a perfect-square trinomial. Why do you think the word "perfect" is used to describe it?

112. Explain why completing the square on $x^2 + 5x$ is more difficult than completing the square on $x^2 + 4x$.

113. Explain the error in the work shown below.

a. $\dfrac{4 \pm \sqrt{3}}{8} = \dfrac{\overset{1}{\cancel{4}} \pm \sqrt{3}}{\underset{1}{\cancel{4} \cdot 2}} = \dfrac{1 \pm \sqrt{3}}{2}$

b. $\dfrac{1 \pm \sqrt{5}}{5} = \dfrac{1 \pm \sqrt{\cancel{5}}}{\underset{1}{\cancel{5}}} = \dfrac{1 \pm 1}{1}$

114. Explain the steps involved in expressing $8 \pm \dfrac{\sqrt{15}}{2}$ as a single fraction with denominator 2.

REVIEW

Simplify each expression. All variables represent positive real numbers.

115. $\sqrt[3]{40a^3 b^6}$

116. $\sqrt[8]{x^{24}}$

117. $\sqrt[4]{\dfrac{16}{625}}$

118. $\sqrt{175a^2 b^3}$

CHALLENGE PROBLEMS

119. What number must be added to $x^2 + \sqrt{3}x$ to make a perfect-square trinomial?

120. Solve $x^2 + \sqrt{3}x - \dfrac{1}{4} = 0$ by completing the square.

SECTION 10.2

The Quadratic Formula

OBJECTIVES

1 Derive the quadratic formula.

2 Solve quadratic equations using the quadratic formula.

3 Write equivalent equations to make quadratic formula calculations easier.

4 Use the quadratic formula to solve application problems.

ARE YOU READY?

The following problems review some basic skills that are needed when solving quadratic equations using the quadratic formula.

1. Evaluate: $\sqrt{5^2 - 4(4)(-6)}$

2. Simplify: $\sqrt{45}$

3. How many terms does $2x^2 - x + 7$ have? What is the coefficient of each term?

4. Evaluate: $\dfrac{-5 \pm 11}{8}$

5. Classify $\sqrt{-28}$ as a rational, irrational, or not a real number.

6. Approximate $\dfrac{6 + \sqrt{3}}{2}$ to the nearest hundredth.

We can solve quadratic equations by completing the square, but that method is often lengthy. In this section, we will develop a formula, called the *quadratic formula,* that enables us to solve quadratic equations with less effort.

1 Derive the Quadratic Formula.

To develop a formula that will produce the solutions of any given quadratic equation, we start with a quadratic equation in **standard form**, $ax^2 + bx + c = 0$, where $a > 0$. We can solve for x by completing the square.

$$ax^2 + bx + c = 0$$

$$\frac{ax^2}{a} + \frac{bx}{a} + \frac{c}{a} = \frac{0}{a}$$ Divide both sides by a so that the coefficient of x^2 is 1.

$$x^2 + \frac{b}{a}x + \frac{c}{a} = 0$$ Simplify: $\frac{ax^2}{a} = x^2$. Write $\frac{bx}{a}$ as $\frac{b}{a}x$

$$x^2 + \frac{b}{a}x = -\frac{c}{a}$$ Subtract $\frac{c}{a}$ from both sides so that only the variable terms are on the left side of the equation and the constant is on the right side.

We can complete the square on $x^2 + \frac{b}{a}x$ by adding the square of one-half of the coefficient of x. Since the coefficient of x is $\frac{b}{a}$, we have $\frac{1}{2} \cdot \frac{b}{a} = \frac{b}{2a}$ and $\left(\frac{b}{2a}\right)^2 = \frac{b^2}{4a^2}$.

$$x^2 + \frac{b}{a}x + \frac{b^2}{4a^2} = -\frac{c}{a} + \frac{b^2}{4a^2}$$ To complete the square, add $\frac{b^2}{4a^2}$ to both sides.

$$x^2 + \frac{b}{a}x + \frac{b^2}{4a^2} = -\frac{4ac}{4aa} + \frac{b^2}{4a^2}$$ On the right side, build $-\frac{c}{a}$ by multiplying it by $\frac{4a}{4a}$. Now the fractions on that side have the common denominator $4a^2$.

$$\left(x + \frac{b}{2a}\right)^2 = \frac{b^2 - 4ac}{4a^2}$$ On the left side, factor the perfect-square trinomial. On the right side, add the fractions. In the numerator, write $-4ac + b^2$ as $b^2 - 4ac$.

$$x + \frac{b}{2a} = \pm\sqrt{\frac{b^2 - 4ac}{4a^2}}$$ Use the square root property.

$$x + \frac{b}{2a} = \pm\frac{\sqrt{b^2 - 4ac}}{\sqrt{4a^2}}$$ On the right side, the square root of a quotient is the quotient of square roots.

$$x + \frac{b}{2a} = \pm\frac{\sqrt{b^2 - 4ac}}{2a}$$ On the right side, simplify the denominator. Since $a > 0$, $\sqrt{4a^2} = 2a$.

$$x = -\frac{b}{2a} \pm \frac{\sqrt{b^2 - 4ac}}{2a}$$ To isolate x, subtract $\frac{b}{2a}$ from both sides.

$$x = \frac{-b \pm \sqrt{b^2 - 4ac}}{2a}$$ Combine the fractions. Write the sum (and difference) over the common denominator $2a$.

This result is called the **quadratic formula.** To develop this formula, we assumed that a was positive. If a is negative, similar steps are used, and we obtain the same result. This formula is very useful and should be memorized.

The Language of Algebra

To **derive** means to obtain by reasoning. To *derive* the quadratic formula means to solve $ax^2 + bx + c = 0$ for x, using the series of steps shown here, to obtain

$$x = \frac{-b \pm \sqrt{b^2 - 4ac}}{2a}$$

The Quadratic Formula

The solutions of $ax^2 + bx + c = 0$, with $a \neq 0$, are given by

$$x = \frac{-b \pm \sqrt{b^2 - 4ac}}{2a}$$ Read as "x equals the opposite of b plus or minus the square root of b squared minus $4ac$, all over $2a$."

The quadratic formula is a compact way of representing two solutions:

$$x = \frac{-b + \sqrt{b^2 - 4ac}}{2a} \qquad \text{or} \qquad x = \frac{-b - \sqrt{b^2 - 4ac}}{2a}$$

2 Solve Quadratic Equations Using the Quadratic Formula.

In the next example, we will use the quadratic formula to solve a quadratic equation.

EXAMPLE 1 Solve $2x^2 - 5x - 3 = 0$ by using the quadratic formula.

Strategy We will begin by comparing $2x^2 - 5x - 3 = 0$ to the standard form $ax^2 + bx + c = 0$.

Why To use the quadratic formula, we need to identify the values of a, b, and c.

Solution

$$2x^2 - 5x - 3 = 0 \quad \text{This is the equation to solve.}$$
$$\uparrow \qquad \uparrow \qquad \uparrow$$
$$ax^2 + bx + c = 0$$

We see that $a = 2$, $b = -5$, and $c = -3$. To find the solutions of the equation, we substitute these values into the quadratic formula and evaluate the right side.

$$x = \frac{-b \pm \sqrt{b^2 - 4ac}}{2a} \qquad \text{This is the quadratic formula.}$$

$$x = \frac{-(-5) \pm \sqrt{(-5)^2 - 4(2)(-3)}}{2(2)} \qquad \text{Substitute 2 for } a, -5 \text{ for } b, \text{ and } -3 \text{ for } c.$$

$$x = \frac{5 \pm \sqrt{25 - (-24)}}{4} \qquad \text{Simplify: } -(-5) = 5. \text{ Evaluate the power and multiply within the radical. Multiply in the denominator.}$$

$$x = \frac{5 \pm \sqrt{49}}{4} \qquad \text{Simplify within the radical.}$$

$$x = \frac{5 \pm 7}{4} \qquad \text{Evaluate the radical: } \sqrt{49} = 7.$$

To find the first solution, we evaluate the expression using the $+$ symbol. To find the second solution, we evaluate the expression using the $-$ symbol.

$$x = \frac{5 + 7}{4} \quad \text{or} \quad x = \frac{5 - 7}{4}$$

$$x = \frac{12}{4} \qquad\qquad x = \frac{-2}{4}$$

$$x = 3 \qquad\qquad x = -\frac{1}{2}$$

The solutions are 3 and $-\frac{1}{2}$ and the solution set is $\left\{3, -\frac{1}{2}\right\}$. Check each solution in the original equation.

Self Check 1 Solve $4x^2 - 7x - 2 = 0$ by using the quadratic formula.

Now Try ▶ Problem 13

Caution

Make sure to include the correct sign when determining a, b, and c. In this example, $b = -5$ and $c = -3$.

Caution

When writing the quadratic formula, be careful to draw the fraction bar so that it includes the entire numerator. Do not write

$$x = -b \pm \frac{\sqrt{b^2 - 4ac}}{2a}$$

or

$$x = -b \pm \sqrt{\frac{b^2 - 4ac}{2a}}$$

To solve a quadratic equation in x using the quadratic formula, we follow these steps.

Solving a Quadratic Equation in x Using the Quadratic Formula	1. Write the equation in standard form: $ax^2 + bx + c = 0$. 2. Identify a, b, and c. 3. Substitute the values for a, b, and c in the quadratic formula and evaluate the right side to obtain the solutions. $$x = \frac{-b \pm \sqrt{b^2 - 4ac}}{2a}$$

EXAMPLE 2   Solve: $2x^2 = -4x - 1$

Strategy   We will write the equation in standard form $ax^2 + bx + c = 0$. Then we will identify the values of a, b, and c, and substitute these values into the quadratic formula.

Why   The quadratic equation must be in standard form to identify the values of a, b, and c.

Solution   To write the equation in standard form, we need to have all nonzero terms on the left side and 0 on the right side.

$$2x^2 = -4x - 1 \qquad \text{This is the equation to solve.}$$
$$2x^2 + 4x + 1 = 0 \qquad \text{To get 0 on the right side, add 4x and 1 to both sides.}$$

In the resulting equivalent equation, $a = 2$, $b = 4$, and $c = 1$.

$$x = \frac{-b \pm \sqrt{b^2 - 4ac}}{2a} \qquad \text{This is the quadratic formula.}$$

$$x = \frac{-4 \pm \sqrt{4^2 - 4(2)(1)}}{2(2)} \qquad \text{Substitute 2 for } a, \text{ 4 for } b, \text{ and 1 for } c.$$

$$x = \frac{-4 \pm \sqrt{16 - 8}}{4} \qquad \begin{array}{l}\text{Evaluate the expression within the radical.}\\ \text{Multiply in the denominator.}\end{array}$$

$$x = \frac{-4 \pm \sqrt{8}}{4} \qquad \text{Do the subtraction within the radical.}$$

$$x = \frac{-4 \pm 2\sqrt{2}}{4} \qquad \text{Simplify the radical: } \sqrt{8} = \sqrt{4 \cdot 2} = 2\sqrt{2}.$$

Success Tip

Perhaps you noticed that Example 1 could be solved by factoring. However, that is not the case for Example 2. These observations illustrate an important fact: The quadratic formula can be used to solve *any* quadratic equation.

We can write the solutions in simpler form by factoring out 2 from the two terms in the numerator and removing the common factor of 2 in the numerator and denominator.

$$x = \frac{-4 \pm 2\sqrt{2}}{4} = \frac{2\left(-2 \pm \sqrt{2}\right)}{4} = \frac{\overset{1}{\cancel{2}}\left(-2 \pm \sqrt{2}\right)}{\underset{1}{\cancel{2} \cdot 2}} = \frac{-2 \pm \sqrt{2}}{2} \qquad \text{Factor first.}$$

Notation

The solutions also can be written:

$$-\frac{2}{2} \pm \frac{\sqrt{2}}{2} = -1 \pm \frac{\sqrt{2}}{2}$$

The two irrational solutions are $\frac{-2 + \sqrt{2}}{2}$ and $\frac{-2 - \sqrt{2}}{2}$ and the solution set is $\left\{\frac{-2 + \sqrt{2}}{2}, \frac{-2 - \sqrt{2}}{2}\right\}$. We can approximate the solutions using a calculator. To the nearest hundredth, they are -0.29 and -1.71.

Self Check 2   Solve $3x^2 = 2x + 3$. Approximate the solutions to the nearest hundredth.

Now Try ▶   Problem 25

EXAMPLE 3 Solve: $m^2 + m = -1$

Strategy We will write the equation in standard form $am^2 + bm + c = 0$. Then we will identify the values of a, b, and c, and substitute these values into the quadratic formula.

Why The quadratic equation must be in standard form to identify the values of a, b, and c.

Solution To write $m^2 + m = -1$ in standard form, we add 1 to both sides, to get

$$m^2 + m + 1 = 0 \quad \text{This is the equation to solve.}$$

In the resulting equivalent equation, $a = 1$, $b = 1$, and $c = 1$:

$$m = \frac{-b \pm \sqrt{b^2 - 4ac}}{2a} \qquad \text{This is the quadratic formula.}$$

$$m = \frac{-1 \pm \sqrt{1^2 - 4(1)(1)}}{2(1)} \qquad \text{Substitute 1 for } a, \text{ 1 for } b, \text{ and 1 for } c.$$

$$m = \frac{-1 \pm \sqrt{1 - 4}}{2} \qquad \begin{array}{l}\text{Evaluate the expression within the radical.}\\\text{Multiply in the denominator.}\end{array}$$

$$m = \frac{-1 \pm \sqrt{-3}}{2} \qquad \text{Do the subtraction within the radical.}$$

$$m = \frac{-1 \pm i\sqrt{3}}{2} \qquad \text{Simplify the radical: } \sqrt{-3} = \sqrt{-1 \cdot 3} = \sqrt{-1}\sqrt{3} = i\sqrt{3}.$$

The solutions are two complex numbers involving i: $-\frac{1}{2} + \frac{\sqrt{3}}{2}i$ and $-\frac{1}{2} - \frac{\sqrt{3}}{2}i$ and the solution set is $\left\{-\frac{1}{2} + \frac{\sqrt{3}}{2}i, -\frac{1}{2} - \frac{\sqrt{3}}{2}i\right\}$.

Self Check 3 Solve: $a^2 + 3a = -5$

Now Try ▶ Problem 29

> **Caution**
>
> Since the variable in the equation is m, not x, we must change the variable in the quadratic formula to reflect this:
>
> $$m = \frac{-b \pm \sqrt{b^2 - 4ac}}{2a}$$

> **Notation**
>
> The solutions are written in complex number form $a + bi$. They also could be written as
>
> $$\frac{-1 \pm i\sqrt{3}}{2}$$

3 Write Equivalent Equations to Make Quadratic Formula Calculations Easier.

When solving a quadratic equation by the quadratic formula, we often can simplify the calculations by solving a simpler, but equivalent equation.

EXAMPLE 4 For each equation below, write an equivalent equation so that the quadratic formula calculations will be simpler.

a. $-2x^2 + 4x - 1 = 0$ **b.** $x^2 + \frac{4}{5}x - \frac{1}{3} = 0$

c. $20x^2 - 60x - 40 = 0$ **d.** $0.03x^2 - 0.04x - 0.01 = 0$

Strategy We will multiply both sides of each equation by a carefully chosen number.

Why In each case, the objective is to find an equivalent equation whose values of a, b, and c are easier to work with than those of the given equation.

Solution **a.** It is often easier to solve a quadratic equation using the quadratic formula if a is positive. If we multiply (or divide) both sides of $-2x^2 + 4x - 1 = 0$ by -1, we obtain an equivalent equation with $a > 0$.

$$-2x^2 + 4x - 1 = 0 \qquad \text{Here, } a = -2.$$

$$-1(-2x^2 + 4x - 1) = -1(0) \qquad \text{Don't forget to multiply each term by } -1.$$

$$2x^2 - 4x + 1 = 0 \qquad \text{Now } a = 2.$$

> **Success Tip**
>
> Unlike completing the square, the quadratic formula does not require the leading coefficient to be 1.

b. For $x^2 + \frac{4}{5}x - \frac{1}{3} = 0$, two coefficients are fractions: $b = \frac{4}{5}$ and $c = -\frac{1}{3}$. We can multiply both sides of the equation by their least common denominator, 15, to obtain an equivalent equation having coefficients that are integers.

$$x^2 + \frac{4}{5}x - \frac{1}{3} = 0 \qquad \text{Here, } a = 1, b = \frac{4}{5}, \text{ and } c = -\frac{1}{3}.$$

$$15\left(x^2 + \frac{4}{5}x - \frac{1}{3}\right) = 15(0)$$

$$15x^2 + 12x - 5 = 0 \qquad \text{On the left side, distribute the multiplication by 15.}$$
$$\text{Now } a = 15, b = 12, \text{ and } c = -5.$$

c. For $20x^2 - 60x - 40 = 0$, the coefficients 20, -60, and -40 have a common factor of 20. If we divide both sides of the equation by their GCF, we obtain an equivalent equation having smaller coefficients.

$$20x^2 - 60x - 40 = 0 \qquad \text{Here, } a = 20, b = -60, \text{ and } c = -40.$$

$$\frac{20x^2}{20} - \frac{60x}{20} - \frac{40}{20} = \frac{0}{20} \qquad \text{The division by 20 is done term-by-term.}$$

$$x^2 - 3x - 2 = 0 \qquad \text{Now } a = 1, b = -3, \text{ and } c = -2.$$

d. For $0.03x^2 - 0.04x - 0.01 = 0$, all three coefficients are decimals. We can multiply both sides of the equation by 100 to obtain an equivalent equation having coefficients that are integers.

$$0.03x^2 - 0.04x - 0.01 = 0 \qquad \text{Here, } a = 0.03, b = -0.04, \text{ and } c = -0.01.$$

$$100(0.03x^2 - 0.04x - 0.01) = 100(0)$$

$$3x^2 - 4x - 1 = 0 \qquad \text{On the left side, distribute 100.}$$
$$\text{Now } a = 3, b = -4, \text{ and } c = -1.$$

Self Check 4 For each equation, write an equivalent equation so that the quadratic formula calculations will be simpler.
   a. $-6x^2 + 7x - 9 = 0$
   b. $\frac{1}{3}x^2 - \frac{2}{3}x - \frac{5}{6} = 0$
   c. $44x^2 + 66x - 99 = 0$
   d. $0.08x^2 - 0.07x - 0.02 = 0$

Now Try ▶ Problems 37 and 39

4 Use the Quadratic Formula to Solve Application Problems.

A variety of real-world applications can be modeled by quadratic equations. However, such equations are often difficult or even impossible to solve using the factoring method. In those cases, we can use the quadratic formula to solve the equation.

EXAMPLE 5

Shortcuts. Instead of using the hallways, students are wearing a path through a planted quad area to walk 195 feet directly from the classrooms to the cafeteria. If the length of the hallway from the office to the cafeteria is 105 feet longer than the hallway from the office to the classrooms, how much walking are the students saving by taking the shortcut?

Analyze The two hallways and the shortcut form a right triangle with a hypotenuse 195 feet long. We will use the Pythagorean theorem to solve this problem.

Assign If we let $x =$ the length (in feet) of the hallway from the classrooms to the office, then the length of the hallway from the office to the cafeteria is $(x + 105)$ feet.

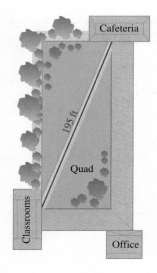

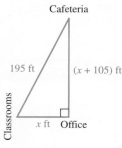

Form   Substituting the lengths into the Pythagorean equation, we have

$$a^2 + b^2 = c^2$$ This is the Pythagorean equation.

$$x^2 + (x + 105)^2 = 195^2$$ Substitute x for a, (x + 105) for b, and 195 for c.

$$x^2 + x^2 + 105x + 105x + 11{,}025 = 38{,}025$$ Find $(x + 105)^2$.

$$2x^2 + 210x + 11{,}025 = 38{,}025$$ Combine like terms.

$$2x^2 + 210x - 27{,}000 = 0$$ To get 0 on the right side, subtract 38,025 from both sides. This is a quadratic equation.

$$x^2 + 105x - 13{,}500 = 0$$ The coefficients have a common factor of 2: Divide both sides by 2.

Solve   To solve $x^2 + 105x - 13{,}500 = 0$, we will use the quadratic formula with $a = 1$, $b = 105$, and $c = -13{,}500$.

$$x = \frac{-b \pm \sqrt{b^2 - 4ac}}{2a}$$ This is the quadratic formula.

$$x = \frac{-105 \pm \sqrt{105^2 - 4(1)(-13{,}500)}}{2(1)}$$ Substitute for a, b, and c.

$$x = \frac{-105 \pm \sqrt{65{,}025}}{2}$$ Evaluate within the radical: $105^2 - 4(1)(-13{,}500) = 11{,}025 + 54{,}000 = 65{,}025$. Multiply in the denominator.

$$x = \frac{-105 \pm 255}{2}$$ Use a calculator: $\sqrt{65{,}025} = 255$.

$$x = \frac{150}{2} \quad \text{or} \quad x = \frac{-360}{2}$$ Add: $-105 + 255 = 150$. Subtract: $-105 - 255 = -360$.

$$x = 75 \quad \mid \quad \cancel{x = -180}$$ Do the division. Since the length of the hallway can't be negative, discard the solution -180.

State   The length of the hallway from the classrooms to the office is 75 feet. The length of the hallway from the office to the cafeteria is $75 + 105 = 180$ feet. Instead of using the hallways, a distance of $75 + 180 = 255$ feet, the students are taking the 195-foot shortcut to the cafeteria, a savings of $(255 - 195)$, or 60 feet.

Check   The length of the 180-foot hallway is 105 feet longer than the length of the 75-foot hallway. The sum of the squares of the lengths of the hallways is $75^2 + 180^2 = 38{,}025$. This equals the square of the length of the 195-foot shortcut: $195^2 = 38{,}025$. The result checks.

Self Check 5   **Right Triangles.**   The hypotenuse of a right triangle is 41 in. long. The longer leg is 31 inches longer than the shorter leg. Find the lengths of the legs of the triangle.

Now Try ▶ Problem 81

EXAMPLE 6   **Mass Transit.**   A bus company has 4,000 passengers daily, each currently paying a 75¢ fare. For each 15¢ fare increase, the company estimates that it will lose 50 passengers. If the company needs to bring in $6,570 per day to stay in business, what fare must be charged to produce this amount of revenue?

©Krivosheev Vitaly/Shutterstock.com

Analyze To understand how a fare increase affects the number of passengers, let's consider what happens if there are two fare increases. We organize the data in a table. The fares are expressed in terms of dollars.

Number of increases	New fare	Number of passengers
One $0.15 increase	$0.75 + $0.15(1) = $0.90	4,000 − 50(1) = 3,950
Two $0.15 increases	$0.75 + $0.15(2) = $1.05	4,000 − 50(2) = 3,900

In general, the new fare will be the old fare ($0.75) plus the number of fare increases times $0.15. The number of passengers who will pay the new fare is 4,000 minus 50 times the number of $0.15 fare increases.

Assign If we let $x =$ the number of $0.15 fare increases necessary to bring in $6,570 daily, then $(0.75 + 0.15x)$ is the fare that must be charged. The number of passengers who will pay this fare is $4,000 - 50x$.

Form We can now form an equation, using the words of the problem.

The bus fare	times	the number of passengers who will pay that fare	equals	$6,570.
$(0.75 + 0.15x)$	·	$(4,000 - 50x)$	=	6,570

Solve

$$(0.75 + 0.15x)(4,000 - 50x) = 6,570$$
$$3,000 - 37.5x + 600x - 7.5x^2 = 6,570 \quad \text{Multiply the binomials on the left side.}$$
$$-7.5x^2 + 562.5x + 3,000 = 6,570 \quad \text{Combine like terms: } -37.5x + 600x = 562.5x.$$
$$-7.5x^2 + 562.5x - 3,570 = 0 \quad \text{To get 0 on the right side, subtract 6,570 from both sides. This is a quadratic equation.}$$
$$7.5x^2 - 562.5x + 3,570 = 0 \quad \text{Multiply both sides by } -1 \text{ so that the value of } a, \ 7.5, \text{ is positive.}$$

To solve this equation, we will use the quadratic formula.

$$x = \frac{-b \pm \sqrt{b^2 - 4ac}}{2a} \qquad \text{This is the quadratic formula.}$$

$$x = \frac{-(-562.5) \pm \sqrt{(-562.5)^2 - 4(7.5)(3,570)}}{2(7.5)} \qquad \text{Substitute 7.5 for } a, \ -562.5 \text{ for } b, \text{ and 3,570 for } c.$$

$$x = \frac{562.5 \pm \sqrt{209,306.25}}{15} \qquad \text{Evaluate within the radical: } (-562.5)^2 - 4(7.5)(3,570) = 316,406.25 - 107.100 = 209,306.25. \text{ Multiply in the denominator.}$$

$$x = \frac{562.5 \pm 457.5}{15} \qquad \text{Use a calculator: } \sqrt{209,306.25} = 457.5.$$

$$x = \frac{1,020}{15} \quad \text{or} \quad x = \frac{105}{15} \qquad \text{Add: } 562.5 + 457.5 = 1,020. \text{ Subtract: } 562.5 - 457.5 = 105.$$
$$x = 68 \qquad \qquad x = 7 \qquad \text{Do the division.}$$

State If there are 7 fifteen-cent increases in the fare, the new fare will be $0.75 + $0.15(7) = $1.80. If there are 68 fifteen-cent increases in the fare, the new fare will be $0.75 + $0.15(68) = $10.95. Although this fare would bring in the necessary revenue, a $10.95 bus fare is unreasonable, so we discard it.

Check A fare of $1.80 will be paid by $[4,000 - 50(7)] = 3,650$ bus riders. The amount of revenue brought in would be $1.80(3,650) = \$6,570$. The result checks.

> **Self Check 6** **Airport Shuttles.** A bus company shuttles 1,120 passengers daily between Rockford, Illinois, and O'Hare Airport. The current one-way fare is $10. For each 25¢ increase in the fare, the company predicts that it will lose 48 passengers. What increase in fare will produce daily revenue of $10, 208?
>
> **Now Try** ▶ Problem 91

EXAMPLE 7 **Lawyers.** The number of lawyers in the United States is approximated by the function $N(x) = 45x^2 + 21,000x + 560,000$, where $N(x)$ is the number of lawyers and x is the number of years after 1980. In what year does this model indicate that the United States had one million lawyers? (Based on data from the American Bar Association)

Strategy We will substitute 1,000,000 for $N(x)$ in the equation and solve for x.

Why The value of x will give the number of years after 1980 that the United States had 1,000,000 lawyers.

Solution

$$N(x) = 45x^2 + 21,000x + 560,000 \quad \text{This is the quadratic function model.}$$
$$1,000,000 = 45x^2 + 21,000x + 560,000 \quad \text{Replace } N(x) \text{ with 1,000,000.}$$
$$0 = 45x^2 + 21,000x - 440,000 \quad \begin{array}{l}\text{To get 0 on the left side, subtract}\\ \text{1,000,000 from both sides.}\end{array}$$

We can simplify the calculations by dividing both sides of the equation by 5, which is the greatest common factor of 45, 21,000, and 440,000.

$$9x^2 + 4,200x - 88,000 = 0 \quad \text{Divide both sides by 5.}$$

We solve this equation using the quadratic formula.

$$x = \frac{-b \pm \sqrt{b^2 - 4ac}}{2a}$$

$$x = \frac{-4,200 \pm \sqrt{(4,200)^2 - 4(9)(-88,000)}}{2(9)} \quad \begin{array}{l}\text{Substitute 9 for } a, 4,200\\ \text{for } b, \text{ and } -88,000 \text{ for } c.\end{array}$$

$$x = \frac{-4,200 \pm \sqrt{20,808,000}}{18} \quad \begin{array}{l}\text{Evaluate the expression within the radical.}\\ \text{Multiply in the denominator.}\end{array}$$

$$x \approx \frac{362}{18} \quad \text{or} \quad x \approx \frac{-8,762}{18} \quad \text{Use a calculator to evaluate each numerator.}$$

$$x \approx 20.1 \qquad x \approx -486.8 \quad \begin{array}{l}\text{Do the division. Since the model is defined for only}\\ \text{positive values of } x, \text{ we discard the second solution.}\end{array}$$

In 20.1 years after 1980, or in early 2000, the model predicts that the United States had approximately 1,000,000 lawyers.

> **Self Check 7** **Lawyers.** See Example 7. In what year does the model indicate that the United States had three-quarters of a million lawyers?
>
> **Now Try** ▶ Problem 95

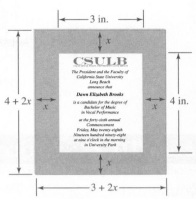

EXAMPLE 8

Graduation Announcements. To create the announcement shown, a graphic artist must follow two design requirements.

- A border of uniform width should surround the text.
- Equal areas should be devoted to the text and to the border.

To meet these requirements, how wide should the border be?

Analyze   The text occupies $4 \cdot 3 = 12$ in.^{2} of space. The border must also have an area of 12 in.^{2}.

Assign   If we let x = the width of the border in inches, the length of the announcement is $(4 + 2x)$ inches and the width is $(3 + 2x)$ inches.

Form   We can now form an equation. Recall that the area of a rectangle is the product of its length and width.

The area of the announcement	minus	the area of the text	equals	the area of the border.
$(4 + 2x)(3 + 2x)$	$-$	12	$=$	12

Solve

$$(4 + 2x)(3 + 2x) - 12 = 12$$

$12 + 8x + 6x + 4x^2 - 12 = 12$ On the left side, multiply the binomials.

$4x^2 + 14x = 12$ Combine like terms. This is a quadratic equation.

$4x^2 + 14x - 12 = 0$ To get 0 on the right side, subtract 12 from both sides.

$2x^2 + 7x - 6 = 0$ The coefficients have a common factor of 2. Divide both sides by 2.

To solve this equation, we will use the quadratic formula with $a = 2$, $b = 7$, and $c = -6$.

$$x = \frac{-b \pm \sqrt{b^2 - 4ac}}{2a}$$

$$x = \frac{-7 \pm \sqrt{7^2 - 4(2)(-6)}}{2(2)}$$ Substitute for a, b, and c.

$$x = \frac{-7 \pm \sqrt{97}}{4}$$ Evaluate within the radical: $7^2 - 4(2)(-6) = 49 + 48 = 97$. Multiply in the denominator.

$$x \approx \frac{-7 + \sqrt{97}}{4} \quad \text{or} \quad x \approx \frac{-7 - \sqrt{97}}{4}$$ These are the two exact solutions.

$$x \approx 0.71 \qquad\qquad\quad x \approx -4.21$$

State   The width of the border should be about 0.71 inch. (We discard the solution $\frac{-7 - \sqrt{97}}{4}$ since it is negative.)

Check   If the border is 0.71 inch wide, the announcement has an area of about $5.42 \cdot 4.42 \approx 23.96$ in.^{2}. If we subtract the area of the text from the area of the announcement, we get $23.96 - 12 = 11.96$ in.^{2}. This represents the area of the border, which was to be 12 in.^{2}. The result seems reasonable.

> **Self Check 8**   **Graduation Announcements.**   See Example 8. Find the width of the border if the text occupies an area 3 inches by 5 inches.
>
> **Now Try ▶**   Problem 97

SECTION 10.2 ▶ STUDY SET

VOCABULARY

Fill in the blanks.

1. The standard form of a _____ equation is $ax^2 + bx + c = 0$.

2. $x = \dfrac{-b \pm \sqrt{b^2 - 4ac}}{2a}$ is called the _____ formula.

CONCEPTS

3. Write each quadratic equation in standard form.

   a. $x^2 + 2x = -5$ **b.** $3x^2 = -2x + 1$

4. For each quadratic equation, find the values of a, b, and c.

   a. $x^2 + 5x + 6 = 0$ **b.** $8x^2 - x = 10$

5. Determine whether each statement is true or false.

   a. Any quadratic equation can be solved by using the quadratic formula.

   b. Any quadratic equation can be solved by completing the square.

   c. Any quadratic equation can be solved by factoring using integers.

6. What is wrong with the beginning of the solution shown below?

   $$\text{Solve:} \quad x^2 - 3x = 2$$
   $$a = 1 \quad b = -3 \quad c = 2$$

7. Evaluate each expression.

   a. $\dfrac{-2 \pm \sqrt{2^2 - 4(1)(-8)}}{2(1)}$

   b. $\dfrac{-(-1) \pm \sqrt{(-1)^2 - 4(2)(-4)}}{2(2)}$

8. A student used the quadratic formula to solve a quadratic equation and obtained $x = \dfrac{-2 \pm \sqrt{3}}{2}$.

   a. How many solutions does the equation have? What are they exactly?

   b. Graph the solutions on a number line.

9. Simplify each of the following.

   a. $\dfrac{3 \pm 6\sqrt{2}}{3}$ **b.** $\dfrac{-12 \pm 4\sqrt{7}}{8}$

10. **a.** Write an expression that represents the width of the larger rectangle shown in red.

    b. Write an expression that represents the length of the larger rectangle shown in red.

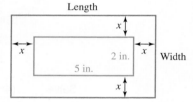

NOTATION

11. On a quiz, students were asked to write the quadratic formula. What is wrong with each answer shown below?

    a. $x = -b \pm \dfrac{\sqrt{b^2 - 4ac}}{2a}$

    b. $x = \dfrac{-b\sqrt{b^2 - 4ac}}{2a}$

12. When reading $\dfrac{-b \pm \sqrt{b^2 - 4ac}}{2a}$, we say, "The _____ of b, plus or _____ the square _____ of b _____ minus ___ times a times c, all _____ $2a$."

GUIDED PRACTICE

Use the quadratic formula to solve each equation. **See Example 1.**

13. $x^2 - 3x + 2 = 0$ 14. $x^2 + 3x + 2 = 0$

15. $x^2 + 12x = -36$ 16. $x^2 - 18x + 81 = 0$

17. $2x^2 + x - 3 = 0$ 18. $6x^2 - x - 1 = 0$

19. $12t^2 - 5t - 2 = 0$ 20. $12z^2 + 5z - 3 = 0$

Solve each equation. Approximate the solutions to the nearest hundredth. **See Example 2.**

21. $x^2 = x + 7$ 22. $t^2 = t + 4$

23. $5x^2 + 5x = -1$ 24. $2x^2 + 7x = -1$

25. $3y^2 + 1 = -6y$

26. $4w^2 + 1 = -6w$

27. $4m^2 = 4m + 19$

28. $3y^2 = 12y - 4$

Solve each equation. See Example 3.

29. $2x^2 + x + 1 = 0$

30. $2x^2 + 3x + 5 = 0$

31. $3x^2 - 2x + 1 = 0$

32. $3x^2 - 2x + 5 = 0$

33. $x^2 - 2x + 2 = 0$

34. $x^2 - 4x + 8 = 0$

35. $4a^2 + 4a + 5 = 0$

36. $4b^2 + 4b + 17 = 0$

For each equation, write an equivalent quadratic equation that will be easier to solve. Do not solve the equation. See Example 4.

37. a. $-5x^2 + 9x - 2 = 0$

b. $1.6t^2 + 2.4t - 0.9 = 0$

38. a. $\dfrac{1}{8}x^2 + \dfrac{1}{2}x - \dfrac{3}{4} = 0$

b. $33y^2 + 99y - 66 = 0$

39. a. $45x^2 + 30x - 15 = 0$

b. $\dfrac{1}{3}m^2 - \dfrac{1}{2}m - \dfrac{1}{3} = 0$

40. a. $0.6t^2 - 0.1t - 0.2 = 0$

b. $-a^2 - 15a + 12 = 0$

TRY IT YOURSELF

Solve each equation. Approximate the solutions to the nearest hundredth when appropriate.

41. $x^2 - \dfrac{14}{15}x = \dfrac{8}{15}$

42. $x^2 = -\dfrac{5}{4}x + \dfrac{3}{2}$

43. $3x^2 - 4x = -2$

44. $2x^2 + 3x = -3$

45. $-16y^2 - 8y + 3 = 0$

46. $-16x^2 - 16x - 3 = 0$

47. $2x^2 - 3x - 1 = 0$

48. $3x^2 - 9x - 2 = 0$

49. $-x^2 + 10x = 18$

50. $-x^2 - 6x - 2 = 0$

51. $x(x - 6) = 391$

52. $x(x - 27) = 280$

53. $x^2 + 5x - 5 = 0$

54. $x^2 - 3x - 27 = 0$

55. $9h^2 - 6h + 7 = 0$

56. $5x^2 = 2x - 1$

57. $50x^2 + 30x - 10 = 0$

58. $120b^2 + 120b - 40 = 0$

59. $0.6x^2 + 0.03 - 0.4x = 0$

60. $2x^2 + 0.1x = 0.04$

61. $\dfrac{1}{8}x^2 - \dfrac{1}{2}x + 1 = 0$

62. $\dfrac{1}{2}x^2 + 3x + \dfrac{13}{2} = 0$

63. $\dfrac{a^2}{10} - \dfrac{3a}{5} + \dfrac{7}{5} = 0$

64. $\dfrac{c^2}{4} + c + \dfrac{11}{4} = 0$

65. $\dfrac{x^2}{2} + \dfrac{5}{2}x = -1$

66. $\dfrac{x^2}{8} - \dfrac{x}{4} = \dfrac{1}{2}$

67. $900x^2 - 8{,}100x = 1{,}800$

68. $14x^2 - 21x = 49$

69. $\dfrac{1}{4}x^2 - \dfrac{1}{6}x - \dfrac{1}{6} = 0$

70. $81x^2 + 12x - 80 = 0$

71. Let $f(x) = 0.7x^2 - 3.5x$ For what value(s) of x is $f(x) = 25$?

72. Let $g(x) = 4.5x^2 + 0.2x$. For what value(s) of x is $g(x) = 3.75$?

Look Alikes . . .

73. a. $a^2 + 4a - 7 = 0$ **b.** $a^2 - 4a - 7 = 0$

74. a. $n^2 + 6n - 2 = 0$ **b.** $n^2 + 6n + 2 = 0$

75. a. $(x + 2)(x - 4) = 16$ **b.** $(x + 2)(x - 4) = -16$

76. a. $5n^2 - 14n - 3 = 0$ **b.** $-5n^2 - 14n - 3 = 0$

77. a. $x^2 - 42x + 441 = 0$ **b.** $x^2 + 42x + 441 = 0$

78. a. $0.3y^2 + 0.6y + 0.5 = 0$

b. $0.003y^2 + 0.006y + 0.005 = 0$

APPLICATIONS

79. Crosswalks. Refer to the illustration below. Instead of using the Main Street and First Avenue crosswalks to get from Nordstrom to Best Buy, a shopper uses the diagonal crosswalk to walk 97 feet directly from one corner to the other. If the length of the Main Street crosswalk is 7 feet longer than the First Avenue crosswalk, how much walking does the shopper save by using the diagonal crosswalk?

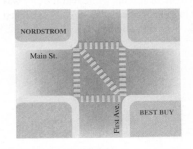

80. Badminton.   The person who wrote the instructions for setting up the badminton net shown below forgot to give the specific dimensions for securing the pole. How long is the support string?

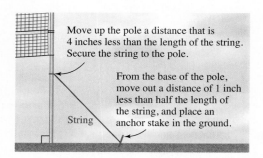

Move up the pole a distance that is 4 inches less than the length of the string. Secure the string to the pole.

From the base of the pole, move out a distance of 1 inch less than half the length of the string, and place an anchor stake in the ground.

String

81. Right Triangles.   The hypotenuse of a right triangle is 2.5 units long. The longer leg is 1.7 units longer than the shorter leg. Find the lengths of the legs of the triangle.

82. Televisions.   The screen size of a television is measured diagonally from one corner to the opposite corner. In 2007, Sharp developed the world's largest TV screen to date—a 108-inch flat-panel liquid crystal display (LCD). Find the width and the height of the rectangular screen if the width were 41 inches greater than the height. Round to the nearest inch.

83. IMAX Screens.   The largest permanent movie screen is in the Panasonic Imax theater at Darling Harbor, Sydney, Australia. The rectangular screen has an area of 11,349 square feet. Find the dimensions of the screen if it is 20 feet longer than it is wide.

84. World's Largest LED Screen.   A huge suspended LED screen is the centerpiece of The Place, a popular mall in Beijing, China. Find the length and width of the rectangular screen if the length is 10 meters more than 8 times its width, and the viewable area is 7,500 square meters.

©China Photos/Alamy

85. Parks.   Central Park is one of New York's best-known landmarks. Rectangular in shape, its length is 5 times its width. When measured in miles, its perimeter numerically exceeds its area by 4.75. Find the dimensions of Central Park if we know that its width is less than 1 mile.

86. History.   One of the important cities of the ancient world was Babylon. Greek historians wrote that the city was square. Measured in miles, its area numerically exceeded its perimeter by about 124. Find its dimensions. (Round to the nearest tenth.)

87. Polygons.   A five-sided polygon, called a *pentagon*, has 5 diagonals. The number of diagonals d of a polygon of n sides is given by the formula $d = \frac{n(n-3)}{2}$. Find the number of sides of a polygon if it has 275 diagonals.

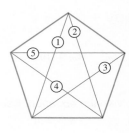

88. Metal Fabrication.   A box with no top is to be made by cutting a 2-inch square from each corner of a square sheet of metal. After bending up the sides, the volume of the box is to be 220 cubic inches. Find the length of a side of the square sheet of metal that should be used in the construction of the box. Round to the nearest hundredth.

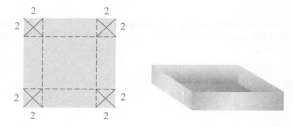

89. Dances.   Tickets to a school dance cost $4 and the projected attendance is 300 people. It is further projected that for every 10¢ increase in ticket price, the average attendance will decrease by 5. At what ticket price will the receipts from the dance be $1,248?

90. Ticket Sales.   A carnival usually sells three thousand 75¢ ride tickets on a Saturday. For each 15¢ increase in price, management estimates that 80 fewer tickets will be sold. What increase in ticket price will produce $2,982 of revenue on Saturday?

91. Magazine Sales.   The *Gazette's* profit is $20 per year for each of its 3,000 subscribers. Management estimates that the profit per subscriber will increase by 1¢ for each additional subscriber over the current 3,000. How many subscribers will bring a total profit of $120,000?

92. Investment Rates.   A woman invests $1,000 in a fund for which interest is compounded annually at a rate r. After one year, she deposits an additional $2,000. After two years, the balance in the account is $1,000(1 + r)^2 + $2,000(1 + r)$. If this amount is $3,368.10, find r.

93.
from **Campus to Careers**
Police Patrol Officer

The number of female police officers (sworn) in the United States is approximated by the function $f(t) = -24t^2 + 1,534t + 72,065$, where t is the number of years after 2000. In what year does the model indicate that the number of female officers reached 75,000? (Source: *Crime in the United States, 2000–2010*)

© Robert E Daemmrich/Getty Images

94. Shopping Centers.   The number of shopping centers in the United States is approximated by the function $s(t) = 48t^2 + 581t + 77{,}383$, where t is the number of years after 1990. In what year does the model indicate that the number of shopping centers reached 100,000? (Source: U.S. Census Bureau)

95. Picture Framing.   The matting around the picture has a uniform width. How wide is the matting if its area equals the area of the picture? Round to the nearest hundredth of an inch.

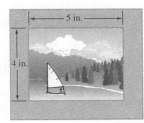

96. Swimming Pools.   In the advertisement shown, how wide will the free concrete decking be if a uniform width is constructed around the perimeter of the pool? Round to the nearest hundredth of a yard. (*Hint:* Note the difference in units. Convert the dimensions of the pool to yards.)

SAHARA POOL & SPA

SUMMER SPECIAL

This 18 ft x 30 ft pool: only $28,500

Buy now and receive 28 square yards of concrete decking *FREE!*

97. Dimensions of Rectangle.   A rectangle is 4 feet longer than it is wide, and its area is 20 square feet. Find its dimensions to the nearest tenth of a foot.

98. Dimensions of a Triangle.   The height of a triangle is 4 meters longer than twice its base. Find the base and height if the area of the triangle is 10 square meters. Round to the nearest hundredth of a meter.

WRITING

99. Explain why the quadratic formula, in most cases, is easier to use to solve a quadratic equation than is the method of completing the square.

100. On an exam, a student was asked to solve the equation $-4w^2 - 6w - 1 = 0$. Her first step was to multiply both sides of the equation by -1. She then used the quadratic formula to solve $4w^2 + 6w + 1 = 0$ instead. Is this a valid approach? Explain.

REVIEW

Change each radical to an exponential expression.

101. $\sqrt{n}$

102. $\sqrt{8r^2s}$

103. $\sqrt[4]{3b}$

104. $3\sqrt[3]{c^2 - d^2}$

Write each expression in radical form.

105. $t^{1/3}$

106. $(3m^2n^2)^{1/5}$

107. $(3t)^{1/4}$

108. $(c^2 + d^2)^{1/2}$

CHALLENGE PROBLEMS

All of the equations we have solved so far have had rational-number coefficients. However, the quadratic formula can be used to solve quadratic equations with irrational or even imaginary coefficients. Solve each equation.

109. $x^2 + 2\sqrt{2}x - 6 = 0$

110. $\sqrt{2}x^2 + x - \sqrt{2} = 0$

111. $x^2 - 3ix - 2 = 0$

112. $100ix^2 + 300x - 200i = 0$

SECTION 10.3

The Discriminant and Equations That Can Be Written in Quadratic Form

OBJECTIVES

1 Use the discriminant to determine number and type of solutions.

2 Solve equations that are quadratic in form.

3 Solve application problems using quadratic equations.

ARE YOU READY?

The following problems review some basic skills that are needed when working with discriminants and equations that can be written in quadratic form.

1. Find the value of the expression within the radical symbol only:

$$\frac{6 \pm \sqrt{(-6)^2 - 4(3)(-4)}}{6}$$

2. Fill in the blanks: **a.** $x^4 = (x^2)$

b. $(x^{1/3})^2 = x$

3. Fill in the blanks: **a.** $\left(\sqrt{x}\right)^2 = \quad$

b. $15a^{-2} = \dfrac{15}{\quad}$

4. Solve: $x^2 = -4$

5. Solve: **a.** $\sqrt{x} = 3$

b. $\sqrt[3]{x} = -\dfrac{1}{2}$

6. Solve: $\dfrac{1}{a} = \dfrac{1}{5}$

We have seen that solutions of the quadratic equation $ax^2 + bx + c = 0$ with $a \neq 0$ are given by the formula

$$x = \frac{-b \pm \sqrt{b^2 - 4ac}}{2a}$$

In this section, we will examine the radicand within the quadratic formula to distinguish or "*discriminate*" among the three types of solutions—rational, irrational, or imaginary.

1 Use the Discriminant to Determine Number and Type of Solutions.

The expression $b^2 - 4ac$ that appears under the radical symbol in the quadratic formula is called the **discriminant.** The discriminant can be used to predict what kind of solutions a quadratic equation has without solving it.

The Discriminant

For a quadratic equation of the form $ax^2 + bx + c = 0$ with rational-number coefficients and $a \neq 0$, the expression $b^2 - 4ac$ is called the **discriminant** and can be used to determine the number and type of the solutions of the equation.

Discriminant: $b^2 - 4ac$	Number and type of solutions
Positive	Two different real numbers
0	One repeated solution, a rational number
Negative.	Two different imaginary numbers that are complex conjugates

Discriminant: $b^2 - 4ac$	Number and type of solutions
A perfect square	Two different rational numbers
Positive and not a perfect square	Two different irrational numbers

---

EXAMPLE 1

Determine the number and type of solutions for each equation:
a. $x^2 + x + 1 = 0$ **b.** $3x^2 + 5x + 2 = 0$

Strategy   We will identify the values of a, b, and c in each equation. Then we will use those values to compute $b^2 - 4ac$, the discriminant.

Why   Once we know whether the discriminant is positive, 0, or negative, and whether it is a perfect square, we can determine the number and type of the solutions of the equation.

Solution   **a.** For $x^2 + x + 1 = 0$, the discriminant is:

$$b^2 - 4ac = 1^2 - 4(1)(1) \qquad \text{Substitute: } a = 1, b = 1, \text{ and } c = 1.$$

$$= -3 \qquad \text{The result is a negative number.}$$

Since $b^2 - 4ac < 0$, the solutions of $x^2 + x + 1 = 0$ are two different imaginary numbers that are complex conjugates.

b. For $3x^2 + 5x + 2 = 0$, the discriminant is:

$$b^2 - 4ac = 5^2 - 4(3)(2) \qquad \text{Substitute: } a = 3, b = 5, \text{ and } c = 2.$$

$$= 25 - 24$$

$$= 1 \qquad \text{The result is a positive number.}$$

Since $b^2 - 4ac > 0$ and $b^2 - 4ac$ is a perfect square, the solutions of $3x^2 + 5x + 2 = 0$ are two different rational numbers.

Success Tip

The discriminant also can be used to determine factorability. The trinomial $ax^2 + bx + c$ with integer coefficients and $a \neq 0$ will factor as the product of two binomials with integer coefficients if the value of $b^2 - 4ac$ is a perfect square. If $b^2 - 4ac = 0$, the factors will be the same.

> **Self Check 1**   Determine the number and type of solutions for:
> **a.** $x^2 + x - 1 = 0$
> **b.** $3x^2 + 4x + 2 = 0$
>
> **Now Try** ▶ Problems 11, 13, and 15

2 Solve Equations That Are Quadratic in Form.

We have discussed four methods that are used to solve quadratic equations. The table below shows some advantages and disadvantages of each method.

Method	Advantages	Disadvantages	Examples
Factoring and the zero-factor property	It can be very fast. When each factor is set equal to 0, the resulting equations are usually easy to solve.	Some polynomials may be difficult to factor and others impossible.	$x^2 - 2x - 24 = 0$ $4a^2 - a = 0$
Square root property	It is the fastest way to solve equations of the form $ax^2 = n$ (n = a number) or $(ax + b)^2 = n$.	It applies only to equations that are in these forms.	$x^2 = 27$ $(2y + 3)^2 = 25$
Completing the square*	It can be used to solve any quadratic equation. It works well with equations of the form $x^2 + bx = n$, where b is even.	It involves more steps than the other methods. The algebra can be cumbersome if the leading coefficient is not 1 or if b is odd or a fraction.	$x^2 + 4x = -1$ $t^2 - 14t - 9 = 0$
Quadratic formula	It can be used to solve any quadratic equation.	It involves several calculations in which sign errors can be made. Often the result must be simplified.	$x^2 + 3x - 33 = 0$ $4s^2 - 10s + 5 = 0$

*The quadratic formula is just a condensed version of completing the square and is usually easier to use. However, you need to know how to complete the square because it is used in more advanced mathematics courses.

Success Tip

The solutions of a quadratic equation can always be found using the quadratic formula. The solutions cannot always be found using factoring.

To determine the most efficient method for a given equation, we can use the following strategy.

Strategy for Solving Quadratic Equations

1. See whether the equation is in a form such that the **square root method** is easily applied.
2. If step 1 does not apply, write the equation in $ax^2 + bx + c = 0$ form.
3. See whether the equation can be solved using the **factoring method.**
4. If you can't factor, solve the equation by the **quadratic formula. Completing the square** can also be used.

Many nonquadratic equations can be written in quadratic form ($ax^2 + bx + c = 0$) and solved using the techniques discussed in previous sections. For example, a careful inspection of the equation $x^4 - 5x^2 + 4 = 0$ leads to the following observations:

The leading term, x^4, is the square of the expression x^2 in the middle term: $x^4 = (x^2)^2$.

$$x^4 - 5x^2 + 4 = 0$$

The last term is a constant.

Equations that contain an expression, the same expression squared, and a constant term are said to be **quadratic in form**. One method used to solve such equations is to make a substitution.

EXAMPLE 2   Solve: $x^4 - 3x^2 - 4 = 0$

Strategy   Since the leading term, x^4, is the square of the expression x^2 in the middle term, we will substitute y for x^2.

Why   Our hope is that such a substitution will produce an equation that we can solve using one of the methods previously discussed.

Solution   If we write x^4 as $(x^2)^2$, the equation takes the form

$$(x^2)^2 - 3x^2 - 4 = 0$$

and it is said to be **quadratic in x^2**. We can solve this equation by letting $y = x^2$.

$$y^2 - 3y - 4 = 0 \qquad \text{Replace each } x^2 \text{ with } y.$$

Notation

The choice of the letter y for the substitution is arbitrary. We could just as well let $b = x^2$.

We can solve the resulting quadratic equation by factoring.

$$(y - 4)(y + 1) = 0 \qquad\qquad \text{Factor } y^2 - 3y - 4.$$
$$y - 4 = 0 \quad \text{or} \quad y + 1 = 0 \qquad \text{Set each factor equal to 0.}$$
$$y = 4 \qquad\qquad\quad y = -1 \qquad \text{Solve for } y.$$

Caution

If you are solving an equation in x, you can't answer with values of y. Remember to reverse (undo) any substitutions, and solve for the variable in the original equation.

These are not the solutions for x. To find x, we reverse the substitution by replacing each y with x^2 and proceed as follows:

$$x^2 = 4 \qquad \text{or} \qquad x^2 = -1 \qquad \text{Undo the substitution. Substitute } x^2 \text{ for } y.$$
$$x = \pm\sqrt{4} \qquad\qquad x = \pm\sqrt{-1} \qquad \text{Use the square root property. Don't forget } \pm.$$
$$x = \pm 2 \qquad\qquad\quad x = \pm i \qquad \text{Simplify each radical.}$$

This equation has four solutions: 2, -2, i, and $-i$. Check each one in the original equation. In general, a fourth-degree polynomial equation, such as this, can have up to four distinct solutions.

Self Check 2   Solve: $x^4 - 5x^2 - 36 = 0$

Now Try ▶ Problem 23

EXAMPLE 3   Solve: $x - 7\sqrt{x} + 12 = 0$

Strategy   Since the leading term, x, is the square of the expression $\sqrt{x}$ in the middle term, we will substitute y for $\sqrt{x}$.

Why   Our hope is that such a substitution will produce an equation that we can solve using one of the methods previously discussed.

Solution   We examine the leading term and the middle term.

The leading term, x, is the square of the expression $\sqrt{x}$ in middle term: $x = \left(\sqrt{x}\right)^2$.

$$x - 7\sqrt{x} + 12 = 0$$

The last term is a constant.

If we write x as $\left(\sqrt{x}\right)^2$, the equation takes the form

$$\left(\sqrt{x}\right)^2 - 7\sqrt{x} + 12 = 0$$

The Language of Algebra

Equations such as $x - 7\sqrt{x} + 12 = 0$ that are quadratic in form are also said to be **reducible** to a quadratic.

and it is said to be **quadratic in $\sqrt{x}$**. We can solve this equation by letting $y = \sqrt{x}$ and factoring.

$$y^2 - 7y + 12 = 0 \qquad \text{Replace each } \sqrt{x} \text{ with } y. \text{ This is a quadratic equation.}$$
$$(y - 3)(y - 4) = 0 \qquad \text{Factor the trinomial.}$$
$$y - 3 = 0 \quad \text{or} \quad y - 4 = 0 \qquad \text{Set each factor equal to 0.}$$
$$y = 3 \qquad\qquad\quad y = 4 \qquad \text{Solve for } y.$$

Success Tip

Recall from Chapter 9 that we must check each proposed solution of a radical equation and eliminate any extraneous solutions.

To find x, we reverse the substitution and replace each y with $\sqrt{x}$. Then we solve the resulting radical equations by squaring both sides.

$$\sqrt{x} = 3 \quad \text{or} \quad \sqrt{x} = 4 \qquad \textit{Undo the substitution.}$$
$$x = 9 \qquad\qquad x = 16$$

The solutions are 9 and 16. Check each solution in the original equation.

Self Check 3 Solve: $x + \sqrt{x} - 6 = 0$

Now Try ▶ Problem 27

EXAMPLE 4 Solve: $2m^{2/3} - 2 = 3m^{1/3}$

Strategy We will write the equation in descending powers of m and look for a possible substitution to make.

Why Our hope is that a substitution will produce an equation that we can solve using one of the methods previously discussed.

Solution After writing the equation in descending powers of m, we see that

$$2m^{2/3} - 3m^{1/3} - 2 = 0$$

The Language of Algebra

Recall that in $2m^{2/3}$, we call 2/3 a **rational** or **fractional exponent**.

is **quadratic in $m^{1/3}$**, because $m^{2/3} = (m^{1/3})^2$. We will use the substitution $y = m^{1/3}$ to write this equation in quadratic form.

$2m^{2/3} - 3m^{1/3} - 2 = 0$	This is the equation to solve.
$2(m^{1/3})^2 - 3m^{1/3} - 2 = 0$	Write $m^{2/3}$ as $(m^{1/3})^2$.
$2y^2 - 3y - 2 = 0$	Substitute: Replace each $m^{1/3}$ with y. This is a quadratic equation.
$(2y + 1)(y - 2) = 0$	Factor $2y^2 - 3y - 2$.
$2y + 1 = 0 \quad \text{or} \quad y - 2 = 0$	Set each factor equal to 0.
$y = -\dfrac{1}{2} \qquad\qquad y = 2$	Solve for y.

To find m, we reverse the substitution and replace each y with $m^{1/3}$. Then we solve the resulting equations by cubing both sides.

Success Tip

We could write $m^{1/3} = -\dfrac{1}{2}$ in the equivalent radical form $\sqrt[3]{m} = -\dfrac{1}{2}$ and solve in the same way—by cubing both sides.

$m^{1/3} = -\dfrac{1}{2} \quad \text{or} \quad m^{1/3} = 2$	Undo the substitution.
$(m^{1/3})^3 = \left(-\dfrac{1}{2}\right)^3 \quad\bigg\vert\quad (m^{1/3})^3 = (2)^3$	Recall that $m^{1/3} = \sqrt[3]{m}$. To solve for m, cube both sides.
$m = -\dfrac{1}{8} \qquad\qquad m = 8$	Find each power.

The solutions are $-\frac{1}{8}$ and 8. Check each solution in the original equation.

Self Check 4 Solve: $a^{2/3} = -3a^{1/3} + 10$

Now Try ▶ Problem 31

EXAMPLE 5 Solve: $(4t + 2)^2 - 30(4t + 2) + 224 = 0$

Strategy Since the leading term, $(4t + 2)^2$, is the square of the expression $4t + 2$ in the middle term, we will substitute y for $4t + 2$.

Why Our hope is that such a substitution will produce an equation that we can solve using one of the methods previously discussed.

Solution This equation is **quadratic in $4t + 2$**. If we make the substitution $y = 4t + 2$, we obtain

$$y^2 - 30y + 224 = 0$$

which can be solved by using the quadratic formula.

$$y = \frac{-b \pm \sqrt{b^2 - 4ac}}{2a}$$

$$y = \frac{-(-30) \pm \sqrt{(-30)^2 - 4(1)(224)}}{2(1)} \qquad \text{Substitute 1 for } a, -30 \text{ for } b, \text{ and 224 for } c.$$

$$y = \frac{30 \pm \sqrt{4}}{2} \qquad \text{Evaluate within the radical.}$$

$$y = \frac{30 \pm 2}{2} \qquad \text{Evaluate the radical: } \sqrt{4} = 2.$$

$$y = 16 \qquad \text{or} \qquad y = 14 \qquad \text{Evaluate: } \frac{30 + 2}{2} = 16 \text{ and } \frac{30 - 2}{2} = 14$$

To find t, we reverse the substitution and replace y with $4t + 2$. Then we solve for t.

$$
\begin{array}{lll}
4t + 2 = 16 & \text{or} \quad 4t + 2 = 14 & \text{Undo the substitution.} \\
4t = 14 & \qquad\quad 4t = 12 & \text{Isolate the variable term, } 4t. \\
t = 3.5 & \qquad\quad\; t = 3 & \text{Solve for } t.
\end{array}
$$

Verify that 3.5 and 3 satisfy the original equation.

Self Check 5 Solve: $(n + 3)^2 - 6(n + 3) = -8$

Now Try ▶ Problem 35

EXAMPLE 6 Solve: $15a^{-2} - 8a^{-1} + 1 = 0$

Strategy We will write the equation with positive exponents and look for a possible substitution to make.

Why Our hope is that a substitution will produce an equation that we can solve using one of the methods previously discussed.

Solution When we write the terms $15a^{-2}$ and $-8a^{-1}$ using positive exponents, we see that this equation is **quadratic in $\frac{1}{a}$**.

Success Tip

We could also solve this equation by multiplying both sides by the LCD, a^2.

$$\frac{15}{a^2} - \frac{8}{a} + 1 = 0 \qquad \text{Think of this equation as } 15 \cdot \left(\frac{1}{a}\right)^2 - 8 \cdot \frac{1}{a} + 1 = 0.$$
$$\text{Note that 0 is not a possible solution.}$$

If we let $y = \frac{1}{a}$, the resulting quadratic equation can be solved by factoring.

$$15y^2 - 8y + 1 = 0 \qquad \text{Substitute } y^2 \text{ for } \frac{1}{a^2} \text{ and } y \text{ for } \frac{1}{a}. \text{ This is a quadratic equation.}$$

$$(5y - 1)(3y - 1) = 0 \qquad \text{Factor } 15y^2 - 8y + 1.$$

$$
\begin{array}{lll}
5y - 1 = 0 & \text{or} \quad 3y - 1 = 0 & \text{Set each factor equal to 0.} \\
y = \dfrac{1}{5} & \qquad\quad y = \dfrac{1}{3} & \text{Solve for } y.
\end{array}
$$

To find a, we reverse the substitution and replace each y with $\frac{1}{a}$. Then we proceed as follows:

$$\frac{1}{a} = \frac{1}{5} \quad \text{or} \quad \frac{1}{a} = \frac{1}{3} \qquad \textit{Undo the substitution.}$$

$$5 = a \qquad\qquad\quad 3 = a \qquad \textit{Solve the proportions by finding the cross products.}$$

The solutions are 5 and 3. Check each solution in the original equation.

Self Check 6 Solve: $28c^{-2} - 3c^{-1} - 1 = 0$

Now Try ▶ Problem 41

3 Solve Application Problems Using Quadratic Equations.

EXAMPLE 7

Electronic Temperature Control

Water Temp

Household Appliances. The illustration shows a temperature control on a washing machine. When the *warm* setting is selected, both the hot and cold water pipes open to fill the tub in 2 minutes 15 seconds. When the *cold* setting is chosen, the tub fills 45 seconds faster than when the *hot* setting is used. How long does it take to fill the washing machine if the *hot* setting is used?

Analyze It is helpful to organize the facts of this shared-work problem in a table. We note that the hot and cold water inlets will be open for the same time: 2 minutes 15 seconds, or 135 seconds.

Assign Let x = the number of seconds it takes to fill the tub with hot water. Since the cold water inlet fills the tub in 45 seconds less time, $x - 45$ = the number of seconds it takes to fill the tub with cold water.

Form To determine the work completed by each inlet, multiply the rate by the time.

	Rate · Time = Work completed		
Hot water	$\frac{1}{x}$	135	$\frac{135}{x}$
Cold water	$\frac{1}{x - 45}$	135	$\frac{135}{x - 45}$

Enter this information first. Multiply to get each of these entries: $W = rt$.

In shared-work problems, 1 represents one whole job completed. So we have

The fraction of tub filled with hot water	plus	the fraction of the tub filled with cold water	equals	1 tub filled.
$\frac{135}{x}$	$+$	$\frac{135}{x - 45}$	$=$	1

Solve

$$\frac{135}{x} + \frac{135}{x - 45} = 1$$

This is a rational equation.

$$x(x - 45)\left(\frac{135}{x} + \frac{135}{x - 45}\right) = x(x - 45)(1)$$

Multiply both sides by the LCD $x(x - 45)$ to clear the equation of fractions.

$$x(x - 45)\frac{135}{x} + x(x - 45)\frac{135}{x - 45} = x(x - 45)(1)$$

Distribute $x(x - 45)$.

$$135(x - 45) + 135x = x(x - 45)$$

Simplify each side.

$$135x - 6{,}075 + 135x = x^2 - 45x$$

Distribute 135 and x.

$$270x - 6{,}075 = x^2 - 45x$$

Combine like terms.

$$0 = x^2 - 315x + 6{,}075$$

Get 0 on the left side.

To solve for x, we will use the quadratic formula: $a = 1$, $b = -315$, and $c = 6{,}075$.

$$x = \frac{-b \pm \sqrt{b^2 - 4ac}}{2a}$$

$$x = \frac{-(-315) \pm \sqrt{(-315)^2 - 4(1)(6{,}075)}}{2(1)}$$

Substitute 1 for a, −315 for b, and 6,075 for c.

$$x = \frac{315 \pm \sqrt{74{,}925}}{2}$$

Evaluate the expression within the radical.

$$x \approx 294 \quad \text{or} \quad \cancel{x \approx 21} \quad \text{Use a calculator to find each solution.}$$

State We can discard the solution of 21 seconds, because this would imply that the cold water inlet fills the tub in a negative number of seconds ($21 - 45 = -24$). Therefore, the hot water inlet fills the washing machine tub in about 294 seconds, which is 4 minutes 54 seconds.

Check Use estimation to check the result. The work completed by the hot water inlet is $\frac{135}{294} \approx 0.46$ and the work completed by the cold water inlet is $\frac{135}{294 - 45} \approx 0.54$. Since $0.46 + 0.54 \approx 1$, the result seems reasonable.

Self Check 7   **Mowing Lawns.**   Carly can mow a lawn in 1 hour less time than her friend Lindsey. Together they can finish the job in 5 hours. How long would it take Carly if she worked alone?

Now Try Problem 87

SECTION 10.3 STUDY SET

VOCABULARY

Fill in the blanks.

1. For the quadratic equation $ax^2 + bx + c = 0$, the _____ is $b^2 - 4ac$.

2. We can solve $x - 2\sqrt{x} - 8 = 0$ by making the _____ $y = \sqrt{x}$.

CONCEPTS

Consider the quadratic equation $ax^2 - bx + c = 0$, where a, b, and c represent rational numbers, and fill in the blanks.

3. If $b^2 - 4ac < 0$, the solutions of the equation are two different imaginary numbers that are complex _____.

4. If $b^2 - 4ac = \blacksquare$, the equation has one repeated rational-number solution.

5. If $b^2 - 4ac$ is a perfect square, the solutions of the equation are two different _____ numbers.

6. If $b^2 - 4ac$ is positive and not a perfect square, the solutions of the equation are two different _____ numbers.

7. For each equation, determine the substitution that should be made to write the equation in quadratic form.

   a. $x^4 - 12x^2 + 27 = 0$ Let $y =$ ▯

   b. $x - 13\sqrt{x} + 40 = 0$ Let $y =$ ▯

   c. $x^{2/3} + 2x^{1/3} - 3 = 0$ Let $y =$ ▯

   d. $x^{-2} - x^{-1} - 30 = 0$ Let $y =$ ▯

   e. $(x + 1)^2 - (x + 1) - 6 = 0$ Let $y =$ ▯

8. Fill in the blanks.

   a. $x^4 = \left(\right)^2$

   b. $x = \left(\right)^2$

   c. $x^{2/3} = \left(\right)^2$

   d. $\dfrac{1}{x^2} = \left(\right)^2$

NOTATION

Complete the solution.

9. To find the type of solutions for the equation $x^2 + 5x + 6 = 0$, we calculate the discriminant.

$$b^2 - \boxed{} = \boxed{}^2 - 4(1)\left(\boxed{}\right)$$
$$= 25 - \boxed{}$$
$$= 1$$

Since a, b, and c are rational numbers and the value of the discriminant is a perfect square, the solutions are two different _____ numbers.

10. Fill in the blanks to write each equation in quadratic form.

   a. $x^4 - 2x^2 - 15 = 0 \rightarrow \left(\boxed{}\right)^2 - 2\boxed{} - 15 = 0$

   b. $x - 2\sqrt{x} + 3 = 0 \rightarrow \left(\boxed{}\right)^2 - 2\boxed{} + 3 = 0$

   c. $8m^{2/3} - 10m^{1/3} - 3 = 0 \rightarrow 8\left(\boxed{}\right)^2 - 10\boxed{} - 3 = 0$

GUIDED PRACTICE

Use the discriminant to determine the number and type of solutions for each equation. Do not solve. See Example 1.

11. $4x^2 - 4x + 1 = 0$

12. $6x^2 - 5x - 6 = 0$

13. $5x^2 + x + 2 = 0$

14. $3x^2 + 10x - 2 = 0$

15. $2x^2 = 4x - 1$

16. $9x^2 = 12x - 4$

17. $x(2x - 3) = 20$

18. $x(x - 3) = -10$

19. $3x^2 - 10 = 0$

20. $5x^2 - 24 = 0$

21. $x^2 - \dfrac{14}{15}x = \dfrac{8}{15}$

22. $x^2 = -\dfrac{5}{4}x + \dfrac{3}{2}$

Solve each equation. See Example 2.

23. $x^4 - 17x^2 + 16 = 0$

24. $x^4 - 10x^2 + 9 = 0$

25. $x^4 + 5x^2 - 36 = 0$

26. $x^4 - 15x^2 - 16 = 0$

Solve each equation. See Example 3.

27. $x - 13\sqrt{x} + 40 = 0$

28. $x - 9\sqrt{x} + 18 = 0$

29. $2x + \sqrt{x} - 3 = 0$

30. $2x - \sqrt{x} - 1 = 0$

Solve each equation. See Example 4.

31. $a^{2/3} - 2a^{1/3} = 3$

32. $r^{2/3} + 4r^{1/3} = 5$

33. $x^{2/3} + 2x^{1/3} - 8 = 0$

34. $x^{2/3} - 7x^{1/3} + 12 = 0$

Solve each equation. See Example 5.

35. $(c + 1)^2 - 4(c + 1) + 3 = 0$

36. $(a - 5)^2 - 4(a - 5) - 21 = 0$

37. $2(2x + 1)^2 - 7(2x + 1) + 6 = 0$

38. $3(2 - x)^2 + 10(2 - x) - 8 = 0$

Solve each equation. See Example 6.

39. $m^{-2} + m^{-1} - 6 = 0$

40. $t^{-2} + t^{-1} - 42 = 0$

41. $8x^{-2} - 10x^{-1} - 3 = 0$

42. $2x^{-2} - 5x^{-1} - 3 = 0$

Solve each equation. See Example 7.

43. $1 - \dfrac{5}{x} = \dfrac{10}{x^2}$

44. $1 - \dfrac{3}{x} = \dfrac{5}{x^2}$

45. $\dfrac{1}{2} + \dfrac{1}{b} = \dfrac{1}{b - 7}$

46. $\dfrac{1}{4} - \dfrac{1}{n} = \dfrac{1}{n + 3}$

TRY IT YOURSELF

Solve each equation.

47. $2x - \sqrt{x} = 3$

48. $3x + 4\sqrt{x} = 4$

49. $x^{-2} + 2x^{-1} - 3 = 0$

50. $x^{-2} + 2x^{-1} - 8 = 0$

51. $x^4 + 19x^2 + 18 = 0$

52. $t^4 + 4t^2 - 5 = 0$

53. $(k - 7)^2 + 6(k - 7) + 10 = 0$

54. $(d + 9)^2 - 4(d + 9) + 8 = 0$

55. $\dfrac{2}{x - 1} + \dfrac{1}{x + 1} = 3$

56. $\dfrac{3}{x - 2} - \dfrac{1}{x + 2} = 5$

57. $x - 6x^{1/2} = -8$

58. $x - 5x^{1/2} + 4 = 0$

59. $(y^2 - 9)^2 + 2(y^2 - 9) - 99 = 0$

60. $(a^2 - 4)^2 - 4(a^2 - 4) - 32 = 0$

61. $x^{-4} - 2x^{-2} + 1 = 0$

62. $4x^{-4} + 1 = 5x^{-2}$

63. $t^4 + 3t^2 = 28$

64. $3h^4 + h^2 - 2 = 0$

65. $2x^{2/5} - 5x^{1/5} = -3$

66. $2x^{2/5} + 3x^{1/5} = -1$

67. $9\left(\dfrac{3m + 2}{m}\right)^2 - 30\left(\dfrac{3m + 2}{m}\right) + 25 = 0$

68. $4\left(\dfrac{c - 7}{c}\right)^2 - 12\left(\dfrac{c - 7}{c}\right) + 9 = 0$

69. $\dfrac{3}{a - 1} = 1 - \dfrac{2}{a}$

70. $1 + \dfrac{4}{x} = \dfrac{3}{x^2}$

71. $\left(8 - \sqrt{a}\right)^2 + 6\left(8 - \sqrt{a}\right) - 7 = 0$

72. $\left(10 - \sqrt{t}\right)^2 - 4\left(10 - \sqrt{t}\right) - 45 = 0$

73. $x + \dfrac{2}{x - 2} = 0$

74. $x + \dfrac{x + 5}{x - 3} = 0$

75. $3x + 5\sqrt{x} + 2 = 0$

76. $3x - 4\sqrt{x} + 1 = 0$

77. $x^4 - 6x^2 + 5 = 0$

78. $2x^4 - 26x^2 + 24 = 0$

79. $8(t + 1)^{-2} - 30(t + 1)^{-1} + 7 = 0$

80. $2(s - 2)^{-2} + 3(s - 2)^{-1} - 5 = 0$

81. $\dfrac{1}{x + 2} + \dfrac{24}{x + 3} = 13$

82. $\dfrac{3}{x} + \dfrac{4}{x + 1} = 2$

Look Alikes . . .

83. a. $y^{2/3} + y^{1/3} - 20 = 0$ **b.** $y^{-2} + y^{-1} - 20 = 0$

84. a. $x + 6\sqrt{x} - 16 = 0$ **b.** $x^{2/3} + 6x^{1/3} - 16 = 0$

85. a. $\dfrac{1}{x} = \dfrac{2x}{x + 1}$ **b.** $\dfrac{1}{x} + \dfrac{2x}{x + 1} = 1$

86. a. $(m^2 - 1)^2 - (m^2 - 1) = 2$ **b.** $m^4 - m^2 = 2$

APPLICATIONS

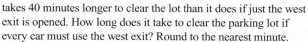

87. from **Campus to Careers**

Police Patrol Officer

Crowd Control. After a sporting event at a stadium, police have found that a public parking lot can be emptied in 60 minutes if both the east and west exits are opened. If just the east exit is used, it takes 40 minutes longer to clear the lot than it does if just the west exit is opened. How long does it take to clear the parking lot if every car must use the west exit? Round to the nearest minute.

88. Paper Routes. When a father, in a car, and his son, on a bicycle, work together to distribute the morning newspaper, it takes them 35 minutes to complete the route. Working alone, it takes the son 25 minutes longer than the father. To the nearest minute, how long does it take the son to cover the route on his bicycle?

89. Assembly Lines. A newly manufactured product traveled 300 feet on a high-speed conveyor belt at a rate of r feet per second. It could have traveled the 300 feet in 3 seconds less time if the speed of the conveyor belt was increased by 5 feet per second. Find r.

90. Bicycling. Tina bicycles 160 miles at the rate of r mph. The same trip would have taken 2 hours longer if she had decreased her speed by 4 mph. Find r.

91. Architecture. A **golden rectangle** is one of the most visually appealing of all geometric forms. The Parthenon, built by the Greeks in the 5th century B.C., fits into a golden rectangle if its ruined triangular pediment is included. See the illustration. In a golden rectangle, the length l and width w must satisfy the equation $\dfrac{l}{w} = \dfrac{w}{l - w}$. If a rectangular billboard is to have a width of 20 feet, what should its length be so that it is a golden rectangle? Round to the nearest tenth.

92. Door Designs. An architect needs to determine the height h of the window shown in the illustration. The radius r, the width w, and the height h of the circular-shaped window are related by the formula $r = \dfrac{4h^2 + w^2}{8h}$. If w is to be 34 inches and r is to be 18 inches, find h to the nearest tenth of an inch.

WRITING

93. Describe how to predict what type of solutions the equation $3x^2 - 4x + 5 = 0$ will have.

94. What **error** is made in the following solution?

Solve: $x^4 - 12x^2 + 27 = 0$

$y^2 - 12y + 27 = 0$ Let $y = x^2$.

$(y - 9)(y - 3) = 0$

$y - 9 = 0$ or $y - 3 = 0$

$y = 9$ | $y = 3$

The solutions of $x^4 - 12x^2 + 27 = 0$ are 9 and 3.

REVIEW

95. Write an equation of the vertical line that passes through $(3, 4)$.

96. Find an equation for a linear function whose graph passes through $(-1, -6)$ and $(-2, -1)$.

97. Write an equation of the line with slope $\frac{2}{3}$ that passes through the origin.

98. Find an equation of the line that passes through $(2, -3)$ and is perpendicular to the line whose equation is $y = \frac{x}{5} + 6$. Write the equation in slope–intercept form.

100. Solve: $x^6 + 17x^3 + 16 = 0$
101. Solve: $x^3 - x^2 + 16x - 16 = 0$
102. Solve: $\sqrt{x^2 + 10} = 4\sqrt{x}$

CHALLENGE PROBLEMS

99. Find the real-number solutions of $x^4 - 3x^2 - 2 = 0$. Rationalize the denominators of the solutions.

SECTION 10.4

Quadratic Functions and Their Graphs

OBJECTIVES

1 Graph functions of the form $f(x) = ax^2$ and $f(x) = ax^2 + k$.

2 Graph functions of the form $f(x) = a(x - h)^2$ and $f(x) = a(x - h)^2 + k$.

3 Graph functions of the form $f(x) = ax^2 + bx + c$ by completing the square.

4 Find the vertex using $-\frac{b}{2a}$.

5 Determine minimum and maximum values.

6 Solve quadratic equations graphically.

ARE YOU READY?

The following problems review some basic skills that are needed when graphing quadratic functions.

1. Graph: $f(x) = x^2$

2. Let $f(x) = 2(x - 3)^2 - 4$. Find $f(4)$.

3. Complete the square on $x^2 + 8x$. Then factor the resulting trinomial.

4. Complete the square on $x^2 + x$. Then factor the resulting trinomial.

5. Solve: $x^2 + 6x + 9 = 0$

6. Solve: $-2x^2 - 8x - 8 = 0$

7. Evaluate $-\frac{b}{2a}$ for $a = -2$ and $b = -20$.

8. Is the graph of $x = -1$ a horizontal or a vertical line?

In this section, we will discuss methods for graphing *quadratic functions*.

Quadratic Functions

A **quadratic function** is a second-degree polynomial function that can be written in the form

$$f(x) = ax^2 + bx + c$$

where a, b, and c are real numbers and $a \neq 0$.

Quadratic functions often are written in another form, called **standard form,**

$$f(x) = a(x - h)^2 + k$$

Notation

Since $y = f(x)$, quadratic functions can also be written as
$y = ax^2 + bx + c$ and
$y = a(x - h)^2 + k$.

where a, h, and k are real numbers and $a \neq 0$. This form is useful because a, h, and k give us important information about the graph of the function. To develop a strategy for graphing quadratic functions written in standard form, we will begin by considering the simplest case, $f(x) = ax^2$.

1 **Graph Functions of the Form $f(x) = ax^2$ and $f(x) = ax^2 + k$.**

One way to graph quadratic functions is to plot points.

EXAMPLE 1   Graph: **a.** $f(x) = x^2$ **b.** $g(x) = 3x^2$ **c.** $s(x) = \frac{1}{3}x^2$

Strategy   We can make a table of values for each function, plot each point, and connect them with a smooth curve.

Why   At this time, this method is our only option.

Solution   After graphing each curve, we see that the graph of $g(x) = 3x^2$ is narrower than the graph of $f(x) = x^2$, and the graph of $s(x) = \frac{1}{3}x^2$ is wider than the graph of $f(x) = x^2$. For $f(x) = ax^2$, the smaller the value of $|a|$, the wider the graph.

$f(x) = x^2$

x	f(x)
−2	4
−1	1
0	0
1	1
2	4

$g(x) = 3x^2$

x	g(x)
−2	12
−1	3
0	0
1	3
2	12

$s(x) = \frac{1}{3}x^2$

x	s(x)
−2	$\frac{4}{3}$
−1	$\frac{1}{3}$
0	0
1	$\frac{1}{3}$
2	$\frac{4}{3}$

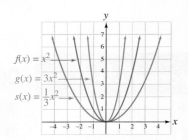

The values of $g(x)$ increase faster than the values of $f(x)$, making its graph steeper.

The values of $s(x)$ increase more slowly than the values of $f(x)$, making its graph flatter.

Self Check 1   Graph: $g(x) = \frac{2}{3}x^2$.

Now Try ▶ Problem 15

EXAMPLE 2   Graph: $f(x) = -3x^2$

Strategy   We make a table of values for the function, plot each point, and connect them with a smooth curve.

Why   At this time, this method is our only option.

Solution   After graphing the curve, we see that it opens downward and has the same shape as the graph of $g(x) = 3x^2$ that was graphed in Example 1.

$f(x) = -3x^2$

x	f(x)	
−2	−12	→ (−2, −12)
−1	−3	→ (−1, −3)
0	0	→ (0, 0)
1	−3	→ (1, −3)
2	−12	→ (2, −12)

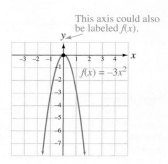

This axis could also be labeled $f(x)$.

Self Check 2   Graph: $f(x) = -\frac{1}{3}x^2$

Now Try ▶ Problem 17

The graphs of functions of the form $f(x) = ax^2$ are **parabolas.** The lowest point on a parabola that opens upward, or the highest point on a parabola that opens downward, is called the **vertex** of the parabola. The vertical line, called an **axis of symmetry,** that passes through the vertex divides the parabola into two congruent halves. If we fold the paper along the axis of symmetry, the two sides of the parabola will match.

The Language of Algebra

An axis of symmetry divides a parabola into two matching sides. The sides are said to be **mirror images** of each other.

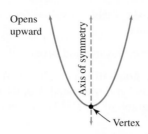

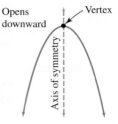

The results from Examples 1 and 2 confirm the following facts.

The Graph of $f(x) = ax^2$	The graph of $f(x) = ax^2$ is a parabola opening upward when $a > 0$ and downward when $a < 0$, with vertex at the point $(0, 0)$ and axis of symmetry the line $x = 0$.

EXAMPLE 3 Graph: **a.** $f(x) = 2x^2$ **b.** $g(x) = 2x^2 + 3$ **c.** $s(x) = 2x^2 - 3$

Strategy We make a table of values for each function, plot each point, and connect them with a smooth curve.

Why At this time, this method is our only option.

Solution After graphing the curves, we see that the graph of $g(x) = 2x^2 + 3$ is identical to the graph of $f(x) = 2x^2$, except that it has been translated 3 units upward. The graph of $s(x) = 2x^2 - 3$ is identical to the graph of $f(x) = 2x^2$, except that it has been translated 3 units downward. In each case, the axis of symmetry is the line $x = 0$.

$f(x) = 2x^2$

x	$f(x)$
-2	8
-1	2
0	0
1	2
2	8

$g(x) = 2x^2 + 3$

x	$g(x)$
-2	11
-1	5
0	3
1	5
2	11

$s(x) = 2x^2 - 3$

x	$s(x)$
-2	5
-1	-1
0	-3
1	-1
2	5

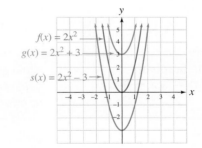

For each x-value, g(x) is 3 more than f(x).

For each x-value, s(x) is 3 less than f(x).

Self Check 3 Graph: $f(x) = 2x^2 + 1$

Now Try ▶ Problem 19

The results of Example 3 confirm the following facts.

The Graph of $f(x) = ax^2 + k$	The graph of $f(x) = ax^2 + k$ is a parabola having the same shape as $f(x) = ax^2$ but translated k units upward if k is positive and $|k|$ units downward if k is negative. The vertex is at the point $(0, k)$, and the axis of symmetry is the line $x = 0$.

2 Graph Functions of the Form $f(x) = a(x - h)^2$ and $f(x) = a(x - h)^2 + k$.

EXAMPLE 4   Graph: **a.** $f(x) = 2x^2$ **b.** $g(x) = 2(x - 3)^2$ **c.** $s(x) = 2(x + 3)^2$

Strategy   We make a table of values for each function, plot each point, and connect them with a smooth curve.

Why   At this time, this method is our only option.

Solution   We note that the graph of $g(x) = 2(x - 3)^2$ below is identical to the graph of $f(x) = 2x^2$, except that it has been translated 3 units to the right. The graph of $s(x) = 2(x + 3)^2$ is identical to the graph of $f(x) = 2x^2$, except that it has been translated 3 units to the left.

$f(x) = 2x^2$

x	$f(x)$
-2	8
-1	2
0	0
1	2
2	8

$g(x) = 2(x - 3)^2$

x	$g(x)$
1	8
2	2
3	0
4	2
5	8

$s(x) = 2(x + 3)^2$

x	$s(x)$
-5	8
-4	2
-3	0
-2	2
-1	8

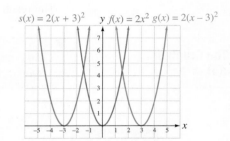

When an x-value is increased by 3, the function's outputs are the same.

When an x-value is decreased by 3, the function's outputs are the same.

Self Check 4   Graph: $g(x) = 2(x + 1)^2$

Now Try ▶   Problem 21

The results of Example 4 confirm the following facts.

The Graph of $f(x) = a(x - h)^2$ The graph of $f(x) = a(x - h)^2$ is a parabola having the same shape as $f(x) = ax^2$ but translated h units to the right if h is positive and $|h|$ units to the left if h is negative. The vertex is at the point $(h, 0)$, and the axis of symmetry is the line $x = h$.

The results of Examples 1–4 suggest a general strategy for graphing quadratic functions that are written in the form $f(x) = a(x - h)^2 + k$.

Graphing a Quadratic Function in Standard Form   The graph of the quadratic function $f(x) = a(x - h)^2 + k$, where $a \neq 0$, is a parabola with vertex at (h, k). The axis of symmetry is the line $x = h$. The parabola opens upward when $a > 0$ and downward when $a < 0$.

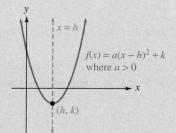

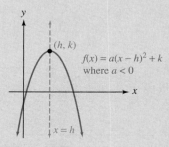

EXAMPLE 5   Graph: $f(x) = 2(x - 3)^2 - 4$. Label the vertex and draw the axis of symmetry.

Strategy   We will determine whether the graph opens upward or downward and find its vertex and axis of symmetry. Then we will plot some points and complete the graph.

Why   This method will be more efficient than plotting many points.

Solution   The graph of $f(x) = 2(x - 3)^2 - 4$ is identical to the graph of $g(x) = 2(x - 3)^2$, except that it has been translated 4 units downward. The graph of $g(x) = 2(x - 3)^2$ is identical to the graph of $s(x) = 2x^2$, except that it has been translated 3 units to the right.

We can learn more about the graph of $f(x) = 2(x - 3)^2 - 4$ by determining a, h, and k.

> **Success Tip**
>
> The most important point to find when graphing a quadratic function is the vertex.

$$f(x) = 2(x - 3)^2 - 4 \atop f(x) = a(x - h)^2 + k \Bigg\} \; a = 2, h = 3, \text{ and } k = -4$$

Upward/downward: Since $a = 2$ and $2 > 0$, the parabola opens upward.

Vertex: The vertex of the parabola is $(h, k) = (3, -4)$, as shown below.

Axis of symmetry: Since $h = 3$, the axis of symmetry is the line $x = 3$, as shown below.

Plotting points: We can construct a table of values to determine several points on the parabola. Since the x-coordinate of the vertex is 3, we choose the x-values of 4 and 5, find $f(4)$ and $f(5)$, and record the results in a table. Then we plot $(4, -2)$ and $(5, 4)$, and use symmetry to locate two other points on the parabola: $(2, -2)$ and $(1, 4)$. Finally, we draw a smooth curve through the points to get the graph.

> **Success Tip**
>
> When graphing, remember that any point on a parabola to the right of the axis of symmetry yields a second point to the left of the axis of symmetry, and vice versa. Think of it as two-for-one.

$$f(x) = 2(x - 3)^2 - 4$$

x	$f(x)$
4	-2	$\rightarrow (4, -2)$
5	4	$\rightarrow (5, 4)$

The x-coordinate of the vertex is 3. Choose values for x close to 3 and on the same side of the axis of symmetry.

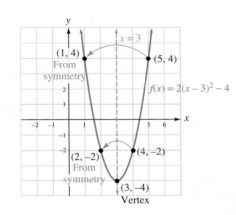

Self Check 5   Graph: $f(x) = 2(x - 1)^2 - 2$. Label the vertex and draw the axis of symmetry.

Now Try ▶   Problems 25 and 31

---

3 **Graph Functions of the Form $f(x) = ax^2 + bx + c$ by Completing the Square.**

To graph functions of the form $f(x) = ax^2 + bx + c$, we can complete the square to write the function in standard form $f(x) = a(x - h)^2 + k$.

EXAMPLE 6   Determine the vertex and the axis of symmetry of the graph of $f(x) = x^2 + 8x + 21$. Will the graph open upward or downward?

Strategy   To find the vertex and the axis of symmetry, we will complete the square on x and write the equation of the function in standard form.

Why Once the equation is written in standard form, we can determine the values of a, h, and k. The coordinates of the vertex will be (h, k) and the equation of the axis of symmetry will be $x = h$. The graph will open upward if $a > 0$ or downward if $a < 0$.

Solution To determine the vertex and the axis of symmetry of the graph, we complete the square on the right side so we can write the function in $f(x) = a(x - h)^2 + k$ form.

$$f(x) = x^2 + 8x + 21$$

$$f(x) = (x^2 + 8x \quad) + 21 \qquad \text{Prepare to complete the square on } x \\ \text{by writing parentheses around } x^2 + 8x.$$

To complete the square on $x^2 + 8x$, we note that one-half of the coefficient of x is $\frac{1}{2} \cdot 8 = 4$, and $4^2 = 16$. If we add 16 to $x^2 + 8x$, we obtain a perfect-square trinomial within the parentheses. Since this step adds 16 to the right side, we must also subtract 16 from the right side so that it remains in an equivalent form.

Success Tip

When a number is added to and that same number is subtracted from one side of an equation, the value of that side of the equation remains the same.

Add 16 to the right side. $\longrightarrow$ Subtract 16 from the right side to counteract the addition of 16.

$$f(x) = (x^2 + 8x + 16) + 21 - 16$$

$$f(x) = (x + 4)^2 + 5 \qquad \text{Factor } x^2 + 8x + 16 \text{ and combine like terms.}$$

The function is now written in standard form, and we can determine a, h, and k.

The standard form requires a minus symbol here.

$$f(x) = \left[(x - (-4)) \right]^2 + 5 \qquad \text{Write } x + 4 \text{ as } x - (-4) \text{ to determine } h.$$

$$a = 1 \qquad h = -4 \qquad k = 5$$

The vertex is $(h, k) = (-4, 5)$ and the axis of symmetry is the line $x = -4$. Since $a = 1$ and $1 > 0$, the parabola opens upward.

Self Check 6 Determine the vertex and the axis of symmetry of the graph of $f(x) = x^2 + 4x + 10$. Will the graph open upward or downward?

Now Try ▶ Problem 39

EXAMPLE 7 Graph: $f(x) = 2x^2 - 4x - 1$

Strategy We will complete the square on x and write the equation of the function in standard form, $f(x) = a(x - h)^2 + k$.

Why When the equation is in standard form, we can identify the values of a, h, and k from the equation. This information will help us sketch the graph.

Solution Recall that to complete the square on $2x^2 - 4x$, the coefficient of x^2 must be equal to 1. Therefore, we factor 2 from $2x^2 - 4x$.

$$f(x) = 2x^2 - 4x - 1$$

$$f(x) = 2(x^2 - 2x \quad) - 1$$

To complete the square on $x^2 - 2x$, we note that one-half of the coefficient of x is $\frac{1}{2}(-2) = -1$, and $(-1)^2 = 1$. If we add 1 to $x^2 - 2x$, we obtain a perfect-square trinomial within the parentheses. Since this step adds 2 to the right side, we must also subtract 2 from the right side so that it remains in an equivalent form.

By the distributive property, when 1 is added to the expression within the parentheses, $2 \cdot 1 = 2$ is added to the right side.   Subtract 2 to counteract the addition of 2 shown in red.

$$f(x) = 2(x^2 - 2x + 1) - 1 - 2$$
$$f(x) = 2(x - 1)^2 - 3 \qquad \text{Factor } x^2 - 2x + 1 \text{ and combine like terms.}$$

We see that $a = 2$, $h = 1$, and $k = -3$. Thus, the vertex is at the point $(1, -3)$, and the axis of symmetry is $x = 1$. Since $a = 2$ and $2 > 0$, the parabola opens upward. We plot the vertex and axis of symmetry as shown below.

Finally, we construct a table of values, plot the points, use symmetry to plot the corresponding points, and then draw the graph.

$$f(x) = 2x^2 - 4x - 1$$
$$\text{or}$$
$$f(x) = 2(x - 1)^2 - 3$$

x	$f(x)$
2	-1	→ $(2, -1)$
3	5	→ $(3, 5)$

The x-coordinate of the vertex is 1. Choose values for x close to 1 and on the same side of the axis of symmetry.

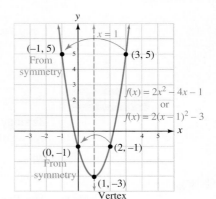

Success Tip

To find additional points on the graph, select values of x that are close to the x-coordinate of the vertex.

Self Check 7   Graph: $f(x) = 3x^2 - 12x + 8$.

Now Try ▶ Problem 45

---

4 Find the Vertex Using $-\dfrac{b}{2a}$.

Because of symmetry, if a parabola has two x-intercepts, the x-coordinate of the vertex is exactly midway between them. We can use this fact to derive a formula to find the vertex of a parabola.

In general, if a parabola has two x-intercepts, they can be found by solving $0 = ax^2 + bx + c$ for x. We can use the quadratic formula to find the solutions. They are

$$x = \frac{-b - \sqrt{b^2 - 4ac}}{2a} \qquad \text{and} \qquad x = \frac{-b + \sqrt{b^2 - 4ac}}{2a}$$

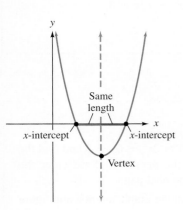

Thus, the parabola's x-intercepts are $\left(\dfrac{-b - \sqrt{b^2 - 4ac}}{2a}, 0\right)$ and $\left(\dfrac{-b + \sqrt{b^2 - 4ac}}{2a}, 0\right)$.

Since the x-value of the vertex of a parabola is halfway between the two x-intercepts, we can find this value by finding the average, or $\frac{1}{2}$ of the sum of the x-coordinates of the x-intercepts.

$$x = \frac{1}{2}\left(\frac{-b - \sqrt{b^2 - 4ac}}{2a} + \frac{-b + \sqrt{b^2 - 4ac}}{2a}\right)$$

$$x = \frac{1}{2}\left(\frac{-b - \sqrt{b^2 - 4ac} + (-b) + \sqrt{b^2 - 4ac}}{2a}\right)$$ Add the numerators and keep the common denominator.

$$x = \frac{1}{2}\left(\frac{-2b}{2a}\right)$$ Combine like terms: $-b + (-b) = -2b$ and $-\sqrt{b^2 - 4ac} + \sqrt{b^2 - 4ac} = 0$.

$$x = -\frac{b}{2a}$$ Remove the common factor of 2 in the numerator and denominator and simplify.

This result is true even if the graph has no x-intercepts.

Formula for the Vertex of a Parabola

The vertex of the graph of the quadratic function $f(x) = ax^2 + bx + c$ is

$$\left(-\frac{b}{2a}, f\left(-\frac{b}{2a}\right)\right)$$

and the axis of symmetry of the parabola is the line $x = -\frac{b}{2a}$.

EXAMPLE 8   Find the vertex of the graph of $f(x) = 2x^2 - 4x - 1$.

Strategy   We will determine the values of a and b and substitute into the formula for the vertex of a parabola.

Why   It is easier to find the coordinates of the vertex using the formula than it is to complete the square on $2x^2 - 4x - 1$.

Solution   The function is written in $f(x) = ax^2 + bx + c$ form, where $a = 2$ and $b = -4$. To find the vertex of its graph, we calculate

Success Tip

We can find the vertex of the graph of a quadratic function by completing the square or by using the formula.

$$-\frac{b}{2a} = -\frac{-4}{2(2)}$$

$$= -\frac{-4}{4}$$

$$= 1 \qquad \text{This is the } x\text{-coordinate of the vertex.}$$

$$f\left(-\frac{b}{2a}\right) = f(1)$$

$$= 2(1)^2 - 4(1) - 1$$

$$= -3 \qquad \text{This is the } y\text{-coordinate of the vertex.}$$

The vertex is the point $(1, -3)$. This agrees with the result we obtained in Example 7 by completing the square.

Self Check 8   Find the vertex of the graph of $f(x) = 3x^2 - 12x + 8$.

Now Try ▶ Problem 55

Using Your Calculator ▶ **Finding the Vertex**

We can use a graphing calculator to graph the function $f(x) = 2x^2 + 6x - 3$ and find the coordinates of the vertex and the axis of symmetry of the parabola. If we enter the function, we will obtain the graph shown in figure (a) on the next page.

We then trace to move the cursor to the lowest point on the graph, as shown in figure (b). By zooming in, we can see that the vertex is the point $(-1.5, -7.5)$, or $\left(-\frac{3}{2}, -\frac{15}{2}\right)$, and that the line $x = -\frac{3}{2}$ is the axis of symmetry.

Some calculators have an fmin or fmax feature that also can be used to find the vertex.

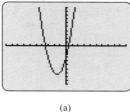

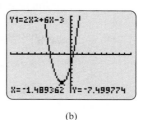

(a)	(b)

We can determine much about the graph of $f(x) = ax^2 + bx + c$ from the coefficients a, b, and c. This information is summarized as follows:

**Graphing a
Quadratic Function
$f(x) = ax^2 + bx + c$**

▼

- Determine whether the parabola opens upward or downward by finding the value of a.
- The x-coordinate of the vertex of the parabola is $x = -\dfrac{b}{2a}$.
- To find the y-coordinate of the vertex, substitute $-\dfrac{b}{2a}$ for x and find $f\left(-\dfrac{b}{2a}\right)$.
- The axis of symmetry is the vertical line passing through the vertex.
- The y-intercept is determined by the value of $f(x)$ when $x = 0$: the y-intercept is $(0, c)$.
- The x-intercepts (if any) are determined by the values of x that make $f(x) = 0$. To find them, solve the quadratic equation $ax^2 + bx + c = 0$.

EXAMPLE 9   Graph: $f(x) = -2x^2 - 8x - 8$

Strategy   We will follow the steps for graphing a quadratic function.

Why   This is the most efficient way to graph a general quadratic function.

Solution   ***Step 1:   Determine whether the parabola opens upward or downward.*** The function is in the form $f(x) = ax^2 + bx + c$, with $a = -2$, $b = -8$, and $c = -8$. Since $a < 0$, the parabola opens downward.

Step 2:   Find the vertex and draw the axis of symmetry. To find the coordinates of the vertex, we calculate

Success Tip

An easy way to remember the vertex formula is to note that $x = \frac{-b}{2a}$ is part of the quadratic formula:

$$x = \frac{-b \pm \sqrt{b^2 - 4ac}}{2a}$$

$$x = -\frac{b}{2a}$$

$$x = -\frac{-8}{2(-2)} \quad \text{Substitute } -2 \text{ for } a \text{ and } -8 \text{ for } b.$$

$$= -2 \quad \begin{array}{l}\text{This is the } x\text{-coordinate}\\\text{of the vertex.}\end{array}$$

$$f\left(-\frac{b}{2a}\right) = f(-2)$$

$$= -2(-2)^2 - 8(-2) - 8$$

$$= -8 + 16 - 8$$

$$= 0 \quad \begin{array}{l}\text{This is the } y\text{-coordinate}\\\text{of the vertex.}\end{array}$$

The vertex of the parabola is the point $(-2, 0)$. This point is in blue on the graph. The axis of symmetry is the line $x = -2$.

Step 3: ***Find the x- and y-intercepts.*** Since $c = -8$, the y-intercept of the parabola is $(0, -8)$. The point $(-4, -8)$, two units to the left of the axis of symmetry, must also be on the graph. We plot both points in black on the graph.

To find the x-intercepts, we set $f(x)$ equal to 0 and solve the resulting quadratic equation.

$$f(x) = -2x^2 - 8x - 8 \qquad \text{This is the function to graph.}$$
$$0 = -2x^2 - 8x - 8 \qquad \text{Set } f(x) = 0.$$
$$0 = x^2 + 4x + 4 \qquad \text{Divide both sides by } -2.$$
$$0 = (x + 2)(x + 2) \qquad \text{Factor the trinomial.}$$
$$x + 2 = 0 \quad \text{or} \quad x + 2 = 0 \qquad \text{Set each factor equal to 0.}$$
$$x = -2 \qquad \qquad x = -2$$

Since the solutions are the same, the graph has only one x-intercept: $(-2, 0)$. This point is the vertex of the parabola and has already been plotted.

Step 4: ***Plot another point.*** Finally, we find another point on the parabola. If $x = -3$, then $f(-3) = -2$. We plot $(-3, -2)$ and use symmetry to determine that $(-1, -2)$ is also on the graph. Both points are in green.

Step 5: ***Draw a smooth curve through the points.***

$$f(x) = -2x^2 - 8x - 8$$

x	$f(x)$
-3	-2	$\rightarrow (-3, -2)$

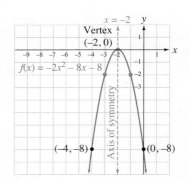

Self Check 9   Graph: $f(x) = -2x^2 + 12x - 16$

Now Try ▶ Problems 59 and 69

---

5 Determine Minimum and Maximum Values.

It is often useful to know the smallest or largest possible value a quantity can assume. For example, companies try to minimize their costs and maximize their profits. If the quantity is expressed by a quadratic function, the y-coordinate of the vertex of the graph of the function gives its minimum or maximum value.

EXAMPLE 10   **Minimizing Costs.**   A glassworks that makes lead crystal vases has daily production costs given by the function $C(x) = 0.2x^2 - 10x + 650$, where x is the number of vases made each day. How many vases should be produced to minimize the per-day costs? What will the costs be?

Strategy   We will find the vertex of the graph of the quadratic function.

Why   The x-coordinate of the vertex indicates the number of vases to make to keep costs at a minimum, and the y-coordinate indicates the minimum cost.

Solution The graph of $C(x) = 0.2x^2 - 10x + 650$ is a parabola opening upward. The vertex is the lowest point on the graph. To find the vertex, we calculate

The Language of Algebra

We say that 25 is the value for which the function $C(x) = 0.2x^2 - 10x + 650$ is a minimum.

$$-\frac{b}{2a} = -\frac{-10}{2(0.2)} \qquad b = -10 \text{ and } a = 0.2.$$

$$= -\frac{-10}{0.4}$$

$$= 25$$

$$f\left(-\frac{b}{2a}\right) = f(25)$$

$$= 0.2(25)^2 - 10(25) + 650$$

$$= 525$$

The vertex is $(25, 525)$, and it indicates that the costs are a minimum of $525 when 25 vases are made daily.

To solve this problem with a graphing calculator, we graph the function $C(x) = 0.2x^2 - 10x + 650$. By using TRACE and ZOOM, we can locate the vertex of the graph. The coordinates of the vertex indicate that the minimum cost is $525 when the number of vases produced is 25.

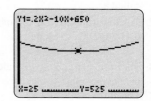

Self Check 10 **Minimizing Costs.** A manufacturing company has a daily production cost of $c(x) = 0.25x^2 - 10x + 800$, where x is the number of items produced and $c(x)$ is the cost. How many items should be produced to minimize the per-day cost? What is the minimum cost?

Now Try ▶ Problem 85

6 Solve Quadratic Equations Graphically.

When solving quadratic equations graphically, we must consider three possibilities. If the graph of the associated quadratic function has two x-intercepts, the quadratic equation has two real-number solutions. Figure (a) shows an example of this. If the graph has one x-intercept, as shown in figure (b), the equation has one repeated real-number solution. Finally, if the graph does not have an x-intercept, as shown in figure (c), the equation does not have any real-number solutions.

Success Tip

Note that the solutions of each quadratic equation are given by the x-coordinate of the x-intercept of each respective graph.

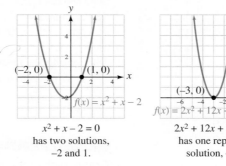

$x^2 + x - 2 = 0$
has two solutions,
-2 and 1.

(a)

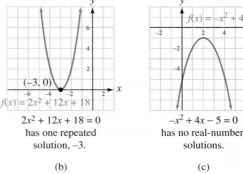

$2x^2 + 12x + 18 = 0$
has one repeated
solution, -3.

(b)

$-x^2 + 4x - 5 = 0$
has no real-number
solutions.

(c)

Using Your Calculator ▶ **Solving Quadratic Equations Graphically**

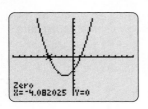

We can use a graphing calculator to find approximate solutions of quadratic equations. For example, the solutions of $0.7x^2 + 2x - 3.5 = 0$ are the numbers x that will make $y = 0$ in the quadratic function $f(x) = 0.7x^2 + 2x - 3.5$. To approximate these numbers, we graph the quadratic function and read the x-intercepts from the graph using the ZERO feature. (The ZERO feature can be found by pressing $\boxed{2^{\text{nd}}}$, CALC, and then 2.) In the figure, we see that the x-coordinate of the left-most x-intercept of the graph is given as -4.082025. This means that an approximate solution of the equation is -4.08. To find the positive x-intercept, we use similar steps.

SECTION 10.4 ▸ STUDY SET

VOCABULARY

Refer to the graph. Fill in the blanks.

1. $f(x) = 2x^2 - 4x + 1$ is called a _____ function. Its graph is a cup-shaped figure called a _____.

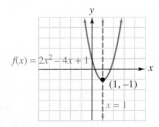
$f(x) = 2x^2 - 4x + 1$
$(1, -1)$
$x = 1$

2. The lowest point on the graph is $(1, -1)$. This is called the _____ of the parabola.

3. The vertical line $x = 1$ divides the parabola into two halves. This line is called the ____ ___ _____.

4. $f(x) = a(x - h)^2 + k$ is called the _____ form of the equation of a quadratic function.

CONCEPTS

5. Refer to the graph.

   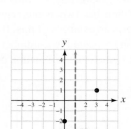

   a. What are the x-intercepts of the graph?

   b. What is the y-intercept of the graph?

   c. What is the vertex?

   d. What is the axis of symmetry?

   e. What are the domain and the range of the function?

6. The vertex of a parabola is at $(1, -3)$, its y-intercept is $(0, -2)$, and it passes through the point $(3, 1)$, as shown in the illustration. Use the axis of symmetry shown in blue to help determine two other points on the parabola.

   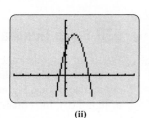
   Vertex

7. Draw the graph of a quadratic function using the given facts about its graph.

   ■ Opens upward   ■ y-intercept: $(0, -3)$
   ■ Vertex: $(-1, -4)$ ■ x-intercepts: $(-3, 0), (1, 0)$
   ■

x	$f(x)$
2	5

8. For $f(x) = -x^2 + 6x - 7$, the value of $-\frac{b}{2a}$ is 3. Find the y-coordinate of the vertex of the graph of this function.

9. Fill in the blanks.

   a. To complete the square on the right side of $f(x) = 2x^2 + 12x + 11$, what should be factored from the first two terms?

   $$f(x) = \boxed{}(x^2 + 6x) + 11$$

   b. To complete the square on $x^2 + 6x$ shown below, what should be added within the parentheses and what should be subtracted outside the parentheses?

   $$f(x) = 2(x^2 + 6x + \boxed{}) + 11 - \boxed{}$$

10. Fill in the blanks. To complete the square on $x^2 + 4x$ shown below, what should be added within the parentheses and what should be added outside the parentheses?

   $$f(x) = -5(x^2 + 4x + \boxed{}) + 7 + \boxed{}$$

11. Use the graph of
   $$f(x) = \tfrac{1}{10}x^2 - \tfrac{1}{5}x - \tfrac{3}{2},$$
   shown here, to estimate the solutions of the equation
   $$\tfrac{1}{10}x^2 - \tfrac{1}{5}x - \tfrac{3}{2} = 0.$$

   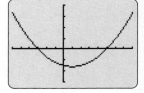

12. Three quadratic equations are to be solved graphically. The graphs of their associated quadratic functions are shown here. Determine which graph indicates that the equation has

   a. two real solutions.

   b. one repeated real solution.

   c. no real solutions.

   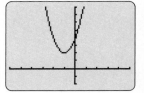
   (i)

   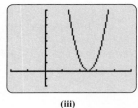
   (ii)   (iii)

NOTATION

13. The function $f(x) = 2(x + 1)^2 + 6$ is written in the form $f(x) = a(x - h)^2 + k$. Is $h = -1$ or is $h = 1$? Explain.

14. Consider the function $f(x) = 2x^2 + 4x - 8$.

   a. What are a, b, and c?

   b. Find $-\dfrac{b}{2a}$.

GUIDED PRACTICE

Graph each group of functions on the same coordinate system. See Example 1.

15. $f(x) = x^2$, $g(x) = 2x^2$, $s(x) = \dfrac{1}{2}x^2$

16. $f(x) = x^2$, $g(x) = 4x^2$, $s(x) = \dfrac{1}{4}x^2$

Graph each pair of functions on the same coordinate system. See Example 2.

17. $f(x) = 2x^2$, $g(x) = -2x^2$

18. $f(x) = \dfrac{1}{2}x^2$, $g(x) = -\dfrac{1}{2}x^2$

Graph each group of functions on the same coordinate system. See Example 3.

19. $f(x) = 4x^2$, $g(x) = 4x^2 + 3$, $s(x) = 4x^2 - 2$

20. $f(x) = \frac{1}{3}x^2$, $g(x) = \frac{1}{3}x^2 + 4$, $s(x) = \frac{1}{3}x^2 - 3$

Graph each group of functions on the same coordinate system and describe how the graphs are similar and how they are different. See Example 4.

21. $f(x) = 3x^2$, $g(x) = 3(x + 2)^2$, $s(x) = 3(x - 3)^2$

22. $f(x) = \frac{1}{2}x^2$, $g(x) = \frac{1}{2}(x + 3)^2$, $s(x) = \frac{1}{2}(x - 2)^2$

Find the vertex and the axis of symmetry of the graph of each function. Do not graph the function, but determine whether the graph will open upward or downward. See Example 5.

23. $f(x) = (x - 1)^2 + 2$

24. $f(x) = 2(x - 2)^2 - 1$

25. $f(x) = -2(x + 3)^2 - 4$

26. $f(x) = -3(x + 1)^2 + 3$

27. $f(x) = -0.5(x - 7.5)^2 + 8.5$

28. $f(x) = -\frac{3}{2}\left(x + \frac{1}{4}\right)^2 + \frac{7}{8}$

29. $f(x) = 2x^2 - 4$

30. $f(x) = 3x^2 - 3$

Determine the vertex and the axis of symmetry of the graph of each function. Then plot several points and complete the graph. See Example 5.

31. $f(x) = (x - 3)^2 + 2$

32. $f(x) = (x + 1)^2 - 2$

33. $f(x) = -(x - 2)^2$

34. $f(x) = -(x + 2)^2$

35. $f(x) = -2(x + 3)^2 + 4$

36. $f(x) = -2(x - 2)^2 - 4$

37. $f(x) = \frac{1}{2}(x + 1)^2 - 3$

38. $f(x) = \frac{1}{3}(x - 1)^2 + 2$

Determine the vertex and the axis of symmetry of the graph of each function. Will the graph open upward or downward? See Example 6.

39. $f(x) = x^2 + 4x + 5$

40. $f(x) = x^2 - 4x - 1$

41. $f(x) = -x^2 + 6x - 15$

42. $f(x) = -x^2 - 6x + 3$

Complete the square to write each function in $f(x) = a(x - h)^2 + k$ form. Determine the vertex and the axis of symmetry of the graph of the function. Then plot several points and complete the graph. See Examples 6 and 7.

43. $f(x) = x^2 + 2x - 3$

44. $f(x) = x^2 + 6x + 5$

45. $f(x) = 4x^2 + 24x + 37$

46. $f(x) = 3x^2 - 12x + 10$

47. $f(x) = x^2 + x - 6$

48. $f(x) = x^2 - x - 6$

49. $f(x) = -4x^2 + 16x - 10$

50. $f(x) = -2x^2 + 4x + 3$

51. $f(x) = 2x^2 + 8x + 6$

52. $f(x) = 3x^2 - 12x + 9$

53. $f(x) = -x^2 - 8x - 17$

54. $f(x) = -x^2 + 6x - 8$

Use the vertex formula to find the vertex of the graph of each function. See Example 8.

55. $f(x) = x^2 + 2x - 5$ **56.** $f(x) = -x^2 + 4x - 5$

57. $f(x) = 2x^2 - 3x + 4$ **58.** $f(x) = 2x^2 - 7x - 4$

Find the x- and y-intercepts of the graph of the quadratic function. See Example 9.

59. $f(x) = x^2 - 2x - 35$ **60.** $f(x) = -x^2 - 10x - 21$

61. $f(x) = -2x^2 + 4x$ **62.** $f(x) = 3x^2 + 6x - 9$

Determine the coordinates of the vertex of the graph of each function using the vertex formula. Then determine the x- and y-intercepts of the graph. Finally, plot several points and complete the graph. See Example 9.

63. $f(x) = x^2 + 4x + 4$

64. $f(x) = x^2 - 6x + 9$

65. $f(x) = -x^2 + 2x - 1$

66. $f(x) = -x^2 - 2x - 1$

67. $f(x) = x^2 - 2x$

68. $f(x) = x^2 + x$

69. $f(x) = 2x^2 - 8x + 6$

70. $f(x) = 3x^2 - 12x + 12$

71. $f(x) = -6x^2 - 12x - 8$

72. $f(x) = -2x^2 + 8x - 10$

73. $f(x) = 4x^2 - 12x + 9$

74. $f(x) = 4x^2 + 4x - 3$

Use a graphing calculator to find the coordinates of the vertex of the graph of each quadratic function. Round to the nearest hundredth. See Using Your Calculator: Finding the Vertex.

75. $f(x) = 2x^2 - x + 1$ **76.** $f(x) = x^2 + 5x - 6$

77. $f(x) = -x^2 + x + 7$ **78.** $f(x) = 2x^2 - 3x + 2$

 Use a graphing calculator to solve each equation. If an answer is not exact, round to the nearest hundredth. **See Using Your Calculator: Solving Quadratic Equations Graphically.**

79. $x^2 + x - 6 = 0$ **80.** $2x^2 - 5x - 3 = 0$

81. $0.5x^2 - 0.7x - 3 = 0$ **82.** $2x^2 - 0.5x - 2 = 0$

APPLICATIONS

83. Crossword Puzzles.   Darken the appropriate squares to the right of the dashed red line so that the puzzle has symmetry with respect to that line.

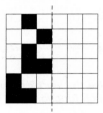

axis of symmetry

84. Graphic Arts.   Draw an axis of symmetry over the letter shown here.

85. Operating Costs.   The cost C in dollars of operating a certain concrete-cutting machine is related to the number of minutes n the machine is run by the function $C(n) = 2.2n^2 - 66n + 655$. For what number of minutes is the cost of running the machine a minimum? What is the minimum cost?

86. Water Usage.   The height (in feet) of the water level in a reservoir over a 1-year period is modeled by the function $H(t) = 3.3(t - 9)^2 + 14$ where $t = 1$ represents January, $t = 2$ represents February, and so on. How low did the water level get that year, and when did it reach the low mark?

87. Fireworks.   A fireworks shell is shot straight up with an initial velocity of 120 feet per second. Its height s in feet after t seconds is approximated by the equation $s = 120t - 16t^2$. If the shell is designed to explode when it reaches its maximum height, how long after being fired, and at what height, will the fireworks appear in the sky?

88. Projectiles.   A ball is thrown straight upward from the top of a building with an initial velocity of 32 feet per second. The equation $s = -16t^2 + 32t + 48$ gives the height s of the ball in feet t seconds after it is thrown. Find the maximum height reached by the ball and the time it takes for the ball to hit the ground.

89. ▶ *from* **Campus to Careers**
··
Police Patrol Officer

Suppose you are a police patrol officer and you have a 300-foot-long roll of yellow "DO NOT CROSS" barricade tape to seal off an automobile accident, as shown in the illustration. What dimensions should you use to seal off the maximum rectangular area around the collision? What is the maximum area?

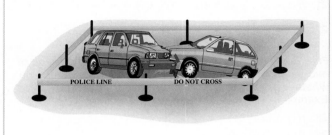

90. Ranching.   See the illustration. A farmer wants to fence in three sides of a rectangular field with 1,000 feet of fencing. The other side of the rectangle will be a river. If the enclosed area is to be maximum, find the dimensions of the field.

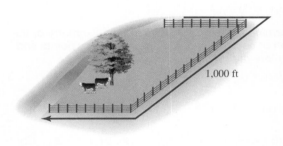

1,000 ft

91. Military History.   The function $N(x) = -0.0534x^2 + 0.337x + 0.97$ gives the number of active-duty military personnel in the United States Army (in millions) for the years 1965–1972, where $x = 0$ corresponds to 1965, $x = 1$ corresponds to 1966, and so on. For this period, when was the army's personnel strength level at its highest, and what was it? Historically, can you explain why?

92. School Enrollment.   After peaking in 1970, school enrollment in the United States fell during the 1970s and 1980s. The total annual enrollment (in millions) in U.S. elementary and secondary schools for the years 1975–1996 is given by the model $E(x) = 0.058x^2 - 1.162x + 50.604$ where $x = 0$ corresponds to 1975, $x = 1$ corresponds to 1976, and so on. For this period, when was enrollment the lowest? What was the enrollment?

93. Maximizing Revenue.   The revenue R received for selling x stereos is given by the formula $R = -\dfrac{x^2}{5} + 80x - 1,000$. How many stereos must be sold to obtain the maximum revenue? Find the maximum revenue.

94. Maximizing Revenue. When priced at $30 each, a toy has annual sales of 4,000 units. The manufacturer estimates that each $1 increase in price will decrease sales by 100 units. Find the unit price that will maximize total revenue. (*Hint:* Total revenue = price · the number of units sold.)

WRITING

95. Use the example of a stream of water from a drinking fountain to explain the concepts of the vertex and the axis of symmetry of a parabola. Draw a picture.

96. What are some quantities that are good to maximize? What are some quantities that are good to minimize?

97. A mirror is held against the *y*-axis of the graph of a quadratic function. What fact about parabolas does this illustrate?

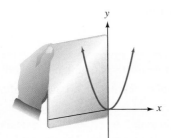

98. The vertex of a quadratic function $f(x) = ax^2 + bx + c$ is given by the formula $\left(-\frac{b}{2a}, f\left(-\frac{b}{2a}\right)\right)$. Explain what is meant by the notation $f\left(-\frac{b}{2a}\right)$.

99. A table of values for $f(x) = 2x^2 - 4x + 3$ is shown. Explain why it appears that the vertex of the graph of f is the point (1, 1).

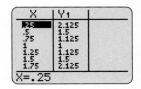

100. The illustration shows the graph of the quadratic function $f(x) = -4x^2 + 12x$ with domain [0, 3]. Explain how the value of $f(x)$ changes as the value of x increases from 0 to 3.

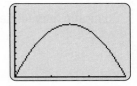

REVIEW

Simplify each expression. Assume all variables represent positive numbers.

101. $\dfrac{\sqrt{3}}{\sqrt{50}}$

102. $\dfrac{3}{\sqrt[3]{9}}$

103. $3\left(\sqrt{5b} - \sqrt{3}\right)^2$

104. $-2\sqrt{5b}\left(4\sqrt{2b} - 3\sqrt{3}\right)$

CHALLENGE PROBLEMS

105. Find a number between 0 and 1 such that the difference of the number and its square is a maximum.

106. Determine a quadratic function whose graph has *x*-intercepts of (2, 0) and (−4, 0).

SECTION 10.5

Quadratic and Other Nonlinear Inequalities

OBJECTIVES

1 Solve quadratic inequalities.

2 Solve rational inequalities.

3 Graph nonlinear inequalities in two variables.

ARE YOU READY?

The following problems review some basic skills that are needed when working with quadratic and nonlinear inequalities?

1. Does $x = -2$ satisfy $x^2 + x - 6 < 0$?

2. Solve: $x^2 - 5x - 50 = 0$

3. Graph the set of real numbers between −3 and 2 on a number line.

4. Graph the set of real numbers greater than 1 or less than or equal to −2 on a number line.

5. What values of *x* make the denominator of $\dfrac{x + 1}{x^2 - 9}$ equal to 0?

6. Graph: $y = -x^2 + 4$

We have previously solved *linear* inequalities in one variable such as $2x + 3 > 8$ and $6x - 7 < 4x - 9$. To find their solution sets, we used properties of inequalities to isolate the variable on one side of the inequality.

In this section, we will solve *quadratic* inequalities in one variable such as $x^2 + x - 6 < 0$ and $x^2 + 4x \geq 5$. We will use an interval testing method on the number line to determine their solution sets.

1 Solve Quadratic Inequalities.

Recall that a quadratic equation can be written in the form $ax^2 + bx + c = 0$. If we replace the $=$ symbol with an inequality symbol, we have a quadratic inequality.

Quadratic Inequalities	▼ A **quadratic inequality** can be written in one of the standard forms
	$$ax^2 + bx + c < 0 \qquad ax^2 + bx + c > 0 \qquad ax^2 + bx + c \leq 0 \qquad ax^2 + bx + c \geq 0$$
	where a, b, and c are real numbers and $a \neq 0$.

To solve a quadratic inequality in one variable, we will use the following steps to find the values of the variable that make the inequality true.

Solving Quadratic Inequalities	▼ 1. Write the inequality in standard form and solve its related quadratic equation.
	2. Locate the solutions (called **critical numbers**) of the related quadratic equation on a number line.
	3. Test each interval on the number line created in step 2 by choosing a test value from the interval and determining whether it satisfies the inequality. The solution set includes the interval(s) whose test value makes the inequality true.
	4. Determine whether the endpoints of the intervals are included in the solution set.

EXAMPLE 1   Solve: $x^2 + x - 6 < 0$

Strategy   We will solve the related quadratic equation $x^2 + x - 6 = 0$ by factoring to determine the critical numbers. These critical numbers will separate the number line into intervals.

Why   We can test each interval to see whether numbers in the interval are in the solution set of the inequality.

Solution   The expression $x^2 + x - 6$ can be positive, negative, or 0, depending on what value is substituted for x. Solutions of the inequality are x-values that make $x^2 + x - 6$ less than 0. To find them, we will follow the steps for solving quadratic inequalities.

Step 1:   Solve the related quadratic equation. For the quadratic inequality $x^2 + x - 6 < 0$, the related quadratic *equation* is $x^2 + x - 6 = 0$.

$$x^2 + x - 6 = 0$$
$$(x + 3)(x - 2) = 0 \qquad \text{Factor the trinomial.}$$
$$x + 3 = 0 \qquad \text{or} \qquad x - 2 = 0 \qquad \text{Set each factor equal to 0.}$$
$$x = -3 \qquad \qquad \qquad x = 2 \qquad \text{Solve each equation.}$$

The solutions of $x^2 + x - 6 = 0$ are -3 and 2. These solutions are the critical numbers.

Step 2:   Locate the critical numbers on a number line. When we highlight -3 and 2 on a number line, they separate the number line into three intervals:

The Language of Algebra

We say that the critical numbers **partition** the real-number line into test intervals. Interior decorators use freestanding screens to *partition* off parts of a room.

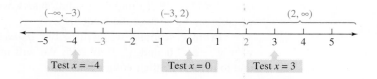

Step 3:   Test each interval. To determine whether the numbers in $(-\infty, -3)$ are solutions of the inequality, we choose a number from that interval, substitute it for x, and see whether it satisfies $x^2 + x - 6 < 0$. *If one number in that interval satisfies the inequality, all numbers in that interval will satisfy the inequality.*

If we choose -4 from $(-\infty, -3)$, we have:

$$x^2 + x - 6 < 0 \qquad \text{This is the original inequality.}$$
$$(-4)^2 + (-4) - 6 \overset{?}{<} 0 \qquad \text{Substitute } -4 \text{ for } x.$$
$$16 + (-4) - 6 \overset{?}{<} 0$$
$$6 < 0 \qquad \text{False}$$

Since -4 does not satisfy the inequality, none of the numbers in $(-\infty, -3)$ are solutions. To test the second interval, $(-3, 2)$, we choose $x = 0$.

$$x^2 + x - 6 < 0 \qquad \text{This is the original inequality.}$$
$$0^2 + 0 - 6 \overset{?}{<} 0 \qquad \text{Substitute 0 for } x.$$
$$-6 < 0 \qquad \text{True}$$

Since 0 satisfies the inequality, all of the numbers in $(-3, 2)$ are solutions. To test the third interval, $(2, \infty)$, we choose $x = 3$.

$$x^2 + x - 6 < 0 \qquad \text{This is the original inequality.}$$
$$3^2 + 3 - 6 \overset{?}{<} 0 \qquad \text{Substitute 3 for } x.$$
$$9 + 3 - 6 \overset{?}{<} 0$$
$$6 < 0 \qquad \text{False}$$

Since 3 does not satisfy the inequality, none of the numbers in $(2, \infty)$ are solutions.

Success Tip

If a quadratic inequality contains $\leq$ or $\geq$, the endpoints of the intervals are included in the solution set. If the inequality contains $<$ or $>$, they are not.

Step 4:   Are the endpoints included? From the interval testing, we see that only numbers from $(-3, 2)$ satisfy $x^2 + x - 6 < 0$. The endpoints -3 and 2 are not included in the solution set because they do not satisfy the inequality. (Recall that -3 and 2 make $x^2 + x - 6$ equal to 0.) The solution set is the interval $(-3, 2)$ as graphed on the right.

Self Check 1   Solve: $x^2 + x - 12 < 0$

Now Try ▶ Problem 15

EXAMPLE 2   Solve: $x^2 + 4x \geq 5$

Strategy   This inequality is not in standard form because it does not have 0 on the right side. We will write it in standard form and solve its related quadratic equation to find any critical numbers. These critical numbers will separate the number line into intervals.

Why   We can then test each interval to see whether numbers in the interval are in the solution set of the inequality.

Solution   To get 0 on the right side, we subtract 5 from both sides.

$$x^2 + 4x \geq 5 \qquad \text{This is the inequality to solve.}$$
$$x^2 + 4x - 5 \geq 0 \qquad \text{Write the inequality in the equivalent form } ax^2 + bx + c \geq 0.$$

We can solve the related quadratic *equation* $x^2 + 4x - 5 = 0$ by factoring.

$$x^2 + 4x - 5 = 0$$
$$(x + 5)(x - 1) = 0 \qquad\qquad\qquad \text{Factor the trinomial.}$$
$$x + 5 = 0 \quad \text{or} \quad x - 1 = 0 \qquad \text{Set each factor equal to 0.}$$
$$x = -5 \quad | \quad\quad\quad x = 1$$

The critical numbers -5 and 1 separate the number line into three intervals. We pick a test value from each interval to see whether it satisfies $x^2 + 4x - 5 \geq 0$.

Success Tip

When choosing a test value from an interval, pick a convenient number that makes the calculations easy. When applicable, 0 is an obvious choice.

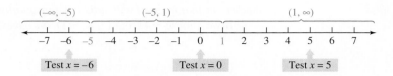

$$x^2 + 4x - 5 \geq 0 \qquad\qquad x^2 + 4x - 5 \geq 0 \qquad\qquad x^2 + 4x - 5 \geq 0$$
$$(-6)^2 + 4(-6) - 5 \overset{?}{\geq} 0 \qquad 0^2 + 4(0) - 5 \overset{?}{\geq} 0 \qquad 5^2 + 4(5) - 5 \overset{?}{\geq} 0$$
$$7 \geq 0 \quad \text{True} \qquad\qquad -5 \geq 0 \quad \text{False} \qquad\qquad 40 \geq 0 \quad \text{True}$$

The numbers in the intervals $(-\infty, -5)$ and $(1, \infty)$ satisfy the inequality. Since the endpoints -5 and 1 also satisfy $x^2 + 4x - 5 \geq 0$, they are included in the solution set. (Recall that -5 and 1 make $x^2 + 4x - 5$ equal to 0.) Thus, the solution set is the union of two intervals: $(-\infty, -5] \cup [1, \infty)$. The graph of the solution set is shown on the right.

Self Check 2   Solve: $\quad x^2 + 3x \geq 40$

Now Try ▶ Problem 19

2   Solve Rational Inequalities.

Rational inequalities in one variable such as $\dfrac{9}{x} < 8$ and $\dfrac{x^2 + x - 2}{x - 4} \geq 0$ can also be solved using the interval testing method.

Solving Rational Inequalities

1. Write the inequality in standard form with a single quotient on the left side and 0 on the right side. Then solve its related rational equation.

2. Set the denominator equal to zero and solve that equation.

3. Locate the solutions (called **critical numbers**) found in steps 1 and 2 on a number line.

4. Test each interval on the number line created in step 3 by choosing a test value from the interval and determining whether it satisfies the inequality. The solution set includes the interval(s) whose test value makes the inequality true.

5. Determine whether the endpoints of the intervals are included in the solution set. Exclude any values that make the denominator 0.

EXAMPLE 3   Solve: $\quad \dfrac{9}{x} < 8$

Strategy   This rational inequality is not in standard form because it does not have 0 on the right side. We will write it in standard form and solve its related rational equation to find any critical numbers. These critical numbers will separate the number line into intervals.

Why   We can test each interval to see whether numbers in the interval are in the solution set of the inequality.

Solution   To get 0 on the right side, we subtract 8 from both sides. We then find a common denominator to write the left side as a single quotient.

$$\frac{9}{x} < 8 \qquad \text{This is the inequality to solve.}$$

$$\frac{9}{x} - 8 < 0 \qquad \text{Subtract 8 from both sides.}$$

$$\frac{9}{x} - 8 \cdot \frac{x}{x} < 0 \qquad \begin{array}{l}\text{To write the left side as a single quotient,}\\ \text{build 8 to a fraction with denominator } x.\end{array}$$

$$\frac{9}{x} - \frac{8x}{x} < 0$$

$$\frac{9 - 8x}{x} < 0 \qquad \text{Subtract the numerators and keep the common denominator, } x.$$

Now we solve the related rational equation.

$$\frac{9 - 8x}{x} = 0$$

$$9 - 8x = 0 \qquad \text{If } x \neq 0, \text{ we can clear the equation of the fraction by multiplying both sides by } x.$$

$$-8x = -9 \qquad \text{To isolate the variable term } -8x, \text{ subtract 9 from both sides.}$$

$$x = \frac{9}{8} \qquad \text{Solve for } x. \text{ This is a critical number.}$$

If we set the denominator of $\frac{9 - 8x}{x}$ equal to 0, we obtain a second critical number, $x = 0$. When graphed, the critical numbers 0 and $\frac{9}{8}$ separate the number line into three intervals. We pick a test value from each interval to see whether it satisfies $\frac{9 - 8x}{x} < 0$.

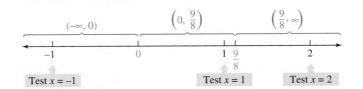

$$\frac{9 - 8x}{x} < 0 \qquad\qquad \frac{9 - 8x}{x} < 0 \qquad\qquad \frac{9 - 8x}{x} < 0$$

$$\frac{9 - 8(-1)}{-1} \overset{?}{<} 0 \qquad\quad \frac{9 - 8(1)}{1} \overset{?}{<} 0 \qquad\quad \frac{9 - 8(2)}{2} \overset{?}{<} 0$$

$$-17 < 0 \quad \text{True} \qquad\qquad 1 < 0 \quad \text{False} \qquad\qquad -\frac{7}{2} < 0 \quad \text{True}$$

The numbers in the intervals $(-\infty, 0)$ and $\left(\frac{9}{8}, \infty\right)$ satisfy the inequality. We do not include the endpoint 0 in the solution set, because it makes the denominator of the original inequality 0. Neither do we include $\frac{9}{8}$, because it does not satisfy $\frac{9 - 8x}{x} < 0$. (Recall that $\frac{9}{8}$ makes $\frac{9 - 8x}{x}$ equal to 0.) Thus, the solution set is the union of two intervals: $(-\infty, 0) \cup \left(\frac{9}{8}, \infty\right)$. Its graph is shown on the right.

Self Check 3   Solve: $\frac{3}{x} < 5$

Now Try ▶ Problem 23

EXAMPLE 4   Solve: $\dfrac{x^2 + x - 2}{x - 4} \geq 0$

Strategy   This inequality is in standard form. We will solve its related rational equation to find any critical numbers. These critical numbers will separate the number line into intervals.

Why   We can test each interval to see whether numbers in the interval are in the solution set of the inequality.

Solution   To solve the related rational equation, we proceed as follows:

$$\frac{x^2 + x - 2}{x - 4} = 0$$

$$x^2 + x - 2 = 0 \qquad \text{If } x \neq 4, \text{ we can clear the equation of the fraction by multiplying both sides by } x - 4.$$

$$(x + 2)(x - 1) = 0 \qquad \text{Factor the trinomial.}$$

$$x + 2 = 0 \quad \text{or} \quad x - 1 = 0 \qquad \text{Set each factor equal to 0.}$$

$$x = -2 \quad \bigg| \qquad x = 1 \qquad \text{These are critical numbers.}$$

> **Caution**
>
> We cannot multiply both sides of the inequality by $x - 4$ to clear it of fractions. We don't know if $x - 4$ is positive or negative, so we don't know whether or not to reverse the inequality symbol.

If we set the denominator of $\dfrac{x^2 + x - 2}{x - 4}$ equal to 0, we see that $x = 4$ is also a critical number. When graphed, the critical numbers, -2, 1, and 4, separate the number line into four intervals. We pick a test value from each interval to see whether it satisfies $\dfrac{x^2 + x - 2}{x - 4} \geq 0$.

$$(-\infty, -2) \qquad (-2, 1) \qquad (1, 4) \qquad (4, \infty)$$

$$\overset{-4 \quad -3 \quad -2 \quad -1 \quad 0 \quad 1 \quad 2 \quad 3 \quad 4 \quad 5 \quad 6 \quad 7 \quad 8}{\longleftrightarrow}$$

$$\text{Test } x = -3 \qquad \text{Test } x = 0 \qquad \text{Test } x = 3 \qquad \text{Test } x = 6$$

$$\frac{(-3)^2 + (-3) - 2}{-3 - 4} \overset{?}{\geq} 0 \qquad \frac{0^2 + 0 - 2}{0 - 4} \overset{?}{\geq} 0 \qquad \frac{3^2 + 3 - 2}{3 - 4} \overset{?}{\geq} 0 \qquad \frac{6^2 + 6 - 2}{6 - 4} \overset{?}{\geq} 0$$

$$-\frac{4}{7} \geq 0 \qquad\qquad \frac{1}{2} \geq 0 \qquad\qquad -10 \geq 0 \qquad\qquad 20 \geq 0$$

$$\text{False} \qquad\qquad \text{True} \qquad\qquad \text{False} \qquad\qquad \text{True}$$

The numbers in the intervals $(-2, 1)$ and $(4, \infty)$ satisfy the inequality. We include the endpoints -2 and 1 in the solution set because they satisfy the inequality. We do not include 4 because it makes the denominator of the fraction 0. Thus, the solution set is the union of two intervals $[-2, 1] \cup (4, \infty)$, as graphed on the right.

Self Check 4   Solve: $\dfrac{x + 2}{x^2 - 2x - 3} \geq 0$

Now Try ▶ Problem 27

EXAMPLE 5   Solve: $\dfrac{3}{x - 1} < \dfrac{2}{x}$

Strategy   We will subtract $\frac{2}{x}$ from both sides to get 0 on the right side and solve the resulting related rational equation to find any critical numbers. These critical numbers will separate the number line into intervals.

Why   We can test each interval to see whether numbers in the interval are in the solution set of the inequality.

Solution

$$\frac{3}{x-1} < \frac{2}{x}$$ *This is the inequality to solve.*

$$\frac{3}{x-1} - \frac{2}{x} < 0$$ *Subtract $\frac{2}{x}$ from both sides.*

$$\frac{3}{x-1} \cdot \frac{x}{x} - \frac{2}{x} \cdot \frac{x-1}{x-1} < 0$$ *To get a single quotient on the left side, build each rational expression to have the common denominator $x(x-1)$.*

$$\frac{3x - 2x + 2}{x(x-1)} < 0$$ *Subtract the numerators and keep the common denominator.*

$$\frac{x+2}{x(x-1)} < 0$$ *Combine like terms.*

The only solution of the related rational equation $\frac{x+2}{x(x-1)} = 0$ is -2. Thus, -2 is a critical number. When we set the denominator equal to 0 and solve $x(x-1) = 0$, we find two more critical numbers, 0 and 1. These three critical numbers create four intervals to test.

Success Tip

When the endpoints of an interval are consecutive integers, such as with the third interval (0, 1), we cannot choose an integer as a test value. For these cases, choose a fraction or decimal that lies within the interval.

$(-\infty, -2)$ $(-2, 0)$ $(0, 1)$ $(1, \infty)$

Test $x = -3$ Test $x = -1$ Test $x = 0.5$ Test $x = 3$

$$\frac{-3+2}{-3(-3-1)} \overset{?}{<} 0 \qquad \frac{-1+2}{-1(-1-1)} \overset{?}{<} 0 \qquad \frac{0.5+2}{0.5(0.5-1)} \overset{?}{<} 0 \qquad \frac{3+2}{3(3-1)} \overset{?}{<} 0$$

$$\frac{-1}{-3(-4)} \overset{?}{<} 0 \qquad\qquad \frac{1}{-1(-2)} \overset{?}{<} 0 \qquad\qquad \frac{2.5}{0.5(-0.5)} \overset{?}{<} 0 \qquad\qquad \frac{5}{3(2)} \overset{?}{<} 0$$

$$-\frac{1}{12} < 0 \qquad\qquad \frac{1}{2} < 0 \qquad\qquad -10 < 0 \qquad\qquad \frac{5}{6} < 0$$

    True   False   True   False

The numbers 0 and 1 are not included in the solution set because they make the denominator 0, and the number -2 is not included because it does not satisfy the inequality. The solution set is the union of two intervals $(-\infty, -2) \cup (0, 1)$, as graphed on the right.

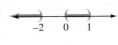

Self Check 5   Solve: $\frac{2}{x+1} > \frac{1}{x}$

Now Try ▶   Problem 31

Using Your Calculator ▶   **Solving Inequalities Graphically**

We can solve $x^2 + 4x \geq 5$ (Example 2) graphically by writing the inequality as $x^2 + 4x - 5 \geq 0$ and graphing the quadratic function $f(x) = x^2 + 4x - 5$, as shown in figure (a) on the next page. The solution set of the inequality will be those values of x for which the graph lies on or above the x-axis. We can trace to determine that this is the union of two intervals: $(-\infty, -5] \cup [1, \infty)$.

To solve $\frac{3}{x-1} < \frac{2}{x}$ (Example 5) graphically, we first write the inequality in the form $\frac{x+2}{x(x-1)} < 0$ and then graph the rational function $f(x) = \frac{x+2}{x(x-1)}$, as shown in figure (b) on the next page. The solution of the inequality will be those values of x for which the graph lies below the axis.

We can trace to see that the graph is below the x-axis when x is less than -2. Since we cannot see the graph in the interval $0 < x < 1$, we redraw the graph using window settings of $[-1, 2]$ for x and $[-25, 10]$ for y, as shown in figure (c).

Now we see that the graph is below the x-axis in the interval $(0, 1)$. Thus, the solution set of the inequality is the union of the two intervals: $(-\infty, -2) \cup (0, 1)$.

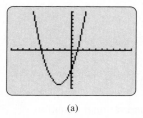   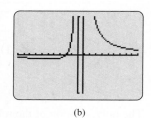   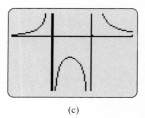

       (a)   (b)   (c)

3 Graph Nonlinear Inequalities in Two Variables.

We have previously graphed linear inequalities in two variables such as $y > 3x + 2$ and $2x - 3y \le 6$ using the following steps.

Graphing Inequalities in Two Variables	
▼	1. Graph the related equation to find the boundary line of the region. If the inequality allows equality (the symbol is either $\le$ or $\ge$), draw the boundary as a solid line. If equality is not allowed ($<$ or $>$), draw the boundary as a dashed line.
	2. Pick a test point that is on one side of the boundary line. (Use the origin if possible.) Replace x and y in the original inequality with the coordinates of that point. If the inequality is satisfied, shade the side that contains that point. If the inequality is not satisfied, shade the other side of the boundary.

We use the same procedure to graph **nonlinear inequalities** in two variables.

EXAMPLE 6   Graph: $y < -x^2 + 4$

Strategy   We will graph the related equation $y = -x^2 + 4$ to establish a boundary parabola. Then we will determine which side of the boundary parabola represents the solution set of the inequality.

Why   To *graph a nonlinear inequality* in two variables means to draw a "picture" of the ordered pairs (x, y) that make the inequality true.

Solution   The graph of the boundary $y = -x^2 + 4$ is a parabola opening downward, with vertex at $(0, 4)$ and axis of symmetry $x = 0$ (the y-axis). Since the inequality contains an $<$ symbol and equality is not allowed, we draw the parabola using a dashed curve.

To determine which region to shade, we pick the test point $(0, 0)$ and substitute its coordinates into the inequality. We shade the region containing $(0, 0)$ because its coordinates satisfy $y < -x^2 + 4$.

Graph the boundary

$$y = -x^2 + 4$$

Compare to $y = a(x - h)^2 + k$

$a = -1$: Opens downward

$h = 0$ and $k = 4$: Vertex $(0, 4)$

Axis of symmetry $x = 0$

x	y
1	3
2	0

Shading: Use the test point (0, 0)

$$y < -x^2 + 4$$
$$0 \overset{?}{<} -0^2 + 4$$
$$0 < 4 \qquad \text{True}$$

Since $0 < 4$ is true, $(0, 0)$ is a solution of $y < -x^2 + 4$.

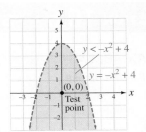

Self Check 6   Graph: $y \geq -x^2 + 4$

Now Try ▶ Problem 35

EXAMPLE 7   Graph: $x \leq |y|$

Strategy   We will graph the related equation $x = |y|$ to establish a boundary. Then we will determine which side of the boundary represents the solution set of the inequality.

Why   To *graph a nonlinear inequality* in two variables means to draw a "picture" of the ordered pairs (x, y) that make the inequality true.

Solution   To graph the boundary, $x = |y|$, we construct a table of solutions, as shown in figure (a). In figure (b), the boundary is a solid line because the inequality contains a $\leq$ symbol and equality is permitted. Since the origin is on the graph, we cannot use it as a test point. However, any other point, such as $(1, 0)$, will do. We substitute 1 for x and 0 for y into the inequality to get

$$x \leq |y| \qquad \text{This is the inequality to graph.}$$
$$1 \overset{?}{\leq} |0| \qquad \text{Substitute.}$$
$$1 \leq 0 \qquad \text{False}$$

Since $1 \leq 0$ is a false statement, the point $(1, 0)$ does not satisfy the inequality and is not part of the graph. Thus, the graph of $x \leq |y|$ is to the left of the boundary.

The complete graph is shown in figure (c).

$$x = |y|$$

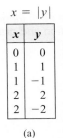

x	y
0	0
1	1
1	-1
2	2
2	-2

(a)

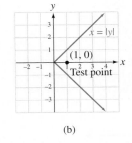

(b)

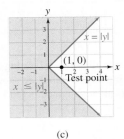

(c)

Self Check 7   Graph: $x \geq -|y|$

Now Try ▶ Problem 39

SECTION 10.5 ▸ STUDY SET

VOCABULARY

Fill in the blanks.

1. $x^2 + 3x - 18 < 0$ is an example of a _____ inequality in one variable.

2. $\frac{x-1}{x^2-x-20} \leq 0$ is an example of a _____ inequality in one variable.

3. $y \leq x^2 - 4x + 3$ is an example of a nonlinear inequality in _____ variables.

4. The set of real numbers greater than 3 can be represented using the _____ notation $(3, \infty)$.

CONCEPTS

5. The critical numbers of a quadratic inequality are highlighted in red on the number line shown below. Use interval notation to represent each interval that must be tested to solve the inequality.

6. Graph each of the following solution sets.

   a. $(-2, 4)$ **b.** $(-\infty, -2) \cup (3,5]$

7. The graph of the solution set of a rational inequality in one variable is shown. Determine whether each of the following numbers is a solution of the inequality.

   a. -10 **b.** -5
   c. 0 **d.** 4

8. What are the critical numbers for each inequality?

   a. $x^2 - 2x - 48 \geq 0$ **b.** $\frac{x-3}{x(x+4)} > 0$

9. **a.** The results after interval testing for a quadratic inequality containing a $>$ symbol are shown below. (The critical numbers are highlighted in red.) What is the solution set?

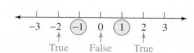

   b. The results after interval testing for a quadratic inequality containing a $\leq$ symbol are shown below. (The critical numbers are highlighted in red.) What is the solution set?

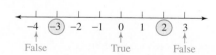

10. Fill in the blank to complete this important fact about the interval testing method discussed in this section: *If one number in an interval satisfies the inequality, _____ numbers in that interval will satisfy the inequality.*

11. **a.** When graphing the solution of $y \leq x^2 + 2x + 1$, should the boundary be solid or dashed?

    b. Does the test point $(0, 0)$ satisfy the inequality?

12. **a.** Estimate the solution of $x^2 - x - 6 > 0$ using the graph of $y = x^2 - x - 6$ shown in figure (a) below.

    b. Estimate the solution of $\frac{x-3}{x} \leq 0$ using the graph of $y = \frac{x-3}{x}$ shown in figure (b) below.

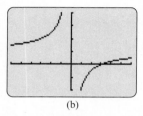
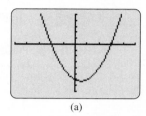

(a)   (b)

NOTATION

13. Write the quadratic inequality $x^2 - 6x \geq 7$ in standard form.

14. The solution set of a rational inequality consists of the intervals $(-1, 4]$ and $(7, \infty)$. When writing the solution set, what symbol is used between the two intervals?

GUIDED PRACTICE

Solve each inequality. Write the solution set in interval notation and graph it. See Example 1.

15. $x^2 - 5x + 4 < 0$ 16. $x^2 + 2x - 8 < 0$

17. $x^2 - 8x + 15 > 0$ 18. $x^2 - 3x - 4 > 0$

Solve each inequality. Write the solution set in interval notation and graph it. See Example 2.

19. $x^2 - x \geq 42$ 20. $x^2 - x \geq 72$

21. $x^2 + x \leq 12$ 22. $x^2 - 8x \leq -15$

Solve each inequality. Write the solution set in interval notation and graph it. See Example 3.

23. $\frac{1}{x} < 2$ 24. $\frac{1}{x} < 3$

25. $\frac{5}{x} \geq -3$ 26. $\frac{4}{x} \geq 8$

Solve each inequality. Write the solution set in interval notation and graph it. See Example 4.

27. $\frac{x^2-x-12}{x-1} < 0$ 28. $\frac{x^2+x-6}{x-4} \geq 0$

29. $\frac{6x^2-5x+1}{2x+1} \geq 0$ 30. $\frac{6x^2+11x+3}{3x-1} < 0$

Solve each inequality. Write the solution set in interval notation and graph it. See Example 5.

31. $\dfrac{3}{x-2} < \dfrac{4}{x}$

32. $\dfrac{-6}{x+1} \geq \dfrac{1}{x}$

33. $\dfrac{7}{x-3} \geq \dfrac{2}{x+4}$

34. $\dfrac{-5}{x-4} < \dfrac{3}{x+1}$

Graph each inequality. See Example 6.

35. $y < x^2 + 1$

36. $y > x^2 - 3$

37. $y \leq x^2 + 5x + 6$

38. $y \geq x^2 + 5x + 4$

Graph each inequality. See Example 7.

39. $y < |x + 4|$

40. $y \leq |x - 3|$

41. $y \geq -|x| + 2$

42. $y > |x| - 2$

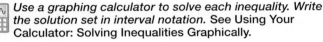 *Use a graphing calculator to solve each inequality. Write the solution set in interval notation. See Using Your Calculator: Solving Inequalities Graphically.*

43. $x^2 - 2x - 3 < 0$

44. $x^2 + x - 6 > 0$

45. $\dfrac{x+3}{x-2} > 0$

46. $\dfrac{3}{x} < 2$

TRY IT YOURSELF

Solve each inequality. Write the solution set in interval notation and graph it.

47. $\dfrac{x}{x+4} \leq \dfrac{1}{x+1}$

48. $\dfrac{x}{x+9} \geq \dfrac{1}{x+1}$

49. $x^2 \geq 9$

50. $x^2 \geq 16$

51. $x^2 + 6x \geq -9$

52. $x^2 + 8x < -16$

53. $\dfrac{x^2 + x - 2}{x - 3} > 0$

54. $\dfrac{x - 2}{x^2 - 1} > 0$

55. $2x^2 - 50 < 0$

56. $3x^2 - 243 < 0$

57. $\dfrac{2x - 3}{3x + 1} < 0$

58. $\dfrac{x - 5}{x + 1} < 0$

59. $x^2 - 6x + 9 < 0$

60. $x^2 + 4x + 4 > 0$

61. $\dfrac{5}{x + 1} > \dfrac{3}{x - 4}$

62. $\dfrac{3}{x - 2} \leq -\dfrac{2}{x + 3}$

APPLICATIONS

63. Bridges. If an x-axis is superimposed over the roadway of the Golden Gate Bridge, with the origin at the center of the bridge, the length L in feet of a vertical support cable can be approximated by the formula

$$L = \dfrac{1}{9{,}000}x^2 + 5$$

For the Golden Gate Bridge, $-2{,}100 < x < 2{,}100$. For what intervals along the x-axis are the vertical cables more than 95 feet long?

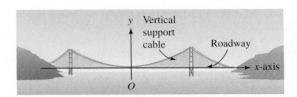

64. Malls. The number of people n in a mall is modeled by the formula

$$n = -100x^2 + 1{,}200x$$

where x is the number of hours since the mall opened. If the mall opened at 9 A.M., when were there 2,000 or more people in it?

WRITING

65. How are critical numbers used when solving a quadratic inequality in one variable?

66. Explain how to graph $y \geq x^2$.

67. The graph of $f(x) = x^2 - 3x + 4$ is shown here. Explain why the quadratic inequality $x^2 - 3x + 4 < 0$ has no solution.

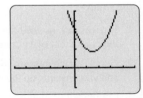

68. Describe the following solution set of a rational inequality in words: $(-\infty, 4] \cup (6, 7)$.

REVIEW

Translate each statement into an equation.

69. x varies directly as y.

70. y varies inversely as t.

71. t varies jointly as x and y.

72. d varies directly as t and inversely as u^2.

CHALLENGE PROBLEMS

73. a. Solve: $x^2 - x - 12 > 0$

b. Find a rational inequality in one variable that has the same solution set as the quadratic inequality in part (a).

74. a. Solve: $\dfrac{1}{x} < 1$

b. Now incorrectly "solve" $\dfrac{1}{x} < 1$ by multiplying both sides by x to clear it of the fraction. What part of the solution set is not obtained with this incorrect approach?

10 Summary & Review

SECTION 10.1 ▶ The Square Root Property and Completing the Square

DEFINITIONS AND CONCEPTS	EXAMPLES
We can use the **square root property** to solve equations of the form $x^2 = c$, where $c > 0$. The two solutions are $\qquad x = \sqrt{c} \qquad$ or $\qquad x = -\sqrt{c}$ We can write $x = \sqrt{c}$ or $x = -\sqrt{c}$ in more compact form using **double-sign notation**: $\qquad x = \pm\sqrt{c}$	Solve: $x^2 = 24$ $\qquad x = \sqrt{24} \qquad$ or $\qquad x = -\sqrt{24}$ Use the square root property. $\qquad x = \pm\sqrt{24}$ Use double-sign notation. $\qquad x = \pm 2\sqrt{6}$ Simplify $\sqrt{24}$. The solutions are $2\sqrt{6}$ and $-2\sqrt{6}$. Verify this using a check. Solve: $(x-3)^2 = -81$ $\qquad x - 3 = \pm\sqrt{-81}$ Use the square root property and double-sign notation. $\qquad x = 3 \pm \sqrt{-81}$ To isolate x, add 3 to both sides. $\qquad x = 3 \pm 9i$ Simplify the radical expression. The solutions are $3 + 9i$ and $3 - 9i$. Verify this using a check.
To **complete the square** on $x^2 + bx$, add the square of one-half of the coefficient of x. $\qquad x^2 + bx + \left(\dfrac{1}{2}b\right)^2$	Complete the square on $x^2 + 8x$ and factor the resulting perfect-square trinomial. $\qquad x^2 + 8x + 16$ The coefficient of x is 8. To complete the square: $\frac{1}{2} \cdot 8 = 4$ and $4^2 = 16$. Add 16 to the binomial. Now we factor: $x^2 + 8x + 16 = (x + 4)^2$
To **solve a quadratic equation in x by completing the square:** 1. If necessary, divide both sides of the equation by the coefficient of x^2 to make its coefficient 1. 2. Get all variable terms on one side of the equation and all constants on the other side. 3. Complete the square. 4. Factor the perfect-square trinomial. 5. Solve the resulting equation by using the square root property. 6. Check your answers in the original equation.	Solve: $3x^2 - 12x + 6 = 0$ $\qquad \dfrac{3x^2}{3} - \dfrac{12x}{3} + \dfrac{6}{3} = \dfrac{0}{3}$ To make the leading coefficient 1, divide both sides by 3, term-by-term. $\qquad x^2 - 4x + 2 = 0$ Do the division. $\qquad x^2 - 4x \quad = -2$ Subtract 2 from both sides so that the constant term, -2, is on the right side. $\qquad x^2 - 4x + 4 = -2 + 4$ The coefficient of x is -4. To complete the square: $\frac{1}{2}(-4) = -2$ and $(-2)^2 = 4$. Add 4 to both sides. $\qquad (x-2)^2 = 2$ Factor the perfect-square trinomial on the left side. Add on the right side. $\qquad x - 2 = \pm\sqrt{2}$ Use the square root property. $\qquad x = 2 \pm \sqrt{2}$ To isolate x, add 2 to both sides. The solutions are $2 + \sqrt{2}$ and $2 - \sqrt{2}$. Verify this using a check.

REVIEW EXERCISES

Solve each equation by factoring.

1. $x^2 + 9x + 20 = 0$ **2.** $6x^2 + 17x + 5 = 0$

Solve each equation using the square root property. Approximate the solutions to the nearest hundredth when appropriate.

3. $x^2 = 28$ **4.** $(t + 2)^2 = 36$

5. $a^2 + 25 = 0$ **6.** $5x^2 - 49 = 0$

7. Solve $A = \pi r^2$ for r. Assume all variables represent positive numbers. Express the result in simplified radical form.

8. Complete the square on $x^2 - x$ and then factor the resulting perfect-square trinomial.

Solve each equation by completing the square. Approximate the solutions to the nearest hundredth when appropriate.

9. $x^2 + 6x + 8 = 0$ **10.** $2x^2 - 6x + 3 = 0$

11. $6a^2 - 12a = -1$ **12.** $x^2 - 2x = -13$

13. Let $f(x) = x^2$. Find all values of x for which $f(x) = 32$.

14. Let $g(x) = (7x - 51)^2$. Find all values of x for which $g(x) = 11$.

15. Explain why completing the square on $x^2 + 7x$ is more difficult than completing the square on $x^2 + 6x$.

16. Happy New Year. As part of a New Year's Eve celebration, a huge ball is to be dropped from the top of a 605-foot-tall building at the proper moment so that it strikes the ground at exactly 12:00 midnight. The distance d in feet traveled by a free-falling object in t seconds is given by the formula $d = 16t^2$. To the nearest second, when should the ball be dropped from the building?

SECTION 10.2 ▶ The Quadratic Formula

DEFINITIONS AND CONCEPTS	EXAMPLES

To **solve a quadratic equation in x using the quadratic formula:**

1. Write the equation in standard form:

$$ax^2 + bx + c = 0$$

2. Identify a, b, and c.

3. Substitute the values for a, b, and c in the quadratic formula

$$x = \frac{-b \pm \sqrt{b^2 - 4ac}}{2a}$$

and evaluate the right side to obtain the solutions.

Solve: $3x^2 - 2x - 2 = 0$

Here, $a = 3$, $b = -2$, and $c = -2$.

$$x = \frac{-b \pm \sqrt{b^2 - 4ac}}{2a} \qquad \text{This is the quadratic formula.}$$

$$x = \frac{-(-2) \pm \sqrt{(-2)^2 - 4(3)(-2)}}{2(3)} \qquad \begin{array}{l}\text{Substitute 3 for } a, -2 \text{ for } b, \\ \text{and } -2 \text{ for } c.\end{array}$$

$$x = \frac{2 \pm \sqrt{28}}{6} \qquad \text{Evaluate the expression within the radical.}$$

$$x = \frac{2 \pm 2\sqrt{7}}{6} \qquad \text{Simplify the radical: } \sqrt{28} = \sqrt{4}\sqrt{7} = 2\sqrt{7}.$$

$$x = \frac{\overset{1}{2(1 \pm \sqrt{7})}}{\underset{1}{2 \cdot 3}} \qquad \begin{array}{l}\text{Factor out the GCF, 2, from the two terms in the} \\ \text{numerator. In the denominator, factor 6 as } 2 \cdot 3. \\ \text{Then remove the common factor, 2.}\end{array}$$

$$x = \frac{1 \pm \sqrt{7}}{3}$$

The exact solutions are $\frac{1 + \sqrt{7}}{3}$ and $\frac{1 - \sqrt{7}}{3}$. We can use a calculator to approximate them. To the nearest hundredth, they are 1.22 and -0.55.

When solving a quadratic equation using the quadratic formula, we can often **simplify the calculations** by solving an equivalent equation that does not involve fractions or decimals, and whose leading coefficient is positive.

Before solving ...	do this ...	to get this
$-3x^2 + 5x - 1 = 0$	Multiply both sides by -1.	$3x^2 - 5x + 1 = 0$
$x^2 + \frac{7}{8}x - \frac{1}{2} = 0$	Multiply both sides by 8.	$8x^2 + 7x - 4 = 0$
$60x^2 - 40x + 90 = 0$	Divide both sides by 10.	$6x^2 - 4x + 9 = 0$
$0.05x^2 + 0.16x + 0.71 = 0$	Multiply both sides by 100.	$5x^2 + 16x + 71 = 0$

REVIEW EXERCISES

Solve each equation using the quadratic formula. Approximate the solutions to the nearest hundredth when appropriate.

17. $2x^2 + 13x = 7$

18. $-x^2 + 10x - 18 = 0$

19. $x^2 - 10x = 0$

20. $3y^2 = 26y - 2$

21. $\frac{1}{3}p^2 + \frac{1}{2}p + \frac{1}{2} = 0$

22. $3{,}000t^2 - 4{,}000t = -2{,}000$

23. $0.5x^2 + 0.3x - 0.1 = 0$

24. $x^2 - 3x - 27 = 0$

25. Let $h(x) = x^2 + 3x - 7$. Find all values of x for which $h(x) = 1$.

26. Let $T(x) = -4x^2 - 2x$. Find all values of x for which $T(x) = -3$.

27. Explain the error: $\dfrac{2 \pm \sqrt{7}}{2} = \dfrac{\overset{1}{2} \pm \sqrt{7}}{\underset{1}{2}}$

28. a. Write an expression that represents the width of the larger rectangle shown in red.

   b. Write an expression that represents the length of the larger rectangle shown in red.

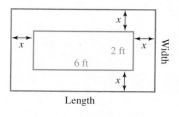

29. **Posters.** The specifications for a poster of Cesar Chavez call for a 615-square-inch photograph to be surrounded by a green border. The borders on the top and bottom of the poster are to be twice as wide as those on the sides. Find the width of each border.

30. **Tutoring.** A private tutoring company charges $20 for a 1-hour session. Currently, 300 students are tutored each week. Since the company is losing money, the owner has decided to increase the price. For each 50¢ increase, she estimates that 5 fewer students will participate. If the company needs to bring in $6,240 per week to stay in business, what price must be charged for a 1-hour tutoring session to produce this amount of revenue?

31. **Acrobats.** To begin his routine on a trapeze, an acrobat is catapulted upward as shown in the illustration. His distance d (in feet) from the arena floor during this maneuver is given by the function $d(t) = -16t^2 + 40t + 5$, where t is the time in seconds since being launched. If the trapeze bar is 25 feet in the air, at what two times will he be able to grab it? Round to the nearest tenth.

32. **Triangles.** The length of the longer leg of a right triangle exceeds the length of the shorter leg by 23 inches and the length of the hypotenuse is 65 inches. Find the length of each leg of the triangle.

SECTION 10.3 ▶ **The Discriminant and Equations That Can Be Written in Quadratic Form**

DEFINITIONS AND CONCEPTS	EXAMPLES
The **discriminant** predicts the type of solutions of $ax^2 + bx + c = 0$, where a, b, and c are rational numbers and $a \neq 0$. Review the table on page 852.	In the quadratic equation $2x^2 - 5x - 3 = 0$, we have $a = 2$, $b = -5$, and $c = -3$. So the value of the discriminant is $$b^2 - 4ac = (-5)^2 - 4(2)(-3) = 25 + 24 = 49$$ Since the value of the discriminant is positive and a perfect square, the equation $2x^2 - 5x - 3 = 0$ has two different rational-number solutions.

Equations that contain an expression, the same expression squared, and a constant term are said to be **quadratic in form.** One method used to solve such equations is to make a **substitution.**

The leading term, x, is the square of the expression $\sqrt{x}$ in the middle term: $x = \left(\sqrt{x}\right)^2$.

$$x - 9\sqrt{x} + 20 = 0$$

The last term is a constant.

Solve: $x^{2/3} - 6x^{1/3} + 5 = 0$

The equation can be written in quadratic form:

$$(x^{1/3})^2 - 6x^{1/3} + 5 = 0 \quad \text{Because } x^{2/3} = (x^{1/3})^2$$

We substitute y for $x^{1/3}$ and use factoring to solve the resulting quadratic equation $y^2 - 6y + 5 = 0$.

$$(y - 1)(y - 5) = 0 \quad \text{Let } y = x^{1/3}.$$
$$y = 1 \quad \text{or} \quad y = 5$$

Now we reverse (undo) the substitution $y = x^{1/3}$ and solve for x.

$$x^{1/3} = 1 \qquad \text{or} \qquad x^{1/3} = 5$$
$$(x^{1/3})^3 = (1)^3 \qquad (x^{1/3})^3 = (5)^3 \quad \text{Recall: } x^{1/3} = \sqrt[3]{x}.$$
$$x = 1 \qquad\qquad x = 125$$

The solutions are 1 and 125. Check both in the original equation.

REVIEW EXERCISES

Use the discriminant to determine the number and type of solutions for each equation.

33. $3x^2 + 4x - 3 = 0$

34. $4x^2 - 5x + 7 = 0$

35. $3x^2 - 4x + \dfrac{4}{3} = 0$

36. $m(2m - 3) = 20$

Solve each equation.

37. $x - 13\sqrt{x} + 12 = 0$

38. $a^{2/3} + a^{1/3} - 6 = 0$

39. $3x^4 + x^2 - 2 = 0$

40. $\dfrac{6}{x + 2} + \dfrac{6}{x + 1} = 5$

41. $(x - 7)^2 + 6(x - 7) + 10 = 0$

42. $m^{-4} - 2m^{-2} + 1 = 0$

43. $4\left(\dfrac{x + 1}{x}\right)^2 + 12\left(\dfrac{x + 1}{x}\right) + 9 = 0$

44. $2m^{2/5} - 5m^{1/5} + 2 = 0$

45. Weekly Chores. Working together, two sisters can do the yard work at their house in 45 minutes. When the older girl does it all herself, she can complete the job in 20 minutes less time than it takes the younger girl working alone. How long does it take the older girl to do the yard work?

46. Road Trips. A woman drives her automobile 150 miles at a rate of r mph. She could have gone the same distance in 2 hours less time if she had increased her speed by 20 mph. Find r.

SECTION 10.4 ▶ Quadratic Functions and Their Graphs

DEFINITIONS AND CONCEPTS	EXAMPLES
A **quadratic function** is a second-degree polynomial function of the form $$f(x) = ax^2 + bx + c$$	Quadratic functions: $$f(x) = 2x^2 - 3x + 5, \qquad g(x) = -x^2 + 4x, \qquad \text{and} \qquad s(x) = \dfrac{1}{4}x^2 - 10$$

The graph of the quadratic function $f(x) = a(x - h)^2 + k$ where $a \neq 0$ is a **parabola** with **vertex** at (h, k). The **axis of symmetry** is the line $x = h$. The parabola opens upward when $a > 0$ and downward when $a < 0$.

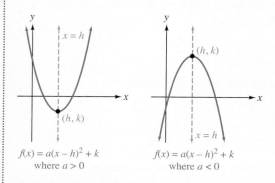

$f(x) = a(x - h)^2 + k$
where $a > 0$

$f(x) = a(x - h)^2 + k$
where $a < 0$

Graph: $f(x) = 2(x + 1)^2 - 8$

$$f(x) = 2[x - (-1)]^2 - 8$$

$$f(x) = a(x - \quad h)^2 + k$$

We see that $a = 2$, $h = -1$, and $k = -8$. The graph is a parabola with vertex $(h, k) = (-1, -8)$ and axis of symmetry $x = -1$. Since a is positive, the parabola opens upward.

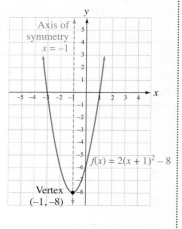

The **vertex** of the graph of $f(x) = ax^2 + bx + c$ is

$$\left(-\frac{b}{2a},\ f\left(-\frac{b}{2a}\right)\right)$$

and the axis of symmetry is the line

$$x = -\frac{b}{2a}$$

The y-coordinate of the vertex of the graph of a quadratic function gives the **minimum or maximum value** of the function.

Graph: $f(x) = -x^2 + 3x + 4$

Here, $a = -1$, $b = 3$, and $c = 4$.

- Since $a < 0$, the graph opens downward.

- The x-coordinate of the vertex of the graph is:

$$-\frac{b}{2a} = -\frac{3}{2(-1)} = \frac{3}{2}$$

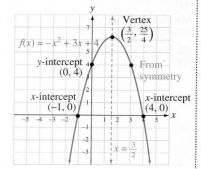

To find the y-coordinate of the vertex, we substitute $\frac{3}{2}$ for x in the function.

$$f\left(\frac{3}{2}\right) = -\left(\frac{3}{2}\right)^2 + 3\left(\frac{3}{2}\right) + 4 = \frac{25}{4}$$

The vertex of the parabola is $\left(\frac{3}{2}, \frac{25}{4}\right)$.

The **y-intercept** is determined by the value of $f(x)$ when $x = 0$: the y-intercept is $(0, c)$.

To find the **x-intercepts**, let $f(x) = 0$ and solve $ax^2 + bx + c = 0$.

- The y-intercept is the value of the function when $x = 0$. Since $f(0) = 4$, the y-intercept is $(0, 4)$.

- To find the x-intercepts, we solve:

$$-x^2 + 3x + 4 = 0 \qquad \text{Let } f(x) = 0.$$

$$x^2 - 3x - 4 = 0 \qquad \text{Multiply both sides by } -1.$$

$$(x + 1)(x - 4) = 0 \qquad \text{Factor.}$$

$$x = -1 \quad \text{or} \quad x = 4$$

The x-intercepts are $(-1, 0)$ and $(4, 0)$.

REVIEW EXERCISES

47. Hospitals. The annual number of in-patient admissions to U.S. community hospitals for the years 1980–2008 can be modeled by the quadratic function $A(x) = 0.03x^2 - 0.88x + 37.3$, where $A(x)$ is the number of admissions in millions and x is the number of years after 1980. Use the function to estimate the number of in-patient admissions for the year 2005. Round to the nearest tenth of one million. (Source: American Hospital Association)

48. Fill in the blanks. The graph of the quadratic function $f(x) = a(x - h)^2 + k$ is a parabola with vertex at ($\quad$, $\quad$). The axis of symmetry is the line $\quad = h$. The parabola opens upward when $a > 0$ and downward when $a < 0$.

Graph each pair of functions on the same coordinate system.

49. $f(x) = 2x^2$, $g(x) = 2x^2 - 3$

50. $f(x) = -\dfrac{1}{4}x^2$, $g(x) = -\dfrac{1}{4}(x + 2)^2$

51. Find the vertex and the axis of symmetry of the graph of $f(x) = -2(x - 1)^2 + 4$. Then plot several points and complete the graph.

52. Complete the square to write $f(x) = 4x^2 + 16x + 9$ in the form $f(x) = a(x - h)^2 + k$. Determine the vertex and the axis of symmetry of the graph. Then plot several points and complete the graph.

53. Find the vertex of the graph of $f(x) = -2x^2 + 4x - 8$ using the vertex formula.

54. First determine the coordinates of the vertex and the axis of symmetry of the graph of $f(x) = x^2 + x - 2$ using the vertex formula. Then determine the x- and y-intercepts of the graph. Finally, plot several points and complete the graph.

55. Farming. The number of farms in the United States for the years 1870–1970 is approximated by

$$N(x) = -1,526x^2 + 155,652x + 2,500,200$$

where $x = 0$ represents 1870, $x = 1$ represents 1871, and so on. For this period, when was the number of U.S. farms a maximum? How many farms were there?

56. Estimate the solutions of $-3x^2 - 5x + 2 = 0$ from the graph of $f(x) = -3x^2 - 5x + 2$, shown here.

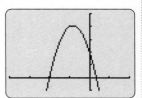

SECTION 10.5 ▶ Quadratic and Other Nonlinear Inequalities

DEFINITIONS AND CONCEPTS	EXAMPLES
To solve a quadratic inequality, get 0 on the right side and solve the related quadratic equation. Then locate the **critical numbers** on a number line, test each interval, and check the endpoints.	To solve $x^2 - x - 6 \geq 0$, we solve the related quadratic equation:

To solve $x^2 - x - 6 \geq 0$, we solve the related quadratic equation:

$$x^2 - x - 6 = 0$$

$$(x - 3)(x + 2) = 0 \qquad \text{Factor.}$$

$$x = 3 \quad \text{or} \quad x = -2 \qquad \text{These are the critical numbers that divide the number line into three intervals.}$$

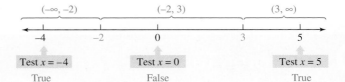

After testing each interval and noting that 3 and -2 satisfy the inequality, we see that the solution set is $(-\infty, -2] \cup [3, \infty)$.

To solve a rational inequality, get 0 on the right side and solve the related rational equation. Then locate the **critical numbers** (including any values that make the denominator 0) on a number line, test each interval, and check the endpoints.

To solve $\frac{x+1}{x-4} < 0$, we solve the related rational equation $\frac{x+1}{x-4} = 0$ to obtain the solution $x = -1$, which is a critical number. Another critical number is $x = 4$, the value that makes the denominator 0. These critical numbers divide the number line into three intervals.

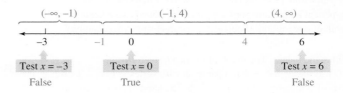

After testing each interval and noting that -1 and 4 do not satisfy the inequality, we see that the solution set is the interval $(-1, 4)$.

To graph a nonlinear inequality in two variables, first graph the boundary. Then use a test point to determine which side of the boundary to shade.

This is the graph of $y \le x^2 + 5x + 4$.

Since the inequality contains the symbol $\le$, and equality is allowed, we draw the parabola determined by $y = x^2 + 5x + 4$ using a **solid curve.**

We shade the region containing the test point $(0, 0)$ because its coordinates satisfy $y \le x^2 + 5x + 4$.

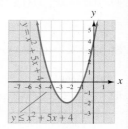

REVIEW EXERCISES

Solve each inequality. Write the solution set in interval notation and graph it.

57. $x^2 + 2x - 35 > 0$

58. $x^2 \le 81$

59. $\frac{3}{x} \le 5$

60. $\frac{2x^2 - x - 28}{x - 1} > 0$

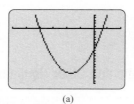
(a)

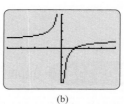
(b)

61. Estimate the solution set of $3x^2 + 10x - 8 \le 0$ from the graph of $f(x) = 3x^2 + 10x - 8$ shown in figure (a).

62. Estimate the solution set of $\frac{x-1}{x} > 0$ from the graph of $f(x) = \frac{x-1}{x}$ shown in figure (b).

Graph each inequality.

63. $y < \frac{1}{2}x^2 - 1$

64. $y \ge -|x|$

---

10 ▸ Chapter Test

1. Fill in the blanks.

  a. An equation of the form $ax^2 + bx + c = 0$, where $a \ne 0$, is called a _____ equation.

  b. When we add 81 to $x^2 + 18x$, we say that we have _____ the _____ on $x^2 + 18x$.

  c. The lowest point on a parabola that opens upward, or the highest point on a parabola that opens downward, is called the _____ of the parabola.

  d. $\frac{x-5}{x^2 - x - 56} > 0$ is an example of a _____ inequality in one variable.

  e. $y \le x^2 - 4x + 3$ is an example of a _____ inequality in two variables.

2. Solve $x^2 - 63 = 0$ using the square root property. Approximate the solutions to the nearest hundredth.

Solve each equation using the square root property.

3. $(a + 7)^2 = 50$

4. $m^2 + 4 = 0$

5. Add a number to make $x^2 + 11x$ a perfect-square trinomial. Then factor the result.

6. Solve $x^2 + 3x - 2 = 0$ by completing the square. Approximate the solutions to the nearest hundredth.

7. Solve $2x^2 + 8x + 12 = 0$ by completing the square.

8. Let $f(x) = (3x - 2)^2$. Find all values of x for which $f(x) = 18$.

Use the quadratic formula to solve each equation. Approximate each solution to the nearest hundredth, when appropriate.

9. $4x^2 + 4x - 1 = 0$

10. $\frac{1}{8}t^2 - \frac{1}{4}t = \frac{1}{2}$

11. $-t^2 + 4t - 13 = 0$ **12.** $0.01x^2 = -0.08x - 0.15$

13. $m^2 - 94m = -2{,}209$

14. Let $g(x) = 3x^2 - 20$. Find all values of x for which $g(x) = 10$.

Solve each equation by any method. Approximate each solution to the nearest hundredth, when appropriate.

15. $2y - 3\sqrt{y} + 1 = 0$ **16.** $3 = m^{-2} - 2m^{-1}$

17. $x^4 - x^2 - 12 = 0$

18. $4\left(\dfrac{x+2}{3x}\right)^2 - 4\left(\dfrac{x+2}{3x}\right) - 3 = 0$

19. $\dfrac{1}{n+2} = \dfrac{1}{3} - \dfrac{1}{n}$

20. $5a^{2/3} + 11a^{1/3} = -2$

21. $10x(x + 1) = -3$

22. $a^3 - 3a^2 + 8a - 24 = 0$

23. Solve $E = mc^2$ for c. Assume that all variables represent positive numbers. Express any radical in simplified form.

24. Use the discriminant to determine the number and type of solutions for each equation.
  a. $3x^2 + 5x + 17 = 0$

  b. $9m^2 - 12m = -4$

25. Tablecloths. In 1990, Sportex of Highland, Illinois, made what was at the time the world's longest tablecloth. Find the dimensions of the rectangular tablecloth if it covered an area of 6,759 square feet and its length was 8 feet more than 332 times its width.

26. Cooking. Working together, a chef and his assistant can make a pastry dessert in 25 minutes. When the chef makes it himself, it takes him 8 minutes less time than it takes his assistant working alone. How long does it take the chef to make the dessert?

27. Drawing. An artist uses four equal-sized right triangles to block out a perspective drawing of an old hotel. See the illustration in the next column. For each triangle, the leg on the horizontal line is 14 inches longer than the leg on the center line. The length of each hypotenuse is 26 inches. On the center line of the drawing, what is the length of the segment extending from the ground to the top of the building?

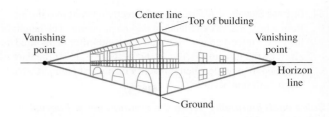

28. Home Decorating. A woman is going to put a cork border of uniform width around an 18-inch by 24-inch wall picture, as shown here. If the area covered by the cork is to be the same as the surface area of the picture, how wide should the border be? Round to the nearest tenth of an inch.

29. ER Rooms. The number of hospital emergency departments in the United States is approximated by the function $E(t) = 2.29t^2 - 75.72t + 5{,}206.95$, where t is the number of years after 1990. In what year does the model indicate that the number of hospital emergency departments was 5,000? (Source: American Hospital Association)

30. Anthropology. Anthropologists refer to the shape of the human jaw as a *parabolic dental arcade*. Which function is the best mathematical model of the parabola shown in the illustration?

  i. $f(x) = -\dfrac{3}{8}(x - 4)^2 + 6$ **ii.** $f(x) = -\dfrac{3}{8}(x - 6)^2 + 4$

  iii. $f(x) = -\dfrac{3}{8}x^2 + 6$ **iv.** $f(x) = \dfrac{3}{8}x^2 + 6$

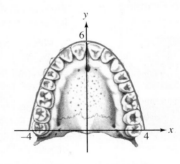

31. Find the vertex and the axis of symmetry of the graph of $f(x) = -3(x - 1)^2 + 2$. Then plot several points and complete the graph.

32. Complete the square to write the function $f(x) = 5x^2 + 10x - 1$ in the form $f(x) = a(x - h)^2 + k$. Determine the vertex and the axis of symmetry of the graph. Then plot several points and complete the graph.

33. First determine the coordinates of the vertex and the axis of symmetry of the graph of $f(x) = 2x^2 + x - 1$ using the vertex formula. Then determine the x- and y-intercepts of the graph. Finally, plot several points and complete the graph.

34. Distress Signals.   A flare is fired directly upward into the air from a boat that is experiencing engine problems. The height of the flare (in feet) above the water, t seconds after being fired, is given by the function $h(t) = -16t^2 + 112t + 15$. If the flare is designed to explode when it reaches its highest point, at what height will this occur?

Solve each inequality. Write the solution set in interval notation and then graph it.

35. $x^2 - 2x > 8$

36. $\dfrac{x - 2}{x + 3} \leq 0$

37. Climate.   The average monthly temperature in San Antonio, Texas, is approximated by the function $T(m) = -1.1m^2 + 15.3m + 29.5$, where m is the number of the month (January = 1, February = 2, and so on). Use the function to approximate the average monthly temperature in July. (Source: cityrating.com)

Average Temperature (°F) San Antonio, Texas

Jan. Feb. Mar. Apr. May. Jun. Jul. Aug. Sep. Oct. Nov. Dec.

38. Graph: $y \leq -x^2 + 3$

39. The graph of a quadratic function of the form $f(x) = ax^2 + bx + c$ is shown. Estimate the solutions of the corresponding quadratic equation $ax^2 + bx + c = 0$.

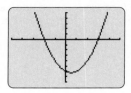

40. See Exercise 39. Estimate the solution of the quadratic inequality $ax^2 + bx + c \leq 0$.

Group Project

Picture Framing

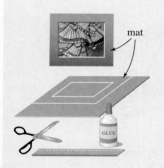

Overview: When framing pictures, mats are often used to enhance the images and give them a sense of depth. In this activity, you will use the quadratic formula to design the matting for several pictures.

Instructions: Form groups of 3 students. Each person in your group is to bring a picture to class. You can use a picture from a magazine or newspaper, a picture postcard, or a photograph that is no larger than 5 in. × 7 in. You will also need a pair of scissors, a ruler, glue, and three pieces of construction paper (12 in. × 18 in.).

Select one of the pictures and find its area. A mat of *uniform* width is to be placed around the picture. The area of the mat should equal the area of the picture. To determine the proper width of the matting, follow the steps of Example 8 in Section 10.2. Once you have determined the proper width, cut out the mat from the construction paper and glue it to the picture.

Then, choose another picture and find its area. Determine the uniform width that a matting should have so that its area is double that of the picture. Cut out the proper-size matting from the construction paper and glue it to the second picture.

Finally, find the area of the third picture and determine the uniform width that a matting should have so that its area is one-half that of the picture. Cut out the proper-size matting from the construction paper and glue it to the third picture.

Is one size matting more visually appealing than another? Discuss this among the members of your group.

CUMULATIVE REVIEW ▶▶ Chapters 1–10

1. Determine whether each statement is true or false.
   [Section 1.3]

   a. All whole numbers are integers.

   b. π is a rational number.

   c. A real number is either rational or irrational.

2. Evaluate: $\dfrac{-3(3 + 2)^2 - (-5)}{17 - |-22|}$ [Section 1.7]

3. Simplify: $-9(3a - 9) - 7(2a - 7)$ [Section 1.9]

4. Use a check to determine whether -11 is a solution of

   $\dfrac{3(b + 2)}{2} = \dfrac{4b - 10}{4}$ [Section 2.2]

5. Solve: $2 - (4x + 7) = 3 + 2(x + 2)$ [Section 2.2]
6. Solve: $2(6n + 5) = 4(3n + 2) + 2$ [Section 2.2]

7. **Backpacks.** Pediatricians advise that children should not carry more than 20% of their own body weight in a backpack. According to this warning, how much weight can a fifth-grade girl who weighs 85 pounds safely carry in her backpack? [Section 2.3]

8. **Surface Area.** The total surface area A of a box with dimensions l, w, and h is given by the formula $A = 2lw + 2wh + 2lh$. If $A = 202$ square inches, $l = 9$ inches, and $w = 5$ inches, find h. [Section 2.4]

   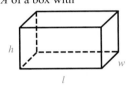

9. **Geometry.** If the vertex angle of an isosceles triangle is $53°$, find the measure of each base angle. [Section 2.5]

10. **Search and Rescue.** Two search and rescue teams leave base at the same time, looking for a lost boy. The first team, on foot, heads north at 2 mph and the other, on horseback, south at 4 mph. How long will it take them to search a distance of 21 miles between them? [Section 2.6]

11. **Pharmacist.** How many liters of a 1% glucose solution should a pharmacist mix with 2 liters of a 5% glucose solution to obtain a 2% glucose solution? [Section 2.6]

12. **Blending Coffee.** A store sells regular coffee for $8 a pound and gourmet coffee for $14 a pound. Using 40 pounds of the gourmet coffee, the owner makes a blend to put on sale for $10 a pound. How many pounds of regular coffee should he use? [Section 2.6]

13. Solve: $3 - 3x \geq 6 + x$. Graph the solution set. Then describe the graph using interval notation. [Section 2.7]

14. Check to determine whether $(-6, -7)$ is a solution of $4x - 3y = -4$. [Section 3.1]

Graph each equation.

15. $y = \dfrac{1}{2}x$ [Section 3.2]

16. $3x - 4y = 12$ [Section 3.3]

17. $x = 5$ [Section 3.3]

18. $y = 2x^2 - 3$ [Section 5.4]

19. Find the x-intercept and the y-intercept of the graph of the linear equation $5x - 3y = 6$. [Section 3.3]

20. **Skype.** The line graph below shows the approximate growth in the number of subscribers to Skype, a software application that allows users to make video calls over the Internet. Find the rate of change in the number of subscribers to Skype during the years 2007–2010 by finding the slope of the line. [Section 3.4]

   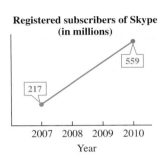

   Registered subscribers of Skype (in millions)

   Source: businessinsider.com

21. What is the slope of the line defined by each equation? [Section 3.5]

   a. $y = 3x - 7$
   b. $5x - 6y = 13$

22. What is the slope of the line whose equation is $y = -3$? [Section 3.5]

Find an equation of the line with the given properties. Write the equation in slope–intercept form.

23. Slope 3, passes through $(-2, -4)$ [Section 3.5]
24. Parallel to the graph of $2x + 3y = 6$ and passes through $(0, -2)$ [Section 3.6]
25. If $f(x) = 2x^2 - 3x + 1$, find $f(-3)$. [Section 3.8]
26. **Boating.** The graph shows the vertical distance from a point on the tip of a propeller to the centerline as the propeller spins. Is this the graph of a function? [Section 3.8]

   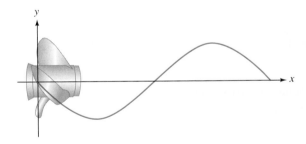

27. Use a check to determine whether $\left(2, \dfrac{1}{3}\right)$ is a solution of

   $\begin{cases} x - 3y = 1 \\ -2x + 6 = -6y \end{cases}$ [Section 4.1]

28. Solve the system $\begin{cases} x + y = 4 \\ y = x + 6 \end{cases}$ by graphing. [Section 4.1]

92. First sketch the graph of the basic function associated with $g(x) = |x - 3| - 4$. Then draw the graph of function g using a translation. Give the domain and range of function g. [Section 8.3]

108. Find the domain of the function $f(x) = \sqrt{0.4x - 36}$. [Section 9.1]

Solve each system of equations.   *Solve each equation.*

Study Skills Workshop ▶ Participating in Class

One of the keys to success in algebra is to learn as much as you can in class. To get the most out of class meetings, and to make them more enjoyable, you should participate in the following ways:

ASK QUESTIONS: During class, clear up any questions that may arise from your homework assignments or from your instructor's lectures. Also, pay close attention when other students ask questions. You never know when you might face the same difficulty.

ANSWER QUESTIONS: Many instructors direct questions to the class while lecturing. Take advantage of this opportunity to increase your knowledge by attempting to answer all such questions from your instructor.

INTERACT WITH CLASSMATES: Before class begins and after class ends, regularly discuss the material that you are studying with fellow classmates.

Now Try This ▶

1. List the reasons why you do not feel comfortable asking questions in class.
2. While working on your next homework assignment, write down any questions that occur to you so that you will not forget to ask them in class.
3. Exchange a written question about a homework problem with a classmate. See if you can answer each other's question.

SECTION 11.1

Algebra and Composition of Functions

OBJECTIVES

1 Add, subtract, multiply, and divide functions.

2 Find the composition of functions.

3 Use graphs to evaluate functions.

4 Use composite functions to solve problems.

ARE YOU READY?

▼ *The following problems review some basic skills that are needed when performing the algebra of functions.*

1. Add:
   $(7x^2 + 5x - 12) + (2x^2 - 3x + 4)$

2. Subtract:
   $(8x^3 - 4x^2) - (6x^3 - 3x^2)$

3. Multiply: $(8x - 5)(9x^2 - 4)$

4. Divide: $(x^2 - x - 6) \div (x - 3)$

Just as it is possible to perform arithmetic operations on real numbers, it is possible to perform those operations on functions. We call the process of adding, subtracting, multiplying, and dividing functions the **algebra of functions.**

1 Add, Subtract, Multiply, and Divide Functions.

We have seen that the sum, difference, product, and quotient of two functions are themselves functions. The new functions that result from such operations can be represented using the following notation.

Operations on Functions

Sum: $(f + g)(x) = f(x) + g(x)$ *Read as "f plus g of x equals f of x plus g of x."*

Difference: $(f - g)(x) = f(x) - g(x)$ *Read as "f minus g of x equals f of x minus g of x."*

Product: $(f \cdot g)(x) = f(x)g(x)$ *Read as "f times g of x equals f of x times g of x."*

Quotient: $(f/g)(x) = \dfrac{f(x)}{g(x)}$ where $g(x) \neq 0$ *Read as "f divided by g of x equals f of x divided by g of x."*

The domain of each sum, difference, and product function shown above is the set of real numbers x that are in the domains of both f and g. The domain of the quotient function is the set of real numbers x that are in the domains of f and g, excluding any values of x where $g(x) = 0$.

EXAMPLE 1   Let $f(x) = 2x^2 + 1$ and $g(x) = 5x - 3$. Find each function and give its domain:
a. $f + g$ **b.** $f - g$ **c.** $f \cdot g$ **d.** f/g

Strategy   We will add, subtract, multiply, and divide the functions as if they were binomials.

Why   We add because of the plus symbol in $f + g$, we subtract because of the minus symbol in $f - g$, we multiply because of the raised dot in $f \cdot g$, and we divide because of the fraction bar in f/g.

Solution   **a.** $(f + g)(x) = f(x) + g(x)$ *This is the definition of a sum function.*

$= (2x^2 + 1) + (5x - 3)$ *Replace $f(x)$ with $2x^2 + 1$ and $g(x)$ with $5x - 3$.*

$= 2x^2 + 5x - 2$ *Drop the parentheses and combine like terms.*

The domain of $f + g$ is the set of real numbers that are in the domain of both f and g. Since the domain of both f and g is $(-\infty, \infty)$, the domain of $f + g$ is the $(-\infty, \infty)$.

b. $(f - g)(x) = f(x) - g(x)$ *This is the definition of a difference function.*

$= (2x^2 + 1) - (5x - 3)$ *Replace $f(x)$ with $2x^2 + 1$ and $g(x)$ with $5x - 3$.*

$= 2x^2 + 1 - 5x + 3$ *Change the sign of each term of $5x - 3$ and drop the parentheses.*

$= 2x^2 - 5x + 4$ *Combine like terms.*

Since the domain of both f and g is $(-\infty, \infty)$, the domain of $f - g$ is $(-\infty, \infty)$.

Notation	**c.** $(f \cdot g)(x) = f(x) \cdot g(x)$ *This is the definition of a product function.*

The parentheses around $\frac{3}{5}$ in the notation $\left(-\infty, \frac{3}{5}\right) \cup \left(\frac{3}{5}, \infty\right)$ indicate that $\frac{3}{5}$ is not included in the domain of f/g. The domain could also be shown graphically:

$= (2x^2 + 1)(5x - 3)$ *Replace $f(x)$ with $2x^2 + 1$ and $g(x)$ with $5x - 3$.*

$= 10x^3 - 6x^2 + 5x - 3$ *Multiply the binomials. There are no like terms.*

The domain of $f \cdot g$ is the set of real numbers that are in the domain of both f and g. Since the domain of both f and g is $(-\infty, \infty)$, the domain of $f \cdot g$ is $(-\infty, \infty)$.

3/5

−1   0   1

d. $(f/g)(x) = \dfrac{f(x)}{g(x)}$ *This is the definition of a quotient function.*

$= \dfrac{2x^2 + 1}{5x - 3}$ *Replace $f(x)$ with $2x^2 + 1$ and $g(x)$ with $5x - 3$. The result does not simplify.*

Since the denominator of the fraction cannot be 0, it follows that this function is undefined if $5x - 3 = 0$. If we solve for x, we see that x cannot be $\frac{3}{5}$. Thus, the domain of f/g is the union of two intervals: $\left(-\infty, \frac{3}{5}\right) \cup \left(\frac{3}{5}, \infty\right)$.

Self Check 1   Let $f(x) = 3x - 2$ and $g(x) = 2x^2 + 3x$. Find each function and give its domain:
a. $f + g$
b. $f - g$
c. $f \cdot g$
d. f/g

Now Try ▶   Problems 13, 15, 17, and 19

EXAMPLE 2   Use the results from Example 1 to find: **a.** $(f + g)(-3)$ **b.** $(f - g)(6)$
c. $(f \cdot g)(0)$ **d.** $(f/g)(10)$

Strategy   We will substitute the given values within the second set of parentheses for each x in the sum, difference, product, and quotient functions found in Example 1. Then we will evaluate the right side of each equation.

Why   The number that is within the second set of parentheses is the input of the function.

Solution   **a.** $(f + g)(x) = 2x^2 + 5x - 2$ This is the sum function found in Example 1, part a.

$(f + g)(-3) = 2(-3)^2 + 5(-3) - 2$ Substitute -3 for each x.

$= 18 + (-15) - 2$ Evaluate the right side.

$= 1$

b. $(f - g)(x) = 2x^2 - 5x + 4$ This is the difference function found in Example 1, part b.

$(f - g)(6) = 2(6)^2 - 5(6) + 4$ Substitute 6 for each x.

$= 72 - 30 + 4$ Evaluate the right side.

$= 46$

c. $(f \cdot g)(x) = 10x^3 - 6x^2 + 5x - 3$ This is the product function found in Example 1, part c.

$(f \cdot g)(0) = 10(0)^3 - 6(0)^2 + 5(0) - 3$ Substitute 0 for each x.

$= -3$ Evaluate the right side.

d. $(f/g)(x) = \dfrac{2x^2 + 1}{5x - 3}$ This is the quotient function found in Example 1, part d.

$(f/g)(10) = \dfrac{2(10)^2 + 1}{5(10) - 3}$ Substitute 10 for each x.

$= \dfrac{2(100) + 1}{50 - 3}$ Evaluate the right side.

$= \dfrac{201}{47}$

Self Check 2   Use the results from Self Check 1 to find: **a.** $(f + g)(5)$
b. $(f - g)(-9)$ **c.** $(f \cdot g)(2)$ **d.** $(f/g)(0)$

Now Try ▶ Problems 29 and 31

There is a relationship that can be seen between the graphs of two functions and the graph of their sum (or difference) function. For example, in the following illustration, the graph of $f + g$, which gives the total number of elementary and secondary students in the United States, can be found by adding the graph of f, which gives the number of secondary students, to the graph of g, which gives the number of elementary students. For any given x-value, we simply add the two corresponding y-values to get the graph of the sum function $f + g$.

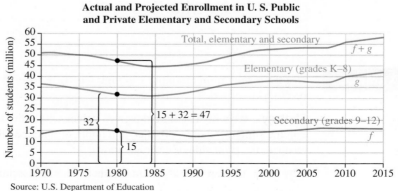

**Actual and Projected Enrollment in U. S. Public
and Private Elementary and Secondary Schools**

To find the total enrollment in 1980, add the elementary enrollment of 32 million to the secondary enrollment of 15 million to get 47 million.

Source: U.S. Department of Education

2 Find the Composition of Functions.

We have seen that a function can be represented by a machine: We put in a number from the domain, and a number from the range comes out. For example, if we put the number 2 into the machine shown on the right, the number $f(2) = 8$ comes out. In general, if we put x into the machine, the value $f(x)$ comes out.

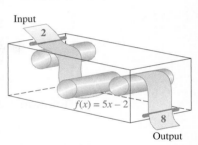

Often one quantity is a function of a second quantity that depends, in turn, on a third quantity. For example, the cost of a car trip is a function of the gasoline consumed. The amount of gasoline consumed, in turn, is a function of the number of miles driven. Such chains of dependence can be analyzed mathematically as **compositions of functions.**

Suppose that $y = f(x)$ and $y = g(x)$ define two functions. Any number x in the domain of g will produce the corresponding value $g(x)$ in the range of g. If $g(x)$ is in the domain of function f, then $g(x)$ can be substituted into f, and a corresponding value $f(g(x))$ will be determined. Because of the **nested parentheses** in $f(g(x))$, we read it as "f of g of x." This two-step process defines a new function, called a **composite function,** denoted by $f \circ g$. (This is read as "f composed with g" or "the composition of f and g" or "f circle g.")

The function machines shown below illustrate the composition $f \circ g$. When we put a number into the function g, a value $g(x)$ comes out. The value $g(x)$ then goes into function f, which transforms $g(x)$ into $f(g(x))$. If the function machines for g and f were connected to make a single machine, that machine would be named $f \circ g$.

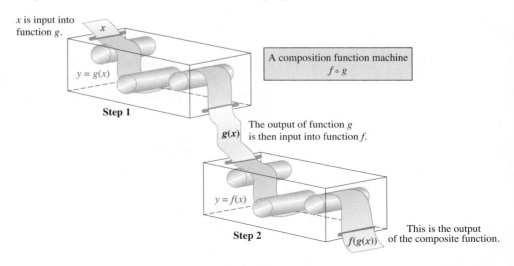

To be in the domain of the composite function $f \circ g$, a number x has to be in the domain of g and the output of g must be in the domain of f. Thus, the domain of $f \circ g$ consists of those numbers x that are in the domain of g, and for which $g(x)$ is in the domain of f.

Composite Functions	▼ The **composite function** $f \circ g$ is defined by $$(f \circ g)(x) = f(g(x))$$

If $f(x) = 4x$ and $g(x) = 3x + 2$, to find $f \circ g$ and $g \circ f$, we proceed as follows.

$$
\begin{aligned}
(f \circ g)(x) &= f(g(x)) \\
&= f(3x + 2) \\
&= 4(3x + 2) \\
&= 12x + 8
\end{aligned}
\qquad
\begin{aligned}
(g \circ f)(x) &= g(f(x)) \\
&= g(4x) \\
&= 3(4x) + 2 \\
&= 12x + 2
\end{aligned}
$$

Different results

The different results illustrate that the composition of functions is not commutative. Usually, we will find that $(f \circ g)(x) \neq (g \circ f)(x)$.

The Language of Algebra

A **composite** is something that is formed by bringing together distinct parts. For example, a police artist creates a *composite* sketch from eyewitness descriptions of the suspect.

The Language of Algebra

$$f(\underbrace{g(x)})$$

We call these **nested parentheses.**

Caution

$$(f \circ g)(x)$$
↑ Composition

does not mean

$$(f \cdot g)(x)$$
↑ Multiplication

EXAMPLE 3   Let $f(x) = 2x + 1$ and $g(x) = x - 4$. Find: **a.** $(f \circ g)(9)$ **b.** $(f \circ g)(x)$ **c.** $(g \circ f)(-2)$

Strategy   In part (a), we will find $f(g(9))$. In part (b), we will find $f(g(x))$. In part (c), we will find $g(f(-2))$.

Why   To evaluate a composite function written with the circle $\circ$ notation, we rewrite it using nested parentheses.

Solution   **a.** $(f \circ g)(9)$ means $f(g(9))$, where the function g is applied first and function f is applied second.

$$(f \circ g)(9) = f(g(9))$$

Apply first

In figure (a) on the next page, we see that function g receives the number 9, subtracts 4, and releases the number $g(9) = 5$. Then 5 goes into the f function, which doubles 5 and adds 1. The final result, 11, is the output of the composite function $f \circ g$.

Read as "f composed   Read as "f
with g of 9."   of g of 9."

$$
\begin{aligned}
(f \circ g)(9) &= f(g(9)) && \text{Change from } \circ \text{ notation to nested parentheses notation.} \\
&= f(5) && \text{Evaluate: } g(9) = 9 - 4 = 5. \\
&= 2(5) + 1 && \text{Evaluate } f(5) \text{ using } f(x) = 2x + 1. \\
&= 11
\end{aligned}
$$

Thus, $(f \circ g)(9) = 11$.

b. $(f \circ g)(x)$ means $f(g(x))$. In figure (a) on the next page, function g receives the number x, subtracts 4, and releases the number $x - 4$. Then $x - 4$ goes into the f function, which doubles $x - 4$ and adds 1. The final result, $2x - 7$, is the output of the composite function $f \circ g$.

Read as "f composed   Read as "f
with g of x."   of g of x."

$$
\begin{aligned}
(f \circ g)(x) &= f(g(x)) && \text{Change from } \circ \text{ notation to nested parentheses notation.} \\
&= f(x - 4) && \text{We are given } g(x) = x - 4. \text{ Replace } g(x) \text{ with } x - 4. \\
&= 2(x - 4) + 1 && \text{Find } f(x - 4) \text{ using } f(x) = 2x + 1. \\
&= 2x - 8 + 1 && \text{Distribute the multiplication by 2.} \\
&= 2x - 7 && \text{Combine like terms.}
\end{aligned}
$$

Thus, $(f \circ g)(x) = 2x - 7$.

c. $(g \circ f)(-2)$ means $g(f(-2))$. In figure (b) on the next page, function f receives the number -2, doubles it and adds 1, and releases -3 into the g function. Function g subtracts 4 from -3 and outputs a final result of -7. Thus,

Read as "g composed   Read as "g
with f of -2."   of f of -2."

$$
\begin{aligned}
(g \circ f)(-2) &= g(f(-2)) && \text{Change from } \circ \text{ notation to nested parentheses notation.} \\
&= g(-3) && \text{Evaluate } f(-2) \text{ using } f(x) = 2x + 1. \\
&= -3 - 4 && \text{Evaluate } g(-3) \text{ using } g(x) = x - 4. \\
&= -7 && \text{Do the subtraction.}
\end{aligned}
$$

Thus, $(g \circ f)(-2) = -7$.

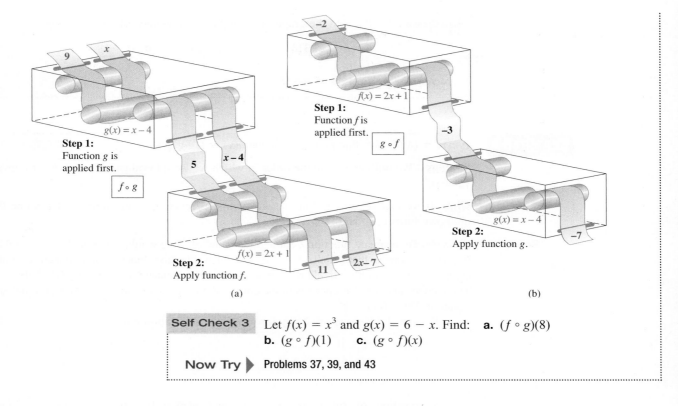

(a)   (b)

Self Check 3 Let $f(x) = x^3$ and $g(x) = 6 - x$. Find: **a.** $(f \circ g)(8)$
b. $(g \circ f)(1)$ **c.** $(g \circ f)(x)$

Now Try ▶ Problems 37, 39, and 43

3 Use Graphs to Evaluate Functions.

EXAMPLE 4 Refer to the graphs of functions f and g on the left to find each of the following.
a. $(f + g)(-4)$ **b.** $(f \cdot g)(2)$ **c.** $(f \circ g)(-3)$

Strategy We will express the sum, product, and composite functions using the functions from which they are formed.

Why We can evaluate sum, product, and composite functions at a given x-value by evaluating each function from which they are formed at that x-value.

Solution **a.** The value of $f(-4)$ is found by looking in quadrant II of the graph and the value of $g(-4)$ by looking in quadrant III.

$$(f + g)(-4) = f(-4) + g(-4)$$
$$= 3 + (-4)$$
$$= -1$$

b. The value of $f(2)$ is found by looking in quadrant IV of the graph and the value of $g(2)$ by looking in quadrant I.

$$(f \cdot g)(2) = f(2) \cdot g(2)$$
$$= -2 \cdot 1$$
$$= -2$$

c. The value of $g(-3)$ is found by looking in quadrant III of the graph and the value of $f(-2)$ by looking in quadrant II.

$$(f \circ g)(-3) = f(g(-3)) \quad \text{Change from } \circ \text{ notation to nested parentheses notation.}$$
$$= f(-2)$$
$$= 3$$

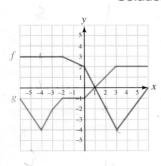

Self Check 4 Refer to the graph in Example 4 to find each of the following.

a. $(f - g)(3)$ **b.** $\left(\dfrac{f}{g}\right)(-2)$ **c.** $(g \circ f)(3)$

Now Try ▶ Problems 45 and 47

EXAMPLE 5 If $h(x) = (4x - 6)^2$, find f and g such that $h(x) = (f \circ g)(x)$.

Strategy We will determine the order in which we would evaluate function h for a given value of x.

Why If we can see the evaluation as a two-step process, it will help us determine the unknown functions f and g.

Solution If we were to evaluate function h for a given value of x, we would first find $4x - 6$, and then we would square that result. This suggests that the first function that operates in the composition, function g, should receive an input x and produce $4x - 6$. Thus, $g(x) = 4x - 6$. The second function that operates in the composition, function f, should receive an input and square it. Thus, $f(x) = x^2$.

We can check these results by forming the composition function.

$$(f \circ g)(x) = f(g(x)) \qquad \text{Change from } \circ \text{ notation to nested parentheses.}$$
$$= f(4x - 6) \qquad \text{Replace } g(x) \text{ with } 4x - 6.$$
$$= (4x - 6)^2 \qquad \text{Find } f(4x - 6) \text{ using } f(x) = x^2.$$

The composition of functions $f(x) = x^2$ and $g(x) = 4x - 6$ does indeed produce $h(x) = (4x - 6)^2$. It is important to note that there are many other possibilities for f and g, but the ones that we found here are the most obvious.

Self Check 5 If $h(x) = \sqrt{x + 15}$, find f and g such that $h(x) = (f \circ g)(x)$.

Now Try ▶ Problems 49 and 51

---

4 Use Composite Functions to Solve Problems.

EXAMPLE 6 **Biological Research.** A specimen is stored in refrigeration at a temperature of 15° Fahrenheit. Biologists remove the specimen and warm it at a controlled rate of 3°F per hour. Express its Celsius temperature as a function of the time t since it was removed from refrigeration.

Strategy We will express the Fahrenheit temperature of the specimen as a function of the time t since it was removed from refrigeration. Then we will express the Celsius temperature of the specimen as a function of its Fahrenheit temperature and find the composition of the two functions.

Why The Celsius temperature of the specimen is a function of its Fahrenheit temperature. Its Fahrenheit temperature is a function of the time since it was removed from refrigeration. This chain of dependence suggests that we write a composition of functions.

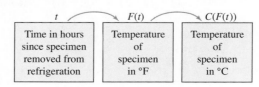

Solution The temperature of the specimen is 15°F when the time $t = 0$. Because it warms at a rate of 3°F per hour, its initial temperature of 15°F increases by $3t$°F in t hours. The Fahrenheit temperature at time t of the specimen is given by the function

$$F(t) = 3t + 15$$

The Celsius temperature C is a function of this Fahrenheit temperature F, given by the function

$$C(F) = \frac{5}{9}(F - 32)$$

To express the specimen's Celsius temperature as a function of *time,* we find the composite function $(C \circ F)(t)$.

$$(C \circ F)(t) = C(F(t)) \qquad \text{Change from } \circ \text{ notation to nested parentheses notation.}$$

$$= C(3t + 15) \qquad \text{Substitute } 3t + 15 \text{ for } F(t).$$

$$= \frac{5}{9}\left(3t + 15 - 32\right) \qquad \begin{array}{l}\text{Find } C(3t + 15) \text{ by substituting } 3t + 15 \text{ for } F \\ \text{in } C(F) = \frac{5}{9}(F - 32).\end{array}$$

$$= \frac{5}{9}(3t - 17) \qquad \text{Subtract within the parentheses: } 15 - 32 = -17.$$

$$= \frac{15}{9}t - \frac{85}{9} \qquad \text{Distribute the multiplication by } \frac{5}{9}.$$

$$= \frac{5}{3}t - \frac{85}{9} \qquad \text{Simplify } \frac{15}{9} : \frac{\overset{1}{\cancel{3}} \cdot 5}{\underset{1}{\cancel{3}} \cdot 3} = \frac{5}{3}.$$

The composite function, $C(t) = \frac{5}{3}t - \frac{85}{9}$, gives the temperature of the specimen in degrees Celsius t hours after it is removed from refrigeration.

Self Check 6 **Weather Forecasting.** A low-pressure area is bringing in colder weather for the next 12 hours. The temperature is now 86° Fahrenheit and is expected to fall 3° every 2 hours. Write a composite function that expresses the Celsius temperature as a function of the number of hours from now.

Now Try ▶ Problem 87

SECTION 11.1 ▶ **STUDY SET**

VOCABULARY

Fill in the blanks.

1. The _____ of f and g, denoted as $f + g$, is defined by $(f + g)(x) =$ _____ and the _____ of f and g, denoted as $f - g$, is defined by $(f - g)(x) =$ _____.

2. The _____ of f and g, denoted as $f \cdot g$, is defined by $(f \cdot g)(x) =$ _____ and the _____ of f and g, denoted as f/g, is defined by $(f/g)(x) =$ _____.

3. The _____ of the function $f + g$ is the set of real numbers x that are in the domain of both f and g.

4. The _____ function $f \circ g$ is defined by $(f \circ g)(x) =$ _____.

5. When we write $(f \circ g)(x)$ as $f(g(x))$, we have changed from $\circ$ notation to _____ parentheses notation.

6. When reading the notation $f(g(x))$, we say "f ____ g ____ x."

CONCEPTS

7. Fill in the blanks.
   a. $(f \circ g)(3) = f($ _____ $)$
   b. To find $f(g(3))$, we first find _____ and then substitute that value for x in $f(x)$.

8. a. If $f(x) = 3x + 1$ and $g(x) = 1 - 2x$, find $f(g(3))$ and $g(f(3))$.
   b. Is the composition of functions commutative?

9. Fill in the three blanks in the drawing of the function machines that show how to compute $g(f(-2))$.

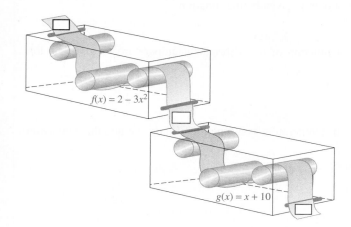

10. If $f(x) = x^2 + 3$ and $g(x) = x - 4$, then $(f/g)(x) = \dfrac{x^2 + 3}{x - 4}$.

    a. What value of x makes $g(x) = 0$?

    b. Fill in the blank: The domain of f/g is $(-\infty, 4)$ ▩ $(4, \infty)$.

NOTATION

Complete each solution.

11. Let $f(x) = 3x - 1$ and $g(x) = 2x + 3$. Find $f \cdot g$.

$$(f \cdot g)(x) = f(x) \cdot \boxed{}$$
$$= \boxed{} \ (2x + 3)$$
$$= 6x^2 + \boxed{} - \boxed{} - 3$$
$$(f \cdot g)(x) = 6x^2 + 7x - 3$$

12. Let $f(x) = 3x - 1$ and $g(x) = 2x + 3$. Find $f \circ g$.

$$(f \circ g)(x) = f(\boxed{})$$
$$= f(\boxed{})$$
$$= 3(\boxed{}) - 1$$
$$= \boxed{} + \boxed{} - 1$$
$$(f \circ g)(x) = 6x + 8$$

GUIDED PRACTICE

Let $f(x) = 2x + 1$ and $g(x) = x - 3$. Find each function and give its domain. **See Example 1.**

13. $f + g$

14. $f - g$

15. $g - f$

16. $g + f$

17. $f \cdot g$

18. f/g

19. g/f

20. $g \cdot f$

Let $f(x) = 3x$ and $g(x) = 4x$. Find each function and give its domain. **See Example 1.**

21. $f + g$
22. $f - g$

23. $g - f$

24. $g + f$

25. $f \cdot g$

26. f/g

27. g/f

28. $g \cdot f$

Let $f(x) = 2x - 5$ and $g(x) = x + 1$. Find each of the following function values. **See Example 2.**

29. $(f + g)(8)$

30. $(f - g)(-4)$

31. $(f \cdot g)(0)$

32. $(f/g)(2)$

Let $s(x) = 3 - x$ and $t(x) = x^2 - x - 6$. Find each function value. **See Example 2.**

33. $(s \cdot t)(-2)$

34. $(s + t)(3)$

35. $(s/t)(1)$

36. $(s - t)(12)$

Let $f(x) = 2x + 1$ and $g(x) = x^2 - 1$. Find each of the following. **See Example 3.**

37. $(f \circ g)(2)$

38. $(g \circ f)(2)$

39. $(g \circ f)(-3)$

40. $(f \circ g)(-3)$

41. $(f \circ g)\left(\dfrac{1}{2}\right)$

42. $(g \circ f)\left(\dfrac{1}{3}\right)$

43. $(g \circ f)(2x)$

44. $(f \circ g)(2x)$

Refer to graphs at the right. Find each function value. **See Example 4.**

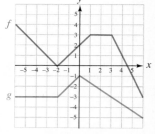

45. a. $(f + g)(-5)$

    b. $(f - g)(3)$

    c. $(f \cdot g)(-3)$

46. a. $(f/g)(0)$

    b. $(f \circ g)(3)$

    c. $(g \circ f)(2)$

Refer to graphs at the right. Find each function value. **See Example 4.**

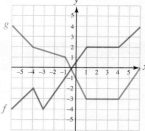

47. a. $(g + f)(2)$

    b. $(g - f)(-5)$

    c. $(g \cdot f)(1)$

48. a. $(g/f)(-6)$

    b. $(g \circ f)(4)$

    c. $(f \circ g)(6)$

Find $f(x)$ and $g(x)$ such that $h(x) = (f \circ g)(x)$. Answers may vary. **See Example 5.**

49. $h(x) = (x + 15)^2$

50. $h(x) = (x - 9)^3$

51. $h(x) = x^5 + 9$

52. $h(x) = x^6 - 100$

53. $h(x) = \sqrt{16x - 1}$

54. $h(x) = \sqrt[3]{10 - x}$

55. $h(x) = \dfrac{1}{x - 4}$

56. $h(x) = \dfrac{1}{3x - 16}$

TRY IT YOURSELF

Let f(x) = 3x − 2 and g(x) = x² + x. Find each of the following.

57. $(f \circ g)(4)$

58. $(g \circ f)(4)$

59. $(g \circ f)(-3)$

60. $(f \circ g)(-3)$

61. $(g \circ f)(0)$

62. $(f \circ g)(0)$

63. $(g \circ f)(x)$

64. $(f \circ g)(x)$

Let f(x) = 3x − 2 and g(x) = 2x² + 1. Find each function and give its domain.

65. $f - g$

66. $f + g$

67. f/g

68. $f \cdot g$

Let f(x) = $\frac{1}{x}$ and g(x) = $\frac{1}{x^2}$. Find each of the following.

69. $(g \circ f)\left(\dfrac{1}{3}\right)$

70. $(g \circ f)\left(\dfrac{1}{10}\right)$

71. $(g \circ f)(8x)$

72. $(f \circ g)(5x)$

Let f(x) = x² − 1 and g(x) = x² − 4. Find each function and give its domain.

73. $f - g$

74. $f + g$

75. g/f

76. $g \cdot f$

Let h(t) = $\sqrt{t + 3}$ and k(t) = t − 5. Find each of the following.

77. $(h \circ k)(18)$

78. $(h \circ k)(11)$

79. $(k \circ h)(22)$

80. $(k \circ h)(-2)$

81. Use the tables of values for functions f and g to find each of the following.

   a. $(f + g)(1)$

   b. $(f - g)(5)$

   c. $(f \cdot g)(1)$

   d. $(g/f)(5)$

x	f(x)
1	3
5	8

x	g(x)
1	4
5	0

82. Use the table of values for functions f and g to find each of the following.

   a. $(f \circ g)(1)$

   b. $(g \circ f)(2)$

x	f(x)
2	5
4	7

x	g(x)
1	2
5	-3

83. If $f(x) = x + 1$ and $g(x) = 2x - 5$, show that $(f \circ g)(x) \neq (g \circ f)(x)$.

84. If $f(x) = x^2 + 1$ and $g(x) = 3x^2 - 2$, show that $(f \circ g)(x) \neq (g \circ f)(x)$.

APPLICATIONS

85. **SAT Scores.**   The graph of function m in the next column gives the average score on the mathematics portion of the SAT college entrance exam, the graph of function r gives the average score on the critical reading portion, and x represents the number of years since 2000.

   a. Find $(m + r)(4)$ and explain what information about SAT scores it gives.

   b. Find $(m - r)(4)$ and explain what information about SAT scores it gives.

   c. Find: $(m + r)(9)$

   d. Find: $(m - r)(9)$

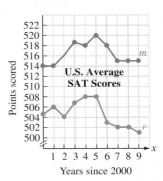

Source: National Center for Education Statistics

86. **Bachelor's Degrees.**   The graph of function m below gives the number of bachelor's degrees awarded to men, and the graph of function w gives the number of bachelor's degrees awarded to women in the U. S. for the years 1990 through 2008.

   a. Estimate $(w + m)(2004)$ and explain what information about bachelor's degrees it gives.

   b. Estimate $(w - m)(2004)$ and explain what information about bachelor's degrees it gives.

   c. Estimate: $(w + m)(1994)$

   d. Estimate: $(w - m)(2000)$

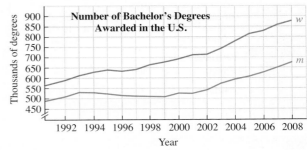

Source: National Center for Education Statistics

87. **Metallurgy.**   A molten alloy must be cooled slowly to control crystallization. When removed from the furnace, its temperature is 2,700°F, and it will be cooled at 200° per hour. Write a composition function that expresses the Celsius temperature as a function of the number of hours t since cooling began. (*Hint*: $C(F) = \frac{5}{9}(F - 32)$.)

88. **Weather Forecasting.**   A high-pressure area promises increasingly warmer weather for the next 48 hours. The temperature is now 34° Celsius and is expected to rise 1° every 6 hours. Write a composition function that expresses the Fahrenheit temperature as a function of the number of hours from now. (*Hint*: $F(C) = \frac{9}{5}C + 32$.)

89. Vacation Mileage Costs.

a. Use the following graphs to determine the cost of the gasoline consumed if a family drove 500 miles on a summer vacation.

b. Write a composition function that expresses the cost of the gasoline consumed on the vacation as a function of the miles driven.

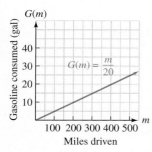
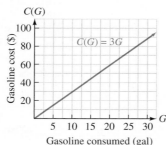

90. Halloween Costumes. The tables on the back of a pattern package can be used to determine the number of yards of material needed to make a rabbit costume for a child.

a. How many yards of material are needed if the child's chest measures 29 inches?

b. In this exercise, one quantity is a function of a second quantity that depends, in turn, on a third quantity. Explain this dependence.

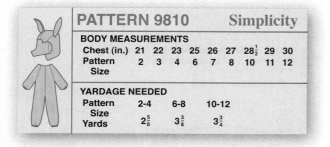

PATTERN 9810   **Simplicity**

BODY MEASUREMENTS

Chest (in.)	21	22	23	25	26	27	28½	29	30
Pattern Size	2	3	4	6	7	8	10	11	12

YARDAGE NEEDED

Pattern Size	2-4	6-8	10-12
Yards	$2\frac{5}{8}$	$3\frac{3}{8}$	$3\frac{3}{4}$

WRITING

91. Exercise 89 illustrates a chain of dependence between the cost of the gasoline, the gasoline consumed, and the miles driven. Describe another chain of dependence that could be represented by a composition function.

92. In this section, what operations are performed on functions? Give an example of each.

93. Write out in words how to say each of the following:

$$(f \circ g)(2) \qquad g(f(-8))$$

94. If $Y_1 = f(x)$ and $Y_2 = g(x)$, explain how to use the following tables to find $g(f(2))$.

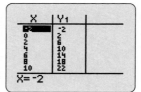

REVIEW

Simplify each complex fraction.

95. $\dfrac{\dfrac{ac - ad - c + d}{a^3 - 1}}{\dfrac{c^2 - 2cd + d^2}{a^2 + a + 1}}$

96. $\dfrac{2 + \dfrac{1}{x^2 - 1}}{1 + \dfrac{1}{x - 1}}$

CHALLENGE PROBLEMS

Fill in the blanks.

97. If $f(x) = x^2$ and $g(x) =$ [blank], then $(f \circ g)(x) = 4x^2 + 20x + 25$.

98. If $f(x) = \sqrt{3x}$ and $g(x) =$ [blank], then $(g \circ f)(x) = 9x^2 + 7$.

Refer to the following graphs of functions f and g.

99. Graph the sum function $f + g$ on the given coordinate system.

100. Graph the difference function $f - g$ on the given coordinate system.

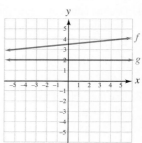

SECTION

Inverse Functions

OBJECTIVES

1 Determine whether a function is a one-to-one function.

2 Use the horizontal line test to determine whether a function is one-to-one.

3 Find the equation of the inverse of a function.

4 Find the composition of a function and its inverse.

5 Graph a function and its inverse.

ARE YOU READY?

The following problems review some basic skills that are needed when working with inverse functions.

1. What are the domain and the range of the function $\{(-2, 8), (3, -3), (5, 10), (9, 1)\}$?

2. Is a parabola that opens upward the graph of a function?

3. Fill in the blank: If y is a _____ of x, the symbols y and $f(x)$ are interchangeable.

4. Let $f(x) = 2x + 6$. Find $f(8x)$.

In the previous section, we created new functions from given functions by using the operations of arithmetic and composition. Another way to create new functions is to find the *inverse of a function*.

1 Determine Whether a Function Is a One-to-One Function.

In figure (a) below, the arrow diagram defines a function f. If we reverse the arrows as shown in figure (b), we obtain a new correspondence where the range of f becomes the domain of the new correspondence, and the domain of f becomes the range. The new correspondence is a function because to each member of the domain, there corresponds exactly one member of the range. We call this new correspondence the **inverse** of f, or f inverse.

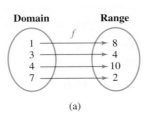

This reversing process does not always produce a function. For example, if we reverse the arrows in function g defined by the diagram in figure (a) below, the resulting correspondence shown in figure (b) is not a function. This is because to the number 2 in the domain, there corresponds two members of the range: 8 and 4.

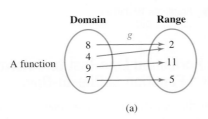
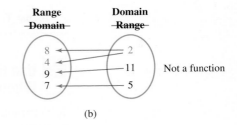

The question that arises is, "What must be true of an original function to guarantee that the reversing process produces a function?" The answer is: *The original function must be one-to-one.*

We have seen that in a function, each input determines exactly one output. For some functions, different inputs determine different outputs, as in figure (a) below. For other functions, different inputs might determine the *same* output, as in figure (b). When a function has the property that different inputs determine different outputs, as in figure (a), we say the function is *one-to-one*.

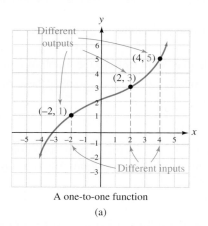

A one-to-one function

(a)

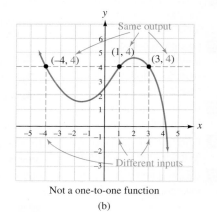

Not a one-to-one function

(b)

One-to-One Functions   ▼   A function is called a **one-to-one function** if different inputs determine different outputs.

EXAMPLE 1   Determine whether each function is one-to-one.   **a.** $f(x) = x^2$ **b.** $f(x) = x^3$

Strategy   We will determine whether different inputs have different outputs.

Why   If different inputs have different outputs, the function is one-to-one. If different inputs have the same output, the function is not one-to-one.

Solution   **a.** Since two different inputs, -3 and 3, have the same output 9, $f(x) = x^2$ is not a one-to-one function.

$$f(-3) = (-3)^2 = 9 \text{ and } f(3) = 3^2 = 9$$

x	$f(x)$
-3	9
3	9

The output 9 does not correspond to exactly one input.

b. Since different numbers have different cubes, each input of $f(x) = x^3$ determines a different output. This function is one-to-one.

Success Tip

Example 1 illustrates that not every function is one-to-one.

Self Check 1   Determine whether each function is one-to-one. If not, find an output that corresponds to more than one input.   **a.** $f(x) = 2x + 3$
b. $f(x) = x^4$

Now Try ▶ Problems 19 and 21

---

2 Use the Horizontal Line Test to Determine Whether a Function Is One-to-One.

To determine whether a function is one-to-one, it is often easier to view its graph rather than its defining equation. If two (or more) points on the graph of a function have the same y-coordinate, the function is not one-to-one. This observation suggests the following **horizontal line test.**

The Horizontal Line Test   ▼   A function is one-to-one if each horizontal line that intersects its graph does so exactly once.

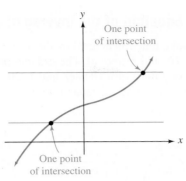

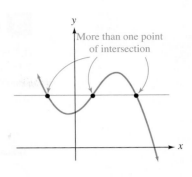

A one-to-one function   Not a one-to-one function

EXAMPLE 2   Use the horizontal line test to determine whether the following graphs of functions represent one-to-one functions.

Strategy   We will draw horizontal lines through the graph of the function and see how many times each line intersects the graph.

Why   If each horizontal line intersects the graph of the function exactly once, the graph represents a one-to-one function. If any horizontal line intersects the graph of the function more than once, the graph does not represent a one-to-one function.

Solution   **a.** Because every horizontal line that intersects the graph of $f(x) = -\frac{3}{4}x - 2$ in figure (a) does so exactly once, the graph represents a one-to-one function. We simply say, the function $f(x) = -\frac{3}{4}x - 2$ is one-to-one.

b. Refer to figure (b). Because we can draw a horizontal line that intersects the graph of $f(x) = x^2 - 4$ twice, the graph does not represent a one-to-one function. We simply say, the function $f(x) = x^2 - 4$ is not one-to-one.

c. Because every horizontal line that intersects the graph of $f(x) = \sqrt{x}$ in figure (c) does so exactly once, the graph represents a one-to-one function. We simply say, the function $f(x) = \sqrt{x}$ is one-to-one.

> **Success Tip**
>
> Recall that we use the **vertical line test** to determine whether a graph represents a function. We use the **horizontal line test** to determine whether the function that is graphed is one-to-one.

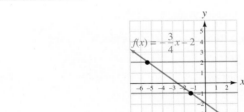

(a)

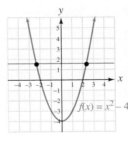

(b)

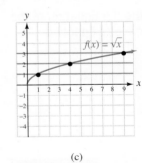

(c)

Self Check 2   Use the horizontal line test to determine whether the graph represents a one-to-one function.

a.

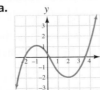

b.

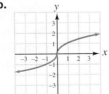

Now Try ▶ Problems 27 and 29

3 Find the Equation of the Inverse of a Function.

If f is the one-to-one function defined by the arrow diagram in figure (a), it turns the number 1 into 10, 2 into 20, and 3 into 30. The ordered pairs that define f can be listed in a table. Since the inverse of f must turn 10 back into 1, 20 back into 2, and 30 back into 3, it consists of the ordered pairs shown in the table in figure (b).

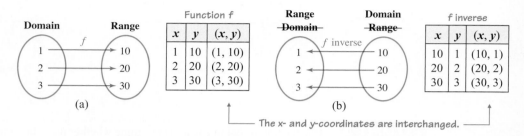

The x- and y-coordinates are interchanged.

Caution

The -1 in the notation $f^{-1}(x)$ is not an exponent:

$$f^{-1}(x) \neq \frac{1}{f(x)}$$

We note that the domain of f and the range of its inverse is $\{1, 2, 3\}$. The range of f and the domain of its inverse is $\{10, 20, 30\}$.

This example suggests that to form the inverse of a function f, we simply interchange the coordinates of each ordered pair that determines f. When the inverse of a function is also a function, we call it **f inverse** and denote it with the symbol f^{-1}. The symbol $f^{-1}(x)$ is read as "the inverse of $f(x)$" or "f inverse of x."

The Inverse of a Function

If f is a one-to-one function consisting of ordered pairs of the form (x, y), **the inverse of** f, denoted f^{-1}, is the one-to-one function consisting of all ordered pairs of the form (y, x).

When a one-to-one function is defined by an equation, we use the following method to find the equation of its inverse.

Finding the Equation of the Inverse of a Function

If a function is one-to-one, we find its inverse as follows:

1. If the function is written using function notation, replace $f(x)$ with y.
2. Interchange the variables x and y.
3. Solve the resulting equation for y.
4. Substitute $f^{-1}(x)$ for y.

EXAMPLE 3 Determine whether each function is one-to-one. If so, find the equation of its inverse.
a. $f(x) = 4x + 2$ **b.** $f(x) = x^3$

Strategy We will determine whether each function is one-to-one. If it is, we can find the equation of its inverse by replacing $f(x)$ with y, interchanging x and y, and solving for y.

Why The reason for interchanging the variables is this: If a one-to-one function takes an input x into an output y, by definition, its inverse function has the reverse effect.

Solution **a.** We recognize $f(x) = 4x + 2$ as a linear function whose graph is a straight line with slope 4 and y-intercept $(0, 2)$. Since such a graph would pass the horizontal line test, we conclude that f is one-to-one.

To find the inverse of function f, we proceed as follows:

$$f(x) = 4x + 2 \qquad \text{Function } f \text{ multiplies all inputs by 4 and then adds 2.}$$

$$y = 4x + 2 \qquad \text{Replace } f(x) \text{ with } y.$$

$$x = 4y + 2 \qquad \text{Interchange the variables } x \text{ and } y.$$

$$x - 2 = 4y \qquad \text{To isolate the term } 4y, \text{ subtract 2 from both sides.}$$

$$\frac{x - 2}{4} = y \qquad \text{To solve for } y, \text{ divide both sides by 4.}$$

$$y = \frac{x - 2}{4} \qquad \text{Write the equation with } y \text{ on the left side.}$$

> **Success Tip**
>
> Recall that $f(x) = 4x + 2$ is a linear function. Every linear function, except those of the form $f(x) = c$, where c is a constant, is one-to-one.

To denote that this equation is the inverse of function f, we replace y with $f^{-1}(x)$.

$$f^{-1}(x) = \frac{x - 2}{4} \qquad \text{Function } f^{-1} \text{ subtracts 2 from each input and then divides by 4.}$$

As an informal check, we see below that if $x = 1$, function f produces an output of 6. And if $x = 6$, function f^{-1} produces an output of 1.

$$f(\mathbf{1}) = 4(\mathbf{1}) + 2 \qquad\qquad f^{-1}(\mathbf{6}) = \frac{\mathbf{6} - 2}{4}$$

$$= 4 + 2 \qquad\qquad\qquad\quad = \frac{4}{4}$$

$$= 6 \qquad\qquad\qquad\qquad = 1$$

$$\text{Ordered pair: } (\mathbf{1}, \mathbf{6}) \qquad\qquad \text{Ordered pair: } (\mathbf{6}, \mathbf{1})$$

The coordinates are interchanged.

> **Success Tip**
>
> Notice that f^{-1} operates on an input using the inverse operations of f in the reverse order.

b. The graph of $f(x) = x^3$ is shown on the right. Since such a graph would pass the horizontal line test, we conclude that f is a one-to-one function.

To find its inverse, we proceed as follows:

$$f(x) = x^3 \qquad \text{Function } f \text{ cubes all inputs.}$$

$$y = x^3 \qquad \text{Replace } f(x) \text{ with } y.$$

$$x = y^3 \qquad \text{Interchange the variables } x \text{ and } y.$$

$$\sqrt[3]{x} = y \qquad \text{To solve for } y, \text{ take the cube root of both sides.}$$

$$y = \sqrt[3]{x} \qquad \text{Write the equation with } y \text{ on the left side.}$$

> **Caution**
>
> Only one-to-one functions have inverse functions.

Replacing y with $f^{-1}(x)$, we have

$$f^{-1}(x) = \sqrt[3]{x} \qquad \text{Function } f^{-1} \text{ finds the cube root of each input.}$$

As an informal check, let $x = 4$ and determine whether f and f^{-1} produce ordered pairs whose coordinates are reversed.

> **Self Check 3**   Determine whether each function is one-to-one. If it is, find the equation of its inverse.   **a.** $f(x) = -5x - 3$
> **b.** $f(x) = x^5$

Now Try ▶   Problems 35 and 45

4   Find the Composition of a Function and Its Inverse.

To emphasize a relationship between a function and its inverse, we substitute some number x, such as $x = 3$, into the function $f(x) = 4x + 2$ of Example 3(a). The corresponding value of y that is produced is

$$f(3) = 4(3) + 2 = 14 \qquad f \text{ determines the ordered pair } (3, 14).$$

If we substitute 14 into the inverse function, $f^{-1}(x) = \frac{x-2}{4}$, the corresponding value of y that is produced is

$$f^{-1}(14) = \frac{14-2}{4} = 3 \quad \text{\small$f^{-1}$ determines the ordered pair (14, 3).}$$

Thus, the function f turns 3 into 14, and the inverse function f^{-1} turns 14 back into 3.

In general, the composition of a function and its inverse function is the identity function, $f(x) = x$, such that any input x has the output x. This fact can be stated symbolically as follows.

The Composition of Inverse Functions	For any one-to-one function f and its inverse, f^{-1}, $$(f \circ f^{-1})(x) = x \quad \text{and} \quad (f^{-1} \circ f)(x) = x$$

We can use this property to determine whether two functions are inverses.

EXAMPLE 4   Show that $f(x) = 4x + 2$ and $f^{-1}(x) = \frac{x-2}{4}$ are inverses.

Strategy   We will find the composition of $f(x)$ and $f^{-1}(x)$ in both directions and show that the result is x.

Why   Only when the result of the composition is x in both directions are the functions inverses.

Solution   To show that $f(x) = 4x + 2$ and $f^{-1}(x) = \frac{x-2}{4}$ are inverses, we must show that for each composition, an input of x gives an output of x.

$$
\begin{aligned}
(f \circ f^{-1})(x) &= f(f^{-1}(x)) & (f^{-1} \circ f)(x) &= f^{-1}(f(x)) \\
&= f\left(\frac{x-2}{4}\right) & &= f^{-1}(4x + 2) \\
&= 4\left(\frac{x-2}{4}\right) + 2 & &= \frac{4x + 2 - 2}{4} \\
&= x - 2 + 2 & &= \frac{4x}{4} \\
&= x & &= x
\end{aligned}
$$

Because $(f \circ f^{-1})(x) = x$ and $(f^{-1} \circ f)(x) = x$, the functions are inverses.

Self Check 4   Show that $f(x) = x - 4$ and $g(x) = x + 4$ are inverses.

Now Try ▶ Problem 55

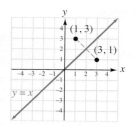

5 Graph a Function and Its Inverse.

If a point (a, b) is on the graph of function f, it follows that the point (b, a) is on the graph of f^{-1}, and vice versa. There is a geometric relationship between a pair of points whose coordinates are interchanged. For example, in the graph, we see that the line segment between $(1, 3)$ and $(3, 1)$ is perpendicular to and cut in half by the line $y = x$. We say that $(1, 3)$ and $(3, 1)$ are mirror images of each other with respect to $y = x$.

Since each point on the graph of f^{-1} is a mirror image of a point on the graph of f, and vice versa, the graphs of f and f^{-1} must be mirror images of each other with respect to $y = x$.

| **EXAMPLE 5** | Find the equation of the inverse of $f(x) = -\frac{3}{2}x + 3$. Then graph f and its inverse on one coordinate system. |

Strategy We will determine whether the function has an inverse. If so, we will replace $f(x)$ with y, interchange x and y, and solve for y to obtain the equation of the inverse.

Why The reason for interchanging the variables is this: If a one-to-one function takes an input x into an output y, by definition, its inverse function has the reverse effect.

Solution Since $f(x) = -\frac{3}{2}x + 3$ is a linear function, it is one-to-one and has an inverse. To find the inverse function, we replace $f(x)$ with y, and interchange x and y to obtain

$$x = -\frac{3}{2}y + 3$$

Then we solve for y to get

$$x - 3 = -\frac{3}{2}y \qquad \text{Subtract 3 from both sides.}$$

$$-\frac{2}{3}x + 2 = y \qquad \text{To isolate } y, \text{ multiply both sides by } -\frac{2}{3}.$$

When we replace y with $f^{-1}(x)$, we have $f^{-1}(x) = -\frac{2}{3}x + 2$.

To graph f, we construct a table of values, plot points, and draw the graph in red as shown below. To graph f^{-1}, we don't need to do any calculations to construct a table of values. We can simply interchange the coordinates of the ordered pairs in the table for f and use them to graph f^{-1}. The result is the graph in blue shown below. Because the functions are inverses of each other, their graphs are **mirror images** about the line $y = x$.

Success Tip

If the graphs of f and f^{-1} intersect, it will always be on the line $y = x$.

$f(x) = -\frac{3}{2}x + 3$ $f^{-1}(x) = -\frac{2}{3}x + 2$

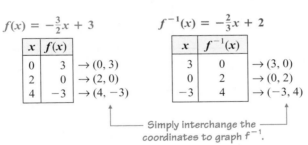

x	$f(x)$	
0	3	$\rightarrow (0, 3)$
2	0	$\rightarrow (2, 0)$
4	-3	$\rightarrow (4, -3)$

x	$f^{-1}(x)$	
3	0	$\rightarrow (3, 0)$
0	2	$\rightarrow (0, 2)$
-3	4	$\rightarrow (-3, 4)$

Simply interchange the coordinates to graph f^{-1}.

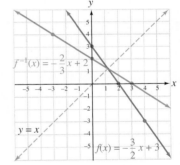

| **Self Check 5** | Find the inverse of $f(x) = \frac{2}{3}x - 2$. Then graph the function and its inverse on one coordinate system. |

Now Try Problem 59

Using Your Calculator ▶ Graphing the Inverse of a Function

We can use a graphing calculator to check the result found in Example 5. First, we enter $f(x) = -\frac{3}{2}x + 3$ and then enter what we believe to be the inverse function, $f^{-1}(x) = -\frac{2}{3}x + 2$, as well as the equation $y = x$. See figure (a) on the next page. Before graphing, we adjust the display so that the graphing grid will be composed of squares. The line of symmetry $y = x$ is then at a 45° angle to the positive x-axis.

In figure (b), it appears that the two graphs are symmetric about the line $y = x$. Although it is not definitive, this visual check does help to validate the result of Example 5.

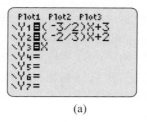

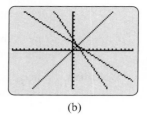

(a)   (b)

EXAMPLE 6   Graph the inverse of function f shown in figure (a).

Strategy   We will find the coordinates of several points on the graph of f in figure (a). After interchanging the coordinates of these points, we will plot them as shown in figure (b).

Why   The reason for interchanging the coordinates is this: If (a, b) is a point on the graph of a one-to-one function, then the point (b, a) is on the graph of its inverse.

Solution   In figure (a), we see that the points $(-5, -3)$, $(-2, -1)$, $(0, 2)$, $(3, 3)$, $(5, 4)$, and $(7, 5)$ lie on the graph of function f. To graph the inverse, we interchange their coordinates, and plot them in blue, as shown in figure (b). Then we graph the line $y = x$ and use symmetry to draw a smooth curve through those points to get the graph of f^{-1}.

The Language of Algebra

We also can say that the graphs of f and f^{-1} are **reflections** of each other about the line $y = x$, or they are **symmetric about** $y = x$.

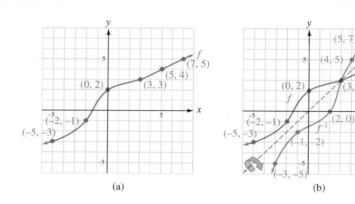

(a)   (b)

Now Try   Problem 65

SECTION 11.2   STUDY SET

VOCABULARY

Fill in the blanks.

1. A function is called a _____ function if different inputs determine different outputs.

2. The _____ line test can be used to determine whether the graph of a function represents a one-to-one function.

3. The functions f and f^{-1} are _____.

4. The graphs of a function and its inverse are _____ images of each other with respect to $y = x$. We also say that their graphs are _____ with respect to the line $y = x$.

CONCEPTS

Fill in the blanks.

5. If any horizontal line that intersects the graph of a function does so more than once, the function is not _____.

6. To find the inverse of the function $f(x) = 2x - 3$, we begin by replacing $f(x)$ with y, and then we _____ x and y.

7. If f is a one-to-one function, the domain of f is the _____ of f^{-1}, and the range of f is the _____ of f^{-1}.

8. If a function turns an input of 2 into an output of 5, the inverse function will turn an input of 5 into the output ▢.

9. If f is a one-to-one function, and if $f(1) = 6$, then $f^{-1}(6) =$ ▢.

10. If the point $(9, -4)$ is on the graph of the one-to-one function f, then the point $($ ▢ , ▢ $)$ is on the graph of f^{-1}.

11. a. Is the correspondence defined by the arrow diagram in figure (a) below a one-to-one function?

  b. Is the correspondence defined by the table in figure (b) below a one-to-one function?

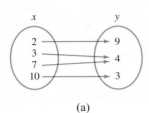

x	$f(x)$
-2	4
-1	1
0	0
2	4
3	9

  (a) (b)

12. Is the inverse of a one-to-one function always a function?

13. Use the table of values of the one-to-one function f to complete a table of values for f^{-1}.

x	$f(x)$
-4	-2
0	0
8	4

x	$f^{-1}(x)$
-2	
0	
4	

14. Redraw the graph of function f. Then graph f^{-1} and the axis of symmetry on the same coordinate system.

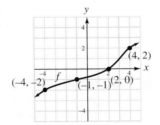

NOTATION

Complete each solution.

15. Find the inverse of $f(x) = 2x - 3$.

$$▢ = 2x - 3$$
$$x = ▢ - 3$$
$$x + ▢ = 2y$$
$$\frac{x + 3}{2} = ▢$$

The inverse of $f(x) = 2x - 3$ is ▢ $(x) = \dfrac{x + 3}{2}$.

16. Find the inverse of $f(x) = \sqrt[3]{x} + 2$.

$$▢ = \sqrt[3]{x} + 2$$
$$x = \sqrt[3]{▢} + 2$$
$$x - ▢ = \sqrt[3]{y}$$
$$(x - 2)^3 = ▢$$

The inverse of $f(x) = \sqrt[3]{x} + 2$ is ▢ $(x) = (x - 2)^3$.

17. The symbol f^{-1} is read as "the _____ of f" or "f _____."

18. Explain the difference in the meaning of the -1 in the notation $f^{-1}(x)$ as compared with a^{-1}.

GUIDED PRACTICE

Determine whether each function is one-to-one. See Example 1.

19. $f(x) = 2x$ **20.** $f(x) = |x|$

21. $f(x) = x^4$ **22.** $f(x) = x^3 + 1$

23. $f(x) = -x^2 + 3x$ **24.** $f(x) = \dfrac{2}{3}x + 8$

25. $\{(1, 1), (2, 1), (3, 1), (4, 1)\}$ **26.** $\{(3, 2), (2, 1), (1, 0)\}$

Each graph represents a function. Use the horizontal line test to determine whether the function is one-to-one. See Example 2.

27.
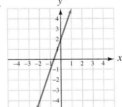

28.
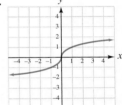

29.
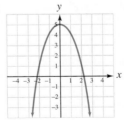

30.
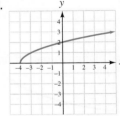

31.
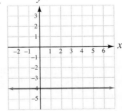

32.
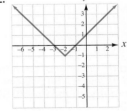

33.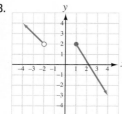

34.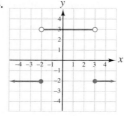

Each of the following functions is one-to-one. Find the inverse of each function and express it using $f^{-1}(x)$ notation. See Example 3.

35. $f(x) = 2x + 4$

36. $f(x) = 5x - 1$

37. $f(x) = \dfrac{x}{5} + \dfrac{4}{5}$

38. $f(x) = \dfrac{x}{3} - \dfrac{1}{3}$

39. $f(x) = \dfrac{x - 4}{5}$

40. $f(x) = \dfrac{2x + 6}{3}$

41. $f(x) = \dfrac{2}{x - 3}$

42. $f(x) = \dfrac{3}{x + 1}$

43. $f(x) = \dfrac{4}{x}$

44. $f(x) = \dfrac{1}{x}$

45. $f(x) = x^3 + 8$

46. $f(x) = x^3 - 4$

47. $f(x) = \sqrt[3]{x}$

48. $f(x) = \sqrt[3]{x - 5}$

49. $f(x) = (x + 10)^3$

50. $f(x) = (x - 9)^3$

51. $f(x) = 2x^3 - 3$

52. $f(x) = \dfrac{3}{x^3} - 1$

53. $f(x) = \dfrac{x^7}{2}$

54. $f(x) = \dfrac{x^9}{4}$

Show that each pair of functions are inverses. See Example 4.

55. $f(x) = 2x + 9,\ f^{-1}(x) = \dfrac{x - 9}{2}$

56. $f(x) = 5x - 1,\ f^{-1}(x) = \dfrac{x + 1}{5}$

57. $f(x) = \dfrac{2}{x - 3},\ f^{-1}(x) = \dfrac{2}{x} + 3$

58. $f(x) = \sqrt[3]{x - 6},\ f^{-1}(x) = x^3 + 6$

Find the inverse of each function. Then graph the function and its inverse on one coordinate system. Show the line of symmetry on the graph. See Examples 5 and 6.

59. $f(x) = 2x$

60. $f(x) = -3x$

61. $f(x) = 4x + 3$

62. $f(x) = \dfrac{x}{3} + \dfrac{1}{3}$

63. $f(x) = -\dfrac{2}{3}x + 3$

64. $f(x) = -\dfrac{1}{3}x + \dfrac{4}{3}$

65. $f(x) = x^3$

66. $f(x) = x^3 + 1$

67. $f(x) = x^2 - 1 \ (x \geq 0)$

68. $f(x) = x^2 + 1 \ (x \geq 0)$

APPLICATIONS

69. Interpersonal Relationships. Feelings of anxiety in a relationship can increase or decrease, depending on what is going on in the relationship. The graph shows how a person's anxiety might vary as a relationship develops over time.

   a. Is this the graph of a function? Is its inverse a function?

   b. Does each anxiety level correspond to exactly one point in time? Use the dashed lined labeled *Maximum threshold* to explain.

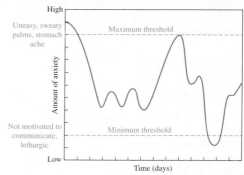

Source: Gudykunst, *Building Bridges: Interpersonal Skills for a Changing World* (Houghton Mifflin, 1994)

70. Lighting Levels. The ability of the eye to see detail increases as the level of illumination increases. This relationship can be modeled by a function E, whose graph is shown here.

   a. From the graph, determine $E(240)$.

   b. Is function E one-to-one? Does E have an inverse?

   c. If the effectiveness of seeing in an office is 7, what is the illumination in the office? How can this question be asked using inverse function notation?

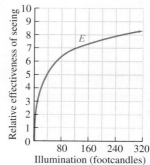

Based on information from *World Book Encyclopedia*

WRITING

71. In your own words, what is a one-to-one function?

72. Two functions are graphed on the square grid on the right along with the line $y = x$. Explain why the functions cannot be inverses of each other.

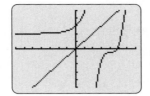

73. Explain how the graph of a one-to-one function can be used to draw the graph of its inverse function.

74. a. Explain the purpose of the vertical line test.

  b. Explain the purpose of the horizontal line test.

75. In the illustration, a function f and its inverse f^{-1} have been graphed on the same coordinate system. Explain what concept can be demonstrated by folding the graph paper on the dashed line.

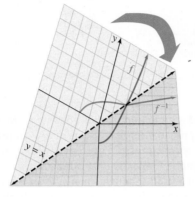

76. Write in words how to read the notation.

  a. $f^{-1}(x) = \dfrac{1}{2}x - 3$

  b. $(f \circ f^{-1})(x) = x$

REVIEW

Simplify. Write the result in the form a + bi.

77. $3 - \sqrt{-64}$

78. $(2 - 3i) + (4 + 5i)$

79. $(3 + 4i)(2 - 3i)$

80. $\dfrac{6 + 7i}{3 - 4i}$

81. $(6 - 8i)^2$

82. i^{100}

CHALLENGE PROBLEMS

83. Find the inverse of $f(x) = \dfrac{x + 1}{x - 1}$.

84. Using the functions of Exercise 83, show that $(f \circ f^{-1})(x) = x$ and $(f^{-1} \circ f)(x) = x$.

85. A table of values for a function f is shown in figure (a). A table of values for f^{-1} is shown in figure (b). Use the tables to find $f^{-1}(f(4))$ and $f(f^{-1}(2))$.

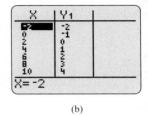

(a)   (b)

86. a. The graph of a one-to-one function lies entirely in quadrant I. In what quadrant does the graph of its inverse lie?

  b. The graph of a one-to-one function lies entirely in quadrant II. In what quadrant does the graph of its inverse lie?

  c. The graph of a one-to-one function lies entirely in quadrant III. In what quadrant does the graph of its inverse lie?

  d. The graph of a one-to-one function lies entirely in quadrant IV. In what quadrant does the graph of its inverse lie?

SECTION 11.3

Exponential Functions

OBJECTIVES

1 Define exponential functions.

2 Graph exponential functions.

3 Use exponential functions in applications involving growth or decay.

ARE YOU READY?

The following problems review some basic skills that are needed when working with exponential functions.

1. Simplify: **a.** $3^4 \cdot 3^8$ 9^{12} **b.** $(3^4)^8$ $(3)^{24}$

2. Evaluate: **a.** 2^3 8 **b.** 2^0 1 **c.** 2^{-2} $\frac{1}{4}$

3. Evaluate: **a.** $\left(\dfrac{1}{3}\right)^2$ $\frac{1}{9}$ **b.** $\left(\dfrac{1}{3}\right)^0$ 1 **c.** $\left(\dfrac{1}{3}\right)^{-3}$ 27

4. Fill in the blanks: The graph of $f(x) = x$ is a $\underline{line}$ and the graph of $f(x) = x^2$ is a $\underline{parabola}$

In previous chapters, we have discussed linear functions, polynomial functions, rational functions, and radical functions. We now begin a study of a new family of functions known as *exponential functions*.

As an example, consider the graph in figure (a) below, which models the soaring popularity of the social network website Twitter in recent years. The rapidly rising red curve is the graph of an exponential function.

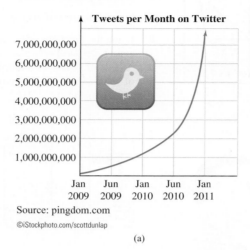

Tweets per Month on Twitter

Source: pingdom.com
©iStockphoto.com/scottdunlap

(a)

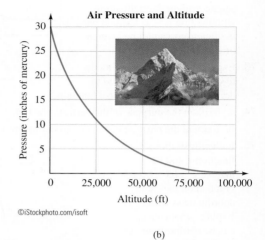

Air Pressure and Altitude

©iStockphoto.com/isoft

(b)

If you have ever climbed a high mountain or gone up in an airplane that does not have a pressurized cabin, you have probably felt the effects of low air pressure. The graph in figure (b) above shows how the atmospheric pressure decreases with increasing altitude. The rapidly falling red curve is also the graph of an exponential function.

Exponential functions are used to model many other situations, such as population growth, the spread of an epidemic, the temperature of a heated object as it cools, and radioactive decay.

1 Define Exponential Functions.

In this course, we have evaluated exponential expressions with integer exponents, such as 2^5, 7^0, and 5^{-1}, and rational number exponents, such as $9^{1/2}$, $64^{3/4}$, and $8^{-2/3}$. To define exponential functions, we also must be able to evaluate exponential expressions that have irrational exponents. For example, let's consider the expression

$$5^{\sqrt{2}} \text{ where } \sqrt{2} \text{ is the irrational number } 1.414213562\ldots$$

We can successively approximate $5^{\sqrt{2}}$ using the following *rational* powers:

$$5^{1.4}, \quad 5^{1.41}, \quad 5^{1.414}, \quad 5^{1.4142}, \quad 5^{1.41421}, \ldots$$

Using concepts from advanced mathematics, it can be shown that there is exactly one number that these powers approach. We define $5^{\sqrt{2}}$ to be that number. This process can be used to approximate $5^{\sqrt{2}}$ to as many decimal places as desired. Any other positive irrational exponent can be defined in the same manner, and negative irrational exponents can be defined using reciprocals.

This discussion leads us to the following conclusion: If b is positive, the exponential expression b^x has meaning and can be evaluated for any real number exponent x. Furthermore, it can be shown that all of the familiar rules of exponents are also true for irrational exponents.

Using Your Calculator ▶ Evaluating Exponential Expressions

We can use a calculator to obtain a very good approximation of an exponential expression with an irrational exponent. To find the value of $5^{\sqrt{2}}$ with a reverse entry scientific calculator, we enter:

$$5 \boxed{y^x} \, 2 \, \boxed{\sqrt{}} \, = \qquad\qquad \boxed{9.738517742}$$

With a direct entry graphing calculator, we enter:

5 $\boxed{\wedge}$ $\boxed{\text{2nd}}$ $\boxed{\sqrt{}}$ 2 $\boxed{)}$ $\boxed{\text{ENTER}}$

```
5^√(2)
          9.738517742
```

If $b > 0$ and $b \neq 1$, the function $f(x) = b^x$ is called an **exponential function.** Since x can be any real number, its domain is the set of real numbers, which can be written as $(-\infty, \infty)$.

Because b is positive, the value of $f(x)$ is positive, and the range is the set of positive numbers, which can be written as $(0, \infty)$.

Since $b \neq 1$, an exponential function cannot be the constant function $f(x) = 1^x$, in which $f(x) = 1$ for every real number x.

Exponential Functions   ▼   An **exponential function with base b** is defined by the equations

$$f(x) = b^x \quad \text{or} \quad y = b^x$$

where $b > 0$, $b \neq 1$, and x is a real number. The domain of $f(x) = b^x$ is the interval $(-\infty, \infty)$, and the range is the interval $(0, \infty)$.

Exponential functions have a *constant base* and a *variable exponent.* Some examples of exponential functions are:

$$f(x) = 2^x \qquad g(x) = \left(\frac{1}{3}\right)^x \qquad s(x) = 4^{x+1} \qquad P(t) = (1.45)^{-3.04t}$$

The base is 2.   The base is $\frac{1}{3}$.   The base is 4.   The base is 1.45.

In the third example, we see that the exponent of an exponential function doesn't have to be just x. It can be a variable expression, such as $x + 1$. In the fourth example, we see that the base can be a positive decimal, and the input variable can be a letter other than x.

The following functions are not exponential functions.

$$f(x) = x^2 \qquad g(x) = x^{1/3} \qquad\qquad h(x) = (-4)^x \qquad\qquad f(x) = 1^x$$

These have a variable base   The base cannot be negative.   The base cannot be 1.
and a constant exponent.

2 Graph Exponential Functions.

Since the domain and range of $f(x) = b^x$ are sets of real numbers, we can graph exponential functions on a rectangular coordinate system. To do this, we will use the familiar **point-plotting method.**

EXAMPLE 1   Graph: $f(x) = 2^x$

Strategy   We will graph the function by creating a table of function values and plotting the corresponding ordered pairs.

Why   After drawing a smooth curve through the plotted points, we will have the graph.

Solution   To graph $f(x) = 2^x$, we select several values for x and find the corresponding values of $f(x)$. If x is -3, and if x is -2, we have:

Caution

We have previously graphed the linear function $f(x) = 2x$ and the squaring function $f(x) = x^2$. For the exponential function $f(x) = 2^x$, note that the variable is in the exponent.

$$f(x) = 2^x$$
$$f(-3) = 2^{-3} \quad \text{Substitute } -3 \text{ for x.}$$
$$= \frac{1}{2^3}$$
$$= \frac{1}{8}$$

$$f(x) = 2^x$$
$$f(-2) = 2^{-2} \quad \text{Substitute } -2 \text{ for x.}$$
$$= \frac{1}{2^2}$$
$$= \frac{1}{4}$$

The points $\left(-3, \frac{1}{8}\right)$ and $\left(-2, \frac{1}{4}\right)$ are on the graph of $f(x) = 2^x$. In a similar way, we find the corresponding values of $f(x)$ for x values of -1, 0, 1, 2, 3, and 4 and list them in a table. Then we plot the ordered pairs and draw a smooth curve through them, as shown below. Notice with the ordered pairs, as the value of x increases, the value of y also increases, but very rapidly as compared with x. This graph is an example of **exponential growth.**

$f(x) = 2^x$

x	$f(x)$	
-3	$\frac{1}{8}$	$\rightarrow \left(-3, \frac{1}{8}\right)$
-2	$\frac{1}{4}$	$\rightarrow \left(-2, \frac{1}{4}\right)$
-1	$\frac{1}{2}$	$\rightarrow \left(-1, \frac{1}{2}\right)$
0	1	$\rightarrow (0, 1)$
1	2	$\rightarrow (1, 2)$
2	4	$\rightarrow (2, 4)$
3	8	$\rightarrow (3, 8)$
4	16	$\rightarrow (4, 16)$

Because of the variable exponent in their equations, the graphs of exponential functions rise or fall sharply. When graphing them, make sure you plot enough points to show this.

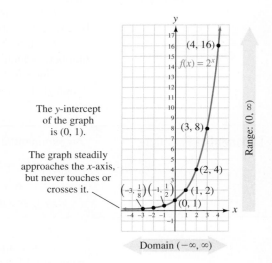

The y-intercept of the graph is (0, 1).

The graph steadily approaches the x-axis, but never touches or crosses it.

Range: $(0, \infty)$

Domain $(-\infty, \infty)$

By the vertical line test, we see that this is indeed the graph of a function. Because the graph extends indefinitely to the left and right, the projection of the graph onto the x-axis includes all real numbers. Thus, the domain of $f(x) = 2^x$ is $(-\infty, \infty)$.

Because the projection of the graph onto the y-axis covers only the positive portion of that axis, the range of the function is $(0, \infty)$. Since the graph passes the horizontal line test, the function is one-to-one.

Note that as x decreases, the values of $f(x)$ decrease and approach 0. Thus, the x-axis is a **horizontal asymptote** of the graph. The graph does not have an x-intercept, the y-intercept is (0, 1), and the graph passes through the point (1, 2).

Self Check 1   Graph: $g(x) = 4^x$

Now Try ▶ Problem 19

Exponential functions can have a base that is a real number between 0 and 1.

EXAMPLE 2   Graph: $f(x) = \left(\frac{1}{3}\right)^x$

Strategy   We will graph the function by creating a table of function values and plotting the corresponding ordered pairs.

Why   After drawing a smooth curve through the plotted points, we will have the graph.

Solution   If $x = -2$ and if $x = -1$, we have

Success Tip

Since $\frac{1}{3} = 3^{-1}$, and since the rules for exponents hold for any real number, we can rewrite this function as:

$$f(x) = \left(\frac{1}{3}\right)^x = (3^{-1})^x = 3^{-x}$$

$$f(x) = \left(\frac{1}{3}\right)^x$$

$$f(-2) = \left(\frac{1}{3}\right)^{-2}$$

$$= \left(\frac{3}{1}\right)^2 \quad \text{Recall: } \left(\frac{x}{y}\right)^{-n} = \left(\frac{y}{x}\right)^n.$$

$$= 9$$

$$f(x) = \left(\frac{1}{3}\right)^x$$

$$f(-1) = \left(\frac{1}{3}\right)^{-1}$$

$$= \left(\frac{3}{1}\right)^1$$

$$= 3$$

The points $(-2, 9)$ and $(-1, 3)$ are on the graph of $f(x) = \left(\frac{1}{3}\right)^x$. In a similar way, we find the corresponding values of $f(x)$ for $x = 0, 1,$ and 2 and list them in a table. Then we plot the ordered pairs and draw a smooth curve through them, as shown below. Notice with the ordered pairs, as the value of x increases, the value of y decreases very rapidly as compared with x. This graph is an example of **exponential decay.**

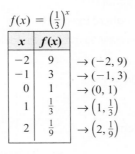

$f(x) = \left(\frac{1}{3}\right)^x$

x	$f(x)$	
-2	9	$\rightarrow (-2, 9)$
-1	3	$\rightarrow (-1, 3)$
0	1	$\rightarrow (0, 1)$
1	$\frac{1}{3}$	$\rightarrow \left(1, \frac{1}{3}\right)$
2	$\frac{1}{9}$	$\rightarrow \left(2, \frac{1}{9}\right)$

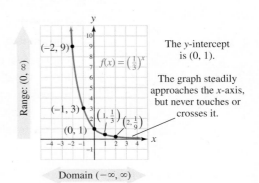

The y-intercept is $(0, 1)$.

The graph steadily approaches the x-axis, but never touches or crosses it.

Domain $(-\infty, \infty)$

The graph passes the vertical line test, and so it is indeed the graph of a function. Because the graph extends indefinitely to the left and right, the projection of the graph onto the x-axis includes all real numbers. Thus, the domain of $f(x) = \left(\frac{1}{3}\right)^x$ is $(-\infty, \infty)$. Because the projection of the graph onto the y-axis covers only the positive portion of that axis, the range of the function is $(0, \infty)$.

Note that as x increases, the values of $f(x)$ decrease and approach 0. Thus, the x-axis is a horizontal asymptote of the graph. The graph does not have an x-intercept, the y-intercept is $(0, 1)$, and the graph passes through the point $\left(1, \frac{1}{3}\right)$.

Self Check 2 Graph: $g(x) = \left(\frac{1}{2}\right)^x$

Now Try ▶ Problem 23

In Example 1 (where $b = 2$), the values of y increase as the values of x increase. Since the graph rises as we move to the right, we call the function an *increasing function*. When $b > 1$, the larger the value of b, the steeper the curve, as shown in figure (a) below.

In Example 2 $\left(\text{where } b = \frac{1}{3}\right)$, the values of y decrease as the values of x increase. Since the graph drops as we move to the right, we call the function a *decreasing function*. When $0 < b < 1$, the smaller the value of b, the steeper the curve, as shown in figure (b) below.

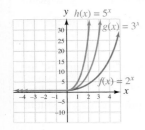

The bases of these exponential functions are 2, 3, and 5. Notice that the largest base, 5, has the steepest graph.

(a)

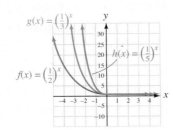

The bases of these exponential functions are $\frac{1}{2}, \frac{1}{3}$, and $\frac{1}{5}$, which are numbers between 0 and 1. Notice that the smallest base, $\frac{1}{5}$, has the steepest graph.

(b)

Examples 1 and 2 illustrate the following properties of exponential functions.

Properties of Exponential Functions

1. The domain of the exponential function $f(x) = b^x$ is the interval $(-\infty, \infty)$ and the range is the interval $(0, \infty)$.

2. The graph has a y-intercept of $(0, 1)$.

3. The x-axis is an asymptote of the graph.

4. The graph of $f(x) = b^x$ passes through the point $(1, b)$.

5. Exponential functions are one-to-one.

6. If $b > 1$, then $f(x) = b^x$ is an **increasing function**.

   If $0 < b < 1$, then $f(x) = b^x$ is a **decreasing function**.

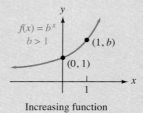

Increasing function

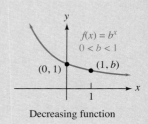

Decreasing function

Using Your Calculator ▶ Graphing Exponential Functions

To use a graphing calculator to graph $f(x) = \left(\frac{2}{3}\right)^x$ and $g(x) = \left(\frac{3}{2}\right)^x$, we enter the right sides of the equations after the symbols $Y_1 =$ and $Y_2 =$. The screen will show the following equations.

$Y_1 = (2/3)\text{^}X$

$Y_2 = (3/2)\text{^}X$

If we press GRAPH, we will obtain the display shown.

We note that the graph of $f(x) = \left(\frac{2}{3}\right)^x$ passes through $(0, 1)$. Since $\frac{2}{3} < 1$, the function is decreasing. The graph of $g(x) = \left(\frac{3}{2}\right)^x$ also passes through $(0, 1)$. Since $\frac{3}{2} > 1$, the function is increasing. Since both graphs pass the horizontal line test, each function is one-to-one.

The graphs of many exponential functions are horizontal and vertical translations of basic graphs.

EXAMPLE 3   Graph each function by using a translation:

a. $g(x) = 2^x - 4$ **b.** $g(x) = \left(\frac{1}{3}\right)^{x+3}$

Strategy   We will graph $g(x) = 2^x - 4$ by translating the graph of $f(x) = 2^x$ downward 4 units. We will graph $g(x) = \left(\frac{1}{3}\right)^{x+3}$ by translating the graph of $f(x) = \left(\frac{1}{3}\right)^x$ to the left 3 units.

Why   The subtraction of 4 in $g(x) = 2^x - 4$ causes a vertical shift of the graph of the base-2 exponential function 4 units downward. The addition of 3 to x in $g(x) = \left(\frac{1}{3}\right)^{x+3}$ causes a horizontal shift of the graph of the base-$\frac{1}{3}$ exponential function 3 units to the left.

Solution   **a.** The graph of $g(x) = 2^x - 4$ will be the same shape as the graph of $f(x) = 2^x$. We call this a **vertical translation.** To graph $g(x) = 2^x - 4$, simply translate each point on the graph of $f(x) = 2^x$ down 4 units. See figure (a) below.

b. The graph of $g(x) = \left(\frac{1}{3}\right)^{x+3}$ will be the same shape as the graph of $f(x) = \left(\frac{1}{3}\right)^x$. We call this a **horizontal translation.** To graph $g(x) = \left(\frac{1}{3}\right)^{x+3}$, simply translate each point on the graph of $f(x) = \left(\frac{1}{3}\right)^x$ to the left 3 units. See figure (b) below.

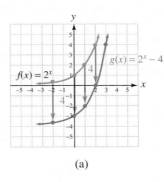

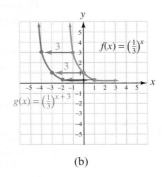

(a)   (b)

Self Check 3   Graph each function by using a translation:

a. $g(x) = \left(\frac{1}{4}\right)^x + 2$ **b.** $g(x) = 4^{x-3}$

Now Try ▶ Problems 27 and 29

3 Use Exponential Functions in Applications Involving Growth or Decay.

Many real-world situations can be modeled by exponential functions that describe how a quantity grows or decays over time. Some examples of this include the studies of populations, bacteria, heat transfer, radioactive substances, drug concentrations, and financial accounts. Two examples of such functions are:

Exponential growth:

$$c(t) = 5(1.034)^t$$

A constant   A base greater than 1

Exponential decay:

$$f(n) = 650(0.94)^n$$

A constant   A base between 0 and 1

EXAMPLE 4   **Professional Baseball Salaries.**   The exponential function $s(t) = 650,000(1.09)^t$ approximates the average annual salary of a major league baseball player, where t is the number of years after 1990. (Source: Baseball Almanac)   **a.** Graph the function.   **b.** Use the function to determine the average annual salary in 2020, if the current trend continues.

Strategy   For part a, we will graph the function by creating a table of function values and plotting the resulting ordered pairs. For part b, we will find $s(30)$.

Why   After drawing a smooth curve through the plotted points, we will have the graph. Since the year 2020 is 30 years after 1990, $t = 30$.

Solution   **a.** The function values for $t = 0$ and $t = 5$ are calculated as follows:

$t = 0$ (*the year 1990*)	$t = 5$ (*the year 1995*)
$s(t) = 650{,}000(1.09)^t$	$s(t) = 650{,}000(1.09)^t$
$s(0) = 650{,}000(1.09)^0$	$s(5) = 650{,}000(1.09)^5$
$= 650{,}000(1)$	$\approx 1{,}000{,}106$ Use a calculator.
$= 650{,}000$	

To approximate $s(5)$, use the keystrokes $650000 \;\boxed{\times}\; 1.09 \;\boxed{y^x}\; 5 \;\boxed{=}$ on a scientific calculator and $650000 \;\boxed{\times}\; 1.09 \;\boxed{\wedge}\; 5 \;\boxed{\text{ENTER}}$ on a graphing calculator.

In a similar way, we find the corresponding values of $s(t)$ for t-values of 10, 15, and 20 and list them in a table. Then we plot the ordered pairs and draw a smooth curve through them to get the graph shown here.

t	$s(t)$
0	650,000
5	1,000,106
10	1,538,786
15	2,367,614
20	3,642,867

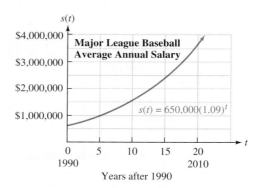

Major League Baseball Average Annual Salary

$s(t) = 650{,}000(1.09)^t$

Years after 1990

b. To estimate the average annual major league baseball salary in 2020, which is 30 years after 1990, we find $s(30)$.

$$s(t) = 650{,}000(1.09)^t \qquad \text{This is the exponential growth model.}$$
$$s(30) = 650{,}000(1.09)^{30} \qquad \text{Substitute 30 for t.}$$
$$\approx 8{,}623{,}991 \qquad \text{Use a calculator.}$$

If the trend continues, in 2020, the average annual salary will be approximately $8,623,991.

Self Check 4   **Salaries.**   Use the function in Example 4 to determine the average annual salary in 2018, if the current trend continues.

Now Try ▶ Problem 43

Using Your Calculator ▶ **Graphing Exponential Functions**

To use a graphing calculator to graph the exponential function $s(t) = 170{,}000(1.12)^t$, we enter the right side of the equation after the symbol $Y_1 =$ and replace the variable t with x. The display will show the equation

$$Y_1 = 170000(1.12^\wedge X)$$

With window settings $[0, 30]$ for x and Xscale $= 5$ and $[0, 3000000]$ for y and Yscale $= 500000$, we obtain the display shown when we press $\boxed{\text{GRAPH}}$.

Up to this point, the financial application problems that we have solved involved **simple interest,** which is calculated using the formula $I = Prt$. However, most savings accounts and investments pay compound interest rather than simple interest. **Compound interest** is paid more than once a year on the principal and *previously earned interest*. The following compound interest formula is a useful application of exponential functions.

Formula for Compound Interest

If $P is deposited in an account and interest is paid k times a year at an annual rate r, the amount A in the account after t years is given by

$$A = P\left(1 + \frac{r}{k}\right)^{kt}$$

EXAMPLE 5   **Educational Savings Plan.**   To save for college, parents of a newborn child invest $12,000 in a mutual fund at 10% interest, compounded quarterly.

a. Find a function for the amount in the account after t years.

b. If the quarterly interest paid is continually reinvested, how much money will be in the account when the child is 18 years old?

Strategy   To write a function for the amount in the account after t years, we will substitute the given values for P, r, and k into the compound interest formula.

Why   The resulting equation will involve only two variables, A and t. Then we can write that equation using function notation.

Solution   **a.** When we substitute 12,000 for P, 0.10 for r, and 4 for k in the formula for compound interest, the resulting formula involves only two variables, A and t.

$$A = P\left(1 + \frac{r}{k}\right)^{kt} \qquad \text{This is the compound interest model.}$$

$$A = 12{,}000\left(1 + \frac{0.10}{4}\right)^{4t} \qquad \begin{array}{l}\text{Since the interest is compounded quarterly, } k = 4.\\ \text{Express } r = 10\% \text{ as a decimal.}\end{array}$$

Since the value of A depends on the value of t, we can express this relationship using function notation.

$$A(t) = 12{,}000\left(1 + \frac{0.10}{4}\right)^{4t}$$

$$A(t) = 12{,}000(1 + 0.025)^{4t} \qquad \text{Evaluate within the parentheses: } \tfrac{0.10}{4} = 0.025.$$

$$A(t) = 12{,}000(1.025)^{4t} \qquad \text{The base of this exponential function is 1.025.}$$

b. To find how much money will be in the account when the child is 18 years old, we need to find $A(18)$.

$$A(t) = 12{,}000(1.025)^{4(t)} \qquad \text{This is the exponential growth model.}$$

$$A(18) = 12{,}000(1.025)^{4(18)} \qquad \text{Substitute 18 for } t.$$

$$= 12{,}000(1.025)^{72} \qquad \text{Evaluate the exponent: } 4(18) = 72.$$

$$\approx 71{,}006.74 \qquad \begin{array}{l}\text{Use a scientific calculator and press these keys:}\\ 12000 \;\boxed{\times}\; 1.025 \;\boxed{y^x}\; 72 \;\boxed{=}\,.\end{array}$$

When the child is 18 years old, the account will contain $71,006.74.

The Language of Algebra

The following words indicate the number of times that interest is paid by a financial institution in one year.

Annually:	1 time
Semiannually:	2 times
Quarterly:	4 times
Monthly:	12 times
Daily:	365 times

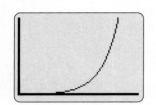

Self Check 5 **Savings Plans.** In Example 5, how much money would be in the account after 18 years if the parents initially invested $20,000?

Now Try ▶ **Problem 53**

Using Your Calculator ▶ **Solving Investment Problems**

Suppose $1 is deposited in an account earning 6% annual interest, compounded monthly. To use a graphing calculator to estimate how much will be in the account in 100 years, we can substitute 1 for P, 0.06 for r, and 12 for k in the formula and simplify.

$$A = P\left(1 + \frac{r}{k}\right)^{kt} = 1\left(1 + \frac{0.06}{12}\right)^{12t} = (1.005)^{12t}$$

We now graph the function $A(t) = (1.005)^{12t}$ using window settings of [0, 120] and [0, 400] with Xscale = 1 and Yscale = 1 to obtain the graph shown. We can then trace and zoom to estimate that $1 grows to be approximately $397 in 100 years. From the graph, we can see that the money grows slowly in the early years and rapidly in the later years.

Examples 4 and 5 are applications illustrating exponential growth. In the next example, we see an application of exponential decay.

EXAMPLE 6

Medications. The most common way people take medications is orally (by mouth). Medications, when swallowed, travel from the stomach or small intestine into the bloodstream, but they are eventually eliminated from the body by the kidneys and the liver. If a patient takes a 250-milligram dose of an antibiotic, the function $A(t) = 250(0.58)^t$ approximates the amount of medication (in milligrams) left in the patient's bloodstream t hours after it is taken.

a. Graph the function.

b. Use the function to determine the amount of medication in the patient's bloodstream 10 hours after taking the dose.

Strategy For part a, we will graph the function by creating a table of function values and plotting the resulting ordered pairs. For part b, we will find $A(10)$.

Why After drawing a smooth curve through the plotted points, we will have the graph. Since the variable t represents the time since taking the dose, $t = 10$.

Solution **a.** The function values for $t = 0$ and $t = 2$ are calculated as follows:

$t = 0$:

$$A(t) = 250(0.58)^t$$
$$A(0) = 250(0.58)^0$$
$$= 250(1)$$
$$= 250$$

$t = 2$:

$$A(t) = 250(0.58)^t$$
$$A(2) = 250(0.58)^2$$
$$\approx 84.1 \quad \text{Use a calculator.}$$

Success Tip

$A(t) = 250(0.58)^t$ is a decreasing function because the base, 0.58, is such that $0 < 0.58 < 1$.

In a similar way, we find the corresponding values of $A(t)$ for t-values of 4 and 6, and list them in a table. Then we plot the ordered pairs and draw a smooth curve through them to get the graph shown below.

t	$A(t)$
0	250
2	84.1
4	28.3
6	9.5

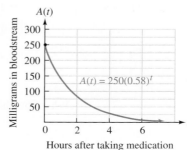

b. To estimate the amount of medication in the patient's bloodstream 10 hours after taking the dose, we find $A(10)$.

$$A(t) = 250(0.58)^t \quad \text{This is the exponential decay model.}$$
$$A(10) = 250(0.58)^{10} \quad \text{Substitute 10 for } t.$$
$$\approx 1.1 \quad \text{Use a calculator.}$$

In 10 hours, there will be approximately 1.1 milligrams of medication in the patient's bloodstream.

Self Check 6 **Medications.** Use the function in Example 6 to determine the amount of medication in the patient's bloodstream $8\frac{1}{2}$ hours after taking the dose.

Now Try ▶ Problem 44

SECTION 11.3 ▶ STUDY SET

VOCABULARY

Fill in the blanks.

1. $f(x) = 2^x$ and $f(x) = \left(\frac{1}{4}\right)^x$ are examples of _____ functions.

2. Exponential functions have a constant base and a variable _____ .

3. The graph of $f(x) = 3^x$ approaches, but never touches, the negative portion of the x-axis. Thus, the x-axis is an _____ of the graph.

4. _____ interest is paid on the principal and previously earned interest.

CONCEPTS

5. Refer to the graph shown at the right.
   a. What type of function is $f(x) = 3^x$?
   b. What is the domain of the function?
   c. What is the range of the function?
   d. What is the y-intercept of the graph? What is the x-intercept of the graph?
   e. Is the function one-to-one?
   f. What is an asymptote of the graph?
   g. Is f an increasing or a decreasing function?
   h. The graph passes through the point $(1, y)$. What is y?

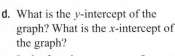

6. Which of the following functions are exponential functions?

   a. $f(x) = x^2$ **b.** $g(x) = 4x$ **c.** $h(x) = 8^x$

   d. $s(x) = \dfrac{1}{x}$ **e.** $T(x) = (0.92)^{x+1}$ **f.** $r(x) = x^3$

   g. $P(x) = \sqrt{x}$ **h.** $d(x) = |x|$

7. Evaluate each expression without a calculator.

   a. 3^{-2} **b.** $\left(\dfrac{1}{2}\right)^4$ **c.** $\left(\dfrac{1}{5}\right)^{-2}$

8. Evaluate each expression using a calculator. Round to the nearest tenth.

   a. $20{,}000(1.036)^{52}$ **b.** $92(0.88)^6$

9. Match each function with its graph shown below.

   a. $f(x) = x^2$ **b.** $f(x) = 2^x$
   c. $f(x) = 2$ **d.** $f(x) = 2x$

   i. 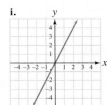   **ii.**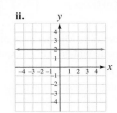

   iii. 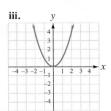   **iv.**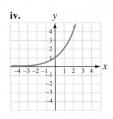

10. a. Two exponential functions of the form $f(x) = b^x$ are graphed in figure (a) below. Which function has the larger base b, the one graphed in red or the one graphed in blue?

   b. Two exponential functions of the form $f(x) = b^x$ are graphed in figure (b) below. Which function has the smaller base b?

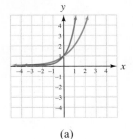

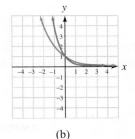

(a)   (b)

11. Determine the domain and range of each exponential function graphed below.

a.

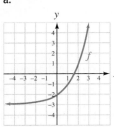

b.

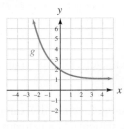

12. Fill in the blanks.

a. The graph of $g(x) = 4^x + 3$ is similar to the graph of $f(x) = 4^x$, but it is translated 3 units _____.

b. The graph of $g(x) = 4^{x-3}$ is similar to the graph of $f(x) = 4^x$, but it is translated 3 units to the _____.

13. Complete the table of function values shown here.

$$f(x) = 5^x$$

x	$f(x)$
-3	
-2	
-1	
0	
1	
2	
3	

14. Determine whether each of the following functions model exponential growth or exponential decay.

a. $D(t) = 150(0.44)^t$ b. $H(t) = 15,000(1.03)^t$

15. Match each situation to the exponential graph that best models it.

a. The number of cell phone subscribers in the world over the past 5 years

b. The level of caffeine in the bloodstream after drinking a cup of coffee

c. The amount of money in a bank account earning interest compounded quarterly

d. The number of rabbits in a population with a high birth rate

e. The amount of water in a shirt that was just washed and hung on a clothesline to dry

i. y

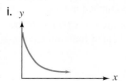

ii. y

16. What formula is used to determine the amount of money in a savings account earning compound interest?

17. For an exponential function of the form $f(x) = b^x$, what are the restrictions on b?

18. In $A(t) = 16,000\left(1 + \frac{0.05}{365}\right)^{365t}$, what is the base and what is the exponent?

GUIDED PRACTICE

Graph each function. **See Examples 1 and 2.**

19. $f(x) = 3^x$ **20.** $f(x) = 6^x$

21. $f(x) = 5^x$ **22.** $f(x) = 7^x$

23. $f(x) = \left(\frac{1}{4}\right)^x$ **24.** $f(x) = \left(\frac{1}{5}\right)^x$

25. $f(x) = \left(\frac{1}{6}\right)^x$ **26.** $f(x) = \left(\frac{1}{8}\right)^x$

Graph each function by plotting points or using a translation. **See Example 4.**

27. $g(x) = 3^x - 2$ **28.** $g(x) = 2^x + 1$

29. $g(x) = 2^{x+1}$ **30.** $g(x) = 3^{x-1}$

31. $g(x) = 4^{x-1} + 2$ **32.** $g(x) = 4^{x+1} - 2$

33. $g(x) = -2^x$ **34.** $g(x) = -3^x$

Use a graphing calculator to graph each function. Determine whether the function is an increasing or a decreasing function. **See Using Your Calculator: Graphing Exponential Functions.**

35. $f(x) = \frac{1}{2}(3^{x/2})$ **36.** $f(x) = -3(2^{x/3})$

37. $f(x) = 2(3^{-x/2})$ **38.** $f(x) = -\frac{1}{4}(2^{-x/2})$

APPLICATIONS

39. **CO_2 Concentration.** The exponential growth model below illustrates the rise in atmospheric carbon dioxide from 1744 to 2006. The historical data (shown with blue points) comes from ice cores, and modern data (shown with red points) was collected from the Mauna Loa Observatory in Hawaii.

a. Estimate the atmospheric carbon dioxide concentrations in 1800, 1900, and 2000.

b. In approximately what year did the concentration surpass 325 parts per million?

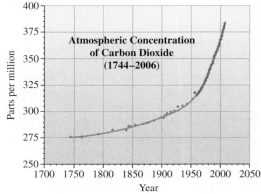

Source: www.eoearth.org

40. Global Warming.   The following graph from the United States Environmental Protection Agency shows the projected sea level changes due to anticipated global warming.

a. What type of function does it appear could be used to model the sea level change?

b. When were the earliest instrumental records of sea level change made?

c. For the year 2100, what is the upper-end projection for sea level change? What is the lower-end projection?

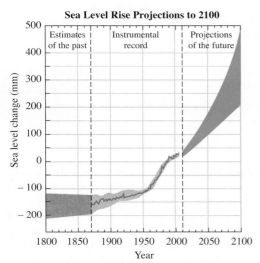

Sea Level Rise Projections to 2100

Source: United States Environmental Protection Agency

41. Value of a Car.   The graph shows how the value of the average car depreciates as a percent of its original value over a 10-year period. It also shows the yearly maintenance costs as a percent of the car's value.

a. When is the car worth half of its purchase price?

b. When is the car worth a quarter of its purchase price?

c. When do the average yearly maintenance costs surpass the value of the car?

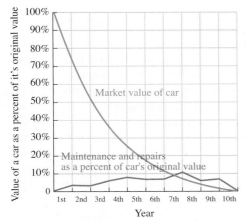

Source: U.S. Department of Transportation

42. Diving.   *Bottom time* is the time a scuba diver spends descending plus the actual time spent at a certain depth. Graph the bottom time limits given in the table as ordered pairs of the form (depth, bottom time). Then draw a smooth curve through the points.

Depth (ft)	Bottom time limit (min)
30	no limit
35	310
40	200
50	100
60	60
70	50

Depth (ft)	Bottom time limit (min)
80	40
90	30
100	25
110	20
120	15
130	10

43. Computer Viruses.   Suppose the number of computers infected by the spread of a virus through an e-mail is described by the exponential function $c(t) = 5(1.034)^t$, where t is the number of minutes since the first infected e-mail was opened.

a. Graph the function. Scale the t-axis from 0 to 400, in units of 50. Scale the $c(t)$-axis from 0 to 800,000 in units of 100,000.

b. Use the function to determine the number of infected computers in 8 hours, which is 480 minutes.

44. Salvage Value.   A small business purchased a computer for $5,000. The value (in dollars) of the computer, t years after its purchase, is given by the exponential function $v(t) = 5,000(0.75)^t$.

a. Graph the function. Scale the t-axis from 0 to 10 in units of 2. Scale the $v(t)$-axis from 0 to 6,000 in units of 1,000.

b. Use the function to determine the value of the computer 12 years after it is purchased.

45. Guitars.   The frets on the neck of a guitar are placed so that pressing a string against them determines the strings' vibrating length. The exponential function $f(n) = 650(0.94)^n$ gives the vibrating length (in millimeters) of a string on a certain guitar for the fret number n. Find the length of the vibrating string when a guitarist holds down a string at the 7th fret.

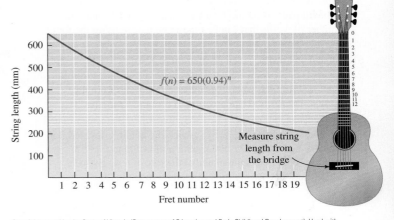

46. Bacterial Cultures.   A colony of 6 million bacteria was determined to be growing in the culture medium shown in illustration (a). If the population P of bacteria after t hours is given by the function $P(t) = 6,000,000(2.3)^t$, find the population in the culture later in the day using the information given in illustration (b).

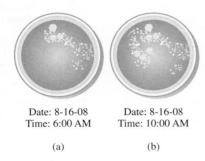

Date: 8-16-08	Date: 8-16-08
Time: 6:00 AM	Time: 10:00 AM
(a)	(b)

47. Radioactive Decay.   Five hundred grams of a radioactive material decays according to the formula $A = 500\left(\frac{2}{3}\right)^t$, where t is measured in years. Find the amount present in 10 years. Round to the nearest one-tenth of a gram.

48. Discharging a Battery.   The charge remaining in a battery decreases as the battery discharges. The charge C (in coulombs) after t days is given by the function $C(t) = 0.0003(0.7)^t$. Find the charge after 5 days.

49. ▶ from **Campus to Careers**

   Social Worker

The function $P(t) = 35.8(1.06)^t$ approximates the number of people (in millions) in the United States living in poverty, where t is the number of years after 2006. Use the function to complete the table below. Round to the nearest tenth. (Source: U.S. Census Bureau)

Year	2006	2007	2008	2009
Number in poverty (in millions)				

50. Publishing Books.   The function $W(f) = 4,066(0.8753)^f$ approximates the number of words that can be typeset on a standard page using the Times Roman font size f. Find the number of words that can be typeset on a page using the font size 12. (Source: writersservices.com)

51. Population Growth.   The population of North Rivers is decreasing exponentially according to the formula $P = 3,745(0.93)^t$, where t is measured in years from the present date. Find the population in 6 years, 9 months.

52. The Louisiana Purchase.   In 1803, the United States negotiated the Louisiana Purchase with France. The country doubled its territory by adding 827,000 square miles of land for $15 million. If the land appreciated at the rate of 6% each year, what would one square mile of land be worth in 2005?

In Exercises 53–58, assume that there are no deposits or withdrawals.

53. Compound Interest.   An initial deposit of $10,000 earns 8% interest, compounded quarterly. How much will be in the account after 10 years?

54. Compound Interest.   An initial deposit of $10,000 earns 8% interest, compounded monthly. How much will be in the account after 10 years?

55. Comparing Interest Rates.   How much more interest could $1,000 earn in 5 years, compounded quarterly, if the annual interest rate were $5\frac{1}{2}\%$ instead of 5%?

56. Comparing Savings Plans.   Which institution in the ads provides the better investment?

Fidelity Savings & Loan
Earn 5.25%
compounded monthly

Union Trust
Money Market Account
paying 5.35%
compounded annually

57. Compound Interest.   If $1 had been invested on July 4, 1776, at 5% interest, compounded annually, what would it be worth on July 4, 2076?

58. Frequency of Compounding. $10,000 is invested in each of two accounts, both paying 6% annual interest. In the first account, interest compounds quarterly, and in the second account, interest compounds daily. Find the difference between the accounts after 20 years.

WRITING

59. If world population is increasing exponentially, why is there cause for concern?

60. How do the graphs of $f(x) = 3^x$ and $g(x) = \left(\frac{1}{3}\right)^x$ differ? How are they similar?

61. A snowball rolling downhill grows *exponentially* with time. Explain what this means. Sketch a simple graph that models the situation.

62. Explain why the change in temperature of a cup of hot coffee left unattended on a kitchen table is an example of exponential decay.

63. Let $f(x) = \left(\frac{1}{5}\right)^x$. Explain why we can rewrite the function equation as $f(x) = 5^{-x}$.

64. Explain why the graph of $f(x) = 3^x$ gets closer and closer to the x-axis as the values of x decrease. Does the graph ever cross the x-axis? Explain why or why not.

65. Describe the graphs of $f(x) = x^2$ and $g(x) = 2^x$ in words.

66. Write a paragraph explaining the concept that is illustrated in the graph.

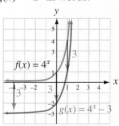

67. In the definition of the exponential function, b could not be negative. Why?

68. How does exponential growth differ from linear growth? Give an example.

REVIEW

In Exercises 69–72, refer to the illustration below in which lines r and s are parallel.

69. Find x.

70. Find the measure of $\angle 1$.

71. Find the measure of $\angle 2$.

72. Find the measure of $\angle 3$.

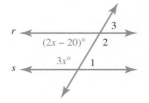

CHALLENGE PROBLEMS

73. Graph $f(x) = 3^x$. Then use the graph to estimate the value of $3^{1.5}$.

74. Graph $y = x^{1/2}$ and $y = \left(\frac{1}{2}\right)^x$ on the same set of coordinate axes. Estimate the coordinates of any point(s) that the graphs have in common.

75. Find the value of b that would cause the graph of $f(x) = b^x$ to look like the graph on the right.

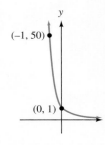

Simplify each expression. Write answers using positive exponents.

76. a. $\left(2^{\sqrt{3}}\right)^{\sqrt{3}}$ **b.** $7^{\sqrt{3}}\, 7^{\sqrt{12}}$

   c. $\dfrac{5^{6\sqrt{2}}}{5^{4\sqrt{2}}}$ **d.** $5^{-\sqrt{5}}$

77. Graph: $f(x) = 2^{|x|}$

78. Graph the inverse of $f(x) = 3^x$.

SECTION 11.4

Logarithmic Functions

OBJECTIVES

1 Define logarithm.

2 Write logarithmic equations as exponential equations.

3 Write exponential equations as logarithmic equations.

4 Evaluate logarithmic expressions.

5 Graph logarithmic functions.

6 Use logarithmic formulas and functions in applications.

ARE YOU READY?

The following problems review some basic skills that are needed when working with logarithmic functions.

1. A table of values for a one-to-one function f is shown below. Complete the table of values for f^{-1}.

x	$f(x)$
0	1
1	2
2	4

x	$f^{-1}(x)$

2. Fill in the blanks: **a.** $5^{-3} = \dfrac{1}{}$ **b.** $3^{} = 27$

3. Fill in the blanks: **a.** $4^{} = 4$ **b.** $7^{} = \sqrt{7}$

4. Evaluate: **a.** 10^3 **b.** 10^{-2}

In this section, we will discuss inverses of exponential functions. These functions are called *logarithmic functions,* and they can be used to solve problems from fields such as electronics, seismology (the study of earthquakes), and business.

1 Define Logarithm.

The graph of the exponential function $f(x) = 2^x$ is shown in red below. Since it passes the horizontal line test, it is a one-to-one function and has an inverse. To graph f^{-1}, we interchange the coordinates of the ordered pairs in the table, plot those points, and draw a smooth curve through them, as shown in blue. As expected, the graphs of f and f^{-1} are symmetric with respect to the line $y = x$.

$f(x) = 2^x$

To graph f^{-1}, interchange each pair of coordinates.

x	$f(x)$
-3	$\frac{1}{8}$	$\to \left(-3, \frac{1}{8}\right)$	$\left(\frac{1}{8}, -3\right)$
-2	$\frac{1}{4}$	$\to \left(-2, \frac{1}{4}\right)$	$\left(\frac{1}{4}, -2\right)$
-1	$\frac{1}{2}$	$\to \left(-1, \frac{1}{2}\right)$	$\left(\frac{1}{2}, -1\right)$
0	1	$\to (0, 1)$	$(1, 0)$
1	2	$\to (1, 2)$	$(2, 1)$
2	4	$\to (2, 4)$	$(4, 2)$
3	8	$\to (3, 8)$	$(8, 3)$

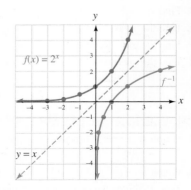

To write an equation for the inverse of $f(x) = 2^x$, we proceed as follows:

$f(x) = 2^x$

$y = 2^x$ Replace f(x) with y.

$x = 2^y$ Interchange the variables x and y.

We cannot solve the equation for y because we have not discussed methods for solving equations with a variable exponent. However, we can translate the relationship $x = 2^y$ into words:

$y =$ the power to which we raise 2 to get x

If we substitute the notation $f^{-1}(x)$ for y, we see that

$f^{-1}(x) =$ the power to which we raise 2 to get x

The Language of Algebra

The abbreviation log is used for the word **logarithm**. A *logarithm* is an exponent.

If we define the symbol $\log_2 x$ to mean *the power to which we raise 2 to get x*, we can write the equation for the inverse as

$f^{-1}(x) = \log_2 x$ Read log₂ x as "the logarithm, base 2, of x" or "log, base 2, of x."

We have found that the inverse of the exponential function $f(x) = 2^x$ is $f^{-1}(x) = \log_2 x$. To find the inverse of exponential functions with other bases, such as $f(x) = 3^x$ and $f(x) = 10^x$, we define *logarithm* in the following way.

Definition of Logarithm

For all positive numbers b, where $b \neq 1$, and all positive numbers x,

$y = \log_b x$ is equivalent to $x = b^y$

Success Tip

Here are two examples of inverses of other exponential functions:

$f(x) = 3^x$ $f^{-1}(x) = \log_3 x$

$g(x) = 10^x$ $g^{-1}(x) = \log_{10} x$

This definition guarantees that any pair (x, y) that satisfies the logarithmic equation $y = \log_b x$ also satisfies the exponential equation $x = b^y$. Because of this relationship, a statement written in logarithmic form can be written in an equivalent exponential form, and vice versa. They are just different ways of expressing the same thing. The following diagram will help you remember the respective positions of the exponent and base in each form.

Exponent

$y = \log_b x$ means $x = b^y$

Base

2 Write Logarithmic Equations as Exponential Equations.

The following table shows the relationship between logarithmic and exponential notation. We need to be able to work in both directions.

Logarithmic equation		*Exponential equation*
$\log_2 8 = 3$		$2^3 = 8$
$\log_3 81 = 4$		$3^4 = 81$
$\log_4 4 = 1$	means	$4^1 = 4$
$\log_5 \dfrac{1}{125} = -3$		$5^{-3} = \dfrac{1}{125}$

EXAMPLE 1   Write each logarithmic equation as an exponential equation:

a. $\log_4 64 = 3$ **b.** $\log_7 \sqrt{7} = \dfrac{1}{2}$ **c.** $\log_6 \dfrac{1}{36} = -2$

Strategy   To write an equivalent exponential equation, we will determine which number will serve as the base and which will serve as the exponent.

Why   We can then use the definition of logarithm to move from one form to the other: $\log_b x = y$ is equivalent to $x = b^y$.

Solution

a. $\log_4 64 = 3$ means $4^3 = 64$.   Read as "log, base 4, of 64 equals 3."
Exponent · Base · The base in each form is the same: 4.

b. $\log_7 \sqrt{7} = \dfrac{1}{2}$ means $7^{1/2} = \sqrt{7}$.   Read as "log, base 7, of $\sqrt{7}$ equals $\frac{1}{2}$."
Exponent · Base · The base in each form is the same: 7.

c. $\log_6 \dfrac{1}{36} = -2$ means $6^{-2} = \dfrac{1}{36}$.   Read as "log, base 6, of $\frac{1}{36}$ equals -2."
Exponent · Base · The base in each form in the same: 6.

Self Check 1   Write $\log_2 128 = 7$ as an exponential equation.

Now Try Problems 23, 27, and 35

3 Write Exponential Equations as Logarithmic Equations.

EXAMPLE 2   Write each exponential equation as a logarithmic equation:

a. $8^0 = 1$ **b.** $6^{1/3} = \sqrt[3]{6}$ **c.** $\left(\dfrac{1}{4}\right)^2 = \dfrac{1}{16}$

Strategy   To write an equivalent logarithmic equation, we will determine which number will serve as the base and where we will place the exponent.

Why   We can then use the definition of logarithm to move from one form to the other: $x = b^y$ is equivalent to $\log_b x = y$.

Solution

a. $8^0 = 1$ means $\log_8 1 = 0$ In each form, the base is 8.

The arrows indicate: Exponent (top), Base (bottom).

b. $6^{1/3} = \sqrt[3]{6}$ means $\log_6 \sqrt[3]{6} = \dfrac{1}{3}$ In each form, the base is 6.

c. $\left(\dfrac{1}{4}\right)^2 = \dfrac{1}{16}$ means $\log_{1/4} \dfrac{1}{16} = 2$ In each form, the base is $\frac{1}{4}$.

Self Check 2 Write $9^{-1} = \frac{1}{9}$ as a logarithmic equation.

Now Try ▶ Problems 39, 43, and 49

Certain logarithmic equations can be solved by writing them as exponential equations.

EXAMPLE 3 Solve each equation for x: **a.** $\log_x 25 = 2$ **b.** $\log_3 x = -3$ **c.** $\log_{1/2} \dfrac{1}{16} = x$

Strategy To solve each logarithmic equation, we will instead write and solve an equivalent exponential equation.

Why The resulting exponential equation is easier to solve because the variable term is often isolated on one side.

Solution

a. Since $\log_x 25 = 2$ is equivalent to $x^2 = 25$, we can solve $x^2 = 25$ to find x.

$$x^2 = 25$$
$$x = \pm\sqrt{25}\quad \text{Use the square root property.}$$
$$x = \pm 5$$

In the expression $\log_x 25$, the base of the logarithm is x. Because the base must be positive, we discard -5 and we have

$$x = 5$$

To check the solution of 5, verify that $\log_5 25 = 2$. The solution set is written as $\{5\}$.

b. Since $\log_3 x = -3$ is equivalent to $3^{-3} = x$, we can instead solve $3^{-3} = x$ to find x.

$$3^{-3} = x$$
$$\frac{1}{3^3} = x$$
$$x = \frac{1}{27}$$

To check the solution of $\frac{1}{27}$, verify that $\log_3 \frac{1}{27} = -3$. The solution set is $\left\{\frac{1}{27}\right\}$.

c. Since $\log_{1/2} \frac{1}{16} = x$ is equivalent to $\left(\frac{1}{2}\right)^x = \frac{1}{16}$, we can instead solve $\left(\frac{1}{2}\right)^x = \frac{1}{16}$ to find x.

$$\left(\frac{1}{2}\right)^x = \frac{1}{16}$$

$$\left(\frac{1}{2}\right)^x = \left(\frac{1}{2}\right)^4 \qquad \text{Write } \tfrac{1}{16} \text{ as a power of } \tfrac{1}{2} \text{ to match the bases: } \tfrac{1}{2} \cdot \tfrac{1}{2} \cdot \tfrac{1}{2} \cdot \tfrac{1}{2} = \tfrac{1}{16}.$$

$$x = 4 \qquad \text{Since the bases are the same, and since exponential}$$
functions are one-to-one, the exponents must be equal.

To check the solution of 4, verify that $\log_{1/2} \frac{1}{16} = 4$. The solution set is $\{4\}$.

Self Check 3 Solve each equation for x: **a.** $\log_x 49 = 2$ **b.** $\log_{1/3} x = 2$ **c.** $\log_6 216 = x$

Now Try ▶ Problems 51, 53, and 55

4 Evaluate Logarithmic Expressions.

In the previous examples, we have seen that the logarithm of a number is an exponent. In fact,

$\log_b x$ is the exponent to which b is raised to get x.

Translating this statement into symbols, we have

$$b^{\log_b x} = x$$

EXAMPLE 4 Evaluate each expression: **a.** $\log_8 64$ **b.** $\log_3 \frac{1}{3}$ **c.** $\log_4 2$

Strategy After identifying the base, we will ask "To what power must the base be raised to get the other number?"

Why That power is the value of the logarithmic expression.

Solution **a.** $\log_8 64 = 2$ Ask: "To what power must we raise 8 to get 64?"
Since $8^2 = 64$, the answer is the 2nd power.

An alternate approach for this evaluation problem is to let $\log_8 64 = x$. When we write the equivalent exponential equation $8^x = 64$, it is easy to see that $x = 2$.

b. $\log_3 \frac{1}{3} = -1$ Ask: "To what power must we raise 3 to get $\frac{1}{3}$?"
Since $3^{-1} = \frac{1}{3}$, the answer is the -1 power.

We could also let $\log_3 \frac{1}{3} = x$. The equivalent exponential equation is $3^x = \frac{1}{3}$. Thus, x must be -1.

c. $\log_4 2 = \frac{1}{2}$ Ask: "To what power must we raise 4 to get 2?"
Since $\sqrt{4} = 4^{1/2} = 2$, the answer is the $\frac{1}{2}$ power.

We could also let $\log_4 2 = x$. Then the equivalent exponential equation is $4^x = 2$. Thus, x must be $\frac{1}{2}$.

Self Check 4 Evaluate each expression: **a.** $\log_9 81$ **b.** $\log_4 \frac{1}{16}$ **c.** $\log_9 3$

Now Try ▶ Problems 75 and 77

The Language of Algebra

London professor Henry Briggs (1561–1630) and Scottish lord John Napier (1550–1617) are credited with developing the concept of **common logarithms.** Their tables of logarithms were useful tools at that time for those performing large calculations.

In many applications, base-10 logarithms (also called **common logarithms**) are used. When the base b is not indicated in the notation $\log x$, we assume that $b = 10$:

$$\log x \quad \text{means} \quad \log_{10} x$$

The table below shows the relationship between base-10 logarithmic notation and exponential notation.

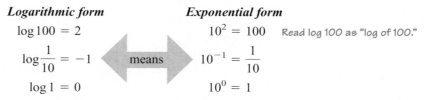

Logarithmic form		*Exponential form*	
$\log 100 = 2$		$10^2 = 100$	Read log 100 as "log of 100."
$\log \dfrac{1}{10} = -1$	**means**	$10^{-1} = \dfrac{1}{10}$	
$\log 1 = 0$		$10^0 = 1$	

In general, we have

$$\boxed{\log 10^x = x}$$

EXAMPLE 5   Evaluate each expression: **a.** $\log 1{,}000$ **b.** $\log \dfrac{1}{100}$ **c.** $\log 10$ **d.** $\log(-10)$

Strategy   After identifying the base, we will ask "To what power must 10 be raised to get the other number?"

Why   That power is the value of the logarithmic expression.

Solution   **a.** $\log 1{,}000 = 3$ Ask: "To what power must we raise 10 to get 1,000?" Since $10^3 = 1{,}000$, the answer is: the 3rd power.

b. $\log \dfrac{1}{100} = -2$ Ask: "To what power must we raise 10 to get $\frac{1}{100}$?" Since $10^{-2} = \frac{1}{100}$, the answer is: the -2 power.

c. $\log 10 = 1$ Ask: "To what power must we raise 10 to get 10?" Since $10^1 = 10$, the answer is: the 1st power.

d. To find $\log(-10)$, we must find a power of 10 such that $10^? = -10$. There is no such number. Thus, $\log(-10)$ is undefined.

Self Check 5   Evaluate each expression: **a.** $\log 10{,}000$ **b.** $\log \dfrac{1}{1{,}000}$
c. $\log 0$

Now Try ▶ Problems 79 and 81

Many logarithmic expressions cannot be evaluated by inspection. For example, to find $\log 2.34$, we ask, "To what power must we raise 10 to get 2.34?" This answer isn't obvious. In such cases, we use a calculator.

Using Your Calculator ▶ Evaluating Logarithms

To find $\log 2.34$ with a scientific calculator we enter

2.34 $\boxed{\text{LOG}}$ .369215857

On some calculators, the $\boxed{10^x}$ key also serves as the $\boxed{\text{LOG}}$ key when $\boxed{\text{2nd}}$ or $\boxed{\text{SHIFT}}$ is pressed. This is because $f(x) = 10^x$ and $f(x) = \log x$ are inverses.

To use a graphing calculator, we enter

$\boxed{\text{LOG}}$ 2.34 $\boxed{)}$ $\boxed{\text{ENTER}}$ log(2.34)
                                                            .369215857

To four decimal places, $\log 2.34 = 0.3692$. This means, $10^{0.3692} \approx 2.34$.

If we attempt to evaluate logarithmic expressions such as log 0, or the logarithm of a negative number, such as $\log(-5)$, an error message like the following will be displayed.

Error

```
ERR:DOMAIN
1:QUIT
2:Go to
```

```
ERR:NONREAL ANS
1:QUIT
2:Go to
```

EXAMPLE 6   Solve $\log x = 0.3568$ and round to four decimal places.

Strategy   To solve this logarithmic equation, we will instead write and solve an equivalent exponential equation.

Why   The resulting exponential equation is easier to solve because the variable term is isolated on one side.

Solution   The equation $\log x = 0.3568$ means $\log_{10} x = 0.3568$, which is equivalent to $10^{0.3568} = x$. Since we cannot determine $10^{0.3568}$ by inspection, we will use a calculator to find an approximate solution. We enter

$$10 \boxed{y^x} .3568 \boxed{=}$$

The display reads $\boxed{2.274049951}$. To four decimal places,

$$x = 2.2740$$

If your calculator has a $\boxed{10^x}$ key, enter .3568 and press it to get the same result. The solution is 2.2740. To check, use your calculator to verify that $\log 2.2740 \approx 0.3568$.

Self Check 6   Solve $\log x = 1.87737$ and round to four decimal places.

Now Try ▶ Problem 91

---

5 Graph Logarithmic Functions.

Because an exponential function defined by $f(x) = b^x$ is one-to-one, it has an inverse function that is defined by $x = b^y$. When we write $x = b^y$ in the equivalent form $y = \log_b x$, the result is called a *logarithmic function*.

Logarithmic Functions   ▼ If $b > 0$ and $b \neq 1$, the **logarithmic function with base b** is defined by the equations

$$f(x) = \log_b x \quad \text{or} \quad y = \log_b x$$

The domain of $f(x) = \log_b x$ is the interval $(0, \infty)$ and the range is the interval $(-\infty, \infty)$.

Caution

Since the domain of the logarithmic function is the set of positive real numbers, it is impossible to find the logarithm of 0 or the logarithm of a negative number. For example, $\log_2 (-4)$ and $\log_2 0$ are undefined.

Since every logarithmic function is the inverse of a one-to-one exponential function, logarithmic functions are one-to-one.

We can plot points to graph logarithmic functions. For example, to graph $f(x) = \log_2 x$, we construct a table of function values, plot the resulting ordered pairs, and draw a smooth curve through the points to get the graph, as shown in figure (a) on the next page. To graph $f(x) = \log_{1/2} x$, we use the same method, as shown in figure (b).

By the vertical line test, we see that each graph is indeed the graph of a function. Because in each case the projection of the graph onto the x-axis covers only the positive portion of that axis, the domain of each function is $(0, \infty)$. Because the graphs extend indefinitely upward and downward, the projection of the graphs onto the y-axis includes all real numbers. Thus, the range of each function is $(-\infty, \infty)$.

$y = \log_b x$

$f(x) = \log_2 x$

x	$f(x)$	
$\frac{1}{4}$	-2	$\rightarrow \left(\frac{1}{4}, -2\right)$
$\frac{1}{2}$	-1	$\rightarrow \left(\frac{1}{2}, -1\right)$
1	0	$\rightarrow (1, 0)$
2	1	$\rightarrow (2, 1)$
4	2	$\rightarrow (4, 2)$
8	3	$\rightarrow (8, 3)$

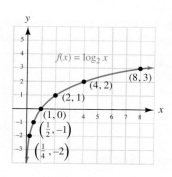

Because the base of the function is 2, choose values for x that are integer powers of 2.

(a)

$f(x) = \log_{1/2} x$

x	$f(x)$	
$\frac{1}{4}$	2	$\rightarrow \left(\frac{1}{4}, 2\right)$
$\frac{1}{2}$	1	$\rightarrow \left(\frac{1}{2}, 1\right)$
1	0	$\rightarrow (1, 0)$
2	-1	$\rightarrow (2, -1)$
4	-2	$\rightarrow (4, -2)$
8	-3	$\rightarrow (8, -3)$

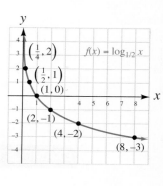

Because the base of the function is $\frac{1}{2}$, choose values for x that are integer powers of $\frac{1}{2}$.

(b)

The graphs of all logarithmic functions are similar to those shown below. If $b > 1$, the logarithmic function is increasing, as in figure (a). If $0 < b < 1$, the logarithmic function is decreasing, as in figure (b).

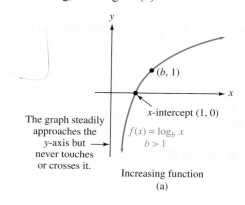

The graph steadily approaches the y-axis but never touches or crosses it.

$(b, 1)$

x-intercept $(1, 0)$

$f(x) = \log_b x$
$b > 1$

Increasing function
(a)

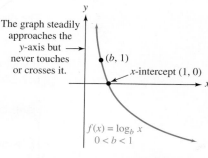

The graph steadily approaches the y-axis but never touches or crosses it.

$(b, 1)$

x-intercept $(1, 0)$

$f(x) = \log_b x$
$0 < b < 1$

Decreasing function
(b)

Properties of Logarithmic Functions

The graph of $f(x) = \log_b x$ (or $y = \log_b x$) has the following properties.

1. It passes through the point $(1, 0)$.
2. It passes through the point $(b, 1)$.
3. The y-axis (the line $x = 0$) is an asymptote.
4. The domain is the interval $(0, \infty)$ and the range is the interval $(-\infty, \infty)$.

The exponential and logarithmic functions are inverses of each other, so their graphs have symmetry about the line $y = x$. The graphs of $f(x) = \log_b x$ and $g(x) = b^x$ are shown in figure (a) when $b > 1$ and in figure (b) when $0 < b < 1$.

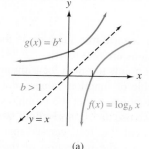
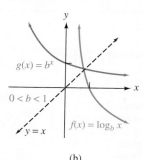

$g(x) = b^x$

$b > 1$

$f(x) = \log_b x$

$y = x$

(a)

$g(x) = b^x$

$0 < b < 1$

$f(x) = \log_b x$

$y = x$

(b)

The graphs of many functions involving logarithms are translations of the basic logarithmic graphs.

EXAMPLE 7 Graph each function by using a translation: **a.** $g(x) = 3 + \log_2 x$
b. $g(x) = \log_{1/2}(x - 1)$

Notation

Since $y = f(x)$, we can write

$$f(x) = \log_2 x$$
$$\text{as}$$
$$y = \log_2 x$$

Strategy We will graph $g(x) = 3 + \log_2 x$ by translating the graph of $f(x) = \log_2 x$ upward 3 units. We will graph $g(x) = \log_{1/2}(x - 1)$ by translating the graph of $f(x) = \log_{1/2} x$ to the right 1 unit.

Why The addition of 3 in $g(x) = \mathbf{3} + \log_2 x$ causes a vertical shift of the graph of the base-2 logarithmic function 3 units upward. The subtraction of 1 from x in $g(x) = \log_{1/2}(x - \mathbf{1})$ causes a horizontal shift of the graph of the base-$\frac{1}{2}$ logarithmic function 1 unit to the right.

Solution **a.** The graph of $g(x) = 3 + \log_2 x$ will be the same shape as the graph of $f(x) = \log_2 x$. We simply translate each point on the graph of $f(x) = \log_2 x$ up 3 units. See figure (a) below.

b. The graph of $g(x) = \log_{1/2}(x - 1)$ will be the same shape as the graph of $f(x) = \log_{1/2} x$. We simply translate each point on the graph of $f(x) = \log_{1/2} x$ to the right 1 unit. See figure (b) below.

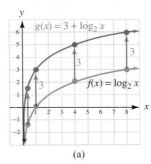
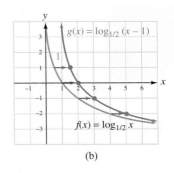

(a)   (b)

Self Check 7 Graph each function by using a translation: **a.** $g(x) = (\log_3 x) - 2$
b. $g(x) = \log_{1/3}(x + 2)$

Now Try ▶ Problems 103 and 105

To graph more complicated logarithmic functions, a graphing calculator is a useful tool.

Using Your Calculator ▶ **Graphing Logarithmic Functions**

To use a calculator to graph the logarithmic function $f(x) = -2 + \log_{10} \frac{x}{2}$, we enter the right side of the equation after the symbol $Y_1 =$. The display will show the equation

$$Y_1 = -2 + \log(X/2)$$

If we use window settings of $[-1, 5]$ for x and $[-4, 1]$ for y and press the $\boxed{\text{GRAPH}}$ key, we will obtain the graph shown.

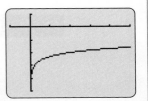

---

6 Use Logarithmic Formulas and Functions in Applications.

Logarithmic functions, like exponential functions, can be used to model certain types of growth and decay. Logarithms are especially useful when measuring a quantity that varies over a very large range of values, such as the intensity of earthquakes, the loudness of sounds, and the brightness of stars.

The following common logarithm formula is used in electrical engineering to express the gain (or loss) of an electronic device such as an amplifier as it takes an input signal and produces an output signal. The unit of gain (or loss) in such cases is called the **decibel,** which is abbreviated **dB.**

Decibel Voltage Gain

If E_O is the output voltage of a device and E_I is the input voltage, the decibel voltage gain of the device (dB gain) is given by

$$\text{dB gain} = 20 \log \frac{E_O}{E_I}$$

EXAMPLE 8   **dB Gain.**   If the input to an amplifier is 0.5 volt and the output is 40 volts, find the decibel voltage gain of the amplifier.

Strategy   We will substitute into the formula for dB gain and evaluate the right side using a calculator.

Why   We can use this formula to find the dB gain because we are given the input voltage E_I and the output voltage E_O.

Solution   We can find the decibel voltage gain by substituting 0.5 for E_I and 40 for E_O into the formula for dB gain:

Notation

$20 \log \dfrac{E_O}{E_I}$ means $20 \cdot \log \dfrac{E_O}{E_I}$

$$\text{dB gain} = 20 \log \frac{E_O}{E_I} \qquad \text{Read as "20 times the log of E sub O divided by E sub I."}$$

$$\text{dB gain} = 20 \log \frac{40}{0.5} \qquad \text{Substitute the input voltage 0.5 for } E_I \text{ and the output voltage 40 for } E_O.$$

$$= 20 \log 80 \qquad \text{Divide: } \tfrac{40}{0.5} = 80.$$

$$\approx 38 \qquad \text{Use a scientific calculator and press: } 20 \;\times\; 80 \;\boxed{\text{LOG}}\; \boxed{=}.$$

The amplifier provides a 38-decibel voltage gain.

Self Check 8   **dB Gain.**   If the input to an amplifier is 0.6 volt and the output is 40 volts, find the decibel voltage gain of the amplifier.

Now Try ▶   Problem 111

EXAMPLE 9   **Stocking Lakes.**   To create the proper environmental balance, 250 hybrid bluegill were introduced into a lake by the local Fish and Game Department. Department biologists found that the number of bluegill in the lake could be approximated by the logarithmic function $f(t) = 250 + 400 \log (t + 1)$, where t is the number of years since the lake was stocked. Find the bluegill population in the lake after 5 years.

Strategy   We will find $f(5)$.

Why   Since the variable t represents the time since the lake was stocked, $t = 5$.

Solution

$$f(t) = 250 + 400 \log (t + 1) \qquad \text{This is the logarithmic growth model.}$$

$$f(5) = 250 + 400 \log (5 + 1) \qquad \text{Substitute 5 for } t.$$

$$= 250 + 400 \log 6 \qquad \text{Do the addition within the parentheses.}$$

$$\approx 561 \qquad \text{Use a scientific calculator and press:}$$
$$\qquad\qquad\qquad 250 \;\boxed{+}\; 400 \;\times\; 6 \;\boxed{\text{LOG}}\; \boxed{=}.$$

There were approximately 561 bluegill in the lake 5 years after it was stocked.

Self Check 9   **Stocking Ponds.** A rancher stocked a pond on his property with 50 catfish. He was told that with the proper care, the catfish population could be approximated by the logarithmic function $f(t) = 50 + 22 \log (t + 1)$, where t is the number of years since the pond was stocked. Find the number of catfish he can expect in the pond in 3 years.

Now Try ▶ Problem 117

SECTION **11.4**   STUDY SET

VOCABULARY

Fill in the blanks.

1. $f(x) = \log_2 x$ and $g(x) = \log x$ are examples of _____ functions.
2. Base-10 logarithms are called _____ logarithms.
3. The graph of $f(x) = \log_2 x$ approaches, but never touches, the negative portion of the y-axis. Thus the y-axis is an _____ of the graph.
4. $\log_x 81 = 4$ is _____ to $x^4 = 81$.

CONCEPTS

5. Refer to the graph on the right.

    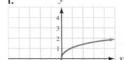

   a. What type of function is $f(x) = \log_4 x$?
   b. What is the domain of the function? What is the range of the function?
   c. What is the y-intercept of the graph? What is the x-intercept of the graph?
   d. Is f a one-to-one function?
   e. What is an asymptote of the graph?
   f. Is f an increasing or a decreasing function?
   g. The graph passes through the point $(4, y)$. What is y?
6. Determine the domain and range of each logarithmic function graphed below.

   a.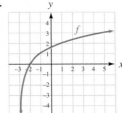

   b.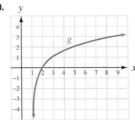

7. Match each function with its graph shown below.

   a. $f(x) = x^3$ b. $f(x) = \log_3 x$
   c. $f(x) = \sqrt[3]{x}$ d. $f(x) = 3x$

   i. 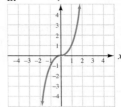   ii.

   iii.   iv.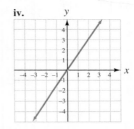

8. a. An exponential function is graphed below. Graph its inverse and the axis of symmetry on the same coordinate system.
   b. What type of function is the inverse function?

   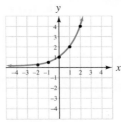

Fill in the blanks.

9. $\log_6 36 = 2$ means ▢ = ▢.
10. $\log x = -2$ is equivalent to ▢ = ▢.
11. $\log_b x$ is the _____ to which b is raised to get x.
12. The functions $f(x) = \log_{10} x$ and $f(x) = 10^x$ are _____ functions.
13. The inverse of an exponential function is called a _____ function.

14. Fill in the blanks.

  a. The graph of $g(x) = 4 + \log x$ is similar to the graph of $f(x) = \log x$, but it is translated 4 units _____.

  b. The graph of $g(x) = \log_4 (x + 2)$ is similar to the graph of $f(x) = \log_4 x$, but it is translated 2 units to the _____.

Complete the table of values.

15. $f(x) = \log x$

x	$f(x)$
100	
$\frac{1}{100}$	

16. $f(x) = \log_5 x$

x	$f(x)$
25	
$\frac{1}{25}$	

17. $f(x) = \log_6 x$

Input	Output
6	
-6	
0	

18. $f(x) = \log_8 x$

Input	Output
8	
-8	
0	

19. a. Use a calculator to complete the table of values for $f(x) = \log x$. Round to the nearest hundredth.

  b. Graph $f(x) = \log x$. Note that the units on the x- and y-axes are different.

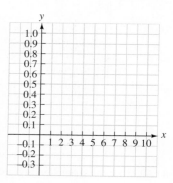

x	$f(x)$
0.5	
1	
2	
4	
6	
8	
10	

20. For each function, determine its inverse, $f^{-1}(x)$.

  a. $f(x) = 10^x$ **b.** $f(x) = 3^x$

  c. $f(x) = \log x$ **d.** $f(x) = \log_2 x$

NOTATION

Fill in the blanks.

21. a. $\log x = \log \_\_ x$ **b.** $\log_{10} 10^x = \_\_$

22. a. We read $\log_5 25$ as "log, __ 5, __ 25."

  b. We read $\log x$ as "__ of x."

GUIDED PRACTICE

Write each logarithmic equation as an exponential equation. See Example 1. Do not solve.

23. $\log_3 81 = 4$

24. $\log_7 7 = 1$

25. $\log_{10} 10 = 1$

26. $\log_{10} 100 = 2$

27. $\log_4 \dfrac{1}{64} = -3$

28. $\log_6 \dfrac{1}{36} = -2$

29. $\log_5 \sqrt{5} = \dfrac{1}{2}$

30. $\log_8 \sqrt[3]{8} = \dfrac{1}{3}$

31. $\log 0.1 = -1$

32. $\log 0.01 = -2$

33. $x = \log_8 64$

34. $x = \log_9 81$

35. $t = \log_b T_1$

36. $n = \log_b R_1$

37. $\log_n C = -42$

38. $\log_m P = 101$

Write each exponential equation as a logarithmic equation. See Example 2.

39. $8^2 = 64$

40. $10^3 = 1{,}000$

41. $4^{-2} = \dfrac{1}{16}$

42. $3^{-4} = \dfrac{1}{81}$

43. $\left(\dfrac{1}{2}\right)^{-5} = 32$

44. $\left(\dfrac{1}{3}\right)^{-3} = 27$

45. $x^y = z$

46. $m^n = p$

47. $y^t = 8.6$

48. $b^r = \dfrac{2}{3}$

49. $7^{4.3} = B + 1$

50. $12^{-2.6} = N + 1$

Solve for x. See Example 3.

51. $\log_x 81 = 2$

52. $\log_x 9 = 2$

53. $\log_8 x = 2$

54. $\log_7 x = 0$

55. $\log_5 125 = x$

56. $\log_4 16 = x$

57. $\log_5 x = -2$

58. $\log_3 x = -4$

59. $\log_{36} x = -\dfrac{1}{2}$

60. $\log_{27} x = -\dfrac{1}{3}$

61. $\log_x 0.01 = -2$

62. $\log_x 0.001 = -3$

63. $\log_{27} 9 = x$

64. $\log_{12} x = 0$

65. $\log_x 5^3 = 3$

66. $\log_x 5 = 1$

67. $\log_{100} x = \dfrac{3}{2}$

68. $\log_x \dfrac{1}{1{,}000} = -\dfrac{3}{2}$

69. $\log_x \dfrac{1}{64} = -3$

70. $\log_x \dfrac{1}{100} = -2$

71. $\log_8 x = 0$

72. $\log_4 8 = x$

73. $\log_x \dfrac{\sqrt{3}}{3} = \dfrac{1}{2}$

74. $\log_x \dfrac{9}{4} = 2$

Evaluate each logarithmic expression. See Examples 4 and 5.

75. $\log_2 8$

76. $\log_3 9$

77. $\log_4 16$

78. $\log_6 216$

79. $\log 1{,}000{,}000$

80. $\log 100{,}000$

81. $\log \dfrac{1}{10}$

82. $\log \dfrac{1}{10{,}000}$

83. $\log_{1/2} \dfrac{1}{32}$

84. $\log_{1/3} \dfrac{1}{81}$

85. $\log_9 3$

86. $\log_{125} 5$

Use a calculator to find each value. Give answers to four decimal places. See Using Your Calculator: Evaluating Logarithms.

87. $\log 3.25$

88. $\log 0.57$

89. $\log 0.00467$

90. $\log 375.876$

Use a calculator to solve each equation. Round answers to four decimal places. See Example 6.

91. $\log x = 3.7813$

92. $\log x = 2.8945$

93. $\log x = -0.7630$

94. $\log x = -1.3587$

95. $\log x = -0.5$

96. $\log x = -0.926$

97. $\log x = -1.71$

98. $\log x = 1.4023$

Graph each function. Determine whether each function is an increasing or a decreasing function. See Objective 5.

99. $f(x) = \log_3 x$

100. $f(x) = \log_{1/3} x$

101. $y = \log_{1/2} x$

102. $y = \log_4 x$

Graph each function by plotting points or by using a translation. (The basic logarithmic functions graphed in Exercises 99–102 will be helpful.) See Example 7.

103. $f(x) = 3 + \log_3 x$

104. $f(x) = (\log_{1/3} x) - 1$

105. $y = \log_{1/2} (x - 2)$

106. $y = \log_4 (x + 2)$

Graph each pair of inverse functions on the same coordinate system. Draw the axis of symmetry. See Objective 1.

107. $f(x) = 6^x$
$f^{-1}(x) = \log_6 x$

108. $f(x) = 3^x$
$f^{-1}(x) = \log_3 x$

109. $f(x) = 5^x$
$f^{-1}(x) = \log_5 x$

110. $f(x) = 8^x$
$f^{-1}(x) = \log_8 x$

APPLICATIONS

111. dB Gain. Find the dB gain of the amplifier shown below. Round to the nearest tenth.

112. Output Voltage. Find the dB gain of an amplifier if the output voltage is 2.8 volts when the input voltage is 0.05 volt. Round to the nearest dB.

113. Earthquakes. Refer to the illustration in the next column. Common logarithms are used to measure the intensity of earthquakes. If R is the intensity of an earthquake on the **Richter scale**, A is the amplitude (measured in micrometers) of the ground motion and P is the period (the time of one oscillation of the Earth's surface measured in seconds), then $R = \log \dfrac{A}{P}$. If an earthquake has amplitude of 5,000 micrometers and a period of 0.2 second, what is its measure on the Richter scale? Round to the nearest tenth.

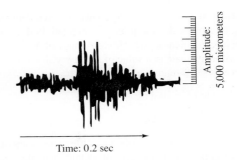

Amplitude: 5,000 micrometers

Time: 0.2 sec

114. Earthquakes. If an earthquake has amplitude of 95,000 micrometers and a period of $\frac{1}{4}$ second, what is its measure on the Richter scale? See problem 113. Round to the nearest tenth.

115. from **Campus to Careers**
Social Worker

The logarithmic function $c(m) = 500 \log (m + 1)$ approximates the total number of cases handled one year by the staff at a county department of social services. The variable m represents the month of the year, where January is 1, February is 2, and so on. Find the total number of cases handled by the department that year by the end of June.

116. Advertising. The dollar amount of sales of a certain new product is approximated by the logarithmic function $D(m) = 20,000 + 100,000 \log (15m + 1)$, where m is the number of minutes of advertising of the product that is shown on cable television. Find the total sales if 30 minutes of cable television advertising time is purchased.

117. Stocking Lakes. A farmer stocked a lake on her property with 75 sunfish. She was told that with the proper oversight, the sunfish population could be approximated by the logarithmic function $f(t) = 75 + 45 \log (t + 1)$, where t is the number of years since the lake was stocked. Find the number of sunfish she can expect in the lake in $2\frac{1}{2}$ years.

118. Zoology. A trap-and-release program run by zoologists found that the ground squirrel population in a wilderness area could be estimated by the logarithmic function $s(t) = 800 + 600 \log (50t + 1)$, where t is the number of months after the program started. Find the ground squirrel population 3 years after the program began. (*Hint*: Be careful to use the correct units in your solution.)

119. Children's Height. The logarithmic function $h(A) = 29 + 48.8 \log (A + 1)$ gives the percent of the adult height a male child A years old has attained. If a boy is 9 years old, what percent of his adult height will he have reached?

120. Depreciation. In business, equipment is often depreciated using the double declining-balance method. In this method, a piece of equipment with a life expectancy of N years, costing $C, will depreciate to a value of $V in n years, where n is given by the formula

$$n = \frac{\log V - \log C}{\log\left(1 - \frac{2}{N}\right)}$$

A computer that cost $37,000 has a life expectancy of 5 years. If it has depreciated to a value of $8,000, how old is it?

121. Investing. If $P is invested at the end of each year in an annuity earning annual interest at a rate r, the amount in the account will be $A after n years, where

$$n = \frac{\log\left(\frac{Ar}{P} + 1\right)}{\log(1 + r)}$$

If $1,000 is invested each year in an annuity earning 12% annual interest, how long will it take for the account to be worth $20,000? Round to the nearest tenth of a year.

122. Growth of Money. If $5,000 is invested each year in an annuity earning 8% annual interest, how long will it take for the account to be worth $50,000? (See Exercise 121.) Round to the nearest tenth of a year.

WRITING

123. Explain the mathematical relationship between $f(x) = \log x$ and $g(x) = 10^x$.

124. Explain why it is impossible to find the logarithm of a negative number.

125. A table of solutions for $f(x) = \log x$ is shown here. As x decreases and gets close to 0, what happens to the values of $f(x)$?

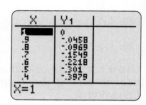

126. What question should be asked when evaluating the expression $\log_4 16$?

REVIEW

Solve each equation.

127. $\sqrt[3]{6x + 4} = 4$

128. $\sqrt{3x + 4} = \sqrt{7x + 2}$

129. $\sqrt{a + 1} - 1 = 3a$

130. $3 - \sqrt{t - 3} = \sqrt{t}$

CHALLENGE PROBLEMS

131. Without graphing, determine the domain of the function $f(x) = \log_5 (x^2 - 1)$. Express the result in interval notation.

132. Evaluate: $\log_6 (\log_5 (\log_4 1{,}024))$

133. Earthquakes. In 1985, Mexico City experienced an earthquake of magnitude 8.1 on the Richter scale. In 1989, the San Francisco Bay area was rocked by an earthquake measuring 7.1. By what factor must the amplitude of an earthquake change to increase its severity by 1 point on the Richter scale? (Assume that the period remains constant.)

134. Graph: $f(x) = \log_2 |x|$

SECTION 11.5

Base-e Exponential and Logarithmic Functions

OBJECTIVES

1 Define the natural exponential function.

2 Graph the natural exponential function.

3 Use base-e exponential formulas and functions in applications.

4 Define base-e logarithms.

5 Evaluate natural logarithmic expressions.

6 Graph the natural logarithmic function.

7 Use base-e logarithmic formulas and functions in applications.

ARE YOU READY?

The following problems review some basic skills that are needed when working with base-e exponential and logarithmic functions.

1. Evaluate $\left(1 + \frac{1}{n}\right)^n$ for $n = 2$.

2. Evaluate: $(2.718)^0$

3. Round 2.718281828459 to the nearest tenth.

4. Use a calculator to evaluate $55(2.718)^{0.4}$. Round to the nearest hundredth.

5. Fill in the blank: $\log_3 x = 6$ is equivalent to ☐ = ☐.

6. Fill in the blank: If $(3, 8)$ is on the graph of a one-to-one function f, then the point (☐, ☐) is on the graph of f^{-1}.

Any positive real number not equal to 1 can be used as a base of an exponential or a logarithmic function. However, some bases are used more often than others. Exponential and logarithmic functions that have many applications are ones whose base is an irrational number represented by the letter e.

n	$\left(1 + \frac{1}{n}\right)^n$
1	2
2	2.25
4	2.44140625 …
12	2.61303529 …
365	2.71456748 …
1,000	2.71692393 …
100,000	2.71826830 …
1,000,000	2.71828137 …

A scientific calculator was used to evaluate the expression.

1 Define the Natural Exponential Function.

The number called e is defined to be the value that $\left(1 + \frac{1}{n}\right)^n$ approaches as n gets larger and larger. The table in the margin shows the value of that expression as n increases from 1 to 1,000,000. It can be shown that as n approaches infinity, the value of $\left(1 + \frac{1}{n}\right)^n$ approaches:

$$e = 2.718281828459 \ldots$$

We give this number a letter-name because it makes communication easier. Reciting its first thirteen digits every time we refer to it would be overwhelming. So, we simply call it by the name "e."

Like π, the number e is an irrational number. That means its decimal representation is nonterminating and nonrepeating. Rounded to four decimal places, $e \approx 2.7183$.

Of all possible bases for an exponential function, e is the most convenient for problems involving growth or decay. Since these situations occur often in natural settings, we call $f(x) = e^x$ the *natural exponential function.*

The Natural Exponential Function	The function defined by $f(x) = e^x$ is the **natural exponential function** (or the **base-e exponential function**) where $e = 2.71828. \ldots$ The domain of $f(x) = e^x$ is the interval $(-\infty, \infty)$. The range is the interval $(0, \infty)$.

The $\boxed{e^x}$ key on a calculator is used to find powers of e.

Using Your Calculator ▶ **Finding powers of e**

To find the value of $\boxed{e^5}$ with a reverse entry scientific calculator, we press:

5 $\boxed{e^x}$

148.4131591

On some calculators, the $\boxed{e^x}$ key also serves as the $\boxed{LN}$ key. (Later in this section we will see why.) To activate the $\boxed{e^x}$ key, we must begin by pressing $\boxed{2nd}$ or $\boxed{SHIFT}$.

With a direct entry graphing calculator, we press:

$\boxed{2nd}$ $\boxed{e^x}$ 5 $\boxed{)}$ $\boxed{ENTER}$

e^(5)
148.4131591

Since powers of e are irrational numbers (nonterminating, nonrepeating decimals), we often round such answers. For example, to the nearest hundredth, $e^5 \approx 148.41$

2 Graph the Natural Exponential Function.

To graph $f(x) = e^x$, we construct a table of function values by choosing several values for x and finding the corresponding values of $f(x)$. For example, if $x = -2$, we have

$$f(x) = e^x$$
$$f(-2) = e^{-2} \qquad \text{Substitute } -2 \text{ for each } x.$$
$$= 0.135335283 \ldots \qquad \text{Use a calculator. On a scientific calculator, press: } 2 \boxed{+/-} \boxed{2nd} \boxed{e^x}.$$
$$\approx 0.1 \qquad \text{Round to the nearest tenth.}$$

Notation

Swiss born Leonhard Euler (1707–1783) is said to have published more than any mathematician in history. Through his work, the symbol e came into common use.

We enter $(-2, 0.1)$ in the table on the next page. Similarly, we find $f(-1)$, $f(0)$, $f(1)$, and $f(2)$, enter each result in the table, and plot the ordered pairs. We draw a smooth curve through the points to get the graph.

From the graph, we can verify that the domain of $f(x) = e^x$ is the interval $(-\infty, \infty)$ and the range is the interval $(0, \infty)$. Since the graph passes the horizontal line test, the function is one-to-one.

Note that as x decreases, the values of $f(x)$ decrease and approach 0. Thus, the x-axis is an asymptote of the graph. The graph does not have an x-intercept, the y-intercept is $(0, 1)$, and the graph passes through the point $(1, e)$.

$f(x) = e^x$

x	$f(x)$	
-2	$\frac{1}{e^2} \approx 0.1$	$\rightarrow (-2, 0.1)$
-1	$\frac{1}{e^1} \approx 0.4$	$\rightarrow (-1, 0.4)$
0	$e^0 = 1$	$\rightarrow (0, 1)$
1	$e^1 \approx 2.7$	$\rightarrow (1, 2.7)$
2	$e^2 \approx 7.4$	$\rightarrow (2, 7.4)$

The outputs can be found using the $\boxed{e^x}$ key on a calculator. In such cases, round to the nearest tenth to make point-plotting easier.

The graph steadily approaches the x-axis, but never touches or crosses it.

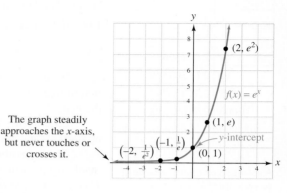

The graph of the natural exponential function can be translated horizontally and vertically, as shown below.

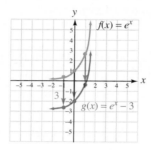

To graph $g(x) = e^x - 3$, translate each point on the graph of $f(x) = e^x$ down 3 units.

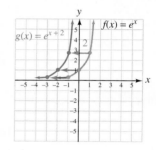

To graph $g(x) = e^{x+2}$, translate each point on the graph of $f(x) = e^x$ to the left 2 units.

We can illustrate the effects of vertical and horizontal translations of the natural exponential function by using a graphing calculator.

Using Your Calculator ▶ Graphing Base e (Natural) Exponential Functions

Figure (a) shows the calculator graphs of $f(x) = e^x$, $g(x) = e^x + 5$, and $h(x) = e^x - 3$. To graph them, we enter the right sides of the equations after $Y_1 =$, $Y_2 =$, and $Y_3 =$. The display will show:

$$Y_1 = e^{\wedge}(X) \qquad Y_2 = e^{\wedge}(X) + 5 \qquad Y_3 = e^{\wedge}(X) - 3$$

The graph of $g(x) = e^x + 5$ is 5 units above the graph of $f(x) = e^x$ and the graph of $h(x) = e^x - 3$ is 3 units below the graph of $f(x) = e^x$.

Figure (b) shows the calculator graphs of $f(x) = e^x$, $g(x) = e^{x+5}$, and $h(x) = e^{x-3}$. The graph of $g(x) = e^{x+5}$ is 5 units to the left of the graph of $f(x) = e^x$ and the graph of $h(x) = e^{x-3}$ is 3 units to the right of the graph of $f(x) = e^x$.

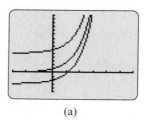

(a)

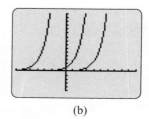

(b)

To graph complicated natural exponential functions, point-plotting can be tedious. In such cases, we will use a graphing calculator. For example, the figure shows the calculator graph of $f(x) = 3e^{-x/2}$. To graph this function, we enter the right side of the equation after the symbol $Y_1 =$. The display will show the equation

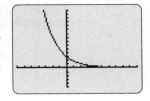

$$Y_1 = 3(e^{\wedge}(-X/2))$$

3 Use Base-e Exponential Formulas and Functions in Applications.

The following formula involving e provides a mathematical model for growth and decay applications. It is used in many areas, such as continuous compound interest, population trends, heat transfer, radioactivity, and learning retention.

Formula for Exponential Growth/Decay	If a quantity P increases or decreases at an annual rate r, compounded continuously, the amount A after t years is given by $A = Pe^{rt}$ Read as "A equals P times e to the rt power."

For the formula above, if the time is measured in years, r is called the **annual growth rate.** If r is negative, the growth represents a decrease.

For a given quantity P, say 10,000, and a given rate r, say 5%, we can write the formula for exponential growth using function notation:

$$A(t) = 10,000e^{0.05t}$$

Recall that if a bank pays interest twice a year, we say the interest is compounded *semiannually.* If it pays interest four times a year, we say the interest is paid *quarterly.* If it pays interest continuously (infinitely many times a year), we say that the interest is **compounded continuously.**

EXAMPLE 1   **Investing.**   If $25,000 accumulates interest at an annual rate of 8%, compounded continuously, find the balance in the account in 50 years.

Strategy   We will substitute 25,000 for P, 0.08 for r, and 50 for t in the formula $A = Pe^{rt}$ and calculate the value of A.

Why   The words *compounded continuously* indicate that we should use the base-e exponential growth/decay formula.

Solution

$A = Pe^{rt}$	This is the formula for continuous compound interest.
$A = 25,000e^{0.08(50)}$	Write 8% as 0.08. Substitute for P, r, and t.
$= 25,000e^{4}$	Evaluate the exponent: 0.08(50) = 4.
$\approx 1,364,953.751$	Use a calculator. On a scientific calculator, press: 25000 $\times$ 4 2nd e^x = .
$\approx 1,364,953.75$	Round to the nearest hundredth.

In 50 years, the balance will be $1,364,953.75—more than a million dollars.

Self Check 1   **Investing.**   In Example 1, find the balance in 60 years.

Now Try ▶   Problems 33 and 73

EXAMPLE 2 **City Planning.** The population of a city is currently 15,000, but economic conditions are causing the population to decrease 3% each year. If this trend continues, find the population in 30 years.

Strategy We will substitute 15,000 for P, -0.03 for r, and 30 for t in the formula $A = Pe^{rt}$ and calculate the value of A.

Why Since the population is decreasing 3% each year, the annual growth rate is -3%, or -0.03.

Solution

$$A = Pe^{rt} \qquad \text{This is the model for population growth/decay.}$$
$$A = 15,000e^{-0.03(30)} \qquad \text{Substitute for } P, r, \text{ and } t.$$
$$= 15,000e^{-0.9} \qquad \text{Evaluate the exponent: } -0.03(30) = -0.9.$$
$$\approx 6,098.544896 \qquad \text{Use a calculator. On a scientific calculator, press:}$$
$$\boxed{15000} \boxed{\times} \boxed{.9} \boxed{+/-} \boxed{2nd} \boxed{e^x} \boxed{=}.$$
$$\approx 6,099 \qquad \text{Round to the nearest whole number.}$$

Success Tip

For quantities that are decreasing, remember to enter a negative value for r, the annual rate, in the formula $A = Pe^{rt}$.

In 30 years, the expected population will be 6,099.

Self Check 2 **City Planning.** In Example 2, find the population in 50 years.

Now Try ▶ Problems 37 and 81

EXAMPLE 3 **Baking.** A mother takes a cake out of the oven and sets it on a rack to cool. The function $T(t) = 68 + 220e^{-0.18t}$ gives the cake's temperature in degrees Fahrenheit after it has cooled for t minutes. If her children will be home from school in 20 minutes, will the cake have cooled enough for the children to eat it? (Assume that 80°F, or cooler, would be a comfortable eating temperature.)

Strategy We will substitute 20 for t in the function $T(t) = 68 + 220e^{-0.18t}$.

Why The variable t represents the number of minutes the cake has cooled.

Solution When the children arrive home, the cake will have cooled for 20 minutes. To find the temperature of the cake at that time, we need to find $T(20)$.

$$T(t) = 68 + 220e^{-0.18t} \qquad \text{This is the cooling model.}$$
$$T(20) = 68 + 220e^{-0.18(20)} \qquad \text{Substitute 20 for } t.$$
$$= 68 + 220e^{-3.6} \qquad \text{Evaluate the exponent: } -0.18(20) = -3.6.$$
$$\approx 74.01121894 \qquad \text{Use a calculator. On a scientific calculator, press:}$$
$$\boxed{68} \boxed{+} \boxed{220} \boxed{\times} \boxed{3.6} \boxed{+/-} \boxed{2nd} \boxed{e^x} \boxed{=}.$$
$$\approx 74.0 \qquad \text{Round to the nearest tenth.}$$

When the children return home, the temperature of the cake will be about 74°, and it can be eaten.

Self Check 3 **Baking.** In Example 3, find the temperature of the cake 10 minutes after it is removed from the oven. Round to the nearest tenth.

Now Try ▶ Problem 91

---

4 **Define Base-e Logarithms.**

Of all possible bases for a logarithmic function, e is the most convenient for problems involving growth or decay. Since these situations occur often in natural settings, base-e

©RoJo Images/Shutterstock.com

logarithms are called **natural logarithms** or **Napierian logarithms** after John Napier (1550–1617). They are usually written as ln x rather than $\log_e x$:

ln x means $\log_e x$ Read ln x letter-by-letter as "ℓ ... n ... of x."

In general, the logarithm of a number is an exponent. For natural logarithms,

ln x is the exponent to which e is raised to get x.

Translating this statement into symbols, we have

$$e^{\ln x} = x$$

Caution

Because of the font used to print the natural log of x, some students initially misread the notation as In x. In handwriting, ln x should look like $\ell n\, x$.

5 Evaluate Natural Logarithmic Expressions.

EXAMPLE 4

Evaluate each natural logarithmic expression:

a. ln e **b.** ln $\dfrac{1}{e^2}$ **c.** ln 1   **d.** ln $\sqrt{e}$

Strategy Since the base is e in each case, we will ask "To what power must e be raised to get the given number?"

Why That power is the value of the logarithmic expression.

Solution

a. ln $e = 1$ Ask: "To what power must we raise e to get e?"
Since $e^1 = e$, the answer is: the 1st power.

b. ln $\dfrac{1}{e^2} = -2$ Ask: "To what power must we raise e to get $\frac{1}{e^2}$?"
Since $e^{-2} = \frac{1}{e^2}$, the answer is: the -2 power.

c. ln $1 = 0$ Ask: "To what power must we raise e to get 1?"
Since $e^0 = 1$, the answer is: the 0 power.

d. ln $\sqrt{e} = \dfrac{1}{2}$ Ask: "To what power must we raise e to get $\sqrt{e}$?"
Since $e^{1/2} = \sqrt{e}$, the answer is: the $\frac{1}{2}$ power.

Success Tip

Every natural logarithmic equation has a corresponding natural exponential equation. For example:

ln $\dfrac{1}{e^2} = -2$ means $e^{-2} = \dfrac{1}{e^2}$

and

ln $\sqrt{e} = \dfrac{1}{2}$ means $e^{1/2} = \sqrt{e}$

Self Check 4   Evaluate each expression: **a.** ln e^3 **b.** ln $\dfrac{1}{e}$ **c.** ln $\sqrt[3]{e}$

Now Try ▶ Problems 41, 45, and 47

Many natural logarithmic expressions are not as easy to evaluate as those in the previous example. For example, to find ln 2.34, we ask, "To what power must we raise e to get 2.34?" The answer isn't obvious. In such cases, we use a calculator.

Using Your Calculator ▶ **Evaluating Base-*e* (Natural) Logarithms**

To find ln 2.34 with a reverse entry scientific calculator, we press:

2.34 ⌊LN⌋   .850150929

On some calculators, the $\boxed{e^x}$ key also serves as the $\boxed{\text{LN}}$ key when $\boxed{\text{2nd}}$ or $\boxed{\text{SHIFT}}$ is pressed. We will see why this is so later in this section.

To use a direct entry graphing calculator, we press:

$\boxed{\text{LN}}$ 2.34 $\boxed{)}$ $\boxed{\text{ENTER}}$ ln(2.34)
                                        .8501509294

To four decimal places, ln 2.34 ≈ 0.8502. This means that $e^{0.8502} \approx 2.34$.

If we attempt to evaluate logarithmic expressions such as $\ln 0$, or the logarithm of a negative number, such as $\ln(-5)$, then one of the following error statements will be displayed.

| Error | ```
ERR:DOMAIN
1:QUIT
2:Go to
``` | ```
ERR:NONREAL ANS
1:QUIT
2:Go to
``` |
|---|---|---|

Certain natural logarithmic equations can be solved by writing them as equivalent natural exponential equations.

EXAMPLE 5   Solve each equation: **a.** $\ln x = 1.335$ and **b.** $\ln x = -5.5$. Give each result to four decimal places.

Strategy   To solve these logarithmic equations, we will instead write and solve equivalent exponential equations.

Why   The resulting exponential equations are easier to solve because the variable term is isolated on one side.

Solution   **a.** Since the base of the natural logarithmic function is e:

$$\ln x = 1.335 \text{ is equivalent to } e^{1.335} = x$$

with *Exponent* labeling the 1.335 and *Base* labeling the e.

To use a reverse entry scientific calculator to find x, press:

1.335 [2nd] [e^x]   `3.799995946`

To four decimal places, $x = 3.8000$. Thus, the solution is 3.8000. To check, use your calculator to verify that $\ln 3.8000 \approx 1.335$.

b. The logarithmic equation $\ln x = -5.5$ is equivalent to the exponential equation $e^{-5.5} = x$. To use a reverse entry scientific calculator to find x, press:

5.5 [+/−] [2nd] [e^x]   `0.004086771`

To four decimal places, $x = 0.0041$. Thus, the solution is 0.0041. To check, use your calculator to verify that $\ln 0.0041 \approx -5.5$.

Self Check 5   Solve each equation. Give each result to four decimal places.
a. $\ln x = 1.9344$ **b.** $-3 = \ln x$

Now Try ▶ Problems 61 and 65

---

6 Graph the Natural Logarithmic Function.

Because the natural exponential function defined by $f(x) = e^x$ is one-to-one, it has an inverse function that is defined by $x = e^y$. When we write $x = e^y$ in the equivalent form $y = \ln x$, the result is called the *natural logarithmic function*.

The Natural Logarithmic Function	The **natural logarithmic function** with base e is defined by the equations $$f(x) = \ln x \text{ or } y = \ln x, \text{ where } \ln x = \log_e x$$ The domain of $f(x) = \ln x$ is the interval $(0, \infty)$, and the range is the interval $(-\infty, \infty)$.

Since the natural logarithmic function is the inverse of the one-to-one natural exponential function, the natural logarithmic function is one-to-one.

To graph $f(x) = \ln x$, we can construct a table of function values, plot the resulting ordered pairs, and draw a smooth curve through the points to get the graph shown in figure (a). Figure (b) shows the calculator graph of $f(x) = \ln x$. We see that the domain of the natural logarithmic function is $(0, \infty)$ and the range is $(-\infty, \infty)$.

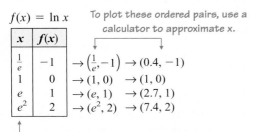

$f(x) = \ln x$

To plot these ordered pairs, use a calculator to approximate x.

x	$f(x)$
$\frac{1}{e}$	-1
1	0
e	1
e^2	2

$\rightarrow \left(\frac{1}{e}, -1\right) \rightarrow (0.4, -1)$
$\rightarrow (1, 0) \quad \rightarrow (1, 0)$
$\rightarrow (e, 1) \quad \rightarrow (2.7, 1)$
$\rightarrow (e^2, 2) \rightarrow (7.4, 2)$

Since the base of the natural logarithmic function is e, choose x-values that are integer powers of e.

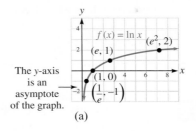

The y-axis is an asymptote of the graph.

(a)

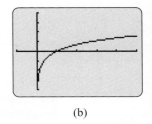

(b)

Notation

If it is helpful, imagine parentheses around the input value in the natural logarithmic function notation.

$$f(e) = 1$$

Function name, Input, Output

$$\ln (e) = 1$$

The natural exponential function and the natural logarithm function are inverse functions. The figure shows that their graphs are symmetric to the line $y = x$.

You may want to confirm that these functions are indeed inverses using the composition of inverses test in Section 11.2.

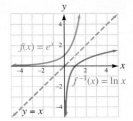

Using Your Calculator ▶ Graphing Base-e Logarithmic Functions

Many graphs of logarithmic functions involve translations of the graph of $f(x) = \ln x$. For example, the figure below shows calculator graphs of the functions $f(x) = \ln x$, $g(x) = (\ln x) + 2$, and $h(x) = (\ln x) - 3$.

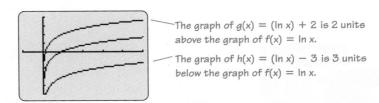

The graph of $g(x) = (\ln x) + 2$ is 2 units above the graph of $f(x) = \ln x$.

The graph of $h(x) = (\ln x) - 3$ is 3 units below the graph of $f(x) = \ln x$.

The next figure shows the calculator graph of the functions $f(x) = \ln x$, $g(x) = \ln (x - 2)$, and $h(x) = \ln (x + 3)$.

The graph of $h(x) = \ln (x + 3)$ is 3 units to the left of the graph of $f(x) = \ln x$.

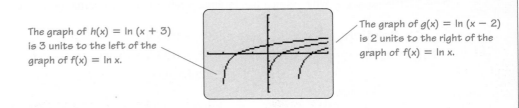

The graph of $g(x) = \ln (x - 2)$ is 2 units to the right of the graph of $f(x) = \ln x$.

7 Use Base-*e* Logarithmic Formulas and Functions in Applications.

If a population grows exponentially at a certain annual rate, the time required for the population to double is called the **doubling time.** It is given by the following formula.

Formula for Doubling Time	If *r* is the annual rate, compounded continuously, and *t* is the time required for a population to double, then
	$$t = \frac{\ln 2}{r}$$

EXAMPLE 6   **Doubling Time.**   The population of the Earth is growing at the approximate rate of 1.133% per year. If this rate continues, how long will it take for the population to double? (Source: CIA World Fact Book, 2009 data)

Strategy   We will substitute 1.133% expressed as a decimal for *r* in the formula for doubling time and evaluate the right side using a calculator.

Why   We can use this formula because we are given the annual rate of continuous compounding.

Solution   Since the population is growing at the rate of 1.133% per year, we substitute 0.0133 for *r* in the formula for doubling time and simplify.

$$t = \frac{\ln 2}{r}$$ Don't forget to substitute the decimal form of 1.133%, which is 0.0133, for r.

$$t = \frac{\ln 2}{0.0133}$$

$$\approx 52.11632937$$ Use a calculator. On a scientific calculator, press: 2 LN ÷ .0033 = .

$$\approx 52$$ Round to the nearest year.

At the current growth rate, the population of the Earth will double in about 52 years.

Self Check 6   **Doubling Time.**   If the annual growth rate of the Earth's population could be reduced to 1.1% per year, what would be the doubling time?

Now Try ▶ Problem 93

EXAMPLE 7   **The Pace of Life.**   A study by psychologists M. H. Bornstein and H. G. Bornstein found that the average walking speed *s*, in feet per second, of a pedestrian in a city of population *p*, is approximated by the natural logarithmic function $s(p) = 0.05 + 0.37 \ln p$. According to this study, what is the average walking speed of a pedestrian in Detroit if its population is 910,000? (Source: *Nature*, Volume 259, Feb. 19, 1976 and infoplease.com)

Strategy   We will find *s*(910,000).

Why   Since the variable *p* represents the population of the city, *p* = 910,000.

Solution
$$s(p) = 0.05 + 0.37 \ln p$$ This is the natural logarithmic model.

$$s(\mathbf{910,000}) = 0.05 + 0.37 \ln \mathbf{910,000}$$ Substitute 910,000 for p.

$$\approx 5.126843955$$ Use a calculator. On a scientific calculator, press: 0.05 + 0.37 × 910000 LN = .

$$\approx 5.1$$ Round to the nearest tenth.

The average walking speed of a pedestrian in Detroit is about 5.1 feet per second.

Self Check 7 **The Pace of Life.** Use the natural logarithmic function from Example 7 to find the average walking speed of a pedestrian in Dallas if its population is 1,300,000.

Now Try ▶ Problem 101

SECTION 11.5 ▶ STUDY SET

VOCABULARY

Fill in the blanks.

1. $f(x) = e^x$ is called the natural _____ function. The base is ____.

2. $f(x) = \ln x$ is called the _____ logarithmic function. The base is ____.

3. If a bank pays interest infinitely many times a year, we say that the interest is compounded _____

4. Like π, the number e is an _____ number. Its decimal representation is nonterminating and _____.

CONCEPTS

5. Refer to the graph on the right.
   a. What is the name of the function $f(x) = e^x$?

   b. What is the domain of the function? What is the range of the function?

   c. What is the y-intercept of the graph? What is the x-intercept of the graph?

   d. Is the function one-to-one?

   e. What is an asymptote of the graph?

   f. Is f an increasing or a decreasing function?

   g. The graph passes through the point $(1, y)$. What is y?

 6. a. Use a calculator to complete the table of values in the next column for $f(x) = \ln x$. Round to the nearest hundredth.

   b. Graph $f(x) = \ln x$. Note that the units on the x- and y-axes are different.

   c. What are the domain and range of the function?

   d. What is the x-intercept of the graph? What is the y-intercept?

   e. What is an asymptote of the graph?

f. Is f increasing or decreasing?

g. Is the function one-to-one?

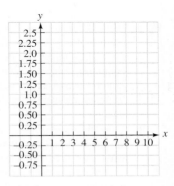

x	$f(x)$
0.5	
1	
2	
4	
6	
8	
10	

Fill in the blanks.

7. $e = $ ___ . ___ ___ ___ ___ ___ ___ ___ ___ ___ ___ ___ ___ ___ ___ ...

8. To two decimal places, the value of e is _____.

9. If n gets larger and larger, the value of $\left(1 + \frac{1}{n}\right)^n$ approaches the value of ____.

10. The formula for exponential growth/decay is $A = $ ____e ____.

11. To find $\ln e^2$, we ask, "To what power must we raise ____ to get e^2?" Since the answer is the 2nd power, $\ln e^2 = $ ____.

12. The logarithmic equation $\ln x = 1.5318$ is equivalent to the exponential equation _____ $= $ ____.

13. Graph each irrational number on the number line: $\left\{\pi, e, \sqrt{2}\right\}$.

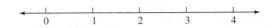

14. Complete the table of values. Use a calculator when necessary and round to the nearest hundredth.

x	-2	-1	0	1	2
e^x					

15. a. The function $f(x) = e^x$ is graphed in figure (a) below and the TRACE feature is used. What is the y-coordinate of the point on the graph having an x-coordinate of 1? What is the symbol that represents this number?

b. Figure (b) below shows a table of values for $f(x) = e^x$. As x decreases, what happens to the values of $f(x)$ listed in the Y_1 column? Will the value of $f(x)$ ever be 0 or negative?

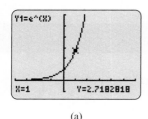

(a)

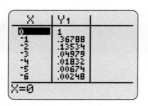

(b)

16. a. The illustration shows the graph of $f(x) = \ln x$, as well as a vertical translation of that graph. Using the notation $g(x)$ for the translation, write the defining equation for that function.

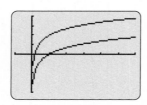

b. In the illustration, $f(x) = \ln x$ was graphed, and the TRACE feature was used. What is the x-coordinate of the point on the graph having a y-coordinate of 1? What is the name given this number?

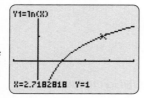

17. What is the inverse of the natural logarithmic function $f(x) = \ln x$?

18. Let $f(x) = 75 + 3{,}570 \ln x$. Find $f(28.1)$. Round to the nearest tenth.

NOTATION

Find A using the formula $A = Pe^{rt}$ given the following values of P, r, and t. Round to the nearest tenth.

19. $P = 1{,}000$, $r = 0.09$, and $t = 10$

$A = \boxed{} e^{(0.09)()}$

$\quad = 1{,}000e^{\boxed{}}$

$\quad \approx \boxed{}$ Use a calculator.

20. $P = 50{,}000$, $r = -0.12$, and $t = 50$

$A = 50{,}000e^{(\boxed{})(50)}$

$\quad = 50{,}000e^{\boxed{}}$

$\quad \approx \boxed{}$ Use a calculator.

Fill in the blanks.

21. We read $\ln x$ letter-by-letter as "$\boxed{}$ ... $\boxed{}$ ... of x."

22. a. $\ln 2$ means $\log_{\boxed{}} 2$.

b. $\log 2$ means $\log_{\boxed{}} 2$.

23. To evaluate a base-10 logarithm with a calculator, use the $\boxed{}$ key. To evaluate the base-e logarithm, use the $\boxed{}$ key.

24. If a population grows exponentially at a rate r, the time it will take the population to double is given by the formula $t = \boxed{}$.

GUIDED PRACTICE

Graph each function. See Objective 2.

25. $f(x) = e^x$ **26.** $f(x) = -e^x$

27. $f(x) = e^x + 1$ **28.** $f(x) = e^x - 2$

29. $y = e^{x+3}$ **30.** $y = e^{x-5}$

31. $f(x) = 2e^x$ **32.** $f(x) = \dfrac{1}{2}e^x$

Find A using the formula $A = Pe^{rt}$ given the following values of P, r, and t. Round to the nearest hundredth. See Example 1.

33. $P = 5{,}000$, $r = 8\%$, $t = 20$ years

34. $P = 15{,}000$, $r = 6\%$, $t = 40$ years

35. $P = 20{,}000$, $r = 10.5\%$, $t = 50$ years

36. $P = 25{,}000$, $r = 6.5\%$, $t = 100$ years

Find A using the formula $A = Pe^{rt}$ given the following values of P, r, and t. Round to the nearest hundredth. See Example 2.

37. $P = 15{,}895$, $r = -2\%$, $t = 16$ years

38. $P = 33{,}999$, $r = -4\%$, $t = 21$ years

39. $P = 565$, $r = -0.5\%$, $t = 8$ years

40. $P = 110$, $r = -0.25\%$, $t = 9$ years

Evaluate each expression without using a calculator. See Example 4.

41. $\ln e^5$ **42.** $\ln e^2$

43. $\ln e^6$ **44.** $\ln e^4$

45. $\ln \dfrac{1}{e}$ **46.** $\ln \dfrac{1}{e^3}$

47. $\ln \sqrt[4]{e}$ **48.** $\ln \sqrt[5]{e}$

49. $\ln \sqrt[3]{e^2}$ **50.** $\ln \sqrt[4]{e^3}$

51. $\ln e^{-7}$ **52.** $\ln e^{-10}$

Use a calculator to evaluate each expression, if possible. Express all answers to four decimal places. See Using Your Calculator: Evaluating Base-e (Natural) Logarithms.

53. $\ln 35.15$ **54.** $\ln 0.675$

55. $\ln 0.00465$ **56.** $\ln 378.96$

57. $\ln 1.72$ **58.** $\ln 2.7$

59. $\ln(-0.1)$ **60.** $\ln(-10)$

Solve each equation. Express all answers to four decimal places. See Example 5.

61. $\ln x = 1.4023$ **62.** $\ln x = 2.6490$

63. $\ln x = 4.24$ **64.** $\ln x = 0.926$

65. $\ln x = -3.71$ **66.** $\ln x = -0.28$

67. $\ln x = 1.001$ **68.** $\ln x = -0.001$

Use a graphing calculator to graph each function. See Objective 2. See Using Your Calculator: Graph Base-e Logarithmic Functions.

69. $f(x) = \ln\left(\dfrac{1}{2}x\right)$ **70.** $f(x) = \ln x^2$

71. $f(x) = \ln(-x)$ **72.** $f(x) = \ln(3x)$

APPLICATIONS

In Exercises 73–78, assume that there are no deposits or withdrawals.

73. **Continuous Compound Interest.** An initial investment of $5,000 earns 8.2% interest, compounded continuously. What will the investment be worth in 12 years?

74. **Continuous Compound Interest.** An initial investment of $2,000 earns 8% interest, compounded continuously. What will the investment be worth in 15 years?

75. **Comparison of Compounding Methods.** An initial deposit of $5,000 grows at an annual rate of 8.5% for 5 years. Compare the final balances resulting from annual compounding and continuous compounding.

76. **Comparison of Compounding Methods.** An initial deposit of $30,000 grows at an annual rate of 8% for 20 years. Compare the final balances resulting from annual compounding and continuous compounding.

77. **Determining the Initial Deposit.** An account now contains $11,180 and has been accumulating interest at 7% annual interest, compounded continuously, for 7 years. Find the initial deposit.

78. **Determining the Previous Balance.** An account now contains $3,610 and has been accumulating interest at 8% annual interest, compounded continuously. How much was in the account 4 years ago?

79. **The 20th Century.** The exponential function $A(t) = 123e^{0.0117t}$ approximates the population of the United States (in millions), where t is the number of years after 1930. Use the function to estimate the U.S. population for these important dates:

   - 1937 The Golden Gate Bridge is completed
   - 1941 The United States enters World War II
   - 1955 Rosa Parks refuses to give up her seat on a Montgomery, Alabama, bus
   - 1969 Astronaut Neil Armstrong walks on the moon
   - 1974 President Nixon resigns
   - 1986 The *Challenger* space shuttle explodes
   - 1997 *The Simpsons* becomes the longest running cartoon television series in history

80. **World Population Growth.** The population of Earth is approximately 6.8 billion people and is growing at an annual rate of 1.133%. Use the exponential growth model to predict the world population in 30 years.

81. **Highs and Lows.** Kuwait, located at the head of the Persian Gulf, has one of the greatest population growth rates in the world. Bulgaria, in southeastern Europe, has one of the smallest. Use an exponential growth/decay model to complete the table.

Country	Population 2010	Annual growth rate	Estimated population 2025
Kuwait	2,789,132	3.501%	
Bulgaria	7,148,785	−0.768%	

Source: CIA World Factbook

82. **Bed Bugs.** If not checked, the population of a colony of bed bugs will grow exponentially at a rate of 65% per week. If a colony currently has 50 bed bugs, how many will there be in 6 weeks?

83. **Epidemics.** The spread of hoof-and-mouth disease through a herd of cattle can be modeled by the function $P(t) = 2e^{0.27t}$ (t is in days). If a rancher does not quickly treat the two cows that now have the disease, how many cattle will have the disease in 12 days?

84. **Oceanography.** The width w (in millimeters) of successive growth spirals of the sea shell *Catapulus voluto,* shown below, is given by the exponential function $w(n) = 1.54e^{0.503n}$ where n is the spiral number. Find the width, to the nearest tenth of a millimeter, of the sixth spiral.

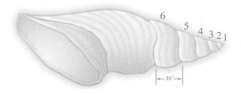

85. **Ants.** Shortly after an explorer ant discovers a food source, a recruitment process begins in which numerous additional ants travel to the source. The number of ants at the source grows exponentially according to the function $a(t) = 1.36\left(\frac{e}{2.5}\right)^t$, where t is the number of minutes since the explorer discovered the food. How many ants will be at the source in 40 minutes?

86. **Half-Life of a Drug.** The quantity of a prescription drug in the bloodstream of a patient t hours after it is administered can be modeled by an exponential function. (See the graph.) From the graph determine the time it takes to eliminate half of the initial dose from the body.

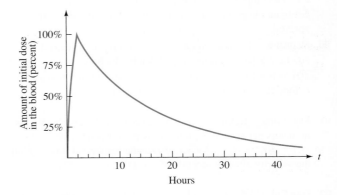

87.

from Campus to Careers

Social Worker

Social workers often use occupational test results when counseling their clients about employment options. The "learning curve" below shows that as a factory trainee assembled more chairs, the assembly time per chair generally decreased. If company standards required an average assembly time of 10 minutes or less, how many chairs did the trainee have to assemble before meeting company standards? (Notice that the graph is a model of exponential decay.)

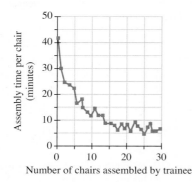

88. Ozone Concentrations. A *Dobson* unit is the most basic measure used in ozone research. Roughly 300 Dobson units are equivalent to the height of 2 pennies stacked on top of each other. Suppose the ozone layer thickness (in Dobsons) over a certain city is modeled by the function $A(t) = 300e^{-0.0011t}$, where t is the number of years after 1990. Estimate how thick the ozone layer will be in 2015.

89. Disinfectants. The exponential function $A(t) = 2,000,000e^{-0.588t}$ approximates the number of germs on a table top, t minutes after disinfectant was sprayed on it. Estimate the germ count on the table 5 minutes after it is sprayed.

90. Medicine. The concentration of a certain prescription drug in an organ after t minutes is modeled by the function $f(t) = 0.08\left(1 - e^{-0.1t}\right)$ where $f(t)$ is the concentration at time t. Find the concentration of the drug at 30 minutes.

91. Sky Diving. Before the parachute opens, a skydiver's velocity in meters per second is modeled by the function $f(t) = 50\left(1 - e^{-0.2t}\right)$ where $f(t)$ is the velocity at time t. Find the velocity after 20 seconds of free fall.

92. Free Fall. After t seconds a certain falling object has a velocity in meters per second given by the function $f(t) = 50\left(1 - e^{-0.3t}\right)$. Which is falling faster after 2 seconds— the object or the skydiver in Exercise 91?

93. The Tarheel State. The 4.3% annual population growth rate for the Raleigh-Cary metropolitan area in North Carolina is one of the largest of any metropolitan area in the United States. If its growth rate remains constant, how long will it take for its population to double? (Source: U.S. Bureau of the Census)

94. The Big Easy. New Orleans has steadily won back some of the population it lost in the wake of Hurricane Katrina in 2005. If the current 8.2% annual increase in population remains constant, how long will it take for its population to double? (Source: money.cnn.com)

95. The Equality State. In 2009, the state with the fastest annual population growth rate was Wyoming. If the 2.13% annual increase in population remains constant, what is the first full year that the population of Wyoming will be double what it was in 2009? (Source: U.S. Bureau of the Census)

96. Doubling Money. How long will it take $1,000 to double if it is invested at an annual rate of 5% compounded continuously?

97. Population Growth. A population growing continuously at an annual rate r will triple in a time t given by the formula $t = \dfrac{\ln 3}{r}$. How long will it take the population of a town to triple if it is growing at the rate of 12% per year?

98. Tripling Money. Find the length of time for $25,000 to triple when it is invested at 6% annual interest, compounded continuously. See Exercise 97.

99. Forensic Medicine. To estimate the number of hours t that a murder victim had been dead, a coroner used the formula $t = \dfrac{1}{0.25} \ln \dfrac{98.6 - T_s}{82 - T_s}$ where T_s is the temperature of the surroundings where the body was found. If the crime took place in an apartment where the thermostat was set at 70°F, approximately how long ago did the murder occur?

100. Making Jello. After the contents of a package of JELL-O are combined with boiling water, the mixture is placed in a refrigerator whose temperature remains a constant 42°F. Estimate the number of hours t that it will take for the JELL-O to cool to 50°F using the formula $t = -\dfrac{1}{0.9} \ln \dfrac{50 - T_r}{200 - T_r}$ where T_r is the temperature of the refrigerator.

101. Cross Country Skiing. The function $H(s) = -47.73 + 107.38 \ln s$ approximates the heart rate (in beats/minute) for an Olympic-class cross country skier traveling at s miles per hour, where $s > 5$ mph. Find the heart rate of a skier traveling at a rate of 7.5 miles per hour. (Source: btc.ontana.edu/Olympics/physiology)

102. Strength Loss. After participating in an eight-week weight training program, a college student was selected to be part of a study to see how much strength he would lose if he discontinued working out. The function $M_B(w) = 225 - 14 \ln (4w + 1)$ approximates his maximum bench press (in pounds) w weeks after stopping weight training. What was his maximum bench press:

a. At the end of the eight-week training course?

b. 6 weeks after stopping the weight training?

103. The Pace of Life. According to the study discussed in Example 7, how much faster does the average pedestrian in New York City (population 8,392,000) walk than the average pedestrian in Atlanta (population 541,000)? (Source: infoplease.com)

104. Maturity Levels. The function $P(a) = 41.0 + 20.4 \ln a$ approximates the percent of adult height attained by an early-maturing girl of age a years, for $1 \le a \le 18$. The function $P(a) = 37.5 + 20.2 \ln a$ does the same for a late-maturing girl. Find the difference in percent of their adult height for both maturity types on their 10th birthday. (Source: Growth, Maturation, and Physical Activity, Human Kinetic Books, Robert Malina)

WRITING

105. Explain why the graph of $y = e^x - 5$ is five units below the graph of $y = e^x$.

106. A feature article in a newspaper stated that the sport of snowboarding was growing *exponentially*. Explain what the author of the article meant by that.

107. As of 2007, the population growth rate for Russia was -0.37% annually. What are some of the consequences for a country that has a negative population growth?

108. What is e?

109. Explain the difference between the functions $f(x) = \log x$ and $g(x) = \ln x$.

110. How are the functions $f(x) = \ln x$ and $g(x) = e^x$ related?

111. Explain why $\ln e = 1$.

112. Why is $f(x) = \ln x$ called the natural logarithmic function?

113. A table of values for $f(x) = \ln x$ is shown in figure (a) below. Explain why ERROR appears in the Y_1 column for the first three entries.

114. The graphs of $f(x) = \ln x$, $g(x) = e^x$, and $y = x$ are shown in figure (b) below. Describe the relationship between the graphs in words.

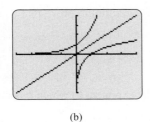

(a)   (b)

REVIEW

Simplify each expression. Assume that all variables represent positive numbers.

115. $\sqrt{240x^5}$

116. $\sqrt[3]{-125x^5y^4}$

117. $4\sqrt{48y^3} - 3y\sqrt{12y}$

118. $\sqrt[4]{48z^5} + \sqrt[4]{768z^5}$

CHALLENGE PROBLEMS

119. Without using a calculator, determine whether the statement $e^e > e^3$ is true or false. Explain your reasoning.

120. Graph the function defined by the equation $f(x) = \dfrac{e^x + e^{-x}}{2}$ from $x = -2$ to $x = 2$. The graph will look like a parabola, but it is not. The graph, called a **catenary**, is important in the design of power distribution networks, because it represents the shape of a uniform flexible cable whose ends are suspended from the same height.

121. If $e^{t+5} = ke^t$, find k.

122. If $e^{5t} = k^t$, find k.

123. Use the formula $P = P_0e^{rt}$ to verify that P will be twice P_0 when $t = \dfrac{\ln 2}{r}$.

124. Use the formula $P = P_0e^{rt}$ to verify that P will be three times as large as P_0 when $t = \dfrac{\ln 3}{r}$.

125. Use a graphing calculator to graph the function $f(x) = \dfrac{1}{1 + e^{-2x}}$. Describe its graph in words.

126. Food Shortages. Suppose that a country with a population of 1,000 people is growing according to the formula $P = 1,000e^{0.02t}$ where t is in years. Furthermore, assume that the food supply F, measured in adequate food per day per person, is growing linearly according to the formula $F = 30.625t + 2,000$ (t is time in years). Use a graphing calculator to determine in how many years the population will outstrip the food supply.

SECTION 11.6

Properties of Logarithms

OBJECTIVES

1 Use the four basic properties of logarithms.

2 Use the product rule for logarithms.

3 Use the quotient rule for logarithms.

4 Use the power rule for logarithms.

5 Write logarithmic expressions as a single logarithm.

6 Use the change-of-base formula.

7 Use properties of logarithms to solve application problems.

ARE YOU READY?

The following problems review some basic skills that are needed when working with properties of logarithms.

1. Evaluate: $\log_2 8 + \log_2 1$

2. Evaluate: $\log 10{,}000 - \log 10$

3. Evaluate: $9 \log_3 \dfrac{1}{3}$

4. Evaluate: $\dfrac{\log_7 49}{\log_7 7}$

5. a. Write $\sqrt{x}$ using a fractional exponent.

b. Write $(x - 2)^{1/2}$ using radical notation.

6. Use a calculator to find $\ln 5$. Round to four decimal places.

Since a logarithm is an exponent, we would expect there to be properties of logarithms just as there are properties of exponents. In this section, we will introduce seven properties of logarithms and use them to simplify and expand logarithmic expressions.

1 Use the Four Basic Properties of Logarithms.

The first four properties of logarithms follow directly from the definition of logarithm.

Properties of Logarithms	For all positive numbers b, where $b \neq 1$,

$$1.\ \log_b 1 = 0 \qquad 2.\ \log_b b = 1 \qquad 3.\ \log_b b^x = x \qquad 4.\ b^{\log_b x} = x \quad (x > 0)$$

We can use the definition of logarithm to prove that these properties are true.

1. $\log_b 1 = 0$, because $b^0 = 1$.   Read as "the log base b of 1 equals 0."
2. $\log_b b = 1$, because $b^1 = b$.   Read as "the log base b of b equals 1."
3. $\log_b b^x = x$, because $b^x = b^x$.   Read as "the log base b of b to the x power equals x."
4. $b^{\log_b x} = x$, because $\log_b x$ is the exponent to which b is raised to get x.
   Read as "b raised to the log base b of x power equals x."

Properties 3 and 4 also indicate that the composition of the exponential and logarithmic functions (in both directions) is the identity function. This is expected, because the exponential and logarithmic functions are inverse functions.

EXAMPLE 1

Simplify: **a.** $\log_5 1$ **b.** $\log_3 3$ **c.** $\ln e^3$ **d.** $6^{\log_6 7}$

Strategy We will compare each logarithmic expression to the left side of the previous four properties of logarithms.

Why When we get a match, the property will provide the answer.

Solution

a. By property 1, $\log_5 1 = 0$, because $5^0 = 1$.

b. By property 2, $\log_3 3 = 1$, because $3^1 = 3$.

c. By property 3, $\ln e^3 = 3$, because $e^3 = e^3$.

d. By property 4, $6^{\log_6 7} = 7$, because $\log_6 7$ is the power to which 6 is raised to get 7.

Self Check 1   Simplify: **a.** $\log_4 1$ **b.** $\log_4 4$ **c.** $\log_2 2^4$ **d.** $5^{\log_5 2}$

Now Try ▶ Problems 19, 21, 23, and 27

2 Use the Product Rule for Logarithms.

The next property of logarithms is related to the product rule for exponents: $x^m \cdot x^n = x^{m+n}$.

The Product Rule for Logarithms	The logarithm of a product equals the sum of the logarithms of the factors. For all positive real numbers M, N, and b, where $b \neq 1$, $$\log_b MN = \log_b M + \log_b N$$ Read as "the log base b of M times N equals the log base b of M plus the log base b of N."

As we apply properties of logarithms to rewrite expressions, we assume that all variables represent positive numbers.

EXAMPLE 2   Write each expression as a sum of logarithms. Then simplify, if possible.   **a.** $\log_2(2 \cdot 7)$
b. $\log 100x$ **c.** $\log_5 125yz$

Strategy   In each case, we will use the product rule for logarithms.

Why   We use the product rule because each of the logarithmic expressions has the form $\log_b MN$.

Solution   **a.** To avoid any confusion, the product $2 \cdot 7$ is written within parentheses.

$$\log_2(2 \cdot 7) = \log_2 2 + \log_2 7 \qquad \text{Read as "the log base 2 of 2 times 7." The log of the product } 2 \cdot 7 \text{ is the sum of the logs of its two factors.}$$

$$= 1 + \log_2 7 \qquad \text{Simplify: By property 2, } \log_2 2 = 1.$$

b. Recall that $100x$ means $100 \cdot x$.

$$\log 100x = \log 100 + \log x \qquad \text{The log of the product 100x is the sum of the logs of its two factors.}$$

$$= 2 + \log x \qquad \text{Simplify: By property 3, } \log 100 = \log 10^2 = 2.$$

c. The product $125yz$ has three factors: $125 \cdot y \cdot z$.

$$\log_5 125yz = \log_5 125 + \log_5 y + \log_5 z \qquad \text{The log of the product 125yz is the sum of the logs of its three factors.}$$

$$= 3 + \log_5 y + \log_5 z \qquad \text{Simplify: By property 3, } \log_5 125 = \log_5 5^3 = 3.$$

Success Tip

Your eyes should go immediately to the "input" of each log function, and then ask:

$$\log 100x$$
$$\uparrow$$
"What are the factors?"
$$\downarrow$$
$$\log_5 125yz$$

Self Check 2   Write each expression as the sum of logarithms. Then simplify, if possible.   **a.** $\log_3(3 \cdot 4)$ **b.** $\log 1{,}000y$
c. $\log_5 25cd$

Now Try ▶   Problems 31 and 35

PROOF   To prove the product rule for logarithms, we let $x = \log_b M$, $y = \log_b N$, and use the definition of logarithm to write each equation in exponential form.

$$M = b^x \text{ and } N = b^y$$

Then $MN = b^x b^y$, and a property of exponents gives

$$MN = b^{x+y} \qquad \text{Keep the base and add the exponents: } b^x b^y = b^{x+y}.$$

We write this exponential equation in logarithmic form as

$$\log_b MN = x + y$$

Substituting the values of x and y completes the proof.

$$\log_b MN = \log_b M + \log_b N \qquad \text{This is the product rule for logarithms.}$$

Caution

The log of a sum **does not equal** the sum of the logs. The log of a difference **does not equal** the difference of the logs.

CAUTION By the product rule, the logarithm of a *product* is equal to the *sum* of the logarithms. The logarithm of a sum or a difference usually does not simplify. **Do not incorrectly apply the distributive property in such cases.** In general,

$$\log_b (M + N) \neq \log_b M + \log_b N \quad \text{and} \quad \log_b (M - N) \neq \log_b M - \log_b N$$

For example,

$$\log_2 (2 + 7) \neq \log_2 2 + \log_2 7 \quad \text{and} \quad \log (100 - y) \neq \log 100 - \log y$$

Using Your Calculator ▶ **Verifying Properties of Logarithms**

We can use a calculator to illustrate the product rule for logarithms by showing that

$$\log (3.7 \cdot 15.9) = \log 3.7 + \log 15.9$$

We calculate the left and right sides of the equation separately and compare the results. To use a scientific calculator to find $\log (3.7 \cdot 15.9)$, we enter

3.7 $\boxed{\times}$ 15.9 $\boxed{=}$ $\boxed{\text{LOG}}$ `1.769598848`

To find $\log 3.7 + \log 15.9$, we enter

3.7 $\boxed{\text{LOG}}$ $\boxed{+}$ 15.9 $\boxed{\text{LOG}}$ $\boxed{=}$ `1.769598848`

Since the screen displays for the left and right sides are equal, that would suggest that the equation $\log (3.7 \cdot 15.9) = \log 3.7 + \log 15.9$ is true.

---

3 **Use the Quotient Rule for Logarithms.**

The next property of logarithms is related to the quotient rule for exponents: $\frac{x^m}{x^n} = x^{m-n}$.

The Quotient Rule for Logarithms

▼ The logarithm of a quotient equals the difference of the logarithms of the numerator and denominator. For all positive real numbers M, N, and b, where $b \neq 1$,

$$\log_b \frac{M}{N} = \log_b M - \log_b N \quad \text{Read as "the log base } b \text{ of } M \text{ divided by } N \text{ equals the log base } b \text{ of } M \text{ minus the log base } b \text{ of } N."$$

The proof of the quotient rule for logarithms is similar to the proof for the product rule for logarithms.

EXAMPLE 3   Write each expression as a difference of logarithms. Then simplify, if possible.

a. $\ln \frac{10}{7}$ **b.** $\log_4 \frac{x}{64}$

Strategy   In both cases, we will apply the quotient rule for logarithms.

Why   We use the quotient rule because each of the logarithmic expressions has the form $\log_b \frac{M}{N}$.

Solution   **a.** $\ln \frac{10}{7} = \ln 10 - \ln 7$ Recall that $\ln \frac{10}{7}$ is a natural logarithm and means $\log_e \frac{10}{7}$. The log of the quotient $\frac{10}{7}$ is the difference of the logs of its numerator and denominator.

b. $\log_4 \dfrac{x}{64} = \log_4 x - \log_4 64$ The log of the quotient $\frac{x}{64}$ is the difference of the logs of its numerator and denominator.

$$= \log_4 x - 3$$ Simplify: $\log_4 64 = \log_4 4^3 = 3$.

Self Check 3 Write each expression as a difference of logarithms. Then simplify, if possible. **a.** $\log_6 \dfrac{6}{5}$ **b.** $\ln \dfrac{y}{100}$

Now Try ▶ Problem 39

CAUTION By the quotient rule, the logarithm of a *quotient* is equal to the *difference* of the logarithms. The logarithm of a quotient is not the quotient of the logarithms:

$$\log_b \frac{M}{N} \neq \frac{\log_b M}{\log_b N}$$

For example,

$$\ln \frac{10}{7} \neq \frac{\ln 10}{\ln 7} \quad \text{and} \quad \log_4 \frac{x}{64} \neq \frac{\log_4 x}{\log_4 64}$$ Using a calculator, we have:
$\ln \frac{10}{7} \approx 0.356674944$
$\frac{\ln 10}{\ln 7} \approx 1.183294662$

In the next example, the product and quotient rules for logarithms are used in combination to rewrite an expression.

EXAMPLE 4 Write $\log \dfrac{xy}{10z}$ as the sum and/or difference of logarithms of a single quantity. Then simplify, if possible.

Strategy We will use the quotient rule for logarithms and then the product rule.

Why We use the quotient rule because $\log \frac{xy}{10z}$ has the form $\log_b \frac{M}{N}$. We later use the product rule because the numerator and denominator of $\frac{xy}{10z}$ contain products.

Solution We begin by applying the quotient rule for logarithms.

$$\log \frac{xy}{10z} = \log xy - \log 10z$$ The log of a quotient is the difference of the logs.

$$= \log x + \log y - (\log 10 + \log z)$$ The log of a product is the sum of the logs.
Write parentheses here so that both terms of the sum $\log 10 + \log z$ are subtracted.

$$= \log x + \log y - \log 10 - \log z$$ Change the sign of each term of $\log 10 + \log z$ and drop the parentheses.

$$= \log x + \log y - 1 - \log z$$ Simplify: $\log 10 = 1$.

Success Tip

Your eyes should go immediately to the "input" of the log function, and identify any quotients and/or products.

$$\log \frac{xy}{10z}$$
↑

Self Check 4 Write $\log_b \dfrac{x}{yz}$ as the sum and/or difference of logarithms of a single quantity. Then simplify, if possible.

Now Try ▶ Problem 45

---

4 Use the Power Rule for Logarithms.

The next property of logarithms is related to the power rule for exponents: $(x^m)^n = x^{mn}$.

The Power Rule for Logarithms	The logarithm of a number raised to a power equals the power times the logarithm of the number.
	For all positive real numbers M and b, where $b \neq 1$, and any real number p,
	$\log_b M^p = p \log_b M$ Read as "the log base b of M to the p power equals p times the log base b of M."

EXAMPLE 5   Write each logarithm without an exponent or a square root: **a.** $\log_5 6^2$ **b.** $\log \sqrt{10}$

Strategy   In each case, we will use the power rule for logarithms.

Why   We use the power rule because $\log_5 6^2$ has the form $\log_b M^p$, as will $\log \sqrt{10}$ if we write $\sqrt{10}$ as $10^{1/2}$.

Solution   **a.** $\log_5 6^2 = 2 \log_5 6$ The log of a power is equal to the power times the log. Write the exponent 2 in front of $\log_5 6$.

      b. $\log \sqrt{10} = \log 10^{1/2}$ Write $\sqrt{10}$ using a fractional exponent: $\sqrt{10} = (10)^{1/2}$.

$$= \frac{1}{2} \log 10 \quad \begin{array}{l} \text{The log of a power is equal to the power times the log.} \\ \text{Write the exponent } \frac{1}{2} \text{ in front of } \log 10. \end{array}$$

$$= \frac{1}{2} \quad \text{Simplify: } \log 10 = 1.$$

Self Check 5   Write each logarithm without an exponent or a cube root:

      a. $\ln x^4$ **b.** $\log_2 \sqrt[3]{3}$

Now Try ▶ Problems 51 and 53

PROOF   To prove the power rule, we let $x = \log_b M$, write the expression in exponential form, and raise both sides to the pth power:

$$M = b^x$$
$$(M)^p = (b^x)^p \quad \text{Raise both sides to the pth power.}$$
$$M^p = b^{px} \quad \text{Keep the base and multiply the exponents.}$$

Using the definition of logarithms gives

$$\log_b M^p = px$$

Substituting $\log_b M$ for x completes the proof.

$$\log_b M^p = p \log_b M \quad \text{This is the power rule.}$$

It is often necessary to use more than one rule for logarithms to **expand a logarithmic expression.**

EXAMPLE 6   Write each expression as the sum and/or difference of logarithms of a single quantity:

      a. $\log_b x^2 y^3 z$ **b.** $\ln \dfrac{y^3 \sqrt[4]{x}}{z}$

Strategy   In part (a), we will use the product rule and the power rules for logarithms. In part (b), we will use the quotient rule, the product rule, and the power rule for logarithms.

Why   In part (a), we first use the product rule because the expression has the form $\log_b MN$. In part (b), we first use the quotient rule because the expression has the form $\log_b \frac{M}{N}$.

Solution

a. The expression $\log_b x^2 y^3 z$ is the logarithm of a product.

$$\log_b x^2 y^3 z = \log_b x^2 + \log_b y^3 + \log_b z \qquad \text{The log of a product is the sum of the logs.}$$
$$= 2\log_b x + 3\log_b y + \log_b z \qquad \text{The log of a power is the power times the log.}$$

b. The expression $\ln \dfrac{y^3 \sqrt[4]{x}}{z}$ is the logarithm of a quotient.

$$\ln \frac{y^3 \sqrt[4]{x}}{z} = \ln y^3 \sqrt[4]{x} - \ln z \qquad \begin{array}{l}\text{This is a natural log expression.}\\ \text{The log of a quotient is the difference of the logs.}\end{array}$$

$$= \ln y^3 + \ln \sqrt[4]{x} - \ln z \qquad \text{The log of a product is the sum of the logs.}$$
$$= \ln y^3 + \ln x^{1/4} - \ln z \qquad \text{Write } \sqrt[4]{x} \text{ as } x^{1/4}.$$
$$= 3\ln y + \frac{1}{4}\ln x - \ln z \qquad \text{The log of a power is the power times the log.}$$

Self Check 6   Expand: $\log \sqrt[4]{\dfrac{x^3 y}{z}}$

Now Try ▶   Problems 59 and 61

---

5 **Write Logarithmic Expressions as a Single Logarithm.**

We also can use properties of logarithms in reverse to **condense logarithmic expressions** having two or more terms.

EXAMPLE 7   Write each logarithmic expression as one logarithm:

a. $16\log_8 x + \frac{1}{3}\log_8 y$ **b.** $\frac{1}{2}\log_b (x - 2) - \log_b y + 3\log_b z$

Strategy   In part (a), we will use the power rule and product rule for logarithms in reverse. In part (b), we will use the power rule, the quotient rule, and the product rule for logarithms in reverse.

Why   We use the power rule because we see expressions of the form $p\log_b M$. The $+$ symbol between logarithmic terms suggests that we use the product rule and the $-$ symbol between such terms suggests that we use the quotient rule.

Solution

a. We begin by using the power rule on both terms of the expression.

$$16\log_8 x + \frac{1}{3}\log_8 y = \log_8 x^{16} + \log_8 y^{1/3} \qquad \text{A power times a log is the log of the power.}$$
$$= \log_8 (x^{16} \cdot y^{1/3}) \qquad \text{The sum of two logs is the log of the product.}$$
$$= \log_8 x^{16} y^{1/3}$$
$$= \log_8 x^{16} \sqrt[3]{y} \qquad \text{Write } y^{1/3} \text{ using radical notation: } \sqrt[3]{y}.$$

The Language of Algebra

In these examples, we use properties of logarithms in "reverse" to **condense** the given expression into a single logarithmic expression. For example:

Condense

$\log_b MN = \log_b M + \log_b N$

b. The first and third terms of this expression can be rewritten using the power rule of logarithms. Note that the base of each logarithm is b. We do not need to know the value of b to apply properties of logarithms.

$$\frac{1}{2} \log_b (x - 2) - \log_b y + 3 \log_b z$$

$$= \log_b (x - 2)^{1/2} - \log_b y + \log_b z^3 \qquad \text{A power times a log is the log of the power.}$$

$$= \log_b \frac{(x - 2)^{1/2}}{y} + \log_b z^3 \qquad \begin{array}{l}\text{The difference of two logs}\\ \text{is the log of the quotient.}\end{array}$$

$$= \log_b \frac{\sqrt{x - 2}}{y} + \log_b z^3 \qquad \text{Write } (x - 2)^{1/2} \text{ using a radical notation: } \sqrt{x - 2}.$$

$$= \log_b \left(\frac{\sqrt{x - 2}}{y} \cdot z^3 \right) \qquad \text{The sum of two logs is the log of the product.}$$

$$= \log_b \frac{z^3 \sqrt{x - 2}}{y}$$

Self Check 7   Write the expression as one logarithm:

$$2 \log_a x + \frac{1}{2} \log_a y - 2 \log_a (x - y)$$

Now Try ▶   Problems 75 and 79

The properties of logarithms can be used when working with numerical values.

EXAMPLE 8   If $\log 2 \approx 0.3010$ and $\log 3 \approx 0.4771$, use properties of logarithms to find approximations for: **a.** $\log 6$ **b.** $\log 18$

Strategy   We will express 6 and 18 using factors of 2 and 3 and then use properties of logarithms to simplify each resulting expression.

Why   We express 6 and 18 using factors of 2 and 3 because we are given values of $\log 2$ and $\log 3$.

Solution   **a.** $\log 6 = \log (2 \cdot 3)$ Write 6 using the factors 2 and 3.

$$= \log 2 + \log 3 \qquad \text{The log of a product is the sum of the logs.}$$

$$\approx 0.3010 + 0.4771 \qquad \begin{array}{l}\text{Substitute the given values for log 2 and log 3.}\\ \text{We must now use an } \approx \text{ symbol. Do the addition.}\end{array}$$

$$\approx 0.7781$$

b. $\log 18 = \log (2 \cdot 3^2)$ Write 18 using the factors 2 and 3.

$$= \log 2 + \log 3^2 \qquad \text{The log of a product is the sum of the logs.}$$

$$= \log 2 + 2 \log 3 \qquad \begin{array}{l}\text{The log of a power is the power times the log.}\\ \text{Write the exponent 2 in front of log 3.}\end{array}$$

$$\approx 0.3010 + 2(0.4771) \qquad \begin{array}{l}\text{Substitute the given value for log 2 and log 3.}\\ \text{We must now use an } \approx \text{ symbol.}\end{array}$$

$$\approx 1.2552 \qquad \text{Evaluate the expression.}$$

Self Check 8   See Example 8. Find approximations for each logarithm.
   a. log 1.5   **b.** log 0.75

Now Try ▶ Problems 87 and 89

We summarize the properties of logarithms as follows.

Properties of Logarithms

If b, M, and N are positive real numbers, $b \neq 1$, and p is any real number,

1. $\log_b 1 = 0$
3. $\log_b b^x = x$

2. $\log_b b = 1$
4. $b^{\log_b x} = x$

5. $\log_b MN = \log_b M + \log_b N$

6. $\log_b \dfrac{M}{N} = \log_b M - \log_b N$

7. $\log_b M^p = p \log_b M$

6   Use the Change-of-Base Formula.

Most calculators can find common logarithms (base 10) and natural logarithms (base e). If we need to find a logarithm with some other base, we can use the following **change-of-base formula.**

Change-of-Base Formula

For any logarithmic bases a and b, and any positive real number x,

$$\log_b x = \frac{\log_a x}{\log_a b}$$ This formula converts a logarithm of one base to a ratio of logarithms of a different base.

We can use any positive number other than 1 for base a in the change-of-base formula. However, we usually use 10 or e because of the capabilities of a standard calculator.

EXAMPLE 9   Find: $\log_3 5$

Strategy   To evaluate this base-3 logarithm, we will substitute into the change-of-base formula.

Why   We assume that the reader does not have a calculator that evaluates base-3 logarithms (at least not directly). Thus, the only alternative is to change the base.

Solution   To find $\log_3 5$, we substitute 3 for b, 10 for a, and 5 for x in the change-of-base formula and simplify:

Caution

Don't misapply the quotient rule: $\dfrac{\log_{10} 5}{\log_{10} 3}$ means $\log_{10} 5 \div \log_{10} 3$. It is the expression $\log_{10} \frac{5}{3}$ that means $\log_{10} 5 - \log_{10} 3$.

$$\log_b x = \frac{\log_a x}{\log_a b}$$ This is the change-of-base formula.

$$\log_3 5 = \frac{\log_{10} 5}{\log_{10} 3}$$ The old base is 3. The new base we want to introduce is 10. Substitute: $b = 3$, $x = 5$, and $a = 10$.

$$\approx 1.464973521$$ Approximate. On a scientific calculator, enter: 5 LOG ÷ 3 LOG = .

To four decimal places, $\log_3 5 = 1.4650$. To check this result, use a calculator to verify that $3^{1.4650} \approx 5$.

We also can use the natural logarithm function (base e) in the change-of-base formula to find a base-3 logarithm.

$$\log_b x = \frac{\log_a x}{\log_a b}$$ This is the change-of-base formula.

$$\log_3 5 = \frac{\log_e 5}{\log_e 3}$$ The old base is 3. The new base we want to introduce is e. Substitute: $b = 3$, $x = 5$, and $a = e$.

$$\log_3 5 = \frac{\ln 5}{\ln 3}$$ Write $\log_e 5$ as $\ln 5$ and $\log_e 3$ as $\ln 3$.

$$\approx 1.464973521$$ Approximate. On a scientific calculator, enter: 5 LN ÷ 3 LN = .

We obtain the same result.

Self Check 9   Find $\log_5 3$ to four decimal places.

Now Try ▶ Problem 95

PROOF   To prove the change-of-base formula, we begin with the equation $\log_b x = y$.

$$y = \log_b x$$
$$x = b^y$$ Change the equation from logarithmic to exponential form.
$$\log_a x = \log_a b^y$$ Take the base-a logarithm of both sides.
$$\log_a x = y \log_a b$$ The log of a power is the power times the log.
$$y = \frac{\log_a x}{\log_a b}$$ Divide both sides by $\log_a b$.
$$\log_b x = \frac{\log_a x}{\log_a b}$$ Refer to the first equation, $y = \log_b x$ and substitute $\log_b x$ for y. This is the change-of-base formula.

7 Use Properties of Logarithms to Solve Application Problems.

In chemistry, common logarithms are used to express how basic or acidic a solution is. The more acidic a solution, the greater the concentration of hydrogen ions. (A **hydrogen ion** is a positively charged hydrogen atom missing its electron.) The concentration of hydrogen ions in a solution is commonly measured using the **pH scale.** The pH of a solution is defined as follows.

pH of a Solution   If $[H^+]$ is the hydrogen ion concentration in gram-ions per liter, then

$$pH = -\log[H^+]$$

EXAMPLE 10   **pH Meters.**   One of the most accurate ways to measure pH is with a probe and meter. What reading should the meter give for lemon juice if it has a hydrogen ion concentration $[H^+]$ of approximately 6.2×10^{-3} gram-ions per liter?

Strategy   We will substitute into the formula for pH and use the power rule for logarithms to simplify the right side.

Why After substituting 6.2×10^{-3} for $[H^+]$ in $-\log[H^+]$, the resulting expression will have the form $\log_b M^p$.

Solution Since lemon juice has approximately 6.2×10^{-3} gram-ions per liter, its pH is

$$pH = -\log[H^+] \qquad \text{This is the formula for pH. Read as "the opposite of the log of the hydrogen ion concentration."}$$

$$pH = -\log(6.2 \times 10^{-3}) \qquad \text{Substitute } 6.2 \times 10^{-3} \text{ for } [H^+].$$
$$= -(\log 6.2 + \log 10^{-3}) \qquad \text{The log of a product is the sum of the logs.}$$
$$= -[\log 6.2 + (-3)\log 10] \qquad \text{The log of a power is the power times the log.}$$
$$= -[\log 6.2 + (-3) \cdot 1] \qquad \text{Evaluate: } \log 10 = 1.$$
$$\approx 2.207608311 \qquad \text{Use a calculator.}$$
$$\approx 2.2 \qquad \text{Round to the nearest tenth.}$$

The meter should give a reading of approximately 2.2.

Self Check 10 **pH Meters.** The hydrogen ion concentration range for a freshwater aquarium has a low-end value of 2.5×10^{-8}. Find the pH level that corresponds to this value.

Now Try ▶ Problem 107

SECTION **11.6** ▶ STUDY SET

VOCABULARY

Fill in the blanks.

1. The logarithm of a _____, such as $\log_3 4x$, equals the sum of the logarithms of the factors.

2. The logarithm of a _____, such as $\log_2 \frac{5}{x}$, equals the difference of the logarithms of the numerator and denominator.

3. The logarithm of a number to a _____, such as $\log_4 5^3$, equals the power times the logarithm of the number.

4. The _____-of-base formula converts a logarithm of one base to a ratio of logarithms of a different base.

CONCEPTS

Fill in the blanks. In problem 6, also give the name of each rule.

5. a. $\log_b 1 = \boxed{\ }$
   b. $\log_b b = \boxed{\ }$
   c. $\log_b b^x = \boxed{\ }$
   d. $b^{\log_b x} = \boxed{\ }$

6. a. $\log_b MN = \log_b \boxed{\ } + \log_b \boxed{\ }$ _____ rule
   b. $\log_b \frac{M}{N} = \log_b M \boxed{\ } \log_b N$ _____ rule
   c. $\log_b M^P = p \log_b \boxed{\ }$ _____ rule
   d. $\log_b x = \dfrac{\log_a \boxed{\ }}{\log \boxed{\ } b}$ _____-of-_____ rule

Use a calculator to verify that each equation is true. See Using Your Calculator: Verifying Properties of Logarithms.

7. $\log(2.5 \cdot 3.7) = \log 2.5 + \log 3.7$
8. $\ln(2.25)^4 = 4 \ln 2.25$
9. $\ln \dfrac{11.3}{6.1} = \ln 11.3 - \ln 6.1$
10. $\log \sqrt{24.3} = \dfrac{1}{2} \log 24.3$

Match each expression with an equivalent expression from the list on the right.

11. $\log_3 10$
12. $\log_3 \dfrac{10}{11}$
13. $\log_3 10^{11}$
14. $\log_3 11$

a. $\dfrac{\log 11}{\log 3}$
b. $11 \log_3 10$
c. $\log_3 5 + \log_3 2$
d. $\log_3 10 - \log_3 11$

NOTATION

Complete each solution.

15. $\log_8 8a^3 = \log_8 \boxed{\ } + \log_8 \boxed{\ }$
    $= \log_8 8 + \boxed{\ } \log_8 a$
    $= \boxed{\ } + 3 \log_8 a$

16. $\log \dfrac{r}{st} = \log r - \log (\boxed{\ })$
    $= \log r - (\log \boxed{\ } + \log t)$
    $= \log r - \log s \boxed{\ }$

17. True or False?

$$\log 10{,}000x = \log (10{,}000x)$$

18. Fill in the blanks:

a. $y^{1/3} = \sqrt{}$ b. $\sqrt[5]{x} = x$

GUIDED PRACTICE

In this Study Set, assume that all variables represent positive numbers and $b \neq 1$.

Evaluate each expression. See Example 1.

19. $\log_6 1$ **20.** $\log_9 9$

21. $\log_4 4^7$ **22.** $\ln e^8$

23. $5^{\log_5 10}$ **24.** $8^{\log_8 10}$

25. $\log_5 5^2$ **26.** $\log_4 4^2$

27. $\ln e$ **28.** $\log_7 1$

29. $\log_3 3^7$ **30.** $5^{\log_5 8}$

Write each logarithm as a sum. Then simplify, if possible. See Example 2.

31. $\log_2 (4 \cdot 5)$ **32.** $\log_3 (27 \cdot 5)$

33. $\log 25y$ **34.** $\log xy$

35. $\log 100pq$

36. $\log 1{,}000rs$

37. $\log 5xyz$

38. $\log 10abc$

Write each logarithm as a difference. Then simplify, if possible. See Example 3.

39. $\log \dfrac{100}{9}$ **40.** $\ln \dfrac{27}{e}$

41. $\log_6 \dfrac{x}{36}$ **42.** $\log_8 \dfrac{y}{8}$

Write each logarithm as the sum and/or difference of logarithms of a single quantity. Then simplify, if possible. See Example 4.

43. $\log \dfrac{7c}{2}$ **44.** $\log \dfrac{9t}{4}$

45. $\log \dfrac{10x}{y}$ **46.** $\log_2 \dfrac{ab}{4}$

47. $\ln \dfrac{exy}{z}$ **48.** $\ln \dfrac{5p}{e}$

49. $\log_8 \dfrac{1}{8m}$ **50.** $\log_6 \dfrac{1}{36r}$

Write each logarithm without an exponent or a radical symbol. Then simplify, if possible. See Example 5.

51. $\ln y^7$ **52.** $\ln z^9$

53. $\log \sqrt{5}$ **54.** $\log \sqrt[3]{7}$

55. $\log e^{-3}$ **56.** $\log e^{-1}$

57. $\log_7 \left(\sqrt[5]{100} \right)^3$ **58.** $\log_3 \left(\sqrt{10} \right)^5$

Write each logarithm as the sum and/or difference of logarithms of a single quantity. Then simplify, if possible. See Example 6.

59. $\log xyz^2$ **60.** $\log 4xz^2$

61. $\log_2 \dfrac{2\sqrt[3]{x}}{y}$ **62.** $\log_3 \dfrac{\sqrt[4]{x}}{yz}$

63. $\log x^3 y^2$ **64.** $\log xy^2 z^3$

65. $\log_b \sqrt{xy}$ **66.** $\log_b x^3 \sqrt{y}$

67. $\log_a \dfrac{\sqrt[3]{x}}{\sqrt[4]{yz}}$

68. $\log_b \sqrt[4]{\dfrac{x^3 y^2}{z^4}}$

69. $\ln x^{20} \sqrt{z}$ **70.** $\ln \sqrt{xy}$

71. $\log_5 \left(\dfrac{1}{t^3} \right)^d$ **72.** $\log_6 \left(\dfrac{1}{x^4} \right)^t$

73. $\ln \sqrt{ex}$ **74.** $\ln \sqrt[3]{e^2 x}$

Write each logarithmic expression as one logarithm. See Example 7.

75. $\log_2 (x + 1) + 9 \log_2 x$

76. $2 \log x + \dfrac{1}{2} \log y$

77. $\log_3 x + \log_3 (x + 2) - \log_3 8$

78. $-2 \log x - 3 \log y + \log z$

79. $-3 \log_b x - 2 \log_b y + \dfrac{1}{2} \log_b z$

80. $3 \log_b (x + 1) - 2 \log_b (x + 2) + \log_b x$

81. $\dfrac{1}{3} \left[\log_b (M^2 - 9) - \log_b (M + 3) \right]$

82. $\dfrac{1}{4} \left[\log_r (n^2 - 16) - \log_r (n - 4) \right]$

83. $\ln \left(\dfrac{x}{z} + x \right) - \ln \left(\dfrac{y}{z} + y \right)$

84. $\ln (xy + y^2) - \ln (xz + yz) + \ln z$

85. $\dfrac{1}{2} \log_6 (x^2 + 1) - \log_6 (x^2 + 2)$

86. $\dfrac{1}{2} \log_8 (x^2 + 5) - \log_8 (x^2 + 5)$

Assume that $\log 4 \approx 0.6021$, $\log 7 \approx 0.8451$, and $\log 9 \approx 0.9542$. Use these values to evaluate each logarithm. See Example 8.

87. $\log_b 28$ **88.** $\log_b \dfrac{7}{4}$

89. $\log_b \dfrac{4}{63}$ **90.** $\log_b 36$

91. $\log_b \dfrac{63}{4}$

92. $\log_b 2.25$

93. $\log_b 64$

94. $\log_b 49$

Use the change-of-base formula to find each logarithm to four decimal places. See Example 9.

95. $\log_3 7$

96. $\log_7 3$

97. $\log_{1/3} 3$

98. $\log_{1/2} 6$

99. $\log_3 8$

100. $\log_5 10$

101. $\log_{\sqrt{2}} \sqrt{5}$

102. $\log_\pi e$

Look Alikes . . .
Which pair of expressions in each list are equivalent?

103. a. $\log (9 \cdot 3)$ **b.** $\log 9 \cdot \log 3$ **c.** $\log 9 + \log 3$

104. a. $\log_6 \dfrac{7}{9}$ **b.** $\dfrac{\log_6 7}{\log_6 9}$ **c.** $\log_6 7 - \log_6 9$

105. a. $\log_2 11^4$ **b.** $4 \log_2 11$ **c.** $(\log_2 11)^4$

106. a. $\ln \sqrt{t}$ **b.** $\sqrt{\ln t}$ **c.** $\dfrac{1}{2} \ln t$

APPLICATIONS

107. pH of a Solution.   Find the pH of a solution with a hydrogen ion concentration of 1.7×10^{-5} gram-ions per liter.

108. pH of Pickles.   The hydrogen ion concentration of sour pickles is 6.31×10^{-4}. Find the pH.

109. Formulas.   Use properties of logarithms to write the right side of each formula in an equivalent condensed form.

   a. From sound engineering: $B = 10(\log I - \log I_0)$

   b. From medicine: $T = \dfrac{1}{k}(\ln C_2 - \ln C_1)$

110. Doubling Time.   The formula $t = \dfrac{\ln 2}{r}$ gives the time t for a population to double, where r is the annual rate of continuous compounding. Write the formula in an equivalent form so that it involves a common logarithm, not a natural logarithm.

WRITING

111. Explain the difference between a logarithm of a product and the product of logarithms.

112. How can the $\boxed{\text{LOG}}$ key on a calculator be used to find $\log_2 7$?

Explain why each statement is false.

113. $\log AB = (\log A)(\log B)$

114. $\log (A + B) = \log A + \log B$

115. $\log_b (A - B) = \dfrac{\log_b A}{\log_b B}$

116. $\dfrac{\log_b A}{\log_b B} = \log_b A - \log_b B$

117. Explain the meaning of the arrow:

   $$\overset{\frown}{\log 7^{15}}$$

118. When is the change-of-base formula helpful?

REVIEW

Consider the line that passes through P(−2, 3) and Q(4, −4).

119. Find the slope of line PQ.

120. Find the distance between P and Q.

121. Find the midpoint of line segment PQ.

122. Write the equation in slope–intercept form of line PQ.

CHALLENGE PROBLEMS

123. Explain why $e^{\ln x} = x$.

124. If $\log_b 3x = 1 + \log_b x$, find b.

125. Show that $\log_{b^2} x = \dfrac{1}{2} \log_b x$.

126. Show that $e^{x \ln a} = a^x$.

SECTION 11.7

Exponential and Logarithmic Equations

OBJECTIVES

1 Solve exponential equations.

2 Solve logarithmic equations.

3 Use exponential and logarithmic equations to solve application problems.

ARE YOU READY?

The following problems review some basic skills that are needed when solving exponential and logarithmic equations.

1. Fill in the blanks: **a.** $16 = 2^{\square}$ **b.** $\dfrac{1}{125} = 5^{\square}$

2. Find $\dfrac{\log 12}{\log 9}$. Round to four decimal places.

3. Use the power rule for logarithms: $\log_3 8^x$

4. Evaluate: $\ln e$

5. Use a property of logarithms to write each expression as a single logarithm:

   a. $\log_2 5 + \log_2 x$

   b. $\ln 10 - \ln (2t + 1)$

6. Evaluate: $\log (-6)$

In earlier chapters, we have solved linear equations, absolute value equations, quadratic equations, rational equations, and radical equations. In this section, we will solve two new types of equations: exponential equations and logarithmic equations.

1 Solve Exponential Equations.

An **exponential equation** contains a variable in one of its exponents. Some examples of exponential equations are

$$3^{x+1} = 81, \qquad 6^{x-3} = 2^x, \qquad \text{and} \qquad e^{0.9t} = 8$$

If both sides of an exponential equation can be expressed as a power of the same base, we can use the following property to solve it.

Exponent Property of Equality	If two exponential expressions with the same base are equal, their exponents are equal. For any real number b, where $b \neq -1$, 0, or 1, $$b^x = b^y \qquad \text{is equivalent to} \qquad x = y$$

EXAMPLE 1   Solve: $3^{x+1} = 81$

Strategy   We will express the right side of the equation as a power of 3.

Why   If each side of the equation is expressed as a power of the *same* base (in this case, 3), we can use the exponent property of equality to set the exponents equal and solve for x.

Solution

$$3^{x+1} = 81 \qquad \text{This is the equation to solve.}$$
$$3^{x+1} = 3^4 \qquad \text{Write 81 as a power of 3: } 81 = 3^4.$$
$$x + 1 = 4 \qquad \text{If two exponential expressions with the same base are equal, their exponents are equal.}$$
$$x = 3 \qquad \text{Solve for x by subtracting 1 from both sides.}$$

The solution is 3 and the solution set is $\{3\}$. To check this result, we substitute 3 for x in the original equation.

Check:
$$3^{x+1} = 81$$
$$3^{3+1} \stackrel{?}{=} 81$$
$$3^4 \stackrel{?}{=} 81$$
$$81 = 81 \qquad \text{True}$$

Self Check 1   Solve: $5^{3x-4} = 25$

Now Try ▶ Problem 21

EXAMPLE 2   Solve: $2^{x^2+2x} = \dfrac{1}{2}$

Strategy   We will express the right side of the equation as a power of 2.

Why   If each side of the equation is expressed as a power of the same base (in this case, 2), we can use the exponent property of equality to set the exponents equal and solve for x.

Solution

$$2^{x^2+2x} = \frac{1}{2}$$ *This is the equation to solve.*

$$2^{x^2+2x} = 2^{-1}$$ *Write $\frac{1}{2}$ as a power of 2: $\frac{1}{2} = 2^{-1}$.*

$$x^2 + 2x = -1$$ *If two exponential expressions with the same base are equal, their exponents are equal.*

$$x^2 + 2x + 1 = 0$$ *Add 1 to both sides.*

$$(x + 1)(x + 1) = 0$$ *Factor the trinomial.*

$$x + 1 = 0 \quad \text{or} \quad x + 1 = 0$$ *Set each factor equal to 0.*

$$x = -1 \quad | \quad x = -1$$ *Solve each linear equation.*

We see that the two solutions are the same. Thus, -1 is a repeated solution and the solution set is $\{-1\}$. Verify that -1 satisfies the original equation.

Self Check 2   Solve: $3^{x^2-2x} = \frac{1}{3}$

Now Try ▶ Problem 25

Using Your Calculator ▶ Solving Exponential Equations Graphically

To use a graphing calculator to approximate the solutions of $2^{x^2+2x} = \frac{1}{2}$ (see Example 2), we can subtract $\frac{1}{2}$ from both sides of the equation to get $2^{x^2+2x} - \frac{1}{2} = 0$ and graph the corresponding function $f(x) = 2^{x^2+2x} - \frac{1}{2}$ as shown in figure (a).

The solutions of $2^{x^2+2x} - \frac{1}{2} = 0$ are the x-coordinates of the x-intercepts of the graph of $f(x) = 2^{x^2+2x} - \frac{1}{2}$. Using the ZERO feature, we see in figure (a) that the graph has only one x-intercept, $(-1, 0)$. Therefore, -1 is the only solution of $2^{x^2+2x} - \frac{1}{2} = 0$.

We also can solve $2^{x^2+2x} = \frac{1}{2}$ using the INTERSECT feature found on most graphing calculators. After graphing $Y_1 = 2^{x^2+2x}$ and $Y_2 = \frac{1}{2}$, we select INTERSECT, which approximates the coordinates of the point of intersection of the two graphs. From the display shown in figure (b), we can conclude that the solution is -1. Verify this by checking.

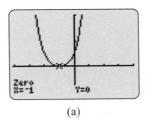   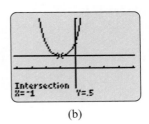

(a)   (b)

When it is difficult or impossible to write each side of an exponential equation as a power of the same base, we often can use the following property of logarithms to solve the equation.

Logarithm Property of Equality	If two positive numbers are equal, the logarithms base-b of the numbers are equal. For any positive number b, where $b \neq 1$, and positive numbers x and y,
	$\log_b x = \log_b y$ is equivalent to $x = y$

EXAMPLE 3   Solve: $3^x = 5$

Strategy   We will take the base-10 logarithm on both sides of the equation.

Why   We can then use the power rule of logarithms to move the variable x from its current position as an exponent to a position as a factor.

Solution

Unlike Example 1, where we solved $3^{x+1} = 81$, it is not possible to write each side of $3^x = 5$ as an integer power of the same base 3. Instead, we use the logarithm property of equality and *take the logarithm on each side* to solve the equation. Although any base logarithm can be chosen, the calculations with a calculator are usually simplest if we use a common or natural logarithm.

<table>
<tr><td>$3^x = 5$</td><td>This is the equation to solve.</td></tr>
<tr><td>$\log 3^x = \log 5$</td><td>Take the common logarithm on each side.</td></tr>
<tr><td>$x \log 3 = \log 5$</td><td>The log of a power is the power times the log: $\log 3^x = x \log 3$. The variable x is now a factor of $x \log 3$ and not an exponent.</td></tr>
<tr><td>$\dfrac{x \log 3}{\log 3} = \dfrac{\log 5}{\log 3}$</td><td>$x \log 3$ means $x \cdot \log 3$. To isolate x, undo the multiplication by $\log 3$ by dividing both sides by $\log 3$.</td></tr>
<tr><td>$\dfrac{x \overset{1}{\cancel{\log 3}}}{\underset{1}{\cancel{\log 3}}} = \dfrac{\log 5}{\log 3}$</td><td>Simplify the left side by removing the common factor of $\log 3$ from the numerator and denominator.</td></tr>
<tr><td>$x = \dfrac{\log 5}{\log 3}$</td><td>This is the exact solution.</td></tr>
<tr><td>$x \approx 1.464973521$</td><td>Approximate. On a reverse-entry scientific calculator, press: 5 LOG ÷ 3 LOG = .</td></tr>
</table>

The exact solution is $\dfrac{\log 5}{\log 3}$ and the solution set is $\left\{ \dfrac{\log 5}{\log 3} \right\}$. Rounded to four decimal places, an approximate solution is 1.4650.

We also can take the natural logarithm on each side of the equation to solve for x.

<table>
<tr><td>$3^x = 5$</td><td></td></tr>
<tr><td>$\ln 3^x = \ln 5$</td><td>Take the natural logarithm on each side.</td></tr>
<tr><td>$x \ln 3 = \ln 5$</td><td>Use the power rule of logarithms: $\ln 3^x = x \ln 3$.</td></tr>
<tr><td>$\dfrac{x \ln 3}{\ln 3} = \dfrac{\ln 5}{\ln 3}$</td><td>$x \ln 3$ means $x \cdot \ln 3$. To isolate x, undo the multiplication by $\ln 3$ by dividing both sides by $\ln 3$.</td></tr>
<tr><td>$\dfrac{x \overset{1}{\cancel{\ln 3}}}{\underset{1}{\cancel{\ln 3}}} = \dfrac{\ln 5}{\ln 3}$</td><td>Simplify the left side by removing the common factor of $\ln 3$ from the numerator and denominator.</td></tr>
<tr><td>$x = \dfrac{\ln 5}{\ln 3}$</td><td>This is the exact solution.</td></tr>
<tr><td>$x \approx 1.464973521$</td><td>Approximate. On a scientific calculator, press: 5 LN ÷ 3 LN = .</td></tr>
</table>

The result is the same using the natural logarithm. To check the approximate solution, we substitute 1.4650 for x in 3^x and see if $3^{1.4650}$ is approximately 5.

Check:

$$3^x = 5$$
$$3^{1.4650} \overset{?}{=} 5$$
$$5.000145454 \approx 5 \quad \text{On a scientific calculator, press: 3 } y^x \text{ 1.4650 = .}$$

The Language of Algebra

Some instructors phrase the first step of the solution process as "taking the logarithm *of* both sides."

Success Tip

The power rule of logarithms provides a way of **moving the variable x from its position in an exponent to a position as a factor** of $x \log 3$.

$$\log 3^x = \log 5$$
$$x \log 3 = \log 5$$

Caution

Don't misuse the quotient rule:

$\dfrac{\ln 5}{\ln 3}$ means $\ln 5 \div \ln 3$

It is the expression $\ln \frac{5}{3}$ that means $\ln 5 - \ln 3$.

Self Check 3   Solve: $5^x = 4$

Now Try ▶   Problem 29

EXAMPLE 4   Solve: $6^{x-3} = 2^x$

Strategy   We will take the common logarithm on both sides of the equation.

Why   We can then use the power rule of logarithms to move the expressions $x - 3$ and x from their current positions as exponents to positions as factors.

Solution

$6^{x-3} = 2^x$	This is the equation to solve.
$\log 6^{x-3} = \log 2^x$	Take the common logarithm on each side.
$(x - 3) \log 6 = x \log 2$	The log of a power is the power times the log. The expression $x - 3$ is now a factor of $(x - 3) \log 6$ and not an exponent.
$x \log 6 - 3 \log 6 = x \log 2$	Distribute the multiplication by $\log 6$.
$x \log 6 - x \log 2 = 3 \log 6$	To get the terms involving x on the left side, add $3 \log 6$ and subtract $x \log 2$ on both sides.
$x(\log 6 - \log 2) = 3 \log 6$	Factor out x on the left side.
$\dfrac{x \, (\cancel{\log 6 - \log 2})}{\cancel{\log 6 - \log 2}} = \dfrac{3 \log 6}{\log 6 - \log 2}$	To isolate x, undo the multiplication by $\log 6 - \log 2$ by dividing both side by $\log 6 - \log 2$. Then simplify the left side.
$x = \dfrac{3 \log 6}{\log 6 - \log 2}$	This is the exact solution.
$x \approx 4.892789261$	Approximate. On a reverse-entry scientific calculator, press: $3 \;\times\; 6 \;\boxed{\text{LOG}}\; \div \;(6\; \boxed{\text{LOG}}\; - \;2\; \boxed{\text{LOG}}\;) =$.

The Language of Algebra

$\dfrac{3 \log 6}{\log 6 - \log 2}$ is the **exact** solution of $6^{x-3} = 2^x$. An **approximate** solution is 4.8928.

The solution is $\dfrac{3 \log 6}{\log 6 - \log 2}$ and the solution set is $\left\{ \dfrac{3 \log 6}{\log 6 - \log 2} \right\}$. To four decimal places, an approximate solution is 4.8928. To check, we substitute 4.8928 for each x in $6^{x-3} = 2^x$. The resulting values on the left and right sides of the equation should be approximately equal.

Self Check 4   Solve: $5^{x-2} = 3^x$

Now Try ▶ Problem 33

When an exponential equation involves an exponential expression with base e, it is easiest to take the natural logarithm on both sides to solve the equation.

EXAMPLE 5   Solve: $e^{0.9t} = 10$

Strategy   We will take the natural (base-e) logarithm on both sides of the equation.

Why   We can then use the power rule of logarithms to move the expression $0.9t$ from its current position as an exponent to a position as a factor.

Solution   The exponential expression on the left side has base e. In such cases, the calculations are easier when we take the natural logarithm of each side.

Success Tip

When we take the natural logarithm of both sides, that conveniently produces the factor ln e, which is equal to 1, on the left side of the equation.

$e^{0.9t} = 10$	This is the equation to solve.
$\ln e^{0.9t} = \ln 10$	Take the natural logarithm on each side.
$0.9t \ln e = \ln 10$	Use the power rule of logarithms: $\ln e^{0.9t} = 0.9t \ln e$. The expression $0.9t$ is now a factor of $0.9t \ln e$ and not an exponent.

$$0.9t \cdot 1 = \ln 10 \qquad \text{Simplify: } \ln e = 1.$$

$$0.9t = \ln 10 \qquad \text{Simplify the left side.}$$

$$t = \frac{\ln 10}{0.9} \qquad \begin{array}{l}\text{To isolate } t \text{, undo the multiplication}\\ \text{by 0.9 by dividing both sides by 0.9.}\end{array}$$

$$t \approx 2.558427881 \qquad \begin{array}{l}\text{Approximate. On a reverse-entry scientific calculator, press:}\\ \text{10 } \boxed{\text{LN}} \div .9 \boxed{=}.\end{array}$$

The exact solution is $\dfrac{\ln 10}{0.9}$. To four decimal places, an approximate solution is 2.5584. Verify this by using a calculator to show that $e^{0.9(2.5584)} \approx 10$.

Self Check 5 Solve: $e^{2.1t} = 35$

Now Try ▶ Problem 37

Strategy for Solving Exponential Equations	1. Isolate one of the exponential expressions in the equation.
	2. If both sides of the equation can be written as exponential expressions with the same base, do so. Then set the exponents equal and solve the resulting equation.
	3. If step 2 is difficult or impossible, take the common or natural logarithm on both sides. Use the power rule of logarithms to write the variable exponent as a factor, and then solve the resulting equation.
	4. Check the results in the original equation.

2 Solve Logarithmic Equations.

A **logarithmic equation** is an equation with a logarithmic expression that contains a variable. Some examples of logarithmic equations are

$$\log 5x = 3, \qquad \log (3x + 2) = \log (2x - 3), \qquad \text{and} \qquad \log_2 7 - \log_2 x = 5$$

Some logarithmic equations can be solved by rewriting them in equivalent exponential form.

EXAMPLE 6 Solve: $\log 5x = 3$

Strategy Recall that $\log 5x = \log_{10} 5x$. To solve $\log 5x = 3$, we will instead write and solve an equivalent base-10 exponential equation.

Why The resulting exponential equation is easier to solve because the variable term is isolated on one side.

Solution

$$\log 5x = 3 \qquad \text{This is the equation to solve.}$$
$$\log_{10} 5x = 3 \qquad \text{The base of the logarithm is 10.}$$
$$10^3 = 5x \qquad \text{Write the equivalent base-10 exponential equation.}$$
$$1{,}000 = 5x \qquad \text{Simplify: } 10^3 = 1{,}000.$$
$$200 = x \qquad \text{To isolate } x \text{, divide both sides by 5.}$$

The solution is 200 and the solution set is $\{200\}$.

Caution

Always check your solutions to a logarithmic equation to identify any extraneous solutions.

Check:
$$\log 5x = 3 \qquad \text{This is the original equation.}$$
$$\log 5(\mathbf{200}) \overset{?}{=} 3 \qquad \text{Substitute 200 for } x.$$
$$\log 1{,}000 \overset{?}{=} 3 \qquad \text{Multiply 5(200) = 1,000.}$$
$$3 = 3 \qquad \text{Evaluate: } \log 1{,}000 = \log 10^3 = 3.$$

Self Check 6   Solve: $\log_2 (x - 3) = -1$

Now Try ▶ Problem 41

There is a possibility of obtaining **extraneous solutions** when solving logarithmic equations. Always discard any possible solutions that produce the logarithm of a negative number or the logarithm of 0 in the original equation.

EXAMPLE 7   Solve: $\log(3x + 2) = \log(2x - 3)$

Strategy   We will use the logarithmic property of equality to see that $3x + 2 = 2x - 3$.

Why   We can use the logarithm property of equality because the given equation, $\log(3x + 2) = \log(2x - 3)$, has the form $\log_b x = \log_b y$.

Solution

$\log(3x + 2) = \log(2x - 3)$	This is the equation to solve.
$3x + 2 = 2x - 3$	If the logarithms of two numbers are equal, the numbers are equal.
$x + 2 = -3$	Subtract 2x from both sides.
$x = -5$	To isolate x, subtract 2 from both sides.

Caution

Don't make this error of trying to "distribute" log:

$$\log (3x + 2)$$

The notation log is not a number, it is the name of a function and cannot be distributed.

Check:

$\log(3x + 2) = \log(2x - 3)$	This is the original equation.
$\log[3(-5) + 2] \stackrel{?}{=} \log[2(-5) - 3]$	Substitute −5 for x.
$\log(-13) \stackrel{?}{=} \log(-13)$	Evaluate within brackets.
	Recall that log(−13) is undefined.

Since the logarithm of a negative number does not exist, the proposed solution of −5 must be discarded. This equation has no solution. Its solution set is $\varnothing$.

Self Check 7   Solve: $\log (5x + 14) = \log (7x - 2)$

Now Try ▶ Problem 49

In Examples 8 and 9, we will use the product and quotient rules of logarithms to "condense" one side of the equation first, before solving for the variable.

EXAMPLE 8   Solve: $\log x + \log (x - 3) = 1$

Strategy   We will use the product rule for logarithms in reverse: The sum of two logarithms is equal to the logarithm of a product. Then we will write and solve an equivalent exponential equation.

Why   We use the product rule of logarithms because the left side of the equation, $\log x + \log (x - 3)$, has the form $\log_b M + \log_b N$.

Solution

Success Tip

The objective is to use the product rule to "condense" the left side of the equation. We want to write an equivalent equation in which the variable x appears in only a single logarithmic expression.

$\log x + \log (x - 3) = 1$	This is the equation to solve.
$\log x(x - 3) = 1$	On the left side, use the product rule of logarithms.
$\log_{10} x(x - 3) = 1$	The base of the logarithm is 10.
$x(x - 3) = 10^1$	Write the equivalent base-10 exponential equation.
$x^2 - 3x - 10 = 0$	Distribute the multiplication by x, and then subtract 10 from both sides.
$(x + 2)(x - 5) = 0$	Factor the trinomial.
$x + 2 = 0$ or $x - 5 = 0$	Set each factor equal to 0.
$x = -2$ $\mid$ $x = 5$	

Caution

Don't automatically discard proposed solutions that are negative. Only discard proposed solutions that produce undefined logarithms in the original equation.

Check: The number -2 is not a solution because it does not satisfy the equation (a negative number does not have a logarithm). We will check the other result, 5.

$$\log x + \log (x - 3) = 1 \quad \text{This is the original equation.}$$
$$\log 5 + \log (5 - 3) \overset{?}{=} 1 \quad \text{Substitute 5 for } x.$$
$$\log 5 + \log 2 \overset{?}{=} 1 \quad \text{Do the subtraction within the parentheses.}$$
$$\log 10 \overset{?}{=} 1 \quad \begin{array}{l}\text{Use the product rule of logarithms:} \\ \log 5 + \log 2 = \log (5 \cdot 2) = \log 10.\end{array}$$
$$1 = 1 \quad \text{Evaluate: } \log 10 = 1.$$

Since 5 satisfies the equation, it is the solution.

Self Check 8   Solve: $\log x + \log (x + 3) = 1$

Now Try ▶ Problem 53

Using Your Calculator ▶ **Solving Logarithmic Equations Graphically**

To use a graphing calculator to approximate the solutions of the logarithmic equation $\log x + \log (x - 3) = 1$ (see Example 8), we can subtract 1 from both sides of the equation to get $\log x + \log (x - 3) - 1 = 0$ and graph the corresponding function $f(x) = \log x + \log (x - 3) - 1$ as shown in figure (a). Since the solution of the equation is the x-value that makes $f(x) = 0$, the solution is the x-coordinate of the x-intercept of the graph. We can use the ZERO feature to find that this x-value is 5.

We also can solve $\log x + \log (x - 3) = 1$ using the INTERSECT feature. After graphing $Y_1 = \log x + \log (x - 3)$ and $Y_2 = 1$, we select INTERSECT, which approximates the coordinates of the point of intersection of the two graphs. From the display shown in figure (b), we can conclude that the solution is 5.

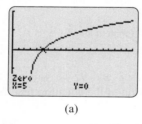
(a)

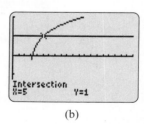
(b)

EXAMPLE 9   Solve: $\log_2 7 - \log_2 x = 5$

Strategy   We will use the quotient rule for logarithms in reverse: The difference of two logarithms is equal to the logarithm of a quotient. Then we will write and solve an equivalent exponential equation.

Why   We use the quotient rule for logarithms because the left side of the equation, $\log_2 7 - \log_2 x$, has the form $\log_b M - \log_b N$.

Solution

Success Tip

The objective is to use the quotient rule to "condense" the left side of the equation. We want to write an equivalent equation in which the variable x appears in only a single logarithmic expression.

$$\log_2 7 - \log_2 x = 5 \quad \text{This is the equation to solve.}$$
$$\log_2 \frac{7}{x} = 5 \quad \text{On the left side, use the quotient rule for logarithms.}$$
$$\frac{7}{x} = 2^5 \quad \text{Write the equivalent base-2 exponential equation.}$$
$$\frac{7}{x} = 32 \quad \text{Evaluate: } 2^5 = 32.$$

$$7 = 32x \qquad \text{To clear the equation of the fraction, multiply both sides by } x.$$

$$\frac{7}{32} = x \qquad \text{To isolate } x, \text{ divide both sides by 32.}$$

The solution is $\frac{7}{32}$. Verify that it satisfies the original equation.

> **Self Check 9**   Solve: $\log_2 9 - \log_2 x = 4$
>
> **Now Try** ▶ Problem 57

3   Use Exponential and Logarithmic Equations to Solve Application Problems.

Recall from Section 11.6 that a **hydrogen ion** [H⁺] is the positively charged nucleus of a hydrogen atom, without its electron. The concentration of hydrogen ions in a solution is commonly measured using the **pH scale.** The pH of a solution is defined as follows.

pH of a Solution	If [H⁺] is the hydrogen ion concentration in gram-ions per liter, then
	$$pH = -\log[H^+]$$

EXAMPLE 10   **Hydrogen Ion Concentration.**   Find the hydrogen ion concentration of seawater if its pH is 8.5.

Strategy   To find the hydrogen ion concentration, we will substitute 8.5 for pH in the formula $pH = -\log[H^+]$ and solve the resulting equation for [H⁺].

Why   After substituting for pH, the resulting logarithmic equation can be solved by solving an equivalent exponential equation.

Solution

$$\begin{aligned}
\mathbf{pH} &= -\log[H^+] && \text{This is the formula for pH.} \\
\mathbf{8.5} &= -\log[H^+] && \text{Substitute 8.5 for pH.} \\
-8.5 &= \log[H^+] && \text{Multiply both sides by } -1. \\
-8.5 &= \log_{10}[H^+] && \text{The base of the logarithm is 10.} \\
[H^+] &= \mathbf{10^{-8.5}} && \text{Write the equivalent base-10 exponential equation.} \\
[H^+] &\approx 0.000000003 && \text{Approximate. On a reverse-entry scientific calculator, press:}
\end{aligned}$$

10 y^x 8.5 +/− = .

Notation

In this logarithmic equation, the variable is the symbol [H⁺].

We can write the result using scientific notation:

$$[H^+] \approx 3.0 \times 10^{-9} \text{ gram-ions per liter}$$

> **Self Check 10**   **Hydrogen Ion Concentration.**   Find the hydrogen ion concentration of a solution with a pH value of 4.8.
>
> **Now Try** ▶ Problem 101

Experiments have determined the time it takes for half of a sample of a radioactive material to decompose. This time is a constant, called the material's **half-life.**

When living organisms die, the oxygen–carbon dioxide cycle common to all living things ceases, and carbon-14, a radioactive isotope with a half-life of 5,700 years, is no longer absorbed. By measuring the amount of carbon-14 present in an ancient object, archaeologists can estimate the object's age by using the radioactive decay formula.

Radioactive Decay Formula ▼ If A is the amount of radioactive material present at time t, A_0 was the amount present at $t = 0$, and h is the material's half-life, then

$$A = A_0 2^{-t/h}$$

EXAMPLE 11   **Carbon-14 Dating.**   How old is a piece of wood that retains only one-third of its original carbon-14 content?

Strategy   If A_0 is the original carbon-14 content, then today's content $A = \frac{1}{3}A_0$. We will substitute $\frac{A_0}{3}$ for A and 5,700 for h in the radioactive decay formula and solve for t.

Why   The value of t is the estimated age of the piece of wood.

Solution   To find the time t when $A = \frac{1}{3}A_0$, we substitute $\frac{A_0}{3}$ for A and 5,700 for h in the radioactive decay formula and solve for t:

$A = A_0 2^{-t/h}$	This is the radioactive decay model.
$\dfrac{A_0}{3} = A_0 2^{-t/5{,}700}$	The half-life of carbon-14 is 5,700 years.
$1 = 3(2^{-t/5{,}700})$	Divide both sides by A_0 and multiply both sides by 3.
$\log 1 = \log 3(2^{-t/5{,}700})$	Take the common logarithm on both sides.
$0 = \log 3 + \log 2^{-t/5{,}700}$	$\log 1 = 0$, and use the product rule for logarithms.
$-\log 3 = -\dfrac{t}{5{,}700}\log 2$	Subtract $\log 3$ from both sides and use the power rule of logarithms.
$5{,}700\left(\dfrac{\log 3}{\log 2}\right) = t$	Multiply both sides by $-\frac{5{,}700}{\log 2}$.
$t \approx 9{,}034.286254$	Approximate. On a reverse-entry scientific calculator, press: 5700 $\boxed{\times}$ 3 $\boxed{\text{LOG}}$ $\boxed{\div}$ 2 $\boxed{\text{LOG}}$ $\boxed{=}$.

The piece of wood is approximately 9,000 years old.

Self Check 11   **Carbon-14 Dating.**   How old is a piece of wood that retains 25% of its original carbon-14 content?

Now Try ▶   Problem 103

Notation

The initial amount of radioactive material is represented by A_0, and it is read as "A sub 0."

When there is sufficient food and space available, populations of living organisms tend to increase exponentially according to the following growth model.

Exponential Growth Model ▼ If P is the population at some time t, P_0 is the initial population at $t = 0$, and k depends on the rate of growth, then

$$P = P_0 e^{kt}$$

EXAMPLE 12   **Population Growth.**   The bacteria in a laboratory culture increased from an initial population of 500 to 1,500 in 3 hours. How long will it take for the population to reach 10,000?

Strategy   We will substitute 500 for P_0, 1,500 for P, and 3 for t in the exponential growth model and solve for k.

Why Once we know the value of k, we can substitute 10,000 for P, 500 for P_0, and the value of k in the exponential growth model and solve for the time t.

Solution

$$P = P_0 e^{kt}$$ This is the population growth formula.

$$1{,}500 = 500(e^{k3})$$ Substitute 1,500 for P, 500 for P_0, and 3 for t.

$$3 = e^{3k}$$ Divide both sides by 500.

$$3k = \ln 3$$ Write the equivalent base-e logarithmic equation.

$$k = \frac{\ln 3}{3}$$ Divide both sides by 3.

Notation

The initial population of bacteria is represented by P_0, and it is read as "P sub 0."

To find when the population will reach 10,000, we substitute 10,000 for P, 500 for P_0, and $\frac{\ln 3}{3}$ for k in the growth model and solve for t:

$$P = P_0 e^{kt}$$

$$10{,}000 = 500 e^{[(\ln 3)/3]t}$$

$$20 = e^{[(\ln 3)/3]t}$$ Divide both sides by 500.

$$\left(\frac{\ln 3}{3}\right)t = \ln 20$$ Write the equivalent base-e logarithmic equation.

$$t = \frac{3 \ln 20}{\ln 3}$$ To isolate t, multiply both sides by the reciprocal of $\frac{\ln 3}{3}$, which is $\frac{3}{\ln 3}$.

$$\approx 8.180499084$$ Approximate. On a reverse-entry scientific calculator, press:
3 × 20 LN ÷ 3 LN = .

The culture will reach 10,000 bacteria in about 8 hours.

Self Check 12 **Population Growth.** In Example 12, how long will it take the population to reach 20,000?

Now Try ▶ Problem 115

SECTION 11.7 ▶ **STUDY SET**

VOCABULARY

Fill in the blanks.

1. An equation with a positive constant base and a variable in its exponent, such as $3^{2x} = 8$, is called an _____ equation.

2. An equation with a logarithmic expression that contains a variable, such as $\log_5 (2x - 3) = \log_5 (x + 4)$, is a _____ equation.

CONCEPTS

Fill in the blanks.

3. a. If two exponential expressions with the same base are equal, their exponents are _____.

   $b^x = b^y$ is equivalent to ☐ = ☐ .

   b. If the logarithms base-b of two numbers are equal, the numbers are _____.

   $\log_b x = \log_b y$ is equivalent to ☐ = ☐ .

4. The right side of the exponential equation $5^{x-3} = 125$ can be written as a power of ☐.

5. If $6^{4x} = 6^{-2}$, then $4x = $ ☐ .

6. a. Write the equivalent base-10 exponential equation for $\log (x + 1) = 2$.

   b. Write the equivalent base-e exponential equation for $\ln (x + 1) = 2$.

Fill in the blanks.

7. To solve $5^x = 2$, we can take the _____ of both sides of the equation to get $\log 5^x = \log 2$.

8. a. For $5^x = 2$, the power rule for logarithms provides a way of moving the variable x from its position as an _____ to a position as a factor.

   b. If the power rule for logarithms is used on the left side of the equation $\log 5^x = 2$, the resulting equation is ☐ $\log 5 = 2$.

9. If $e^{x+2} = 4$, then $\ln e^{x+2} = $ ☐ .

10. Perform a check to determine whether -2 is a solution of $5^{2x+3} = \frac{1}{5}$.

11. Perform a check to determine whether 4 is a solution of $\log_5 (x + 1) = 2$.

12. Use a calculator to determine whether 2.5646 is an approximate solution of $2^{2x+1} = 70$.

13. a. How do we solve $x \ln 3 = \ln 5$ for x?

   b. What is the exact solution?

   c. What is an approximate solution to four decimal places?

14. Use a property of logarithms to condense the left side of each equation to a single logarithm. **Do not solve.**

   a. $\log_5 x + \log_5 \cdot (4x - 1) = 1$

   b. $\log_3 4x - \log_3 7 = 2$

15. a. Find $\dfrac{\log 8}{\log 5}$. Round to four decimal places.

   b. Find $\dfrac{3 \ln 12}{\ln 4 - \ln 2}$. Round to four decimal places.

16. Does $\dfrac{\log 7}{\log 3} = \log 7 - \log 3$?

17. Complete each formula.

   a. pH $= -$ ▢ $[H^+]$

   b. Radioactive decay: $A =$ ▢

   c. Population growth: $P =$ ▢

18. Use the graphs below to estimate the solution of each equation.

   a. $2^x = 3^{-x+3}$

   b. $3 \log (x - 1) = 2 \log x$

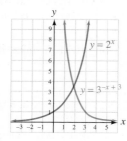
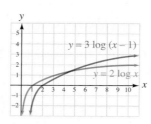

Complete each solution.

19. Solve: $2^x = 7$

   ▢ $2^x = \log 7$

   x ▢ $= \log 7$

   $x = \dfrac{\log 7}{\log 2}$

   $x \approx$ ▢

20. Solve: $\log_2 (2x - 3) = \log_2 (x + 4)$

   ▢ $= x + 4$

   $x =$ ▢

GUIDED PRACTICE

Solve each equation. **See Example 1.**

21. $6^{x-2} = 36$

22. $3^{x+1} = 27$

23. $5^{4x} = \dfrac{1}{125}$

24. $8^{-2x+1} = \dfrac{1}{64}$

Solve each equation. **See Example 2.**

25. $2^{x^2 - 2x} = 8$

26. $3^{x^2 - 3x} = 81$

27. $3^{x^2 + 4x} = \dfrac{1}{81}$

28. $7^{x^2 + 3x} = \dfrac{1}{49}$

Solve each equation. Give the exact solution and an approximation to four decimal places. **See Example 3.**

29. $4^x = 5$

30. $7^x = 12$

31. $13^{x-1} = 2$

32. $5^{x+1} = 3$

Solve each equation. Give the exact solution and an approximation to four decimal places. **See Example 4.**

33. $2^{x+1} = 3^x$

34. $6^x = 7^{x-4}$

35. $5^{x-3} = 3^{2x}$

36. $8^{3x} = 9^{x+1}$

Solve each equation. Give the exact solution and an approximation to four decimal places. **See Example 5.**

37. $e^{2.9x} = 4.5$

38. $e^{3.3t} = 9.1$

39. $e^{-0.2t} = 14.2$

40. $e^{-0.7x} = 6.2$

Solve each equation. **See Example 6.**

41. $\log 2x = 4$

42. $\log 5x = 4$

43. $\log_3 (x - 3) = 2$

44. $\log_4 (2x - 1) = 3$

45. $\log (7 - x) = 2$

46. $\log (2 - x) = 3$

47. $\log \dfrac{1}{8} x = -2$

48. $\log \dfrac{1}{5} x = -3$

Solve each equation. **See Example 7.**

49. $\log (3 - 2x) = \log (x + 24)$

50. $\log (3x + 5) = \log (2x + 6)$

51. $\ln (3x + 1) = \ln (x + 7)$

52. $\ln (x^2 + 4x) = \ln (x^2 + 16)$

Solve each equation. **See Example 8.**

53. $\log x + \log (x - 48) = 2$

54. $\log x + \log (x + 9) = 1$

55. $\log_5 (4x - 1) + \log_5 x = 1$

56. $\log_2 (x - 7) + \log_2 x = 3$

Solve each equation. **See Example 9.**

57. $\log 5 - \log x = 1$

58. $\log 11 - \log x = 2$

59. $\log_3 4x - \log_3 7 = 2$

60. $\log_2 5x - \log_2 3 = 4$

Solve each equation. Give the exact solution and, when appropriate, an approximation to four decimal places.

61. $\log 2x = \log 4$

62. $\log 3x = \log 9$

63. $\ln x = 1$

64. $\ln x = 5$

65. $7^{x^2} = 10$

66. $8^{x^2} = 11$

67. $\log (x + 90) + \log x = 3$

68. $\log (x - 90) + \log x = 3$

69. $3^{x-6} = 81$

70. $5^{x+4} = 125$

71. $\log \dfrac{4x + 1}{2x + 9} = 0$

72. $\log \dfrac{2 - 5x}{2(x + 8)} = 0$

73. $15 = 9^{x+2}$

74. $29 = 5^{x-6}$

75. $\log x^2 = 2$

76. $\log x^3 = 3$

77. $\log (x - 6) - \log (x - 2) = \log \dfrac{5}{x}$

78. $\log (3 - 2x) - \log (x + 9) = 0$

79. $\log_3 x = \log_3 \left(\dfrac{1}{x}\right) + 4$

80. $\log_5 (7 + x) + \log_5 (8 - x) - \log_5 2 = 2$

81. $2 \log_2 x = 3 + \log_2 (x - 2)$

82. $2 \log_3 x - \log_3 (x - 4) = 2 + \log_3 2$

83. $\log (7y + 1) = 2 \log (y + 3) - \log 2$

84. $2 \log (y + 2) = \log (y + 2) - \log 12$

85. $e^{3x} = 9$

86. $e^{4x} = 60$

87. $\dfrac{\log (5x + 6)}{2} = \log x$

88. $\dfrac{1}{2} \log (4x + 5) = \log x$

Look Alikes . . .

89. a. $\log 5x = 1.7$ **b.** $\ln 5x = 1.7$

90. a. $\log_2 (x^2 - x) = 1$ **b.** $\log_6 (x^2 - x) = 1$

91. a. $4^{3x-5} = 90$ **b.** $e^{3x-5} = 90$

92. a. $\log x + 2 \log x = \log 8$ **b.** $\log x - 2 \log x = \log 8$

93. a. $\log_2 (x + 5) - \log_2 4x = \log_2 x$

    b. $\ln (x + 5) - \ln 4x = \ln x$

94. a. $5^{9x-1} = 125$ **b.** $5^{9x-1} = 124$

95. a. $\left(\dfrac{2}{3}\right)^{6-x} = \dfrac{8}{27}$ **b.** $\left(\dfrac{2}{3}\right)^{6-x} = \dfrac{16}{81}$

96. a. $\log x - \log (x + 7) = -1$ **b.** $\log x - \log (x + 7) = 1$

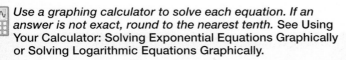

Use a graphing calculator to solve each equation. If an answer is not exact, round to the nearest tenth. **See Using Your Calculator: Solving Exponential Equations Graphically or Solving Logarithmic Equations Graphically.**

97. $2^{x+1} = 7$

98. $3^x - 10 = 3^{-x}$

99. $\log x + \log (x - 15) = 2$

100. $\ln (2x + 5) - \ln 3 = \ln (x - 1)$

APPLICATIONS

101. Hydrogen Ion Concentration. Find the hydrogen ion concentration of a saturated solution of calcium hydroxide whose pH is 13.2.

102. Aquariums. The safe pH range for a freshwater aquarium is shown on the scale in the next column. Find the corresponding hydrogen ion concentration.

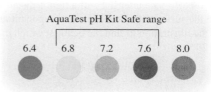

AquaTest pH Kit Safe range

6.4   6.8   7.2   7.6   8.0

103. Tritium Decay. The half-life of tritium is 12.4 years. How long will it take for 25% of a sample of tritium to decompose?

104. Radioactive Decay. In 2 years, 20% of a radioactive element decays. Find its half-life.

105. Thorium Decay. An isotope of thorium, written as ^{227}Th, has a half-life of 18.4 days. How long will it take for 80% of the sample to decompose?

106. Lead Decay. An isotope of lead, written as ^{201}Pb, has a half-life of 8.4 hours. How many hours ago was there 30% more of the substance?

107. Carbon-14 Dating. A bone fragment analyzed by archaeologists contains 60% of the carbon-14 that it is assumed to have had initially. How old is it?

108. Carbon-14 Dating. Only 10% of the carbon-14 in a small wooden bowl remains. How old is the bowl?

109. Compound Interest. If $500 is deposited in an account paying 8.5% annual interest, compounded semiannually, how long will it take for the account to increase to $800?

110. Continuous Compound Interest. In Exercise 109, how long will it take if the interest is compounded continuously?

111. Compound Interest. If $1,300 is deposited in a savings account paying 9% interest, compounded quarterly, how long will it take the account to increase to $2,100?

112. Compound Interest. A sum of $5,000 deposited in an account grows to $7,000 in 5 years. Assuming annual compounding, what interest rate is being paid?

113. Rule of Seventy. A rule of thumb for finding how long it takes an investment to double is called the **rule of seventy.** To apply the rule, divide 70 by the interest rate written as a percent. At 5%, an investment takes $\dfrac{70}{5} = 14$ years to double. At 7%, it takes $\dfrac{70}{7} = 10$ years. Explain why this formula works.

114. Bacterial Growth. A bacterial culture grows according to the function $P(t) = P_0 a^t$. If it takes 5 days for the culture to triple in size, how long will it take to double in size?

115. Rodent Control. The rodent population in a city is currently estimated at 30,000. If it is expected to double every 5 years, when will the population reach 1 million?

116. Population Growth. The population of a city is expected to triple every 15 years. When can the city planners expect the present population of 140 persons to double?

117. Bacterial Culture. A bacteria culture doubles in size every 24 hours. By how much will it have increased in 36 hours?

118. Oceanography. The intensity I of a light a distance x meters beneath the surface of a lake decreases exponentially. Use the data in the illustration to find the depth at which the intensity will be 20%.

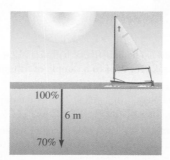

100%

6 m

70% ↓

119. Newton's Law of Cooling. Water initially at 100°C is left to cool in a room at temperature 60°C. After 3 minutes, the water temperature is 90°. The water temperature T is a function of time t given by the formula $T = 60 + 40e^{kt}$. Find k.

120. Newton's Law of Cooling. Refer to Exercise 119 and find the time for the water temperature to reach 70°C.

WRITING

121. Explain how to solve the equation $2^{x+1} = 31$.

122. Explain how to solve the equation $2^{x+1} = 32$.

123. Write a justification for each step of the solution.

$15^x = 9$ This is the equation to solve.

$\log 15^x = \log 9$ _____.

$x \log 15 = \log 9$ _____.

$x = \dfrac{\log 9}{\log 15}$ _____.

124. What is meant by the term *half-life*?

REVIEW

125. Find the length of leg AC.

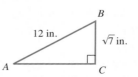

126. Dosages. The amount of medicine a patient should take is often proportional to his or her weight. If a patient weighing 83 kilograms needs 150 milligrams of medicine, how much will be needed by a person weighing 99.6 kilograms?

CHALLENGE PROBLEMS

Solve each equation.

127. $\log_3 x + \log_3 (x + 2) = 2$

128. $x^{\log x} = 10,000$

129. $\dfrac{\log_2 (6x - 8)}{\log_2 x} = 2$

130. $\dfrac{\log (3x - 4)}{\log x} = 2$

11 Summary & Review

SECTION 11.1 ▶ Algebra and Composition of Functions

DEFINITIONS AND CONCEPTS	EXAMPLES
Just as it is possible to perform arithmetic operations on real numbers, it is possible to perform those operations on functions. The **sum, difference, product,** and **quotient functions** are defined as: $(f + g)(x) = f(x) + g(x)$ $(f - g)(x) = f(x) - g(x)$ $(f \cdot g)(x) = f(x)g(x)$ $(f/g)(x) = \dfrac{f(x)}{g(x)},$ with $g(x) \ne 0$	Let $f(x) = 2x + 1$ and $g(x) = x^2$. $\begin{aligned}(f + g)(x) &= f(x) + g(x) \\ &= 2x + 1 + x^2 \\ &= x^2 + 2x + 1\end{aligned}$ $\begin{aligned}(f - g)(x) &= f(x) - g(x) \\ &= 2x + 1 - x^2 \\ &= -x^2 + 2x + 1\end{aligned}$ $\begin{aligned}(f \cdot g)(x) &= f(x) \cdot g(x) \\ \\ &= (2x + 1)x^2 \\ \\ &= 2x^3 + x^2\end{aligned}$ $\begin{aligned}(f/g)(x) &= \dfrac{f(x)}{g(x)} \\ \\ &= \dfrac{2x + 1}{x^2}\end{aligned}$

Often one quantity is a function of a second quantity that depends, in turn, on a third quantity. Such chains of dependence can be modeled by a **composition of functions.**

Read as "f of g of x."
$$\downarrow$$
$$(f \circ g)(x) = f(g(x))$$
$$\uparrow$$
Read as "f composed with g of x."

Let $f(x) = 4x - 9$ and $g(x) = x^3$. Find $(f \circ g)(2)$ and $(f \circ g)(x)$.

$$(f \circ g)(2) = f(g(2)) \qquad \textit{Change to nested parentheses notation.}$$
$$= f(8) \qquad \textit{Evaluate: } g(2) = 2^3 = 8.$$
$$= 4(8) - 9 \qquad \textit{Evaluate f(8) using f(x) = 4x - 9.}$$
$$= 23$$
$$(f \circ g)(x) = f(g(x)) = f(x^3) = 4x^3 - 9$$

REVIEW EXERCISES

Let $f(x) = 2x$ and $g(x) = x + 1$. Find each function and give its domain.

1. $f + g$
2. $f - g$
3. $f \cdot g$
4. f/g

Let $f(x) = x^2 + 2$ and $g(x) = 2x + 1$. Find each of the following.

5. $(f \circ g)(-1)$
6. $(g \circ f)(0)$
7. $(f \circ g)(x)$
8. $(g \circ f)(x)$

9. Use the graphs of functions f and g to find each of the following.

   a. $(f + g)(2)$
   b. $(f \cdot g)(-4)$
   c. $(f \circ g)(4)$
   d. $(g \circ f)(6)$

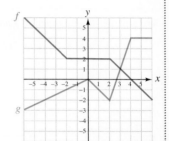

10. **Mileage Costs.** The function $f(m) = \frac{m}{8}$ gives the number of gallons of fuel consumed if a bus travels m miles. The function $C(f) = 3.25f$ gives the cost (in dollars) of f gallons of fuel. Write a composition function that expresses the cost of the fuel consumed as a function of the number of miles driven.

SECTION 11.2 ▶ Inverse Functions

DEFINITIONS AND CONCEPTS	EXAMPLES
A function is called a **one-to-one function** if different inputs determine different outputs.	The function $f(x) = 3x - 5$ is a one-to-one function because different inputs have different outputs. Since two different inputs, -2 and 2, have the same output 16, the function $f(x) = x^4$ is not one-to-one.
Horizontal line test: A function is one-to-one if every horizontal line intersects the graph of the function at most once.	The function $f(x) = |x| - 2$ is not a one-to-one function because we can draw a horizontal line that intersects its graph twice. 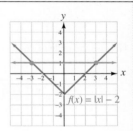
To find the inverse of a function, replace $f(x)$ with y, interchange the variables x and y, solve for y, and then replace y with $f^{-1}(x)$.	Find the inverse of the one-to-one function $f(x) = 2x + 1$. $f(x) = 2x + 1$ $y = 2x + 1$ *Replace f(x) with y.* $x = 2y + 1$ *Interchange the variables x and y.* $\dfrac{x - 1}{2} = y$ *Solve for y.* $f^{-1}(x) = \dfrac{x - 1}{2}$ *Replace y with f⁻¹(x).*

If a point (a, b) is on the graph of function f, it follows that the point (b, a) is on the graph of f^{-1}, and vice versa.

The graph of a function and its inverse are **symmetric about the line $y = x$.**

The graphs of $f(x) = 2x + 1$ and $f^{-1}(x) = \frac{x-1}{2}$ are symmetric about the line $y = x$ as shown in the illustration.

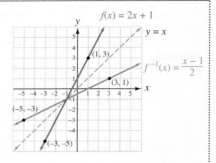

For any one-to-one function f and its inverse, f^{-1},

$$(f \circ f^{-1})(x) = x \quad \text{and} \quad (f^{-1} \circ f)(x) = x$$

The composition of $f(x) = 2x + 1$ and its inverse $f^{-1}(x) = \frac{x-1}{2}$ is the identity function $f(x) = x$.

$$(f \circ f^{-1})(x) = f(f^{-1}(x)) = f\left(\frac{x-1}{2}\right) = 2\left(\frac{x-1}{2}\right) + 1 = x - 1 + 1 = x$$

$$(f^{-1} \circ f)(x) = f^{-1}(f(x)) = f^{-1}(2x + 1) = \frac{2x + 1 - 1}{2} = \frac{2x}{2} = x$$

REVIEW EXERCISES

In Exercises 11–16, determine whether the function is one-to-one.

11. $f(x) = x^2 + 3$

12. $f(x) = \frac{1}{3}x - 8$

13. $\{(3, 4), (5, 10), (10, -1), (6, 6)\}$

14.

x	f(x)
0	-5
2	10
4	-5
6	15

15.

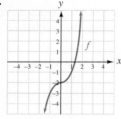

16.

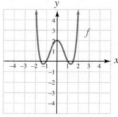

17. Use the table of values of the one-to-one function f to complete a table of values for f^{-1}.

x	f(x)
-6	-6
-1	-3
7	12
20	3

x	f⁻¹(x)
-6	
-3	
12	
3	

18. Given the graph of function f, graph f^{-1} on the same coordinate axes. Label the axis of symmetry.

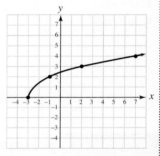

Find the inverse of each function.

19. $f(x) = 6x - 3$

20. $f(x) = \dfrac{4}{x - 1}$

21. $f(x) = (x + 2)^3$

22. $f(x) = \dfrac{x}{6} - \dfrac{1}{6}$

23. Find the inverse of $f(x) = \sqrt[3]{x - 1}$. Then graph the function and its inverse on one coordinate system. Show the axis of symmetry on the graph.

24. Use composition to show that $f(x) = 5 - 4x$ and $f^{-1}(x) = -\frac{x-5}{4}$ are inverse functions.

SECTION 11.3 ▶ Exponential Functions

DEFINITIONS AND CONCEPTS	EXAMPLES

Exponential functions have a *constant base* and a *variable exponent* and are defined by the equation

$$f(x) = b^x, \quad \text{with } b > 0, b \neq 1$$

Properties of an exponential function $f(x) = b^x$:

The **domain** is the interval $(-\infty, \infty)$.

The **range** is the interval $(0, \infty)$.

Its graph has a **y-intercept** of $(0, 1)$.

The x-axis is an **asymptote** of its graph.

The graph **passes through** the point $(1, b)$.

If $b > 1$, then $f(x) = b^x$ is an **increasing function.**

If $0 < b < 1$, then $f(x) = b^x$ is a **decreasing function.**

The graphs of $f(x) = 2^x$ and $g(x) = \left(\frac{1}{2}\right)^x$ are shown below.

$g(x) = \left(\frac{1}{2}\right)^x$

x	$g(x)$
-3	8
-2	4
-1	2
0	1
1	$\frac{1}{2}$
2	$\frac{1}{4}$

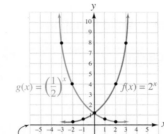

$f(x) = 2^x$

x	$f(x)$
-2	$\frac{1}{4}$
-1	$\frac{1}{2}$
0	1
1	2
2	4
3	8

The x-axis is an asymptote of each graph.

Since the base 2 is greater than 1, the function $f(x) = 2^x$ is an increasing function.

Since the base $\frac{1}{2}$ is such that $0 < \frac{1}{2} < 1$, the function $g(x) = \left(\frac{1}{2}\right)^x$ is a decreasing function.

The graphs of exponential functions can be **translated** horizontally and vertically.

$h(x) = 2^{x+3}$ The graph of $f(x) = 2^x$ is moved 3 units to the left.

$s(x) = \left(\frac{1}{2}\right)^x - 4$ The graph of $g(x) = \left(\frac{1}{2}\right)^x$ is moved 4 units downward.

Exponential functions are used to model many situations, such as population **growth,** the spread of an epidemic, the temperature of a heated object as it cools, and radioactive **decay.**

Exponential functions are suitable models for describing **compound interest.**

If P is the deposit, and interest is paid k times a year at an annual rate r, the amount A in the account after t years is given by

$$A = P\left(1 + \frac{r}{k}\right)^{kt}$$

If \$15,000 is deposited in an account paying an annual interest rate of 7.5%, compounded monthly, how much will be in the account in 60 years?

$$A(t) = 15,000\left(1 + \frac{0.075}{12}\right)^{12t}$$

To write the formula in function notation, substitute for P, r, and k.

$$A(60) = 15,000\left(1 + \frac{0.075}{12}\right)^{12(60)}$$

Substitute 60 for the time t.

$$= 15,000\left(1 + \frac{0.075}{12}\right)^{720}$$

Evaluate the exponent: 12(60) = 720.

$$\approx 1,331,479.52$$

Use a calculator with an exponential key: y^x or $\wedge$.

In 60 years, the account will contain about \$1,331,479.52.

REVIEW EXERCISES

25. a. Which of the following are exponential functions?

$$f(x) = 2x \qquad g(x) = x^2 \qquad h(a) = \sqrt{a}$$

$$n(x) = 2^x \qquad t(x) = \frac{1}{x} \qquad s(t) = 1.08^t$$

b. Use a calculator to find $0.9(1.42)^{14}$. Round to four decimal places.

26. Determine whether each application is an example of exponential growth or decay.

a.

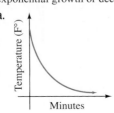

Temperature (F°)

Minutes

b.

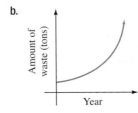

Amount of waste (tons)

Year

Graph each function and give the domain and the range. Label the y-intercept.

27. $f(x) = 3^x$

28. $f(x) = \left(\frac{1}{3}\right)^x$

29. $f(x) = \left(\frac{1}{2}\right)^x - 2$

30. $f(x) = 3^{x-1}$

31. In Exercise 30, what is the asymptote of the graph of $f(x) = 3^{x-1}$?

32. Coal Production.   The function $c(t) = 128,000\,(1.08)^t$ approximates the number of tons of coal produced in the United States for the years 1800–1910, where t is the number of years after 1800. How many tons of coal did the U.S. produce in:

a. 1800?   **b.** 1900?

33. Compound Interest. How much will \$10,500 become if it earns 9% annual interest, compounded quarterly, for 60 years?

34. Depreciation. The value (in dollars) of a certain model car is given by the function $V(t) = 12,000\left(10^{-0.155t}\right)$, where t is the number of years from the present. Find the value of the car in 5 years.

SECTION 11.4 ▶ Logarithmic Functions

DEFINITIONS AND CONCEPTS	EXAMPLES
Definition of logarithm: If $b > 0$, $b \neq 1$, and x is positive, then Exponent $y = \log_b x$ is equivalent to $x = b^y$ Base	**Logarithmic form Exponential form** Exponent $\log_5 125 = 3$ means $5^3 = 125$ Base Exponent $\log_2 \dfrac{1}{16} = -4$ means $2^{-4} = \dfrac{1}{16}$ Base
$\log_b x$ is the exponent to which b is raised to get x. $b^{\log_b x} = x$	To evaluate $\log_4 16$ we ask: "To what power must we raise 4 to get 16?" Since $4^2 = 16$, the answer is: the 2nd power. Thus, $\log_4 16 = 2$.
We cannot find the logarithm of 0 or a negative number.	$\log_4 0$ is undefined. $\log_8 (-64)$ is undefined.
For calculation purposes and in many applications, we use base-10 logarithms, called **common logarithms.** $\log x$ means $\log_{10} x$	$\log 1,000,000 = 6$ because $10^6 = 1,000,000$. $\log \dfrac{1}{1,000} = -3$ because $10^{-3} = \dfrac{1}{1,000}$.
If $b > 0$ and $b \neq 1$, the **logarithmic function with base b** is defined by $f(x) = \log_b x$. The domain is $(0, \infty)$ and the range is $(-\infty, \infty)$. If $b > 1$, then $f(x) = \log_b x$ is an increasing function. If $0 < b < 1$, then $f(x) = \log_b x$ is a decreasing function. The graphs of logarithmic functions can be **translated** horizontally and vertically.	The graph of the logarithmic function $f(x) = \log_2 x$ is shown at the right. From the graph, we see that $f(x) = \log_2 x$ is an increasing function. To graph $g(x) = \log_2 (x - 3)$, move the graph of $f(x) = \log_2 x$ to the right 3 units. 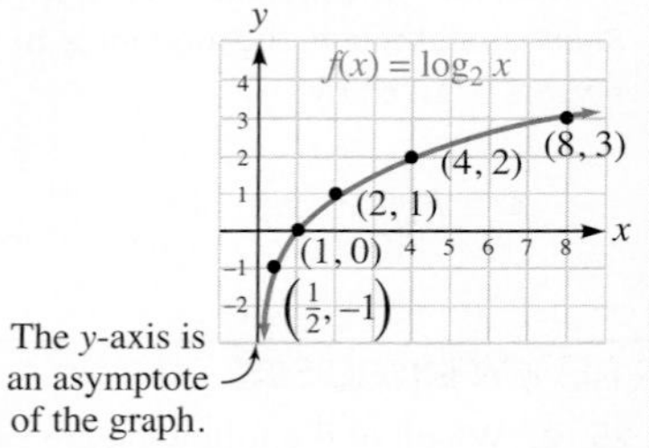 The y-axis is an asymptote of the graph.
The exponential function $f(x) = b^x$ and the logarithmic function $f(x) = \log_b x$ are inverses of each other.	$f(x) = 3^x$ and $f^{-1}(x) = \log_3 x$ are inverses of each other. Their graphs are symmetric about the line $y = x$. Similarly, $f(x) = 10^x$ and $f^{-1}(x) = \log x$ are inverses. 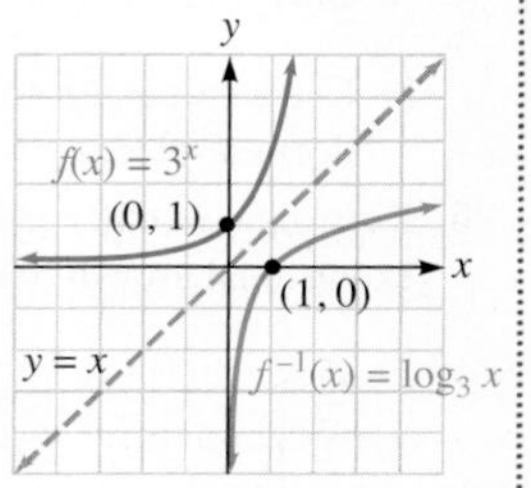

Logarithmic functions, like exponential functions, can be used to **model** certain types of growth and decay.

Decibel voltage gain: dB gain $= 20 \log \dfrac{E_O}{E_I}$

The Richter scale: $R = \log \dfrac{A}{P}$

The input to an amplifier is 0.4 volt and the output is 30 volts. Find the dB gain.

$$\text{dB gain} = 20 \log \dfrac{E_O}{E_I}$$

$$= 20 \log \dfrac{30}{0.4} \qquad \text{Substitute 30 for } E_O \text{ and 0.4 for } E_I.$$

$$\approx 37.50122527 \qquad \text{Use a calculator with a } \boxed{\text{LOG}} \text{ key.}$$

The dB gain is about 38 decibels.

REVIEW EXERCISES

35. Give the domain and range of $f(x) = \log x$.

36. Explain why a student got an error message when she used a calculator to evaluate $\log 0$.

37. Write the statement $\log_4 64 = 3$ in exponential form.

38. Write the statement $7^{-1} = \frac{1}{7}$ in logarithmic form.

Evaluate.

39. $\log_3 9$

40 $\log_9 \frac{1}{81}$

41. $\log_{1/2} 1$

42. $\log_5 (-25)$

43. $\log_6 \sqrt{6}$

44. $\log 1{,}000$

Solve for x.

45. $\log_2 x = 5$

46. $\log_3 x = -4$

47. $\log_x 16 = 2$

48. $\log_x \frac{1}{100} = -2$

49. $\log_9 3 = x$

50. $\log_{27} 3 = x$

Use a calculator to find the value of x to four decimal places.

51. $\log 4.51 = x$

52. $\log x = 1.43$

Graph each function and its inverse on the same coordinate system. Draw the axis of symmetry.

53. $f(x) = \log_4 x$ and $g(x) = 4^x$

54. $f(x) = \log_{1/3} x$ and $g(x) = \left(\frac{1}{3}\right)^x$

Graph each function. Label the x-intercept.

55. $f(x) = \log (x - 2)$

56. $f(x) = 3 + \log x$

57. Electrical Engineering.   Find the dB gain of an amplifier with an output of 18 volts and an input of 0.04 volt.

58. Earthquakes.   An earthquake had a period of 0.3 second and an amplitude of 7,500 micrometers. Use the formula $R = \log \frac{A}{P}$ to find its measure on the Richter scale.

59. Organ Pipes.   The design for a set of brass pipes for a church organ is shown below. The function $h(n) = 52 + 25 \log n$ approximates the height (in centimeters) of the pipe with number n. Find the height of

  a. Pipe 1

  b. Pipe 8

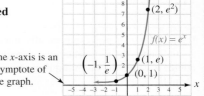

Pipe number

60. Girls' Heights.   The function $P(A) = 61.8 + 34.9 \log(A - 4)$ approximates the percent of the adult height a female child A years old has attained, where $5 \le A \le 15$. What percent of her adult height will a girl have reached the day she first becomes a teenager?

SECTION 11.5 ▶ Base-*e* Exponential and Logarithmic Functions

DEFINITIONS AND CONCEPTS	EXAMPLES

Of all possible bases for an exponential function, *e* is the most convenient for problems involving growth or decay.

$$e = 2.718281828459 \ldots$$

As n approaches infinity, the value of $\left(1 + \frac{1}{n}\right)^n$ approaches e.

The function defined by $f(x) = e^x$ is called the **natural exponential function.** It is called this because it can be applied to many natural settings.

From the graph, we see that the domain of the natural exponential function is $(-\infty, \infty)$ and the range is $(0, \infty)$.

The graph of $f(x) = e^x$ can be **translated** horizontally and vertically.

The *x*-axis is an asymptote of the graph.

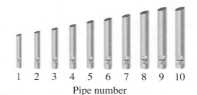

Exponential growth/decay: If a quantity increases or decreases at an annual rate r, **compounded continuously,** the amount A after t years is given by

$$A = Pe^{rt}$$

If r is negative, the amount decreases.

If interest is paid coutinuously (infinitely many times a year), we say that the interest is **compounded continuously.**

If \$30,000 accumulates interest at an annual rate of 9%, compounded continuously, find the amount in the account after 25 years.

$A = Pe^{rt}$ This is the formula for continuous compound interest.

$= 30{,}000e^{0.09 \cdot 25}$ Substitute 30,000 for P, 0.09 for r, and 25 for t.

$= 30{,}000e^{2.25}$ Evaluate the exponent: $0.09 \cdot 25 = 2.25$

$\approx 284{,}632.08$ Use a calculator with an e^x key.

In 30 years, the account will contain \$284,632.08.

Suppose the population of a city of 50,000 people is decreasing exponentially according to the function $P(t) = 50{,}000e^{-0.003t}$, where t is measured in years from the present date. Find the expected population of the city in 20 years.

$P(t) = 50{,}000e^{-0.003t}$ Since r is negative, this is the exponential decay model.

$P(20) = 50{,}000e^{-0.003(20)}$ Substitute 20 for t.

$= 50{,}000e^{-0.06}$ Evaluate the exponent: $-0.003\,(20) = -0.06$.

$\approx 47{,}088$ Use a calculator with an e^x key.

After 20 years, the expected population will be about 47,088 people.

Of all possible bases for a logarithmic function, e is the most convenient for problems involving growth or decay. Since these situations occur often in natural settings, base-e logarithms are called **natural logarithms:**

$\ln x$ means $\log_e x$

To evaluate $\ln \frac{1}{e^4}$ we ask: "To what power must we raise e to get $\frac{1}{e^4}$?"

Since $e^{-4} = \frac{1}{e^4}$, the answer is: the -4th power. Thus,

$$\ln \frac{1}{e^4} = -4$$

$\ln 0$ and $\ln(-5)$ are undefined.

$\ln x$ is the exponent to which e is raised to get x.

$\ln 9 \approx 2.1972$ means $e^{2.1972} \approx 9$

The **natural logarithmic function** with base e is defined by

$$f(x) = \ln x$$

The domain is the interval $(0, \infty)$ and the range is the interval $(-\infty, \infty)$.

The graph of the natural logarithmic function $f(x) = \ln x$ is shown on the right.

From the graph, we see that $f(x) = \ln x$ is an increasing function.

The graph of $f(x) = \ln x$ can be translated horizontally and vertically.

The y-axis is an asymptote of the graph.

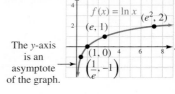

The natural exponential function $f(x) = e^x$ and the natural logarithmic function $f^{-1}(x) = \ln x$ are **inverses** of each other.

The graphs are symmetric about the line $y = x$.

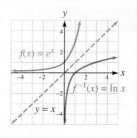

If a population grows exponentially at a certain annual rate r, the time required for the population to double is called the **doubling time.** It is given by the formula:

$$t = \frac{\ln 2}{r}$$

The population of a town is growing at a rate of 3% per year. If this rate continues, how long will it take the population to double?

We substitute 0.03 for r and use a calculator to perform the calculation.

$$t = \frac{\ln 2}{r} = \frac{\ln 2}{0.03} \approx 23.10490602$$ Use a calculator with an $\boxed{\text{LN}}$ key.

The population will double in about 23.1 years.

REVIEW EXERCISES

61. a. Approximate e to the nearest hundredth.

   b. Fill in the blanks:

   $\ln 15 \approx 2.7081$ means $e^{\quad} \approx \quad$

62. Use a calculator to find $16.4 + 252.7e^{-0.76(9)}$. Round to four decimal places.

Graph each function, and give the domain and the range.

63. $f(x) = e^x + 1$

64. $f(x) = e^{x-3}$

65. Interest Compounded Continuously.   If \$10,500 accumulates interest at an annual rate of 9%, compounded continuously, how much will be in the account in 60 years?

66. The Sooner State.   In 2009, Oklahoma had the largest *gross domestic product* growth rate of all fifty states: 6.6%. (The GDP, as it is called, is the value of all goods and services produced within a state.) If the 2009 GDP totaled \$142.5 billion, predict Oklahoma's GDP in 2015, assuming the growth rate remains the same. (Source: huffingtonpost.com)

67. Mortgage Rates.   There was the housing boom in the 1980s as the baby boomers (those born from 1946 through 1964) bought their homes. The average annual interest rate in percent on a 30-year fixed-rate home mortgage for the years 1980–1996 can be approximated by the function $r(t) = 13.9e^{-0.035t}$, where t is the number of years since 1980. To the nearest hundredth of a percent, what does this model predict was the 30-year fixed rate in 1980? In 1985? In 1990?

68. Medical Tests.   A radioactive dye is injected into a patient as part of a test to detect heart disease. The amount of dye remaining in his bloodstream t hours after the injection is given by the function $f(t) = 10e^{-0.27t}$. How can you determine from the function that the amount of dye in the bloodstream is decreasing?

Evaluate each expression. Do not use a calculator.

69. $\ln e$

70. $\ln e^2$

71. $\ln \frac{1}{e^5}$

72. $\ln \sqrt{e}$

73. $\ln (-e)$

74. $\ln 0$

75. $\ln 1$

76. $\ln e^{-7}$

Use a calculator to evaluate each expression. Express all answers to four decimal places.

77. $\ln 452$

78. $\ln 0.85$

Solve each equation. Express all answers to four decimal places.

79. $\ln x = 2.336$

80. $\ln x = -8.8$

81. Explain the difference between the functions $f(x) = \log x$ and $g(x) = \ln x$.

82. What function is the inverse of $f(x) = \ln x$?

Graph each function.

83. $f(x) = 1 + \ln x$

84. $f(x) = \ln (x + 1)$

85. Population Growth.   How long will it take the population of Mexico to double if the growth rate is currently about 1.118%? (Source: CIA World Fact Book)

86. Botany.   The height (in inches) of a certain plant is approximated by the function $H(a) = 13 + 20.03 \ln a$, where a is its age in years. How tall will it be when it is 19 years old?

SECTION 11.6 ▶ **Properties of Logarithms**

DEFINITIONS AND CONCEPTS	EXAMPLES
Properties of logarithms: If M, N, and b are positive real numbers, $b \neq 1$	Apply a property of logarithms and then simplify, if possible.
1. $\log_b 1 = 0$ $\qquad$ **2.** $\log_b b = 1$ **3.** $\log_b b^x = x$ $\qquad$ **4.** $b^{\log_b x} = x$	**1.** $\log_3 1 = 0$ $\qquad$ **2.** $\log_7 7 = 1$ **3.** $\log_5 5^3 = 3$ $\qquad$ **4.** $9^{\log_9 10} = 10$
5. *Product rule for logarithms:* $\quad \log_b MN = \log_b M + \log_b N$	**5.** $\log_2 (6 \cdot 8) = \log_2 6 + \log_2 8$ $\qquad\qquad\quad = \log_2 6 + 3$
6. *Quotient rule for logarithms:* $\quad \log_b \frac{M}{N} = \log_b M - \log_b N$	**6.** $\log_3 \dfrac{81}{x} = \log_3 81 - \log_3 x$ $\qquad\qquad = 4 - \log_3 x$
7. *Power rule for logarithms:* $\quad \log_b M^p = p \log_b M$	**7.** $\log_8 7^3 = 3 \log_8 7$ $\quad$ and $\quad$ $\log \sqrt[4]{x} = \log x^{\frac{1}{4}} = \dfrac{1}{4} \log x$

Properties of logarithms can be used to **expand** logarithmic expressions.	Write $\log_3 (x^2 y^3)$ as the sum and/or difference of logarithms of a single quantity. $\log_3 (x^2 y^3) = \log_3 x^2 + \log_3 y^3$ The log of a product is the sum of the logs. $ = 2 \log_3 x + 3 \log_3 y$ The log of a power is the power times the log.
Properties of logarithms can be used to **condense** certain logarithmic expressions. To condense, apply the power rule first to make the coefficients of logarithms 1. Then use the product and quotient rules.	Write $3 \ln x - \frac{1}{2} \ln y$ as a single logarithm. $3 \ln x - \frac{1}{2} \ln y = \ln x^3 - \ln y^{1/2}$ A power times a log is the log of the power. $\phantom{3 \ln x - \frac{1}{2} \ln y} = \ln \dfrac{x^3}{y^{1/2}}$ The difference of two logs is the log of the quotient. $\phantom{3 \ln x - \frac{1}{2} \ln y} = \ln \dfrac{x^3}{\sqrt{y}}$ Write $y^{1/2}$ as $\sqrt{y}$.
If we need to find a logarithm with some base other than 10 or e, we can use a conversion formula. **Change-of-base formula:** $\log_b x = \dfrac{\log_a x}{\log_a b}$	Find $\log_7 6$ to four decimal places. $\log_7 6 = \dfrac{\log 6}{\log 7} \approx 0.920782221$ Change to the ratio of base-10 logarithms. To four decimal places, $\log_7 6 = 0.9208$. To check, verify that $7^{0.9208}$ is approximately 6.
In chemistry, common logarithms are used to express the acidity of solutions using pH. **pH scale:** $pH = -\log[H^+]$ where the symbol $[H^+]$ represents the hydrogen ion concentration in gram-ions per liter.	Find the pH of a liquid with a hydrogen ion concentration of 10^{-8} gram-ions per liter. $pH = -\log [H^+]$ This is the pH formula. $pH = -\log 10^{-8}$ Substitute 10^{-8} for $[H^+]$. $ = -(-8) \log 10$ The log of a power is the power times the log. $ = 8$ Simplify: $\log 10 = 1$.

REVIEW EXERCISES

Simplify each expression.

87. $\log_2 1$

88. $\log_9 9$

89. $\log 10^3$

90. $7^{\log_7 4}$

Write each logarithm as the sum and/or difference of logarithms of a single quantity. Then simplify, if possible.

91. $\log_3 27x$

92. $\log \dfrac{100}{x}$

93. $\log_5 \sqrt{27}$

94. $\log_b 10ab$

Write each logarithm as the sum and/or difference of logarithms of a single quantity.

95. $\log_b \dfrac{x^2 y^3}{z}$

96. $\ln \sqrt{\dfrac{x}{yz^2}}$

Write each logarithmic expression as one logarithm.

97. $3 \log_2 x - 5 \log_2 y + 7 \log_2 z$

98. $-3 \log_b y - 7 \log_b z + \frac{1}{2} \log_b (x + 2)$

99. $\log_b (a^2 - 25) - \log_b (a + 5)$

100. $3 \log_8 x + 4 \log_8 x$

Assume that $\log_b 5 = 1.1609$ and $\log_b 8 = 1.5000$ and find each value to four decimal places.

101. $\log_b 40$

102. $\log_b 64$

103. Find $\log_5 17$ to four decimal places.

104. pH of Grapefruit. Find the pH of grapefruit juice if its hydrogen ion concentration is 7.9×10^{-4} gram-ions per liter. Round to the nearest tenth.

SECTION 11.7 ▶ Exponential and Logarithmic Equations

DEFINITIONS AND CONCEPTS	EXAMPLES
An **exponential equation** contains a variable in one of its exponents. Two examples are: $6^{x-3} = 9$ and $e^{-2.5t} = 56$ If both sides of an exponential equation can be expressed as a power of the same base, we can use the following property to solve it: $b^x = b^y$ is equivalent to $x = y$	Solve: $3^{x+2} = 27$ $3^{x+2} = 3^3$ Express the right side of the equation as a power of 3: $27 = 3^3$. $x + 2 = 3$ If two exponential expressions with the same base are equal, their exponents are equal. $x = 1$ The solution is 1. Check it in the original equation.
When it is difficult to write each side of an exponential equation as a power of the same base, **take the logarithm on each side.** With this method, we often obtain **exact solutions** involving logarithms that we can **approximate.**	Solve: $4^x = 7$. Give an approximate solution to four decimal places. $\log 4^x = \log 7$ Take the base-10 logarithm on both sides of the equation. $x \log 4 = \log 7$ The log of a power is the power times the log. $x = \dfrac{\log 7}{\log 4}$ To isolate x, divide both sides by log 4. This is the exact solution. $x \approx 1.4037$ Use a calculator with a LOG key. To four decimal places, the approximate solution is 1.4037. To check it, we substitute 1.4037 for x in $4^x = 7$ and use a calculator to evaluate the left side: $4^{1.4037} \approx 7$
To solve an exponential equation that contains a base-e exponential expression, take the natural logarithm on both sides of the equation.	Solve: $e^{5t} = 11$ $\ln e^{5t} = \ln 11$ Take the base-e logarithm on both sides. $5t \ln e = \ln 11$ The log of a power is the power times the log. $5t \cdot 1 = \ln 11$ Simplify: $\ln e = 1$. $5t = \ln 11$ Simplify the left side. $t = \dfrac{\ln 11}{5}$ This is the exact solution. An approximate solution to four decimal places is 0.4796.
A **logarithmic equation** is an equation containing a variable in a logarithmic expression. Two examples are: $2 \log_3 x + \log_3 5x = 4$ and $\ln (x + 1) = \ln (3x - 4)$ Certain logarithmic equations can be solved using the following property: $\log_b x = \log_b y$ is equivalent to $x = y$	Solve: $\log(4x - 3) = \log(2x + 7)$ $4x - 3 = 2x + 7$ If the logarithms of two numbers are equal, the numbers are equal. $2x = 10$ $x = 5$ The solution is 5. Check it in the original equation.
To solve some logarithmic equations, we write and solve an equivalent exponential equation.	Solve: $\log_4(x + 1) = 2$ $x + 1 = 4^2$ Write the equivalent base-4 exponential equation. $x + 1 = 16$ $x = 15$ The solution is 15. Check it in the original equation.

To solve some logarithmic equations, we first apply properties of logarithms, such as:

- The product rule
- The quotient rule
- The power rule

Solve: $\log_2 (x + 14) - \log_2 x = 3$

$$\log_2 \frac{x + 14}{x} = 3 \qquad \text{On the left side, use the quotient rule for logarithms.}$$

$$\frac{x + 14}{x} = 2^3 \qquad \text{Write the equivalent base-2 exponential equation.}$$

$$\frac{x + 14}{x} = 8 \qquad \text{Evaluate: } 2^3 = 8.$$

$$x + 14 = 8x \qquad \text{Multiply both sides by x.}$$

$$14 = 7x \qquad \text{Subtract x from both sides.}$$

$$2 = x \qquad \text{Divide both sides by 7.}$$

The solution is 2. Check by substituting it into the original equation.

When there is sufficient food and space available, populations of living organisms tend to increase exponentially according to the following **growth model.**

$$\textit{Population growth:} \quad P = P_0 e^{kt}$$

Find the number of bacteria in a culture of 1,000 bacteria if they are allowed to reproduce for 5 hours. Assume $k = \frac{\ln 3}{3}$.

$$P = P_0 e^{kt} \qquad \text{This is the population growth model.}$$

$$= 1,000 e^{\frac{\ln 3}{3} \cdot 5} \qquad \text{Substitute for } P_0, k, \text{ and } t.$$

$$\approx 6,240 \qquad \text{Use a calculator with } \boxed{\text{LN}} \text{ and } \boxed{e^x} \text{ keys.}$$

In 5 hours, there will be approximately 6,240 bacteria.

Solve each equation. Give the exact solution and an approximate solution to four decimal places, when appropriate.

105. $5^{x+6} = 25$

106. $2^{x^2 + 4x} = \frac{1}{8}$

107. $3^x = 7$

108. $2^x = 3^{x-4}$

109. $e^x = 7$

110. $e^{-0.4t} = 25$

Solve each equation.

111. $\left(\frac{2}{5}\right)^{3x-4} = \frac{8}{125}$

112. $9^{x^2} = 33$

113. $\log (x - 4) = 2$

114. $\ln (2x - 3) = \ln 15$

115. $\log x + \log (29 - x) = 2$

116. $\log_2 x + \log_2 (x - 2) = 3$

117. $\dfrac{\log (7x - 12)}{\log x} = 2$

118. $\log_2 (x + 2) + \log_2 (x - 1) = 2$

119. $\log x + \log (x - 5) = \log 6$

120. $\log 3 - \log (x - 1) = -1$

121. Evaluate both sides of the statement $\frac{\log 8}{\log 15} \neq \log 8 - \log 15$ to show that the sides are indeed not equal.

122. Carbon-14 Dating.   A wooden statue found in Egypt has a carbon-14 content that is two-thirds of that found in living wood. If the half-life of carbon-14 is 5,700 years, how old is the statue?

123. Ants.   The number of ants in a colony is estimated to be 800. If the ant population is expected to triple every 14 days, how long will it take for the population to reach one million?

124. The approximate coordinates of the points of intersection of the graphs of $f(x) = \log x$ and $g(x) = 1 - \log (7 - x)$ are shown in parts (a) and (b) of the illustration. Use the graphs to estimate the solutions of the logarithmic equation $\log x = 1 - \log (7 - x)$. Then check your answers.

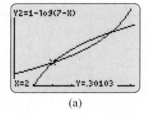
(a)

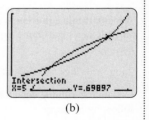
(b)

11 ▸ Chapter Test

1. Fill in the blanks.
   a. A _____ function is denoted by $f \circ g$.
   b. $f(x) = e^x$ is the _____ exponential function.
   c. In _____ compound interest, the number of compoundings is infinitely large.
   d. The functions $f(x) = \log_{10} x$ and $f(x) = 10^x$ are _____ functions.
   e. $f(x) = \log_4 x$ is a _____ function.

2. Write out in words how to say each of the following:
   a. $(f \circ g)(x)$
   b. $g(f(8))$
   c. $f^{-1}(x)$

Let f(x) = x + 9 and g(x) = 4x² − 3x + 2. Find each function and give its domain.

3. $f + g$

4. g/f

Let f(x) = 2x² + 3 and g(x) = 4x − 8. Find each composition.

5. $(g \circ f)(-3)$

6. $(f \circ g)(x)$

Use the tables of values for functions f and g to find each of the following.

7. a. $(f \cdot g)(9)$
   b. $(f \circ g)(-3)$

x	$f(x)$
9	−1
10	17

x	$g(x)$
−3	10
9	16

8. Refer to the graphs of functions f and g below to find each of the following.
   a. $(g/f)(-4)$
   b. $(f \circ g)(1)$
   c. $(f + g)(2)$
   d. $(f \cdot g)(0)$
   e. $(g - f)(1)$

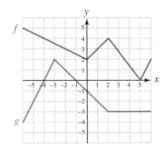

9. Determine whether each function is one-to-one.
   a. $f(x) = |x|$
   b. {(1,7), (7,1), (2,8), (8,2)}
   c.
   d.

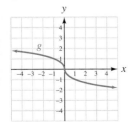

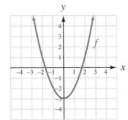

10. Find the inverse of $f(x) = -\frac{1}{3}x$ and then graph f and its inverse on the same coordinate axes. Label the axis of symmetry.

11. Determine whether $f(x) = \frac{1}{3}x + 2$ is a one-to-one function. If it is, find its inverse.

12. Find the inverse of $f(x) = (x - 15)^3$.

13. Use composition to show that $f(x) = 4x + 4$ and $f^{-1}(x) = \frac{x - 4}{4}$ are inverse functions.

14. Consider the following graph of the function f.
    a. Is f a one-to-one function?
    b. Is its inverse a function?
    c. What is $f^{-1}(260)$? What information does it give?

Relationship Between Car Speed and Tire Temperature

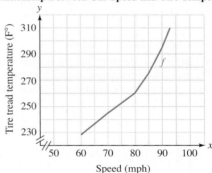

Graph each function and give the domain and the range.

15. $f(x) = 2^x + 1$

16. $f(x) = 3^{-x}$

17. **Radioactive Decay.** A radioactive material decays according to the formula $A = A_0(2)^{-t}$. How much of a 3-gram sample will be left in 6 years?

18. **Compound Interest.** An initial deposit of $1,000 earns 6% interest, compounded twice a year. How much will be in the account in one year?

19. a. Graph $f(x) = e^x$. Label the y-intercept and the asymptote of the graph.
    b. Give the domain and range.
    c. What is the inverse of $f(x) = e^x$?

20. **Population Growth.** As of July 2010, the population of India was estimated to be 1,173,108,018, with an annual growth rate of 1.376%. If the growth rate remains the same, how large will the population be in July, 2020? Round to the nearest thousand. (Source: CIA World Fact Book)

21. Biology. Human growth hormone, known as HGH, is produced by the pituitary gland in the brain and released into the blood stream. It stimulates growth and cell production. After the age of 20, levels of HGH in the body decrease dramatically, as shown in the graph. Use the given function to approximate the amount of HGH produced per day by a person 55 years old.

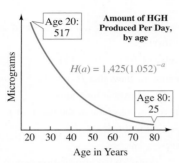

Source: Aging Well, James L. Holly, MD

22. Write the statement $\log_6 \frac{1}{36} = -2$ in exponential form.

23. a. What are the domain and range of the function
$f(x) = \log x$?
   b. What is the inverse of $f(x) = \log x$?

24. Botany. Which phrase best describes the relationship between the rate of photosynthesis in plants and light intensity that is graphed below: linear growth, exponential growth, or logarithmic growth?

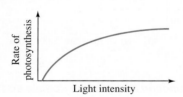

Evaluate each logarithmic expression, if possible.

25. $\log_5 25$

26. $\log_9 \frac{1}{81}$

27. $\log(-100)$

28. $\ln \frac{1}{e^6}$

29. $\log_4 2$

30. $\log_{1/3} 1$

Solve for x.

31. $\log_x 32 = 5$

32. $\log_8 x = \frac{4}{3}$

33. $\log_3 x = -3$

34. $\ln x = 1$

Graph each function.

35. $f(x) = -\log_3 x$

36. $f(x) = \ln x$

37. Chemistry. Find the pH of a solution with a hydrogen ion concentration of 3.7×10^{-7} gram-ions per liter. (*Hint:* pH $= -\log [H^+]$.)

38. Electronics. Find the dB gain of an amplifier when $E_O = 60$ volts and $E_I = 0.3$ volt. *Hint:* dB gain $= 20 \log \frac{E_O}{E_I}$.

39. Use a calculator to find x to four decimal places: $\log x = -1.06$

40. Use the change-of-base formula to find $\log_7 3$ to four decimal places.

41. Write the expression $\log_b a^2 b c^3$ as the sum and/or difference of logarithms of a single quantity. Then simplify, if possible.

42. Write the expression $\frac{1}{2} \ln (a + 2) + \ln b - 3 \ln c$ as a logarithm of a single quantity.

Solve each equation. Give the exact solution and an approximate solution to four decimal places, when appropriate.

43. $5^x = 3$

44. $3^{x-1} = 27$

45. $\left(\frac{3}{2}\right)^{6x+2} = \frac{27}{8}$

46. $e^{0.08t} = 4$

47. $2 \log x = \log 25$

48. $\log_2 (x + 2) - \log_2 (x - 5) = 3$

49. $\ln (5x + 2) = \ln (2x + 5)$

50. $\log x + \log (x - 9) = 1$

51. The illustration shows the graphs of $y = \frac{1}{2} \ln (x - 1)$ and $y = \ln 2$ and the approximate coordinates of their point of intersection. Estimate the solution of the logarithmic equation $\frac{1}{2} \ln (x - 1) = \ln 2$. Then check the result.

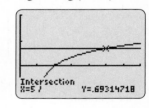

52. Insects. The number of insects attracted to a bright light is currently 5. If the number is expected to quadruple every 6 minutes, how long will it take for the number to reach 500?

Group Project

The Number e

Overview: In this activity, you will use a calculator to find progressively more accurate approximations of e.

Instructions: Form groups of two students. Each student will need a scientific calculator.

Begin by finding an approximation of e using the $\boxed{e^x}$ key on your calculator. Copy the table shown below, and write the number displayed on the calculator screen at the top of the table.

The value of e can be calculated to any degree of accuracy by adding the terms of the following pattern:

$$e = 1 + 1 + \frac{1}{2} + \frac{1}{2 \cdot 3} + \frac{1}{2 \cdot 3 \cdot 4} + \frac{1}{2 \cdot 3 \cdot 4 \cdot 5} + \cdots$$

The more terms that are added, the closer the sum will be to e.

You are to add as many terms as necessary until you obtain a sum that matches the value of e, given by the $\boxed{e^x}$ key on your calculator. Work together as a team. One member of the group should compute the fractional form of the term to be added. (See the middle column of the table.) The other member should take that information and calculate the cumulative sum. (See the right column of the table.)

How many terms must be added so that the cumulative sum approximation and the $\boxed{e^x}$ key approximation match in each decimal place?

Approximation of e found using the $\boxed{e^x}$ key: $e \approx$ _____

Number of terms in the sum	Term (expressed as a fraction)	Cumulative sum (an approximation of e)
1	1	1
2	1	2
3	$\frac{1}{2}$	2.5
4	$\frac{1}{2 \cdot 3} = \frac{1}{6}$	2.666666667
⋮	⋮	⋮

Final exams can be stressful for many students because the number of topics to study can seem overwhelming. Here are some suggestions to help reduce the stress and prepare you for the test.

GET ORGANIZED: Gather all of your notes, study sheets, homework assignments, and especially all of your returned tests to review.

TALK WITH YOUR INSTRUCTOR: Ask your instructor to list the topics that may appear on the final and those that won't be covered.

MANAGE YOUR TIME: Adjust your daily schedule 1 week before the final so that it includes extended periods of study time.

Now Try This ▶

1. Review your old tests. Make a list of the test problems that you are still unsure about and see a tutor or your instructor to get help.
2. Make a practice final exam that includes one or more of each type of problem that may appear on the test.
3. Make a detailed study plan. Determine when, where, and what you will study each day for 1 week before the final.

SECTION 12.1

Solving Systems of Equations in Two Variables; Applications

OBJECTIVES

1. Determine whether an ordered pair is a solution of a system.
2. Solve systems of linear equations by graphing.
3. Use graphing to identify inconsistent systems and dependent equations.
4. Solve systems of linear equations by substitution.
5. Solve systems of linear equations by the elimination (addition) method.
6. Use substitution and elimination (addition) to identify inconsistent systems and dependent equations.
7. Solve application problems using systems of equations.

ARE YOU READY?

▼ *The following problems review some basic skills that are needed when solving systems of linear equations in two variables.*

1. Is $(-1, 4)$ a solution of $y = 3x - 1$?
2. Use the slope and the y-intercept to graph $y = -4x + 2$.
3. Graph $3x + 4y = 12$ by finding the x- and y-intercepts.
4. Solve $5x - y = -4$ for y.
5. Substitute 4 for x in $y = -2x - 1$ and find y.
6. Multiply both sides of the equation $7x - y = 9$ by -4.

In this section, we will review graphical and algebraic methods for solving systems of two linear equations in two variables.

Determine Whether an Ordered Pair Is a Solution of a System.

When two equations with the same variables are considered simultaneously (at the same time), we say that they form a **system of equations.** We will use a left brace { when writing a system of equations. An example is

$$\begin{cases} 2x + 5y = -1 \\ x - y = -4 \end{cases}$$ Read as "the system of equations $2x + 5y = -1$ and $x - y = -4$."

A **solution of a system** of equations in two variables is an ordered pair that satisfies both equations of the system.

<table>
<tr><td>**EXAMPLE 1**</td><td>Determine whether $(-3, 1)$ is a solution of each system of equations.</td></tr>
</table>

a. $\begin{cases} 2x + 5y = -1 \\ x - y = -4 \end{cases}$ **b.** $\begin{cases} 5y = 2 - x \\ y = 3x \end{cases}$

Strategy We will substitute the x- and y-coordinates of $(-3, 1)$ for the corresponding variables in both equations of the system.

Why If both equations are satisfied (made true) by the x- and y-coordinates, the ordered pair is a solution of the system.

Solution **a.** To determine whether $(-3, 1)$ is a solution, we substitute -3 for x and 1 for y in each equation.

The Language of Algebra

A system of equations is two (or more) equations that are considered **simultaneously**—at the same time. On June 3, 2007, in Kansas City, more than 1,680 guitarists set a world record for the most people playing the same song *simultaneously*. The song was Deep Purple's *Smoke on the Water*.

$$\text{Check:} \quad 2x + 5y = -1 \quad \text{First equation} \qquad x - y = -4 \quad \text{Second equation}$$
$$2(-3) + 5(1) \overset{?}{=} -1 \qquad\qquad\qquad -3 - 1 \overset{?}{=} -4$$
$$-6 + 5 \overset{?}{=} -1 \qquad\qquad\qquad\qquad -4 = -4 \quad \text{True}$$
$$-1 = -1 \quad \text{True}$$

Since $(-3, 1)$ satisfies both equations, it is a solution of the system.

b. We substitute -3 for x and 1 for y in each equation in the second system.

The Language of Algebra

We say that $(-3, 1)$ **satisfies** both equations because it makes both equations true. To *satisfy* means to make content, as in *satisfy* your thirst or a *satisfied* customer.

$$\text{Check:} \quad 5y = 2 - x \quad \text{First equation} \qquad y = 3x \quad \text{Second equation}$$
$$5(1) \overset{?}{=} 2 - (-3) \qquad\qquad\qquad 1 \overset{?}{=} 3(-3)$$
$$5 \overset{?}{=} 2 + 3 \qquad\qquad\qquad\qquad 1 = -9 \quad \text{False}$$
$$5 = 5 \qquad \text{True}$$

Although $(-3, 1)$ satisfies the first equation, it does not satisfy the second. Because it does not satisfy both equations, $(-3, 1)$ is *not a solution* of the system.

Self Check 1	Determine whether $(6, -2)$ is a solution of $\begin{cases} x - 2y = 10 \\ y = 3x - 20 \end{cases}$.

Now Try ▶ Problem 13

2 Solve Systems of Linear Equations by Graphing.

To **solve a system** of equations means to find all of the solutions of the system. One way to solve a system of linear equations in two variables is to graph each equation and find where the graphs intersect.

The Graphing Method	1. Carefully graph each equation on the same rectangular coordinate system.
	2. If the lines intersect, determine the coordinates of the point of intersection of the graphs. That ordered pair is the solution of the system.
	3. If the graphs have no point in common, the system has no solution.
	4. Check the proposed solution in each equation of the original system.

A system of two linear equations can have exactly one solution, no solution, or infinitely many solutions. When a system of equations (as in Example 2) has at least one solution, the system is called a **consistent system.**

EXAMPLE 2 Solve the system by graphing: $\begin{cases} x + 2y = 4 \\ 2x - y = 3 \end{cases}$

Strategy We will graph both equations on the same coordinate system.

Why The graph of a linear equation is a picture of its solutions. If both equations are graphed on the same coordinate system, we can see whether they have any common solutions.

Solution The intercept method is a convenient way to graph equations such as $x + 2y = 4$ and $2x - y = 3$, because they are in standard $Ax + By = C$ form.

Success Tip

Since accuracy is crucial when using the graphing method to solve a system:
- Use graph paper.
- Use a sharp pencil.
- Use a straightedge.

$x + 2y = 4$

x	y	(x, y)
4	0	$(4, 0)$
0	2	$(0, 2)$
-2	3	$(-2, 3)$

$2x - y = 3$

x	y	(x, y)
$\frac{3}{2}$	0	$\left(\frac{3}{2}, 0\right)$
0	-3	$(0, -3)$
-1	-5	$(-1, -5)$

Success Tip

When determining the coordinates of a point of intersection from a graph, realize that they are simply estimates. Only after algebraically checking a proposed solution can we be sure that it is an actual solution.

Although infinitely many ordered pairs (x, y) satisfy $x + 2y = 4$, and infinitely many ordered pairs (x, y) satisfy $2x - y = 3$, only the coordinates of the point where the graphs intersect satisfy both equations. From the graph, it appears that the intersection point has coordinates $(2, 1)$. To verify that it is the solution, we substitute 2 for x and 1 for y in both equations and show that $(2, 1)$ satisfies each one.

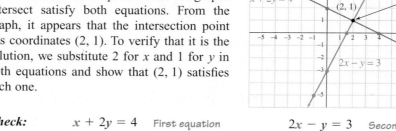

The point of intersection gives the solution of the system.

Check:

$x + 2y = 4$	First equation	$2x - y = 3$	Second equation
$2 + 2(1) \overset{?}{=} 4$		$2(2) - 1 \overset{?}{=} 3$	
$2 + 2 \overset{?}{=} 4$		$4 - 1 \overset{?}{=} 3$	
$4 = 4$	True	$3 = 3$	True

Since $(2, 1)$ makes both equations true, it is the solution of the system. The solution set is $\{(2, 1)\}$.

Self Check 2 Solve the system by graphing: $\begin{cases} x - 3y = -5 \\ 2x + y = 4 \end{cases}$

Now Try ▶ Problem 21

3 Use Graphing to Identify Inconsistent Systems and Dependent Equations.

When a system has no solution (as in Example 3), it is called an **inconsistent system**.

EXAMPLE 3 Solve the system $\begin{cases} 2x + 3y = 6 \\ 4x + 6y = 24 \end{cases}$ by graphing, if possible.

Strategy We will graph both equations on the same coordinate system.

Why If both equations are graphed on the same coordinate system, we can see whether they have any common solutions.

Solution   Using the intercept method, we graph both equations on one set of coordinate axes, as shown on the right.

$2x + 3y = 6$

x	y	(x, y)
3	0	$(3, 0)$
0	2	$(0, 2)$
-3	4	$(-3, 4)$

$4x + 6y = 24$

x	y	(x, y)
6	0	$(6, 0)$
0	4	$(0, 4)$
-3	6	$(-3, 6)$

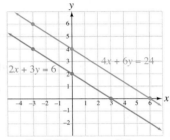

Parallel lines — no solution

Caution

A common error is to graph the parallel lines, but forget to answer with the words

no solution

In this example, the graphs are parallel, because the slopes of the two lines are equal and they have different y-intercepts. We can see that the slope of each line is $-\frac{2}{3}$ by writing the equations in slope–intercept form. To do that, we solve each for y.

$2x + 3y = 6$	First equation	$4x + 6y = 24$	Second equation
$3y = -2x + 6$		$6y = -4x + 24$	
$y = -\dfrac{2}{3}x + 2$	Divide both sides by 3 and simplify.	$y = -\dfrac{2}{3}x + 4$	Divide both sides by 6 and simplify.

Because the lines are parallel, there is no point of intersection. Such a system has *no solution* and it is called an **inconsistent system.** The solution set is the empty set, which is written $\varnothing$.

Self Check 3   Solve the system $\begin{cases} 3y - 2x = 6 \\ 2x - 3y = 6 \end{cases}$ by graphing, if possible.

Now Try ▶ Problem 23

When the equations of a system have different graphs (as in Examples 2 and 3), the equations are called **independent equations.**

EXAMPLE 4   Solve the system by graphing: $\begin{cases} y = \dfrac{1}{2}x + 2 \\ 2x + 8 = 4y \end{cases}$

Strategy   We will graph both equations on the same coordinate system.

Why   If both equations are graphed on the same coordinate system, we can see whether they have any common solutions.

Solution   We graph each equation on one set of coordinate axes, as shown below.

The Language of Algebra

Here the graphs of the lines **coincide.** That is, they occupy the same location. To illustrate this concept, think of a clock. At noon and midnight, the hands of the clock *coincide.*

Graph using the slope and y-intercept.

$y = \dfrac{1}{2}x + 2$

$m = \dfrac{1}{2}$

y-intercept: $(0, 2)$

Graph using the intercept method.

$2x + 8 = 4y$

x	y	(x, y)
-4	0	$(-4, 0)$
0	2	$(0, 2)$
2	3	$(2, 3)$

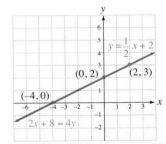

The same line — infinitely many solutions

The graphs appear to be identical. We can verify this by writing the second equation in slope–intercept form and observing that it is the same as the first equation.

$$y = \frac{1}{2}x + 2 \quad \text{First equation} \qquad\qquad 2x + 8 = 4y \quad \text{Second equation}$$

$$\frac{2x}{4} + \frac{8}{4} = \frac{4y}{4} \quad \text{Divide both sides by 4.}$$

$$\frac{1}{2}x + 2 = y$$

We see that the equations of the system are equivalent. Because $y = \frac{1}{2}x + 2$ and $2x + 8 = 4y$ are different forms of the same equation, they are called **dependent equations.**

Since the graphs are the same line, they have infinitely many points in common. All of the points that lie on the common line are solutions because the coordinates of each of those points satisfy both equations of the system. In cases like this, we say that there are *infinitely many solutions*. The solution set can be written using **set-builder notation** as

$$\left\{ (x, y) \,\middle|\, y = \frac{1}{2}x + 2 \right\} \quad \begin{array}{l}\text{Read as, "the set of all ordered pairs } (x, y),\\ \text{such that } y = \frac{1}{2}x + 2."\end{array}$$

Caution

A common error is to graph the identical lines, but forget to answer with the words *infinitely many solutions* and the set-builder notation.

We also can express the solution set using the second equation of the system in the set-builder notation: $\{(x, y) \,|\, 2x + 8 = 4y\}$.

Some instructors prefer that the set-builder notation use an equation in standard form with coefficients that are integers having no common factor other than 1. Such an equation that is equivalent to $y = \frac{1}{2}x + 2$ and $2x + 8 = 4y$ is $x - 2y = -4$. The set-builder notation solution for this example could, therefore, be written as $\{(x, y) \,|\, x - 2y = -4\}$.

From the graph, it appears that three of the infinitely many solutions are $(-4, 0)$, $(0, 2)$, and $(2, 3)$. Check each of them to verify that both equations of the system are satisfied.

Self Check 4 Solve the system by graphing: $\begin{cases} 2x - y = 4 \\ y = 2x - 4 \end{cases}$

Now Try ▶ Problem 25

We now summarize the possibilities that can occur when two linear equations, each with two variables, are graphed.

Solving a System of Equations by the Graphing Method

If the lines are different and intersect, the equations are independent, and the system is consistent. **One solution exists.** It is the point of intersection.

If the lines are different and parallel, the equations are independent, and the system is inconsistent. **No solution exists.**

If the lines are identical, the equations are dependent, and the system is consistent. **Infinitely many solutions exist.** Any point on the line is a solution.

If each equation in one system is equivalent to a corresponding equation in another system, the systems are called **equivalent systems.**

EXAMPLE 5   Solve the system by graphing: $\begin{cases} \dfrac{3}{2}x - y = \dfrac{5}{2} \\ \dfrac{1}{8}y = 1 - \dfrac{x}{4} \end{cases}$

Strategy   We will use the multiplication property of equality to clear both equations of fractions and solve the resulting equivalent system by graphing.

Why   It is usually easier to solve systems of equations that do not contain fractions.

Solution   We multiply both sides of $\frac{3}{2}x - y = \frac{5}{2}$ by 2 to eliminate the fractions and obtain the equation $3x - 2y = 5$. We multiply both sides of $\frac{1}{8}y = 1 - \frac{x}{4}$ by 8 to eliminate the fractions and obtain the equation $y = 8 - 2x$.

The original system   *An equivalent system*

$\begin{cases} \dfrac{3}{2}x - y = \dfrac{5}{2} \\ \dfrac{1}{8}y = 1 - \dfrac{x}{4} \end{cases}$ $\xrightarrow[\text{Multiply by 8}]{\text{Multiply by 2}}$ $\begin{aligned} 2\left(\dfrac{3}{2}x - y\right) &= 2\left(\dfrac{5}{2}\right) \\ 8\left(\dfrac{1}{8}y\right) &= 8\left(1 - \dfrac{x}{4}\right) \end{aligned}$ $\xrightarrow[\text{Simplify}]{\text{Simplify}}$ $\begin{cases} 3x - 2y = 5 \\ y = 8 - 2x \end{cases}$

Since the new system is equivalent to the original system, they have the same solution. If we graph the equations of the new system, it appears that the point where the lines intersect is $(3, 2)$.

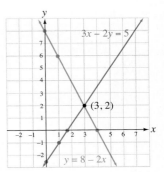

Graph using the   Graph using the slope
intercept method.   and y-intercept.

$3x - 2y = 5$ $y = 8 - 2x$

x	y	(x, y)
$\frac{5}{3}$	0	$\left(\frac{5}{3}, 0\right)$
0	$-\frac{5}{2}$	$\left(0, -\frac{5}{2}\right)$
1	-1	$(1, -1)$

Slope $= -2$
y-intercept: $(0, 8)$

Caution

When checking the solution of a system of equations, always substitute the values of the variables into the original equations.

To verify that $(3, 2)$ is the solution, we substitute 3 for x and 2 for y in each equation of the original system.

Check:

$\dfrac{3}{2}x - y = \dfrac{5}{2}$ First equation

$\dfrac{3}{2}(3) - 2 \overset{?}{=} \dfrac{5}{2}$

$\dfrac{9}{2} - \dfrac{4}{2} \overset{?}{=} \dfrac{5}{2}$

$\dfrac{5}{2} = \dfrac{5}{2}$ True

$\dfrac{1}{8}y = 1 - \dfrac{x}{4}$ Second equation

$\dfrac{1}{8}(2) \overset{?}{=} 1 - \dfrac{3}{4}$

$\dfrac{2}{8} \overset{?}{=} \dfrac{1}{4}$

$\dfrac{1}{4} = \dfrac{1}{4}$ True

Self Check 5   Solve the system by graphing: $\begin{cases} \dfrac{1}{2}x + \dfrac{1}{2}y = -1 \\ \dfrac{1}{3}x - \dfrac{1}{2}y = -4 \end{cases}$

Now Try ▶ Problem 29

Using Your **Calculator** ▶ Solving Systems by Graphing

The TRACE and INTERSECT features found on most graphing calculators enable us to get very good approximations of solutions of systems of two linear equations. To illustrate this, consider the following system. To graph the equations, we must first solve each equation for y.

To solve the system $\begin{cases} 3x + 2y = 12 \\ 2x - 3y = 12 \end{cases}$ $\xrightarrow[\text{Solve for } y]{\text{Solve for } y}$ $\begin{cases} y = -\frac{3}{2}x + 6 \\ y = \frac{2}{3}x - 4 \end{cases}$

Next, we press $\boxed{Y =}$ and enter the right side of each equation of the equivalent system after the symbols Y_1 and Y_2, as shown in figure (a) below. Then we press $\boxed{\text{GRAPH}}$. If we use window settings of $[-10, 10]$ for x and for y, the graphs of the equations will look like those in figure (b). If we zoom in on the intersection point of the two lines and trace, we will get an approximate solution like the one shown in figure (c). To get better results, we can do more zooms. We would then find that, to the nearest hundredth, the solution is $(4.63, -0.94)$. Verify that this is reasonable.

A more efficient method for finding the intersection point of two lines uses the INTERSECT feature. With this feature, the cursor automatically highlights the intersection point, and the x- and y-coordinates are displayed. To locate INTERSECT, press $\boxed{\text{2nd}}$, $\boxed{\text{CALC}}$, 5, followed by $\boxed{\text{ENTER}}$. The result is a graph similar to figure (d). The display shows the approximate coordinates of the point of intersection.

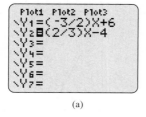

(a)

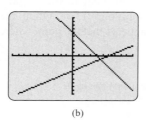

(b)

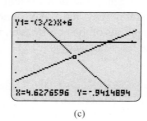

(c)

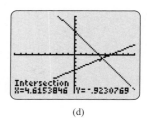

(d)

4 Solve Systems of Linear Equations by Substitution.

The graphing method enables us to visualize the process of solving systems of equations. However, it can be difficult to determine the exact coordinates of the point of intersection. We now review an algebraic method that we can use to find the exact solutions of systems of equations.

The **substitution method** works well for solving systems where one equation is solved, or can be easily solved, for one of the variables. To solve a system of two linear equations in x and y by the substitution method, we can follow these steps.

The Substitution Method

1. Solve one of the equations for either x or y—preferably a variable with a coefficient of 1 or -1. If this is already done, go to step 2. (We call this equation the **substitution equation.**)

2. Substitute the expression for x or for y obtained in step 1 into the other equation and solve that equation.

3. Substitute the value of the variable found in step 2 into the substitution equation to find the value of the remaining variable.

4. Check the proposed solution in each equation of the original system. Write the solution as an ordered pair.

EXAMPLE 6   Solve the system by substitution: $\begin{cases} 4x + y = 13 \\ -2x + 3y = -17 \end{cases}$

Strategy   We will use the substitution method. Since the system does not contain an equation solved for x or y, we must choose an equation and solve it for x or y. It is easiest to solve for y in the first equation, because y has a coefficient of 1.

Why   Solving $4x + y = 13$ for x or solving $-2x + 3y = -17$ for x or y would involve working with cumbersome fractions.

Solution   **Step 1:** We solve the first equation for y, because y has a coefficient of 1.

$$4x + y = 13$$

$$4x + y - 4x = -4x + 13 \qquad \text{To isolate y, subtract 4x from both sides.}$$

$$y = -4x + 13 \qquad \text{This is the substitution equation.}$$
$$\text{It could also be written: } y = 13 - 4x.$$

The Language of Algebra

Since substitution involves algebra and not graphing, it is called an **algebraic** method for solving a system.

Success Tip

Throughout the course, we have been substituting numbers for variables. With this method, we substitute a *variable expression for a variable*. The objective is to use an appropriate substitution to obtain *one* equation in *one* variable.

Because y and $-4x + 13$ are equal, we can substitute $-4x + 13$ for y in the second equation of the system.

$$y = \boxed{-4x + 13} \qquad -2x + 3y = -17$$

Step 2: We then substitute $-4x + 13$ for y in the second equation to eliminate the variable y from that equation. The result will be an equation containing only one variable, x.

$$-2x + 3y = -17 \qquad \text{This is the second equation of the system.}$$

$$-2x + 3(-4x + 13) = -17 \qquad \text{Substitute } -4x + 13 \text{ for y. Write the parentheses so}$$
$$\text{that the multiplication by 3 is distributed over both}$$
$$\text{terms of } -4x + 13.$$

$$-2x - 12x + 39 = -17 \qquad \text{Distribute the multiplication by 3.}$$

$$-14x + 39 = -17 \qquad \text{Combine like terms.}$$

$$-14x = -56 \qquad \text{Subtract 39 from both sides.}$$

$$x = 4 \qquad \text{To solve for x, divide both sides by } -14.$$
$$\text{This is the x-value of the solution.}$$

The Language of Algebra

The phrase **back-substitute** can also be used to describe step 3 of the substitution method. To find y, we *back-substitute* 4 for x in the equation $y = -4x + 13$.

Step 3: To find y, we substitute 4 for x in the substitution equation and evaluate the right side.

$$y = -4x + 13 \qquad \text{This is the substitution equation.}$$

$$y = -4(4) + 13$$

$$y = -16 + 13 \qquad \text{Multiply: } -4(4) = -16.$$

$$y = -3 \qquad \text{This is the y-value of the solution.}$$

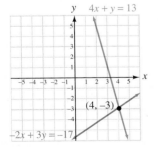

Step 4: To verify that $(4, -3)$ satisfies both equations, we substitute 4 for x and -3 for y into each equation of the original system and simplify.

Check:

$$4x + y = 13 \quad \text{First equation} \qquad\qquad -2x + 3y = -17 \quad \text{Second equation}$$

$$4(4) + (-3) \overset{?}{=} 13 \qquad\qquad\qquad -2(4) + 3(-3) \overset{?}{=} -17$$

$$16 - 3 \overset{?}{=} 13 \qquad\qquad\qquad\qquad -8 - 9 \overset{?}{=} -17$$

$$13 = 13 \quad \text{True} \qquad\qquad\qquad\qquad -17 = -17 \quad \text{True}$$

Since $(4, -3)$ satisfies both equations of the system, it is the solution of the system. The solution set is $\{(4, -3)\}$. The graphs of the equations of the system help to verify this—they appear to intersect at $(4, -3)$, as shown on the left.

Self Check 6   Solve the system by substitution: $\begin{cases} x + 3y = 9 \\ 2x - y = -10 \end{cases}$

Now Try ▶   Problem 35

5 Solve Systems of Linear Equations by the Elimination (Addition) Method.

Recall that with the **elimination (addition) method,** we combine the equations of the system in a way that will eliminate terms involving one of the variables.

The Elimination (Addition) Method

1. Write both equations of the system in standard form: $Ax + By = C$.

2. If necessary, multiply one or both of the equations by a nonzero number chosen to make the coefficients of x (or the coefficients of y) opposites.

3. Add the equations to eliminate the terms involving x (or y).

4. Solve the equation resulting from step 3.

5. Find the value of the remaining variable by substituting the solution found in step 4 into any equation containing both variables. Or, repeat steps 2–4 to eliminate the other variable.

6. Check the proposed solution in each equation of the original system. Write the solution as an ordered pair.

EXAMPLE 7   Solve: $\begin{cases} \dfrac{4}{3}x + \dfrac{1}{2}y = -\dfrac{2}{3} \\ 0.3x + 0.4y = 1 \end{cases}$

Strategy   We will find an equivalent system without fractions or decimals and use the elimination method to solve it.

Why   It's usually easier to solve a system of equations that involves only integers.

Solution   **Step 1:** To clear the first equation of the fractions, we multiply both sides by 6. To clear the second equation of decimals, we multiply both sides by 10.

$$\begin{cases} \dfrac{4}{3}x + \dfrac{1}{2}y = -\dfrac{2}{3} \\ 0.3x + 0.4y = 1 \end{cases} \xrightarrow{\text{Multiply by 6}} \ 6\left(\dfrac{4}{3}x + \dfrac{1}{2}y\right) = 6\left(-\dfrac{2}{3}\right) \xrightarrow{\text{Simplify}} \begin{cases} 8x + 3y = -4 \\ 3x + 4y = 10 \end{cases}$$

$$10(0.3x + 0.4y) = 10(1)$$

Multiply by 10   Simplify

Step 2: To make the y-terms drop out when we add the equations, we multiply both sides of $8x + 3y = -4$ by 4 and both sides of $3x + 4y = 10$ by -3 to get

$$\begin{cases} 8x + 3y = -4 \\ 3x + 4y = 10 \end{cases} \xrightarrow[\text{Multiply by } -3]{\text{Multiply by 4}} \begin{cases} 32x + 12y = -16 \\ -9x - 12y = -30 \end{cases}$$

Success Tip

The basic objective of the elimination method is to obtain two equations whose sum will be *one* equation in *one* variable.

Step 3: When these equations are added, the y-terms drop out.

$$\begin{array}{r} 32x + 12y = -16 \\ \underline{-9x - 12y = -30} \\ 23x \qquad\quad = -46 \end{array}$$

Add the like terms, column by column: $32x + (-9x) = 23x$,

$12y + (-12y) = 0$, and $-16 + (-30) = -46$.

Step 4: We solve the resulting equation to find x.

$$23x = -46$$

$$x = -2$$ To solve for x, divide both sides by 23. This is the x-value of the solution.

Step 5: To find y, we can substitute -2 for x in either of the equations of the original system or either of the equations of the equivalent system. It appears the calculations will be the simplest if we use $3x + 4y = 10$.

$$3x + 4y = 10 \quad \text{This is the second equation of the equivalent system.}$$
$$3(-2) + 4y = 10 \quad \text{Substitute } -2 \text{ for } x.$$
$$-6 + 4y = 10 \quad \text{Simplify.}$$
$$4y = 16 \quad \text{To isolate the variable term, add 6 to both sides.}$$
$$y = 4 \quad \text{To solve for } y, \text{ divide both sides by 4. This is the } y\text{-value of the solution.}$$

Step 6: The solution is $(-2, 4)$ and the solution set is $\{(-2, 4)\}$. Verify that the solution checks using the original equations.

Self Check 7   Solve the system: $\begin{cases} \dfrac{2}{3}x - \dfrac{2}{5}y = 10 \\ 0.3x + 0.4y = -4.2 \end{cases}$

Now Try ▶ Problem 49

6   Use Substitution and Elimination (Addition) to Identify Inconsistent Systems and Dependent Equations.

We have solved inconsistent systems and systems of dependent equations by graphing. We also can solve these systems using the substitution and elimination methods.

EXAMPLE 8   Solve the system: $\begin{cases} y = 2x + 4 \\ 8x - 4y = 7 \end{cases}$

Strategy   We will use the substitution method to solve this system.

Why   The substitution method works well when one of the equations of the system (in this case, $y = 2x + 4$) is solved for a variable.

Solution   Since the first equation is solved for y, we will use the substitution method.

$$y = 2x + 4 \quad \text{This is the substitution equation.}$$
$$8x - 4y = 7 \quad \text{This is the second equation of the system.}$$
$$8x - 4(2x + 4) = 7 \quad \text{Substitute } 2x + 4 \text{ for } y.$$

Now we can try to solve this equation for x:

$$8x - 8x - 16 = 7 \quad \text{Distribute the multiplication by } -4.$$
$$-16 = 7 \quad \text{Simplify the left side: } 8x - 8x = 0.$$

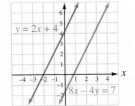

Here, the terms involving x drop out, and we get $-16 = 7$. This false statement indicates that the system has *no solution* and is, therefore, inconsistent. The solution set is $\varnothing$. The graphs of the equations of the system help to verify this—they appear to be parallel lines, as shown on the left.

Self Check 8   Solve the system: $\begin{cases} x = -2.5y + 8 \\ y = -0.4x + 2 \end{cases}$

Now Try ▶ Problem 51

EXAMPLE 9   Solve: $\begin{cases} 2(2x + 3y) = 12 \\ -2x = 3y - 6 \end{cases}$

Strategy   We will write each equation in standard (general) form $Ax + By = C$ and use the elimination (addition) method to solve the resulting equivalent system.

Why   Since no variable has a coefficient of 1 or −1, it would be difficult to solve this system using substitution.

Solution   To write the first equation in standard (general) form, we use the distributive property. To write the second equation in standard form, we subtract 3y from both sides.

The first equation	*The second equation*
$2(2x + 3y) = 12$	$-2x = 3y - 6$
$4x + 6y = 12$	$-2x - 3y = -6$

We now copy $4x + 6y = 12$ and multiply both sides of $-2x - 3y = -6$ by 2 to get

$$
\begin{array}{r}
4x + 6y = 12 \\
-4x - 6y = -12 \\
\hline
0 = 0
\end{array}
$$

When we add like terms, column by column, the result is $0x + 0y = 0$, which simplifies to $0 = 0$.

Here, both the x- and y-terms drop out. The resulting true statement $0 = 0$ indicates that the equations are dependent and that the system has an *infinitely many solutions*. The solution set is written using set-builder notation as $\{(x, y) \mid 4x + 6y = 12\}$ and is read as "the set of all ordered pairs (x, y) such that $4x + 6y = 12$."

Note that the equations of the system are dependent equations, because when the second equation is multiplied by −2, it becomes the first equation. The graphs of these equations are, therefore, the same line. To find some of the infinitely many solutions of the system, we can substitute 0, 3, and −3 for x in either equation to obtain $(0, 2)$, $(3, 0)$, and $(-3, 4)$.

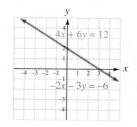

Self Check 9   Solve the system: $\begin{cases} 2x = 5(y + 2) \\ -4x + 10y = -20 \end{cases}$

Now Try ▶   Problem 53

Examples 8 and 9 illustrate the following facts.

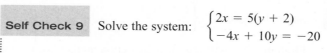

Inconsistent Systems and Dependent Equations

When solving a system of two linear equations in two variables using substitution or elimination (addition):

1. If the variables drop out and a true statement (identity) is obtained, the system has an infinite number of solutions. The equations are dependent and the system is consistent.

2. If the variables drop out and a false statement (contradiction) is obtained, the system has no solution and is inconsistent.

▇7 Solve Application Problems Using Systems of Equations.

We have solved applied problems involving two unknown quantities by modeling the situation with an equation in one variable. It's often easier to solve such problems using a two-variable approach. We write two equations in two variables to model the situation, and then we use the methods of this section to solve the system formed by the pair of equations.

EXAMPLE 10   **Wedding Pictures.**   A professional photographer offers two different packages for wedding pictures. Use the information in the illustration on the next page to determine the cost of one 8 × 10-inch photograph and the cost of one 5 × 7-inch photograph.

Wedding Pictures

Package 1
8 - 8 x 10's
12 - 5 x 7's
Only $133.00

Package 2
6 - 8 x 10's
22 - 5 x 7's
Only $168.00

© Carlush/Shutterstock.com

Analyze

- Eight 8×10 and twelve 5×7 pictures cost $133.
- Six 8×10 and twenty-two 5×7 pictures cost $168.
- Find the cost of one 8×10 photograph and the cost of one 5×7 photograph.

Assign Let x = the cost of one 8×10 photograph (in dollars), and let y = the cost of one 5×7 photograph (in dollars).

Form We can use the fact that **Number · value = total value** to construct tables that model the cost of each package.

Package 1

Size of photo	Number	· Value	= Total value
8×10	8	x	$8x$
5×7	12	y	$12y$

Total: $133

↑
One equation comes
from this column.

Package 2

Size of photo	Number	· Value	= Total value
8×10	6	x	$6x$
5×7	22	y	$22y$

Total: $168

↑
The second equation
comes from this column.

From the *Total value column* of the first table:

The cost of eight 8×10 photographs	plus	the cost of twelve 5×7 photographs	is	the cost of the first package.
$8x$	$+$	$12y$	$=$	133

From the *Total value column* of the second table:

The cost of six 8×10 photographs	plus	the cost of twenty-two 5×7 photographs	is	the cost of the second package.
$6x$	$+$	$22y$	$=$	168

The resulting system is:
$$\begin{cases} 8x + 12y = 133 & \textbf{(1)} \\ 6x + 22y = 168 & \textbf{(2)} \end{cases}$$

Solve We will use elimination to solve this system. To make the x-terms drop out, we multiply both sides of equation 1 by 3. Then we multiply both sides of equation 2 by -4, add the resulting equations, and solve for y:

$$24x + 36y = 399 \qquad \text{This is } 3(8x + 12y) = 3(133).$$
$$\underline{-24x - 88y = -672} \qquad \text{This is } -4(6x + 22y) = -4(168).$$
$$-52y = -273 \qquad \text{Add the terms, column by column. The x-terms drop out.}$$
$$y = 5.25 \qquad \text{Divide both sides by } -52. \text{ This is the cost of one } 5 \times 7 \text{ photograph.}$$

To find x, we substitute 5.25 for y in equation 1 and solve for x:

$$8x + 12y = 133$$
$$8x + 12(\mathbf{5.25}) = 133 \qquad \text{Substitute 5.25 for y.}$$
$$8x + 63 = 133 \qquad \text{Do the multiplication.}$$
$$8x = 70 \qquad \text{Subtract 63 from both sides.}$$
$$x = 8.75 \qquad \text{Divide both sides by 8. This is the cost of one } 8 \times 10 \text{ photograph.}$$

State The cost of one 8×10 photo is $8.75, and the cost of one 5×7 photo is $5.25.

Check If the first package contains eight 8×10 and twelve 5×7 photographs, the value of the package is $8(\$8.75) + 12(\$5.25) = \$70 + \$63 = \$133$. If the second package contains six 8×10 and twenty-two 5×7 photographs, the value of the package is $6(\$8.75) + 22(\$5.25) = \$52.50 + \$115.50 = \$168$. The results check.

Solve each system by any method. If a system is inconsistent or if the equations are dependent, so indicate.

67. $\begin{cases} 2x + 3y = 8 \\ 3x - 2y = -1 \end{cases}$

68. $\begin{cases} x = \dfrac{3}{2}y + 5 \\ 2x - 3y = 8 \end{cases}$

69. $\begin{cases} 4(x - 2) = -9y \\ 2(x - 3y) = -3 \end{cases}$

70. $\begin{cases} 2(2x + 3y) = 5 \\ 8x = 3(1 + 3y) \end{cases}$

71. $\begin{cases} 0.3a + 0.1b = 0.5 \\ \dfrac{4}{3}a + \dfrac{1}{3}b = 3 \end{cases}$

72. $\begin{cases} 0.9p + 0.2q = 1.2 \\ \dfrac{2}{3}p + \dfrac{1}{9}q = 1 \end{cases}$

73. $\begin{cases} \dfrac{x}{2} + \dfrac{y}{2} = 6 \\ \dfrac{x}{3} + \dfrac{y}{3} = 4 \end{cases}$

74. $\begin{cases} \dfrac{x}{2} - \dfrac{y}{3} = -4 \\ \dfrac{x}{2} + \dfrac{y}{9} = 0 \end{cases}$

75. $\begin{cases} x = \dfrac{2}{3}y \\ y = 4x + 5 \end{cases}$

76. $\begin{cases} 5x - 2y = 19 \\ y = \dfrac{1 - 3x}{4} \end{cases}$

77. $\begin{cases} 3x - 4y = 9 \\ x + 2y = 8 \end{cases}$

78. $\begin{cases} 3x - 2y = -10 \\ 6x + 5y = 25 \end{cases}$

79. $\begin{cases} x - \dfrac{4y}{5} = 4 \\ \dfrac{y}{3} = \dfrac{x}{2} - \dfrac{5}{2} \end{cases}$

80. $\begin{cases} 3x - 2y = \dfrac{9}{2} \\ \dfrac{x}{2} - \dfrac{3}{4} = 2y \end{cases}$

81. $\begin{cases} \dfrac{2}{3}x - \dfrac{1}{4}y = -8 \\ 0.5x - 0.375y = -9 \end{cases}$

82. $\begin{cases} 0.5x + 0.5y = 6 \\ \dfrac{x}{2} - \dfrac{y}{2} = -2 \end{cases}$

83. $\begin{cases} \dfrac{3}{2}p + \dfrac{1}{3}q = 2 \\ \dfrac{2}{3}p + \dfrac{1}{9}q = 1 \end{cases}$

84. $\begin{cases} a + \dfrac{b}{3} = \dfrac{5}{3} \\ \dfrac{a + b}{3} = 3 - a \end{cases}$

85. $\begin{cases} \dfrac{m - n}{5} + \dfrac{m + n}{2} = 6 \\ \dfrac{m - n}{2} - \dfrac{m + n}{4} = 3 \end{cases}$

86. $\begin{cases} \dfrac{r - 2}{5} + \dfrac{s + 3}{2} = 5 \\ \dfrac{r + 3}{2} + \dfrac{s - 2}{3} = 6 \end{cases}$

Solve each system. To do so, substitute a for $\dfrac{1}{x}$ and b for $\dfrac{1}{y}$ and solve for a and b. Then find x and y using the fact that $a = \dfrac{1}{x}$ and $b = \dfrac{1}{y}$.

87. $\begin{cases} \dfrac{1}{x} + \dfrac{1}{y} = \dfrac{5}{6} \\ \dfrac{1}{x} - \dfrac{1}{y} = \dfrac{1}{6} \end{cases}$

88. $\begin{cases} \dfrac{1}{x} + \dfrac{1}{y} = \dfrac{9}{20} \\ \dfrac{1}{x} - \dfrac{1}{y} = \dfrac{1}{20} \end{cases}$

89. $\begin{cases} \dfrac{1}{x} + \dfrac{2}{y} = -1 \\ \dfrac{2}{x} - \dfrac{1}{y} = -7 \end{cases}$

90. $\begin{cases} \dfrac{3}{x} - \dfrac{2}{y} = -30 \\ \dfrac{2}{x} - \dfrac{3}{y} = -30 \end{cases}$

APPLICATIONS

91. ▶

from **Campus to Careers**

Fashion Designer

One of the line graphs below gives the percent share of the U.S. footwear market for shoes produced in the United States. The other line gives the percent share of the U.S. footwear market for imports.

a. Estimate the coordinates of the point of intersection of the graphs.

b. What important percent-of-the-market information does your answer to part a give?

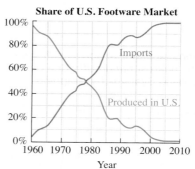

Share of U.S. Footware Market

Source: Americal Apparel and Footwear Association

92. The Internet.

The graph on the next page shows the growing importance of the Internet in the daily lives of Americans. Determine when the time spent on the following activities was the same. Approximately how many hours per year were spent on each?

a. Internet and reading magazines

b. Internet and reading newspapers

c. Internet and reading books

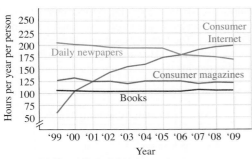

Source: Vernois Suhler Stevenson

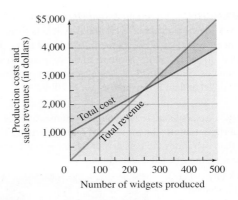

93. Law of Supply and Demand. The demand function, graphed below, describes the relationship between the price x of a certain camera and the demand for the camera.

a. The supply function, $S(x) = \frac{25}{4}x - 525$, describes the relationship between the price x of the camera and the number of cameras the manufacturer is willing to supply. Graph this function in the illustration.

b. For what price will the supply of cameras equal the demand?

c. As the price of the camera is increased, what happens to supply and what happens to demand?

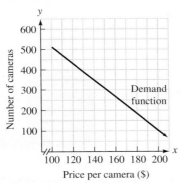

94. Cost and Revenue. The function $C(x) = 200x + 400$ gives the cost for a college to offer x sections of an introductory class in CPR (cardiopulmonary resuscitation). The function $R(x) = 280x$ gives the amount of revenue the college brings in when offering x sections of CPR.

a. Find the *break-even point* (where cost = revenue) by graphing each function on the same coordinate system.

b. How many sections does the college need to offer to make a profit on the CPR training course?

95. Business. Estimate the break-even point (where cost = revenue) on the graph in the next column. Explain why it is called the *break-even point.*

96. Navigation. The paths of two ships are tracked on the same coordinate system. One ship is following a path described by the equation $2x + 3y = 6$, and the other is following a path described by the equation $y = \frac{2}{3}x - 3$.

a. Is there a possibility of a collision?

b. What are the coordinates of the danger point?

c. Is a collision a certainty?

In Exercises 97–112, write a system of two equations in two variables to solve each problem.

97. Ticket Sales. The ticket prices for a Halloween haunted house were $5 for adults and $3 for children. On a day when a total of 390 tickets were purchased, the receipts were $1,470. How many of each type of ticket were sold?

98. Advertising. Use the information in the ad to find the cost of a 15-second and the cost of a 30-second radio commercial on radio station KLIZ.

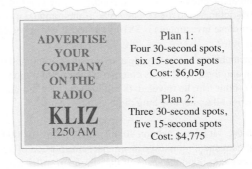

99.   from **Campus to Careers**

Fashion Designer

In 2009, there was a combined total of 4,046 Gap and Aéropostale clothing stores worldwide. The number of Gap stores was $3\frac{1}{4}$ times more than the number of Aéropostale stores. How many Gap stores and how many Aéropostale stores were there that year? (Source: wikinvest.com)

©iStockphoto.com/CandyBox Photography

100. Summer Concerts. According to *StubHub.com,* in 2009, two tickets to a Jonas Brothers concert and two tickets to an Elton John concert cost, on average, a total of $560. At those prices, four tickets to see the Jonas Brothers and two tickets to see Elton John cost $806. What was the average cost of a Jonas Brothers ticket and an Elton John ticket in 2009?

101. Geometry. An acute angle is an angle with measure less than 90°. In a right triangle, the measure of one acute angle is 15° greater than two times the measure of the other acute angle. Find the measure of each acute angle.

102. New York City. The triangular-shaped Flatiron Building in Manhattan has a perimeter of 499 feet at its base. It is bordered on each side by a street. The 5th Avenue front of the building is 198 feet long. The Broadway front is 43 feet more than twice as long as the East 22nd Street front. Find the length of the Broadway front and East 22nd Street front. (Source: New York Public Library)

©Songquan Deng/Shutterstock.com

103. Investment Clubs. Part of $8,000 was invested by an investment club at 10% interest and the rest at 12%. If the annual income from these investments is $900, how much was invested at each rate?

104. Retirement Income. A retired couple invested part of $12,000 at 6% interest and the rest at 7.5%. If their annual income from these investments is $810, how much was invested at each rate?

105. Snowmobiling. A man rode a snowmobile at the rate of 20 mph and then skied cross country at the rate of 4 mph. During the 6-hour trip, he traveled 48 miles. How long did he snowmobile, and how long did he ski?

106. Salmon. It takes a salmon 40 minutes to swim 10,000 feet upstream and 8 minutes to swim that same portion of a river downstream. Find the speed of the salmon in still water and the speed of the current.

107. Production Planning. A manufacturer builds racing bikes and mountain bikes, with the per unit manufacturing costs shown in the table. The company has budgeted $26,150 for materials and $31,800 for labor. How many bicycles of each type can be built?

Model	Cost of materials	Cost of labor
Racing	$110	$120
Mountain	$140	$180

108. Farming. A farmer keeps some animals on a strict diet. Each animal is to receive 15 grams of protein and 7.5 grams of carbohydrates. The farmer uses two food mixes, with nutrients as shown in the table. How many grams of each mix should be used to provide the correct nutrients for each animal?

Mix	Protein	Carbohydrates
Mix A	12%	9%
Mix B	15%	5%

109. Cosmotology. A beauty shop specializing in permanents has fixed costs of $2,101.20 per month. The owner estimates that the cost for each permanent is $23.60, which covers labor, chemicals, and electricity. If her shop can give as many permanents as she wants at a price of $44 each, how many must be given each month for her to break even?

110. Mixing Candy. How many pounds of each candy shown in the illustration must be mixed to obtain 60 pounds of candy that would be worth $4 per pound?

Gummy Bears $3.50/lb   Jelly Beans $5.50/lb

111. Dermatology. Tests of an antibacterial face-wash cream showed that a mixture containing 0.3% Triclosan (active ingredient) gave the best results. How many grams of cream from each tube should be used to make an equal-size tube of the 0.3% cream?

Contents: 185 g — **Daily Face Wash** — 0.2% Triclosan

Contents: 185 g — **Daily Face Wash** — 0.7% Triclosan

112. Mixing Solutions. How many ounces of the two alcohol solutions in the illustration must be mixed to obtain 100 ounces of a 12.2% solution?

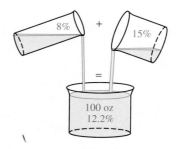

8% + 15% = 100 oz 12.2%

WRITING

113. Which method would you use to solve the system? Explain.

$$\begin{cases} y - 1 = 3x \\ 3x + 2y = 12 \end{cases}$$

114. Which method would you use to solve the system? Explain.

$$\begin{cases} 2x + 4y = 9 \\ 3x - 5y = 20 \end{cases}$$

115. When solving a system, what advantages are there with the substitution and elimination methods compared with the graphing method?

116. When using the elimination (addition) method, how can you tell whether

  a. a system of linear equations has no solution?

  b. a system of linear equations has infinitely many solutions?

REVIEW

Solve each formula for the specified variable.

117. $\dfrac{V_2}{V_1} = \dfrac{P_1}{P_2}$ for P_1

118. $\dfrac{1}{r} = \dfrac{1}{r_1} + \dfrac{1}{r_2}$ for r

119. $S = \dfrac{a - lr}{1 - r}$ for r

120. $P = \dfrac{Q_1}{Q_2 - Q_1}$ for Q_1

CHALLENGE PROBLEMS

121. If the solution of the system $\begin{cases} Ax + By = -2 \\ Bx - Ay = -26 \end{cases}$ is $(-3, 5)$, find the values of A and B.

122. Solve $\begin{cases} 2ab - 3cd = 1 \\ 3ab - 2cd = 1 \end{cases}$ and assume that b and d are constants.

SECTION 12.2

Solving Systems of Equations in Three Variables

OBJECTIVES

1 Determine whether an ordered triple is a solution of a system.

2 Solve systems of three linear equations in three variables.

3 Solve systems of equations with missing variable terms.

4 Identify inconsistent systems and dependent equations.

ARE YOU READY?

The following problems review some basic skills that are needed when solving systems of equations in three variables.

1. What is the coefficient of each term on the left side of the equation $x - 4y + 5z = 2$?

2. For $6x + y + 2z = 36$, if $x = 5$ and $y = -2$, what is z?

3. Write the equation $7x + 5y = z + 9$ so that all three variable terms are on the left side.

4. Solve the system by elimination: $\begin{cases} 5x + 2y = -5 \\ -6x - 2y = 10 \end{cases}$

In previous sections, we solved systems of linear equations in two variables. We will now extend this discussion to consider systems of linear equations in *three* variables.

1 Determine Whether an Ordered Triple Is a Solution of a System.

The equation $x - 5y + 7z = 10$, where each variable is raised to the first power, is an example of a linear equation in three variables. In general, we have the following definition.

Standard Form	▼ A **linear equation in three variables** is an equation that can be written in the form $$Ax + By + Cz = D$$ where A, B, C, and D are real numbers and A, B, and C are not all 0.

A solution of a linear equation in three variables is an **ordered triple** of numbers of the form (x, y, z) whose coordinates satisfy the equation. For example, $(2, 0, 1)$ is a solution of $x + y + z = 3$ because a true statement results when we substitute 2 for x, 0 for y, and 1 for z: $2 + 0 + 1 = 3$.

A **solution of a system of three linear equations** in three variables is an ordered triple that satisfies each equation of the system.

EXAMPLE 1   Determine whether $(-4, 2, 5)$ is a solution of the system:

$$\begin{cases} 2x + 3y + 4z = 18 \\ 3x + 4y + z = 1 \\ x + y + 3z = 13 \end{cases}$$

Strategy   We will substitute the x-, y-, and z-coordinates of $(-4, 2, 5)$ for the corresponding variables in each equation of the system.

Why   If each equation is satisfied by the x-, y-, and z-coordinates, the ordered triple is a solution of the system.

Solution   We substitute -4 for x, 2 for y, and 5 for z in each equation.

The first equation	*The second equation*	*The third equation*
$2x + 3y + 4z = 18$	$3x + 4y + z = 1$	$x + y + 3z = 13$
$2(-4) + 3(2) + 4(5) \overset{?}{=} 18$	$3(-4) + 4(2) + 5 \overset{?}{=} 1$	$-4 + 2 + 3(5) \overset{?}{=} 13$
$-8 + 6 + 20 \overset{?}{=} 18$	$-12 + 8 + 5 \overset{?}{=} 1$	$-4 + 2 + 15 \overset{?}{=} 13$
$18 = 18$ True	$1 = 1$ True	$13 = 13$ True

Since $(-4, 2, 5)$ satisfies each equation, it is a solution of the system.

Self Check 1   Is $(6, -3, 1)$ a solution of: $\begin{cases} x - y + z = 10 \\ x + 4y - z = -7 \\ 3x - y + 4z = 24 \end{cases}$

Now Try ▶ Problem 11

The graph of an equation of the form $Ax + By + Cz = D$ can be drawn on a coordinate system with three axes. The graph of such an equation is a flat surface called a **plane.** A system of three linear equations with three variables is consistent or inconsistent, depending on how the three planes corresponding to the three equations intersect. The following illustration shows some of the possibilities. Just as in the case of two variables, a system of three linear equations in three variables can have exactly one solution, no solution, or infinitely many solutions, as shown below.

A consistent system

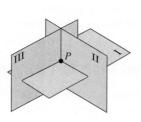

The three planes intersect at a single point: The system has **one solution**.

(a)

A consistent system

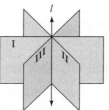

The three planes have a line l in common. The system has **infinitely many solutions**.

(b)

Three types of inconsistent systems

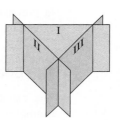

The three planes have no point in common to all three. The system has **no solutions**.

(c)

2 Solve Systems of Three Linear Equations in Three Variables.

To **solve a system of three linear equations** in three variables means to find all of the solutions of the system. Solving such a system by graphing is not practical because it requires a three-dimensional coordinate system.

The substitution method is useful to solve systems of three equations where one or more equations have only two variables. However, the best way to solve systems of three linear equations in three variables is usually the elimination method.

Solving a System of Three Linear Equations by Elimination	1. Write each equation in standard form $Ax + By + Cz = D$ and clear any decimals or fractions.
	2. Pick any two equations and eliminate a variable.
	3. Pick a different pair of equations and eliminate the same variable as in step 1.
	4. Solve the resulting pair of two equations in two variables.
	5. To find the value of the third variable, substitute the values of the two variables found in step 4 into any equation containing all three variables and solve the equation.
	6. Check the proposed solution in all three of the original equations. Write the solution as an ordered triple.

EXAMPLE 2   Solve the system: $\begin{cases} 2x + y + 4z = 12 \\ x + 2y + 2z = 9 \\ 3x - 3y - 2z = 1 \end{cases}$

Strategy   Since the coefficients of the z-terms are opposites in the second and third equations, we will add the left and right sides of those equations to eliminate z. Then we will choose another pair of equations and eliminate z again.

Why   The result will be a system of two equations in x and y that we can solve by elimination.

Solution

Step 1: We can skip step 1 because each equation is written in standard form and there are no fractions or decimals to clear. We will number each equation and move to step 2.

(1) $\quad\begin{cases} 2x + y + 4z = 12 \\ x + 2y + 2z = 9 \\ 3x - 3y - 2z = 1 \end{cases}$
(2)
(3)

Step 2: If we pick equations 2 and 3 and add them, the variable z is eliminated.

(2) $\quad x + 2y + 2z = 9$
(3) $\quad \underline{3x - 3y - 2z = 1}$
(4) $\quad 4x - y = 10$ *This equation does not contain z.*

Step 3: We now pick a different pair of equations (equations 1 and 3) and eliminate z again. If each side of equation 3 is multiplied by 2, and the resulting equation is added to equation 1, z is eliminated.

(1) $\quad 2x + y + 4z = 12$
$\quad \underline{6x - 6y - 4z = 2}$ *This is 2(3x − 3y − 2z) = 2(1).*
(5) $\quad 8x - 5y = 14$ *This equation does not contain z.*

Step 4: Equations 4 and 5 form a system of two equations in x and y.

(4) $\quad\begin{cases} 4x - y = 10 \\ 8x - 5y = 14 \end{cases}$
(5)

To solve this system, we multiply equation 4 by -5 and add the resulting equation to equation 5 to eliminate y.

$\quad -20x + 5y = -50$ *This is −5(4x − y) = −5(10).*
(5) $\quad \underline{8x - 5y = 14}$
$\quad -12x = -36$
$\quad\quad\quad\quad x = 3$ *Divide both sides by −12. This is the x-value of the solution.*

To find y, we substitute 3 for x in any equation containing x and y (such as equation 5) and solve for y:

(5) $\quad 8x - 5y = 14$

$\qquad 8(3) - 5y = 14 \qquad$ Substitute 3 for x.

$\qquad\quad 24 - 5y = 14 \qquad$ Simplify.

$\qquad\qquad\quad -5y = -10 \qquad$ Subtract 24 from both sides.

$\qquad\qquad\qquad y = 2 \qquad$ Divide both sides by −5. This is the y-value of the solution.

Step 5: To find z, we substitute 3 for x and 2 for y in any equation containing x, y, and z (such as equation 1) and solve for z:

(1) $\quad 2x + y + 4z = 12$

$\qquad 2(3) + 2 + 4z = 12 \qquad$ Substitute 3 for x and 2 for y.

$\qquad\qquad\; 8 + 4z = 12 \qquad$ Simplify.

$\qquad\qquad\qquad\; 4z = 4 \qquad$ Subtract 8 from both sides.

$\qquad\qquad\qquad\quad z = 1 \qquad$ Divide both sides by 4. This is the z-value of the solution.

Step 6: To verify that the solution is $(3, 2, 1)$, we substitute 3 for x, 2 for y, and 1 for z in the three equations of the original system. The solution set is written as $\{(3, 2, 1)\}$. Since this system has a solution, it is a consistent system.

Self Check 2 Solve the system: $\begin{cases} 2x - 3y + 2z = -7 \\ x + 4y - z = 10 \\ 3x + 2y + z = 4 \end{cases}$

Now Try ▶ Problem 15

3 Solve Systems of Equations with Missing Variable Terms.

When one or more of the equations of a system is missing a variable term, the elimination of a variable that is normally performed in step 2 of the solution process can be skipped.

EXAMPLE 3 Solve the system: $\begin{cases} 3x = 6 - 2y + z \\ -y - 2z = -8 - x \\ x = 1 - 2z \end{cases}$

Strategy Since the third equation does not contain the variable y, we will work with the first and second equations to obtain another equation that does not contain y.

Why Then we can use the elimination method to solve the resulting system of two equations in x and z.

Solution **Step 1:** We use the addition property of equality to write each equation in the standard form $Ax + By + Cz = D$ and number each equation.

(1) $\begin{cases} 3x + 2y - z = 6 \quad$ Add 2y and subtract z from both sides of 3x = 6 − 2y + z.
(2) $\phantom{\begin{cases}} x - y - 2z = -8 \quad$ Add x to both sides of −y − 2z = −8 − x.
(3) $\phantom{\begin{cases}} x + 2z = 1 \quad$ Add 2z to both sides of x = 1 − 2z.

Step 2: Since equation 3 does not have a y-term, we can skip to step 3, where we will find another equation that does not contain a y-term.

Step 3: If each side of equation 2 is multiplied by 2 and the resulting equation is added to equation 1, y is eliminated.

(1) $3x + 2y - z = 6$
$\underline{2x - 2y - 4z = -16}$ This is $2(x - y - 2z) = 2(-8)$.
(4) $5x \qquad -5z = -10$

Step 4: Equations 3 and 4 form a system of two equations in x and z:

(3) $\begin{cases} x + 2z = 1 \\ (4) \quad 5x - 5z = -10 \end{cases}$

Success Tip

We don't have to find the values of the variables in alphabetical order. In step 2, choose the variable that is the easiest to eliminate. In this example, the value of z is found first.

To solve this system, we multiply equation 3 by -5 and add the resulting equation to equation 4 to eliminate x:

$-5x - 10z = -5$ This is $-5(x + 2z) = -5(1)$.
(4) $\underline{5x - 5z = -10}$
$-15z = -15$
$z = 1$ Divide both sides by -15. This is the z-value of the solution.

To find x, we substitute 1 for z in equation 3.

(3) $x + 2z = 1$
$x + 2(1) = 1$ Substitute 1 for z.
$x + 2 = 1$ Multiply.
$x = -1$ Subtract 2 from both sides.

Step 5: To find y, we substitute -1 for x and 1 for z in equation 1:

(1) $3x + 2y - z = 6$
$3(-1) + 2y - 1 = 6$ Substitute -1 for x and 1 for z.
$-3 + 2y - 1 = 6$ Multiply.
$2y = 10$ Simplify and add 4 to both sides.
$y = 5$ Divide both sides by 2.

The solution of the system is $(-1, 5, 1)$ and the solution set is $\{(-1, 5, 1)\}$.

Step 6: Check the proposed solution in all three of the original equations.

Self Check 3   Solve the system: $\begin{cases} x + 2y = 1 + z \\ 2x = 3 + y - z \\ x + z = 3 \end{cases}$

Now Try ▶ Problem 23

EXAMPLE 4   Solve the system: $\begin{cases} x - y + 4z = -30 & \text{(1)} \\ x + 2y = 200 & \text{(2)} \\ y + z = 30 & \text{(3)} \end{cases}$

Strategy   Since the second equation does not contain the variable z, we will work with the first and third equations to obtain another equation that does not contain z.

Why   Then we can use the elimination method to solve the resulting system of two equations in x and y.

Solution   **Step 1:** Each of the equations is written in standard form, however, two of the equations are missing variable terms.

Step 2: Since equation 2 does not have a z-term, we can skip to step 3, where we will find another equation that does not contain a z-term.

Step 3: If each side of equation 3 is multiplied by -4 and the resulting equation is added to the equation 1, z is eliminated.

(1) $\quad x - y + 4z = -30$

$\quad\quad\;\; \underline{-4y - 4z = -120}\quad$ This is $-4(y + z) = -4(30)$.

(4) $\quad x - 5y \quad\quad\;\; = -150$

Step 4: Equations 2 and 4 form a system of two equations in x and y.

(2) $\begin{cases} x + 2y = 200 \\ x - 5y = -150 \end{cases}$
(4)

To solve this system, we multiply equation 4 by -1 and add the resulting equation to equation 2 to eliminate x.

(2) $\quad\;\; x + 2y = 200$

$\quad\quad\; \underline{-x + 5y = 150}\quad$ This is $-1(x - 5y) = -1(-150)$.

$\quad\quad\quad\quad\; 7y = 350$

$\quad\quad\quad\quad\;\; y = 50 \quad\quad$ To find y, divide both sides by 7.

We then find the value of x to complete step 4 and the value of z (step 5) in the same way as in Examples 2 and 3.

Step 6: Use a check to verify that the solution is $(100, 50, -20)$.

Self Check 4 Solve the system: $\begin{cases} x + y + 3z = 35 \\ x + 3y = -20 \\ 2y + z = -35 \end{cases}$

Now Try ▶ **Problem 27**

In the following example, we will solve the same system from Example 4 using a different approach.

EXAMPLE 5 Use substitution to solve the system: $\begin{cases} x - y + 4z = -30 \\ x + 2y = 200 \\ y + z = 30 \end{cases}$

Strategy We will solve the second equation for x and the third equation for z. This creates two substitution equations. Then we will substitute the results for x and for z in the first equation.

Why These substitutions will produce one equation in the variable y.

Solution The method we will use is much like solving systems of two equations by substitution. However, we must find two substitution equations, instead of one.

$\begin{cases} x - y + 4z = -30 \\ x + 2y = 200 \\ y + z = 30 \end{cases}$ $\begin{matrix} \xrightarrow{\text{Solve for } x} \\ \\ \xrightarrow[\text{Solve for } z]{} \end{matrix}$ $\begin{cases} x - y + 4z = -30 & \textbf{(1)} \\ x = \boxed{200 - 2y} & \textbf{(2)} \\ z = \boxed{30 - y} & \textbf{(3)} \end{cases}$

Since the variable x is isolated in equation 2, we will substitute $200 - 2y$ for x in equation 1, and since the variable z is isolated in equation 3, we will substitute $30 - y$ for z in equation 1. These substitutions will eliminate x and z from equation 1, leaving an equation in one variable, y.

$$x - y + 4z = -30 \qquad \text{This is equation 1.}$$
$$200 - 2y - y + 4(30 - y) = -30 \qquad \text{Substitute } 200 - 2y \text{ for } x \text{ and } 30 - y \text{ for } z.$$
$$200 - 2y - y + 120 - 4y = -30 \qquad \text{Distribute the multiplication by 4.}$$
$$320 - 7y = -30 \qquad \text{On the left side, combine like terms.}$$
$$-7y = -350 \qquad \text{Subtract 320 from both sides.}$$
$$y = 50 \qquad \text{To solve for } y, \text{ divide both sides by } -7.$$

As expected, this is the same value for y that we obtained using elimination in Example 4. We can substitute 50 for y in equation 2 to find that $x = 100$ and 50 for y in equation 3 to find that $z = -20$. Using elimination or substitution, we find that the solution is $(100, 50, -20)$.

Self Check 5 Use substitution to solve the system: $\begin{cases} x + y - 4z = -54 \\ x - y = -6 \\ 3y + z = 12 \end{cases}$

Now Try ▶ Problem 31

4 Identify Inconsistent Systems and Dependent Equations.

We have seen that a system of three linear equations in three variables represents three planes. If the planes have no common point of intersection, the system is said to be **inconsistent** with no solution. Illustrations of these types of inconsistent systems are shown in figure c on page 1020.

EXAMPLE 6 Solve the system: $\begin{cases} 2a + b - 3c = -3 & \textbf{(1)} \\ 3a - 2b + 4c = 2 & \textbf{(2)} \\ 4a + 2b - 6c = -7 & \textbf{(3)} \end{cases}$

Strategy Since the coefficients of the b-terms are opposites in the second and third equations, we will add the left and right sides of those equations to eliminate b. Then we will choose another pair of equations and eliminate b again.

Why The result will be a system of two equations in a and c that we can attempt to solve by elimination.

Solution We add equations 2 and 3 of the system to eliminate b.

(2) $\quad 3a - 2b + 4c = 2$
(3) $\quad \underline{4a + 2b - 6c = -7}$
(4) $\quad 7a \qquad - 2c = -5$

We can multiply both sides of equation 1 by 2 and add the resulting equation to equation 2 to eliminate b again:

$$4a + 2b - 6c = -6 \qquad \text{This is } 2(2a + b - 3c) = 2(-3).$$
(2) $\quad \underline{3a - 2b + 4c = 2}$
(5) $\quad 7a \qquad - 2c = -4$

Equations 4 and 5 form a system in a and c.

(4) $\quad \begin{cases} 7a - 2c = -5 \\ \end{cases}$
(5) $\quad \begin{cases} 7a - 2c = -4 \end{cases}$

If we multiply both sides of equation 5 by -1 and add the result to equation 4, the terms involving a and c are both eliminated.

(4)
$$7a - 2c = -5$$
$$\underline{-7a + 2c = 4} \quad \text{This is } -1(7a - 2c) = -1(-4).$$
$$0 = -1$$

Note that in the solution process, all three variables have been eliminated. The false statement $0 = -1$ indicates that the system has *no solution* and is, therefore, inconsistent. The solution set is $\varnothing$.

Self Check 6 Solve the system:
$$\begin{cases} 2a + b - 3c = 8 \\ 3a - 2b + 4c = 10 \\ 4a + 2b - 6c = -5 \end{cases}$$

Now Try ▶ Problems 33 and 35

When the equations in a system of *two* equations with *two* variables are dependent, the system has infinitely many solutions. In such cases, we classify the system as consistent. This is not always true for systems of three equations with three variables. In fact, a system can have dependent equations* and still be inconsistent. The following illustration shows the different possibilities.

A consistent system

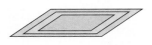

When three planes coincide, the equations are dependent, and there are **infinitely many solutions**.

(a)

A consistent system

When three planes intersect in a common line, the equations are dependent, and there are **infinitely many solutions**.

(b)

An inconsistent system

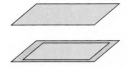

When two planes coincide and are parallel to a third plane, the system is inconsistent, and there are **no solutions**.

(c)

*A set of equations is dependent if at least one equation can be expressed as a sum of multiples of other equations in that set.

EXAMPLE 7 Solve the system:
$$\begin{cases} \dfrac{4}{5}x - y + z = \dfrac{53}{5} \\ x - 2y - z = 8 \\ 0.2x - 0.3y + 0.1z = 2.3 \end{cases}$$

Strategy We will find an equivalent system without fractions or decimals and use elimination to solve it.

Why It's easier to solve a system of equations that involves only integers.

Solution To clear equation 1 of fractions, we multiply both sides by the LCD of the fractions, which is 5. To clear equation 3 of decimals, we multiply both sides by 10.

(1) $\begin{cases} \dfrac{4}{5}x - y + z = \dfrac{53}{5} \end{cases}$ $\xrightarrow{\text{Multiply by 5}}$ $\begin{cases} 4x - 5y + 5z = 53 \quad \textbf{(4)} \end{cases}$

(2) $\begin{cases} x - 2y - z = 8 \end{cases}$ $\xrightarrow{\text{Unchanged}}$ $\begin{cases} x - 2y - z = 8 \qquad \textbf{(2)} \end{cases}$

(3) $\begin{cases} 0.2x - 0.3y + 0.1z = 2.3 \end{cases}$ $\xrightarrow{\text{Multiply by 10}}$ $\begin{cases} 2x - 3y + z = 23 \qquad \textbf{(5)} \end{cases}$

If each side of equation 2 is multiplied by 5 and the resulting equation is added to equation 4, the variable z is eliminated.

(4) $\quad 4x - 5y + 5z = 53$

$\quad\quad\underline{5x - 10y - 5z = 40}$ $\quad$ This is $5(x - 2y - z) = 5(8)$.

(6) $\quad 9x - 15y \quad\quad = 93$

If we add equations 2 and 5, the variable z is eliminated again.

(2) $\quad x - 2y - z = 8$

(5) $\quad\underline{2x - 3y + z = 23}$

(7) $\quad 3x - 5y \quad\quad = 31$

Equations 6 and 7 form a system in x and y. If each side of equation 7 is multiplied by -3 and the resulting equation is added to equation 6, both x and y are eliminated.

(6) $\quad 9x - 15y = 93$

$\quad\quad\underline{-9x + 15y = -93}$ $\quad$ This is $-3(3x - 5y) = -3(31)$.

$\quad\quad\quad\quad\quad\quad 0 = 0$

Note that in the solution process, all three variables are eliminated. The resulting true statement, $0 = 0$, indicates that we are working with a set of dependent equations and that the system has an infinite number of solutions.

> **Success Tip**
>
> If you obtain a true statement at any time in the solution process, you need not proceed. Such an outcome indicates that the system contains dependent equations.

Self Check 7 $\quad$ Solve the system: $\quad\begin{cases} x - 2y - z = 1 \\ x + \dfrac{4}{3}y + z = \dfrac{5}{3} \\ 0.02x + 0.01y + 0.01z = 0.03 \end{cases}$

Now Try ▶ Problems 33 and 35

SECTION 12.2 ▶ STUDY SET

VOCABULARY

Fill in the blanks.

1. $\begin{cases} 2x + y - 3z = 0 \\ 3x - y + 4z = 5 \\ 4x + 2y - 6z = 0 \end{cases}$ is called a _____ of three linear

   equations in three variables. Each equation is written in
   _____ $Ax + By + Cz = D$ form.

2. If the first two equations of the system in Exercise 1 are added, the variable y is _____.

3. Solutions of a system of three equations in three variables, x, y, and z, are written in the form (x, y, z) and are called ordered _____.

4. The graph of the equation $2x + 3y + 4z = 5$ is a flat surface called a _____.

5. When three planes coincide, the equations of the system are _____, and there are infinitely many solutions.

6. When three planes intersect in a line, the system will have _____ many solutions.

CONCEPTS

7. For each graph of a system of three equations, determine whether the solution set contains one solution, infinitely many solutions, or no solution.

   a. 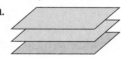 $\quad\quad$ **b.**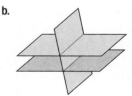

8. Consider the system: $\quad\begin{array}{l}(1) \\ (2) \\ (3)\end{array}\begin{cases} -2x + y + 4z = 3 \\ x - y + 2z = 1 \\ x + y - 3z = 2 \end{cases}$

   a. What is the result if equation 1 and equation 2 are added?

   b. What is the result if equation 2 and equation 3 are added?

   c. What variable was eliminated in the steps performed in parts (a) and (b)?

NOTATION

9. For the following system, clear the equations of any fractions or decimals and write each equation in $Ax + By + Cz = D$ form.

$$\begin{cases} x + y = 3 - 4z \\ 0.7x - 0.2y + 0.8z = 1.5 \\ \dfrac{x}{2} + \dfrac{y}{3} - \dfrac{z}{6} = \dfrac{2}{3} \end{cases} \longrightarrow \begin{cases} \\ \\ \end{cases}$$

10. What is the purpose of the numbers shown in red in front of the equations below?

(1) $\begin{cases} x + y - z = 6 \\ (2) & 2x - y + z = 3 \\ (3) & 5x + 3y - z = -2 \end{cases}$

GUIDED PRACTICE

Use a check to determine whether the ordered triple is a solution of the system. See Example 1.

11. $(2, 1, 1)$
$$\begin{cases} x - y + z = 2 \\ 2x + y - z = 4 \\ 2x - 3y + z = 2 \end{cases}$$

12. $(-3, 2, -1)$
$$\begin{cases} 3x + y - z = -6 \\ 2x + 2y + 3z = -1 \\ x + y + 2z = 1 \end{cases}$$

13. $(6, -7, -5)$
$$\begin{cases} 3x - 2y - z = 37 \\ x - 3y = 27 \\ 2x + 7y + 2z = -48 \end{cases}$$

14. $(-4, 0, 9)$
$$\begin{cases} x + 2y - 3z = -31 \\ 2x + 6z = 46 \\ 3x - y = -12 \end{cases}$$

Solve each system. See Example 2.

15. $\begin{cases} x + y + z = 4 \\ 2x + y - z = 1 \\ 2x - 3y + z = 1 \end{cases}$

16. $\begin{cases} x + y + z = 4 \\ x - y + z = 2 \\ x - y - 2z = -1 \end{cases}$

17. $\begin{cases} 3x + 2y - 5z = 3 \\ 4x - 2y - 3z = -10 \\ 5x - 2y - 2z = -11 \end{cases}$

18. $\begin{cases} 5x + 4y + 2z = -2 \\ 3x + 4y - 3z = -27 \\ 2x - 4y - 7z = -23 \end{cases}$

19. $\begin{cases} 2x + 6y + 3z = 9 \\ 5x - 3y - 5z = 3 \\ 4x + 3y + 2z = 15 \end{cases}$

20. $\begin{cases} 4x - 3y + 5z = 23 \\ 2x - 5y - 3z = 13 \\ -4x - 6y + 7z = 7 \end{cases}$

21. $\begin{cases} 4x - 5y - 8z = -52 \\ 2x - 3y - 4z = -26 \\ 3x + 7y + 8z = 31 \end{cases}$

22. $\begin{cases} 2x + 6y + 3z = -20 \\ 5x - 3y - 5z = 47 \\ 4x + 3y + 2z = 4 \end{cases}$

Solve each system. See Example 3.

23. $\begin{cases} 3x + 3z = 6 - 4y \\ 7x - 5z = 46 + 2y \\ 4x = 31 - z \end{cases}$

24. $\begin{cases} 5x + 6z = 4y - 21 \\ 9x + 2y = 3z - 47 \\ 3x + y = -19 \end{cases}$

25. $\begin{cases} 2x + z = -2 + y \\ 8x - 3y = -2 \\ 6x - 2y + 3z = -4 \end{cases}$

26. $\begin{cases} 3y + z = -1 \\ -x + 2z = -9 + 6y \\ 9y + 3z = -9 + 2x \end{cases}$

Solve each system using elimination. See Example 4.

27. $\begin{cases} x + y + 3z = 35 \\ -x - 3y = 20 \\ 2y + z = -35 \end{cases}$

28. $\begin{cases} x + 2y + 3z = 11 \\ 5x - y = 13 \\ 2x - 3z = -11 \end{cases}$

29. $\begin{cases} 3x + 2y - z = 7 \\ 6x - 3y = -2 \\ 3y - 2z = 8 \end{cases}$

30. $\begin{cases} 2x + y = 4 \\ -x - 2y + 8z = 7 \\ -y + 4z = 5 \end{cases}$

Solve each system using substitution. See Example 5.

31. $\begin{cases} r + s - 3t = 21 \\ r + 4s = 9 \\ 5s + t = -4 \end{cases}$

32. $\begin{cases} r - s + 6t = 12 \\ r + 6s = -28 \\ 7s + t = -26 \end{cases}$

33. $\begin{cases} x - 8z = -30 \\ 3x + y - 4z = 5 \\ y + 7z = 30 \end{cases}$

34. $\begin{cases} x + 6z = -36 \\ 5x + 3y - 2z = -20 \\ y + 4z = -20 \end{cases}$

Solve each system. If a system is inconsistent or if the equations are dependent, state this. See Examples 6 and 7.

35. $\begin{cases} 7a + 9b - 2c = -5 \\ 5a + 14b - c = -11 \\ 2a - 5b - c = 3 \end{cases}$

36. $\begin{cases} 3x + 4y + z = 10 \\ x - 2y + z = -3 \\ 2x + y + z = 5 \end{cases}$

37. $\begin{cases} 7x - y - z = 10 \\ x - 3y + z = 2 \\ x + 2y - z = 1 \end{cases}$

38. $\begin{cases} 2a - b + c = 6 \\ -5a - 2b - 4c = -30 \\ a + b + c = 8 \end{cases}$

TRY IT YOURSELF

Solve each system, if possible. If a system is inconsistent or if the equations are dependent, state this.

39. $\begin{cases} 2a + 3b - 2c = 18 \\ 5a - 6b + c = 21 \\ 4b - 2c - 6 = 0 \end{cases}$

40. $\begin{cases} r - s + t = 4 \\ r + 2s - t = -1 \\ r + s - 3t = -2 \end{cases}$

41. $\begin{cases} 2x + 2y - z = 2 \\ x + 3z - 24 = 0 \\ y = 7 - 4z \end{cases}$

42. $\begin{cases} r - 3t = -11 \\ r + s + t = 13 \\ s - 4t = -12 \end{cases}$

43. $\begin{cases} b + 2c = 7 - a \\ a + c = 2(4 - b) \\ 2a + b + c = 9 \end{cases}$

44. $\begin{cases} 0.02a = 0.02 - 0.03b - 0.01c \\ 4a + 6b + 2c - 5 = 0 \\ a + c = 3 + 2b \end{cases}$

45. $\begin{cases} 2x + y - z = 1 \\ x + 2y + 2z = 2 \\ 4x + 5y + 3z = 3 \end{cases}$

46. $\begin{cases} 2x + 2y + 3z = 10 \\ 3x + y - z = 0 \\ x + y + 2z = 6 \end{cases}$

47. $\begin{cases} 0.4x + 0.3z = 0.4 \\ 2y - 6z = -1 \\ 4(2x + y) = 9 - 3z \end{cases}$

48. $\begin{cases} a + b + c = 180 \\ \dfrac{a}{4} + \dfrac{b}{2} + \dfrac{c}{3} = 60 \\ 2b + 3c - 330 = 0 \end{cases}$

49. $\begin{cases} r + s + 4t = 3 \\ 3r + 7t = 0 \\ 3s + 5t = 0 \end{cases}$

50. $\begin{cases} x - y = 3 \\ 2x - y + z = 1 \\ x + z = -2 \end{cases}$

51. $\begin{cases} 0.5a + 0.3b = 2.2 \\ 1.2c - 8.5b = -24.4 \\ 3.3c + 1.3a = 29 \end{cases}$

52. $\begin{cases} 4a - 3b = 1 \\ 6a - 8c = 1 \\ 2b - 4c = 0 \end{cases}$

53. $\begin{cases} 2x + 3y = 6 - 4z \\ 2x + 3y + 4z - 4 \\ 4x + 6y + 8z = 12 \end{cases}$

54. $\begin{cases} -x + 5y - 7z = 0 \\ 4x + y - z = 0 \\ x + y - 4z = 0 \end{cases}$

55. $\begin{cases} a + b = 2 + c \\ a = 3 + b - c \\ -a + b + c - 4 = 0 \end{cases}$

56. $\begin{cases} 0.1x - 0.3y + 0.4z = 0.2 \\ 2x + y + 2z = 3 \\ 4x - 5y + 10z = 7 \end{cases}$

57. $\begin{cases} x + \dfrac{1}{3}y + z = 13 \\ \dfrac{1}{2}x - y + \dfrac{1}{3}z = -2 \\ x + \dfrac{1}{2}y - \dfrac{1}{3}z = 2 \end{cases}$

58. $\begin{cases} x - \dfrac{1}{5}y - z = 9 \\ \dfrac{1}{4}x + \dfrac{1}{5}y - \dfrac{1}{2}z = 5 \\ 2x + y + \dfrac{1}{6}z = 12 \end{cases}$

APPLICATIONS

59. Graphs of Systems. Explain how each of the following pictures is an example of the graph of a system of three equations. Then describe the solution, if there is any.

a.

b.

c.

d.

60. Zoology. An X-ray of a mouse revealed a cancerous tumor located at the intersection of the coronal, sagittal, and transverse planes. From this description, would you expect the tumor to be at the base of the tail, on the back, in the stomach, on the tip of the right ear, or in the mouth of the mouse?

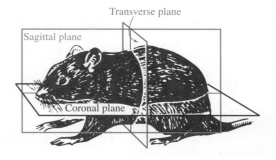

61. NBA Records. The three highest one-game point totals by one player in a National Basketball Association game are shown below. Solve the following system to find x, y, and z.

$\begin{cases} x + y + z = 259 \\ x - y = 19 \\ x - z = 22 \end{cases}$

Pts	Player, team	Date
x	Wilt Chamberlain, Philadelphia	3/2/1962
y	Kobe Bryant, Los Angeles	1/22/2006
z	Wilt Chamberlain, Philadelphia	12/8/1961

62. Bicycle Frames. The angle measures of the triangular part of the bicycle frame shown can be found by solving the following system. Find x, y, and z.

$\begin{cases} x + y + z = 180 \\ x + y = 120 \\ y + z = 135 \end{cases}$

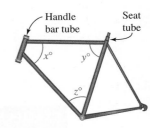

WRITING

63. Explain how a system of three equations in three variables can be reduced to a system of two equations in two variables.

64. What makes a system of three equations with three variables inconsistent?

65. What does the graph of a linear equation in three variables such as $2x - 3y + 9z = 10$ look like?

66. What situation discussed in this section looks like two walls of a room and the floor meeting in a corner?

REVIEW

Graph each of the basic functions.

67. $f(x) = |x|$

68. $g(x) = x^2$

69. $h(x) = x^3$

70. $S(x) = x$

CHALLENGE PROBLEMS

Solve each system.

71.
$$\begin{cases} w + x + y + z = 3 \\ w - x + y + z = 1 \\ w + x - y + z = 1 \\ w + x + y - z = 3 \end{cases}$$

72.
$$\begin{cases} \dfrac{1}{x} + \dfrac{1}{y} + \dfrac{1}{z} = 3 \\ \dfrac{2}{x} + \dfrac{1}{y} - \dfrac{1}{z} = 0 \\ \dfrac{1}{x} - \dfrac{2}{y} + \dfrac{4}{z} = 21 \end{cases}$$

73.
$$\begin{cases} 4a + b + 2c - 3d = -16 \\ 3a - 3b + c - 4d = -20 \\ a - 2b - 5c - d = 4 \\ 5a + 4b + 3c - d = -10 \end{cases}$$

74.
$$\begin{cases} a + c + 2d = -4 \\ b - 2c = 1 \\ a + 2b - c = -2 \\ 2a + b + 3c - 2d = -4 \end{cases}$$

SECTION 12.3

Problem Solving Using Systems of Three Equations

OBJECTIVES

1 Assign variables to three unknowns.

2 Use systems to solve curve-fitting problems.

ARE YOU READY?

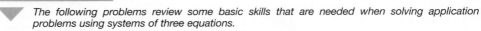

The following problems review some basic skills that are needed when solving application problems using systems of three equations.

1. Translate to mathematical symbols: 75 more than the number n.

2. Write an algebraic expression that represents the value of x coats, if each coat has a value of $150.

3. Write an algebraic expression that represents the value (in cents) of n nickels.

4. Solve the system $\begin{cases} x - y + 6z = 12 \\ x + 6y = -28 \\ 7y + z = -26 \end{cases}$ by substitution.

In this section, we will solve application problems involving three unknown quantities.

1 Assign Variables to Three Unknowns.

The six step problem-solving strategy that was used to solve application problems involving two unknowns in Section 4.4 can be extended to situations involving three unknowns. In the Assign step, we assign *three* variables to represent *three* unknown quantities. In the Form and Solve steps, we form a system of three equations in three variables and solve it using the methods of the previous section.

EXAMPLE 1

Tool Manufacturing.   A company makes three types of hammers, which are marketed as "good," "better," and "best." The cost of manufacturing each type of hammer is $4, $6, and $7, respectively, and the hammers sell for $6, $9, and $12. Each day, the cost of manufacturing 100 hammers is $520, and the daily revenue from their sale is $810. How many hammers of each type are manufactured per day?

Analyze   We need to find how many of each type of hammer are manufactured daily. Since there are three unknowns, we must write three equations to find them.

Assign   Let x = the number of good hammers
y = the number of better hammers
z = the number of best hammers

Form   We can organize the facts of the problem in a table, as shown below. To fill in the "Cost to manufacture" column, we multiply the number of good hammers, x, by the cost to manufacture a good hammer, $4, to find that it costs $4 \cdot x$, or $4x$, to manufacture the good hammers. Similarly, we use multiplication to find that the manufacturing cost for y better hammers is $6y$ and for z best hammers is $7z$. The total manufacturing cost of $520 is entered at the bottom of that column.

To complete the "Revenue received" column, we again use multiplication. The revenue received from the sale of x good hammers, sold for \$6 per hammer, is $\$6 \cdot x$, or $\$6x$. Similarly, the revenue received from the sale of y better hammers is $\$9y$, and the revenue received from the sale of z best hammers is $\$12z$. The total revenue received of \$810 is entered at the bottom of that column.

We can use the facts of the problem to write three equations.

Type of hammer	Number	Cost to manufacture	Revenue received
Good	x	$4x$	$6x$
Better	y	$6y$	$9y$
Best	z	$7z$	$12z$

Total: 100   Total: \$520   Total: \$810

↑ | ↑ | ↑

One equation comes from this column. | A second equation comes from this column. | A third equation comes from this column.

The resulting system is:
$$\begin{cases} x + y + z = 100 & \textbf{(1)} \\ 4x + 6y + 7z = 520 & \textbf{(2)} \\ 6x + 9y + 12z = 810 & \textbf{(3)} \end{cases}$$

Solve   We will use the elimination method to solve this system of three equations in three variables. If we multiply equation 1 by -7 and add the result to equation 2, we get

$$-7x - 7y - 7z = -700 \quad \text{This is } -7(x + y + z) = -7(100).$$

(2) $\underline{\quad 4x + 6y + 7z = \quad\; 520 \quad}$

(4) $\quad -3x - \; y \qquad\quad = -180$

If we multiply equation 1 by -12 and add the result to equation 3, we get

$$-12x - 12y - 12z = -1{,}200 \quad \text{This is } -12(x + y + z) = -12(100).$$

(3) $\underline{\quad 6x + \; 9y + 12z = \qquad 810 \quad}$

(5) $\quad -6x - \; 3y \qquad\qquad = \;\; -390$

We can multiply equation 4 by -3 and add it to equation 5 to eliminate y.

$$9x + 3y = \quad 540 \quad \text{This is } -3(-3x - y) = -3(-180).$$

(5) $\underline{-6x - 3y = -390}$

$\qquad\; 3x \qquad\; = 150$

$\qquad\qquad x = 50 \qquad$ To solve for x, divide both sides by 3.
$\qquad\qquad\qquad\qquad$ This is the number of good hammers manufactured.

To find y, we substitute 50 for x in equation 4:

$\qquad -3x - y = -180$

$\quad -3(50) - y = -180 \qquad$ Substitute 50 for x.

$\qquad -150 - y = -180$

$\qquad\qquad\quad -y = -30 \qquad$ Add 150 to both sides.

$\qquad\qquad\quad\; y = 30 \qquad$ To solve for y, divide both sides by -1.
$\qquad\qquad\qquad\qquad\qquad$ This is the number of better hammers manufactured.

To find z, we substitute 50 for x and 30 for y in equation 1:

$\qquad x + y + z = 100$

$\quad \mathbf{50 + 30} + z = 100$

$\qquad\qquad\quad z = 20 \qquad$ To solve for z, subtract 80 from both sides.
$\qquad\qquad\qquad\qquad$ This is the number of best hammers manufactured.

State   Each day, the company manufactures 50 good hammers, 30 better hammers, and 20 best hammers.

Check   If the company manufactures **50** good hammers, **30** better hammers, and **20** best hammers each day, that is a total of **50** + **30** + **20** = 100 hammers. The cost of manufacturing the three types of hammers is $4(**50**) + $6(**30**) + $7(**20**) = $200 + $180 + $140 or $520. The revenue from the sale of the hammers is $6(**50**) + $9(**30**) + $12(**20**) = $300 + $270 + $240 or $810. The results check.

Self Check 2   **Computer Storage.**   A manufacturer of memory cards makes 1-GB, 2-GB, and 4-GB storage size cards. The cost of manufaturing each is $2, $3, and $5, respectively. Each day the cost of manufacturing 500 cards is $1,500. The cards sell for $15, $20, and $30, respectively, with a daily revenue of $10,000. How many memory cards of each type are manufactured?

Now Try ▶   Problem 7

EXAMPLE 2   **The Olympics.**   The three countries that won the most medals in the 2008 summer Olympic games were the United States, China, and Russia, in that order. Together they won a total of 282 medals, with the U.S. medal count 10 more than China's and China's medal count 28 more than Russia's. Find the number of medals won by each country. (Source: sportsillustrated.cnn.com)

Analyze   We need to find how many medals the United States, China, and Russia won. Since there are three unknowns, we must write three equations to find them.

Assign   Let x = the number of medals won by the United States
y = the number of medals won by China
z = the number of medals won by Russia

Form   We can use the facts of the problem to write three equations.

| The number of medals won by the United States | plus | the number of medals won by China | plus | the number of medals won by Russia | was | 282. |
| x | $+$ | y | $+$ | z | $=$ | 282 |

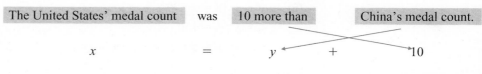

The United States' medal count   was   10 more than   China's medal count.

$$x \quad = \quad y \quad + \quad 10$$

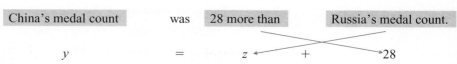

China's medal count   was   28 more than   Russia's medal count.

$$y \quad = \quad z \quad + \quad 28$$

Solve   We can use substitution to solve the resulting system of three equations. If we solve equation 3 for z, then the resulting equation 4 and equation 2 can serve as substitution equations.

$$
\begin{array}{lll}
\textbf{(1)} & \begin{cases} x + y + z = 282 \\ x = y + 10 \\ y = z + 28 \end{cases} & \begin{array}{l} \text{Unchanged} \\ \text{Unchanged} \\ \text{Solve for } z \end{array} \rightarrow \begin{cases} x + y + z = 282 \\ x = \boxed{y + 10} \\ z = \boxed{y - 28} \end{cases} & \begin{array}{l} \textbf{(1)} \\ \textbf{(2)} \\ \textbf{(4)} \end{array}
\end{array}
$$

When we substitute for x and z in equation 1, we obtain an equation in one variable, y.

$$x + y + z = 282 \qquad \text{This is equation 1.}$$
$$y + 10 + y + y - 28 = 282 \qquad \text{Substitute } y + 10 \text{ for } x \text{ and } y - 28 \text{ for } z.$$
$$3y - 18 = 282 \qquad \text{On the left side, combine like terms.}$$
$$3y = 300 \qquad \text{Add 18 to both sides.}$$
$$y = 100 \qquad \text{To solve for } y, \text{ divide both sides by 3.}$$
$$\text{This is the number of medals won by China.}$$

To find x, we substitute 100 for y in equation 2. To find z, we substitute 100 for y in equation 4.

$x = y + 10$ This is equation 2.	$z = y - 28$ This is equation 4.
$x = 100 + 10$	$z = 100 - 28$
$x = 110$ This is the U.S. medal count.	$z = 72$ Russia's medal count

State   In the 2008 summer Olympics, the United States won 110 medals, China won 100, and Russia won 72.

Check   The sum of $110 + 100 + 72$ is 282. Furthermore, 110 is 10 more than 100, and 100 is 28 more than 72. The results check.

Self Check 2   **The Winter Olympics.**   The three countries that are at the top of the list for the most all-time medal wins are Norway, the United States, and Austria, in that order. Together they have won a total of 618 medals, with Norway's medal count 70 more than the U.S., and the U.S. medal count 31 more than Austria's. Find the number of medals won by each country.   (Source: nationmaster.com)

Now Try ▶ Problems 33 and 35

---

2 Use Systems to Solve Curve-Fitting Problems.

The process of determining an equation whose graph contains given points is called **curve fitting.**

EXAMPLE 3   The equation of a parabola opening upward or downward is of the form $y = ax^2 + bx + c$. Find the equation of the parabola graphed on the left by determining the values of a, b, and c.

Strategy   We will substitute the x- and y-coordinates of three points that lie on the graph into the equation $y = ax^2 + bx + c$. This will produce a system of three equations in three variables that we can solve to find a, b, and c.

Why   Once we know a, b, and c, we can write the equation.

Solution   Since the parabola passes through the points $(-1, 5), (1, 1)$, and $(2, 2)$, each pair of coordinates must satisfy the equation $y = ax^2 + bx + c$. If we substitute each pair into $y = ax^2 + bx + c$, we will get a system of three equations in three variables.

Substitute $(-1, 5)$	**Substitute $(1, 1)$**	**Substitute $(2, 2)$**
$y = ax^2 + bx + c$	$y = ax^2 + bx + c$	$y = ax^2 + bx + c$
$5 = a(-1)^2 + b(-1) + c$	$1 = a(1)^2 + b(1) + c$	$2 = a(2)^2 + b(2) + c$
$5 = a - b + c$	$1 = a + b + c$	$2 = 4a + 2b + c$
This is equation 1.	This is equation 2.	This is equation 3.

The three equations above give the system, which we can solve to find a, b, and c.

(1)
(2)
(3)
$$\begin{cases} a - b + c = 5 \\ a + b + c = 1 \\ 4a + 2b + c = 2 \end{cases}$$

If we add equations 1 and 2, we obtain

$$
\begin{array}{l}
 a - b + c = 5 \\
 \underline{a + b + c = 1} \\
\textbf{(4)}\ \ 2a + 2c = 6
\end{array}
$$

If we multiply equation 1 by 2 and add the result to equation 3, we get

$$
\begin{array}{l}
 2a - 2b + 2c = 10 \\
\textbf{(3)}\ \ \underline{4a + 2b + c = 2} \\
\textbf{(5)}\ \ 6a + 3c = 12
\end{array}
$$

We can then divide both sides of equation 4 by 2 to get equation 6 and divide both sides of equation 5 by 3 to get equation 7. We now have the system

(6)
(7)
$$\begin{cases} a + c = 3 \\ 2a + c = 4 \end{cases}$$

To eliminate c, we multiply equation 6 by -1 and add the result to equation 7. We get

$$
\begin{array}{l}
-a - c = -3 \quad \text{This is } -1(a + c) = -1(3). \\
\underline{2a + c = 4} \\
a = 1
\end{array}
$$

To find c, we can substitute 1 for a in equation 6 and find that $c = 2$. To find b, we can substitute 1 for a and 2 for c in equation 2 and find that $b = -2$.

After we substitute these values of a, b, and c into the equation $y = ax^2 + bx + c$, we have the equation of the parabola.

$$y = ax^2 + bx + c$$
$$y = 1x^2 - 2x + 2$$
$$y = x^2 - 2x + 2 \quad \text{This is the equation of the parabola graphed above.}$$

Self Check 3   Find the equation of the parabola, $y = ax^2 + bx + c$, that passes through $(1, 6)$, $(-4, 1)$, and $(-3, -2)$.

Now Try ▶ Problem 27

SECTION **12.3** ▶ STUDY SET

VOCABULARY

Fill in the blanks.

1. If a point lies on the graph of an equation, it is a solution of the equation, and the coordinates of the point _____ the equation.
2. The process of determining an equation whose graph contains given points is called curve _____.

CONCEPTS

Write a system of three equations in three variables that models the situation. Do not solve the system.

3. **Desserts.**   A bakery makes three kinds of pies: chocolate cream, which sells for $5; apple, which sells for $6; and cherry, which sells for $7. The cost to make the pies is $2, $3, and $4, respectively. Let x = the number of chocolate cream pies made daily, y = the number of apple pies made daily, and z = the number of cherry pies made daily.

   ■ Each day, the bakery makes 50 pies.
   ■ Each day, the revenue from the sale of the pies is $295.
   ■ Each day, the cost to make the pies is $145.

4. Fast Foods. Let x = the number of calories in a Big Mac hamburger, y = the number of calories in a small order of French fries, and z = the number of calories in a medium Coca-Cola.

- The total number of calories in a Big Mac hamburger, a small order of French fries, and a medium Coke is 1,000.
- The number of calories in a Big Mac is 260 more than in a small order of French fries.
- The number of calories in a small order of French fries is 40 more than in a medium Coke. (Source: McDonald's USA)

5. What equation results when the coordinates of the point $(2, -3)$ are substituted into $y = ax^2 + bx + c$?

6. The equation $y = 5x^2 - 6x + 1$ is written in the form $y = ax^2 + bx + c$. What are a, b, and c?

APPLICATIONS

7. Making Statues. An artist makes three types of ceramic statues (large, medium, and small) at a monthly cost of $650 for 180 statues. The manufacturing costs for the three types are $5, $4, and $3. If the statues sell for $20, $12, and $9, respectively, how many of each type should be made to produce $2,100 in monthly revenue?

8. Puppets. A toy company makes a total of 500 puppets in three sizes during a production run. The small puppets cost $5 to make and sell for $8 each, the standard-size puppets cost $10 to make and sell for $16 each, and the super-size puppets cost $15 to make and sell for $25. The total cost to make the puppets is $4,750 and the revenue from their sale is $7,700. How many small, standard, and super-size puppets are made during a production run?

9. Nutrition. A dietician is to design a meal using Foods A, B, and C that will provide a patient with exactly 14 grams of fat, 13 grams of carbohydrates, and 9 grams of protein.

- Each ounce of Food A contains 2 grams of fat, 3 grams of carbohydrates, and 2 grams of protein.
- Each ounce of Food B contains 3 grams of fat, 2 grams of carbohydrates, and 1 gram of protein.
- Each ounce of Food C contains 1 gram of fat, 1 gram of carbohydrates, and 2 grams of protein.

a. Complete the following table and then form a system of three equations that could be used to determine how many ounces of each food should be used in the meal.

Name of food	Number of ounces used	Grams of fat	Grams of carbohydrates	Grams of protein
A	a	$2a$	$3a$	
B	b	$3b$		b
C	c		c	$2c$
		Total: 14	Total:	Total: 9

b. Solve the system from part a.

10. Nutritional Planning. One ounce of each of three foods has the vitamin and mineral content shown in the table. How many ounces of each must be used to provide exactly 22 milligrams (mg) of niacin, 12 mg of zinc, and 20 mg of vitamin C?

Milligrams per ounce in each food type

Food	Niacin	Zinc	Vitamin C
A	1 mg	1 mg	2 mg
B	2 mg	1 mg	1 mg
C	2 mg	1 mg	2 mg

from **Campus to Careers**

11. ▶

Fashion Designer

A clothing manufacturer makes coats, shirts, and slacks. The time required for cutting, sewing, and packaging each item is shown in the table. How many of each should be made to use all available labor hours?

	Coats	Shirts	Slacks	Time available
Cutting	20 min	15 min	10 min	115 hr
Sewing	60 min	30 min	24 min	280 hr
Packaging	5 min	12 min	6 min	65 hr

12. Sculpting. A wood sculptor carves three types of statues with a chainsaw. The number of hours required for carving, sanding, and painting a totem pole, a bear, and a deer are shown in the table. How many of each should be produced to use all available labor hours?

	Totem pole	Bear	Deer	Time available
Carving	2 hr	2 hr	1 hr	14 hr
Sanding	1 hr	2 hr	2 hr	15 hr
Painting	3 hr	2 hr	2 hr	21 hr

13. NFL Records. Jerry Rice, who played the majority of his career with the San Francisco 49ers and the Oakland Raiders, holds the all-time record for touchdown (TD) passes caught. Here are some interesting facts about this feat.

- He caught 30 more TD passes from Steve Young than he did from Joe Montana.
- He caught 39 more TD passes from Joe Montana than he did from Rich Gannon.
- He caught a total of 156 TD passes from Young, Montana, and Gannon.

Determine the number of touchdown passes Rice has caught from Young, from Montana, and from Gannon.

14. Hot Dogs. In 10 minutes, the top three finishers in the 2010 Nathan's Hot Dog Eating Contest consumed a total of 136 hot dogs. The winner, Joey Chestnut, ate 9 more hot dogs than the runner-up, Tim Janus. Pat Bertoletti finished a distant third, 8 hot dogs behind Janus. How many hot dogs did each person eat? (Source: nathansfamous.com)

15. **Earth's Atmosphere.** Use the information in the circle graph to determine what percent of Earth's atmosphere is nitrogen, is oxygen, and is other gases.

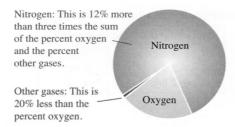

Nitrogen: This is 12% more than three times the sum of the percent oxygen and the percent other gases.

Other gases: This is 20% less than the percent oxygen.

16. **Deceased Celebrities.** Between October 2009 and October 2010, the estates of Michael Jackson, Elvis Presley, and J.R.R. Tolkien (author of *Lord of the Rings*) earned a total of $385 million. Together, the Presley and Tolkien estates earned $165 million less than the Jackson estate. The Jackson estate earned 5.5 times as much as the Tolkien estate. Use this information to label each bar on the graph below. (Source: Forbes.com)

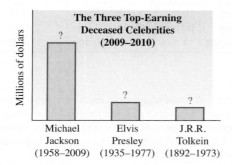

17. **Triangles.** The sum of the measures of the angles of any triangle is 180°. In $\triangle ABC$, $\angle A$ measures 100° less than the sum of the measures of $\angle B$ and $\angle C$, and the measure of $\angle C$ is 40° less than twice the measure of $\angle B$. Find the measure of each angle of the triangle.

18. **Quadrilaterals.** A quadrilateral is a four-sided polygon. The sum of the measures of the angles of any quadrilateral is 360°. In the illustration, the measures of $\angle A$ and $\angle B$ are the same. The measure of $\angle C$ is 20° greater than the measure of $\angle A$, and the measure of $\angle D$ is 60° less than $\angle B$. Find the measure of $\angle A$, $\angle B$, $\angle C$, and $\angle D$.

19. **TV History.** *X-Files, Will & Grace,* and *Seinfeld* are three of the most popular television shows of all time. The total number of episodes of these three shows is 575. There are 21 more episodes of *X-Files* than *Seinfeld,* and the difference between the number of episodes of *Will & Grace* and *Seinfeld* is 14. Find the number of episodes of each show.

20. **Traffic Lights.** At a traffic light, one cycle through green-yellow-red lasts for 80 seconds. The green light is on eight times longer than the yellow light, and the red light is on eleven times longer than the yellow light. For how long is each colored light on during one cycle?

21. **Ice Skating.** Three circles are traced out by a figure skater during her performance as shown below. If the centers of the circles are the given distances apart (10 yd, 14 yd, and 18 yd), find the radius of each circle. (*Hint:* Each red line segment is composed of two radii. Label the radii r_1, r_2, *and* r_3.)

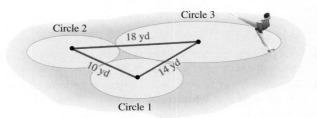

22. **NBA Centers.** Together, Shaquille O'Neil (Boston Celtics) and Dwight Howard (Orlando Magic) weigh 590 pounds. Together O'Neil and Yao Ming (Houston Rockets) weigh 635 pounds. Together, Howard and Yao Ming weigh 575 pounds. Find the weight of each center.

23. **Potpourri.** The owner of a home decorating shop wants to mix dried rose petals selling for $6 per pound, dried lavender selling for $5 per pound, and buckwheat hulls selling for $4 per pound to get 10 pounds of a mixture that would sell for $5.50 per pound. She wants to use twice as many pounds of rose petals as lavender. How many pounds of each should she use?

24. **Mixing Nuts.** The owner of a candy store wants to mix some peanuts worth $3 per pound, some cashews worth $9 per pound, and some Brazil nuts worth $9 per pound to get 50 pounds of a mixture that will sell for $6 per pound. She uses 15 fewer pounds of cashews than peanuts. How many pounds of each did she use?

25. **Piggy Banks.** When a child breaks open her piggy bank, she finds a total of 64 coins, consisting of nickels, dimes, and quarters. The total value of the coins is $6. If the nickels were dimes, and the dimes were nickels, the value of the coins would be $5. How many nickels, dimes, and quarters were in the piggy bank?

26. **Theater Seating.** The illustration shows the cash receipts and the ticket prices from two sold-out Sunday performances of a play. Find the number of seats in each of the three sections of the 800-seat theater.

Sunday Ticket Receipts

Matinee	$13,000
Evening	$23,000

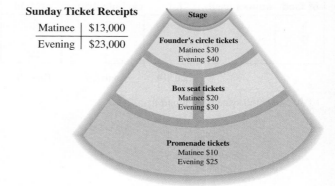

27. Astronomy. Comets have elliptical orbits, but the orbits of some comets are so large that they look much like a parabola. Find an equation of the form $y = ax^2 + bx + c$ for the parabola that closely describes the orbit of the comet shown in the illustration.

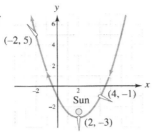

28. Curve Fitting. Find an equation of the form $y = ax^2 + bx + c$ for the parabola shown in the illustration.

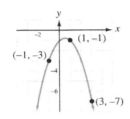

29. Walkways. A circular sidewalk is to be constructed in a city park. The walk is to pass by three particular areas of the park, as shown in the illustration. If an equation of a circle is of the form $x^2 + y^2 + Cx + Dy + E = 0$, find an equation that describes the path of the sidewalk by determining C, D, and E.

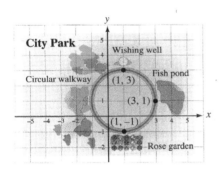

30. Curve Fitting. The equation of a circle is of the form $x^2 + y^2 + Cx + Dy + E = 0$. Find an equation of the circle shown in the illustration by determining C, D, and E.

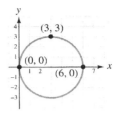

WRITING

31. Explain why the following problem does not give enough information to answer the question: The sum of three integers is 48. If the first integer is doubled, the sum is 60. Find the integers.

32. Write an application problem that can be solved using a system of three equations in three variables.

REVIEW

Determine whether each equation defines y to be a function of x. If it does not, find two ordered pairs where more than one value of y corresponds to a single value of x.

33. $y = \dfrac{1}{x}$

34. $y^4 = x$

35. $xy = 9$

36. $y = |x|$

37. $x + 1 = |y|$

38. $y = \dfrac{1}{x^2}$

39. $y^2 = x$

40. $x = |y|$

CHALLENGE PROBLEMS

41. Digits Problems. The sum of the digits of a three-digit number is 8. Twice the hundreds digit plus the tens digit is equal to the ones digit. If the digits of the number are reversed, the new number is 82 more than twice the original number. What is the three-digit number?

42. Purchasing Pets. A pet store owner spent $100 to buy 100 animals. He bought at least one iguana, one guinea pig, and one mouse, but no other kinds of animals. If an iguana cost $10.00, a guinea pig cost $3.00, and a mouse cost $0.50, how many of each did he buy?

ARE YOU READY? 1.1 (page 2)

1. 210 **2.** 1,750 **3.** 1,092 **4.** 9

SELF CHECKS 1.1

1. 350 calories **2.** The product of 22 and 11 equals 242.
3. $u = 500 - p$ (Answers may vary depending on the variables used.) **4.** 480 calories **5.**

m	c
8	80
75	750

STUDY SET SECTION 1.1 (page 7)

1. sum, difference, product, quotient **3.** constant
5. equation; expression **7.** horizontal **9. a.** Equation
b. Algebraic Expression **11. a.** Algebraic Expression
b. Equation **13.** Addition, multiplication, division; t

15.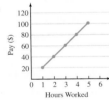

17. is not equal to
19. $5 \cdot 6, 5(6)$ **21.** $4x$
23. $2w$ **25.** $\frac{32}{x}$ **27.** $\frac{55}{5}$
29. 15-year-old machinery is worth $35,000. **31.** $250
33. The product of 8 and 2 equals 16.
35. The difference of 11 and 9 equals 2.
37. The sum of x and 2 equals 10.
39. The quotient of 66 and 11 equals 6. **41.** $p = 100 - d$
43. $7d = h$ **45.** $s = 3c$ **47.** $w = e + 1,200$
49. $p = r - 600$ **51.** $\frac{l}{4} = m$ **53.** 390, 400, 405
55. 1,300; 1,200; 1,100 **57.** 12 **59.** 2

61. a. The number of calories burned is the product of 3 and the number of minutes cleaning. **b.** $c = 3m$
c. 30, 60, 90, 120, 150, 180

ARE YOU READY? 1.2 (page 9)

1. 1 **2.** 150 **3.** Yes **4.** four-fifths

SELF CHECKS 1.2

1. $189 = 3 \cdot 3 \cdot 3 \cdot 7$ **2.** $\frac{10}{27}$ **3.** $\frac{12}{25}$ **4.** $\frac{15}{24}$ **5. a.** $\frac{3}{7}$
b. In simplest form **6.** $\frac{9}{5}$ **7.** $\frac{13}{240}$ **8. a.** 28 **b.** $\frac{4}{5}$ **9.** $\frac{81}{8} = 10\frac{1}{8}$
10. $6\frac{11}{24}$

STUDY SET SECTION 1.2 (page 20)

1. multiplied **3.** prime-factored **5.** equivalent
7. least or lowest **9. a.** 1 **b.** a **c.** $\frac{a \cdot c}{b \cdot d}$ **d.** $\frac{a \cdot d}{b \cdot c}$ **e.** $\frac{a + b}{d}$
f. $\frac{a - b}{d}$ **11. a.** 1 **b.** 1 **13. a.** $\frac{5}{5}, \frac{25}{30}$ **b.** $2, 7, \frac{2}{7}$
15. $3 \cdot 5 \cdot 5$ **17.** $2 \cdot 2 \cdot 7$ **19.** $3 \cdot 3 \cdot 3 \cdot 3$ **21.** $3 \cdot 3 \cdot 13$
23. $2 \cdot 2 \cdot 5 \cdot 11$ **25.** $2 \cdot 3 \cdot 11 \cdot 19$ **27.** $\frac{5}{48}$ **29.** $\frac{21}{55}$ **31.** $\frac{15}{8}$
33. $\frac{42}{25}$ **35.** $\frac{3}{9}$ **37.** $\frac{24}{54}$ **39.** $\frac{35}{5}$ **41.** $\frac{35}{7}$ **43.** $\frac{1}{3}$ **45.** $\frac{6}{7}$
47. $\frac{3}{8}$ **49.** Simplest form **51.** $\frac{2}{3}$ **53.** $\frac{4}{25}$ **55.** $\frac{6}{5}$ **57.** $\frac{4}{7}$
59. $\frac{5}{24}$ **61.** $\frac{22}{35}$ **63.** $\frac{41}{45}$ **65.** $\frac{5}{12}$ **67.** 24 **69.** 4 **71.** $\frac{7}{9}$
73. $\frac{7}{20}$ **75.** $32\frac{2}{3}$ **77.** $2\frac{1}{2}$ **79.** $\frac{5}{9}$ **81.** $5\frac{19}{48}$ **83.** $\frac{19}{15}$
85. 70 **87.** $13\frac{3}{4}$ **89.** $\frac{1}{2}$ **91.** $\frac{14}{5}$ **93.** $\frac{8}{5}$ **95.** $\frac{3}{35}$ **97.** $\frac{9}{4}$
99. $\frac{3}{25}$ **101.** $1\frac{9}{11}$ **103.** $\frac{1}{7}$ **105.** 0 **107.** 14 **109. a.** $\frac{55}{63}$
b. $\frac{1}{63}$ **c.** $\frac{4}{21}$ **d.** $\frac{28}{27}$ **111. a.** $\frac{7}{32}$ in. **b.** $\frac{3}{32}$ in.
113. $63\frac{1}{8}$ in. **115.** $40\frac{1}{2}$ in. **121.** Variables

ARE YOU READY? 1.3 (page 22)

1. 28 **2.** -10 **3.** a decimal (3.5 GPA)
4. a fraction ($\frac{3}{4}$ cup of sugar)

SELF CHECKS 1.3

1. Natural numbers: 45; whole numbers: 45; integers: 45, -2; rational numbers: 0.1, $-\frac{2}{7}$, 45, -2, $\frac{13}{4}$, $-6\frac{7}{8}$; irrational numbers: none; real numbers: all **2. a.** > **b.** < **c.** > **d.** <
3.

$$-1\frac{3}{4} \quad\quad 0.\overline{6} \;\; 1.7 \;\; \frac{5}{2} \;\; \pi$$

number line from -3 to 4

4. a. 100 **b.** 4.7 **c.** $\sqrt{2}$

STUDY SET SECTION 1.3 (page 29)

1. whole **3.** number line **5.** signed **7.** inequality
9. terminating; repeating **11.** decimal **13. a.** $-\$15$ million
b. $\frac{5}{16}$ in. or $+\frac{5}{16}$ in. **15. a.** -20 **b.** $\frac{2}{3}$ **17.** -14 and -4
19. square, root **21.** is approximately equal to **23.** Greek
25. $-4, -5$

27.

	5	0	-3	$\frac{7}{8}$	0.17	$-9\frac{1}{4}$	$\sqrt{2}$	π
Real	✓	✓	✓	✓	✓	✓	✓	✓
Irrational							✓	✓
Rational	✓	✓	✓	✓	✓	✓		
Integer	✓	✓	✓					
Whole	✓	✓						
Natural	✓							

29. True **31.** False **33.** True **35.** True **37.** > **39.** <
41. > **43.** < **45.** > **47.** < **49.** 0.625 **51.** $0.0\overline{3}$
53. $0.01\overline{6}$ **55.** 0.42
57.

59.

61. 83 **63.** $\frac{4}{3}$ **65.** 11 **67.** 6.1 **69.** >
71. < **73.** = **75.** = **77.** < **79.** >
81. Natural, whole, integers: 9; rational: $9, \frac{15}{16}, 3\frac{1}{8}, 1.765$; irrational:
$2\pi, 3\pi, \sqrt{89}$; real: all **83.** iii
85. a. 2006; $-\$90$ billion **b.** 2009; $-\$45$ billion **93.** $\frac{4}{9}$
95. $2\frac{5}{23}$

ARE YOU READY? 1.4 (page 32)

1. $3, 5; -5$ has the larger absolute value. **2.** 7.17 **3.** 621 **4.** $\frac{2}{15}$

SELF CHECKS 1.4

1. a. -60 **b.** -13.18 **c.** $-\frac{11}{12}$ **2. a.** -24 **b.** 1.73 **c.** $\frac{2}{5}$
3. 569 **4.** 139 **5.** -5 **6.** 11

STUDY SET SECTION 1.4 (page 37)

1. sum **3.** commutative, associative **5. a.** 6 **b.** -9.2
7. a. Negative **b.** Positive **9. a.** $1 + (-5)$ **b.** $-80.5 + 15$
c. $20 + 4$ **d.** $3 + 2.1$ **11.** Step 1: Commutative Property of
Addition; Step 2: Associative Property of Addition
13. a. $x + y = y + x$ **b.** $(x + y) + z = x + (y + z)$ **15.** -9
17. -17 **19.** -74 **21.** -10.3 **23.** $-\frac{17}{12}$ **25.** $-\frac{7}{20}$ **27.** -3
29. 39 **31.** 0 **33.** 2.25 **35.** $-\frac{4}{15}$ **37.** $\frac{3}{8}$ **39.** 16 **41.** -15
43. -21 **45.** 195 **47.** 215 **49.** -112 **51.** $1\frac{2}{3}$ **53.** 15.4
55. 9 **57.** 1 **59.** 70 **61.** -6.6 **63.** $-\frac{1}{8}$ **65.** -14 **67.** 0
69. -26 **71.** 0.67 **73.** -5 **75.** -22.1 **77.** 2,167 **79.** -1.7
81. 68 **83.** $-\frac{15}{28}$ **85.** -0.9 **87. a.** 27 **b.** 3 **c.** -27 **d.** -3
89. a. $\frac{13}{18}$ **b.** $-\frac{5}{18}$ **c.** $-\frac{13}{18}$ **d.** $\frac{5}{18}$ **91.** 2,150 m
93. Yang: -8, Woods: -5, Westwood: -3, McIlroy: -3
95. 1,242.86 **97.** $-\$99,650,000$ **99.** $-1, 3$
101. 79 feet above sea level **103.** $\$6,276$ million **107.** True
109. -9 and 3

ARE YOU READY? 1.5 (page 40)

1. $-6, 15$ **2.** $22 - 6$ **3.** 12 **4.** -9

SELF CHECKS 1.5

1. a. 1 **b.** y **c.** -500 **2. a.** -57 **b.** 2.9 **c.** $\frac{5}{12}$ **3. a.** 2.7
b. -2.7 **4.** -8 **5.** $41°F$ **6.** -11 ft

STUDY SET SECTION 1.5 (page 44)

1. Subtraction **3.** range **5. a.** -12 **b.** $\frac{1}{5}$ **c.** -2.71 **d.** 0
7. $+, 9, 10$ **9.** $-10 + (-8) + (-23) + 5 + 34$ **11. a.** $-6 \ominus (-4)$
b. $7 + (-3) \ominus 5 \ominus (-2)$ **13. a.** $1 - (-7) = 8$ **b.** $-(-2) = 2$
c. $-|-3| = -3$ **d.** $2 - 6 = -4$ **15.** 55 **17.** x **19.** -25
21. $-\frac{3}{16}$ **23.** -3 **25.** -10 **27.** 11 **29.** -6 **31.** 2
33. 40 **35.** 5 **37.** 12 **39.** -6.9 **41.** -2.31 **43.** $-\frac{1}{2}$ **45.** $-\frac{5}{12}$
47. 22 **49.** -25 **51.** -7 **53.** -1 **55.** 256 **57.** 0 **59.** -2.1
61. $\frac{47}{56}$ **63.** 3 **65.** -47.5 **67.** 149 **69.** -171 **71.** 4.63

73. $-\frac{19}{12}$ **75.** -11 **77.** -88 **79.** -1.1 **81.** -50 **83.** -3.5
85. $-\frac{5}{16}$ **87.** 1 **89.** -13 **91. a.** -53 **b.** -47 **93. a.** $-\frac{13}{18}$
b. $-\frac{7}{18}$ **95.** $160°F$ **97.** 21 points **99.** Orlando: $-115,000$
passengers; Ft Lauderdale: $-50,000$ passengers **101.** 1,030 ft
103. an increase of $315°F$ **105.** $-179, -206$ **111.** $2 \cdot 3 \cdot 5$
113. True

ARE YOU READY? 1.6 (page 47)

1. 14, 6.75 **2.** Different signs **3.** $\frac{5}{16}$ **4.** 3.7

SELF CHECKS 1.6

1. a. -60 **b.** -15 **c.** -11.18 **d.** $-\frac{2}{5}$ **2. a.** 120 **b.** $\frac{1}{12}$
3. a. -300 **b.** 18 **4. a.** $-\frac{16}{15}$ **b.** $\frac{16}{15}$ **c.** $-\frac{1}{27}$ **5. a.** 7 **b.** -3
c. -0.2 **d.** $-\frac{6}{5}$ **6.** The house depreciated $\$2,250$ per year.
7. a. Undefined **b.** 0

STUDY SET SECTION 1.6 (page 55)

1. product, quotient **3.** associative **5. a.** positive **b.** negative
7. a. $-3, 3, -9$ **b.** $0, 8, 0$ **9. a.** a **b.** 1 **c.** 0
d. Undefined **11. a.** Positive **b.** Negative **c.** Negative
13. a. $8 \cdot 5$ **b.** $(-2 \cdot 6)9$ **c.** $\frac{1}{5}$ **d.** 1 **15. a.** NEG
b. Not possible to tell **c.** POS **d.** NEG **17.** $-4(-5) = 20$
19. -4 **21.** -16 **23.** -60 **25.** -66 **27.** -0.48 **29.** $-\frac{1}{4}$
31. 7 **33.** 54 **35.** 9 **37.** -441 **39.** 2.4 **41.** $\frac{1}{12}$
43. 66 **45.** -720 **47.** -861 **49.** -216 **51.** $\frac{9}{7}; 1$
53. $-\frac{1}{13}; 1$ **55.** 10 **57.** 3 **59.** -17 **61.** 1 **63.** -9
65. -0.005 **67.** $-\frac{5}{12}$ **69.** $\frac{15}{4}$ **71.** 0 **73.** Undefined
75. -4 **77.** -1 **79.** 16 **81.** 0 **83.** -4.7 **85.** -520
87. $\frac{1}{24}$ **89.** -11 **91.** $1\frac{1}{2}$ **93.** 30.24 **95.** $-\frac{3}{8}$
97. $-\frac{3}{20}$ **99.** 30.3 **101.** $\frac{15}{16}$ **103. a.** 1.8 **b.** 3.6 **c.** -2.43
d. -3 **105.** -67 **107.** 6 **109.** $-\$8,000$ per year **111.** $-72°$
113. a. ii **b.** 36 lb **115.** $-51°F$ **117.** (160), (250), (800)
119. a. $5, -10$ **b.** $2.5, -5$ **c.** $7.5, -15$ **d.** $10, -20$
125. -5 **127.** $1.08\overline{3}$

ARE YOU READY? 1.7 (page 58)

1. Subtraction, multiplication **2.** Addition, multiplication,
division **3.** 81 **4.** -125

SELF CHECKS 1.7

1. a. 12^3 **b.** $2 \cdot 9^4$ **c.** $(-30)^2$ **d.** y^6 **e.** $8b^3c$ **2. a.** 32
b. $-\frac{27}{64}$ **c.** 9 **d.** 0.09 **e.** 36 **f.** -125 **3.** -625 **4. a.** 35
b. -66 **c.** 27 **d.** 256 **5. a.** 216 **b.** -35 **6.** -130 **7.** -1
8. 1,003 **9.** 2

STUDY SET SECTION 1.7 (page 65)

1. base, exponent, power **3.** exponent **5.** order
7. a. Subtraction **b.** Division **c.** Addition **d.** Power
9. a. Parentheses, brackets, braces, absolute value symbols, fraction
bar **b.** Innermost: parentheses; outermost: brackets **11. a.** -5
b. 5 **13.** $3, 9, 27, 54, -73$ **15.** 8^3 **17.** $7^3 12^2$ **19.** x^3 **21.** $r^4 s^2$
23. 49 **25.** 216 **27.** 625 **29.** 0.01 **31.** $-\frac{1}{64}$ **33.** $\frac{8}{27}$
35. $36, -36$ **37.** $64, -64$ **39.** -17 **41.** 30 **43.** 43
45. 8 **47.** -34 **49.** -118 **51.** -44 **53.** 0 **55.** -148

57. 100   **59.** 53   **61.** -86 **63.** -392 **65.** 3   **67.** $\frac{1}{2}$ **69.** 0
71. $-\frac{8}{9}$ **73.** 13   **75.** 2   **77.** -31 **79.** 11   **81.** 1   **83.** -32
85. 86   **87.** -8 **89.** -19 **91.** -500 **93.** -376 **95.** 12
97. 39   **99.** Undefined   **101.** -275 **103.** -54 **105.** $\frac{1}{8}$ **107.** 10
109. -1 **111. a.** 22   **b.** -13 **113. a.** -40 **b.** -10
115. 2^2 square units, 3^2 square units, 4^2 square units   **117.** 12 min
119. a. \$11,875   **b.** \$95   **121.** 81 in.   **127.** $-17, -5$

ARE YOU READY? 1.8 (page 68)

1. $9x$ **2.** m **3.** $-t$ **4.** $\frac{7}{8}y$ **5.** Quotient   **6.** Difference
7. Product   **8.** Sum

SELF CHECKS 1.8

1. $1, -12, 3, -4$ **2. a.** Factor   **b.** Term   **3. a.** $t - 80$ **b.** $\frac{2}{3}T$
c. $(2a - 15)^2$ **4.** $(m + 15)$ min   **5.** $s =$ amount donated to
scholarship fund in dollars; $900 - s =$ amount donated to building
fund in dollars   **6.** $x =$ number of votes received by the challenger;
$3x - 55 =$ number of votes received by the incumbent
7. Daughter's: x; Kayla's: $x + 5$; Son's: $x + 2$ **8.** $\frac{h}{24}$ days
9. a. \$300   **b.** \$100t **c.** \$1,000$(x - 4)$ **10. a.** 17   **b.** -18
c. 0   **11.** 96 ft

STUDY SET SECTION 1.8 (page 75)

1. expressions   **3.** terms   **5.** coefficient   **7.** $7, 14, 21, 7w$
9. $12 - h$ **11.** $x + 20$ **13. a.** $b - 15$
b. $p + 15$ **15.** $5, 25, 45$ **17. a.** $8y$ **b.** $2cd$ **c.** Commutative
19. a. 4   **b.** $3, 11, -1, 9$ **21.** Term   **23.** Factor   **25.** $l + 15$
27. $50x$ **29.** $\frac{w}{l}$ **31.** $P + \frac{2}{3}p$ **33.** $k^2 - 2{,}005$ **35.** $2a - 1$
37. $\frac{1{,}000}{n}$ **39.** $2p + 90$ **41.** $3(35 + h + 300)$ **43.** $p - 680$
45. $4d - 15$ **47.** $2(200 + t)$ **49.** $|a - 2|$ **51.** $0.1d$ or $\frac{1}{10}d$
53. Three-fourths of r **55.** 50 less than t
57. The product of x, y, and z **59.** Twice m, increased by 5
61. $x + 2$ **63.** $36 - x$ **65.** $60h$ **67.** $\frac{i}{12}$ **69.** \$8x
71. $49x$¢   **73.** \$2t **75.** \$25$(x + 2)$ **77.** 2   **79.** 13   **81.** 20
83. -12 **85.** -5 **87.** $-\frac{1}{5}$ **89.** 17   **91.** 36   **93.** 255
95. 8   **97.** $-1, -2, -28$ **99.** $41, 11, 2$ **101.** $150, -450$
103. $0, 0, 5$ **105. a.** $x + 7^2$ **b.** $(x + 7)^2$ **107. a.** $4(x + 2)$
b. $4x + 2$ **109. a.** Let $x =$ weight of the Element, $2x - 340 =$
weight of the Hummer   **b.** 6,400 lb   **111. a.** Let $x =$ age of Apple;
$x + 80 =$ age of IBM; $x - 9 =$ age of Dell
b. IBM: 112 yr; Dell: 23 yr   **117.** 60   **119.** $\frac{8}{27}$

ARE YOU READY? 1.9 (page 78)

1. The terms are in a different order.   **2.** The position of the
parentheses is different.   **3.** 30, 30; same result   **4.** Different
variable factors (x and y); the same coefficient (4)

SELF CHECKS 1.9

1. a. $(5x + 3x) + 1$ **b.** $-15a$ **2. a.** $54s$ **b.** $48u$ **c.** m **d.** $8y$
3. a. $7m + 14$ **b.** $-640x - 240$ **c.** $4y + 9$ **4. a.** $10x - 5$
b. $9y + 36$ **c.** $-c + 22$ **5. a.** $-2x - 8$ **b.** $54c - 108d$
c. $-1.4r - 3.5s + 5.6$ **6.** $5x - 18$ **7. a.** $-2y$ and $7y$
b. $5p^2$ and $17p^2$; -12 and 2   **8. a.** $8x$ **b.** $-3y$ **c.** $0.5s^4$
d. Doesn't simplify   **e.** $\frac{6}{7}c$ **9. a.** $8h$ **b.** $10h$ **c.** h **d.** $-h$
10. $7y^2 + 19y - 6$ **11.** $21y - 8$

STUDY SET SECTION 1.9 (page 86)

1. simplify   **3.** distributive   **5.** like   **7. a.** 4, 9, 36
b. Associative Property of Multiplication   **9. a.** +   **b.** −   **c.** −
d. +   **11. a.** $10x$ **b.** Can't be simplified   **c.** $-42x$
d. Can't be simplified   **e.** $18x$ **f.** $3x + 5$ **13. a.** $6(h - 4)$
b. $-(z + 16)$ **15.** $(8 + 7) + a$ **17.** $11y$ **19.** $8d(2 \cdot 6)$
21. $t + 4$ **23.** $12t$ **25.** $-35q$ **27.** $11.2x$ **29.** $60c$ **31.** g
33. $5x$ **35.** $5x + 15$ **37.** $-12x - 27$ **39.** $9x + 10$
41. $0.4x + 1.6$ **43.** $36c - 42$ **45.** $-78c + 18$ **47.** $30t + 90$
49. $4a - 1$ **51.** $24t + 16$ **53.** $2w - 4$ **55.** $56y + 32$
57. $5a - 7.5b + 2.5$ **59.** $-x + 7$ **61.** $5.6y - 7$
63. $3x$ and $-2x$ **65.** $-3m^3$ and $-m^3$ **67.** $10x$ **69.** $20b^2$
71. $28y$ **73.** $\frac{4}{5}t$ **75.** r **77.** $-s^3$ **79.** $-6y - 10$ **81.** $-2x + 5$
83. $9m^2 + 6m - 4$ **85.** $4x^2 - 3x + 9$ **87.** $7z - 25$
89. $s^2 - 12$ **91.** $-\frac{5}{8}x$ **93.** $-3.6c$ **95.** $-96m$ **97.** 0   **99.** $0.4r$
101. $6y$ **103.** $-41r + 130$ **105.** $63m$ **107.** $12c + 34$
109. $300t$ **111.** $8x - 9$ **113.** $-10r$ **115.** $-20r$ **117.** $3a$
119. $9r - 16$ **121.** Doesn't simplify   **123.** $c - 13$ **125.** $a^3 - 8$
127. a. $70x$ **b.** $14x + 10$ **129.** $12x$ in.   **133.** 2

CHAPTER 1 REVIEW (page 89)

1. 1 hr; 100 cars   **2.** 100   **3.** 7 P.M.   **4.** 12 A.M. (midnight)
5. The difference of 15 and 3 equals 12.
6. The sum of 15 and 3 equals 18.
7. The quotient of 15 and 3 equals 5.
8. The product of 15 and 3 equals 45.   **9. a.** $4 \cdot 9$; $4(9)$
b. $\frac{9}{3}$ **10. a.** $8b$ **b.** Prt **11. a.** Equation
b. Expression   **12.** 10, 15, 25   **13. a.** $2 \cdot 12$, $3 \cdot 8$ (Answers may
vary)   **b.** $2 \cdot 2 \cdot 6$ (Answers may vary)   **c.** 1, 2, 3, 4, 6, 8, 12, 24
14. Equivalent   **15.** $2 \cdot 3^3$ **16.** $3 \cdot 7^2$ **17.** $5 \cdot 7 \cdot 11$
18. Prime   **19.** $\frac{4}{7}$ **20.** $\frac{4}{3}$ **21.** $\frac{40}{64}$ **22.** $\frac{36}{45}$ **23.** 90
24. 210   **25.** $\frac{7}{64}$ **26.** $\frac{5}{21}$ **27.** $\frac{16}{45}$ **28.** $3\frac{1}{4}$ **29.** $\frac{2}{5}$ **30.** $\frac{5}{22}$
31. $\frac{59}{60}$ **32.** $\frac{5}{18}$ **33.** $52\frac{1}{2}$ million   **34.** $\frac{17}{96}$ in.   **35. a.** 0
b. $\{\ldots, -2, -1, 0, 1, 2, \ldots\}$ **36.** -206 ft   **37. a.** $<$
b. $>$ **38. a.** $\frac{7}{10}$ **b.** $\frac{14}{3}$ **39.** 0.004   **40.** $0.7\overline{72}$
41.

$$-\frac{17}{4} \qquad 0.333\ldots \quad \frac{7}{8} \quad \sqrt{2} \qquad \pi \quad 3.75$$

-5	-4	-3	-2	-1	0	1	2	3	4	5

42. Natural: 8; whole: 0, 8; integers: 0, -12, 8; rational: $-\frac{4}{5}$, 99.99,
0, -12, $4\frac{1}{2}$, 0.666 $\ldots$, 8; irrational: $\sqrt{2}$; real: all
43. False   **44.** False   **45.** True   **46.** True   **47.** $>$ **48.** $<$
49. -82 **50.** 12   **51.** -7 **52.** 0   **53.** -11 **54.** -12.3
55. $-\frac{3}{16}$ **56.** 11   **57. a.** Commutative Property of Addition
b. Associative Property of Addition   **c.** Addition Property of
Opposites (Inverse Property of Addition)   **d.** Addition Property of
0 (Identity Property of Addition)   **58.** 118°F   **59. a.** -10 **b.** 3
60. a. $\frac{9}{16}$ **b.** -4 **61.** -19 **62.** $-\frac{14}{15}$ **63.** 5   **64.** 5.7
65. -10 **66.** -29 **67.** 65,233 ft; $65{,}233 + (-36{,}205) = 29{,}028$
68. 287 B.C.; (-287); $-287 + 75 = -212$ **69.** -56 **70.** 1
71. 12   **72.** -12 **73.** 6.36   **74.** -2 **75.** $-\frac{2}{15}$ **76.** 0
77. High: 3, low: -4.5 **78. a.** Associative Property of
Multiplication   **b.** Commutative Property of Multiplication
c. Multiplication Property of 1 (Identity Property of Multiplication)
d. Inverse Property of Multiplication   **79.** -1 **80.** -17 **81.** 3
82. $-\frac{6}{5}$ **83.** Undefined   **84.** -4.5 **85.** 0, 18, 0   **86.** $-\$360$
87. a. 8^5 **b.** $9\pi r^2$ **88. a.** 81   **b.** $-\frac{8}{27}$ **c.** 32   **d.** 50
89. 17   **90.** -36 **91.** -169 **92.** 23   **93.** -420 **94.** $-\frac{7}{19}$
95. 113   **96.** Undefined   **97. a.** $(-9)^2 = 81$ **b.** $-9^2 = -81$

98. $20 **99. a.** 3 **b.** 1 **100. a.** $16, -5, 25$ **b.** $\frac{1}{2}, 1$
101. $h + 25$ **102.** $3s - 15$ **103.** $\frac{1}{2}t - 6$
104. $|2 - a^2|$ **105.** $n + 4$ **106.** $b - 4$ **107.** $10d$
108. $x - 5$ **109.** $30, 10d$ **110.** $0, 19, -16$ **111.** 40
112. -36 **113.** $150a$ **114.** $(9 + 1) + 7y$ **115.** $(2.7 \cdot 10)b$
116. $2x^2 + x$ **117.** $-28w$ **118.** $24x$ **119.** $2.08f$ **120.** r
121. $5x + 15$ **122.** $-2x - 3 + y$ **123.** $3c - 6$
124. $12.6c + 29.4$ **125.** $9p$ **126.** $-7m$ **127.** $4n$
128. $-p - 18$ **129.** $0.1k^2$ **130.** $8a^3 - 1$ **131.** w
132. $4h - 15$ **133.** $4.6t - 7.7$ **134. a.** x **b.** $-x$
c. $4x + 1$ **d.** $4x - 1$

CHAPTER 1 TEST (page 98)

1. a. equivalent **b.** product **c.** reciprocal **d.** like terms
e. undefined **2. a.** $24 **b.** 5 hr **3.** $3, 20, 70$
4. $2 \cdot 2 \cdot 3 \cdot 3 \cdot 5 = 2^2 \cdot 3^2 \cdot 5$ **5.** $\frac{2}{5}$ **6.** $\frac{3}{2} = 1\frac{1}{2}$ **7.** $\frac{27}{35}$ **8.** $6\frac{11}{15}$
9. a. $4\frac{1}{4}$ lb **b.** $3.57 **10.** $0.8\overline{3}$
11. a.

$$-3.75 \qquad -1\frac{1}{4} \quad 0 \; 0.5 \; \sqrt{2} \qquad \frac{7}{2}$$

number line from -5 to 5

b. Natural numbers: 2; whole numbers: 0, 2; integers: $0, 2, -3$;
rational numbers: $-1\frac{1}{4}, 0, -3.75, 2, \frac{7}{2}, 0.5, -3$; irrational numbers:
$\sqrt{2}$; real numbers: all **12. a.** True **b.** False **c.** True **d.** True
e. True **13. a.** $>$ **b.** $<$ **c.** $<$ **d.** $>$
14. A gain of 0.6 of a rating point **15.** -7.6 **16.** -2 **17.** $\frac{3}{8}$
18. a. -6 **b.** $-6 + (-4) = -10$ **19. a.** 14
b. $14(-0.9) = -12.6$ **20.** -30 **21.** -2.44 **22.** 0 **23.** $-\frac{27}{125}$
24. 0 **25.** -3 **26.** 50 **27.** 14 **28.** a net loss of 78 in.
29. $-$1,275 **30. a.** $-12 + (97 + 3)$ **b.** $2x + 14$ **c.** $-2(5)m$
d. 1 **e.** $15x$ **31. a.** 9^5 **b.** $3x^2z^3$ **32.** $4, 17, -59$ **33.** 170
34. -12 **35.** -99 **36.** -351 **37.** 20 **38.** -60 **39.** $2w - 7$
40. a. $x - 2$ **b.** $25q¢$ **41.** 3 **42.** $1, -6, -1, 10$ **43.** $-20x$
44. $224t$ **45.** $-4a + 4$ **46.** $-5.9d^3$ **47.** $14x + 3$
48. $3m^2 + 2m - 4$ **49. a.** True **b.** False **c.** False **d.** False
e. True **f.** False

ARE YOU READY? 2.1 (page 102)

1. $-$ **2.** $+$ **3.** 7 **4.** $\cdot$ **5.** $\frac{2}{5}$ **6.** $-\frac{8}{9}$

SELF CHECKS 2.1

1. Yes **2.** 49 **3. a.** 33 **b.** 49 **4. a.** $\frac{29}{15}$ **b.** -0.5 **5.** 72
6. a. 6 **b.** $-\frac{11}{21}$ **7. a.** 11 **b.** -25.1 **8.** 12

STUDY SET SECTION 2.1 (page 110)

1. equation **3.** solve **5.** equivalent **7. a.** $x + 6$ **b.** Neither
c. No **d.** Yes **9. a.** c, c **b.** c, c **11. a.** x **b.** y **c.** t
d. h **13.** $5, 5, 50, 50, \stackrel{?}{=}, 45, 50$ **15. a.** Is possibly equal to
b. Yes **17.** No **19.** No **21.** No **23.** No **25.** Yes **27.** No
29. No **31.** Yes **33.** Yes **35.** Yes **37.** 71 **39.** 18 **41.** -12
43. 3 **45.** $\frac{11}{10}$ **47.** -2.3 **49.** 45 **51.** -48 **53.** 20 **55.** $-\frac{5}{42}$
57. 4 **59.** 0.5 **61.** -18 **63.** $-\frac{4}{21}$ **65.** 7 **67.** $\frac{8}{9}$ **69.** 0
71. -0.9 **73.** 15 **75.** 20 **77.** $-\frac{1}{25}$ **79.** 21 **81.** 0 **83.** -2.64
85. 1 **87.** 4 **89.** 13 **91.** 2.5 **93.** $-\frac{8}{3}$ **95.** $-\frac{21}{16}$ **97.** -5
99. -200 **101.** $\frac{4}{3}$ **103.** 4 **105. a.** $\frac{13}{20}$ **b.** $\frac{17}{20}$ **c.** $\frac{15}{2}$ **d.** $\frac{3}{40}$
107. $65°$ **109.** $6,000,000 **115.** 0 **117.** $45 - x$

ARE YOU READY? 2.2 (page 112)

1. -12 **2.** $2a$ **3.** $-7m + 18$ **4.** $3x$ **5.** $24n$ **6.** 8

SELF CHECKS 2.2

1. 7 **2.** -36 **3.** -3.9 **4. a.** 1 **b.** -11 **5.** -16 **6.** $-\frac{5}{2}$
7. 6,000 **8.** 0 **9.** All real numbers; the equation is an identity.
10. No solution; the equation is a contradiction.

STUDY SET SECTION 2.2 (page 120)

1. equation **3.** identity **5. a.** subtraction, multiplication
b. addition, division **7.** No **9. a.** 6 **b.** 10
11. $7, 7, 2, 2, 14, \stackrel{?}{=}, 28, 21, 14$ **13.** -9 **15.** -5 **17.** 18 **19.** 16
21. -4 **23.** 2.9 **25.** $\frac{11}{5}$ **27.** -6 **29.** -21 **31.** 1 **33.** $\frac{2}{15}$
35. 6 **37.** 5 **39.** 200 **41.** -4 **43.** -1 **45.** All real numbers
47. No solution **49.** $\frac{1}{4}$ **51.** 12 **53.** -1 **55.** 6 **57.** 1 **59.** 30
61. No solution **63.** -11 **65.** 7 **67.** -11 **69.** $\frac{9}{2}$ **71.** $-\frac{12}{5}$
73. -0.25 **75.** -7 **77.** $\frac{10}{3}$ **79.** 5 **81.** 1,000 **83.** -3 **85.** $\frac{27}{5}$
87. 200 **89.** -11 **91.** 3 **93.** $\frac{52}{9}$ **95.** 0.04 **97.** 80 **99.** $-\frac{5}{2}$
101. -20 **103.** No solution **105.** All real numbers **107.** -6
109. -6 **111. a.** $x - 20$ **b.** -5 **113. a.** $0.4 - 0.2x$ **b.** 0
119. Commutative property of multiplication **121.** Associative
property of addition

ARE YOU READY? 2.3 (page 122)

1. 61 **2.** 2 **3.** $0.5, 0.75$ **4.** 0.27 **5.** 3.72 **6.** 49.5

SELF CHECKS 2.3

1. 2.24 **2.** 570 million **3.** 1.45% **4.** 21% **5.** $120 **6.** $600

STUDY SET SECTION 2.3 (page 127)

1. Percent **3.** multiplication, is **5.** $\frac{51}{100}, 0.51, 51\%$
7. amount, percent, base **9. a.** 639 **b.** 639, what, 3,618
11. a. 0.35 **b.** 0.085 **c.** 1.5 **d.** 0.0275 **e.** 0.0925 **f.** 0.015
13. 312 **15.** 46.2 **17.** 300 **19.** 1,464 **21.** 26% **23.** 2.5%
25. 0.48 oz **27. a.** $1,102.6 billion **b.** $715.2 billion **29.** $10.45
31. $24.20 **33.** 60%, 40% **35.** 19% **37.** No (66%)
39. 120 children **41. a.** 5 g; 25% **b.** 20 g **43. a.** 11% **b.** 46%
45. 12% **47. a.** 6% **b.** 23.5 mpg **49.** $75 **51.** $300
53. $95,000 **55.** $25,600 **61.** $\frac{12}{5} = 2\frac{2}{5}$ **63.** No

ARE YOU READY? 2.4 (page 130)

1. a. one **b.** three **2.** d **3.** x **4.** $8c - cx$ **5.** Yes **6.** 1

SELF CHECKS 2.4

1. $1,510.50 **2.** 2.5 yr **3.** 1.25 min **4.** $-283°F$ **5.** 230 ft
6. 62.83 in. **7.** $1,357.2$ m^3 **8.** $c = r - p$ **9.** $a = \frac{2A}{r^2}$
10. $c = \frac{B - 4d}{3}$ **11.** $y = 4 - \frac{1}{3}x$ or $y = -\frac{1}{3}x + 4$
12. $s = \frac{A + 3xy}{xy}$

STUDY SET SECTION 2.4 (page 137)

1. formula **3.** volume **5. a.** $d = rt$ **b.** $r = c + m$
c. $p = r - c$ **d.** $I = Prt$ **7.** 11,176,920 mi, 65,280 ft
9. Ax, Ax, B, B, B **11. a.** $\pi r^2 h$ **b.** The radius of a cylinder;
the height of a cylinder **13.** $240 million **15.** $931 **17.** 3.5%
19. $6,000 **21.** 2.5 mph **23.** 4.5 hours **25.** $185°C$

27. $-454°F$ **29.** 20 in. **31.** 1,885 mm³ **33.** $c = r - m$
35. $b = P - a - c$ **37.** $h = \frac{3V}{B}$ **39.** $R = \frac{E}{I}$ **41.** $r = \frac{T - 2t}{2}$
43. $x = \frac{C - By}{A}$ **45.** $y = -\frac{2}{7}x + 3$ **47.** $y = \frac{9}{2}x + 4$
49. $m = \frac{T - 4ab}{4ab}$ **51.** $r = \frac{G + g}{4g}$ **53.** $c = 3A - a - b$
55. $y = -3x + 9$ **57.** $m = \frac{2K}{v^2}$ **59.** $r = \frac{C}{2\pi}$ **61.** $M = 4.2B + 19.8$
63. $f = \frac{s}{w}$ **65.** $y = \frac{1}{3}x + 3$ **67.** $b = \frac{2A}{h} - d$ or $b = \frac{2A - hd}{h}$
69. $a^2 = c^2 - b^2$ **71.** $c = \frac{72 - 8w}{7}$ **73.** $b = \frac{m - 70 - at}{t}$
75. $l = \frac{V}{wh}$ **77.** $t = T - 18E$ **79.** $r^2 = \frac{s}{4\pi}$ **81. a.** $R = A - ab$
b. $a = \frac{A - R}{b}$ **83. a.** $h = \frac{S - 4lw}{2w}$ **b.** $l = \frac{S - 2wh}{4w}$
85. Horsepower $= \frac{RPM \cdot Torque}{5,252}$ **87.** 168.4, 192.8 **89.** 14 in.
91. 50 in. **93.** 25 in., 2.5 in. **95.** 18.1 in.² **97.** 2,463 ft²
99. 3,150 cm² **101.** 6 in. **103.** 8 ft **105.** 348 ft³ **107.** 254 in.²
109. $R = \frac{L - 2D - 3.25r}{3.25}$ or $R = \frac{L - 2D}{3.25} - r$ **115.** 137.76
117. 15%

ARE YOU READY? 2.5 (page 142)

1. $4x + 4$ **2.** 49 **3.** $39.15 **4.** $0.28x$ **5.** $P = 2l + 2w$
6. 180° **7.** $2x - 8$ **8.** 0.06

SELF CHECKS 2.5

1. 16 mi, 18 mi, 20 mi, and 22 mi **2.** 47 shirts **3.** $2,762.77
4. Page 579 **5.** 5 ft by 11 ft **6.** 12 cm, 12 cm

STUDY SET SECTION 2.5 (page 147)

1. consecutive **3.** vertex, base **5.** $17, x + 2, 3x$ **7.** $0.03x$
9. 180° **11. a.** $x + 1$ **b.** $x + 2$ **c.** $x + 2, x + 4$ **13.** 4 ft, 8 ft
15. Day 1: 102 mi; day 2: 108 mi; day 3: 114 mi; day 4: 120 mi
17. 7.3 ft, 10.7 ft **19.** *Guitar Hero:* $2.99; *Call of Duty:
World at War: Zombies II:* $9.99; *Tom Tom USA:* $39.99
21. 250 calories in ice cream, 600 calories in pie **23.** 7 hr
25. 580 mi **27.** 20 hr **29.** $50,000 **31.** $240 **33.** $5,250
35. Ronaldo: 15 goals; Mueller: 14 goals
37. *Friends:* 236 episodes; *Leave It to Beaver:* 234 episodes
39. July 22, 24, 26 **41.** Width: 27 ft; length: 78 ft
43. 21 in. by 30.25 in. **45.** 7 ft, 7 ft; 11 ft **47.** 20°
49. At steering column: 42.5°; at seat support: 70°;
at pedal gear: 67.5° **51.** $x = 11°; 22°, 68°$
53. Maximum stride angle: 106° **59.** -24 **61.** $-\frac{40}{37}$

ARE YOU READY? 2.6 (page 151)

1. $400 **2.** 135 mi **3.** 3.6 gal of antifreeze **4.** $19.60
5. $14,000 **6.** $3x$

SELF CHECKS 2.6

1. $2,400 ar 2%, $1,800 at 3% **2.** 3.5 hr **3.** 1.5 hr **4.** 10 gal
5. 40 lb **6.** 12 iPods, 4 skins, 24 cards

STUDY SET SECTION 2.6 (page 158)

1. investment, motion **3.** $30,000 - x$ **5.** $r - 150$
7. $35t; t; 45t; 80; 35t + 45t = 80$
9. a. $0.25x, 0.50(6), 6 + x, 0.30(6 + x)$,
$0.25x + 0.50(6) = 0.30(6 + x)$
b. $10 - x, 0.06x, 0.03(10 - x), 0.05(10)$,
$0.03(10 - x) + 0.06x = 0.05(10)$ **11.** 0.06, 0.152 **13.** 4
15. 6,000 **17.** $15,000 at 4%; $10,000 at 7% **19.** Silver: $1,500;
gold: $2,000 **21.** $26,000 **23.** 822: $9,000; 721: $6,000 **25.** $4,900
27. Credit union: $13,500; stocks: $4,500 **29.** 2 hr

31. $\frac{1}{4}$ hr = 15 min **33.** 1 hr **35.** 4 hr **37.** 55 mph
39. 50 gal **41.** 4%: 5 gal; 1%: 10 gal
43. 32 ounces of 8%; 32 ounces of 22% **45.** 6 gal **47.** 50 lb
49. 20 scoops **51.** 15 **53.** $4.25 **55.** 17 **57.** 90
59. 40 pennies, 20 dimes, 60 nickels
61. 2-pointers: 50; 3-pointers: 4 **67.** $-36a - 48b + 384$
69. $30t + 6$

ARE YOU READY? 2.7 (page 162)

1. is less than **2.** True **3.**

4. $0 < 10$

SELF CHECKS 2.7

1. Yes **2.** $[0, \infty)$
3. $(-\infty, 1)$
4. a. $[-200, \infty)$
b. $(-\infty, 12)$
5. $(-3, \infty)$
6. $(-\infty, 2.1)$
7. $\left[\frac{13}{4}, \infty\right)$
8. $\left(-\infty, \frac{21}{2}\right)$
9. $[-2, 1)$
10. $[-4, 0]$ **11.** 84% or better

STUDY SET SECTION 2.7 (page 171)

1. inequality **3.** interval **5. a.** both **b.** positive
c. negative **7.** $x > 32$ **9. a.** $-1, -\infty$ **b.** $2, \infty$ **11. a.** $\leq$
b. ∞ **c.** $[$ or $]$ **d.** $>$ **13.** 5, 5, 12, 4, 4, 3 **15. a.** Yes **b.** No
17. a. No **b.** Yes **19.** $(-\infty, 5)$
21. $(-3, 1]$ **23.** $(3, \infty)$
25. $[10, \infty)$ **27.** $(-\infty, 48]$
29. $[3, \infty)$ **31.** $[2, \infty)$
33. $(-\infty, 6)$ **35.** $(7, \infty)$
37. $(-\infty, -5]$ **39.** $(-\infty, 0.4]$
41. $(2.4, \infty)$ **43.** $(-5, \infty)$
45. $\left[-\frac{5}{3}, \infty\right)$ **47.** $\left(\frac{5}{4}, \infty\right)$

49. $(-\infty, 15]$

51. $[-2, 3)$

53. $\left(-\frac{7}{4}, 2\right)$

55. $(7, 10)$

57. $[-10, 0]$

59. $[2, 3)$

61. $(-3, 6]$

63. $\left(-\infty, \frac{3}{2}\right]$

65. $(-\infty, 12]$

67. $(-2, 1]$

69. $(-\infty, 1.5]$

71. $\left(-\infty, \frac{1}{8}\right]$

73. $(-\infty, 0)$

75. $\left[\frac{9}{4}, \infty\right)$

77. $(-5, -2)$

79. $(-\infty, 2]$

81. $(-\infty, -27)$

83. $\left(-\infty, \frac{17}{21}\right]$

85. $[-13, \infty)$

87. $(6, \infty)$

89. $[-32, 48]$

91. $(-\infty, 1.5]$

93. $\left[-\frac{3}{8}, \infty\right)$

95. $\left(-\infty, \frac{1}{2}\right)$

97. $(-\infty, -1]$

99. a. $\left(\frac{1}{8}, \infty\right)$ **b.** $\frac{1}{8}$

101. a. $[5, \infty)$ **b.** $[5, 12)$

103. 98% or better   **105.** More than 27 mpg   **107.** 19 ft or less
109. More than 5 ft   **111.** 40 or less   **113.** 12.5 in. or less
115. 26, 27, 28, 29, 30   **119.** 1, −3, 6

CHAPTER 2 REVIEW (page 175)

1. Yes   **2.** No   **3.** No   **4.** No   **5.** Yes   **6.** Yes
7. equation   **8.** True   **9.** 21   **10.** 32   **11.** −20.6
12. 107   **13.** 24   **14.** $\frac{16}{21}$ **15.** −9   **16.** −7.8   **17.** 0
18. $-\frac{16}{5}$ **19.** 2   **20.** −30.6   **21.** 30   **22.** −19   **23.** 4
24. 1   **25.** $\frac{5}{4}$ **26.** $\frac{47}{13}$ **27.** 6   **28.** $-\frac{22}{75}$ **29.** 5   **30.** 1
31. Identity; all real numbers   **32.** Contradiction; no solution
33. a. Percent   **b.** discount   **c.** commission   **34.** 192.4
35. 142.5   **36.** 12%   **37. a.** 28.8%   **b.** 221 million
38. $26.74   **39.** No   **40.** $450   **41.** $150   **42.** 1,567%
43. $176   **44.** $11,800   **45.** 8 min   **46.** 4.5%
47. 1,949°F   **48. a.** 168 in.   **b.** 1,440 in.²   **c.** 4,320 in.³
49. 76.5 m²   **50.** 144 in.²   **51. a.** 50.27 cm
b. 201 cm²   **52.** 9.4 ft³   **53.** 381.70 in.³   **54.** 120 ft³
55. $h = \frac{A}{2\pi r}$ **56.** $G = 3A - 3BC + K$ **57.** $t = \frac{4C}{s} + d$
58. $y = \frac{3}{4}x + 4$ **59.** 8 ft   **60.** 200 signatures   **61.** $2,500,000
62. Labonte: 43; Petty: 45
63. 24.875 in. × 29.875 in. $\left(24\frac{7}{8} \text{ in.} \times 29\frac{7}{8} \text{ in.}\right)$

64. 76.5°, 76.5°   **65.** $16,000 at 7%, $11,000 at 9%   **66.** 20 min
67. $1\frac{2}{3}$ hr = 1 hr 40 min   **68.** TV celebrities: 12 autographs;
movie stars: 4 autographs   **69.** 10 lb of each   **70.** 2 gal

71. $(-\infty, 1)$

72. $(-\infty, 12]$ **73.** $\left(\frac{5}{4}, \infty\right)$

74. $[3, \infty)$ **75.** $(-\infty, 40]$

76. $(7, \infty)$ **77.** $(6, 11)$

78. $\left(-\frac{7}{2}, \frac{3}{2}\right]$

79. 2.40 g ≤ w ≤ 2.53 g   **80.** 0 in. < l ≤ 48 in.; 48 inches or less

CHAPTER 2 TEST (page 182)

1. a. solve   **b.** Percent   **c.** circumference   **d.** inequality
e. multiplication, equality   **2.** No   **3.** 2   **4.** 22   **5.** −5
6. $\frac{12}{7}$ **7.** 1,336   **8.** All real numbers (an identity)   **9.** $\frac{7}{4}$ **10.** 55
11. 0   **12.** 0   **13.** −4   **14.** No solution (a contradiction)
15. 12.16   **16.** $76,000   **17.** 6%   **18.** $30   **19.** $295
20. −10°C   **21.** 66,480 ft   **22.** 393 in.³   **23.** $h = \frac{V}{\pi r^2}$
24. $r = \frac{A - P}{Pt}$ **25.** $c = 4A - a - b - d$ **26.** $y = \frac{2}{3}x - 3$
27. 20 in.²   **28.** Programming: 22 min; commercials: 8 min
29. $40.55   **30.** 80 balcony seats, 800 floor seats   **31.** $120,000
32. 380 mi, 280 mi   **33.** Green: 16 lb; herbal: 4 lb   **34.** 412, 413
35. $\frac{3}{5}$ hr   **36.** 10 liters   **37.** $\frac{1}{3}$ hr = 20 min   **38.** 68°   **39.** $5,250
40. No   **41.** $[-3, \infty)$

42. $(-\infty, 6.4)$ **43.** $[-7, 4)$

44. $(-\infty, -13)$

45. $(-\infty, 5]$ **46.** 180 words

ARE YOU READY? 3.1 (page 186)

1. 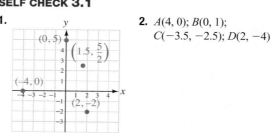   **2. a.** 8   **b.** −3.5

3. I, II, III, IV   **4.** $4\frac{1}{2}$, $-3\frac{2}{3}$

SELF CHECK 3.1

1.

2. $A(4, 0)$; $B(0, 1)$;
$C(-3.5, -2.5)$; $D(2, -4)$

3. a. 30 min before and 85 min after taping began   **b.** 200
c. 40 min before taping began

STUDY SET SECTION 3.1 (page 191)

1. ordered   **3.** axis, axis, origin   **5.** rectangular
7. a. origin, left, up   **b.** origin, right, down   **9. a.** I and II
b. II and III   **c.** IV   **d.** The y-axis
11. (3, 5) is an ordered pair, 3(5) = 3 · 5
13. Yes   **15.** Horizontal
17.

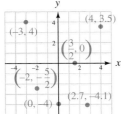

19. (4, 3), (0, 4), (−5, 0), (−4, −5), (3, −3)
21. a. 60 beats/min   **b.** 10 min
23. a. 5 min and 50 min after starting   **b.** 20 min
25. a. 2 hr   **b.** −1,000 ft   **27. a.** It ascends (rises) 500 ft
b. −500 ft   **29.** Rivets: (−60, 0), (−20, 0), (20, 0), (60, 0); welds:
(−40, 30), (0, 30), (40, 30); anchors: (−60, −30), (60, −30)
31. (G, 2), (G, 3), (G, 4)   **33. a.** 8 teeth   **b.** It represents the
patient's left side.   **35. a.** 60°; 4 ft   **b.** 30°; 4 ft   **37.** 10 square units
39.

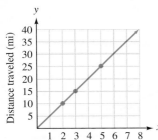

a. 20 mi.   **b.** 6 gal
c. 35 mi

41.

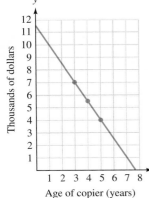

a. A 3-yr-old copier
is worth $7,000.   **b.** $1,000
c. 6 yr
47. $h = \frac{3(AC + T)}{2}$ or $h = \frac{3AC + 3T}{2}$
49. −1

ARE YOU READY? 3.2 (page 195)

1. False   **2.** 5   **3.** 2   **4.** $y = -\frac{4}{5}x - 3$ **5.** 3   **6.** −5

SELF CHECK 3.2

1. Yes   **2.** (−2, −10)   **3.**

x	y	(x, y)
3	−2	(3, −2)
5	−5	(5, −5)

4.

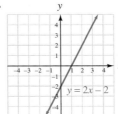

5.

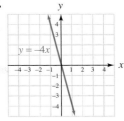

6.

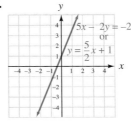

7. $c = 15 + 10n$

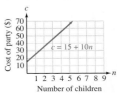

STUDY SET SECTION 3.2 (page 203)

1. two   **3.** table   **5.** linear   **7. a.** 2   **b.** Yes   **c.** No
d. Infinitely many   **9.** solution, point
11. a. −5, 0, 5 (Answers may vary)
b. −10, 0, 10 (Answers may vary)   **13.** 6, −2, 2, 6
15. a. 1's   **b.** The exponent on x is not 1.   **17.** Yes
19. No   **21.** Yes   **23.** Yes   **25.** No   **27.** No   **29.** 11
31. 4   **33.** 13   **35.** $-\frac{8}{7}$
37.

x	y	(x, y)
8	12	(8, 12)
6	8	(6, 8)

39.

x	y	(x, y)
−5	−13	(−5, −13)
−1	−1	(−1, −1)

41.

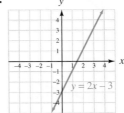

43.

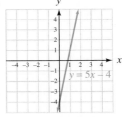

45.

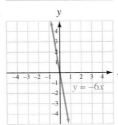

47.

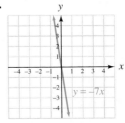

49.

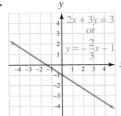

51.

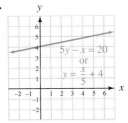

53.
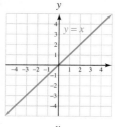

55.
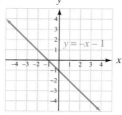

81.
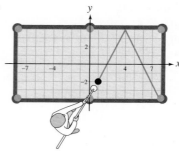

57.
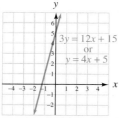

59.
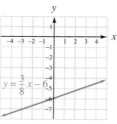

83. About 125 hr
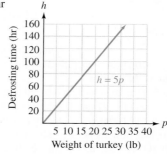

61.
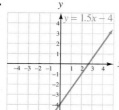

63.
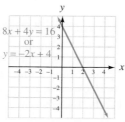

85. About 3 oz
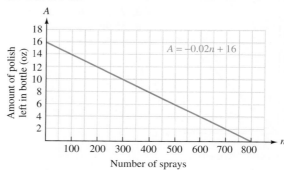

65.
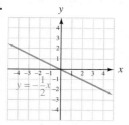

67.
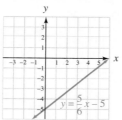

87. About $100
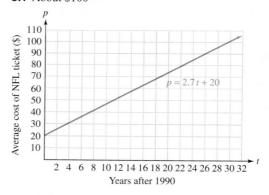

69.
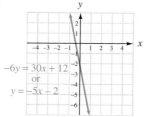

71.
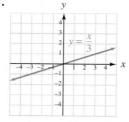

73.
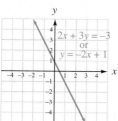

75.
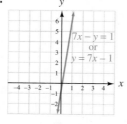

89. About 180 tickets
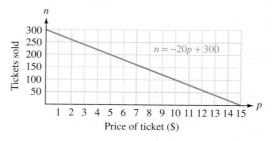

77.
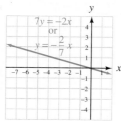

79.
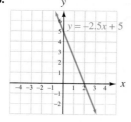

91. 2030

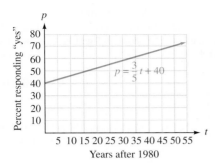

101. $5 + 4c$ or $4c + 5$ **103.** 904.8 ft^3

ARE YOU READY? 3.3 (page 206)

1.

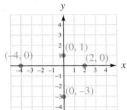

2. 0   **3.** The origin $(0, 0)$ **4.** 5

SELF CHECK 3.3

1. $(-1, 0)$; $(0, -3)$

2.

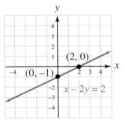

3.

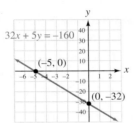

4.

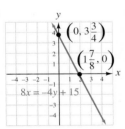

5.

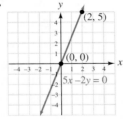

6.

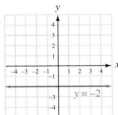

7.

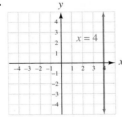

STUDY SET SECTION 3.3 (page 214)

1. x-intercept   **3.** horizontal, vertical   **5. a.** $0, y$ **b.** $0, x$
7. a. y-intercept: $(0, 80{,}000)$; $\$80{,}000$
b. x-intercept: $(30, 0)$;   30 years after purchase   **9.** $y = 0$; $x = 0$
11. x-intercept: $(4, 0)$, y-intercept: $(0, 3)$
13. x-intercept: $(-5, 0)$, y-intercept: $(0, -4)$
15. No x-intercept, y-intercept: $(0, 2)$

17. x-intercept: $\left(-2\frac{1}{2}, 0\right)$; y-intercept: $\left(0, \frac{2}{3}\right)$ (Answers may vary)
19. $(3, 0)$; $(0, 8)$ **21.** $(4, 0)$; $(0, -14)$ **23.** $(-2, 0)$; $\left(0, -\frac{10}{3}\right)$
25. $\left(\frac{3}{2}, 0\right)$; $(0, 9)$

27.

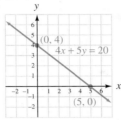

29.

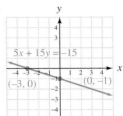

31.

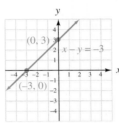

33.

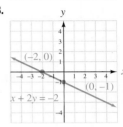

35.

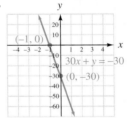

37.

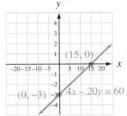

39.

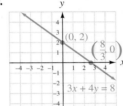

41.

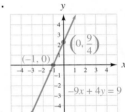

43.

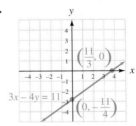

45.

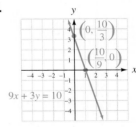

47.

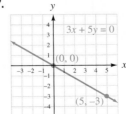

49.

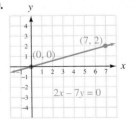

51.
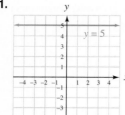

53.
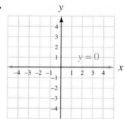

55.
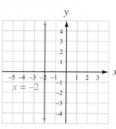

57.
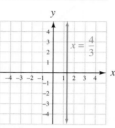

59. $y = 2$
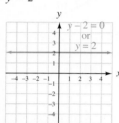

61. $x = 1.5$
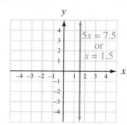

63.
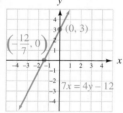

65.
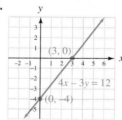

67.
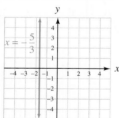

69.
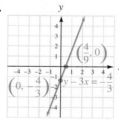

71.
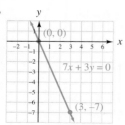

73.
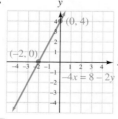

75.
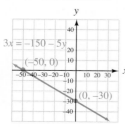

77.
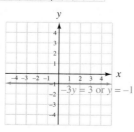

79. a. About $-270°C$ **b.** 0 milliliters

81. The g-intercept is $(0, 5)$: Before any cups of water have been served from the bottle, it contains 5 gallons of water. The c-intercept is $\left(106\frac{2}{3}, 0\right)$: The bottle will be empty after $106\frac{2}{3}$ six-ounce cups of water have been served from it.

83.
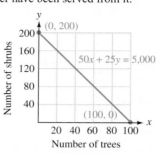

a. If only shrubs are purchased, he can buy 200.

b. If only trees are purchased, he can buy 100.

89. $\frac{1}{5}$ **91.** $2x - 6$

ARE YOU READY? 3.4 (page 217)

1. $\frac{3}{5}$ **2.** undefined   **3.** -1 **4.** $\frac{5}{6}$

SELF CHECK 3.4

1. $-\frac{1}{2}$ **2.** 5   **3.** $-\frac{5}{2}$ **4.** 0   **5.** Undefined slope   **6.** $\frac{5}{12}$
7. An increase of 650 million bushels per year   **8.** Neither
9. $-\frac{13}{4}$

STUDY SET SECTION 3.4 (page 225)

1. slope, ratio   **3.** change   **5. a.** Line 2   **b.** Line 1   **c.** Line 4
d. Line 3   **7. a.** Line 1   **b.** Line 1   **c.** Line 2   **9. a.** $\frac{1}{3}$
b. $\frac{4}{12} = \frac{1}{3}$ **c.** same   **11. a.** 0   **b.** Undefined   **c.** $\frac{1}{4}$ **d.** 2
13. 40%   **15. a.** $-\frac{1}{6}$ **b.** $\frac{8}{7}$ **c.** 1   **17. a.** $m = \frac{y_2 - y_1}{x_2 - x_1}$
b. sub, sub, over (divided by), two, one   **19.** 1   **21.** $\frac{2}{3}$ **23.** $\frac{4}{3}$
25. -2 **27.** 0   **29.** $-\frac{1}{5}$ **31.** $\frac{1}{2}$ **33.** 1   **35.** -3 **37.** $\frac{5}{4}$
39. $-\frac{1}{2}$ **41.** $\frac{3}{5}$ **43.** 0   **45.** Undefined   **47.** $-\frac{2}{3}$ **49.** -4.75
51. 0   **53.** $\frac{7}{5}$ **55.** $-\frac{2}{5}$ **57.** $\frac{3}{4}$ **59.** 0   **61.** 0   **63.** 0
65. Undefined   **67.** Undefined   **69.** 0   **71.** Undefined
73. Parallel   **75.** Perpendicular   **77.** Neither   **79.** Perpendicular
81. Parallel   **83.** Neither   **85.** $\frac{5}{9}$ **87.** $-\frac{2}{3}$ **89.** -1 **91.** $\frac{1}{2}$
93. $-\frac{2}{5}$ **95.** $\frac{1}{20}$; 5%   **97.** $\frac{3}{25}$; 12%   **99.** Front: $\frac{3}{2}$; side: $\frac{3}{5}$
101. a decrease of 875 gal per hour (-875 gal per hr)
103. 319 lb per yr   **105.** An increase of 325 students per year
111. 40 lb licorice; 20 lb gumdrops

ARE YOU READY? 3.5 (page 230)

1. a. $3x, -6$ **b.** 3   **2.** $y = -\frac{2}{5}x + 3$ **3.** True   **4.** $\frac{3}{1}$
5. the y-axis   **6.** True

SELF CHECK 3.5

1. a. $m = -9$; $(0, 4)$ **b.** $m = \frac{1}{11}$; $(0, -2)$ **c.** $m = -5$; $\left(0, -\frac{7}{2}\right)$
2. $y = x - 12$ **3.** $y = -\frac{3}{2}x + 2$

4.
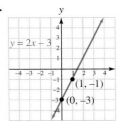

5.
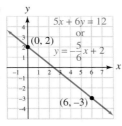

6. Neither   **7.** $c = -10.50p + 4,500$

STUDY SET SECTION 3.5 (page 237)

1. slope–intercept   **3. a.** No   **b.** No   **c.** Yes   **d.** No

5. a. $y = 2x + 8$ **b.** $y = -5x - 3$ **c.** $y = \frac{1}{3}x - 1$

d. $y = \frac{9}{5}x + 4$ **7.** $-2x, 5y, 5, 5, 5, -\frac{2}{5}, 3, -\frac{2}{5}, 0, 3$ **9.** $-2, -3$

11. $4, (0, 2)$ **13.** $-5, (0, -8)$ **15.** $25, (0, -9)$ **17.** $-1, (0, 11)$

19. $\frac{1}{2}, (0, 6)$ **21.** $\frac{1}{4}, \left(0, -\frac{1}{2}\right)$ **23.** $-5, (0, 0)$ **25.** $1, (0, 0)$

27. $0, (0, -2)$ **29.** $0, \left(0, -\frac{2}{5}\right)$ **31.** $-1, (0, 8)$ **33.** $\frac{1}{6}, (0, -1)$

35. $-\frac{3}{2}, (0, 1)$ **37.** $-\frac{2}{3}, (0, 2)$ **39.** $\frac{3}{5}, (0, -3)$ **41.** $1, \left(0, -\frac{11}{6}\right)$

43. $y = 5x - 3$ **45.** $y = -3x + 6$

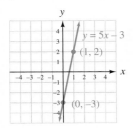

47. $y = \frac{1}{4}x - 2$ **49.** $y = -\frac{8}{3}x + 5$

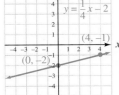

51. $y = \frac{6}{5}x$ **53.** $y = -2x + \frac{1}{2}$

55. $y = 5x - 1$ **57.** $y = -2x + 3$ **59.** $y = \frac{4}{5}x - 2$

61. $y = -\frac{5}{3}x + 2$

63. $3, (0, 3)$ **65.** $\frac{1}{2}, (0, 2)$

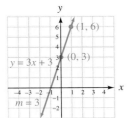
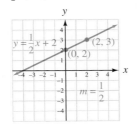

67. $-3, (0, 0)$ **69.** $-4, (0, -4)$

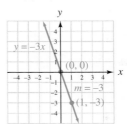
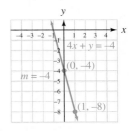

71. $-\frac{3}{4}, (0, 4)$ **73.** $2, (0, -1)$

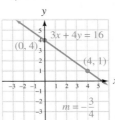
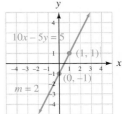

75. Parallel   **77.** Perpendicular   **79.** Parallel   **81.** Neither
83. Perpendicular   **85.** Parallel   **87.** Perpendicular   **89.** Neither
91. a. $c = 2,000h + 5,000$ **b.** $21,000$ **93.** $F = 5t - 10$
95. $c = -20m + 500$ **97.** $c = 5x + 20$
99. a. $c = 14.95m + 629.99$ **b.** 988.79
101. a. When there are no head waves, the ship can travel at
18 knots.   **b.** $-\frac{1}{2}$ knot/ft   **c.** $y = -\frac{1}{2}x + 18$
105. 42 ft, 45 ft, 48 ft, 51 ft

ARE YOU READY? 3.6 (page 240)

1. $\frac{4}{5}$ **2.** $x + 5$ **3.** $y = 6x - 44$ **4.** $\frac{29}{4}$

SELF CHECK 3.6

1. $y = -2x + 5$ **2.** $y = -\frac{10}{13}x + \frac{2}{13}$ **3. a.** $y = 2$ **b.** $x = -1$
4.   **5.** $F = \frac{9}{5}C + 32$ **6.** $c = 5n + 12$

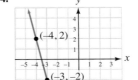
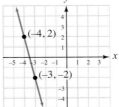

STUDY SET SECTION 3.6 (page 246)

1. point–slope, sub, times, minus, one   **3. a.** point–slope
b. slope–intercept   **5. a.** $(-2, -3)$ **b.** $\frac{5}{6}$ **c.** $y + 3 = \frac{5}{6}(x + 2)$
7. $(67, 170), (79, 220)$ **9.** $5, -1, +, 2, 3$
11. point–slope, slope–intercept   **13.** $y - 1 = 3(x - 2)$
15. $y + 1 = \frac{4}{5}(x + 5)$ **17.** $y = 2x - 1$ **19.** $y = -5x - 37$
21. $y = -3x$ **23.** $y = \frac{1}{5}x - 1$ **25.** $y = -\frac{4}{3}x + 4$
27. $y = -\frac{11}{6}x - \frac{7}{3}$ **29.** $y = 2x + 5$ **31.** $y = -\frac{1}{2}x + 1$
33. $y = 5$ **35.** $y = \frac{1}{10}x + \frac{1}{2}$ **37.** $x = -8$ **39.** $y = \frac{1}{2}x$
41. $x = 4$ **43.** $y = 5$

45.
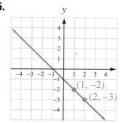

47.
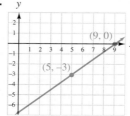

5.
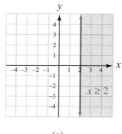

      (a)   (b)

6. $x + 15y \le 150$

49.
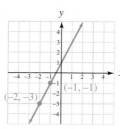

51.
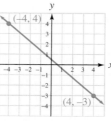

STUDY SET SECTION 3.7 (page 255)

1. inequality **3.** satisfies **5.** half-planes **7.** Yes
9. dashed, solid **11.** The half-plane opposite that in which the test point lies **13. a.** Yes **b.** No **c.** No **d.** Yes
15. a. Is less than **b.** Is greater than or equal to
c. Is less than or equal to **d.** Is possibly greater than **17.** $=, <$
19. Yes **21.** No **23.** No **25.** Yes

53. $y = \frac{1}{4}x - \frac{5}{4}$ **55.** $y = 12$ **57.** $y = -\frac{1}{4}x + \frac{7}{8}$
59. $y = -\frac{2}{3}x + 2$ **61.** $y = 8x + 4$ **63.** $x = -3$ **65.** $y = 7x - 11$
67. $y = -4x - 9$ **69.** $y = \frac{2}{7}x - 2$ **71.** $y = \frac{1}{10}x$ **73.** $x = -\frac{1}{8}$
75. $y = 1.7x - 2.8$ **77.** $h = 3.9r + 28.9$
79. $y = -\frac{2}{5}x + 4, y = -7x + 70, x = 10$

81. a. $y = -40m + 920$ **b.** 440 yd³ **83.** $l = \frac{25}{4}r + \frac{1}{4}$

85. a. $y = -\frac{3}{10}x + \frac{283}{10}$ or $y = -0.3x + 28.3$ **b.** 16.3 gal
91. 17 in. by 39 in.

27.
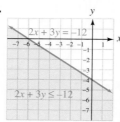

29.
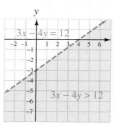

ARE YOU READY? 3.7 (page 249)

1. False **2.** True **3.**
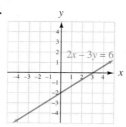

4. a. Below **b.** On **c.** Above

31.
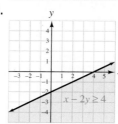

33.
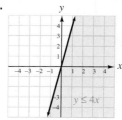

SELF CHECK 3.7

1. a. Not a solution **b.** Solution **c.** Solution **d.** Solution
2.
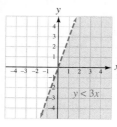

3.
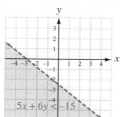

35.
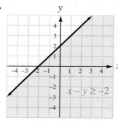

37.
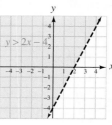

4.

39.
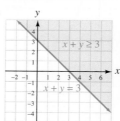

41.
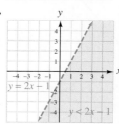

43.
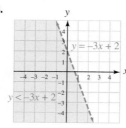

45.
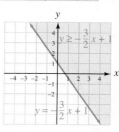

47.

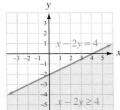

49.

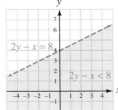

73. a.

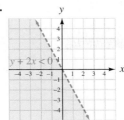

b.

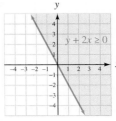

51.

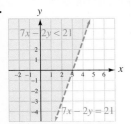

53.

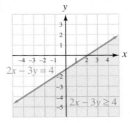

75. No **77.** (2, 7), (4, 6), (9, 2); answers may vary.

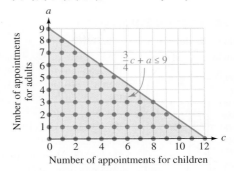

Number of appointments for children

79. (10, 10), (20, 10), (10, 20); Answers may vary

55.

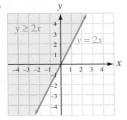

57.

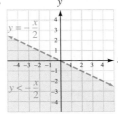

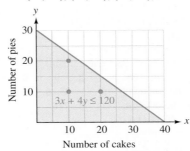

59.

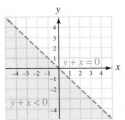

61.

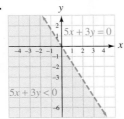

81. (40, 30), (30, 40), (40, 20); Answers may vary

63.

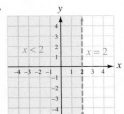

65.

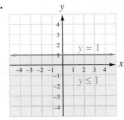

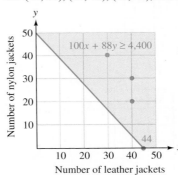

87. $t = \dfrac{A - P}{Pr}$

89. $15x + 22$

67.

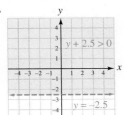

69.

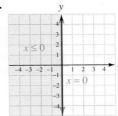

ARE YOU READY? 3.8 (page 258)

1. 17 **2.** (3, 5), (3, 0) **3.** (8, 4), (−3, 4) **4. a.** 5 **b.** 2

SELF CHECK 3.8

1. Domain: $\{-5, -1, 6, 8\}$; range: $\{-5, 2, 10\}$
2. a. Not a function, $-1 \rightarrow 4$ and $-1 \rightarrow 5$ **b.** Function; domain: $\{-6, 4, 5\}$; range: $\{-6, 5, 8\}$ **c.** Function; domain: $\{1, 3, 4, 9\}$; range: $\{4, 9\}$ **3. a.** -5 **b.** 5 **c.** 3 **4.** 3, 79

71. a.

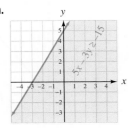

b.

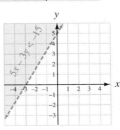

5.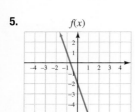

6.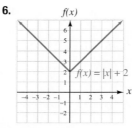

7. a. Function   **b.** Not a function   **8.** $140

STUDY SET SECTION 3.8 (page 266)

1. relation   **3.** domain, range   **5.** value

7.

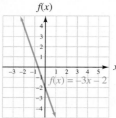

Domain	Range
1992	4.25
1994	
1996	4.75
1998	5.15
2000	
2002	
2004	
2006	
2008	6.55
2010	7.25

9. 33   **11.** of   **13.** 4, 5, 4, 5
15. Domain: $\{-6, -1, 6, 8\}$; range: $\{-10, -5, -1, 2\}$
17. Domain: $\{-8, 0, 6\}$; range: $\{9, 50\}$
19. Yes; domain: $\{10, 20, 30\}$; range: $\{20, 40, 60\}$
21. No; (4, 2), (4, 4), (4, 6) (Answers may vary)
23. Yes; domain: $\{1, 2, 3, 4, 5\}$; range: $\{7, 8, 15, 16, 23\}$
25. No; (-1, 0), (-1, 2)

27. No; (3, 4), (3, -4) or (4, 3), (4, -3)
29. Yes; domain: $\{-3, 1, 5, 6\}$; range: $\{-8, 0, 4, 9\}$
31. No, (3, 4), (3, -4) or (4, 3), (4, -3)   **33.** Yes; domain: $\{-2, -1, 0, 1\}$; range: $\{7, 10, 13, 16\}$ **35. a.** 3   **b.** -9   **c.** 0
d. 199   **37. a.** 0.32   **b.** 18   **c.** 2,000,000   **d.** $\frac{1}{32}$ **39. a.** 7
b. 14   **c.** 0   **d.** 1   **41. a.** 0   **b.** 990   **c.** -24   **d.** 210
43. a. 36   **b.** 0   **c.** 9   **d.** 4   **45.** 1.166

47.

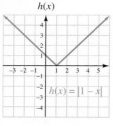

x	f(x)
-2	4
-1	1
0	-2
1	-5

49.

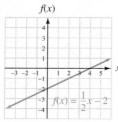

x	h(x)
-2	3
-1	2
0	1
1	0
2	1
3	2
4	3

51.

53.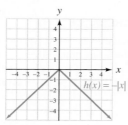

55. Yes   **57.** No; (3, 4), (3, -1) (Answers may vary)
59. No; (0, 2), (0, -4) (Answers may vary)

61. No; (3, 0), (3, 1) (Answers may vary)   **63.** $f(x) = |x|$
65. $900   **67.** 78.5 ft², 1,256.6 ft²   **69.** Yes   **77.** 80 lb of regular coffee

CHAPTER 3 REVIEW (page 270)

1.

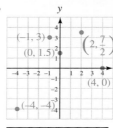

2. (158, 21.5)   **3.** Quadrant III
4. (0, 0)   **5.** (1, 4); 36 square units
6. a. 2,500; week 2   **b.** 1,000
c. 1st week and 5th week
7. Yes

8.

x	y	(x, y)
-2	-6	(-2, -6)
-8	3	(-8, 3)

9. $y = x^2 + 1$ and $y - x^3 = 0$ **10. a.** True   **b.** False
11.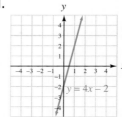

12.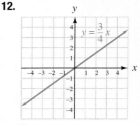

13.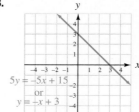

14.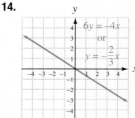

15. About $190

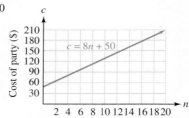

16. a. False   **b.** True   **17.** (-3, 0), (0, 2.5)
18. (0, 25,000); the equipment was originally valued at $25,000. (10, 0); in 10 years, the sound equipment had no value.
19. x-intercept: (-2, 0);   **20.** x-intercept: $\left(\frac{13}{5}, 0\right)$;
y-intercept: (0, 4)   y-intercept: $\left(0, -\frac{13}{4}\right)$

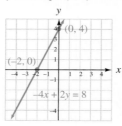

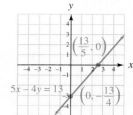

21. 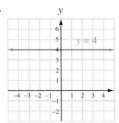   **22.**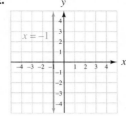

23. $\frac{1}{4}$ **24.** $-\frac{7}{8}$ **25.** -7 **26.** $-\frac{3}{2}$

27.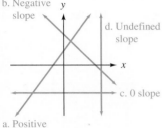

b. Negative slope
d. Undefined slope
c. 0 slope
a. Positive slope

28. $\frac{3}{4}$ **29.** 8.3%   **30.** 1.5 gal/yr   **31.** They are neither.

32. $-\frac{7}{5}$ **33.** $m = \frac{3}{4}$; y-intercept: $(0, -2)$

34. $m = -4$; y-intercept: $(0, 0)$ **35.** $m = \frac{1}{8}$; y-intercept: $(0, 10)$

36. $m = -\frac{7}{5}$; y-intercept: $\left(0, -\frac{21}{5}\right)$

37. $y = -4x - 1$ **38.** $y = \frac{3}{2}x - 3$

39. $m = 3$; y-intercept: $(0, -5)$

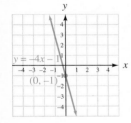   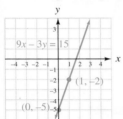

40. a. $c = 300w + 75{,}000$ **b.** 90,600 copies   **41.** Parallel

42. Perpendicular

43. $y = 3x + 2$ **44.** $y = -\frac{1}{2}x - 3$

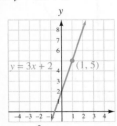   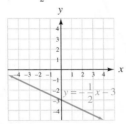

45. $y = \frac{2}{3}x + 5$ **46.** $y = -8$ **47.** $f = -35x + 450$

48. a. $P = \frac{3}{2}t + 310$ **b.** 400 parts per million

49. a. Yes   **b.** Yes   **c.** Yes   **d.** No   **50.** $=, >$

51. 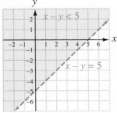   **52.**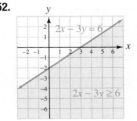

53. 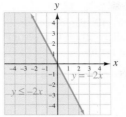   **54.**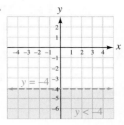

55. a. True   **b.** False   **c.** False

56. $(2, 4), (5, 3), (6, 2)$; answers may vary

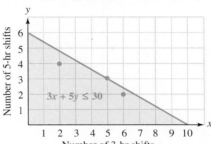

57. Domain: $\{-5, 0, 4, 7\}$; range: $\{-11, -3, 4, 9\}$

58. Domain: $\{-6, 1, 2, 15\}$; range: $\{-8, -2, 9\}$

59. Yes; domain: $\{1, 4, 8\}$; range: $\{0, 6, 9\}$

60. Yes; domain: $\{2, 3, 5, 6\}$; range: $\{1, 4\}$

61. Yes; domain: $\{3, 5, 7, 9\}$; range: $\{9, 25, 49, 81\}$

62. No; $(-1, 2), (-1, 4)$ **63.** Yes; domain: $\{-1, 0, 1, 2\}$; range: $\{6\}$

64. No; $(4, 4), (4, 6)$ **65.** domain, range   **66.** $f(x)$ **67.** -3

68. 0   **69.** 21   **70.** $-\frac{7}{4}$ **71.** -5 **72.** 37   **73.** -2

74. -8 **75.** No; $(1, 0.5), (1, 4)$, (answers may vary)   **76.** Yes

77.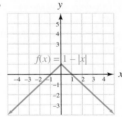

x	$f(x)$
0	1
1	0
3	-2
-1	0
-3	-2

78. $1{,}004.8$ in.^{3}

CHAPTER 3 TEST (page 279)

1. a. axis, axis   **b.** solution   **c.** linear   **d.** slope   **e.** function

2. 10 dogs   **3.** 60 dogs   **4.** 1 day before and the 3rd day of the holiday   **5.** 50 dogs were in the kennel when the holiday began.

6.

7. $A(2, 4), B(-3, 3), C(-2, -3),$ $D(4, -3), E(-4, 0), F(3.5, 1.5)$

8. a. III   **b.** IV

9. Yes

10.

x	y	(x, y)
2	1	$(2, 1)$
-6	3	$(-6, 3)$

11. a. False   **b.** True   **12.**

13. x-intercept: $(3, 0)$; y-intercept: $(0, -2)$

14.

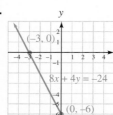

15. $\frac{8}{7}$ **16.** -1 **17.** 0
18. 10% **19.** Perpendicular
20. Parallel **21.** -15 ft per mi
22. 25 ft per mi

23.

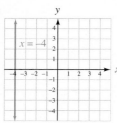

24.

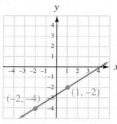

25. $m = -\frac{1}{2}$; $(0, 4)$ **26.** $y = 7x + 19$ **27.** $y = -2x - 5$
28. a. $v = -1,500x + 15,000$ **b.** \$3,000 **29.** Yes
30. $y = -\frac{1}{5}T + 41$ **31. a.** Yes **b.** No **c.** No **32.** Yes

33.

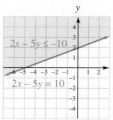

34. Domain: $\{-4, 0, 1, 5\}$;
range: $\{-8, 3, 12\}$
35. Yes; domain: $\{1, 2, 3, 4\}$;
range: $\{1, 2, 3, 4\}$
36. No; $(-3, 9)$, $(-3, -7)$;
37. Yes; domain: $\{6, 7, 8, 9, 10\}$;
range: $\{5\}$ **38.** No; $(2, 6)$, $(2, 2)$
39. No; $(2, 3.5)$, $(2, -3.5)$; (answers
may vary) **40.** No; $(-2, 2)$,
$(-2, -1)$; (answers may vary)
41. -13 **42.** 756
43. $C(45) = 28.50$; it costs \$28.50 to
make 45 calls.

44.

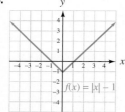

CUMULATIVE REVIEW CHAPTERS 1–3 (page 281)

1. $2^2 \cdot 3^3$ **2.** 0.004 **3. a.** True **b.** True **c.** True **4.** -15
5. -0.77 **6.** -945 **7.** 30 **8.** 2 **9.** 32 **10.** $500 - x$
11. $3, -2$ **12. a.** $2x + 8$ **b.** $-2x + 8$ **13.** $4a + 10$
14. $-63t$ **15.** $4b^2$ **16.** 0 **17.** 4 **18.** $-160a$ **19.** $-3y$
20. $7x - 12$ **21.** 6 **22.** 2.9 **23.** 9 **24.** -19 **25.** $\frac{1}{7}$
26. 1 **27.** $-\frac{55}{6}$ **28.** No solution, contradiction **29.** -99
30. $-\frac{1}{4}$ **31.** 1,100 **32.** $h = \frac{S - 2\pi r^2}{2\pi r}$ **33.** $3\frac{1}{8}$ in., $\frac{39}{64}$ in.^{2}
34. 45°

35.

	% acid	Liters	Amount of acid
50% solution	0.50	x	$0.50x$
25% solution	0.25	$13 - x$	$0.25(13 - x)$
30% mixture	0.30	13	$0.30(13)$

36. 7.5 hr **37.** 80 lb candy corn, 120 lb gumdrops
38. $(-\infty, 48]$ **39.** $(0, \infty)$

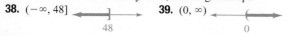

40. I and II **41.** No
42.

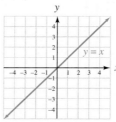

43.

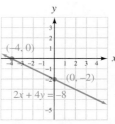

44. 0 **45.** $-\frac{10}{7}$ **46.** $\frac{7}{12}$ **47.** $\frac{2}{3}$, $(0, 2)$ **48.** $y = -2x + 1$
49. $y + 9 = -\frac{7}{8}(x - 2)$; $y = -\frac{7}{8}x - \frac{29}{4}$ **50.** Yes
51.

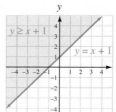

52.

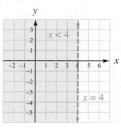

53. 78 **54.** No

ARE YOU READY? 4.1 (page 284)

1. Not a solution
2.

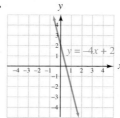

3.

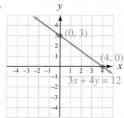

4. Parallel

SELF CHECKS 4.1

1. Not a solution
2. $(-2, 1)$

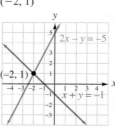

3. No solution

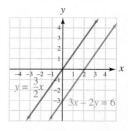

4. Infinitely many solutions

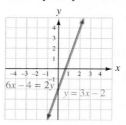

5. No solution

STUDY SET SECTION 4.1 (page 290)

1. system **3.** intersection **5.** consistent, inconsistent
7. a. True **b.** True **9. a.** $-5, 2$ **b.** $3, 3, (0, -2)$ **11.** No
solution; independent **13.** A solution **15.** A solution

17. Not a solution   **19.** Not a solution   **21.** Not a solution
23. A solution   **25.** (3, 2)

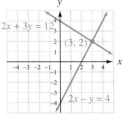

27. (−1, 5)   **29.** No solution

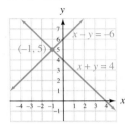   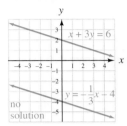

31. No solution   **33.** Infinitely many solutions

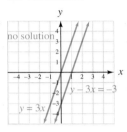   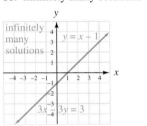

35. Infinitely many solutions

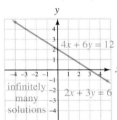

37. 1 solution   **39.** Infinitely many
solutions   **41.** No solution
43. 1 solution   **45.** (1, 3)
47. No solution

49. (−2, 0)   **51.** No solution

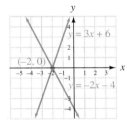   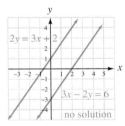

53. (3, −1)   **55.** (3, 0)

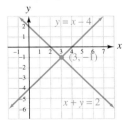   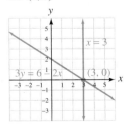

57. (−4, 0)   **59.** (4, −6)

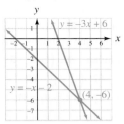   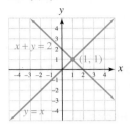

61. (5, −2)   **63.** (1, 1)

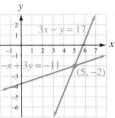   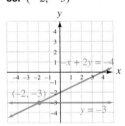

65. Infinitely many solutions   **67.** (−6, 1)

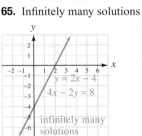   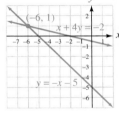

69. (−2, −3)   **71.** (4, −4)

   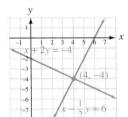

73. May '09; about 70 million   **75. a.** Houston, New Orleans,
St. Augustine   **b.** St. Louis, Memphis, New Orleans
c. New Orleans   **77. a.** The incumbent; 7%   **b.** November 2
c. The challenger; 3   **79.** (6, 4), (6, 8), (12, 4), (12, 8); yes
87. $[-3, \infty)$

89. $(-\infty, 2]$

ARE YOU READY? 4.2 (page 294)

1. 1   **2.** $y = 2x + 3$ **3.** 18   **4.** 17   **5.** $3x$

SELF CHECKS 4.2

1. (3, 1)   **2.** (−8, 2)   **3.** (5, 0)   **4.** $\left(\frac{18}{7}, \frac{8}{7}\right)$ **5.** (−3, −3)
6. No solution   **7.** Infinitely many solutions

STUDY SET SECTION 4.2 (page 301)

1. substituting   **3.** $y = -3x$ **5.** $x + 3(x - 4) = 8$
7. Substitute 3 for a in the second equation.   **9. a.** No   **b.** ii
11. $3x, 4, -2, -2, -6, -2, -6$ **13.** (2, 4)   **15.** (3, 0)

89. 1 **91.** $\frac{64s^2}{81t^4}$ **93.** $\frac{32v^{25}}{u^{10}}$ **95.** $\frac{9}{y^8}$ **97.** $-15y$ **99.** $\frac{h^{20}}{16}$ **101.** $\frac{1}{x^6}$

103. $\frac{c^{12}}{d^{27}}$ **105.** 15 **107.** $\frac{9}{4g^2}$ **109.** $\frac{125}{d^6}$ **111.** $\frac{x^{28}}{y^{20}}$ **113.** $\frac{32x^{15}}{y^{10}}$

115. t^{10} **117.** $-\frac{4t^2}{s^5}$ **119.** $\frac{1}{x^3}$ **121. a.** $\frac{1}{8}$ **b.** $-\frac{1}{8}$ **c.** $-\frac{1}{8}$ **d.** $\frac{1}{8}$

123. a. $\frac{4x}{y^2}$ **b.** $\frac{1}{16x^2y^2}$ **c.** $\frac{4y}{x^2}$ **d.** $\frac{xy}{16}$

125.

Type of Sound	Intensity
Front row rock concert	10^{-1}
Normal conversation	10^{-6}
Vacuum cleaner	10^{-4}
Military jet takeoff	10^{2}
Whisper	10^{-10}

129. $-\frac{3}{2}$ **131.** $y = \frac{3}{4}x - 5$

ARE YOU READY? 5.3 (page 369)

1. 100 **2.** 4,528 **3.** $\frac{1}{10}$ **4.** 0.0622

SELF CHECKS 5.3

1. a. 4,880,000 **b.** 0.0098 **2. a.** 9.3×10^7 **b.** 9.055×10^{-5}
c. 8.5×10^{-2} **3.** 1.0414×10^9 **4.** 3.3×10^{-22} g

STUDY SET SECTION 5.3 (page 374)

1. scientific, standard **3.** right, left **5. a.** positive **b.** negative
7. a. 7.7 **b.** 5.0 **c.** 8 **9. a.** $(5.1 \times 1.5)(10^9 \times 10^{22})$
b. $\frac{8.8}{2.2} \times \frac{10^{30}}{10^{19}}$ **11.** 1, 10, integer **13.** 230 **15.** 812,000
17. 0.00115 **19.** 0.000976 **21.** 6,001,000 **23.** 2.718
25. 0.06789 **27.** 0.00002 **29.** 2.3×10^4 **31.** 1.7×10^6
33. 6.2×10^{-2} **35.** 5.1×10^{-6} **37.** 5.0×10^9
39. 3.0×10^{-7} **41.** 9.09×10^8 **43.** 3.45×10^{-2}
45. 9.0×10^0 **47.** 1.1×10^1 **49.** 1.718×10^{18}
51. 1.23×10^{-14} **53.** 7.3×10^5 **55.** 2.018×10^{17}
57. 7.3×10^{-5} **59.** 3.602×10^{-19} **61.** 7.14×10^5; 714,000
63. 4.032×10^{-3}; 0.004032 **65.** 4.0×10^{-4}; 0.0004
67. 3.0×10^4; 30,000 **69.** 4.3×10^{-3}; 0.0043
71. 3.08×10^{-2}; 0.0308 **73.** 2.0×10^5; 200,000
75. 7.5×10^{-11}; 0.000000000075 **77.** $9.038030748 \times 10^{15}$
79. $1.734152992 \times 10^{-12}$ **81.** 2.57×10^{13} mi
83. 197,000,000 mi²; 109,000,000,000,000,000 mi²;
14,600,000 mi² **85.** 4.5×10^{-10} oz **87.** g, x, u, v, i, m, r
89. 3.3×10^{-1} km/sec **91.** 3.09936×10^{16} ft
93. 3.04×10^{11} dollars
95. 1.0×10^6, 1.0×10^9, 1.0×10^{12}, 1.0×10^{15}, 1.0×10^{18}
101. 5 **103.** $c = 30t + 45$

ARE YOU READY? 5.4 (page 376)

1. 3 terms **2.** 6 **3.** $5b^4$ **4.** -26

SELF CHECKS 5.4

1. a. A trinomial in one variable of degree 2 written in descending
powers of x; terms: x^2, $4x$, -16; coefficients: 1, 4, -16; degree of
terms: 2, 1, 0 **b.** A binomial in two variables of degree 7 written in
descending powers of s and ascending powers of t; terms: $-14s^5t$, s^4t^3;
coefficients: -14, 1; degree of terms: 6, 7 **2.** 33 **3.** 55 cans **4.** 16

5.

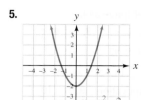

6.

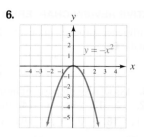

7.

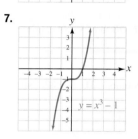

STUDY SET SECTION 5.4 (page 382)

1. polynomial **3.** one, descending, two, ascending
5. monomial, binomial, trinomial **7.** evaluate **9. a.** Yes **b.** No
c. No **d.** Yes **e.** Yes **f.** Yes **11.**

Term	Coefficient	Degree
$8x^2$	8	2
x	1	1
-7	-7	0

Degree of the polynomial: 2

13.

Term	Coefficient	Degree
$8a^6b^3$	8	9
$-27ab$	-27	2

Degree of the polynomial: 9
15. a. $5x^3 + 3x^2 + x - 9$ **b.** $x^2 - 2xy + y^2$ **17.** Binomial
19. Trinomial **21.** Monomial **23.** Binomial **25.** Trinomial
27. None of these **29.** None of these **31.** Trinomial **33.** 4th
35. 2nd **37.** 1st **39.** 4th **41.** 12th **43.** 0th **45.** 18th
47. 3rd **49. a.** 3 **b.** 13 **51. a.** -6 **b.** -8 **53. a.** 7 **b.** 34
55. a. -11.6 **b.** -40.2 **57. a.** 28 **b.** 4 **59. a.** 2 **b.** 0
61. 72 **63.** 19 **65.** -35 **67.** -257

69.

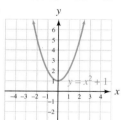

71.

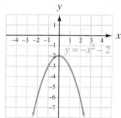

73.

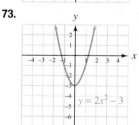

75.

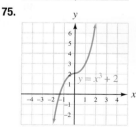

77.

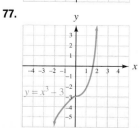

79.

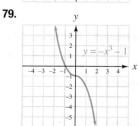

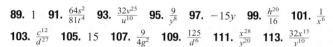

81. 91 cantaloupes **83.** 63 ft **85.** 28.6 billion downloads
87.

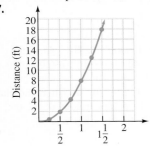

93. $[-3, \infty)$ 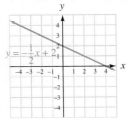 **95.** x^{18} **97.** y^9

-3

ARE YOU READY? 5.5 (page 385)

1. $17x$ **2.** $1.2a^3$ **3.** $5t^2u$ **4.** Does not simplify
5. $-4b^2 + 9b - 1$ **6.** -8

SELF CHECKS 5.5

1. a. $9m^4$ **b.** x **c.** $1.1s^3t + 0.3s^2t$ **d.** $\frac{11}{8}c^5 - \frac{4}{15}d^5 - 8$
2. a. $7a^2 + 5a - 1$ **b.** $\frac{9}{4}b^3 - \frac{3}{10}b - 3$ **c.** $11x^2 - 2xy - 2y^2$
3. $(29h^2 - 15h)$ in. **4.** $6q^2 - 8q + 2$ **5. a.** $7a^3 - 4a^2 + 12$
b. $x^2y - 8x - 8y$ **6. a.** $3p^2 - 8p + 15$
b. $-12m^3 + 6m^2 + 9m$ **7.** $0.6q^2 - 0.3q$
8. $\$(7,000x + 220,000)$

STUDY SET SECTION 5.5 (page 391)

1. polynomials **3.** Like **5.** combine **7. a.** $5x^2$ **b.** $14m^3$
c. $7a^3b$ **d.** $6cd + 4c^2d$ **9. a.** $-5x^2 + 8x - 23$
b. $5y^4 - 3y^2 + 7$ **11.** $4x^2, 2x, 1, 10x^2, 4$ **13.** $12t^2$
15. $20x^2 - 19x$ **17.** $x^2 + x$ **19.** $\frac{13}{15}x^2 - \frac{1}{8}x$ **21.** $1.3x^3$
23. $2st$ **25.** $-ab$ **27.** $-4x^3y + x^2y + 5$ **29.** $5q^2 - 4q - 5$
31. $y^3 + \frac{19}{20}y^2 + \frac{1}{3}$ **33.** $0.7p - 0.9q$ **35.** $7x^2 + xy + 2y^2$
37. $(3x^2 + 6x - 2)$ yd **39.** $(7x^2 + 5x + 6)$ mi **41.** $5x^2 + x + 11$
43. $-3a^2 + 7a + 7$ **45.** $10z^3 + z - 2$
47. $-x^3y^2 + 4x^2y + 5x + 6$ **49.** $2a^2 + a - 3$
51. $-5h^3 + 5h^2 + 30$ **53.** $\frac{1}{24}s^8 - \frac{19}{20}s^7$ **55.** $b^2 + 4ab - 2$
57. $x^2 + 6x + 2$ **59.** $4s^2 - 4s + 7$ **61.** $9a^3 - 8a^2 + 28a - 11$
63. $0.6x^3 + 1.2x^2 + 1.3x - 0.3$ **65.** $-9x^2 - 3x + 1$
67. $t^3 + 3t^2 + 6t - 5$ **69.** $13a^2 + a$ **71.** $3y^5 - 6y^4 + 1.2$
73. $10r^4 - 4r$ **75.** $-0.14f^2 + 0.25f + 2.09$ **77.** $\frac{5}{4}r^4 + \frac{11}{9}r^2 - 2$
79. $9c^2 - 6c - 14$ **81.** $19.4h^3 + 11h^2$ **83.** $-5r^2t - 9rt + 30$
85. $6x^2 + x - 5$ **87.** $\frac{7}{12}c^2 - \frac{1}{2}cd + d^2$ **89.** $7x + 4$
91. $-1.3t^2 + 0.7t + 0.6$ **93.** $-48u^3$ **95.** $5d^2 + 14d$
97. $7x^3y^2 - 2x^2y - 2x + 15$ **99.** $3x + 1$
101. $9x^3 + 2x^2 - 7x + 6$ **103. a.** $-19x^2 + 3x + 10$
b. $3x^2 - 9x - 10$ **105. a.** $(x^2 - 8x + 12)$ ft **b.** $(x^2 + 2x - 8)$ ft
107. $(2a^2 + 6a + 5)$ in. **109. a.** $(22t + 20)$ ft **b.** 108 ft
117. 180° **119.**

$y = -\frac{1}{2}x + 2$

ARE YOU READY? 5.6 (page 394)

1. $50a$ **2.** $10x - 15$ **3.** $28y + 56$ **4.** x^{14} **5.** -30
6. $9x^2 + 3x + 2$

SELF CHECKS 5.6

1. a. $18t^2$ **b.** $60d^{11}$ **c.** $4y^{14}$ **d.** $-30a^7b^8$ **2. a.** $220x^6 + 22x^5$
b. $20c^5 - 45c^3 - 40c^2$ **c.** $s^6t^4 - s^5t^5 + s^4t^6 - 7s^3t^2$
d. $6w^{12} - 12w^6$ **3.** $(3n^5 + 2n^4 - 9n^3)$ m^2 **4.** $9y^2 - 33y - 12$
5. a. $y^2 + 4y + 3$ **b.** $6a^2 + a - 2$ **c.** $16x^2 + x - \frac{3}{8}$
d. $10y^6 - 39by^3 + 14b^2$ **6.** $6a^6 - 5a^4 - 3a^3 + a^2 + a$
7. a. $6x^3 - 8x^2 + 7x + 10$ **b.** $-4x^4 + 8x^3 + 8x^2 - 12x - 3$
8. $-6y^3 - 14y^2 + 12y$

STUDY SET SECTION 5.6 (page 400)

1. monomials, binomials **3.** first, outer, inner, last **5. a.** each,
each **b.** any, third **7. a.** $6x^2 + x - 12$ **b.** $5x^4 + 8ax^2 + 3a^2$
9. $8, n^3, 72n^5$ **11.** $2x, 5, 5, 4x, 15x, 11x$ **13.** $5m^2$ **15.** $12x^5$
17. $6c^6$ **19.** $-24b^6$ **21.** $8x^5y^5$ **23.** $-2a^{11}$ **25.** $3x^2 + 12x$
27. $-4t^3 + 28t$ **29.** $-6x^5 + 2x^4 - 2x^3$ **31.** $\frac{5}{8}t^8 + 5t^4$
33. $-12x^4z - 4x^2z^3 - 4x^3z^2 + 4x^2z$ **35.** $6x^{14} - 72x^{13}$
37. $(7h^2 + 3h)$ in.^{2} **39.** $(4w^2 - 2w)$ ft^2 **41.** $y^2 + 8y + 15$
43. $m^2 - 3m - 54$ **45.** $4y^2 + 23y - 35$ **47.** $12x^2 - 28x + 15$
49. $7.6y^2 - 5.8y + 1$ **51.** $18m^2 - 10m + \frac{8}{9}$ **53.** $t^4 - 7t^2 + 12$
55. $12a^2 - 5ab - 2b^2$ **57.** $x^3 - x + 6$
59. $4t^3 + 11t^2 + 18t + 9$ **61.** $2x^3 + 7x^2 - 16x - 35$
63. $r^4 - 5r^3 + 2r^2 - 7r - 15$ **65.** $x^3 - 3x + 2$
67. $12x^3 + 17x^2 - 6x - 8$ **69.** $8x^3 - 12x^2 - 8x$
71. $-3a^3 + 3ab^2$ **73.** $18a^6 - 12a^5$ **75.** $x^3 - 6x^2 + 5x + 12$
77. $30x^2 - 17x + 2$ **79.** $6x^4 + 8x^3 - 14x^2$ **81.** $2t^2 + 2t - 24$
83. $6a^4 + 5a^3 + 5a^2 + 10a + 4$ **85.** $9t^2 + 15st - 6s^2$ **87.** $2a^{10}$
89. $16a^2 - 2ar - \frac{15}{16}r^2$ **91.** $a^2 + 2ab + b^2$
93. $x^4 + 11x^3 + 26x^2 - 28x - 24$ **95.** $9x^4 - 18x^3 + 54x^2$
97. $4y^3 + 40y^2 + 84y$ **99.** $0.12p^9 - 1.8p^7$
101. $16.4p^2q^2 - 24.6p^2q + 41pq^2$
103. $-3x^3 + 25x^2y - 56xy^2 + 16y^3$ **105. a.** $x^2 + 3x + 2$
b. $x^3 - 8$ **107. a.** Does not simplify **b.** $-18x^3z^8$
109. a. $-x^2 + 2x$ **b.** $6x^4 - 9x^3 + 3x^2$ **111. a.** $13a + 1$
b. $72a^3 + 6a^2 - 6a$ **113.** $(6x^2 + x - 1)$ cm^2
115. $(0.785x^2 - 0.785)$ in.^{2} **117.** $(2x^3 - 4x^2 - 6x)$ in.^{3}
125. a. 1 **b.** Undefined **c.** $-\frac{2}{3}$ **d.** 0

ARE YOU READY? 5.7 (page 403)

1. $x^2 + 4x + 4$ **2. a.** Base: $x + 4$; exponent: 2 **b.** Base: $x - 1$;
exponent: 3 **3.** $a^2 + 10a + 25$ **4.** $a^2 - 25$

SELF CHECKS 5.7

1. a. $r^2 + 12r + 36$ **b.** $49g^2 - 28g + 4$ **c.** $v^2 + 1.6v + 0.64$
d. $w^8 - 3w^4y + \frac{9}{4}y^2$ **2. a.** $b^2 - 16$ **b.** $25m^2 - 81$ **c.** $s^2 - \frac{9}{16}$
d. $c^6 - 4d^2$ **3.** $n^3 - 9n^2 + 27n - 27$ **4. a.** $7a^2 + 4a$
b. $11x^2 - 3x - 24$ **c.** $-3a^2 + 16a - 97$ **5.** $(72a^2 - 2)$ ft^2

STUDY SET SECTION 5.7 (page 409)

1. products **3. a.** square, Twice, first **b.** second, square
5. $x, 4, 4, 8x$ **7.** $s, 5, 25$ **9.** $x^2 + 2x + 1$ **11.** $m^2 - 12m + 36$
13. $16x^2 + 40x + 25$ **15.** $49m^2 - 28m + 4$ **17.** $1 - 6y + 9y^2$
19. $y^2 + 1.8y + 0.81$ **21.** $a^4 + 2a^2b^2 + b^4$ **23.** $s^2 + \frac{3}{2}s + \frac{9}{16}$
25. $x^2 - 9$ **27.** $4p^2 - 49$ **29.** $9n^2 - 1$ **31.** $c^2 - \frac{9}{16}$

33. $0.16 - 81m^4$ **35.** $25 - 36g^2$ **37.** $x^3 + 12x^2 + 48x + 64$
39. $n^3 - 18n^2 + 108n - 216$ **41.** $8g^3 - 36g^2 + 54g - 27$
43. $a^3 + 3a^2b + 3ab^2 + b^3$ **45.** $-x^2 + 20x - 8$
47. $4x^2 - 5x - 11$ **49.** $-80d^3 + 40d^2 - 5d$ **51.** $4d^5 - 4dg^6$
53. $(2x^2 - 2)$ yd^2 **55.** $(9x^2 + 6x + 1)$ ft^2 **57.** $4v^6 - 32v^3 + 64$
59. $12x^3 + 36x^2 + 27x$ **61.** $16f^2 - 0.16$
63. $r^4 + 20r^2s + 100s^2$ **65.** $6x - 2$ **67.** $d^8 + \frac{1}{2}d^4 + \frac{1}{16}$
69. $d^2 - 49$ **71.** $4a^2 - 12ab + 9b^2$ **73.** $n^2 - 36$ **75.** $36m + 36$
77. $8m^3 + 12m^2n + 6mn^2 + n^3$ **79.** $25m^2 - 12m + \frac{36}{25}$
81. $r^4 - 2r^2s^2 + s^4$ **83.** $x^2 - 4x + 4$ **85.** $r^2 + 4r + 4$
87. $n^4 - 8n^3 + 24n^2 - 32n + 16$ **89.** $17y^2 + 2y - 60$
91. $13x^2 - 8x + 5$ **93.** $f^2 - 16f + 64$ **95.** $36b^2 - \frac{1}{4}$
97. $4y^2 + 6y - 1$ **99.** $36 - 24d^3 + 4d^6$
101. $8e^3 + 12e^2 + 6e + 1$ **103.** $64x^2 + 48x + 9$
105. a. x^2y^2 **b.** $x^2 + 2xy + y^2$ **107. a.** $4b^4d^2$
b. $4b^4 + 4b^2d + d^2$ **109.** $(x^2 + 12x + 36)$ in.^{2}
111. $\pi hR^2 - \pi hr^2$ **117.** $\frac{5}{6}$ **119.** $\frac{21}{40}$

ARE YOU READY? 5.8 (page 411)

1. a. $\frac{2}{5}$ **b.** a^2 **2.** $\frac{a+b}{d}$ **3.** 36 **4.** $2x^2$

SELF CHECKS 5.8

1. a. $6y^2$ **b.** $\frac{d^4}{4c^3}$ **2. a.** $10h + 1$ **b.** $2s^3 - \frac{s^2t}{11} + 4t^2$ **3.** $x + 4$
4. $4x - 3 + \frac{6}{2x+3}$ **5.** $3x^2 + 2x - 4$ **6.** $x + 3$ **7.** $(9x + 3)$ in.

STUDY SET SECTION 5.8 (page 417)

1. monomial **3.** binomial **5.** Divide, multiply, subtract, bring
down **7.** quotient, dividend **9.** $7x^2, x^3, 7x^2, 5, 2, 7, 2, 2, 4x^3, 5, 7$
11. $5x^4 + 0x^3 + 2x^2 + 0x - 1$ **13.** x^3 **15.** $\frac{4h^2}{3}$ **17.** $-\frac{1}{5d^4}$
19. $\frac{10}{s}$ **21.** $\frac{x^2}{5y^4}$ **23.** $\frac{4r}{y^5}$ **25.** $2x + 1$ **27.** $\frac{1}{a^3} - \frac{1}{a} + 1$
29. $\frac{h^2}{4} + \frac{2}{h}$ **31.** $3s^5 - 6s^2 + 4s$ **33.** $c^3 + 3c^2 - 2c - \frac{5}{c}$
35. $5y - \frac{6}{x} + \frac{1}{xy}$ **37.** $x + 6$ **39.** $x - 2$ **41.** $x + 1 + \frac{-1}{2x+3}$
43. $2x - 3 + \frac{-1}{3x-1}$ **45.** $2x - 1$ **47.** $2x + 1$ **49.** $a - 5$
51. $x + 1$ **53.** $2x - 3$ **55.** $9b + 7$ **57.** $y + 12 + \frac{1}{y+1}$
59. $3a^5 - \frac{2b^3}{a}$ **61.** $2x^2 + 2x + 1$ **63.** $2x^5 - 8x^2$
65. $3a - 2$ **67.** $5m^5$ **69.** $b + 3$ **71.** $x + 3$ **73.** $x^2 - x + 1$
75. $-\frac{13}{3rs^3}$ **77.** $-2w^2 - \frac{1}{w^4}$ **79.** $9 - \frac{6}{m}$
81. $y^2 + 2y + 5 + \frac{10}{y-2}$ **83.** $\frac{x}{5} - \frac{2}{5x^2}$ **85.** $x^2 - 2x + 1$
87. $x + 1 + \frac{10}{x+5}$ **89.** $3x^2y - 2x - \frac{1}{y}$ **91.** $a - 12 + \frac{4}{a-5}$
93. $a^2 + a + 1$ **95.** $2x^2 + x + 1 + \frac{2}{3x-1}$ **97.** $\frac{x^2}{2y^{10}}$
99. $3m - 8$ **101. a.** $4x - 4 - \frac{5}{4x}$ **b.** $4x - 5$ **103.** $(x - 6)$ in.
105. $(2x^2 - x + 3)$ in. **111.** $y = -\frac{11}{6}x - \frac{7}{3}$

CHAPTER 5 REVIEW (page 420)

1. a. Base n, exponent 12 **b.** Base $2x$, exponent 6 **c.** Base r,
exponent 4 **d.** Base $y - 7$, exponent 3 **2. a.** m^5 **b.** $-3x^4$
c. $(x + 8)^2$ **d.** $\left(\frac{1}{2}pq\right)^3$ **3.** 7^{12} **4.** m^2n^2 **5.** y^{21} **6.** $81x^4$
7. b^9 **8.** $-b^{12}$ **9.** $256s^{10}$ **10.** $4.41x^4y^2$ **11.** $(-9)^{15}$
12. a^{23} **13.** $\frac{1}{8}x^{15}$ **14.** $\frac{x^{12}}{9y^2}$ **15.** $(m - 25)^{12}$ **16.** $125yz^4$
17. a^{11} **18.** c^5d^5 **19.** $64x^{12}$ in.^{3} **20.** y^4 ft^2 **21.** 1 **22.** 1
23. 3 **24.** $\frac{1}{1,000}$ **25.** $-\frac{1}{25}$ **26.** $\frac{1}{t^6}$ **27.** $8x^5$ **28.** $-\frac{6}{y}$

29. $\frac{8}{49}$ **30.** x^{14} **31.** $-\frac{27}{r^9}$ **32.** $\frac{1}{16z^2}$ **33.** $\frac{8c}{9d^5}$ **34.** t^{30}
35. w^{22} **36.** $\frac{f^{40}}{4^{10}}$ **37.** 7.2×10^8 **38.** 9.37×10^{15}
39. 9.42×10^{-9} **40.** 1.3×10^{-4} **41.** 1.8×10^{-4}
42. 8.53×10^5 **43.** $126,000$ **44.** 0.00000003919 **45.** 2.68
46. 57.6 **47.** $3.0 \times 10^{-4}; 0.0003$ **48.** $1.6 \times 10^8; 160,000,000$
49. $6,570,000,000; 6.57 \times 10^9$ **50.** $1.0 \times 10^5 = 100,000$
51. a. 4 **b.** $3x^3$ **c.** $3, -1, 1, 10$ **d.** 10 **52. a.** 7th, monomial
b. 3rd, monomial **c.** 2nd, binomial **d.** 5th, trinomial **e.** 6th,
binomial **f.** 4th, none of these **53.** $3, -13$ **54.** 8 in.
55.   **56.**

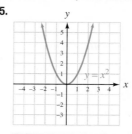

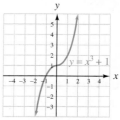

x	-2	-1	0	1	2
y	4	1	0	1	4

x	-2	-1	0	1	2
y	-7	0	1	2	9

57. $13y^3$ **58.** $-4a^3b + a^2b + 6$ **59.** $\frac{7}{12}x^2 - \frac{3}{4}xy + y^2$
60. $6.7c^5 + 8.1c^4 - 2.1c^3$ **61.** $25r^6 + 9r^3 + 5r$
62. $3.7a^2 + 6.1a - 17.6$ **63.** $4r^3s - 7r^2s^2 - 7rs^3 - 2s^4$
64. $\frac{5}{8}m^4 - m^3$ **65.** $-z^3 + 2z^2 + 5z - 17$ **66.** $(x^2 + x + 3)$ in.
67. $4x^2 + 2x + 8$ **68.** $8x^3 - 7x^2 + 19x$ **69.** $10x^3$
70. $-6x^{10}z^5$ **71.** $120b^{11}$ **72.** $2h^{14} + 8h^{11}$
73. $9n^4 - 15n^3 + 6n^2$ **74.** $x^2y^3 - x^3y^2$ **75.** $6x^6 + 12x^5$
76. $a^6b^4 - a^5b^5 + a^3b^6 - 7a^3b^2$ **77.** $x^2 + 5x + 6$
78. $2x^2 - x - 1$ **79.** $6t^2 - 6$ **80.** $6n^8 - 13n^6 + 5n^4$
81. $-5a^9 + 4a^7b + a^5b^2$ **82.** $6.6a^2 - 6.6$ **83.** $18t^2 + 3t - \frac{5}{9}$
84. $24b^2 - 34b + 11$ **85.** $8a^3 - 27$
86. $56x^4 + 15x^3 - 21x^2 - 3x + 2$ **87.** $8x^3 + 1$
88. a. $(6x + 10)$ in. **b.** $(2x^2 + 11x - 6)$ in.^{2}
c. $(6x^3 + 33x^2 - 18x)$ in.^{3} **89.** $a^2 - 6a + 9$
90. $m^3 + 6m^2 + 12m + 8$ **91.** $x^2 - 49$ **92.** $4x^2 - 0.81$
93. $4y^2 + 4y + 1$ **94.** $y^4 - 1$ **95.** $36r^4 + 120r^2s + 100s^2$
96. $-64a^2 + 48ac - 9c^2$ **97.** $80r^4s - 80s^5$
98. $36b^3 - 96b^2 + 64b$ **99.** $t^2 - \frac{3}{2}t + \frac{9}{16}$ **100.** $x^2 + \frac{8}{3}x + \frac{16}{9}$
101. $5x^2 + 19x + 3$ **102.** $24c^2 - 10c + 37$ **103.** $(x^2 - 4)$ in.^{2}
104. $(50x^2 - 8)$ in.^{2} **105.** $2n^3$ **106.** $-\frac{2x}{3y^2}$ **107.** $\frac{a^3}{6} - \frac{4}{a^4}$
108. $3a^3 + \frac{b}{5a} - \frac{5}{a^2}$ **109.** $x - 5$ **110.** $2x + 1$
111. $5x - 6 + \frac{4}{3x+2}$ **112.** $5y - 3$ **113.** $3x^2 - x - 4$
114. $3x^2 + 2x + 1 + \frac{2}{2x-1}$
115. $(y + 3)(3y + 2) = 3y^2 + 11y + 6$ **116.** $(2x^2 + 3x - 4)$ in.

CHAPTER 5 TEST (page 427)

1. a. base, exponent **b.** monomial, binomial, trinomial
c. degree **d.** special **2.** $2x^3y^4$ **3.** y^6 **4.** $\frac{1}{32}x^{21}$ **5.** 3.5 **6.** $\frac{2}{y^3}$
7. $\frac{1}{125}$ **8.** $(x + 1)^9$ **9.** y^{21} **10.** $\frac{b^3}{64a^3}$ **11.** $\frac{m^{12}}{64}$ **12.** $-6ab^9$
13. $1,000y^{12}$ in.^{3} **14.** 6.25×10^{18} **15.** 0.000093
16. $9.2 \times 10^3; 9,200$ **17.** Trinomial

Term	Coefficient	Degree
x^4	1	4
$8x^2$	8	2
-12	-12	0

Degree of the polynomial: 4

18. 5th degree **19.**

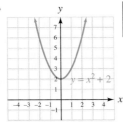

x	-2	-1	0	1	2
y	6	3	2	3	6

20. 0 ft; the rock hits the canyon floor 18 seconds after being dropped.
21. $\frac{1}{10}x^2 + \frac{7}{12}x - 2$ **22.** $-4a^3b + a^2b + 5$
23. $19.4h^3 - 11.1h^2 - 0.6$ **24.** $6b^3c - 2bc - 12$
25. $-3y^3 + 18y^2 - 17y + 35$ **26.** $(10a^2 + 8a - 20)$ in.
27. $10x^5y^{11}$ **28.** $-72b^8$ **29.** $3y^4 - 6y^3 + 9y^2$
30. $0.24p^{11} - 0.54p^8$ **31.** $\frac{3}{4}s^7t^{17} + 12s^4t^{10}$
32. $3x^2 - 11x - 20$ **33.** $12t^2 - 8t - \frac{3}{4}$
34. $7.6m^2 - 5.8m + 1$ **35.** $a^6 + a^3 - 42$
36. $2x^3 - 7x^2 + 14x - 12$ **37.** $1 - 100c^2$
38. $49b^6 - 42b^3t + 9t^2$ **39.** $2.2a^3 + 4.4a^2 - 33a$
40. $2x^2 + 2xy$ **41.** $\frac{a}{4b} - \frac{b}{2a}$ **42.** $x - 2$
43. $3x^2 + 2x + 1 + \frac{2}{2x-1}$ **44.** $(x - 5)$ ft
45. Yes; $(5m + 1)(m - 6) = 5m^2 - 29m - 6$
46. No; $(a + b)^2 = a^2 + 2ab + b^2$

CUMULATIVE REVIEW CHAPTERS 1–5 (page 429)

1. $2 \cdot 3^3 \cdot 5$ **2. a.** $a + b = b + a$ **b.** $(xy)z = x(yz)$ **3.** -37
4. 28 **5.** $18x$ **6.** 0 **7.** -2 **8.** 15 **9.** \$2.21 billion
10. 1.2 ft³ **11.** 30° **12.** \$6,250 **13.** Mutual fund: \$25,000;
bonds: \$20,000 **14.** $\left(-\infty, -\frac{11}{4}\right)$

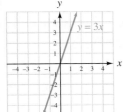

15. 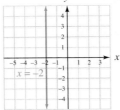 **16.**

17. $-\frac{4}{9}$ **18.** 0.75 million people per year or $\frac{3}{4}$ million people per
year **19.** $m = 3, (0, -2); y = 3x - 2$ **20.** Perpendicular
21. $y = -4x + 2$ **22.** No **23.** 26 **24.** Not a function; (1, 2),
(1, −2); answers may vary. **25.** No
26. (4, 1) **27.** $(-4, 3)$ **28.** $(-2, 4)$
29. Adult: \$61; child: \$51

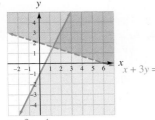

30.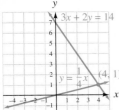
31. $9x^4y^8$ **32.** v^{22}
33. $a^2b^7c^6$ **34.** $\frac{64t^{12}}{27}$
35. $\frac{1}{16y^4}$ **36.** a^7 **37.** $-\frac{1}{25}$
38. $\frac{x^{10}}{a^{10}}$ **39.** 6.15×10^5
40. 1.3×10^{-6}

41.

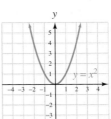

42. 1.5 in. **43.** $7c^2 + 7c$
44. $-6x^4 - 17x^2 - 68x + 11$
45. $6t^2 + 7st - 3s^2$
46. $12x^3 + 36x^2 + 27x$
47. $2x + 1$ **48.** $\frac{1}{8} - \frac{2}{x}$

ARE YOU READY? 6.1 (page 432)

1. $2 \cdot 3 \cdot 3 \cdot 3 = 2 \cdot 3^3$ **2.** a^6 **3.** $-x + 7$ **4.** 4
5. $4d^4 + 8d^2$ **6.** $x^3 + x^2 - 3x - 3$

SELF CHECKS 6.1

1. a. 2 **b.** 1 **c.** 15 **2. a.** $11c$ **b.** $21s^2t^2$ **3. a.** $6(f + 6)$
b. $6s^2t(4t - 7s)$ **c.** $y^3(y^3 - 10y - 1)$ **4. a.** $-(b^4 + 3b^2 - 2)$
b. $-(t - 9)$ **5.** $-11(4c - 5)$ **6.** $(y - 1)(2y + 7)$
7. a. $(3n + 2)(n^2 + 3)$ **b.** $(x - y)(7 + y)$
8. a. $(a + 11)(a^4 + 1)$ **b.** $(b - c)(b - 1)$ **9.** $(y + 3)(y^2 - 2)$
10. $4(t + s)(1 + z)$

STUDY SET SECTION 6.1 (page 440)

1. factor **3.** grouping **5. a.** 3 **b.** $7, h$ **c.** $3, y, y$
7. a. $2x + 4$ (Answers may vary) **b.** $x^3 + x^2 + x$ (Answers may
vary) **9.** $2x, x + 3$ **11. a.** 4 **b.** No **c.** $2; h$ **13.** 8
15. $b^2, 2, b - 6$ **17.** 2 **19.** 6 **21.** 7 **23.** 8 **25.** m^3
27. 5 **29.** $4c$ **31.** $9a^3$ **33.** $8a$ **35.** $3m^3n$ **37.** $x + 7$
39. $p - t$ **41.** $3(x + 2)$ **43.** $9(2m - 1)$ **45.** $d(d - 7)$
47. $5(3c^3 + 5)$ **49.** $8a(3 - 2a)$ **51.** $7(2x^2 - x - 1)$
53. $t^2(t^2 + t + 2)$ **55.** $3xy^2(7xy + 1)$ **57.** $-(a + b)$
59. $-(x^2 + x - 16)$ **61.** $-(-5 + x)$ or $-(x - 5)$
63. $-(-9 + 4a)$ or $-(4a - 9)$ **65.** $-3x(x + 2)$
67. $-4a^2(b - 3a)$ **69.** $-12x^2(2x^2 + 4x - 3)$
71. $-2ab^2(2a^2 - 7a + 5)$ **73.** $(x + 2)(y + 3)$
75. $(p - q)(m - 5)$ **77.** $(x + y)(2 + a)$ **79.** $(s - u)(r + 8w)$
81. $(7m - 2)(m^2 + 2)$ **83.** $(5x - 1)(x^2 + 2)$ **85.** $(b + c)(a + 1)$
87. $(r + 4s)(s - 1)$ **89.** $(2x - 3)(a + b)$ **91.** $(m - n)(p - q)$
93. $(m + 1)(5m^2 + 6)$ **95.** $(y^2 + 3)(y - 4)$
97. $a(x - 2)(x^2 + 5)$ **99.** $6(x^2 + 2)(x - 1)$
101. $(14 + r)(h^2 + 5)$ **103.** $11a^2(2a - 3)$ **105.** $(a + b)(x - 1)$
107. $3r^5(5r^3 - 6r - 10)$ **109.** $3(3p + q)(3m - n)$
111. $-20pt^2(3p + 4t)$ **113.** $-(2x - 5)$ **115.** $(3x - y)(2x - 5)$
117. $2z(x - 2)(x^2 + 16)$ **119.** $6uvw^2(2w - 9v)$
121. $(x + 1)(x^2 + 1)$ **123.** $-(3r - 2s + 3)$
125. a. $(5t + 6)(t^2 + 3)$ **b.** $3(t^3 + 2t^2 + 5t + 6)$
127. $(x^2 + 5)$ ft; $(x + 4)$ ft **129. a.** $V = \pi r^2\left(h_1 + \frac{1}{3}h_2\right)$
b. A 40 in.³ block of wax is needed. **135.** 12%

ARE YOU READY? 6.2 (page 443)

1. 1 **2.** $x^2 + 7x - 8$ **3.** 2 **4.** 2 **5.** 2 and 4 **6.** -3 and 5

SELF CHECKS 6.2

1. $(y + 2)(y + 5)$ **2.** $(p - 2)(p - 4)$ **3.** $(m + 7)(m - 6)$
4. $(q + 4)(q - 6)$ **5.** $-(x - 4)(x - 7)$ **6.** $(s + 7t)(s - t)$
7. $4m^3(m + 4)(m - 2)$ **8.** $t(t - 2)(t + 6)$ **9.** Prime trinomial
10. $(m + 7)(m - 6)$ **11.** $(q + 4t)(q - 6t)$
12. $3m(m - 8)(m - 1)$

STUDY SET SECTION 6.2 (page 452)

1. factors **3.** leading **5. a.** descending **b.** common **7.** 3, 5
9. a. No **b.** Yes **11. a.** They are both positive or both negative.
b. One will be positive, the other negative. **13.** $+3, -2$
15. $(x + 2)(x + 1)$ **17.** $(z + 4)(z + 3)$ **19.** $(m - 3)(m - 2)$
21. $(t - 7)(t - 4)$ **23.** $(x + 8)(x - 3)$ **25.** $(t - 3)(t + 16)$
27. $(a - 8)(a + 2)$ **29.** $(b - 12)(b + 3)$ **31.** $-(x + 5)(x + 2)$
33. $-(t + 6)(t - 5)$ **35.** $-(r + 9)(r - 6)$
37. $-(m - 7)(m - 11)$ **39.** $(a + 3b)(a + b)$
41. $(x - 7y)(x + y)$ **43.** $(r + 2s)(r - s)$ **45.** $(a - 3b)(a - 2b)$
47. $2(x + 3)(x + 2)$ **49.** $6(a - 4)(a - 1)$ **51.** $5(a - 3)(a - 2)$
53. $-z(z - 4)(z - 25)$ **55.** $(x - 4)(x - 20)$ **57.** $(y + 9)(y + 1)$
59. $r(r - 2)(r + 8)$ **61.** $r(r + 3x)(r + x)$ **63.** Prime
65. Prime **67.** $(x + 3)(5 + y)$ **69.** $2n(13n - 4)$
71. $(a - 5)(a + 1)$ **73.** $-(x - 22)(x + 1)$ **75.** $4(y - 1)(x + 7)$
77. $12b^2(b^2 - 4b - 3)$ **79.** $(r - 3)(r - 6)$
81. $-n^2(n - 30)(n + 2)$ **83.** $(x + 2y)(x + 2y) = (x + 2y)^2$
85. $(a - 6b)(a + 2b)$ **87.** $4x^2(x + 2)(x + 2) = 4x^2(x + 2)^2$
89. $(a - 45)(a - 1)$ **91.** Prime **93.** $(x + 2)(t + 7)$
95. $s^2(s + 13)(s - 2)$ **97.** $15(s^3 + 5)$ **99.** $(y - 14)(y + 1)$
101. $2(x - 2)(x - 4)$ **103. a.** $(x - 4)(x - 6)$

b. $(x - 12)(x + 2)$ **105.** $(x + 9)$ in., x in., $(x + 3)$ in. **113.** $\frac{1}{x^2}$

115. $\frac{1}{x^{10}}$

ARE YOU READY? 6.3 (page 454)

1. 3 **2.** $5y^2$ **3.** $6x^2 - 13x - 5$ **4.** $1(-3)$ and $-1(3)$
5. $6, -3, 7$ **6.** $(2b + 3)(5b - 1)$

SELF CHECKS 6.3

1. $(2x + 1)(x + 2)$ **2.** $(6b - 1)(b - 3)$ **3.** $(5t + 2)(t - 5)$
4. $(2x + 3y)(2x - y)$ **5.** $-2y(7y + 3)(y - 2)$
6. $(3a + 4)(5a - 1)$ **7.** $a^2(7a - 2)(3a - 1)$

STUDY SET SECTION 6.3 (page 462)

1. leading **3.** $5y, y, 1, 3$ **5.** $10x$ and x, $5x$ and $2x$
7. a. descending, GCF, coefficient **b.** $3s^2$ **c.** $-(2d^2 - 19d + 8)$
9. negative **11.** different **13.** $-13; -6, -8; -3, -7$
15. a. $12, 20, -9$ **b.** -108 **17.** $3t, 2, 4t + 3$
19. $(2x + 1)(x + 1)$ **21.** $(3a + 1)(a + 3)$ **23.** $(5x + 2)(x + 1)$
25. $(7x + 11)(x + 1)$ **27.** $(2x - 3)(2x - 1)$
29. $(4x - 1)(2x - 5)$ **31.** $(5t - 7)(3t - 1)$ **33.** $(6y - 1)(y - 2)$
35. $(3x + 7)(x - 3)$ **37.** $(5m + 3)(m - 2)$ **39.** $(7y - 1)(y + 8)$
41. $(11y - 4)(y + 1)$ **43.** $(3r + 2s)(2r - s)$
45. $(2x + 3y)(2x + y)$ **47.** $(8m + 3n)(m + 11n)$
49. $(5x + 3y)(3x - 2y)$ **51.** $2(3x + 2)(x - 5)$
53. $a(2a - 5)(4a - 3)$ **55.** $(2u + 3v)(u - 2v)$
57. $4(9y - 4)(y - 2)$ **59.** $(2t - 5)(3t + 4)$
61. $(3p - q)(5p + q)$ **63.** $(2t - 1)(2t - 7)$
65. $10(13r - 11)(r + 1)$ **67.** $(4y + 1)(2y - 1)$
69. $(18x - 5)(x + 2)$ **71.** $-y(y + 12)(y + 1)$ **73.** Prime
75. $-3x^2(2x + 1)(x - 3)$ **77.** $(3p - q)(2p + q)$
79. $3r^3(5r - 2)(2r + 5)$ **81.** $2mn(4m + 3n)(2m + n)$
83. Prime **85.** $-(4y - 3)(3y - 4)$ **87.** $(m + 7)(m - 4)$
89. $3a^2(2a + 5)$ **91.** $(x - 2)(x^2 + 5)$ **93.** $(5y - 3)(y - 1)$
95. $-2(x + 2)(x + 3)$ **97.** $3x^2y^2(4xy - 6y + 5)$
99. $(a - 5b)(a - 2b)$ **101.** $u^4(9u + 1)(u - 8)$
103. $(2x + 11)$ in., $(2x - 1)$ in. **109.** -49 **111.** 1 **113.** 49

ARE YOU READY? 6.4 (page 464)

1. $9y^2 + 12y + 4$ **2.** $m^2 - 81$ **3.** $64d^2$ **4.** $x^2 + 25$

SELF CHECKS 6.4

1. a. Yes **b.** No **c.** No **d.** No **2. a.** $(x + 9)^2$
b. $(4x - y)^2$ **3.** $x(7x - 1)^2$ **4. a.** $(c + 2)(c - 2)$
b. $(11 + t)(11 - t)$ **c.** Prime **d.** Prime
5. a. $(4y + 3)(4y - 3)$ **b.** $(3m + 8n^2)(3m - 8n^2)$
c. $(10 + a^2)(10 - a^2)$ or $-1(a^2 + 10)(a^2 - 10)$
6. $2(p + 10)(p - 10)$ **7.** $(a^2 + 9)(a + 3)(a - 3)$

STUDY SET SECTION 6.4 (page 470)

1. perfect **3. a.** $5x$ **b.** 3 **c.** $5x, 3$ **5. a.** x, y **b.** $-$
c. $+, x, y$ **7.** 1, 4, 9, 16, 25, 36, 49, 64, 81, 100, 121, 144, 169,
196, 225, 256, 289, 324, 361, 400 **9.** 2 **11.** $+, -$ **13.** Yes
15. No **17.** No **19.** Yes **21.** $(x + 3)^2$ **23.** $(b + 1)^2$
25. $(c - 6)^2$ **27.** $(2x + 3)^2$ **29.** $(6m + 5n)^2$ **31.** $(9x - 4y)^2$
33. $3(u - 3)^2$ **35.** $x(6x + 1)^2$ **37.** $(x + 2)(x - 2)$
39. $(x + 4)(x - 4)$ **41.** $(6 + y)(6 - y)$ **43.** $(t + 5)(t - 5)$
45. Prime **47.** Prime **49.** $(5t + 8)(5t - 8)$
51. $(9y + 1)(9y - 1)$ **53.** $(3x^2 + y)(3x^2 - y)$
55. $(4c + 7d^2)(4c - 7d^2)$ or $-(7d^2 + 4c)(7d^2 - 4c)$
57. $8(x + 2y)(x - 2y)$ **59.** $7(3a + 1)(3a - 1)$
61. $(9 + s^2)(3 + s)(3 - s)$ **63.** $(b^2 + 16)(b + 4)(b - 4)$
65. $(a^2 + 12b)(a^2 - 12b)$ **67.** $(3xy + 5)^2$
69. $16(t^2 + s^2)(t + s)(t - s)$ **71.** $(t - 10)^2$
73. $(3y - 4)^2$ **75.** $(z + 8)(z - 8)$ **77.** $25(m^2 + 1)(m + 1)(m - 1)$
79. $2a^3(3a + 7b)^2$ **81.** $x(x + 12)(x - 12)$ **83.** $(7t - 2s)^2$
85. $3(m^2 + n^2)(m + n)(m - n)$ **87.** $(5m + 7)^2$ **89.** $-(10t - 1)^2$
91. $6x^2(x + y)(x - y)$ **93.** Prime **95.** $(5x + 13)(5x - 13)$ or
$-(13 + 5x)(13 - 5x)$ **97.** $(x + 7)(x - 6)$ **99.** $(x + 3)(x - 3)$
101. $8a^2b(3a - 2)$ **103.** $-2(r - 10)(r - 4)$ **105.** $(x + 3)(x^2 + 4)$
107. $(2b - 5)^2$ **109.** $(p + q)^2$ **111.** $0.5g(t_1 + t_2)(t_1 - t_2)$
117. $3cd + \frac{3c}{2} + d$

ARE YOU READY? 6.5 (page 472)

1. $x^3 + 64$ **2.** $8h^3 - 1$ **3. a.** 27 **b.** 125 **4.** There are no two
integers whose product is 4 and whose sum is -2.

SELF CHECKS 6.5

1. $(h + 3)(h^2 - 3h + 9)$ **2.** $(2c - 1)(4c^2 + 2c + 1)$
3. $4(c + d)(c^2 - cd + d^2)$

STUDY SET SECTION 6.5 (page 475)

1. sum, cubes **3. a.** F, L **b.** $-, F^2, L^2$ **5.** $6n, 5$ **7.** 1, 8, 27,
64, 125, 216, 343, 512, 729, 1,000 **9.** No **11.** $2a$ **13.** $b + 3$
15. a. $x^3 + 8$ (Answers may vary.) **b.** $(x + 8)^3$
17. $(y + 5)(y^2 - 5y + 25)$ **19.** $(a + 4)(a^2 - 4a + 16)$
21. $(n + 8)(n^2 - 8n + 64)$ **23.** $(2 + t)(4 - 2t + t^2)$
25. $(a + 10b)(a^2 - 10ab + 100b^2)$
27. $(5c + 3d)(25c^2 - 15cd + 9d^2)$ **29.** $(a - 3)(a^2 + 3a + 9)$
31. $(m - 7)(m^2 + 7m + 49)$ **33.** $(6 - v)(36 + 6v + v^2)$
35. $(2s - t)(4s^2 + 2st + t^2)$ **37.** $(10a - w)(100a^2 + 10aw + w^2)$
39. $(4x - 3y)(16x^2 + 12xy + 9y^2)$ **41.** $2(x + 1)(x^2 - x + 1)$
43. $3(d + 3)(d^2 - 3d + 9)$ **45.** $x(x - 6)(x^2 + 6x + 36)$
47. $8x(2m - n)(4m^2 + 2mn + n^2)$ **49.** $(x + 4)^2$
51. $(3r + 4s)(3r - 4s)$ **53.** $(x - t)(y + s)$
55. $4(p + 2q)(p^2 - 2pq + 4q^2)$ **57.** $2ct^2(4c + 3t)(2c + t)$
59. $36(e^2 + 1)(e + 1)(e - 1)$ **61.** $7a^2b^2(5a - 2b + 2ab)$
63. $(6r + 5s)^2$ **65. a.** $(x + 1)(x - 1)$
b. $(x - 1)(x^2 + x + 1)$ **67. a.** $x(x + 2)$ **b.** $(x + 1)^2$
69. $(1,000 - x^3)$ in.^{3}; $(10 - x)(100 + 10x + x^2)$ **73.** Repeating
75. -3

ARE YOU READY? **6.6** (page 477)

1. a. 4 **b.** 3 **2.** No **3.** $3n^3 - 27n^2 - 210n$ **4.** $5cd^2$

SELF CHECKS **6.6**

1. $11a^2(a^2 + 1)(a + 1)(a - 1)$ **2.** $-2h^2(4h + 5)^2$
3. $(b + 1)(b + 2)(b^2 - 2b + 4)$ **4.** $6m(m^2 + m - 9)$
5. $3y(2y - 1)(y + 4)$

STUDY SET SECTION **6.6** (page 481)

1. product **3.** Factor out the GCF **5.** Perfect-square trinomial
7. Sum of two cubes **9.** Trinomial factoring **11.** Is there a
common factor? **13.** $14m, m$ **15.** $2(b + 6)(b - 2)$
17. $4p^2q^3(2pq^4 + 1)$ **19.** $2(2y + 1)(10y + 1)$
21. $8(x^2 + 1)(x + 1)(x - 1)$ **23.** $(c + 21)(c - 7)$ **25.** Prime
27. $-2x^2(x - 4)(x^2 + 4x + 16)$ **29.** $(c + d^2)(a^2 + b)$
31. $-(3x - 1)^2$ **33.** $-5m(2m + 5)^2$ **35.** $(2c + d)(c - 3d)$
37. $(p - 2)^2(p^2 + 2p + 4)$ **39.** $(x - a)(a + b)(a - b)$
41. $(ab + 12)(ab - 12)$ **43.** $(x + 5)(2x^2 + 1)$
45. $v^2(v^2 - 14v + 8)$ **47.** $2(3a - b)(3a + 7c)$
49. $2x(2ax + b)(2ax - b)$ **51.** $2(3x - 4)(x - 1)$
53. $y^2(2x + 1)^2$ **55.** $4m^2(m + 5)(m^2 - 5m + 25)$
57. $(a + 6)(a + 2)(a - 2)$ **59.** Prime
61. $2a^2(2a - 3)(4a^2 + 6a + 9)$ **63.** $27(x - y - z)$
65. $(x - t)(y + s)$ **67.** $x^6(7x + 1)(5x - 1)$
69. $5(x - 2)(1 + 2y)$ **71.** $(7p + 2q)^2$ **73.** $4(t^2 + 9)$
75. $(n + 3)(n - 3)(m^2 + 3)$
81.

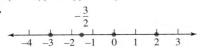

83.

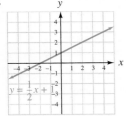

ARE YOU READY? **6.7** (page 482)

1. 0 **2.** 0 **3.** -4 **4.** 0 **5.** $(x - 3)(x + 2)$
6. $(3n + 2)(n - 1)$

SELF CHECKS **6.7**

1. $12, -\frac{6}{5}$ **2.** $-2, -3$ **3.** $-7, 7$ **4.** $0, 5$ **5.** $\frac{2}{3}, -4$ **6.** $-\frac{3}{2}$
repeated **7.** $0, \frac{2}{5}, -\frac{1}{2}$

STUDY SET SECTION **6.7** (page 487)

1. quadratic **3.** zero-factor, $0, 0$ **5. a.** Yes **b.** No **c.** Yes
d. No **7.** $-\frac{4}{5}$ **9. a.** Add 6 to both sides. **b.** Distribute the
multiplication by x and subtract 3 from both sides.
11. $0, x + 7, -7$ **13.** $p, p - 3, 0, 3, -2$ **15.** $3, 2$ **17.** $-7, 7$
19. $0, \frac{5}{2}$ **21.** $0, -\frac{10}{3}$ **23.** $0, 6, -8$ **25.** $1, -2, 3$
27. $12, 1$ **29.** $-3, 7$ **31.** $8, 1$ **33.** $-3, -5$ **35.** $-9, 9$
37. $-5, 5$ **39.** $-\frac{1}{2}, \frac{1}{2}$ **41.** $-\frac{7}{3}, \frac{7}{3}$ **43.** $0, 7$ **45.** $0, 16$
47. $0, 3$ **49.** $0, -\frac{8}{3}$ **51.** $-2, \frac{1}{3}$ **53.** $-\frac{3}{2}, 1$ **55.** $\frac{1}{5}, 1$
57. $-\frac{5}{2}, 4$ **59.** $-\frac{7}{2}$ repeated **61.** $\frac{5}{3}$ repeated **63.** $0, -1, -2$
65. $0, 9, -3$ **67.** $-\frac{9}{2}, \frac{9}{2}$ **69.** 8 repeated **71.** $\frac{5}{2}, -6$ **73.** $2, 10$

75. $0, -5, 4$ **77.** $-10, 10$ **79.** $3, 4$ **81.** $-\frac{1}{3}, 5$ **83.** $2, 7, 1$
85. $-3, -2$ **87.** $0, 3$ repeated **89.** $0, 2$ **91.** $-\frac{2}{3}, -\frac{3}{2}$
93. $0, -1, -\frac{1}{3}$ **95.** $0, -1, 2$ **97.** $\frac{2}{3}, -\frac{1}{5}$ **99.** $-\frac{11}{2}, \frac{11}{2}$ **101.** $\frac{1}{8}, 1$
103. a. $(x + 7)(x - 3)$ **b.** $-7, 3$ **105. a.** $(4n + 1)(3n - 2)$
b. $-\frac{1}{4}, \frac{2}{3}$ **113.** 15 min $\le t <$ 30 min

ARE YOU READY? **6.8** (page 490)

1. $A = lw$ **2.** $A = \frac{1}{2}bh$ **3.** $x + 1$ **4.** 3

SELF CHECKS **6.8**

1. Width: 5 m; length: 11 m **2.** Base: 3 yd; height: 10 yd
3. 23 and 24 **4.** 8 in., 15 in., and 17 in. **5.** 5 sec

STUDY SET SECTION **6.8** (page 495)

1. consecutive **3.** hypotenuse, legs **5.** ii. **7.** $20 = b(b + 5)$
9. a. A right triangle **b.** x ft; $(x + 1)$ ft **c.** 9 ft
11. $-16, 1, 0, 0, 3, -1$ **13.** Width: 3 ft; length: 6 ft **15.** 8 in.,
10 in. **17.** 3 ft by 9 ft **19.** Base: 6 cm; height: 5 cm
21. Foot: 4 ft; luff: 12 feet **23.** Kahne: 9; Riggs: 10 **25.** 12
27. $(11, 13)$ **29.** 10 yd **31.** 8 ft **33.** 5 m, 12 m, 13 m
35. 5 sec **37.** 4 sec **39.** 1 sec **41.** 8 **47.** $25b^2 - 20b + 4$
49. $s^4 + 8s^2 + 16$ **51.** $81x^2 - 36$

CHAPTER 6 REVIEW (page 499)

1. $5 \cdot 7$ **2.** $2^5 \cdot 3$ **3.** 7 **4.** $18a^3$ **5.** $3(x + 3y)$
6. $5a(x^2 + 3)$ **7.** $7s^3(s^2 + 2)$ **8.** $\pi a(b - c)$
9. $12x(2x^2 + 5x - 4)$ **10.** $xy^3z^2(x^4 + y^2z - 1)$
11. $-5ab(b - 2a + 3)$ **12.** $(x - 2)(4 - x)$ **13.** $-(a + 7)$
14. $-(4t^2 - 3t + 1)$ **15.** $(c + d)(2 + a)$ **16.** $(y + 6)(3x - 5)$
17. $(a + 1)(2a^2 - 1)$ **18.** $4m(n + 3)(m - 2)$ **19.** 1
20.

Factors of 6	Sum of the factors of 6
1(6)	7
2(3)	5
$-1(-6)$	-7
$-2(-3)$	-5

21. $(x + 6)(x - 4)$
22. $(x - 20)(x + 2)$
23. $(x - 5)(x - 9)$
24. Prime
25. $-(y - 8)(y - 7)$
26. $(y + 9)(y + 1)$
27. $(c + 5d)(c - 2d)$

28. $(m - 2n)(m - n)$ **29.** Multiply **30.** There are no two
integers whose product is 11 and whose sum is 7.
31. $5a^3(a + 10)(a - 1)$ **32.** $-4x(x + 3y)(x - 2y)$
33. $(2x + 1)(x - 3)$ **34.** $(7y + 5)(5y - 2)$
35. $-(3x + 5)(x - 6)$ **36.** $3p(6p + 1)(p - 2)$
37. $(4b - c)(b - 4c)$ **38.** Prime **39.** $(4x + 1)$ in., $(3x - 1)$ in.
40. The signs of the second terms must be negative. **41.** $(x + 5)^2$
42. $(3y - 4)^2$ **43.** $-(z - 1)^2$ **44.** $(5a + 2b)^2$
45. $(x + 3)(x - 3)$ **46.** $(7t + 11y)(7t - 11y)$
47. $(xy + 20)(xy - 20)$ **48.** $8a(t + 2)(t - 2)$
49. $(c^2 + 16)(c + 4)(c - 4)$ **50.** Prime
51. $(b + 1)(b^2 - b + 1)$ **52.** $(x - 6)(x^2 + 6x + 36)$
53. $(p + 5q)(p^2 - 5pq + 25q^2)$
54. $2x^2(2x - 3y)(4x^2 + 6xy + 9y^2)$ **55.** $2y^2(3y - 5)(y + 4)$
56. $5(t + u^2)(s^2 + v)$ **57.** $(j^2 + 4)(j + 2)(j - 2)$
58. $-3(j + 2)(j^2 - 2j + 4)$ **59.** $(x + 1)(20 + m)(20 - m)$
60. $3w^2(2w - 3)^2$ **61.** $2(t^3 + 5)$ **62.** Prime **63.** $z(x + 8y)^2$
64. $6c^2d(3cd - 2c - 4)$ **65.** $0, 6$ **66.** $\frac{7}{4}, -1$ **67.** $0, -2$
68. $-3, 3$ **69.** $-\frac{5}{12}, \frac{5}{12}$ **70.** $3, 4$ **71.** -7 repeated
72. $6, -4$ **73.** $1, \frac{1}{5}$ **74.** $0, -1, 2$ **75.** Width: 9 in.;
length: 11 in. **76.** 15 m **77.** $x + 1; x + 2; x + 2$

78. Jackson: 12 nominations; West: 10 nominations **79.** 5 m
80. 10 sec

CHAPTER 6 TEST (page 505)

1. a. greatest, common, factor **b.** product **c.** Pythagorean
d. difference **e.** binomials **2. a.** $45 = 3^2 \cdot 5; 30 = 2 \cdot 3 \cdot 5$
b. $15x^3$ **3.** $4(x + 4)$ **4.** $(q + 9)(q - 9)$
5. $5ab(6ab^2 - 4a^2b + 1)$ **6.** Prime **7.** $(x + 1)(2x + 3)$
8. $(x + 3)(x + 1)$ **9.** $-(x - 11)(x + 2)$ **10.** $x^2(x - 30)(x - 2)$
11. $(a - b)(9 + x)$ **12.** $(2a - 3)(a + 4)$ **13.** $2(3x + 5y)^2$
14. $(x + 2)(x^2 - 2x + 4)$ **15.** $15m^6(4m^2 - 3)$
16. $3(a - 3)(a^2 + 3a + 9)$ **17.** $(4x^2 + 9)(2x + 3)(2x - 3)$
18. $(a + 5)(a^2 + 1)$ **19.** $(a + 6)(a^3 - 4)$
20. $(5d + 4)(2d - 1)$ **21.** $8(m + 10)(m - 10)$ **22.** $(6n - 7)^2$
23. $(4r - 1)(2r - 3)$ **24.** Prime **25.** $(5x - 4)$ in.
26. $(x - 9)(x + 6); x^2 + 6x - 9x - 54 = x^2 - 3x - 54$
27. $-3, 2$ **28.** $-5, 5$ **29.** $0, \frac{1}{6}$ **30.** -3 repeated **31.** $\frac{1}{3}, -\frac{1}{2}$
32. $9, -2$ **33.** $0, -1, -6$ **34.** 6 ft by 9 ft **35.** 5 sec
36. Base: 6 in.; height: 11 in. **37.** 12, 13 **38.** 10
39. A quadratic equation is an equation that can be written in the
form $ax^2 + bx + c = 0; x^2 - 2x + 1 = 0.$ (Answers may vary.)
40. At least one of them is 0.

CUMULATIVE REVIEW CHAPTERS 1–6 (page 508)

1. About 35 beats/min difference **2.** $2 \cdot 5^3$ **3.** $\frac{24}{25}$ **4.** 0.992
5. a. False **b.** True **c.** True **6.** $\frac{5}{0}$ **7.** -39 **8.** -5
9. -27 **10.** \$20x **11.** 3 **12.** $8, -1, 9$ **13.** $-13y^2 + 6$
14. $3y + z$ **15.** $-\frac{3}{2}$ **16.** -2 **17.** 9 **18.** $-\frac{55}{6}$ **19.** 248 lb
20. 330 mi **21.** $I = Prt$ **22.** 12.6 in.² **23.** $t = \frac{A - P}{Pr}$
24. 22nd president, 24th president **25.** Los Angeles: 6 wk; Las
Vegas: 4 wk; Dallas: 7 wk **26.** 4 L **27.** 5 lb apple slices, 5 lb
banana chips **28.** $(-\infty, -2)$ **29.** Yes

30.
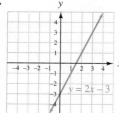

31. Vertical line **32.** They are the
same. **33.** An increase of 536,000
articles per year **34.** 1; $(0, -2)$
35. $y = 7x + 19$

36.
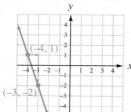

37.
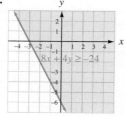

38. 17 **39.** Yes **40.**
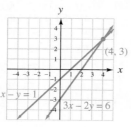

41. $\left(\frac{3}{4}, -2\right)$ **42.** $\left(-2, \frac{2}{3}\right)$ **43.** Newspaper: 8 tons; cardboard:
6 tons **44.** **45.** $-4y^5$

46. x^4y^{23} **47.** b^7 **48.** 2 **49.** 9.011×10^{-5} **50.** 1.7×10^6
51. 3 **52.** **53.** $-2x^2 - 4x + 5$
54. $8b^5 - 8b^4$
55. $3x^2 + 10x - 8$
56. $y^2 - 12y + 36$
57. $3ab - 2a - 1$
58. $2x + 1$
59. a. $(4x + 8)$ in.
b. $(x^2 + 4x + 3)$ in.²
c. $(x^3 + 4x^2 + 3x)$ in.³
60. $6x^5y$ **61.** $9b^2(b - 3)$ **62.** $(x + y)(a + b)$
63. $(u + 3)(u - 1)$ **64.** $(2x + 1)(5x - 2)$ **65.** $(2a - 3)^2$
66. $(3z + 1)(3z - 1)$ **67.** $(t - 2)(t^2 + 2t + 4)$
68. $3(b^2 - 2)(a + 1)(a - 1)$ **69.** $0, \frac{4}{3}$ **70.** $\frac{1}{2}, 2$ **71.** $0, -1, -2$
72. 9 in. by 12 in.

ARE YOU READY? **7.1** (page 512)

1. a. 0 **b.** Undefined **2. a.** $\frac{3}{4}$ **b.** $\frac{1}{9}$ **3.** $4(3x - 2)$
4. $(a + 4)(a - 4)$ **5.** $(5x + 2)(x - 5)$ **6.** -1

SELF CHECKS **7.1**

1. $\frac{13}{50}, -1$ **2. a.** -9 **b.** $-5, 5$ **c.** None **d.** None **3.** $\frac{4a^2}{3}$
4. a. $\frac{t - 5}{3}$ **b.** $\frac{x + 2}{x}$ **c.** $2x^3$ **5. a.** $\frac{2x + 3}{2x(2x + 5)}$ **b.** $(a + 3b)^3$
6. $\frac{4}{3}$ **7.** -1 **8. a.** $-\frac{m + 10}{m}$ **b.** Does not simplify

STUDY SET SECTION **7.1** (page 519)

1. rational **3.** undefined **5.** $\frac{6}{24} = \frac{1}{4}$ **7. a.** 1 **b.** -1 **c.** 1
d. Does not simplify **9.** $x, 1, x + 1, x + 3$ **11.** 4 **13.** 0
15. Undefined **17.** $-\frac{2}{11}$ **19.** $\frac{1}{6}$ **21.** Undefined **23.** 2
25. 0 **27.** None **29.** $\frac{1}{2}$ **31.** None **33.** $-6, 6$ **35.** $-2, 1$
37. 20 **39.** $\frac{5}{a}$ **41.** $\frac{3x^2}{2}$ **43.** $\frac{2x + 1}{3}$ **45.** $\frac{1}{3}$ **47.** $\frac{x + 2}{x - 4}$
49. $\frac{x + 1}{x}$ **51.** $\frac{m - n}{7(m + n)}$ or $\frac{m - n}{7m + 7n}$ **53.** $\frac{1}{2b + 1}$ **55.** $\frac{10}{3}$
57. $\frac{2x}{x - 6}$ **59.** -1 **61.** $-\frac{1}{2}$ **63.** $-\frac{1}{a + 1}$ **65.** $-\frac{5}{m + 5}$ **67.** $\frac{1}{a}$
69. $-\frac{x + 2}{x + 1}$ **71.** -6 **73.** $\frac{x + 1}{x - 1}$ **75.** $\frac{3x}{y}$ **77.** x^7 **79.** $\frac{4 - x}{4 + x}$ or
$-\frac{x - 4}{x + 4}$ **81.** 4 **83.** $\frac{3(x + 3)}{2x + 1}$ or $\frac{3x + 9}{2x + 1}$ **85.** $-\frac{3x + 11}{x + 3}$ **87.** $\frac{7c^2}{3d^2}$
89. Does not simplify **91.** $\frac{2u - 3}{u^3}$ **93.** $(2x + 3)^2$ **95.** 9
97. $\frac{3x}{5y}$ **99.** Does not simplify **101.** $\frac{2}{x - 9}$ **103.** $85\frac{1}{3}$
105. 2, 1.6, and 1.2 milligrams per liter
113. a. $(a + b) + c = a + (b + c)$ **b.** $ab = ba$

ARE YOU READY? **7.2** (page 522)

1. $\frac{3}{20}$ **2.** $\frac{9}{8}$ **3.** $\frac{11}{14}$ **4.** $x(1 - x)$

SELF CHECKS 7.2

1. a. $\frac{6(a+7)}{5a^4}$ **b.** $\frac{3a}{11}$ **2. a.** $\frac{(n-3)(3n-2)}{2}$ **b.** $-\frac{2(m+1)}{3m+1}$
3. a. 6 **b.** $4x+12$ **4.** $\frac{3b}{2a}$ **5.** $\frac{z+1}{z}$ **6.** $-a$ **7.** 600 yd^2
8. 36,000 beats per minute

STUDY SET SECTION 7.2 (page 528)

1. reciprocal **3. a.** numerators, denominators, reciprocal
b. AC, BD, D, C **5.** $-\frac{y^2}{y+1}$ **7.** 1 **9.** ft **11.** $\frac{3y}{14}$
13. $\frac{3(y+2)}{y^3}$ or $\frac{3y+6}{y^3}$ **15.** $\frac{20}{3n}$ **17.** $x^2 y^2$ **19.** $\frac{x}{5}$
21. $\frac{3}{2x}$ **23.** $x+1$ **25.** $-(x-2)$ or $-x+2$ **27.** $\frac{(x-2)^2}{x}$
29. $\frac{(m-2)(m-3)}{2(m+2)}$ **31.** 35 **33.** $3x+3$ **35.** $10y-16$
37. $\frac{36a-60}{a}$ **39.** $\frac{3}{2y}$ **41.** $\frac{3a}{5}$ **43.** $\frac{x^2}{3}$ **45.** $\frac{9p^3}{5}$ **47.** $\frac{5(a-2)}{4a^3}$
49. $-\frac{x+2}{3}$ **51.** $\frac{3x}{x+7}$ **53.** $-(m+5)$ or $-m-5$ **55.** $t+7$
57. $\frac{2(x-7)}{x+9}$ **59.** $\frac{1}{3}$ **61.** 1 **63.** $\frac{1}{12(2r-3s)}$ **65.** $\frac{4(n-1)}{3n}$
67. 450 ft **69.** $\frac{3}{4}$ gal **71.** $\frac{1}{2}$ mi per min **73.** 1,800 m per min
75. $\frac{b-3}{b}$ **77.** $\frac{1}{(x+1)^2}$ **79.** $\frac{3(a+3)^2}{2a^3}$ **81.** $\frac{d(6c-7d)}{6}$
83. $25h-15$ **85.** $n-1$ **87.** $\frac{5r^3}{2s^2}$
89. $\frac{7(p+2)}{3p^4}$ or $\frac{7p+14}{3p^4}$ **91.** $\frac{x-2}{x-3}$ **93.** $\frac{2x-3y}{y(2x+3y)}$ **95.** -2
97. a. $(x+2)^2$ **b.** $\frac{9}{16}$ **99. a.** $\frac{(x-3)^2}{x-2}$ **b.** $\frac{x-2}{4}$ **101.** $\frac{x^2}{10}$ ft^2
103. 4,380,000 **105.** 8 yd^2
107. $\frac{1}{2}$ mi per min **109.** $\frac{1}{4}$ mi^2 **115.** $w=6$ in., $l=10$ in.

ARE YOU READY? 7.3 (page 531)

1. $\frac{8}{11}$ **2.** $\frac{1}{3}$ **3.** x^2+5x+1 **4.** $\frac{1}{x-7}$ **5.** $2\cdot2\cdot2\cdot3\cdot x\cdot x$
6. $5(x+1)$

SELF CHECKS 7.3

1. a. $\frac{2x}{5}$ **b.** $\frac{3m-6}{23n}$ or $\frac{3(m-2)}{23n}$ **2. a.** $\frac{2}{3}$ **b.** $\frac{2c^2-11c}{(c-1)(c+2)}$ or
$\frac{c(2c-11)}{(c-1)(c+2)}$ **3.** $\frac{1}{n+4}$ **4. a.** $x-1$ **b.** $\frac{6y^2-y}{(y+3)(y-3)}$
5. a. $150y^3$ **b.** $a(a+3)$ **6. a.** $2x(x-6)$
b. $(m+3)(m-3)^2$ **7. a.** $\frac{21m}{60m^3}$ **b.** $\frac{2c^2+6c}{(c+1)(c+3)}$
8. $\frac{x^2+5x-24}{x(x-4)(x+8)}$

STUDY SET SECTION 7.3 (page 538)

1. denominator **3.** build **5.** numerators, denominator,
$A+B, D, A-B, D$ **7.** $\frac{4}{5}$ **9. a.** Twice **b.** Once
11. $3, 4a+1, 2, 4a+1, 2$ **13.** $\frac{11}{x}$ **15.** $\frac{x+5}{18}$ **17.** $\frac{1}{3a^2}$
19. $\frac{x+4}{y}$ **21.** $\frac{1}{r-5}$ **23.** 9 **25.** $\frac{x}{25}$ **27.** $\frac{m-6}{6m^2}$ **29.** $\frac{1}{t+2}$
31. $\frac{2}{w(w-9)}$ **33.** $\frac{1}{2}$ **35.** $2x-5$ **37.** $\frac{1}{y}$ **39.** 0 **41.** $6x$
43. $30a^3$ **45.** $3a^2 b^3$ **47.** $c(c+2)$ **49.** $12(x-1)$
51. $12(b+2)$ **53.** $8k(k+2)$ **55.** $(x+1)(x-1)$
57. $(x+1)(x+5)(x-5)$ **59.** $(2n+5)(n+4)^2$ **61.** $\frac{50}{10r}$
63. $\frac{8xy}{x^2 y}$ **65.** $\frac{27b}{12b^2}$ **67.** $\frac{3x^2+3x}{(x+1)^2}$ **69.** $\frac{x^2+9x}{x^2(x+5)}$
71. $\frac{t^2+14t+45}{4(t+2)(t+9)}$ **73.** $\frac{4y^2+12y}{4y(y-2)(y-3)}$ **75.** $\frac{36-3h}{3(h+9)(h-9)}$
77. $\frac{3}{t-7}$ **79.** $\frac{1}{c+d}$ **81.** $\frac{3}{4}$ **83.** $\frac{5a}{a+2}$ **85.** $\frac{2x}{3-x^2}$

87. $\frac{7n+1}{(n+4)(n-2)}$ **89.** $\frac{3}{r}$ **91.** $\frac{5}{9y}$ **93.** $-\frac{1}{3x-1}$ **95.** $3x-2$
97. a. $\frac{t}{6}$ **b.** $\frac{5t^2}{144}$ **c.** $\frac{1}{5}$ **99. a.** $\frac{4}{5}$ **b.** $\frac{m^2+8m+12}{25}$ **c.** $\frac{m+6}{m+2}$
101. $\frac{2x+6}{x+2}$ ft **109. a.** $I=Prt$ **b.** $A=\frac{1}{2}bh$ **c.** $P=2l+2w$

ARE YOU READY? 7.4 (page 540)

1. $\frac{20a}{16a^2}$ **2.** $2\cdot2\cdot3\cdot3\cdot x\cdot x\cdot x$ **3.** $\frac{11x}{9}$ **4.** $t-8$

SELF CHECKS 7.4

1. $\frac{19y}{14}$ **2.** $\frac{20-9z}{84z^2}$ **3.** $\frac{2}{5(x-5)}$ **4.** $\frac{6x+63}{(x+9)(x+8)}$
5. $\frac{b+3}{(b+2)(b+5)}$ **6.** $\frac{14y+ny}{n+4}$ **7.** $\frac{n-12}{n-8}$

STUDY SET SECTION 7.4 (page 546)

1. unlike **3. a.** $2\cdot2\cdot5\cdot x\cdot x$ **b.** $(x-2)(x+6)$
5. $(x+6)(x+3)$ **7.** $\frac{5}{5}$ **9.** $3x, 5, 15x, 15x, 35$ **11.** $\frac{13x}{21}$
13. $\frac{67a}{40}$ **15.** $\frac{7-2m}{m^2}$ **17.** $\frac{6-5p}{10p^2}$ **19.** $\frac{4t^2-33}{24t^3}$
21. $\frac{3-16c^2}{18c^4}$ **23.** $\frac{a+8}{2(a+2)(a-2)}$ **25.** $\frac{6a+9}{(3a+2)(3a-2)}$
27. $\frac{4a+1}{(a+2)^2}$ **29.** $\frac{6-3m}{5m(m-1)}$ **31.** $\frac{17t+42}{(t+3)(t+2)}$
33. $\frac{2x^2+11x}{(2x-1)(2x+3)}$ **35.** $\frac{14s+58}{(s+3)(s+7)}$ **37.** $\frac{2m^2+20m-6}{(m-2)(m+5)}$
39. $\frac{s^2+8s+4}{(s+4)(s+1)(s+1)}$ **41.** $\frac{2x+13}{(x-8)(x-1)(x+2)}$ **43.** $\frac{1}{a+1}$
45. $\frac{1}{(y+3)(y+4)}$ **47.** $\frac{5y+xy}{x-4}$ **49.** $\frac{8+xz}{x}$ **51.** $\frac{2}{a-4}$ **53.** $\frac{c+d}{7c-d}$
55. $\frac{1}{(x-1)(x-2)}$ **57.** $\frac{6d-3}{d-9}$ **59.** $\frac{xy-y+10}{x-1}$
61. $\frac{2b+1}{(b+1)(b+2)}$ **63.** $\frac{1}{g+2}$ **65.** $\frac{5y}{2}$ **67.** $\frac{35x^2+x+5}{5x(x+5)}$
69. $\frac{41}{30x}$ **71.** $\frac{2x^2-1}{x(x+1)}$ **73.** $\frac{y+4}{y-1}$ **75.** $\frac{2n+2}{15}$ **77.** $\frac{y^2+7y+6}{15y^2}$
79. $\frac{x+2}{x-2}$ **81.** $\frac{a^2 b-3}{a^2}$ **83.** $\frac{10a-14}{3a(a-2)}$ **85.** $\frac{17x+3}{x^2}$
87. $\frac{-4x-3}{x+1}$ or $-\frac{4x+3}{x+1}$ **89.** $\frac{11b}{12}$ **91. a.** $\frac{75+8x^2}{30x}$ **b.** $\frac{2}{3}$
93. a. $\frac{t^2+4t}{(t-5)(t+5)}$ **b.** $t+5$ **95.** $\frac{20x+9}{6x^2}$ cm
101. $8; (0, 2)$ **103.** 0

ARE YOU READY? 7.5 (page 549)

1. Division **2.** $\frac{3}{2}$ **3.** $2x$ **4.** $8a-10$

SELF CHECKS 7.5

1. $\frac{5y}{6}$ **2.** $\frac{10x+30}{6x^2-15x}$ **3.** $\frac{b}{a}$ **4.** $\frac{15x-60}{12x^2+20x}$ **5.** $-\frac{2}{n}$ **6.** $\frac{2x+4}{2x+5}$

STUDY SET SECTION 7.5 (page 555)

1. complex, complex **3.** single, division, reciprocal
5. a. $\frac{x-3}{4}$, yes **b.** $\frac{1}{12}-\frac{x}{6}$; no **7.** $\div$ **9.** $\frac{8}{9}$ **11.** $\frac{5x}{12}$ **13.** $\frac{x^2}{y}$
15. $\frac{n^3}{8}$ **17.** $\frac{10}{3a^3}$ **19.** $-\frac{x^2}{14}$ **21.** $\frac{5}{7}$ **23.** $\frac{3y+12}{4y^2-6y}$ **25.** $\frac{2-5y}{6}$
27. $\frac{24-c^2}{12}$ **29.** $\frac{5}{4}$ **31.** $\frac{1-3x}{5+2x}$ **33.** $\frac{1+x}{2+x}$ **35.** $\frac{3-x}{x-1}$
37. $\frac{x-12}{x+6}$ **39.** $a-7$ **41.** $\frac{5d^2+16d}{10d+10}$ **43.** $\frac{y}{x-2y}$ **45.** $\frac{1}{x+2}$
47. $\frac{1}{x+3}$ **49.** $\frac{q+p}{q}$ **51.** $18x$ **53.** $\frac{2c}{2-c}$ **55.** $\frac{r-1}{r+1}$ **57.** $\frac{b+9}{8a}$
59. $\frac{5x}{3}$ **61.** $\frac{32h-1}{96h+6}$ **63.** $\frac{m^2+n^2}{m^2-n^2}$ **65.** $\frac{8}{4c+5c^2}$ **67.** $\frac{t^3}{2}$
69. $\frac{s^2-s}{2+2s}$ **71.** $\frac{t+2}{t-3}$ **73.** $\frac{xy}{y+x}$ **75.** $-\frac{10x^3}{3}$ **77.** $\frac{x}{x-2}$

79. $\frac{d-3}{2d}$ **81.** $\frac{b-5ab}{3ab-7a}$ **83.** $2m-1$ **85.** $\frac{7}{6}$ **87.** $\frac{R_1R_2}{R_2+R_1}$

93. 1   **95.** $\frac{25}{16x^{12}}$

ARE YOU READY? 7.6 (page 557)

1. $18x$ **2.** $5x$ **3.** $-7, 8$ **4.** -8

SELF CHECKS 7.6

1. 1   **2.** 22   **3.** $3, -8$ **4.** No solution, 6 is extraneous   **5.** $\frac{5}{2}$

6. $S = \frac{RT - 10R}{e}$ **7.** $p = \frac{fq}{q-f}$

STUDY SET SECTION 7.6 (page 564)

1. rational   **3.** clear   **5. a.** Yes   **b.** No   **7. a.** $3, 0$
b. $3, 0$ **c.** $3, 0$ **9. a.** y **b.** $(x+2)(x-2)$ **11. a.** 3
b. $3x+18$ **13.** $2a, 2a, 2a, 2a, 2a, 4, 7, 4, 3$ **15.** 1   **17.** 0
19. $\frac{3}{5}$ **21.** 9   **23.** $-\frac{4}{3}$ **25.** $-\frac{12}{7}$ **27.** -48 **29.** $\frac{3}{10}$ **31.** $2, 4$
33. $-5, 2$ **35.** $-4, -5$ **37.** $3, -\frac{5}{3}$ **39.** No solution; 5 is
extraneous   **41.** No solution; -2 is extraneous   **43.** $\frac{5}{2}$ **45.** $0, 3$
47. $A = \frac{h(b+d)}{2}$ **49.** $r = \frac{E-IR}{I}$ **51.** $x = \frac{5yz}{5y+4z}$
53. $r = \frac{st}{s-t}$ **55.** $P = nrt$ **57.** $d = \frac{bc}{a}$ **59.** $a = \frac{b}{b-1}$
61. $L^2 = 6dF - 3d^2$ **63.** 6   **65.** 1   **67.** $-1, 6$ **69.** -40
71. No solution; -1 is extraneous   **73.** 7   **75.** 1   **77.** $-4, 3$
79. 1   **81.** 3   **83.** No solution; 2 is extraneous   **85.** $\frac{9}{40}$ **87.** 0
89. -3 **91.** $1, 2$ **93.** 7   **95. a.** $\frac{2a+3}{5}$ **b.** $-\frac{9}{4}$
97. a. $\frac{x^2-4x+2}{(x-2)(x-3)}$ **b.** 4   **99.** $R = \frac{HB}{B-H}$ **101.** $r = \frac{r_1r_2}{r_2+r_1}$
107. 20

ARE YOU READY? 7.7 (page 566)

1. $t = \frac{d}{r}$ **2.** $\frac{x}{5}$ **3.** $I = Prt$ **4.** 63

SELF CHECKS 7.7

1. 9   **2.** 4 mph   **3.** $\frac{3}{4}$ of the job   **4.** $3\frac{3}{7}$ hr   **5.** 1%

STUDY SET SECTION 7.7 (page 573)

1. motion, investment, work   **3.** iii   **5. a.** $\frac{1}{45}$ of the job per minute
b. $\frac{x}{4}$ **7. a.** $t = \frac{d}{r}$ **b.** $P = \frac{I}{rt}$ **9.** $\frac{x}{15}, \frac{x}{8}$ **11.** $6\frac{1}{9}$ days   **13.** 4
15. 2   **17.** 5   **19.** $\frac{2}{3}$ or $\frac{3}{2}$ **21.** 8   **23.** Garin: 16 mph; Armstrong:
26 mph   **25.** 1st: $1\frac{1}{2}$ ft per sec; 2nd: $\frac{1}{2}$ ft per sec   **27.** Canada
goose: 30 mph; great blue heron: 20 mph   **29.** $\frac{300}{255+x}, \frac{210}{255-x}$;
45 mph   **31.** $2\frac{6}{11}$ days   **33.** No, after the pipes are opened, the
swimming is scheduled to take place in 6 hours. It takes 7.2 hr
(7 hr 12 min) to fill the pool.   **35.** 8 hr   **37.** 20 min
39. $1\frac{4}{5}$ hr $= 1.8$ hr   **41.** Credit union: 4%; bonds: 6%
43. 7% and 8%   **47.** $(1, 3)$ **49.** Yes

ARE YOU READY? 7.8 (page 576)

1. $\frac{7}{9}$ **2. a.** ab **b.** bc **3.** 8.5   **4.** $-2, 9$

SELF CHECKS 7.8

1. a. $\frac{15}{2}$ **b.** $\frac{1}{4}$ **2.** No   **3.** 24   **4.** $-5, 6$ **5.** $187.50   **6.** 30 ft
7. 3 lb for $6.89   **8.** 66 ft

STUDY SET SECTION 7.8 (page 583)

1. ratio, rate   **3.** extremes, means   **5.** unit   **7.** equal, ad, bc
9. $2, 1,000, x$ **11.** $2.19, 1$ **13.** $x, 288, 18, 18, 16$ **15.** as, to
17. $\frac{4}{15}$ **19.** $\frac{3}{4}$ **21.** $\frac{5}{4}$ **23.** $\frac{1}{2}$ **25.** $\frac{1}{2}$ **27.** $\frac{25}{22}$ **29.** Yes
31. No   **33.** 4   **35.** 14   **37.** 0   **39.** $-\frac{3}{2}$ **41.** -2 **43.** -27
45. $2, -2$ **47.** $6, -1$ **49.** $-1, 16$ **51.** $-\frac{5}{2}, -1$ **53.** 15
55. 8   **57.** $-\frac{1}{3}, 2$ **59.** 2   **61.** $-\frac{27}{2}$ **63.** $-10, 10$ **65.** $-4, 3$
67. $\frac{26}{9}$ **69. a.** $-\frac{15}{8}$ **b.** $\frac{65}{8}$ **71. a.** $\frac{8}{5}$ **b.** $\frac{2}{3}, 4$ **73.** $62.50
75. 14 breaths   **77. a.** 462   **b.** $\frac{11}{12}$; 11:12   **79.** $309
81. 45,000 tweets   **83.** 568, 13, 14   **85.** Not exactly, but close
87. 140   **89.** 522 in.; 43.5 ft   **91.** 10 ft   **93.** 45 min for $25
95. 150 for $12.99   **97.** 6-pack for $1.50   **99.** Four 4-oz cartons
101. 39 ft   **103.** $46\frac{7}{8}$ ft   **105.** 8   **111.** 90%   **113.** 480

CHAPTER 7 REVIEW (page 587)

1. $4, -4$ **2.** $-\frac{3}{7}$ **3.** $\frac{1}{2x}$ **4.** $\frac{5}{2x}$ **5.** $\frac{x}{x+1}$ **6.** $a-2$ **7.** -1
8. $-\frac{1}{x+3}$ **9.** $\frac{x}{x-1}$ **10.** Does not simplify   **11.** $\frac{1}{x-y}$ **12.** $\frac{4}{3}$
13. x is not a common factor of the numerator and the denominator; x
is a term of the numerator.   **14.** 150 mg   **15.** $\frac{3x}{y}$ **16.** 96
17. $\frac{x-1}{x+2}$ **18.** $\frac{2x}{x+1}$ **19.** $\frac{3y}{2}$ **20.** $-x-2$ **21. a.** Yes
b. No   **c.** Yes   **d.** Yes   **22.** $\frac{1}{3}$ mi per min   **23.** $\frac{1}{3d}$ **24.** 1
25. $\frac{2x+2}{x-7}$ **26.** $\frac{1}{a-4}$ **27.** $9x$ **28.** $8x^3$ **29.** $m(m-8)$
30. $(5x+1)(5x-1)$ **31.** $(a+5)(a-5)$ **32.** $(2t+7)(t+5)^2$
33. $\frac{63}{7a}$ **34.** $\frac{2xy+x}{x(x-9)}$ **35.** $\frac{2b+14}{6(b-5)}$ **36.** $\frac{9r^2-36r}{(r+1)(r-4)(r+5)}$
37. $\frac{a-7}{7a}$ **38.** $\frac{x^2+x-1}{x(x-1)}$ **39.** $\frac{1}{t+1}$ **40.** $\frac{x^2+4x-4}{2x^2}$
41. $\frac{b+6}{b-1}$ **42.** $\frac{6c+8}{c}$ **43.** $\frac{14n+58}{(n+3)(n+7)}$ **44.** $\frac{4t+1}{(t+2)^2}$
45. $\frac{1}{(a+3)(a+2)}$ **46.** $\frac{17y-2}{12(y-2)(y+2)}$ **47.** Yes
48. $\frac{14x+28}{(x+6)(x-1)}$ units, $\frac{12}{(x+6)(x-1)}$ square units   **49.** $\frac{n^3}{14}$
50. $\frac{r+9}{8s}$ **51.** $\frac{1+y}{1-y}$ **52.** $\frac{21}{3a+10a^2}$ **53.** x^2+3 **54.** $\frac{y-5xy}{3xy-7x}$
55. 3   **56.** No solution; 5 is extraneous   **57.** 3   **58.** $2, 4$
59. 0   **60.** $-4, 3$ **61.** $T_1 = \frac{T_2}{1-E}$ **62.** $y = \frac{xz}{z-x}$ **63.** 3
64. 5 mph   **65.** $\frac{1}{4}$ of the job per hr   **66.** $5\frac{5}{6}$ days   **67.** 5%
68. 40 mph   **69.** No   **70.** Yes   **71.** $\frac{9}{2}$ **72.** 0   **73.** 7
74. $4, -\frac{3}{2}$ **75.** 255   **76.** 20 ft   **77.** 5 ft 6 in.   **78.** 250 for $98

CHAPTER 7 TEST (page 595)

1. a. rational   **b.** similar   **c.** proportion   **d.** build   **e.** factors
2. 10 words   **3.** 0   **4.** $-3, 2$ **5.** 3,360,000 or 3,360K bits per
minute   **6.** 5 is not a common factor of the numerator, and therefore
cannot be removed. 5 is a term of the numerator.   **7.** $\frac{8x}{9y}$ **8.** -7
9. $\frac{x+1}{2x+3}$ **10.** 1   **11.** $3c^2d^3$ **12.** $(n+1)(n+5)(n-5)$
13. $\frac{5y^2}{4}$ **14.** $\frac{x+1}{3(x-2)}$ **15.** $-\frac{x^2}{3}$ **16.** $\frac{1}{6}$ **17.** 3   **18.** $\frac{4n-5mn}{10m}$
19. $\frac{2x^2+x+1}{x(x+1)}$ **20.** $\frac{2a+7}{a-1}$ **21.** $\frac{c^2-4c+9}{c-4}$ **22.** $\frac{1}{(t+3)(t+2)}$
23. $\frac{12}{5m}$ **24.** $\frac{a+2s}{2as^2-3a^2}$ **25.** 11   **26.** No solution; 6 is extraneous
27. 1   **28.** $1, 2$ **29.** $\frac{2}{3}$ **30.** -10; 3 is extraneous
31. $B = \frac{HR}{R-H}$ **32.** $s = \frac{rt}{r-t}$ **33.** Yes   **34.** 1,785

35. 171 ft **36.** 80 sheets for $3.89 **37.** $3\frac{15}{16}$ hr **38.** 4 mph

39. 2 **40.** To simplify $\frac{1}{x} + \frac{1}{4}$, we build each fraction to have the LCD of $4x$. To solve $\frac{1}{x} + \frac{1}{4} = \frac{1}{2}$, we multiply both sides by the LCD $4x$ to eliminate the denominators and clear the equation of fractions.

CUMULATIVE REVIEW CHAPTERS 1–7 (page 597)

1. a. False **b.** False **c.** True **d.** True **2.** $<$ **3.** 36
4. 77 **5.** $6c + 62$ **6.** -5 **7.** 3 **8.** About 26%
9. $B = \frac{A - c - r}{2}$ **10.** 104°F **11.** 240 ft³ **12.** 12 lb of the $6.40 tea and 8 lb of the $4 tea **13.** 500 mph
14. $[-1, \infty)$  **15.**

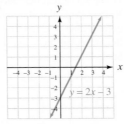

16. -1 **17.** 0.008 mm/m **18.** $\frac{8}{7}$ **19.** $y = 3x + 2$
20.

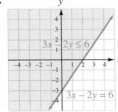

21. 0 **22.** domain, range

23.

24. $(5, 2)$ **25.** $(1, -1)$ **26.** Red: 8, blue: 15 **27.** x^7 **28.** x^{25}
29. $\frac{y^3}{8}$ **30.** $-\frac{32a^5}{b^5}$ **31.** $\frac{a^8}{b^{12}}$
32. $3b^2$ **33.** 2.9×10^5 **34.** 3

35.

36. $A = \pi R^2 - \pi r^2$
37. $6x^2 + x - 5$
38. $-\frac{1}{2}t^3 - \frac{7}{4}t^2 - \frac{1}{12}$ **39.** $6x^4 y^5$
40. $6y^2 - y - 35$
41. $-12x^4 z + 4x^2 z^2$
42. $9a^2 - 24a + 16$
43. $2x + 3$ **44.** $x^2 + 2x - 1$
45. $k^2 t(k - 3)$
46. $(b + c)(2a + 3)$ **47.** $(u - 9)^2$
48. $-(r - 2)(r + 1)$ **49.** Prime **50.** $(2x - 9)(3x + 7)$
51. $2(a + 10b)(a - 10b)$ **52.** $(b + 5)(b^2 - 5b + 25)$
53. $0, -\frac{1}{5}$ **54.** $\frac{1}{3}, \frac{1}{2}$ **55.** 16 in., 10 in. **56.** $5, -5$ **57.** $\frac{2x}{x - 2}$
58. $-\frac{x^3}{3}$ **59.** $2m - 5$ **60.** $-\frac{1}{x - 3}$ **61.** $\frac{m - 3}{(m + 3)(m + 1)}$
62. $\frac{x^2}{(x + 1)^2}$ **63.** $\frac{17}{25}$ **64.** 2 **65.** $14\frac{2}{5}$ hr **66.** 34.8 ft

ARE YOU READY? 8.1 (page 600)

1. $-11m + 8$ **2.** $18n$ **3.** 27 **4.** True
5. (number line) **6.** $x < 6$

SELF CHECKS 8.1

1. -3 **2.** $-\frac{53}{37}$ **3. a.** All real numbers, $\mathbb{R}$; identity
b. No solution, $\varnothing$; contradiction **4.** $r = \frac{A - P}{Pt}$ **5.** $t = \frac{7S + 360}{180}$
6. $(-8, \infty)$ (number line: −9 −8 −7) **7.** $[1, \infty)$ (number line: 0 1 2)
8. $(-\infty, \infty)$ (number line: −1 0 1) **9.** 30 people

10. Be Thrifty's plan is better if the car is going to be driven more than 100 miles that day.

STUDY SET SECTION 8.1 (page 609)

1. equation **3.** solution **5.** identity **7.** inequality **9. a.** same
b. same **11. a.** No **b.** Yes **13. a.** iii **b.** i **c.** ii **15.** 3
17. 4 **19.** -2 **21.** 1 **23.** -2 **25.** 24 **27.** 18 **29.** $-\frac{1}{6}$
31. No solution, $\varnothing$; contradiction **33.** All real numbers, $\mathbb{R}$; identity
35. All real numbers, $\mathbb{R}$; identity
37. No solution, $\varnothing$; contradiction
39. $w = \frac{P - 2l}{2}$ **41.** $B = \frac{3V}{h}$ **43.** $W = T - ma$
45. $x = z\sigma + \mu$ **47.** $l = \frac{2S - na}{n}$ or $l = \frac{2S}{n} - a$ **49.** $d = \frac{l - a}{n - 1}$
51. $(2, \infty)$ (number line: 2) **53.** $(-\infty, 2]$ (number line: 2)
55. $(-\infty, 20]$ (number line: 20) **57.** $(0, \infty)$ (number line: 0)
59. $[-2, \infty)$ (number line: −2) **61.** $\left[-\frac{2}{5}, \infty\right)$ (number line: −1 0, −2/5)
63. $(-\infty, 3)$ (number line: 3) **65.** $(-\infty, 7]$ (number line: 7)
67. $(-\infty, \infty)$; $\mathbb{R}$ (number line: −1 0 1)
69. No solution; $\varnothing$ **71.** 2 **73.** -11 **75.** $-\frac{5}{2}$
77. $-\frac{1}{2}$ **79.** All real numbers, $\mathbb{R}$; identity **81.** 2 **83.** $\frac{21}{19}$
85. No solution, $\varnothing$; contradiction **87.** 1,000 **89.** $\frac{9}{13}$
91. $\left(-\infty, -\frac{8}{5}\right)$ (number line: −2 −8/5 −1) **93.** $(-\infty, 6]$ (number line: 6)
95. $(-\infty, \infty)$; $\mathbb{R}$ (number line: −1 0 1) **97.** $(-\infty, 1.5]$ (number line: 1 1.5 2)
99. $[-36, \infty)$ (number line: −36) **101.** $(6, \infty)$ (number line: 6)
103. a. $-x$ **b.** $\frac{12}{7}$ **105. a.** $(-\infty, 3.25)$ **b.** $(3.25, \infty)$ **107.** 20
109. 310 mi **111.** 20 ft by 45 ft **113.** 9,431,000 views **115.** 8 hr
117. 7 hr **121.** $\frac{1}{t^{12}}$

ARE YOU READY? 8.2 (page 613)

1. $(3, 5), (3, 0)$ **2.** 7 **3.** $3, (0, -8)$ **4.** $-\frac{3}{2}$

SELF CHECKS 8.2

1. D: $\{-12, -6, 5, 8\}$; R: $\{-6, 4, 6\}$ **2. a.** No; $(0, 2), (0, 3)$
b. Yes **c.** No; $(4, -1), (4, 4)$ **d.** Yes **3. a.** Yes **b.** No;
$(1, 2), (1, -2)$ **4. a.** -5 **b.** 5 **c.** $2t - 1$ **d.** 0.42 **5.** -27
6. a. The set of real numbers **b.** The set of all real numbers
except -3 **7. a.** $f(x) = -\frac{1}{5}x + 9$ **b.** $f(x) = 2x - 13$

c. $f(x) = \frac{1}{10}x - 2$ **8. a.** $E(t) = 8t + 398$ **b.** 638 quadrillion Btu
9. 96 in.^{3}

STUDY SET SECTION 8.2 (page 624)

1. relation, domain, range **3.** function, variable, dependent
5. linear, one **7. a.** {(2000, 63), (2001, 56), (2002, 54), (2003, 50), (2004, 52), (2005, 51), (2006, 51)}
b. D: {2000, 2001, 2002, 2003, 2004, 2005, 2006};
R: {50, 51, 52, 54, 56, 63}
c.

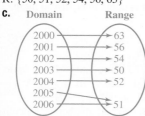

Domain	Range
2000 → 63
2001 → 56
2002 → 54
2003 → 50
2004 → 52
2005 → 51
2006 → 51

9. If $x = -4$, the denominator of $\frac{1}{x+4}$ is 0 and the fraction is undefined.
11. a. $(0, -4)$ **b.** $\left(-\frac{2}{3}, 0\right)$
13. a. of **b.** of **15.** $f(8)$
17. $f(x), y$ **19.** D: $\{-5, -1, 7, 8\}$; R: $\{-11, -6, -1, 3\}$
21. D: $\{-23, 0, 7\}$; R: $\{1, 35\}$
23. Yes **25.** No; (4, 2), (4, 4), (4, 6) **27.** No; (3, 4), (3, −4) or (4, 3), (4, −3) **29.** Yes **31.** Yes **33.** No; (−1, 0), (−1, 2)
35. Yes **37.** Yes **39.** No; (1, 1), (1, −1) **41.** Yes **43.** Yes
45. No; (1, 1), (1, −1) **47.** 9, −3 **49.** 3, −5 **51.** −6, −1
53. −6, −24 **55.** 9, 16 **57.** 7, 16 **59.** 7, 4 **61.** $\frac{1}{8}$, 1
63. $\frac{5}{2}, \frac{2}{5}$ **65.** 0, undefined **67.** 3.7, 1.1, 3.4
69. $-\frac{27}{64}, \frac{1}{216}, \frac{125}{8}$ **71.** $2w, 2w + 2$ **73.** $3w - 5, 3w - 2$
75. 0 **77.** 1 **79. a.** The set of real numbers **b.** The set of all real numbers except 4 **81. a.** The set of real numbers **b.** The set of all real numbers except $-\frac{1}{2}$

83.

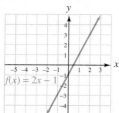

$f(x) = 2x - 1$

85.

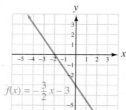

$f(x) = -\frac{3}{2}x - 3$

87.

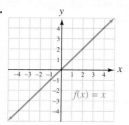

$f(x) = x$

89.

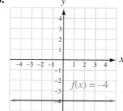

$f(x) = -4$

91.

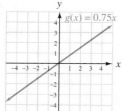

$g(x) = 0.75x$

93.

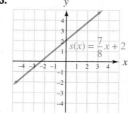

$s(x) = \frac{7}{8}x + 2$

95. $f(x) = 5x - 3$ **97.** $f(x) = \frac{1}{5}x - 1$ **99.** $f(x) = 2x + 5$
101. $f(x) = -\frac{2}{3}x + 2$ **103.** $f(x) = 6x - 4$ **105.** $f(x) = 12$
107. 105.17 million websites **109. a.** $p(b) = 4.75b - 125$
b. $397.50 **111. a.** $N(t) = 41,100t + 1,970,000$ **b.** 2,997,500 registered nurses **113. a.** $L(a) = -1.2a + 132$ **b.** 36%

115. a. $3,331.25; the tax on an adjusted gross income of $25,000 is $ 3,331.25. **b.** $T(a) = 4,681.25 + 0.25(a - 34,000)$
117. 10 m, 42 m, 26 m, 10 m **119.** 2,160 in.^{3}
125. No solution, $\varnothing$; contradiction

ARE YOU READY? 8.3 (page 628)

1. 3, 9 **2.** 1, 1 **3.** −8, 8 **4.** 4, 4

SELF CHECKS 8.3

1. a. −2 **b.** 2
2. D: the set of real numbers, R: the set of all real numbers greater than or equal to −2; the graph has the same shape, but is 2 units lower.

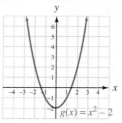

$g(x) = x^2 - 2$

3. D: the set of real numbers, R: the set of all real numbers; the graph has the same shape, but is 1 unit higher.

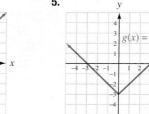

$g(x) = x^3 + 1$

4. D: the set of real numbers, R: the set of nonnegative real numbers; the graph has the same shape, but is 2 units to the right.

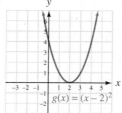

$g(x) = |x - 2|$

5.

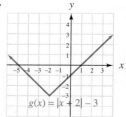

$g(x) = |x| - 3$

6.

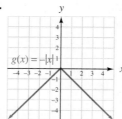

$g(x) = (x - 2)^2$

7.

$g(x) = |x + 2| - 3$

8.

$g(x) = -|x| + 1$

9. a. −10 **b.** −2, 0.2, 4.8
10. Not a function

STUDY SET SECTION 8.3 (page 638)

1. nonlinear   **3.** nonnegative

5. a. The squaring function

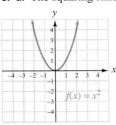

$f(x) = x^2$

b. The cubing function

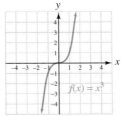

$f(x) = x^3$

c. The absolute value function

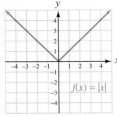

$f(x) = |x|$

7. reflection

9. a.

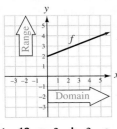

Range

Domain

f

b. D: the set of nonnegative real numbers, R: the set of real numbers greater than or equal to 2   **11. a.** 4 **b.** 0 **c.** -2 **13. a.** $(-2, 4), (-2, -4)$ **b.** No; to the x-value -2, there corresponds more than one y-value (4 and -4).   **15. a.** 4, left **b.** 4, up   **17. a.** -4 **b.** 0 **c.** 2 **d.** -1 **19. a.** 2 **b.** 2 **c.** -1 **d.** $-3, 1$ **21.** D: the set of real numbers, R: the set of real numbers   **23.** D: the set of real numbers, R: the set of real numbers less than or equal to 5   **25.** D: the set of real numbers, R: the set of real numbers greater than or equal to -4 **27.** D: the set of nonnegative real numbers, R: the set of nonnegative real numbers

29. D: the set of real numbers, R: the set of real numbers greater than or equal to 2

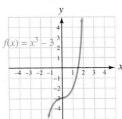

$f(x) = x^2 + 2$

31. D: the set of real numbers, R: the set of real numbers

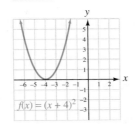

$f(x) = x^3 - 3$

33. D: the set of real numbers, R: the set of nonnegative real numbers

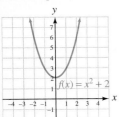

$f(x) = |x - 1|$

35. D: the set of real numbers, R: the set of nonnegative real numbers

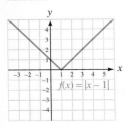

$f(x) = (x + 4)^2$

37. D: the set of real numbers, R: the set of real numbers greater than or equal to -2

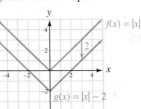

$f(x) = |x|$

$g(x) = |x| - 2$

39. D: the set of real numbers, R: the set of real numbers

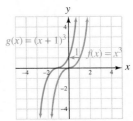

$g(x) = (x + 1)^3$

$f(x) = x^3$

41. D: the set of real numbers, R: the set of all real numbers greater than or equal to -3

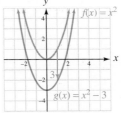

$f(x) = x^2$

$g(x) = x^2 - 3$

43. D: the set of real numbers, R: the set of real numbers

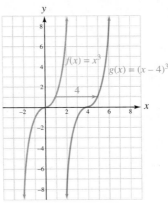

$f(x) = x^3$

$g(x) = (x - 4)^3$

45. D: the set of real numbers, R: the set of real numbers

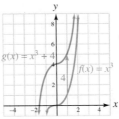

$g(x) = x^3 + 4$

$f(x) = x^3$

47. D: the set of real numbers, R: the set of nonnegative real numbers

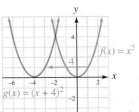

$f(x) = x^2$

$g(x) = (x + 4)^2$

49.

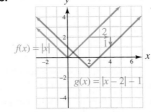

$f(x) = |x|$

$g(x) = |x - 2| - 1$

51.

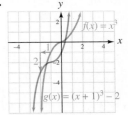

$f(x) = x^3$

$g(x) = (x + 1)^3 - 2$

53.

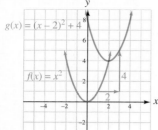

55.

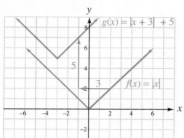

57.   **59.**

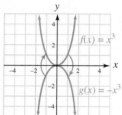   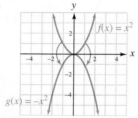

61.

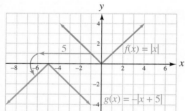

63.

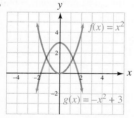

65. a. 15   **b.** 5   **c.** 0, −2, −4   **d.** D: $(-\infty, \infty)$; R: $(-\infty, \infty)$
67. a. 2   **b.** −5   **c.** −2, 2   **d.** D: $(-\infty, \infty)$; R: $(-\infty, 4]$
69. No, (0, 2), (0, −2)   **71.** Yes   **73.** Yes   **75.** No, (3, 0), (3, 1)
77.   **79.**   **81.**

83.   **85.** $f(x) = |x|$ **87.** A parabola

89. a. $J(9) \approx 12.2$; in 2009, there were about 12.2
        million manufacturing jobs in the U.S.
b. $x \approx 3$; in 2003, there were about 14.5 million manufacturing jobs
in the U.S.   **97.** $W = T - ma$ **99.** $g = \frac{2(s - vt)}{t^2}$

ARE YOU READY? 8.4 (page 643)

1. 3 and 4   **2.** $[-7, \infty)$ **3.** Yes
                                    −7

4.
        −1   2

SELF CHECKS 8.4

1. a. {9}   **b.** {3, 6, 8, 9, 10, 11, 12, 15}
2. $(-6, 10]$ **3.** $\left(\frac{1}{2}, \infty\right)$
        −6 0   10   0 1/2 1
4. No solution; $\varnothing$ **5.** $[1, 5]$
                                        0 1   5
6. $(-\infty, 2) \cup (4, \infty)$
                0   2   4
7. $(-\infty, \infty)$
        −1   0   1

STUDY SET SECTION 8.4 (page 651)

1. intersection, union   **3.** double   **5. a.** both   **b.** one, both
7. a. intersection   **b.** union   **9. a.** No   **b.** Yes
11. a. $[-2, 1)$ **b.** $[2, 2]$ **c.** $\varnothing$ **13.** union, intersection
15. All real numbers   **17.** {4, 6}   **19.** {−3, 1, 2}
                −1 0 1
21. {−3, −1, 0, 1, 2, 4, 6, 8, 10}   **23.** {−3, 0, 1, 2, 3, 4, 5, 6, 8}
25. $(-2, 5]$ **27.** $(2, 3]$
        −2   5   2   3
29. $(-\infty, -6]$
                −6
31. No solution; $\varnothing$
33. $[1, 4]$
        1   4
35. $(0.8, 1.1)$
        0.8   1.1
37. $(-\infty, -2] \cup (6, \infty)$
                −2   6
39. $(-\infty, -1) \cup (2, \infty)$
                −1   2
41. $(-\infty, 2) \cup (7, \infty)$
                2   7
43. $(-\infty, \infty)$ **45.** $(-\infty, 1)$
        −1   0   1   1
47. $(-10, -9)$
        −10   −9
49. $(-2, 5)$ **51.** $(-\infty, \infty)$
        −2   5   −1   0   1
53. $[2, \infty)$ **55.** No solution; $\varnothing$
        2
57. $[-4, 6)$ **59.** $[2, 2]$
        −4   6   2
61. $(-\infty, 4.8) \cup (6.5, \infty)$
                4.8   6.5
63. $(-0.7, 0.2]$
        −0.7   0.2
65. $(-12, -6]$
        −12   −6

67. $\left(-\infty, \frac{1}{6}\right] \cup (2, \infty)$

69. $[-2, 4]$ **71.** $[4, 4]$

73. $(1, 3]$ **75.** $(3, 6)$

77. a. $[6, \infty)$ **b.** $[2, \infty)$

79. a. No solution; $\varnothing$ **b.** $(-\infty, 3] \cup [6, \infty)$

81. a. 128, 192   **b.** $32 \le s \le 48$, [32, 48]   **83. a.** (67, 77)
b. (62, 82)   **85. a.** 2004   **b.** 2004, 2005, 2006, 2007   **c.** 2006,
2007   **d.** 2007   **87. a.**   **b.**
95. B747:
403 passengers;
B777: 278 passengers

ARE YOU READY? 8.5 (page 655)

1. a. 12   **b.** 7.5   **2. a.** True   **b.** False
3. $(-\infty, -3] \cup [1, \infty)$

4. $(-8, 4)$

SELF CHECKS 8.5

1. a. $\frac{1}{2}, -\frac{1}{2}$ **b.** 5, -2 **c.** No solution, $\varnothing$ **2.** 7.5, 2.5   **3.** -6
4. 7, -15 **5.** $-1, -6$ **6.** $\left(-2, \frac{2}{3}\right)$

7. [2.8985, 2.9015]   **8.** No solution, $\varnothing$
9. $(-\infty, -2] \cup [6, \infty)$

10. $(-\infty, -8) \cup \left(\frac{8}{3}, \infty\right)$

11. $(-\infty, \infty)$

STUDY SET SECTION 8.5 (page 664)

1. absolute value   **3.** isolate   **5.** compound   **7.** compound
9. a. $-2, 2$ **b.** $-1.99, -1, 0, 1, 1.99$ **c.** $-3, -2.01, 2.01, 3$
11. a. 8, -8 **b.** $x - 3, -(x - 3)$ **13. a.** $x = 8$ or $x = -8$
b. $x \le -8$ or $x \ge 8$ **c.** $-8 \le x \le 8$ **d.** $5x - 1 = x + 3$ or
$5x - 1 = -(x + 3)$ **15. a.** No solution   **b.** No solution
c. All real numbers   **17. a.** ii   **b.** iii   **c.** i   **19.** 23, -23
21. 13, -3 **23.** $\frac{14}{3}, -6$ **25.** 50, -50 **27.** 3.1, -6.7
29. No solution; $\varnothing$ **31.** 25, -19 **33.** 7, $-\frac{7}{3}$ **35.** 2, $-\frac{1}{2}$
37. $\frac{32}{7}, -16$ **39.** -10 **41.** -8 **43.** $\frac{9}{2}$ **45.** $-\frac{1}{2}$ **47.** $-4, \frac{28}{9}$
49. $-2, \frac{18}{11}$ **51.** 0, -2 **53.** 11, $\frac{1}{3}$
55. $(-4, 4)$

57. $[-21, 3]$

59. $\left(-\frac{8}{3}, 4\right)$ **61.** No solution; $\varnothing$

63. $(-\infty, -3) \cup (3, \infty)$

65. $(-\infty, -12) \cup (36, \infty)$

67. $\left(-\infty, -\frac{1}{5}\right] \cup \left[\frac{3}{5}, \infty\right)$

69. $(-\infty, \infty)$ **71.** 0, -6 **73.** $(-3, 1)$

75. $\left(-\infty, -\frac{16}{3}\right) \cup (4, \infty)$

77. $[-10, 14]$ **79.** 40, -20

81. $(-\infty, \infty)$ **83.** $-3, -\frac{3}{4}$

85. $\frac{2}{3}$ **87.** No solution; $\varnothing$ **89.** $\frac{12}{11}, -\frac{12}{11}$

91. $(-\infty, -2) \cup (5, \infty)$ **93.** No solution; $\varnothing$

95. a. 20   **b.** 20, 0   **c.** $(20, \infty)$

d. $(-\infty, 0) \cup (20, \infty)$

97. a. -25 **b.** $-25, 31$ **c.** $(-\infty, -25)$

d. $(-\infty, -25) \cup (31, \infty)$

99. a. $[3, 7]$ **b.** $(-\infty, 3] \cup [7, \infty)$

101. a. $(-\infty, -8) \cup (10, \infty)$

b. $[-8, 10]$

103. $70° \le t \le 86°$ **105. a.** $|c - 0.6°| \le 0.5°$ **b.** $[0.1°, 1.1°]$
107. 26.45%, 24.76%   **113.** First piece: 9 in.; middle piece: 14 in.;
last piece: 6 in.

ARE YOU READY? 8.6 (page 667)

1. $2 \cdot 2 \cdot 3 \cdot 3 \cdot 3 = 2^2 \cdot 3^3$ **2.** $6b^4 + 12b^2 + 24b$
3. $x^2 + 2x - 48$ **4.** $m^2 - 3m - 10$ **5.** 2 and 5   **6.** -3 and 6

SELF CHECKS 8.6

1. $2ab^2(3a - 2b + 1)$ **2.** $-3p^2q(p - 2q)$ **3.** $(y^2 + 1)(c^2 + d^2)$
4. $(m - n)(7 + n)$ **5.** $ab(3a - 2b)(a + 1)$ **6.** $f_1 = \frac{ff_2}{f_2 - f}$
7 $(a - 4)(a - 3)$ **8.** $3(p + 4q)(p - 2q)$ **9.** $(4q + 3)(q - 3)$
10. $b(2a^2 + 1)(3a^2 + 4)$ **11.** $(a + b + 2)(a + b - 5)$
12. a. $(m + 7)(m + 6)$ **b.** $(3a + 4b)(5a - b)$

STUDY SET SECTION 8.6 (page 674)

1. factored   **3.** greatest common factor   **5.** grouping
7. leading, coefficient, 2   **9.** $6xy^2$ **11.** 9, 6, -9, -6
13. $-1 + (-12) = -13, -2(-6) = 12, -2 + (-6) = -8$,
$-3 + (-4) = -7$ **15.** $5c^2d^4$ **17.** $3m, 3$ **19.** $2x(x - 3)$
21. $5x^2y(3 - 2y)$ **23.** $3z(9z^2 + 4z + 1)$

25. $6s(4s^2 - 2st + t^2)$　**27.** Prime　**29.** Prime　**31.** $-8(a + 2)$
33. $-3x(2x + y)$　**35.** $-6ab(3a - 2b)$
37. $-4a^2c^8(2a^2 - 7a + 5c)$　**39.** $(x + y)(u + v)$
41. $(a - b + c)(5 - t)$　**43.** $(x + y)(a + b)$　**45.** $(x + y)(x - 1)$
47. $(t - 3)(t^2 - 7)$　**49.** $(a + b)(a - 4)$　**51.** $6(x - 1)(x^2 + 2)$
53. $2c(2b^3 + 1)(7a^3 - 1)$　**55.** $h = \frac{2g}{c + d}$　**57.** $r_1 = \frac{rr_2}{r_2 - r}$
59. $a^2 = \frac{b^2x^2}{b^2 - y^2}$　**61.** $n = \frac{360}{180 - S}$　**63.** $(x - 3)(x - 2)$
65. $(x + 6)(x - 5)$　**67.** $3(x + 7y)(x - 3y)$
69. $6(a - 4b)(a - b)$　**71.** $n^2(n - 30t)(n + 2t)$
73. $-3(x - 3y)(x - 2y)$　**75.** $(5x + 3)(x + 2)$
77. $(7a + 5)(a + 1)$　**79.** $(11y - 1)(y + 3)$
81. $(4x - 1)(2x - 5)$　**83.** $(3y - 2)(2y - 3)$
85. $(5b - 2)(3b + 2)$　**87.** $5(3x^2 - 4)(2x^2 + 1)$
89. $8(2x^2 - 3)^2$　**91.** $4h(8h^2 - 1)(2h^2 + 1)$
93. $-(3a^2 + 2b^2)(a^2 + b^2)$　**95.** $(a + b + 4)(a + b - 6)$
97. $(x + a + 1)^2$　**99.** $(m + n + p)(3 + x)$
101. $-7u^2v^3(9uv^3 - 4v^4 + 3u)$　**103.** $x^2(b^2 - 7)(b^2 - 5)$
105. $(1 - n)(1 - m)$　**107.** $-(x + 3y)(x - 7y)$
109. $(a^2 + b)(x - 1)$　**111.** $(2y + 1)^2$　**113.** Prime
115. $(3r - 2)(r + 5)$　**117.** $(y^2 + 3)(y - 4)$
119. $2y(y^2 - 10)(y^2 - 3)$　**121.** $(7q - 7r + 2)(2q - 2r - 3)$
123. $\pi r^2\left(h_1 + \frac{1}{3}h_2\right)$　**125.** $x + 3$　**129. a.** 2　**b.** 3　**c.** $-1, 1, 5$
d. 3

63. $(4 - a - b)(16 + 4a + 4b + a^2 + 2ab + b^2)$
65. $(x + 1)(x^2 - x + 1)(x - 1)(x^2 + x + 1)$
67. $(x^2 + y)(x^4 - x^2y + y^2)(x^2 - y)(x^4 + x^2y + y^2)$
69. $5(x + 5)(x^2 - 5x + 25)$　**71.** $4x^2(x - 4)(x^2 + 4x + 16)$
73. $(4a - 5b^2)(16a^2 + 20ab^2 + 25b^4)$
75. $2b^2(12 + b^2)(12 - b^2)$　**77.** $(x + y)(x - y + 8)$
79. $(x + y)(x^2 - xy + y^2)(x^6 - x^3y^3 + y^6)$
81. $(12at + 13b^3)(12at - 13b^3)$　**83.** Prime
85. $(9c^2d^2 + 4t^2)(3cd + 2t)(3cd - 2t)$
87. $2u^2(4v - t)(16v^2 + 4tv + t^2)$　**89.** $(y + 2x - t)(y - 2x + t)$
91. $(x + 10 + 3z)(x + 10 - 3z)$
93. $(c - d + 6)(c^2 - 2cd + d^2 - 6c + 6d + 36)$
95. $\left(\frac{1}{6} + y^2\right)\left(\frac{1}{6} - y^2\right)$
97. $(m + 2)(m^2 - 2m + 4)(m - 2)(m^2 + 2m + 4)$
99. $(a + b)(x + 3)(x^2 - 3x + 9)$
101. $(x^3 - y^4z^5)(x^6 + x^3y^4z^5 + y^8z^{10})$　**103. a.** $(q + 8)(q - 8)$
b. $(q - 4)(q^2 + 4q + 16)$　**105. a.** $(d + 5)(d - 5)$
b. $(d - 5)(d^2 + 5d + 25)$　**107. a.** $(a^2 - b)(a^4 + a^2b + b^2)$
b. $(a^2 + b)(a^4 - a^2b + b^2)$
109. a. $(5m + 2n)(25m^2 - 10mn + 4n^2)$
b. $(5m - 2n)(25m^2 + 10mn + 4n^2)$
111. $\frac{4}{3}\pi(r_1 - r_2)(r_1{}^2 + r_1r_2 + r_2{}^2)$
117. 45 minutes for $25

ARE YOU READY? 8.7 (page 677)

1. $n^2 - 81$　**2.** $64d^2$　**3. a.** 27　**b.** 216　**4.** $64a^3$　**5.** $b^3 + 64$
6. $8a^3 - 1$

SELF CHECKS 8.7

1. $(9p + 5)(9p - 5)$　**2.** $(6r^2 + s)(6r^2 - s)$
3. $(a^2 + 9)(a + 3)(a - 3)$
4. $(a^2 - 2ab + b^2 + c^2)(a - b + c)(a - b - c)$
5. $3(a^2 + 1)(a + 1)(a - 1)$　**6. a.** $(a + b)(a - b + 1)$
b. $(a + 2 + b)(a + 2 - b)$　**7.** $(p + 3)(p^2 - 3p + 9)$
8. $(2c^2 - 5d)(4c^4 + 10c^2d + 25d^2)$
9. $(p + q - r)(p^2 + 2pq + q^2 + pr + qr + r^2)$
10. $(1 + x)(1 - x + x^2)(1 - x)(1 + x + x^2)$
11. $3x^2(x + 2)(x^2 - 2x + 4)$

STUDY SET SECTION 8.7 (page 683)

1. squares　**3. a.** 1, 4, 9, 16, 25, 36, 49, 64, 81, 100
b. 1, 8, 27, 64, 125, 216, 343, 512, 729, 1,000　**5. a.** $F - L$
b. $F^2 - FL + L^2$　**c.** $F^2 + FL + L^2$　**7. a.** $x^2 - 4$ (Answers
may vary)　**b.** $(x - 4)^2$ (Answers may vary)　**c.** $x^2 + 4$
(Answers may vary)　**d.** $x^3 + 8$ (Answers may vary)　**e.** $(x + 8)^3$
(Answers may vary)　**9.** $(x + 4)(x - 4)$　**11.** $(3y + 8)(3y - 8)$
13. $(12 + c)(12 - c)$　**15.** $(10m + 1)(10m - 1)$
17. $(9a + 7b)(9a - 7b)$　**19.** Prime　**21.** $(3r^2 + 11s)(3r^2 - 11s)$
23. $(4t + 5w^2)(4t - 5w^2)$　**25.** $(10rs^2 + t^2)(10rs^2 - t^2)$
27. $(6x^2y + 7z^3)(6x^2y - 7z^3)$　**29.** $(x^2 + y^2)(x + y)(x - y)$
31. $(4a^2 + 9b^2)(2a + 3b)(2a - 3b)$　**33.** $(x + y + z)(x + y - z)$
35. $(r - s + t^2)(r - s - t^2)$　**37.** $2(x + 12)(x - 12)$
39. $3x(x + 9)(x - 9)$　**41.** $5a(b^2 + 1)(b + 1)(b - 1)$
43. $4b(4 + b^2)(2 + b)(2 - b)$　**45.** $(c + d)(c - d + 1)$
47. $(a - b)(a + b + 2)$　**49.** $(x + 6 + y)(x + 6 - y)$
51. $(x - 1 + 3z)(x - 1 - 3z)$　**53.** $(a + 5)(a^2 - 5a + 25)$
55. $(2r + s)(4r^2 - 2rs + s^2)$
57. $(4t^2 - 3v)(16t^4 + 12t^2v + 9v^2)$
59. $(x - 6y^2)(x^2 + 6xy^2 + 36y^4)$
61. $(a - b + 3)(a^2 - 2ab + b^2 - 3a + 3b + 9)$

ARE YOU READY? 8.8 (page 686)

1. a. 0　**b.** Undefined　**2.** $\frac{9}{7}$　**3.** $\frac{x + 5}{4(x - 5)}$　**4.** $\frac{3x}{2}$　**5. a.** $\frac{3}{56}$　**b.** $\frac{9}{5}$
6. a. $\frac{8}{11}$　**b.** $\frac{7}{15}$

SELF CHECKS 8.8

1. $1.56 per hour　**2.** The domain is set of all real numbers except
-7 and 7: $(-\infty, -7) \cup (-7, 7) \cup (7, \infty)$　**3.** $\frac{3a^3}{5b^2}$　**4. a.** $\frac{2x + 1}{3x - 1}$
b. $\frac{-2a + 3b}{b}$ or $\frac{-2a - 3b}{b}$　**5. a.** $\frac{a^2(a + 3)}{6}$　**b.** $-x(x + 3)$
6. $\frac{x(x - 2)}{3}$　**7.** $\frac{b}{b - 2}$　**8.** $\frac{9 + 20xz^2}{84z^3}$　**9.** $\frac{9a - 2}{(a - 2)(a - 2)(a + 2)}$
10. $-\frac{5}{2}, 1$

STUDY SET SECTION 8.8 (page 696)

1. rational　**3.** domain　**5.** simplify　**7.** factor　**9.** build
11. a. $-\frac{1}{4}$　**b.** $\frac{5}{6}$　**c.** Undefined　**13. a.** -1　**b.** 2　**c.** 2　**d.** 5
15. numerators, denominators, reciprocal　**17.** factor, greatest
19. a. Twice　**b.** Once　**21. a.** 3a　**b.** $(x - 2)(x + 5)$
23. a. $\frac{5x^2 + 35x}{1}$　**b.** $\frac{1}{5x^2 + 35x}$
25. All real numbers except 0; $(-\infty, 0) \cup (0, \infty)$
27. All real numbers except -2; $(-\infty, -2) \cup (-2, \infty)$
29. All real numbers except 0 and 1; $(-\infty, 0) \cup (0, 1) \cup (1, \infty)$
31. All real numbers except -7 and 8;
$(-\infty, -7) \cup (-7, 8) \cup (8, \infty)$
33. $\frac{3}{5a^6}$　**35.** $\frac{4y}{9x}$　**37.** $\frac{5x}{x - 2}$　**39.** $\frac{3x - 5}{x + 2}$　**41.** $-\frac{x + 2}{x + 1}$
43. $-\frac{p + 2q}{q + 2p}$　**45.** $\frac{8}{b}$　**47.** $\frac{p(p - 4)}{12}$　**49.** $\frac{x + 1}{9}$　**51.** 1
53. $-\frac{a^4}{a^2 + 3}$　**55.** $-\frac{(x + 1)^2(x + 2)}{2c + x}$　**57.** $\frac{3m}{2n^2}$　**59.** $\frac{x - 4}{x + 5}$
61. $\frac{c + 1}{25c^2 - 5c + 1}$　**63.** $\frac{n + 2}{n + 1}$　**65.** $\frac{3}{x + 3}$　**67.** $\frac{1}{2}$　**69.** $\frac{17}{12x}$
71. $\frac{16y^2 + 3}{18y^4}$　**73.** $\frac{3a - 10b}{4a^2b^2}$　**75.** $-\frac{y^2 + 5y + 14}{2y^2}$　**77.** $\frac{8x - 2}{(x + 2)(x - 4)}$
79. $\frac{7x + 29}{(x + 5)(x + 7)}$　**81.** $\frac{2x^2 + x}{(x + 3)(x + 2)(x - 2)}$
83. $\frac{-x^2 + 11x + 8}{(3x + 2)(x + 1)(x - 3)}$　**85.** $\frac{6 - 3d}{5d(d - 1)}$　**87.** $\frac{m - 5}{(m + 3)(m + 5)}$

89. $\frac{1}{2}$ **91.** $-\frac{1}{2}$ **93.** 1, 2 **95.** 4, −1

97. $f(x) = \frac{x+8}{x+2}$, provided $x \neq -2, x \neq 2$ **99.** $g(x) = \frac{x^2 - 4x + 16}{x^2 + 3}$,

provided $x \neq -4$ **101.** $-\frac{q}{p}$ **103.** $\frac{t-3}{(t+3)(t+1)}$ **105.** 26

107. $\frac{-x^2 + 3x + 2}{(x-1)(x+1)^2}$ **109.** $x - 5$ **111.** $\frac{y^2 + xy + x^2}{x+y}$ **113.** $\frac{3n}{2n+3}$

115. $\frac{x^2 - 5x - 5}{x - 5}$ **117.** $\frac{x+y}{a-b}$ **119.** 1 **121.** 2, −5 **123.** $\frac{x}{x-3}$

125. a. \$50,000 **b.** \$200,000 **127. a.** $c(n) = 0.09n + 7.50$

b. $c(n) = \frac{0.09n + 7.50}{n}$ **c.** About 10¢ **133.** $-\frac{1}{4}$

ARE YOU READY? 8.9 (page 700)

1. 450 **2.** 5 **3.** 1,620 **4. a.** $\frac{2}{13}$ **b.** 200

SELF CHECKS 8.9

1. 735 British pounds **2.** 16 foot-candles
3. Approximately 1,055 lb **4.** 20 weeks

STUDY SET SECTION 8.9 (page 705)

1. direct, increases **3.** joint, combined **5. a.** Direct **b.** Inverse
7. Direct **9.** Inverse **11.** Direct **13.** Inverse **15. a.** Yes
b. No **c.** No **d.** Yes **17.** $A = kp^2$ **19.** $z = \frac{k}{t^3}$
21. $C = kxyz$ **23.** $P = \frac{ka^2}{j^3}$ **25.** r varies directly as t.
27. b varies inversely as h. **29.** U varies jointly as r, the square of s,
and t. **31.** P varies directly as m and inversely as n.
33. a. False **b.** False **c.** True **35.** 117.6 newtons
37. 432 mi **39.** 25 days **41.** 12 in.³ **43.** \$9,000 **45.** 3 ohms
47. 0.275 in. **49.** 1.4 ohms **51.** 12.8 lb

55. $(2, 5)$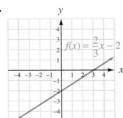

57. $(-\infty, 6) \cup (9, \infty)$

CHAPTER 8 REVIEW (page 708)

1. $-\frac{12}{5}$ **2.** −9 **3.** 8 **4.** $\frac{11}{7}$ **5.** $\frac{88}{17}$ **6.** 12 **7.** All real
numbers, $\mathbb{R}$; identity **8.** No solution, $\varnothing$; contradiction **9.** −8
10. 0 **11.** $h = \frac{V}{\pi r^2}$ **12.** $x = \frac{6v - aby}{ab}$ or $x = \frac{6v}{ab} - y$

13. $[4, \infty)$ **14.** $\left(-\infty, -\frac{51}{11}\right)$

15. $(-\infty, 20)$ **16.** $(-\infty, \infty), \mathbb{R}$

17. 5 ft from one end **18.** Length: 9 m, width: 5 m
19. D: $\{-4, -1, 2, 5\}$, R: $\{-2, 0, 16\}$ **20. a.** function
b. function, variable, dependent **21. a.** Yes
b. No; $(-1, 8), (-1, 9)$ **c.** Yes **22.** 0 **23.** Yes **24.** Yes
25. No; $(25, 5), (25, -5)$ **26.** No; $(3, 4), (3, -4)$
27. −7 **28.** 18 **29.** 8 **30.** $3t + 8$ **31.** 3 **32.** $\frac{4}{3}$
33. The set of real numbers **34.** The set of real numbers
35. The set of all real numbers except 2 **36.** The set of all real
numbers except −5 **37.** −2, $(0, -16)$

38.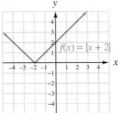

39. $f(x) = \frac{9}{10}x + \frac{7}{8}$
40. $f(x) = \frac{1}{5}x - 1$ **41.** $f(x) = 12$
42. $f(x) = 4x - 3$
43. $f(x) = \frac{1}{3}x + 5$
44. a. $R(t) = 0.02t + 5.05$
b. 7.05 milliohms
45. 134 in.³ **46.** $\frac{65}{24} = 2\frac{17}{24}$
47. a. −4 **b.** 3 **c.** 1
48. a. 4 **b.** 1 **c.** −4, 2
49. a. −1 **b.** −2, −1, 1 **c.** D: $(-\infty, \infty)$; R: $[-1, \infty)$
50. The real numbers greater than or equal to 0
51. D: the set of real numbers, R: the set of real numbers
52. D: the set of real numbers, R: the set of real numbers greater
than or equal to 1
53. D: the set of real numbers, R: the set of nonnegative real
numbers **54. a.** 6, up **b.** 6, left

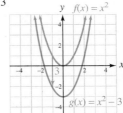

55. D: the set of real numbers, R: the set of real numbers greater
than or equal to −3

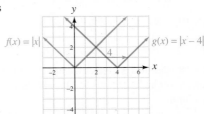

56. D: the set of real numbers, R: the set of nonnegative real
numbers

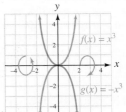

57. D: the set of real numbers, **58.** D: the set of real numbers,
R: the set of real numbers R: the set of real numbers

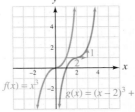

59. Function **60.** Not a function; $(0, 2), (0, 3)$ **61.** $\{-3, 3\}$
62. $\{-6, -5, -3, 0, 3, 6, 8\}$ **63.** Yes **64.** No
65. **66.**

67. $[-10, -4)$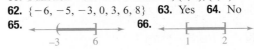

68. $(-\infty, -11)$

69. No solution; $\varnothing$

70. $[0, 0]$

71. $\left(-\frac{1}{3}, 2\right)$

72. $[1, 9]$

73. Yes   **74.** No

75. $(-\infty, -5) \cup (4, \infty)$

76. $(-\infty, \infty)$

77. $17 \le 4x \le 25$, 4.25 ft $\le x \le 6.25$ ft, $[4.25, 6.25]$

78. a. ii, iv   **b.** i, iii   **79.** $(-\infty, 73.6) \cup [137.6, \infty)$

80. $\left(-\frac{7}{3}, \frac{1}{3}\right]$ **81.** $2, -2$ **82.** $3, -\frac{11}{3}$ **83.** $\frac{26}{3}, -\frac{10}{3}$

84. No solution; $\varnothing$ **85.** 3 **86.** $\frac{1}{8}, -\frac{19}{8}$ **87.** $\frac{1}{5}, -5$ **88.** $\frac{13}{12}$

89. $[-3, 3]$

90. $(-5, -2)$

91. $\left[-3, \frac{19}{3}\right]$ **92.** No solution; $\varnothing$

93. $(-\infty, -1) \cup (1, \infty)$

94. $(-\infty, -4] \cup \left[\frac{22}{5}, \infty\right)$

95. $\left(-\infty, \frac{4}{3}\right) \cup (4, \infty)$

96. $(-\infty, \infty)$, $\mathbb{R}$

97. a. $8, 2$ **b.** $[6, 10]$ **98.** $3, -3$ **99.** $0, -8$
100. $(2, 12)$

101. Since $|0.04x - 8.8|$ is always greater than or equal to 0 for any real number x, it can never be less than -2. This absolute value inequality has no solution.
102. Since $\left|\frac{3x}{50} + \frac{1}{45}\right|$ is always greater than or equal to 0 for any real number x, it will always be greater than or equal to $-\frac{4}{5}$. This absolute value inequality is true for all real numbers.
103. $(z - 5)(z - 6)$ **104.** $(x^2 + 4)(x^2 + y)$
105. $(4a - 1)(a - 1)$ **106.** $9x^2y^3z^2(3xz + 9x^2y^2 - 10z^5)$
107. $(5b - 2)(3b + 2)$ **108.** $-(x + 7)(x - 4)$
109. $3(5x + y)(x - 4y)$ **110.** $(w^4 - 10)(w^4 + 9)$
111. $(ry - a + 1)(r - 1)$ **112.** $(7a^3 + 6b^2)^2$ **113.** Prime
114. $2a^2(a + 3)(a - 1)$ **115.** $(s + t - 1)^2$ **116.** $m_1 = \frac{mm_2}{m_2 - m}$
117. $(z + 4)(z - 4)$ **118.** $(xy^2 + 8z^3)(xy^2 - 8z^3)$ **119.** Prime
120. $(c + a + b)(c - a - b)$
121. $2c(4a^2 + 9b^2)(2a + 3b)(2a - 3b)$
122. $(k + 1 + 3m)(k + 1 - 3m)$ **123.** $(m + n)(m - n - 1)$
124. $(t + 4)(t^2 - 4t + 16)$
125. $(2a - 5b^3)(4a^2 + 10ab^3 + 25b^6)$
126. $\frac{\pi}{2}h(r_1 + r_2)(r_1 - r_2)$ **127. a.** 1 **b.** $-\frac{1}{2}$ **c.** 0 **128.** The domain is the set of all real numbers except -6 and 4: $(-\infty, -6) \cup (-6, 4) \cup (4, \infty)$.

129. $n(3) = 8.4$; Three hours after the injection, the concentration of pain medication in the patient's bloodstream was 8.4 milligrams per liter.   **130.** Undefined   **131.** $\frac{31x}{72y}$ **132.** -2 **133.** $\frac{cd}{7x^2}$
134. $\frac{2a - 1}{a + 2}$ **135.** $\frac{a + b}{(m + p)(m - 3)}$ **136.** $\frac{3x(x - 1)}{(x - 3)(x + 1)}$ **137.** $\frac{1}{c - d}$
138. $-\frac{2}{t - 3}$ **139.** $\frac{40x + 7y^2z}{112z^2}$ **140.** $\frac{12y + 20}{15y(x - 2)}$ **141.** $\frac{14y + 58}{(y + 3)(y + 7)}$
142. $\frac{5x^2 + 11x}{(x + 1)(x + 2)}$ **143.** 5 **144.** $-2, 3$ **145.** $-1, -2$ **146.** $\frac{3}{2}$

147. 0 **148.** No solution; 3 is extraneous   **149.** $\$5,460$

150. 1.25 amps   **151.** $\frac{1}{32}$ **152.** 126.72 lb   **153.** Inverse variation
154. 0.2

CHAPTER 8 TEST (page 723)

1. a. solve   **b.** inequality   **c.** factors   **d.** reciprocal
e. function   **f.** domain, range   **2.** Yes   **3.** $\frac{21}{5}$ **4.** -1

5. No solution, $\varnothing$; contradiction   **6.** $x_1 = \frac{y_1 + mx - y}{m}$ **7.** 8
8. More than 78   **9. a.** No; $(1, -8), (1, 6)$ **b.** Yes   **c.** Yes
d. No; $(4, -4), (4, 4)$ **10.** The set of all real numbers except 6
11. -20 **12.** $8, (0, -9)$ **13.** $f(x) = -\frac{5}{4}x + \frac{5}{2}$

14. a. $T(m) = -0.16m + 331.3$ **b.** 8.9 sec   **15.** 10   **16.** 49
17. $\frac{9}{16}$ **18.** $3r + 25$ **19.** 110 ft   **20. a.** 0   **b.** 2, 6
c. D: $(-\infty, \infty)$; R: $(-\infty, 2]$ **21.** Function   **22.** Not a function; $(2, 2), (2, -2)$ **23.** D: the set of real numbers, R: the set of real numbers greater than or equal to 3

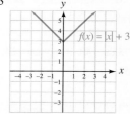

24.

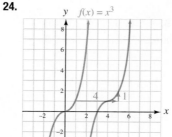

D: the set of real numbers, R: the set of real numbers

25. $(-\infty, -5]$

26. $(-2, 16)$

27. $\left[1, \frac{9}{4}\right]$

28. $(-\infty, -3) \cup (8, \infty)$

29. $(-\infty, -9) \cup (13, \infty)$

30. $\left[\frac{4}{3}, \frac{8}{3}\right]$ **31.** $8, -11$ **32.** $4, -4$

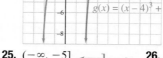

33. $3abc(4a^2b - abc + 2c^2)$

34. $4(y^2 + 4)(y + 2)(y - 2)$
35. $(b + 5)(b^2 - 5b + 25)$ **36.** $3(u + 2)(2u - 1)$
37. $(a - y)(x + y)$ **38.** $(5m^4 - 6n^2)^2$ **39.** Prime
40. $(x + 3 + y)(x + 3 - y)$
41. $(4a - 5b^2)(16a^2 + 20ab^2 + 25b^4)$
42. $(x - y + 5)(x - y - 2)$ **43. a.** 1   **b.** $-\frac{1}{2}$ **c.** -1 **d.** 2
44. $p(7) = 175$ **45.** No   **46.** The set of all real numbers except 0
and 1; $(-\infty, 0) \cup (0, 1) \cup (1, \infty)$ **47.** -3 **48.** $\frac{2x + y}{4y}$
49. $\frac{(x + y)^2}{2}$ **50.** $\frac{13}{x + 1}$ **51.** $\frac{2}{t - 4}$ **52.** $\frac{6a - 17}{(a + 1)(a - 2)(a - 3)}$
53. 40   **54.** 5; 3 is extraneous   **55.** 6, -1 **56.** 26   **57.** $\frac{6}{5}$
58. 25 decibels

ARE YOU READY? **9.1** (page 728)

1. a. 225   **b.** 64   **2. a.** $\frac{49}{25}$ **b.** 0.04   **3. a.** -216 **b.** 81
4. a. a^8 **b.** x^9 **5.** $x^2 + 16x + 64$ **6.** 5

SELF-CHECKS **9.1**

1. a. 8   **b.** -1 **c.** $\frac{1}{4}$ **d.** 0.3   **2. a.** $5|a|$ **b.** $|b^7|$ **c.** $|x - 9|$
d. $10n^4$ **3.**

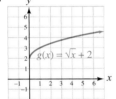

D: $[0, \infty)$; R: $[2, \infty)$; the graph
is 2 units higher

4. a. $[2, \infty)$ **b.**

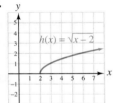

c. $[0, \infty)$

5. 1.92 sec   **6. a.** 4   **b.** $-\frac{1}{10}$ **c.** $-5a$ **d.** $3m^2n^3$
7. a.

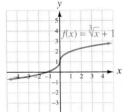

b. D: $(-\infty, \infty)$; R: $(-\infty, \infty)$

8. a. $\frac{1}{3}$ **b.** 10   **c.** Not a real number   **9. a.** $|x|$ **b.** $a + 5$
c. $2a^2$

STUDY SET SECTION **9.1** (page 739)

1. square, cube   **3.** positive   **5.** principal   **7.** simplified
9. radical   **11.** a **13.** squared   **15.** $|x|, x$ **17. a.** 3   **b.** 0
c. Undefined   **d.** 6   **e.** None   **f.** D: $[2, \infty)$; R: $[0, \infty)$ **19. a.** -5
b. -3 **c.** 1   **d.** D: $(-\infty, \infty)$, R: $(-\infty, \infty)$ **21. a.** $\sqrt{x^2} = |x|$
b. $\sqrt[3]{x^3} = x$ **c.** $\sqrt[5]{-32} = -2$ **23.** 10   **25.** -8 **27.** $\frac{1}{3}$
29. 0.5   **31.** Not a real number   **33.** 11   **35.** 3.4641
37. 26.0624   **39.** $2|x|$ **41.** $9h^2$ **43.** $6|s^3|$ **45.** $12m^4$
47. $|y - 1|$ **49.** $a^2 + 3$

51. 0, -1, -2, -3, -4;
D: $[0, \infty)$; R: $(-\infty, 0]$

53. D: $[-4, \infty)$; R: $[0, \infty)$

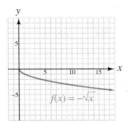

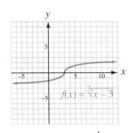

55. D: $[-6, \infty)$ **57.** D: $(-\infty, 4]$ **59.** D: $\left[\frac{4}{9}, \infty\right)$ **61.** D: $[40, \infty)$
63. a. 5   **b.** Undefined   **65. a.** 2   **b.** -3 **67. a.** 4.1231
b. 2.5539   **69. a.** 3.3322   **b.** 7.7543   **71.** 1   **73.** -5 **75.** $\frac{2}{3}$
77. 4   **79.** $-6a$ **81.** $-10p^2q$
83. -5, -4, -3, -2, -1;   **85.** D: $(-\infty, \infty)$; R: $(-\infty, \infty)$
D: $(-\infty, \infty)$; R: $(-\infty, \infty)$

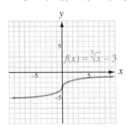

87. 3   **89.** -3 **91.** Not a real number   **93.** $-\frac{1}{2}$ **95.** $2a$
97. $3|a|$ **99.** k^2 **101.** $(m + 4)^2$ **103.** $4s^3t^2$ **105.** $-7b^4$
107. $\frac{1}{2}$ **109.** $-5m^2$ **111.** $20m^8|n|$ **113.** $2|ab|$ **115.** Not a real
number   **117.** $|n + 6|$ **119. a.** 8   **b.** 4   **121. a.** 9   **b.** 3
123. 7.0 in.   **125.** 1,138.5 mm   **127.** About 58.6 beats/min
129. 13.4 ft   **131.** 3.5%   **137.** $\frac{(x - 4y)^2}{(x - 2y)(x - 3y)}$

ARE YOU READY? **9.2** (page 743)

1. a. 8   **b.** -4 **2. a.** 3   **b.** $\frac{1}{2}$ **3. a.** $|x + 5|$ **b.** $3a^2$ **4.** 216
5. $\frac{1}{49}$ **6.** x^9

SELF-CHECKS **9.2**

1. a. 4   **b.** $-\frac{3}{2}$ **c.** -3 **d.** 1   **2. a.** $-2n$ **b.** $5|a|$ **c.** b^2
d. Not a real number   **3. a.** 64   **b.** 625   **c.** 36   **d.** $-\frac{1}{16}$
4. a. $8c^6$ **b.** $9m^2n^2$ **c.** $-8a^6$ **5.** $(7ab)^{1/6}$ **6.** $\sigma = \sqrt{\frac{\Sigma(x - \mu)^2}{N}}$
7. a. $\frac{1}{3}$ **b.** $\frac{1}{216}$ **c.** $\frac{1}{9a^2}$ **d.** -27 **8. a.** $2^{3/5}$ **b.** $12^{4/3}$ **c.** x^2y^9
d. x^2 **9.** $t - 1$ **10. a.** $\sqrt{3}$ **b.** $\sqrt{7xy}$ **c.** $\sqrt[12]{m}$

STUDY SET SECTION **9.2** (page 751)

1. rational (or fractional)   **3.** negative   **5.** index, radicand
7.

Radical form	Exponential form	Base	Exponent
$\sqrt[5]{25}$	$25^{1/5}$	25	$\frac{1}{5}$
$\left(\sqrt[3]{-27}\right)^2$	$(-27)^{2/3}$	-27	$\frac{2}{3}$
$\left(\sqrt[4]{16}\right)^{-3}$	$16^{-3/4}$	16	$-\frac{3}{4}$
$\left(\sqrt{81}\right)^3$	$81^{3/2}$	81	$\frac{3}{2}$
$-\sqrt{\frac{9}{64}}$	$-\left(\frac{9}{64}\right)^{1/2}$	$\frac{9}{64}$	$\frac{1}{2}$

27. D: $[0, \infty)$; R: $[0, \infty)$

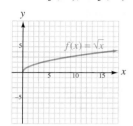

28. D: $(-\infty, \infty)$; R: $(-\infty, \infty)$

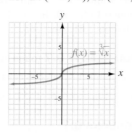

29. D: $[-2, \infty)$; R: $[0, \infty)$

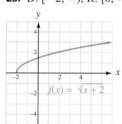

30. D: $(-\infty, \infty)$; R: $(-\infty, \infty)$

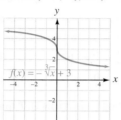

31. $\sqrt{t}$ **32.** $\sqrt[4]{5xy^3}$ **33.** 5 **34.** -6 **35.** Not a real number
36. 1 **37.** $\frac{3}{x}$ **38.** -2 **39.** 5 **40.** $3cd$ **41.** 27 **42.** $\frac{1}{4}$
43. $-16,807$ **44.** 10 **45.** $\frac{27}{8}$ **46.** $\frac{1}{3,125}$ **47.** $125x^3y^6$
48. $\frac{1}{4u^4v^2}$ **49.** $5^{3/4}$ **50.** $a^{1/7}$ **51.** k^8 **52.** $3^{2/3}$ **53.** $u - 1$
54. $v + v^2$ **55.** $\sqrt{a}$ **56.** $\sqrt[6]{c}$ **57.** 183 mi **58.** Two true
statements result: $32 = 32$. **59.** $4\sqrt{5}$ **60.** $3\sqrt[3]{2}$ **61.** $2\sqrt[4]{10}$
62. $-2\sqrt[5]{3}$ **63.** $2x^2\sqrt{2x}$ **64.** $r^4\sqrt[4]{r}$ **65.** $-3j^2\sqrt[3]{jk}$
66. $-2xy\sqrt[3]{2x^2y}$ **67.** $\frac{\sqrt{m}}{12n^6}$ **68.** $\frac{\sqrt{17xy}}{8a^2}$ **69.** $2x$ **70.** $3x^3$
71. $3\sqrt{2}$ **72.** $11\sqrt{5}$ **73.** 0 **74.** $-8a\sqrt[4]{2a}$ **75.** $29x\sqrt{2}$
76. $13x\sqrt[3]{2}$ **77.** $9\sqrt[4]{2t^3} - 8\sqrt[4]{6t^3}$ **78.** $12x^2\sqrt[4]{x} + 5x\sqrt[4]{x}$
80. $\left(6\sqrt{2} + 2\sqrt{10}\right)$ in., 14.8 in. **81.** 7 **82.** $6\sqrt{10}$ **83.** 32
84. $6\sqrt{10}$ **85.** $3x$ **86.** $x + 1$ **87.** $-2x^3\sqrt[3]{x}$ **88.** 3
89. $42t + 9t\sqrt{21t}$ **90.** $-2x^3y^3\sqrt[4]{2x^2y^2}$ **91.** $3b + 6\sqrt{b} + 3$
92. $\sqrt[3]{9p^2} - \sqrt[3]{6p} - 2\sqrt[3]{4}$ **93.** $\frac{10\sqrt{3}}{3}$ **94.** $\frac{\sqrt{15xy}}{5xy}$ **95.** $\frac{\sqrt[3]{6u^2}}{u^2}$
96. $\frac{\sqrt[4]{27ab^2}}{3b}$ **97.** $2\left(\sqrt{2} + 1\right)$ or $2\sqrt{2} + 2$
98. $\frac{12\sqrt{xz} - 16x - 2z}{z - 16x}$ **99.** $\frac{a - b}{a + \sqrt{ab}}$ **100.** $r = \frac{\sqrt[3]{6\pi^2 V}}{2\pi}$
101. 22 **102.** 16, 9 **103.** $\frac{13}{2}$ **104.** $\frac{9}{16}$ **105.** 2, -4 **106.** 7
107. 1 **108.** $-\frac{3}{2}$, 1 **109.** $\cancel{3}$, no solution **110.** 6, $\cancel{-2}$ **111.** 0, 3
112. $-\frac{1}{2}$, 4 **113.** $P = \frac{A}{(r + 1)^2}$ **114.** $I = \frac{h^3 b}{12}$
115. 17 ft **116.** 88 yd **117.** $7\sqrt{2}$ m ≈ 9.90 m
118. $\frac{15\sqrt{2}}{2}$ yd ≈ 10.61 yd **119.** Shorter leg: 6 cm, longer leg:
$6\sqrt{3}$ cm ≈ 10.39 cm **120.** $40\sqrt{3}$ ft ≈ 69.28 ft,
$20\sqrt{3}$ ft ≈ 34.64 ft **121.** $x = 5\sqrt{2} \approx 7.07$, $y = 5$
122. $x = 25\sqrt{3} \approx 43.30$, $y = 25$ **123.** 13 **124.** $2\sqrt{2}$
125. $(7, -3)$ **126.** $(2, -2)$ **127.** $5i$ **128.** $3i\sqrt{2}$ **129.** $-i\sqrt{6}$
130. $\frac{3}{8}i$ **131.** Real, Imaginary **132. a.** True **b.** True **c.** False
d. False **133. a.** $3 - 6i$ **b.** $0 - 19i$ **134. a.** $-1 + 7i$
b. $0 + i$ **135.** $8 - 2i$ **136.** $3 - 5i$ **137.** $3 + 6i$
138. $22 + 29i$ **139.** $-3\sqrt{3} + 0i$ **140.** $-81 + 0i$ **141.** $4 + i$
142. $0 - \frac{3}{11}i$ **143.** -1 **144.** i

CHAPTER 9 TEST (page 821)

1. a. radical **b.** imaginary **c.** extraneous **d.** isosceles
e. rationalize **f.** complex **2. a.** If $\sqrt[n]{a}$ and $\sqrt[n]{b}$ are real
numbers, then $\sqrt[n]{ab} = \sqrt[n]{a}\sqrt[n]{b}$. **b.** If $\sqrt[n]{a}$ and $\sqrt[n]{b}$ are real
numbers, then $\sqrt[n]{\frac{a}{b}} = \frac{\sqrt[n]{a}}{\sqrt[n]{b}}$, $(b \neq 0)$. **c.** No real number raised to
the fourth power is -16.
3. D: $[1, \infty)$; R: $[0, \infty)$

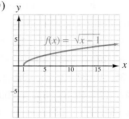

4. 46 ft/sec **5. a.** -1 **b.** 2 **c.** 1 **d.** D: $(-\infty, \infty)$;
R: $(-\infty, \infty)$ **6.** $[-5, \infty)$ **7.** $7x^2$ **8.** -9 **9.** $\frac{1}{216}$ **10.** $\frac{25n^4}{4}$
11. $2^{4/3}$ **12.** $a^{1/9}$ **13.** $|x|$ **14.** $|y - 5|$ **15.** $-4xy^2$ **16.** $\frac{2}{3}a$
17. $t + 8$ **18.** $6xy^2\sqrt{15xy}$ **19.** $2x^5y\sqrt[3]{3}$ **20.** $2\sqrt[4]{2}$
21. $2y^2\sqrt{3y}$ **22.** $14\sqrt[3]{5}$ **23.** $5z^3\sqrt[4]{3z}$ **24.** $-6x\sqrt{y} - 2xy^2$
25. $3 - 7\sqrt{6}$ **26.** $\sqrt[3]{4a^2} + 18\sqrt[3]{2a} + 81$ **27.** $\frac{4\sqrt{10}}{5}$
28. $\frac{x + 2\sqrt{xy} + y}{x - y}$ **29.** $\frac{\sqrt[3]{18a^2}}{2a}$ **30.** $\frac{1}{\sqrt{2}(\sqrt{5} - 3)} = \frac{1}{\sqrt{10} - 3\sqrt{2}}$
31. $\frac{1}{15}$ **32.** 10 **33.** $\cancel{4}$, no solution **34.** 3, $\cancel{-3}$ **35.** 2, 3
36. $\cancel{108}$, no solution **37.** -2 **38.** $G = \frac{4\pi^2 r^3}{Mt^2}$
39. $x = \frac{8\sqrt{3}}{3}$ cm ≈ 4.62 cm, $h = \frac{16\sqrt{3}}{3}$ cm ≈ 9.24 cm
40. $x = 6.13\sqrt{2}$ in. ≈ 8.67 in., $y = 6.13\sqrt{2}$ in. ≈ 8.67 in.
41. 25 **42.** $\left(\frac{5}{2}, -8\right)$ **43.** $(7, 3)$ **44.** 28 in. **45.** $3i\sqrt{5}$
46. -1 **47.** $-4 + 11i$ **48.** $4 - 7i$ **49.** $75 + 45i$
50. $-46 - 78i$ **51.** $0 - \frac{\sqrt{2}}{2}i$ **52.** $\frac{1}{2} + \frac{1}{2}i$

ARE YOU READY? 10.1 (page 826)

1. a. $2\sqrt{7}$ **b.** $6i$ **2.** $\frac{\sqrt{30}}{6}$ **3.** $\frac{9}{2}$ **4.** $\frac{49}{4}$ **5.** 169 **6.** $(x - 4)^2$

SELF CHECKS 10.1

1. $\pm 3\sqrt{2}$ **2.** $\sqrt{\frac{14}{\pi}}$ ft ≈ 2.11 ft **3.** $\pm \frac{7}{4}i$ **4.** 1, -5
5. $\frac{-11 \pm \sqrt{3}}{4}$ **6.** $a^2 - 5a + \frac{25}{4} = \left(a - \frac{5}{2}\right)^2$
7. $5 \pm \sqrt{29}$; 10.39, -0.39 **8.** $\frac{4}{3}$, -2
9. $\frac{-3 \pm \sqrt{6}}{3}$; -0.18, -1.82 **10. a.** $3 \pm 3i\sqrt{2}$ **b.** $-\frac{1}{5} \pm \frac{i\sqrt{74}}{5}$

STUDY SET SECTION 10.1 (page 836)

1. quadratic **3.** square **5.** $\sqrt{c}$, $-\sqrt{c}$ **7. a.** 36 **b.** $\frac{25}{4}$
9. a. Subtract 7 from both sides. **b.** Divide both sides by 4.
11. It is a solution. **13.** plus or minus **15.** $\pm \sqrt{11}$
17. $\pm \sqrt{35}$ **19.** $\pm 5\sqrt{2}$ **21.** $\pm \frac{4\sqrt{3}}{3}$ **23.** $\pm 4i$ **25.** $\pm 2i\sqrt{2}$
27. $\pm \frac{9}{2}i$ **29.** $\pm 2i\sqrt{6}$ **31.** -8, 2 **33.** 0, -8
35. $-5 \pm \sqrt{3}$ **37.** $\frac{2 \pm 2\sqrt{2}}{7}$ **39.** $x^2 + 24x + 144 = (x + 12)^2$
41. $a^2 - 7a + \frac{49}{4} = \left(a - \frac{7}{2}\right)^2$ **43.** $x^2 + \frac{2}{3}x + \frac{1}{9} = \left(x + \frac{1}{3}\right)^2$
45. $m^2 - \frac{5}{6}m + \frac{25}{144} = \left(m - \frac{5}{12}\right)^2$ **47.** $2 \pm \sqrt{6}$; 4.45, -0.45
49. $6 \pm \sqrt{35}$; 11.92, 0.08 **51.** $-10 \pm 5\sqrt{3}$; -1.34, -18.66

53. $-8 \pm 4\sqrt{5}$; 0.94, -16.94 **55.** $-\frac{1}{2}, 1$ **57.** $\frac{3}{4}, -\frac{1}{3}$

59. $\frac{6 \pm \sqrt{33}}{3}$; 3.91, 0.09   **61.** $\frac{-5 \pm \sqrt{41}}{4}$; 0.35, -2.85

63. $-1 \pm i$ **65.** $-4 \pm i\sqrt{2}$ **67.** $-\frac{1}{3} \pm \frac{i\sqrt{62}}{3}$ **69.** $\frac{1}{4} \pm \frac{i\sqrt{15}}{4}$

71. $2, -\frac{4}{3}$ **73.** $\frac{3 \pm 2\sqrt{3}}{3}$; 2.15, -0.15 **75.** $-4 \pm \sqrt{10}$;
$-7.16, -0.84$ **77.** $\pm 2i\sqrt{3}$ **79.** $1 \pm 3\sqrt{2}$; 5.24, -3.24

81. $\frac{7 \pm \sqrt{37}}{2}$; 6.54, 0.46   **83.** $\pm\sqrt{5}$; ± 2.24

85. $\frac{-7 \pm \sqrt{29}}{10}$; $-0.16, -1.24$ **87.** $-\frac{1}{2} \pm \frac{\sqrt{11}}{2}i$

89. $\frac{-5 \pm 2\sqrt{6}}{8}$; $-1.24, -0.01$ **91.** $-3, 9$ **93.** $-\frac{1}{4} \pm \frac{\sqrt{11}}{4}i$

95. a. $\pm 2\sqrt{6}$; ± 4.90 **b.** $\pm 2i\sqrt{6}$ **97. a.** 0, 4
b. $\frac{4 \pm 3\sqrt{2}}{2}$; 4.12, -0.12 **99. a.** $2 \pm 4i$
b. $2 \pm 2\sqrt{6}$; 6.90, -2.90

101. a. $\frac{2 \pm i\sqrt{2}}{2}$ **b.** $\frac{2 \pm \sqrt{10}}{2}$; 2.58, -0.58 **103.** 4.4 sec

105. 1.6 sec   **107.** 1.70 in.   **109.** $c = \frac{\sqrt{Em}}{m}$ **115.** $2ab^2\sqrt[3]{5}$

117. $\frac{2}{5}$

ARE YOU READY? 10.2 (page 838)

1. 11   **2.** $3\sqrt{5}$ **3.** 3; 2, $-1, 7$ **4.** $\frac{3}{4}, -2$ **5.** Not a real
number   **6.** 3.87

SELF CHECKS 10.2

1. $2, -\frac{1}{4}$ **2.** $\frac{1 \pm \sqrt{10}}{3}$; $-0.72, 1.39$ **3.** $-\frac{3}{2} \pm \frac{\sqrt{11}}{2}i$
4. a. $6x^2 - 7x + 9 = 0$ **b.** $2x^2 - 4x - 5 = 0$
c. $4x^2 + 6x - 9 = 0$ **d.** $8x^2 - 7x - 2 = 0$ **5.** 9 in., 40 in.
6. $1   **7.** Late 1988   **8.** $\frac{4 + \sqrt{31}}{2}$ in. ≈ 0.78 in.

STUDY SET SECTION 10.2 (page 848)

1. quadratic   **3. a.** $x^2 + 2x + 5 = 0$ **b.** $3x^2 + 2x - 1 = 0$
5. a. True   **b.** True   **c.** False   **7. a.** 2, -4 **b.** $\frac{1 \pm \sqrt{33}}{4}$
9. a. $1 \pm 2\sqrt{2}$ **b.** $\frac{-3 \pm \sqrt{7}}{2}$ **11. a.** The fraction bar wasn't
drawn under both terms of the numerator.
b. A $\pm$ sign wasn't written between $-b$ and the radical.   **13.** 1, 2
15. A repeated solution of -6 **17.** $-\frac{3}{2}, 1$ **19.** $\frac{2}{3}, -\frac{1}{4}$

21. $\frac{1 \pm \sqrt{29}}{2}$; 3.19, -2.19 **23.** $\frac{-5 \pm \sqrt{5}}{10}$; $-0.28, -0.72$

25. $\frac{-3 \pm \sqrt{6}}{3}$; $-0.18, -1.82$ **27.** $\frac{1 \pm 2\sqrt{5}}{2}$; 2.74, -1.74

29. $-\frac{1}{4} \pm \frac{\sqrt{7}}{4}i$ **31.** $\frac{1}{3} \pm \frac{\sqrt{2}}{3}i$ **33.** $1 \pm i$ **35.** $-\frac{1}{2} \pm i$
37. a. $5x^2 - 9x + 2 = 0$ **b.** $16t^2 + 24t - 9 = 0$
39. a. $3x^2 + 2x - 1 = 0$ **b.** $2m^2 - 3m - 2 = 0$ **41.** $\frac{4}{3}, -\frac{2}{5}$

43. $\frac{2}{3} \pm \frac{\sqrt{2}}{3}i$ **45.** $\frac{1}{4}, -\frac{3}{4}$ **47.** $\frac{3 \pm \sqrt{17}}{4}$; 1.78; -0.28

49. $5 \pm \sqrt{7}$; 2.35, 7.65   **51.** 23, -17

53. $\frac{-5 \pm 3\sqrt{5}}{2}$; 0.85, -5.85 **55.** $\frac{1}{3} \pm \frac{\sqrt{6}}{3}i$

57. $\frac{-3 \pm \sqrt{29}}{10}$; 0.24, -0.84 **59.** $\frac{10 \pm \sqrt{55}}{30}$; 0.58, 0.09

61. $2 \pm 2i$ **63.** $3 \pm i\sqrt{5}$ **65.** $\frac{-5 \pm \sqrt{17}}{2}$; $-0.44, -4.56$

67. $\frac{9 \pm \sqrt{89}}{2}$; 9.22, -0.22 **69.** $\frac{1 \pm \sqrt{7}}{3}$; 1.22, -0.55

71. $\frac{35 \pm 5\sqrt{329}}{14}$; 8.98, -3.98 **73. a.** $-2 \pm \sqrt{11}$; 1.32, -5.32

b. $2 \pm \sqrt{11}$; 5.32, -1.32 **75. a.** 6, -4 **b.** $1 \pm i\sqrt{7}$
77. a. A repeated solution of 21   **b.** A repeated solution of -21
79. 40 ft   **81.** 0.7 units, 2.4 units   **83.** 97 ft by 117 ft
85. About 0.5 mi by 2.5 mi   **87.** 25 sides   **89.** \$4.80 or \$5.20
91. 4,000 subscribers   **93.** 2002   **95.** 0.92 in.   **97.** 2.9 ft, 6.9 ft
101. $n^{1/2}$ **103.** $(3b)^{1/4}$ **105.** $\sqrt[3]{t}$ **107.** $\sqrt[4]{3t}$

ARE YOU READY? 10.3 (page 851)

1. 84   **2. a.** 2   **b.** 2/3   **3. a.** x **b.** a^2 **4.** $\pm 2i$ **5. a.** 9
b. $-\frac{1}{8}$ **6.** 5

SELF CHECKS 10.3

1. a. Two different irrational numbers   **b.** Two different imaginary
numbers that are complex conjugates
2. 3, -3, $2i$, $-2i$ **3.** 4, -9 does not check   **4.** $-125, 8$
5. $-1, 1$ **6.** $-7, 4$ **7.** About 9.5 hours

STUDY SET SECTION 10.3 (page 858)

1. discriminant   **3.** conjugates   **5.** rational   **7. a.** x^2 **b.** $\sqrt{x}$
c. $x^{1/3}$ **d.** $\frac{1}{x}$ **e.** $x + 1$ **9.** $4ac$, 5, 6, 24, rational
11. One repeated rational-number solution   **13.** Two imaginary-
number solutions (complex conjugates)   **15.** Two different
irrational-number solutions   **17.** Two different rational-number
solutions   **19.** Two different irrational-number solutions
21. Two different rational-number solutions   **23.** $-1, 1, -4, 4$
25. 2, -2, $3i$, $-3i$ **27.** 25, 64   **29.** 1, $\frac{9}{4}$ is extraneous

31. $-1, 27$ **33.** $-64, 8$ **35.** 0, 2   **37.** $\frac{1}{4}, \frac{1}{2}$ **39.** $-\frac{1}{3}, \frac{1}{2}$

41. $-4, \frac{2}{3}$ **43.** $\frac{5 \pm \sqrt{65}}{2}$ **45.** $\frac{7 \pm \sqrt{105}}{2}$ **47.** $\frac{9}{4}$, 1 is extraneous

49. $-\frac{1}{3}, 1$ **51.** $-i, i, -3i\sqrt{2}, 3i\sqrt{2}$ **53.** $4 \pm i$

55. $\frac{3 \pm \sqrt{57}}{6}$ **57.** 16, 4   **59.** $\pm i\sqrt{2}, \pm 3\sqrt{2}$

61. Repeated solutions of 1 and -1 **63.** 2, -2, $i\sqrt{7}, -i\sqrt{7}$
65. $\frac{243}{32}$, 1   **67.** A repeated solution of $-\frac{3}{2}$ **69.** $3 \pm \sqrt{7}$
71. 49, 225   **73.** $1 \pm i$ **75.** No solution   **77.** 1, -1, $\sqrt{5}, -\sqrt{5}$
79. $-\frac{5}{7}, 3$ **81.** $-1, -\frac{27}{13}$ **83. a.** 64, -125 **b.** $\frac{1}{4}, -\frac{1}{5}$
85. a. 1, $-\frac{1}{2}$ **b.** $\pm i$ **87.** 103 min   **89.** 20 feet per second
91. 32.4 ft   **95.** $x = 3$ **97.** $y = \frac{2}{3}x$

ARE YOU READY? 10.4 (page 861)

1.
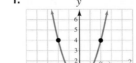
2. -2
3. $x^2 + 8x + 16 = (x + 4)^2$
4. $x^2 + x + \frac{1}{4} = \left(x + \frac{1}{2}\right)^2$
5. A repeated solution of -3
6. A repeated solution of -2
7. -5 **8.** A vertical line

SELF CHECKS 10.4

1.
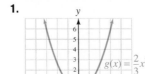
2.
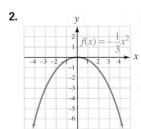

3.

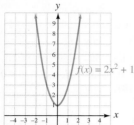

$f(x) = 2x^2 + 1$

4.

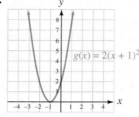

$g(x) = 2(x + 1)^2$

5.

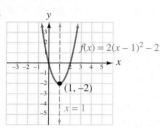

$f(x) = 2(x - 1)^2 - 2$

$(1, -2)$

$x = 1$

6. $(-2, 6)$; $x = -2$; opens upward   **7.**

8. $(2, -4)$

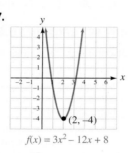

$(2, -4)$

$f(x) = 3x^2 - 12x + 8$

9.

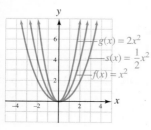

$f(x) = -2x^2 + 12x - 16$

10. 20, $700

STUDY SET SECTION 10.4 (page 872)

1. quadratic, parabola   **3.** axis of symmetry
5. a. $(1, 0)$, $(3, 0)$ **b.** $(0, -3)$ **c.** $(2, 1)$ **d.** $x = 2$
e. Domain: $(-\infty, \infty)$; range: $(-\infty, 1]$
7.

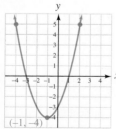

$(-1, -4)$

9. a. 2   **b.** 9, 18   **11.** $-3, 5$
13.
$h = -1$; $f(x) = 2[x - (-1)]^2 + 6$

15.

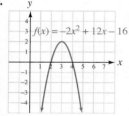

$g(x) = 2x^2$

$s(x) = \frac{1}{2}x^2$

$f(x) = x^2$

17.

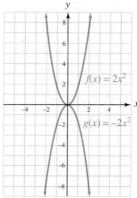

$f(x) = 2x^2$

$g(x) = -2x^2$

19.

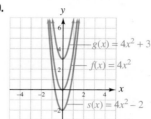

$g(x) = 4x^2 + 3$

$f(x) = 4x^2$

$s(x) = 4x^2 - 2$

21.

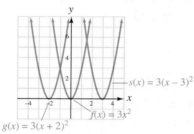

$s(x) = 3(x - 3)^2$

$f(x) = 3x^2$

$g(x) = 3(x + 2)^2$

23. $(1, 2)$; $x = 1$; upward   **25.** $(-3, -4)$; $x = -3$; downward
27. $(7.5, 8.5)$; $x = 7.5$; downward   **29.** $(0, -4)$; $x = 0$; upward
31. $(3, 2)$, $x = 3$ **33.** $(2, 0)$, $x = 2$

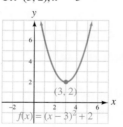

$(3, 2)$

$f(x) = (x - 3)^2 + 2$

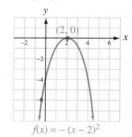

$(2, 0)$

$f(x) = -(x - 2)^2$

35. $(-3, 4)$, $x = -3$ **37.** $(-1, -3)$, $x = 1$

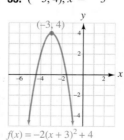

$(-3, 4)$

$f(x) = -2(x + 3)^2 + 4$

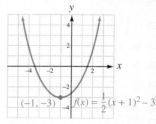

$(-1, -3)$ $f(x) = \frac{1}{2}(x + 1)^2 - 3$

39. $(-2, 1)$; $x = -2$; upward   **41.** $(3, -6)$; $x = 3$; downward

43. $f(x) = (x + 1)^2 - 4$; $(-1, -4)$, $x = -1$

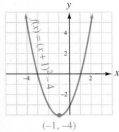

45. $f(x) = 4(x + 3)^2 + 1$; $(-3, 1)$, $x = -3$

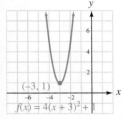

47. $f(x) = \left(x + \frac{1}{2}\right)^2 - \frac{25}{4}$; $\left(-\frac{1}{2}, -\frac{25}{4}\right)$; $x = -\frac{1}{2}$

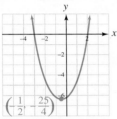

49. $f(x) = -4(x - 2)^2 + 6$; $(2, 6)$, $x = 2$

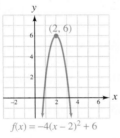

51. $f(x) = 2(x + 2)^2 - 2$; $(-2, -2)$, $x = -2$

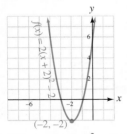

53. $f(x) = -(x + 4)^2 - 1$; $(-4, -1)$, $x = -4$

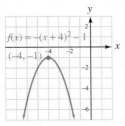

55. $(-1, -6)$ **57.** $\left(\frac{3}{4}, \frac{23}{8}\right)$ **59.** $(-5, 0), (7, 0)$; $(0, -35)$
61. $(0, 0), (2, 0)$; $(0, 0)$
63. $(-2, 0)$; $(-2, 0)$; $(0, 4)$

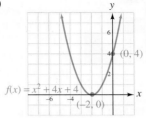

65. $(1, 0)$; $(1, 0)$; $(0, -1)$

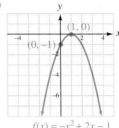

67. $(1, -1)$; $(0, 0), (2, 0)$; $(0, 0)$

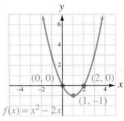

69. $(2, -2)$; $(1, 0), (3, 0)$; $(0, 6)$

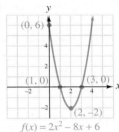

71. $(-1, -2)$; no x-intercept; $(0, -8)$

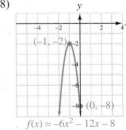

73. $\left(\frac{3}{2}, 0\right)$; $\left(\frac{3}{2}, 0\right)$; $(0, 9)$

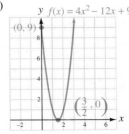

75. $(0.25, 0.88)$ **77.** $(0.50, 7.25)$ **79.** $2, -3$ **81.** $-1.85, 3.25$

83.

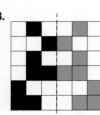

axis of symmetry

85. 15 min, $160
87. 3.75 sec, 225 ft
89. 75 ft by 75 ft, 5,625 ft^2
91. 1968, about 1.5 million; the U.S. involvement in the war in Vietnam was at its peak
93. 200, $7,000   **101.** $\frac{\sqrt{6}}{10}$
103. $15b - 6\sqrt{15b} + 9$

ARE YOU READY? 10.5 (page 875)

1. Yes   **2.** $-5, 10$ **3.**

4.

5. $-3, 3$ **6.**

$y = -x^2 + 4$

SELF CHECKS 10.5

1. $(-4, 3)$

2. $(-\infty, -8] \cup [5, \infty)$

3. $(-\infty, 0) \cup \left(\frac{3}{5}, \infty\right)$

4. $[-2, -1) \cup (3, \infty)$

5. $(-1, 0) \cup (1, \infty)$

6.

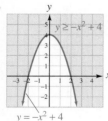

$y \geq -x^2 + 4$

$y = -x^2 + 4$

7.

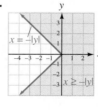

$x = -|y|$

$x \geq -|y|$

STUDY SET SECTION 10.5 (page 884)

1. quadratic   **3.** two   **5.** $(-\infty, -1), (-1, 4), (4, \infty)$
7. a. Yes **b.** No **c.** Yes **d.** No
9. a. $(-3, 2)$ **b.** $(-\infty, -1] \cup [1, \infty)$ **11. a.** Solid
b. Yes   **13.** $x^2 - 6x - 7 \geq 0$ **15.** $(1, 4)$

17. $(-\infty, 3) \cup (5, \infty)$

19. $(-\infty, -6] \cup [7, \infty)$

21. $[-4, 3]$

23. $(-\infty, 0) \cup \left(\frac{1}{2}, \infty\right)$

25. $\left(-\infty, -\frac{5}{3}\right] \cup (0, \infty)$

27. $(-\infty, -3) \cup (1, 4)$

29. $\left(-\frac{1}{2}, \frac{1}{3}\right] \cup \left[\frac{1}{2}, \infty\right)$

31. $(0, 2) \cup (8, \infty)$

33. $\left[-\frac{34}{5}, -4\right) \cup (3, \infty)$

35.

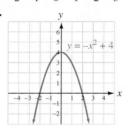

$y = x^2 + 1$

$y < x^2 + 1$

37.

$y = x^2 + 5x + 6$

$y \leq x^2 + 5x + 6$

39.

$y = |x + 4|$

$y < |x + 4|$

41.

$y = -|x| + 2$

$y \geq -|x| + 2$

43. $(-1, 3)$ **45.** $(-\infty, -3) \cup (2, \infty)$
47. $(-4, -2] \cup (-1, 2]$

49. $(-\infty, -3] \cup [3, \infty)$

51. $(-\infty, \infty)$

53. $(-2, 1) \cup (3, \infty)$

55. $(-5, 5)$

57. $\left(-\frac{1}{3}, \frac{3}{2}\right)$ **59.** No solutions

61. $(-1, 4) \cup \left(\frac{23}{2}, \infty\right)$

63. $(-2,100, -900) \cup (900, 2,100)$ **69.** $x = ky$ **71.** $t = kxy$

CHAPTER 10 REVIEW (page 886)

1. $-5, -4$ **2.** $-\frac{1}{3}, -\frac{5}{2}$ **3.** $\pm 2\sqrt{7}; \pm 5.29$ **4.** $4, -8$
5. $\pm 5i$ **6.** $\pm \frac{7\sqrt{5}}{5}; \pm 3.13$ **7.** $r = \frac{\sqrt{\pi A}}{\pi}$
8. $x^2 - x + \frac{1}{4} = \left(x - \frac{1}{2}\right)^2$ **9.** $-4, -2$ **10.** $\frac{3 \pm \sqrt{3}}{2}; 2.37, 0.63$
11. $\frac{6 \pm \sqrt{30}}{6}; 1.91, 0.09$ **12.** $1 \pm 2i\sqrt{3}$ **13.** $\pm 4\sqrt{2}$
14. $\frac{51 \pm \sqrt{11}}{7}$ **15.** Because 7 is an odd number and not divisible by 2, the calculations involved in completing the square on $x^2 + 7x$ involve fractions. The calculations involved in completing the square on $x^2 + 6x$ do not.   **16.** 6 seconds before midnight

17. $\frac{1}{2}, -7$ **18.** $5 \pm \sqrt{7}$; 7.65, 2.35 **19.** 0, 10

20. $\frac{13 \pm \sqrt{163}}{3}$; 8.59, 0.08 **21.** $-\frac{3}{4} \pm \frac{\sqrt{15}}{4}i$ **22.** $\frac{2}{3} \pm \frac{\sqrt{2}}{3}i$

23. $\frac{-3 \pm \sqrt{29}}{10}$; 0.24, −0.84 **24.** $\frac{3 \pm 3\sqrt{13}}{2}$; 6.91, −3.91

25. $\frac{-3 \pm \sqrt{41}}{2}$ **26.** $\frac{-1 \pm \sqrt{13}}{4}$ **27.** 2 is not a factor of the numerator—it is a term. Only common factors of the numerator and denominator can be removed. **28. a.** $(2 + 2x)$ ft **b.** $(6 + 2x)$ ft

29. Sides: 1.25 in. wide; top/bottom: 2.5 in. wide

30. $24 or $26 **31.** 0.7 sec, 1.8 sec **32.** 33 in., 56 in.

33. Two different irrational-number solutions

34. Two imaginary-number solutions that are complex conjugates

35. One repeated solution, a rational number **36.** Two different rational-number solutions **37.** 1, 144 **38.** 8, −27

39. $i, -i, \frac{\sqrt{6}}{3}, -\frac{\sqrt{6}}{3}$ **40.** $1, -\frac{8}{5}$ **41.** $4 \pm i$ **42.** Repeated solutions of −1 and 1 **43.** A repeated solution of $-\frac{2}{5}$ **44.** $\frac{1}{32}$, 32

45. About 81 min **46.** 30 mph **47.** 34.1 million **48.** h, k, x

49.

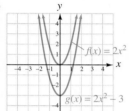

50.

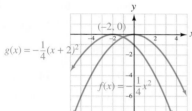

51. $(1, 4), x = 1$

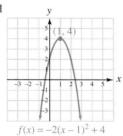

52. $f(x) = 4(x + 2)^2 - 7$; $(-2, -7)$, $x = -2$

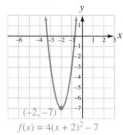

53. $(1, -6)$

54. $\left(-\frac{1}{2}, -\frac{9}{4}\right)$; $x = -\frac{1}{2}$; $(-2, 0)$, $(1, 0)$; $(0, -2)$

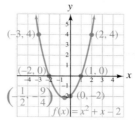

55. 1921; 6,469,326 **56.** $-2, \frac{1}{3}$

57. $(-\infty, -7) \cup (5, \infty)$

58. $[-9, 9]$

59. $(-\infty, 0) \cup \left[\frac{3}{5}, \infty\right)$

60. $\left(-\frac{7}{2}, 1\right) \cup (4, \infty)$

61. $\left[-4, \frac{2}{3}\right]$ **62.** $(-\infty, 0) \cup (1, \infty)$

63.

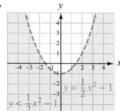

64.

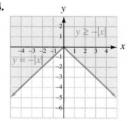

CHAPTER 10 TEST (page 892)

1. a. quadratic **b.** completed, square **c.** vertex **d.** rational **e.** nonlinear **2.** $\pm 3\sqrt{7} \approx \pm 7.94$ **3.** $-7 \pm 5\sqrt{2}$ **4.** $\pm 2i$

5. $x^2 + 11x + \frac{121}{4} = \left(x + \frac{11}{2}\right)^2$ **6.** $\frac{-3 \pm \sqrt{17}}{2}$; −3.56; 0.56

7. $-2 \pm i\sqrt{2}$ **8.** $\frac{2 \pm 3\sqrt{2}}{3}$ **9.** $\frac{-1 \pm \sqrt{2}}{2}$; −1.21; 0.21

10. $1 \pm \sqrt{5}$; −1.24; 3.24 **11.** $2 \pm 3i$ **12.** $-5, -3$

13. A repeated solution of 47 **14.** $\pm\sqrt{10}$ **15.** $1, \frac{1}{4}$ **16.** $-1, \frac{1}{3}$

17. $2, -2, i\sqrt{3}, -i\sqrt{3}$ **18.** $-\frac{4}{5}, \frac{4}{7}$ **19.** $2 \pm \sqrt{10}$; 5.16, −1.16

20. $-8, -\frac{1}{125}$ **21.** $-\frac{1}{2} \pm \frac{\sqrt{5}}{10}i$ **22.** $3, \pm 2i\sqrt{2}$ **23.** $c = \frac{\sqrt{Em}}{m}$

24. a. Two different imaginary-number solutions that are complex conjugates **b.** One repeated solution, a rational number

25. 4.5 ft by 1,502 ft **26.** About 46 min **27.** 20 in. **28.** 4.3 in.

29. 1993 **30.** iii

31. $(1, 2), x = 1$

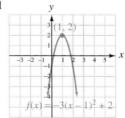

32. $f(x) = 5(x + 1)^2 - 6$; $(-1, -6)$, $x = -1$

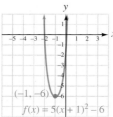

33. $\left(-\frac{1}{4}, -\frac{9}{8}\right)$, $x = -\frac{1}{4}$, $(-1, 0)$, $\left(\frac{1}{2}, 0\right)$; $(0, -1)$

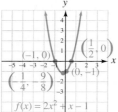

34. 211 ft   **35.** $(-\infty, -2) \cup (4, \infty)$

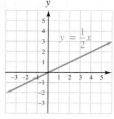

36. $(-3, 2]$

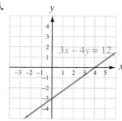

37. 82.7° F

38.

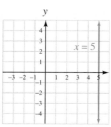

39. $-2, 3$ **40.** $[-2, 3]$

CUMULATIVE REVIEW CHAPTERS 1–10 (page 895)

1. a. True   **b.** False   **c.** True   **2.** 14   **3.** $-41a + 130$
4. It is a solution.   **5.** -2 **6.** All real numbers   **7.** 17 lb
8. 4 in.   **9.** 63.5°   **10.** 3.5 hr   **11.** 6 L   **12.** 80 lb
13. $\left(-\infty, -\frac{3}{4}\right]$

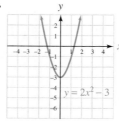

14. No

15.

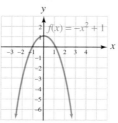

16.

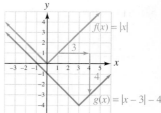

17.

18.

19. x-intercept: $\left(\frac{6}{5}, 0\right)$; y-intercept: $(0, -2)$
20. An increase of 114 million subscribers per year   **21. a.** 3
b. $\frac{5}{6}$ **22.** 0   **23.** $y = 3x + 2$ **24.** $y = -\frac{2}{3}x - 2$

25. 28   **26.** Yes   **27.** It is not a solution.
28. $(-1, 5)$

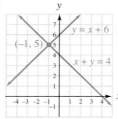

29. $(3, -1)$ **30.** $(-1, 2)$ **31.** 6%: \$3,000; 12%: \$3,000

32.

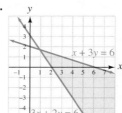

33. x^{31} **34.** $\frac{a^{15}b^5}{c^{20}}$ **35.** 1
36. $\frac{125c^{21}}{8a^{12}b^{12}}$ **37.** 5   **38.** $\frac{4}{a^{10}b^4}$
39. 1.44×10^{10}; 14,400,000,000
40. $\frac{1}{10}s^2 - st - \frac{2}{5}t^2$
41. $-11t^3 + 0.8t^2 - 1.4t$
42. $8a^3 - b^3$
43. $-6t^2 + 13st - 6s^2$
44. $16b^2 - 64b + 64$
45. $36b^2 - \frac{1}{4}$ **46.** $2x - 1$ **47.** $6uvw^2(2w - 3v)$
48. $(x - y)(x - 4)$ **49.** $(x + 5)(x + 2)$ **50.** Prime
51. $(3a + 4)(2a - 5)$ **52.** $2a^2(3a + 2)(5a - 4)$
53. $(7s^3 - 6n^2)^2$ **54.** $(x^2 + 4y^2)(x + 2y)(x - 2y)$
55. $(x - 4)(x^2 + 4x + 16)$ **56.** $(2x^2 + 5y)(4x^4 - 10x^2y + 25y^2)$
57. $-1, -2$ **58.** $0, 2$ **59.** $\frac{2}{3}, -\frac{1}{2}$ **60.** $-5, 5$ **61.** $2, -\frac{5}{2}$
62. $0, \frac{2}{3}, -\frac{1}{2}$ **63.** 5 cm   **64.** $\frac{x + 1}{x - 1}$ **65.** $\frac{(p - 3)(p + 2)}{3(p + 3)}$ **66.** $-\frac{3}{5x}$
67. $\frac{1}{3a}$ **68.** $\frac{7x + 29}{(x + 5)(x + 7)}$ **69.** $\frac{3 - 16b^2}{18b^4}$ **70.** $\frac{y + x}{y - x}$ **71.** 1
72. 5; 3 is extraneous   **73.** $R = \frac{R_1 R_2 R_3}{R_2 R_3 + R_1 R_3 + R_1 R_2}$ **74.** $2\frac{2}{9}$ hr
75. 6,480   **76.** 20   **77.** 18   **78.** All real numbers, $\mathbb{R}$; identity
79. 83 or better   **80.** function   **81. a.** 0   **b.** 2
82. D: The set of real numbers, R: The set of real numbers
83. D: $\{-6, 0, 1, 5\}$, R: $\{-12, 4, 7, 8\}$; no   **84.** No;
$(4, 2), (4, -2)$ **85.** -60 **86. a.** 3   **b.** $3r^2 + 2$
87. The set of all real numbers except -1 **88.** 6, $(0, 15)$
89. $f(x) = -\frac{7}{8}$ **90. a.** $M(t) = 0.17t + 4.06$
b. 10.86 billion vehicle miles
91. D: the set of real numbers,   **92.** D: the set of real numbers,
R: the set of real numbers less   R: the set of real numbers
than or equal to 1   greater than or equal to -4

93. $3, -\frac{3}{2}$ **94.** $-5, -\frac{3}{5}$ **95.** $\left(-\infty, -\frac{10}{9}\right)$

96. $(-\infty, -2) \cup (2, \infty)$

97. $\left[1, \frac{9}{4}\right]$

98. $(-\infty, -10] \cup [15, \infty)$

99. $\left[-\frac{2}{3}, 2\right]$ 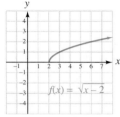　**100.** No solution

101. $(x + y + 4)(x + y + 3)$　**102.** $f = \frac{d_1 d_2}{d_2 + d_1}$

103. $(x + 1)(x^2 - x + 1)(x - 1)(x^2 + x + 1)$

104. All real numbers except 0 and 2;
$(-\infty, 0) \cup (0, 2) \cup (2, \infty)$　**105. a.** iii.　**b.** i.　**c.** iv.　**d.** ii.

106. \$9,000

107. D: $[2, \infty)$; R: $[0, \infty)$

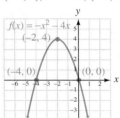

108. D: $[90, \infty)$　**109.** $-3x$　**110.** $4t\sqrt{3t}$　**111.** $\frac{1}{16}$　**112.** $x^{17/12}$

113. $-12\sqrt[4]{2} + 10\sqrt[4]{3}$　**114.** $-18\sqrt{6}$　**115.** $\frac{x + 3\sqrt{x} + 2}{x - 1}$

116. $\frac{5\sqrt[3]{x^2}}{x}$　**117.** 2, 7　**118.** $\frac{1}{4}$　**119.** 2, 4　**120. a.** $3\sqrt{2}$ in.

b. $2\sqrt{3}$ in.　**121. a.** 10　**b.** $\left(-\frac{3}{2}, \frac{5}{2}\right)$　**122.** $-i$　**123.** $-5 + 17i$

124. $\frac{3}{2} + \frac{1}{2}i$　**125.** $3 + 4i$　**126.** $0 - \frac{2}{3}i$　**127.** $\pm 2\sqrt{7}$

128. $19 \pm i\sqrt{5}$　**129.** $\frac{3 \pm \sqrt{3}}{2}$　**130.** $\frac{1}{5} \pm \frac{2}{5}i$　**131.** 10 ft by 18 ft

132. 50 m and 120 m　**133.** $-8, 27$

134. Repeated solutions of -1 and 1

135. $(-2, 4), x = -2; (-4, 0), (0, 0); (0, 0)$

136. $(-9, 9)$

137. $(-4, -2] \cup (-1, 2]$

138. a. $-\frac{3}{4}$　**b.** No solution

ARE YOU READY? 11.1 (page 900)

1. $9x^2 + 2x - 8$　**2.** $2x^3 - x^2$　**3.** $72x^3 - 45x^2 - 32x + 20$

4. $x + 2$

SELF CHECKS 11.1

1. a. $(f + g)(x) = 2x^2 + 6x - 2$; D: $(-\infty, \infty)$

b. $(f - g)(x) = -2x^2 - 2$; D: $(-\infty, \infty)$

c. $(f \cdot g)(x) = 6x^3 + 5x^2 - 6x$; D: $(-\infty, \infty)$

d. $(f/g)(x) = \frac{3x - 2}{2x^2 + 3x}$; $\left(-\infty, -\frac{3}{2}\right) \cup \left(-\frac{3}{2}, 0\right) \cup (0, \infty)$　**2. a.** 78

b. -164　**c.** 56　**d.** Undefined　**3. a.** -8　**b.** 5

c. $(g \circ f)(x) = 6 - x^3$　**4. a.** -6　**b.** -3　**c.** -4

5. $f(x) = \sqrt{x}, g(x) = x + 15$　**6.** $C(t) = -\frac{5}{6}t + 30$

STUDY SET SECTION 11.1 (page 907)

1. sum, $f(x) + g(x)$, difference, $f(x) - g(x)$　**3.** domain

5. nested　**7. a.** $g(3)$　**b.** $g(3)$

9.

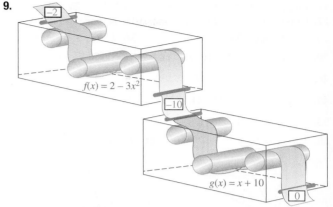

11. $g(x), (3x - 1), 9x, 2x$　**13.** $(f + g)(x) = 3x - 2, (-\infty, \infty)$

15. $(g - f)(x) = -x - 4, (-\infty, \infty)$

17. $(f \cdot g)(x) = 2x^2 - 5x - 3, (-\infty, \infty)$

19. $(g/f)(x) = \frac{x - 3}{2x + 1}, \left(-\infty, -\frac{1}{2}\right) \cup \left(-\frac{1}{2}, \infty\right)$

21. $(f + g)(x) = 7x, (-\infty, \infty)$　**23.** $(g - f)(x) = x, (-\infty, \infty)$

25. $(f \cdot g)(x) = 12x^2, (-\infty, \infty)$

27. $(g/f)(x) = \frac{4}{3}, (-\infty, 0) \cup (0, \infty)$　**29.** 20　**31.** -5　**33.** 0

35. $-\frac{1}{3}$　**37.** 7　**39.** 24　**41.** $-\frac{1}{2}$　**43.** $(g \circ f)(2x) = 16x^2 + 8x$

45. a. 0　**b.** 6　**c.** -3　**47. a.** -1　**b.** 6　**c.** -6

49. $f(x) = x^2; g(x) = x + 15$　**51.** $f(x) = x + 9; g(x) = x^5$

53. $f(x) = \sqrt{x}; g(x) = 16x - 1$　**55.** $f(x) = \frac{1}{x}; g(x) = x - 4$

57. 58　**59.** 110　**61.** 2　**63.** $(g \circ f)(x) = 9x^2 - 9x + 2$

65. $(f - g)(x) = -2x^2 + 3x - 3, (-\infty, \infty)$

67. $(f/g)(x) = \frac{3x - 2}{2x^2 + 1}, (-\infty, \infty)$　**69.** $\frac{1}{9}$

71. $(g \circ f)(8x) = 64x^2$　**73.** $(f - g)(x) = 3, (-\infty, \infty)$

75. $(g/f)(x) = \frac{x^2 - 4}{x^2 - 1}, (-\infty, -1) \cup (-1, 1) \cup (1, \infty)$　**77.** 4

79. 0　**81. a.** 7　**b.** 8　**c.** 12　**d.** 0　**85. a.** 1,026; in 2004, the average combined math and reading score was 1,026.　**b.** 10; in 2004, the average difference in the math and reading scores was 10.

c. 1,016　**d.** 14　**87.** $C(t) = \frac{5}{9}(2,668 - 200t)$　**89. a.** About \$75

b. $C(m) = \frac{3m}{20} = 0.15m$　**95.** $\frac{1}{c - d}$

ARE YOU READY? 11.2 (page 911)

1. D: $\{-2, 3, 5, 9\}$, R: $\{-3, 1, 8, 10\}$　**2.** Yes　**3.** function

4. $16x + 6$

SELF CHECKS 11.2

1. a. Yes　**b.** No, $(-1, 1), (1, 1)$　**2. a.** No　**b.** Yes

3. a. $f^{-1}(x) = \frac{-x - 3}{5}$　**b.** $f^{-1}(x) = \sqrt[5]{x}$

5.

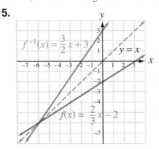

STUDY SET SECTION 11.2 (page 918)

1. one-to-one **3.** inverses **5.** one-to-one **7.** range, domain
9. 1 **11. a.** No **b.** No **13.** $-4, 0, 8$ **15.** $y, 2y, 3, y, f^{-1}$
17. inverse, inverse **19.** Yes **21.** No **23.** No **25.** No
27. One-to-one **29.** Not one-to-one **31.** Not one-to-one
33. One-to-one **35.** $f^{-1}(x) = \frac{x-4}{2}$ **37.** $f^{-1}(x) = 5x - 4$
39. $f^{-1}(x) = 5x + 4$ **41.** $f^{-1}(x) = \frac{2}{x} + 3$ **43.** $f^{-1}(x) = \frac{4}{x}$
45. $f^{-1}(x) = \sqrt[3]{x - 8}$ **47.** $f^{-1}(x) = x^3$
49. $f^{-1}(x) = \sqrt[3]{x} - 10$ **51.** $f^{-1}(x) = \sqrt[3]{\frac{x+3}{2}}$
53. $f^{-1}(x) = \sqrt[7]{2x}$
59. $f^{-1}(x) = \frac{1}{2}x$ **61.** $f^{-1}(x) = \frac{x-3}{4}$

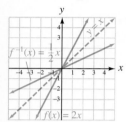
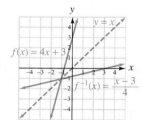

63. $f^{-1}(x) = -\frac{3}{2}x + \frac{9}{2}$ **65.** $f^{-1}(x) = \sqrt[3]{x}$

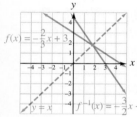
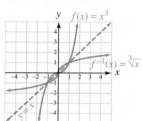

67. $f^{-1}(x) = \sqrt{x + 1}$

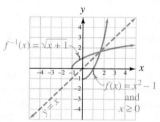

69. a. Yes; no **b.** No. Twice during this period, the person's anxiety level was at the maximum threshold value. **77.** $3 - 8i$
79. $18 - i$ **81.** $-28 - 96i$

ARE YOU READY? 11.3 (page 921)

1. a. 3^{12} **b.** 3^{32} **2. a.** 8 **b.** 1 **c.** $\frac{1}{4}$ **3. a.** $\frac{1}{9}$ **b.** 1 **c.** 27
4. line, parabola

SELF CHECKS 11.3

1.   **2.**

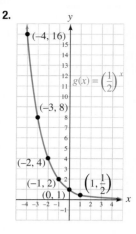

3. a.   **b.**

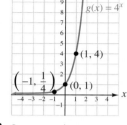
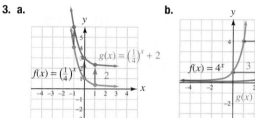

4. $\$7,258,641$ **5.** $\$118,344.56$ **6.** About 2.4 milligrams

STUDY SET SECTION 11.3 (page 931)

1. exponential **3.** asymptote **5. a.** Exponential **b.** $(-\infty, \infty)$
c. $(0, \infty)$ **d.** $(0, 1)$, none **e.** Yes **f.** The x-axis ($y = 0$)
g. Increasing **h.** 3 **7. a.** $\frac{1}{9}$ **b.** $\frac{1}{16}$ **c.** 25 **9. a.** iii **b.** iv
c. ii **d.** i **11. a.** D: $(-\infty, \infty)$, R: $(-3, \infty)$
b. D: $(-\infty, \infty)$, R: $(1, \infty)$ **13.** $f(x) = 5^x$

x	$f(x)$
-3	$\frac{1}{125}$
-2	$\frac{1}{25}$
-1	$\frac{1}{5}$
0	1
1	5
2	25
3	125

15. a. ii **b.** i **c.** ii **d.** ii
e. i **17.** $b > 0, b \neq 1$
19.   **21.**

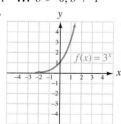
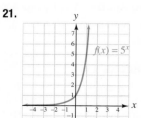

23.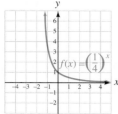

25.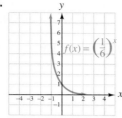

27.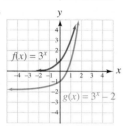

29.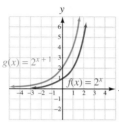

31.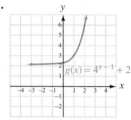

33.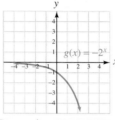

35. Increasing   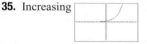   **37.** Decreasing

39. a. 280 ppm, 295 ppm, 370 ppm   **b.** About 1970
41. a. At the end of the 2nd year   **b.** At the end of the 4th year
c. During the 7th year
43. a.

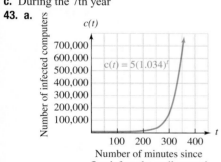

b. About 46,650,000 computers   **45.** About 422 mm   **47.** 8.7 gm

49.

Year	2006	2007	2008	2009
Number in poverty (in millions)	35.8	37.9	40.2	42.6

51. 2,295   **53.** $22,080.40   **55.** $32.03   **57.** $2,273,996.13
69. 40   **71.** 120°

ARE YOU READY? 11.4 (page 935)

1.

x	$f^{-1}(x)$
1	0
2	1
4	2

2. a. 125   **b.** 3   **3. a.** 1   **b.** 1/2
4. a. 1,000   **b.** $\frac{1}{100}$

SELF CHECKS 11.4

1. $2^7 = 128$ **2.** $\log_9 \frac{1}{9} = -1$ **3. a.** 7   **b.** $\frac{1}{9}$ **c.** 3   **4. a.** 2
b. -2 **c.** $\frac{1}{2}$ **5. a.** 4   **b.** -3 **c.** Undefined   **6.** 75.3998
7. a. 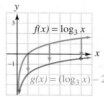   **b.**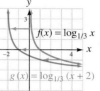

8. About 36 dB   **9.** About 63 catfish

STUDY SET SECTION 11.4 (page 945)

1. logarithmic   **3.** asymptote   **5. a.** Logarithmic
b. D: $(0, \infty)$; R: $(-\infty, \infty)$ **c.** None, $(1, 0)$ **d.** Yes
e. The y-axis $(x = 0)$ **f.** Increasing   **g.** 1   **7. a.** ii   **b.** iii   **c.** i
d. iv   **9.** $6^2, 36$ **11.** exponent   **13.** logarithmic
15. 2, -2 **17.** 1, undefined, undefined
19. a. $-0.30, 0, 0.30, 0.60, 0.78, 0.90, 1$
b.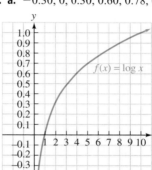

21. a. 10   **b.** x
23. $3^4 = 81$
25. $10^1 = 10$
27. $4^{-3} = \frac{1}{64}$
29. $5^{1/2} = \sqrt{5}$
31. $10^{-1} = 0.1$
33. $8^x = 64$
35. $b^t = T_1$
37. $n^{-42} = C$
39. $\log_8 64 = 2$
41. $\log_4 \frac{1}{16} = -2$
43. $\log_{1/2} 32 = -5$

45. $\log_x z = y$ **47.** $\log_y 8.6 = t$ **49.** $\log_7 (B + 1) = 4.3$
51. 9   **53.** 64   **55.** 3   **57.** $\frac{1}{25}$ **59.** $\frac{1}{6}$ **61.** 10   **63.** $\frac{2}{3}$
65. 5   **67.** 1,000   **69.** 4   **71.** 1   **73.** $\frac{1}{3}$ **75.** 3   **77.** 2
79. 6   **81.** -1 **83.** 5   **85.** $\frac{1}{2}$ **87.** 0.5119   **89.** -2.3307
91. 6,043.6597   **93.** 0.1726   **95.** 0.3162   **97.** 0.0195
99. Increasing   **101.** Decreasing

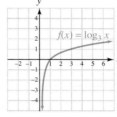   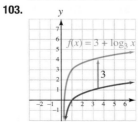

103. 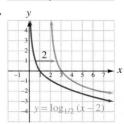   **105.**

107.

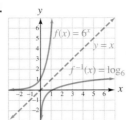

109.

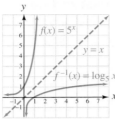

111. 49.5 dB   **113.** 4.4   **115.** About 423 cases
117. About 99 sunfish   **119.** 77.8%   **121.** 10.8 yr   **127.** 10
129. 0; $-\frac{5}{9}$ is extraneous

ARE YOU READY? **11.5** (page 948)

1. 2.25   **2.** 1   **3.** 2.7   **4.** 82.05   **5.** $3^6, x$ **6.** 8, 3

SELF CHECKS **11.5**

1. \$3,037,760.44   **2.** 3,347   **3.** 104.4°   **4. a.** 3   **b.** -1 **c.** $\frac{1}{3}$
5. a. 6.9199   **b.** 0.0498   **6.** About 63 years
7. About 5.3 feet per second

STUDY SET SECTION **11.5** (page 957)

1. exponential; e **3.** continuously   **5. a.** The natural exponential
function   **b.** D: $(-\infty, \infty)$; R: $(0, \infty)$ **c.** (0, 1), none   **d.** Yes
e. The x-axis $(y = 0)$ **f.** Increasing   **g.** e **7.** 2.718281828459
9. e **11.** $e, 2$
13.

15. a. 2.7182818 . . .; e **b.** They decrease, no   **17.** $f^{-1}(x) = e^x$
19. 1,000, 10, 0.9, 2,459.6   **21.** l, n **23.** LOG, LN
25.

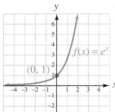

27.

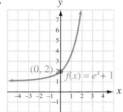

29.

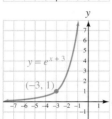

31.

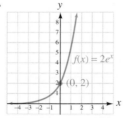

33. 24,765.16   **35.** 3,811,325.37   **37.** 11,542.14   **39.** 542.85
41. 5   **43.** 6   **45.** -1 **47.** $\frac{1}{4}$ **49.** $\frac{2}{3}$ **51.** -7 **53.** 3.5596
55. -5.3709 **57.** 0.5423   **59.** Undefined   **61.** 4.0645
63. 69.4079   **65.** 0.0245   **67.** 2.7210
69.

71.

73. \$13,375.68   **75.** \$7,518.28 from annual compounding,
\$7,647.95 from continuous compounding   **77.** \$6,849.16
79. 133 million, 140 million, 165 million, 194 million, 206 million,
237 million, 269 million   **81.** 4,715,620; 6,370,911
83. About 51   **85.** About 39   **87.** 14 chairs   **89.** 105,731 germs
91. About 49 meters per second   **93.** About 16 years
95. The year 2042   **97.** About 9.2 yr   **99.** About 3.5 hr

101. About 169 beats per minute   **103.** About 1 foot per second
faster (5.9 ft/sec $-$ 4.9 ft/sec)   **115.** $4x^2\sqrt{15x}$ **117.** $10y\sqrt{3y}$

ARE YOU READY? **11.6** (page 962)

1. 3   **2.** 3   **3.** -9 **4.** 2   **5. a.** $x^{1/2}$ **b.** $\sqrt{x-2}$ **6.** 1.6094

SELF CHECKS **11.6**

1. a. 0   **b.** 1   **c.** 4   **d.** 2   **2. a.** $1 + \log_3 4$ **b.** $3 + \log y$
c. $2 + \log_5 c + \log_5 d$ **3. a.** $1 - \log_6 5$ **b.** $\ln y - \ln 100$
4. $\log_b x - \log_b y - \log_b z$ **5. a.** $4 \ln x$ **b.** $\frac{1}{3}\log_2 3$

6. $\frac{3}{4}\log x + \frac{1}{4}\log y - \frac{1}{4}\log z$ **7.** $\log_a \frac{x^2\sqrt{y}}{(x-y)^2}$ **8. a.** 0.1761
b. -0.1249 **9.** 0.6826   **10.** 7.6

STUDY SET SECTION **11.6** (page 971)

1. product   **3.** power   **5. a.** 0   **b.** 1   **c.** x **d.** x **11.** c   **13.** b
15. $8, a^3, 3, 1$ **17.** True   **19.** 0   **21.** 7   **23.** 10   **25.** 2   **27.** 1
29. 7   **31.** $2 + \log_2 5$ **33.** $\log 25 + \log y$
35. $2 + \log p + \log q$ **37.** $\log 5 + \log x + \log y + \log z$
39. $2 - \log 9$ **41.** $\log_6 x - 2$ **43.** $\log 7 + \log c - \log 2$
45. $1 + \log x - \log y$ **47.** $1 + \ln x + \ln y - \ln z$
49. $-1 - \log_8 m$ **51.** $7 \ln y$ **53.** $\frac{1}{2}\log 5$ **55.** $-3 \log e$
57. $\frac{3}{5}\log_7 100$ **59.** $\log x + \log y + 2 \log z$
61. $1 + \frac{1}{3}\log_2 x - \log_2 y$ **63.** $3 \log x + 2 \log y$
65. $\frac{1}{2}\log_b x + \frac{1}{2}\log_b y$ **67.** $\frac{1}{3}\log_a x - \frac{1}{4}\log_a y - \frac{1}{4}\log_a z$
69. $20 \ln x + \frac{1}{2}\ln z$ **71.** $-3d \log_5 t$ **73.** $\frac{1}{2} + \frac{1}{2}\ln x$
75. $\log_2 x^9(x + 1)$ **77.** $\log_3 \frac{x(x + 2)}{8}$ **79.** $\log_b \frac{\sqrt{z}}{x^3 y^2}$

81. $\log_b \sqrt[3]{M - 3}$ **83.** $\ln \frac{\frac{x}{z} + x}{\frac{y}{z} + y} = \ln \frac{x}{y}$ **85.** $\log_6 \frac{\sqrt{x^2 + 1}}{x^2 + 2}$

87. 1.4472   **89.** -1.1972 **91.** 1.1972   **93.** 1.8063   **95.** 1.7712
97. -1.0000 **99.** 1.8928   **101.** 2.3219   **103.** a, c   **105.** a, b
107. About 4.8   **109. a.** $B = \log\left(\frac{I}{I_0}\right)^{10}$ **b.** $T = \ln\sqrt[k]{\frac{C_2}{C_1}}$
119. $-\frac{7}{6}$ **121.** $\left(1, -\frac{1}{2}\right)$

ARE YOU READY? **11.7** (page 973)

1. a. 4   **b.** -3 **2.** 1.1309   **3.** $x \log_3 8$ **4.** 1   **5. a.** $\log_2 5x$
b. $\ln \frac{10}{2t + 1}$ **6.** Undefined

SELF CHECKS **11.7**

1. 2   **2.** A repeated solution of 1   **3.** $\frac{\log 4}{\log 5} \approx 0.8614$
4. $\frac{2 \log 5}{\log 5 - \log 3} \approx 6.3013$ **5.** $\frac{\ln 35}{2.1} \approx 1.6930$ **6.** $\frac{7}{2}$ **7.** 8   **8.** 2
9. $\frac{9}{16}$ **10.** About 1.58×10^{-5} gram-ions per liter
11. About 11,400 years   **12.** About 10 hours

STUDY SET SECTION **11.7** (page 983)

1. exponential   **3. a.** equal; x, y **b.** equal; x, y **5.** -2
7. logarithm   **9.** $\ln 4$ **11.** Not a solution   **13. a.** Divide both
sides by $\ln 3$.   **b.** $\frac{\ln 5}{\ln 3}$ **c.** 1.4650   **15. a.** 1.2920   **b.** 10.7549
17. a. log   **b.** $A_0 2^{-t/h}$ **c.** $P_0 e^{kt}$ **19.** log, log 2, 2.8074
21. 4   **23.** $-\frac{3}{4} = -0.75$ **25.** 3, -1
27. A repeated solution of -2 **29.** $\frac{\log 5}{\log 4} \approx 1.1610$
31. $\frac{\log 2 + \log 13}{\log 13} \approx 1.2702$ **33.** $\frac{\log 2}{\log 3 - \log 2} \approx 1.7095$
35. $\frac{3 \log 5}{\log 5 - 2 \log 3} \approx -8.2144$ **37.** $\frac{\ln 4.5}{2.9} \approx 0.5186$

39. $-\frac{\ln 14.2}{0.2} \approx -13.2662$ **41.** 5,000 **43.** 12 **45.** -93
47. 0.08 **49.** -7 **51.** 3 **53.** 50 **55.** $\frac{5}{4} = 1.25$ **57.** 0.5
59. 15.75 **61.** 2 **63.** $e \approx 2.7183$ **65.** $\pm\sqrt{\frac{\log 10}{\log 7}} \approx \pm 1.0878$
67. 10 **69.** 10 **71.** 4 **73.** $\frac{\log 15 - 2\log 9}{\log 9} \approx -0.7675$
75. 10, -10 **77.** 10 **79.** 9 **81.** A repeated solution of 4
83. 1, 7 **85.** $\frac{\ln 9}{3} \approx 0.7324$ **87.** 6 **89. a.** $\frac{10^{1.7}}{5} \approx 10.0237$
b. $\frac{e^{1.7}}{5} \approx 1.0948$ **91. a.** $\frac{\log 90 + 5\log 4}{3\log 4} \approx 2.7486$
b. $\frac{5 + \ln 90}{3} \approx 3.1666$ **93. a.** $\frac{5}{4}$ **b.** $\frac{5}{4}$ **95. a.** 3 **b.** 2 **97.** 1.8
99. 20 **101.** About 6.3×10^{-14} gram-ions per liter
103. About 5.1 yr **105.** About 42.7 days **107.** About 4,200 yr
109. About 5.6 yr **111.** About 5.4 yr **113.** Because $\ln 2 \approx 0.7$
115. About 25.3 yr **117.** 2.828 times larger
119. $\frac{1}{3}\ln 0.75 \approx -0.0959$ **125.** $\sqrt{137}$ in.

CHAPTER 11 REVIEW (page 986)

1. $(f + g)(x) = 3x + 1, (-\infty, \infty)$
2. $(f - g)(x) = x - 1, (-\infty, \infty)$
3. $(f \cdot g)(x) = 2x^2 + 2x, (-\infty, \infty)$
4. $(f/g)(x) = \frac{2x}{x + 1}, (-\infty, -1) \cup (-1, \infty)$ **5.** 3 **6.** 5
7. $(f \circ g)(x) = 4x^2 + 4x + 3$ **8.** $(g \circ f)(x) = 2x^2 + 5$
9. a. 0 **b.** -8 **c.** 0 **d.** -1 **10.** $C(m) = \frac{3.25m}{8}$
11. No **12.** Yes **13.** Yes **14.** No **15.** Yes **16.** No
17. $-6, -1, 7, 20$ **18.**

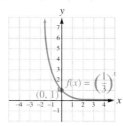

19. $f^{-1}(x) = \frac{x + 3}{6}$ **20.** $f^{-1}(x) = \frac{4}{x} + 1$ **21.** $f^{-1}(x) = \sqrt[3]{x} - 2$
22. $f^{-1}(x) = 6x + 1$
23. $f^{-1}(x) = x^3 + 1$

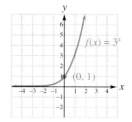

25. a. $n(x) = 2^x, s(t) = 1.08^t$ **b.** 121.9774
26. a. Exponential decay **b.** Exponential growth
27. D: $(-\infty, \infty)$; R: $(0, \infty)$ **28.** D: $(-\infty, \infty)$; R: $(0, \infty)$

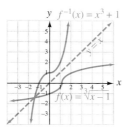

29. D: $(-\infty, \infty)$; R: $(-2, \infty)$ **30.** D: $(-\infty, \infty)$; R: $(0, \infty)$

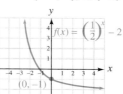
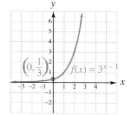

31. The x-axis $(y = 0)$ **32. a.** 128,000 tons
b. About 281,569,441 tons **33.** About \$2,189,703.45
34. About \$2,015 **35.** D: $(0, \infty)$; R: $(-\infty, \infty)$ **36.** Since there is
no real number such that $10^? = 0$, log 0 is undefined. **37.** $4^3 = 64$
38. $\log_7 \frac{1}{7} = -1$ **39.** 2 **40.** -2 **41.** 0 **42.** Undefined
43. $\frac{1}{2}$ **44.** 3 **45.** 32 **46.** $\frac{1}{81}$ **47.** 4 **48.** 10 **49.** $\frac{1}{2}$
50. $\frac{1}{3}$ **51.** 0.6542 **52.** 26.9153
53.

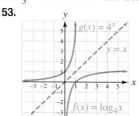

54. **55.**

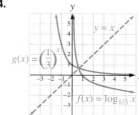
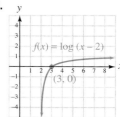

56.

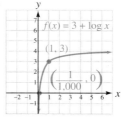

57. About 53 dB **58.** About 4.4 **59. a.** 52 cm **b.** About 74.6 cm
60. About 95% **61. a.** $e \approx 2.72$ **b.** 2.7081, 15 **62.** 16.6704
63. D: $(-\infty, \infty)$; R: $(1, \infty)$ **64.** D: $(-\infty, \infty)$; R: $(0, \infty)$

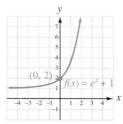
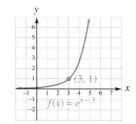

65. \$2,324,767.37 **66.** About \$211.7 billion **67.** 13.9%,
11.67%, 9.80% **68.** The exponent on the base e is negative.
69. 1 **70.** 2 **71.** -5 **72.** $\frac{1}{2}$ **73.** Undefined **74.** Undefined
75. 0 **76.** -7 **77.** 6.1137 **78.** -0.1625 **79.** 10.3398
80. 0.0002
81. They have different bases: $\log x = \log_{10} x$ and $\ln x = \log_e x$.

17.

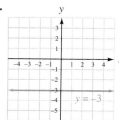

18.

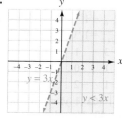

19. $\frac{3}{5}$ **20.** A decrease of 900,000 viewers per year **21.** $-\frac{4}{5}$

22. $y = -2x + 1$ **23.** Perpendicular **24.** $y = \frac{1}{4}x - 1$

25.

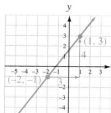

26. -8

27. Domain: $\{-4, 1, 4, 5\}$; range: $\{-3, 2, 8\}$

28. a. Yes **b.** No; (0, 10), (0, 12)

29. $(-2, 3)$

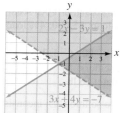

30. $(-3, -1)$
31. $(-1, 2)$ **32.** 550 mph
33. 36 lb of hard candy, 12 lb soft candy

34.

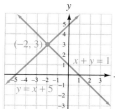

35. y^9 **36.** $\frac{b^6}{27a^3}$ **37.** 2
38. $\frac{x^{10}z^4}{9y^6}$ **39.** 2,600,000
40. 7.3×10^{-4}

41.

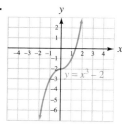

42. $6x^3 + 4x$
43. $6x^3 + 8x^2 + 3x - 72$
44. $-6a^5$ **45.** $6b^2 + 5b - 4$
46. $6x^3 - 7x^2y + y^3$
47. $4x^2 + 20xy + 25y^2$
48. $81m^4 - 1$ **49.** $2a - \frac{3}{2}b + \frac{1}{2a}$
50. $2x + 1$
51. $6a(a - 2a^2b + 6b)$
52. $(x + y)(2 + a)$

53. $(x + 2)(x - 8)$ **54.** $3y^3(5y - 2)(2y + 5)$
55. $(t^2 + 4)(t + 2)(t - 2)$ **56.** $(b + 5)(b^2 - 5b + 25)$
57. $0, -\frac{8}{3}$ **58.** $\frac{2}{3}, -\frac{1}{5}$ **59.** 5 in. **60.** -8 **61.** $\frac{3(x + 3)}{x + 6}$
62. -1 **63.** $\frac{x - 3}{x - 5}$ **64.** $\frac{1}{s - 5}$ **65.** $\frac{x^2 + 4x + 1}{x^2y}$ **66.** $\frac{x^2 + 5x}{x^2 - 4}$
67. $\frac{9m^2}{2}$ **68.** $\frac{9y + 5}{4 - y}$ **69.** 3 **70.** 1 **71.** $a = \frac{b}{b - 1}$
72. $2\frac{6}{11}$ days **73.** 875 days **74.** 39 **75.** 1 **76.** No solution
77. $b_1 = \frac{2A - hb_2}{h}$ **78.** 20 students
79. $(-\infty, \infty)$; $\mathbb{R}$
80. Years after 2002 **81. a.** -105 **b.** $-r^2 - \frac{r}{2}$
82. a. $A(t) = -170t + 5,350$ **b.** 1,100 accidents

83. a. 4 **b.** 5 **c.** $-2, 1$ **d.** Domain: $(-\infty, \infty)$; range: $(-\infty, \infty)$
84. 288 ft **85. a.** Yes **b.** No. It does not pass the vertical line test. $(-2, 6), (-2, 2)$ **86. a.** D: the set of real numbers; R: the set of real numbers greater than or equal to 0.

b. $g(x) = |x| + 3$

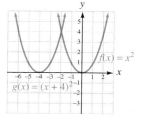

87. $[-10, 14]$

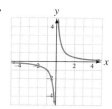

88. $(-\infty, 2) \cup (7, \infty)$

89. $(x + 2 + y)(x + 2 - y)$ **90.** $(b + 1)(b - 1)(b + 4)(b - 4)$
91. All real numbers except 0 and 3; $(-\infty, 0) \cup (0, 3) \cup (3, \infty)$
92. $-\frac{n^6}{n^2 - 2}$ **93.** $\frac{2x - 3}{3x - 1}$
94.

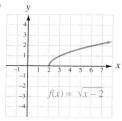

95. 9 **96.** 1.2 revolutions per second
97. D: $[2, \infty)$; R: $[0, \infty)$

98. About 3.2 meters per sec **99.** $2|x|$
100. $\frac{1}{16}$ **101.** $10a^3b^2$ **102.** $2xy\sqrt[4]{x^3}$ **103.** $9\sqrt{6}$
104. $-12\sqrt[4]{2} + 10\sqrt[4]{3}$ **105.** $\frac{6x\sqrt{2x}}{y}$
106. $\frac{3m}{2n^2}$ **107.** $\frac{2\sqrt[3]{a^2}}{a}$ **108.** $\frac{x - 2\sqrt{xy} + y}{x - y}$ **109.** 1, 9
110. 21.2 in. **111.** $7i$ **112.** $3i\sqrt{6}$
113. a. $1 + 5i$ **b.** $16 - 2i$ **114. a.** $6 - 17i$ **b.** $1 - i$
115. $-2, -6$ **116.** $\frac{1 \pm \sqrt{33}}{8}$; $-0.59, 0.84$ **117.** $0 \pm 4i$
118. $2 \pm i$ **119.** $8, -27$ **120.**

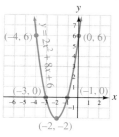

121. 16 **122.** $f^{-1}(x) = -\frac{2}{3}x + 2$

123. D: $(-\infty, \infty)$; R: $(0, \infty)$ **124.** D: $(0, \infty)$; R: $(-\infty, \infty)$

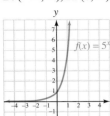

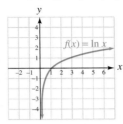

125. 2.7   **126.** About 8.6 billion   **127.** 5   **128.** 64   **129.** -2
130. 1   **131.** $3 \ln y + \frac{1}{2} \ln x - \ln z$ **132.** $\log \frac{x^2 z}{y^3}$ **133.** -8.2144
134. 10   **135.** $(2, -1, 1)$ **136.** $\angle D$: $40°$, $\angle E$: $60°$, $\angle F$: $80°$
137. $(2, -3)$ **138.** $\left(5, \frac{3}{2}\right)$

ARE YOU READY? 13.1 (page 1076)

1. $x^2 - 16x + 64$ **2.** $x^2 - 6x + 9 = (x - 3)^2$ **3.** $(y + 5)^2$
4. $-3(y^2 + 4y)$

SELF CHECK 13.1

1. a. 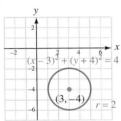   **b.**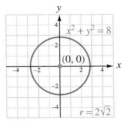

2. $(x + 7)^2 + (y - 1)^2 = 100$ **3.**

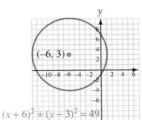

4. 9 ft   **5.**

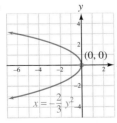

6. 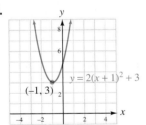   **7.**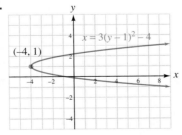

STUDY SET SECTION 13.1 (page 1086)

1. conic sections   **3.** circle, radius
5. a. $(x - h)^2 + (y - k)^2 = r^2$ **b.** $x^2 + y^2 = r^2$
7. a. $(2, -1)$; $r = 4$ **b.** $(x - 2)^2 + (y + 1)^2 = 16$

9. a. $y = a(x - h)^2 + k$ **b.** $x = a(y - k)^2 + h$
11. a. Circle   **b.** Parabola   **c.** Parabola   **d.** Circle
13. $6, -2, 3$ **15.** $(0, 0), r = 3$

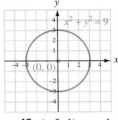

17. $(0, -3), r = 1$ **19.** $(-3, 1), r = 4$

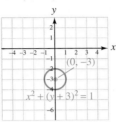   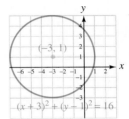

21. $(0, 0), r = \sqrt{6} \approx 2.4$

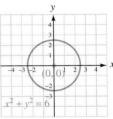

23. $x^2 + y^2 = 1$ **25.** $(x - 6)^2 + (y - 8)^2 = 25$
27. $(x + 2)^2 + (y - 6)^2 = 144$ **29.** $x^2 + y^2 = \frac{1}{16}$
31. $\left(x - \frac{2}{3}\right)^2 + \left(y + \frac{7}{8}\right)^2 = 2$ **33.** $x^2 + y^2 = 8$
35. $(x - 1)^2 + (y + 2)^2 = 4$; $(1, -2), r = 2$

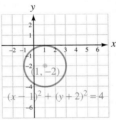

37. $(x + 2)^2 + (y + 1)^2 = 9$; $(-2, -1), r = 3$

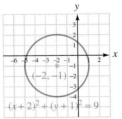

39. $y = 2(x - 1)^2 + 3$; vertex: $(1, 3)$

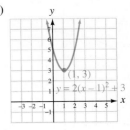

41. $y = -(x + 1)^2 + 4$; vertex: $(-1, 4)$

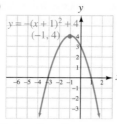

43. Vertex: $(0, 0)$

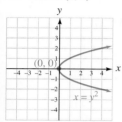

45. Vertex: $(3, -1)$

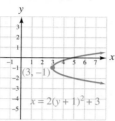

47. $x = (y - 1)^2 + 4$; vertex: $(4, 1)$

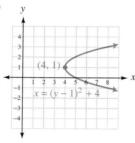

49. $x = -3(y - 3)^2 + 2$; vertex: $(2, 3)$

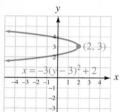

51.

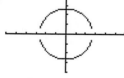

53.

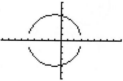

55.

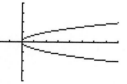

57.

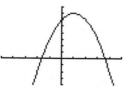

59. $x = (y - 3)^2 - 5$; vertex: $(-5, 3)$

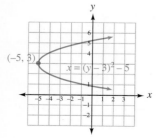

61. $(2, 0)$; $r = 5$

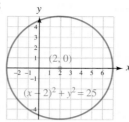

63. $(x - 3)^2 + (y + 4)^2 = 7$; $(3, -4)$; $r = \sqrt{7} \approx 2.6$

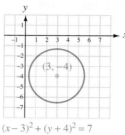

65. $y = 4(x - 2)^2 + 1$; vertex: $(2, 1)$

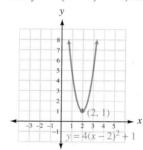

67. $(1, 3)$; $r = \sqrt{15} \approx 3.9$

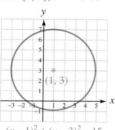

69. Vertex: $(1, 0)$

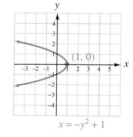

71. $(2, 4)$; $r = 6$

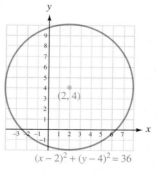

73. Vertex: $(0, 0)$

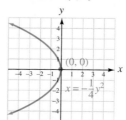

75. Vertex: $(3, 1)$

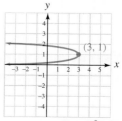

77. $(x + 1)^2 + y^2 = 9$; $(-1, 0)$; $r = 3$

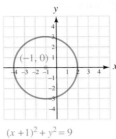

$(x +1)^2 + y^2 = 9$

79. $x = \frac{1}{2}(y + 2)^2 - 2$; vertex: $(-2, -2)$

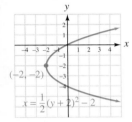

$x = \frac{1}{2}(y + 2)^2 - 2$

81. Vertex: $(-5, 5)$

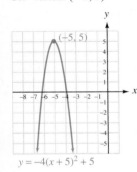

$y = -4(x + 5)^2 + 5$

83. a. $(4, -7)$; $r = 2\sqrt{7} \approx 5.3$
b. $(-4, 7)$; $r = 2\sqrt{7} \approx 5.3$
85. a. $V(3, 6)$; opens upward
b. $V(6, 3)$; opens to the right
87. No **89. a.** 8 mi
b. 9 mi **91.** 5 ft
93. 2 AU **99.** $5, -\frac{7}{3}$ **101.** $3, -\frac{1}{4}$

ARE YOU READY? 13.2 (page 1089)

1. ± 9 **2.** $y + 4$ **3.** $4x^2 + y^2$ **4.** $2\sqrt{2}$

SELF CHECK 13.2

1.

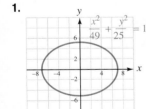

$\frac{x^2}{49} + \frac{y^2}{25} = 1$

2.

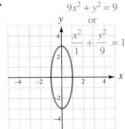

$9x^2 + y^2 = 9$
or
$\frac{x^2}{1} + \frac{y^2}{9} = 1$

3.

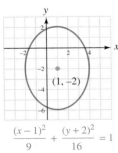

$\frac{(x - 1)^2}{9} + \frac{(y + 2)^2}{16} = 1$

4.

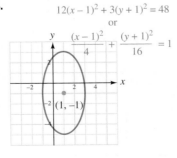

$12(x - 1)^2 + 3(y + 1)^2 = 48$
or
$\frac{(x - 1)^2}{4} + \frac{(y + 1)^2}{16} = 1$

5. $\frac{x^2}{324} + \frac{y^2}{576} = 1$

STUDY SET SECTION 13.2 (page 1095)

1. ellipse **3.** foci, focus **5.** major **7.** $\frac{x^2}{a^2} + \frac{y^2}{b^2} = 1$
9. x-intercepts: $(a, 0)$, $(-a, 0)$; y-intercepts: $(0, b)$, $(0, -b)$
11. a. $(-2, 1)$; $a = 2, b = 5$ **b.** Vertical
c. $\frac{(x + 2)^2}{4} + \frac{(y - 1)^2}{25} = 1$ **13.** $\frac{(x - 1)^2}{16} + \frac{(y + 5)^2}{1} = 1$
15. $h = -8, k = 6, a = 10, b = 12$ **17.**

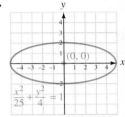

$\frac{x^2}{25} + \frac{y^2}{4} = 1$

19.

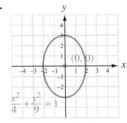

$\frac{x^2}{4} + \frac{y^2}{9} = 1$

21.

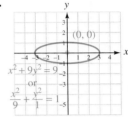

$x^2 + 9y^2 = 9$
or
$\frac{x^2}{9} + \frac{y^2}{1} = 1$

23.

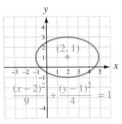

$16x^2 + 4y^2 = 64$
or
$\frac{x^2}{4} + \frac{y^2}{16} = 1$

25.

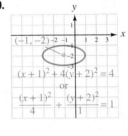

$\frac{(x - 2)^2}{9} + \frac{(y - 1)^2}{4} = 1$

27.

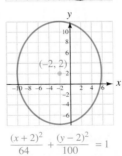

$\frac{(x + 2)^2}{64} + \frac{(y - 2)^2}{100} = 1$

29.

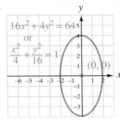

$(x + 1)^2 + 4(y + 2)^2 = 4$
or
$\frac{(x + 1)^2}{4} + \frac{(y + 2)^2}{1} = 1$

31.

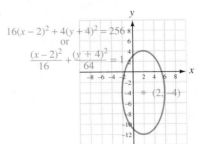

$16(x - 2)^2 + 4(y + 4)^2 = 256$
or
$\frac{(x - 2)^2}{16} + \frac{(y + 4)^2}{64} = 1$

33.

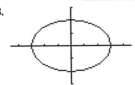

35.

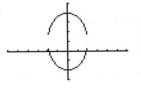

37.

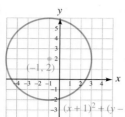

$(x + 1)^2 + (y - 2)^2 = 16$

39.

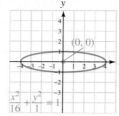

$\dfrac{x^2}{16} + \dfrac{y^2}{1} = 1$

SELF CHECKS 13.3

1.

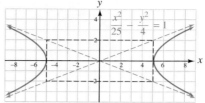

$\dfrac{x^2}{25} - \dfrac{y^2}{4} = 1$

41.

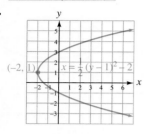

$x = \frac{1}{2}(y - 1)^2 - 2$

$(-2, 1)$

43. $x^2 + y^2 = 25$

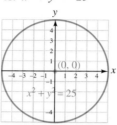

$x^2 + y^2 = 25$

2.

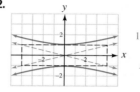

$16y^2 - x^2 = 16$
or
$\dfrac{y^2}{1} - \dfrac{x^2}{16} = 1$

45.

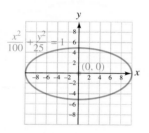

$\dfrac{x^2}{100} + \dfrac{y^2}{25} = 1$

47.

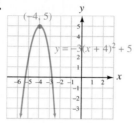

$(-4, 5)$

$y = -3(x + 4)^2 + 5$

3. a.

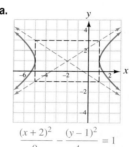

$\dfrac{(x + 2)^2}{9} - \dfrac{(y - 1)^2}{4} = 1$

b.

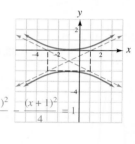

$\dfrac{(y + 1)^2}{1} - \dfrac{(x + 1)^2}{4} = 1$

49.

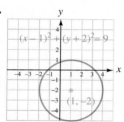

$(x - 1)^2 + (y + 2)^2 = 9$

$(1, -2)$

51.

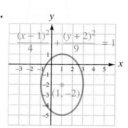

$\dfrac{(x - 1)^2}{4} + \dfrac{(y + 2)^2}{9} = 1$

$(1, -2)$

4.

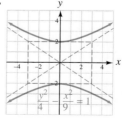

$xy = 6$

5. 1×10^9 mi

53.

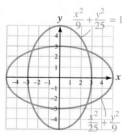

$\dfrac{x^2}{9} + \dfrac{y^2}{25} = 1$

$\dfrac{x^2}{25} + \dfrac{y^2}{9} = 1$

55.

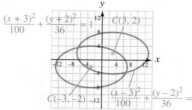

$\dfrac{(x + 3)^2}{100} + \dfrac{(y + 2)^2}{36} = 1$ $C(3, 2)$

$C(-3, -2)$ $\dfrac{(x - 3)^2}{100} + \dfrac{(y - 2)^2}{36} = 1$

STUDY SET SECTION 13.3 (page 1104)

1. hyperbola **3.** vertices **5.** diagonals **7.** $\dfrac{x^2}{a^2} - \dfrac{y^2}{b^2} = 1$
9. $\dfrac{(x - h)^2}{a^2} - \dfrac{(y - k)^2}{b^2} = 1$ **11. a.** $(-1, -2)$; $a = 3, b = 1$
b. $\dfrac{(y + 2)^2}{9} - \dfrac{(x + 1)^2}{1} = 1$ **13.** $\dfrac{(x + 1)^2}{1} - \dfrac{(y - 5)^2}{4} = 1$
15. $h = 5, k = -11, a = 5, b = 6$

57. a. $\dfrac{x^2}{400} + \dfrac{y^2}{100} = 1$ **b.** $5\sqrt{3}$ ft ≈ 8.7 ft

59. $\dfrac{x^2}{1,600} + \dfrac{y^2}{1,225} = 1$ **61.** 12π sq. units ≈ 37.7 sq. units

67. $12y^2 + \dfrac{9}{x^2}$ **69.** $\dfrac{y^2 + x^2}{y^2 - x^2}$

17.

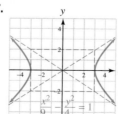

$\dfrac{x^2}{9} - \dfrac{y^2}{4} = 1$

19.

$\dfrac{y^2}{4} - \dfrac{x^2}{9} = 1$

ARE YOU READY? 13.3 (page 1098)

1. ± 4 **2.** $x + 2$ **3.** $\dfrac{2}{3}$ **4.** -10

21.
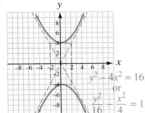
$y^2 - 4x^2 = 16$ or $\dfrac{y^2}{16} - \dfrac{x^2}{4} = 1$

23.
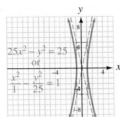
$25x^2 - y^2 = 25$ or $\dfrac{x^2}{1} - \dfrac{y^2}{25} = 1$

45.
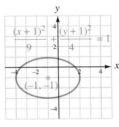
$\dfrac{(x+1)^2}{9} + \dfrac{(y+1)^2}{4} = 1$
$(-1, -1)$

47.
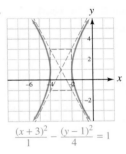
$\dfrac{(x+3)^2}{1} - \dfrac{(y-1)^2}{4} = 1$

25.
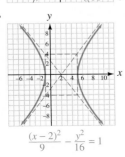
$\dfrac{(x-2)^2}{9} - \dfrac{y^2}{16} = 1$

27.
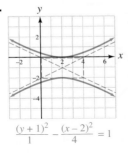
$\dfrac{(y+1)^2}{1} - \dfrac{(x-2)^2}{4} = 1$

49.
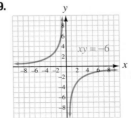
$xy = -6$

51.
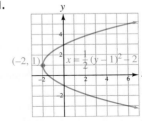
$x = \dfrac{1}{2}(y-1)^2 - 2$
$(-2, 1)$

29.
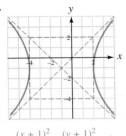
$\dfrac{(x+1)^2}{9} - \dfrac{(y+1)^2}{9} = 1$

31.
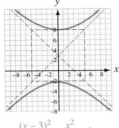
$\dfrac{(y-3)^2}{25} - \dfrac{x^2}{25} = 1$

53.
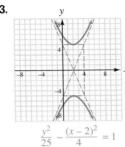
$\dfrac{y^2}{25} - \dfrac{(x-2)^2}{4} = 1$

55.
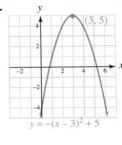
$(3, 5)$
$y = -(x-3)^2 + 5$

33.
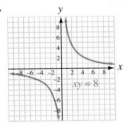
$xy = 8$

35.
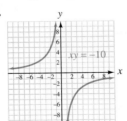
$xy = -10$

57.
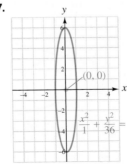
$(0, 0)$
$\dfrac{x^2}{1} + \dfrac{y^2}{36} = 1$

59.
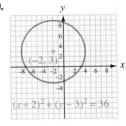
$(-2, 3)$
$(x+2)^2 + (y-3)^2 = 36$

37.

39.

61. 3 units **63.** $10\sqrt{3}$ miles ≈ 17.3 miles **65.** A hyperbola
71. 64 **73.** 3 **75.** $\frac{3}{2}$ **77.** 10

ARE YOU READY? 13.4 (page 1107)

1.
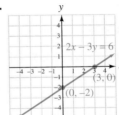
$2x - 3y = 6$
$(3, 0)$
$(0, -2)$

2. $-1, \frac{5}{9}$ **3.** $(4, 12)$
4. a. $\pm\dfrac{\sqrt{5}}{3}$ **b.** $\pm 3\sqrt{2}$

41.
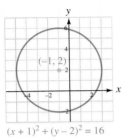
$(-1, 2)$
$(x+1)^2 + (y-2)^2 = 16$

43.
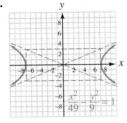
$\dfrac{x^2}{49} - \dfrac{y^2}{9} = 1$

SELF CHECK 13.4

1. $(-4, 3), (0, -5)$

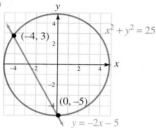

2. $(1, 3), (-3, -1)$ **3.** $(2, 4), (-2, 4)$
4. $\left(2, \sqrt{3}\right), \left(2, -\sqrt{3}\right), \left(-2, \sqrt{3}\right), \left(-2, -\sqrt{3}\right)$

STUDY SET SECTION 13.4 (page 1111)

1. system   **3.** intersection   **5.** secant   **7. a.** two   **b.** four
c. four   **d.** four   **9.** $(-3, 2), (3, 2), (-3, -2), (3, -2)$
11. a. -4 **b.** -2 **13.** $2x, 5, 5, 1, 1, -1, -2$
15. $(0, 3), (-3, 0)$ **17.** $(-4, 0), (4, 0)$

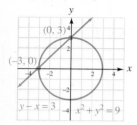

19. $(0, 0), (2, -4)$ **21.** $(-2, 0), (0, -1), (0, 1)$

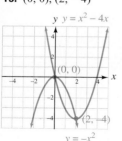

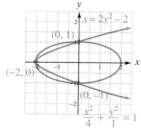

23. $(1, 2), (2, 1)$ **25.** $(-6, 7), (-2, -1)$ **27.** $(-2, 3), (2, 3)$
29. $(\sqrt{5}, 5), (-\sqrt{5}, 5)$ **31.** $(2, 4), (2, -4), (-2, 4), (-2, -4)$
33. $(3, 0), (-3, 0)$ **35.** $(\sqrt{3}, 0), (-\sqrt{3}, 0)$
37. $(-2, 3), (2, 3), (-2, -3), (2, -3)$
39. $(1, 0), (5, 0)$

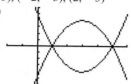

41. $(2, 1), (-2, 1), (2, -1), (-2, -1)$ **43.** $(0, -4), (-3, 5), (3, 5)$
45. $(6, 2), (-6, -2), \left(-\sqrt{42}, 0\right), \left(\sqrt{42}, 0\right)$
47. $\left(-\sqrt{15}, 5\right), \left(\sqrt{15}, 5\right), (-2, -6), (2, -6)$
49. $(0, 3), \left(-\frac{25}{12}, -\frac{13}{4}\right)$ **51.** $(0, 0), (2, 4)$ **53.** No solution, $\varnothing$
55. $(3, 5)$
57. $\left(\frac{\sqrt{10}}{4}, \frac{3\sqrt{6}}{4}\right), \left(\frac{\sqrt{10}}{4}, -\frac{3\sqrt{6}}{4}\right), \left(-\frac{\sqrt{10}}{4}, \frac{3\sqrt{6}}{4}\right), \left(-\frac{\sqrt{10}}{4}, -\frac{3\sqrt{6}}{4}\right)$
59. $\left(\frac{1}{2}, \frac{1}{3}\right), \left(\frac{1}{3}, \frac{1}{2}\right)$ **61.** $(-1, 3), (1, 3)$ **63.** $\left(\frac{5}{2}, \frac{3}{2}\right)$ **65.** $4, 8$
67. $\left(10, \frac{10}{3}\right); \frac{10}{3}\sqrt{10}$ m   **69.** 80 ft by 100 ft or 50 ft by 160 ft
71. \$2,500 at 9%   **75.** 2,000   **77.** 7

CHAPTER 13 REVIEW (page 1114)

1.   **2.**

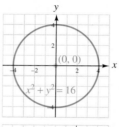   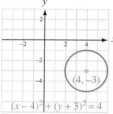

3.

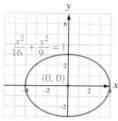

4. $(x - 9)^2 + (y - 9)^2 = 9^2$ or $(x - 9)^2 + (y - 9)^2 = 81$
5. $(-6, 0); r = 2\sqrt{6}$ **6.** center, radius
7. $(0, 0)$ **8.** $(-2, -1)$

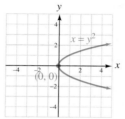

9.   **10.**

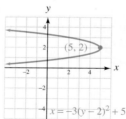   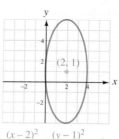

11. $(2, -2), (8, -3)$
12. When $x = 22$, $y = 0$: $-\frac{5}{121}(22 - 11)^2 + 5 = 0$
13.   **14.**

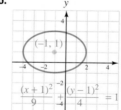

$$\frac{(x - 2)^2}{4} + \frac{(y - 1)^2}{25} = 1$$

15.   **16.** $\frac{x^2}{12^2} + \frac{y^2}{1^2} = 1$ **17. a.** Circle
                          b. Ellipse   **c.** Parabola
                          d. Ellipse   **18.** $\frac{x^2}{25} + \frac{y^2}{9} = 1$
                          19. ellipse, focus

20.

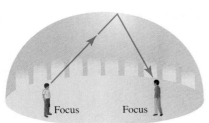

Answers may vary.

21.

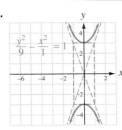

$$\frac{y^2}{9} - \frac{x^2}{1} = 1$$

22.

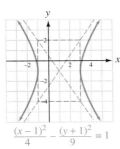

$$\frac{(x-1)^2}{4} - \frac{(y+1)^2}{9} = 1$$

23.

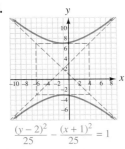

$$\frac{(y-2)^2}{25} - \frac{(x+1)^2}{25} = 1$$

24.

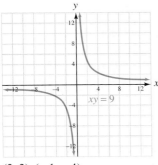

$xy = 9$

25. 4 units **26. a.** Ellipse
b. Hyperbola **c.** Parabola
d. Circle **27.** Yes
28. $(0, 3), (0, -3)$

29. $(2, 2), (-1, -4)$

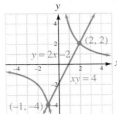

$y = 2x - 2$
$xy = 4$

30. a. 2 **b.** 4
c. 4 **d.** 4
31. $(0, 1), (0, -1)$
32. $y = 3x - 1$

33. $(0, -4), (-3, 5), (3, 5)$ **34.** $\left(\sqrt{2}, 0\right), \left(-\sqrt{2}, 0\right)$
35. $(2, 2), \left(-\frac{2}{9}, -\frac{22}{9}\right)$ **36.** $(4, 2), (4, -2), (-4, 2), (-4, -2)$
37. $(2, 3), (2, -3), (-2, 3), (-2, -3)$
38. $\left(2\sqrt{2}, \sqrt{2}\right), \left(-2\sqrt{2}, -\sqrt{2}\right), (1, 4), (-1, -4)$
39. No solution, $\varnothing$ **40.** $(-2, 1)$

CHAPTER 13 TEST (page 1119)

1. a. conic **b.** center, radius **c.** hyperbola **d.** nonlinear

e. ellipse **2.** $(0, 0); r = 10$

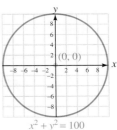

$x^2 + y^2 = 100$

3. $(-2, 3), r = 3\sqrt{2}$ **4.** $(x - 4)^2 + (y - 3)^2 = 9$
5. $\frac{21}{2}$ in. $= 10.5$ in. **6.** 16, 16, 4, 6
7.

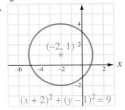

$(x + 2)^2 + (y - 1)^2 = 9$

8.

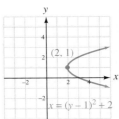

$x = (y - 1)^2 + 2$

9.

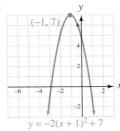

$y = -2(x + 1)^2 + 7$

10.

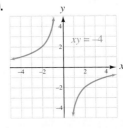

$xy = -4$

11.

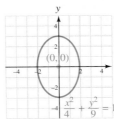

$$\frac{x^2}{4} + \frac{y^2}{9} = 1$$

12.

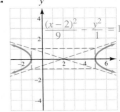

$$\frac{(x-2)^2}{9} - \frac{y^2}{1} = 1$$

13.

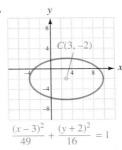

$$\frac{(x-3)^2}{49} + \frac{(y+2)^2}{16} = 1$$

14.

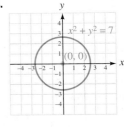

$x^2 + y^2 = 7$

15.

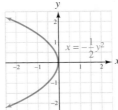

$x = -\frac{1}{2}y^2$

16.

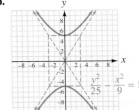

$$\frac{y^2}{25} - \frac{x^2}{9} = 1$$

17. $\frac{(x-1)^2}{16} + \frac{(y+2)^2}{9} = 1$ **18.** 2.5 in.
19. $\frac{x^2}{784} + \frac{y^2}{256} = 1$

20. $(-1, 1)$; length: 4 units, width: 4 units **21.** $\frac{y^2}{16} - \frac{x^2}{36} = 1$
22. a. Ellipse **b.** Hyperbola **c.** Circle **d.** Parabola
23. $(-4, -3), (3, 4)$

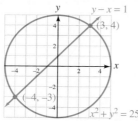

24. $(2, 6), (-2, -2)$
25. $\left(1, \sqrt{2}\right), \left(1, -\sqrt{2}\right), \left(-1, \sqrt{2}\right), \left(-1, -\sqrt{2}\right)$
26. $\left(-1, \frac{9}{2}\right), \left(3, -\frac{3}{2}\right)$ **27.** $(-1, 0)$ **28.** No solution; $\varnothing$

ARE YOU READY? 14.1 (page 1122)

1. $1, 4, 6, 4, 1$ **2.** $a^2 + 2ab + b^2$ **3.** 120 **4.** 30

SELF CHECK 14.1

1. $x^4 + 4x^3y + 6x^2y^2 + 4xy^3 + y^4$
2. $x^5 - 5x^4y + 10x^3y^2 - 10x^2y^3 + 5xy^4 - y^5$ **3. a.** $5,040$
b. 144 **c.** 1 **4. a.** 4 **b.** 21
5. $a^4 + 4a^3b + 6a^2b^2 + 4ab^3 + b^4$ **6.** $x^3 - 3x^2y + 3xy^2 - y^3$
7. $64a^3 - 240a^2b + 300ab^2 - 125b^3$ **8.** $36a^7b^2$ **9.** $\frac{35}{81}c^6d^4$

STUDY SET SECTION 14.1 (page 1129)

1. binomial **3.** binomial **5.** factorial, decreasing **7.** one
9. $20, 20$ **11.** $1, 1$ **13.** $n, 1$ **15.** 1 **17.** $9, 3$ **19.** $2, 4$
21. $3, 3, y, 2, 2, 3$ **23.** $n, 1$ **25.** $a^3 + 3a^2b + 3ab^2 + b^3$
27. $m^5 - 5m^4p + 10m^3p^2 - 10m^2p^3 + 5mp^4 - p^5$ **29.** 6
31. 120 **33.** 30 **35.** 144 **37.** $40,320$ **39.** $2,352$
41. $\frac{1}{110}$ **43.** 72 **45.** 5 **47.** 10 **49.** $\frac{1}{168}$ **51.** 21
53. $39,916,800$ **55.** $2.432902008 \times 10^{18}$
57. $m^4 + 4m^3n + 6m^2n^2 + 4mn^3 + n^4$
59. $c^5 - 5c^4d + 10c^3d^2 - 10c^2d^3 + 5cd^4 - d^5$
61. $a^9 - 9a^8b + 36a^7b^2 - 84a^6b^3 + 126a^5b^4 - 126a^4b^5 + 84a^3b^6 - 36a^2b^7 + 9ab^8 - b^9$
63. $s^6 + 6s^5t + 15s^4t^2 + 20s^3t^3 + 15s^2t^4 + 6st^5 + t^6$
65. $8x^3 + 12x^2y + 6xy^2 + y^3$
67. $32t^5 - 240t^4 + 720t^3 - 1,080t^2 + 810t - 243$
69. $625m^4 - 1,000m^3n + 600m^2n^2 - 160mn^3 + 16n^4$
71. $\frac{x^3}{27} + \frac{x^2y}{6} + \frac{xy^2}{4} + \frac{y^3}{8}$ **73.** $\frac{x^4}{81} - \frac{2x^3y}{27} + \frac{x^2y^2}{6} - \frac{xy^3}{6} + \frac{y^4}{16}$
75. $c^{10} - 5c^8d^2 + 10c^6d^4 - 10c^4d^6 + 5c^2d^8 - d^{10}$ **77.** $28x^6y^2$
79. $15r^2s^4$ **81.** $78x^{11}$ **83.** $-12x^3y$ **85.** $810xy^4$
87. $-\frac{1}{6}c^3d$ **89.** $-70,000t^4$ **91.** $6a^{10}b^2$ **97.** $\log x^2y^{1/2}$ or
$\log x^2\sqrt{y}$ **99.** $\ln y$

ARE YOU READY? 14.2 (page 1131)

1. 21 **2. a.** 1 **b.** -1 **3.** 8 **4.** 52

SELF CHECK 14.2

1. a. $8, 11, 14$ **b.** 305 **2.** $-1, \frac{1}{2}, -\frac{1}{3}, \frac{1}{4}$
3. $10, 18, 26, 34, 42; 242$ **4.** 879 **5.** $15, 22, 29, 36$ **6.** $20, 32$
7. $6,275$ **8.** 140 members **9.** 52

STUDY SET SECTION 14.2 (page 1138)

1. sequence **3.** arithmetic **5.** mean **7.** $1, 7, 13$
9. a. $a_n = a_1 + (n - 1)d$ **b.** $S_n = \frac{n(a_1 + a_n)}{2}$ **11.** nth
13. sigma **15.** summation, runs **17.** $3, 7, 11, 15, 19; 159$
19. $-2, -5, -8, -11, -14; -89$
21. $-1, -4, -9, -16, -25; -400$ **23.** $0, \frac{1}{2}, \frac{2}{3}, \frac{3}{4}, \frac{4}{5}; \frac{11}{12}$
25. $-\frac{1}{3}, \frac{1}{9}, -\frac{1}{27}, \frac{1}{81}$ **27.** $-7, 8, -9, 10$ **29.** $3, 5, 7, 9, 11; 21$
31. $-5, -8, -11, -14, -17; -47$ **33.** $7, 19, 31, 43, 55; 355$
35. $-7, -9, -11, -13, -15; -35$ **37.** 88 **39.** 59
41. $5, 11, 17, 23, 29$ **43.** $-4, -11, -18, -25, -32$ **45.** $5, 8$
47. $12, 14, 16, 18$ **49.** $\frac{45}{2}, 25, \frac{55}{2}$ **51.** $\frac{5}{4}$ **53.** $2,555$
55. $2,920$ **57.** $3 + 6 + 9 + 12$ **59.** $4 + 9 + 16$ **61.** 60
63. 91 **65.** 31 **67.** 12 **69.** 70 **71.** 57 **73.** 12 **75.** 354
77. $-118, -111, -104, -97, -90$ **79.** $34, 31, 28, 25, 22, 19$
81. $1,398$ **83.** $1,275$ **85.** -179 **87.** -23 **89.** -3
91. $2,500$ **93.** $\$60, \$110, \$160, \$210, \$260, \$310; \$6,060$
95. $11,325$ **97.** 78 gifts **103.** $1 + \log_2 x - \log_2 y$
105. $3 \log x + 2 \log y$

ARE YOU READY? 14.3 (page 1141)

1. 48 **2. a.** 625 **b.** $\frac{1}{27}$ **3.** $\frac{1}{4}$ **4.** ± 12

SELF CHECK 14.3

1. a. $3, 12, 48, 192$ **b.** $49,152$ **2.** $\frac{1}{625}$
3. $-2, -6, -18, -54, -162$ **4.** $1, 2, 4, 8, 16$ **5.** 20
6. 124.96 **7.** 125 **8.** $\frac{243}{4}$ **9.** $\frac{2}{3}$ **10.** About $\$763$
11. 135 in.

STUDY SET SECTION 14.3 (page 1150)

1. geometric **3.** mean **5.** $16, 4, 1$ **7.** $a_n = a_1r^{n-1}$
9. a. Yes **b.** No **c.** No **d.** Yes **11.** r^2, a_1r^4 **13.** n
15. $3, 6, 12, 24, 48; 768$ **17.** $-5, -1, -\frac{1}{5}, -\frac{1}{25}, -\frac{1}{125}; -\frac{1}{15,625}$
19. $1,458$ **21.** $-\frac{3,125}{2}$ **23.** $2, 6, 18, 54, 162$
25. $3, 6, 12, 24, 48$ **27.** $6, 18, 54$
29. $-20, -100, -500, -2,500$
31. -16 or 16 **33.** $-10\sqrt{2}$ or $10\sqrt{2}$ **35.** 728 **37.** 122
39. -255 **41.** 381 **43.** 16 **45.** 81 **47.** $-\frac{81}{2}$ **49.** No sum
51. 8 **53.** $-\frac{135}{4}$ **55.** $\frac{1}{9}$ **57.** $\frac{1}{3}$ **59.** $\frac{4}{33}$ **61.** $\frac{25}{33}$ **63.** 3
65. $-64, 32, -16, 8, -4$ **67.** No geometric mean exists.
69. $3,584$ **71.** $-64, -32, -16, -8$ **73.** 4 **75.** $\frac{1}{27}$ **77.** 93
79. $\$1,469.74$ **81.** About $\$539,731$
83. $\left(\frac{1}{2}\right)^{11} \approx 0.0005$ square unit **85.** 30 m **87.** $5,000$
93. $[-1, 6]$ **95.** $(-\infty, -3) \cup (4, \infty)$

CHAPTER 14 REVIEW (page 1153)

1. $1, 3, 1, 1, 10, 15; 1, 5, 10, 10, 5, 1$ **2. a.** 13 **b.** 12
c. a^{12}, b^{12} **d.** a: decrease; b: increase **3.** 144 **4.** 20
5. 15 **6.** 220 **7.** 1 **8.** 8
9. $x^5 + 5x^4y + 10x^3y^2 + 10x^2y^3 + 5xy^4 + y^5$
10. $x^9 - 9x^8y + 36x^7y^2 - 84x^6y^3 + 126x^5y^4 - 126x^4y^5 + 84x^3y^6 - 36x^2y^7 + 9xy^8 - y^9$
11. $64x^3 - 48x^2y + 12xy^2 - y^3$
12. $\frac{c^4}{16} + \frac{c^3d}{6} + \frac{c^2d^2}{6} + \frac{2cd^3}{27} + \frac{d^4}{81}$ **13.** $6x^2y^2$ **14.** $-20x^3y^3$
15. $-108x^2y$ **16.** $5u^2v^{12}$ **17.** $-2, 0, 2, 4$
18. $-\frac{1}{2}, \frac{1}{3}, -\frac{1}{4}, \frac{1}{5}, -\frac{1}{6}$ **19.** 75 **20.** 42
21. $122, 137, 152, 167, 182$ **22.** $-1,194$ **23.** -5

24. $\frac{41}{3}, \frac{58}{3}$ **25.** $-\frac{45}{2}$ **26.** 1,568   **27.** $\frac{15}{2}$ **28.** 378
29. 14   **30.** 360   **31.** 20,100   **32.** 1,170   **33.** 4
34. 24, 12, 6, 3, $\frac{3}{2}$ **35.** $\frac{1}{27}$ **36.** 24, -96 **37.** $\frac{2,186}{9}$
38. $-\frac{85}{8}$ **39.** About 1.6 lb   **40.** 125   **41.** $\frac{5}{99}$ **42.** 190 ft

CHAPTER 14 TEST (page 1157)

1. a. Pascal's   **b.** alternate   **c.** arithmetic   **d.** series
e. geometric   **2.** 2, -4, -10, -16 **3.** $-1, \frac{1}{8}, -\frac{1}{27}, \frac{1}{64}, -\frac{1}{125}$
4. 210
5. $a^6 - 6a^5b + 15a^4b^2 - 20a^3b^3 + 15a^2b^4 - 6ab^5 + b^6$
6. $24x^4y^2$ **7.** 66   **8.** 306   **9.** 34, 66   **10.** $\frac{1}{4}$ **11.** $-1,377$
12. 205 pipes   **13.** 1,600 ft   **14.** 3   **15.** -81 **16.** $\frac{364}{27}$ **17.** 6
18. 18, 108   **19.** $\frac{27}{2}$ **20.** About \$651,583   **21.** 2,000 in.   **22.** $\frac{7}{9}$

GROUP PROJECT (page 1158)

1. g   **2.** o   **3.** i   **4.** l   **5.** u   **6.** y   **7.** p   **8.** x   **9.** m   **10.** d
11. f   **12.** c   **13.** w   **14.** b   **15.** j   **16.** s   **17.** e   **18.** z
19. n   **20.** k   **21.** h   **22.** v   **23.** q   **24.** a   **25.** r   **26.** t

CUMULATIVE REVIEW CHAPTERS 1–14 (page 1159)

1. a. 0   **b.** $-\frac{4}{3}, 5.6, 0, -23$ **c.** $\pi, \sqrt{2}, e$
d. $-\frac{4}{3}, \pi, 5.6, \sqrt{2}, 0, -23, e$ **2.** 0
3. $b_2 = \frac{2A - b_1h}{h}$ or $b_2 = \frac{2A}{h} - b_1$ **4.** 85°, 80°, 15°   **5.** \$8,250
6. $[-1, \infty)$ 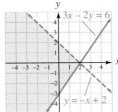   **7.** 12.5 in. or less
8. $\frac{1}{120}$ decibels/rpm   **9. a.** Parallel   **b.** Perpendicular
10. $y = -3,400x + 28,000$ **11.** $y = -2x + 5$
12. $y = -\frac{9}{13}x + \frac{7}{13}$ **13.** It doesn't pass the vertical line test.

The graph passes through $(0, 2)$ and $(0, -2)$.   **14.** $-4; 3a^5 - 2a^2 + 1$
15. $(-7, 7)$ **16.** $\left(\frac{4}{5}, \frac{3}{4}\right)$ **17.** Regular: $29\frac{1}{3}$ lb; Brazilian: $10\frac{2}{3}$ lb

18. 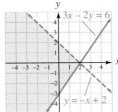   **19.** x^8y^{10} **20.** $\frac{16}{y^{16}}$

21. 1.73×10^{14}; 4.6×10^{-8} **22.** 1.44×10^{-3}; 0.00144
23. $\frac{7}{4}rt^2 - \frac{5}{6}rt$ **24.** $5x^2 - 11x - 5$ **25.** $2x^2y^3 + 13xy + 3y^2$
26. $x^3 - 27y^3$ **27.** $6m^{10} - 23m^5 + 7$
28. $81a^2b^4 - 72ab^2 + 16$ **29.** $(b - 4)(b^2 - 3)$
30. $(3y + 2)(4y + 5)$ **31.** $(12x + y)(12x - y)$
32. $(3t + u)(9t^2 - 3tu + u^2)$
33. $b^2(a + 4)(a - 4)(a + 2)(a - 2)$
34. $-2, \frac{1}{3}$ **35.** A repeated solution of -8 **36.** 0, 1, -9
37. Length: 21 ft; width: 4 ft   **38.** 5 sec   **39.** 6, 8, 10   **40.** $\frac{x - 3}{6x + 1}$
41. $-\frac{q}{p}$ **42.** $\frac{1}{(x^2 + 9)(x - 3)}$ **43.** $\frac{4a - 1}{(a + 2)(a - 2)}$ **44.** $y - x$

45. $\frac{11}{4}$ **46.** $R = \dfrac{R_1R_2R_3}{R_2R_3 + R_1R_3 + R_1R_2}$ **47.** $2\frac{2}{5}$ hr = 2.4 hr
48. 93 squirrels   **49.** No solution, $\varnothing$; contradiction
50. It is not a solution.   **51.** 10 hr   **52.** No; $(2, 2)$, $(2, -2)$
53. a. 4   **b.** 3   **c.** 0, 2   **d.** 1   **54. a.** $P(t) = -0.26t + 11.6$
b. 1.2%   **55.** 91 cantaloupes
56. D: the set of real numbers $(-\infty, \infty)$; R: the set of nonnegative real numbers $[0, \infty)$

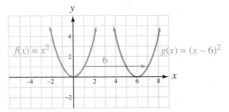

57. $(-\infty, -2)$
58. $(-\infty, -12] \cup [2, \infty)$
59. $(-\infty, -15)$
60. $\left[-3, \frac{19}{3}\right]$ **61.** $-2, -\frac{4}{5}$
62. $(7x - 7t + 2)(2x - 2t - 3)$ **63.** $\lambda = \frac{4d - 2}{A - 6}$
64. $(x + 5 + 4z)(x + 5 - 4z)$
65. $(4a^2 - 3b)(16a^4 + 12a^2b + 9b^2)$ **66.** $g(x) = \frac{x^2 - 4x + 16}{x^2 + 3}$
provided $x \neq -4$ **67.** $-\frac{7}{5}$ **68.** All real numbers except -5 and 5
69. 2 lumens   **70.** $[-3, \infty)$ **71.** 4 ft
72. D: $[0, \infty)$; R: $[2, \infty)$ **73.** $\frac{343}{125}$ **74.** $4ab^2\sqrt{7ab}$ **75.** $5\sqrt{2}$
76. $81x\sqrt[3]{3x}$ **77.** $13 - \sqrt{7}$
78. $15x - 6\sqrt{15x} + 9$ **79.** $\frac{\sqrt[3]{4b^2}}{b}$
80. $\sqrt{3t} - 1$ **81.** 1, 3   **82.** 5   **83.** 0

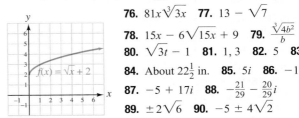

84. About $22\frac{1}{2}$ in.   **85.** $5i$ **86.** -1
87. $-5 + 17i$ **88.** $-\frac{21}{29} - \frac{20}{29}i$
89. $\pm 2\sqrt{6}$ **90.** $-5 \pm 4\sqrt{2}$
91. $\frac{-3 \pm \sqrt{5}}{4}$ **92.** $\frac{2}{3} \pm \frac{\sqrt{2}}{3}i$ **93.** $\frac{1}{4}, \frac{1}{2}$
94. $-i, i, -3i\sqrt{2}, 3i\sqrt{2}$ **95. a.** A quadratic function
b. At about 85% and 120% of the suggested inflation
96. $(-1, -2)$; $(0, -8)$; no x-intercepts

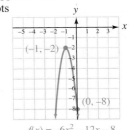

97. $[3, 5]$ **98. a.** $x^2 + 2x - 1$
b. $2x^3 + x^2 - 4x - 2$ **c.** $4x^2 + 4x - 1$ **99.** $f^{-1}(x) = \sqrt[3]{\frac{x + 1}{2}}$

100. D: $(-\infty, \infty)$; R: $(0, \infty)$

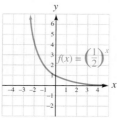

101.

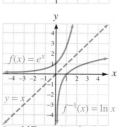

102. About 150 million
103. 3 **104.** 2 **105.** $\frac{1}{27}$ **106.** 5
107. 1 **108.** -1 **109.** Undefined
110. $2 - 3\log_6 x$ **111.** $\ln \frac{y\sqrt{x}}{z}$
112. About 13.4 hr **113.** $-\frac{3}{4}$
114. 3.4190
115. 1, -10 does not check
116. 9 **117. a.** ii **b.** iv **c.** i **d.** iii **118.** $(2, -3)$
119. $\left(-2, \frac{3}{2}\right)$ **120.** $(3, 2, 1)$ **121.** Ankle: 100 pair; low cut, 150 pair; crew: 250 pair
122. $(x - 1)^2 + (y + 3)^2 = 4$

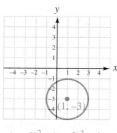

123. $x = -\frac{1}{4}(y - 3)^2 + 2$; $(2, 3)$; $y = 3$

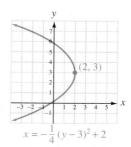

124.

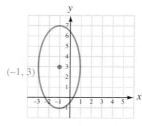

$$\frac{(x + 1)^2}{4} + \frac{(y - 3)^2}{16} = 1$$

125.

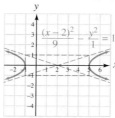

$$\frac{(x - 2)^2}{9} - \frac{y^2}{1} = 1$$

126. $81a^4 - 108a^3b + 54a^2b^2 - 12ab^3 + b^4$ **127.** $112x^2y^6$
128. 66 **129.** 103 **130.** 690 **131.** 27
132. \$2,848.31 **133.** $\frac{1,023}{64}$ **134.** $\frac{27}{2}$

SELF CHECK APPENDIX 2
1. $5x + 11 + \frac{35}{x - 3}$ **2.** $x^2 + 4x + 19 - \frac{14}{x - 4}$

3. $3x^2 - 7x + 9 - \frac{12}{x + 1}$ **4.** 9 **5.** Since $P(-1) = 0, x + 1$ is a factor of $P(x)$.

APPENDIX 2 (page A-7)
1. synthetic **3.** divisor **5.** theorem
7. a. $(5x^3 + x - 3) \div (x + 2)$ **b.** $5x^2 - 10x + 21 - \frac{45}{x + 2}$
9. $6x^3 - x^2 - 17x + 9, x - 8$ **11.** 2, 1, 12, 26, 6, 8 **13.** $x + 2$
15. $x - 3$ **17.** $x + 2$ **19.** $x - 7 + \frac{28}{x + 2}$ **21.** $3x^2 - x + 2$
23. $2x^2 + 4x + 3$ **25.** $6x^2 - x + 1 + \frac{3}{x + 1}$ **27.** $t^2 + 1 + \frac{1}{t + 1}$
31. $-5x^4 + 11x^3 - 3x^2 - 7x - 1$ **33.** $8t^2 + 2$
35. $x^3 + 7x^2 - 2$ **37.** $7.2x - 0.66 + \frac{0.368}{x - 0.2}$
39. $9x^2 - 513x + 29,241 + \frac{1,666,762}{x + 57}$ **41.** -1 **43.** -37
45. 23 **47.** -1 **49.** 2 **51.** -1 **53.** 18 **55.** 174
57. -8 **59.** 59 **61.** 44 **63.** $\frac{29}{32}$ **65.** yes **67.** no
73. 0 **75.** 2

INDEX